OXFORD PAPERBACK REFERENCE

The Oxford Dictionary of
Quotations by Subject

Susan Ratcliffe is an Associate Editor for Oxford Quotations
Dictionaries. Her previous publications include *The Little Oxford
Dictionary of Quotations* and *The Oxford Dictionary of Phrase, Saying,
and Quotation.*

The Oxford Dictionary of

Quotations by Subject

Edited by
SUSAN RATCLIFFE

OXFORD
UNIVERSITY PRESS

OXFORD
UNIVERSITY PRESS

Great Clarendon Street, Oxford OX2 6DP

Oxford University Press is a department of the University of Oxford.
It furthers the University's objective of excellence in research, scholarship,
and education by publishing worldwide in

Oxford New York

Auckland Bangkok Buenos Aires Cape Town Chennai
Dar es Salaam Delhi Hong Kong Istanbul Karachi Kolkata
Kuala Lumpur Madrid Melbourne Mexico City Mumbai Nairobi
São Paulo Shanghai Taipei Tokyo Toronto

Oxford is a registered trade mark of Oxford University Press
in the UK and in certain other countries

Published in the United States
by Oxford University Press Inc., New York
British Library Cataloguing in Publication Data

Data available

Library of Congress Cataloging in Publication Data

Data available

ISBN 0-19-860750-4

2

Designed by Jane Stevenson
Typeset in Minion and Frutiger
by Interactive Sciences Ltd, Gloucester
Printed at Clays Ltd
St Ives plc

Project Team

Managing Editor	Elizabeth Knowles
Editor	Susan Ratcliffe
Index Editor	Christina Malkowska Zaba
Library Research	Ralph Bates
	Marie G. Diaz
Reading Programme	Verity Mason
	Helen Rappaport
Data Capture	Muriel Summersgill
Proof-reading	Kim Allen
	Fabia Claris
	Penny Trumble

We are grateful to Charlotte Graves Taylor and Jean Harker for additional contributions to the Reading Programme.

Introduction

Originally, dictionaries of quotations were intended to answer the question 'Who said that?'. Today, a question which is more frequently asked is 'What has been said about this?'. This perhaps reflects a modern society with a much more varied cultural and educational experience, where quotations are not restricted to an established literary and political background, and spring from a bewildering variety of media. *Oxford Quotations by Subject* sets out to offer some lively and diverse answers to today's question.

The dictionary is arranged by themes, ranging from traditonal ones such as **Chance** and **Courage** to more recent topics such as **Genetic Engineering** and **The Internet**. While some major themes on which a great deal has been said, such as **Love** and **Death**, are inevitably large, wherever possible more specific themes have been chosen. Thus there are separate but related themes for **Journalism**, **News**, **Newspapers**, and **Press Photographers**. Cross-references lead the reader to such related themes, so that for example **Warfare** links to **The Army**, **Weapons**, and individual wars such as the **Gulf War** or **World War II**, while **World War II** leads on to **Genocide**. Elsewhere, quotations about people such as **Poets** are brought together, while a few characters such as **Ronald Reagan** and **Diana, Princess of Wales**, who have attracted a great deal of comment, form the subject of separate themes.

Within each theme, a major consideration in the selection of quotations has been topicality. Sometimes, words from the past remain as relevant as ever and demand inclusion. Thus Shakespeare's 'To be, or not to be' stands alongside Margaret Thatcher's 'There is no real alternative' at **Choice**. Jeremy Bentham's 'The question is not, Can they reason? nor, Can they talk? but, Can they suffer?' is still quoted on the issue of **Animal Rights**, while Horace's 'We are just statistics, born to consume resources' might have been written yesterday, rather than 2,000 years ago. But in most cases the quotations which reflect today's world are recent, and nowhere more so than in the field of information technology. Francis Fukuyama tells us that 'Silicon Valley is the Florence of the late 20th century' and the world of **Computers** and **The Internet** contributes plenty of ideas. Esther Dyson sums up her **Self**: 'I think of who I am as what I've done', while Andrew Grove says 'Technology happens. It's not good, it's not bad. Is steel good or bad?'. Thirty years before, Marshall McLuhan had a question which perhaps replies to that: 'When this circuit learns your job, what are you going to do?'.

The authors in this book range from poets and scientists to politicians and singers. Grouping the quotations by themes means that there are often insights from unexpected quarters—two differing views on **Colours** from amateur artists better known in another field are illuminating: Winston Churchill's 'I cannot pretend to feel impartial about the colours. I rejoice with the brilliant ones, and am genuinely sorry for the poor browns' contrasts with Adolf Hitler's 'If artists do see fields blue they are deranged and should go to an asylum. If they only pretend to see them blue, they are criminals and should go to prison'. Other politicians contribute elsewhere. Tessa Jowell gives us an unusual analysis of **Parliament**: 'In the last Parliament, the House of Commons had more MPs called John than all the women MPs put together', while George Bush has an unexpected view on the advantages of his position: 'I'm President of the United States, and I'm not going to eat any more broccoli'. More seriously, on the same topic of **Food**, the writer Joanna Trollope asks 'What makes food such a tyranny for women? A man, after all, may in times of crisis, hit the bottle (or another person), but he rarely hits the fridge'.

Often, the quotations within a theme cast a light on very different aspects of it. The former slave Frederick Douglass looks at gaining **Power**: 'Power concedes nothing without a demand. It never did, and it never will' while General H. Norman Schwarzkopf III reflects on its loss 'Seven months ago I could give a single command and 541,000 people would immediately obey it. Today I can't get a plumber to come to my house'. Harry S. Truman thought a similar problem would afflict his successor in **The Presidency**: 'He'll sit right here and he'll say do this, do that! And nothing will happen. Poor Ike—it won't be a bit like the Army'. But it seems that Eisenhower had his own realistic view: 'No easy problems ever come to the President of the United States. If they are easy to solve, somebody else has solved them'.

There are many strong **Opinions**: some, like those of A. J. P. Taylor are 'Extreme views, weakly held', others agreeing with the American politician Jim Hightower that 'There's nothing in the middle of the road but yellow stripes and dead armadillos'. Gerry Robinson said of the Arts Council that 'The most excited voice I heard in the building when I came here was the automated voice in the lift', and perhaps it is as well to be reminded by Ben Elton that 'Uncool people never hurt anybody—all they do is collect stamps, read science-fiction books and stand on the end of railway platforms staring at trains'.

That well-known railway enthusiast, the Revd W. Awdry, thought that 'Railways and the Church have their critics, but both are the best ways of getting a man to his ultimate destination', and both topics are covered here, along with such competing attractions as **Air Travel** and **Crime**. Crime, of course, means breaking **Laws**, and T. H. White offers a stark choice: 'Everything not forbidden is compulsory'. At **Cinema**, Frank Capra has a more relaxed attitude: 'There are no rules in filmmaking. Only sins. And the cardinal sin is dullness'. When it comes to boredom, Julie Burchill has a poor opinion of 'relationship', but Michael Heseltine is in favour of interaction: 'You can't wield a handbag from an empty chair'.

What makes a quotation? Tony Benn thinks that it is 'what a speaker wants to say—unlike a soundbite which is all that an interviewer allows you to say'. But, as the March Hare pointed out to Alice, meaning what you say is not the same as saying what you mean, and some words may come back to haunt their author—one thinks of Jonathan Aitken and the 'simple sword of truth and the trusty shield of British fair play'. Trials often bring out unintentionally memorable remarks: Christine Keeler's recent comment on Monica Lewinsky links the 1960s scandal which produced Mandy Rice-Davies' immortal 'He would, wouldn't he?' with Bill Clinton's 1990s reflection on the meaning of 'is'.

Where further information may be necessary to an understanding of the context of a remark this has been added, and a brief source is given for each quotation, but such supplementary material has been kept to a minimum. After all, while one can agree with

Chesterton that 'There is no such thing on earth as an uninteresting subject; the only thing that can exist is an uninterested person', Quentin Tarantino undoubtedly has a valid point 'That was a little bit more information than I needed to know'.

Although the main use of this book is to suggest quotations on a particular subject, it is also possible to trace quotations by an individual. The author index includes a short description of each author, and a brief line from each of their quotations, together with an indication of which theme will give the full text. The index gives a flavour of the range and variety of the book, offering '19th century beer bottles' (Loren Eiseley), '87% of all mosquitoes' (Jeremy Clarkson), and '246 varieties of cheese' (Charles de Gaulle). Richard Nixon talks of 'whitewash at the White House' and Joseph Heller of what is 'as good as *Catch-22*'. You can find out what Tony Blair has to say about 'sex and sleaze', Elizabeth II's views on 'surfing the Net', and why Maureen Lipman thinks 'Awards are like piles'.

The Japanese monk Hakuin said 'If someone claps his hands a sound arises. Listen to the sound of the single hand'. This book would not have been possible without the contributions of many people, and I should like to thank them all. As Chinua Achebe tells us, 'The world is like a Mask dancing. If you want to see it well you do not stand in one place'. The authors of the quotations included here stand in many places, and I hope that the variety and contrast of their viewpoints mean that anyone can find a quotation to agree—or indeed disagree—with on most subjects.

SUSAN RATCLIFFE

List of themes

Ability

....

see also **Achievement**

1 Prisoner, God has given you good abilities, instead of which you go about the country stealing ducks.
   William Arabin 1773–1841: Frederick Pollock *Essays in the Law* (1922); sometimes attributed to a Revd Mr Alderson

2 If a man write a better book, preach a better sermon, or make a better mouse-trap than his neighbour, tho' he build his house in the woods, the world will make a beaten path to his door.
   Ralph Waldo Emerson 1803–82: attributed

3 This very remarkable man
   Commends a most practical plan:
   You can do what you want
   If you don't think you can't,
   So don't think you can't think you can.
   Charles Inge 1868–1957: 'On Monsieur Coué' (1928); cf. **Medicine 4**

4 I'm usually called a jack of all trades by people who are scarcely jacks of one.
   Jonathan Miller 1934– : in *Daily Telegraph* 24 December 1988

5 *Non omnia possumus omnes.*
   We can't all do everything.
   Virgil 70–19 BC: *Eclogues*

Absence

....

see also **Meeting, Parting**

1 When I came back to Dublin, I was courtmartialled in my absence and sentenced to death in my absence, so I said they could shoot me in my absence.
   Brendan Behan 1923–64: *Hostage* (1958)

2 The heart may think it knows better: the senses know that absence blots people out. We have really no absent friends.
   Elizabeth Bowen 1899–1973: *Death of the Heart* (1938)

3 *Partir c'est mourir un peu.*
   To go away is to die a little.
   Edmond Haraucourt 1856–1941: 'Rondel de l'Adieu' (1891)

4 I wish you could invent some means to make me at all happy without you. Every hour I am more and more concentrated in you; every thing else tastes like chaff in my mouth.
   John Keats 1795–1821: letter to Fanny Brawne, August 1820

5 Absence diminishes commonplace passions and increases great ones, as the wind extinguishes candles and kindles fire.
   Duc de la Rochefoucauld 1613–80: *Maximes* (1678)

6 The more he looked inside the more Piglet wasn't there.
   A. A. Milne 1882–1956: *The House at Pooh Corner* (1928)

7 Most of what matters in your life takes place in your absence.
   Salman Rushdie 1947– : *Midnight's Children* (1981)

8 I am reduced to a thing that wants Virginia.
   Vita Sackville-West 1892–1962: letter to Virginia Woolf, 21 January 1926

Achievement

....

see also **Ability, Ambition, Effort, Greatness, Success**

1 That's one small step for man, one giant leap for mankind.
   ■ *stepping onto the moon*
   Neil Armstrong 1930– : in *New York Times* 21 July 1969; interference in the transmission obliterated 'a' between 'for' and 'man'

2 The desire accomplished is sweet to the soul.
   Bible: Proverbs

3 When people are put into positions slightly above what they would expect, they're apt to excel.
   Richard Branson 1950– : in *Success* November 1992

4 That low man seeks a little thing to
  do,
  Sees it and does it:
  This high man, with a great thing to
  pursue,
  Dies ere he knows it.
  That low man goes on adding one to
  one,
  His hundred's soon hit:
  This high man, aiming at a million,
  Misses an unit.

  Robert Browning 1812–89: 'A Grammarian's
  Funeral' (1855)

5 Here is the answer which I will give to
  President Roosevelt . . . Give us the
  tools and we will finish the job.

  Winston Churchill 1874–1965: radio broadcast,
  9 February 1941

6 None climbs so high as he who knows
  not whither he is going.

  Oliver Cromwell 1599–1658: attributed

7 The trouble with fulfilling your
  ambitions is you think you will be
  transformed into some sort of
  archangel and you're not. You still
  have to wash your socks.

  Louis de Bernières 1954– : in *Independent*
  14 February 1999

8 I feel for eight minutes on screen, I
  should only get a little bit of him.

  ■ *accepting an Oscar for her role as Queen
  Elizabeth in* Shakespeare in Love
  Judi Dench 1934– : at the Academy Awards,
  Los Angeles, 21 March 1999

9 The distance is nothing; it is only the
  first step that is difficult.

  ■ *commenting on the legend that St Denis,
  carrying his head in his hands, walked two
  leagues*
  Mme Du Deffand 1697–1780: letter to Jean Le
  Rond d'Alembert, 7 July 1763

10 Seriously, though, he's doing a grand
  job!

  David Frost 1939– : catch-phrase in 'That
  Was The Week That Was', on BBC
  Television, 1962–3

11 Just as Oliver Cromwell aimed to
  bring about the kingdom of God on
  earth and founded the British Empire,

so Bunyan wanted the millennium
  and got the novel.

  Christopher Hill 1912– : *A Turbulent,
  Seditious, and Factious People: John Bunyan
  and his Church, 1628-1688* (1988)

12 Those who believe that they are
  exclusively in the right are generally
  those who achieve something.

  Aldous Huxley 1894–1963: *Proper Studies*
  (1927) 'Note on Dogma'

13 He has, indeed, done it very well; but
  it is a foolish thing well done.

  ■ *on Goldsmith's apology in the* London
  Chronicle *for assaulting Thomas Evans*
  Samuel Johnson 1709–84: James Boswell *Life
  of Johnson* (1791) 3 April 1773

14 I would much rather be known as the
  mother of a great son than the author
  of a great book or the painter of a
  great masterpiece.

  Rose Kennedy 1890–1995: attributed

15 It is sobering to consider that when
  Mozart was my age he had already
  been dead for a year.

  Tom Lehrer 1928– : attributed

16 Think nothing done while aught
  remains to do.

  Samuel Rogers 1763–1855: 'Human Life'
  (1819)

17 There are two tragedies in life. One is
  not to get your heart's desire. The
  other is to get it.

  George Bernard Shaw 1856–1950: *Man and
  Superman* (1903)

Acting

see also **Actors**, **The Cinema**, **Films**,
Shakespeare, **The Theatre**

1 When I read 'Be real, don't get caught
  acting,' I thought, 'How the hell do
  you do that?'

  Billy Connolly 1942– : John Miller *Judi
  Dench: With a Crack in Her Voice* (1998)

2 Just say the lines and don't trip over
  the furniture.

  ■ *advice on acting*
  Noël Coward 1899–1973: D. Richards *The Wit
  of Noël Coward* (1968)

3 'Playing our parts.' Yes, we all have to do that and from childhood on, I have found that my own character has been much harder to play worthily and far harder at times to comprehend than any of the roles I have portrayed.

   Bette Davis 1908–89: in *New York Herald Tribune* 22 July 1956

4 Acting is a masochistic form of exhibitionism. It is not quite the occupation of an adult.

   Laurence Olivier 1907–89: in *Time* 3 July 1978

5 Acting is pretending to be someone else.

   Anna Paquin 1982– : in *Guardian* 24 January 1997

6 Acting is merely the art of keeping a large group of people from coughing.

   Ralph Richardson 1902–83: in *New York Herald Tribune* 19 May 1946

7 Be not too tame neither, but let your own discretion be your tutor: suit the action to the word, the word to the action; with this special observance, that you o'erstep not the modesty of nature; for anything so overdone is from the purpose of playing, whose end, both at the first and now, was and is, to hold, as 'twere, the mirror up to nature.

   William Shakespeare 1564–1616: *Hamlet* (1601)

8 They say an actor is only as good as his parts. Well, my parts have done me pretty well, darling.

   Barbara Windsor 1937– : in *The Times* 13 February 1999

Action

see also **Idleness, Words and Deeds**

1 Under conditions of tyranny it is far easier to act than to think.

   Hannah Arendt 1906–75: W. H. Auden *A Certain World* (1970)

2 But men must know, that in this theatre of man's life it is reserved only for God and angels to be lookers on.

   Francis Bacon 1561–1626: *The Advancement of Learning* (1605)

3 Enough of talking—it is time now to do.

   ■ *taking office as Prime Minister*
   Tony Blair 1953– : on the steps of 10 Downing Street, 2 May 1997

4 My parents brought me up with this philosophy; you must *do* things—you mustn't watch what other people are doing; you mustn't listen to what other people are doing.

   Richard Branson 1950– : in *Vanity Fair* May 1992

5 The world can only be grasped by action, not by contemplation . . . The hand is the cutting edge of the mind.

   Jacob Bronowski 1908–74: *The Ascent of Man* (1973)

6 It is vain to say that human beings ought to be satisfied with tranquillity: they must have action; and they will make it if they cannot find it.

   Charlotte Brontë 1816–55: *Jane Eyre* (1847)

7 Action is consolatory. It is the enemy of thought and the friend of flattering illusions.

   Joseph Conrad 1857–1924: *Nostromo* (1904)

8 You have sat too long here for any good you have been doing. Depart, I say, and let us have done with you. In the name of God, go!

   ■ *addressing the Rump Parliament, 20 April 1653; quoted by Leo Amery to Neville Chamberlain in the House of Commons, 7 May 1940*
   Oliver Cromwell 1599–1658: oral tradition

9 Gentlemen, I think it is about time we 'pulled our fingers out' . . . If we want to be more prosperous we've simply got to get down to it and work for it. The rest of the world does not owe us a living.

   Prince Philip, Duke of Edinburgh 1921– : speech in London, 17 October 1961

10 If it were done when 'tis done, then 'twere well
It were done quickly.

   William Shakespeare 1564–1616: *Macbeth* (1606)

Actors
....
see also **Acting, The Cinema, The Theatre**

1 How different, how very different
from the home life of our own dear
Queen!

■ *comment overheard at a performance of
Cleopatra by Sarah Bernhardt*
Anonymous: Irvin S. Cobb *A Laugh a Day*
(1924); probably apocryphal

2 For an actress to be a success, she
must have the face of a Venus, the
brains of a Minerva, the grace of
Terpsichore, the memory of a
Macaulay, the figure of Juno, and the
hide of a rhinoceros.

Ethel Barrymore 1879–1959: George Jean
Nathan *The Theatre in the Fifties* (1953)

3 Don't put your daughter on the stage,
Mrs Worthington.

Noël Coward 1899–1973: 'Mrs Worthington'
(1935 song)

4 Garbo's visage had a kind of
emptiness into which anything could
be projected—nothing can be read
into Bardot's face.

Simone de Beauvoir 1908–86: *Brigitte Bardot
and the Lolita Syndrome* (1959)

5 It was better in the old days when the
public didn't know so much about
actors. There was a wonderful
mystery about them.

Judi Dench 1934– : in *Radio Times* 11 April
1998

6 Is it Colman's smile
That makes life worth while
Or Crawford's significant form?
Is it Lombard's lips
Or Mae West's hips
That carry you through the storm?

Gavin Ewart 1916–95: 'Verse from an Opera'
(1939)

7 An actor is a kind of a guy who if you
ain't talking about him ain't listening.

George Glass 1910–84: Bob Thomas *Brando*
(1973); often quoted by Marlon Brando, 1956
onwards

8 Actors are cattle.

Alfred Hitchcock 1899–1980: in *Saturday
Evening Post* 22 May 1943

9 I have pale blue eyes and I was
receding in my late twenties. And if
you look like this and you're twenty-
eight, you play rapists.

Patrick Malahide 1945– : in *Daily Telegraph*
20 July 1996

10 When you do Shakespeare they think
you must be intelligent because they
think you understand what you're
saying.

Helen Mirren 1945– : interviewed on *Ruby
Wax Meets . . .* , 1997

11 She ran the whole gamut of the
emotions from A to B.

■ *of Katharine Hepburn at a Broadway first
night, 1933*
Dorothy Parker 1893–1967: attributed

12 There are times when Richard Gere
has the warm effect of a wind tunnel
at dawn, waiting for work, all sheen,
inner curve, and posed emptiness.

David Thomson 1941– : *A Biographical
Dictionary of Film* (1994)

13 Ladies, just a little more virginity, if
you don't mind.

■ *to a motley collection of women, assembled to
play ladies-in-waiting to a queen*
Herbert Beerbohm Tree 1852–1917: Alexander
Woollcott *Shouts and Murmurs* (1923)

Administration
....
see also **Bureaucracy, The Civil Service,
Committees**

1 A memorandum is written not to
inform the reader but to protect the
writer.

Dean Acheson 1893–1971: in *Wall Street
Journal* 8 September 1977

2 I have in general no very exalted
opinion of the virtue of paper
government.

Edmund Burke 1729–97: *On Conciliation with
America* (1775)

3 Thank heavens we do not get all of the
government that we are made to pay
for.

Milton Friedman 1912– : quoted in the House
of Lords, 24 November 1994

4 *when his secretary suggested throwing away out-of-date files:*

A good idea, only be sure to make a copy of everything before getting rid of it.

Sam Goldwyn 1882–1974: Michael Freedland *The Goldwyn Touch* (1986)

5 Let's find out what everyone is doing, And then stop everyone from doing it.

A. P. Herbert 1890–1971: 'Let's Stop Somebody from Doing Something!' (1930)

6 For forms of government let fools contest;
Whate'er is best administered is best.

Alexander Pope 1688–1744: *An Essay on Man* Epistle 3 (1733)

7 Are you labouring under the impression that I read these memoranda of yours? I can't even lift them.

Franklin D. Roosevelt 1882–1945: J. K. Galbraith *Ambassador's Journal* (1969)

8 If any man will draw up his case, and put his name at the foot of the first page, I will give him an immediate reply. Where he compels me to turn over the sheet, he must wait my leisure.

■ *on appeals made by officers to the Navy Board*
Lord Sandwich 1718–92: N. W. Wraxall *Memoirs* (1884)

Adversity

see also **Misfortunes**, **Suffering**

1 Adversity is sometimes hard upon a man; but for one man who can stand prosperity, there are a hundred that will stand adversity.

Thomas Carlyle 1795–1881: *On Heroes, Hero-Worship, and the Heroic* (1841)

2 But there, everything has its drawbacks, as the man said when his mother-in-law died, and they came down upon him for the funeral expenses.

Jerome K. Jerome 1859–1927: *Three Men in a Boat* (1889)

3 A woman is like a teabag—only in hot water do you realise how strong she is.

Nancy Reagan 1923– : in *Observer* 29 March 1981

4 Sweet are the uses of adversity, Which like the toad, ugly and venomous,
Wears yet a precious jewel in his head.

William Shakespeare 1564–1616: *As You Like It* (1599)

5 By trying we can easily learn to endure adversity. Another man's, I mean.

Mark Twain 1835–1910: *Following the Equator* (1897)

6 The heart *prefers* to move against the grain of circumstance; perversity is the soul's very life.

John Updike 1932– : *Assorted Prose* (1965) 'More Love in the Western World'

Advertising

1 The cheap contractions and revised spellings of the advertising world which have made the beauty of the written word almost unrecognizable—surely any society that permits the substitution of 'kwik' for 'quick' and 'e.z.' for 'easy' does not deserve Shakespeare, Eliot or Michener.

Russell Baker 1925– : column in *New York Times*; Ned Sherrin *Cutting Edge* (1984)

2 A good poster is a visual telegram.

A. M. Cassandre 1901–68: attributed

3 You can tell the ideals of a nation by its advertisements.

Norman Douglas 1868–1952: *South Wind* (1917)

4 It is not necessary to advertise food to hungry people, fuel to cold people, or houses to the homeless.

J. K. Galbraith 1908– : *American Capitalism* (1952)

5 It is far easier to write ten passably effective sonnets, good enough to take in the not too enquiring critic, than one effective advertisement that will take in a few thousand of the uncritical buying public.

Aldous Huxley 1894–1963: *On the Margin* (1923) 'Advertisement'

6 Promise, large promise, is the soul of an advertisement.

Samuel Johnson 1709–84: in *The Idler* 20 January 1759

7 Society drives people crazy with lust and calls it advertising.

John Lahr 1941– : in *Guardian* 2 August 1989

8 Advertising may be described as the science of arresting human intelligence long enough to get money from it.

Stephen Leacock 1869–1944: *Garden of Folly* (1924) 'The Perfect Salesman'

9 Half the money I spend on advertising is wasted, and the trouble is I don't know which half.

Lord Leverhulme 1851–1925: David Ogilvy *Confessions of an Advertising Man* (1963)

10 Good wine needs no bush,
   And perhaps products that people really want need no hard-sell or soft-sell TV push.
   Why not?
   Look at pot.

Ogden Nash 1902–71: 'Most Doctors Recommend or Yours For Fast, Fast, Fast Relief' (1972)

11 The consumer isn't a moron; she is your wife.

David Ogilvy 1911–99: *Confessions of an Advertising Man* (1963)

12 Advertising is the rattling of a stick inside a swill bucket.

George Orwell 1903–50: attributed

13 Those who prefer their English sloppy have only themselves to thank if the advertisement writer uses his mastery of vocabulary and syntax to mislead their weak minds . . . The moral of all this . . . is that we have the kind of advertising we deserve.

Dorothy L. Sayers 1893–1957: in *Spectator* 19 November 1937

14 As advertising blather becomes the nation's normal idiom, language becomes printed noise.

George F. Will 1941– : *The Pursuit of Happiness and Other Sobering Thoughts* (1976)

Advice

1 Don't panic.

Douglas Adams 1952–2001: *Hitch Hiker's Guide to the Galaxy* (1979)

2 It was, perhaps, one of those cases in which advice is good or bad only as the event decides.

Jane Austen 1775–1817: *Persuasion* (1818)

3 Books will speak plain when counsellors blanch.

Francis Bacon 1561–1626: *Essays* (1625) 'Of Counsel'

4 Well, if you knows of a better 'ole, go to it.

Bruce Bairnsfather 1888–1959: *Fragments from France* (1915)

5 Of all the horrid, hideous notes of woe,
   Sadder than owl-songs or the midnight blast,
   Is that portentous phrase, 'I told you so.'

Lord Byron 1788–1824: *Don Juan* (1819–24)

6 In matters of religion and matrimony I never give any advice; because I will not have anybody's torments in this world or the next laid to my charge.

Lord Chesterfield 1694–1773: letter to Arthur Charles Stanhope, 12 October 1765

7 It's the worst thing that can ever happen to you in all your life, and you've got to mind it . . . They'll come saying, 'Bear up—trust to time.' No, no; they're wrong. Mind it.

E. M. Forster 1879–1970: *The Longest Journey* (1907)

8 On Venus it is considered a loving gesture to offer advice. But on Mars it is not. Women need to remember that

Martians do not offer advice unless it is directly requested.

John Gray 1951– : *Men are from Mars, Women are from Venus* (1992)

9 Get the advice of everybody whose advice is worth having—they are very few—and then do what you think best yourself.

Charles Stewart Parnell 1846–91: Conor Cruise O'Brien *Parnell* (1957)

10 I shan't be pulling the levers there but I shall be a very good back-seat driver.

■ *on the appointment of John Major as Prime Minister*

Margaret Thatcher 1925– : in *Independent* 27 November 1990

11 The Miss Lonelyhearts are the priests of twentieth-century America.

Nathaniel West 1903–40: *Miss Lonelyhearts* (1933)

12 I always pass on good advice. It is the only thing to do with it. It is never of any use to oneself.

Oscar Wilde 1854–1900: *An Ideal Husband* (1895)

Africa

1 I am a woman and a woman of Africa. I am a daughter of Nigeria and if she is in shame, I shall stay and mourn with her in shame.

Buchi Emecheta 1944– : *Destination Biafra* (1982)

2 We are . . . a nation of dancers, singers and poets.

■ *of the Ibo people*

Olaudah Equiano c.1745–c.1797: *Narrative of the Life of Olaudah Equiano* (1789)

3 The shape of Africa resembles a revolver, and Zaire is the trigger.

Frantz Fanon 1925–61: attributed

4 Are you there . . . Africa of the millions of royal slaves, deported Africa, drifting continent, are you there? Slowly you vanish, you withdraw into the past, into the tales of castaways, colonial museums, the works of scholars.

Jean Genet 1910–86: *The Blacks* (1959)

5 Westerners have aggressive problem-solving minds; Africans experience people.

Kenneth Kaunda 1924– : attributed, 1990

6 I have dedicated my life to this struggle of the African people. I have fought against white domination, and I have fought against black domination. I have cherished the ideal of a democratic and free society in which all persons live together in harmony with equal opportunities. It is an ideal which I hope to live for, and to see realized. But my lord, if needs be, it is an ideal for which I am prepared to die.

Nelson Mandela 1918– : speech in Pretoria, 20 April 1964, which he quoted on his release in Cape Town, 11 February 1990

7 Hopeless doomed continent! Only lies flourished here. Africa was swaddled in lies—the lies of an aborted European civilisation; the lies of liberation. Nothing but lies.

Shiva Naipaul 1945–85: *North of South* (1978)

8 *Semper aliquid novi Africam adferre.*
Africa always brings [us] something new.

■ *often quoted as* 'Ex Africa semper aliquid novi [Always something new out of Africa]'

Pliny the Elder AD 23–79: *Historia Naturalis*

9 I who have cursed
The drunken officer of British rule, how choose
Between this Africa and the English tongue I love?

Derek Walcott 1930– : 'A Far Cry From Africa' (1962)

Ageing

see also **Old Age**

1 I recently turned sixty. Practically a third of my life is over.

Woody Allen 1935– : in *Observer* 10 March 1996

2 With full-span lives having become the norm, people may need to learn

how to be aged as they once had to
learn how to be adult.
Ronald Blythe 1922– : *The View in Winter*
(1979)

3 The man who works and is not bored
is never old.
Pablo Casals 1876–1973: J. Lloyd Webber (ed.)
Song of the Birds (1985)

4 Considering the alternative, it's not
too bad at all.
■ *when asked what he felt about the advancing
years on his seventy-second birthday*
Maurice Chevalier 1888–1972: Michael
Freedland *Maurice Chevalier* (1981)

5 Oh, to be seventy again!
■ *on seeing a pretty girl on his eightieth birthday*
Georges Clemenceau 1841–1929: James Agate
diary, 19 April 1938; also attributed to Oliver
Wendell Holmes Jnr.

6 The paradox of ageing is that every
generation perceives itself as
justifiably different from its
predecessor, but plans as if its
successor generation will be the same
as them.
Charles Handy 1932– : *The Empty Raincoat*
(1994)

7 You will recognize, my boy, the first
sign of old age: it is when you go out
into the streets of London and realize
for the first time how young the
policemen look.
Seymour Hicks 1871–1949: C. R. D. Pulling
They Were Singing (1952)

8 The unending problem of growing
old was not how he changed, but how
things did.
Toni Morrison 1931– : *Tar Baby* (1981)

9 Every man desires to live long; but no
man would be old.
Jonathan Swift 1667–1745: *Thoughts on
Various Subjects* (1727 ed.)

10 Do not go gentle into that good night,
Old age should burn and rave at close
of day;
Rage, rage against the dying of the
light.
Dylan Thomas 1914–53: 'Do Not Go Gentle
into that Good Night' (1952)

11 Hope I die before I get old.
Pete Townshend 1945– : 'My Generation'
(1965 song)

12 The tragedy of old age is not that one
is old, but that one is young.
Oscar Wilde 1854–1900: *The Picture of Dorian
Grey* (1891)

Aid and Development

see also **Famine**

1 Foreign aid is a system of taking
money from poor people in rich
countries and giving it to rich people
in poor countries.
Lord Bauer 1915– : attributed

2 That will make some sense out of the
nonsense of the millennium.
■ *urging cancellation of Third World debt*
Bono 1960– : in *Independent* 14 June 1999

3 Feed the world
Let them know it's Christmas time
again.
Bob Geldof 1954– and **Midge Ure** 1953– : 'Do
They Know it's Christmas?' (1984 song)

4 To help the hungry we should feed
them this year and teach them to farm
organically next. And stop
encouraging them to grow cash crops
for export instead of food for their
own nationals.
Paul Heiney: *Farming Times* (1992)

5 The most important determinant of
the technology's future is the Western
consumer, yet its potential is greatest
for tropical countries. If GM foods
become uneconomic because they are
mishandled in the first world, they
will not be developed for the third
world . . . what is needed are proper
experiments and a somewhat less
Gadarene rush hoping for instant
profits from soya beans.
■ *of genetically modified foods*
Steve Jones 1944– : in *Times Higher
Education Supplement* 27 August 1999

6 The Third World never sold a newspaper.

    Rupert Murdoch 1931– : in *Observer* 1 January 1978

7 The Third World is an artificial construction of the West—an ideological empire on which the sun is always setting.

    Shiva Naipaul 1945–85: *An Unfinished Journey* (1986)

8 It will be golden elephants next.

    ■ *suggesting that the government of Montserrat was 'talking mad money' in claiming assistance for evacuating the island*

    Clare Short 1946– : in *Observer* 24 August 1997

Aids

1 and I swear sometimes
when I put my head to his chest
I can hear the virus humming
like a refrigerator.

    Mark Doty 1953– : 'Atlantis' (1996)

2 An illness in stages, a very long flight of steps that led assuredly to death, but whose every step represented a unique apprenticeship. It was a disease that gave death time to live and its victims time to die, time to discover time, and in the end to discover life.

    Hervé Guibert 1955–91: *To the Friend who did not Save my Life* (1991)

3 Sometimes I have a terrible feeling that I am dying not from the virus, but from being untouchable.

    Amanda Heggs: in *Guardian* 12 June 1989

4 We used to say: How can we live like this? And now the question really is: How can we die like this?

    Gary Indiana: *Horse Crazy* (1989)

5 Would someone turn the lights back on please? I can hear the splash and swish of car tyres on wet tarmac outside my window, and I can hear rain rapping like fingernails on the glass, but I cannot see across the room, let alone outside, into the street.

    ■ *on his blindness in the final stages of Aids*

    Oscar Moore 1960–96: in *Guardian* 10 August 1996

6 The NBA players are smart enough to know you get the virus from unprotected sex, and we're not going to have unprotected sex on the basketball court.

    ■ *on the return of Earvin 'Magic' Johnson, who is HIV-positive*

    Rony Seikaly: in *San Francisco Chronicle* 8 February 1996

7 Societies need to have one illness which becomes identified with evil, and attaches blame to its 'victims'.

    Susan Sontag 1933– : *AIDS and its Metaphors* (1989)

8 The Aids epidemic has rolled back a big rotting log and revealed all the squirming life underneath it, since it involves, all at once, the main themes of our existence: sex, death, power, money, love, hate, disease and panic. No American phenomenon has been so compelling since the Vietnam War.

    Edmund White 1940– : *States of Desire: Travels in Gay America* (afterword to 1986 edition)

The Air Force

1 The bomber will always get through. The only defence is in offence, which means that you have to kill more women and children more quickly than the enemy if you want to save yourselves.

    Stanley Baldwin 1867–1947: speech, House of Commons, 10 November 1932

2 Never in the field of human conflict was so much owed by so many to so few.

    ■ *on the skill and courage of British airmen*

    Winston Churchill 1874–1965: speech, House of Commons, 20 August 1940

3 In bombers named for girls, we burned

The cities we had learned about in
  school—
Till our lives wore out; our bodies lay
  among
The people we had killed and never
  seen.
When we lasted long enough they
  gave us medals;
When we died they said, 'Our
  casualties were low.'
  Randall Jarrell 1914–65: 'Losses' (1963)

4 Nor law, nor duty bade me fight,
Nor public men, nor cheering crowds,
A lonely impulse of delight
Drove to this tumult in the clouds;
I balanced all, brought all to mind,
The years to come seemed waste of
  breath,
A waste of breath the years behind
In balance with this life, this death.
  W. B. Yeats 1865–1939: 'An Irish Airman
  Foresees his Death' (1919)

Air Travel

1 Had I been a man I might have
explored the Poles, or climbed Mount
Everest, but as it was, my spirit found
outlet in the air.
  Amy Johnson 1903–41: Margot Asquith (ed.)
  Myself When Young (1938)

2 I feel about airplanes the way I feel
about diets. It seems to me that they
are wonderful things for other people
to go on.
  Jean Kerr 1923–2003: *The Snake Has All the
  Lines* (1958)

3 Oh! I have slipped the surly bonds of
  earth
And danced the skies on laughter-
  silvered wings; . . .
And, while with silent lifting mind
  I've trod
The high, untrespassed sanctity of
  space,
Put out my hand and touched the face
  of God.
  John Gillespie Magee 1922–41: 'High Flight'
  (1943)

4 I did not fully understand the dread
term 'terminal illness' until I saw
Heathrow for myself.
  Dennis Potter 1935–94: in *Sunday Times*
  4 June 1978

5 The Devil himself had probably re-
designed Hell in the light of
information he had gained from
observing airport layouts.
  Anthony Price 1928– : *The Memory Trap*
  (1989)

6 Anything that is white is sweet.
Anything that is brown is meat.
Anything that is grey, don't eat.
  ■ *on airline food*
  Stephen Sondheim 1930– : 'Do I Hear a
  Waltz?' (1965 song)

7 There are only two emotions in a
plane: boredom and terror.
  Orson Welles 1915–85: interview in *The Times*
  6 May 1985

Alcohol

see also **Drunkenness**, **Teetotalism**

1 The light did him harm, but not as
much as looking at things did; he
resolved, having done it once, never to
move his eyeballs again. A dusty
thudding in his head made the scene
before him beat like a pulse. His
mouth had been used as a latrine by
some small creature of the night, and
then as its mausoleum.
  Kingsley Amis 1922–95: *Lucky Jim* (1953)

2 Let's get out of these wet clothes and
into a dry Martini.
  Anonymous: line coined in the 1920s by
  Robert Benchley's press agent and adopted
  by Mae West in *Every Day's a Holiday*
  (1937 film)

3 Freedom and Whisky gang thegither!
  Robert Burns 1759–96: 'The Author's Earnest
  Cry and Prayer' (1786)

4 Alcohol is like love: the first kiss is
magic, the second is intimate, the
third is routine. After that you just
take the girl's clothes off.
  Raymond Chandler 1888–1959: *The Long
  Good-Bye* (1953)

5 I have taken more out of alcohol than
alcohol has taken out of me.

Winston Churchill 1874–1965: Quentin
Reynolds *By Quentin Reynolds* (1964)

6 A man shouldn't fool with booze until
he's fifty; then he's a damn fool if he
doesn't.

William Faulkner 1897–1962: James M. Webb
and A. Wigfall Green *William Faulkner of
Oxford* (1965)

7 Some weasel took the cork out of my
lunch.

W. C. Fields 1880–1946: *You Can't Cheat an
Honest Man* (1939 film)

8 A medium Vodka dry Martini—with
a slice of lemon peel. Shaken and not
stirred.

Ian Fleming 1908–64: *Dr No* (1958)

9 And malt does more than Milton can
To justify God's ways to man.
Ale, man, ale's the stuff to drink
For fellows whom it hurts to think.

A. E. Housman 1859–1936: *A Shropshire Lad*
(1896); see **Writing** 26

10 We drink one another's healths, and
spoil our own.

Jerome K. Jerome 1859–1927: *Idle Thoughts of
an Idle Fellow* (1886)

11 Claret is the liquor for boys; port, for
men; but he who aspires to be a hero
(smiling) must drink brandy.

Samuel Johnson 1709–84: James Boswell *Life
of Johnson* (1791) 7 April 1779

12 O for a beaker full of the warm South,
Full of the true, the blushful
Hippocrene,
With beaded bubbles winking at the
brim,
And purple-stainèd mouth.

John Keats 1795–1821: 'Ode to a Nightingale'
(1820)

13 I've made it a rule never to drink by
daylight and never to refuse a drink
after dark.

H. L. Mencken 1880–1956: in *New York Post*
18 September 1945

14 A good general rule is to state that the
bouquet is better than the taste, and
vice versa.

■ *on wine-tasting*
Stephen Potter 1900–69: *One-Upmanship*
(1952)

15 Wine is for drinking and enjoying,
talking about it is deadly dull.

Jancis Robinson 1950– : in *Daily Mail*
19 October 1995

16 Fifteen men on the dead man's chest
Yo-ho-ho, and a bottle of rum!
Drink and the devil had done for the
rest—
Yo-ho-ho, and a bottle of rum!

Robert Louis Stevenson 1850–94: *Treasure
Island* (1883)

17 It's a naïve domestic Burgundy
without any breeding, but I think
you'll be amused by its presumption.

James Thurber 1894–1961: cartoon caption in
New Yorker 27 March 1937

18 A drink that tasted, she thought, like
weak vinegar mixed with a packet of
pins.

■ *of champagne*
H. G. Wells 1866–1946: *Joan and Peter* (1918)

Alzheimer's Disease

1 It is rather like falling from stair to
stair in a series of bumps.

■ *on his wife Iris Murdoch's progressive loss of
memory from Alzheimer's disease*
John Bayley 1925– : in an interview, *Daily
Telegraph* 8 February 1997

2 She is not sailing into the dark: the
voyage is over, and under the dark
escort of Alzheimer's she has arrived
somewhere. So have I.

John Bayley 1925– : *Iris: A memoir of Iris
Murdoch* (1998)

3 I now begin the journey that will lead
me into the sunset of my life.

■ *statement to the American people revealing
that he had Alzheimer's disease, 1994*
Ronald Reagan 1911– : in *Daily Telegraph*
5 January 1995

Ambition

....

see also **Achievement**, **Success**

1 *Aut Caesar, aut nihil.*
Caesar or nothing.
Cesare Borgia 1476–1507: motto inscribed on his sword

2 Ah, but a man's reach should exceed his grasp,
Or what's a heaven for?
Robert Browning 1812–89: 'Andrea del Sarto' (1855)

3 Well is it known that ambition can creep as well as soar.
Edmund Burke 1729–97: *Third Letter . . . on the Proposals for Peace with the Regicide Directory* (1797)

4 [I] had rather be first in a village than second at Rome.
Julius Caesar 100–44 BC: Plutarch *Parallel Lives*

5 I had rather be right than be President.
Henry Clay 1777–1852: S. W. McCall *Life of Thomas Brackett Reed* (1914)

6 All ambitions are lawful except those which climb upwards on the miseries or credulities of mankind.
Joseph Conrad 1857–1924: *Some Reminiscences* (1912)

7 Do you sincerely want to be rich?
■ *stock question to salesmen*
Bernard Cornfeld 1927– : Charles Raw et al. *Do You Sincerely Want to be Rich?* (1971)

8 At the age of six I wanted to be a cook. At seven I wanted to be Napoleon. And my ambition has been growing steadily ever since.
Salvador Dali 1904–89: *The Secret Life of Salvador Dali* (1948)

9 He is loyal to his own career but only incidentally to anything or anyone else.
■ *of Richard Crossman*
Hugh Dalton 1887–1962: diary, 17 September 1941

10 Wish to be like Tina Brown, though not, obviously, quite so hardworking.
Helen Fielding 1958– : *Bridget Jones's Diary* (1996)

11 Remember that there is not one of you who does not carry in his cartridge-pouch the marshal's baton of the duke of Reggio; it is up to you to bring it forth.
Louis XVIII 1755–1824: speech to Saint-Cyr cadets, 9 August 1819

12 Better to reign in hell, than serve in heaven.
John Milton 1608–74: *Paradise Lost* (1667)

13 The worst fault of the working classes is telling their children they're not going to succeed, saying: 'There is life, but it's not for you.'
John Mortimer 1923– : in *Daily Mail* 31 May 1988

14 Before this time to-morrow I shall have gained a peerage, or Westminster Abbey.
Horatio, Lord Nelson 1758–1805: before the battle of the Nile, 1 August 1798

15 It is better to be a has-been than a never-was.
Cecil Parkinson 1932– : in *Guardian* 29 June 1990

16 Fain would I climb, yet fear I to fall.
■ *line written on a window-pane; Queen Elizabeth I (1533–1603) replied 'If thy heart fails thee, climb not at all'*
Walter Ralegh *c.*1552–1618: Thomas Fuller *Worthies of England* (1662)

17 Yo I'll tell you what I want, what I really really want
so tell me what you want, what you really really want.
The Spice Girls: 'Wannabe' (1996 song, with Matthew Rowbottom and Richard Stannard)

18 Cromwell, I charge thee, fling away ambition:
By that sin fell the angels.
William Shakespeare 1564–1616: *Henry VIII* (1613)

19 There is always room at the top.
Daniel Webster 1782–1852: attributed

American Cities and States

see also **United States**

1 California is a fine place to live—if you happen to be an orange.
Fred Allen 1894–1956: *American Magazine* December 1945

2 A Boston man is the east wind made flesh.
Thomas Gold Appleton 1812–84: attributed

3 New York makes one think of the collapse of civilization, about Sodom and Gomorrah, the end of the world. The end wouldn't come as a surprise here. Many people already bank on it.
Saul Bellow 1915– : *Mr Sammler's Planet* (1970)

4 The state with the prettiest name, the state that floats in brackish water, held together by mangrove roots.
Elizabeth Bishop 1911–79: 'Florida' (1946)

5 And this is good old Boston,
The home of the bean and the cod,
Where the Lowells talk to the Cabots
And the Cabots talk only to God.
John Collins Bossidy 1860–1928: verse spoken at Holy Cross College alumni dinner in Boston, Massachusetts, 1910

6 I had forgotten just how flat and empty it is. Stand on two phone books almost anywhere in Iowa and you get a view.
■ *of middle America*
Bill Bryson 1951– : *The Lost Continent* (1989)

7 A big hard-boiled city with no more personality than a paper cup.
■ *of Los Angeles*
Raymond Chandler 1888–1959: *The Little Sister* (1949)

8 New York, New York,—a helluva town,
The Bronx is up but the Battery's down.
Betty Comden 1919– and **Adolph Green** 1915– : 'New York, New York' (1945 song)

9 I left my heart in San Francisco
High on a hill it calls to me.

To be where little cable cars climb half-way to the stars,
The morning fog may chill the air—
I don't care!
Douglas Cross: 'I Left My Heart in San Francisco' (1954 song)

10 Last week, I went to Philadelphia, but it was closed.
W. C. Fields 1880–1946: Richard J. Anobile *Godfrey Daniels* (1975)

11 Washington is a city of southern efficiency and northern charm.
John F. Kennedy 1917–63: Arthur M. Schlesinger Jr. *A Thousand Days* (1965)

12 This is Red Hook, not Sicily . . . This is the gullet of New York swallowing the tonnage of the world.
Arthur Miller 1915– : *A View from the Bridge* (1955)

13 A trip through a sewer in a glass-bottomed boat.
■ *of Hollywood*
Wilson Mizner 1876–1933: Alva Johnston *The Legendary Mizners* (1953)

14 Hog Butcher for the World,
Tool Maker, Stacker of Wheat,
Player with Railroads and the
　Nation's Freight Handler;
Stormy, husky, brawling,
City of the Big Shoulders.
Carl Sandburg 1878–1967: 'Chicago' (1916)

American Civil War

1 Give them the cold steel, boys!
Lewis Addison Armistead 1817–63: attributed during the American Civil War, 1863

2 There is Jackson with his Virginians, standing like a stone wall. Let us determine to die here, and we will conquer.
■ *referring to General T. J. ('Stonewall') Jackson*
Barnard Elliott Bee 1823–61: at the battle of Bull Run, 21 July 1861

3 All quiet along the Potomac to-night,
No sound save the rush of the river,
While soft falls the dew on the face of the dead—

The picket's off duty forever.
Ethel Lynn Beers 1827–79: 'The Picket Guard' (1861); the first line is also attributed to George B. McClellan (1826–85)

4 Hold out. Relief is coming.
■ *usually quoted as 'Hold the fort! I am coming!'*
William Sherman 1820–91: flag signal from Kennesaw Mountain to General John Murray Corse at Allatoona Pass, 5 October 1864

American War of Independence

1 What a glorious morning is this.
■ *traditionally quoted 'What a glorious morning for America'*
Samuel Adams 1722–1803: on hearing gunfire at Lexington, 19 April 1775

2 Men, you are all marksmen—don't one of you fire until you see the white of their eyes.
Israel Putnam 1718–90: at Bunker Hill, 1775; also attributed to William Prescott, 1726–95

3 We beat them to-day or Molly Stark's a widow.
John Stark 1728–1822: before the battle of Bennington, 16 August 1777

Anger

1 A soft answer turneth away wrath.
Bible: Proverbs

2 The tygers of wrath are wiser than the horses of instruction.
William Blake 1757–1827: *The Marriage of Heaven and Hell* (1790–3)

3 We boil at different degrees.
Ralph Waldo Emerson 1803–82: *Society and Solitude* (1870)

4 Anger is never without an argument, but seldom with a good one.
Lord Halifax 1633–95: *Political, Moral, and Miscellaneous Thoughts and Reflections* (1750)

5 When you get angry, they tell you, count to five before you reply. Why should I count to five? It's what happens *before* you count to five which makes life interesting.
David Hare 1947– : *The Secret Rapture* (1988)

6 *Ira furor brevis est.*
Anger is a short madness.
Horace 65–8 BC: *Epistles*

7 It's my rule never to lose me temper till it would be dethrimental to keep it.
Sean O'Casey 1880–1964: *The Plough and the Stars* (1926)

8 When angry, count four; when very angry, swear.
Mark Twain 1835–1910: *Pudd'nhead Wilson* (1894)

Animal Rights

1 It takes 40 dumb animals to make a fur coat, but only one to wear it.
Anonymous: slogan of an anti-fur campaign poster, 1980s, sometimes attributed to David Bailey

2 The question is not, Can they reason? nor, Can they talk? but, Can they suffer?
Jeremy Bentham 1748–1832: *Principles of Morals and Legislation* (1789)

3 A righteous man regardeth the life of his beast: but the tender mercies of the wicked are cruel.
Bible: Proverbs

4 A robin red breast in a cage
Puts all Heaven in a rage.
William Blake 1757–1827: 'Auguries of Innocence' (*c*.1803)

5 Animals, whom we have made our slaves, we do not like to consider our equal.
Charles Darwin 1809–82: Notebook B (1837–8)

6 If our history of bear-baiting, pit ponies and ejected Christmas puppies can honestly be called a great British love affair with animals then the average praying mantis and her husband are Darby and Joan.
Stephen Fry 1957– : *Paperweight* (1992)

7 'Twould ring the bells of Heaven
    The wildest peal for years,
    If Parson lost his senses
    And people came to theirs,
    And he and they together
    Knelt down with angry prayers
    For tamed and shabby tigers
    And dancing dogs and bears,
    And wretched, blind, pit ponies,
    And little hunted hares.
    Ralph Hodgson 1871–1962: 'Bells of Heaven'
    (1917)

8 Mankind's true moral test, its
    fundamental test (which lies deeply
    buried from view) consists of its
    attitudes towards those who are at its
    mercy: animals.
    Milan Kundera 1929– : *The Unbearable
    Lightness of Being* (1984)

9 If patenting animals is allowed it will
    mark the lowest status granted to
    animals in the history of European
    ethics.
    Andrew Linzey 1952– : Danny Penman *The
    Price of Meat* (1996)

10 Death may be inevitable but cruelty is
    not. If we must eat meat, then we
    must ensure that the animals we kill
    for our food live the best possible lives
    before they die.
    Desmond Morris 1928– : *The Animal
    Contract* (1990)

11 A creature with rights is duty-bound
    to respect the rights of others. The fox
    would be duty-bound to respect the
    right to life of the chicken, and whole
    species would be condemned out of
    hand as criminal by nature.
    Roger Scruton 1944– : *Animal Rights and
    Wrongs* (1996)

Animals

see also **Animal Rights, Birds, Cats, Dogs,
Horses**

1 The rabbit has a charming face:
    Its private life is a disgrace.
    I really dare not name to you
    The awful things that rabbits do.
    Anonymous: 'The Rabbit' (1925)

2 I'm not over-fond of animals. I am
    merely astounded by them.
    David Attenborough 1926– : in *Independent*
    14 January 1995

3 Old pond,
    leap-splash—
    a frog.
    Matsuo Basho 1644–94: translated by Lucien
    Stryk

4 When people call this beast to mind,
    They marvel more and more
    At such a little tail behind,
    So large a trunk before.
    Hilaire Belloc 1870–1953: 'The Elephant'
    (1896)

5 The Llama is a woolly sort of fleecy
    hairy goat,
    With an indolent expression and an
    undulating throat
    Like an unsuccessful literary man.
    Hilaire Belloc 1870–1953: 'The Llama' (1897)

6 Tyger Tyger, burning bright,
    In the forests of the night;
    What immortal hand or eye,
    Could frame thy fearful symmetry?
    William Blake 1757–1827: 'The Tiger' (1794)

7 A four-legged friend, a four-legged
    friend,
    He'll never let you down.
    ■ *sung by Roy Rogers about his horse Trigger*
    J. Brooks: 'A Four Legged Friend' (1952 song)

8 To my mind, the only possible pet is a
    cow. Cows love you . . . They will
    listen to your problems and never ask
    a thing in return. They will be your
    friends for ever. And when you get
    tired of them, you can kill and eat
    them. Perfect.
    Bill Bryson 1951– : *Neither Here Nor There*
    (1991)

9 All animals, except man, know that
    the principal business of life is to
    enjoy it—and they do enjoy it as
    much as man and other
    circumstances will allow.
    Samuel Butler 1835–1902: *The Way of All Flesh*
    (1903)

10   Giraffes!—a People
    Who live between the earth and skies,

Each in his lone religious steeple,
Keeping a light-house with his eyes.
Roy Campbell 1901–57: 'Dreaming Spires'
(1946)

11 With monstrous head and sickening
    cry
    And ears like errant wings,
    The devil's walking parody
    On all four-footed things.
    G. K. Chesterton 1874–1936: 'The Donkey'
    (1900)

12 I am fond of pigs. Dogs look up to us.
    Cats look down on us. Pigs treat us as
    equals.
    Winston Churchill 1874–1965: attributed

13 The giraffe, in their queer, inimitable,
    vegetative gracefulness . . . a family of
    rare, long-stemmed, speckled gigantic
    flowers slowly advancing.
    Isak Dinesen 1885–1962: *Out of Africa* (1937)

14 I hate a word like 'pets': it sounds so
    much
    Like something with no living of its
    own.
    Elizabeth Jennings 1926–2001: 'My Animals'
    (1966)

15 The turtle lives 'twixt plated decks
    Which practically conceal its sex.
    I think it clever of the turtle
    In such a fix to be so fertile.
    Ogden Nash 1902–71: 'Autres Bêtes, Autres
    Moeurs' (1931)

16 God in His wisdom made the fly
    And then forgot to tell us why.
    Ogden Nash 1902–71: 'The Fly' (1942)

17 Cats is 'dogs' and rabbits is 'dogs' and
    so's Parrats, but this 'ere 'Tortis' is a
    insect, and there ain't no charge for
    it.
    Punch: 6 March 1869

18 It is part of the pathos of a pet, that it
    always stands on the edge of the moral
    dialogue, staring from beyond an
    impassable barrier at the life which is
    now everything to it, and which yet it
    cannot comprehend.
    Roger Scruton 1944– : *Animal Rights and
    Wrongs* (1996)

19 I think I could turn and live with
    animals, they are so placid and self-
    contained,
    I stand and look at them long and
    long.
    They do not sweat and whine about
    their condition,
    They do not lie awake in the dark and
    weep for their sins,
    They do not make me sick discussing
    their duty to God,
    Not one is dissatisfied, not one is
    demented with the mania of owning
    things.
    Walt Whitman 1819–92: 'Song of Myself'
    (written 1855)

20 But I freely admit that the best of my
    fun
    I owe it to horse and hound.
    George John Whyte-Melville 1821–78: 'The
    Good Grey Mare' (1933)

21 Whales play, in an amniotic paradise.
    Their light minds shaped by
    buoyancy, unrestricted by gravity,
    Somersaulting.
    Like angels, or birds;
    Like our own lives, in the womb.
    Heathcote Williams 1941– : *Whale Nation*
    (1988)

Apology and Excuses

1 Very sorry can't come. Lie follows by
   post.
   ■ *telegraphed message to the Prince of Wales, on
   being summoned to dine at the eleventh hour*
   Lord Charles Beresford 1846–1919: Ralph
   Nevill *The World of Fashion 1837–1922* (1923)

2 Never make a defence or apology
   before you be accused.
   Charles I 1600–49: letter to Lord Wentworth,
   3 September 1636

3 As I waited I thought that there's
   nothing like a confession to make one
   look mad; and that of all confessions a
   written one is the most detrimental all
   round. Never confess! Never, never!
   Joseph Conrad 1857–1924: *Chance* (1913)

4 Never complain and never explain.
   Benjamin Disraeli 1804–81: J. Morley *Life of
   William Ewart Gladstone* (1903)

5 The most important thing a man can learn—the importance of three little words: 'I was wrong.' These words will get you much further than 'I love you.'

Charlton Heston 1924– : in *Independent* 21 July 1999

6 Never explain—your friends do not need it and your enemies will not believe you anyway.

Elbert Hubbard 1859–1915: *The Motto Book* (1907)

7 Several excuses are always less convincing than one.

Aldous Huxley 1894–1963: *Point Counter Point* (1928)

8 A man should never be ashamed to own he has been in the wrong, which is but saying, in other words, that he is wiser to-day than he was yesterday.

Alexander Pope 1688–1744: *Miscellanies* (1727) vol. 2 'Thoughts on Various Subjects'

9 It is a good rule in life never to apologize. The right sort of people do not want apologies, and the wrong sort take a mean advantage of them.

P. G. Wodehouse 1881–1975: *The Man Upstairs* (1914)

Appearance
....
see also **The Body**, **Cosmetics**, **The Face**, **Fat**

1 Though I yield to no one in my admiration for Mr Coolidge, I do wish he did not look as if he had been weaned on a pickle.

Anonymous: Alice Roosevelt Longworth *Crowded Hours* (1933)

2 Have you ever noticed, Harry, that many jewels make women either incredibly fat or incredibly thin?

J. M. Barrie 1860–1937: *The Twelve-Pound Look and Other Plays* (1921)

3 It's as large as life, and twice as natural!

Lewis Carroll 1832–98: *Through the Looking-Glass* (1872)

4 Glamour is on a life-support machine and not expected to live.

Joan Collins 1933– : in *Independent* 24 April 1999

5 Like the silver plate on a coffin.
■ *describing Robert Peel's smile*

John Philpot Curran 1750–1817: quoted by Daniel O'Connell, House of Commons, 26 February 1835

6 She may very well pass for forty-three In the dusk with a light behind her!

W. S. Gilbert 1836–1911: *Trial by Jury* (1875)

7 The photograph is not quite true to my own notion of my gentleness and sweetness of nature, but neither perhaps is my external appearance.

A. E. Housman 1859–1936: letter 12 June 1922

8 She was a gordian shape of dazzling hue,
Vermilion-spotted, golden, green, and blue;
Striped like a zebra, freckled like a pard,
Eyed like a peacock, and all crimson barred.

John Keats 1795–1821: 'Lamia' (1820)

9 The most common error made in matters of appearance is the belief that one should disdain the superficial and let the true beauty of one's soul shine through. If there are places on one's body where this is a possibility, you are not attractive—you are leaking.

Fran Lebowitz 1946– : *Metropolitan Life* (1978)

10 The Lord prefers common-looking people. That is why he makes so many of them.

Abraham Lincoln 1809–65: attributed; James Morgan *Our Presidents* (1928)

11 No power on earth, however, can abolish the merciless class distinction between those who are physically desirable and the lonely, pallid, spotted, silent, unfancied majority.

John Mortimer 1923– : *Clinging to the Wreckage* (1982)

12 Sure, deck your lower limbs in pants;
Yours are the limbs, my sweeting.

You look divine as you advance—
Have you seen yourself retreating?
Ogden Nash 1902–71: 'What's the Use?' (1940)

13 Men seldom make passes
At girls who wear glasses.
Dorothy Parker 1893–1967: 'News Item' (1937)

14 An unforgiving eye, and a damned
disinheriting countenance!
Richard Brinsley Sheridan 1751–1816: *The School for Scandal* (1777)

15 You can never be too rich or too thin.
Duchess of Windsor 1896–1986: attributed

Archaeology

1 Every woman should marry an
archaeologist because she grows
increasingly attractive to him as she
grows increasingly to resemble a ruin.
Agatha Christie 1890–1976: Russell H.
Fitzgibbon *The Agatha Christie Companion*
(1980); attributed, perhaps apocryphal

2 A man who has once looked with the
archaeological eye will never see quite
normally. He will be wounded by
what other men call trifles. It is
possible to refine the sense of time
until an old show in the grass or a pile
of nineteenth century beer bottles in
an abandoned mining town tolls in
one's head like a hall clock.
Loren Eiseley 1907–77: *The Night Country*
(1971)

3 Why read when you can pick up a
spade and find out for yourself?
Penelope Fitzgerald 1916–2000: *The Golden
Child* (1977)

4 Industrial archaeology . . . believes
that a thing that doesn't work any
more is far more interesting than a
thing that still works.
Miles Kington 1941– : *Nature Made
Ridiculously Simple* (1983)

5 Dead archaeology is the driest dust
that blows.
Mortimer Wheeler 1890–1976: Glyn Daniel *A
Short History of Archaeology* (1981)

Architecture

see also **Buildings**

1 In my experience, if you have to keep
the lavatory door shut by extending
your left leg, it's modern architecture.
Nancy Banks-Smith: in *Guardian* 20 February
1979

2 Official designs are aggressively
neuter,
The Puritan work of an eyeless
computer.
John Betjeman 1906–84: 'The Newest Bath
Guide' (1974)

3 He builded better than he knew;—
The conscious stone to beauty grew.
Ralph Waldo Emerson 1803–82: 'The Problem'
(1847)

4 Light (God's eldest daughter) is a
principal beauty in building.
Thomas Fuller 1608–61: *The Holy State and the
Profane State* (1642)

5 Architecture is the art of how to waste
space.
Philip Johnson 1906– : in *New York Times*
27 December 1964

6 A house is a machine for living in.
Le Corbusier 1887–1965: *Vers une architecture*
(1923)

7 God is in the details.
Mies van der Rohe 1886–1969: in *New York
Times* 19 August 1969

8 I am proud to be an Eskimo, but I
think we can improve on the igloo as a
permanent dwelling.
Abraham Okpik d. 1997: in *Northern Affairs
Bulletin* March 1960

9 A bicycle shed is a building; Lincoln
Cathedral is a piece of architecture.
Nearly everything that encloses space
on a scale sufficient for a human being
to move in is a building; the term
architecture applies only to buildings
designed with a view to aesthetic
appeal.
Nikolaus Pevsner 1902–83: *An Outline of
European Architecture* (1943)

10 Little boxes on the hillside . . .
And they're all made out of ticky-
tacky

And they all look just the same.

■ *on the tract houses in the hills to the south of San Francisco*
Malvina Reynolds 1900–78: 'Little Boxes' (1962 song)

11 You should be able to read a building. It should be what it does.
Richard Rogers 1933– : lecture, London, March 1990

12 When we build, let us think that we build for ever.
John Ruskin 1819–1900: *Seven Lamps of Architecture* (1849)

13 Architecture in general is frozen music.
Friedrich von Schelling 1775–1854: *Philosophie der Kunst* (1809)

14 Form follows function.
Louis Henri Sullivan 1856–1924: *The Tall Office Building Artistically Considered* (1896)

15 Less is a bore.
Robert Venturi 1925– : *Complexity and Contradiction in Architecture* (1966); cf. **Simplicity** 3

16 The physician can bury his mistakes, but the architect can only advise his client to plant vines—so they should go as far as possible from home to build their first buildings.
Frank Lloyd Wright 1867–1959: in *New York Times* 4 October 1953

Argument

see also **Compromise**, **Opinion**

1 Our disputants put me in mind of the skuttle fish, that when he is unable to extricate himself, blackens all the water about him, till he becomes invisible.
Joseph Addison 1672–1719: in *The Spectator* 5 September 1712

2 You cannot argue with someone who denies the first principles.
Anonymous: *Auctoritates Aristotelis*: a compilation of medieval propositions

3 I've never won an argument with her; and the only times I thought I had I found out the argument wasn't over yet.
Jimmy Carter 1924– : in *Reader's Digest* March 1979

4 I'll thcream and thcream and thcream till I'm thick.
■ *Violet Elizabeth's threat*
Richmal Crompton 1890–1969: *Still—William* (1925)

5 I am continually fascinated at the difficulty intelligent people have in distinguishing what is controversial from what is merely offensive.
Nora Ephron 1941– : in *Esquire* January 1976

6 Persuasion is the resource of the feeble; and the feeble can seldom persuade.
Edward Gibbon 1737–94: *The Decline and Fall of the Roman Empire* (1776–88)

7 Making noise is an effective means of opposition.
Joseph Goebbels 1897–1945: Ernest K. Bramsted *Goebbels and National Socialist Propaganda 1925–45* (1965)

8 There is no arguing with Johnson; for when his pistol misses fire, he knocks you down with the butt end of it.
Oliver Goldsmith 1730–74: James Boswell *Life of Johnson* (1791) 26 October 1769

9 Any stigma, as the old saying is, will serve to beat a dogma.
Philip Guedalla 1889–1944: *Masters and Men* (1923)

10 The concept of two people living together for 25 years without having a cross word suggests a lack of spirit only to be admired in sheep.
A. P. Herbert 1890–1971: in *News Chronicle*, 1940

11 It takes in reality only one to make a quarrel. It is useless for the sheep to pass resolutions in favour of vegetarianism, while the wolf remains of a different opinion.
William Ralph Inge 1860–1954: *Outspoken Essays: First Series* (1919) 'Patriotism'

12 I hate a fellow whom pride, or cowardice, or laziness drives into a corner, and who does nothing when he is there but sit and *growl*; let him come out as I do, and *bark*.

Samuel Johnson 1709–84: James Boswell *Life of Johnson* 10 October 1782

13 There is no good in arguing with the inevitable. The only argument available with an east wind is to put on your overcoat.

James Russell Lowell 1819–91: *Democracy and other Addresses* (1887)

14 Conflicts, like living organisms, had a natural lifespan. The trick was to know when to let them die.

Ian McEwan 1948– : *Enduring Love* (1998)

15 That happy sense of purpose people have when they are standing up for a principle they haven't really been knocked down for yet.

P. J. O'Rourke 1947– : *Give War a Chance* (1992)

16 The Catholic and the Communist are alike in assuming that an opponent cannot be both honest and intelligent.

George Orwell 1903–50: in *Polemic* January 1946

17 Who can refute a sneer?

William Paley 1743–1805: *Principles of Moral and Political Philosophy* (1785)

18 The argument of the broken window pane is the most valuable argument in modern politics.

Emmeline Pankhurst 1858–1928: George Dangerfield *The Strange Death of Liberal England* (1936)

19 'Yes, but not in the South', with slight adjustments, will do for any argument about any place, if not about any person.

Stephen Potter 1900–69: *Lifemanship* (1950)

20 My uncle Toby would never offer to answer this by any other kind of argument, than that of whistling half a dozen bars of Lillabullero.

Laurence Sterne 1713–68: *Tristram Shandy* (1759–67)

21 I maintain that two and two would continue to make four, in spite of the whine of the amateur for three, or the cry of the critic for five.

James McNeill Whistler 1834–1903: *Whistler v. Ruskin. Art and Art Critics* (1878)

22 I am not arguing with you—I am telling you.

James McNeill Whistler 1834–1903: *The Gentle Art of Making Enemies* (1890)

23 Get your tanks off my lawn, Hughie.

■ *to the trade union leader Hugh Scanlon, at Chequers in June 1969*

Harold Wilson 1916–95: Peter Jenkins *The Battle of Downing Street* (1970)

Aristocracy

see also **Class, Titles**

1 The rank is but the guinea's stamp, The man's the gowd for a' that!

Robert Burns 1759–96: 'For a' that and a' that' (1790)

2 The Stately Homes of England, How beautiful they stand, To prove the upper classes Have still the upper hand.

Noël Coward 1899–1973: 'The Stately Homes of England' (1938 song); see 5 below

3 I can trace my ancestry back to a protoplasmal primordial atomic globule. Consequently, my family pride is something in-conceivable. I can't help it. I was born sneering.

W. S. Gilbert 1836–1911: *The Mikado* (1885)

4 I am a well-known élitist. I don't even own a pair of trainers. If I did, I am sure they would be very fragrant.

Lord Gowrie 1939– : in *Independent* 24 January 1998

5 The stately homes of England, How beautiful they stand! Amidst their tall ancestral trees, O'er all the pleasant land.

Felicia Hemans 1793–1835: 'The Homes of England' (1849); cf. 2 above

6 As far as the fourteenth earl is concerned, I suppose Mr Wilson, when you come to think of it, is the fourteenth Mr Wilson.

■ *replying to Harold Wilson's remark (on Home's becoming leader of the Conservative party) that 'the whole [democratic] process has ground to a halt with a fourteenth Earl'*

Lord Home 1903–95: in *Daily Telegraph* 22 October 1963

7 I agree with you that there is a natural aristocracy among men. The grounds of this are virtue and talents.

Thomas Jefferson 1743–1826: letter to John Adams, 28 October 1813

8 I am an ancestor.

■ *reply when taunted on his lack of ancestry having been made Duke of Abrantes, 1807*

Marshal Junot 1771–1813: attributed

9 A fully-equipped duke costs as much to keep up as two Dreadnoughts; and dukes are just as great a terror and they last longer.

David Lloyd George 1863–1945: speech at Newcastle, 9 October 1909

10 An aristocracy in a republic is like a chicken whose head has been cut off: it may run about in a lively way, but in fact it is dead.

Nancy Mitford 1904–73: *Noblesse Oblige* (1956)

11 Kind hearts are more than coronets, And simple faith than Norman blood.

Alfred, Lord Tennyson 1809–92: 'Lady Clara Vere de Vere' (1842)

The Army

see also **The Air Force**, **The Navy**, **Warfare**

1 Lions led by donkeys.

■ *associated with British soldiers during the First World War*

Anonymous: attributed to Max Hoffman (1869–1927) in Alan Clark *The Donkeys* (1961); this attribution has not been traced elsewhere, and the phrase is of much earlier origin

2 O Death, where is thy sting-a-ling-a-ling,
O grave, thy victory?
The bells of Hell go ting-a-ling-a-ling For you but not for me.

Anonymous: 'For You But Not For Me' (First World War song); see **Death 4**

3 To save your world you asked this man to die:
Would this man, could he see you now, ask why?

W. H. Auden 1907–73: 'Epitaph for the Unknown Soldier' (1955)

4 *C'est magnifique, mais ce n'est pas la guerre.*
It is magnificent, but it is not war.

■ *on the charge of the Light Brigade*

Pierre Bosquet 1810–61: at Balaclava, 25 October 1854

5 For here the lover and killer are mingled
who had one body and one heart.
And death, who had the soldier singled
has done the lover mortal hurt.

Keith Douglas 1920–44: 'Vergissmeinnicht, 1943'

6 The sergeant is the army.

Dwight D. Eisenhower 1890–1969: attributed

7 Old soldiers never die,
They simply fade away.

J. Foley 1906–70: 'Old Soldiers Never Die' (1920 song); possibly a 'folk-song' from the First World War

8 Rascals, would you live for ever?

■ *to hesitant Guards at Kolin, 18 June 1757*

Frederick the Great 1712–86: attributed

9 Their shoulders held the sky suspended;
They stood, and earth's foundations stay;
What God abandoned, these defended,
And saved the sum of things for pay.

A. E. Housman 1859–1936: 'Epitaph on an Army of Mercenaries' (1922)

10 You'll get no promotion this side of the ocean,
So cheer up, my lads, Bless 'em all!
Bless 'em all! Bless 'em all! The long and the short and the tall.

Jimmy Hughes and **Frank Lake**: 'Bless 'Em All' (1940 song)

11 For it's Tommy this, an' Tommy that, an' 'Chuck him out, the brute!'

But it's 'Saviour of 'is country' when
   the guns begin to shoot.
   Rudyard Kipling 1865–1936: 'Tommy' (1892)

12 An army marches on its stomach.
   Napoleon I 1769–1821: attributed, 1816; also
   attributed to Frederick the Great

13 What passing-bells for these who die
   as cattle?
   Only the monstrous anger of the
   guns.
   Only the stuttering rifles' rapid rattle
   Can patter out their hasty orisons.
   Wilfred Owen 1893–1918: 'Anthem for
   Doomed Youth' (written 1917)

14 I saw him stab
   And stab again
   A well-killed Boche.
   This is the happy warrior,
   This is he . . .
   Herbert Read 1893–1968: 'The Happy
   Warrior' (1919)

15 Today we have naming of parts.
      Yesterday,
   We had daily cleaning. And tomorrow
      morning,
   We shall have what to do after firing.
      But today,
   Today we have naming of parts.
   Henry Reed 1914–86: 'Lessons of the War: 1,
   Naming of Parts' (1946)

16 If these gentlemen had their way, they
   would soon be asking me to defend
   the moon against a possible attack
   from Mars.
   ■ *of his senior military advisers, and their
   tendency to see threats which did not exist*
   Lord Salisbury 1830–1903: Robert Taylor *Lord
   Salisbury* (1975)

17 If I were fierce, and bald, and short of
      breath,
   I'd live with scarlet Majors at the Base,
   And speed glum heroes up the line to
      death.
   Siegfried Sassoon 1886–1967: 'Base Details'
   (1918)

18 Who will remember, passing through
   this Gate,
   The unheroic Dead who fed the guns?
   Who shall absolve the foulness of
   their fate,—

Those doomed, conscripted,
   unvictorious ones?
   Siegfried Sassoon 1886–1967: 'On Passing the
   New Menin Gate' (1928)

19 I don't consider myself dovish and I
   certainly don't consider myself
   hawkish. Maybe I would describe
   myself as owlish—that is, wise
   enough to understand that you want
   to do everything possible to avoid
   war.
   H. Norman Schwarzkopf III 1934– : in *New
   York Times* 28 January 1991

20 You can always tell an old soldier by
   the inside of his holsters and cartridge
   boxes. The young ones carry pistols
   and cartridges; the old ones, grub.
   George Bernard Shaw 1856–1950: *Arms and
   the Man* (1898)

21 Theirs not to make reply,
   Theirs not to reason why,
   Theirs but to do and die:
   Into the valley of Death
   Rode the six hundred.
   Alfred, Lord Tennyson 1809–92: 'The Charge
   of the Light Brigade' (1854)

22 I didn't fire him because he was a
   dumb son of a bitch, although he was,
   but that's not against the law for
   generals. If it was, half to three-
   quarters of them would be in jail.
   ■ *of General MacArthur*
   Harry S. Truman 1884–1972: Merle Miller *Plain
   Speaking* (1974)

23 As Lord Chesterfield said of the
   generals of his day, 'I only hope that
   when the enemy reads the list of their
   names, he trembles as I do.'
   ■ *usually quoted as 'I don't know what effect
   these men will have upon the enemy, but, by
   God, they frighten me'*
   Duke of Wellington 1769–1852: letter,
   29 August 1810

24 Ours [our army] is composed of the
   scum of the earth—the mere scum of
   the earth.
   Duke of Wellington 1769–1852: Philip Henry
   Stanhope *Notes of Conversations with the
   Duke of Wellington* (1888) 4 November 1831

25 I have fewer disciplinary problems
   commanding a third of a million

troops now than I did in
1973 commanding 1,000 men.
John J. Yeosock 1937– : in *Time* 18 March 1991

Art
....

see also **Acting, Art and Society, Artists,
Arts and Sciences, Drawing, Literature,
Music, Painting, Photography,
Sculpture, The Theatre**

1 Art is born of humiliation.
W. H. Auden 1907–73: Stephen Spender *World
Within World* (1951)

2 Do not imagine that Art is something
which is designed to give gentle uplift
and self-confidence. Art is not a
brassière. At least, not in the English
sense. But do not forget that *brassière*
is the French for life-jacket.
Julian Barnes 1946– : *Flaubert's Parrot* (1984)

3 I suppose art is the only thing that can
go on mattering once it has stopped
hurting.
Elizabeth Bowen 1899–1973: *Heat of the Day*
(1949)

4 The history of art is the history of
revivals.
Samuel Butler 1835–1902: *Notebooks* (1912)

5 Art for art's sake, with no purpose, for
any purpose perverts art. But art
achieves a purpose which is not its
own.
Benjamin Constant 1767–1834: diary
11 February 1804

6 Art is vice. You don't marry it
legitimately, you rape it.
Edgar Degas 1834–1917: Paul Lafond *Degas*
(1918)

7 I always said God was against art and I
still believe it.
Edward Elgar 1857–1934: letter to A. J. Jaeger,
9 October 1900

8 Art is a jealous mistress.
Ralph Waldo Emerson 1803–82: *The Conduct
of Life* (1860)

9 Human life is a sad show,
undoubtedly: ugly, heavy and
complex. Art has no other end, for
people of feeling, than to conjure
away the burden and bitterness.
Gustave Flaubert 1821–80: letter to Amelie
Bosquet, July 1864

10 The artist must be in his work as God
is in creation, invisible and all-
powerful; one must sense him
everywhere but never see him.
Gustave Flaubert 1821–80: letter to
Mademoiselle Leroyer de Chantepie,
18 March 1857

11 Art is significant deformity.
Roger Fry 1866–1934: Virginia Woolf *Roger
Fry* (1940)

12 Then a sentimental passion of a
vegetable fashion must excite your
languid spleen,
An attachment à la Plato for a bashful
young potato, or a not too French
French bean!
Though the Philistines may jostle, you
will rank as an apostle in the high
aesthetic band,
If you walk down Piccadilly with a
poppy or a lily in your medieval
hand.
W. S. Gilbert 1836–1911: *Patience* (1881)

13 In art the best is good enough.
Johann Wolfgang von Goethe 1749–1832:
Italienische Reise (1816–17) 3 March 1787

14 Art is not a mirror but a hammer.
John Grierson 1888–1972: H. Forsyth Hardy
(ed.) *Grierson on Documentary* (1946, 1966)

15 Art has to move you and design does
not, unless it's a good design for a bus.
David Hockney 1937– : in *Guardian*
26 October 1988

16 We work in the dark—we do what we
can—we give what we have. Our
doubt is our passion and our passion
is our task. The rest is the madness of
art.
Henry James 1843–1916: 'The Middle Years'
(short story, 1893)

17 Life being all inclusion and confusion,
and art being all discrimination and
selection.
Henry James 1843–1916: *The Spoils of Poynton*
(1909 ed.)

18 The artist, like the God of the creation, remains within or behind or beyond or above his handiwork, invisible, refined out of existence, indifferent, paring his fingernails.
   James Joyce 1882–1941: *A Portrait of the Artist as a Young Man* (1916)

19 All art, permanent or temporary, has a life in the immediate experience, but then has a life in the imagination.
   Anish Kapoor 1954– : in *Sunday Times* 11 July 1999

20 We know that the tail must wag the dog, for the horse is drawn by the cart;
   But the Devil whoops, as he whooped of old: 'It's clever, but is it Art?'
   Rudyard Kipling 1865–1936: 'The Conundrum of the Workshops' (1892)

21 Art is the objectification of feeling, and the subjectification of nature.
   Susanne Langer 1895–1985: in *Mind* (1967)

22 Art is a revolt against fate.
   André Malraux 1901–76: *Les Voix du silence* (1951)

23 We all know that Art is not truth. Art is a lie that makes us realize truth.
   Pablo Picasso 1881–1973: Dore Ashton *Picasso on Art* (1972)

24 Art for art's sake is an empty phrase. Art for the sake of the true, art for the sake of the good and the beautiful, that is the faith I am searching for.
   George Sand 1804–76: letter to Alexandre Saint-Jean, 1872

25 I don't know what art is, but I do know what it isn't.
   Brian Sewell: in *Independent* 26 April 1999

26 Airing one's dirty linen never makes for a masterpiece.
   François Truffaut 1932–84: *Bed and Board* (1972)

27 An artist is someone who produces things that people don't need to have but that he—for *some reason*—thinks it would be a good idea to give them.
   Andy Warhol 1927–87: *Philosophy of Andy Warhol* (*From A to B and Back Again*) (1975)

28 Another unsettling element in modern art is that common symptom of immaturity, the dread of doing what has been done before.
   Edith Wharton 1862–1937: *The Writing of Fiction* (1925)

29 Listen! There never was an artistic period. There never was an Art-loving nation.
   James McNeill Whistler 1834–1903: *Mr Whistler's 'Ten O'Clock'* (1885)

30 All that I desire to point out is the general principle that Life imitates Art far more than Art imitates Life.
   Oscar Wilde 1854–1900: *Intentions* (1891)

Art and Society

1 The proletarian state must bring up thousands of excellent 'mechanics of culture', 'engineers of the soul'.
   Maxim Gorky 1868–1936: speech at the Writers' Congress 1934

2 In free society art is not a weapon . . . Artists are not engineers of the soul.
   John F. Kennedy 1917–63: speech at Amherst College, Mass., 26 October 1963

3 God help the Minister that meddles with art!
   Lord Melbourne 1779–1848: Lord David Cecil *Lord M* (1954)

4 Artists are the antennae of the race, but the bullet-headed many will never learn to trust their great artists.
   Ezra Pound 1885–1972: *Literary Essays* (1954)

5 The true artist will let his wife starve, his children go barefoot, his mother drudge for his living at seventy, sooner than work at anything but his art.
   George Bernard Shaw 1856–1950: *Man and Superman* (1903)

6 Politics in the middle of things that concern the imagination are like a pistol-shot in the middle of a concert.
   Stendhal 1783–1842: *Scarlet and Black* (1830)

Artists

see also **Art**, **Drawing**, **Painting**

1 Monet is only an eye, but what an eye!
   Paul Cézanne 1839–1906: attributed

2 In Claude's landscape all is lovely—all amiable—all is amenity and repose;—the calm sunshine of the heart.
   John Constable 1776–1837: lecture, 2 June 1836

3 Picasso is Spanish, I am too. Picasso is a genius. I am too. Picasso will be seventy-two and I about forty-eight. Picasso is known in every country of the world; so am I. Picasso is a Communist; I am not.
   Salvador Dali 1904–89: lecture in Madrid, 12 October 1951

4 It's amazing what you can do with an E in A-level art, twisted imagination and a chainsaw.
   ■ *after winning the 1995 Turner Prize*
   Damien Hirst 1965– : in *Observer* 3 December 1995

5 If Botticelli were alive today he'd be working for *Vogue*.
   Peter Ustinov 1921– : in *Observer* 21 October 1962

6 A genius with the IQ of a moron.
   ■ *of Andy Warhol*
   Gore Vidal 1925– : in *Observer* 18 June 1989

Arts and Sciences

1 The true men of action in our time, those who transform the world, are not the politicians and statesmen, but the scientists. Unfortunately poetry cannot celebrate them, because their deeds are concerned with things, not persons, and are, therefore, speechless. When I find myself in the company of scientists, I feel like a shabby curate who has strayed by mistake into a drawing room full of dukes.
   W. H. Auden 1907–73: *The Dyer's Hand* (1963) 'The Poet and the City'

2 A contemporary poet has characterized this sense of the personality of art and of the impersonality of science in these words—'Art is myself; science is ourselves'.
   Claude Bernard 1813–78: *Introduction à l'Étude de la Médecin Expériméntale* (1865)

3 Art is meant to disturb, science reassures.
   Georges Braque 1882–1963: *Le Jour et la nuit: Cahiers 1917–52*

4 In science, read, by preference, the newest works; in literature, the oldest.
   Edward Bulwer-Lytton 1803–73: *Caxtoniana* (1863) 'Hints on Mental Culture'

5 Poets do not go mad; but chess-players do. Mathematicians go mad, and cashiers; but creative artists very seldom. I am not, as will be seen, in any sense attacking logic: I only say that this danger does lie in logic, not in imagination.
   G. K. Chesterton 1874–1936: *Orthodoxy* (1908)

6 Even if I could be Shakespeare, I think I should still choose to be Faraday.
   Aldous Huxley 1894–1963: in 1925, attributed; Walter M. Elsasser *Memoirs of a Physicist in the Atomic Age* (1978)

7 Shakespeare would have grasped wave functions, Donne would have understood complementarity and relative time. They would have been excited. What richness! They would have plundered this new science for their imagery. And they would have educated their audiences too. But you 'arts' people, you're not only ignorant of these magnificent things, you're rather proud of knowing nothing.
   Ian McEwan 1948– : *The Child in Time* (1987)

8 If a scientist were to cut his ear off, no one would take it as evidence of a heightened sensibility.
   Peter Medawar 1915–87: 'J. B. S.' (1968)

9 During the 1950s, the first great age of molecular biology, the English Schools of Oxford and particularly of Cambridge produced more than a score of graduates of quite outstanding ability—much more brilliant, inventive, articulate and

dialectically skilful than most young scientists; right up in the Watson class. But Watson had one towering advantage over all of them: in addition to being extremely clever he had something important to be clever *about*.

Peter Medawar 1915–87: review of James D. Watson's *The Double Helix* in *New York Review of Books* 28 March 1968

10 Science must begin with myths, and with the criticism of myths.

Karl Popper 1902–94: 'The Philosophy of Science'; C. A. Mace (ed.) *British Philosophy in the Mid-Century* (1957)

11 We believe a scientist because he can substantiate his remarks, not because he is eloquent and forcible in his enunciation. In fact, we distrust him when he seems to be influencing us by his manner.

I. A. Richards 1893–1979: *Science and Poetry* (1926)

12 If Watson and Crick had not discovered the nature of DNA, one can be virtually certain that other scientists would eventually have determined it. With art—whether painting, music or literature—it is quite different. If Shakespeare had not written *Hamlet*, no other playwright would have done so.

Lewis Wolpert 1929– : *The Unnatural Nature of Science* (1993)

Asia

1 The Japanese are full of surprises, because the women are so refined and elegant and the men fundamentally so crude and tough.

Harold Acton 1904–94: Naim Attallah *Singular Encounters* (1990)

2 Nothing and no one can destroy the Chinese people. They are relentless survivors. They are the oldest civilized people on earth. Their civilization passes through phases but its basic characteristics remain the same. They yield, they bend to the wind, but they do not break.

Pearl S. Buck 1892–1973: *China, Past and Present* (1972)

3 Match me such marvel, save in Eastern clime,—
A rose-red city—half as old as Time!

John William Burgon 1813–88: *Petra* (1845)

4 Nothing in India is identifiable, the mere asking of a question causes it to disappear or to merge in something else.

E. M. Forster 1879–1970: *A Passage to India* (1924)

5 India . . . is not a place that one can pick up and put down again as if nothing had happened. In a way it's not so much a country as an experience, and whether it turns out to be a good or a bad one depends, I suppose, on oneself.

Ruth Prawer Jhabvala 1927– : *Travellers* (1973)

6 The Japanese have perfected good manners and made them indistinguishable from rudeness.

Paul Theroux 1941– : *The Great Railway Bazaar* (1975)

Assertiveness

see **Self-Esteem and Assertiveness**

Atheism

see also **Belief**

1 An atheist is a man who has no invisible means of support.

John Buchan 1875–1940: H. E. Fosdick *On Being a Real Person* (1943)

2 Thanks to God, I am still an atheist.

Luis Buñuel 1900–83: in *Le Monde* 16 December 1959

3 When men stop believing in God they don't believe in nothing; they believe in anything.

G. K. Chesterton 1874–1936: widely attributed, although not traced in his works

4 A young man who wishes to remain a sound atheist cannot be too careful of his reading.

C. S. Lewis 1898–1963: *Surprised by Joy* (1955)

5 He was an embittered atheist (the sort of atheist who does not so much disbelieve in God as personally dislike Him), and took a sort of pleasure in thinking that human affairs would never improve.

George Orwell 1903–50: *Down and Out in Paris and London* (1933)

6 God can stand being told by Professor Ayer and Marganita Laski that He doesn't exist.

J. B. Priestley 1894–1984: in *Listener* 1 July 1965

7 I was told that the Chinese said they would bury me by the Western Lake and build a shrine to my memory. I have some slight regret that this did not happen as I might have become a god, which would have been very *chic* for an atheist.

Bertrand Russell 1872–1970: *Autobiography* (1968)

Jane Austen 1775–1817

1 What should I do with your strong, manly, spirited sketches, full of variety and glow?—How could I possibly join them on to the little bit (two inches wide) of ivory on which I work with so fine a brush, as produces little effect after much labour?

Jane Austen 1775–1817: letter to J. Edward Austen, 16 December 1816

2 Jane Austen finds sex as demonic as Sade does. She finds it demonic and therefore locks it out.

J. M. Coetzee 1940– : *Giving Offence* (1996)

3 The Big Bow-Wow strain I can do myself like any now going; but the exquisite touch, which renders ordinary commonplace things and characters interesting, from the truth of the description and the sentiment, is denied to me.

Sir Walter Scott 1771–1832: diary 14 March 1826

4 When I take up one of Jane Austen's books . . . I feel like a barkeeper entering the kingdom of heaven. I know what his sensation would be and his private comments. He would not find the place to his taste, and he would probably say so.

Mark Twain 1835–1910: Q. D. Leavis *Fiction and the Reading Public* (1932)

Australia

1 We wish no harm to England's native people. We are here to bring you good manners, refinement and an opportunity to make a *Koompartoo*, a fresh start.

■ *planting an Aboriginal flag on the white cliffs of Dover and 'claiming' England for the Aboriginal people*

Burnum Burnum 1936–97: on 26 January 1988, the year of Australia's bicentenary

2 True patriots we; for be it understood, We left our country for our country's good.

Henry Carter d. 1806: prologue, written for, but not recited at, the opening of the Playhouse, Sydney, New South Wales, 16 January 1796, when the actors were principally convicts; previously attributed to George Barrington (b. 1755)

3 Australia is a huge rest home, where no unwelcome news is ever wafted on to the pages of the worst newspapers in the world.

Germaine Greer 1939– : in *Observer* 1 August 1982

4 And her five cities, like teeming sores, Each drains her: a vast parasite robber-state Where second-hand Europeans pullulate Timidly on the edge of alien shores.

A. D. Hope 1907– : 'Australia' (1939)

5 Australia is a lucky country run mainly by second-rate people who share its luck.

Donald Richmond Horne 1921– : *The Lucky Country: Australia in the Sixties* (1964)

6 A broad school of Australian writing has based itself on the assumption

that Australia not only has a history worth bothering about, but that all the history worth bothering about happened in Australia.
Clive James 1939– : *The Dreaming Swimmer* (1992)

7 Earth is here so kind, that just tickle her with a hoe and she laughs with a harvest.
Douglas Jerrold 1803–57: *The Wit and Opinions of Douglas Jerrold* (1859)

8 Even as it [Great Britain] walked out on you and joined the Common Market, you were still looking for your MBEs and your knighthoods, and all the rest of the regalia that comes with it. You would take Australia right back down the time tunnel to the cultural cringe where you have always come from.
■ *addressing Australian Conservative supporters of Great Britain*
Paul Keating 1944– : on 27 February 1992

9 Australia has a marvellous sky and air and blue clarity, and a hoary sort of land beneath it, like a Sleeping Princess on whom the dust of ages has settled.
D. H. Lawrence 1885–1930: letter to Jan Juta, 20 May 1922

10 What Great Britain calls the Far East is to us the near north.
Robert Gordon Menzies 1894–1978: in *Sydney Morning Herald* 27 April 1939

11 I have been disappointed in all my expectations of Australia, except as to its wickedness; for it is far more wicked than I have conceived it possible for any place to be, or than it is possible for me to describe to you in England.
Henry Parkes 1815–95: letter, 1 May 1840

12 The crimson thread of kinship runs through us all.
■ *on Australian federation*
Henry Parkes 1815–95: speech at banquet in Melbourne, 6 February 1890

13 Once a jolly swagman camped by a billabong,
Under the shade of a coolibah tree;

And he sang as he watched and waited till his 'Billy' boiled:
'You'll come a-waltzing, Matilda, with me.'
'Banjo' Paterson 1864–1941: 'Waltzing Matilda' (1903 song)

14 Above our writers—and other artists—looms the intimidating mass of Anglo-Saxon culture. Such a situation almost inevitably produces the characteristic Australian Cultural Cringe—appearing either as the Cringe Direct, or as the Cringe Inverted, in the attitude of the Blatant Blatherskite, the God's-Own-Country and I'm-a-better-man-than-you-are Australian bore.
Arthur Angell Phillips 1900–85: *Meanjin* (1950) 'The Cultural Cringe'

15 In all directions stretched the great Australian Emptiness, in which the mind is the least of possessions.
Patrick White 1912–90: *The Vital Decade* (1968) 'The Prodigal Son'

16 By God what a site! By man what a mess!
■ *of Sydney*
Clough Williams-Ellis 1883–1978: *Architect Errant* (1971)

17 Australia is the flattest, driest, ugliest place on earth. Only those who can be possessed by her can know what secret beauty she holds.
Eric Paul Willmot 1936– : *Australia The Last Experiment* (1987)

Autobiography

see also **Biography**

1 I used to think I was an interesting person, but I must tell you how sobering a thought it is to realize your life's story fills about thirty-five pages and you have, actually, not much to say.
Roseanne Barr 1953– : *Roseanne* (1990)

2 An autobiography is an obituary in serial form with the last instalment missing.
Quentin Crisp 1908–99: *The Naked Civil Servant* (1968)

3 He made the books and he died.
- *his own 'sum and history of my life'*
  William Faulkner 1897–1962: letter to
  Malcolm Cowley, 11 February 1949

4 Autobiography is now as common as
adultery and hardly less
reprehensible.
  John Grigg 1924– : in *Sunday Times*
  28 February 1962

5 I should be trading on the blood of
my men.
- *refusing an offer to write his memoirs*
  Robert E. Lee 1807–70: attributed, perhaps
  apocryphal

6 I write no memoirs. I'm a gentleman.
I cannot bring myself to write nastily
about persons whose hospitality I
have enjoyed.
  John Pentland Mahaffy 1839–1919: W. B.
  Stanford and R. B. McDowell *Mahaffy* (1971)

7 Every autobiography . . . becomes an
absorbing work of fiction, with
something of the charm of a
cryptogram.
  H. L. Mencken 1880–1956: *Minority Report*
  (1956)

8 To write one's memoirs is to speak ill
of everybody except oneself.
  Henri Philippe Pétain 1856–1951: in *Observer*
  26 May 1946

9 If you really want to hear about it, the
first thing you'll probably want to
know is where I was born, and what
my lousy childhood was like, and how
my parents were occupied and all
before they had me, and all that David
Copperfield kind of crap, but I don't
feel like going into it.
  J. D. Salinger 1919– : *Catcher in the Rye* (1951)

10 Only when one has lost all curiosity
about the future has one reached the
age to write an autobiography.
  Evelyn Waugh 1903–66: *A Little Learning*
  (1964)

11 A man who publishes his letters
becomes a nudist—nothing shields

him from the world's gaze except his
bare skin.
  E. B. White 1899–1985: letter to Corona
  Machemer, 11 June 1975

Autumn
....

1 But it's a long, long while
From May to December;
And the days grow short
When you reach September.
  Maxwell Anderson 1888–1959: 'September
  Song' (1938 song)

2 Early autumn—
rice field, ocean,
one green.
  Matsuo Basho 1644–94: translated by Lucien
  Stryk

3 Now is the time for the burning of the
leaves.
  Laurence Binyon 1869–1943: 'The Ruins'
  (1942)

4 Season of mists and mellow
fruitfulness,
Close bosom-friend of the maturing
sun;
Conspiring with him how to load and
bless
With fruit the vines that round the
thatch-eaves run.
  John Keats 1795–1821: 'To Autumn' (1820)

5 I want to go south, where there is no
autumn, where the cold doesn't
crouch over one like a snow-leopard
waiting to pounce. The heart of the
North is dead, and the fingers of cold
are corpse fingers.
  D. H. Lawrence 1885–1930: letter to J.
  Middleton Murry, 3 October 1924

6 What of October, that ambiguous
month, the month of tension, the
unendurable month?
  Doris Lessing 1919– : *Martha Quest* (1952)

7 For man, autumn is a time of harvest,
of gathering together. For nature, it is
a time of sowing, of scattering abroad.
  Edwin Way Teale 1899–1980: *Autumn Across
  America* (1956)

Awards

1 Prizes are like sashes, you can wear ~~them and be Miss World for a bit~~ . . . I've been royally dissed by prizes.
Martin Amis 1949– : interview in *Waterstone's Quarterly Guide* Spring/ Summer 1996

2 Members [of civil service orders] rise from CMG (known sometimes in Whitehall as 'Call Me God') to the KCMG ('Kindly Call Me God') to— for a select few governors and super-ambassadors—the GCMG ('God Calls Me God').
Anonymous: Anthony Sampson *Anatomy of Britain* (1962)

3 The whole idea of an award just for women fills me with horror.
■ *on the Orange prize for women's fiction*
Anita Brookner 1928– : in *Sunday Times* 21 April 1996

4 A medal glitters, but it also casts a shadow.
■ *a reference to the envy caused by the award of honours*
Winston Churchill 1874–1965: in 1941; Kenneth Rose *King George V* (1983)

5 It's about money and power, and that's what gets the column inches.
■ *on establishing the Orange prize for women's fiction*
Sarah Dunant 1950– : in *Sunday Times* 21 April 1996

6 The Nobel is a ticket to one's funeral. No one has ever done anything after he got it.
T. S. Eliot 1888–1965: attributed

7 Awards are like piles. Sooner or later, every bum gets one.
Maureen Lipman 1946– : in *Independent* 31 July 1999

8 She says 'Men are monopolists of "stars, garters, buttons and other shining baubles."'
Marianne Moore 1887–1972: 'Marriage' (1935)

9 People fail you, children disappoint you, thieves break in, moths corrupt, but an OBE goes on for ever.
Fay Weldon 1931– : *Praxis* (1978)

Johann Sebastian Bach
1685–1750
see also **Mozart**

1 Too much counterpoint; what is worse, Protestant counterpoint.
Thomas Beecham 1879–1961: in *Guardian* 8 March 1971

2 The immortal god of harmony.
Ludwig van Beethoven 1770–1827: letter to Breitkopf und Härtel, 22 April 1801

3 Bach almost persuades me to be a Christian.
Roger Fry 1866–1934: Virginia Woolf *Roger Fry* (1940)

Bachelors
see also **Marriage**, **Men**

1 It is a truth universally acknowledged, that a single man in possession of a good fortune, must be in want of a wife.
Jane Austen 1775–1817: *Pride and Prejudice* (1813)

2 A man in love is incomplete until he has married. Then he's finished.
Zsa Zsa Gabor 1919– : in *Newsweek* 28 March 1960

3 We are a select group, without personal obligation, social encumbrance, or any socks that match.
P. J. O'Rourke 1947– : *The Bachelor Home Companion* (1987)

4 Somehow a bachelor never quite gets over the idea that he is a thing of beauty and a boy forever.
Helen Rowland 1875–1950: *A Guide to Men* (1922); see **Beauty 14**

5 Nothing perhaps is so efficacious in preventing men from marrying as the tone in which married women speak of the struggles made in that direction by their unmarried friends.
Anthony Trollope 1815–82: *The Way We Live Now*

The Balkans

1 Not worth the healthy bones of a single Pomeranian grenadier.
   ■ *of possible German involvement in the Balkans*
   Otto von Bismarck 1815–98: George O. Kent *Bismarck and his Times* (1978)

2 If there is ever another war in Europe, it will come out of some damned silly thing in the Balkans.
   Otto von Bismarck 1815–98: quoted in speech, House of Commons, 16 August 1945

3 Balkan graveyards are full of the broken promises of Slobodan Milosevic.
   Bill Clinton 1946– : statement in Washington, 13 October 1998

4 No history much? Perhaps. Only this ominous
   Dark beauty flowering under veils,
   Trapped in the spectrum of a dying style:
   A village like an instinct left to rust,
   Composed around the echo of a pistol-shot.
   Lawrence Durrell 1912–90: 'Sarajevo' (1951)

5 Serbs out, Nato in, refugees back.
   George Robertson 1946– : summing up the Nato objective in Kosovo, 7 June 1999

6 The name is history.
   The thick Miljacka flows
   Under its bridges through a canyon's breadth
   Fretted with minarets and plump with domes,
   Cupped in its mountains, caught on a drawn breath.
   Anthony Thwaite 1930– : 'Sarajevo: I' (1973)

Baseball

see also **Sports and Games**

1 Think! How the hell are you gonna think and hit at the same time?
   Yogi Berra 1925– : *Nice Guys Finish Seventh* (1976)

2 A ball player's got to be kept hungry to become a big leaguer. That's why no boy from a rich family ever made the big leagues.
   Joe DiMaggio 1914–99: in *New York Times* 30 April 1961

3 [Baseball] breaks your heart. It is designed to break your heart. The game begins in the spring, when everything else begins again, and it blossoms in the summer, filling the afternoons and evenings, and then as soon as the chill rains come, it stops and leaves you to face the fall alone.
   A. Bartlett Giamatti 1938–89: *The Green Fields of the Mind* (1977)

4 Baseball is very big with my people. It figures. It's the only way we can get to shake a bat at a white man without starting a riot.
   Dick Gregory 1932– : D. H. Nathan (ed.) *Baseball Quotations* (1991)

5 Take me out to the ball game,
   Take me out with the crowd.
   Buy me some peanuts and cracker-jack—
   I don't care if I never get back.
   Jack Norworth 1879–1959: 'Take Me Out to the Ball Game' (1908 song)

6 All you have to do is keep the five players who hate your guts away from the five who are undecided.
   Casey Stengel 1891–1975: attributed

7 Baseball, it is said, is only a game. True. And the Grand Canyon is only a hole in Arizona. Not all holes, or games, are created equal.
   George F. Will 1941– : *Men At Work: The Craft of Baseball* (1990)

8 Baseball gives every American boy a chance to excel. Not just to be as good as someone else, but to be better. This is the nature of man and the name of the game.
   Ted Williams 1918– : *Baseball* (1994)

Beauty

....

see also **The Body**, **Cosmetics**

1 A pretty girl is like a melody
That haunts you night and day.
Irving Berlin 1888–1989: 'A Pretty Girl is like a Melody' (1919 song)

2 Consider the lilies of the field, how they grow; they toil not, neither do they spin:
And yet I say unto you, That even Solomon in all his glory was not arrayed like one of these.
Bible: St Matthew

3 She walks in beauty, like the night
Of cloudless climes and starry skies;
And all that's best of dark and bright
Meet in her aspect and her eyes.
Lord Byron 1788–1824: 'She Walks in Beauty' (1815)

4 And she was fayr as is the rose in May.
Geoffrey Chaucer c.1343–1400: *The Legend of Good Women* 'Cleopatra'

5 When a woman isn't beautiful, people always say, 'You have lovely eyes, you have lovely hair.'
Anton Chekhov 1860–1904: *Uncle Vanya* (1897)

6 There is nothing ugly; *I never saw an ugly thing in my life*: for let the form of an object be what it may,—light, shade, and perspective will always make it beautiful.
John Constable 1776–1837: C. R. Leslie *Memoirs of the Life of John Constable* (1843)

7 Love built on beauty, soon as beauty, dies.
John Donne 1572–1631: *Elegies* 'The Anagram' (c.1595)

8 The awful thing is that beauty is mysterious as well as terrible. God and devil are fighting there, and the battlefield is the heart of man.
Fedor Dostoevsky 1821–81: *The Brothers Karamazov* (1879–80)

9 He was afflicted by the thought that where Beauty was, nothing ever ran quite straight, which, no doubt, was why so many people looked on it as immoral.
John Galsworthy 1867–1933: *In Chancery* (1920)

10 I have a left shoulder-blade that is a miracle of loveliness. People come miles to see it. My right elbow has a fascination that few can resist.
W. S. Gilbert 1836–1911: *The Mikado* (1885)

11 Is it too much to ask that women be spared the daily struggle for superhuman beauty in order to offer it to the caresses of a subhumanly ugly mate?
Germaine Greer 1939– : *The Female Eunuch* (1970)

12 All things counter, original, spare, strange;
Whatever is fickle, freckled (who knows how?)
With swift, slow; sweet, sour; adazzle, dim;
He fathers-forth whose beauty is past change:
Praise him.
Gerard Manley Hopkins 1844–89: 'Pied Beauty' (written 1877)

13 Beauty is no quality in things themselves. It exists merely in the mind which contemplates them.
David Hume 1711–76: 'Of the Standard of Taste' (1757)

14 A thing of beauty is a joy for ever:
Its loveliness increases; it will never
Pass into nothingness.
John Keats 1795–1821: *Endymion* (1818)

15 'Beauty is truth, truth beauty,'—that is all
Ye know on earth, and all ye need to know.
John Keats 1795–1821: 'Ode on a Grecian Urn' (1820)

16 I'm tired of all this nonsense about beauty being only skin-deep. That's deep enough. What do you want—an adorable pancreas?
Jean Kerr 1923–2003: *The Snake has all the Lines* (1958)

17 At some point in life the world's beauty becomes enough. You don't

need to photograph, paint or even remember it. It is enough.

Toni Morrison 1931– : *Tar Baby* (1981)

18 Beauty is handed out as undemocratically as inherited peerages, and beautiful people have done nothing to deserve their astonishing reward.

John Mortimer 1923– : in *Observer* 21 March 1999

19 'Form follows profit' is the aesthetic principle of our times.

Richard Rogers 1933– : in *The Times* 13 February 1991

20 Remember that the most beautiful things in the world are the most useless; peacocks and lilies for instance.

John Ruskin 1819–1900: *Stones of Venice* vol. 1 (1851)

21 O! she doth teach the torches to burn bright.
It seems she hangs upon the cheek of night
Like a rich jewel in an Ethiop's ear;
Beauty too rich for use, for earth too dear.

William Shakespeare 1564–1616: *Romeo and Juliet* (1595)

22 Beauty is all very well at first sight; but who ever looks at it when it has been in the house three days?

George Bernard Shaw 1856–1950: *Man and Superman* (1903)

23 I do not know which to prefer,
The beauty of inflections
Or the beauty of innuendoes,
The blackbird whistling
Or just after.

Wallace Stevens 1879–1955: 'Thirteen Ways of Looking at a Blackbird' (1923)

24 The beauty myth moves for men as a mirage; its power lies in its ever-receding nature. When the gap is closed, the lover embraces only his own disillusion.

Naomi Wolf 1962– : *The Beauty Myth* (1990)

25 A woman of so shining loveliness
That men threshed corn at midnight by a tress,

A little stolen tress.

W. B. Yeats 1865–1939: 'The Secret Rose' (1899)

Ludwig van Beethoven
1770–1827

1 Everything will pass, and the world will perish but the Ninth Symphony will remain.

Michael Bakunin 1814–76: Edmund Wilson *To The Finland Station* (1940)

2 It will be generally admitted that Beethoven's Fifth Symphony is the most sublime noise that has ever penetrated into the ear of man.

E. M. Forster 1879–1970: *Howards End* (1910)

3 To us musicians the work of Beethoven parallels the pillars of smoke and fire which led the Israelites through the desert.

Franz Liszt 1811–86: letter to Wilhelm von Lenz, 1852

Beginning
see also **Change**, **Ending**

1 In the beginning God created the heaven and the earth. And the earth was without form, and void; and darkness was upon the face of the deep. And the Spirit of God moved upon the face of the waters.
And God said, Let there be light: and there was light.

Bible: Genesis

2 Everything has already begun before, the first line of the first page of every novel refers to something that has already happened outside the book.

Italo Calvino 1923–85: *If on a Winter's Night a Traveller* (1979)

3 'Where shall I begin, please your Majesty?' he asked. 'Begin at the beginning,' the King said, gravely, 'and go on till you come to the end: then stop.'

Lewis Carroll 1832–98: *Alice's Adventures in Wonderland* (1865)

4 when god decided to invent
everything he took one
breath bigger than a circustent
and everything began
e. e. cummings 1894–1962: *1 x 1* (1944) no. 26

5 In my beginning is my end.
T. S. Eliot 1888–1965: *Four Quartets* 'East Coker' (1940)

6 All this will not be finished in the first 100 days. Nor will it be finished in the first 1,000 days, nor in the life of this Administration, nor even perhaps in our lifetime on this planet. But let us begin.
John F. Kennedy 1917–63: inaugural address, 20 January 1961

7 A tower of nine storeys begins with a heap of earth.
The journey of a thousand *li* starts from where one stands.
Lao Tzu c.604–c.531 BC: *Tao-te Ching*

8 I've started so I'll finish.
■ *said when a contestant's time runs out while a question is being put*
Magnus Magnusson 1929– : *Mastermind*, BBC television (1972–97)

9 Ere time and place were, time and place were not;
Where primitive nothing something straight begot;
Then all proceeded from the great united what.
Lord Rochester 1647–80: 'Upon Nothing' (1680)

Behaviour

see also **Manners, Vulgarity, Words and Deeds**

1 When I go to Rome, I fast on Saturday, but here [Milan] I do not. Do you also follow the custom of whatever church you attend, if you do not want to give or receive scandal.
■ *usually quoted as 'When in Rome, do as the Romans do'*
St Ambrose c.339–97: 'Letter 54 to Januarius' (AD c.400)

2 Private faces in public places
Are wiser and nicer

Than public faces in private places.
W. H. Auden 1907–73: *Orators* (1932)

3 When people are on their best behaviour they aren't always at their best.
Alan Bennett 1934– : *Dinner at Noon* (BBC television, 1988)

4 He only does it to annoy,
Because he knows it teases.
Lewis Carroll 1832–98: *Alice's Adventures in Wonderland* (1865)

5 Take the tone of the company that you are in.
Lord Chesterfield 1694–1773: *Letters to his Son* (1774) 16 October 1747

6 *O tempora, O mores!*
Oh, the times! Oh, the manners!
Cicero 106–43 BC: *In Catilinam*

7 Being tactful in audacity is knowing how far one can go too far.
Jean Cocteau 1889–1963: *Le Rappel à l'ordre* (1926)

8 Careless she is with artful care,
Affecting to seem unaffected.
William Congreve 1670–1729: 'Amoret'

9 I get too hungry for dinner at eight.
I like the theatre, but never come late.
I never bother with people I hate.
That's why the lady is a tramp.
Lorenz Hart 1895–1943: 'The Lady is a Tramp' (1937 song)

10 Already at four years of age I had begun to apprehend that refinement was very often an extenuating virtue; one that excused and eclipsed almost every other unappetizing trait.
Barry Humphries 1934– : *More Please* (1992)

11 They teach the morals of a whore, and the manners of a dancing master.
■ *of the Letters of Lord Chesterfield*
Samuel Johnson 1709–84: James Boswell *Life of Samuel Johnson* (1791) 1754

12 Be a good animal, true to your instincts.
D. H. Lawrence 1885–1930: *The White Peacock* (1911)

13 There was a little girl
Who had a little curl

Right in the middle of her forehead,
When she was good
She was very, very good,
But when she was bad she was horrid.

■ *composed for, and sung to, his second daughter while a babe in arms, c.1850*

Henry Wadsworth Longfellow 1807–82: B. R. Tucker-Macchetta *The Home Life of Henry W. Longfellow* (1882)

14 Go directly—see what she's doing, and tell her she mustn't.

Punch: 16 November 1872

Belief

....

see also **Atheism**, **Doubt**, **Faith**

1 Of course, Behaviourism 'works'. So does torture. Give me a no-nonsense, down-to-earth behaviourist, a few drugs, and simple electrical appliances, and in six months I will have him reciting the Athanasian Creed in public.

W. H. Auden 1907–73: *A Certain World* (1970)

2 For what a man would like to be true, that he more readily believes.

Francis Bacon 1561–1626: *Novum Organum* (1620)

3 Lord, I believe; help thou mine unbelief.

Bible: St Mark

4 Of course not, but I am told it works even if you don't believe in it.

■ *when asked whether he really believed a horseshoe hanging over his door would bring him luck, c.1930*

Niels Bohr 1885–1962: A. Pais *Inward Bound* (1986)

5 Just when we are safest, there's a sunset-touch,
A fancy from a flower-bell, some one's death,
A chorus-ending from Euripides,—
And that's enough for fifty hopes and fears
As old and new at once as nature's self . . .
The grand Perhaps!

Robert Browning 1812–89: 'Bishop Blougram's Apology' (1855)

6 Why, sometimes I've believed as many as six impossible things before breakfast.

Lewis Carroll 1832–98: *Through the Looking-Glass* (1872)

7 plato told

him: he couldn't
believe it (jesus

told him; he
wouldn't believe
it)

e. e. cummings 1894–1962: *1 x 1* (1944) no. 13

8 I do not pretend to know where many ignorant men are sure—that is all that agnosticism means.

Clarence Darrow 1857–1938: speech at the trial of John Thomas Scopes, 15 July 1925

9 No matter how I probe and prod
I cannot quite believe in God.
But oh! I hope to God that he
Unswervingly believes in me.

E. Y. Harburg 1898–1981: 'The Agnostic' (1965)

10 It is harder for some people to believe that God loves them than to believe that he exists.

Basil Hume 1923–99: in *Guardian* 18 June 1999

11 I do not believe . . . I know.

Carl Gustav Jung 1875–1961: L. van der Post *Jung and the Story of our Time* (1976)

12 Credulity is the man's weakness, but the child's strength.

Charles Lamb 1775–1834: *Essays of Elia* (1823) 'Witches, and Other Night-Fears'

13 There is a great deal of difference between *still* believing something, and *again* believing it.

Georg Christoph Lichtenberg 1742–99: Notebook E no. 8 1775–6

14 If it were an innocent, passive gullibility it would be excusable; but all too clearly, alas, it is an active willingness to be deceived.

Peter Medawar 1915–87: review of Teilhard de Chardin *The Phenomenon of Man* (1961)

15 *We can believe what we choose.* We are answerable for what we choose to believe.

John Henry Newman 1801–90: letter to Mrs William Froude, 27 June 1848

16 George [Gershwin] died on July 11, 1937, but I don't have to believe that if I don't want to.

John O'Hara 1905–70: in *Newsweek* 15 July 1940

17 The big issue of our times is surely not the absence of a set of common values in a multicultural society. It is rather a battle between people who believe in something and those who believe in nothing: not in knowledge, not in authority, not in moral absolutes, and above all, not in themselves.

Melanie Phillips: *All Must Have Prizes* (1996)

18 Man is a credulous animal, and must believe *something*; in the absence of good grounds for belief, he will be satisfied with bad ones.

Bertrand Russell 1872–1970: *Unpopular Essays* (1950) 'Outline of Intellectual Rubbish'

19 I confused things with their names: that is belief.

Jean-Paul Sartre 1905–80: *Les Mots* (1964)

20 *Certum est quia impossibile est.*
It is certain because it is impossible.
■ *often quoted as* 'Credo quia impossibile [I believe because it is impossible]'
Tertullian AD c.160–c.225: *De Carne Christi*

21 There is a lot to be said in the Decade of Evangelism for believing more and more in less and less.

John Yates 1925– : in *Gloucester Diocesan Gazette* August 1991

Bereavement

see also **Death**, **Sorrow**

1 Do not stand at my grave and weep:
I am not there. I do not sleep.
I am a thousand winds that blow.
I am the diamond glints on snow . . .
Do not stand at my grave and cry;
I am not there, I did not die.
■ *quoted in letter left by British soldier Stephen Cummins when killed by the IRA, March 1989*
Anonymous: origin uncertain; attributed to various authors

2 He was my North, my South, my East and West,
My working week and my Sunday rest,
My noon, my midnight, my talk, my song;
I thought that love would last for ever: I was wrong.
W. H. Auden 1907–73: 'Funeral Blues' (1936)

3 Blessed are they that mourn: for they shall be comforted.
Bible: St Matthew

4 The Bustle in a House
The Morning after Death
Is solemnest of industries
Enacted upon Earth—
The Sweeping up the Heart
And putting Love away
We shall not want to use again
Until Eternity.
Emily Dickinson 1830–86: 'The Bustle in a House' (*c.*1866)

5 How small and selfish is sorrow. But it bangs one about until one is senseless.
■ *shortly after the death of George VI*
Queen Elizabeth, the Queen Mother 1900–2002: letter to Edith Sitwell, 1952; Victoria Glendinning *Edith Sitwell* (1983)

6 I feel the loss more than I had thought I should . . . Without my wishing it she chose to lose herself in me, and the result was she became truly my better half.
■ *on the death of his wife Kasturba*
Mahatma Gandhi 1869–1948: Arun Gandhi *Daughter of Midnight: The Child Bride of Gandhi* (1998)

7 Woman much missed, how you call to me, call to me.
Saying that now you are not as you were
When you had changed from the one who was all to me,
But as at first, when our day was fair.
Thomas Hardy 1840–1928: 'The Voice' (1914)

8 All I have I would have given gladly not to be standing here today.
■ *following the assassination of John F. Kennedy*
Lyndon Baines Johnson 1908–73: first speech to Congress as President, 27 November 1963

9 For a season there must be pain—
For a little, little space

I shall lose the sight of her face,
Take back the old life again
While She is at rest in her place.
   Rudyard Kipling 1865–1936: 'The Widower'

10 Bereavement is a universal and
integral part of our experience of love.
It follows marriage as normally as
marriage follows courtship or as
autumn follows summer.
   C. S. Lewis 1898–1963: *A Grief Observed* (1961)

11 A man's dying is more the survivors'
affair than his own.
   Thomas Mann 1875–1955: *The Magic Mountain* (1924)

12 Time does not bring relief; you all
have lied
Who told me time would ease me of
my pain!
I miss him in the weeping of the rain;
I want him at the shrinking of the
tide.
   Edna St Vincent Millay 1892–1950: 'Time does not bring relief'

13 I can't think of a more wonderful
thanksgiving for the life I have had
than that everyone should be jolly at
my funeral.
   Lord Mountbatten 1900–79: Richard Hough *Mountbatten* (1980)

14 I thought of you tonight, *a leanbh*,
lying there in your long barrow,
colder and dumber than a fish by
Francisco de Herrera.
   Paul Muldoon 1951– : 'Incantata' (1994)

15 Forgive me.
If you are not living,
If you, beloved, my love,
If you have died
All the leaves will fall on my breast
It will rain on my soul, all night, all
day
My feet will want to march to where
you are sleeping
But I shall go on living.
   Pablo Neruda 1904–73: 'The Dead Woman'

16 Widow. The word consumes itself.
   Sylvia Plath 1932–63: 'Widow' (1971)

17 People are mourning on both sides of
this conflict. In our prayers we shall
quite rightly remember those who are
bereaved in our own country and the
relations of the young Argentinian
soldiers who were killed. Common
sorrow could do something to reunite
those who were engaged in this
struggle. A shared anguish can be a
bridge of reconciliation. Our
neighbours are indeed like us.
   Robert Runcie 1921–99: sermon in St. Paul's Cathedral, service of thanksgiving at the end of the Falklands war, 26 July 1982

18 Beloved, come to me often in my
dreams. No, not that. Live in my
dreams.
   Marina Tsvetaeva 1892–1941: letter to Rainer Maria Rilke, 31 December 1926, after hearing of his death

19 He first deceased; she for a little tried
To live without him: liked it not, and
died.
   Henry Wotton 1568–1639: 'Upon the Death of Sir Albertus Moreton's Wife' (1651)

Best-sellers

see also **Books**

1 The most important thing is to avoid
making an enormous amount of
money before you're forty.
   V. S. Naipaul 1932– : Paul Theroux *Sir Vidia's Shadow* (1998)

2 The principle of procrastinated rape is
said to be the ruling one in all the
great best-sellers.
   V. S. Pritchett 1900–97: *The Living Novel* (1946) 'Clarissa'

3 Revolts may come, revolts may go, but
brats go on forever. And I would like
to do a perfectly stunning brat book!
   Arthur Ransome 1884–1967: A. N. Wilson *Penfriends from Porlock* (1988)

4 A best-seller is the gilded tomb of a
mediocre talent.
   Logan Pearsall Smith 1865–1946: *Afterthoughts* (1931)

Betrayal

see also **Sacrifice**, **Trust**

1 Just for a handful of silver he left us,
Just for a riband to stick in his coat.

   ■ *of Wordsworth's apparent betrayal of his
   radical principles by accepting the position of
   poet laureate*
   Robert Browning 1812–89: 'The Lost Leader'
   (1845)

2 *Et tu, Brute?*
You too, Brutus?

   Julius Caesar 100–44 BC: traditional
   rendering of Suetonius *Lives of the Caesars*
   'Divus Julius'

3 Anyone can rat, but it takes a certain
amount of ingenuity to re-rat.

   ■ *on rejoining the Conservatives twenty years
   after leaving them for the Liberals, c.1924*
   Winston Churchill 1874–1965: Kay Halle
   Irrepressible Churchill (1966)

4 Anyone who hasn't experienced the
ecstasy of betrayal knows nothing
about ecstasy at all.

   Jean Genet 1910–86: *Prisoner of Love* (1986)

5 Treason doth never prosper, what's
the reason?
For if it prosper, none dare call it
treason.

   John Harington 1561–1612: *Epigrams* (1618)

6 He who wields the knife never wears
the crown.

   Michael Heseltine 1933– : in *New Society*
   14 February 1986

7 The night of the long knives.

   Adolf Hitler 1889–1945: phrase given to the
   massacre of Ernst Roehm and his associates
   by Hitler on 29–30 June 1934, taken from an
   early Nazi marching song; subsequently
   associated with Harold Macmillan's Cabinet
   dismissals of 13 July 1962

8 It is rather like sending your opening
batsmen to the crease only for them to
find the moment that the first balls
are bowled that their bats have been
broken before the game by the team
captain.

   Geoffrey Howe 1926– : resignation speech as
   Deputy Prime Minister, House of
   Commons, 13 November 1990

9 To betray, you must first belong.

   Kim Philby 1912–88: in *Sunday Times*
   17 December 1967

10 Judas was paid! I am sacrificing my
whole political life.

   ■ *response to a heckler's call of 'Judas', having
   advised Conservatives to vote Labour at the
   coming general election*
   Enoch Powell 1912–98: speech at Bull Ring,
   Birmingham, 23 February 1974

11 *to the Emperor of Russia, who had spoken
bitterly of those who had betrayed the cause of
Europe:*
That, Sire, is a question of dates.

   ■ *often quoted as, 'treason is a matter of dates'*
   Charles-Maurice de Talleyrand 1754–1838:
   Duff Cooper *Talleyrand* (1932)

12 Greater love hath no man than this,
that he lay down his friends for his
life.

   ■ *on Harold Macmillan sacking seven of his
   Cabinet on 13 July 1962*
   Jeremy Thorpe 1929– : D. E. Butler and
   Anthony King *The General Election of 1964*
   (1965); see **Sacrifice** 1

13 Having watched the form of our
traitors for a number of years, I
cannot think that espionage can be
recommended as a technique for
building an impressive civilization.
It's a lout's game.

   Rebecca West 1892–1983: *The Meaning of
   Treason* (1982 ed.)

The Bible

1 The pencil of the Holy Ghost hath
laboured more in describing the
afflictions of Job than the felicities of
Solomon.

   Francis Bacon 1561–1626: *Essays* (1625) 'Of
   Adversity'

2 There's a great text in Galatians,
Once you trip on it, entails
Twenty-nine distinct damnations,
One sure, if another fails.

   Robert Browning 1812–89: 'Soliloquy of the
   Spanish Cloister' (1842)

3 An apology for the Devil: It must be
remembered that we have only heard

one side of the case. God has written all the books.
  Samuel Butler 1835–1902: *Notebooks* (1912)

4 The English Bible, a book which, if everything else in our language should perish, would alone suffice to show the whole extent of its beauty and power.
  Lord Macaulay 1800–59: 'John Dryden' (1828)

5 I know of no book which has been a source of brutality and sadistic conduct, both public and private, that can compare with the Bible.
  Reginald Paget 1908–90: in *Observer* 28 June 1964

6 The devil can cite Scripture for his purpose.
  William Shakespeare 1564–1616: *The Merchant of Venice* (1596–8)

7 LORD ILLINGWORTH: The Book of Life begins with a man and a woman in a garden.
  MRS ALLONBY: It ends with Revelations.
  Oscar Wilde 1854–1900: *A Woman of No Importance* (1893)

Biography
....
see also **Autobiography**

1 To be more interested in the writer than the writing is just eternal human vulgarity.
  Martin Amis 1949– : on BBC2 *Bookmark*, 9 March 1996

2 Nobody likes being written about in their lifetime, it's as though the FBI and the CIA were suddenly to splash your files in the paper.
  ■ *on his forthcoming biography*
  Saul Bellow 1915– : in *Guardian* 10 September 1997

3 And kept his heart a secret to the end From all the picklocks of biographers.
  ■ *of Robert E. Lee*
  Stephen Vincent Benét 1898–1943: *John Brown's Body* (1928)

4 The Art of Biography Is different from Geography.

Geography is about Maps, But Biography is about Chaps.
  Edmund Clerihew Bentley 1875–1956: *Biography for Beginners* (1905)

5 A well-written Life is almost as rare as a well-spent one.
  Thomas Carlyle 1795–1881: *Critical and Miscellaneous Essays* (1838) 'Jean Paul Friedrich Richter'

6 Reformers are always finally neglected, while the memoirs of the frivolous will always eagerly be read.
  Henry ('Chips') Channon 1897–1958: diary 7 July 1936

7 It's an excellent life of somebody else. But I've really lived inside myself, and she can't get in there.
  ■ *on a biography of himself*
  Robertson Davies 1913–95: interview in *The Times* 4 April 1995

8 But that perhaps is the point of any memoir—to walk with the dead and yet see them with our eyes, from our vantage point.
  Margaret Forster 1938– : *Hidden Lives: A Family Memoir* (1995)

9 The facts of life are to the biographer what the text of a novel is to the critic.
  Victoria Glendinning 1937– : attributed, in *Times Literary Supplement* 23 February 1996

10 Nobody can write the life of a man, but those who have eat and drunk and lived in social intercourse with him.
  Samuel Johnson 1709–84: James Boswell *Life of Samuel Johnson* (1791) 31 March 1772

11 Lives of great men all remind us We can make our lives sublime, And, departing, leave behind us Footprints on the sands of time.
  Henry Wadsworth Longfellow 1807–82: 'A Psalm of Life' (1838)

12 I have done my best to die before this book is published. It now seems possible that I may not succeed.
  Robert Runcie 1921–99: letter to Humphrey Carpenter, July 1996, in H. Carpenter *Robert Runcie* (1996)

13 Discretion is not the better part of biography.

> **Lytton Strachey** 1880–1932: Michael Holroyd *Lytton Strachey* vol. 1 (1967)

14 Then there is my noble and biographical friend who has added a new terror to death.

> ■ *on Lord Campbell's* Lives of the Lord Chancellors *being written without the consent of heirs or executors*
> **Charles Wetherell** 1770–1846: Lord St Leonards *Misrepresentations in Campbell's Lives of Lyndhurst and Brougham* (1869); also attributed to Lord Lyndhurst (1772–1863)

15 Every great man nowadays has his disciples, and it is always Judas who writes the biography.

> **Oscar Wilde** 1854–1900: *Intentions* (1891) 'The Critic as Artist'

Birds
....
see also **Animal Rights**

1 That's the wise thrush; he sings each song twice over,
Lest you should think he never could recapture
The first fine careless rapture!

> **Robert Browning** 1812–89: 'Home-Thoughts, from Abroad' (1845)

2 It was the Rainbow gave thee birth,
And left thee all her lovely hues.

> **W. H. Davies** 1871–1940: 'Kingfisher' (1910)

3 At once a voice outburst among
The bleak twigs overhead
In a full-hearted evensong
Of joy illimited;
An aged thrush, frail, gaunt, and small,
In blast-beruffled plume,
Had chosen thus to fling his soul
Upon the growing gloom.

> **Thomas Hardy** 1840–1928: 'The Darkling Thrush' (1902)

4 I caught this morning morning's minion, kingdom of daylight's dauphin, dapple-dawn-drawn Falcon.

> **Gerard Manley Hopkins** 1844–89: 'The Windhover' (written 1877)

5 It took the whole of Creation
To produce my foot, my each feather:
Now I hold Creation in my foot.

> **Ted Hughes** 1930–98: 'Hawk Roosting' (1960)

6 Oh, a wondrous bird is the pelican!
His beak holds more than his belican.
He takes in his beak
Food enough for a week.
But I'll be darned if I know how the helican.

> **Dixon Lanier Merritt** 1879–1972: in *Nashville Banner* 22 April 1913

7 The Ostrich roams the great Sahara.
Its mouth is wide, its neck is narra.
It has such long and lofty legs,
I'm glad it sits to lay its eggs.

> **Ogden Nash** 1902–71: 'The Ostrich' (1957)

8 Hail to thee, blithe Spirit!
Bird thou never wert,
That from Heaven, or near it,
Pourest thy full heart
In profuse strains of unpremeditated art.

> **Percy Bysshe Shelley** 1792–1822: 'To a Skylark' (1819)

9 Blackbirds are the cellos of the deep farms.

> **Anne Stevenson** 1933– : 'Green Mountain, Black Mountain' (1982)

10 Alone and warming his five wits,
The white owl in the belfry sits.

> **Alfred, Lord Tennyson** 1809–92: 'Song—The Owl' (1830)

11 I once had a sparrow alight upon my shoulder for a moment while I was hoeing in a village garden, and I felt that I was more distinguished by that circumstance than I should have been by any epaulette I could have worn.

> **Henry David Thoreau** 1817–62: *Walden* (1854) 'Winter Animals'

12 O blithe new-comer! I have heard,
I hear thee and rejoice:
O Cuckoo! Shall I call thee bird,
Or but a wandering voice?

> **William Wordsworth** 1770–1850: 'To the Cuckoo' (1807)

Birth

see also **Pregnancy**

1 No phallic hero, no matter what he does to himself or to another to prove his courage, ever matches the solitary, existential courage of the woman who gives birth.
   Andrea Dworkin 1946– : *Our Blood* (1976)

2 With its heart bursting, the infant sinks into hell . . . the mother is driving it out. At the same time she is holding it in, preventing its passage. It is she who is the enemy. She who stands between the child and life. Only one of them can prevail. It is mortal combat.
   Frederick Leboyer: *Birth Without Violence* (1975)

3 Death and taxes and childbirth! There's never any convenient time for any of them.
   Margaret Mitchell 1900–49: *Gone with the Wind* (1936)

4 Good work, Mary. We all knew you had it in you.
   ■ *telegram to Mrs Sherwood on the arrival of her baby*
   Dorothy Parker 1893–1967: Alexander Woollcott *While Rome Burns* (1934)

5 Love set you going like a fat gold watch.
   The midwife slapped your footsoles, and your bald cry
   Took its place among the elements.
   Sylvia Plath 1932–63: 'Morning Song' (1965)

6 I s'pect I growed. Don't think nobody never made me.
   ■ *said by Topsy*
   Harriet Beecher Stowe 1811–96: *Uncle Tom's Cabin* (1852)

7 What you say of the pride of giving life to an immortal soul is very fine, dear, but I own I can not enter into that; I think much more of our being like a cow or a dog at such moments; when our poor nature becomes so very animal and unecstatic.
   Queen Victoria 1819–1901: letter to the Princess Royal, 15 June 1858

8 Our birth is but a sleep and a forgetting . . .
   Not in entire forgetfulness,
   And not in utter nakedness,
   But trailing clouds of glory do we come.
   William Wordsworth 1770–1850: 'Ode. Intimations of Immortality' (1807)

Birth Control

see also **Pregnancy**

1 A fast word about oral contraception. I asked a girl to go to bed with me and she said 'no'.
   Woody Allen 1935– : at a nightclub in Washington, April 1965

2 It is now quite lawful for a Catholic woman to avoid pregnancy by a resort to mathematics, though she is still forbidden to resort to physics and chemistry.
   H. L. Mencken 1880–1956: *Notebooks* (1956)

3 Contraceptives should be used on all conceivable occasions.
   Spike Milligan 1918–2002: *The Last Goon Show of All* (1972)

4 We want better reasons for having children than not knowing how to prevent them.
   Dora Russell 1894–1986: *Hypatia* (1925)

5 Impotence and sodomy are socially O.K. but birth control is flagrantly middle-class.
   Evelyn Waugh 1903–66: 'An Open Letter' in Nancy Mitford (ed.) *Noblesse Oblige* (1956)

Bisexuality

1 On bisexuality: It immediately doubles your chances for a date on Saturday night.
   Woody Allen 1935– : in *New York Times* 1 December 1975

2 A gender bender I
   A creature of illusion,
   Of genital confusion,
   A gorgeous butterfly.
   Alistair Beaton and **Ned Sherrin** 1931– : *The Metropolitan Mikado* (1985)

3 Bisexuality is not so much a cop-out
as a fearful compromise.

Jill Johnston 1929– : *Lesbian Nature: The
Feminist Solution* (1973)

Boats

see also **The Sea**

1 Jolly boating weather,
And a hay harvest breeze,
Blade on the feather,
Shade off the trees
Swing, swing together
With your body between your knees.

William Cory 1823–92: 'Eton Boating Song' in
Eton Scrap Book (1865)

2 A wet sheet and a flowing sea,
A wind that follows fast
And fills the white and rustling sail
And bends the gallant mast.

Allan Cunningham 1784–1842: 'A Wet Sheet
and a Flowing Sea' (1825)

3 There is *nothing*—absolutely
nothing—half so much worth doing
as simply messing about in boats.

Kenneth Grahame 1859–1932: *The Wind in the
Willows* (1908)

4 Ocean racing is like standing under a
cold shower tearing up £5 notes.

Edward Heath 1916– : attributed

5 Quinquireme of Nineveh from distant
Ophir
Rowing home to haven in sunny
Palestine,
With a cargo of ivory,
And apes and peacocks,
Sandalwood, cedarwood, and sweet
white wine.

John Masefield 1878–1967: 'Cargoes' (1903)

6 Dirty British coaster with a salt-caked
smoke stack,
Butting through the Channel in the
mad March days,
With a cargo of Tyne coal,
Road-rails, pig lead,
Firewood, ironware, and cheap tin
trays.

John Masefield 1878–1967: 'Cargoes' (1903)

The Body

see also **Appearance**, **The Face**, **Fat**, **Hair**,
Health, **The Senses**

1 My brain? It's my second favourite
organ.

Woody Allen 1935– : *Sleeper* (1973 film, with
Marshall Brickman)

2 I let my body do what it wants. When
you are in love, you cannot organize
your body.

Roberto Benigni 1952– : at the Academy
Awards, Los Angeles, 21 March 1999

3 Entrails don't care for travel,
Entrails don't care for stress:
Entrails are better kept folded inside
you
For outside, they make a mess.

Connie Bensley 1929– : 'Entrails' (1987)

4 I'm the female equivalent of a
counterfeit $20 bill. Half of what you
see is a pretty good reproduction, the
rest is a fraud.

Cher 1946– : Doug McClelland *Star Speak:
Hollywood on Everything* (1987)

5 A woman watches her body uneasily,
as though it were an unreliable ally in
the battle for love.

Leonard Cohen 1934– : *The Favourite Game*
(1963)

6 Anatomy is destiny.

Sigmund Freud 1856–1939: *Collected Writings*
(1924)

7 I travel light; as light,
That is, as a man can travel who will
Still carry his body around because
Of its sentimental value.

Christopher Fry 1907– : *The Lady's not for
Burning* (1949)

8 I came in here in all good faith to help
my country. I don't mind giving a
reasonable amount [of blood], but a
pint . . . why that's very nearly an
armful.

Ray Galton 1930– and **Alan Simpson** 1929– :
The Blood Donor (1961 BBC television
programme) words spoken by Tony
Hancock

9 I have gone marking the blank atlas of
  your body
  with crosses of fire.
  My mouth went across: a spider,
  trying to hide.
  In you, behind you, timid, driven by
  thirst.
  Pablo Neruda 1904–73: 'I Have Gone
  Marking' (1924)

10 Modern body building is ritual,
  religion, sport, art, and science, awash
  in Western chemistry and
  mathematics. Defying nature, it
  surpasses it.
  Camille Paglia 1947– : *Sex, Art, and American
  Culture* (1992)

11 I don't really like knees.
  Yves Saint Laurent 1936– : in *Observer*
  3 August 1958

12 The body of a young woman is God's
  greatest achievement . . . Of course,
  He could have built it to last longer
  but you can't have everything.
  Neil Simon 1927– : *The Gingerbread Lady*
  (1970)

13 This Englishwoman is so refined
  She has no bosom and no behind.
  Stevie Smith 1902–71: 'This Englishwoman'
  (1937)

14 An impersonal and scientific
  knowledge of the structure of our
  bodies is the surest safeguard against
  prurient curiosity and lascivious
  gloating.
  Marie Stopes 1880–1958: *Married Love* (1918)

15 Our body is a machine for living. It is
  organized for that, it is its nature. Let
  life go on in it unhindered and let it
  defend itself, it will do more than if
  you paralyse it by encumbering it
  with remedies.
  Leo Tolstoy 1828–1910: *War and Peace*
  (1865–9)

16 The hands are a sort of feet, which
  serve us in our passage towards
  Heaven, curiously distinguished into
  joints and fingers, and fit to be applied
  to any thing which reason can
  imagine or desire.
  Thomas Traherne *c*.1637–74: *Meditations on
  the Six Days of Creation* (1717)

17 I sing the body electric.
  Walt Whitman 1819–92: title of poem (1855)

18 She fitted into my biggest armchair as
  if it had been built round her by
  someone who knew they were
  wearing armchairs tight about the
  hips that season.
  P. G. Wodehouse 1881–1975: *My Man Jeeves*
  (1919)

Books

see also **Best-sellers**, **Crime Fiction**,
Dictionaries, **Fantasy**, **Fiction**, **Libraries**,
Literature, **Publishing**, **Reading**,
Reviews, **Science Fiction**, **Writing**

1 Some books are undeservedly
  forgotten; none are undeservedly
  remembered.
  W. H. Auden 1907–73: *The Dyer's Hand* (1963)
  'Reading'

2 Some books are to be tasted, others to
  be swallowed, and some few to be
  chewed and digested.
  Francis Bacon 1561–1626: *Essays* (1625) 'Of
  Studies'

3 Books say: she did this because. Life
  says: she did this. Books are where
  things are explained to you; life is
  where things aren't . . . Books make
  sense of life. The only problem is that
  the lives they make sense of are other
  people's lives, never your own.
  Julian Barnes 1946– : *Flaubert's Parrot* (1984)

4 Of making many books there is no
  end; and much study is a weariness of
  the flesh.
  Bible: Ecclesiastes

5 The possession of a book becomes a
  substitute for reading it.
  Anthony Burgess 1917–93: in *New York Times
  Book Review* 4 December 1966

6 'What is the use of a book', thought Alice, 'without pictures or conversations?'
Lewis Carroll 1832–98: *Alice's Adventures in Wonderland* (1865)

7 The good of a book lies in its being read.
Umberto Eco 1932– : *The Name of the Rose* (1981)

8 Books are made not like children but like pyramids . . . and they're just as useless! and they stay in the desert! . . . Jackals piss at their foot and the bourgeois climb up on them.
Gustave Flaubert 1821–80: letter to Ernest Feydeau, November/December 1857

9 I suggest that the only books that influence us are those for which we are ready, and which have gone a little farther down our particular path than we have yet got ourselves.
E. M. Forster 1879–1970: *Two Cheers for Democracy* (1951)

10 Long books, when read, are usually overpraised, because the reader wishes to convince others and himself that he has not wasted his time.
E. M. Forster 1879–1970: note from commonplace book; O. Stallybrass (ed.) *Aspects of the Novel and Related Writings* (1974)

11 A bad book is as much of a labour to write as a good one; it comes as sincerely from the author's soul.
Aldous Huxley 1894–1963: *Point Counter Point* (1928)

12 Your *borrowers of books*—those mutilators of collections, spoilers of the symmetry of shelves, and creators of odd volumes.
Charles Lamb 1775–1834: *Essays of Elia* (1823) 'The Two Races of Men'

13 All books are either dreams or swords, You can cut, or you can drug, with words.
Amy Lowell 1874–1925: 'Sword Blades and Poppy Seed' (1914)

14 The book is the greatest interactive medium of all time. You can underline it, write in the margins, fold down a page, skip ahead. And you can take it anywhere.
■ *on taking over as head of Penguin Books*
Michael Lynton: in *Daily Telegraph* 19 August 1996

15 A good book is the precious life-blood of a master spirit, embalmed and treasured up on purpose to a life beyond life.
John Milton 1608–74: *Areopagitica* (1644)

16 I opened it at page 96—the secret page on which I write my name to catch out borrowers and book-sharks.
Flann O'Brien 1911–66: *Myles Away from Dublin* (1990)

17 This is not a novel to be tossed aside lightly. It should be thrown with great force.
Dorothy Parker 1893–1967: R. E. Drennan *Wit's End* (1973)

18 Books can not be killed by fire. People die, but books never die. No man and no force can abolish memory . . . In this war, we know, books are weapons. And it is a part of your dedication always to make them weapons for man's freedom.
Franklin D. Roosevelt 1882–1945: 'Message to the Booksellers of America' 6 May 1942

19 No furniture so charming as books.
Sydney Smith 1771–1845: Lady Holland *Memoir* (1855)

20 Books that told me everything about the wasp, except why.
Dylan Thomas 1914–53: *A Child's Christmas in Wales* (1954)

21 A good book is the best of friends, the same to-day and for ever.
Martin Tupper 1810–89: *Proverbial Philosophy* Series I (1838) 'Of Reading'

22 '*Classic*'. A book which people praise and don't read.
Mark Twain 1835–1910: *Following the Equator* (1897)

23 There is no such thing as a moral or an immoral book. Books are well written, or badly written.
Oscar Wilde 1854–1900: *The Picture of Dorian Gray* (1891)

Boredom

1 Nothing happens, nobody comes, nobody goes, it's awful!
Samuel Beckett 1906–89: *Waiting for Godot* (1955)

2 Life, friends, is boring. We must not say so . . .
And moreover my mother taught me as a boy
(repeatedly) 'Ever to confess you're bored
means you have no
Inner Resources.' I conclude now I have no
inner resources, because I am heavy bored.
John Berryman 1914–72: *77 Dream Songs* (1964) no. 14

3 What's wrong with being a boring kind of guy?
■ *during the campaign for the Republican nomination*
George Bush 1924– : in *Daily Telegraph* 28 April 1988

4 Someone has somewhere commented on the fact that millions long for immortality who don't know what to do with themselves on a rainy Sunday afternoon.
Susan Ertz 1894–1985: *Anger in the Sky* (1943)

5 Nothing, like something, happens anywhere.
Philip Larkin 1922–85: 'I Remember, I Remember' (1955)

6 Boredom is . . . a vital problem for the moralist, since half the sins of mankind are caused by the fear of it.
Bertrand Russell 1872–1970: *The Conquest of Happiness* (1930)

7 A desire for desires—boredom.
Leo Tolstoy 1828–1910: *Anna Karenina* (1873–6)

8 He is an old bore. Even the grave yawns for him.
■ *of Israel Zangwill*
Herbert Beerbohm Tree 1852–1917: Max Beerbohm *Herbert Beerbohm Tree* (1920)

9 A healthy male adult bore consumes *each year* one and a half times his own weight in other people's patience.
John Updike 1932– : *Assorted Prose* (1965) 'Confessions of a Wild Bore'

10 The secret of being a bore . . . is to tell everything.
Voltaire 1694–1778: *Discours en vers sur l'homme* (1737)

Boxing

see also **Sports and Games**

1 Float like a butterfly, sting like a bee.
■ *summary of his boxing strategy*
Muhammad Ali 1942– : G. Sullivan *Cassius Clay Story* (1964); probably originated by Drew 'Bundini' Brown

2 Boxing's just show business with blood.
Frank Bruno 1961– : in *Guardian* 20 November 1991; also attributed to David Belasco in 1915

3 Women are made for loving not hitting.
■ *on female boxing*
Henry Cooper 1934– : in *Independent on Sunday* 5 October 1997

4 Honey, I just forgot to duck.
■ *on losing the World Heavyweight title*
Jack Dempsey 1895–1983: to his wife, 23 September 1926; after a failed attempt on his life in 1981, Ronald Reagan quipped to his wife 'Honey, I forgot to duck'

5 We was robbed!
■ *after Jack Sharkey beat Max Schmeling (of whom Jacobs was manager) in the heavyweight title fight, 21 June 1932*
Joe Jacobs 1896–1940: Peter Heller *In This Corner* (1975)

6 He can run. But he can't hide.
■ *of Billy Conn, his opponent*
Joe Louis 1914–81: before a heavyweight title fight, 19 June 1946; *Louis: My Life Story* (1947)

7 *when asked by the coroner if he had intended to 'get Doyle in trouble':*
Mister, it's my *business* to get him in trouble.
■ *following the death of Jimmy Doyle from his injuries after fighting Robinson, 24 June 1947*
Sugar Ray Robinson 1920–89: *Sugar Ray* (1970, with Dave Anderson)

Britain

see also **British Cities and Towns**, **England**

1 Great Britain has lost an empire and has not yet found a role.

Dean Acheson 1893–1971: speech at the Military Academy, West Point, 5 December 1962

2 When I think of Cool Britannia, I think of old people dying of hypothermia.

Tony Benn 1925– : at the Labour Party Conference, in *Daily Star* 30 September 1998

3 The American dream is that any citizen can rise to the highest office in the land. The British dream is that the Queen drops in for tea.

Michael Bywater: in *Independent* 20 October 1997

4 The British nation is unique in this respect. They are the only people who like to be told how bad things are, who like to be told the worst.

Winston Churchill 1874–1965: speech in the House of Commons, 10 June 1941

5 We did have a form of Afro-Asian studies which consisted of colouring bits of the map red to show the British Empire.

Michael Green 1927– : *The Boy Who Shot Down an Airship* (1988)

6 Britain will be honoured by historians more for the way she disposed of an empire than for the way in which she acquired it.

Lord Harlech 1918–85: in *New York Times* 28 October 1962

7 Britain is no longer totally a white place where people ride horses, wear long frocks and drink tea. The national dish is no longer fish and chips, it's curry.

Marianne Jean-Baptiste: in *Observer* 18 May 1997

8 Fifty years on from now, Britain will still be the country of long shadows on county [cricket] grounds, warm beer, invincible green suburbs, dog lovers, and—as George Orwell said—old maids bicycling to Holy Communion through the morning mist.

John Major 1943– : speech to the Conservative Group for Europe, 22 April 1993; cf. **England 14**

9 He [the Briton] is a barbarian, and thinks that the customs of his tribe and island are the laws of nature.

George Bernard Shaw 1856–1950: *Caesar and Cleopatra* (1901)

10 Rule, Britannia, rule the waves;
Britons never will be slaves.

James Thomson 1700–48: *Alfred: a Masque* (1740)

11 A soggy little island huffing and puffing to keep up with Western Europe.

John Updike 1932– : 'London Life' (written 1969)

12 Other nations use 'force'; we Britons alone use 'Might'.

Evelyn Waugh 1903–66: *Scoop* (1938)

British Cities and Towns

see also **London**, **Oxford**

1 Oh! who can ever be tired of Bath?

Jane Austen 1775–1817: *Northanger Abbey* (1818)

2 One has no great hopes from Birmingham. I always say there is something direful in the sound.

Jane Austen 1775–1817: *Emma* (1816)

3 Come, friendly bombs, and fall on Slough!
It isn't fit for humans now,
There isn't grass to graze a cow.
Swarm over, Death!

John Betjeman 1906–84: 'Slough' (1937)

4 O the bricks they will bleed and the rain it will weep
And the damp Lagan fog lull the city to sleep;
It's to hell with the future and live on the past:

May the Lord in His mercy be kind to
Belfast.

■ *based on the traditional refrain 'May God in
His mercy look down on Belfast'*
   Maurice James Craig 1919– : 'Ballad to a
   Traditional Refrain' (1974)

5 Bugger Bognor.

■ *comment made either in 1929, when it was
proposed that the town be renamed Bognor Regis
following the king's convalescence there; or on
his deathbed when someone said 'Cheer up, your
Majesty, you will soon be at Bognor again.'*
   George V 1865–1936: Kenneth Rose *King
   George V* (1983)

6 With the possible exceptions of
Jerusalem and Mecca, Belfast must be
the most religion-conscious city in
the world.
   Tyrone Guthrie 1900–71: *A Life in the Theatre*
   (1959)

7 City of perspiring dreams.

■ *of Cambridge*
   Frederic Raphael 1931– : *The Glittering Prizes*
   (1976); see **Oxford** 2

8 It is from the midst of this putrid
sewer that the greatest river of human
industry springs up and carries
fertility to the whole world. From this
foul drain pure gold flows forth.

■ *of Manchester*
   Alexis de Tocqueville 1805–59: *Voyage en
   Angleterre et en Irlande de 1835* 2 July 1835

Buildings
....
see also **Architecture**

1 The existence of St Sophia is
atmospheric; that of St Peter's,
overpoweringly, imminently
substantial. One is a church to God:
the other a salon for his agents. One is
consecrated to reality, the other, to
illusion. St Sophia in fact is large, and
St Peter's is vilely, tragically small.
   Robert Byron 1905–41: *The Road to Oxiana*
   (1937)

2 A monstrous carbuncle on the face of
a much-loved and elegant friend.

■ *on the proposed extension to the National
Gallery, London*
   Charles, Prince of Wales 1948– : speech to the
   Royal Institute of British Architects, 30 May
   1984

3 Our cathedrals are like abandoned
computers now, but they used to be
prayer factories once.
   Lawrence Durrell 1912–90: in *Listener* 20 April
   1978

4 Who would guess that those gloomy
bunkers were built to celebrate the
pleasures of the senses?

■ *of the Hayward Gallery complex, London*
   Lord Esher 1913– : *A Broken Wave* (1987)

5 It looks like a portable typewriter full
of oyster shells, and to the contention
that it echoes the sails of yachts on the
harbour I can only point out that the
yachts on the harbour don't waste any
time echoing opera houses.

■ *of the Sydney Opera House*
   Clive James 1939– : *Flying Visits* (1984)

6 That temple of silence and
reconciliation where the enmities of
twenty generations lie buried.

■ *of Westminster Abbey*
   Lord Macaulay 1800–59: *Essays Contributed to
   the Edinburgh Review* (1843) 'Warren
   Hastings'

7 As if St Paul's had come down and
littered.

■ *on Brighton Pavilion*
   Sydney Smith 1771–1845: Peter Virgin *Sydney
   Smith* (1994)

8 To people who laugh at the
Millennium Dome as not just over-
priced but 'pretentious', I'd say that's
precisely why I love it—because it
combines with such insouciance the
qualities of biblical crown of thorns,
royal crown and crown roast of lamb.
   John Walsh 1937– : in *Independent*
   30 September 1998

Bureaucracy
....
see also **Administration**, **Committees**

1 It is an inevitable defect, that
bureaucrats will care more for routine
than for results.
   Walter Bagehot 1826–77: *The English
   Constitution* (1867)

2 Guidelines for bureaucrats: (1) When
in charge, ponder. (2) When in

trouble, delegate. (3) When in doubt, mumble.

James H. Boren 1925– : in *New York Times* 8 November 1970

3 Whatever was required to be done, the Circumlocution Office was beforehand with all the public departments in the art of perceiving—HOW NOT TO DO IT.

Charles Dickens 1812–70: *Little Dorrit* (1857)

4 Where there is officialism every human relationship suffers.

E. M. Forster 1879–1970: *A Passage to India* (1924)

5 What is official
Is incontestable. It undercuts
The problematical world and sells us life
At a discount.

Christopher Fry 1907– : *The Lady's not for Burning* (1949)

6 Official dignity tends to increase in inverse ratio to the importance of the country in which the office is held.

Aldous Huxley 1894–1963: *Beyond the Mexique Bay* (1934)

7 The truth in these matters may be stated as a scientific law: 'The persistence of public officials varies inversely with the importance of the matter on which they are persisting.'

Bernard Levin 1928– : *In These Times* (1986)

8 The man who is denied the opportunity of taking decisions of importance begins to regard as important the decisions he is allowed to take.

C. Northcote Parkinson 1909–93: *Parkinson's Law* (1958)

9 Back in the East you can't do much without the right papers, but *with* the right papers you can do *anything*. They *believe* in papers. Papers are power.

Tom Stoppard 1937– : *Neutral Ground* (1983)

10 The concept of the 'official secret' is its [bureaucracy's] specific invention.

Max Weber 1864–1920: 'Politik als Beruf' (1919)

Business

see also **Economics**, **Shopping**

1 There is nothing more requisite in business than dispatch.

Joseph Addison 1672–1719: *The Drummer* (1716)

2 A merchant shall hardly keep himself from doing wrong.

Bible: Ecclesiasticus

3 NINOTCHKA: Why should you carry other people's bags?
PORTER: Well, that's my business, Madame.
NINOTCHKA: That's no business. That's social injustice.
PORTER: That depends on the tip.

Charles Brackett 1892–1969 and **Billy Wilder** 1906–2002: *Ninotchka* (1939 film, with Walter Reisch)

4 Here's the rule for bargains: 'Do other men, for they would do you.' That's the true business precept.

Charles Dickens 1812–70: *Martin Chuzzlewit* (1844)

5 *Knowledge is the only meaningful resource today.* The traditional 'factors of production'—land (i.e. natural resources), labour and capital—have not disappeared. But they have become secondary.

Peter F. Drucker 1909– : *Post-Capitalist Society* (1993)

6 The salary of the chief executive of the large corporation is not a market reward for achievement. It is frequently in the nature of a warm personal gesture by the individual to himself.

J. K. Galbraith 1908– : *Annals of an Abiding Liberal* (1979)

7 Only the paranoid survive.

■ *dictum on which he has long run his company, the Intel Corporation*

Andrew Grove 1936– : in *New York Times* 18 December 1994

8 To say that profit is a means to other ends and not an end in itself is not a

semantic quibble, it is a serious moral point. A requirement is not a purpose.
Charles Handy 1932– : *The Empty Raincoat* (1994)

9 Accountants are the witch-doctors of the modern world and willing to turn their hands to any kind of magic.
Charles Eustace Harman 1894–1970: speech, February 1964

10 If I have to intervene to help British companies . . . I'll intervene—before breakfast, before lunch, before tea and before dinner. And I'll get up the next morning and I'll start all over again.
■ *of his role as President of the Board of Trade*
Michael Heseltine 1933– : to the Conservative Party Conference, 7 October 1992

11 In a sense, every business today, not just those in the garment trade, is a 'fashion' business. To compete effectively, companies must innovate continually and in ever shorter cycles.
Rosabeth Moss Kanter 1943– : *World Class* (1995)

12 The green shoots of economic spring are appearing once again.
■ *often quoted as 'the green shoots of recovery'*
Norman Lamont 1942– : speech at Conservative Party Conference, 9 October 1991

13 Doing well by doing good.
■ *now the slogan of Monsanto*
Tom Lehrer 1928– : 'The Old Dope Peddler' (1953 song)

14 How to succeed in business without really trying.
Shepherd Mead 1914– : title of book (1952)

15 For a salesman, there is no rock bottom to the life . . . A salesman is got to dream, boy. It comes with the territory.
Arthur Miller 1915– : *Death of a Salesman* (1949)

16 Could Henry Ford produce the Book of Kells? Certainly not. He would quarrel initially with the advisability of such a project and then prove it was impossible.
Flann O'Brien 1911–66: *Myles Away from Dublin* (1990)

17 Jane Austen doesn't sell hi-tech cars. We do the past very well in this country but how can we compete from a high-tech point of view when the rest of the world sees us dressed up in top hats and crinolines all the time?
Roger Puttnam: in *Independent* 7 June 1997

18 We even sell a pair of earrings for under £1, which is cheaper than a prawn sandwich from Marks & Spencers. But I have to say the earrings probably won't last as long.
Gerald Ratner 1949– : speech to the Institute of Directors, Albert Hall, 23 April 1991

19 The customer is never wrong.
César Ritz 1850–1918: R. Nevill and C. E. Jerningham *Piccadilly to Pall Mall* (1908)

20 I think that business practices would improve immeasurably if they were guided by 'feminine' principles— qualities like love and care and intuition.
Anita Roddick 1942– : *Body and Soul* (1991)

21 Running a company on market research is like driving while looking in the rear view mirror.
Anita Roddick 1942– : in *Independent* 22 August 1997

22 The most striking thing about modern industry is that it requires so much and accomplishes so little. Modern industry seems to be inefficient to a degree that surpasses one's ordinary powers of imagination. Its inefficiency therefore remains unnoticed.
E. F. Schumacher 1911–77: *Small is Beautiful* (1973)

23 People of the same trade seldom meet together, even for merriment and diversion, but the conversation ends in a conspiracy against the public, or in some contrivance to raise prices.
Adam Smith 1723–90: *Wealth of Nations* (1776)

24 To found a great empire for the sole purpose of raising up a people of customers, may at first sight appear a project fit only for a nation of

shopkeepers. It is, however, a project altogether unfit for a nation of shopkeepers; but extremely fit for a nation whose government is influenced by shopkeepers.

Adam Smith 1723–90: *Wealth of Nations* (1776)

25 Corporations have neither bodies to be punished, nor souls to be condemned, they therefore do as they like.

■ *often quoted as 'Did you ever expect a corporation to have a conscience, when it has no soul to be damned, and no body to be kicked?'*

Lord Thurlow 1731–1806: John Poynder *Literary Extracts* (1844)

26 Deals are my art form. Other people paint beautifully on canvas or write wonderful poetry. I like making deals, preferably big deals. That's how I get my kicks.

Donald Trump 1946– : Donald Trump and Tony Schwartz *The Art of the Deal* (1987)

27 The public be damned! I'm working for my stockholders.

William H. Vanderbilt 1821–85: comment to a news reporter, 2 October 1882

28 Being good in business is the most fascinating kind of art.

Andy Warhol 1927–87: *Philosophy of Andy Warhol (From A to B and Back Again)* (1975)

29 You cannot be a success in any business without believing that it is the greatest business in the world . . . You have to put your heart in the business and the business in your heart.

Thomas Watson Snr. 1874–1956: Robert Sobel *IBM: Colossus in Transition* (1981)

30 For years I thought what was good for our country was good for General Motors and vice versa.

Charles E. Wilson 1890–1961: testimony to the Senate Armed Services Committee on his proposed nomination for Secretary of Defence, 15 January 1953

31 Nothing is illegal if one hundred well-placed business men decide to do it.

Andrew Young 1932– : Morris K. Udall *Too Funny to be President* (1988)

Canada

1 A Canadian is somebody who knows how to make love in a canoe.

Pierre Berton 1920– : in *The Canadian* 22 December 1973

2 We French, we English, never lost our civil war,
endure it still, a bloodless civil bore;
no wounded lying about, no Whitman wanted.
It's only by our lack of ghosts we're haunted.

Earle Birney 1904– : 'Can.Lit.' (1962)

3 Dusty, cobweb-covered, maimed, and set at naught,
Beauty crieth in an attic, and no man regardeth.
O God! O Montreal!

Samuel Butler 1835–1902: 'Psalm of Montreal' (1878)

4 Canada could have enjoyed:
English government,
French culture,
and American know-how.
Instead it ended up with:
English know-how,
French government,
and American culture.

■ *a similar (prose) summary has been attributed to Lester Pearson (1897–1972)*

John Robert Colombo 1936– : 'O Canada' (1965)

5 I see Canada as a country torn between a very northern, rather extraordinary, mystical spirit which it fears and its desire to present itself to the world as a Scotch banker.

Robertson Davies 1913–95: *The Enthusiasms of Robertson Davies* (1990)

6 *Vive Le Québec Libre.*
Long Live Free Quebec.

Charles de Gaulle 1890–1970: speech in Montreal, 24 July 1967

7 If some countries have too much history, we have too much geography.

William Lyon Mackenzie King 1874–1950: speech on Canada as an international power, 18 June 1936

8 The nineteenth century was the
century of the United States. I think
we can claim that it is Canada that
shall fill the twentieth century.

■ *usually quoted as 'The twentieth century
belongs to Canada'*
Wilfrid Laurier 1841–1919: speech in Ottawa,
18 January 1904

9 Canadians are Americans with no
Disneyland.
Margaret Mahy 1936– : *The Changeover*
(1984)

10 There are very few Eskimos, but
millions of Whites, just like
mosquitoes. It is something very
special and wonderful to be an
Eskimo—they are like the snow geese.
If an Eskimo forgets his language and
Eskimo ways, he will be nothing but
just another mosquito.
Abraham Okpik d. 1997: attributed

11 I have to spend so much time
explaining to Americans that I am not
English and to Englishmen that I am
not American that I have little time
left to be Canadian.
Laurence J. Peter 1919–90: *Quotations for our
Time* (1977)

12 Ours is a sovereign nation
Bows to no foreign will
But whenever they cough in
Washington
They spit on Parliament Hill.
Joe Wallace: attributed

13 Canadians do not like heroes, and so
they do not have them.
George Woodcock 1912–95: *Canada and the
Canadians* (1970)

Cancer

see also **Sickness**

1 The best sentence in the English
language is not 'I love you' but 'It's
benign'.
Woody Allen 1935– : *Deconstructing Harry*
(1998 film)

2 My final word, before I'm done,
Is 'Cancer can be rather fun'.

Thanks to the nurses and Nye Bevan
The NHS is quite like heaven
Provided one confronts the tumour
With a sufficient sense of humour.
J. B. S. Haldane 1892–1964: 'Cancer's a Funny
Thing' (1968)

3 Human nature seldom walks up to the
word 'cancer'.
Rudyard Kipling 1865–1936: *Debits and Credits*
(1926)

Capitalism

see also **Class**, **Communism**

1 There is a good deal of solemn cant
about the common interests of capital
and labour. As matters stand, their
only common interest is that of
cutting each other's throat.
Brooks Atkinson 1894–1984: *Once Around the
Sun* (1951)

2 The worker is the slave of capitalist
society, the female worker is the slave
of that slave.
James Connolly 1868–1916: *The Re-conquest of
Ireland* (1915)

3 History suggests that capitalism is a
necessary condition for political
freedom. Clearly it is not a sufficient
condition for it.
Milton Friedman 1912– : *Capitalism and
Freedom* (1962)

4 The unpleasant and unacceptable face
of capitalism.

■ *on the Lonrho affair*
Edward Heath 1916– : speech, House of
Commons, 15 May 1973

5 There is a permanent tension in a
capitalist economy between the
desirability of forming committed
relationships where both parties
cooperate and don't cheat on each
other—and the temptation to cut and
run, attempting to find a better deal
elsewhere.
Will Hutton 1950– : *The State We're In* (1995)

6 Yes to the market economy, No to the market society.

Lionel Jospin 1937– : in *Independent*
16 September 1998

7 Whether you like it or not, history is on our side. We will bury you.

Nikita Khrushchev 1894–1971: speech to
Western diplomats in Moscow, 18 November
1956

8 Imperialism is the monopoly stage of capitalism.

Lenin 1870–1924: *Imperialism as the Last Stage
of Capitalism* (1916) 'Briefest possible
definition of imperialism'

9 He enjoys prophesying the imminent fall of the capitalist system and is prepared to play a part, any part, in its burial, except that of mute.

■ *of Aneurin Bevan*

Harold Macmillan 1894–1986: Michael Foot
Aneurin Bevan (1962)

10 Normally speaking, it may be said that the forces of a capitalist society, if left unchecked, tend to make the rich richer and the poor poorer and thus increase the gap between them.

Jawaharlal Nehru 1889–1964: 'Basic
Approach' in Vincent Shean *Nehru . . .*
(1960)

11 In the first stone which he [the savage] flings at the wild animals he pursues, in the first stick that he seizes to strike down the fruit which hangs above his reach, we see the appropriation of one article for the purpose of aiding in the acquisition of another, and thus discover the origin of capital.

Robert Torrens 1780–1864: *An Essay on the
Production of Wealth* (1821)

12 You have riches and freedom here but I feel no sense of faith or direction. You have so many computers, why don't you use them in the search for love?

Lech Wałęsa 1943– : in Paris, on his first
journey outside the Soviet area, in *Daily
Telegraph* 14 December 1988

Careers
....
see also **Ambition**, **Work**

1 For promotion cometh neither from the east, nor from the west: nor yet from the south.

Bible: Psalm 75

2 Most twentieth-century authors, and in particular the greats like Yeats, Eliot and Lawrence, who regularly feature in A-level and undergraduate syllabuses, inculcate an attitude of contempt for ordinary, bread-earning citizens, which must inevitably unsettle youngsters who are on the point of choosing a career, unless they are mercifully too dense to get the modernists' message at all.

John Carey 1934– : in *Listener* 1974

3 Your work parallels your life, but in the sense of a glass full of water where people look at it and say, 'Oh, the water's the same shape as the glass!'

Francis Ford Coppola 1939– : in *Guardian*
15 October 1988

4 McJob: A low-pay, low-prestige, low-dignity, low benefit, no-future job in the service sector.

Douglas Coupland 1961– : *Generation X*
(1991)

5 To do nothing and get something, formed a boy's ideal of a manly career.

Benjamin Disraeli 1804–81: *Sybil* (1845)

6 Don't worry me—I am an 8 ulcer man on 4 ulcer pay.

Stephen T. Early 1889–1951: letter to Harry S.
Truman; William Hillman *Mr President*
(1952)

7 If I would be a young man again and had to decide how to make my living, I would not try to become a scientist or scholar or teacher. I would rather choose to be a plumber or a peddler in the hope to find that modest degree of independence still available under present circumstances.

Albert Einstein 1879–1955: in *Reporter*
18 November 1954

8 By working faithfully eight hours a day, you may eventually get to be a boss and work twelve hours a day.
Robert Frost 1874–1963: attributed

9 I didn't get where I am today without . . . .
■ *catch-phrase used by the manager C. J.*
David Nobbs 1935– : *The Death of Reginald Perrin* (1975); and subsequently the BBC TV series *The Fall and Rise of Reginald Perrin* (1976–80)

10 I have that normal male thing of valuing myself according to the job I do. When I can't tell someone in one word what I am, then something is missing. I don't represent anything any more.
Michael Portillo 1953– : in *Independent on Sunday* 20 June 1999

11 Thou art not for the fashion of these times,
Where none will sweat but for promotion.
William Shakespeare 1564–1616: *As You Like It* (1599)

12 All professions are conspiracies against the laity.
George Bernard Shaw 1856–1950: *The Doctor's Dilemma* (1911)

13 The test of a vocation is the love of the drudgery it involves.
Logan Pearsall Smith 1865–1946: *Afterthoughts* (1931) 'Art and Letters'

14 How to be an effective secretary is to develop the kind of lonely self-abnegating sacrificial instincts usually possessed only by the early saints on their way to martyrdom.
Jill Tweedie 1936–93: *It's Only Me* (1980)

Cars

see also **Speed**

1 A car standing alone can be a beautiful and emotive object, but wherever two or three are gathered together, in my view, you have ugliness.
Rowan Atkinson 1955– : in *Sunday Times* 3 October 1999

2 A car crash harnesses elements of eroticism, aggression, desire, speed, drama, kinaesthetic factors, the stylizing of motion, consumer goods, status—all these in one event. I myself see the car crash as a tremendous sexual event really: a liberation of human and machine libido (if there is such a thing).
J. G. Ballard 1930– : interview in *Penthouse* September 1970

3 I think that cars today are almost the exact equivalent of the great Gothic cathedrals: I mean the supreme creation of an era, conceived with passion by unknown artists, and consumed in image if not in usage by a whole population which appropriates them as a purely magical object.
Roland Barthes 1915–80: *Mythologies* (1957) 'La nouvelle Citroën'

4 We have now to plan no longer for soft little animals pottering about on their own two legs, but for hard steel canisters hurtling about with these same little animals inside them.
Hugh Casson 1910–99: Clough Williams-Ellis *Around the World in 90 Years* (1978)

5 The poetry of motion! The *real* way to travel! The *only* way to travel! Here today—in next week tomorrow! Villages skipped, towns and cities jumped—always somebody else's horizon! O bliss! O poop-poop! O my! O my!
■ *on the car*
Kenneth Grahame 1859–1932: *The Wind in the Willows* (1908)

6 The automobile changed our dress, manners, social customs, vacation habits, the shape of our cities, consumer purchasing patterns, common tastes and positions in intercourse.
John Keats 1920– : *The Insolent Chariots* (1958)

7 To George F. Babbitt, as to most prosperous citizens of Zenith, his motor car was poetry and tragedy, love and heroism. The office was his pirate ship but the car his perilous excursion ashore.

Sinclair Lewis 1885–1951: *Babbitt* (1922)

8 The car has become an article of dress without which we feel uncertain, unclad and incomplete in the urban compound.

Marshall McLuhan 1911–80: *Understanding Media* (1964)

9 Beneath this slab
John Brown is stowed.
He watched the ads,
And not the road.

Ogden Nash 1902–71: 'Lather as You Go' (1942)

10 You have your own company, your own temperature control, your own music—and don't have to put up with dreadful human beings sitting alongside you.

■ *on cars compared to public transport*
Steven Norris 1945– : comment to Commons Environment Select Committee, in *Daily Telegraph* 9 February 1995

11 It looks like a poached egg—we can't make that.

■ *on seeing the Morris Minor prototype in 1945*
Lord Nuffield 1877–1963: attributed

12 At 60 miles an hour the loudest noise in this new Rolls-Royce comes from the electric clock.

David Ogilvy 1911–99: advertising slogan for the Silver Cloud, 1959

13 Though the various scents of garages, showrooms, and racetracks have pleasing associations for me, I've yet to hear a woman say, 'Mmmmmmm, you smell like a car.'

P. J. O'Rourke 1947– : in *Automobile*, 1993

14 When a man opens the car door for his wife, it's either a new car or a new wife.

Prince Philip, Duke of Edinburgh 1921– : in *Today* 2 March 1988

15 No other man-made device since the shields and lances of ancient knights fulfils a man's ego like an automobile.

Lord Rootes 1894–1964: attributed, 1958

Cats

············

see also **Animals**

1 Macavity, Macavity, there's no one like Macavity,
There never was a Cat of such deceitfulness and suavity.
He always has an alibi, and one or two to spare:
At whatever time the deed took place—MACAVITY WASN'T THERE!

T. S. Eliot 1888–1965: 'Macavity: the Mystery Cat' (1939)

2 The Naming of Cats is a difficult matter,
It isn't just one of your holiday games;
You may think at first I'm as mad as a hatter
when I tell you, a cat must have THREE DIFFERENT NAMES.

T. S. Eliot 1888–1965: 'The Naming of Cats' (1939)

3 Daylong this tomcat lies stretched flat
As an old rough mat, no mouth and no eyes,
Continual wars and wives are what
Have tattered his ears and battered his head.

Ted Hughes 1930–98: 'Esther's Tomcat' (1960)

4 He walked by himself, and all places were alike to him.

Rudyard Kipling 1865–1936: *Just So Stories* (1902) 'The Cat that Walked by Himself'

5 Cats seem to go on the principle that it never does any harm to ask for what you want.

Joseph Wood Krutch 1893–1970: *Twelve Seasons* (1949)

6 When I play with my cat, who knows whether she isn't amusing herself with me more than I am with her?

Montaigne 1533–92: *Essais* (1580)

7 The trouble with a kitten is
THAT
Eventually it becomes a
CAT.

Ogden Nash 1902–71: 'The Kitten' (1940)

8 The greater cats with golden eyes
Stare out between the bars.

Deserts are there, and different skies,
And night with different stars.
Vita Sackville-West 1892–1962: *The King's Daughter* (1929)

9 For I will consider my Cat
Jeoffrey. . . .
For he counteracts the powers of
darkness by his electrical skin and
glaring eyes.
For he counteracts the Devil, who is
death, by brisking about the life.
Christopher Smart 1722–71: *Jubilate Agno* (*c.*1758–63)

10 Cats, no less liquid than their
shadows,
Offer no angles to the wind.
They slip, diminished, neat, through
loopholes
Less than themselves.
A. S. J. Tessimond 1902–62: *Cats* (1934)

Causes and Consequences

1 The present contains nothing more
than the past, and what is found in the
effect was already in the cause.
Henri Bergson 1859–1941: *L'Évolution créatrice* (1907)

2 Whatsoever a man soweth, that shall
he also reap.
Bible: Galatians

3 One leak will sink a ship, and one sin
will destroy a sinner.
John Bunyan 1628–88: *The Pilgrim's Progress* (1684)

4 You have broader considerations that
might follow what you might call the
'falling domino' principle. You have a
row of dominoes set up. You knock
over the first one, and what will
happen to the last one is that it will go
over very quickly. So you have the
beginning of a disintegration that
would have the most profound
influences.
Dwight D. Eisenhower 1890–1969: speech at
press conference, 7 April 1954

5 Whoever wills the end, wills also (so
far as reason decides his conduct) the
means in his power which are
indispensably necessary thereto.
Immanuel Kant 1724–1804: *Fundamental
Principles of the Metaphysics of Ethics* (1785)

6 As it will be in the future, it was at the
birth of Man—
There are only four things certain
since Social Progress began:
That the Dog returns to his Vomit and
the Sow returns to her Mire,
And the burnt Fool's bandaged finger
goes wabbling back to the Fire;
And that after this is accomplished,
and the brave new world begins
When all men are paid for existing
and no man must pay for his sins,
As surely as Water will wet us, as
surely as Fire will burn,
The Gods of the Copybook Headings
with terror and slaughter return!
Rudyard Kipling 1865–1936: 'The Gods of the
Copybook Headings' (1919)

7 The English . . . are paralysed by fear.
That is what thwarts and distorts the
Anglo-Saxon existence . . . Nothing
could be more lovely and fearless than
Chaucer. But already Shakespeare is
morbid with fear, fear of
consequences. That is the strange
phenomenon of the English
Renaissance: this mystic terror of the
consequences, the consequences of
action.
D. H. Lawrence 1885–1930: *Phoenix* (1936)

8 The structure of a play is always the
story of how the birds came home to
roost.
Arthur Miller 1915– : in *Harper's Magazine*
August 1958

9 Every positive value has its price in
negative terms . . . The genius of
Einstein leads to Hiroshima.
Pablo Picasso 1881–1973: F. Gilot and C. Lake
Life With Picasso (1964)

10 Sow an act, and you reap a habit. Sow
a habit and you reap a character. Sow
a character, and you reap a destiny.
Charles Reade 1814–84: attributed

Caution

····················

see also **Danger, Risk**

1 Happy is that city which in time of peace thinks of war.
■ *inscription found in the armoury of Venice*
Anonymous: Robert Burton *The Anatomy of Melancholy* (1621–51)

2 And always keep a-hold of Nurse
For fear of finding something worse.
Hilaire Belloc 1870–1953: *Cautionary Tales* (1907) 'Jim'

3 Prudence is a rich, ugly, old maid courted by Incapacity.
William Blake 1757–1827: *The Marriage of Heaven and Hell* (1790–3)

4 Beware of desperate steps. The darkest day
(Live till tomorrow) will have passed away.
William Cowper 1731–1800: 'The Needless Alarm' (written *c.*1790)

5 Tar-baby ain't sayin' nuthin', en Brer Fox, he lay low.
Joel Chandler Harris 1848–1908: *Uncle Remus and His Legends of the Old Plantation* (1881)

6 Them that asks no questions isn't told a lie.
Watch the wall, my darling, while the Gentlemen go by!
Rudyard Kipling 1865–1936: 'A Smuggler's Song' (1906)

7 All the security around the American president is just to make sure the man who shoots him gets caught.
Norman Mailer 1923– : in *Sunday Telegraph* 4 March 1990

8 Of all forms of caution, caution in love is perhaps the most fatal to true happiness.
Bertrand Russell 1872–1970: *The Conquest of Happiness* (1930)

9 Put all your eggs in the one basket, and—WATCH THAT BASKET.
Mark Twain 1835–1910: *Pudd'nhead Wilson* (1894)

Celebrations

····················

see also **Christmas**

1 Never ask the children to tell the class what they did for Easter or Christmas or Confirmation or St Patrick's Day . . . Nothing points up the inequality of people's lives more starkly than asking innocent children to tell you how they spent what was meant to be a festival.
Maeve Binchy 1940– : in *Irish Times* 14 March 1998

2 A diplomat is a man who always remembers a woman's birthday but never remembers her age.
Robert Frost 1874–1963: attributed

3 If there is a project that can pump a bit of excitement into the big depressed sponge that is the core of English negativity, then it will be worth doing.
■ *on being appointed musical director of the Millennium Experience*
Peter Gabriel 1950– : in *Independent* on 16 January 1999

4 The holiest of all holidays are those
Kept by ourselves in silence and apart;
The secret anniversaries of the heart.
Henry Wadsworth Longfellow 1807–82: 'Holidays' (1877)

5 Time has no divisions to mark its passage, there is never a thunderstorm or blare of trumpets to announce the beginning of a new month or year. Even when a new century begins it is only we mortals who ring bells and fire off pistols.
Thomas Mann 1875–1955: *The Magic Mountain* (1924)

6 For every year of life we light
A candle on your cake
To mark the simple sort of progress
Anyone can make,
And then, to test your nerve or give
A proper view of death,
You're asked to blow each light, each year,
Out with your own breath.
James Simmons 1933–2001: 'A Birthday Poem' (1969)

7 Ring out the old, ring in the new,
Ring, happy bells, across the snow:
The year is going, let him go;
Ring out the false, ring in the true.
Alfred, Lord Tennyson 1809–92: *In Memoriam
A. H. H.* (1850)

8 Millennium Eve, the way things are
going, seems as good a night as any to
stay in and whitewash the spare
bedroom.
Keith Waterhouse 1929– : in *Sunday Times*
17 January 1999

9 Seasons pursuing each other the
indescribable
crowd is gathered, it is the fourth of
Seventh-
month, (what salutes of cannon and
small-arms!)
Walt Whitman 1819–92: 'Song of Myself'
(written 1855)

Celibacy

1 Nobody dies from lack of sex. It's lack
of love we die from.
Margaret Atwood 1939– : *The Handmaid's
Tale* (1986)

2 I am that twentieth-century failure, a
happy undersexed celibate.
Denise Coffey: Ned Sherrin *Cutting Edge*
(1984)

3 Being an old maid is like death by
drowning, a really delightful sensation
after you cease to struggle.
Edna Ferber 1887–1968: R. E. Drennan *Wit's
End* (1973)

4 Deep down, we remain human, very
human and have all the desires to love
and be loved by one person . . . Every
time I did a marriage, every time I see
people married, I say: 'That could
have been me.'
Basil Hume 1923–99: attributed; in 1992

5 Chastity—the most unnatural of all
the sexual perversions.
Aldous Huxley 1894–1963: *Eyeless in Gaza*
(1936)

6 Marriage has many pains, but celibacy
has no pleasures.
Samuel Johnson 1709–84: *Rasselas* (1759)

7 By staying single I have one saintly
virtue as far as men are concerned,
even though it is by default: I can't be
unfaithful to one of their sex.
Irma Kurtz: *Malespeak* (1986)

Censorship

see also **Pornography**

1 So cryptic as to be almost
meaningless. If there is a meaning, it
is doubtless objectionable.
■ *banning the film* The Seashell and the
Clergyman
Anonymous: British Board of Film Censors,
1929

2 Everybody favours free speech in the
slack moments when no axes are
being ground.
Heywood Broun 1888–1939: in *New York
World* 23 October 1926

3 The reading or non-reading a book—
will never keep down a single
petticoat.
Lord Byron 1788–1824: letter to Richard
Hoppner, 29 October 1819

4 One does not put Voltaire in the
Bastille.
■ *when asked to arrest Sartre, in the 1960s*
Charles de Gaulle 1890–1970: in *Encounter*
June 1975

5 Modern technology endows the
individual with the means to
circumvent totalitarian controls on
information.
Peter F. Drucker 1909– : *Post-Capitalist
Society* (1993)

6 It's red hot, mate. I hate to think of
this sort of book getting into the
wrong hands. As soon as I've finished
this, I shall recommend they ban it.
Ray Galton 1930– and **Alan Simpson** 1929– :
The Missing Page (1960 BBC television
programme) words spoken by Tony
Hancock

7 Is it a book you would even wish your
wife or your servants to read?
■ *of D. H. Lawrence's* Lady Chatterley's Lover
Mervyn Griffith-Jones 1909–79: speech for the
prosecution at the Central Criminal Court,
Old Bailey, 20 October 1960

8 To portray only what you would like to be true is the beginning of censorship.
  David Hare 1947– : *The History Plays* (1984)

9 Wherever books will be burned, men also, in the end, are burned.
  Heinrich Heine 1797–1856: *Almansor* (1823)

10 One has to multiply thoughts to the point where there aren't enough policemen to control them.
  Stanislaw Lec 1909–66: *Unkempt Thoughts* (1962)

11 We have long passed the Victorian Era when asterisks were followed after a certain interval by a baby.
  W. Somerset Maugham 1874–1965: *The Constant Wife* (1926)

12 You have not converted a man, because you have silenced him.
  Lord Morley 1838–1923: *On Compromise* (1874)

13 If these writings of the Greeks agree with the book of God, they are useless and need not be preserved; if they disagree, they are pernicious and ought to be destroyed.
  ■ *on burning the library of Alexandria,* AD *c.641*
  Caliph Omar d. 644: Edward Gibbon *The Decline and Fall of the Roman Empire* (1776–88)

14 Don't you see that the whole aim of Newspeak is to narrow the range of thought? In the end we shall make thoughtcrime literally impossible, because there will be no words in which to express it.
  George Orwell 1903–50: *Nineteen Eighty-Four* (1949)

15 What is freedom of expression? Without the freedom to offend, it ceases to exist.
  Salman Rushdie 1947– : in *Weekend Guardian* 10 February 1990

16 Assassination is the extreme form of censorship.
  George Bernard Shaw 1856–1950: *The Showing-Up of Blanco Posnet* (1911)

17 If decade after decade the truth cannot be told, each person's mind begins to roam irretrievably. One's fellow countrymen become harder to understand than Martians.
  Alexander Solzhenitsyn 1918– : *Cancer Ward* (1968)

18 We are paid to have dirty minds.
  ■ *on British Film Censors*
  John Trevelyan: in *Observer* 15 November 1959

19 The state has no place in the nation's bedrooms.
  Pierre Trudeau 1919–2000: interview, Ottawa, 22 December 1967

20 Those who want the Government to regulate matters of the mind and spirit are like men who are so afraid of being murdered that they commit suicide to avoid assassination.
  Harry S. Truman 1884–1972: address at the National Archives, Washington, D.C., 15 December 1952

21 I disapprove of what you say, but I will defend to the death your right to say it.
  ■ *his attitude towards Helvétius following the burning of the latter's* De l'esprit *in 1759*
  Voltaire 1694–1778: attributed to Voltaire, the words are in fact S. G. Tallentyre's summary; *The Friends of Voltaire* (1907)

22 The Khomeini cry for the execution of Rushdie is an infantile cry. From the beginning of time we have seen that. To murder the thinker does not murder the thought.
  Arnold Wesker 1932– : in *Weekend Guardian* 3 June 1989

23 God forbid that any book should be banned. The practice is as indefensible as infanticide.
  Rebecca West 1892–1983: *The Strange Necessity* (1928)

Certainty
see also **Doubt**, **Fanaticism**

1 My mind is not a bed to be made and re-made.
  James Agate 1877–1947: *Ego 6* (1944) 9 June 1943

2 I beseech you, in the bowels of Christ, think it possible you may be mistaken.
Oliver Cromwell 1599–1658: letter to the General Assembly of the Kirk of Scotland, 3 August 1650

3 What, never?
No, never!
What, *never*?
Hardly ever!
W. S. Gilbert 1836–1911: *HMS Pinafore* (1878)

4 When a Southern Irishman says 'Not an inch', he means no more than four or five inches, and certainly not, at any rate for the next five or six years. But when an Ulsterman says 'Not an inch', that's it: he means not the tiniest fraction of an inch, from now until the last syllable of recorded time. And when he says 'No Surrender' he means just that, no surrender, ever.
Tony Gray 1928– : *St Patrick's People* (1996)

5 I wish I was as cocksure of anything as Tom Macaulay is of everything.
Lord Melbourne 1779–1848: Lord Cowper's preface to *Lord Melbourne's Papers* (1889)

6 Ah, what a dusty answer gets the soul When hot for certainties in this our life!
George Meredith 1828–1909: *Modern Love* (1862)

7 Human beings are perhaps never more frightening than when they are convinced beyond doubt that they are right.
Laurens van der Post 1906–96: *The Lost World of the Kalahari* (1958)

Chance

see also **Luck**

1 I come from a vertiginous country where the lottery forms a principal part of reality.
Jorge Luis Borges 1899–1986: *Fictions* (1956) 'The Babylon Lottery'

2 The chapter of knowledge is a very short, but the chapter of accidents is a very long one.
Lord Chesterfield 1694–1773: letter to Solomon Dayrolles, 16 February 1753

3 If an army of monkeys were strumming on typewriters they *might* write all the books in the British Museum.
Arthur Eddington 1882–1944: *The Nature of the Physical World* (1928)

4 At any rate, I am convinced that *He* [God] does not play dice.
■ *often quoted as 'God does not play dice'*
Albert Einstein 1879–1955: letter to Max Born, 4 December 1926

5 The ball no question makes of Ayes and Noes,
But here or there as strikes the player goes.
Edward Fitzgerald 1809–83: *The Rubáiyát of Omar Khayyám* (4th ed., 1879)

6 Mr Bond, they have a saying in Chicago: 'Once is happenstance. Twice is coincidence. The third time it's enemy action.'
Ian Fleming 1908–64: *Goldfinger* (1959)

7 A million million spermatozoa,
All of them alive:
Out of their cataclysm but one poor Noah
Dare hope to survive.
And among that billion minus one
Might have chanced to be Shakespeare, another Newton, a new Donne—
But the One was Me.
Aldous Huxley 1894–1963: 'Fifth Philosopher's Song' (1920)

8 The chance of winning the lottery jackpot is less than that of being struck by lightning. I have never bought a ticket and plan to buy an insulating rubber helmet with the money I save. It will increase my life expectancy by precisely one fourteen-millionth.
Steve Jones 1944– : in *Independent on Sunday* 5 November 1995

9 Predictability: Does the flap of a butterfly's wings in Brazil set off a tornado in Texas?
Edward N. Lorenz 1944– : title of paper given to the American Association for the Advancement of Science, Washington, 29 December 1979

10 A throw of the dice will never eliminate chance.
Stéphane Mallarmé 1842–98: title of poem (1897)

11 O! many a shaft, at random sent, Finds mark the archer little meant! And many a word, at random spoken, May soothe or wound a heart that's broken.
Sir Walter Scott 1771–1832: *The Lord of the Isles* (1813)

Change

....

see also **Progress**

1 But catastrophes only encouraged experiment.
As a rule, it was the fittest who perished, the mis-fits, forced by failure to emigrate to unsettled niches, who altered their structure and prospered.
W. H. Auden 1907–73: 'Unpredictable but Providential (for Loren Eiseley)' (1976)

2 He that will not apply new remedies must expect new evils; for time is the greatest innovator.
Francis Bacon 1561–1626: *Essays* (1625) 'Of Innovations'

3 There is in all change something at once sordid and agreeable, which smacks of infidelity and household removals. This is sufficient to explain the French Revolution.
Charles Baudelaire 1821–67: *Journaux intimes* (1887) 'Mon coeur mis à nu'

4 Can the Ethiopian change his skin, or the leopard his spots?
Bible: Jeremiah

5 'Yes,' I answered you last night; 'No,' this morning, sir, I say. Colours seen by candle-light Will not look the same by day.
Elizabeth Barrett Browning 1806–61: 'The Lady's Yes' (1844)

6 And now for something completely different.
Graham Chapman 1941–89, **John Cleese** 1939– , et al.: *Monty Python's Flying Circus* (BBC TV programme, 1970)

7 All conservatism is based upon the idea that if you leave things alone you leave them as they are. But you do not. If you leave a thing alone you leave it to a torrent of change.
G. K. Chesterton 1874–1936: *Orthodoxy* (1908)

8 Variety's the very spice of life, That gives it all its flavour.
William Cowper 1731–1800: *The Task* (1785)

9 Change is inevitable in a progressive country. Change is constant.
Benjamin Disraeli 1804–81: speech at Edinburgh, 29 October 1867

10 I sometimes sense the world is changing almost too fast for its inhabitants, at least for us older ones.
Elizabeth II 1926– : on a tour of Pakistan, 8 October 1997

11 When it is not necessary to change, it is necessary not to change.
Lucius Cary, Lord Falkland 1610–43: speech, 1641

12 Most of the change we think we see in life
Is due to truths being in and out of favour.
Robert Frost 1874–1963: 'The Black Cottage' (1914)

13 Everything flows and nothing stays . . . You can't step twice into the same river.
Heraclitus c.540–c.480 BC: Plato *Cratylus*

14 There is a certain relief in change, even though it be from bad to worse . . . it is often a comfort to shift one's position and be bruised in a new place.
Washington Irving 1783–1859: *Tales of a Traveller* (1824)

15 Change is not made without inconvenience, even from worse to better.
Samuel Johnson 1709–84: *A Dictionary of the English Language* (1755)

16 *Plus ça change, plus c'est la même chose.*

The more things change, the more they are the same.
Alphonse Karr 1808–90: *Les Guêpes* January 1849

17 There is nothing stable in the world—uproar's your only music.
John Keats 1795–1821: letter to George and Thomas Keats, 13 January 1818

18 If we want things to stay as they are, things will have to change.
Giuseppe di Lampedusa 1896–1957: *The Leopard* (1957)

19 Change and decay in all around I see;
O Thou, who changest not, abide with me.
Henry Francis Lyte 1793–1847: 'Abide with Me' (*c.*1847)

20 The wind of change is blowing through this continent.
Harold Macmillan 1894–1986: speech at Cape Town, 3 February 1960

21 At last he rose, and twitched his mantle blue:
Tomorrow to fresh woods, and pastures new.
John Milton 1608–74: 'Lycidas' (1638)

22 God, give us the serenity to accept what cannot be changed;
Give us the courage to change what should be changed;
Give us the wisdom to distinguish one from the other.
Reinhold Niebuhr 1892–1971: prayer said to have been first published in 1951; Richard Wightman Fox *Reinhold Niebuhr* (1985)

23 Forward, forward let us range,
Let the great world spin for ever down the ringing grooves of change.
Alfred, Lord Tennyson 1809–92: 'Locksley Hall' (1842)

24 The old order changeth, yielding place to new,
And God fulfils himself in many ways,
Lest one good custom should corrupt the world.
Alfred, Lord Tennyson 1809–92: *Idylls of the King* 'The Passing of Arthur' (1869)

25 If we do not find anything pleasant, at least we shall find something new.
Voltaire 1694–1778: *Candide* (1759)

Chaos

1 Chaos often breeds life, when order breeds habit.
Henry Brooks Adams 1838–1918: *The Education of Henry Adams* (1907)

2 With ruin upon ruin, rout on rout, Confusion worse confounded.
John Milton 1608–74: *Paradise Lost* (1667)

3 The whole worl's in a state o' chassis!
Sean O'Casey 1880–1964: *Juno and the Paycock* (1925)

4 Things fall apart; the centre cannot hold;
Mere anarchy is loosed upon the world,
The blood-dimmed tide is loosed, and everywhere
The ceremony of innocence is drowned.
W. B. Yeats 1865–1939: 'The Second Coming' (1921)

Character

see also **Human Nature**

1 It is not in the still calm of life, or the repose of a pacific station, that great characters are formed . . . Great necessities call out great virtues.
Abigail Adams 1744–1818: letter to John Quincy Adams, 19 January 1780

2 A thick skin is a gift from God.
Konrad Adenauer 1876–1967: in *New York Times* 30 December 1959

3 There exists a great chasm between those, on one side, who relate everything to a single central vision . . . and, on the other side, those who pursue many ends, often unrelated and even contradictory . . . The first kind of intellectual and artistic personality belongs to the hedgehogs, the second to the foxes.
Isaiah Berlin 1909–97: *The Hedgehog and the Fox* (1953); cf. **Knowledge 2**

4 I am not at all the sort of person you and I took me for.
Jane Carlyle 1801–66: letter to Thomas Carlyle, 7 May 1822

5 Qualities too elevated often unfit a
man for society. We don't take ingots
with us to market; we take silver or
small change.
   Nicolas-Sébastien Chamfort 1741–94:
   Maximes et Pensées (1796)

6 We are all worms. But I do believe that
I am a glow-worm.
   Winston Churchill 1874–1965: Violet Bonham-
   Carter *Winston Churchill as I Knew Him*
   (1965)

7 If you have bright plumage, people
will take pot shots at you.
   Alan Clark 1928–99: in *Independent* 25 June
   1994

8 Claudia's the sort of person who goes
through life holding on to the sides.
   Alice Thomas Ellis 1932– : *The Other Side of
   the Fire* (1983)

9 Talent develops in quiet places,
character in the full current of human
life.
   Johann Wolfgang von Goethe 1749–1832:
   Torquato Tasso (1790)

10 Those who stand for nothing fall for
anything.
   Alex Hamilton 1936– : 'Born Old' (radio
   broadcast), in *Listener* 9 November 1978

11 A man's character is his fate.
   Heraclitus *c.*540–*c.*480 BC: *On the Universe*

12 Before you judge me, try hard to love
me, look within your heart
Then ask,—have you seen my
childhood?
   Michael Jackson 1958– : 'Childhood'
   (1995 song)

13 Though I've belted you and flayed
you,
By the livin' Gawd that made you,
You're a better man than I am, Gunga
Din!
   Rudyard Kipling 1865–1936: 'Gunga Din'
   (1892)

14 If you can trust yourself when all men
doubt you,
But make allowance for their
doubting too;
If you can wait and not be tired by
waiting,

Or being lied about, don't deal in lies,
Or being hated, don't give way to
hating,
And yet don't look too good, nor talk
too wise.
   Rudyard Kipling 1865–1936: 'If—' (1910)

15 Underneath this flabby exterior is an
enormous lack of character.
   Oscar Levant 1906–72: *Memoirs of an
   Amnesiac* (1965)

16 Nice guys, when we turn nasty, can
make a terrible mess of it, usually
because we've had so little practice,
and have bottled it up for too long.
   Matthew Parris 1949– : in *The Spectator*
   27 February 1993

17 You can tell a lot about a fellow's
character by his way of eating
jellybeans.
   Ronald Reagan 1911– : in *New York Times*
   15 January 1981

18   My nature is subdued
To what it works in, like the dyer's
hand.
   William Shakespeare 1564–1616: sonnet 111

19 A man of great common sense and
good taste, meaning thereby a man
without originality or moral courage.
   George Bernard Shaw 1856–1950: *Notes to
   Caesar and Cleopatra* (1901) 'Julius Caesar'

20 Fame vaporizes, money goes with the
wind, and all that's left is character.
   O. J. Simpson 1947– : *Juice: O. J. Simpson's
   Life* (1977)

21 Slice him where you like, a hellhound
is always a hellhound.
   P. G. Wodehouse 1881–1975: *The Code of the
   Woosters* (1938)

22 The Child is father of the Man.
   William Wordsworth 1770–1850: 'My heart
   leaps up when I behold' (1807)

Charity

see also **Giving**, **Goodness**

1 The living need charity more than the
dead.
   George Arnold 1834–65: 'The Jolly Old
   Pedagogue' (1866)

2 Without trampling down twelve
others
You cannot help one poor man.
Bertolt Brecht 1898–1956: *The Good Woman of Setzuan* (1938)

3 People often feed the hungry so that
nothing may disturb their own
enjoyment of a good meal.
W. Somerset Maugham 1874–1965: *A Writer's Notebook* (1949) written in 1896

4 Much benevolence of the passive
order may be traced to a
disinclination to inflict pain upon
oneself.
George Meredith 1828–1909: *Vittoria* (1866)

5 Keeping books on charity is capitalist
nonsense! I just use the money for the
poor. I can't stop to count it.
Eva Perón 1919–52: Fleur Cowles *Bloody Precedent: the Peron Story* (1952)

6 Let humble Allen, with an awkward
shame,
Do good by stealth, and blush to find
it fame.
Alexander Pope 1688–1744: *Imitations of Horace* (1738)

7 The Christian usually tries to give
away his own money, whilst the
philosopher usually tries to give away
the money of someone else.
Lord Salisbury 1830–1903: C. S. Kenny *Property for Charitable Uses* (1880)

8 'Tis not enough to help the feeble up,
But to support him after.
William Shakespeare 1564–1616: *Timon of Athens* (c.1607)

9 Thy necessity is yet greater than mine.
■ *on giving his water-bottle to a dying soldier on the battle-field of Zutphen, 1586; commonly quoted as 'thy need is greater than mine'*
Philip Sidney 1554–86: Fulke Greville *Life of Sir Philip Sidney* (1652)

10 For Charity is cold in the multitude of
possessions, and the rich are covetous
of their crumbs.
Christopher Smart 1722–71: *Jubilate Agno* (c.1758–63)

11 Oh I am a cat that likes to
Gallop about doing good.
Stevie Smith 1902–71: 'The Galloping Cat' (1972)

12 We ourselves feel that what we are
doing is just a drop in the ocean. But
if that drop was not in the ocean, I
think the ocean would be less because
of that missing drop. I do not agree
with the big way of doing things.
Mother Teresa 1910–97: *A Gift for God* (1975)

13 No one would remember the Good
Samaritan if he'd only had good
intentions. He had money as well.
Margaret Thatcher 1925– : television interview, 6 January 1980

14 Friends, I have lost a day.
■ *on reflecting that he had done nothing to help anybody all day*
Titus AD 39–81: Suetonius *Lives of the Caesars* 'Titus'

15 I have always depended on the
kindness of strangers.
Tennessee Williams 1911–83: *A Streetcar Named Desire* (1947)

Charm

1 Charm . . . it's a sort of bloom on a
woman. If you have it, you don't need
to have anything else; and if you don't
have it, it doesn't much matter what
else you have.
J. M. Barrie 1860–1937: *What Every Woman Knows* (1918)

2 You know what charm is: a way of
getting the answer yes without having
asked any clear question.
Albert Camus 1913–60: *The Fall* (1957)

3 Oozing charm from every pore,
He oiled his way around the floor.
Alan Jay Lerner 1918–86: 'You Did It' (1956 song) from *My Fair Lady*

4 What is charm then? The free giving
of a grace, the spending of something
given by nature in her role of
spendthrift . . . something extra,

superfluous, unnecessary, essentially a power thrown away.
Doris Lessing 1919– : *Particularly Cats* (1967)

5 Charm is the great English blight. It does not exist outside these damp islands. It spots and kills anything it touches. It kills love, it kills art.
Evelyn Waugh 1903–66: *Brideshead Revisited* (1945)

Childhood

see also **Children**

1 Childhood is measured out by sounds and smells
And sights before the dark of reason grows.
John Betjeman 1906–84: *Summoned by Bells* (1960)

2 Lord knows what incommunicable small terrors infants go through, unknown to all. We disregard them, we say they forget, because they have not the words to make us remember . . . By the time they learn to speak they have forgotten the details of their complaints, and so we never know. They forget so quickly we say, because we cannot contemplate the fact that they never forget.
Margaret Drabble 1939– : *The Millstone* (1965)

3 All childhood is an emigration. Some are slow,
leaving you standing, resigned, up an avenue
where no one you know stays. Others are sudden.
You accent wrong. Corners, which seem familiar,
leading to unimagined, pebble-dashed estates, big boys
eating worms and shouting words you don't understand.
Carol Ann Duffy 1965– : 'Originally' (1990)

4 Alas, regardless of their doom,
The little victims play!
No sense have they of ills to come,
Nor care beyond to-day.
Thomas Gray 1716–71: *Ode on a Distant Prospect of Eton College* (1747)

5 There is always one moment in childhood when the door opens and lets the future in.
Graham Greene 1904–91: *The Power and the Glory* (1940)

6 When I look back on my childhood I wonder how I managed to survive at all. It was, of course, a miserable childhood: the happy childhood is hardly worth your while. Worse than the ordinary miserable childhood is the miserable Irish childhood, and worse yet is the miserable Irish Catholic childhood.
Frank McCourt 1930– : *Angela's Ashes* (1996)

7 For children, childhood is timeless. It's always the present. Everything is in the present tense. Of course they have memories. Of course, time shifts a little for them and Christmas comes round in the end. But they don't *feel* it.
Ian McEwan 1948– : *The Child in Time* (1987)

8 Childhood is the kingdom where nobody dies.
Nobody that matters, that is.
Edna St Vincent Millay 1892–1950: 'Childhood is the Kingdom where Nobody dies' (1934)

9 Sam will not enjoy his childhood . . . Sam is being educated not so as to enjoy himself, but so other people will enjoy him.
■ *on his son, aged five months*
Roger Scruton 1944– : in *The Times* 1 May 1999

10 Childhood is Last Chance Gulch for happiness. After that, you know too much.
Tom Stoppard 1937– : *Where Are They Now?* (1973)

11 The summer that I was ten—
Can it be there was only one summer that I was ten? It must have been a long one then.
May Swenson 1919–89: 'The Centaur' (1958)

Children

see also **Childhood**, **The Family**, **Parents**, **Schools**, **Youth**

1 I don't work that way . . . The very idea that all children want to be cuddled by a complete stranger, I find completely amazing.
■ *on her work for Save the Children*
Anne, Princess Royal 1950– : in *Daily Telegraph* 17 January 1998

2 Children sweeten labours, but they make misfortunes more bitter.
Francis Bacon 1561–1626: *Essays* (1625) 'Of Parents and Children'

3 There is no end to the violations committed by children on children, quietly talking alone.
Elizabeth Bowen 1899–1973: *The House in Paris* (1935)

4   Go practise if you please
With men and women: leave a child alone
For Christ's particular love's sake!
Robert Browning 1812–89: *The Ring and the Book* (1868–9)

5 The place is very well and quiet and the children only scream in a low voice.
Lord Byron 1788–1824: letter to Lady Melbourne, 21 September 1813

6 There is no finer investment for any community than putting milk into babies.
Winston Churchill 1874–1965: radio broadcast, 21 March 1943

7 There is no such thing as other people's children.
Hillary Rodham Clinton 1947– : in *Newsweek* 15 January 1996

8 There never was a child so lovely but his mother was glad to get asleep.
Ralph Waldo Emerson 1803–82: *Journal* 1836

9 If there is anything that we wish to change in the child, we should first examine it and see whether it is not something that could better be changed in ourselves.
Carl Gustav Jung 1875–1961: 'Vom Werden der Persönlichkeit' (1932)

10 A child is owed the greatest respect; if you ever have something disgraceful in mind, don't ignore your son's tender years.
Juvenal AD *c.*60–*c.*130: *Satires*

11 Literature is mostly about having sex and not much about having children. Life is the other way round.
David Lodge 1935– : *The British Museum is Falling Down* (1965)

12 I've never outgrown that feeling of mild pride, of acceptance, when children take your hand.
Ian McEwan 1948– : *Enduring Love* (1998)

13 With the birth of each child, you lose two novels.
Candia McWilliam 1955– : in *Guardian* 5 May 1993

14 It should be noted that children at play are not playing about; their games should be seen as their most serious-minded activity.
Montaigne 1533–92: *Essais* (1580)

15 The first child is made of glass, the second porcelain, the rest of rubber, steel, and granite.
Richard J. Needham 1939– : in *Toronto Globe and Mail* 25 January 1977

16 The art of dealing with children might be defined as *knowing what not to say.*
A. S. Neill 1883–1973: Jonathan Croall *Neill of Summerhill: The Permanent Rebel* (1983)

17 If you have a great passion it seems that the logical thing is to see the fruit of it, and the fruit are children.
Roman Polanski 1933– : in *Independent on Sunday* 12 May 1991

18 Behold the child, by Nature's kindly law
Pleased with a rattle, tickled with a straw.
Alexander Pope 1688–1744: *An Essay on Man* Epistle 2 (1733)

19 A child is not a vase to be filled, but a fire to be lit.
François Rabelais *c.*1494–*c.*1553: attributed

20 Children are given us to discourage our better emotions.
Saki 1870–1916: *Reginald* (1904)

21 A child becomes an adult when he realizes that he has a right not only to be right but also to be wrong.
Thomas Szasz 1920– : *The Second Sin* (1973)

22 You will find as the children grow up that as a rule children are a bitter disappointment—their greatest object being to do precisely what their parents do not wish and have anxiously tried to prevent.
Queen Victoria 1819–1901: letter to the Crown Princess of Prussia, 5 January 1876

23 He says that when men first meet women they want to be getting the sort of signals that say, 'I can't wait to be naked with you.' He says I look like I'm thinking, 'Do you fancy a stroll past the local Mothercare?' He also said I hadn't got 'bedroom eyes', I'd got 'pram eyes'.
Arabella Weir: *Does My Bum Look Big in This?* (1997)

Choice
········

see also **Compromise, Indecision**

1 Whose finger do you want on the trigger?
■ *headline alluding to the atom bomb, apropos the failure of both the Labour and Conservative parties to purge their leaders of proven failures*
Anonymous: in *Daily Mirror* 21 September 1951

2 From this day you must be a stranger to one of your parents.—Your mother will never see you again if you do *not* marry Mr Collins, and I will never see you again if you *do*.
Jane Austen 1775–1817: *Pride and Prejudice* (1813)

3 For many are called, but few are chosen.
Bible: St Matthew

4 White shall not neutralize the black, nor good
Compensate bad in man, absolve him so:
Life's business being just the terrible choice.
Robert Browning 1812–89: *The Ring and the Book* (1868–9)

5 If it has to choose who is to be crucified, the crowd will always save Barabbas.
Jean Cocteau 1889–1963: *Le Rappel à l'ordre* (1926)

6 Was there ever in anyone's life span a point free in time, devoid of memory, a night when choice was any more than the sum of all the choices gone before?
Joan Didion 1934– : *Run River* (1963)

7 A woman can hardly ever choose . . . she is dependent on what happens to her. She must take meaner things, because only meaner things are within her reach.
George Eliot 1819–80: *Felix Holt* (1866)

8 Any customer can have a car painted any colour that he wants so long as it is black.
■ *on the Model T Ford, 1909*
Henry Ford 1863–1947: *My Life and Work* (with Samuel Crowther, 1922)

9 Two roads diverged in a wood, and I—
I took the one less travelled by,
And that has made all the difference.
Robert Frost 1874–1963: 'The Road Not Taken' (1916)

10 How happy could I be with either,
Were t'other dear charmer away!
John Gay 1685–1732: *The Beggar's Opera* (1728)

11 Many men would take the death-sentence without a whimper to escape the life-sentence which fate carries in her other hand.
T. E. Lawrence 1888–1935: *The Mint* (1955)

12 Which do you want? A whipping and no turnips or turnips and no whipping?
Toni Morrison 1931– : *The Bluest Eye* (1961)

13 When I go into the voting booth, do I vote for the person who is the best President? Or the slime bucket who will make my life as a cartoonist wonderful?
Mike Peters: in *Wall Street Journal* 20 January 1993

14 I'll make him an offer he can't refuse.
Mario Puzo 1920–99: *The Godfather* (1969)

15 To be, or not to be: that is the question.
William Shakespeare 1564–1616: *Hamlet* (1601)

16 There is no real alternative.
■ *popularly encapsulated in the acronym* TINA
Margaret Thatcher 1925– : speech at Conservative Women's Conference, 21 May 1980

17 Chips with everything.
Arnold Wesker 1932– : title of play (1962)

18 Between two evils, I always pick the one I never tried before.
Mae West 1892–1980: *Klondike Annie* (1936 film)

Christianity

see also **The Church**, **Clergy**, **God**, **Religion**

1 Christians have burnt each other, quite persuaded
That all the Apostles would have done as they did.
Lord Byron 1788–1824: *Don Juan* (1819–24)

2 The Christian ideal has not been tried and found wanting. It has been found difficult; and left untried.
G. K. Chesterton 1874–1936: *What's Wrong with the World* (1910)

3 He who begins by loving Christianity better than Truth will proceed by loving his own sect or church better than Christianity, and end by loving himself better than all.
Samuel Taylor Coleridge 1772–1834: *Aids to Reflection* (1825)

4 His Christianity was muscular.
Benjamin Disraeli 1804–81: *Endymion* (1880)

5 The Christian religion not only was at first attended with miracles, but even at this day cannot be believed by any reasonable person without one.
David Hume 1711–76: *An Enquiry Concerning Human Understanding* (1748)

6 We are an Easter people and Alleluia is our song.
Pope John Paul II 1920– : speech in Harlem, New York, 2 October 1979

7 The chief contribution of Protestantism to human thought is its massive proof that God is a bore.
H. L. Mencken 1880–1956: *Minority Report* (1956)

8 The sinner is at the heart of Christianity . . . No one is as competent as the sinner in matters of Christianity. No one, except a saint.
Charles Péguy 1873–1914: *Basic Verities* (1943) 'Un Nouveau théologien . . . ' (1911)

9 People may say what they like about the decay of Christianity; the religious system that produced green Chartreuse can never really die.
Saki 1870–1916: *Reginald* (1904)

10 Perhaps it is no wonder that the women were first at the Cradle and last at the Cross. They had never known a man like this Man—there never has been such another . . . who never made arch jokes about them, never treated them either as 'The women, God help us', or 'The ladies, God bless them!'
Dorothy L. Sayers 1893–1957: *Unpopular Opinions* (1946)

11 If you're going to do a thing, you should do it thoroughly. If you're going to be a Christian, you may as well be a Catholic.
Muriel Spark 1918– : in *Independent* 2 August 1989

12 Christianity is the most materialistic of all great religions.
William Temple 1881–1944: *Readings in St John's Gospel* vol. 1 (1939)

13 You have no idea how much nastier I would be if I was not a Catholic. Without supernatural aid I would hardly be a human being.
Evelyn Waugh 1903–66: Noel Annan *Our Age* (1990)

14 The Gospel of Christ knows of no
religion but social; no holiness but
social holiness.
John Wesley 1703–91: *Hymns and Sacred Poems* (1739) preface

15 Scratch the Christian and you find the
pagan—spoiled.
Israel Zangwill 1864–1926: *Children of the Ghetto* (1892)

Christmas

1 I'm dreaming of a white Christmas,
Just like the ones I used to know,
Where the tree-tops glisten
And children listen
To hear sleigh bells in the snow.
Irving Berlin 1888–1989: 'White Christmas' (1942 song)

2 And girls in slacks remember Dad,
And oafish louts remember Mum,
And sleepless children's hearts are
glad,
And Christmas-morning bells say
'Come!'
John Betjeman 1906–84: 'Christmas' (1954)

3 She brought forth her firstborn son,
and wrapped him in swaddling
clothes, and laid him in a manger;
because there was no room for them
in the inn.
Bible: St Luke

4 Yes, Virginia, there is a Santa Claus.
■ *replying to a letter from eight-year-old Virginia O'Hanlon*
Francis Pharcellus Church 1839–1906: editorial in New York *Sun*, 21 September 1897

5 Christmas is the Disneyfication of
Christianity.
Don Cupitt 1934– : in *Independent* 19 December 1996

6 'Bah,' said Scrooge. 'Humbug!'
Charles Dickens 1812–70: *A Christmas Carol* (1843)

7 'Twas the night before Christmas,
when all through the house
Not a creature was stirring, not even a
mouse;
The stockings were hung by the
chimney with care,

In hopes that St Nicholas soon would
be there.
Clement C. Moore 1779–1863: 'A Visit from St Nicholas' (December 1823)

8 Christmas begins about the first of
December with an office party and
ends when you finally realize what
you spent, around April fifteenth of
the next year.
P. J. O'Rourke 1947– : *Modern Manners* (1984)

9 Still xmas is a good time with all those
presents and good food and i hope it
will never die out or at any rate not
until i am grown up and hav to pay
for it all.
Geoffrey Willans 1911–58 and **Ronald Searle** 1920– : *How To Be Topp* (1954)

10 The darkness drops again; but now I
know
That twenty centuries of stony sleep
Were vexed to nightmare by a rocking
cradle,
And what rough beast, its hour come
round at last,
Slouches towards Bethlehem to be
born?
W. B. Yeats 1865–1939: 'The Second Coming' (1921)

The Church
see also **Christianity, Clergy**

1 I see it as an elderly lady, who mutters
away to herself in a corner, ignored
most of the time.
■ *on the Church of England*
George Carey 1935– : in *Readers Digest* (British ed.) March 1991

2 We must recall that the Church is
always 'one generation away from
extinction.'
George Carey 1935– : Working Party Report *Youth A Part: Young People and the Church* (1996) foreword

3 The two dangers which beset the
Church of England are good music
and bad preaching.
Lord Hugh Cecil 1869–1956: K. Rose *The Later Cecils* (1975)

4 He cannot have God for his father who has not the church for his mother.
St Cyprian c.AD 200–258: *De Ecclesiae Catholicae Unitate*

5 If Christ were to return today, the Church of England would ask him to set out his ideas on a single sheet of A4.
David Hare 1947– : *Racing Demon* (1990)

6 The crisis of the Church of England is that too many of its bishops, and some would say of its archbishops, don't quite realise that they are atheists, but have begun to suspect it.
Clive James 1939– : *The Dreaming Swimmer* (1992)

7 I want to throw open the windows of the Church so that we can see out and the people can see in.
Pope John XXIII 1881–1963: attributed

8 A serious house on serious earth it is,
In whose blent air all our compulsions meet,
Are recognised, and robed as destinies.
Philip Larkin 1922–85: 'Church Going' (1955)

9 The Church should go forward along the path of progress and be no longer satisfied only to represent the Conservative Party at prayer.
Maude Royden 1876–1956: address at Queen's Hall, London, 16 July 1917

10 The Church can no longer contain the fizzy, explosive stuff that the true wine of the bottle ought to be.
Donald Soper 1903–98: in *Methodist Recorder* 18 January 1968

11 As often as we are mown down by you, the more we grow in numbers; the blood of Christians is the seed.
■ traditionally 'The blood of the martyrs is the seed of the Church'
Tertullian AD c.160–c.225: *Apologeticus*

12 The Catholic Church has never really come to terms with women. What I object to is being treated either as Madonnas or Mary Magdalenes.
Shirley Williams 1930– : in *Observer* 22 March 1981

Winston Churchill
1874–1965

1 Winston is back.
■ on Churchill's reappointment as First Sea Lord
Anonymous: Board of Admiralty signal to the Fleet, 3 September 1939

2 I thought he was a young man of promise, but it appears he is a young man of promises.
Arthur James Balfour 1848–1930: Winston Churchill *My Early Life* (1930)

3 The greatest adventurer of modern political history.
R. A. Butler 1902–82: John Colville's diary, 10 May 1940

4 The first time you meet Winston you see all his faults and the rest of your life you spend in discovering his virtues.
Lady Lytton 1874–1971: letter to Sir Edward Marsh, December 1905

5 He mobilized the English language and sent it into battle to steady his fellow countrymen and hearten those Europeans upon whom the long dark night of tyranny had descended.
Ed Murrow 1908–65: broadcast, 30 November 1954

The Cinema
see also **Actors**, **Films**

1 [The camera] is so refined that it makes it possible for us to shed light on the human soul, to reveal it the more brutally and thereby add to our knowledge new dimensions of the 'real'.
Ingmar Bergman 1918– : in *New York Times* 22 January 1978

2 After years of playing with images of life and death, life has made me shy.
■ message sent on winning the Palme of Palmes at the Cannes Film Festival
Ingmar Bergman 1918– : in *Observer* 18 May 1997

3 JOE GILLIS: You used to be in pictures. You used to be big.

NORMA DESMOND: I am big. It's the pictures that got small.
Charles Brackett 1892–1969 and **Billy Wilder** 1906–2002: *Sunset Boulevard* (1950 film, with D. M. Marshman Jr.)

4 There are no rules in filmmaking. Only sins. And the cardinal sin is dullness.
Frank Capra 1897–1991: in *People* 16 September 1991

5 If my books had been any worse, I should not have been invited to Hollywood, and if they had been any better, I should not have come.
Raymond Chandler 1888–1959: letter to Charles W. Morton, 12 December 1945

6 Words are cheap. The biggest thing you can say is 'elephant'.
■ *on the universality of silent films*
Charlie Chaplin 1889–1977: B. Norman *The Movie Greats* (1981)

7 Bring on the empty horses!
■ *said while directing the 1936 film* The Charge of the Light Brigade
Michael Curtiz 1888–1962: David Niven *Bring on the Empty Horses* (1975)

8 Sexuality is such a part of life, but sexuality in the movies—I have a hard time finding it.
Catherine Deneuve 1943– : in *Première* April 1993

9 *on being asked which film he would like to see while convalescing:*
Anything except that damned Mouse.
George V 1865–1936: George Lyttelton, letter to Rupert Hart-Davis, 12 November 1959

10 Photography is truth. The cinema is truth 24 times per second.
Jean-Luc Godard 1930– : *Le Petit Soldat* (1960 film)

11 *Ce n'est pas une image juste, c'est juste une image.*
This is not a just image, it is just an image.
Jean-Luc Godard 1930– : Colin MacCabe *Godard: Images, Sounds, Politics* (1980)

12 GEORGES FRANJU: Movies should have a beginning, a middle and an end.

JEAN-LUC GODARD: Certainly. But not necessarily in that order.
Jean-Luc Godard 1930– : in *Time* 14 September 1981

13 Why should people go out and pay to see bad movies when they can stay at home and see bad television for nothing?
Sam Goldwyn 1882–1974: in *Observer* 9 September 1956

14 Pictures are for entertainment, messages should be delivered by Western Union.
Sam Goldwyn 1882–1974: Arthur Marx *Goldwyn* (1976)

15 What we need is a story that starts with an earthquake and works its way up to a climax.
Sam Goldwyn 1882–1974: attributed, perhaps apocryphal

16 In sponsored film work the price to be paid for the privilege of aesthetic experiment is the discipline of public service.
John Grierson 1888–1972: attributed

17 [Goldwyn] filled the room with wonderful panic and beat at your mind like a man in front of a slot machine, shaking it for a jackpot.
Ben Hecht 1894–1964: A. Scott Berg *Goldwyn* (1989)

18 If I made Cinderella, the audience would immediately be looking for a body in the coach.
Alfred Hitchcock 1899–1980: in *Newsweek* 11 June 1956

19 If you gave him a good script, actors and technicians, Mickey Mouse could direct a movie.
Nicholas Hytner 1956– : interview, in *Daily Telegraph* 24 February 1994

20 The words 'Kiss Kiss Bang Bang' which I saw on an Italian movie poster, are perhaps the briefest statement imaginable of the basic appeal of movies.
Pauline Kael 1919– : *Kiss Kiss Bang Bang* (1968)

21 Don't forget the Western is not only the history of this country, it is what

the Saga of the Nibelungen is for the European.
Fritz Lang 1890–1976: Peter Bogdanovich *Fritz Lang in America* (1967)

22 Hollywood money isn't money. It's congealed snow, melts in your hand, and there you are.
Dorothy Parker 1893–1967: Malcolm Cowley *Writers at Work* 1st Series (1958)

23 There is only one thing that can kill the movies, and that is education.
Will Rogers 1879–1935: *Autobiography of Will Rogers* (1949)

24 The lunatics have taken charge of the asylum.
■ *on the take-over of United Artists by Charles Chaplin, Mary Pickford, Douglas Fairbanks and D. W. Griffith*
Richard Rowland c.1881–1947: Terry Ramsaye *A Million and One Nights* (1926)

25 Once a month the sky falls on my head, I come to, and I see another movie I want to make.
Steven Spielberg 1947– : in *Time* 8 June 1998

26 The biggest electric train set any boy ever had!
■ *of the RKO studios*
Orson Welles 1915–85: Peter Noble *The Fabulous Orson Welles* (1956)

27 From the movies we learn precisely how to hold a champagne flute, kiss a mistress, pull a trigger, turn a phrase . . . [but] the movies spoil us for life; nothing ever lives up to them.
Edmund White 1940– : *Genet* (1993)

28 I wouldn't say when you've seen one Western you've seen the lot; but when you've seen the lot you get the feeling you've seen one.
Katharine Whitehorn 1928– : *Sunday Best* (1976) 'Decoding the West'

Circumstance and Situation
··············
see also **Fate**

1 As if I were a river
The harsh age changed my course,
Replaced one life with another,
Flowing in a different channel
And I do not recognize my shores.
Anna Akhmatova 1889–1966: 'As if I were a River' (1944)

2 To every thing there is a season, and a time to every purpose under the heaven:
A time to be born, and a time to die . . .
A time to weep, and a time to laugh; a time to mourn, and a time to dance.
Bible: Ecclesiastes

3 But for the grace of God there goes John Bradford.
■ *on seeing a group of criminals being led to their execution; usually quoted as, 'There but for the grace of God go I'*
John Bradford c.1510–55: in *Dictionary of National Biography* (1917–)

4 People should be taught what is, not what should be. All my humour is based on destruction and despair. If the whole world were tranquil, without disease and violence, I'd be standing in the breadline.
Lenny Bruce 1925–66: *The Essential Lenny Bruce* (1967)

5 I love to feel events overlapping each other, crawling over one another like wet crabs in a basket.
Lawrence Durrell 1912–90: *Balthazar* (1958)

6 The whole world seemed so unequal, so unfair. Some people were created with all the good things ready-made for them, others were just created like mistakes. God's mistakes.
Buchi Emecheta 1944– : *Second-Class Citizen* (1974)

7 We are so made, that we can only derive intense enjoyment from a contrast, and only very little from a state of things.
Sigmund Freud 1856–1939: *Civilization and its Discontents* (1930)

8 *No se puede mirar.*
One cannot look at this.
Goya 1746–1828: *The Disasters of War* (1863) title of etching

9 If, of all words of tongue and pen, The saddest are, 'It might have been,'

More sad are these we daily see:
'It is, but hadn't ought to be!'
Bret Harte 1836–1902: 'Mrs Judge Jenkins'
(1867); cf. 14 below

10 Anyone who isn't confused doesn't
really understand the situation.
■ *on the Vietnam War*
Ed Murrow 1908–65: Walter Bryan *The
Improbable Irish* (1969)

11 And, spite of Pride, in erring Reason's
spite,
One truth is clear, 'Whatever IS, is
RIGHT.'
Alexander Pope 1688–1744: *An Essay on Man*
Epistle 1 (1733)

12 The time is out of joint; O cursèd
spite,
That ever I was born to set it right!
William Shakespeare 1564–1616: *Hamlet*
(1601)

13 We shall generally find that the
triangular person has got into the
square hole, the oblong into the
triangular, and a square person has
squeezed himself into the round hole.
The officer and the office, the doer
and the thing done, seldom fit so
exactly that we can say they were
almost made for each other.
Sydney Smith 1771–1845: *Sketches of Moral
Philosophy* (1849)

14 For of all sad words of tongue or pen,
The saddest are these: 'It might have
been!'
John Greenleaf Whittier 1807–92: 'Maud
Muller' (1854)

Cities

see also **American Cities and States**,
British Cities and Towns, **The Country**

1 A city is in many respects a great
business corporation, but in other
respects it is enlarged
housekeeping . . . May we not say that
city housekeeping has failed partly
because women, the traditional
housekeepers, have not been

consulted as to its multiform
activities?
Jane Addams 1860–1935: *Newer Ideals of Peace*
(1907) 'Utilization of Women in City
Government'

2 Woe unto them that join house to
house, that lay field to field, till there
be no place.
Bible: Isaiah

3 Slums may well be breeding-grounds
of crime, but middle-class suburbs are
incubators of apathy and delirium.
Cyril Connolly 1903–74: *The Unquiet Grave*
(1944)

4 God made the country, and man
made the town.
William Cowper 1731–1800: *The Task* (1785)

5 It is not what they built. It is what they
knocked down.
It is not the houses. It is the spaces
between the houses.
It is not the streets that exist. It is the
streets that no longer exist.
James Fenton 1949– : *German Requiem*
(1981)

6 'You are a pretty urban sort of person
though, wouldn't you say?'
'Only nor'nor'east,' I said. 'I know a
fox from a fax-machine.'
Stephen Fry 1957– : *The Hippopotamus*
(1994)

7 Ever since I have been old enough to
understand what it means to be
suburban I have wanted to come from
somewhere else.
Nick Hornby 1957– : *Fever Pitch* (1992)

8 The materials of city planning are sky,
space, trees, steel and cement in that
order and in that hierarchy.
Le Corbusier 1887–1965: in *The Times* 1965

9 A city is a place where there is no need
to wait for next week to get the answer
to a question, to taste the food of any
country, to find new voices to listen to
and familiar ones to listen to again.
Margaret Mead 1901–78: *World Enough* (1975)

10 Judaism, Christianity and Islam all
took root among nomads who had

recently settled, and all three characterize nomadic traits—the shepherd, the pilgrim, the wanderer in the wilderness—as godly, and the life of the city as degenerate.
George Monbiot: *No Man's Land* (1994)

11 The city is not a concrete jungle, it is a human zoo.
Desmond Morris 1928– : *The Human Zoo* (1969)

12 I come from suburbia . . . and I don't ever want to go back. It's the one place in the world that's further away than anywhere else.
Frederic Raphael 1931– : *The Glittering Prizes* (1976)

13 What is the city but the people?
William Shakespeare 1564–1616: *Coriolanus* (1608)

14 The modern city is a place for banking and prostitution and very little else.
Frank Lloyd Wright 1867–1959: Robert C. Twombly *Frank Lloyd Wright* (1973)

Civilization
....
see also **Culture**

1 The three great elements of modern civilization, Gunpowder, Printing, and the Protestant Religion.
Thomas Carlyle 1795–1881: *Critical and Miscellaneous Essays* (1838) 'The State of German Literature'

2 All civilization has from time to time become a thin crust over a volcano of revolution.
Havelock Ellis 1859–1939: *Little Essays of Love and Virtue* (1922)

3 JOURNALIST: Mr Gandhi, what do you think of modern civilization?
GANDHI: That would be a good idea.
■ *on arriving in England in 1930*
Mahatma Gandhi 1869–1948: E. F. Schumacher *Good Work* (1979)

4 If a nation expects to be ignorant and free, in a state of civilization, it expects what never was and never will be.
Thomas Jefferson 1743–1826: letter to Colonel Charles Yancey, 6 January 1816

5 If civilization had been left in female hands, we would still be living in grass huts.
Camille Paglia 1947– : *Sexual Personae* (1990)

6 'Sergeant Pepper'—a decisive moment in the history of Western Civilisation.
Kenneth Tynan 1927–80: in 1967; Howard Elson *McCartney* (1986)

7 Civilization advances by extending the number of important operations which we can perform without thinking about them.
Alfred North Whitehead 1861–1947: *Introduction to Mathematics* (1911)

8 The soul of any civilization on earth has ever been and still is Art and Religion, but neither has ever been found in commerce, in government or the police.
Frank Lloyd Wright 1867–1959: *A Testament* (1957)

The Civil Service
....

1 A mechanism that prides itself on being a Rolls-Royce appeared more like an old banger.
■ *of the Foreign Office's handling of the arms-to-Africa affair*
Donald Anderson 1939– : in *Guardian* 10 February 1999

2 The Civil Service is a bit like a Rolls-Royce—you know it's the best machine in the world, but you're not quite sure what to do with it.
R. A. Butler 1902–82: Anthony Sampson *Anatomy of Britain* (1962)

3 Give a civil servant a good case and he'll wreck it with clichés, bad punctuation, double negatives and convoluted apology.
Alan Clark 1928–99: diary 22 July 1983

4 The Civil Service is profoundly deferential—'Yes, Minister! No, Minister! If you wish it, Minister!'
Richard Crossman 1907–74: diary, 22 October 1964

5 Sack the lot!
■ *on overmanning and overspending within government departments*
John Arbuthnot Fisher 1841–1920: letter to *The Times*, 2 September 1919

6 This high official, all allow,
Is grossly overpaid;
There wasn't any Board, and now
There isn't any Trade.
A. P. Herbert 1890–1971: 'The President of the Board of Trade' (1922)

7 A civil servant doesn't make jokes.
Eugène Ionesco 1912–94: *The Killer* (1958)

8 In the case of nutrition and health, just as in the case of education, the gentleman in Whitehall really does know better what is good for people than the people know themselves.
Douglas Jay 1907–96: *The Socialist Case* (1939)

9 I think it will be a clash between the political will and the administrative won't.
Jonathan Lynn 1943– and **Antony Jay** 1930– : *Yes Prime Minister* (1987) vol. 2

10 By the time the civil service has finished drafting a document to give effect to a principle, there may be little of the principle left.
Lord Reith 1889–1971: *Into the Wind* (1949)

Class

see also **Communism**

1 The rich man in his castle,
The poor man at his gate,
God made them, high or lowly,
And ordered their estate.
Cecil Frances Alexander 1818–95: 'All Things Bright and Beautiful' (1848)

2 *Il faut épater le bourgeois.*
One must astonish the bourgeois.
Charles Baudelaire 1821–67: attributed

3 The real solvent of class distinction is a proper measure of self-esteem—a kind of unselfconsciousness. Some people are at ease with themselves, so the world is at ease with them. My

parents thought this kind of ease was produced by education . . . they didn't see that what disqualified them was temperament—just as, though educated up to the hilt, it disqualifies me. What keeps us in our place is embarrassment.
Alan Bennett 1934– : *Dinner at Noon* (BBC television, 1988)

4 The essence of servanthood is the servant's intimacy with the master's dirt.
J. M. Coetzee 1940– : *In the Heart of the Country* (1977)

5 Destroy him as you will, the bourgeois always bounces up—execute him, expropriate him, starve him out *en masse*, and he reappears in your children.
Cyril Connolly 1903–74: in *Observer* 7 March 1937

6 Dear me, I never knew that the lower classes had such white skins.
■ *supposedly said when watching troops bathing during the First World War*
Lord Curzon 1859–1925: K. Rose *Superior Person* (1969)

7 O let us love our occupations,
Bless the squire and his relations,
Live upon our daily rations,
And always know our proper stations.
Charles Dickens 1812–70: *The Chimes* (1844) 'The Second Quarter'

8 All the world over, I will back the masses against the classes.
W. E. Gladstone 1809–98: speech in Liverpool, 28 June 1886

9 The bourgeois prefers comfort to pleasure, convenience to liberty, and a pleasant temperature to the deathly inner consuming fire.
Hermann Hesse 1877–1962: *Der Steppenwolf* (1927)

10 There are those who think that Britain is a class-ridden society, and those who think it doesn't matter either way as long as you know your place in the set-up.
Miles Kington 1941– : *Welcome to Kington* (1989)

11 How beastly the bourgeois is
Especially the male of the species.
D. H. Lawrence 1885–1930: 'How Beastly the
Bourgeois Is' (1929)

12 The proletarians have nothing to lose
but their chains. They have a world to
win. WORKING MEN OF ALL
COUNTRIES, UNITE!
■ *commonly rendered as* 'Workers of the world,
unite!'
Karl Marx 1818–83 and **Friedrich Engels**
1820–95: *The Communist Manifesto* (1848)

13 We of the sinking middle class . . .
may sink without further struggles
into the working class where we
belong, and probably when we get
there it will not be so dreadful as we
feared, for, after all, we have nothing
to lose but our aitches.
George Orwell 1903–50: *The Road to Wigan
Pier* (1937)

14 I am pretty middle class.
John Prescott 1938– : on BBC Radio Four
Today programme; April 1996

15 You can be in the Horseguards and
still be common, dear.
Terence Rattigan 1911–77: *Separate Tables*
(1954)

16 Ladies were ladies in those days; they
did not do things themselves.
Gwen Raverat 1885–1957: *Period Piece* (1952)

17 The bourgeois are other people.
Jules Renard 1864–1910: diary, 28 January
1890

18 When Adam dalfe and Eve spane
Go spire if thou may spede,
Where was than the pride of man
That now merres his mede?
■ *traditionally taken by John Ball as the text of
his revolutionary sermon on the outbreak of the
Peasants' Revolt, 1381, in the form* 'When Adam
delved and Eve span, who was then the
gentleman?'
Richard Rolle de Hampole c.1290–1349: G. G.
Perry *Religious Pieces* (1914)

19 You may tempt the upper classes
With your villainous demi-tasses,
But; Heaven will protect a working-
girl!
Edgar Smith 1857–1938: 'Heaven Will Protect
the Working-Girl' (1909 song)

20 Civilization has made the peasantry
its pack animal. The bourgeoisie in
the long run only changed the form of
the pack.
Leon Trotsky 1879–1940: *History of the
Russian Revolution* (1933)

21 The so called immorality of the lower
classes is not to be named on the same
day with that of the higher and
highest. This is a thing which makes
my blood boil, and they will pay for it.
Queen Victoria 1819–1901: letter to the Crown
Princess of Prussia, 26 June 1872

22 Any who have heard that sound will
shrink at the recollection of it; it is the
sound of English county families
baying for broken glass.
Evelyn Waugh 1903–66: *Decline and Fall*
(1928)

Clergy

see also **Christianity**, **The Church**

1 Don't like bishops. Fishy lot. Blessed
are the meek my foot! They're all on
the climb. Ever heard of meekness
stopping a bishop from becoming a
bishop? Nor have I.
Maurice Bowra 1898–1971: Arthur Marshall
Life's Rich Pageant (1984)

2 Pray remember, Mr Dean, no dogma,
no Dean.
Benjamin Disraeli 1804–81: W. Monypenny
and G. Buckle *Life of Benjamin Disraeli* vol. 4
(1916)

3 Pastors need to start where people are
and not where we think they should
be.
Basil Hume 1923–99: in *Independent* 18 June
1999

4 In all ages of the world, priests have
been enemies of liberty.
David Hume 1711–76: 'Of the Parties of Great
Britain' (1741–2)

5 Anybody can be pope; the proof of
this is that I have become one.
   Pope John XXIII 1881–1963: Henri Fesquet *Wit and Wisdom of Good Pope John* (1964)

6 As the French say, there are three
sexes—men, women, and clergymen.
   Sydney Smith 1771–1845: Lady Holland *Memoir* (1855)

7 How can a bishop marry? How can he
flirt? The most he can say is, 'I will see
you in the vestry after service.'
   Sydney Smith 1771–1845: Lady Holland *Memoir* (1855)

8 I never saw, heard, nor read, that the
clergy were beloved in any nation
where Christianity was the religion of
the country. Nothing can render them
popular, but some degree of
persecution.
   Jonathan Swift 1667–1745: *Thoughts on Religion* (1765)

9 There is a species of person called a
'Modern Churchman' who draws the
full salary of a beneficed clergyman
and need not commit himself to any
religious belief.
   Evelyn Waugh 1903–66: *Decline and Fall* (1928)

10 I asked why he was a priest, and he
said if you have to work for anybody
an absentee boss is best.
   Jeanette Winterson 1959– : *The Passion* (1987)

Clothes
....
see also **Fashion**

1 It is totally impossible to be well
dressed in cheap shoes.
   Hardy Amies 1909– : *The Englishman's Suit* (1994)

2 The trick of wearing mink is to look as
though you were wearing a cloth coat.
The trick of wearing a cloth coat is to
look as though you are wearing mink.
   Pierre Balmain 1914–82: in *Observer* 25 December 1955

3 From the cradle to the grave,
underwear first, last and all the time.
   Bertolt Brecht 1898–1956: *The Threepenny Opera* (1928)

4 Clothes are our weapons, our
challenges, our visible insults.
   Angela Carter 1940–92: *Nothing Sacred* (1982)

5 When I began, at least women dressed
to please men. Now, they dress to
astonish one another.
   Coco Chanel 1883–1971: attributed

6 A good uniform must work its way
with the women, sooner or later.
   Charles Dickens 1812–70: *Pickwick Papers* (1837)

7 When I was young, I found out that
the big toe always ends up making a
hole in a sock. So I stopped wearing
socks.
   Albert Einstein 1879–1955: to Philippe Halsman; A. P. French *Einstein: A Centenary Volume* (1979)

8 The sense of being well-dressed gives
a feeling of inward tranquillity which
religion is powerless to bestow.
   Miss C. F. Forbes 1817–1911: R. W. Emerson *Letters and Social Aims* (1876)

9 The origins of clothing are not
practical. They are mystical and
erotic. The primitive man in the wolf-
pelt was not keeping dry; he was
saying: 'Look what I killed. Aren't I
the best?'
   Katherine Hamnett 1948– : in *Independent on Sunday* 10 March 1991

10 Whenas in silks my Julia goes,
Then, then (methinks) how sweetly
   flows
That liquefaction of her clothes.
Next, when I cast mine eyes and see
That brave vibration each way free;
O how that glittering taketh me!
   Robert Herrick 1591–1674: 'Upon Julia's Clothes' (1648)

11 You should never have your best
trousers on when you go out to fight
for freedom and truth.
   Henrik Ibsen 1828–1906: *An Enemy of the People* (1882)

12 If people don't want to listen to *you*, what makes you think they want to hear from your sweater?

■ *on slogans on clothing*
Fran Lebowitz 1946– : *Metropolitan Life* (1978)

13 *on being asked what she wore in bed:*
Chanel No. 5.
Marilyn Monroe 1926–62: Pete Martin *Marilyn Monroe* (1956)

14 Where's the man could ease a heart like a satin gown?
Dorothy Parker 1893–1967: 'The Satin Dress' (1937)

15 My closet looks like a convention of multiple-personality cases.
Anna Quindlen 1953– : *Newsmakers* (1993)

16 His socks compelled one's attention without losing one's respect.
Saki 1870–1916: *Chronicles of Clovis* (1911)

17 Costly thy habit as thy purse can buy,
But not expressed in fancy; rich, not gaudy;
For the apparel oft proclaims the man.
William Shakespeare 1564–1616: *Hamlet* (1601)

18 Beware of all enterprises that require new clothes.
Henry David Thoreau 1817–62: *Walden* (1854) 'Economy'

19 Clothes don't make the man . . . but they go a long way toward making a businessman.
Thomas Watson Snr. 1874–1956: Robert Sobel *IBM: Colossus in Transition* (1981)

20 Does my bum look big in this?
Arabella Weir: title of book (1997)

21 Every time you open your wardrobe, you look at your clothes and you wonder what you are going to wear. What you are really saying is 'Who am I going to be today?'
Fay Weldon 1931– : in *New Yorker* 26 June 1995

22 When you're all dressed up and have no place to go.
George Whiting: title of song (1912)

23 The Right Hon. was a tubby little chap who looked as if he had been poured into his clothes and had forgotten to say 'When!'
P. G. Wodehouse 1881–1975: *Very Good, Jeeves* (1930)

Colours

1 I was shown round Tutankhamun's tomb in the 1920s. I saw all this wonderful pink on the walls and the artefacts. I was so impressed that I vowed to wear it for the rest of my life.
Barbara Cartland 1901–2000: in *Irish Times* 28 March 1998

2 I cannot pretend to feel impartial about the colours. I rejoice with the brilliant ones, and am genuinely sorry for the poor browns.
Winston Churchill 1874–1965: *Thoughts and Adventures* (1932)

3 Green how I love you green.
Green wind.
Green boughs.
The ship on the sea
and the horse on the mountain.
Federico García Lorca 1899–1936: *Romance sonámbulo* (1924–7)

4 Grass-green and aspen-green,
Laurel-green and sea-green,
Fine-emerald-green,
And many another hue:
As green commands the variables of green
So love my loves of you.
Robert Graves 1895–1985: 'Variables of Green'

5 If artists do see fields blue they are deranged and should go to an asylum. If they only pretend to see them blue, they are criminals and should go to prison.
Adolf Hitler 1889–1945: speech in Munich, July 1937

6 Colour has taken hold of me; no longer do I have to chase after it. I know that it has hold of me for ever.

That is the significance of this blessed moment.

■ *on a visit to Tunis in 1914*
  Paul Klee 1879–1940: Herbert Read *A Concise History of Modern Painting* (1968)

7 She favoured sensible shades:
  Moss Green, Mustard, Beige.
  I dreamt a robe of a colour
  so pure it became a word.
  Paula Meehan 1955– : 'The Pattern' (1991)

8 I own I like definite form in what my eyes are to rest upon; and if landscapes were sold, like the sheets of characters of my boyhood, one penny plain and twopence coloured, I should go the length of twopence every day of my life.
  Robert Louis Stevenson 1850–94: *Travels with a Donkey* (1879)

9 If I could find anything blacker than black, I'd use it.
  J. M. W. Turner 1775–1851: remark, 1844

10 Pink is the navy blue of India.
  Diana Vreeland 1903–89: attributed, 1977

11 I think it pisses God off if you walk by the colour purple in a field somewhere and don't notice it.
  Alice Walker 1944– : *The Colour Purple* (1982)

Comedy

see also **Humour**

1 Comedy is tragedy that happens to *other* people.
  Angela Carter 1940–92: *Wise Children* (1991)

2 All I need to make a comedy is a park, a policeman and a pretty girl.
  Charlie Chaplin 1889–1977: *My Autobiography* (1964)

3 The funniest thing about comedy is that you never know why people laugh. I know *what* makes them laugh but trying to get your hands on the *why* of it is like trying to pick an eel out of a tub of water.
  W. C. Fields 1880–1946: R. J. Anobile *A Flask of Fields* (1972)

4 It is intriguing to win the prize for best comedy, as I thought I was writing a tragedy.
  ■ *on winning the Evening Standard Award for her play* Art
  Yasmina Reza 1969– : comment, 1996

5 Your anger can be 49 per cent and your comedy 51 per cent, and you are okay. If the anger is 51 per cent, the comedy is gone.
  Joan Rivers 1939– : *Enter Talking* (1986)

6 The difference between my generation and the current comics is that comedy was always at our expense. Now it's at somebody else's.
  Eric Sykes 1923– : in *Independent* 31 October 1998

Commitment

see also **Faithfulness**

1 'I will love You for ever,' swears the poet. I find this easy to swear too. *I will love You at 4.15 p.m. next Tuesday*: is that still as easy?
  W. H. Auden 1907–73: attributed

2 My commitment is such that under John Major my hair went grey, and now William Hague is leader I am going bald.
  Gyles Brandreth 1948– : in *Sunday Times* 4 April 1999

3 My tongue swore, but my mind's unsworn.
  ■ *on the breaking of an oath*
  Euripides *c.*485–*c.*406 BC: *Hippolytus*

4 With malice toward none; with charity for all; with firmness in the right, as God gives us to see the right, let us strive on to finish the work we are in.
  Abraham Lincoln 1809–65: Second Inaugural Address, 4 March 1865

5 The most excited voice I heard in the building when I came here was the automated voice in the lift.
  ■ *on the Arts Council*
  Gerry Robinson 1948– : in *Independent* 30 July 1999

Committees

see also **Administration**, **Management**

1 Committee—a group of men who individually can do nothing but as a group decide that nothing can be done.
   Fred Allen 1894–1956: attributed

2 No academic person is ever voted into the chair until he has reached an age at which he has forgotten the meaning of the word 'irrelevant'.
   Francis M. Cornford 1874–1943: *Microcosmographia Academica* (1908)

3 No grand idea was ever born in a conference, but a lot of foolish ideas have died there.
   F. Scott Fitzgerald 1896–1940: Edmund Wilson (ed.) *The Crack-Up* (1945) 'Note-Books E'

4 A camel is a horse designed by a committee.
   Alec Issigonis 1906–88: attributed

5 The committee divided between the theorists, who had done all their thinking long ago, or had had it done for them, and the pragmatists, who hoped to discover what it was they thought in the process of saying it.
   Ian McEwan 1948– : *The Child in Time* (1987)

6 Oh for just
   one
   more conference
   regarding the eradication of all conferences!
   Vladimir Mayakovsky 1893–1930: 'In Re Conferences'

7 Time spent on any item of the agenda will be in inverse proportion to the sum involved.
   C. Northcote Parkinson 1909–93: *Parkinson's Law* (1958)

8 The length of a meeting rises with the square of the number of people present.
   Eileen Shanahan: in *New York Times Magazine* 17 March 1968

Communism

see also **Capitalism**, **Class**, **Russia**

1 Capitalism, it is said, is a system wherein man exploits man. And communism—is vice versa.
   ■ *quoting 'a Polish intellectual'*
   Daniel Bell 1919– : *The End of Ideology* (1960)

2 It is as wholly wrong to blame Marx for what was done in his name, as it is to blame Jesus for what was done in his.
   Tony Benn 1925– : Alan Freeman *The Benn Heresy* (1982)

3 Capitalism is using its money; we socialists throw it away.
   Fidel Castro 1927– : in *Observer* 8 November 1964

4 From Stettin in the Baltic to Trieste in the Adriatic an iron curtain has descended across the Continent.
   ■ *the expression 'iron curtain' previously had been applied by others to the Soviet Union or her sphere of influence*
   Winston Churchill 1874–1965: speech at Westminster College, Fulton, Missouri, 5 March 1946

5 M is for Marx
   And Movement of Masses
   And Massing of Arses.
   And Clashing of Classes.
   Cyril Connolly 1903–74: 'Where Engels Fears to Tread' (1945)

6 In the service of the people we followed such a policy that socialism would not lose its human face.
   Alexander Dubček 1921–92: in *Rudé Právo* 19 July 1968

7 The Soviet Union has indeed been our greatest menace, not so much because of what it has done, but because of the excuses it has provided us for our failures.
   J. William Fulbright 1905–95: in *Observer* 21 December 1958

8 It would be simplistic to say that Divine Providence caused the fall of communism. It fell by itself as a consequence of its own mistakes and

abuses. It fell by itself because of its own inherent weaknesses.

Pope John Paul II 1920– : Carl Bernstein and Marco Politi *His Holiness: John Paul II and the Hidden History of our Time* (1996)

9 The trouble with Communism is that it accepts too much of today's furniture. I hate furniture.

T. E. Lawrence 1888–1935: letter to Cecil Day Lewis, 20 December 1934

10 Communism is Soviet power plus the electrification of the whole country.

Lenin 1870–1924: Report to 8th Congress, 1920

11 All I know is that I am not a Marxist.

Karl Marx 1818–83: attributed in a letter from Friedrich Engels to Conrad Schmidt, 5 August 1890

12 A spectre is haunting Europe—the spectre of Communism.

Karl Marx 1818–83 and **Friedrich Engels** 1820–95: *The Communist Manifesto* (1848)

13 Communism is like prohibition, it's a good idea but it won't work.

Will Rogers 1879–1935: in 1927; *Weekly Articles* (1981)

14 The clock of communism has stopped striking. But its concrete building has not yet come crashing down. For that reason, instead of freeing ourselves, we must try to save ourselves being crushed by the rubble.

Alexander Solzhenitsyn 1918– : in *Komsomolskaya Pravda* 18 September 1990

15 The State is an instrument in the hands of the ruling class, used to break the resistance of the adversaries of that class.

Joseph Stalin 1879–1953: *Foundations of Leninism* (1924)

16 I have seen the future; and it works.

▪ *following a visit to the Soviet Union in 1919*
Lincoln Steffens 1866–1936: *Letters* (1938)

Compassion

see also **Sorrow, Suffering**

1 Intellectual disgrace
Stares from every human face,
And the seas of pity lie
Locked and frozen in each eye.

W. H. Auden 1907–73: 'In Memory of W. B. Yeats' (1940)

2 Nobody can tell what I suffer! But it is always so. Those who do not complain are never pitied.

Jane Austen 1775–1817: *Pride and Prejudice* (1813)

3 Hatred is a tonic, it makes one live, it inspires vengeance; but pity kills, it makes our weakness weaker.

Honoré de Balzac 1799–1850: *La Peau de Chagrin* (1831)

4 Then cherish pity, lest you drive an angel from your door.

William Blake 1757–1827: 'Holy Thursday' (1789)

5 O divine Master, grant that I may not so much seek
To be consoled as to console;
To be understood as to understand.

St Francis of Assisi 1181–1226: 'Prayer of St Francis'; attributed

6 Our sympathy is cold to the relation of distant misery.

Edward Gibbon 1737–94: *The Decline and Fall of the Roman Empire* (1776–88)

7 Any victim demands allegiance.

Graham Greene 1904–91: *The Heart of the Matter* (1948)

8 If a madman were to come into this room with a stick in his hand, no doubt we should pity the state of his mind; but our primary consideration would be to take care of ourselves. We should knock him down first, and pity him afterwards.

Samuel Johnson 1709–84: House of Commons, 3 April 1776

9 We are all strong enough to bear the misfortunes of others.

Duc de la Rochefoucauld 1613–80: *Maximes* (1678)

10 The fact that I have no remedy for the sorrows of the world is no reason for my accepting yours. It simply

supports the strong probability that
yours is a fake.

H. L. Mencken 1880–1956: *Minority Report*
(1956)

11 Only the hopeless are starkly sincere
and . . . only the unhappy can either
give or take sympathy.

Jean Rhys c.1890–1979: *The Left Bank* (1927)

12 But yet the pity of it, Iago! O! Iago, the
pity of it, Iago!

William Shakespeare 1564–1616: *Othello*
(1602–4)

13 If you see anybody fallen by the
wayside and lying in the ditch, it isn't
much good climbing into the ditch
and lying by his side.

Dick Sheppard 1880–1937: Carolyn Scott *Dick
Sheppard* (1977)

14 When times get rough,
And friends just can't be found
Like a bridge over troubled water
I will lay me down.

Paul Simon 1942– : 'Bridge over Troubled
Water' (1970 song)

Compromise

see also **Argument**, **Choice**, **Tolerance**

1 An agreement between two men to do
what both agree is wrong.

Lord Edward Cecil 1867–1918: letter,
3 September 1911

2 When compromise goes out of
fashion among the young, so do
babies.

Charles Handy 1932– : *The Empty Raincoat*
(1994)

3 He never wants anything but what's
right and fair; only when you come to
settle what's right and fair, it's
everything that he wants and nothing
that you want. And that's his idea of a
compromise. Give me the Brown
compromise when I'm on his side.

Thomas Hughes 1822–96: *Tom Brown's
Schooldays* (1857)

4 If one cannot catch the bird of
paradise, better take a wet hen.

Nikita Khrushchev 1894–1971: in *Time*
6 January 1958

5 A compromise in the sense that being
bitten in half by a shark is a
compromise with being swallowed
whole.

P. J. O'Rourke 1947– : *Parliament of Whores*
(1991)

Computers

see also **The Internet**

1 To err is human but to really foul
things up requires a computer.

Anonymous: *Farmers' Almanac for 1978*
'Capsules of Wisdom'

2 Computers are composed of nothing
more than logic gates stretched out to
the horizon in a vast numerical
irrigation system.

Stan Augarten: *State of the Art: A
Photographic History of the Integrated Circuit*
(1983)

3 A modern computer hovers between
the obsolescent and the nonexistent.

Sydney Brenner 1927– : attributed in *Science*
5 January 1990

4 Computers are anti-Faraday
machines. He said he couldn't
understand anything until he could
count it, while computers count
everything and understand nothing.

Ralph Cornes: in *Guardian* 28 March 1991

5 Silicon Valley is the Florence of the
late 20th century.

Francis Fukuyama 1952– : in *Independent*
19 June 1999

6 If they want we will give them a
sleeping bag, but there is something
romantic about sleeping under the
desk. They want to do it.

■ *on his young software programmers*
Bill Gates 1955– : in *Independent*
18 November 1995

7 The PC is the LSD of the '90s.

Timothy Leary 1920–96: remark made in the
early 1990s; in *Guardian* 1 June 1996

8 The Analytical Engine weaves
algebraic patterns just as the Jacquard
loom weaves flowers and leaves.
  ▪ *of Babbage's mechanical computer*
  Ada Lovelace 1815–52: Luigi Menabrea *Sketch
  of the Analytical Engine invented by Charles
  Babbage* (1843), translated and annotated by
  Ada Lovelace, Note A

9 A sort of cognitive equivalent of a
condom—it's a layer of contraceptive
rubber between the direct experience
and the cognitive system.
  ▪ *of reading text from a computer screen*
  Jonathan Miller 1934– : in *Independent on
  Sunday* 14 January 1996

10 Like the anthropologist returning
home from a foreign culture, the
voyager in virtuality can return home
to a real world better equipped to
understand its artifices.
  Sherry Turkle 1948– : *Life on the Screen:
  Identity in the Age of the Internet* (1995)

11 We used to have lots of questions to
which there were no answers. Now
with the computer there are lots of
answers to which we haven't thought
up the questions.
  Peter Ustinov 1921– : in *Illustrated London
  News* 1 June 1968

Conformity

see also **Individuality**

1 You cannot make a man by standing a
sheep on its hind-legs. But by
standing a flock of sheep in that
position you can make a crowd of
men.
  Max Beerbohm 1872–1956: *Zuleika Dobson*
  (1911)

2 My parents were convinced that I
would one day become Mr Average,
but almost 30 years on I am still an
A1 freak.
  Boy George 1961– : in *Independent on
  Sunday* 28 March 1999

3 'It's always best on these occasions to
do what the mob do.' 'But suppose
there are two mobs?' suggested Mr

Snodgrass. 'Shout with the largest,'
replied Mr Pickwick.
  Charles Dickens 1812–70: *Pickwick Papers*
  (1837)

4 The Party line is that there is no Party
line.
  Milovan Djilas 1911– : comment on reforms
  of the Yugoslavian Communist Party,
  November 1952; Fitzroy Maclean *Disputed
  Barricade* (1957)

5 Whoso would be a man must be a
nonconformist.
  Ralph Waldo Emerson 1803–82: *Essays* (1841)
  'Self-Reliance'

6 Imitation lies at the root of most
human actions. A respectable person
is one who conforms to custom.
People are called good when they do
as others do.
  Anatole France 1844–1924: *Crainquebille*
  (1923)

7 I've broken Anne of gathering
bouquets.
It's not fair to the child. It can't be
helped though:
Pressed into service means pressed
out of shape.
  Robert Frost 1874–1963: 'The Self-Seeker'
  (1914)

8 These are the days when men of all
social disciplines and all political
faiths seek the comfortable and the
accepted; when the man of
controversy is looked upon as a
disturbing influence; when originality
is taken to be a mark of instability;
and when, in minor modification of
the scriptural parable, the bland lead
the bland.
  J. K. Galbraith 1908– : *The Affluent Society*
  (1958)

9 Never forget that only dead fish swim
with the stream.
  Malcolm Muggeridge 1903–90: quoting a
  supporter; in *Radio Times* 9 July 1964

10 Her exotic daydreams do not prevent
her from being small-town bourgeois
at heart, clinging to conventional
ideas or committing this or that
conventional violation of the
conventional, adultery being a most

conventional way to rise above the conventional.

Vladimir Nabokov 1899–1977: *Lectures on Literature* (1980) 'Madame Bovary'

11 While we were talking came by several poor creatures carried by, by constables, for being at a conventicle . . . I would to God they would either conform, or be more wise, and not be catched!

Samuel Pepys 1633–1703: diary 7 August 1664

12 The Normal is the good smile in a child's eyes—all right. It is also the dead stare in a million adults. It both sustains and kills—like a God. It is the Ordinary made beautiful; it is also the Average made lethal.

Peter Shaffer 1926– : *Equus* (1983 ed.)

13 Teach him to think for himself? Oh, my God, teach him rather to think like other people!

■ *on her son's education*
Mary Shelley 1797–1851: Matthew Arnold *Essays in Criticism* Second Series (1888) 'Shelley'

14 If a man does not keep pace with his companions, perhaps it is because he hears a different drummer. Let him step to the music which he hears, however measured or far away.

Henry David Thoreau 1817–62: *Walden* (1854)

Conscience

see also **Forgiveness**, **Sin**

1 Conscience is thoroughly well-bred and soon leaves off talking to those who do not wish to hear it.

Samuel Butler 1835–1902: *Further Extracts from Notebooks* (1934)

2 I cannot and will not cut my conscience to fit this year's fashions.

Lillian Hellman 1905–84: letter to John S. Wood, 19 May 1952

3 Sufficient conscience to bother him, but not sufficient to keep him straight.

■ *of Ramsay MacDonald*
David Lloyd George 1863–1945: A. J. Sylvester *Life with Lloyd George* (1975)

4 Conscience: the inner voice which warns us that someone may be looking.

H. L. Mencken 1880–1956: *A Little Book in C major* (1916)

5 If I am obliged to bring religion into after-dinner toasts (which indeed does not seem quite the thing) I shall drink—to the Pope, if you please— still, to Conscience first, and to the Pope afterwards.

John Henry Newman 1801–90: *A Letter Addressed to the Duke of Norfolk . . .* (1875)

6 Thus conscience doth make cowards of us all.

William Shakespeare 1564–1616: *Hamlet* (1601)

7 Most people sell their souls, and live with a good conscience on the proceeds.

Logan Pearsall Smith 1865–1946: *Afterthoughts* (1931)

Consequences

see **Causes and Consequences**

Consistency

1 A foolish consistency is the hobgoblin of little minds, adored by little statesmen and philosophers and divines. With consistency a great soul has simply nothing to do.

Ralph Waldo Emerson 1803–82: *Essays* (1841) 'Self-Reliance'

2 Consistency is contrary to nature, contrary to life. The only completely consistent people are the dead.

Aldous Huxley 1894–1963: *Do What You Will* (1929)

3 Do I contradict myself?
Very well then I contradict myself,
(I am large, I contain multitudes.)

Walt Whitman 1819–92: 'Song of Myself' (written 1855)

Consumer Society

see also **Business, Possessions, Shopping**

1 The source of status is no longer the ability to make things but simply the ability to purchase them.
   Harry Braverman: *Labour and Monopoly Capital* (1974)

2 Consumer wants can have bizarre, frivolous, or even immoral origins, and an admirable case can still be made for a society that seeks to satisfy them. But the case cannot stand if it is the process of satisfying wants that creates the wants.
   J. K. Galbraith 1908– : *The Affluent Society* (1958)

3 Just as the great shopping centres have become the new cathedrals of our age, so the lottery is a variant on a religious theme. The form of redemption offered by the lottery is utterly consistent with the underlying creed of consumer populism; redemption through money, through getting something for nothing.
   John Humphrys: *Devil's Advocate* (1999)

4 In a consumer society there are inevitably two kinds of slaves: the prisoners of addiction and the prisoners of envy.
   Ivan Illich 1926– : *Tools for Conviviality* (1973)

5 Transformations in Eastern Europe seem to have been fuelled by people's desire to buy rather than their desire to vote, by dreams of purchasing rather than dreams of participating.
   Rosabeth Moss Kanter 1943– : *World Class* (1995)

6 The metamorphosis of consumption from vice to virtue is one of the most important yet least examined phenomena of the twentieth century.
   Jeremy Rifkin 1945– : *The End of Work* (1995)

7 The consumer, so it is said, is the king . . . each is a voter who uses his money as votes to get the things done that he wants done.
   Paul A. Samuelson 1915– : *Economics* (8th ed., 1970)

Conversation

see also **Gossip, Speech**

1 On every formal visit a child ought to be of the party, by way of provision for discourse.
   Jane Austen 1775–1817: *Sense and Sensibility* (1811)

2 JOHNSON: Well, we had a good talk.
   BOSWELL: Yes, Sir; you tossed and gored several persons.
   James Boswell 1740–95: *Life of Samuel Johnson* (1791) Summer 1768

3 Although there exist many thousand subjects for elegant conversation, there are persons who cannot meet a cripple without talking about feet.
   Ernest Bramah 1868–1942: *The Wallet of Kai Lung* (1900)

4 'The time has come,' the Walrus said,
   'To talk of many things:
   Of shoes—and ships—and sealing wax—
   Of cabbages—and kings—
   And why the sea is boiling hot—
   And whether pigs have wings.'
   Lewis Carroll 1832–98: *Through the Looking-Glass* (1872)

5 Religion is by no means a proper subject of conversation in a mixed company.
   Lord Chesterfield 1694–1773: *Letters . . . to his Godson and Successor* (1890)

6 I see people in terms of dialogue and I believe that people are their talk.
   Roddy Doyle 1958– : John Ardagh *Ireland and the Irish* (1994)

7 Two may talk and one may hear, but three cannot take part in a conversation of the most sincere and searching sort.
   Ralph Waldo Emerson 1803–82: *Essays* (1841) 'Friendship'

8 How time flies when you's doin' all the talking.
   Harvey Fierstein 1954– : *Torch Song Trilogy* (1979)

9 It is the province of knowledge to
speak and it is the privilege of wisdom
to listen.

Oliver Wendell Holmes 1809–94: *The Poet at
the Breakfast-Table* (1872)

10 And, when you stick on
conversation's burrs,
Don't strew your pathway with those
dreadful *urs*.

Oliver Wendell Holmes 1809–94: 'A Rhymed
Lesson' (1848)

11 If you are ever at a loss to support a
flagging conversation, introduce the
subject of eating.

Leigh Hunt 1784–1859: attributed

12 Questioning is not the mode of
conversation among gentlemen. It is
assuming a superiority.

Samuel Johnson 1709–84: James Boswell *Life
of Samuel Johnson* (1791) 25 March 1776

13 The opposite of talking isn't listening.
The opposite of talking is waiting.

Fran Lebowitz 1946– : *Social Studies* (1981)

14 I am not bound to please thee with
my answer.

William Shakespeare 1564–1616: *The
Merchant of Venice* (1596–8)

15 He speaks to Me as if I was a public
meeting.

■ *of Gladstone*

Queen Victoria 1819–1901: G. W. E. Russell
Collections and Recollections (1898)

16 There is no such thing as
conversation. It is an illusion. There
are intersecting monologues, that is
all.

Rebecca West 1892–1983: *There is No
Conversation* (1935)

Cooking
....
see also **Eating**, **Food and Drink**

1 There are few virtues a man can
possess more erotic than culinary
skill. The first thing that attracted me
to my husband was his incredible life
story, but I actually fell in love with

him several hours later as I was
watching him prepare dinner for me.

Isabel Allende 1942– : in *The Times* 25 April
1998

2 Anyone who tells a lie has not a pure
heart, and cannot make a good soup.

Ludwig van Beethoven 1770–1827: Ludwig
Nohl *Beethoven Depicted by his
Contemporaries* (1880)

3 Be content to remember that those
who can make omelettes properly can
do nothing else.

Hilaire Belloc 1870–1953: *A Conversation with
a Cat* (1931)

4 Cooking is the most ancient of the
arts, for Adam was born hungry.

Anthelme Brillat-Savarin 1755–1826:
Physiologie du Goût (1825)

5 The difference between a chef and a
cook is the difference between a wife
and a prostitute. Cooks do meals for
people they know and love. Chefs do
it anonymously for anyone who's got
the price.

A. A. Gill 1954– : in *Independent* 4 November
1998

6 Hot on Sunday,
Cold on Monday,
Hashed on Tuesday,
Minced on Wednesday,
Curried Thursday,
Broth on Friday,
Cottage pie Saturday.

Dorothy Hartley 1893–1985: *Food in England*
(1954) 'Vicarage Mutton'

7 Home-made dishes that drive one
from home.

Thomas Hood 1799–1845: *Miss Kilmansegg
and her Precious Leg* (1841–3)

8 Kissing don't last: cookery do!

George Meredith 1828–1909: *The Ordeal of
Richard Feverel* (1859)

9 On the Continent people have good
food; in England people have good
table manners.

George Mikes 1912– : *How to be an Alien*
(1946)

10 I never see any home cooking. All I get is fancy stuff.
   Prince Philip, Duke of Edinburgh 1921– : in *Observer* 28 October 1962

11 Her cooking is the missionary position of cooking. That is how everybody starts.
   ■ *defending Delia Smith*
   Egon Ronay: in *Independent on Sunday* 1 November 1998

12 The cook was a good cook, as cooks go; and as cooks go, she went.
   Saki 1870–1916: *Reginald* (1904)

13 You won't be surprised that diseases are innumerable—count the cooks.
   Seneca *c*.4 BC–AD 65: *Epistles*

14 I discovered that dinners follow the order of creation—fish first, then entrées, then joints, lastly the apple as dessert. The soup is chaos.
   Sylvia Townsend Warner 1893–1978: diary, 26 May 1929

Cooperation

1 The lion and the calf shall lie down together but the calf won't get much sleep.
   Woody Allen 1935– : in *New Republic* 31 August 1974

2 If a house be divided against itself, that house cannot stand.
   Bible: St Mark

3 When bad men combine, the good must associate; else they will fall, one by one, an unpitied sacrifice in a contemptible struggle.
   Edmund Burke 1729–97: *Thoughts on the Cause of the Present Discontents* (1770)

4 Then join hand in hand, brave Americans all,—
   By uniting we stand, by dividing we fall.
   John Dickinson 1732–1808: 'The Liberty Song' (1768)

5 All for one, one for all.
   ■ *motto of the Three Musketeers*
   Alexandre Dumas 1802–70: *Les Trois Mousquetaires* (1844)

6 We must indeed all hang together, or, most assuredly, we shall all hang separately.
   Benjamin Franklin 1706–90: at the signing of the Declaration of Independence, 4 July 1776; possibly not original

7 Before I built a wall I'd ask to know What I was walling in or walling out, And to whom I was like to give offence.
   Robert Frost 1874–1963: 'Mending Wall' (1914)

8 If someone claps his hand a sound arises. Listen to the sound of the single hand!
   Hakuin 1686–1769: attributed

9 We must learn to live together as brothers or perish together as fools.
   Martin Luther King 1929–68: speech at St Louis, 22 March 1964

10 Why don't you do something to *help* me?
   Stan Laurel 1890–1965: *Drivers' Licence Sketch* (1947 film); words spoken by Oliver Hardy

11 In a place where 'please' is pronounced 'I s'pose you couldn't' it is rare to meet with any belief in help.
   Les A. Murray 1938– : *The Boys Who Stole the Funeral* (1989)

12 You may call it combination, you may call it the accidental and fortuitous concurrence of atoms.
   ■ *on a projected Palmerston–Disraeli coalition*
   Lord Palmerston 1784–1865: speech, House of Commons, 5 March 1857

13 Government and co-operation are in all things the laws of life; anarchy and competition the laws of death.
   John Ruskin 1819–1900: *Unto this Last* (1862)

14 To my daughter Leonora without whose never-failing sympathy and encouragement this book would have been finished in half the time.
   P. G. Wodehouse 1881–1975: *The Heart of a Goof* (1926) dedication

Corruption

1 When their lordships asked Bacon
How many bribes he had taken
He had at least the grace
To get very red in the face.
Edmund Clerihew Bentley 1875–1956: 'Bacon'
(1939)

2 I stuffed their mouths with gold.
■ *on his handling of the consultants during the
establishment of the National Health Service*
Aneurin Bevan 1897–1960: Brian Abel-Smith
The Hospitals 1800–1948 (1964)

3 I got fed up with all the sex and sleaze
and backhanders of rock 'n' roll so I
went into politics.
Tony Blair 1953– : in *Independent*
12 November 1994

4 Nothing to be done without a bribe I
find, in love as well as law.
Susannah Centlivre c.1669–1723: *The Perjured
Husband* (1700)

5 Men are more often bribed by their
loyalties and ambitions than money.
Robert H. Jackson 1892–1954: dissenting
opinion in *United States v. Wunderlich* 1951

6 . . . *Omnia Romae*
Cum pretio.
Everything in Rome—at a price.
Juvenal AD c.60–c.130: *Satires*

7 I am not worth purchasing, but such
as I am, the King of Great Britain is
not rich enough to do it.
■ *replying to an offer from Governor George
Johnstone of £10,000, and any office in the
Colonies in the King's gift, if he were able
successfully to promote a Union between Britain
and America*
Joseph Reed 1741–85: W. B. Read *Life and
Correspondence of Joseph Reed* (1847)

8 I note with considerable satisfaction
that I am whiter than white.
■ *of the inquiry into fraud at the European
Commission*
Jacques Santer 1937– : at a news conference,
16 March 1999

9 But the jingling of the guinea helps
the hurt that Honour feels.
Alfred, Lord Tennyson 1809–92: 'Locksley Hall'
(1842)

10 All those men have their price.
■ *of fellow parliamentarians*
Robert Walpole 1676–1745: W. Coxe *Memoirs
of Sir Robert Walpole* (1798)

11 The flood of money that gushes into
politics today is a pollution of
democracy.
Theodore H. White 1915–86: in *Time*
19 November 1984

Cosmetics

1 Women have been trained to speak
softly and carry lipstick. Those days
are over.
Bella Abzug 1920–98: attributed; in *Times*
2 April 1998

2 You look rather rash my dear your
colors dont quite match your face.
Daisy Ashford 1881–1972: *The Young Visiters*
(1919)

3 Most women are not so young as they
are painted.
Max Beerbohm 1872–1956: *The Yellow Book*
(1894)

4 So much lipstick must rot the brain.
■ *of Suzanne Moore*
Germaine Greer 1939– : in *Daily Mail* 17 May
1995

5 A girl whose cheeks are covered with
paint
Has an advantage with me over one
whose ain't.
Ogden Nash 1902–71: 'Biological Reflection'
(1931)

6 In the factory we make cosmetics; in
the store we sell hope.
Charles Revson 1906–75: A. Tobias *Fire and
Ice* (1976)

7 How do you ennoble the spirit when
you are selling something as
inconsequential as a cosmetic cream?
Anita Roddick 1942– : *Body and Soul* (1991)

8 There are no ugly women, only lazy
ones.
Helena Rubinstein 1882–1965: *My Life for
Beauty* (1966)

9 I was tired of being a woman,
tired of the spoons and the pots,

tired of my mouth and my breasts
tired of the cosmetics and silks . . .
I was tired of the gender of things.
Anne Sexton 1928–74: 'Consorting with
angels' (1967)

Counselling

see also **Advice, The Mind**

1 Therapy has become what I think of
as the tenth American muse.
Jacob Bronowski 1908–74: attributed

2 He had polyester sheets and I wanted
to get cotton sheets. He discussed it
with his shrink many times before he
made the switch.
■ *of her former partner, Woody Allen*
Mia Farrow 1945– : in *Independent*
8 February 1997

3 Before I went into analysis I told
everyone lies—but when you spend
all that money, you tell the truth.
Jane Fonda 1937– : Thomas Kiernan *Jane: An
Intimate Biography of Jane Fonda* (1973)

4 People go into counselling and never
emerge. I wonder if counselling isn't
the new religion.
Rajen Persaud: in *Independent* 13 September
1997

5 We didn't have counsellors rushing
around every time somebody let off a
gun, you know, asking 'Are you all
right—are you sure you don't have a
ghastly problem?' You just got on with
it.
■ *on his shipmates in the Second World War*
Prince Philip, Duke of Edinburgh 1921– : BBC
TV interview, August 1999

6 Why waste money on psychotherapy
when you can listen to the B Minor
Mass?
Michael Torke 1961– : in *Observer*
23 September 1990

The Country

see also **Cities, Farming**

1 Nothing can be said in his
vindication, but that his abolishing

Religious Houses and leaving them to
the ruinous depredations of time has
been of infinite use to the landscape of
England in general.
■ *of Henry VIII*
Jane Austen 1775–1817: *The History of England*
(written 1791)

2 'Tis distance lends enchantment to
the view,
And robes the mountain in its azure
hue.
Thomas Campbell 1777–1844: *Pleasures of
Hope* (1799)

3 O fat white woman whom nobody
loves,
Why do you walk through the fields in
gloves . . .
Missing so much and so much?
Frances Cornford 1886–1960: 'To a Fat Lady
seen from the Train' (1910)

4 It is my belief, Watson, founded upon
my experience, that the lowest and
vilest alleys in London do not present
a more dreadful record of sin than
does the smiling and beautiful
countryside.
Arthur Conan Doyle 1859–1930: *The
Adventures of Sherlock Holmes* (1892) 'The
Copper Beeches'

5 Green belts should be the start of the
countryside, not a ditch between
Subtopias.
Hugh Gaitskell 1906–63: in *Observer* 1 January
1961

6 There is nothing good to be had in the
country, or if there is, they will not let
you have it.
William Hazlitt 1778–1830: *The Round Table*
(1817)

7 It will be said of this generation that it
found England a land of beauty and
left it a land of 'beauty spots'.
C. E. M. Joad 1891–1953: *The Horrors of the
Countryside* (1931)

8 So *that's* what hay looks like.
■ *said at Badminton House, where she was
evacuated during the Second World War*
Queen Mary 1867–1953: James Pope-
Hennessy *Life of Queen Mary* (1959)

9 Sylvia . . . was accustomed to nothing
much more sylvan than 'leafy

Kensington'. She looked on the country as something excellent and wholesome in its way, which was apt to become troublesome if you encouraged it overmuch.

Saki 1870–1916: *The Chronicles of Clovis* (1911)

10 I have no relish for the country; it is a kind of healthy grave.

Sydney Smith 1771–1845: letter to Miss G. Harcourt, 1838

11 Anybody can be good in the country.

Oscar Wilde 1854–1900: *The Picture of Dorian Gray* (1891)

Courage

see also **Cowardice, Fear**

1 Courage is the thing. All goes if courage goes!

J. M. Barrie 1860–1937: Rectorial Address at St Andrews, 3 May 1922

2 No coward soul is mine,
No trembler in the world's storm-troubled sphere:
I see Heaven's glories shine,
And faith shines equal, arming me from fear.

Emily Brontë 1818–48: 'No coward soul is mine' (1846)

3 Boldness, and again boldness, and always boldness!

Georges Jacques Danton 1759–94: speech to the Legislative Committee of General Defence, 2 September 1792

4 None but the brave deserves the fair.

John Dryden 1631–1700: *Alexander's Feast* (1697)

5 Grace under pressure.

■ *when asked what he meant by 'guts', in an interview with Dorothy Parker*

Ernest Hemingway 1899–1961: in *New Yorker* 30 November 1929

6 In the fell clutch of circumstance,
I have not winced nor cried aloud:
Under the bludgeonings of chance
My head is bloody, but unbowed.

W. E. Henley 1849–1903: 'Invictus. In Memoriam R.T.H.B.' (1888)

7 Tender-handed stroke a nettle,
And it stings you for your pains;

Grasp it like a man of mettle,
And it soft as silk remains.

Aaron Hill 1685–1750: 'Verses Written on a Window in Scotland'

8 Courage is not simply *one* of the virtues but the form of every virtue at the testing point.

C. S. Lewis 1898–1963: Cyril Connolly *The Unquiet Grave* (1944)

9 As to moral courage, I have very rarely met with two o'clock in the morning courage: I mean instantaneous courage.

Napoleon I 1769–1821: E. A. de Las Cases *Mémorial de Ste-Hélène* (1823) 4–5 December 1815

10 Had we lived, I should have had a tale to tell of the hardihood, endurance, and courage of my companions which would have stirred the heart of every Englishman. These rough notes and our dead bodies must tell the tale.

Robert Falcon Scott 1868–1912: 'Message to the Public' in late editions of *The Times* 11 February 1913

11 Boldness be my friend!
Arm me, audacity.

William Shakespeare 1564–1616: *Cymbeline* (1609–10)

12 My valour is certainly going!—it is sneaking off!—I feel it oozing out as it were at the palms of my hands!

Richard Brinsley Sheridan 1751–1816: *The Rivals* (1775)

13 Perhaps those, who, trembling most, maintain a dignity in their fate, are the bravest: resolution on reflection is real courage.

Horace Walpole 1717–97: *Memoirs of the Reign of King George II* (1757)

Courtship

see also **Love**

1 Woe betide the man who dares to pay a woman a compliment today . . .
Forget the flowers, the chocolates, the soft word—rather woo her with a self-

defence manual in one hand and a family planning leaflet in the other.
Alan Ayckbourn 1939– : *Round and Round the Garden* (1975)

2 Ten years of courtship is carrying celibacy to extremes.
Alan Bennett 1934– : *Habeas Corpus* (1973)

3 I asked her to put me on a quest because she didn't believe me when I told her I wanted to marry her. And she made this list of almost impossible things to achieve. They were very creative things, which made me love her even more.
Nicolas Cage 1964– : in *The Times* 17 June 1998

4 I certainly didn't go down on one knee. I think she said it's about time we got married.
■ *on his diamond wedding day, remembering his proposal*
James Callaghan 1912– : in *Daily Telegraph* 29 July 1998

5 Courtship to marriage, as a very witty prologue to a very dull play.
William Congreve 1670–1729: *The Old Bachelor* (1693)

6 Everyone knows that dating in your thirties is not the happy-go-lucky free-for-all it was when you were twenty-two.
Helen Fielding 1958– : *Bridget Jones's Diary* (1996)

7 Holding hands at midnight
'Neath a starry sky,
Nice work if you can get it,
And you can get it if you try.
Ira Gershwin 1896–1983: 'Nice Work If You Can Get It' (1937 song)

8 I can't get no satisfaction
I can't get no girl reaction.
Mick Jagger 1943– and **Keith Richards** 1943– : '(I Can't Get No) Satisfaction' (1965 song)

9 Had we but world enough, and time,
This coyness, lady, were no crime.
Andrew Marvell 1621–78: 'To His coy Mistress' (1681)

10 Wooing, so tiring.
Nancy Mitford 1904–73: *The Pursuit of Love* (1945)

11 Dating is a social engagement with the threat of sex at its conclusion.
P. J. O'Rourke 1947– : *Modern Manners* (1984)

12 I court others in verse: but I love thee in prose:
And they have my whimsies, but thou hast my heart.
Matthew Prior 1664–1721: 'A Better Answer' (1718)

13 She is a woman, therefore may be wooed;
She is a woman, therefore may be won.
William Shakespeare 1564–1616: *Titus Andronicus* (1590)

14 You think that you are Ann's suitor; that you are the pursuer and she the pursued . . . Fool: it is you who are the pursued, the marked down quarry, the destined prey.
George Bernard Shaw 1856–1950: *Man and Superman* (1903)

15 Why so pale and wan, fond lover?
Prithee, why so pale?
Will, when looking well can't move her,
Looking ill prevail?
Prithee, why so pale?
John Suckling 1609–42: *Aglaura* (1637)

16 She knew how to allure by denying, and to make the gift rich by delaying it.
Anthony Trollope 1815–82: *Phineas Finn* (1869)

17 We've got to have
We plot to have
For it's so dreary not to have
That certain thing called the Boy Friend.
Sandy Wilson 1924– : 'The Boyfriend' (1954 song)

Cowardice

see also **Courage, Fear**

1 Cowardice, as distinguished from panic, is almost always simply a lack

of ability to suspend the functioning of the imagination.

Ernest Hemingway 1899–1961: *Men at War* (1942)

2 It is thus that mutual cowardice keeps us in peace. Were one half of mankind brave and one half cowards, the brave would be always beating the cowards. Were all brave, they would lead a very uneasy life; all would be continually fighting: but being all cowards, we go on very well.

Samuel Johnson 1709–84: James Boswell *Life of Samuel Johnson* (1791) 28 April 1778

3 For all men would be cowards if they durst.

Lord Rochester 1647–80: 'A Satire against Mankind' (1679)

4 Cowards die many times before their deaths;
The valiant never taste of death but once.

William Shakespeare 1564–1616: *Julius Caesar* (1599)

5 As an old soldier I admit the cowardice: it's as universal as sea sickness, and matters just as little.

George Bernard Shaw 1856–1950: *Man and Superman* (1903)

Creativity

1 The urge for destruction is also a creative urge!

Michael Bakunin 1814–76: *Jahrbuch für Wissenschaft und Kunst* (1842) 'Die Reaktion in Deutschland' (under the pseudonym 'Jules Elysard')

2 If the devil doesn't exist, but man has created him, he has created him in his own image and likeness.

Fedor Dostoevsky 1821–81: *The Brothers Karamazov* (1879–80)

3 Think before you speak is criticism's motto; speak before you think creation's.

E. M. Forster 1879–1970: *Two Cheers for Democracy* (1951)

4 Like a piece of ice on a hot stove the poem must ride on its own melting. A poem may be worked over once it is in being, but may not be worried into being.

Robert Frost 1874–1963: *Collected Poems* (1939) 'The Figure a Poem Makes'

5 Birds build—but not I build; no, but strain,
Time's eunuch, and not breed one work that wakes.
Mine, O thou lord of life, send my roots rain.

Gerard Manley Hopkins 1844–89: 'Thou art indeed just, Lord' (written 1889)

6 There is, perhaps, no more dangerous man in the world than the man with the sensibilities of an artist but without creative talent. With luck such men make wonderful theatrical impresarios and interior decorators, or else they become mass murderers or critics.

Barry Humphries 1934– : *More Please* (1992)

7 Poems are made by fools like me,
But only God can make a tree.

Joyce Kilmer 1886–1918: 'Trees' (1914)

8 Nothing can be created out of nothing.

Lucretius c.94–55 BC: *De Rerum Natura*

9 An artist has no need to express his thought directly in his work for the latter to reflect its quality; it has even been said that the highest praise of God consists in the denial of Him by the atheist who finds creation so perfect that it can dispense with a creator.

Marcel Proust 1871–1922: *Guermantes Way* (1921)

10 Why does my Muse only speak when she is unhappy?
She does not, I only listen when I am unhappy
When I am happy I live and despise writing
For my Muse this cannot but be dispiriting.

Stevie Smith 1902–71: 'My Muse' (1964)

11 Our current obsession with creativity is the result of our continued striving

for immortality in an era when most people no longer believe in an after-life.

Arianna Stassinopoulos 1950– : *The Female Woman* (1973)

12 The worst crime is to leave a man's hands empty.
Men are born makers, with that primal simplicity
In every maker since Adam.

Derek Walcott 1930– : *Omeros* (1990)

13 Urge and urge and urge,
Always the procreant urge of the world.

Walt Whitman 1819–92: 'Song of Myself' (written 1855)

Cricket

1   In Affectionate Remembrance
of
ENGLISH CRICKET,
Which Died at The Oval
on
29th August, 1882.
Deeply lamented by a large circle of sorrowing friends and acquaintances.
R. I. P.
N. B.—The body will be cremated
and
the ashes taken to Australia.

■ *following England's defeat by the Australians*
Anonymous: in *Sporting Times* September 1882

2 They have paid to see Dr Grace bat, not to see you bowl.

■ *said to the bowler when the umpire had called 'not out' after W. G. Grace was unexpectedly bowled first ball*
Anonymous: Harry Furniss *A Century of Grace* (1985); perhaps apocryphal

3 If everything else in this nation of ours were lost but cricket—her Constitution and the laws of England of Lord Halsbury—it would be possible to reconstruct from the theory and practice of cricket all the eternal Englishness which has gone to the establishment of that Constitution and the laws aforesaid.

Neville Cardus 1889–1975: *Cricket* (1930)

4 I couldn't bat for the length of time required to score 500. I'd get bored and fall over.

Denis Compton 1918– : in *Daily Telegraph* 27 June 1994

5 Never read print, it spoils one's eye for the ball.

■ *habitual advice to his players*
W. G. Grace 1848–1915: Harry Furniss *A Century of Grace* (1985)

6 It's more than a game. It's an institution.

■ *of cricket*
Thomas Hughes 1822–96: *Tom Brown's Schooldays* (1857)

7 Cricket—a game which the English, not being a spiritual people, have invented in order to give themselves some conception of eternity.

Lord Mancroft 1914–87: *Bees in Some Bonnets* (1979)

8 Cricket civilizes people and creates good gentlemen. I want everyone to play cricket in Zimbabwe; I want ours to be a nation of gentlemen.

Robert Mugabe 1924– : in *Sunday Times* 26 February 1984

9 There's a breathless hush in the Close to-night—
Ten to make and the match to win—
A bumping pitch and a blinding light,
An hour to play and the last man in.

Henry Newbolt 1862–1938: 'Vitaï Lampada' (1897)

10 It is hard to tell where the MCC ends and the Church of England begins.

J. B. Priestley 1894–1984: in *New Statesman* 20 July 1962

11 I don't think I can be expected to take seriously any game which takes less than three days to reach its conclusion.

■ *a cricket enthusiast on baseball*
Tom Stoppard 1937– : in *Guardian* 24 December 1984

12 Personally, I have always looked on cricket as organized loafing.

William Temple 1881–1944: attributed

13 It's a well-known fact that, when I'm on 99, I'm the best judge of a run in all the bloody world.

Alan Wharton 1923– : Freddie Trueman *You Nearly Had Me That Time* (1978)

Crime

see also **Laws**, **Murder**, **Police**, **Punishment**

1 Labour is the party of law and order in Britain today. Tough on crime and tough on the causes of crime.

Tony Blair 1953– : speech at the Labour Party Conference, 30 September 1993

2 The fear of burglars is not only the fear of being robbed, but also the fear of a sudden and unexpected clutch out of the darkness.

Elias Canetti 1905–94: *Crowds and Power* (1960)

3 Once in the racket you're always in it.

Al Capone 1899–1947: in *Philadelphia Public Ledger* 18 May 1929

4 Crime isn't a disease, it's a symptom. Cops are like a doctor that gives you aspirin for a brain tumour.

Raymond Chandler 1888–1959: *The Long Good-Bye* (1953)

5 Thieves respect property. They merely wish the property to become their property that they may more perfectly respect it.

G. K. Chesterton 1874–1936: *The Man who was Thursday* (1908)

6 Thou shalt not steal; an empty feat, When it's so lucrative to cheat.

Arthur Hugh Clough 1819–61: 'The Latest Decalogue' (1862)

7 Singularity is almost invariably a clue. The more featureless and commonplace a crime is, the more difficult is it to bring it home.

Arthur Conan Doyle 1859–1930: *The Adventures of Sherlock Holmes* (1892) 'The Boscombe Valley Mystery'

8 Major Strasser has been shot. Round up the usual suspects.

Julius J. Epstein 1909–2001 et al.: *Casablanca* (1942 film)

9 Even the most hardened criminal a few years ago would help an old lady across the road and give her a few quid if she was skint.

Charlie Kray c.1930–2000: in *Observer* 28 December 1986

10 A clever theft was praiseworthy amongst the Spartans; and it is equally so amongst Christians, provided it be on a sufficiently large scale.

Herbert Spencer 1820–1903: *Social Statics* (1850)

Crime Fiction

1 Sapper, Buchan, Dornford Yates, practitioners in that school of Snobbery with Violence that runs like a thread of good-class tweed through twentieth-century literature.

Alan Bennett 1934– : *Forty Years On* (1969)

2 When in doubt have a man come through the door with a gun in his hand.

Raymond Chandler 1888–1959: attributed

3 Detection is, or ought to be, an exact science, and should be treated in the same cold and unemotional manner. You have attempted to tinge it with romanticism, which produces much the same effect as if you worked a love-story or an elopement into the fifth proposition of Euclid.

Arthur Conan Doyle 1859–1930: *The Sign of Four* (1890)

4 What the detective story is about is not murder but the restoration of order.

P. D. James 1920– : in *Face* December 1986

5 I had an interest in death from an early age. It fascinated me. When I heard 'Humpty Dumpty sat on a wall,' I thought, 'Did he fall or was he pushed?'

P. D. James 1920– : in *Paris Review* 1995

6 The detective novel is the art-for-art's-sake of our yawning

Philistinism, the classic example of a specialized form of art removed from contact with the life it pretends to build on.

V. S. Pritchett 1900–97: in *New Statesman* 16 June 1951

Crises

1 Comin' in on a wing and a pray'r.

■ *the contemporary comment of a war pilot, speaking from a disabled plane to ground control*
Harold Adamson 1906–80: title of song (1943)

2 We won't make a drama out of a crisis.

Advertising slogan: Commercial Union insurance

3 Crisis? What Crisis?

■ *headline summarizing James Callaghan's remark of 10 January 1979: 'I don't think other people in the world would share the view there is mounting chaos'*
Anonymous: in *Sun* 11 January 1979

4 The die is cast.

■ *at the crossing of the Rubicon*
Julius Caesar 100–44 BC: Suetonius *Lives of the Caesars* 'Divus Julius'; Plutarch *Parallel Lives* 'Pompey'

5 I felt as if I was walking with destiny, and that all my past life had been but a preparation for this hour and this trial.

Winston Churchill 1874–1965: on becoming Prime Minister, 10 May 1940

6 We do not experience and thus we have no measure of the disasters we prevent.

J. K. Galbraith 1908– : *A Life in our Times* (1981)

7 Swimming for his life, a man does not see much of the country through which the river winds.

W. E. Gladstone 1809–98: diary, 31 December 1868

8 The illustrious bishop of Cambrai was of more worth than his chambermaid, and there are few of us that would hesitate to pronounce, if his palace were in flames, and the life of only one

of them could be preserved, which of the two ought to be preferred.

William Godwin 1756–1836: *An Enquiry concerning the Principles of Political Justice* (1793)

9 In bygone days, commanders were taught that when in doubt, they should march their troops towards the sound of gunfire. I intend to march my troops towards the sound of gunfire.

Jo Grimond 1913–93: speech at Liberal Party Annual Assembly, 14 September 1963

10 Don't have a cow, man.

Matt Groening 1954– : catchphrase associated with Bart Simpson; *The Simpsons* (American TV series, 1990–)

11 For it is your business, when the wall next door catches fire.

Horace 65–8 BC: *Epistles*

12 We have the wolf by the ears; and we can neither hold him, nor safely let him go. Justice is in one scale, and self-preservation in the other.

■ *on slavery*
Thomas Jefferson 1743–1826: letter to John Holmes, 22 April 1820

13 As someone pointed out recently, if you can keep your head when all about you are losing theirs, it's just possible you haven't grasped the situation.

Jean Kerr 1923–2003: *Please Don't Eat the Daisies* (1957)

14 If you can keep your head when all about you
Are losing theirs and blaming it on you . . .

Rudyard Kipling 1865–1936: 'If—' (1910)

15 There cannot be a crisis next week. My schedule is already full.

Henry Kissinger 1923– : in *New York Times Magazine* 1 June 1969

16 We're eyeball to eyeball, and I think the other fellow just blinked.

■ *on the Cuban missile crisis*
Dean Rusk 1909– : comment, 24 October 1962

17 Whatever might be the extent of the individual calamity, I do not consider

it of a nature worthy to interrupt the proceedings on so great a national question.

■ *on hearing that his theatre was on fire, during a debate on the campaign in Spain*

Richard Brinsley Sheridan 1751–1816: speech, House of Commons 24 February 1809

18 It is exciting to have a real crisis on your hands, when you have spent half your political life dealing with humdrum issues like the environment.

■ *on the Falklands campaign, 1982*

Margaret Thatcher 1925– : speech to Scottish Conservative Party conference, 14 May 1982

19 I myself have always deprecated . . . in crisis after crisis, appeals to the Dunkirk spirit as an answer to our problems.

Harold Wilson 1916–95: in the House of Commons, 26 July 1961

20 I'm at my best in a messy, middle-of-the-road muddle.

Harold Wilson 1916–95: remark in Cabinet, 21 January 1975

Critics

....

see also Likes and Dislikes, Reviews, Taste

1 A critic is a bundle of biases held loosely together by a sense of taste.

Whitney Balliett 1926– : *Dinosaurs in the Morning* (1962)

2 She was one of the people who say 'I don't know anything about music really, but I know what I like.'

Max Beerbohm 1872–1956: *Zuleika Dobson* (1911)

3 A man must serve his time to every trade
Save censure—critics all are ready made.

Lord Byron 1788–1824: *English Bards and Scotch Reviewers* (1809)

4 Whom the gods wish to destroy they first call promising.

Cyril Connolly 1903–74: *Enemies of Promise* (1938)

5 *Il n'y a pas de hors-texte.*
There is nothing outside of the text.

Jacques Derrida 1930– : *Of Grammatology* (1967)

6 You know who the critics are? The men who have failed in literature and art.

Benjamin Disraeli 1804–81: *Lothair* (1870)

7 Long experience has taught me that to be criticized is not always to be wrong.

■ *speech at Lord Mayor's Guildhall banquet during the Suez crisis*

Anthony Eden 1897–1977: in *Daily Herald* 10 November 1956

8 If there's 10,000 people of all ages and races screaming and dancing and going wild out there, and one person in the audience decides to do a hatchet job, how could that be right?

Michael Flatley: in *Irish Times* 1 November 1997

9 The good critic is he who relates the adventures of his soul in the midst of masterpieces.

Anatole France 1844–1924: *La Vie littéraire* (1888)

10 When I read something saying I've not done anything as good as *Catch-22* I'm tempted to reply, 'Who has?'

Joseph Heller 1923–99: in *The Times* 9 June 1993

11 Parodies and caricatures are the most penetrating of criticisms.

Aldous Huxley 1894–1963: *Point Counter Point* (1928)

12 We must grant the artist his subject, his idea, his *donnée*: our criticism is applied only to what he makes of it.

Henry James 1843–1916: *Partial Portraits* (1888) 'Art of Fiction'

13 You *may* abuse a tragedy, though you cannot write one. You may scold a carpenter who has made you a bad table, though you cannot make a table. It is not your trade to make tables.

■ *on literary criticism*

Samuel Johnson 1709–84: James Boswell *Life of Samuel Johnson* (1791) 25 June 1763

14 I have always suspected that the reading is right, which requires many words to prove it wrong; and the emendation wrong, that cannot without so much labour appear to be right.
Samuel Johnson 1709–84: *Plays of William Shakespeare . . .* (1765)

15 Never trust the artist. Trust the tale. The proper function of a critic is to save the tale from the artist who created it.
D. H. Lawrence 1885–1930: *Studies in Classic American Literature* (1923)

16 People ask you for criticism, but they only want praise.
W. Somerset Maugham 1874–1965: *Of Human Bondage* (1915)

17 One should look long and carefully at oneself before one considers judging others.
Molière 1622–73: *Le Misanthrope* (1666)

18 You don't expect me to know what to say about a play when I don't know who the author is, do you?
George Bernard Shaw 1856–1950: *Fanny's First Play* (1914)

19 Remember, a statue has never been set up in honour of a critic!
Jean Sibelius 1865–1957: Bengt de Törne *Sibelius: A Close-Up* (1937)

20 Interpretation is the revenge of the intellect upon art.
Susan Sontag 1933– : in *Evergreen Review* December 1964

21 It is an open question whether it is *ever* productive to discard courtesy, humaneness, a complete alertness to the vulnerabilities involved, when one is writing criticism.
George Steiner 1926– : open letter to *New Review*, 1974

22 Yet malice never was his aim;
He lashed the vice, but spared the name;
No individual could resent,
Where thousands equally were meant.
Jonathan Swift 1667–1745: 'Verses on the Death of Dr Swift' (1731)

23 He *sees* more in my pictures than I ever painted!
■ *of John Ruskin*
J. M. W. Turner 1775–1851: Mary Lloyd *Sunny Memories* (1879)

24 A critic is a man who knows the way but can't drive the car.
Kenneth Tynan 1927–80: in *New York Times Magazine* 9 January 1966

25 [Roger Fry] gave us the term 'Post-Impressionist', without realising that the late twentieth century would soon be entirely fenced in with posts.
Jeanette Winterson 1959– : *Art Objects* (1995)

26 Literature is strewn with the wreckage of men who have minded beyond reason the opinions of others.
Virginia Woolf 1882–1941: *A Room of One's Own* (1929)

27 You who scribble, yet hate all who write . . .
And with faint praises one another damn.
■ *of theatre critics*
William Wycherley c.1640–1716: *The Plain Dealer* (1677)

Cruelty

1 Boys throw stones at frogs for fun, but the frogs don't die for 'fun', but in sober earnest.
Bion c.325–c.255 BC: Plutarch *Moralia*

2 The wish to hurt, the momentary intoxication with pain, is the loophole through which the pervert climbs into the minds of ordinary men.
Jacob Bronowski 1908–74: *The Face of Violence* (1954)

3 Man's inhumanity to man
Makes countless thousands mourn!
Robert Burns 1759–96: 'Man was made to Mourn' (1786)

4 *There* were his young barbarians all at play,
There was their Dacian mother—he, their sire,

Butchered to make a Roman holiday.
Lord Byron 1788–1824: *Childe Harold's Pilgrimage* (1812–18)

5 Strike him so that he can feel that he is dying.
Caligula AD 12–41: Suetonius *Lives of the Caesars* 'Gaius Caligula'

6 Being cruel to be kind is just ordinary cruelty with an excuse made for it . . . And it is right that it should be more resented, as it is.
Ivy Compton-Burnett 1884–1969: *Daughters and Sons* (1937)

7 Cruelty, like every other vice, requires no motive outside itself—it only requires opportunity.
George Eliot 1819–1880: *Scenes of Clerical Life* (1858)

8 The infliction of cruelty with a good conscience is a delight to moralists. That is why they invented Hell.
Bertrand Russell 1872–1970: *Sceptical Essays* (1928) 'On the Value of Scepticism'

9 I must be cruel only to be kind.
William Shakespeare 1564–1616: *Hamlet* (1601)

Culture

see also **Civilization**, **Museums**

1 I must study politics and war that my sons may have liberty to study mathematics and philosophy. My sons ought to study mathematics and philosophy, geography, natural history, naval architecture, navigation, commerce, and agriculture, in order to give their children a right to study painting, poetry, music, architecture, statuary, tapestry, and porcelain.
John Adams 1735–1826: letter to Abigail Adams, 12 May 1780

2 Some refer to it as a cultural Chernobyl. I think of it as a cultural Stalingrad.
■ *of Euro Disney*
J. G. Ballard 1930– : in *Daily Telegraph* 2 July 1994; cf. 13 below

3 Rousseau was the first militant lowbrow.
Isaiah Berlin 1909–97: in *Observer* 9 November 1952

4 I love *East Enders*; it's the next best thing to Chekhov.
David Bowie 1947– : in *Observer* 3 January 1999

5 What are we waiting for, gathered in the market-place?
The barbarians are to arrive today.
Constantine Cavafy 1863–1933: 'Waiting for the Barbarians' (1904)

6 Cultured people are merely the glittering scum which floats upon the deep river of production.
■ *on hearing his son Randolph criticize the lack of culture of the Calgary oil magnates, probably c.1929*
Winston Churchill 1874–1965: Martin Gilbert *In Search of Churchill* (1994)

7 Culture may even be described simply as that which makes life worth living.
T. S. Eliot 1888–1965: *Notes Towards a Definition of Culture* (1948)

8 When politicians and civil servants hear the word 'culture' they feel for their blue pencils.
Lord Esher 1913– : speech, House of Lords, 2 March 1960; cf. 11 below

9 Is there a culture where there is corporal punishment for delinquency . . . where female circumcision is practised, where mixed marriages are forbidden and polygamy authorized? Multi-culturalism requires that we respect all these practices . . . In a world which has lost its transcendental significance, cultural identity serves to sanction those barbarous traditions which God is no longer in a position to endorse. Fanaticism is indefensible when it appeals to heaven, but beyond reproach when it is grounded in antiquity and cultural distinctiveness.
Alain Finkielkraut: *The Undoing of Thought* (1988)

10 It is unlikely that the government reaches for a revolver when it hears

the word culture. The more likely response is to search for a dictionary.

David Glencross 1936– : Royal Television Society conference on the future of television, 26-27 November 1988; cf. 11 below

11 Whenever I hear the word culture . . . I release the safety-catch of my Browning!

■ *often quoted as: 'Whenever I hear the word culture, I reach for my pistol!'*

Hanns Johst 1890–1978: *Schlageter* (1933); often attributed to Hermann Goering

12 We would prefer to see the House run by a philistine with the requisite financial acumen than by the succession of opera and ballet lovers who have brought a great and valuable institution to its knees.

Gerald Kaufman 1930– : report of the Commons' Culture, Media and Sport select committee on Covent Garden, 3 December 1997

13 A cultural Chernobyl.

■ *of Euro Disney*

Ariane Mnouchkine 1934– : in *Harper's Magazine* July 1992

14 All my wife has ever taken from the Mediterranean—from that whole vast intuitive culture—are four bottles of Chianti to make into lamps.

Peter Shaffer 1926– : *Equus* (1973)

15 In Italy for thirty years under the Borgias they had warfare, terror, murder, bloodshed—they produced Michelangelo, Leonardo da Vinci and the Renaissance. In Switzerland they had brotherly love, five hundred years of democracy and peace and what did that produce . . . ? The cuckoo clock.

Orson Welles 1915–85: *The Third Man* (1949 film); words added by Welles to Graham Greene's script

16 Popular culture is a contradiction in terms. If it's popular, it's not culture. If everyone loves it, it's not original.

Vivienne Westwood 1941– : in *Independent on Sunday* 8 November 1998

17 Mrs Ballinger is one of the ladies who pursue Culture in bands, as though it were dangerous to meet it alone.

Edith Wharton 1862–1937: *Xingu and Other Stories* (1916)

Cynicism

see also **Disillusion**

1 Kill them all; God will recognize his own.

■ *when asked how the true Catholics could be distinguished from the heretics at the massacre of Béziers, 1209*

Arnald-Amaury d. 1225: Jonathan Sumption *The Albigensian Crusade* (1978)

2 CYNIC, *n.* A blackguard whose faulty vision sees things as they are, not as they ought to be.

Ambrose Bierce 1842–*c*.1914: *Cynic's Word Book* (1906)

3 What makes all doctrines plain and clear?
About two hundred pounds a year.
And that which was proved true before,
Prove false again? Two hundred more.

Samuel Butler 1612–80: *Hudibras* pt. 3 (1680)

4 *when asked why he was begging for alms from a statue:*
To get practice in being refused.

Diogenes 404–323 BC: Diogenes Laertius *Lives of the Philosophers*

5 Cynicism is an unpleasant way of saying the truth.

Lillian Hellman 1905–84: *The Little Foxes* (1939)

6 Paris is well worth a mass.

■ *a Huguenot view on becoming King of France*

Henri IV 1553–1610: attributed; alternatively attributed to his minister Sully, in conversation with Henri

7 If someone tells you he is going to make a 'realistic decision', you immediately understand that he has resolved to do something bad.

Mary McCarthy 1912–89: *On the Contrary* (1961) 'American Realist Playwrights'

8 'Blessed is the man who expects nothing, for he shall never be disappointed' was the ninth beatitude.

Alexander Pope 1688–1744: letter to Fortescue, 23 September 1725

9 A man who knows the price of everything and the value of nothing.
  ■ *definition of a cynic*
  Oscar Wilde 1854–1900: *Lady Windermere's Fan* (1892)

Dance

1 Can't act. Slightly bald. Also dances.
  ■ *studio official's comment on Fred Astaire*
  Anonymous: Bob Thomas *Astaire* (1985)

2 He had the charisma and the simplicity of a man of the earth and the untouchable arrogance of the gods.
  ■ *of Rudolf Nureyev*
  Mikhail Baryshnikov 1948– : attributed, Diane Solway *Nureyev: His Life* (1998)

3 There may be trouble ahead,
  But while there's moonlight and music and love and romance,
  Let's face the music and dance.
  Irving Berlin 1888–1989: 'Let's Face the Music and Dance' (1936 song)

4 Heaven—I'm in Heaven—And my heart beats so that I can hardly speak;
  And I seem to find the happiness I seek
  When we're out together dancing cheek-to-cheek.
  Irving Berlin 1888–1989: 'Cheek-to-Cheek' (1935 song)

5 On with the dance! let joy be unconfined;
  No sleep till morn, when Youth and Pleasure meet
  To chase the glowing Hours with flying feet.
  Lord Byron 1788–1824: *Childe Harold's Pilgrimage* (1812–18)

6 The truest expression of a people is in its dances and its music. Bodies never lie.
  Agnes de Mille 1908–93: in *New York Times Magazine* 11 May 1975

7 Dance is the hidden language of the soul.
  Martha Graham 1894–1991: *Blood Memory* (1991)

8 So gay the band,
  So giddy the sight,
  Full evening dress is a must,
  But the zest goes out of a beautiful waltz
  When you dance it bust to bust.
  Joyce Grenfell 1910–79: 'Stately as a Galleon' (1978 song)

9 Come, and trip it as ye go
  On the light fantastic toe.
  John Milton 1608–74: 'L'Allegro' (1645)

10 I wish I could shimmy like my sister Kate,
  She shivers like the jelly on a plate.
  Armand J. Piron: *Shimmy like Kate* (1919 song)

11 [Dancing is] a perpendicular expression of a horizontal desire.
  George Bernard Shaw 1856–1950: in *New Statesman* 23 March 1962

12 O body swayed to music, O brightening glance,
  How can we know the dancer from the dance?
  W. B. Yeats 1865–1939: 'Among School Children' (1928)

Danger

see also **Risk**, **Security**

1 Dangers by being despised grow great.
  Edmund Burke 1729–97: speech on the Petition of the Unitarians, 11 May 1792

2 When there is no peril in the fight, there is no glory in the triumph.
  Pierre Corneille 1606–84: *Le Cid* (1637)

3 In skating over thin ice, our safety is in our speed.
  Ralph Waldo Emerson 1803–82: *Essays* (1841) 'Prudence'

4 Fasten your seat-belts, it's going to be a bumpy night.
  Joseph L. Mankiewicz 1909– : *All About Eve* (1950 film); spoken by Bette Davis

5 Out of this nettle, danger, we pluck this flower, safety.
  William Shakespeare 1564–1616: *Henry IV, Part 1* (1597)

Day

see also **Evening, Night**

1 Morning has broken
 Like the first morning,
 Blackbird has spoken
 Like the first bird.
 Eleanor Farjeon 1881–1965: 'A Morning Song
 (for the First Day of Spring)' (1957)

2 Awake! for Morning in the bowl of
 night
 Has flung the stone that puts the stars
 to flight:
 And Lo! the Hunter of the East has
 caught
 The Sultan's turret in a noose of light.
 Edward Fitzgerald 1809–83: *The Rubáiyát of
 Omar Khayyám* (1859)

3 What are days for?
 Days are where we live.
 They come, they wake us
 Time and time over.
 They are to be happy in:
 Where can we live but days?
 Philip Larkin 1922–85: 'Days' (1964)

4 Night's candles are burnt out, and
 jocund day
 Stands tiptoe on the misty mountain
 tops.
 William Shakespeare 1564–1616: *Romeo and
 Juliet* (1595)

5 And ghastly through the drizzling
 rain
 On the bald street breaks the blank
 day.
 Alfred, Lord Tennyson 1809–92: *In Memoriam
 A. H. H.* (1850)

Death

see also **Bereavement, Dying, Epitaphs,
Last Words, Murder, Suicide**

1 Death has got something to be said
 for it:
 There's no need to get out of bed for
 it;
 Wherever you may be,
 They bring it to you, free.
 Kingsley Amis 1922–95: 'Delivery Guaranteed'
 (1979)

2 I would like my love to die
 and the rain to be falling on the
 graveyard
 and on me walking the streets
 mourning she who sought to love me.
 Samuel Beckett 1906–89: 'I would like my
 love to die'

3 Even death is unreliable: instead of
 zero it may be some ghastly
 hallucination, such as the square root
 of minus one.
 Samuel Beckett 1906–89: attributed

4 O death, where is thy sting? O grave,
 where is thy victory?
 Bible: I Corinthians

5 In the midst of life we are in death.
 The Book of Common Prayer 1662: *The Burial
 of the Dead*

6 Forasmuch as it hath pleased
 Almighty God of his great mercy to
 take unto himself the soul of our dear
 brother here departed, we therefore
 commit his body to the ground; earth
 to earth, ashes to ashes, dust to dust;
 in sure and certain hope of the
 Resurrection to eternal life.
 The Book of Common Prayer 1662: *The Burial
 of the Dead* Interment

7 He shouts play death more sweetly
 this Death is a master from
 Deutschland
 he shouts scrape your strings darker
 you'll rise then as smoke to the sky
 you'll have a grave then in the clouds
 there you won't lie too cramped.
 Paul Celan 1920–70: 'Deathfugue' (written
 1944)

8 This parrot is no more! It has ceased
 to be! It's expired and gone to meet its
 maker! This is a late parrot! It's a stiff!
 Bereft of life it rests in peace—if you
 hadn't nailed it to the perch it would
 be pushing up the daisies! It's rung
 down the curtain and joined the choir
 invisible! THIS IS AN EX-PARROT!
 Graham Chapman 1941–89, **John Cleese**
 1939– , et al.: *Monty Python's Flying Circus*
 (BBC TV programme, 1969)

9 Death be not proud, though some
 have called thee

Mighty and dreadful, for thou art not so.
John Donne 1572–1631: *Holy Sonnets* (1609)

10 Any man's death diminishes me, because I am involved in Mankind; And therefore never send to know for whom the bell tolls; it tolls for thee.
John Donne 1572–1631: *Devotions upon Emergent Occasions* (1624)

11 The bodies of those that made such a noise and tumult when alive, when dead, lie as quietly among the graves of their neighbours as any others.
Jonathan Edwards 1703–58: *Miscellaneous Discourses* sermon on procrastination

12 Webster was much possessed by death And saw the skull beneath the skin; And breastless creatures underground Leaned backward with a lipless grin.
T. S. Eliot 1888–1965: 'Whispers of Immortality' (1919)

13 My thoughts are crowded with death and it draws so oddly on the sexual that I am confused confused to be attracted by, in effect, my own annihilation.
Thom Gunn 1929– : 'In Time of Plague' (1992)

14 Death is nothing at all; it does not count. I have only slipped away into the next room.
Henry Scott Holland 1847–1918: sermon preached on Whitsunday 1910

15 *Non omnis moriar.*
I shall not altogether die.
Horace 65–8 BC: *Odes*

16 So here it is at last, the distinguished thing!
■ *on experiencing his first stroke*
Henry James 1843–1916: Edith Wharton *A Backward Glance* (1934)

17 Darkling I listen; and, for many a time I have been half in love with easeful Death,
Called him soft names in many a musèd rhyme,
To take into the air my quiet breath;
Now more than ever seems it rich to die,

To cease upon the midnight with no pain.
John Keats 1795–1821: 'Ode to a Nightingale' (1820)

18 The dead don't die. They look on and help.
D. H. Lawrence 1885–1930: letter to J. Middleton Murry, 2 February 1923

19   This is death.
To die and know it. This is the Black Widow, death.
Robert Lowell 1917–77: 'Mr Edwards and the Spider' (1950)

20 There are no dead.
Maurice Maeterlinck 1862–1949: *L'Oiseau bleu* (1909)

21 Let me die a youngman's death
Not a clean & in-between-
The-sheets, holy-water death,
Not a famous-last-words
Peaceful out-of-breath death.
Roger McGough 1937– : 'Let Me Die a Youngman's Death' (1967)

22 I am not afraid of death. When I have to confront the Great Reaper, I'd like to recall Bernanos' words—'And now—just the two of us!'
Jean Mercure 1909–98: attributed

23 Life is a great surprise. I do not see why death should not be an even greater one.
Vladimir Nabokov 1899–1977: *Pale Fire* (1962)

24 And all our calm is in that balm—
Not lost but gone before.
Caroline Norton 1808–77: 'Not Lost but Gone Before'

25 We die containing a richness of lovers and tribes, tastes we have swallowed, bodies we have plunged into and swum up as if rivers of wisdom, characters we have climbed into as if trees, fears we have hidden into as if in caves.
Michael Ondaatje 1943– : *The English Patient* (1992)

26 The pallor of girls' brows shall be their pall;
Their flowers the tenderness of patient minds,

And each slow dusk a drawing-down
of blinds.
Wilfred Owen 1893–1918: 'Anthem for
Doomed Youth' (written 1917)

27 We shall die alone.
Blaise Pascal 1623–62: *Pensées* (1670)

28 Only we die in earnest, that's no jest.
Walter Ralegh c.1552–1618: 'On the Life of
Man'

29 Anyone can stop a man's life, but no
one his death; a thousand doors open
on to it.
Seneca c.4 BC–AD 65: *Phoenissae*

30 I care not; a man can die but once; we
owe God a death.
William Shakespeare 1564–1616: *Henry IV,
Part 2* (1597)

31　　　　　To die, to sleep;
To sleep: perchance to dream: ay,
there's the rub;
For in that sleep of death what dreams
may come
When we have shuffled off this mortal
coil,
Must give us pause.
William Shakespeare 1564–1616: *Hamlet*
(1601)

32 In the arts of life man invents nothing;
but in the arts of death he outdoes
Nature herself, and produces by
chemistry and machinery all the
slaughter of plague, pestilence and
famine.
George Bernard Shaw 1856–1950: *Man and
Superman* (1903)

33 The cemetery is an open space among
the ruins, covered in winter with
violets and daisies. It might make one
in love with death, to think that one
should be buried in so sweet a place.
Percy Bysshe Shelley 1792–1822: *Adonais*
(1821)

34 If there wasn't death, I think you
couldn't go on.
Stevie Smith 1902–71: in *Observer*
9 November 1969

35 Death must be distinguished from
dying, with which it is often confused.
Sydney Smith 1771–1845: H. Pearson *The
Smith of Smiths* (1934)

36 One death is a tragedy, a million
deaths a statistic.
Joseph Stalin 1879–1953: attributed

37 For though from out our bourne of
time and place
The flood may bear me far,
I hope to see my pilot face to face
When I have crossed the bar.
Alfred, Lord Tennyson 1809–92: 'Crossing the
Bar' (1889)

38 Though lovers be lost love shall not;
And death shall have no dominion.
Dylan Thomas 1914–53: 'And death shall have
no dominion' (1936)

39 Just try and set death aside. It sets you
aside, and that's the end of it!
Ivan Turgenev 1818–83: *Fathers and Sons*
(1862)

40 He knows death to the bone—
Man has created death.
W. B. Yeats 1865–1939: 'Death' (1933)

Debt

see also **Lending**, **Money**

1 Dreading that climax of all human
ills,
The inflammation of his weekly bills.
Lord Byron 1788–1824: *Don Juan* (1819–24)

2 They hired the money, didn't they?
■ *on the subject of war debts incurred by
England and others*
Calvin Coolidge 1872–1933: John H. McKee
Coolidge: Wit and Wisdom (1933)

3 Annual income twenty pounds,
annual expenditure nineteen nineteen
six, result happiness. Annual income
twenty pounds, annual expenditure
twenty pounds nought and six, result
misery.
Charles Dickens 1812–70: *David Copperfield*
(1850)

4 Should we really let our people starve
so we can pay our debts?
Julius Nyerere 1922–99: in *Guardian* 21 March
1985

5 You can't put your VISA bill on your
American Express card.
P. J. O'Rourke 1947– : *The Bachelor Home
Companion* (1987)

6 All decent people live beyond their incomes nowadays, and those who aren't respectable live beyond other peoples'.
   Saki 1870–1916: *Chronicles of Clovis* (1911)

7 The National Debt is a very Good Thing and it would be dangerous to pay it off, for fear of Political Economy.
   W. C. Sellar 1898–1951 and **R. J. Yeatman** 1898–1968: *1066 and All That* (1930)

8 Sixteen tons, what do you get? Another day older and deeper in debt. Say brother, don't you call me 'cause I can't go
I owe my soul to the company store.
   Merle Travis 1917–83: 'Sixteen Tons' (1947 song)

9 One must have some sort of occupation nowadays. If I hadn't my debts I shouldn't have anything to think about.
   Oscar Wilde 1854–1900: *A Woman of No Importance* (1893)

Deception

see also **Hypocrisy**, **Lies**

1 Doubtless the pleasure is as great
Of being cheated, as to cheat.
As lookers-on feel most delight,
That least perceive a juggler's sleight.
   Samuel Butler 1612–80: *Hudibras* pt. 2 (1664)

2 It was the men I deceived the most that I loved the most.
   Marguerite Duras 1914–96: *Practicalities* (1990)

3 An open foe may prove a curse, But a pretended friend is worse.
   John Gay 1685–1732: *Fables* (1727) 'The Shepherd's Dog and the Wolf'

4 It was beautiful and simple as all truly great swindles are.
   O. Henry 1862–1910: *Gentle Grafter* (1908)

5 You may fool all the people some of the time; you can even fool some of the people all the time; but you can't fool all of the people all the time.
   Abraham Lincoln 1809–65: Alexander K. McClure *Lincoln's Yarns and Stories* (1904); also attributed to Phineas Barnum

6 And if, to be sure, sometimes you need to conceal a fact with words, do it in such a way that it does not become known, or, if it does become known, that you have a ready and quick defence.
   Niccolò Machiavelli 1469–1527: 'Advice to Raffaello Girolami when he went as Ambassador to the Emperor' (October 1522)

7 O what a tangled web we weave, When first we practise to deceive!
   Sir Walter Scott 1771–1832: *Marmion* (1808)

Deeds

see **Words and Deeds**

Defeat

see also **Failure**, **Winning**

1 History to the defeated
May say Alas but cannot help or pardon.
   W. H. Auden 1907–73: 'Spain 1937' (1937)

2 Victory has a hundred fathers, but no-one wants to recognise defeat as his own.
   Count Galeazzo Ciano 1903–44: diary, 9 September 1942

3 'The game,' said he, 'is never lost till won.'
   George Crabbe 1754–1832: *Tales of the Hall* (1819) 'Gretna Green'

4 Man is not made for defeat. A man can be destroyed but not defeated.
   Ernest Hemingway 1899–1961: *The Old Man and the Sea* (1952)

5 The war situation has developed not necessarily to Japan's advantage.
   Emperor Hirohito 1901–89: announcing Japan's surrender on 15 August 1945

6 A man able to think isn't defeated— even when he is defeated.
   Milan Kundera 1929– : in *Sunday Times* 20 May 1984

7 *Vae victis.*
Down with the defeated!
   ■ *cry (already proverbial) of the Gallic King, Brennus, on capturing Rome (390 BC)*
   Livy 59 BC–AD 17: *Ab Urbe Condita*

8 Defeat doesn't finish a man—quit does. A man is not finished when he's defeated. He's finished when he quits.
   Richard Nixon 1913–94: William Safire *Before the Fall* (1975)

9 We are not interested in the possibilities of defeat; they do not exist.
   ■ *on the Boer War during 'Black Week', December 1899*
   Queen Victoria 1819–1901: Lady Gwendolen Cecil *Life of Robert, Marquis of Salisbury* (1931)

10 The only safe course for the defeated is to expect no safety.
   Virgil 70–19 BC: *Aeneid*

11 It is a terrible shame for me—I came back, still alive, without having won the war.
   ■ *on returning to Japan after surviving for 28 years in the jungles of Guam before surrendering to the Americans in 1972*
   Shoichi Yokoi 1915–97: in *Independent* 26 September 1997

Defiance

see also **Determination**

1 No surrender!
   ■ *the defenders of the besieged city of Derry to the army of James II, April 1689*
   Anonymous: adopted as a slogan of Protestant Ulster

2 I was ever a fighter, so—one fight more,
The best and the last!
I would hate that death bandaged my eyes, and forbore,
And bade me creep past.
   Robert Browning 1812–89: 'Prospice' (1864)

3 She won't go quietly, that's the problem. I'll fight to the end.
   Diana, Princess of Wales 1961–97: interview on *Panorama*, BBC1 TV, 20 November 1995

4 He will give him seven feet of English ground, or as much more as he may be taller than other men.
   ■ *his offer to the invader Harald Hardrada, before the battle of Stamford Bridge, 1066*
   Harold II c.1019–66: Snorri Sturluson *Heimskringla* (c.1260) 'King Harald's Saga'

5 *No pasarán.*
They shall not pass.
   Dolores Ibarruri 1895–1989: radio broadcast, Madrid, 19 July 1936

6 Nuts!
   Anthony McAuliffe 1898–1975: replying to the German demand for surrender at Bastogne, Belgium, 22 December 1944

7 Get up, stand up
Stand up for your rights
Get up, stand up
Never give up the fight.
   Bob Marley 1945–81: 'Get up, Stand up' (1973 song)

8 . . . What though the field be lost?
All is not lost; the unconquerable will,
And study of revenge, immortal hate,
And courage never to submit or yield:
And what is else not to be overcome?
   John Milton 1608–74: *Paradise Lost* (1667)

9 I grow, I prosper;
Now, gods, stand up for bastards!
   William Shakespeare 1564–1616: *King Lear* (1605–6)

Delay

see also **Idleness**, **Punctuality**, **Waiting**

1 Hesitating doesn't matter if only you win out.
   Bertolt Brecht 1898–1956: *The Good Woman of Setzuan* (1938)

2 No admittance till the week after next!
   Lewis Carroll 1832–98: *Through the Looking-Glass* (1872)

3 A wrong decision isn't forever; it can always be reversed. The losses from a delayed decision *are* forever; they can never be retrieved.
   J. K. Galbraith 1908– : *A Life in our Times* (1981)

4 He gave her a bright fake smile; so much of life was a putting-off of unhappiness for another time. Nothing was ever lost by delay.
   Graham Greene 1904–91: *The Heart of the Matter* (1948)

5 procrastination is the
art of keeping

up with yesterday.
Don Marquis 1878–1937: *archy and mehitabel* (1927)

6 Never do to-day what you can put off till to-morrow.
Punch: 22 December 1849

7 He who hesitates is sometimes saved.
James Thurber 1894–1961: *The Thurber Carnival* (1945)

Democracy

see also **Elections, Minorities and Majorities, Politics**

1 After each war there is a little less democracy to save.
Brooks Atkinson 1894–1984: *Once Around the Sun* (1951)

2 Democracy means government by discussion, but it is only effective if you can stop people talking.
Clement Attlee 1883–1967: speech at Oxford, 14 June 1957

3 No one pretends that democracy is perfect or all-wise. Indeed, it has been said that democracy is the worst form of Government except all those other forms that have been tried from time to time.
Winston Churchill 1874–1965: speech, House of Commons, 11 November 1947

4 So Two cheers for Democracy: one because it admits variety and two because it permits criticism. Two cheers are quite enough: there is no occasion to give three. Only Love the Beloved Republic deserves that.
E. M. Forster 1879–1970: *Two Cheers for Democracy* (1951)

5 No, Democracy is *not* identical with majority rule. Democracy is a *State* which recognizes the subjection of the minority to the majority, that is, an organization for the systematic use of *force* by one class against the other, by one part of the population against another.
Lenin 1870–1924: *State and Revolution* (1919)

6 Fourscore and seven years ago our fathers brought forth upon this continent a new nation, conceived in liberty, and dedicated to the proposition that all men are created equal . . . we here highly resolve that the dead shall not have died in vain, that this nation, under God, shall have a new birth of freedom; and that government of the people, by the people, and for the people, shall not perish from the earth.

■ *the Lincoln Memorial inscription reads 'by the people, for the people'*
Abraham Lincoln 1809–65: address at the Dedication of the National Cemetery at Gettysburg, 19 November 1863, as reported the following day

7 Democracy is the theory that the common people know what they want, and deserve to get it good and hard.
H. L. Mencken 1880–1956: *A Little Book in C major* (1916)

8 Man's capacity for justice makes democracy possible, but man's inclination to injustice makes democracy necessary.
Reinhold Niebuhr 1892–1971: *Children of Light and Children of Darkness* (1944)

9 Democracy substitutes election by the incompetent many for appointment by the corrupt few.
George Bernard Shaw 1856–1950: *Man and Superman* (1903) 'Maxims: Democracy'

10 It's not the voting that's democracy, it's the counting.
Tom Stoppard 1937– : *Jumpers* (1972)

11 The world must be made safe for democracy.
Woodrow Wilson 1856–1924: speech to Congress, 2 April 1917

12 For many Chinese, the Russian lesson appears to be that only after a nation achieves a relatively high level of economic prosperity can it afford the fruit and peril of democracy.
Xiao-Huang Yin: in *Independent* 8 October 1993

Depression

see also **Despair**

1 One's upbringing and early experiences can leave a sort of 'gunpowder' that accumulates in the mind. In some people, the gunpowder is never lit; in others, a particular event can spark a fuse.
   Derek Draper: in *Daily Telegraph* 3 March 1999

2 Frozen anger.
   ■ *his definition of depression*
   Sigmund Freud 1856–1939: attributed

3 When you're depressed, there *are* no molehills.
   Randall Jarrell 1914–65: William H. Pritchard *Randall Jarrell: A Literary Life* (1990)

4 The black dog I hope always to resist, and in time to drive, though I am deprived of almost all those that used to help me . . . When I rise my breakfast is solitary, the black dog waits to share it, from breakfast to dinner he continues barking, except that Dr Brocklesby for a little keeps him at a distance . . . Night comes at last, and some hours of restlessness and confusion bring me again to a day of solitude. What shall exclude the black dog from a habitation like this?
   ■ *on his attacks of melancholia; more recently associated with Winston Churchill, who used the phrase 'black dog' when alluding to his own periodic bouts of depression*
   Samuel Johnson 1709–84: letter to Mrs Thrale, 28 June 1783

5 I am in that temper that if I were under water I would scarcely kick to come to the top.
   John Keats 1795–1821: letter to Benjamin Bailey, 25 May 1818

6 I was aware of a little grey shadow, as it might have been a snowflake seen against the light, floating at an immense distance in the background of my brain.
   Rudyard Kipling 1865–1936: *Actions and Reactions* (1909) 'The House Surgeon'

Despair

see also **Hope, Pessimism, Sorrow**

1 My God, my God, look upon me; why hast thou forsaken me?
   Bible: Psalm 22

2 I give the fight up: let there be an end, A privacy, an obscure nook for me. I want to be forgotten even by God.
   Robert Browning 1812–89: *Paracelsus* (1835)

3 In despair there are the most intense enjoyments, especially when one is very acutely conscious of the hopelessness of one's position.
   Fedor Dostoevsky 1821–81: *Notes from Underground* (1864)

4 There is no despair so absolute as that which comes with the first moments of our first great sorrow, when we have not yet known what it is to have suffered and be healed, to have despaired and have recovered hope.
   George Eliot 1819–80: *Adam Bede* (1859)

5 In a real dark night of the soul it is always three o'clock in the morning.
   F. Scott Fitzgerald 1896–1940: 'Handle with Care' in *Esquire* March 1936

6 Despair is the price one pays for setting oneself an impossible aim.
   Graham Greene 1904–91: *Heart of the Matter* (1948)

7 Not, I'll not, carrion comfort, Despair, not feast on thee; Not untwist—slack they may be— these last strands of man In me or, most weary, cry *I can no more*. I can; Can something, hope, wish day come, not choose not to be.
   Gerard Manley Hopkins 1844–89: 'Carrion Comfort' (written 1885)

8 Human life begins on the far side of despair.
   Jean-Paul Sartre 1905–80: *Les Mouches* (1943)

9 Everywhere I see bliss, from which I alone am irrevocably excluded.
   Mary Shelley 1797–1851: *Frankenstein* (1818)

Determination

see also **Defiance, Persistence, Strength and Weakness**

1 Thought shall be the harder, heart the keener, courage the greater, as our might lessens.
Anonymous: *The Battle of Maldon* (*c*.1000)

2 It's a great life if you don't weaken.
John Buchan 1875–1940: *Mr Standfast* (1919)

3 I will fight for what I believe in until I drop dead. And that's what keeps you alive.
Barbara Castle 1910–2002: in *Guardian* 14 January 1998

4 The best way out is always through.
Robert Frost 1874–1963: 'A Servant to Servants' (1914)

5 Climb ev'ry mountain, ford ev'ry stream
Follow ev'ry rainbow, till you find your dream!
Oscar Hammerstein II 1895–1960: *Climb Ev'ry Mountain* (1959 song)

6 I have not yet begun to fight.
■ *as his ship was sinking, 23 September 1779, having been asked whether he had lowered his flag*
John Paul Jones 1747–92: Mrs Reginald De Koven *Life and Letters of John Paul Jones* (1914)

7 Here stand I. I can do no other. God help me. Amen.
Martin Luther 1483–1546: speech at the Diet of Worms, 18 April 1521; attributed

8 There comes a time in a man's life when to get where he has to go—if there are no doors or windows—he walks through a wall.
Bernard Malamud 1914–86: *Rembrandt's Hat* (1972)

9 One man that has a mind and knows it can always beat ten men who haven't and don't.
George Bernard Shaw 1856–1950: *The Apple Cart* (1930)

10 She's as headstrong as an allegory on the banks of the Nile.
Richard Brinsley Sheridan 1751–1816: *The Rivals* (1775)

11 That which we are, we are;
One equal temper of heroic hearts,
Made weak by time and fate, but strong in will
To strive, to seek, to find, and not to yield.
Alfred, Lord Tennyson 1809–92: 'Ulysses' (1842)

12 We shall not be diverted from our course. To those waiting with bated breath for that favourite media catch-phrase, the U-turn, I have only this to say. 'You turn if you want; the lady's not for turning.'
■ *final line from alteration of the title of Christopher Fry's 1949 play* The Lady's Not For Burning
Margaret Thatcher 1925– : speech at Conservative Party Conference in Brighton, 10 October 1980

Development

see **Aid and Development**

Diana, Princess of Wales 1961–97

see also **Press Photographers**

1 She was the People's Princess, and that is how she will stay . . . in our hearts and in our memories forever.
Tony Blair 1953– : on hearing of the death of Diana, Princess of Wales, 31 August 1997

2 Now, at last, this sad, glittering century has an image worthy of it: a wandering, wondering girl, a silly Sloane turned secular saint, coming home in her coffin to RAF Northolt like the good soldier she was.
Julie Burchill 1960– : in *Guardian* 2 September 1997

3 I'd like to be a queen in people's hearts but I don't see myself being Queen of this country.
Diana, Princess of Wales 1961–97: interview on *Panorama*, BBC1 TV, 20 November 1995

4 The Princess of Wales was the queen of surfaces, ruling over a kingdom

where fame was the highest value and glamour the most cherished attribute.
Maureen Dowd 1952– : in *New York Times* 3 September 1997

5 Whatever 'in love' means, true love is talented. Someone vividly gifted in love has gone.
■ *on the death of Diana, Princess of Wales*
Carol Ann Duffy 1965– : 'September, 1997' (1997); cf. **Love** 15

6 Goodbye England's rose; May you ever grow in our hearts.
Elton John 1947– and **Bernie Taupin** 1950– : 'Candle in the Wind' (song, revised version, 1997); cf. **Singing** 10

7 And it seems to me you lived your life Like a candle in the wind: Never fading with the sunset When the rain set in.
Elton John 1947– and **Bernie Taupin** 1950– : 'Candle in the Wind' (song, revised version, 1997)

8 Beside the river, swerving under ground.
your future tracked you, snapping at your heels:
Diana, breathless, hunted by your own quick hounds.
Andrew Motion 1952– : 'Mythology' (1997)

Diaries

1 Now that I am finishing the damned thing I realise that diary-writing isn't wholly good for one, that too much of it leads to living for one's diary instead of living for the fun of living as ordinary people do.
James Agate 1877–1947: letter, 7 December 1946

2 What is more dull than a discreet diary? One might just as well have a discreet soul.
Henry ('Chips') Channon 1897–1958: diary, 26 July 1935

3 I want to go on living even after death!
Anne Frank 1929–45: diary, 4 April 1944

4 Ten years after your death I meet on a page of your journal, as never before,

The shock of your joy.
Ted Hughes 1930–98: *Birthday Letters* (1998) 'Visit'

5 To be a good diarist one must have a little snouty, sneaky mind.
Harold Nicolson 1886–1968: diary, 9 November 1947

6 To write a diary every day is like returning to one's own vomit.
Enoch Powell 1912–98: interview in *Sunday Times* 6 November 1977

7 I have decided to keep a full journal, in the hope that my life will perhaps seem more interesting when it is written down.
Sue Townsend 1946– : *Adrian Mole: The Wilderness Years* (1993)

8 One need not write in a diary what one is to remember for ever.
Sylvia Townsend Warner 1893–1978: diary, 22 October 1930

9 I always say, keep a diary and some day it'll keep you.
Mae West 1892–1980: *Every Day's a Holiday* (1937 film)

10 I never travel without my diary. One should always have something sensational to read in the train.
Oscar Wilde 1854–1900: *The Importance of Being Earnest* (1895)

11 What sort of diary should I like mine to be? . . . I should like it to resemble some deep old desk, or capacious hold-all, in which one flings a mass of odds and ends without looking them through.
Virginia Woolf 1882–1941: diary, 20 April 1919

Dictionaries

1 The greatest masterpiece in literature is only a dictionary out of order.
Jean Cocteau 1889–1963: attributed

2 *Lexicographer.* A writer of dictionaries, a harmless drudge.
Samuel Johnson 1709–84: *A Dictionary of the English Language* (1755)

3 Dictionaries are like watches, the worst is better than none, and the best cannot be expected to go quite true.
Samuel Johnson 1709–84: letter to Francesco Sastres, 21 August 1784

4 [The] collective unconscious of the race is the OED.
James Merrill 1926– : in *American Poetry Review* September/October 1979

5 I suppose that so long as there are people in the world, they will publish dictionaries defining what is unknown in terms of something equally unknown.
Flann O'Brien 1911–66: *Myles Away from Dublin* (1990)

6 I've been in *Who's Who*, and I know what's what, but it'll be the first time I ever made the dictionary.
■ *on having an inflatable life jacket named after her*
Mae West 1892–1980: letter to the RAF, early 1940s; Fergus Cashin *Mae West* (1981)

Diets

see also **Eating, Fat**

1 I repent of my diets, the delicious dishes rejected out of vanity, as much as I lament the opportunities for making love that I let go by because of pressing tasks or puritanical virtue.
Isabel Allende 1942– : in *The Times* 25 April 1998

2 The first law of dietetics seems to be: if it tastes good, it's bad for you.
Isaac Asimov 1920–92: attributed

3 The right diet directs sexual energy into the parts that matter.
Barbara Cartland 1901–2000: in *Observer* 11 January 1981

4 Give me a dozen heart-breaks like that if you think it would help me lose one pound.
Colette 1873–1954: *Chéri* (1920)

5 Food is an important part of a balanced Diet.
Fran Lebowitz 1946– : *Metropolitan Life* (1978)

6 On this twelfth day of my diet I would rather die satiated than slim.
Marge Piercy 1936– : 'On Mental Corsets' (1983)

7 I have lost half a stone. The Lead Plan Diet I call it.
■ *after recovering from being shot in the chest*
Frank Warren: attributed, 1989

Difference

see **Similarity and Difference**

Diplomacy

see also **International Relations**

1 I do not regard the procuring of peace as a matter in which we should play the role of arbiter between different opinions . . . more that of an honest broker who really wants to press the business forward.
Otto von Bismarck 1815–98: speech to the Reichstag, 19 February 1878

2 An appeaser is one who feeds a crocodile hoping it will eat him last.
Winston Churchill 1874–1965: in the House of Commons, January 1940

3 To jaw-jaw is always better than to war-war.
Winston Churchill 1874–1965: speech at White House, 26 June 1954

4 The gentleman can not have forgotten his own sentiment, uttered even on the floor of this House, 'peaceably if we can, forcibly if we must'.
Henry Clay 1777–1852: speech in Congress, 8 January 1813

5 Personally I feel happier now that we have no allies to be polite to and to pamper.
George VI 1895–1952: to Queen Mary, 27 June 1940; John Wheeler-Bennett *King George VI* (1958)

6 American *diplomacy*. It's like watching somebody trying to do joinery with a chainsaw.
James Hamilton-Paterson 1941– : *Griefwork* (1993)

7 It's no good ceasing to be the world's policeman in order to become the world's parson instead.

Denis Healey 1917– : at a meeting of the Cabinet, 17 November 1974

8 If you can prevent the deaths of people still alive, you're not doing a disservice to those already killed.

■ *on dealing with Balkan leaders*
Richard Holbrooke 1941– : attributed, summer 1998

9 Let us never negotiate out of fear. But let us never fear to negotiate.

John F. Kennedy 1917–63: inaugural address, 20 January 1961

10 Negotiating with de Valera . . . is like trying to pick up mercury with a fork.

■ *to which de Valera replied, 'Why doesn't he use a spoon?'*
David Lloyd George 1863–1945: M. J. MacManus *Eamon de Valera* (1944)

11 We are prepared to go to the gates of Hell—but no further.

■ *attempting to reach an agreement with Napoleon, c.1800–1*
Pope Pius VII 1742–1823: J. M. Robinson *Cardinal Consalvi* (1987)

12 There is a homely old adage which runs: 'Speak softly and carry a big stick; you will go far.' If the American nation will speak softly, and yet build and keep at a pitch of the highest training a thoroughly efficient navy, the Monroe Doctrine will go far.

Theodore Roosevelt 1858–1919: speech in Chicago, 3 April 1903

13 A diplomat . . . is a person who can tell you to go to hell in such a way that you actually look forward to the trip.

Caskie Stinnett 1911– : *Out of the Red* (1960)

14 A diplomat these days is nothing but a head-waiter who's allowed to sit down occasionally.

Peter Ustinov 1921– : *Romanoff and Juliet* (1956)

15 An ambassador is an honest man sent to lie abroad for the good of his country.

Henry Wotton 1568–1639: written in the album of Christopher Fleckmore in 1604

Disability

1 Does he take sugar?

Anonymous: title of programme, BBC Radio 4

2 If Hoddle is right, I must have been a failed football coach in a previous incarnation.

David Blunkett 1947– : in *Sunday Times* 31 January 1999; cf. 5 below

3 And now she is like everyone else.

■ *on the death of his daughter, who had been born with Down's Syndrome*
Charles de Gaulle 1890–1970: attributed

4 If we are all unique creatures of God, as Christians affirm, normality becomes a meaningless concept.

Ted Harrison 1948– : *Disability: Rights and Wrongs* (1995)

5 You and I have been physically given two hands and two legs and half-decent brains. Some people have not been born like that for a reason. The karma is working from another lifetime.

Glenn Hoddle 1957– : in *The Times* 30 January 1999; cf. 2 above

6 When I consider how my light is spent,
E're half my days, in this dark world and wide,
And that one talent which is death to hide
Lodged with me useless.

■ *on his blindness*
John Milton 1608–74: 'When I consider how my light is spent' (1673)

7 My real motive is to describe how my brain-damaged life is as normal for me as my friends' able-bodied life is to them. My mind is just like a spin-dryer at full speed; my thoughts fly around my skull while millions of beautiful words cascade down into my lap. Images gunfire across my consciousness and while trying to discipline them I jump in awe at the soulfilled bounty of my mind's expanse. Try then to imagine how frustrating it is to give expression to that avalanche in efforts of one great nod after the other.

Christopher Nolan 1965– : in *Observer* 8 November 1987

8 And so I betake myself to that course, which is almost as much as to see myself go into my grave—for which, and all the discomforts that will accompany my being blind, the good God prepare me!

Samuel Pepys 1633–1703: diary 31 May 1669, closing words

9 'You haven't got a husband? Well build a social life—
Perhaps you'll find a crippled man who wants a crippled wife!'
I found this quite offensive, and told her so, at length,
She said, 'My dear, I understand—you've lost your health and strength.'

Janice Pink: Lois Keith (ed.) *Mustn't Grumble* (1994)

10 You play the hand you're dealt, and I think the game's worthwhile.

Christopher Reeve 1952– : in *Irish Times* 6 February 1999

11 Does it matter?—losing your sight? . . .
There's such splendid work for the blind;
And people will always be kind,
As you sit on the terrace remembering
And turning your face to the light.

Siegfried Sassoon 1886–1967: 'Does it Matter?' (1918)

12 Deafness is not by nature part of the fall—but the social stigma, prejudice, exclusion, and other deaf-related suffering certainly is!

Mary Weir: address at Canterbury, September 1994

Discontent

1 When you don't have any money, the problem is food. When you have money, it's sex. When you have both it's health.

J. P. Donleavy 1926– : *The Ginger Man* (1955)

2 It is an uneasy lot at best, to be what we call highly taught and yet not to enjoy: to be present at this great spectacle of life and never to be liberated from a small hungry shivering self.

George Eliot 1819–80: *Middlemarch* (1871–2)

3 Modern man lives under the illusion that he knows what he wants, while he actually wants what he is supposed to want.

Erich Fromm 1900–80: *The Fear of Freedom* (1942)

4 I've had this business that anything is better than nothing. There are times when nothing has to be better than anything.

Penelope Gilliatt 1933–93: *Sunday, Bloody Sunday* (1971)

5   It is a flaw
In happiness, to see beyond our bourn—
It forces us in summer skies to mourn:
It spoils the singing of the nightingale.

John Keats 1795–1821: 'To J. H. Reynolds, Esq.' (written 1818)

6 It is better to be a human being dissatisfied than a pig satisfied; better to be Socrates dissatisfied than a fool satisfied.

John Stuart Mill 1806–73: *Utilitarianism* (1863)

7 The heart is a small thing, but desireth great matters. It is not sufficient for a kite's dinner, yet the whole world is not sufficient for it.

Francis Quarles 1592–1644: *Emblems* (1635)

8 As long as I have a want, I have a reason for living. Satisfaction is death.

George Bernard Shaw 1856–1950: *Overruled* (1916)

9 The stoical scheme of supplying our wants, by lopping off our desires, is like cutting off our feet when we want shoes.

Jonathan Swift 1667–1745: *Thoughts on Various Subjects* (1711)

10 'Tis just like a summer birdcage in a garden; the birds that are without

despair to get in, and the birds that are within despair, and are in a consumption, for fear they shall never get out.
John Webster c.1580–c.1625: *The White Devil* (1612)

11 He spoke with a certain what-is-it in his voice, and I could see that, if not actually disgruntled, he was far from being gruntled.
P. G. Wodehouse 1881–1975: *The Code of the Woosters* (1938)

12 Content is disillusioning to behold: what is there to be content about?
Virginia Woolf 1882–1941: diary 5 May 1920

Discoveries
....
see **Inventions and Discoveries**

Disillusion
....
see also **Cynicism**

1 Never glad confident morning again!
Robert Browning 1812–89: 'The Lost Leader' (1845)

2 I never nursed a dear Gazelle, to glad me with its soft black eye, but when it came to know me well, and love me, it was sure to marry a market-gardener.
Charles Dickens 1812–70: *The Old Curiosity Shop* (1841); see **Transience** 12

3 And nothing to look backward to with pride,
And nothing to look forward to with hope.
Robert Frost 1874–1963: 'The Death of the Hired Man' (1914)

4 Take the life-lie away from the average man and straight away you take away his happiness.
Henrik Ibsen 1828–1906: *The Wild Duck* (1884)

5 Man hands on misery to man.
It deepens like a coastal shelf.
Get out as early as you can,
And don't have any kids yourself.
Philip Larkin 1922–85: 'This Be The Verse' (1974)

6 The flesh, alas, is wearied; and I have read all the books there are.
Stéphane Mallarmé 1842–98: 'Brise Marin' (1887)

7 Reason and Progress, the old firm, is selling out! Everyone get out while the going's good. Those forgotten shares you had in the old traditions, the old beliefs are going up—up and up and up.
John Osborne 1929–94: *Look Back in Anger* (1956)

8 Oh, life is a glorious cycle of song,
A medley of extemporanea;
And love is a thing that can never go wrong;
And I am Marie of Roumania.
Dorothy Parker 1893–1967: 'Comment' (1937)

9 Like all dreamers, I mistook disenchantment for truth.
Jean-Paul Sartre 1905–80: *Les Mots* (1964) 'Écrire'

10 Disillusionment in living is the finding out nobody agrees with you not those that are and were fighting with you. Disillusionment in living is the finding out nobody agrees with you not those that are fighting for you. Complete disillusionment is when you realise that no one can for they can't change.
Gertrude Stein 1874–1946: *Making of Americans* (1934)

11 If he paid for each day's comfort with the small change of his illusions, he grew daily to value the comfort more and set less store upon the coin.
Edith Wharton 1862–1937: *The Descent of Man* (1904)

Dislikes
....
see **Likes and Dislikes**

Divorce
....

1 Divorce and suicide have many characteristics in common and one crucial difference: although both are devastatingly public admissions of

failure, divorce, unlike suicide, has to be lived through.

Alfred Alvarez 1929– : *Life After Marriage* (1982)

2 A divorce is like an amputation; you survive, but there's less of you.

Margaret Atwood 1939– : in *Time*, 1973

3 Mention of divorce and avenues open up all round.

Alan Bennett 1934– : *Habeas Corpus* (1973)

4 The figure is unbelievable—just because she cooked a few meals now and again and wrote a few books.

■ *on the £10 million divorce settlement awarded to Caroline Conran*

Terence Conran 1931– : in *Mail on Sunday* 6 July 1997

5 He taught me housekeeping; when I divorce I keep the house.

■ *of her fifth husband*

Zsa Zsa Gabor 1919– : Ned Sherrin *Cutting Edge* (1984)

6 A TV host asked my wife, 'Have you ever considered divorce?' She replied: 'Divorce never, murder often.'

Charlton Heston 1924– : in *Independent* 21 July 1999

7 There is a rhythm to the ending of a marriage just like the rhythm of a courtship—only backward. You try to start again but get into blaming over and over. Finally you are both worn out, exhausted, hopeless. Then the lawyers are called in to pick clean the corpses. The death has occurred much earlier.

Erica Jong 1942– : *How To Save Your Own Life* (1977)

8 There are four stages to a marriage. First there's the affair, then the marriage, then children and finally the fourth stage, without which you cannot know a woman, the divorce.

Norman Mailer 1923– : in *Nova*, 1969

9 Women will only leave a marriage if it's unbearable, whereas men will split if they get a better offer.

Andrea Newman 1938– : in *Sunday Times* 23 May 1999

10 Staying married may have long-term benefits. You can elicit much more sympathy from friends over a bad marriage than you ever can from a good divorce.

P. J. O'Rourke 1947– : *Modern Manners* (1984)

11 However often marriage is dissolved, it remains indissoluble. Real divorce, the divorce of heart and nerve and fibre, does not exist, since there is no divorce from memory.

Virgilia Peterson 1904–66: *A Matter of Life and Death* (1961)

12 Love the quest; marriage the conquest; divorce the inquest.

Helen Rowland 1875–1950: *Reflections of a Bachelor Girl* (1903)

Dogs

see also **Animals**

1 The great pleasure of a dog is that you may make a fool of yourself with him and not only will he not scold you, but he will make a fool of himself too.

Samuel Butler 1835–1902: *Notebooks* (1912)

2 Near this spot are deposited the remains of one who possessed beauty without vanity, strength without insolence, courage without ferocity, and all the virtues of Man, without his vices.

Lord Byron 1788–1824: 'Inscription on the Monument of a Newfoundland Dog' (1808)

3 Brothers and Sisters, I bid you beware Of giving your heart to a dog to tear.

Rudyard Kipling 1865–1936: 'The Power of the Dog' (1909)

4 I'm a lean dog, a keen dog, a wild dog, and lone; I'm a rough dog, a tough dog, hunting on my own.

Irene Rutherford McLeod 1891–1964: 'Lone Dog' (1915)

5 A door is what a dog is perpetually on the wrong side of.

Ogden Nash 1902–71: 'A Dog's Best Friend is his Illiteracy' (1953)

6 Any man who hates dogs and babies can't be all bad.

■ *of W. C. Fields, and often attributed to him*
Leo Rosten 1908–97: speech at Masquers' Club dinner, 16 February 1939

7 That indefatigable and unsavoury engine of pollution, the dog.
John Sparrow 1906–92: letter to *The Times* 30 September 1975

8 The more one gets to know of men, the more one values dogs.

■ *also attributed to Mme Roland in the form 'The more I see of men, the more I like dogs'*
A. Toussenel 1803–85: *L'Esprit des bêtes* (1847)

Doubt

see also **Belief, Certainty, Faith, Indecision**

1 If a man will begin with certainties, he shall end in doubts; but if he will be content to begin with doubts, he shall end in certainties.
Francis Bacon 1561–1626: *The Advancement of Learning* (1605)

2 Oh! let us never, never doubt
What nobody is sure about!
Hilaire Belloc 1870–1953: 'The Microbe' (1897)

3 How long halt ye between two opinions?
Bible: I Kings

4 I am too much of a sceptic to deny the possibility of anything.
T. H. Huxley 1825–95: letter to Herbert Spencer, 22 March 1886

5 I respect faith but doubt is what gets you an education.
Wilson Mizner 1876–1933: H. L. Mencken *A New Dictionary of Quotations* (1942)

6 Ten thousand difficulties do not make one doubt.
John Henry Newman 1801–90: *Apologia pro Vita Sua* (1864)

7 It was not the power of the Spaniards that destroyed the Aztec Empire but the disbelief of the Aztecs in themselves.
E. F. Schumacher 1911–77: *Roots of Economic Growth* (1962)

8 There lives more faith in honest doubt,
Believe me, than in half the creeds.
Alfred, Lord Tennyson 1809–92: *In Memoriam A. H. H.* (1850)

9 Life is doubt,
And faith without doubt is nothing but death.
Miguel de Unamuno 1864–1937: 'Salmo II' (1907)

Drawing

see also **Artists, Art, Painting**

1 I rarely draw what I see—I draw what I feel in my body.
Barbara Hepworth 1903–75: Alan Bowness *Barbara Hepworth—Drawings from a Sculptor's Landscape* (1966)

2 *Le dessin est la probité de l'art.*
Drawing is the true test of art.
J. A. D. Ingres 1780–1867: *Pensées d'Ingres* (1922)

3 An active line on a walk, moving freely without a goal. A walk for walk's sake.
Paul Klee 1879–1940: *Pedagogical Sketchbook* (1925)

4 As in the fourteen lines of a sonnet, a few strokes of the pencil can hold immensity.
Laura Knight 1877–1970: *The Magic of a Line* (1965)

5 When I was the age of these children I could draw like Raphael: it took me many years to learn how to draw like these children.

■ *to Herbert Read, when visiting an exhibition of childen's drawings*
Pablo Picasso 1881–1973: quoted in letter from Read to *The Times* 27 October 1956

6 I find a particular delight in taking the caricature as far as I can. It satisfies me to stretch the human frame about and recreate it and yet keep a likeness.
Gerald Scarfe 1936– : *Scarfe by Scarfe* (1986)

Dreams

see also **Sleep**

1 Have you noticed . . . there is never any third act in a nightmare? They bring you to a climax of terror and then leave you there. They are the work of poor dramatists.
Max Beerbohm 1872–1956: S. N. Behrman *Conversations with Max* (1960)

2 The armoured cars of dreams, contrived to let us do
so many a dangerous thing.
Elizabeth Bishop 1911–79: 'Sleeping Standing Up' (1946)

3 All the things one has forgotten scream for help in dreams.
Elias Canetti 1905–94: *Die Provinz der Menschen* (1973)

4 When we dream that we are dreaming, the moment of awakening is at hand.
J. M. Coetzee 1940– : *In the Heart of the Country* (1977)

5 The interpretation of dreams is the royal road to a knowledge of the unconscious activities of the mind.
■ *often quoted as, 'Dreams are the royal road to the unconscious'*
Sigmund Freud 1856–1939: *The Interpretation of Dreams* (2nd ed., 1909)

6 The dream of reason produces monsters.
Goya 1746–1828: *Los Caprichos* (1799)

7 Was it a vision, or a waking dream? Fled is that music:—do I wake or sleep?
John Keats 1795–1821: 'Ode to a Nightingale' (1820)

8 O God! I could be bounded in a nut-shell, and count myself a king of infinite space, were it not that I have bad dreams.
William Shakespeare 1564–1616: *Hamlet* (1601)

9 How many of our daydreams would darken into nightmares if there seemed any danger of their coming true!
Logan Pearsall Smith 1865–1946: *Afterthoughts* (1931)

10 I have spread my dreams under your feet;
Tread softly because you tread on my dreams.
W. B. Yeats 1865–1939: 'He Wishes for the Cloths of Heaven' (1899)

Drink

see **Food and Drink**

Drugs

1 LSD? Nothing much happened, but I did get the distinct impression that some birds were trying to communicate with me.
W. H. Auden 1907–73: George Plimpton (ed.) *The Writer's Chapbook* (1989)

2 Cocaine habit-forming? Of course not. I ought to know. I've been using it for years.
Tallulah Bankhead 1903–68: *Tallulah* (1952)

3 Alcohol didn't cause the high crime rates of the '20s and '30s, Prohibition did. Drugs don't cause today's alarming crime rates, but drug prohibition does.
David Boaz 1953– : 'The Legalization of Drugs' 27 April 1988; quoted by Judge James C. Paine, addressing the Federal Bar Association in Miami, 1991

4 I'll die young, but it's like kissing God.
■ *on his drug addiction*
Lenny Bruce 1925–66: attributed

5 Junk is the ideal product . . . the ultimate merchandise. No sales talk necessary. The client will crawl through a sewer and beg to buy.
William S. Burroughs 1914–97: *The Naked Lunch* (1959)

6 I experimented with marijuana a time or two. And I didn't like it, and I didn't inhale.
Bill Clinton 1946– : in *Washington Post* 30 March 1992

7 Thou hast the keys of Paradise, oh
just, subtle, and mighty opium!
Thomas De Quincey 1785–1859: *Confessions of
an English Opium Eater* (1822)

8 Drugs is like getting up and having a
cup of tea in the morning.
Noel Gallagher 1967– : radio interview,
28 January 1997

9 I saw the best minds of my generation
destroyed by madness, starving
hysterical naked,
dragging themselves through the
negro streets at dawn looking for an
angry fix,
angelheaded hipsters burning for the
ancient heavenly connection to the
starry dynamo in the machinery of
the night.
Allen Ginsberg 1926–97: *Howl* (1956)

10 LSD reminds me of the minks that
escape from mink-farms and breed in
the forest and become dangerous and
destructive. It has escaped from the
drug factory and gets made in college
laboratories.
Robert Graves 1895–1985: George Plimpton
(ed.) *The Writer's Chapbook* (1989)

11 In this country, don't forget, a habit is
no damn private hell. There's no
solitary confinement outside of jail. A
habit is hell for those you love.
Billie Holiday 1915–59: *Lady Sings the Blues*
(1956, with William F. Duffy)

12 Every form of addiction is bad, no
matter whether the narcotic is
alcohol or morphine or idealism.
Carl Gustav Jung 1875–1961: *Erinnerungen,
Träume, Gedanken* (1962)

13 Sure thing, man. I used to be a
laboratory myself once.
■ *on being asked to autograph a fan's school
chemistry book*
Keith Richards 1943– : in *Independent on
Sunday* 7 August 1994

14 We can no more hope to end drug
abuse by eliminating heroin and
cocaine than we could alter the
suicide rate by outlawing high
buildings or the sale of rope.
Ben Whittaker 1934– : *The Global Fix* (1987)

15 A drug is neither moral or immoral—
it's a chemical compound. The
compound itself is not a menace to
society until a human being treats it as
if consumption bestowed a temporary
licence to act like an asshole.
Frank Zappa 1940–93: *The Real Frank Zappa
Book* (1989)

Drunkenness

see also **Alcohol**

1 BESSIE BRADDOCK: Winston, you're
drunk.
CHURCHILL: Bessie, you're ugly. But
tomorrow I shall be sober.
Winston Churchill 1874–1965: J. L. Lane (ed.)
Sayings of Churchill (1992)

2 After a man has had his coffee it's
tomorrow: it has to be! . . . And
tomorrow it's just a hangover; you
ain't still drunk tomorrow.
William Faulkner 1897–1962: *Pylon* (1935)

3 Licker talks mighty loud w'en it git
loose fum de jug.
Joel Chandler Harris 1848–1908: *Uncle Remus:
His Songs and His Sayings* (1880)

4 Grape is my mulatto mother
In this frozen whited country. Her
veined interior
Hangs hot open for me to re-enter
The blood-coloured glasshouse
against which the stone world
Thins to a dew and steams off.
Ted Hughes 1930–98: 'Wino' (1967)

5 A man who exposes himself when he
is intoxicated, has not the art of
getting drunk.
Samuel Johnson 1709–84: James Boswell *Life
of Samuel Johnson* (1791) 24 April 1779

6 You're not drunk if you can lie on the
floor without holding on.
Dean Martin 1917– : Paul Dickson *Official
Rules* (1978)

7 One more drink and I'd have been
under the host.
Dorothy Parker 1893–1967: Howard
Teichmann *George S. Kaufman* (1972)

8 Drink, sir, is a great provoker of three
things . . . nose-painting, sleep, and

urine. Lechery, sir, it provokes, and
unprovokes; it provokes the desire,
but it takes away the performance.
William Shakespeare 1564–1616: *Macbeth*
(1606)

9 But I'm not so think as you drunk I
am.
J. C. Squire 1884–1958: 'Ballade of Soporific
Absorption' (1931)

10 A man you don't like who drinks as
much as you do.
■ *definition of an alcoholic*
Dylan Thomas 1914–53: Constantine
Fitzgibbon *Life of Dylan Thomas* (1965)

Duty

see also **Responsibility**

1 Do your duty, and leave the outcome
to the Gods.
Pierre Corneille 1606–84: *Horace* (1640)

2 Duty is what no-one else will do at the
moment.
Penelope Fitzgerald 1916–2000: *Offshore*
(1979)

3 Let no guilty man escape, if it can be
avoided . . . No personal
consideration should stand in the way
of performing a public duty.
■ *on the implication of his private secretary in a
tax fraud*
Ulysses S. Grant 1822–85: endorsement of a
letter relating to the Whiskey Ring received
29 July 1875

4 Do the work that's nearest,
Though it's dull at whiles,
Helping, when we meet them,
Lame dogs over stiles.
Charles Kingsley 1819–75: 'The Invitation. To
Tom Hughes' (1856)

5 I could not love thee, Dear, so much,
Loved I not honour more.
Richard Lovelace 1618–58: 'To Lucasta, Going
to the Wars' (1649)

6 If we believe a thing to be bad, and if
we have a right to prevent it, it is our
duty to try to prevent it and to damn
the consequences.
Lord Milner 1854–1925: speech in Glasgow,
26 November 1909

7 England expects that every man will
do his duty.
Horatio, Lord Nelson 1758–1805: at the battle
of Trafalgar, 21 October 1805

8 A sense of duty is useful in work, but
offensive in personal relations. People
wish to be liked, not to be endured
with patient resignation.
Bertrand Russell 1872–1970: *The Conquest of
Happiness* (1930)

9 When a stupid man is doing
something he is ashamed of, he always
declares that it is his duty.
George Bernard Shaw 1856–1950: *Caesar and
Cleopatra* (1901)

10 I know this—a man got to do what he
got to do.
John Steinbeck 1902–68: *Grapes of Wrath*
(1939)

11 On an occasion of this kind it
becomes more than a moral duty to
speak one's mind. It becomes a
pleasure.
Oscar Wilde 1854–1900: *The Importance of
Being Earnest* (1895)

Dying

see also **Death**

1 It's not that I'm afraid to die. I just
don't want to be there when it
happens.
Woody Allen 1935– : *Death* (1975)

2 To die will be an awfully big
adventure.
J. M. Barrie 1860–1937: *Peter Pan* (1928)

3 The American daydream, as in Twain
(and Hemingway), is about re-
building after the flood, about being
better off than before, about
outwitting this or that challenge, up
to and including death. Well, how do
you manage to be optimistic for the
moment? Without hope?
Harold Brodkey 1930–96: *This Wild Darkness:
The Story of My Death* (1996)

4 Death is nothing if one can approach it as such. I was just a tiny night-light, suffocated in its own wax, and on the point of expiring.
E. M. Forster 1879–1970: Philip Gardner (ed.) *E. M. Forster: Commonplace Book* (1985)

5 When we die, all we are possessed of is our experience. It is one part of our lives that is largely in our own control.
Marilyn French 1929– : *A Season in Hell* (1998)

6 My breath is folded up
Like sheets in lavender.
The end for me
Arrives like nursery tea.
Graham Greene 1904–91: *A World of My Own* (1992)

7 I have received two wonderful graces. First, I have been given time to prepare for a new future. Secondly, I find myself—uncharacteristically—calm and at peace.
■ *breaking the news of his imminent death from cancer*
Basil Hume 1923–99: letter to priests of Westminster diocese, 16 April 1999

8 It matters not how a man dies, but how he lives. The act of dying is not of importance, it lasts so short a time.
Samuel Johnson 1709–84: James Boswell *Life of Samuel Johnson* (1791) 26 October 1769

9 The key to dying well is for you to decide where, when, how and whom to invite to the last party.
Timothy Leary 1920–96: in *Daily Telegraph* 3 May 1996

10 Dying is a very dull, dreary affair. And my advice to you is to have nothing whatever to do with it.
W. Somerset Maugham 1874–1965: Robin Maugham *Conversations with Willie* (1978)

11 Dying,
Is an art, like everything else.
Sylvia Plath 1932–63: 'Lady Lazarus' (1963)

12 Deception is not as creative as truth. We do best in life if we look at it with clear eyes, and I think that applies to coming up to death as well.
■ *of the Hospice movement*
Cicely Saunders 1916– : in *Time* 5 September 1988

13 Nothing in his life
Became him like the leaving it.
William Shakespeare 1564–1616: *Macbeth* (1606)

14 Nor dread nor hope attend
A dying animal;
A man awaits his end
Dreading and hoping all.
W. B. Yeats 1865–1939: 'Death' (1933)

The Earth

see also **The Environment, Maps, Nature, Pollution, The Universe**

1 Praise the green earth. Chance has appointed her
home, workshop, larder, middenpit.
Her lousy skin scabbed here and there by
cities provides us with name and nation.
Basil Bunting 1900–85: 'Attis: or, Something Missing' (1931)

2 How inappropriate to call this planet Earth when it is clearly Ocean.
Arthur C. Clarke 1917– : in *Nature* 1990; attributed

3 Villages, unlike towns, have always been ruled by conformism, isolation, petty surveillance, boredom and repetitive malicious gossip about the same families. Which is a precise enough description of the global spectacle's present vulgarity.
■ *on the concept of the 'global village'*
Guy Debord 1931–94: *Comments on the Society of the Spectacle* (1988); cf. 6 below

4 Now there is one outstandingly important fact regarding Spaceship Earth, and that is that no instruction book came with it.
R. Buckminster Fuller 1895–1983: *Operating Manual for Spaceship Earth* (1969)

5 Let me enjoy the earth no less
Because the all-enacting Might

That fashioned forth its loveliness
Had other aims than my delight.
Thomas Hardy 1840–1928: 'Let me Enjoy'
(1909)

6 The new electronic interdependence
recreates the world in the image of a
global village.
Marshall McLuhan 1911–80: *The Gutenberg
Galaxy* (1962)

7 Gaia is a tough bitch. People think the
earth is going to die and they have to
save it, that's ridiculous . . . There's
no doubt that Gaia can compensate
for our output of greenhouse gases,
but the environment that's left will
not be happy for any people.
Lynn Margulis 1938– : in *New York Times
Biographical Service* January 1996

8 God owns heaven
but He craves the earth.
Anne Sexton 1928–74: 'The Earth' (1975)

9 We have a beautiful
mother
Her green lap
immense
Her brown embrace
eternal
Her blue body
everything
we know.
Alice Walker 1944– : 'We Have a Beautiful
Mother' (1991)

10 The earth does not argue,
Is not pathetic, has no arrangements,
Does not scream, haste, persuade,
threaten, promise,
Makes no discriminations, has no
conceivable failures,
Closes nothing, refuses nothing, shuts
none out.
Walt Whitman 1819–92: 'A Song of the Rolling
Earth' (1881)

11 From space, the planet is blue.
From space, the planet is the territory
Not of humans, but of the whale.
Blue seas cover seven-tenths of the
earth's surface,
And are the domain of the largest
brain ever created,

With a fifty-million-year-old smile.
Heathcote Williams 1941– : *Whale Nation*
(1988)

Eating

see also **Cooking, Diets, Food and Drink**

1 Tell me what you eat and I will tell you
what you are.
Anthelme Brillat-Savarin 1755–1826:
Physiologie du Goût (1825)

2 Some have meat and cannot eat,
Some cannot eat that want it:
But we have meat and we can eat,
Sae let the Lord be thankit.
Robert Burns 1759–96: 'The Kirkudbright
Grace' (1790), also known as 'The Selkirk
Grace'

3 The healthy stomach is nothing if not
conservative. Few radicals have good
digestions.
Samuel Butler 1835–1902: *Notebooks* (1912)

4 It's a very odd thing—
As odd as can be—
That whatever Miss T eats
Turns into Miss T.
Walter de la Mare 1873–1956: 'Miss T' (1913)

5 Gluttony is an emotional escape, a
sign something is eating us.
Peter De Vries 1910–93: *Comfort Me With
Apples* (1956)

6 It [bingeing] gives you a feeling of
comfort. It's like having a pair of arms
around you, but it's temporary. Then
you're disgusted at the bloatedness of
your stomach, and then you bring it
all up again.
Diana, Princess of Wales 1961–97: interview
on *Panorama*, BBC1 TV, 20 November 1995

7 Self-starvation is above all a
performance. Like Hamlet's mouse-
trap, it is staged to trick the
conscience of its viewers, forcing
them to recognize that they are
implicated in the spectacle that they
behold.
Maud Ellman 1954– : *The Hunger Artists:
Starving, Writing and Imprisonment* (1993)

8 I do wish we could chat longer, but I'm having an old friend for dinner.
Thomas Harris 1940– and **Ted Tally** 1952– : *The Silence of the Lambs* (1991 film)

9 Time for a little something.
A. A. Milne 1882–1956: *Winnie-the-Pooh* (1926)

10 Now good digestion wait on appetite, And health on both!
William Shakespeare 1564–1616: *Macbeth* (1606)

11 We each day dig our graves with our teeth.
Samuel Smiles 1812–1904: *Duty* (1880)

12 He sows hurry and reaps indigestion.
Robert Louis Stevenson 1850–94: *Virginibus Puerisque* (1881) 'An Apology for Idlers'

13 I'll fill hup the chinks wi' cheese.
R. S. Surtees 1805–64: *Handley Cross* (1843)

Economics
....
see also **Business**, **Debt**, **Money**

1 There's no such thing as a free lunch.
Anonymous: colloquial axiom in US economics from the 1960s, much associated with Milton Friedman; recorded from 1938

2 Everyone is always in favour of general economy and particular expenditure.
Anthony Eden 1897–1977: in *Observer* 17 June 1956

3 Inflation is the one form of taxation that can be imposed without legislation.
Milton Friedman 1912– : in *Observer* 22 September 1974

4 Trickle-down theory—the less than elegant metaphor that if one feeds the horse enough oats, some will pass through to the road for the sparrows.
J. K. Galbraith 1908– : *The Culture of Contentment* (1992)

5 In a community where public services have failed to keep abreast of private consumption things are very different. Here, in an atmosphere of private opulence and public squalor, the private goods have full sway.
J. K. Galbraith 1908– : *The Affluent Society* (1958)

6 I could seek to ease his pain, but only by giving him an aspirin.
■ *the Governor of the Bank of England on economic problems of small businessmen*
Eddie George 1938– : interview on *The Money Programme* BBC2 TV, 28 February 1999

7 Balancing the budget is like going to heaven. Everybody wants to do it, but nobody wants to do what you have to do to get there.
Phil Gramm 1942– : in a television interview, 16 September 1990

8 The best of all monopoly profits is a quiet life.
J. R. Hicks 1904– : *Econometrica* (1935)

9 Lenin was right. There is no subtler, no surer means of overturning the existing basis of society than to debauch the currency.
John Maynard Keynes 1883–1946: *The Economic Consequences of the Peace* (1919)

10 First of all the Georgian silver goes, and then all that nice furniture that used to be in the saloon. Then the Canalettos go.
■ *on privatization; often quoted as 'selling the family silver'*
Harold Macmillan 1894–1986: speech to the Tory Reform Group, 8 November 1985

11 If the policy isn't hurting, it isn't working.
■ *on controlling inflation*
John Major 1943– : speech in Northampton, 27 October 1989

12 Expenditure rises to meet income.
C. Northcote Parkinson 1909–93: *The Law and the Profits* (1960)

13 Small is beautiful. A study of economics as if people mattered.
E. F. Schumacher 1911–77: title of book (1973)

14 Call a thing immoral or ugly, soul-destroying or a degradation of man, a peril to the peace of the world or to the well-being of future generations: as long as you have not shown it to be 'uneconomic' you have not really questioned its right to exist, grow, and prosper.

E. F. Schumacher 1911–77: *Small is Beautiful* (1973)

15 The cold metal of economic theory is in Marx's pages immersed in such a wealth of steaming phrases as to acquire a temperature not naturally its own.

Joseph Alois Schumpeter 1883–1950: *Capitalism, Socialism and Democracy* (1942)

16 A continually 'growing economy' is no longer healthy but a cancer.

Gary Snyder 1930– : *A Place in Space* (1995)

17 What a country calls its vital economic interests are not the things which enable its citizens to live, but the things which enable it to make war.

Simone Weil 1909–43: W. H. Auden *A Certain World* (1971)

Education

see also **Examinations, Schools, Teaching, Universities**

1 I read Shakespeare and the Bible and I can shoot dice. That's what I call a liberal education.

Tallulah Bankhead 1903–68: attributed

2 Ask me my three main priorities for Government, and I tell you: education, education and education.

Tony Blair 1953– : speech at the Labour Party Conference, 1 October 1996

3 The liberally educated person is one who is able to resist the easy and preferred answers, not because he is obstinate but because he knows others worthy of consideration.

Allan Bloom 1930–92: *The Closing of the American Mind* (1987)

4 Education makes a people easy to lead, but difficult to drive; easy to govern, but impossible to enslave.

Lord Brougham 1778–1868: attributed

5 To live for a time close to great minds is the best kind of education.

John Buchan 1875–1940: *Memory Hold-the-Door* (1940)

6 Gie me ae spark o' Nature's fire, That's a' the learning I desire.

Robert Burns 1759–96: 'Epistle to J. L[aprai]k' (1786)

7 The empires of the future are the empires of the mind.

Winston Churchill 1874–1965: speech at Harvard, 6 September 1943

8 In education there should be no class distinction.

Confucius 551–479 BC: *Analects*

9 Education is the ability to listen to almost anything without losing your temper or your self-confidence.

Robert Frost 1874–1963: in *Reader's Digest* April 1960

10 The aim of education is the knowledge not of facts but of values.

William Ralph Inge 1860–1954: 'The Training of the Reason' in A. C. Benson (ed.) *Cambridge Essays on Education* (1917)

11 If you are truly serious about preparing your child for the future, don't teach him to subtract—teach him to deduct.

Fran Lebowitz 1946– : *Social Studies* (1981)

12 People like me were branded, pigeon-holed, a ceiling put on our ambitions.

■ *on failing his 11-plus*

John Prescott 1938– : speech at Ruskin College, Oxford, 13 June 1996

13 Education is what survives when what has been learned has been forgotten.

B. F. Skinner 1904–90: in *New Scientist* 21 May 1964

14 It [education] has produced a vast population able to read but unable to distinguish what is worth reading, an easy prey to sensations and cheap appeals.

G. M. Trevelyan 1876–1962: *English Social History* (1942)

15 Soap and education are not as sudden as a massacre, but they are more deadly in the long run.

Mark Twain 1835–1910: *A Curious Dream* (1872) 'Facts concerning the Recent Resignation'

16 Education ent only books and music—it's asking questions, all the

time. There are millions of us, all over the country, and no one, not one of us, is asking questions, we're all taking the easiest way out.

Arnold Wesker 1932– : *Roots* (1959)

17 The best thing for being sad . . . is to learn something.

T. H. White 1906–64: *The Sword in the Stone* (1938)

18 Education is an admirable thing, but it is well to remember from time to time that nothing that is worth knowing can be taught.

Oscar Wilde 1854–1900: *Intentions* (1891)

Effort

1 For twenty years he has held a season-ticket on the line of least resistance and has gone wherever the train of events has carried him, lucidly justifying his position at whatever point he has happened to find himself.

■ *of Herbert Asquith*
Leo Amery 1873–1955: in *Quarterly Review* July 1914

2 Now, *here*, you see, it takes all the running *you* can do, to keep in the same place. If you want to get somewhere else, you must run at least twice as fast as that!

Lewis Carroll 1832–98: *Through the Looking-Glass* (1872)

3 Say not the struggle naught availeth, The labour and the wounds are vain, The enemy faints not, nor faileth, And as things have been, things remain.

Arthur Hugh Clough 1819–61: 'Say not the struggle naught availeth' (1855)

4 Also say to them, that they suffre hym this day to wynne his spurres, for if god be pleased, I woll this journey be his, and the honoure therof.

■ *commonly quoted as 'Let the boy win his spurs'*
Edward III 1312–77: speaking of the Black Prince at the battle of Crécy, 1346; *The Chronicle of Froissart* (translated by John Bourchier 1523–5)

5 *Parturient montes, nascetur ridiculus mus.*

Mountains will go into labour, and a silly little mouse will be born.

Horace 65–8 BC: *Ars Poetica*

6 I had done all that I could; and no man is well pleased to have his all neglected, be it ever so little.

Samuel Johnson 1709–84: letter to Lord Chesterfield, 7 February 1755

7 The world is an oyster, but you don't crack it open on a mattress.

Arthur Miller 1915– : *Death of a Salesman* (1949)

8 But the fruit that can fall without shaking,
Indeed is too mellow for me.

Lady Mary Wortley Montagu 1689–1762: 'Answered, for Lord William Hamilton' (1758)

9 The world is divided into people who do things and people who get the credit. Try, if you can, to belong to the first class. There's far less competition.

Dwight Morrow 1873–1931: letter to his son; Harold Nicolson *Dwight Morrow* (1935)

10 Things won are done; joy's soul lies in the doing.

William Shakespeare 1564–1616: *Troilus and Cressida* (1602)

11 It is a folly to expect men to do all that they may reasonably be expected to do.

Richard Whately 1787–1863: *Apophthegms* (1854)

Elections

see also **Democracy**

1 It's The Sun Wot Won It.

■ *following the 1992 general election*
Anonymous: headline in *Sun* 11 April 1992

2 Vote for the man who promises least; he'll be the least disappointing.

Bernard Baruch 1870–1965: Meyer Berger *New York* (1960)

3 The accursed power which stands on Privilege

(And goes with Women, and
  Champagne, and Bridge)
Broke—and Democracy resumed her
  reign:
(Which goes with Bridge, and Women
  and Champagne).
Hilaire Belloc 1870–1953: 'On a Great
Election' (1923)

4 You campaign in poetry. You govern
in prose.
Mario Cuomo 1932– : in *New Republic*,
Washington, DC, 8 April 1985

5 An election is coming. Universal
peace is declared, and the foxes have a
sincere interest in prolonging the lives
of the poultry.
George Eliot 1819–80: *Felix Holt* (1866)

6 Hell, I never vote *for* anybody. I always
vote *against*.
W. C. Fields 1880–1946: Robert Lewis Taylor
W. C. Fields (1950)

7 Don't buy a single vote more than
necessary. I'll be damned if I'm going
to pay for a landslide.
■ *telegraphed message from his father, read at a
Gridiron dinner in Washington, 15 March 1958,
and almost certainly JFK's invention*
John F. Kennedy 1917–63: J. F. Cutler *Honey
Fitz* (1962)

8 To give victory to the right, not
bloody bullets, but peaceful ballots
only, are necessary.
■ *usually quoted 'The ballot is stronger than the
bullet'*
Abraham Lincoln 1809–65: speech, 18 May
1858

9 If voting changed anything, they'd
abolish it.
Ken Livingstone 1945– : title of book, 1987

10 If there had been any formidable body
of cannibals in the country he would
have promised to provide them with
free missionaries fattened at the
taxpayer's expense.
■ *of Harry Truman's success in the
1948 presidential campaign*
H. L. Mencken 1880–1956: in *Baltimore Sun*
7 November 1948

11 You won the elections, but I won the
count.
■ *replying to an accusation of ballot-rigging*
Anastasio Somoza 1925–80: in *Guardian*
17 June 1977

Emotions

1 The desires of the heart are as crooked
as corkscrews.
W. H. Auden 1907–73: 'Death's Echo' (1937)

2 One mad magenta moment and I
have paid for it all my life.
Alan Bennett 1934– : *Habeas Corpus* (1973)

3 Passion always goes, and boredom
stays.
Coco Chanel 1883–1971: Frances Kennett *Coco:
the Life and Loves of Gabrielle Chanel* (1989)

4 The world of the emotions that are so
lightly called physical.
Colette 1873–1954: *Le Blé en herbe* (1923)

5 The human heart likes a little disorder
in its geometry.
Louis de Bernières 1954– : *Captain Corelli's
Mandolin* (1994)

6 As you pass from the tender years of
youth into harsh and embittered
manhood, make sure you take with
you on your journey all the human
emotions! Don't leave them on the
road, for you will not pick them up
afterwards!
Nikolai Gogol 1809–52: *Dead Souls* (1842)

7 They had been corrupted by money,
and he had been corrupted by
sentiment. Sentiment was the more
dangerous, because you couldn't
name its price. A man open to bribes
was to be relied upon below a certain
figure, but sentiment might uncoil in
the heart at a name, a photograph,
even a smell remembered.
Graham Greene 1904–91: *The Heart of the
Matter* (1948)

8 A man who has not passed through
the inferno of his passions has never
overcome them.
Carl Gustav Jung 1875–1961: *Erinnerungen,
Träume, Gedanken* (1962)

9 The trumpets came out brazenly with the last post. We all swallowed our spittle, chokingly, while our eyes smarted against our wills. A man hates to be moved to folly by a noise.
T. E. Lawrence 1888–1935: *The Mint* (1955)

10 There is no such thing as inner peace. There is only nervousness or death.
Fran Lebowitz 1946– : *Metropolitan Life* (1978)

11 Sentimentality is the emotional promiscuity of those who have no sentiment.
Norman Mailer 1923– : *Cannibals and Christians* (1966)

12 Calm of mind, all passion spent.
John Milton 1608–74: *Samson Agonistes* (1671)

13 The heart is an organ of fire.
Michael Ondaatje 1943– : *The English Patient* (1992)

14 Oh heavens, how I long for a little ordinary human enthusiasm. Just enthusiasm—that's all. I want to hear a warm, thrilling voice cry out Hallelujah! Hallelujah! I'm alive!
John Osborne 1929–94: *Look Back in Anger* (1956)

15 *on being told there was no English word equivalent to* sensibilité:
Yes we have. Humbug.
Lord Palmerston 1784–1865: attributed

16 The heart has its reasons which reason knows nothing of.
Blaise Pascal 1623–62: *Pensées* (1670)

17 The ruling passion, be it what it will, The ruling passion conquers reason still.
Alexander Pope 1688–1744: *Epistles to Several Persons* 'To Lord Bathurst' (1733)

18 Our passions are most like to floods and streams;
The shallow murmur, but the deep are dumb.
Walter Ralegh *c.*1552–1618: 'Sir Walter Ralegh to the Queen' (1655)

19 Do you know what 'le vice Anglais'— the English vice—really is? Not flagellation, not pederasty—whatever the French believe it to be. It's our refusal to admit our emotions. We think they demean us, I suppose.
Terence Rattigan 1911–77: *In Praise of Love* (1973)

20 One must have a heart of stone to read the death of Little Nell without laughing.
Oscar Wilde 1854–1900: Ada Leverson *Letters to the Sphinx* (1930)

21 Now that my ladder's gone
I must lie down where all the ladders start
In the foul rag-and-bone shop of the heart.
W. B. Yeats 1865–1939: 'The Circus Animals' Desertion' (1939)

Employment

see also **Careers, Management, Trade Unions, Unemployment, Work**

1 A professional is a man who can do his job when he doesn't feel like it. An amateur is a man who can't do his job when he does feel like it.
James Agate 1877–1947: diary 19 July 1945

2 Lord Finchley tried to mend the Electric Light
Himself. It struck him dead: And serve him right!
It is the business of the wealthy man
To give employment to the artisan.
Hilaire Belloc 1870–1953: 'Lord Finchley' (1911)

3 We spend most of our lives working. So why do so few people have a good time doing it? Virgin is the possibility of good times.
Richard Branson 1950– : interview in *New York Times* 28 February 1993

4 How I love a colleague-free day! Then I can really get on with the job.
Hugh Dalton 1887–1962: diary 17 September 1941

5 Knowledge employees cannot, in effect, be supervised. Unless they know more than anybody else in the

organization, they are useless to all intents and purposes.

Peter F. Drucker 1909– : *Post-Capitalist Society* (1993)

6 Sex suppressed will go berserk,
But it keeps us all alive.
It's a wonderful change from wives and work
And it ends at half past five.

Gavin Ewart 1916–95: 'Office Friendships' (1966)

7 Dr—well remembered that he had a salary to receive, and only forgot that he had a duty to perform.

Edward Gibbon 1737–94: *Memoirs of My Life* (1796)

8 That state is a state of slavery in which a man does what he likes to do in his spare time and in his working time that which is required of him.

Eric Gill 1882–1940: *Art-nonsense and Other Essays* (1929)

9 It is wonderful, when a calculation is made, how little the mind is actually employed in the discharge of any profession.

Samuel Johnson 1709–84: James Boswell *Life of Samuel Johnson* (1791) 6 April 1775

10 If there is one word that sums up the modern workforce that word is flexibility.

Bill Morris 1938– : speech to trade unionists, London, February 1994

11 Professional men, they have no cares;
Whatever happens, they get theirs.

Ogden Nash 1902–71: 'I Yield to My Learned Brother' (1935)

12 Which of us . . . is to do the hard and dirty work for the rest—and for what pay? Who is to do the pleasant and clean work, and for what pay?

John Ruskin 1819–1900: *Sesame and Lilies* (1865)

13 Work is of two kinds: first, altering the position of matter at or near the earth's surface relatively to other such matter; second, telling other people to do so. The first kind is unpleasant and ill paid; the second is pleasant and highly paid.

Bertrand Russell 1872–1970: *In Praise of Idleness and Other Essays* (1986) title essay (1932)

14 When domestic servants are treated as human beings it is not worth while to keep them.

George Bernard Shaw 1856–1950: *Man and Superman* (1903)

Ending

1 It ain't over till it's over.

Yogi Berra 1925– : comment on National League pennant race, 1973, quoted in many versions

2 Better is the end of a thing than the beginning thereof.

Bible: Ecclesiastes

3 All tragedies are finished by a death,
All comedies are ended by a marriage;
The future states of both are left to faith.

Lord Byron 1788–1824: *Don Juan* (1819–24)

4 Now this is not the end. It is not even the beginning of the end. But it is, perhaps, the end of the beginning.

■ *on the Battle of Egypt*

Winston Churchill 1874–1965: speech at the Mansion House, London, 10 November 1942

5 The party's over, it's time to call it a day.

Betty Comden 1919– and **Adolph Green** 1915– : 'The Party's Over' (1956 song)

6 What if this present were the world's last night?

John Donne 1572–1631: *Holy Sonnets* (after 1609)

7 This is the way the world ends
Not with a bang but a whimper.

T. S. Eliot 1888–1965: 'The Hollow Men' (1925)

8 Some say the world will end in fire,
Some say in ice.
From what I've tasted of desire
I hold with those who favour fire.

Robert Frost 1874–1963: 'Fire and Ice' (1923)

9 You cannot reheat a soufflé.
- *discounting rumours of a Beatles reunion*
Paul McCartney 1942– : attributed; L. Botts
Loose Talk (1980)

10 In my end is my beginning.
Mary, Queen of Scots 1542–87: motto; letter
from William Drummond of Hawthornden
to Ben Jonson in 1619

11 *Dies irae, dies illa,*
Solvet saeclum in favilla,
Teste David cum Sibylla.
That day, the day of wrath, will turn
the universe to ashes, as David
foretells (and the Sibyl too).
The Missal: *Order of Mass for the Dead*
'Sequentia' (commonly known as *Dies Irae*);
attributed to Thomas of Celano, *c.*1190–1260

12 The rest is silence.
William Shakespeare 1564–1616: *Hamlet*
(1601)

13 This is the beginning of the end.
- *on the announcement of Napoleon's Pyrrhic*
victory at Borodino, 1812
Charles-Maurice de Talleyrand 1754–1838:
attributed; Sainte-Beuve *M. de Talleyrand*
(1870)

14 They think it's all over—it is now.
Kenneth Wolstenholme 1920–2002: television
commentary in closing moments of the
World Cup Final, 30 July 1966

Enemies
....
see also **Hatred**

1 *on someone observing that Nye Bevan was*
sometimes his own worst enemy:
Not while I'm alive 'e ain't!
Ernest Bevin 1881–1951: Roderick Barclay
Ernest Bevin and the Foreign Office (1975)

2 He that is not with me is against me.
Bible: St Matthew

3 Love your enemies, do good to them
which hate you.
Bible: St Luke

4 He that wrestles with us strengthens
our nerves, and sharpens our skill.
Our antagonist is our helper.
Edmund Burke 1729–97: *Reflections on the*
Revolution in France (1790)

5 Fidel Castro is right. You do not
quieten your enemy by talking with
him like a priest, but by burning him.
Nicolae Ceauşescu 1918–89: at a Communist
Party meeting, 17 December 1989

6 You shall judge of a man by his foes as
well as by his friends.
Joseph Conrad 1857–1924: *Lord Jim* (1900)

7 Better to have him inside the tent
pissing out, than outside pissing in.
- *of J. Edgar Hoover*
Lyndon Baines Johnson 1908–73: David
Halberstam *The Best and the Brightest* (1972)

8 People wish their enemies dead—but
I do not; I say give them the gout, give
them the stone!
Lady Mary Wortley Montagu 1689–1762: letter
from Horace Walpole to George Harcourt,
17 September 1778

9 I am the enemy you killed, my friend.
I knew you in this dark: for you so
frowned
Yesterday through me as you jabbed
and killed . . .
Let us sleep now.
Wilfred Owen 1893–1918: 'Strange Meeting'
(written 1918)

10 Scratch a lover, and find a foe.
Dorothy Parker 1893–1967: 'Ballade of a Great
Weariness' (1937)

11 There is nothing in the whole world
so painful as feeling that one is not
liked. It always seems to me that
people who hate me must be suffering
from some strange form of lunacy.
Sei Shōnagon *c.*966–*c.*1013: *The Pillow Book of*
Sei Shōnagon

12 Heat not a furnace for your foe so hot
That it do singe yourself.
William Shakespeare 1564–1616: *Henry VIII*
(1613)

13 He makes no friend who never made a
foe.
Alfred, Lord Tennyson 1809–92: *Idylls of the*
King 'Lancelot and Elaine' (1859)

14 A man cannot be too careful in the
choice of his enemies.
Oscar Wilde 1854–1900: *The Picture of Dorian*
Gray (1891)

England

see also **Britain**, **British Cities and Towns**

1 Think of what our Nation stands for,
  Books from Boots' and country lanes,
  Free speech, free passes, class
    distinction,
  Democracy and proper drains.
  John Betjeman 1906–84: 'In Westminster
  Abbey' (1940)

2 I will not cease from mental fight,
  Nor shall my sword sleep in my hand,
  Till we have built Jerusalem,
  In England's green and pleasant land.
  William Blake 1757–1827: *Milton* (1804–10)
  'And did those feet in ancient time'

3 God! I will pack, and take a train,
  And get me to England once again!
  For England's the one land, I know,
  Where men with Splendid Hearts may
    go.
  Rupert Brooke 1887–1915: 'The Old Vicarage,
  Grantchester' (1915)

4 In England there are sixty different
  religions, and only one sauce.
  Francesco Caracciolo 1752–99: attributed

5 Mad dogs and Englishmen
  Go out in the midday sun.
  Noël Coward 1899–1973: 'Mad Dogs and
  Englishmen' (1931 song)

6 England's not a bad country . . . It's
  just a mean, cold, ugly, divided, tired,
  clapped-out, post-imperial, postindustrial slag-heap covered in
  polystyrene hamburger cartons.
  Margaret Drabble 1939– : *A Natural
  Curiosity* (1989)

7 It is not that the Englishman can't
  feel—it is that he is afraid to feel. He
  has been taught at his public school
  that feeling is bad form. He must not
  express great joy or sorrow, or even
  open his mouth too wide when he
  talks—his pipe might fall out if he
  did.
  E. M. Forster 1879–1970: *Abinger Harvest*
  (1936) 'Notes on English Character'

8 An Englishman, even if he is alone,
  forms an orderly queue of one.
  George Mikes 1912– : *How to be an Alien*
  (1946)

9 I am American bred,
  I have seen much to hate here—much
    to forgive,
  But in a world where England is
    finished and dead,
  I do not wish to live.
  Alice Duer Miller 1874–1942: *The White Cliffs*
  (1940)

10 The English are busy; they don't have
   time to be polite.
   Montesquieu 1689–1755: *Pensées et fragments
   inédits . . .* vol. 2 (1901)

11 England is a nation of shopkeepers.
   ■ *the phrase 'nation of shopkeepers' had been
   used earlier by Samuel Adams and Adam Smith*
   Napoleon I 1769–1821: Barry E. O'Meara
   Napoleon in Exile (1822)

12 Let us pause to consider the English,
   Who when they pause to consider
     themselves they get all reticently
     thrilled and tinglish,
   Because every Englishman is
     convinced of one thing, viz.:
   That to be an Englishman is to belong
     to the most exclusive club there is.
   Ogden Nash 1902–71: 'England Expects'
   (1938)

13 Down here it was still the England I
   had known in my childhood: the
   railway cuttings smothered in wild
   flowers . . . the red buses, the blue
   policemen—all sleeping the deep,
   deep sleep of England, from which I
   sometimes fear that we shall never
   wake till we are jerked out of it by the
   roar of bombs.
   George Orwell 1903–50: *Homage to Catalonia*
   (1938)

14 Old maids biking to Holy
   Communion through the mists of the
   autumn mornings . . . these are not
   only fragments, but *characteristic*
   fragments, of the English scene.
   George Orwell 1903–50: *The Lion and the
   Unicorn* (1941) 'England Your England'; cf.
   Britain 8

15 This is a letter of hate. It is for you my
countrymen, I mean those men of my
country who have defiled it. The men
with manic fingers leading the
sightless, feeble, betrayed body of my
country to its death . . . damn you
England.
  John Osborne 1929–94: in *Tribune* 18 August
  1961

16 There'll always be an England
While there's a country lane,
Wherever there's a cottage small
Beside a field of grain.
  Ross Parker 1914–74 and **Hugh Charles**
  1907– : 'There'll always be an England' (1939
  song)

17 Ask any man what nationality he
would prefer to be, and ninety-nine
out of a hundred will tell you that they
would prefer to be Englishmen.
  Cecil Rhodes 1853–1902: Gordon Le Sueur
  Cecil Rhodes (1913)

18 This royal throne of kings, this
    sceptered isle,
This earth of majesty, this seat of
    Mars . . .
This blessèd plot, this earth, this
    realm, this England.
  William Shakespeare 1564–1616: *Richard II*
  (1595)

19 Englishmen never will be slaves: they
are free to do whatever the
Government and public opinion
allow them to do.
  George Bernard Shaw 1856–1950: *Man and
  Superman* (1903)

20 America is a land whose centre is
nowhere; England one whose centre is
everywhere.
  John Updike 1932– : *Picked Up Pieces* (1976)
  'London Life' (written 1969)

21 You never find an Englishman among
the under-dogs—except in England,
of course.
  Evelyn Waugh 1903–66: *The Loved One* (1948)

22 We must be free or die, who speak the
    tongue
That Shakespeare spake; the faith and
    morals hold

Which Milton held.
  William Wordsworth 1770–1850: 'It is not to be
  thought of that the Flood' (1807)

The Environment

see also **Cities**, **The Earth**, **Pollution**

1 Think globally, act locally.
  Anonymous: Friends of the Earth slogan,
  c.1985

2 The desert shall rejoice, and blossom
as the rose.
  Bible: Isaiah

3 I do not know of any environmental
group in any country that does not
view its government as an adversary.
  Gro Harlem Brundtland 1939– : in *Time*
  25 September 1989

4 Man has been endowed with reason,
with the power to create, so that he
can add to what he's been given. But
up to now he hasn't been a creator,
only a destroyer. Forests keep
disappearing, rivers dry up, wild life's
become extinct, the climate's ruined
and the land grows poorer and uglier
every day.
  Anton Chekhov 1860–1904: *Uncle Vanya*
  (1897)

5 Mankind has probably done more
damage to the earth in the 20th
century than in all of previous human
history.
  Jacques Cousteau 1910–97: 'Consumer
  Society is the Enemy' in *New Perspectives
  Quarterly* Summer 1996

6 Make it a *green* peace.
  ■ *at a meeting of the Don't Make a Wave
  Committee, which preceded the formation of
  Greenpeace*
  Bill Darnell: in Vancouver, 1970; Robert
  Hunter *The Greenpeace Chronicle* (1979)

7 The poor tread lightest upon the
earth. The higher our income, the
more resources we control and the
more havoc we wreak.
  Paul Harrison 1936– : in *Guardian* 1 May 1992

8 What would the world be, once bereft
Of wet and wildness? Let them be left,

O let them be left, wildness and wet;
Long live the weeds and the
wilderness yet.

   Gerard Manley Hopkins 1844–89: 'Inversnaid'
   (written 1881)

9 The word *Greenpeace* had a ring to
it—it conjured images of Eden; it said
ecology and antiwar in two syllables;
it fit easily into even a one-column
headline.

   Robert Hunter 1941– : *Warriors of the
   Rainbow* (1979)

10 The greenest political party there has
ever been was the Nazi party. The
Nazis were great believers in purity,
that nature should not be interfered
with.

   Steve Jones 1944– : in *Times Higher
   Education Supplement* 27 August 1999

11   All that remains
For us will be concrete and tyres.

   Philip Larkin 1922–85: 'Going, Going' (1974)

12 They paved paradise
And put up a parking lot,
With a pink hotel,
A boutique, and a swinging hot spot.

   Joni Mitchell 1945– : 'Big Yellow Taxi' (1970
   song)

13 Conservation has gone astray because
it has failed to confront the disease
that is causing all the trouble. The
organizers of the movement have
been too embarrassed to face the
simple truth: if human breeding is not
restricted, wildlife will disappear.

   Desmond Morris 1928– : *The Animal
   Contract* (1990)

14 What have they done to the earth?
What have they done to our fair sister?
Ravaged and plundered and ripped
her and did her,
Stuck her with knives in the side of
the dawn,
And tied her with fences and dragged
her down.

   Jim Morrison 1943–71: 'When the Music's
   Over' (1967 song)

15 I think that I shall never see
A billboard lovely as a tree.
Perhaps, unless the billboards fall,

I'll never see a tree at all.

   Ogden Nash 1902–71: 'Song of the Open
   Road' (1933); see **Trees 9**

16 If I were a Brazilian without land or
money or the means to feed my
children, I would be burning the rain
forest too.

   Sting 1951– : in *International Herald Tribune*
   14 April 1989

Envy

1 May good confront the man on top
and the man below. But let him who is
jealous of another's position choke
with his envy.

   Chinua Achebe 1930– : *Arrow of God* (1988)

2 Thou shalt not covet; but tradition
Approves all forms of competition.

   Arthur Hugh Clough 1819–61: 'The Latest
   Decalogue' (1862)

3 Fools out of favour grudge at knaves
in place.

   Daniel Defoe 1660–1731: *The True-Born
   Englishman* (1701)

4 Do we want laurels for ourselves
most,
Or most that no one else shall have
any?

   Amy Lowell 1874–1925: 'La Ronde du Diable'
   (1925)

5 If something pleasant happens to you,
don't forget to tell it to your friends,
to make them feel bad.

   Casimir, Comte de Montrond 1768–1843:
   attributed; Comte J. d'Estourmel *Derniers
   Souvenirs* (1860)

Epitaphs

see also **Death**

1 Commander Jacques-Yves Cousteau
has rejoined the world of silence.

   ■ *Cousteau* (1910–97) *published* The Silent
   World *in 1953*

   Anonymous: announcement by the Cousteau
   Foundation, Paris, 25 June 1997

2 Free at last, free at last
Thank God almighty

We are free at last.

■ *epitaph of Martin Luther King (1929–68), Atlanta, Georgia*

Anonymous: spiritual, with which he ended his 'I have a dream' speech

3 I will return. And I will be millions.

Anonymous: inscription on the tomb of Eva Perón (1919–52), Buenos Aires

4 Rest in peace. The mistake shall not be repeated.

Anonymous: inscription on the cenotaph at Hiroshima, Japan

5 A soldier of the Great War known unto God.

■ *standard epitaph for the unidentified dead of World War One*

Anonymous: adopted by the War Graves Commission

6 Timothy has passed . . .

■ *announcing the death of Timothy Leary (1920–96)*

Anonymous: message on his Internet home page, 31 May 1996

7 Hereabouts died a very gallant gentleman, Captain L. E. G. Oates of the Inniskilling Dragoons. In March 1912, returning from the Pole, he walked willingly to his death in a blizzard to try and save his comrades, beset by hardships.

E. L. Atkinson 1882–1929 and **Apsley Cherry-Garrard** 1882–1959: epitaph on cairn erected in the Antarctic, 15 November 1912

8 I should like my epitaph to say, 'He helped people see God in the ordinary things of life, and he made children laugh.'

Revd W. Awdry 1911–97: in *Independent* 22 March 1997

9 When I am dead, I hope it may be said:
'His sins were scarlet, but his books were read.'

Hilaire Belloc 1870–1953: 'On His Books' (1923)

10 Their bodies are buried in peace; but their name liveth for evermore.

Bible: Ecclesiasticus

11 They shall grow not old, as we that are left grow old.

Age shall not weary them, nor the years condemn.
At the going down of the sun and in the morning
We will remember them.

■ *particularly associated with Remembrance Day services*

Laurence Binyon 1869–1943: 'For the Fallen' (1914)

12 Alan died suddenly at Saltwood on Sunday 5th September. He said he would like it to be stated that he regarded himself as having gone to join Tom and the other dogs.

Alan Clark 1928–99: announcement in *The Times* 8 September 1999

13 The only thing that really saddens me over my demise is that I shall not be here to read the nonsense that will be written about me . . . There will be lists of apocryphal jokes I never made and gleeful misquotations of words I never said. *What* a pity I shan't be here to enjoy them!

Noël Coward 1899–1973: diary 19 March 1955

14 When you go home, tell them of us and say,
'For your tomorrows these gave their today.'

■ *particularly associated with the dead of the Burma campaign of the Second World War, in the form 'For your tomorrow we gave our today.'*

John Maxwell Edmonds 1875–1958: *Inscriptions Suggested for War Memorials* (1919)

15 Here lies W. C. Fields. I would rather be living in Philadelphia.

■ *suggested epitaph for himself*

W. C. Fields 1880–1946: in *Vanity Fair* June 1925

16 Life is a jest; and all things show it.
I thought so once; but now I know it.

John Gay 1685–1732: 'My Own Epitaph' (1720)

17 His foe was folly and his weapon wit.

Anthony Hope 1863–1933: inscription on W. S. Gilbert's memorial on the Victoria Embankment, London, 1915

18 Here lies one whose name was writ in water.

■ *epitaph for himself*
John Keats 1795–1821: Richard Monckton Milnes *Life, Letters and Literary Remains of John Keats* (1848)

19 John Le Mesurier wishes it to be known that he conked out on November 15th. He sadly misses family and friends.

John Le Mesurier 1912–83: obituary notice in *The Times* 16 November 1983

20 Here lie I, Martin Elginbrodde:
Hae mercy o' my soul, Lord God;
As I wad do, were I Lord God,
And ye were Martin Elginbrodde.

George MacDonald 1824–1905: *David Elginbrod* (1863)

21 Excuse My Dust.

■ *suggested epitaph for herself* (1925)
Dorothy Parker 1893–1967: Alexander Woollcott *While Rome Burns* (1934)

22 Here was the world's worst wound.
And here with pride
'Their name liveth for ever' the
Gateway claims.
Was ever an immolation so belied
As these intolerably nameless names?

Siegfried Sassoon 1886–1967: 'On Passing the New Menin Gate' (1928)

23 Good friend, for Jesu's sake forbear
To dig the dust enclosed here.
Blest be the man that spares these stones,
And curst be he that moves my bones.

William Shakespeare 1564–1616: epitaph on his tomb, probably composed by himself

24 Go, tell the Spartans, thou who passest by,
That here obedient to their laws we lie.

■ *epitaph for the Spartans who died at Thermopylae*
Simonides *c.*556–468 BC: attributed; Herodotus *Histories*

25 Without you, Heaven would be too dull to bear,

And Hell would not be Hell if you are there.

■ *epitaph for Maurice Bowra (1898–1971)*
John Sparrow 1906–92: in *Times Literary Supplement* 30 May 1975

26 This be the verse you grave for me:
'Here he lies where he longed to be;
Home is the sailor, home from sea,
And the hunter home from the hill.'

Robert Louis Stevenson 1850–94: 'Requiem' (1887)

27 Where fierce indignation can no longer tear his heart.

■ *Swift's epitaph*
Jonathan Swift 1667–1745: S. Leslie *The Skull of Swift* (1928)

28 I always thought I'd like my tombstone to be blank. No epitaph, and no name. Well, actually I'd like it to say 'figment'.

Andy Warhol 1927–87: *America* (1985)

Equality

see also **Human Rights**

1 There is no method by which men can be both free and equal.

Walter Bagehot 1826–77: in *The Economist* 5 September 1863

2 He maketh his sun to rise on the evil and on the good, and sendeth rain on the just and on the unjust.

Bible: St Matthew

3 A man's a man for a' that.

Robert Burns 1759–96: 'For a' that and a' that' (1790)

4 You can have equality or equality of opportunity; you cannot have both. Equality will mean the holding back (or the new deprivation) of the brighter children.

Brian Cox 1928– and **Rhodes Boyson** 1925– : *Black Paper 1975* (1975)

5 While there is a lower class, I am in it; while there is a criminal element, I am of it; while there is a soul in prison, I am not free.

Eugene Victor Debs 1855–1926: speech at his trial for sedition in Cleveland, Ohio, 14 September 1918

6 When every one is somebodee,
Then no one's anybody.
W. S. Gilbert 1836–1911: *The Gondoliers* (1889)

7 Sir, there is no settling the point of
precedency between a louse and a flea.
■ *on the relative merits of two minor poets*
Samuel Johnson 1709–84: James Boswell *Life
of Samuel Johnson* (1791) 1783

8 I have a dream that one day on the red
hills of Georgia the sons of former
slaves and the sons of former slave
owners will be able to sit down
together at the table of brotherhood.
Martin Luther King 1929–68: speech at Civil
Rights March in Washington, 28 August 1963

9 Oh, East is East, and West is West, and
never the twain shall meet,
Till Earth and Sky stand presently at
God's great Judgement Seat;
But there is neither East nor West,
Border, nor Breed, nor Birth,
When two strong men stand face to
face, tho' they come from the ends
of earth!
Rudyard Kipling 1865–1936: 'The Ballad of
East and West' (1892)

10 All animals are equal but some
animals are more equal than others.
George Orwell 1903–50: *Animal Farm* (1945)

11 Hath not a Jew eyes? hath not a Jew
hands, organs, dimensions, senses,
affections, passions? fed with the same
food, hurt with the same weapons,
subject to the same diseases, healed by
the same means, warmed and cooled
by the same winter and summer, as a
Christian is? If you prick us, do we not
bleed? if you tickle us, do we not
laugh? if you poison us, do we not die?
and if you wrong us, shall we not
revenge?
William Shakespeare 1564–1616: *The
Merchant of Venice* (1596–8)

12 Those who dread a dead-level of
income or wealth . . . do not dread, it
seems, a dead-level of law and order,
and of security for life and property.
R. H. Tawney 1880–1962: *Equality* (4th ed.,
1931)

13 Make all men equal today, and God
has so created them that they shall all
be unequal tomorrow.
Anthony Trollope 1815–82: *Autobiography*
(1883)

14 The constitution does not provide for
first and second class citizens.
Wendell Willkie 1892–1944: *An American
Programme* (1944)

Europe

see also **European Community**, **France**,
Greece, **International Relations**, **Italy**

1 It's where they commit suicide and
the king rides a bicycle, Sweden.
Alan Bennett 1934– : *Enjoy* (1980)

2 If you open that Pandora's Box, you
never know what Trojan 'orses will
jump out.
■ *on the Council of Europe*
Ernest Bevin 1881–1951: Roderick Barclay
Ernest Bevin and the Foreign Office (1975)

3 Whoever speaks of Europe is wrong,
[it is] a geographical concept.
Otto von Bismarck 1815–98: marginal note on
a letter from the Russian Chancellor
Gorchakov, November 1876

4 Fog in Channel—Continent isolated.
Russell Brockbank 1913– : newspaper placard
in cartoon, *Round the Bend with Brockbank*
(1948)

5 Belgium has only one real claim to
fame. Thanks to all the wars that have
been fought on its soil, there are more
dead people there than anywhere else
in the world. So, while there's no
quality of life in Belgium, there is a
simply wonderful quality of death.
Jeremy Clarkson 1960– : in *Sunday Times*
18 July 1999

6 They're Germans. Don't mention the
war.
John Cleese 1939– and **Connie Booth**: *Fawlty
Towers* 'The Germans' (BBC TV
programme, 1975)

7 Yes, it is Europe, from the Atlantic to
the Urals, it is Europe, it is the whole

of Europe, that will decide the fate of the world.

Charles de Gaulle 1890–1970: speech to the people of Strasbourg, 23 November 1959

8 Without Britain Europe would remain only a torso.

Ludwig Erhard 1897–1977: remark on West German television, 27 May 1962

9 Leave this Europe where they are never done talking of Man, yet murder men everywhere they find them.

Frantz Fanon 1925–61: *The Wretched of the Earth* (1961)

10 Purity of race does not exist. Europe is a continent of energetic mongrels.

H. A. L. Fisher 1856–1940: *A History of Europe* (1935)

11 What cleanliness everywhere! You dare not throw your cigarette into the lake. No graffiti in the urinals. Switzerland is proud of this; but I believe this is just what she lacks: manure.

André Gide 1869–1951: diary, Lucerne, 10 August 1917

12 The forest is the spiritual, mystical heart of Germany, the engine and the ultimate metaphor of their literature, poetry and music.

A. A. Gill 1954– : in *Sunday Times* 11 July 1999

13 In the eighteenth and nineteenth centuries you weren't considered cultured unless you made the European tour, and so it should be.

Edward Heath 1916– : in *Observer* 18 November 1990

14 The European view of a poet is not of much importance unless the poet writes in Esperanto.

A. E. Housman 1859–1936: in *Cambridge Review* 1915

15 We are part of the community of Europe and we must do our duty as such.

Lord Salisbury 1830–1903: speech at Caernarvon, 10 April 1888

16 Europe is in danger of plunging into a cold peace.

Boris Yeltsin 1931– : at the summit meeting of the Conference on Security and Co-operation in Europe, December 1994

The European Community

1 The EEC is a horse and carriage: Germany is the horse and France is the coachman.

Charles de Gaulle 1890–1970: attributed; Bernard Connolly *The Rotten Heart of Europe* (1995)

2 It means the end of a thousand years of history.

■ *on a European federation*
Hugh Gaitskell 1906–63: speech at Labour Party Conference, 3 October 1962

3 You can't wield a handbag from an empty chair.

Michael Heseltine 1933– : at the launch of Britain in Europe, 14 October 1999

4 The policy of European integration is in reality a question of war and peace in the 21st century.

Helmut Kohl 1930– : speech at Louvain University, 2 February 1996

5 'We went in ,' he said, 'to screw the French by splitting them off from the Germans. The French went in to protect their inefficient farmers from commercial competition. The Germans went in to cleanse themselves of genocide and apply for readmission to the human race.'

Jonathan Lynn 1943– and **Antony Jay** 1930– : *Yes, Minister* (1982) vol. 2

6 Whereas in England all is permitted that is not expressly prohibited, it has been said that in Germany all is prohibited unless expressly permitted and in France all is permitted that is expressly prohibited. In the European Common Market (as it then was) no-one knows what is permitted and it all costs more.

Robert Megarry 1910– : lecture, London, 22 March 1972

7 We should not create a nation Europe instead of a nation France.
   Jean Monnet 1888–1979: François Duchêne *Jean Monnet* (1994)

8 We have not successfully rolled back the frontiers of the State in Britain only to see them reimposed at European level, with a European super-State exercising a new dominance from Brussels.
   Margaret Thatcher 1925– : speech in Bruges, 20 September 1988

9 This 'going into Europe' will not turn out to be the thrilling mutual exchange supposed. It is more like nine middle-aged couples with failing marriages meeting in a darkened bedroom in a Brussels hotel for a Group Grope.
   E. P. Thompson 1924– : in *Sunday Times* 27 April 1975

Evening

see also **Day**, **Night**

1 Let us go then, you and I,
   When the evening is spread out against the sky
   Like a patient etherized upon a table.
   T. S. Eliot 1888–1965: 'The Love Song of J. Alfred Prufrock' (1917)

2 The curfew tolls the knell of parting day,
   The lowing herd wind slowly o'er the lea,
   The ploughman homeward plods his weary way,
   And leaves the world to darkness and to me.
   Thomas Gray 1716–71: *Elegy Written in a Country Churchyard* (1751)

3 I have a horror of sunsets, they're so romantic, so operatic.
   Marcel Proust 1871–1922: *Cities of the Plain* (1922)

4 It is a beauteous evening, calm and free;
   The holy time is quiet as a nun Breathless with adoration.
   William Wordsworth 1770–1850: 'It is a beauteous evening, calm and free' (1807)

Evil

see also **Sin**, **Virtue**

1 It was as though in those last minutes he [Eichmann] was summing up the lessons that this long course in human wickedness had taught us—the lesson of the fearsome, word-and-thought-defying *banality of evil*.
   Hannah Arendt 1906–75: *Eichmann in Jerusalem* (1963)

2 I and the public know
   What all schoolchildren learn,
   Those to whom evil is done
   Do evil in return.
   W. H. Auden 1907–73: 'September 1, 1939' (1940)

3 It's very different from living in academia in Oxford. We called someone vicious in the *Times Literary Supplement*. We didn't know what vicious was.
   ■ *on returning to Burma (Myanmar)*
   Aung San Suu Kyi 1945– : in *Observer* 25 September 1988

4 It is necessary only for the good man to do nothing for evil to triumph.
   Edmund Burke 1729–97: attributed (in a number of forms) to Burke, but not found in his writings

5 The face of 'evil' is always the face of total need.
   William S. Burroughs 1914–97: *The Naked Lunch* (1959)

6 As soon as men decide that all means are permitted to fight an evil, then their good becomes indistinguishable from the evil that they set out to destroy.
   Christopher Dawson 1889–1970: *The Judgement of the Nations* (1942)

7 Imagine that you are creating a fabric of human destiny with the object of making men happy in the end, giving them peace and rest at last, but that it was essential and inevitable to torture to death only one tiny creature . . . and to found that edifice on its unavenged tears, would you consent

to be the architect on those
conditions?

Fedor Dostoevsky 1821–81: *The Brothers
Karamazov* (1879–80)

8 What we call evil is simply ignorance
bumping its head in the dark.

Henry Ford 1863–1947: in *Observer* 16 March
1930

9 In my humble opinion, non-
cooperation with evil is as much a
duty as is cooperation with good.

Mahatma Gandhi 1869–1948: speech in
Ahmadabad, 23 March 1922

10 To respond to evil by committing
another evil does not eliminate evil
but allows it to go on forever.

Václav Havel 1936– : letter, 5 November 1989

11 Farewell remorse! All good to me is
lost;
Evil, be thou my good.

John Milton 1608–74: *Paradise Lost* (1667)

12 There is nothing either good or bad,
but thinking makes it so.

William Shakespeare 1564–1616: *Hamlet*
(1601)

Examinations

1 I wrote my name at the top of the
page. I wrote down the number of the
question '1'. After much reflection I
put a bracket round it thus '(1)'. But
thereafter I could not think of
anything connected with it that was
either relevant or true. . . . It was from
these slender indications of
scholarship that Mr Welldon drew the
conclusion that I was worthy to pass
into Harrow. It is very much to his
credit.

Winston Churchill 1874–1965: *My Early Life*
(1930)

2 Examinations are formidable even to
the best prepared, for the greatest fool
may ask more than the wisest man
can answer.

Charles Caleb Colton c.1780–1832: *Lacon*
(1820)

3 I evidently knew more about
economics than my examiners.

■ *explaining why he performed badly in the
Civil Service examinations*

John Maynard Keynes 1883–1946: Roy Harrod
Life of John Maynard Keynes (1951)

4 Four times, under our educational
rules, the human pack is shuffled and
cut—at eleven-plus, sixteen-plus,
eighteen-plus and twenty-plus—and
happy is he who comes top of the deck
on each occasion, but especially the
last. This is called Finals, the very
name of which implies that nothing of
importance can happen after it.

David Lodge 1935– : *Changing Places* (1975)

5 If we have to have an exam at 11, let us
make it one for humour, sincerity,
imagination, character—and where is
the examiner who could test such
qualities.

A. S. Neill 1883–1973: letter to *Daily Telegraph*,
1957

6 In examinations those who do not
wish to know ask questions of those
who cannot tell.

Walter Raleigh 1861–1922: *Laughter from a
Cloud* (1923)

7 Do not on any account attempt to
write on both sides of the paper at
once.

W. C. Sellar 1898–1951 and **R. J. Yeatman**
1898–1968: *1066 and All That* (1930) 'Test
Paper 5'

8 Had silicon been a gas, I would have
been a major-general by now.

■ *having been found 'deficient in chemistry' in a
West Point examination*

James McNeill Whistler 1834–1903: E. R. and J.
Pennell *The Life of James McNeill Whistler*
(1908)

Excellence

see also **Perfection**

1 The dullard's envy of brilliant men is
always assuaged by the suspicion that
they will come to a bad end.

Max Beerbohm 1872–1956: *Zuleika Dobson*
(1911)

2 The danger chiefly lies in acting well;
No crime's so great as daring to excel.
Charles Churchill 1731–64: *An Epistle to William Hogarth* (1763)

3 The pretension is nothing; the performance every thing. A good apple is better than an insipid peach.
Leigh Hunt 1784–1859: *The Story of Rimini* (1832 ed.)

4 The best is the best, though a hundred judges have declared it so.
Arthur Quiller-Couch 1863–1944: *Oxford Book of English Verse* (1900) preface

5 The best is the enemy of the good.
Voltaire 1694–1778: *Contes* (1772) 'La Begueule'; derived from an Italian proverb

6 The best lack all conviction, while the worst
Are full of passionate intensity.
W. B. Yeats 1865–1939: 'The Second Coming' (1921)

Excuses
see **Apology and Excuses**

Executions

1 Let's do it!
■ *to the firing squad at his execution; after his conviction for murder, Gilmore had refused to appeal, and petitioned the Supreme Court that the execution should be carried out*
Gary Gilmore 1941–77: Norman Mailer *The Executioner's Song* (1979)

2 Depend upon it, Sir, when a man knows he is to be hanged in a fortnight, it concentrates his mind wonderfully.
■ *on the execution of Dr Dodd*
Samuel Johnson 1709–84: James Boswell *Life of Samuel Johnson* (1791) 19 September 1777

3 No more hanging? . . . What's this country coming to!
Patrick McCabe 1955– : *The Butcher Boy* (1992)

4 We were terribly lucky to catch
The Ceauşescus' execution, being
By sheer chance that Christmas Day
In the only house for twenty miles
With satellite TV. We sat,
Cradling brandies, by the fire
Watching those two small, cranky autocrats
Lying in snow against a blood-spattered wall,
Hardly able to believe our good fortune.
Bernard O'Donoghue 1945– : 'Carolling' (1995)

5 This is the death I should have asked for if God had given me the choice of all deaths—to die a soldier's death for Ireland and freedom.
Patrick Pearse 1879–1916: letter to his mother, May 1916

6 I went out to Charing Cross, to see Major-general Harrison hanged, drawn, and quartered; which was done there, he looking as cheerful as any man could do in that condition.
Samuel Pepys 1633–1703: diary 13 October 1660

7 'Tis a sharp remedy, but a sure one for all ills.
■ *on feeling the edge of the axe prior to his execution*
Walter Ralegh *c.*1552–1618: D. Hume *History of Great Britain* (1754)

8 I hate victims who respect their executioners.
Jean-Paul Sartre 1905–80: *Les Séquestrés d'Altona* (1960)

Exercise
see also **Health**

1 If you walk hard enough, you probably don't need any other God.
Bruce Chatwin 1940–89: *In Patagonia* (1977)

2 Exercise is the yuppie version of bulimia.
Barbara Ehrenreich 1941– : *The Worst Years of Our Lives* (1991) 'Food Worship'

3 Exercise is bunk. If you are healthy, you don't need it: if you are sick you shouldn't take it.
Henry Ford 1863–1947: attributed

4 The sovereign invigorator of the body is exercise, and of all the exercises, walking is best.

Thomas Jefferson 1743–1826: letter to Thomas Mann Randolph Jr., 27 August 1786

5 The only exercise I take is walking behind the coffins of friends who took exercise.

Peter O'Toole 1932– : in *Mail on Sunday* 27 December 1998

Exile

1 Once we had a country and we thought it fair,
Look in the atlas and you'll find it there:
We cannot go there now, my dear, we cannot go there now.

W. H. Auden 1907–73: 'Refugee Blues' (1940)

2 No longer shall our children, like our cattle, be brought up for export.

Eamon de Valera 1882–1975: speech in Dáil Éireann, 1934

3 The country wears their going like a scar.
Today their relatives save to support and
Send others in planes for the new diaspora.

Sean Dunne 1956–97: 'Letter from Ireland' (1991)

4 Fair these broad meads, these hoary woods are grand;
But we are exiles from our fathers' land.

John Galt 1779–1839: 'Canadian Boat Song' (1829); translated from the Gaelic; attributed

5 For an exile, there are no continuities, merely succession.

Candia McWilliam 1955– : *Debatable Land* (1994)

6 What captivity was to the Jews, exile has been to the Irish. America and American influence has educated them.

Oscar Wilde 1854–1900: in *Pall Mall Gazette* 13 April 1889

Experience

see also **Maturity**

1 All experience is an arch to build upon.

Henry Brooks Adams 1838–1918: *The Education of Henry Adams* (1907)

2 You should make a point of trying every experience once, excepting incest and folk-dancing.

Anonymous: Arnold Bax (1883–1953), quoting 'a sympathetic Scot'; *Farewell My Youth* (1943)

3 Experience isn't interesting till it begins to repeat itself—in fact, till it does that, it hardly *is* experience.

Elizabeth Bowen 1899–1973: *Death of the Heart* (1938)

4 I learned . . . that one can never go back, that one should not ever try to go back—that the essence of life is going forward. Life is really a One Way Street.

Agatha Christie 1890–1976: *At Bertram's Hotel* (1965)

5 The light which experience gives is a lantern on the stern, which shines only on the waves behind us!

Samuel Taylor Coleridge 1772–1834: *Table Talk* (1835) 18 December 1831

6 The courtiers who surround him have forgotten nothing and learnt nothing.

■ *of Louis XVIII*

Charles François du Périer Dumouriez 1739–1823: at the time of the Declaration of Verona, September 1795; quoted by Napoleon in his Declaration to the French on his return from Elba; a similar saying is attributed to Talleyrand

7 We had the experience but missed the meaning.

T. S. Eliot 1888–1965: *Four Quartets* 'The Dry Salvages' (1941)

8 The years teach much which the days never know.

Ralph Waldo Emerson 1803–82: *Essays. Second Series* (1844) 'Experience'

9 Damaged people are dangerous. They know they can survive.

Josephine Hart: *Damage* (1991)

10 Experience is not what happens to a man; it is what a man does with what happens to him.
Aldous Huxley 1894–1963: *Texts and Pretexts* (1932)

11 I've looked at life from both sides now,
From win and lose and still somehow
It's life's illusions I recall;
I really don't know life at all.
Joni Mitchell 1945– : 'Both Sides Now' (1967 song)

12 *after George Bush had laid stress on the value of experience in the 1992 presidential debates:*
I don't have any experience in running up a $4 trillion debt.
H. Ross Perot 1930– : in *Newsweek* 19 October 1992

13 Education is when you read the fine print; experience is what you get when you don't.
Pete Seeger 1919– : L. Botts *Loose Talk* (1980)

14 *Experto credite.*
Trust one who has gone through it.
Virgil 70–19 BC: *Aeneid*

15 I've been things and seen places.
Mae West 1892–1980: *I'm No Angel* (1933 film)

16 *replying to the question: 'For two days' labour, you ask two hundred guineas?':*
No, I ask it for the knowledge of a lifetime.
James McNeill Whistler 1834–1903: in his case against Ruskin; D. C. Seitz *Whistler Stories* (1913)

17 Experience is the name every one gives to their mistakes.
Oscar Wilde 1854–1900: *Lady Windermere's Fan* (1892)

Experiment

see also **Facts**, **Science**, **Theory**

1 Nothing is too wonderful to be true, if it be consistent with the laws of nature, and in such things as these, experiment is the best test of such consistency.
Michael Faraday 1791–1867: diary, 19 March 1849

2 The best scale for an experiment is 12 inches to a foot.
John Arbuthnot Fisher 1841–1920: *Memories* (1919)

3 It may be so, there is no arguing against facts and experiments.
■ *when told of an experiment which appeared to destroy his theory*
Isaac Newton 1642–1727: reported by John Conduit, 1726

4 Where observation is concerned, chance favours only the prepared mind.
Louis Pasteur 1822–95: address given on the inauguration of the Faculty of Science, University of Lille, 7 December 1854

5 Aristotle maintained that women have fewer teeth than men; although he was twice married, it never occurred to him to verify this statement by examining his wives' mouths.
Bertrand Russell 1872–1970: *The Impact of Science on Society* (1952)

6 It is much easier to make measurements than to know exactly what you are measuring.
J. W. N. Sullivan 1886–1937: comment, 1928

7 An experiment is a device to make Nature speak intelligibly. After that one has only to listen.
George Wald 1904–97: in *Science* vol. 162 (1968)

Experts

see also **Knowledge**

1 Too bad that all the people who know how to run the country are busy driving taxicabs and cutting hair.
George Burns 1896–1996: in *Life* December 1979

2 An expert is one who knows more and more about less and less.
Nicholas Murray Butler 1862–1947: commencement address at Columbia University; attributed

3 Experts have their expert fun

ex-cathedra
telling one
just how nothing
can be done.
Piet Hein 1905– : 'Experts' (1966)

4 An expert is someone who knows
some of the worst mistakes that can be
made in his subject and who manages
to avoid them.
Werner Heisenberg 1901–76: *Der Teil und das
Ganze* (1969)

5 No lesson seems to be so deeply
inculcated by the experience of life as
that you never should trust experts. If
you believe the doctors, nothing is
wholesome: if you believe the
theologians, nothing is innocent: if
you believe the soldiers, nothing is
safe. They all require to have their
strong wine diluted by a very large
admixture of insipid common sense.
Lord Salisbury 1830–1903: letter to Lord
Lytton, 15 June 1877

Exploration

see also **Maps**, **Travel**

1 Why do people so love to wander? I
think the civilized parts of the world
will suffice for me in the future.
Mary Cassatt 1844–1926: letter to Louisine
Havemeyer, 11 February 1911

2 Polar exploration is at once the
cleanest and most isolated way of
having a bad time which has been
devised.
Apsley Cherry-Garrard 1882–1959: *The Worst
Journey in the World* (1922)

3 It was a melancholy day for human
nature when that stupid Lord Anson,
after beating about for three years,
found himself again at Greenwich.
The circumnavigation of our globe
was accomplished, but the illimitable
was annihilated and a fatal blow
[dealt] to all imagination.
Benjamin Disraeli 1804–81: written 1860, in
Reminiscences (ed. H. and M. Swartz, 1975)

4 We shall not cease from exploration
And the end of all our exploring

Will be to arrive where we started
And know the place for the first time.
T. S. Eliot 1888–1965: *Four Quartets* 'Little
Gidding' (1942)

5 Everybody in fifteenth-century Spain
was wrong about where China was
and as a result, Columbus discovered
Caribbean vacations.
P. J. O'Rourke 1947– : *Parliament of Whores*
(1991)

6 These are the voyages of the starship
Enterprise. Its five-year mission . . . to
boldly go where no man has gone
before.
Gene Roddenberry 1921–91: *Star Trek*
(television series, from 1966)

7 Great God! this is an awful place.
■ *of the South Pole*
Robert Falcon Scott 1868–1912: diary
17 January 1912

8 Go West, young man, go West!
John L. B. Soule 1815–91: in *Terre Haute*
[Indiana] *Express* (1851)

9   I am become a name;
For always roaming with a hungry
heart
Alfred, Lord Tennyson 1809–92: 'Ulysses'
(1842)

10 There is no land unhabitable nor sea
innavigable.
Robert Thorne d. 1527: Richard Hakluyt *The
Principal Navigations, Voyages, and
Discoveries of the English Nation* (1589)

The Face

see also **Cosmetics**

1 My face looks like a wedding-cake left
out in the rain.
W. H. Auden 1907–73: Humphrey Carpenter
W. H. Auden (1981)

2 I think your whole life shows in your
face and you should be proud of that.
Lauren Bacall 1924– : in *Daily Telegraph*
2 March 1988

3 A merry heart maketh a cheerful
countenance.
Bible: Proverbs

4 Was this the face that launched a
thousand ships,
And burnt the topless towers of Ilium?
Sweet Helen, make me immortal with
a kiss!
Christopher Marlowe 1564–93: *Doctor Faustus*
(1604)

5 At 50, everyone has the face he
deserves.
George Orwell 1903–50: last words in his
notebook, 17 April 1949

6 Had Cleopatra's nose been shorter,
the whole face of the world would
have changed.
Blaise Pascal 1623–62: *Pensées* (1670)

7 Her face, at first . . . just ghostly
Turned a whiter shade of pale.
Keith Reid 1946– : 'A Whiter Shade of Pale'
(1967 song)

8 A large nose is in fact the sign of an
affable man, good, courteous, witty,
liberal, courageous, such as I am.
Edmond Rostand 1868–1918: *Cyrano de
Bergerac* (1897)

9 There's no art
To find the mind's construction in the
face.
William Shakespeare 1564–1616: *Macbeth*
(1606)

10 Bah! the thing is not a nose at all, but
a bit of primordial chaos clapped on
to my face.
H. G. Wells 1866–1946: *Select Conversations
with an Uncle* (1895) 'The Man with a Nose'

Facts

see also **Theory**

1 Now, what I want is, Facts . . . Facts
alone are wanted in life.
Charles Dickens 1812–70: *Hard Times* (1854)

2 Facts do not cease to exist because
they are ignored.
Aldous Huxley 1894–1963: *Proper Studies*
(1927)

3 Roundabout the accredited and
orderly fact of every science there ever
floats a sort of dust cloud of

exceptional observations, of
occurences minute and irregular and
seldom met with, which it always
proves more easy to ignore than to
attend to.
William James 1842–1910: attributed

4 If it looks like a duck, walks like a
duck and quacks like a duck, then it
just may be a duck.
■ *as a test, during the McCarthy era, of
Communist affiliations*
Walter Reuther 1907–70: attributed

5 Some circumstantial evidence is very
strong, as when you find a trout in the
milk.
Henry David Thoreau 1817–62: diary,
11 November 1850

Failure

see also **Defeat, Success**

1 Ever tried. Ever failed. No matter. Try
again. Fail again. Fail better.
Samuel Beckett 1906–89: *Worstward Ho*
(1983)

2 The world is made of people who
never quite get into the first team and
who just miss the prizes at the flower
show.
Jacob Bronowski 1908–74: *Face of Violence*
(1954)

3 The conduct of a losing party never
appears right: at least it never can
possess the only infallible criterion of
wisdom to vulgar judgements—
success.
Edmund Burke 1729–97: *Letter to a Member of
the National Assembly* (1791)

4 'Tis better to have fought and lost,
Than never to have fought at all.
Arthur Hugh Clough 1819–61: 'Peschiera'
(1854)

5 And all my endeavours are unlucky
explorers
come back, abandoning the
expedition.
Keith Douglas 1920–44: 'On Return from
Egypt, 1943–4' (1946)

6 I don't think we have failed, we have just found another way that doesn't work.

■ *on the ending of an attempted round-the-world balloon flight*

Andy Elson: comment, Hamamatsu, Japan, 7 March 1999

7 There is only one step from the sublime to the ridiculous.

■ *to De Pradt, Polish ambassador, after the retreat from Moscow in 1812*

Napoleon I 1769–1821: D. G. De Pradt *Histoire de l'Ambassade dans le grand-duché de Varsovie en 1812* (1815)

8 MACBETH: If we should fail,—
LADY MACBETH: We fail!
But screw your courage to the sticking-place,
And we'll not fail.

William Shakespeare 1564–1616: *Macbeth* (1606)

9 You [the Mensheviks] are pitiful isolated individuals; you are bankrupts; your role is played out. Go where you belong from now on—into the dustbin of history!

Leon Trotsky 1879–1940: *History of the Russian Revolution* (1933)

10 Anybody seen in a bus over the age of 30 has been a failure in life.

Loelia, Duchess of Westminster 1902–93: in *The Times* 4 November 1993; habitual remark

Faith

....

see also **Belief**

1 The Sea of Faith
Was once, too, at the full, and round earth's shore
Lay like the folds of a bright girdle furled.
But now I only hear
Its melancholy, long, withdrawing roar.

Matthew Arnold 1822–88: 'Dover Beach' (1867)

2 We're now paying the price for the Eighties and Lord Runcie's kind of effete, liberal elitism amongst bishops which also spread into the theological colleges. There is now a big gap between the faith of those in the pulpit and those in the pews.

George Austin 1931– : in *Guardian* 7 February 1997

3 A faith is something you die for; a doctrine is something you kill for: there is all the difference in the world.

Tony Benn 1925– : in *Observer* 16 April 1989

4 Yes, I believe in God.

■ *reply to gunman*

Cassie Bernall 1981–99: attributed last words, Columbine High School, Littleton, Colorado, 20 April 1999; the words have also been attributed to a survivor

5 Faith without works is dead.

Bible: James

6 The faith that stands on authority is not faith.

Ralph Waldo Emerson 1803–82: *Essays* (1841) 'The Over-Soul'

7 And I said to the man who stood at the gate of the year: 'Give me a light that I may tread safely into the unknown.'
And he replied:
'Go out into the darkness and put your hand into the Hand of God. That shall be to you better than light and safer than a known way.'

■ *quoted by King George VI in his Christmas broadcast, 25 December 1939*

Minnie Louise Haskins 1875–1957: *Desert* (1908) 'God Knows'

8 The great act of faith is when a man decides he is not God.

Oliver Wendell Holmes Jr. 1841–1935: letter to William James, 24 March 1907

9 A man with God is always in the majority.

John Knox c.1505–72: inscription on the Reformation Monument, Geneva

10 Faith may be defined briefly as an illogical belief in the occurrence of the improbable.

H. L. Mencken 1880–1956: *Prejudices* (1922)

11 A miracle, my friend, is an event which creates faith. That is the purpose and nature of miracles....Frauds deceive. An event

which creates faith does not deceive:
therefore it is not a fraud, but a
miracle.

George Bernard Shaw 1856–1950: *Saint Joan*
(1924)

12 'Tis not the dying for a faith that's so
hard, Master Harry—every man of
every nation has done that—'tis the
living up to it that is difficult.

William Makepeace Thackeray 1811–63: *The
History of Henry Esmond* (1852)

13 In the darkness . . . the sound of a
man
Breathing, testing his faith
On emptiness, nailing his questions
One by one to an untenanted cross.

R. S. Thomas 1913–2000: 'Pietà' (1966)

Faithfulness
....

see also **Commitment**, **Loyalty**

1 I'll love you, dear, I'll love you
Till China and Africa meet
And the river jumps over the
mountain
And the salmon sing in the street,

I'll love you till the ocean
Is folded and hung up to dry
And the seven stars go squawking
Like geese about the sky.

W. H. Auden 1907–73: 'As I Walked Out One
Evening' (1940)

2 Sexual fidelity is more important in a
homosexual relationship than in any
other. In other relationships there are
a variety of ties. But here, fidelity is
the only bond.

W. H. Auden 1907–73: Nicholas Jenkins (ed.)
Table Talk of W. H. Auden (1990) 20 October
1947

3 There is no infidelity when there has
been no love.

Honoré de Balzac 1799–1850: letter to Mme
Hanska, August 1833

4 It is better to be unfaithful than
faithful without wanting to be.

Brigitte Bardot 1934– : in *Observer*
18 February 1968

5 The highest level of sexual excitement
is in a monogamous relationship.

Warren Beatty 1937– : in *Observer*
27 October 1991

6 You're . . . turning into a kind of serial
monogamist.

Richard Curtis 1956– : *Four Weddings and a
Funeral* (1994 film)

7 But I was desolate and sick of an old
passion,
Yea, all the time, because the dance
was long:
I have been faithful to thee, Cynara! in
my fashion.

Ernest Dowson 1867–1900: 'Non Sum Qualis
Eram' (1896); also known as 'Cynara'

8 Bright star, would I were steadfast as
thou art—.

John Keats 1795–1821: 'Bright star, would I
were steadfast as thou art' (written 1819)

9 No, the heart that has truly loved
never forgets,
But as truly loves on to the close,
As the sun-flower turns on her god,
when he sets,
The same look which she turned
when he rose.

Thomas Moore 1779–1852: 'Believe me, if all
those endearing young charms' (1807)

10 But I'm always true to you, darlin', in
my fashion.
Yes I'm always true to you, darlin', in
my way.

Cole Porter 1891–1964: 'Always True to You in
my Fashion' (1949 song)

11 But true love is a durable fire,
In the mind ever burning,
Never sick, never old, never dead,
From itself never turning.

Walter Ralegh *c.*1552–1618: 'Walsinghame'

12 Your idea of fidelity is not having
more than one man in bed at the same
time.

Frederic Raphael 1931– : *Darling* (1965)

13 If I could pray to move, prayers would
move me;

But I am constant as the northern star.
William Shakespeare 1564–1616: *Julius Caesar* (1599)

14 My true love hath my heart and I have his,
By just exchange one for the other giv'n.
Philip Sidney 1554–86: *Arcadia* (1581)

15 His honour rooted in dishonour stood,
And faith unfaithful kept him falsely true.
Alfred, Lord Tennyson 1809–92: *Idylls of the King* 'Lancelot and Elaine' (1859)

Falklands War 1982

1 GOTCHA!
Anonymous: headline on the sinking of the *General Belgrano*, in *Sun* 4 May 1982

2 The Falklands thing was a fight between two bald men over a comb.
Jorge Luis Borges 1899–1986: in *Time* 14 February 1983

3 I counted them all out and I counted them all back.
■ *on the number of British aeroplanes (which he was not permitted to disclose) joining the raid on Port Stanley in the Falkland Islands*
Brian Hanrahan 1949– : BBC broadcast report, 1 May 1982

4 This was the kind of war which existed in order to produce victory parades.
■ *of the Falklands War*
Eric Hobsbawm 1917– : in *Marxism Today* January 1983

5 Just rejoice at that news and congratulate our forces and the Marines . . . Rejoice!
■ *on the recapture of South Georgia; usually quoted as 'Rejoice, rejoice'*
Margaret Thatcher 1925– : to newsmen outside Downing Street, 25 April 1982

6 We have to see that the spirit of the South Atlantic—the real spirit of Britain—is kindled not only by war but can now be fired by peace. We have the first prerequisite. We know

that we can do it—we haven't lost the ability. That is the Falklands Factor.
Margaret Thatcher 1925– : speech in Cheltenham, 3 July 1982

Fame

see also **Reputation**

1 What price glory?
Maxwell Anderson 1888–1959: title of play (1924, with Lawrence Stallings)

2 Now who is responsible for this work of development on which so much depends? To whom must the praise be given? To the boys in the back rooms. They do not sit in the limelight. But they are the men who do the work.
Lord Beaverbrook 1879–1964: in *Listener* 27 March 1941

3 There's no such thing as bad publicity except your own obituary.
Brendan Behan 1923–64: Dominic Behan *My Brother Brendan* (1965)

4 Oh, the self-importance of fading stars. Never mind, they will be black holes one day.
Jeffrey Bernard 1932–97: in *The Spectator* 18 July 1992

5 He's always backing into the limelight.
■ *of T. E. Lawrence*
Lord Berners 1883–1950: oral tradition

6 The celebrity is a person who is known for his well-knownness.
Daniel J. Boorstin 1914– : *The Image* (1961)

7 I awoke one morning and found myself famous.
■ *on the instantaneous success of* Childe Harold
Lord Byron 1788–1824: Thomas Moore *Letters and Journals of Lord Byron* (1830)

8 If Oasis are bigger than God, what does that make us? Bigger than Buddha?
■ *asserting that the Spice Girls are 'a darn sight bigger than Oasis'*
Melanie ('Mel C.') Chisholm 1974– : in *Independent* 16 August 1997; cf. **Rock and Pop Music** 2

9 I don't care what you say about me, as long as you say *something* about me,

and as long as you spell my name right.

■ *said to a newspaperman in 1912*
George M. Cohan 1878–1942: John McCabe *George M. Cohan* (1973)

10 Fancy being remembered around the world for the invention of a mouse!
Walt Disney 1901–66: during his last illness; Leonard Mosley *Disney's World* (1985)

11 The deed is all, the glory nothing.
Johann Wolfgang von Goethe 1749–1832: *Faust* pt. 2 (1832)

12 Full many a flower is born to blush unseen,
And waste its sweetness on the desert air.
Thomas Gray 1716–71: *Elegy Written in a Country Churchyard* (1751)

13 Every man has a lurking wish to appear considerable in his native place.
Samuel Johnson 1709–84: letter to Joshua Reynolds, 17 July 1771

14 O the flummery of a birth place! Cant! Cant! Cant! It is enough to give a spirit the guts-ache.
■ *on visiting Burns's birthplace*
John Keats 1795–1821: letter to John Hamilton Reynolds, 11 July 1818

15 Being in the public eye, as Monica Lewinsky will be for the rest of her life, is like being the lady with the moustache at the circus. You're a curiosity—and you will never stop being one.
Christine Keeler 1942– : attributed, in *The Times* 13 March 1999

16 The best fame is a writer's fame: it's enough to get a table at a good restaurant, but not enough that you get interrupted when you eat.
Fran Lebowitz 1946– : in *Observer* 30 May 1993

17 We're more popular than Jesus now; I don't know which will go first—rock 'n' roll or Christianity.
■ *of The Beatles*
John Lennon 1940–80: interview in *Evening Standard* 4 March 1966

18 When . . . you're first famous and you're flush with your influence and you say something whimsical, at a party or something to be cool, it gets reported for real.
Courtney Love 1965– : interview in *Guardian* 28 February 1997

19 Fame is the spur that the clear spirit doth raise
(That last infirmity of noble mind)
To scorn delights, and live laborious days.
John Milton 1608–74: 'Lycidas' (1638)

20 A very quiet and tasteful way to be famous is to have a famous relation. Then you can not only be nothing, you can do nothing, too.
P. J. O'Rourke 1947– : *Modern Manners* (1984)

21 So long as men can breathe, or eyes can see,
So long lives this, and this gives life to thee.
William Shakespeare 1564–1616: sonnet 18

22 Martyrdom . . . the only way in which a man can become famous without ability.
George Bernard Shaw 1856–1950: *The Devil's Disciple* (1901)

23 Celebrity is good for kick-starting ideas, but often celebrity is a lead weight around your neck. It's like you pointing at the moon, but people are looking at your finger.
■ *on campaigning*
Sting 1951– : in *Mojo* February 1995

24 Celebrity is a mask that eats into the face.
John Updike 1932– : *Self-Consciousness: Memoirs* (1989)

25 In the future everybody will be world famous for fifteen minutes.
Andy Warhol 1927–87: *Andy Warhol* (1968)

26 It's better to be looked over than overlooked.
Mae West 1892–1980: *Belle of the Nineties* (1934 film)

Familiarity

1 A prophet is not without honour, save in his own country, and in his own house.
   Bible: St Matthew

2 Think you, if Laura had been Petrarch's wife,
   He would have written sonnets all his life?
   Lord Byron 1788–1824: *Don Juan* (1819–24)

3 There is nothing that God hath established in a constant course of nature, and which therefore is done every day, but would seem a Miracle, and exercise our admiration, if it were done but once.
   John Donne 1572–1631: *LXXX Sermons* (1640) Easter Day, 25 March 1627

4 A maggot must be born i' the rotten cheese to like it.
   George Eliot 1819–80: *Adam Bede* (1859)

5 I've grown accustomed to the trace Of something in the air;
   Accustomed to her face.
   Alan Jay Lerner 1918–86: 'I've Grown Accustomed to her Face' (1956 song)

6 Old friends are best. King James used to call for his old shoes; they were easiest for his feet.
   John Selden 1584–1654: *Table Talk* (1689) 'Friends'

7 There are no conditions of life to which a man cannot get accustomed, especially if he sees them accepted by everyone about him.
   Leo Tolstoy 1828–1910: *Anna Karenina* (1875–7)

8 Familiarity breeds contempt—and children.
   Mark Twain 1835–1910: *Notebooks* (1935)

The Family

see also **Children**, **In-Laws**, **Parents**

1 He that hath wife and children hath given hostages to fortune; for they are impediments to great enterprises, either of virtue or mischief.
   Francis Bacon 1561–1626: *Essays* (1625) 'Of Marriage and the Single Life'

2 The worst families are those in which the members never really speak their minds to one another; they maintain an atmosphere of unreality, and everyone always lives in an atmosphere of suppressed ill-feeling.
   Walter Bagehot 1826–77: *The English Constitution* (ed. 2, 1872) introduction

3 I have never understood this liking for war. It panders to instincts already catered for within the scope of any respectable domestic establishment.
   Alan Bennett 1934– : *Forty Years On* (1969)

4 We begin our public affections in our families. No cold relation is a zealous citizen.
   Edmund Burke 1729–97: *Reflections on the Revolution in France* (1790)

5 The truth is that it is not the sins of the fathers that descend unto the third generation, but the sorrows of the mothers.
   Marilyn French 1929– : *Her Mother's Daughter* (1987)

6 I am the family face;
   Flesh perishes, I live on,
   Projecting trait and trace
   Through time to times anon,
   And leaping from place to place
   Over oblivion.
   Thomas Hardy 1840–1928: 'Heredity' (1917)

7 Far from being the basis of the good society, the family, with its narrow privacy and tawdry secrets, is the source of all our discontents.
   Edmund Leach 1910– : BBC Reith Lectures, 1967

8 One would be in less danger
   From the wiles of the stranger
   If one's own kin and kith
   Were more fun to be with.
   Ogden Nash 1902–71: 'Family Court' (1931)

9 Family history, of course, has its proper dietary laws. One is supposed to swallow and digest only the

permitted parts of it, the halal portions of the past, drained of their redness, their blood.
Salman Rushdie 1947– : *Midnight's Children* (1981)

10 In each family some emotions are regarded as 'good' and some as 'bad'. The bad ones get put behind the screen and the entire family has a kind of unspoken but very powerful agreement that the feelings behind the screen mustn't be noticed.
Robin Skynner 1922– and **John Cleese** 1939– : *Families and How to Survive Them* (1983)

11 I detest collaterals. Blood may be thicker than water, but it is also a great deal nastier.
Edith Œ Somerville 1858–1949 and **Martin Ross** 1862–1915: *Some Experiences of an Irish R.M.* (1899)

12 She knew one of the great family truths, that aunts always help, while moms always think it would be good for you if you did it yourself.
Jane Smiley 1949– : *A Thousand Acres* (1991)

13 Family! . . . the home of all social evil, a charitable institution for comfortable women, an anchorage for house-fathers, and a hell for children.
August Strindberg 1849–1912: *The Son of a Servant* (1886)

14 If a man's character is to be abused, say what you will, there's nobody like a relation to do the business.
William Makepeace Thackeray 1811–63: *Vanity Fair* (1847–8)

15 All happy families resemble one another, but each unhappy family is unhappy in its own way.
Leo Tolstoy 1828–1910: *Anna Karenina* (1875–7)

16 Relations are simply a tedious pack of people, who haven't got the remotest knowledge of how to live, nor the smallest instinct about when to die.
Oscar Wilde 1854–1900: *The Importance of Being Earnest* (1899)

17 No test tube can breed love and affection. No frozen packet of semen ever read a story to a sleepy child.
Shirley Williams 1930– : in *Daily Mirror* 2 March 1978

18 It is no use telling me that there are bad aunts and good aunts. At the core, they are all alike. Sooner or later, out pops the cloven hoof.
P. G. Wodehouse 1881–1975: *The Code of the Woosters* (1938)

Famine

see also **Aid and Development**

1 They that die by famine die by inches.
Matthew Henry 1662–1714: *An Exposition on the Old and New Testament* (1710)

2 Clay is the word and clay is the flesh Where the potato-gatherers like mechanized scarecrows move Along the side-fall of the hill— Maguire and his men.
Patrick Kavanagh 1904–67: 'The Great Hunger' (1947)

3 There's famine in the land, its grip is tightening still! There's trouble, black and bitter, on every side I glance.
Emily Lawless 1845–1913: 'An Exile's Mother'

4 How can you frighten a man whose hunger is not only in his own cramped stomach but in the wretched bellies of his children? You can't scare him—he has known a fear beyond every other.
John Steinbeck 1902–68: *The Grapes of Wrath* (1939)

5 Famine sighs like scythe across the field of statistics and the desert is a moving mouth.
Derek Walcott 1930– : 'The Fortunate Traveller' (1981)

Fanaticism

see also **Certainty, Ideas**

1 Just as every conviction begins as a whim so does every emancipator

serve his apprenticeship as a crank. A fanatic is a great leader who is just entering the room.

Heywood Broun 1888–1939: in *New York World* 6 February 1928

2 A fanatic is one who can't change his mind and won't change the subject.
Winston Churchill 1874–1965: attributed

3 I would remind you that extremism in the defence of liberty is no vice! And let me remind you also that moderation in the pursuit of justice is no virtue!
Barry Goldwater 1909–98: accepting the presidential nomination, 16 July 1964

4 What is objectionable, what is dangerous about extremists is not that they are extreme but that they are intolerant.
Robert Kennedy 1925–68: *The Pursuit of Justice* (1964)

5 Fanaticism consists in redoubling your effort when you have forgotten your aim.
George Santayana 1863–1952: *The Life of Reason* (1905)

Fantasy
....
see also **Fiction**, **Imagination**

1 All fantasy should have a solid base in reality.
Max Beerbohm 1872–1956: *Zuleika Dobson* (1946 ed.) note

2 Fantasy deals with things that are not and cannot be. Science fiction deals with things that can be, that some day may be.
Frederic Brown 1906–72: *Angels and Spaceships* (1955)

3 We need metaphors of magic and monsters in order to understand the human condition.
Stephen Donaldson 1947– : Stan Nicholls (ed.) *Wordsmiths of Wonder* (1993)

4 Most modern fantasy just rearranges the furniture in Tolkien's attic.
Terry Pratchett 1948– : Stan Nicholls (ed.) *Wordsmiths of Wonder* (1993)

Farming
....
see also **The Country**

1 We plough the fields, and scatter
The good seed on the land,
But it is fed and watered
By God's almighty hand.
Jane Montgomery Campbell 1817–78: 'We plough the fields, and scatter' (1861 hymn)

2 Farming looks mighty easy when your plough is a pencil, and you're a thousand miles from the corn field.
Dwight D. Eisenhower 1890–1969: speech, Peoria, 25 September 1956

3 Few people these days seem to like farmers very much, which is unhealthy. They feed us cheaply and plentifully and we ought to be able to trust them.
Paul Heiney: *Farming Times* (1992)

4 The Farmer will never be happy again;
He carries his heart in his boots;
For either the rain is destroying his grain
Or the drought is destroying his roots.
A. P. Herbert 1890–1971: 'The Farmer' (1922)

5 Farm animals have become nothing more than meat on legs.
Desmond Morris 1928– : *The Animal Contract* (1990)

6 If it is necessary to remove something as basic to a bird as part of its beak, then there must be something fundamentally wrong with the agricultural system that is in operation.
Desmond Morris 1928– : *The Animal Contract* (1990)

7 A farm is an irregular patch of nettles bounded by short-term notes, containing a fool and his wife who didn't know enough to stay in the city.
S. J. Perelman 1904–79: *The Most of S. J. Perelman* (1959) 'Acres and Pains'

8 O farmers excessively fortunate if only they recognized their blessings!
Virgil 70–19 BC: *Georgics*

Fashion

....
see also **Clothes**

1 I never cared for fashion much. Amusing little seams and witty little pleats. It was the girls I liked.
    David Bailey 1938– : in *Independent* 5 November 1990

2 Uncool people never hurt anybody— all they do is collect stamps, read science-fiction books and stand on the end of railway platforms staring at trains.
    Ben Elton 1959– : in *Radio Times* 18/24 April 1998

3 Haute Couture should be fun, foolish and almost unwearable.
    Christian Lacroix 1951– : attributed, 1987

4 Hip is the sophistication of the wise primitive in a giant jungle.
    Norman Mailer 1923– : *Voices of Dissent* (1959)

5 Fashion is more usually a gentle progression of revisited ideas.
    Bruce Oldfield 1950– : in *Independent* 9 September 1989

6 Fashion is something barbarous, for it produces innovation without reason and imitation without benefit.
    George Santayana 1863–1952: *The Life of Reason* (1905)

7 You cannot be both fashionable and first-rate.
    Logan Pearsall Smith 1865–1946: *Afterthoughts* (1931)

8 I like to dress egos. If you haven't got an ego today, you can forget it.
    Gianni Versace 1949–96: in *Guardian* 16 July 1997; obituary

9 It is charming to totter into vogue.
    Horace Walpole 1717–97: letter to George Selwyn, 2 December 1765

10 Radical Chic . . . is only radical in Style; in its heart it is part of Society and its tradition—Politics, like Rock, Pop, and Camp, has its uses.
    Tom Wolfe 1931– : in *New York* 8 June 1970

Fat

....
see also **Appearance**, **Diets**

1 Outside every fat man there was an even fatter man trying to close in.
    Kingsley Amis 1922–95: *One Fat Englishman* (1963)

2 Imprisoned in every fat man a thin one is wildly signalling to be let out.
    Cyril Connolly 1903–74: *The Unquiet Grave* (1944)

3 As long as a woman's flesh is clean and healthy what does it matter what shape she is?
    Ian Fleming 1908–64: from his private notebooks; Frank Pepper (ed.) *20th Century Quotations* (1984)

4 it's a sex object if you're pretty and no love
  or love and no sex if you're fat
    Nikki Giovanni 1943– : 'Woman Poem' (1970)

5 Fat is a feminist issue.
    Susie Orbach 1946– : title of book (1978)

6 When self-indulgence has reduced a man to the shape of Lord Hailsham, sexual continence requires no more than a sense of the ridiculous.
    Reginald Paget 1908–90: speech in the House of Commons during the Profumo affair, 17 June 1963

7 CARRIER: Try zideways, Mrs Jones, try zideways!
  MRS JONES: Lar' bless 'ee John, I ain't got no zideways!
    ■ *cartoon of a stout lady trying to enter a doorway*
    Punch: 17 October 1900

8 I would rather be round and jolly than thin and cross.
    Ann Widdecombe 1947– : in *Independent* 13 June 1998

9 To ask women to become unnaturally thin is to ask them to relinquish their sexuality.
    Naomi Wolf 1962– : *The Beauty Myth* (1990)

Fate

....

see also **Circumstance and Situation**, **Necessity**

1 The spring is wound up tight. It will uncoil of itself. That is what is so convenient in tragedy. The least little turn of the wrist will do the job. Anything will set it going.
   Jean Anouilh 1910–87: *Antigone* (1944)

2 Must it be? It must be.
   Ludwig van Beethoven 1770–1827: String Quartet in F Major, Opus 135, epigraph

3 Canst thou bind the sweet influences of Pleiades, or loose the bands of Orion?
   Bible: Job

4 Fate is not an eagle, it creeps like a rat.
   Elizabeth Bowen 1899–1973: *The House in Paris* (1935)

5 It was inevitable the Titanic was going to set sail, but that doesn't mean it was a good idea to be on it.
   ■ *on his opposition to joining the single currency*
   William Hague 1961– : in *Mail on Sunday* 11 January 1998

6 There once was an old man who said, 'Damn!
   It is borne in upon me I am
   An engine that moves
   In determinate grooves,
   I'm not even a bus, I'm a tram.'
   Maurice Evan Hare 1886–1967: 'Limerick' (1905)

7 I go the way that Providence dictates with the assurance of a sleepwalker.
   Adolf Hitler 1889–1945: speech in Munich, 15 March 1936

8 It's no go my honey love, it's no go my poppet;
   Work your hands from day to day, the winds will blow the profit.
   The glass is falling hour by hour, the glass will fall for ever,
   But if you break the bloody glass you won't hold up the weather.
   Louis MacNeice 1907–63: 'Bagpipe Music' (1938)

9 I [Death] was astonished to see him in Baghdad, for I had an appointment with him tonight in Samarra.
   W. Somerset Maugham 1874–1965: *Sheppey* (1933)

10 There's a divinity that shapes our ends,
   Rough-hew them how we will.
   William Shakespeare 1564–1616: *Hamlet* (1601)

11 We are merely the stars' tennis-balls, struck and bandied
   Which way please them.
   John Webster c.1580–c.1625: *The Duchess of Malfi* (1623)

12 Every bullet has its billet.
   William III 1650–1702: John Wesley's diary, 6 June 1765

Fathers

....

see also **Parents**

1 I feel like the roots of a great bunch of flowers. The grower gets all the praise, the flowers get the adoration, while the roots that started it all must remain under the ground unnoticed.
   ■ *view of the father of Noel and Liam*
   Thomas Gallagher: in *Independent* 23 August 1997

2 There must be many fathers around the country who have experienced the cruellest, most crushing rejection of all: their children have ended up supporting the wrong team.
   Nick Hornby 1957– : *Fever Pitch* (1992)

3 If I'm more of an influence to your son as a rapper than you are as a father . . . you got to look at yourself as a parent.
   Ice Cube 1970– : in *Rolling Stone* 4 October 1990

4 The fundamental defect of fathers, in our competitive society, is that they want their children to be a credit to them.
   Bertrand Russell 1872–1970: *Sceptical Essays* (1928) 'Freedom versus Authority in Education'

5 There is no good father, that's the rule. Don't lay the blame on men but on the bond of paternity, which is rotten. To beget children, nothing better; to *have* them, what iniquity!
Jean-Paul Sartre 1905–80: *Les Mots* (1964)

6 It doesn't matter who my father was; it matters who I remember he was.
Anne Sexton 1928–74: diary, 1 January 1972

Fear

....

see also **Courage, Cowardice**

1 Most people go through life dreading they'll have a traumatic experience. Freaks are born with their trauma. They've already passed it. They're aristocrats.
Diane Arbus 1923–71: *Diane Arbus* (1972)

2 Now a man talks frankly only with his wife, at night, with the blanket over his head.
Isaac Babel 1894–1940: remark *c.*1937; Solomon Volkov *St Petersburg* (1996)

3 We must travel in the direction of our fear.
John Berryman 1914–72: 'A Point of Age' (1942)

4 No passion so effectually robs the mind of all its powers of acting and reasoning as fear.
Edmund Burke 1729–97: *On the Sublime and Beautiful* (1757)

5 Wee, sleekit, cow'rin', tim'rous beastie,
O what a panic's in thy breastie!
Robert Burns 1759–96: 'To a Mouse' (1786)

6 The horror! The horror!
Joseph Conrad 1857–1924: *Heart of Darkness* (1902)

7 I will show you fear in a handful of dust.
T. S. Eliot 1888–1965: *The Waste Land* (1922)

8 They cannot scare me with their empty spaces
Between stars—on stars where no human race is.

I have it in me so much nearer home
To scare myself with my own desert places.
Robert Frost 1874–1963: 'Desert Places' (1936)

9 There is no terror in a bang, only in the anticipation of it.
Alfred Hitchcock 1899–1980: attributed

10 Terror . . . often arises from a pervasive sense of disestablishment; that things are in the unmaking.
Stephen King 1947– : *Danse Macabre* (1981)

11 When it comes to sex, and everything else, the male's great fear is of failure, and the female's is of not being loved.
Irma Kurtz: *Malespeak* (1986)

12 Anxiety is love's greatest killer. It makes others feel as you might when a drowning man holds on to you. You want to save him, but you know he will strangle you with his panic.
Anais Nin 1903–77: *The Diary of Anais Nin* vol. 4 (1944–7)

13 The only thing we have to fear is fear itself.
Franklin D. Roosevelt 1882–1945: inaugural address, 4 March 1933

14 To fear love is to fear life, and those who fear life are already three parts dead.
Bertrand Russell 1872–1970: *Marriage and Morals* (1929)

15 Present fears
Are less than horrible imaginings.
William Shakespeare 1564–1616: *Macbeth* (1606)

16 Better be killed than frightened to death.
R. S. Surtees 1805–64: *Mr Facey Romford's Hounds* (1865)

17 Every drop of ink in my pen ran cold.
Horace Walpole 1717–97: letter to George Montagu, 30 July 1752

Fiction

....

see also **Crime Fiction, Fantasy, Science Fiction, Writers, Writing**

1 Andrew Davies said adapting *Middlemarch* was like getting an

elephant into a suitcase; Jane Austen is much easier. In *Pride and Prejudice* the plot works like a Swiss clock.

■ *on adapting for television*
Sue Birtwistle 1945– : in *Guardian* 13 October 1995

2 I hate things all *fiction* . . . there should always be some foundation of fact for the most airy fabric and pure invention is but the talent of a liar.
Lord Byron 1788–1824: letter to John Murray, 2 April 1817

3 Literature is a luxury; fiction is a necessity.
G. K. Chesterton 1874–1936: *The Defendant* (1901) 'A Defence of Penny Dreadfuls'

4 The central function of imaginative literature is to make you realize that other people act on moral convictions different from your own.
William Empson 1906–84: *Milton's God* (1981)

5 Yes—oh dear yes—the novel tells a story.
E. M. Forster 1879–1970: *Aspects of the Novel* (1927)

6 Merely corroborative detail, intended to give artistic verisimilitude to an otherwise bald and unconvincing narrative.
W. S. Gilbert 1836–1911: *The Mikado* (1885)

7 The Story is just the spoiled child of art.
Henry James 1843–1916: *The Ambassadors* (1909 ed.) preface

8 What is character but the determination of incident? What is incident but the illustration of character?
Henry James 1843–1916: *Partial Portraits* (1888) 'The Art of Fiction'

9 A beginning, a muddle, and an end.
■ *on the 'classic formula' for a novel*
Philip Larkin 1922–85: in *New Fiction* January 1978

10 If you try to nail anything down in the novel, either it kills the novel, or the novel gets up and walks away with the nail.
D. H. Lawrence 1885–1930: *Phoenix* (1936) 'Morality and the Novel'

11 The things I like to find in a story are punch and poetry.
Sean O'Faolain 1900–91: *The Short Story* (1948) foreword

12 As artists they're rot, but as providers they're oil wells; they gush.
■ *on lady novelists*
Dorothy Parker 1893–1967: Malcolm Cowley *Writers at Work* 1st Series (1958)

13 A novel is a mirror which passes over a highway. Sometimes it reflects to your eyes the blue of the skies, at others the churned-up mud of the road.
Stendhal 1783–1842: *Le Rouge et le noir* (1830)

14 Sex is more exciting on the screen and between the pages than between the sheets.
Andy Warhol 1927–87: *Philosophy of Andy Warhol (From A to B and Back Again)* (1975)

15 The good ended happily, and the bad unhappily. That is what fiction means.
Oscar Wilde 1854–1900: *The Importance of Being Earnest* (1895)

Field Sports
....
see also **Fishing**, **Hunting**

1 A sportsman is a man who, every now and then, simply has to get out and kill something. Not that he's cruel. He wouldn't hurt a fly. It's not big enough.
Stephen Leacock 1869–1944: *My Remarkable Uncle* (1942)

2 I don't think doing it [killing animals] for money makes it any more moral. I don't think a prostitute is more moral than a wife, but they are doing the same thing.
■ *comparing participation in blood sports to selling slaughtered meat*
Prince Philip, Duke of Edinburgh 1921– : speech in London, 6 December 1988

3 When a man wants to murder a tiger he calls it sport; when a tiger wants to murder him, he calls it ferocity.
George Bernard Shaw 1856–1950: *Man and Superman* (1903)

4 The fascination of shooting as a sport depends almost wholly on whether you are at the right or wrong end of a gun.
P. G. Wodehouse 1881–1975: attributed

Films

see also **Cinema**

1 Just when you thought it was safe to go back in the water.
Advertising slogan: publicity for *Jaws 2* (1978 film)

2 It would have been cheaper to lower the Atlantic!
■ *of the disaster movie* Raise the Titanic
Lew Grade 1906–98: *Still Dancing: My Story* (1987)

3 If we'd had as many soldiers as that, we'd have won the war!
■ *on seeing the number of Confederate troops in* Gone with the Wind *at the 1939 premiere*
Margaret Mitchell 1900–49: W. G. Harris *Gable and Lombard* (1976)

4 You come out of *Gone With the Wind* feeling that history isn't so disturbing after all. One can always make a dress out of a curtain.
Dilys Powell 1902–95: in *Independent on Sunday* 29 April 1990

5 [*Gandhi*] looms over the real world like an abandoned space station— eternal, expensive and forsaken.
David Thomson 1941– : *A Biographical Dictionary of Film* (1994)

6 Fiction is the great virus waiting to do away with fact—that is one of the most ominous meanings of the film.
■ *of* Citizen Kane
David Thomson 1941– : *Rosebud: the Story of Orson Welles* (1996)

7 It is like writing history with lightning. And my only regret is that it is all so terribly true.
■ *on seeing D. W. Griffith's film* The Birth of a Nation
Woodrow Wilson 1856–1924: at the White House, 18 February 1915

Fishing

see also **Field Sports**

1 Fishing is unquestionably a form of madness but, happily, for the once-bitten there is no cure.
Lord Home 1903–95: *The Way the Wind Blows* (1976)

2 Fly fishing may be a very pleasant amusement; but angling or float fishing I can only compare to a stick and a string, with a worm at one end and a fool at the other.
Samuel Johnson 1709–84: attributed; Hawker *Instructions to Young Sportsmen* (1859); also attributed to Jonathan Swift, in *The Indicator* 27 October 1819

3 As no man is born an artist, so no man is born an angler.
Izaak Walton 1593–1683: *The Compleat Angler* (1653)

Flattery

see also **Praise**

1 If you are flattering a woman, it pays to be a little more subtle. You don't have to bother with men, they believe any compliment automatically.
Alan Ayckbourn 1939– : *Round and Round the Garden* (1975)

2 I can't think of many toadies that have prospered, or many toadies who have become household names.
Betty Boothroyd 1929– : in *Mail on Sunday* 12 April 1998

3 Everyone likes flattery; and when you come to Royalty you should lay it on with a trowel.
Benjamin Disraeli 1804–81: to Matthew Arnold; G. W. E. Russell *Collections and Recollections* (1898); cf. **Prime Ministers** 3

4 Please don't be too effusive.
■ *to the Prime Minister, on the speech he was to make to celebrate her golden wedding*
Elizabeth II 1926– : in *Daily Telegraph* 21 November 1997; cf. **Prime Ministers** 3

5 Madam, before you flatter a man so grossly to his face, you should consider whether or not your flattery is worth his having.

Samuel Johnson 1709–84: Fanny Burney's diary, August 1778

6 But when I tell him he hates flatterers, He says he does, being then most flattered.

William Shakespeare 1564–1616: *Julius Caesar* (1599)

7 I suppose flattery hurts no one, that is, if he doesn't inhale.

Adlai Stevenson 1900–65: television broadcast, 30 March 1952

Flowers

....

see also **Gardens**

1 Unkempt about those hedges blows An English unofficial rose.

Rupert Brooke 1887–1915: 'The Old Vicarage, Grantchester' (1915)

2 Oh, no man knows Through what wild centuries Roves back the rose.

Walter de la Mare 1873–1956: 'All That's Past' (1912)

3 Here are sweet peas, on tip-toe for a flight.

John Keats 1795–1821: 'I stood tip-toe upon a little hill' (1817)

4 Hey, buds below, up is where to grow, Up with which below can't compare with.
Hurry! It's lovely up here! *Hurry*!

Alan Jay Lerner 1918–86: 'It's Lovely Up Here' (1965)

5 The rose of all the world is not for me. I want for my part Only the little white rose of Scotland That smells sharp and sweet—and breaks the heart.

Hugh MacDiarmid 1892–1978: 'The Little White Rose' (1934)

6 People from a planet without flowers would think we must be mad with joy the whole time to have such things about us.

Iris Murdoch 1919–99: *A Fairly Honourable Defeat* (1970)

7 Flowers are for wrapping in cellophane to present as a bouquet;
Flowers are for prize arrangements in vases and silver tea-pots;
Flowers are for plaiting into funeral wreaths.
You can keep your flowers.
Give me weeds.

Norman Nicholson 1914–87: 'Weeds' (1981)

8 I know a bank whereon the wild thyme blows,
Where oxlips and the nodding violet grows
Quite over-canopied with luscious woodbine,
With sweet musk-roses, and with eglantine:

William Shakespeare 1564–1616: *A Midsummer Night's Dream* (1595–6)

9   Daffodils,
That come before the swallow dares, and take
The winds of March with beauty; violets dim,
But sweeter than the lids of Juno's eyes.

William Shakespeare 1564–1616: *The Winter's Tale* (1610–11)

10 From my experience of life I believe my personal motto should be 'Beware of men bearing flowers.'

Muriel Spark 1918– : *Curriculum Vitae* (1992)

11 As well as any bloom upon a flower I like the dust on the nettles, never lost Except to prove the sweetness of a shower.

Edward Thomas 1878–1917: 'Tall Nettles' (1917)

12 Summer set lip to earth's bosom bare, And left the flushed print in a poppy there.

Francis Thompson 1859–1907: 'The Poppy' (1913)

13 I wandered lonely as a cloud That floats on high o'er vales and hills,
When all at once I saw a crowd, A host, of golden daffodils;
Beside the lake, beneath the trees,

Fluttering and dancing in the breeze.
William Wordsworth 1770–1850: 'I wandered lonely as a cloud' (1815 ed.)

14 I never see a flower that pleases me, but I wish for you.
William Wordsworth 1770–1850: letter to his wife Mary, 1810

Fog

see also **Weather**

1 This is a London particular . . . A fog, miss.
Charles Dickens 1812–70: *Bleak House* (1853)

2 The yellow fog that rubs its back upon the window-panes.
T. S. Eliot 1888–1965: 'The Love Song of J. Alfred Prufrock' (1917)

3 The fog comes
on little cat feet.
It sits looking
over harbour and city
on silent haunches
and then moves on.
Carl Sandburg 1878–1967: 'Fog' (1916)

Food and Drink

see also **Alcohol, Cooking, Diets, Eating**

1 Shake and shake
The catsup bottle.
None will come,
And then a lot'll.
Richard Armour 1906–89: 'Going to Extremes' (1949)

2 An egg boiled very soft is not unwholesome.
Jane Austen 1775–1817: *Emma* (1816)

3 Salad. I can't bear salad. It grows while you're eating it, you know. Have you noticed? You start one side of your plate and by the time you've got to the other, there's a fresh crop of lettuce taken root and sprouted up.
Alan Ayckbourn 1939– : *Living Together* (1975)

4 The restaurant is like a theatre: we do two shows a day and when you are doing Shakespeare you don't want to throw in something out of Walt Disney.
■ *on tomato ketchup*
Philip Britten 1957– : in *Evening Standard* 4 February 1999

5 Fair fa' your honest, sonsie face, Great chieftain o' the puddin'-race!
Robert Burns 1759–96: 'To a Haggis' (1787)

6 I'm President of the United States, and I'm not going to eat any more broccoli!
George Bush 1924– : in *New York Times* 23 March 1990

7 Doubtless God could have made a better berry, but doubtless God never did.
■ *on the strawberry*
William Butler 1535–1618: Izaak Walton *The Compleat Angler* (3rd ed., 1661)

8 Tea, although an Oriental,
Is a gentleman at least;
Cocoa is a cad and coward,
Cocoa is a vulgar beast.
G. K. Chesterton 1874–1936: 'Song of Right and Wrong' (1914)

9 Take away that pudding—it has no theme.
Winston Churchill 1874–1965: Lord Home *The Way the Wind Blows* (1976)

10 Milk's leap toward immortality.
■ *of cheese*
Clifton Fadiman 1904– : *Any Number Can Play* (1957)

11 Roast Beef, Medium, is not only a food. It is a philosophy.
Edna Ferber 1887–1968: *Roast Beef, Medium* (1911)

12 Last night we went to a Chinese dinner at six and a French dinner at nine, and I can feel the sharks' fins navigating unhappily in the Burgundy.
Peter Fleming 1907–71: letter from Yunnanfu, 20 March 1938

13 The ethical value of uncooked food is incomparable. Economically this food has possibilities which no cooked food can have.

Mahatma Gandhi 1869–1948: in *Young India* 13 June 1929

14 I ate his liver with some fava beans and a nice chianti.

Thomas Harris 1940– and **Ted Tally** 1952– : *The Silence of the Lambs* (1991 film)

15 A cucumber should be well sliced, and dressed with pepper and vinegar, and then thrown out, as good for nothing.

Samuel Johnson 1709–84: James Boswell *Journal of a Tour to the Hebrides* (1785) 5 October 1773

16 *What* is the matter with Mary Jane?
She's perfectly well and she hasn't a pain,
And it's lovely rice pudding for dinner again!
What *is* the matter with Mary Jane?

A. A. Milne 1882–1956: 'Rice Pudding' (1924)

17 Parsley
Is gharsley.

Ogden Nash 1902–71: 'Further Reflections on Parsley' (1942)

18 A fruit is a vegetable with looks and money. Plus, if you let fruit rot, it turns into wine, something Brussels sprouts never do.

P. J. O'Rourke 1947– : *The Bachelor Home Companion* (1987)

19 The ordinary human being would sooner starve than live on brown bread and raw carrots. And the peculiar evil is this, that the less money you have, the less inclined you feel to spend it on wholesome food. A millionaire may enjoy breakfasting off orange juice and ryvita biscuits; [but] . . . When you are underfed, harassed, bored and miserable, you don't *want* to eat dull wholesome food. You want something a little bit 'tasty.'

George Orwell 1903–50: *The Road to Wigan Pier* (1937)

20 Coffee, (which makes the politician wise,

And see thro' all things with his half-shut eyes).

Alexander Pope 1688–1744: *The Rape of the Lock* (1714)

21 It is said that the effect of eating too much lettuce is 'soporific'.

Beatrix Potter 1866–1943: *The Tale of the Flopsy Bunnies* (1909)

22 Look here, Steward, if this is coffee, I want tea; but if this is tea, then I wish for coffee.

Punch: 23 July 1902

23 Methinks sometimes I have no more wit than a Christian or an ordinary man has; but I am a great eater of beef, and I believe that does harm to my wit.

William Shakespeare 1564–1616: *Twelfth Night* (1601)

24 A hen's egg is, quite simply, a work of art, a masterpiece of design and construction with, it has to be said, brilliant packaging.

Delia Smith: *How To Cook* (1998)

25 Let onion atoms lurk within the bowl, And, scarce-suspected, animate the whole.

Sydney Smith 1771–1845: Lady Holland *Memoir* (1855) 'Receipt for a Salad'

26 Many's the long night I've dreamed of cheese—toasted, mostly.

Robert Louis Stevenson 1850–94: *Treasure Island* (1883)

27 What makes food such a tyranny for women? A man, after all, may in times of crisis, hit the bottle (or another person), but he rarely hits the fridge.

Joanna Trollope 1943– : in *Independent* 28 November 1998

28 Cauliflower is nothing but cabbage with a college education.

Mark Twain 1835–1910: *Pudd'nhead Wilson* (1894)

29 MOTHER: It's broccoli, dear.
CHILD: I say it's spinach, and I say the hell with it.

E. B. White 1899–1985: *New Yorker* 8 December 1928 (cartoon caption)

30 *to a waiter:*

When I ask for a watercress sandwich, I do not mean a loaf with a field in the middle of it.

Oscar Wilde 1854–1900: Max Beerbohm, letter to Reggie Turner, 15 April 1893

Fools

see also **Intelligence**

1 The world is full of fools, and he who would not see it should live alone and smash his mirror.

Anonymous: adaptation from an original form attributed to Claude Le Petit (1640–65)

2 There's a sucker born every minute.

Phineas T. Barnum 1810–91: attributed

3 A fool sees not the same tree that a wise man sees.

William Blake 1757–1827: *The Marriage of Heaven and Hell* (1790–3)

4 A fool can always find a greater fool to admire him.

Nicolas Boileau 1636–1711: *L'Art poétique* (1674)

5 'Tis hard if all is false that I advance A fool must now and then be right, by chance.

William Cowper 1731–1800: 'Conversation' (1782)

6 Never give a sucker an even break.

W. C. Fields 1880–1946: title of a W. C. Fields film (1941); the catch-phrase (Fields's own) is said to have originated in the musical comedy *Poppy* (1923)

7 So dumb he can't fart and chew gum at the same time.

■ *of Gerald Ford*

Lyndon Baines Johnson 1908–73: Richard Reeves *A Ford, not a Lincoln* (1975)

8 A knowledgeable fool is a greater fool than an ignorant fool.

Molière 1622–73: *Les Femmes savantes* (1672)

9 For fools rush in where angels fear to tread.

Alexander Pope 1688–1744: *An Essay on Criticism* (1711)

10 The follies which a man regrets most, in his life, are those which he didn't commit when he had the opportunity.

Helen Rowland 1875–1950: *A Guide to Men* (1922)

11 With stupidity the gods themselves struggle in vain.

Friedrich von Schiller 1759–1805: *Die Jungfrau von Orleans* (1801)

12 The ae half of the warld thinks the tither daft.

Sir Walter Scott 1771–1832: *Redgauntlet* (1824)

13 The ultimate result of shielding men from the effects of folly, is to fill the world with fools.

Herbert Spencer 1820–1903: *Essays* (1891) vol. 3 'State Tamperings with Money and Banks'

14 Better to keep your mouth shut and appear stupid than to open it and remove all doubt.

Mark Twain 1835–1910: attributed, perhaps apocryphal

15 Be wise with speed; A fool at forty is a fool indeed.

Edward Young 1683–1765: *The Love of Fame* (1725–8)

Football

see also **Sports and Games**

1 The great fallacy is that the game is first and last about winning. It is nothing of the kind. The game is about glory, it is about doing things in style and with a flourish, about going out and beating the lot, not waiting for them to die of boredom.

Danny Blanchflower 1926–93: attributed, 1972

2 Football, wherein is nothing but beastly fury, and extreme violence, whereof proceedeth hurt, and consequently rancour and malice do remain with them that be wounded.

Thomas Elyot 1499–1546: *Book of the Governor* (1531)

3 Football is an art more central to our culture than anything the Arts Council deigns to recognize.

Germaine Greer 1939– : in *Independent* 28 June 1996

4 The natural state of the football fan is bitter disappointment, no matter what the score.
Nick Hornby 1957– : *Fever Pitch* (1992)

5 The nice aspect about football is that, if things go wrong, it's the manager who gets the blame.
■ *before his first match as captain of England*
Gary Lineker 1960– : in *Independent* 12 September 1990

6 Oh, he's football crazy, he's football mad
And the football it has robbed him o' the wee bit sense he had.
And it would take a dozen skivvies, his clothes to wash and scrub,
Since our Jock became a member of that terrible football club.
Jimmie McGregor 1932– : 'Football Crazy' (1960 song)

7 The goal was scored a little bit by the hand of God, another bit by head of Maradona.
■ *on his controversial goal against England in the 1986 World Cup*
Diego Maradona 1960– : in *Guardian* 1 July 1986

8 Nobody cares if Le Saux is gay or not. It is the fact that he openly admits to reading *The Guardian* that makes him the most reviled man in football.
Piers Morgan 1965– : letter to *Guardian*, 5 March 1999; cf. **Intellectuals 4**

9 Football? It's the beautiful game.
Pelé 1940– : attributed; his autobiography (1977) was *My Life and the Beautiful Game*

10 To say that these men paid their shillings to watch twenty-two hirelings kick a ball is merely to say that a violin is wood and catgut, that *Hamlet* is so much paper and ink. For a shilling the Bruddersford United AFC offered you Conflict and Art.
J. B. Priestley 1894–1984: *Good Companions* (1929)

11 For when the One Great Scorer comes to mark against your name,
He writes—not that you won or lost—but how you played the Game.
Grantland Rice 1880–1954: 'Alumnus Football' (1941)

12 Some people think football is a matter of life and death . . . I can assure them it is much more serious than that.
Bill Shankly 1914–81: in *Sunday Times* 4 October 1981

13 Football and cookery are the two most important subjects in the country.
Delia Smith: in *Observer* 23 February 1997

Foresight

see also **The Future**

1 Science fiction writers foresee the inevitable, and although problems and catastrophes may be inevitable, solutions are not.
Isaac Asimov 1920–92: in *Natural History* April 1975

2 Some of the jam we thought was for tomorrow, we've already eaten.
Tony Benn 1925– : attributed, 1969

3 It was déjà vu all over again.
Yogi Berra 1925– : attributed

4 You can never plan the future by the past.
Edmund Burke 1729–97: *Letter to a Member of the National Assembly* (1791)

5 The best laid schemes o' mice an' men
Gang aft a-gley.
Robert Burns 1759–96: 'To a Mouse' (1786)

6 She felt that those who prepared for all the emergencies of life beforehand may equip themselves at the expense of joy.
E. M. Forster 1879–1970: *Howards End* (1910)

7 The best way to suppose what may come, is to remember what is past.
Lord Halifax 1633–95: *Political, Moral, and Miscellaneous Thoughts and Reflections* (1750) 'Miscellaneous: Experience'

8 What all the wise men promised has not happened, and what all the d—d fools said would happen has come to pass.
■ *of the Catholic Emancipation Act* (1829)
Lord Melbourne 1779–1848: H. Dunckley *Lord Melbourne* (1890)

9 The man who has fed the chicken every day throughout its life at last wrings its neck instead, showing that a more refined view as to the uniformity of nature would have been useful to the chicken.
Bertrand Russell 1872–1970: *The Problems of Philosophy* (1912)

10 Prognostics do not always prove prophecies,—at least the wisest prophets make sure of the event first.
Horace Walpole 1717–97: letter to Thomas Walpole, 19 February 1785

11 God damn you all: I told you so.
■ *suggestion for his own epitaph, 1939*
H. G. Wells 1866–1946: Ernest Barker *Age and Youth* (1953)

Forgiveness

1 You ought certainly to forgive them as a Christian, but never to admit them in your sight, or allow their names to be mentioned in your hearing.
Jane Austen 1775–1817: *Pride and Prejudice* (1813)

2 I never forgive but I always forget.
Arthur James Balfour 1848–1930: R. Blake *Conservative Party* (1970)

3 I believe any person who asks for forgiveness has to be prepared to give it.
Bill Clinton 1946– : statement after being acquitted by the Senate, 12 February 1999

4 I ain't sayin' you treated me unkind
You could have done better but I don't mind
You just kinda wasted my precious time
But don't think twice, it's all right.
Bob Dylan 1941– : 'Don't Think Twice, It's All Right' (1963 song)

5 After such knowledge, what forgiveness?
T. S. Eliot 1888–1965: 'Gerontion' (1920)

6 God will pardon me, it is His trade.
■ *on his deathbed*
Heinrich Heine 1797–1856: Alfred Meissner *Heinrich Heine. Erinnerungen* (1856)

7 True reconciliation does not consist in merely forgetting the past.
Nelson Mandela 1918– : speech, 7 January 1996

8 We read that we ought to forgive our enemies; but we do not read that we ought to forgive our friends.
Cosimo de' Medici 1389–1464: Francis Bacon *Apophthegms* (1625)

9 Only a culture without hope cannot forgive—a culture that doesn't believe in progress or redemption. Have we so little faith in ourselves we can't accept the possibility of maturation, change, cure?
■ *on the killing of James Bulger*
Blake Morrison 1950– : *As If* (1997)

10 To err is human; to forgive, divine.
Alexander Pope 1688–1744: *An Essay on Criticism* (1711)

11 The stupid neither forgive nor forget; the naïve forgive and forget; the wise forgive but do not forget.
Thomas Szasz 1920– : *The Second Sin* (1973)

12 And blessings on the falling out
That all the more endears,
When we fall out with those we love
And kiss again with tears!
Alfred, Lord Tennyson 1809–92: *The Princess* (1847), song (added 1850)

13 God of forgiveness, do not forgive those murderers of Jewish children here.
Elie Wiesel 1928– : at an unofficial ceremony at Auschwitz, 26 January 1995

France

see also **International Relations**

1 France was long a despotism tempered by epigrams.
Thomas Carlyle 1795–1881: *History of the French Revolution* (1837)

2 France is the only place where you can make love in the afternoon without people hammering on your door.
Barbara Cartland 1901–2000: in *Guardian* 24 December 1984

3 How can you govern a country which has 246 varieties of cheese?
Charles de Gaulle 1890–1970: Ernest Mignon *Les Mots du Général* (1962)

4 The last time I saw Paris
Her heart was warm and gay,
I heard the laughter of her heart in ev'ry street café.
Oscar Hammerstein II 1895–1960: 'The Last Time I saw Paris' (1941 song)

5 Paris is a movable feast.
Ernest Hemingway 1899–1961: *A Movable Feast* (1964)

6 Yet, who can help loving the land that has taught us
Six hundred and eighty-five ways to dress eggs?
Thomas Moore 1779–1852: *The Fudge Family in Paris* (1818)

7 The French are a logical people, which is one reason the English dislike them so intensely. The other is that they own France, a country which we have always judged to be much too good for them.
Robert Morley 1908–92: *A Musing Morley* (1974)

8 They order, said I, this matter better in France.
Laurence Sterne 1713–68: *A Sentimental Journey* (1768)

9 If the French noblesse had been capable of playing cricket with their peasants, their chateaux would never have been burnt.
G. M. Trevelyan 1876–1962: *English Social History* (1942)

Friendship

see also **Relationships**

1 One friend in a lifetime is much; two are many; three are hardly possible. Friendship needs a certain parallelism of life, a community of thought, a rivalry of aim.
Henry Brooks Adams 1838–1918: *The Education of Henry Adams* (1907)

2 Oh, the comfort—the inexpressible comfort of feeling safe with a person, having neither to weigh thoughts, nor measure words, but pouring them all out, just as they are, chaff and grain together; knowing that a faithful hand will take and sift them—keep what is worth keeping—and with the breath of kindness blow the rest away.
Anonymous: 'Friendship'; often attributed to George Eliot or Dinah Mulock Craik (1826–87)

3 *when asked 'What is a friend?':*
One soul inhabiting two bodies.
Aristotle 384–322 BC: Diogenes Laertius *Lives of Philosophers*

4 Who can I tear to pieces, if not my friends? . . . If they were not my friends, I could not do such violence to them.
Francis Bacon 1909–92: John Russell *Francis Bacon* (1979)

5 There is a friend that sticketh closer than a brother.
Bible: Proverbs

6 Should auld acquaintance be forgot And never brought to mind?
Robert Burns 1759–96: 'Auld Lang Syne' (1796)

7 Friendship is Love without his wings!
Lord Byron 1788–1824: 'L'Amitié est l'amour sans ailes' (written 1806)

8 Give me the avowed, erect and manly foe;
Firm I can meet, perhaps return the blow;
But of all plagues, good Heaven, thy wrath can send,
Save me, oh, save me, from the candid friend.
George Canning 1770–1827: 'New Morality' (1821)

9 A woman can become a man's friend only in the following stages—first an acquaintance, next a mistress, and only then a friend.
Anton Chekhov 1860–1904: *Uncle Vanya* (1897)

10 The man that hails you Tom or Jack, And proves by thumps upon your back

How he esteems your merit,
Is such a friend, that one had need
Be very much his friend indeed
To pardon or to bear it.
   William Cowper 1731–1800: 'Friendship'
   (1782)

11 To find a friend one must close one
   eye. To keep him—two.
   Norman Douglas 1868–1952: *Almanac* (1941)

12 Friendships begin with liking or
   gratitude—roots that can be pulled
   up.
   George Eliot 1819–80: *Daniel Deronda* (1876)

13 No man can be friends with a woman
   he finds attractive. He always wants to
   have sex with her. Sex is always out
   there. Friendship is ultimately
   doomed and that is the end of the
   story.
   Nora Ephron 1941– : *When Harry Met Sally*
   (1989 film)

14 My life is spent in a perpetual
   alternation between two rhythms, the
   rhythm of attracting people for fear I
   may be lonely, and the rhythm of
   trying to get rid of them because I
   know that I am bored.
   C. E. M. Joad 1891–1953: in *Observer*
   12 December 1948

15 If a man does not make new
   acquaintance as he advances through
   life, he will soon find himself left
   alone. A man, Sir, should keep his
   friendship in constant repair.
   Samuel Johnson 1709–84: James Boswell *Life
   of Samuel Johnson* (1791) 1755

16 God's apology for relations.
   ■ *on friends*
   Hugh Kingsmill 1889–1949: Michael Holroyd
   The Best of Hugh Kingsmill (1970)

17 Oh I get by with a little help from my
   friends.
   John Lennon 1940–80 and **Paul McCartney**
   1942– : 'With a Little Help From My
   Friends' (1967 song)

18 In any social network there are always
   some people who are as it were
   'friends' by social compulsion, though
   if the net fell apart they would seldom
   or never see each other.
   Alison Lurie 1926– : *Foreign Affairs* (1984)

19 Levin wanted friendship and got
   friendliness; he wanted steak and they
   offered spam.
   Bernard Malamud 1914–86: *A New Life* (1961)

20 I count myself in nothing else so
   happy
   As in a soul remembering my good
   friends.
   William Shakespeare 1564–1616: *Richard II*
   (1595)

21 I do not believe that friends are
   necessarily the people you like best,
   they are merely the people who got
   there first.
   Peter Ustinov 1921– : *Dear Me* (1977)

22 I have lost friends, some by death . . .
   others through sheer inability to cross
   the street.
   Virginia Woolf 1882–1941: *The Waves* (1931)

23 Think where man's glory most begins
   and ends,
   And say my glory was I had such
   friends.
   W. B. Yeats 1865–1939: 'The Municipal Gallery
   Re-visited' (1939)

Futility

1 O plunge your hands in water,
   Plunge them in up to the wrist;
   Stare, stare in the basin
   And wonder what you've missed.
   The glacier knocks in the cupboard,
   The desert sighs in the bed,
   And the crack in the tea-cup opens
   A lane to the land of the dead.
   W. H. Auden 1907–73: 'As I Walked Out One
   Evening' (1940)

2 It seems that I have spent my entire
   time trying to make life more rational
   and that it was all wasted effort.
   A. J. Ayer 1910–89: in *Observer* 17 August 1986

3 Nothing to be done.
   Samuel Beckett 1906–89: *Waiting for Godot*
   (1955)

4 Vanity of vanities, saith the Preacher,
vanity of vanities; all is vanity.
Bible: Ecclesiastes

5 We are the hollow men
We are the stuffed men
Leaning together
Headpiece filled with straw. Alas!
T. S. Eliot 1888–1965: 'The Hollow Men' (1925)

6 Pathos, piety, courage—they exist, but
are identical, and so is filth.
Everything exists, nothing has value.
E. M. Forster 1879–1970: *A Passage to India* (1924)

7 He's a real nowhere man
Sitting in his nowhere land
Making all his nowhere plans for
nobody.
John Lennon 1940–80 and **Paul McCartney** 1942– : 'Nowhere Man' (1966 song)

8 I'm not going to rearrange the
furniture on the deck of the Titanic.
■ *having lost five of the last six primaries as President Ford's campaign manager*
Rogers Morton 1914–79: *Washington Post* 16 May 1976

9 There aren't any good, brave causes
left. If the big bang does come, and we
all get killed off, it won't be in aid of
the old-fashioned, grand design. It'll
just be for the Brave New-nothing-
very-much-thank-you. About as
pointless and inglorious as stepping
in front of a bus.
John Osborne 1929–94: *Look Back in Anger* (1956)

10 'Strange friend,' I said, 'here is no
cause to mourn.'
'None,' said that other, 'save the
undone years,
The hopelessness. Whatever hope is
yours,
Was my life also.'
Wilfred Owen 1893–1918: 'Strange Meeting' (written 1918)

11 Who breaks a butterfly upon a wheel?
Alexander Pope 1688–1744: 'An Epistle to Dr Arbuthnot' (1735)

12 Nothingness haunts being.
Jean-Paul Sartre 1905–80: *Being and Nothingness* (1956)

13 How weary, stale, flat, and
unprofitable
Seem to me all the uses of this world.
William Shakespeare 1564–1616: *Hamlet* (1601)

14 'My name is Ozymandias, king of
kings:
Look on my works, ye Mighty, and
despair!'
Nothing beside remains. Round the
decay
Of that colossal wreck, boundless and
bare
The lone and level sands stretch far
away.
Percy Bysshe Shelley 1792–1822: 'Ozymandias' (1819)

The Future

see also **Foresight**

1 'We are always doing', says he,
'something for Posterity, but I would
fain see Posterity do something for
us.'
Joseph Addison 1672–1719: in *The Spectator* 20 August 1714

2 More than any other time in history,
mankind faces a crossroads. One path
leads to despair and utter
hopelessness. The other, to total
extinction. Let us pray we have the
wisdom to choose correctly.
Woody Allen 1935– : *Side Effects* (1980) 'My Speech to the Graduates'

3 The future ain't what it used to be.
Yogi Berra 1925– : attributed

4 People will not look forward to
posterity, who never look backward to
their ancestors.
Edmund Burke 1729–97: *Reflections on the Revolution in France* (1790)

5 And now, we can see a new world
coming into view. A world in which
there is the very real prospect of a new
world order.
George Bush 1924– : speech, in *New York Times* 7 March 1991

6 He seems to think that posterity is a pack-horse, always ready to be loaded.
Benjamin Disraeli 1804–81: speech, 3 June 1862; attributed

7 I never think of the future. It comes soon enough.
Albert Einstein 1879–1955: in an interview given on the *Belgenland*, December 1930

8 You cannot fight against the future. Time is on our side.
W. E. Gladstone 1809–98: speech on the Reform Bill, House of Commons, 27 April 1866

9 You will eat, bye and bye,
In that glorious land above the sky;
Work and pray, live on hay,
You'll get pie in the sky when you die.
Joe Hill 1879–1915: 'Preacher and the Slave' (1911 song)

10 *In the long run* we are all dead.
John Maynard Keynes 1883–1946: *A Tract on Monetary Reform* (1923)

11 *announcing that he had ended his association with the cryonics movement, and abandoned his plan to have his head cryonically preserved:*
They have no sense of humour. I was worried I would wake up in fifty years surrounded by people with clipboards.
Timothy Leary 1920–96: in *Daily Telegraph* 10 May 1996

12 We have trained them [men] to think of the Future as a promised land which favoured heroes attain—not as something which everyone reaches at the rate of sixty minutes an hour, whatever he does, whoever he is.
C. S. Lewis 1898–1963: *The Screwtape Letters* (1942)

13 If you want a picture of the future, imagine a boot stamping on a human face—for ever.
George Orwell 1903–50: *Nineteen Eighty-Four* (1949)

14 They spend their time mostly looking forward to the past.
John Osborne 1929–94: *Look Back in Anger* (1956)

15 Lord! we know what we are, but know not what we may be.
William Shakespeare 1564–1616: *Hamlet* (1601)

16 Make me a beautiful word for doing things tomorrow; for that surely is a great and blessed invention.
George Bernard Shaw 1856–1950: *Back to Methuselah* (1921)

17 I guess—what may happen is what keeps us alive. We want to see tomorrow.
John Steinbeck 1902–68: letter to Carlton Sheffield, 16 October 1952

18 So many worlds, so much to do,
So little done, such things to be.
Alfred, Lord Tennyson 1809–92: *In Memoriam A. H. H.* (1850)

19 We are YOUTH chiz chiz whether we like it or not and as every weed who come to give us prizes sa—The Future is in yore Keeping.
n.b. it is no use saing We don't want it. You can keep it etc. *Nobody* wants the future and we are left holding the baby chiz chiz chiz.
Geoffrey Willans 1911–58 and **Ronald Searle** 1920– : *Whizz for Atomms* (1956)

Games

see **Sports and Games**

Gardens

see also **Flowers**

1 I'm not a dirt gardener. I sit with my walking stick and point things out that need to be done. After many years, the garden is now totally obedient.
Hardy Amies 1909– : in *Sunday Times* 11 July 1999

2 Tradition dictates that we have a lawn—but do we really need one? Why not increase the size of your borders or replace lawned areas with paving stones or gravel?
Anonymous: Severn Trent Water 'The Gardener's Water Code' (1996)

3 God Almighty first planted a garden; and, indeed, it is the purest of human pleasures.
Francis Bacon 1561–1626: *Essays* (1625) 'Of Gardens'

4 Nothing is more pleasant to the eye than green grass kept finely shorn.
Francis Bacon 1561–1626: *Essays* (1625) 'Of Gardens'

5 I just come and talk to the plants, really—very important to talk to them, they respond I find.
Charles, Prince of Wales 1948– : television interview, 21 September 1986

6 What is a weed? A plant whose virtues have not been discovered.
Ralph Waldo Emerson 1803–82: *Fortune of the Republic* (1878)

7 I will keep returning to the virtues of sharp and swift drainage, whether a plant prefers to be wet or dry . . . I would have called this book Better Drains, but you would never have bought it or borrowed it for bedtime.
Robin Lane Fox 1946– : *Better Gardening* (1982)

8 The kiss of the sun for pardon, The song of the birds for mirth, One is nearer God's Heart in a garden Than anywhere else on earth.
Dorothy Frances Gurney 1858–1932: 'God's Garden' (1913)

9 Among man's immemorial consolations is undoubtedly the company of green and growing things, no less than the melancholy comforts of scholarship.
James Hamilton-Paterson 1941– : *Griefwork* (1993)

10 But though an old man, I am but a young gardener.
Thomas Jefferson 1743–1826: letter to Charles Willson Peale, 20 August 1811

11 The Glory of the Garden lies in more than meets the eye.
Rudyard Kipling 1865–1936: 'The Glory of the Garden' (1911)

12 A garden was the primitive prison till man with Promethean felicity and boldness luckily sinned himself out of it.
Charles Lamb 1775–1834: letter to William Wordsworth, 22 January 1830

13 Weeds are not supposed to grow, But by degrees Some achieve a flower, although No one sees.
Philip Larkin 1922–85: 'Modesties' (1951)

14 Annihilating all that's made To a green thought in a green shade.
Andrew Marvell 1621–78: 'The Garden' (1681)

15 There can be no other occupation like gardening in which, if you were to creep behind someone at their work, you would find them smiling.
Mirabel Osler: *A Gentle Plea for Chaos* (1989)

16 All gardening is landscape-painting.
Alexander Pope 1688–1744: Joseph Spence *Anecdotes* (1966)

17 All really grim gardeners possess a keen sense of humus.
W. C. Sellar 1898–1951 and **R. J. Yeatman** 1898–1968: *Garden Rubbish* (1930)

18 Gardening is the new rock'n'roll. When I was little, it was all fuddy-duddy Percy Thrower. Now it's very social and very, very fashionable.
Ali Ward: in *Independent* 13 June 1998

19 Perennials are the ones that grow like weeds, biennials are the ones that die this year instead of next and hardy annuals are the ones that never come up at all.
Katharine Whitehorn 1928– : *Observations* (1970)

The Generation Gap

see also **Old Age**, **Youth**

1 Each year brings new problems of Form and Content, new foes to tug with: at Twenty I tried to vex my elders, past Sixty it's the young whom

I hope to bother.
W. H. Auden 1907–73: 'Shorts I' (1969)

2 It is the one war in which everyone changes sides.
Cyril Connolly 1903–74: Tom Driberg, speech in House of Commons, 30 October 1959

3 Grown-ups never understand anything for themselves, and it is tiresome for children to be always and forever explaining things to them.
Antoine de Saint-Exupéry 1900–44: *Le Petit Prince* (1943)

4 Come mothers and fathers,
Throughout the land
And don't criticize
What you can't understand.
Your sons and your daughters
Are beyond your command
Your old road is
Rapidly agin'
Please get out of the new one
If you can't lend your hand
For the times they are a-changin'!
Bob Dylan 1941– : 'The Times They Are A-Changing' (1964 song)

5 *Si jeunesse savait; si vieillesse pouvait.*
If youth knew; if age could.
Henri Estienne 1531–98: *Les Prémices* (1594)

6 When I was young, the old regarded me as an outrageous young fellow, and now that I'm old the young regard me as an outrageous old fellow.
Fred Hoyle 1915–2001: in *Scientific American* March 1995

7 There's an uneasiness I have to conceal when I meet a child. I see myself through that child's eyes and remember how I regarded adults when I was small. They seemed a grey crew to me, too fond of sitting down, too keen on small talk, too accustomed to having nothing to look forward to.
Ian McEwan 1948– : *Enduring Love* (1998)

8 Every generation revolts against its fathers and makes friends with its grandfathers.
Lewis Mumford 1895–1990: *The Brown Decades* (1931)

9 The young have aspirations that never come to pass, the old have reminiscences of what never happened.
Saki 1870–1916: *Reginald* (1904)

10 The young man who has not wept is a savage, and the old man who will not laugh is a fool.
George Santayana 1863–1952: *Dialogues in Limbo* (1925)

11 Crabbed age and youth cannot live together:
Youth is full of pleasance, age is full of care.
William Shakespeare 1564–1616: *The Passionate Pilgrim* (1599)

12 Youth, which is forgiven everything, forgives itself nothing: age, which forgives itself everything, is forgiven nothing.
George Bernard Shaw 1856–1950: *Man and Superman* (1903)

13 When I was a boy of 14, my father was so ignorant I could hardly stand to have the old man around. But when I got to be 21, I was astonished at how much the old man had learned in seven years.
Mark Twain 1835–1910: attributed in *Reader's Digest* September 1939, but not traced in his works

14 O Man! that from thy fair and shining youth
Age might but take the things Youth needed not!
William Wordsworth 1770–1850: 'The Small Celandine' (1807)

Genetic Engineering
....
see also **Life Sciences**, **Science and Society**

1 Perhaps what is considered natural is in reality merely what has become familiar.
Anonymous: OECD report *Biotechnology, Agriculture and Food* (1992)

2 Men will not be content to manufacture life: they will want to improve on it.

J. D. Bernal 1901–71: *The World, the Flesh and the Devil* (1929)

3 The mindset that leads to and validates genetic engineering is *genetic determinism*—the idea that organisms are determined by their genetic make-up, or the totality of their genes.

Mae-Wan Ho: *Genetic Engineering: Dream or Nightmare?* (1998)

4 Tony Blair and his ministers are operating on a 'pollute now, pay later' policy. Farm-scale trial plots are rather like letting a rat with bubonic plague out into the environment and then seeing what happens.

■ *on GM foods*

Patrick Holden 1937– : in *Independent* 18 June 1999

5 People in the forefront of environmental causes are destroying experimental crops. That's not logical. That's Luddite.

Douglas Hurd 1930– : in *Sunday Times* 19 September 1999

6 Students accept astonishing things happening in human genetics without turning a hair but worry about GM soya beans.

Steve Jones 1944– : in *Times Higher Education Supplement* 27 August 1999

7 Animals have the right to be animals. Once one claims the right to redesign them then one is doing something that challenges their integrity. The genetic engineers are suggesting that there is nothing in nature that has integrity.

Andrew Linzey 1952– : Danny Penman *The Price of Meat* (1996)

8 We ought not to permit a cottage industry in the God business.

■ *on hearing that British scientists had successfully cloned a lamb*

John Marchi 1948– : in *Guardian* 28 February 1997

9 Many of the products bought at the chemist, such as vitamins, are the result of genetic engineering. Is a vitamin that's been made by yeast better or worse than one that's been synthesized by chemists?

David Sherratt 1945– : in *Oxford Today* Trinity 1999

10 Some day a child is going to sue its parents for being born. They will say, my life is so awful with these terrible genetic defects and you just callously didn't find out.

■ *on the question of genetic screening of foetuses*

James D. Watson 1928– : interview in *Sunday Telegraph* 16 February 1997

11 Genetic control will be the weapon of the future.

Jeanette Winterson 1959– : *Art and Lies* (1994)

Genius

see also **Greatness**

1 There is more beauty in the works of a great genius who is ignorant of all the rules of art, than in the works of a little genius, who not only knows but scrupulously observes them.

Joseph Addison 1672–1719: in *The Spectator* 10 September 1714

2 Geniuses are the luckiest of mortals because what they must do is the same as what they most want to do.

W. H. Auden 1907–73: Dag Hammarskjöld *Markings* (1964)

3 Since when was genius found respectable?

Elizabeth Barrett Browning 1806–61: *Aurora Leigh* (1857)

4 Great wits are sure to madness near allied,
And thin partitions do their bounds divide.

John Dryden 1631–1700: *Absalom and Achitophel* (1681)

5 Genius is one per cent inspiration, ninety-nine per cent perspiration.

Thomas Alva Edison 1847–1931: said *c.*1903, in *Harper's Monthly Magazine* September 1932

6 Little minds are interested in the extraordinary; great minds in the commonplace.

Elbert Hubbard 1859–1915: *Thousand and One Epigrams* (1911)

7 The true genius is a mind of large general powers, accidentally determined to some particular direction.

Samuel Johnson 1709–84: *Lives of the English Poets* (1779–81) 'Cowley'

8 A man of genius makes no mistakes. His errors are volitional and are the portals of discovery.

James Joyce 1882–1941: *Ulysses* (1922)

9 Genius does what it must, and Talent does what it can.

Owen Meredith 1831–91: 'Last Words of a Sensitive Second-Rate Poet' (1868)

10 When a true genius appears in the world, you may know him by this sign, that the dunces are all in confederacy against him.

Jonathan Swift 1667–1745: *Thoughts on Various Subjects* (1711)

11 I have nothing to declare except my genius.

■ *at the New York Custom House*
Oscar Wilde 1854–1900: Frank Harris *Oscar Wilde* (1918)

Genocide

1 This happened near the core
Of a world's culture. This
Occurred among higher things.
This was a philosophical conclusion.
Everybody gets what he deserves.
The bare drab rubble of the place.
The dull damp stone. The rain.
The emptiness. The human lack.

Alan Bold 1943– : 'June 1967 at Buchenwald' (1969); cf. **Justice 2**

2 I herewith commission you to carry out all preparations with regard to . . . a *total solution* of the Jewish question in those territories of Europe which are under German influence.

Hermann Goering 1893–1946: instructions to Heydrich, 31 July 1941; W. L. Shirer *The Rise and Fall of the Third Reich* (1962)

3 Behind my voice lay the suffering of the thousands of prisoners who had not survived to bear witness as I have.

■ *of the people of Tibet*
Palden Gyatso: *Fire Under the Snow* (1997)

4 After all, who remembers today the extermination of the Armenians?

Adolf Hitler 1889–1945: comment, 22 August 1939

5 Our language lacks words to express this offence, the demolition of a man.

■ *of a year spent in Auschwitz*
Primo Levi 1919–87: *If This is a Man* (1958)

6 We know that a man can read Goethe or Rilke in the evening, that he can play Bach and Schubert, and go to his day's work at Auschwitz in the morning.

George Steiner 1926– : *Language and Silence* (1967)

Giving

see also **Charity**

1 It is more blessed to give than to receive.

Bible: Acts of the Apostles

2 They gave it me,—for an un-birthday present.

Lewis Carroll 1832–98: *Through the Looking-Glass* (1872)

3 CHAIRMAN: What is service?
CANDIDATE: The rent we pay for our room on earth.

■ *admission ceremony of Toc H*
Tubby Clayton 1885–1972: Tresham Lever *Clayton of Toc H* (1971)

4 When a woman keeps score, no matter how big or small a gift of love is, it scores one point; each gift has equal value . . . A man, however, thinks he scores one point for a small gift and thirty points for a big gift.

John Gray 1951– : *Men are from Mars, Women are from Venus* (1992)

5 Teach us, good Lord, to serve Thee as Thou deservest:
To give and not to count the cost;
To fight and not to heed the wounds;

To toil and not to seek for rest;
To labour and not to ask for any
  reward
Save that of knowing that we do Thy
will.
St Ignatius Loyola 1491–1556: 'Prayer for
Generosity' (1548)

6 I know it's not much, but it's the best
I can do,
My gift is my song and this one's for
you.
Elton John 1947– and **Bernie Taupin** 1950– :
'Your Song' (1970 song)

7 Presents, I often say, endear Absents.
Charles Lamb 1775–1834: *Essays of Elia* (1823)
'A Dissertation upon Roast Pig'

8 Giving presents is one of the most
possessive of things we do . . . It's the
way we keep a hold on other people.
Plant ourselves in their lives.
Penelope Lively 1933– : *Moon Tiger* (1987)

9 Why is it no one ever sent me yet
One perfect limousine, do you
  suppose?
Ah no, it's always just my luck to get
One perfect rose.
Dorothy Parker 1893–1967: 'One Perfect Rose'
(1937)

10   *Equo ne credite, Teucri.*
Quidquid id est, timeo Danaos et dona
  ferentes.
Do not trust the horse, Trojans.
Whatever it is, I fear the Greeks even
when they bring gifts.
Virgil 70–19 BC: *Aeneid*

11 Behold, I do not give lectures or a
little charity,
When I give I give myself.
Walt Whitman 1819–92: 'Song of Myself'
(written 1855)

God

see also **Atheism, Belief, The Bible,
Christianity, Religion**

1 If only God would give me some clear
sign! Like making a large deposit in
my name at a Swiss bank.
Woody Allen 1935– : in *New Yorker*
5 November 1973

2 The nature of God is a circle of which
the centre is everywhere and the
circumference is nowhere.
Anonymous: said to have been traced to a lost
treatise of Empedocles; quoted in the *Roman
de la Rose*, and by St Bonaventura in
Itinerarius Mentis in Deum

3 God has been replaced, as he has all
over the West, with respectability and
air-conditioning.
Imamu Amiri Baraka 1934– : *Midstream*
(1963)

4 If I were Her what would really piss
me off the worst is that they cannot
even get My gender right for
Christsakes.
Roseanne Barr 1953– : *Roseanne* (1990)

5 With men this is impossible; but with
God all things are possible.
Bible: St Matthew

6 He that loveth not knoweth not God;
for God is love.
Bible: I John

7 And almost every one when age,
Disease, or sorrows strike him,
Inclines to think there is a God,
Or something very like Him.
Arthur Hugh Clough 1819–61: *Dipsychus* (1865)

8 God moves in a mysterious way
His wonders to perform.
William Cowper 1731–1800: 'Light Shining out
of Darkness' (1779 hymn)

9 It is the final proof of God's
omnipotence that he need not exist in
order to save us.
Peter De Vries 1910–93: *The Mackerel Plaza*
(1958)

10 But I can't think for you
You'll have to decide,
Whether Judas Iscariot
Had God on his side.
Bob Dylan 1941– : 'With God on our Side'
(1963 song)

11 God is subtle but he is not malicious.
Albert Einstein 1879–1955: remark made at
Princeton University, May 1921

12 'I didn't exist at Creation
I didn't exist at the Flood,

And I won't be around for Salvation
To sort out the sheep from the cud—
'Or whatever the phrase is. The fact is
In soteriological terms
I'm a crude existential malpractice
And you are a diet of worms.'
James Fenton 1949– : 'God, A Poem' (1983)

13 Forgive, O Lord, my little jokes on
Thee
And I'll forgive Thy great big one on
me.
Robert Frost 1874–1963: 'Cluster of Faith'
(1962)

14 God, to me, it seems,
is a verb
not a noun,
proper or improper.
R. Buckminster Fuller 1895–1983: *No More
Secondhand God* (1963)

15 Mine eyes have seen the glory of the
coming of the Lord:
He is trampling out the vintage where
the grapes of wrath are stored;
He hath loosed the fateful lightning of
his terrible swift sword:
His truth is marching on.
Julia Ward Howe 1819–1910: 'Battle Hymn of
the Republic' (1862)

16 Operationally, God is beginning to
resemble not a ruler but the last
fading smile of a cosmic Cheshire cat.
Julian Huxley 1887–1975: *Religion without
Revelation* (1957 ed.)

17 I am not clear that God manoeuvres
physical things . . . After all, a
conjuring trick with bones only
proves that it is as clever as a
conjuring trick with bones.
■ *of the Resurrection*
David Jenkins 1925– : 'Poles Apart' (BBC
radio, 4 October 1984)

18 God seems to have left the receiver off
the hook, and time is running out.
Arthur Koestler 1905–83: *The Ghost in the
Machine* (1967)

19 God is love, but get it in writing.
Gypsy Rose Lee 1914–70: attributed

20 Though the mills of God grind slowly,
yet they grind exceeding small;

Though with patience He stands
waiting, with exactness grinds He
all.
Henry Wadsworth Longfellow 1807–82:
translation of *Sinngedichte* (1654) by
Friedrich von Logau (1604–55), of classical
origin

21 Better authentic mammon than a
bogus god.
Louis MacNeice 1907–63: *Autumn Journal*
(1939)

22 If the triangles were to make a God
they would give him three sides.
Montesquieu 1689–1755: *Lettres Persanes*
(1721)

23 God is dead: but considering the state
the species Man is in, there will
perhaps be caves, for ages yet, in
which his shadow will be shown.
Friedrich Nietzsche 1844–1900: *Die fröhliche
Wissenschaft* (1882)

24 'God is or he is not.' But to which side
shall we incline? . . . Let us weigh the
gain and the loss in wagering that God
is. Let us estimate the two chances. If
you gain, you gain all; if you lose, you
lose nothing. Wager then without
hesitation that he is.
■ *known as Pascal's wager*
Blaise Pascal 1623–62: *Pensées* (1670)

25 God is really only another artist. He
invented the giraffe, the elephant, and
the cat. He has no real style. He just
goes on trying other things.
Pablo Picasso 1881–1973: F. Gilot and C. Lake
Life With Picasso (1964)

26 Liszt said to me today that God alone
deserves to be loved. It may be true,
but when one has loved a man it is
very difficult to love God. It is so
different.
George Sand 1804–76: Marie Jenny Howe *The
Intimate Journal of George Sand* (1929) 1834

27 God heard the embattled nations sing
and shout
'Gott strafe England!' and 'God save
the King!'
God this, God that, and God the other
thing—

'Good God!' said God, 'I've got my work cut out.'

J. C. Squire 1884–1958: 'The Dilemma' (1916)

28 It is a mistake to suppose that God is only, or even chiefly, concerned with religion.

William Temple 1881–1944: R. V. C. Bodley *In Search of Serenity* (1955)

29 If God did not exist, it would be necessary to invent him.

Voltaire 1694–1778: *Épîtres* no. 96 'A l'Auteur du livre des trois imposteurs'

30 Any God I ever felt in church I brought in with me. And I think all the other folks did too. They come to church to *share* God not find God.

Alice Walker 1944– : *The Colour Purple* (1982)

31 Even God has become female. God is no longer the bearded patriarch in the sky. He has had a sex change and turned into Mother Nature.

Fay Weldon 1931– : in *The Times* 29 August 1998

32 If God is your emotional role model, very few human relationships will match up to it.

Jeanette Winterson 1959– : *Oranges are Not the Only Fruit* (1985)

Golf

1 If you watch a game, it's fun. If you play it, it's recreation. If you work at it, it's golf.

Bob Hope 1903– : in *Reader's Digest* October 1958

2 A decision of the courts decided that the game of golf may be played on Sunday, not being a game within the view of the law, but being a form of moral effort.

Stephen Leacock 1869–1944: *Over the Footlights* (1923)

3 Golf is a good walk spoiled.

Mark Twain 1835–1910: attributed

4 The least thing upset him on the links. He missed short putts because of the uproar of the butterflies in the adjoining meadows.

P. G. Wodehouse 1881–1975: *The Clicking of Cuthbert* (1922)

5 Golf . . . is the infallible test. The man who can go into a patch of rough alone, with the knowledge that only God is watching him, and play his ball where it lies, is the man who will serve you faithfully and well.

P. G. Wodehouse 1881–1975: *The Clicking of Cuthbert* (1922)

Goodness

see also **Charity**, **Evil**, **Sin**

1 I'm as pure as the driven slush.

Tallulah Bankhead 1903–68: in *Saturday Evening Post* 12 April 1947

2 Terrible is the temptation to be good.

Bertolt Brecht 1898–1956: *The Caucasian Chalk Circle* (1948)

3 No people do so much harm as those who go about doing good.

Mandell Creighton 1843–1901: *The Life and Letters of Mandell Creighton* by his wife (1904)

4 What after all
Is a halo? It's only one more thing to keep clean.

Christopher Fry 1907– : *The Lady's not for Burning* (1949)

5 The virtue which requires to be ever guarded is scarce worth the sentinel.

Oliver Goldsmith 1728–74: *The Vicar of Wakefield* (1766)

6 I expect to pass through this world but once; any good thing therefore that I can do, or any kindness that I can show to any fellow-creature, let me do it now; let me not defer or neglect it, for I shall not pass this way again.

Stephen Grellet 1773–1855: attributed; there are many other claimants to authorship

7 Good, but not religious-good.

Thomas Hardy 1840–1928: *Under the Greenwood Tree* (1872)

8 If some great Power would agree to make me always think what is true

and do what is right, on condition of being turned into a sort of clock and wound up every morning before I got out of bed, I should instantly close with the offer.
T. H. Huxley 1825–95: 'On Descartes' *Discourse on Method*' (written 1870)

9 Be good, sweet maid, and let who will be clever.
Charles Kingsley 1819–75: 'A Farewell' (1858)

10 Our intentions make blackguards of us all; our weakness in carrying them out we call probity.
Pierre Choderlos de Laclos 1741–1803: *Les Liaisons Dangereuses* (1782) letter 66

11 Mostly, we are good when it makes sense. A good society is one that makes sense of being good.
Ian McEwan 1948– : *Enduring Love* (1998)

12 The only way for goodness to be carried out is with the unconsciousness of habit.
Candia McWilliam 1955– : *Debatable Land* (1994)

13 When men grow virtuous in their old age, they only make a sacrifice to God of the devil's leavings.
Alexander Pope 1688–1744: *Miscellanies* (1727) 'Thoughts on Various Subjects'

14 How far that little candle throws his beams!
So shines a good deed in a naughty world.
William Shakespeare 1564–1616: *The Merchant of Venice* (1596–8)

15 More people are flattered into virtue than bullied out of vice.
R. S. Surtees 1805–64: *The Analysis of the Hunting Field* (1846)

16 My strength is as the strength of ten, Because my heart is pure.
Alfred, Lord Tennyson 1809–92: 'Sir Galahad' (1842)

17 Would that we had spent one whole day well in this world!
Thomas à Kempis c.1380–1471: *The Imitation of Christ*

18 Few things are harder to put up with than the annoyance of a good example.
Mark Twain 1835–1910: *Pudd'nhead Wilson* (1894)

19 Virtue knows to a farthing what it has lost by not having been vice.
Horace Walpole 1717–97: L. Kronenberger *The Extraordinary Mr Wilkes* (1974)

20 'Goodness, what beautiful diamonds!' 'Goodness had nothing to do with it.'
Mae West 1892–1980: *Night After Night* (1932 film)

21 I used to be Snow White . . . but I drifted.
Mae West 1892–1980: Joseph Weintraub *Peel Me a Grape* (1975)

22 It is better to be beautiful than to be good. But . . . it is better to be good than to be ugly.
Oscar Wilde 1854–1900: *The Picture of Dorian Gray* (1891)

23 If all the good people were clever, And all clever people were good, The world would be nicer than ever We thought that it possibly could. But somehow, 'tis seldom or never The two hit it off as they should; The good are so harsh to the clever, The clever so rude to the good!
Elizabeth Wordsworth 1840–1932: 'Good and Clever'

24 That best portion of a good man's life,
His little, nameless, unremembered, acts
Of kindness and of love.
William Wordsworth 1770–1850: 'Lines composed a few miles above Tintern Abbey' (1798)

Gossip
see also **Reputation**

1 Every man is surrounded by a neighbourhood of voluntary spies.
Jane Austen 1775–1817: *Northanger Abbey* (1818)

2 I make my boyfriends famous.
Naomi Campbell 1970– : attributed; in *Guardian* 25 June 1998

3 Gossip is a sort of smoke that comes from the dirty tobacco-pipes of those who diffuse it: it proves nothing but the bad taste of the smoker.
George Eliot 1819–80: *Daniel Deronda* (1876)

4 Love and scandal are the best sweeteners of tea.
Henry Fielding 1707–54: *Love in Several Masques* (1728)

5 Like all gossip—it's merely one of those half-alive things that try to crowd out real life.
E. M. Forster 1879–1970: *A Passage to India* (1924)

6 Blood sport is brought to its ultimate refinement in the gossip columns.
Bernard Ingham 1932– : speech, 5 February 1986

7 Men have always detested women's gossip because they suspect the truth: their measurements are being taken and compared.
Erica Jong 1942– : *Fear of Flying* (1973)

8 Prince or commoner, tenor or bass, Painter or plumber or never-do-well, Do me a favour and shut your face— Poets alone should kiss and tell.
Dorothy Parker 1893–1967: 'Ballade of a Talked-Off Ear'

9 I hope there's a tinge of disgrace about me. Hopefully, there's one good scandal left in me yet.
Diana Rigg 1938– : in *The Times* 3 May 1999

10 Be thou as chaste as ice, as pure as snow, thou shalt not escape calumny.
William Shakespeare 1564–1616: *Hamlet* (1601)

11 It takes your enemy and your friend, working together, to hurt you to the heart: the one to slander you and the other to get the news to you.
Mark Twain 1835–1910: *Following the Equator* (1897)

12 There is only one thing in the world worse than being talked about, and that is not being talked about.
Oscar Wilde 1854–1900: *The Picture of Dorian Gray* (1891)

Government

see also **Civil Service**, **International Relations**, **Parliament**, **Politics**, **Society**

1 Let them hate, so long as they fear.
Accius 170–c.86 BC: from *Atreus*; Seneca *Dialogues*

2 A government of laws, and not of men.
John Adams 1735–1826: *Boston Gazette* (1774) 'Novanglus' papers; later incorporated in the Massachusetts Constitution (1780)

3 The happiness of society is the end of government.
John Adams 1735–1826: *Thoughts on Government* (1776)

4 My faith in the people governing is, on the whole, infinitesimal; my faith in The People governed is, on the whole, illimitable.
Charles Dickens 1812–70: speech at Birmingham and Midland Institute, 27 September 1869

5 No Government can be long secure without a formidable Opposition.
Benjamin Disraeli 1804–81: *Coningsby* (1844)

6 Though God hath raised me high, yet this I count the glory of my crown: that I have reigned with your loves.
Elizabeth I 1533–1603: The Golden Speech, 1601

7 The State is not 'abolished', *it withers away*.
Friedrich Engels 1820–95: *Anti-Dühring* (1878)

8 Why do we not rage against those who accept the shameful idea that sickness must be 'incurable', that our betters know what they are doing when they prefer missiles to medicine?
Robert Fisk 1946– : in *Independent* 30 September 1998

9 If the Government is big enough to give you everything you want, it is big enough to take away everything you have.

Gerald Ford 1909– : John F. Parker *If Elected* (1960)

10 The state is like the human body. Not all of its functions are dignified.

Anatole France 1844–1924: *Les Opinions de M. Jerome Coignard* (1893)

11 The English and, more latterly, the British, have the habit of acquiring their institutions by chance or inadvertence, and shedding them in a fit of absent-mindedness.

Lord Hailsham 1907–2001: 'The Granada Guildhall Lecture' 10 November 1987

12 Many journalists have fallen for the conspiracy theory of government. I do assure you that they would produce more accurate work if they adhered to the cock-up theory.

Bernard Ingham 1932– : in *Observer* 17 March 1985

13 I would not give half a guinea to live under one form of government rather than another. It is of no moment to the happiness of an individual.

Samuel Johnson 1709–84: James Boswell *Life of Samuel Johnson* (1791) 31 March 1772

14 I work for a Government I despise for ends I think criminal.

John Maynard Keynes 1883–1946: letter to Duncan Grant, 15 December 1917

15 How is the world ruled and how do wars start? Diplomats tell lies to journalists and then believe what they read.

Karl Kraus 1874–1936: *Aphorisms and More Aphorisms* (1909)

16 We give the impression of being in office but not in power.

Norman Lamont 1942– : speech, House of Commons, 9 June 1993

17 While the State exists, there can be no freedom. When there is freedom there will be no State.

Lenin 1870–1924: *State and Revolution* (1919)

18 To govern is to choose.

Duc de Lévis 1764–1830: *Maximes et Réflexions* (1812 ed.)

19 The reluctant obedience of distant provinces generally costs more than it [the territory] is worth.

Lord Macaulay 1800–59: *Essays Contributed to the Edinburgh Review* (1843) 'The War of Succession in Spain'

20 Because it is difficult to join them together, it is much safer for a prince to be feared than loved, if he is to fail in one of the two.

Niccolò Machiavelli 1469–1527: *The Prince* (written 1513)

21 BIG BROTHER IS WATCHING YOU.

George Orwell 1903–50: *Nineteen Eighty-Four* (1949)

22 Government, even in its best state, is but a necessary evil . . . Government, like dress, is the badge of lost innocence; the palaces of kings are built upon the ruins of the bowers of paradise.

Thomas Paine 1737–1809: *Common Sense* (1776)

23 When, in countries that are called civilized, we see age going to the workhouse and youth to the gallows, something must be wrong in the system of government.

Thomas Paine 1737–1809: *The Rights of Man* pt. 2 (1792)

24 Government of the busy by the bossy for the bully.

■ *on over-government*
Arthur Seldon 1916– : *Capitalism* (1990)

25 A government which robs Peter to pay Paul can always depend on the support of Paul.

George Bernard Shaw 1856–1950: *Everybody's Political What's What?* (1944)

26 A fainéant government is not the worst government that England can have. It has been the great fault of our politicians that they have all wanted to do something.

Anthony Trollope 1815–82: *Phineas Finn* (1869)

27 Governments need both shepherds and butchers.

Voltaire 1694–1778: 'The Piccini Notebooks' (c.1735–50)

Grammar

1 Would you convey my compliments to the purist who reads your proofs and tell him or her that I write in a sort of broken-down patois which is something like the way a Swiss waiter talks, and that when I split an infinitive, God damn it, I split it so it will stay split.
Raymond Chandler 1888–1959: letter to Edward Weeks, 18 January 1947

2 Colourless green ideas sleep furiously.
■ *illustrating that grammatical structure is independent of meaning*
Noam Chomsky 1928– : *Syntactic Structures* (1957)

3 This is the sort of English up with which I will not put.
Winston Churchill 1874–1965: Ernest Gowers *Plain Words* (1948)

4 I will not go down to posterity talking bad grammar.
■ *while correcting proofs of his last Parliamentary speech, 31 March 1881*
Benjamin Disraeli 1804–81: Robert Blake *Disraeli* (1966)

5 The English-speaking world may be divided into (1) those who neither know nor care what a split infinitive is; (2) those who do not know, but care very much; (3) those who know and condemn; (4) those who know and distinguish. Those who neither know nor care are the vast majority, and are a happy folk, to be envied by most of the minority classes.
H. W. Fowler 1858–1933: *Modern English Usage* (1926)

6 Every sentence he manages to utter scatters its component parts like pond water from a verb chasing its own tail.
■ *of George Bush*
Clive James 1939– : *The Dreaming Swimmer* (1992)

7 The subjunctive mood is in its death throes, and the best thing to do is to put it out of its misery as soon as possible.
W. Somerset Maugham 1874–1965: *A Writer's Notebook* (1949) written in 1941

8 I don't want to talk grammar, I want to talk like a lady.
George Bernard Shaw 1856–1950: *Pygmalion* (1916)

9 Save the gerund and screw the whale.
Tom Stoppard 1937– : *The Real Thing* (1988 rev. ed.)

Gratitude
see also **Ingratitude**

1 Maybe the only thing worse than having to give gratitude constantly all the time, is having to accept it.
William Faulkner 1897–1962: *Requiem for a Nun* (1951)

2 The obligation of gratitude may easily become a trap, and the young are often caught and maimed in it.
Eric Gill 1882–1940: *Autobiography* (1940)

3 There are minds so impatient of inferiority, that their gratitude is a species of revenge, and they return benefits, not because recompense is a pleasure, but because obligation is a pain.
Samuel Johnson 1709–84: in *The Rambler* 15 January 1751

4 In most of mankind gratitude is merely a secret hope for greater favours.
Duc de la Rochefoucauld 1613–80: *Maximes* (1678)

5 [Gratitude] is a sickness suffered by dogs.
Joseph Stalin 1879–1953: Nikolai Tolstoy *Stalin's Secret War* (1981)

Greatness
see also **Achievement**, **Genius**

1 A man is seldom ashamed of feeling that he cannot love a woman so well when he sees a certain greatness in her: nature having intended greatness for men.
George Eliot 1819–80: *Middlemarch* (1871–2)

2 Is it so bad, then, to be misunderstood? Pythagoras was

misunderstood, and Socrates, and Jesus, and Luther, and Copernicus, and Galileo, and Newton, and every pure and wise spirit that ever took flesh. To be great is to be misunderstood.

Ralph Waldo Emerson 1803–82: *Essays* (1841) 'Self-Reliance'

3 A man does not attain the status of Galileo merely because he is persecuted; he must also be right.

Stephen Jay Gould 1941–2002: *Ever since Darwin* (1977)

4 If I am a great man, then all great men are frauds.

Andrew Bonar Law 1858–1923: Lord Beaverbrook *Politicians and the War* (1932)

5 Everything we think of as great has come to us from neurotics. It is they and they alone who found religions and create great works of art. The world will never realise how much it owes to them and what they have suffered in order to bestow their gifts on it.

Marcel Proust 1871–1922: *Guermantes Way* (1921)

6 But be not afraid of greatness: some men are born great, some achieve greatness, and some have greatness thrust upon them.

William Shakespeare 1564–1616: *Twelfth Night* (1601)

7 All the world's great have been little boys who wanted the moon.

John Steinbeck 1902–68: *Cup of Gold* (1953)

8   In me there dwells
No greatness, save it be some far-off touch
Of greatness to know well I am not great.

Alfred, Lord Tennyson 1809–92: *Idylls of the King* 'Lancelot and Elaine' (1859)

Greece
....

1 The isles of Greece, the isles of Greece!
Where burning Sappho loved and sung,

Where grew the arts of war and peace,
Where Delos rose, and Phoebus sprung!
Eternal summer gilds them yet,
But all, except their sun, is set!

Lord Byron 1788–1824: *Don Juan* (1819–24)

2 If you take Greece apart, in the end you will see remaining to you an olive tree, a vineyard and a ship. Which means: with just so much you can put her back together.

Odysseus Elytis 1911– : 'The Little Seafarer' (1988)

3 Except the blind forces of Nature, nothing moves in this world which is not Greek in its origin.

Henry Maine 1822–88: *Village Communities* (3rd ed., 1876)

4 Let there be light! said Liberty,
And like sunrise from the sea,
Athens arose!

Percy Bysshe Shelley 1792–1822: *Hellas* (1822)

Greed
....

see also **Money**

1 Greed is all right . . . Greed is healthy. You can be greedy and still feel good about yourself.

Ivan F. Boesky 1937– : commencement address, Berkeley, California, 18 May 1986

2 You shall not crucify mankind upon a cross of gold.

William Jennings Bryan 1860–1925: speech at the Democratic National Convention, Chicago, 1896

3 There is enough in the world for everyone's need, but not enough for everyone's greed.

Frank Buchman 1878–1961: *Remaking the World* (1947)

4 Please, sir, I want some more.

Charles Dickens 1812–70: *Oliver Twist* (1838)

5 But the music that excels is the sound of oil wells
As they slurp, slurp, slurp into the barrels . . .
I want an old-fashioned house

With an old-fashioned fence
And an old-fashioned millionaire.
Marve Fisher: 'An Old-Fashioned Girl' (1954
song)

6 *in reply to his mother's warning 'You'll be sick
tomorrow', when stuffing himself with cakes at
tea:*
I'll be sick tonight.
Jack Llewelyn-Davies 1894–1959: Andrew
Birkin *J. M. Barrie and the Lost Boys* (1979);
Barrie used the line in *Little Mary* (1903)

7 If all the rich people in the world
divided up their money among
themselves there wouldn't be enough
to go round.
Christina Stead 1902–83: *House of All Nations*
(1938)

8 To what do you not drive human
hearts, cursed craving for gold!
Virgil 70–19 BC: *Aeneid*

9 Greed—for lack of a better word—is
good. Greed is right. Greed works.
Stanley Weiser and **Oliver Stone** 1946– : *Wall
Street* (1987 film)

Guests
··················
see also **Parties**

1 Mankind is divisible into two great
classes: hosts and guests.
Max Beerbohm 1872–1956: *And Even Now*
(1920)

2 Guests can be, and often are,
delightful, but they should never be
allowed to get the upper hand.
Elizabeth, Countess von Arnim 1866–1941: *All
the Dogs in My Life* (1936)

3 It's life's losers who really want to
please—and wanting to please is a
prerequisite of hospitality.
A. A. Gill 1954– : in *Sunday Times*
19 September 1999

4 Some people can stay longer in an
hour than others can in a week.
William Dean Howells 1837–1920: attributed

5 My father used to say,
'Superior people never make long
visits,

have to be shown Longfellow's grave
or the glass flowers at Harvard.'
Marianne Moore 1887–1972: 'Silence' (1935)

6 I suppose you are decorating the
house with guests for Christmas?
Toni Morrison 1931– : *Tar Baby* (1981)

7 For I, who hold sage Homer's rule the
best,
Welcome the coming, speed the going
guest.
Alexander Pope 1688–1744: *Imitations of
Horace* (1734); 'speed the parting guest' in
Pope's translation of *The Odyssey* (1725–6)

8 Unbidden guests
Are often welcomest when they are
gone.
William Shakespeare 1564–1616: *Henry VI,
Part 1* (1592)

Guilt
··············
see also **Innocence**

1 He that is without sin among you, let
him first cast a stone at her.
Bible: St John

2 Good women always think it is their
fault when someone else is being
offensive. Bad women never take the
blame for anything.
Anita Brookner 1928– : *Hotel du Lac* (1984)

3 In former days, everyone found the
assumption of innocence so easy;
today we find fatally easy the
assumption of guilt.
Amanda Cross 1926– : *Poetic Justice* (1970)

4 Of all means to regeneration Remorse
is surely the most wasteful. It cuts
away healthy tissue with the poisoned.
It is a knife that probes far deeper
than the evil.
E. M. Forster 1879–1970: *Howards End* (1910)

5 To be absolutely honest, what I feel
really bad about is that I don't feel
worse. That's the ineffectual liberal's
problem in a nutshell.
Michael Frayn 1933– : in *Observer* 8 August
1965

6 True guilt is guilt at the obligation one
owes to oneself to be oneself. False

guilt is guilt felt at not being what
other people feel one ought to be or
assume that one is.

R. D. Laing 1927–89: *Self and Others* (1961)

7 Guilt feelings so often arise from
accusations rather than from crimes.

Iris Murdoch 1919–99: *The Sea, The Sea* (1978)

8 I brought myself down. I gave them a
sword. And they stuck it in.

Richard Nixon 1913–94: television interview,
19 May 1977

9 One thing that the Roman Catholic
Church and the West Midlands
Serious Crimes Squad have in
common—well, one of many things
actually—is the shrewd professional
understanding that given the right
circumstances people will always want
to confess, whether guilty or not.

Joseph O'Connor 1963– : *The Secret World of
the Irish Male* (1994)

10 *to Albert Speer, who having always denied
knowledge of the Holocaust had said that he was
at fault in having 'looked away':*
You cannot look away from
something you don't know. If you
looked away, then you knew.

Gitta Sereny 1923– : recalled on BBC2
Reputations, 2 May 1996

11 Here's the smell of the blood still: all
the perfumes of Arabia will not
sweeten this little hand.

William Shakespeare 1564–1616: *Macbeth*
(1606)

12 What hangs people . . . is the
unfortunate circumstance of guilt.

Robert Louis Stevenson 1850–94: *The Wrong
Box* (with Lloyd Osbourne, 1889)

13 *Non! rien de rien,
Non! je ne regrette rien.*
No, no regrets,
No, we will have no regrets.

Michel Vaucaire: 'Non, je ne regrette rien'
(1960 song); sung by Edith Piaf

Gulf War 1991

1 That killed head straining through the
windscreen

with its frill of bubbles in the eye-
sockets
is not trying to tell you something—
it is telling you something.

Helen Dunmore 1952– : 'Poem on the
Obliteration of 100,000 Iraqi Soldiers' (1994)

2 Let them remember, all those who
celebrate,
that their good news is someone else's
bad.

Tony Harrison 1953– : 'Initial Illumination'
(1991)

3 The mother of battles.

■ *popular interpretation of his description of the
approaching Gulf War*

Saddam Hussein 1937– : speech in Baghdad,
6 January 1991; *The Times*, 7 January 1991,
reported that Saddam had no intention of
relinquishing Kuwait and was ready for the
'mother of all wars'

4 If Kuwait grew carrots we wouldn't
give a damn.

Lawrence Korb 1939– : in *International
Herald Tribune* 21 August 1990

5 First, we are going to cut it off, and
then, we are going to kill it.

■ *strategy for dealing with the Iraqi Army in the
Gulf War*

Colin Powell 1937– : at a press conference,
23 January 1991

Habit

1 Routine, in an intelligent man, is a
sign of ambition.

W. H. Auden 1907–73: 'The Life of That-There
Poet' (1958)

2 The air is full of our cries. (*He listens*)
But habit is a great deadener.

Samuel Beckett 1906–89: *Waiting for Godot*
(1955)

3 Custom reconciles us to everything.

Edmund Burke 1729–97: *On the Sublime and
Beautiful* (1757)

4 A leopard does not change his spots,
or change his feeling that spots are
rather a credit.

Ivy Compton-Burnett 1884–1969: *More
Women than Men* (1933)

5 Habit with him was all the test of
truth,
'It must be right: I've done it from my
youth.'
George Crabbe 1754–1832: *The Borough* (1810)

6 People wish to be settled: only as far as
they are unsettled is there any hope
for them.
Ralph Waldo Emerson 1803–82: *Essays* (1841)
'Circles'

Hair

1 It was a blonde. A blonde to make a
bishop kick a hole in a stained glass
window.
Raymond Chandler 1888–1959: *Farewell, My
Lovely* (1940)

2 Being blonde is definitely a different
state of mind. I can't really put my
finger on it, but the artifice of being
blonde has some incredible sort of
sexual connotation.
Madonna 1958– : in *Rolling Stone* 23 March
1989

3 When I had curls
I knew more girls.
I do more reading
Now my hair is receding.
James Simmons 1933–2001: 'Epigrams'

4 There is more felicity on the far side of
baldness than young men can possibly
imagine.
Logan Pearsall Smith 1865–1946:
Afterthoughts (1931)

5 In England and America a beard
usually means that its owner would
rather be considered venerable than
virile; on the continent of Europe it
often means that its owner makes a
special claim to virility.
Rebecca West 1892–1983: *The Thinking Reed*
(1936)

6 Only God, my dear,
Could love you for yourself alone
And not your yellow hair.
W. B. Yeats 1865–1939: 'Anne Gregory' (1932)

Happiness

see also **Pleasure**

1 A large income is the best recipe for
happiness I ever heard of. It certainly
may secure all the myrtle and turkey
part of it.
Jane Austen 1775–1817: *Mansfield Park* (1814)

2 You ask if they were happy. This is not
a characteristic of a European. To be
contented—that's for the cows.
Coco Chanel 1883–1971: A. Madsen *Coco
Chanel* (1990)

3 For all the happiness mankind can
gain
Is not in pleasure, but in rest from
pain.
John Dryden 1631–1700: *The Indian Emperor*
(1665)

4 The happiest women, like the
happiest nations, have no history.
George Eliot 1819–80: *The Mill on the Floss*
(1860)

5 We have lived through the era when
happiness was a warm puppy, and the
era when happiness was a dry martini,
and now we have come to the era
when happiness is 'knowing what
your uterus looks like'.
Nora Ephron 1941– : *Crazy Salad* (1975)
'Vaginal Politics'

6 Happiness makes up in height for
what it lacks in length.
Robert Frost 1874–1963: title of poem (1942)

7 Point me out the happy man and I
will point you out either egotism,
selfishness, evil—or else an absolute
ignorance.
Graham Greene 1904–91: *The Heart of the
Matter* (1948)

8 Happiness is not an ideal of reason
but of imagination.
Immanuel Kant 1724–1804: *Fundamental
Principles of the Metaphysics of Ethics* (1785)

9 One is never as unhappy as one
thinks, nor as happy as one hopes.
Duc de la Rochefoucauld 1613–80: *Sentences et
Maximes de Morale* (1664)

10 Happiness is a warm gun.
John Lennon 1940–80: title of song (1968)

11 Ask yourself whether you are happy, and you cease to be so.
John Stuart Mill 1806–73: *Autobiography* (1873)

12 But headlong joy is ever on the wing.
John Milton 1608–74: 'The Passion' (1645)

13 Not to admire, is all the art I know, To make men happy, and to keep them so.
Alexander Pope 1688–1744: *Imitations of Horace*

14 For if unhappiness develops the forces of the mind, happiness alone is salutary to the body.
Marcel Proust 1871–1922: *Time Regained* (1926)

15 I always say I don't think everyone has the right to happiness or to be loved. Even the Americans have written into their constitution that you have the right to the 'pursuit of happiness'. You have the right to try but that is all.
Claire Rayner 1931– : G. Kinnock and F. Miller (eds.) *By Faith and Daring* (1993)

16 Pleasure comes with the fulfilment of desire—getting what you want and wanting what you get. Happiness comes with the fulfilment of the person. And much of our moral confusion comes from the fact that we no longer know what happiness is, nor how to obtain it.
Roger Scruton 1944– : *The Good Life* (1998)

17 We have no more right to consume happiness without producing it than to consume wealth without producing it.
George Bernard Shaw 1856–1950: *Candida* (1898)

18 But a lifetime of happiness! No man alive could bear it: it would be hell on earth.
George Bernard Shaw 1856–1950: *Man and Superman* (1903)

19 Happiness is an imaginary condition, formerly often attributed by the living to the dead, now usually attributed by adults to children, and by children to adults.
Thomas Szasz 1920– : *The Second Sin* (1973)

Hatred

see also **Enemies**

1 Now hatred is by far the longest pleasure;
Men love in haste, but they detest at leisure.
Lord Byron 1788–1824: *Don Juan* (1819–24)

2 I tell you there is such a thing as creative hate!
Willa Cather 1873–1947: *The Song of the Lark* (1915)

3 I never hated a man enough to give him diamonds back.
Zsa Zsa Gabor 1919– : in *Observer* 25 August 1957

4 We can scarcely hate any one that we know.
William Hazlitt 1778–1830: *Table Talk* (1822) 'On Criticism'

5 If you hate a person, you hate something in him that is part of yourself. What isn't part of ourselves doesn't disturb us.
Hermann Hesse 1877–1962: *Demian* (1919)

6 Hating gets going, it goes round, it gets older and tighter and older and tighter, until it holds a person inside it like a fist holds a stick.
Ursula K. Le Guin 1929– : *Always Coming Home* (1985)

7 No one is born hating another person because of the colour of his skin, or his background, or his religion. People must learn to hate, and if they can learn to hate, they can be taught to love, for love comes more naturally to the human heart than its opposite.
Nelson Mandela 1918– : *Long Walk to Freedom* (1994)

8 Any kiddie in school can love like a fool,
But hating, my boy, is an art.
Ogden Nash 1902–71: 'Plea for Less Malice Toward None' (1933)

9 Always give your best, never get
discouraged, never be petty; always
remember, others may hate you.
Those who hate you don't win unless
you hate them. And then you destroy
yourself.

Richard Nixon 1913–94: address to staff,
9 August 1974

10 I have loved him too much not to feel
any hatred for him.

Jean Racine 1639–99: *Andromaque* (1667)

11 Hate takes a long time
To grow in, and mine
Has increased from birth;
Not for the brute earth . . .
. . . I find
This hate's for my own kind . . .

R. S. Thomas 1913–2000: 'Those Others' (1961)

12 One cannot overestimate the power of
a good rancorous hatred on the part
of the *stupid*. The stupid have so
much more industry and energy to
expend on hating. They build it up
like coral insects.

Sylvia Townsend Warner 1893–1978: diary
26 September 1954

Health

see also **The Body**, **Exercise**, **Medicine**,
Sickness

1 In the face of such overwhelming
statistical possibilities, hypochondria
has always seemed to me to be the
only rational position to take on life.

John Diamond: *C: Because Cowards Get
Cancer Too* (1998)

2 Aromatherapy is like going into the
countryside and smelling flowers. It
should be available in Parliament.
They already have it in some mental
hospitals.

Simon Hughes 1951– : in *Independent*
24 January 1998

3 *Orandum est ut sit mens sana in
corpore sano.*
You should pray to have a sound mind
in a sound body.

Juvenal AD c.60–c.130: *Satires*

4 Life's not just being alive, but being
well.

Martial AD c.40–c.104: *Epigrammata*

5 A man dies and is buried, and all his
words and actions are forgotten, but
the food he has eaten lives after him in
the sound or rotten bones of his
children.

George Orwell 1903–50: *The Road to Wigan
Pier* (1937)

6 At 70, I'm in fine fettle for my age,
sleep like a babe and feel around 12.
The secret? Lots of meat, drink and
cigarettes and not giving in to things.

Jennifer Paterson 1928–99: in *Daily Mail*
18 August 1998

7 Look to your health; and if you have
it, praise God, and value it next to a
good conscience; for health is the
second blessing that we mortals are
capable of; a blessing that money
cannot buy.

Izaak Walton 1593–1683: *The Compleat Angler*
(1653)

8 When people discussed tonics, pick-
me-ups after a severe illness, she kept
to herself the prescription of a quick
dip in bed with someone you liked
but were not in love with. A shock of
sexual astonishment which could
make you feel astonishingly well and
high spirited.

Mary Wesley 1912– : *Not That Sort of Girl*
(1987)

9 To get back my youth I would do
anything in the world, except take
exercise, get up early, or be
respectable.

Oscar Wilde 1854–1900: *The Picture of Dorian
Grey* (1891)

Heaven

1 Whose love is given over-well
Shall look on Helen's face in hell
Whilst they whose love is thin and
wise
Shall see John Knox in Paradise.

Dorothy Parker 1893–1967: 'Partial Comfort'
(1937)

2 The true paradises are the paradises
that we have lost.
Marcel Proust 1871–1922: *Time Regained*
(1926)

3 My idea of heaven is, eating *pâté de
foie gras* to the sound of trumpets.
■ *the view of Smith's friend Henry Luttrell*
Sydney Smith 1771–1845: H. Pearson *The
Smith of Smiths* (1934)

4 I will spend my heaven doing good on
earth.
St Teresa of Lisieux 1873–97: T. N. Taylor
(ed.) *Soeur Thérèse of Lisieux* (1912)

5 There is no expeditious road
To pack and label men for God,
And save them by the barrel-load.
Some may perchance, with strange
surprise,
Have blundered into Paradise.
Francis Thompson 1859–1907: 'A Judgement in
Heaven' (1913)

Hell

1 Hell, madam, is to love no more.
Georges Bernanos 1888–1948: *Journal d'un
curé de campagne* (1936)

2 Then I saw that there was a way to
Hell, even from the gates of heaven.
John Bunyan 1628–88: *The Pilgrim's Progress*
(1678)

3 LASCIATE OGNI SPERANZA VOI
CH'ENTRATE!
Abandon all hope, you who enter!
■ *inscription at the entrance to Hell; now often
quoted as 'Abandon hope, all ye who enter here'*
Dante Alighieri 1265–1321: *Divina Commedia*
'Inferno'

4 What is hell?
Hell is oneself,
Hell is alone, the other figures in it
Merely projections.
T. S. Eliot 1888–1965: *The Cocktail Party* (1950)

5 Hell is other people.
Jean-Paul Sartre 1905–80: *Huis Clos* (1944)

Heroes

1 In such a regime, I say, you died a
good death if your life had inspired

someone to come forward and shoot
your murderer in the chest—without
asking to be paid.
Chinua Achebe 1930– : *A Man of the People*
(1966)

2 Faster than a speeding bullet! . . .
Look! Up in the sky! It's a bird! It's a
plane! It's Superman! Yes, it's
Superman! Strange visitor from
another planet . . . Who can change
the course of mighty rivers, bend steel
with his bare hands, and who—
disguised as Clark Kent, mild-
mannered reporter for a great
metropolitan newspaper—fights a
never ending battle for truth, justice
and the American way!
Anonymous: *Superman* (US radio show, 1940
onwards)

3 People always complain about muck-
raking biographers saying 'Leave us
our heroes.' 'Leave us our villains' is
just as important.
■ *of an attempt to rehabilitate Earl Haig*
Alan Bennett 1934– : diary, 11 February 1996

4 ANDREA: Unhappy the land that has
no heroes! . . .
GALILEO: No. Unhappy the land that
needs heroes.
Bertolt Brecht 1898–1956: *The Life of Galileo*
(1939)

5 Down these mean streets a man must
go who is not himself mean, who is
neither tarnished nor afraid.
Raymond Chandler 1888–1959: in *Atlantic
Monthly* December 1944 'The Simple Art of
Murder'

6 No man is a hero to his valet.
Mme Cornuel 1605–94: *Lettres de Mlle Aïssé à
Madame C* (1787) Letter 13 'De Paris, 1728'

7 Men reject their prophets and slay
them, but they love their martyrs and
honour those whom they have slain.
Fedor Dostoevsky 1821–81: *The Brothers
Karamazov* (1879–80)

8 Every hero becomes a bore at last.
Ralph Waldo Emerson 1803–82: *Representative
Men* (1850)

9 Show me a hero and I will write you a tragedy.

F. Scott Fitzgerald 1896–1940: Edmund Wilson (ed.) *The Crack-Up* (1945) 'Note-Books E'

10 If the myth gets bigger than the man, print the myth.

Dorothy Johnson 1905–84: *Indian Country* (1953) 'The Man Who Shot Liberty Valance'

11 It was involuntary. They sank my boat.

■ *on being asked how he became a war hero*
John F. Kennedy 1917–63: Arthur M. Schlesinger Jr. *A Thousand Days* (1965)

12 Many people see Eva Perón as either a saint or the incarnation of Satan. That means I can definitely identify with her.

■ *on playing the starring role in the film* Evita
Madonna 1958– : in *Newsweek* 5 February 1996

13 Ultimately a hero is a man who would argue with the Gods, and so awakens devils to contest his vision.

Norman Mailer 1923– : *The Presidential Papers* (1976)

14 Go to Spain and get killed. The movement needs a Byron.

■ *on being asked by Stephen Spender in the 1930s how best a poet could serve the Communist cause*

Harry Pollitt 1890–1960: Frank Johnson *Out of Order* (1982); attributed, perhaps apocryphal

15 Heroing is one of the shortest-lived professions there is.

Will Rogers 1879–1935: newspaper article, 15 February 1925

16 Hero-worship is strongest where there is least regard for human freedom.

Herbert Spencer 1820–1903: *Social Statics* (1850)

17 In this world I would rather live two days like a tiger, than two hundred years like a sheep.

Tipu Sultan c.1750–99: Alexander Beatson *A View of the Origin and Conduct of the War with Tippoo Sultaun* (1800)

History

see also **Archaeology, The Past**

1 Does history repeat itself, the first time as tragedy, the second time as farce? No, that's too grand, too considered a process. History just burps, and we taste again that raw-onion sandwich it swallowed centuries ago.

Julian Barnes 1946– : *A History of the World in 10½ Chapters* (1989)

2 That great dust-heap called 'history'.

Augustine Birrell 1850–1933: *Obiter Dicta* (1884)

3 It has been said that though God cannot alter the past, historians can; it is perhaps because they can be useful to Him in this respect that He tolerates their existence.

Samuel Butler 1835–1902: *Erewhon Revisited* (1901); see **The Past** 1

4 A people without history
Is not redeemed from time, for history is a pattern
Of timeless moments. So, while the light fails
On a winter's afternoon, in a secluded chapel
History is now and England.

T. S. Eliot 1888–1965: *Four Quartets* 'Little Gidding' (1942)

5 Living in history is a bit like finding oneself in a shuttered mansion to which one has been brought blindfold, and trying to imagine what it might look like from the outside.

Garret Fitzgerald 1926– : in *Irish Times* 9 May 1998

6 History is more or less bunk.

Henry Ford 1863–1947: interview with Charles N. Wheeler in *Chicago Tribune* 25 May 1916

7 History is past politics, and politics is present history.

E. A. Freeman 1823–92: *Methods of Historical Study* (1886)

8 What experience and history teach is this—that nations and governments have never learned anything from

history, or acted upon any lessons they might have drawn from it.
G. W. F. Hegel 1770–1831: *Lectures on the Philosophy of World History: Introduction* (1830)

9 Hegel says somewhere that all great events and personalities in world history reappear in one fashion or another. He forgot to add: the first time as tragedy, the second as farce.
Karl Marx 1818–83: *The Eighteenth Brumaire of Louis Bonaparte* (1852)

10 Happy the people whose annals are blank in history-books!
Montesquieu 1689–1755: attributed; in Thomas Carlyle *History of Frederick the Great*

11 History, like wood, has a grain in it which determines how it splits; and those in authority, besides trying to shape and direct events, sometimes find it more convenient just to let them happen.
Malcolm Muggeridge 1903–90: *The Infernal Grove* (1975)

12 And even I can remember
A day when the historians left blanks in their writings,
I mean for things they didn't know.
Ezra Pound 1885–1972: *Draft of XXX Cantos* (1930)

13 History is not what you thought. *It is what you can remember.*
W. C. Sellar 1898–1951 and **R. J. Yeatman** 1898–1968: *1066 and All That* (1930)

14 History gets thicker as it approaches recent times.
A. J. P. Taylor 1906–90: *English History 1914–45* (1965) bibliography

15 Human history becomes more and more a race between education and catastrophe.
H. G. Wells 1866–1946: *The Outline of History* (1920)

Adolf Hitler 1889–1945

1 I, and many others who had interviews with him, were at first impressed by his sincerity, and later realized that he was sincere only in his belief that he was destined to rule the world.
Vernon Bartlett 1894–1983: *I Know What I Liked* (1974)

2 I thank heaven for a man like Adolf Hitler, who built a front line of defence against the anti-Christ of Communism.
Frank Buchman 1878–1961: in *New York World-Telegram* 26 August 1936

3 A monster of wickedness, insatiable in his lust for blood and plunder . . . this bloodthirsty guttersnipe.
Winston Churchill 1874–1965: radio broadcast, 26 June 1941

4 That man for a Chancellor? I'll make him a postmaster and he can lick the stamps with my head on them.
Paul von Hindenburg 1847–1934: to Meissner, 13 August 1932

5 A racing tipster who only reached Hitler's level of accuracy would not do well for his clients.
A. J. P. Taylor 1906–90: *The Origins of the Second World War* (1961)

Holidays

see also **Leisure**, **Travel**

1 May I ask what you were hoping to see out of a Torquay bedroom window? Sydney Opera House, perhaps? The Hanging Gardens of Babylon? Herds of wildebeeste sweeping majestically . . .
John Cleese 1939– and **Connie Booth**: *Fawlty Towers* 'Communication Problems' (BBC TV programme, 1979)

2 There's sand in the porridge and sand in the bed,
And if this is pleasure we'd rather be dead.
Noël Coward 1899–1973: 'The English Lido' (1928)

3 Cannot avoid contrasting deliriously rapid flight of time when on a holiday with very much slower passage of

days, and even hours, in other and more familiar surroundings.

E. M. Delafield 1890–1943: *The Diary of a Provincial Lady* (1930)

4 A perpetual holiday is a good working definition of hell.

George Bernard Shaw 1856–1950: *Parents and Children* (1914)

5 We're all going on a summer holiday, No more worries for a week or two.

Bruce Welch and **Brian Bennett**: 'Summer Holiday' (1963 song)

Home

1 It is a most miserable thing to feel ashamed of home.

Charles Dickens 1812–70: *Great Expectations* (1861)

2 'Home is the place where, when you have to go there, They have to take you in.' 'I should have called it Something you somehow haven't to deserve.'

Robert Frost 1874–1963: 'The Death of the Hired Man' (1914)

3 The best Thing we can do is to make wherever we're lost in Look as much like home as we can.

Christopher Fry 1907– : *The Lady's not for Burning* (1949)

4 What's the good of a home if you are never in it?

George and **Weedon Grossmith** 1847–1912, 1854–1919: *The Diary of a Nobody* (1894)

5 Any old place I can hang my hat is home sweet home to me.

William Jerome 1865–1932: title of song (1901)

6 The accent of one's birthplace lingers in the mind and in the heart as it does in one's speech.

Duc de la Rochefoucauld 1613–80: *Maximes* (1678)

7 There is scarcely any less bother in the running of a family than in that of an entire state. And domestic business is

no less importunate for being less important.

Montaigne 1533–92: *Essais* (1580)

8 Mid pleasures and palaces though we may roam, Be it ever so humble, there's no place like home.

J. H. Payne 1791–1852: 'Home, Sweet Home' (1823 song)

9 Home is the girl's prison and the woman's workhouse.

George Bernard Shaw 1856–1950: *Man and Superman* (1903) 'Maxims: Women in the Home'

10 Show me a man who cares no more for one place than another, and I will show you in that same person one who loves nothing but himself. Beware of those who are homeless by choice.

Robert Southey 1774–1843: *The Doctor* (1812)

11 Home is where you come to when you have nothing better to do.

Margaret Thatcher 1925– : in *Vanity Fair* May 1991

12 I'm not living with you. We occupy the same cage.

Tennessee Williams 1911–83: *Cat on a Hot Tin Roof* (1955)

Homosexuality

see also **Lesbianism**, **Sex**

1 My dear fellow, buggers can't be choosers.

■ *on being told he should not marry anyone as plain as his fiancée*

Maurice Bowra 1898–1971: Hugh Lloyd-Jones *Maurice Bowra: a Celebration* (1974); possibly apocryphal

2 The world dictates that heteros make love while gays have sex.

Boy George 1961– : in *New Musical Express Book of Quotes* (1995)

3 If homosexuality were the normal way, God would have made Adam and Bruce.

Anita Bryant 1940– : in *New York Times* 5 June 1977

4 In homosexual sex you know exactly what the other person is feeling, so you are identifying with the other person completely. In heterosexual sex you have no idea what the other person is feeling.
William S. Burroughs 1914–97: Victor Bockris *With William Burroughs: A Report from the Bunker* (1981)

5 The worst part of being gay in the twentieth century is all that damn disco music to which one has to listen.
Quentin Crisp 1908–99: *Manners From Heaven* (1984)

6 I am the Love that dare not speak its name.
Lord Alfred Douglas 1870–1945: 'Two Loves' (1896)

7 In homosexual love the passion is homosexuality itself. What a homosexual loves, as if it were his lover, his country, his art, his land, is homosexuality.
Marguerite Duras 1914–96: *Practicalities* (1990)

8 For men who want to flee Family Man America and never come back, there is a guaranteed solution: homosexuality is the new French Foreign Legion.
Florence King 1936– : *Reflections in a Jaundiced Eye* (1989)

9 There is probably no sensitive heterosexual alive who is not preoccupied with his latent homosexuality.
Norman Mailer 1923– : *Advertisement for Myself* (1959)

10 When I was in the military, they gave me a medal for killing two men and a discharge for loving one.
Leonard Matlovich d. 1988: attributed

11 I have heard some say . . . [homosexual] practices are allowed in France and in other NATO countries. We are not French, and we are not other nationals. We are British, thank God!
■ *on the 2nd reading of the Sexual Offences Bill*
Lord Montgomery 1887–1976: speech, House of Lords, 24 May 1965

12 Don't ask, don't tell.
■ *summary of the Clinton administration's compromise policy on homosexuals serving in the armed forces*
Sam Nunn 1938– : in *New York Times* 12 May 1993

Honesty

see also **Deception**, **Lies**, **Truth**

1 Remark all these roughnesses, pimples, warts, and everything as you see me; otherwise I will never pay a farthing for it.
■ *to Lely, commonly quoted as 'warts and all'*
Oliver Cromwell 1599–1658: Horace Walpole *Anecdotes of Painting in England* vol. 3 (1763)

2 The louder he talked of his honour, the faster we counted our spoons.
Ralph Waldo Emerson 1803–82: *The Conduct of Life* (1860)

3 In all life one should comfort the afflicted but verily, also, one should afflict the comfortable, especially when they are comfortably, contentedly, even happily wrong.
J. K. Galbraith 1908– : in *Observer* 30 July 1989

4 It is always the best policy to speak the truth—unless, of course, you are an exceptionally good liar.
Jerome K. Jerome 1859–1927: in *The Idler* February 1892

5 Honesty is praised and left to shiver.
Juvenal AD c.60–c.130: *Satires*

6 I write the truth and it kills me.
Sarah Kane 1971–99: *Crave* (1998)

7 honesty is a good
thing but
it is not profitable to
its possessor
unless it is
kept under control.
Don Marquis 1878–1937: *archys life of mehitabel* (1933)

8 An honest man's the noblest work of God.
Alexander Pope 1688–1744: *An Essay on Man* Epistle 4 (1734)

9 There was altogether too much candour in married life; it was an indelicate modern idea, and frequently led to upsets in a household, if not divorce.
Muriel Spark 1918– : *Memento Mori* (1959)

10 Always be sincere, even if you don't mean it.
Harry S. Truman 1884–1972: attributed

11 Honesty is the best policy; but he who is governed by that maxim is not an honest man.
Richard Whately 1787–1863: *Apophthegms* (1854)

12 A little sincerity is a dangerous thing, and a great deal of it is absolutely fatal.
Oscar Wilde 1854–1900: *Intentions* (1891)

Hope

see also **Despair, Optimism, Pessimism**

1 Providence has given human wisdom the choice between two fates: either hope and agitation, or hopelessness and calm.
Yevgeny Baratynsky 1800–44: 'Two Fates' (1823)

2 What is hope? nothing but the paint on the face of Existence; the least touch of truth rubs it off, and then we see what a hollow-cheeked harlot we have got hold of.
Lord Byron 1788–1824: letter to Thomas Moore, 28 October 1815

3 If hopes were dupes, fears may be liars.
Arthur Hugh Clough 1819–61: 'Say not the struggle naught availeth' (1855)

4 Hope raises no dust.
Paul Éluard 1895–1952: 'Ailleurs, ici, partout' (1946)

5 He that lives upon hope will die fasting.
Benjamin Franklin 1706–90: *Poor Richard's Almanac* (1758)

6 Walk on, walk on, with hope in your heart,

And you'll never walk alone.
Oscar Hammerstein II 1895–1960: 'You'll never walk alone' (1945 song)

7 Hope is definitely not the same thing as optimism. It is not the conviction that something will turn out well, but the certainty that something makes sense, regardless of how it turns out.
Václav Havel 1936– : *Disturbing the Peace* (1986)

8 *Nil desperandum.*
Never despair.
Horace 65–8 BC: *Odes*

9 After all, tomorrow is another day.
Margaret Mitchell 1900–49: *Gone with the Wind* (1936)

10 Hope sleeps in our bones like a bear waiting for spring to rise and walk.
Marge Piercy 1936– : 'Stone, Paper, Knife' (1983)

11 Hope springs eternal in the human breast:
Man never Is, but always To be blest.
Alexander Pope 1688–1744: *An Essay on Man* Epistle 1 (1733)

12 He who has never hoped can never despair.
George Bernard Shaw 1856–1950: *Caesar and Cleopatra* (1901)

13 I think it's a fresh, clean page. I think I go onwards and upwards.
■ *the day before her divorce was made absolute*
Sarah, Duchess of York 1959– : interview on *Sky News* 29 May 1996

Horses

1 Where in this wide world can man find nobility without pride, Friendship without envy, or beauty without vanity?
Ronald Duncan 1914–82: 'In Praise of the Horse' (1962)

2   I saw the horses:
Huge in the dense grey—ten together—
Megalith-still. They breathed, making no move,

With draped manes and tilted hind-
hooves,
Making no sound.
I passed: not one snorted or jerked its
head.
Grey silent fragments
Of a grey silent world.
Ted Hughes 1930–98: 'The Horses' (1957)

3 Cheltenham is the Irish Lourdes. It is
the racing people's Lourdes. It is the
Mecca of jump racing.
Peter O'Sullevan 1918– : in *Irish Post*
14 March 1998

4 I know two things about the horse
And one of them is rather coarse.
Naomi Royde-Smith c.1875–1964: *Weekend
Book* (1928)

Housework

see also **Home**

1 Conran's Law of Housework—it
expands to fill the time available plus
half an hour.
Shirley Conran 1932– : *Superwoman 2* (1977)

2 There was no need to do any
housework at all. After the first four
years the dirt doesn't get any worse.
Quentin Crisp 1908–99: *The Naked Civil
Servant* (1968)

3 Few tasks are more like the torture of
Sisyphus than housework, with its
endless repetition . . . The housewife
wears herself out marking time: she
makes nothing, simply perpetuates
the present.
Simone de Beauvoir 1908–86: *The Second Sex*
(1949)

4 'I hate discussions of feminism that
end up with who does the dishes,' she
said. So do I. But at the end, there are
always the damned dishes.
Marilyn French 1929– : *The Women's Room*
(1977)

5 The dust comes secretly day after day,
Lies on my ledge and dulls my shining
things.
But O this dust that I shall drive away
Is flowers and Kings,

Is Solomon's temple, poets, Nineveh.
Viola Meynell 1886–1956: 'Dusting' (1919)

6 How often does a house need to be
cleaned, anyway? As a general rule,
once every girlfriend.
P. J. O'Rourke 1947– : *The Bachelor Home
Companion* (1987)

7 MR PRITCHARD: I must dust the blinds
and then I must raise them.
MRS OGMORE-PRITCHARD: And before
you let the sun in, mind it wipes its
shoes.
Dylan Thomas 1914–53: *Under Milk Wood*
(1954)

8 Hatred of domestic work is a natural
and admirable result of civilization.
Rebecca West 1892–1983: in *The Freewoman*
6 June 1912

Human Nature

see also **Behaviour, Character, The
Human Race**

1 Civilized ages inherit the human
nature which was victorious in
barbarous ages, and that nature is, in
many respects, not at all suited to
civilized circumstances.
Walter Bagehot 1826–77: *Physics and Politics*
(1872)

2 That is ever the way. 'Tis all jealousy
to the bride and good wishes to the
corpse.
J. M. Barrie 1860–1937: *Quality Street* (1913)

3 There's a man all over for you,
blaming on his boots the faults of his
feet.
Samuel Beckett 1906–89: *Waiting for Godot*
(1955)

4 By nature men are alike. Through
practice they have become far apart.
Confucius 551–479 BC: *Analects*

5 The terrorist and the policeman both
come from the same basket.
Joseph Conrad 1857–1924: *The Secret Agent*
(1907)

6 Subdue your appetites my dears, and
you've conquered human natur.
Charles Dickens 1812–70: *Nicholas Nickleby*
(1839)

7 Goodness has only once found a perfect incarnation in a human body and never will again, but evil can always find a home there. Human nature is not black and white but black and grey.
   Graham Greene 1904–91: 'The Lost Childhood' (1951)

8 But good God, people don't do such things!
   Henrik Ibsen 1828–1906: *Hedda Gabler* (1890)

9 The natural man has only two primal passions, to get and beget.
   William Osler 1849–1919: *Science and Immortality* (1904)

10 It is part of human nature to hate the man you have hurt.
   Tacitus AD c.56–after 117: *Agricola*

11 Adam was but human—this explains it all. He did not want the apple for the apple's sake; he wanted it only because it was forbidden.
   Mark Twain 1835–1910: *Pudd'nhead Wilson* (1894)

The Human Race

see also **Human Nature**, **Life Sciences**

1 In all my work what I try to say is that as human beings we are more alike than we are unalike.
   Maya Angelou 1928– : interview in *New York Times* 20 January 1993

2 Drinking when we are not thirsty and making love all year round, madam; that is all there is to distinguish us from other animals.
   Pierre-Augustin Caron de Beaumarchais 1732–99: *Le Mariage de Figaro* (1785)

3 We carry within us the wonders we seek without us: there is all Africa and her prodigies in us.
   Thomas Browne 1605–82: *Religio Medici* (1643)

4 I hate 'Humanity' and all such abstracts: but I love *people*. Lovers of 'Humanity' generally hate *people and children*, and keep parrots or puppy dogs.
   Roy Campbell 1901–57: *Light on a Dark Horse* (1951)

5 Nobody's perfect. Now and then, my pet,
   You're almost human. You could make it yet.
   Wendy Cope 1945– : 'Faint Praise' (1992)

6 What is man, when you come to think upon him, but a minutely set, ingenious machine for turning, with infinite artfulness, the red wine of Shiraz into urine?
   Isak Dinesen 1885–1962: *Seven Gothic Tales* (1934) 'The Dreamers'

7 Is man an ape or an angel? Now I am on the side of the angels.
   Benjamin Disraeli 1804–81: speech at Oxford, 25 November 1864; see **Life Sciences** 17

8   Human kind
   Cannot bear very much reality.
   T. S. Eliot 1888–1965: *Four Quartets* 'Burnt Norton' (1936)

9 Man is a tool-making animal.
   Benjamin Franklin 1706–90: James Boswell *Life of Samuel Johnson* (1791) 7 April 1778

10 Here you could love human beings nearly as God loved them, knowing the worst; you didn't love a pose, a pretty dress, a sentiment artfully assumed.
   Graham Greene 1904–91: *The Heart of the Matter* (1948)

11 I am all at once what Christ is, since he was what I am, and
   This Jack, joke, poor potsherd, patch, matchwood, immortal diamond,
   Is immortal diamond.
   Gerard Manley Hopkins 1844–89: 'That Nature is a Heraclitean Fire' (written 1888)

12 Many people believe that they are attracted by God, or by Nature, when they are only repelled by man.
   William Ralph Inge 1860–1954: *More Lay Thoughts of a Dean* (1931)

13 Man, biologically considered, and whatever else he may be into the bargain, is simply the most

formidable of all the beasts of prey, and, indeed, the only one that preys systematically on its own species.
William James 1842–1910: in *Atlantic Monthly* December 1904

14 Taking a very gloomy view of the future of the human race, let us suppose that it can only expect to survive for two thousand million years longer, a period about equal to the past age of the earth. Then, regarded as a being destined to live for three-score years and ten, humanity, although it has been born in a house seventy years old, is itself only three days old.
James Jeans 1877–1946: *Eos* (1928)

15 Out of the crooked timber of humanity no straight thing can ever be made.
Immanuel Kant 1724–1804: *Idee zu einer allgemeinen Geschichte in weltbürgerlicher Absicht* (1784)

16 Only human beings guide their behaviour by a knowledge of what happened before they were born and a preconception of what may happen after they are dead; thus only humans find their way by a light that illuminates more than the patch of ground they stand on.
Peter Medawar 1915–87 and **Jean Medawar** 1913– : *The Life Science* (1977)

17 To say, for example, that a man is made up of certain chemical elements is a satisfactory description only for those who intend to use him as a fertilizer.
H. J. Muller 1890–1967: *Science and Criticism* (1943)

18 I teach you the superman. Man is something to be surpassed.
Friedrich Nietzsche 1844–1900: *Also Sprach Zarathustra* (1883)

19 Man is only a reed, the weakest thing in nature; but he is a thinking reed.
Blaise Pascal 1623–62: *Pensées* (1670)

20 Know then thyself, presume not God to scan;

The proper study of mankind is man.
Alexander Pope 1688–1744: *An Essay on Man* Epistle 2 (1733)

21 Man is the measure of all things.
Protagoras b. *c.*485 BC: Plato *Theaetetus*

22 I wish I loved the Human Race;
I wish I loved its silly face;
I wish I liked the way it walks;
I wish I liked the way it talks;
And when I'm introduced to one
I wish I thought *What Jolly Fun!*
Walter Raleigh 1861–1922: 'Wishes of an Elderly Man' (1923)

23 Man must be invented each day.
Jean-Paul Sartre 1905–80: *Qu'est-ce que la littérature?* (1948)

24 What a piece of work is a man! How noble in reason! how infinite in faculty! in form, in moving, how express and admirable! in action how like an angel! in apprehension how like a god! the beauty of the world! the paragon of animals! And yet, to me, what is this quintessence of dust?
William Shakespeare 1564–1616: *Hamlet* (1601)

25 There are many wonderful things, and nothing is more wonderful than man.
Sophocles *c.*496–406 BC: *Antigone*

26 Man, unlike any other thing organic or inorganic in the universe, grows beyond his work, walks up the stairs of his concepts, emerges ahead of his accomplishments.
John Steinbeck 1902–68: *The Grapes of Wrath* (1939)

27 Notwithstanding, if he could be reincarnated and placed in a New York subway—provided that he were bathed, shaved, and dressed in modern clothing—it is doubtful whether he would attract any more attention than some of its other denizens.
■ *of Neanderthal man*
William L. Strauss and **A. J. E. Cave**: in *Quarterly Review of Biology* Winter 1957

28 Principally I hate and detest that animal called man; although I heartily

love John, Peter, Thomas, and so forth.

Jonathan Swift 1667–1745: letter to Pope, 29 September 1725

29 I am a man, I count nothing human foreign to me.

Terence c.190–159 BC: *Heauton Timorumenos*

30 Man is the Only Animal that Blushes. Or needs to.

Mark Twain 1835–1910: *Following the Equator* (1897)

31 We're all of us guinea pigs in the laboratory of God. Humanity is just a work in progress.

Tennessee Williams 1911–83: *Camino Real* (1953)

Human Rights

see also **Equality**, **Justice**

1 We hold these truths to be self-evident, that all men are created equal, that they are endowed by their Creator with certain unalienable rights, that among these are life, liberty and the pursuit of happiness.

Anonymous: The American Declaration of Independence, 4 July 1776; from a draft by Thomas Jefferson (1743–1826)

2 *Liberté! Égalité! Fraternité!* Freedom! Equality! Brotherhood!

Anonymous: motto of the French Revolution, but of earlier origin

3 All human beings are born free and equal in dignity and rights.

Anonymous: *Universal Declaration of Human Rights* (1948) article 1

4 Natural rights is simple nonsense: natural and imprescriptible rights, rhetorical nonsense—nonsense upon stilts.

Jeremy Bentham 1748–1832: *Anarchical Fallacies* (1843)

5 I would like to see a time when man loves his fellow man and forgets his colour or his creed. We will never be civilized until that time comes. I know the Negro race has a long road to go. I believe that the life of the Negro race has been a life of tragedy, of injustice, of oppression. The law has made him equal, but man has not.

Clarence Darrow 1857–1938: speech in Detroit, 19 May 1926

6 No man can put a chain about the ankle of his fellow man without at last finding the other end fastened about his own neck.

Frederick Douglass c.1818–95: speech at Civil Rights Mass Meeting, Washington, DC, 22 October 1883

7 We have talked long enough in this country about equal rights. We have talked for a hundred years or more. It is time now to write the next chapter, and to write it in the books of law.

Lyndon Baines Johnson 1908–73: speech to Congress, 27 November 1963

8 No free man shall be taken or imprisoned or dispossessed, or outlawed or exiled, or in any way destroyed, nor will we go upon him, nor will we send against him except by the lawful judgement of his peers or by the law of the land.

Magna Carta 1215: clause 39

9 The price of championing human rights is a little inconsistency at times.

David Owen 1938– : speech, House of Commons, 30 March 1977

10 Any law which violates the inalienable rights of man is essentially unjust and tyrannical; it is not a law at all.

Maximilien Robespierre 1758–94: *Déclaration des droits de l'homme* 24 April 1793

11 We look forward to a world founded upon four essential human freedoms. The first is freedom of speech and expression—everywhere in the world. The second is freedom of every person to worship God in his own way—everywhere in the world. The third is freedom from want . . . everywhere in the world. The fourth is freedom from fear . . . anywhere in the world.

Franklin D. Roosevelt 1882–1945: message to Congress, 6 January 1941

12 A right is not effectual by itself, but only in relation to the obligation to

which it corresponds . . . An obligation which goes unrecognized by anybody loses none of the full force of its existence. A right which goes unrecognized by anybody is not worth very much.
Simone Weil 1909–43: *L'Enracinement* (1949)

Humility

········

see also **Self-Esteem and Assertiveness**

1 Blessed are the meek: for they shall inherit the earth.
Bible: St Matthew

2 He that is down needs fear no fall,
He that is low no pride.
He that is humble ever shall
Have God to be his guide.
John Bunyan 1628–88: *The Pilgrim's Progress* (1684) 'Shepherd Boy's Song'

3 We are so very 'umble.
Charles Dickens 1812–70: *David Copperfield* (1850)

4 The tumult and the shouting dies—
The captains and the kings depart—
Still stands Thine ancient Sacrifice,
An humble and a contrite heart.
Lord God of Hosts, be with us yet,
Lest we forget—lest we forget!
Rudyard Kipling 1865–1936: 'Recessional' (1897)

5 In 1969 I published a small book on Humility. It was a pioneering work which has not, to my knowledge, been superseded.
Lord Longford 1905–2001: in *Tablet* 22 January 1994

6 We have the highest authority for believing that the meek shall inherit the earth; though I have never found any particular corroboration of this aphorism in the records of Somerset House.
F. E. Smith 1872–1930: *Contemporary Personalities* (1924); see 1 above

Humour

········

see also **Comedy**, **Wit and Satire**

1 Among all kinds of writing, there is none in which authors are more apt to miscarry than in works of humour, as there is none in which they are more ambitious to excel.
Joseph Addison 1672–1719: in *The Spectator* 10 April 1711

2 The marvellous thing about a joke with a double meaning is that it can only mean one thing.
Ronnie Barker 1929– : *Sauce* (1977)

3 I make myself laugh at everything, for fear of having to weep at it.
Pierre-Augustin Caron de Beaumarchais 1732–99: *Le Barbier de Séville* (1775)

4 Mark my words, when a society has to resort to the lavatory for its humour, the writing is on the wall.
Alan Bennett 1934– : *Forty Years On* (1969)

5 Freud's theory was that when a joke opens a window and all those bats and bogeymen fly out, you get a marvellous feeling of relief and elation. The trouble with Freud is that he never had to play the old Glasgow Empire on a Saturday night after Rangers and Celtic had both lost.
Ken Dodd 1931– : in *Guardian* 30 April 1991; quoted in many, usually much contracted, forms since the mid-1960s

6 Nothing is so impenetrable as laughter in a language you don't understand.
William Golding 1911–93: *An Egyptian Journal* (1985)

7 What do you mean, funny? Funny-peculiar or funny ha-ha?
Ian Hay 1876–1952: *The Housemaster* (1938)

8 Laughter is nothing else but sudden glory arising from some sudden conception of some eminency in ourselves, by comparison with the infirmity of others, or with our own formerly.
Thomas Hobbes 1588–1679: *Human Nature* (1650)

9 Fun is fun but no girl wants to laugh all of the time.
Anita Loos 1893–1981: *Gentlemen Prefer Blondes* (1925)

10 Good taste and humour . . . are a contradiction in terms, like a chaste whore.
Malcolm Muggeridge 1903–90: in *Time* 14 September 1953

11 Whatever is funny is subversive, every joke is ultimately a custard pie . . . A dirty joke is a sort of mental rebellion.
George Orwell 1903–50: in *Horizon* September 1941 'The Art of Donald McGill'

12 Everything is funny as long as it is happening to Somebody Else.
Will Rogers 1879–1935: *The Illiterate Digest* (1924)

13 People sometimes divide others into those you laugh at and those you laugh with. The young Auden was someone you could laugh-at-with.
Stephen Spender 1909–95: *W. H. Auden* (1973)

14 Humour is emotional chaos remembered in tranquillity.
James Thurber 1894–1961: in *New York Post* 29 February 1960; see **Poetry 32**

15 Laughter would be bereaved if snobbery died.
Peter Ustinov 1921– : in *Observer* 13 March 1955

16 We are not amused.
Queen Victoria 1819–1901: attributed; Caroline Holland *Notebooks of a Spinster Lady* (1919) 2 January 1900

17 I love such mirth as does not make friends ashamed to look upon one another next morning.
Izaak Walton 1593–1683: *The Compleat Angler* (1653)

Hunting

see also **Animal Rights, Field Sports**

1 I do not see why I should break my neck because a dog chooses to run after a nasty smell.
■ *on being asked why he did not hunt*
Arthur James Balfour 1848–1930: Ian Malcolm *Lord Balfour: A Memory* (1930)

2 If killing foxes is necessary for the safety and survival of other species, I—and several million others—will vote for it to continue. But the slaughter ought not to be fun.
Roy Hattersley 1932– : in *Guardian* 21 April 1990

3 It is very strange, and very melancholy, that the paucity of human pleasures should persuade us ever to call hunting one of them.
Samuel Johnson 1709–84: Hester Lynch Piozzi *Anecdotes of . . . Johnson* (1786)

4 They do you a decent death on the hunting-field.
John Mortimer 1923– : *Paradise Postponed* (1985)

5 Most of their discourse was about hunting, in a dialect I understand very little.
Samuel Pepys 1633–1703: diary 22 November 1663

6 It is my belief that six out of every dozen people who go out hunting are disagreeably conscious of a nervous system, and two out of six are in what is brutally called 'a blue funk'.
Edith Œ Somerville 1858–1949 and **Martin Ross** 1862–1915: *Some Experiences of an Irish R.M.* (1899)

7 It ar'n't that I loves the fox less, but that I loves the 'ound more.
R. S. Surtees 1805–64: *Handley Cross* (1843)

8 'Unting is all that's worth living for—all time is lost wot is not spent in 'unting—it is like the hair we breathe—if we have it not we die—it's the sport of kings, the image of war without its guilt, and only five-and-twenty per cent of its danger.
R. S. Surtees 1805–64: *Handley Cross* (1843)

9 The English country gentleman galloping after a fox—the unspeakable in full pursuit of the uneatable.
Oscar Wilde 1854–1900: *A Woman of No Importance* (1893)

Husbands

....
see also **Marriage**, **Men**

1 You may marry the man of your
dreams, ladies, but 14 years later
you're married to a couch that burps.
   Roseanne Barr 1953– : *Roseanne* (American
   TV series, 1988–)

2 Being a husband is a whole-time job.
That is why so many husbands fail.
They cannot give their entire
attention to it.
   Arnold Bennett 1867–1931: *The Title* (1918)

3 Never marry a man who hates his
mother, because he'll end up hating
you.
   Jill Bennett 1931–90: in *Observer*
   12 September 1982

4 Even quarrels with one's husband are
preferable to the ennui of a solitary
existence.
   Elizabeth Patterson Bonaparte 1785–1879:
   Eugene L. Didier *The Life and Letters of
   Madame Bonaparte* (1879)

5 Why should marriage bring only
   tears?
All I wanted was a man
With a single heart,
And we would stay together
As our hair turned white,
Not somebody always after wriggling
fish
With his big bamboo rod.
   Chuo Wen-chun *c*.179–117 BC: 'A Song of
   White Hair'

6 I've never yet met a man who could
look after me. I don't need a husband.
What I need is a wife.
   Joan Collins 1933– : in *Sunday Times*
   27 December 1987

7 I never married because there was no
need. I have three pets at home which
answer the same purpose as a
husband. I have a dog which growls
every morning, a parrot which swears
all the afternoon, and a cat that comes
home late at night.
   Marie Corelli 1855–1924: attributed

8 Husbands are like fires. They go out
when unattended.
   Zsa Zsa Gabor 1919– : in *Newsweek* 28 March
   1960

9 The men that women marry,
And why they marry them, will always
be
A marvel and a mystery to the world.
   Henry Wadsworth Longfellow 1807–82:
   Michael Angelo (1883)

10 He tells you when you've got on too
much lipstick,
And helps you with your girdle when
your hips stick.
   Ogden Nash 1902–71: 'The Perfect Husband'
   (1949)

11 No matter how liberated she is every
woman still wants a husband.
   P. J. O'Rourke 1947– : *Modern Manners*
   (1984)

12 A husband is what is left of a lover,
after the nerve has been extracted.
   Helen Rowland 1875–1950: *A Guide to Men*
   (1922)

13 If you cannot have your dear husband
for a comfort and a delight, for a
breadwinner and a crosspatch, for a
sofa, chair or a hot-water bottle, one
can use him as a Cross to be Borne.
   Stevie Smith 1902–71: *Novel on Yellow Paper*
   (1936)

14 Chumps always make the best
husbands. When you marry, Sally,
grab a chump. Tap his forehead first,
and if it rings solid, don't hesitate. All
the unhappy marriages come from
the husbands having brains.
   P. G. Wodehouse 1881–1975: *The Adventures of
   Sally* (1920)

Hypocrisy

....
see also **Deception**

1 Conventionality is not morality. Self-
righteousness is not religion. To
attack the first is not to assail the last.
To pluck the mask from the face of the
Pharisee, is not to lift an impious
hand to the Crown of Thorns.
   Charlotte Brontë 1816–55: *Jane Eyre* (2nd ed.,
   1848)

2 Keep up appearances; there lies the
test;
The world will give thee credit for the
rest.
Outward be fair, however foul within;
Sin if thou wilt, but then in secret sin.
Charles Churchill 1731–64: *Night* (1761)

3 Hypocrisy is a tribute which vice pays
to virtue.
Duc de la Rochefoucauld 1613–80: *Maximes*
(1678)

4 In the mouths of many men soft
words are like roses that soldiers put
into the muzzles of their muskets on
holidays.
Henry Wadsworth Longfellow 1807–82: *Table-
Talk* (1857) 'Driftwood'

5 Hypocrisy is the most difficult and
nerve-racking vice that any man can
pursue; it needs an unceasing
vigilance and a rare detachment of
spirit. It cannot, like adultery or
gluttony, be practised at spare
moments; it is a whole-time job.
W. Somerset Maugham 1874–1965: *Cakes and
Ale* (1930)

6   I want that glib and oily art
To speak and purpose not.
William Shakespeare 1564–1616: *King Lear*
(1605–6)

7 All Reformers, however strict their
social conscience, live in houses just as
big as they can pay for.
Logan Pearsall Smith 1865–1946:
Afterthoughts (1931) 'Other People'

8 I sit on a man's back, choking him
and making him carry me, and yet
assure myself and others that I am
very sorry for him and wish to ease his
lot by all possible means—except by
getting off his back.
Leo Tolstoy 1828–1910: *What Then Must We
Do?* (1886)

9 I hope you have not been leading a
double life, pretending to be wicked
and being really good all the time.
That would be hypocrisy.
Oscar Wilde 1854–1900: *The Importance of
Being Earnest* (1895)

Idealism
....

1 A cause may be inconvenient, but it's
magnificent. It's like champagne or
high heels, and one must be prepared
to suffer for it.
Arnold Bennett 1867–1931: *The Title* (1918)

2 Where there is no vision, the people
perish.
Bible: Proverbs

3 Oh, the vision thing.
■ *responding to the suggestion that he turn his
attention from short-term campaign objectives
and look to the longer term*
George Bush 1924– : in *Time* 26 January 1987

4 You never reach the promised land.
You can march towards it.
James Callaghan 1912– : television interview,
20 July 1978

5 To dream the impossible dream,
To reach the unreachable star!
Joe Darion 1917–2001: 'The Impossible
Dream' (1965 song)

6 Hitch your wagon to a star.
Ralph Waldo Emerson 1803–82: *Society and
Solitude* (1870)

7 I submit to you that if a man hasn't
discovered something he will die for,
he isn't fit to live.
Martin Luther King 1929–68: speech in
Detroit, 23 June 1963

8 I am an idealist. I don't know where
I'm going but I'm on the way.
Carl Sandburg 1878–1967: *Incidentals* (1907)

9 When they come downstairs from
their Ivory Towers, Idealists are very
apt to walk straight into the gutter.
Logan Pearsall Smith 1865–1946:
Afterthoughts (1931) 'Other People'

10 We are all in the gutter, but some of us
are looking at the stars.
Oscar Wilde 1854–1900: *Lady Windermere's
Fan* (1892)

11 Plain living and high thinking are no
more:
The homely beauty of the good old
cause

Is gone.
William Wordsworth 1770–1850: 'O friend! I
know not which way I must look' (1807)

12 We were the last romantics—chose
for theme
Traditional sanctity and loveliness.
W. B. Yeats 1865–1939: 'Coole and Ballylee,
1931' (1933)

Ideas

see also **Facts**, **The Mind**, **Problems and
Solutions**, **Theories**, **Thinking**

1 Nothing is more dangerous than an
idea, when you have only one idea.
Alain 1868–1951: *Propos sur la religion* (1938)

2 Our ideas are only intellectual
instruments which we use to break
into phenomena; we must change
them when they have served their
purpose, as we change a blunt lancet
that we have used long enough.
Claude Bernard 1813–78: *An Introduction to
the Study of Experimental Medicine* (1865)

3 You can't stop. Composing's not
voluntary, you know. There's no
choice, you're not free. You're landed
with an idea and you have
responsibility to that idea.
Harrison Birtwistle 1934– : in *Observer*
14 April 1996

4 What we need is hatred. From it our
ideas are born.
Jean Genet 1910–86: *The Blacks* (1959);
epigraph

5 A stand can be made against invasion
by an army; no stand can be made
against invasion by an idea.
Victor Hugo 1802–85: *Histoire d'un Crime*
(1877)

6 It is better to entertain an idea than to
take it home to live with you for the
rest of your life.
Randall Jarrell 1914–65: *Pictures from an
Institution* (1954)

7 Madmen in authority, who hear
voices in the air, are distilling their

frenzy from some academic scribbler
of a few years back.
John Maynard Keynes 1883–1946: *General
Theory* (1947 ed.)

8 New opinions are always suspected,
and usually opposed, without any
other reason but because they are not
already common.
John Locke 1632–1704: *An Essay concerning
Human Understanding* (1690)

9 General notions are generally wrong.
Lady Mary Wortley Montagu 1689–1762: letter
to her husband Edward Wortley Montagu,
28 March 1710

10 The English approach to ideas is not
to kill them, but to let them die of
neglect.
Jeremy Paxman 1950– : *The English: a
portrait of a people* (1998)

11 For an idea ever to be fashionable is
ominous, since it must afterwards be
always old-fashioned.
George Santayana 1863–1952: *Winds of
Doctrine* (1913)

12 You see things; and you say 'Why?'
But I dream things that never were;
and I say 'Why not?'
George Bernard Shaw 1856–1950: *Back to
Methuselah* (1921)

13 I share no one's ideas. I have my own.
Ivan Turgenev 1818–83: *Fathers and Sons*
(1862)

14 *Ideas won't keep.* Something must be
done about them.
Alfred North Whitehead 1861–1947: *Dialogues*
(1954) 28 April 1938

Idleness

see also **Delay**, **Words and Deeds**

1 A man who has nothing to do with his
own time has no conscience in his
intrusion on that of others.
Jane Austen 1775–1817: *Sense and Sensibility*
(1811)

2 Oh! how I hate to get up in the
morning,
Oh! how I'd love to remain in bed.
Irving Berlin 1888–1989: *Oh! How I Hate to
Get Up in the Morning* (1918 song)

3 The foul sluggard's comfort: 'It will last my time.'
   Thomas Carlyle 1795–1881: *Critical and Miscellaneous Essays* (1838)

4 Idleness is only the refuge of weak minds.
   Lord Chesterfield 1694–1773: *Letters to his Son* (1774) 20 July 1749

5 I do nothing, granted. But I see the hours pass—which is better than trying to fill them.
   E. M. Cioran 1911–95: in *Guardian* 11 May 1993

6 It is impossible to enjoy idling thoroughly unless one has plenty of work to do.
   Jerome K. Jerome 1859–1927: *Idle Thoughts of an Idle Fellow* (1886)

7 If you are idle, be not solitary; if you are solitary, be not idle.
   Samuel Johnson 1709–84: letter to Boswell, 27 October 1779

8 I was raised to feel that doing nothing was a sin. I had to learn to do nothing.
   Jenny Joseph 1932– : in *Observer* 19 April 1998

9 Henry has always led what could be called a sedentary life, if only he'd ever got as far as actually sitting up.
   Henry Reed 1914–86: *Not a Drum was Heard* (unpublished radio play, 1959)

10 Some people are born slack—others have slacking thrust upon them.
   Will Self 1961– : in *Observer* 2 January 1994

11 How dull it is to pause, to make an end,
   To rust unburnished, not to shine in use!
   As though to breathe were life.
   Alfred, Lord Tennyson 1809–92: 'Ulysses' (1842)

Ignorance

see also **Knowledge**

1 Happy the hare at morning, for she cannot read
   The Hunter's waking thoughts.
   W. H. Auden 1907–73: *Dog beneath the Skin* (with Christopher Isherwood, 1935)

2 Where people wish to attach, they should always be ignorant. To come with a well-informed mind, is to come with an inability of administering to the vanity of others, which a sensible person would always wish to avoid. A woman especially, if she have the misfortune of knowing any thing, should conceal it as well as she can.
   Jane Austen 1775–1817: *Northanger Abbey* (1818)

3 Ignorance is an evil weed, which dictators may cultivate among their dupes, but which no democracy can afford among its citizens.
   William Henry Beveridge 1879–1963: *Full Employment in a Free Society* (1944)

4 Too many people in Britain say with almost a badge of pride that they never did understand maths properly.
   David Blunkett 1947– : comment, 16 March 1999

5 Ignorance is not innocence but sin.
   Robert Browning 1812–89: *The Inn Album* (1875)

6 I know nothing—nobody tells me anything.
   John Galsworthy 1867–1933: *Man of Property* (1906)

7   Where ignorance is bliss,
   'Tis folly to be wise.
   Thomas Gray 1716–71: *Ode on a Distant Prospect of Eton College* (1747)

8 Ignorance, madam, pure ignorance.
   ■ *on being asked why he had defined* pastern *as the 'knee' of a horse*
   Samuel Johnson 1709–84: James Boswell *Life of Samuel Johnson* (1791) 1755

9 Nothing in all the world is more dangerous than sincere ignorance and conscientious stupidity.
   Martin Luther King 1929–68: *Strength to Love* (1963)

10 A bishop wrote gravely to the *Times* inviting all nations to destroy 'the formula' of the atomic bomb. There is no simple remedy for ignorance so abysmal.
   Peter Medawar 1915–87: *The Hope of Progress* (1972)

11 You know everybody is ignorant, only on different subjects.
Will Rogers 1879–1935: in *New York Times* 31 August 1924

12 For most men, an ignorant enjoyment is better than an informed one; it is better to conceive the sky as a blue dome than a dark cavity; and the cloud as a golden throne than a sleety mist.
John Ruskin 1819–1900: *Modern Painters* (1856)

13 If one does not know to which port one is sailing, no wind is favourable.
Seneca *c.*4 BC–AD 65: *Epistulae Morales*

14 It was absolutely marvellous working for Pauli. You could ask him anything. There was no worry that he would think a particular question was stupid, since he thought *all* questions were stupid.
Victor Weisskopf 1908–2002: in *American Journal of Physics* 1977

15 Ignorance is like a delicate exotic fruit; touch it and the bloom is gone. The whole theory of modern education is radically unsound. Fortunately, in England, at any rate, education produces no effect whatsoever.
Oscar Wilde 1854–1900: *The Importance of Being Earnest* (1895)

16 As any fule kno.
Geoffrey Willans 1911–58 and **Ronald Searle** 1920– : *Down with Skool!* (1953)

Imagination

see also **Fantasy**

1 To see a world in a grain of sand
And a heaven in a wild flower
Hold infinity in the palm of your hand
And eternity in an hour.
William Blake 1757–1827: 'Auguries of Innocence' (*c.*1803)

2 When the imagination sleeps, words are emptied of their meaning.
Albert Camus 1913–60: *Resistance, Rebellion and Death* (1961)

3 An adventure is only an inconvenience rightly considered. An inconvenience is only an adventure wrongly considered.
G. K. Chesterton 1874–1936: *All Things Considered* (1908) 'On Running after one's Hat'

4 Where there is no imagination there is no horror.
Arthur Conan Doyle 1859–1930: *A Study in Scarlet* (1888)

5 He said he should prefer not to know the sources of the Nile, and that there should be some unknown regions preserved as hunting-grounds for the poetic imagination.
George Eliot 1819–80: *Middlemarch* (1871–2)

6 Imagination isn't merely a surplus mental department meant for entertainment, but the most essential piece of machinery we have if we are going to live the lives of human beings.
Ted Hughes 1930–98: in *Children's Literature in Education* March 1970

7 Were it not for imagination, Sir, a man would be as happy in the arms of a chambermaid as of a Duchess.
Samuel Johnson 1709–84: James Boswell *Life of Samuel Johnson* (1791) 9 May 1778

8 The same that oft-times hath
Charmed magic casements, opening on the foam
Of perilous seas, in faery lands forlorn.
John Keats 1795–1821: 'Ode to a Nightingale' (1820)

9 His imagination resembled the wings of an ostrich. It enabled him to run, though not to soar.
Lord Macaulay 1800–59: T. F. Ellis (ed.) *Miscellaneous Writings of Lord Macaulay* (1860) 'John Dryden' (1828)

10 Must then a Christ perish in torment in every age to save those that have no imagination?
George Bernard Shaw 1856–1950: *Saint Joan* (1924)

11 Though our brother is on the rack, as long as we ourselves are at our ease,

our senses will never inform us of what he suffers . . . It is by imagination that we can form any conception of what are his sensations.
Adam Smith 1723–90: *Theory of Moral Sentiments* (2nd ed., 1762)

12 Fantasy love is much better than reality love. Never doing it is very exciting. The most exciting attractions are between two opposites that never meet.
Andy Warhol 1927–87: *Philosophy of Andy Warhol* (*From A to B and Back Again*) (1975)

13 Whither is fled the visionary gleam? Where is it now, the glory and the dream?
William Wordsworth 1770–1850: 'Ode. Intimations of Immortality' (1807)

Impartiality

see also **Indifference**

1 I decline utterly to be impartial as between the fire brigade and the fire.
■ *replying to complaints of his bias in editing the* British Gazette *during the General Strike*
Winston Churchill 1874–1965: speech, House of Commons, 7 July 1926

2 When people feel deeply, impartiality is bias.
Lord Reith 1889–1971: *Into the Wind* (1945)

3 Take sides. Neutrality helps the oppressor, never the victim. Silence encourages the tormentor, never the tormented.
■ *accepting the Nobel Peace Prize*
Elie Wiesel 1928– : in *New York Times* 11 December 1986

Impulsiveness

1 May I ask whether these pleasing attentions proceed from the impulse of the moment, or are the result of previous study?
Jane Austen 1775–1817: *Pride and Prejudice* (1813)

2 A first impulse was never a crime.
Pierre Corneille 1606–84: *Horace* (1640)

3 Have no truck with first impulses for they are always generous ones.
Casimir, Comte de Montrond 1768–1843: attributed; Comte J. d'Estourmel *Derniers Souvenirs* (1860)

4 Impulse has more effect than conscious purpose in moulding men's lives.
Bertrand Russell 1872–1970: *Autobiography* (1967)

Indecision

see also **Certainty**, **Doubt**

1 The Flying Scotsman is no less splendid a sight when it travels north to Edinburgh than when it travels south to London. Mr Baldwin denouncing sanctions was as dignified as Mr Baldwin imposing them.
Lord Beaverbrook 1879–1964: in *Daily Express* 29 May 1937

2 Often undecided whether to desert a sinking ship for one that might not float, he would make up his mind to sit on the wharf for a day.
■ *of Lord Curzon*
Lord Beaverbrook 1879–1964: *Men and Power* (1956)

3 The archbishop is usually to be found nailing his colours to the fence.
■ *of Archbishop Runcie*
Frank Field 1942– : attributed in *Crockfords* 1987/88 (1987)

4 I'll give you a definite maybe.
Sam Goldwyn 1882–1974: attributed

5 A very weak-minded fellow I am afraid, and, like the feather pillow, bears the marks of the last person who has sat on him!
■ *of Lord Derby*
Earl Haig 1861–1928: letter to Lady Haig, 14 January 1918

6 There is no more miserable human being than one in whom nothing is habitual but indecision.
William James 1842–1910: *The Principles of Psychology* (1890)

7 The tragedy of a man who could not make up his mind.
   Laurence Olivier 1907–89: introduction to his 1948 screen adaptation of *Hamlet*

8 She floats, she hesitates; in a word, she's a woman.
   Jean Racine 1639–99: *Athalie* (1691)

9 I must have a prodigious quantity of mind; it takes me as much as a week, sometimes, to make it up.
   Mark Twain 1835–1910: *The Innocents Abroad* (1869)

Indifference

see also **Impartiality**

1 All colours will agree in the dark.
   Francis Bacon 1561–1626: *Essays* (1625) 'Of Unity in Religion'

2 There is nothing upon the face of the earth so insipid as a medium. Give me love or hate! a friend that will go to jail for me, or an enemy that will run me through the body!
   Fanny Burney 1752–1840: *Camilla* (1796)

3 Catholics and Communists have committed great crimes, but at least they have not stood aside, like an established society, and been indifferent. I would rather have blood on my hands than water like Pilate.
   Graham Greene 1904–91: *The Comedians* (1966)

4 Science may have found a cure for most evils; but it has found no remedy for the worst of them all—the apathy of human beings.
   Helen Keller 1880–1968: *My Religion* (1927)

5 I wish I could care what you do or where you go but I can't . . . My dear, I don't give a damn.
   ■ 'Frankly, my dear, I don't give a damn!' in the 1939 screen version by Sidney Howard
   Margaret Mitchell 1900–49: *Gone with the Wind* (1936)

6 When Hitler attacked the Jews I was not a Jew, therefore, I was not concerned. And when Hitler attacked the Catholics, I was not a Catholic, and therefore, I was not concerned. And when Hitler attacked the unions and the industrialists, I was not a member of the unions and I was not concerned. Then, Hitler attacked me and the Protestant church—and there was nobody left to be concerned.
   ■ often quoted in the form 'In Germany they came first for the Communists, and I didn't speak up because I wasn't a Communist . . .' and so on
   Martin Niemöller 1892–1984: in *Congressional Record* 14 October 1968

7 Vacant heart and hand, and eye,— Easy live and quiet die.
   Sir Walter Scott 1771–1832: *The Bride of Lammermoor* (1819)

8 The worst sin towards our fellow creatures is not to hate them, but to be indifferent to them: that's the essence of inhumanity.
   George Bernard Shaw 1856–1950: *The Devil's Disciple* (1901)

9 The opposite of love is not hate, it's indifference. The opposite of art is not ugliness, it's indifference. The opposite of faith is not heresy, it's indifference. And the opposite of life is not death, it's indifference.
   Elie Wiesel 1928– : in *U.S. News and World Report* 27 October 1986

10 Cast a cold eye
   On life, on death.
   Horseman, pass by!
   W. B. Yeats 1865–1939: 'Under Ben Bulben' (1939)

Individuality

see also **Conformity**, **The Self**

1 PERSONALITY TITHE: A price paid for becoming a couple.
   Douglas Coupland 1961– : *Generation X* (1991)

2 It is easier to live through someone else than to become complete yourself.
   Betty Friedan 1921– : *The Feminine Mystique* (1963)

3 No human relation gives one possession in another—every two souls are absolutely different. In

friendship or in love, the two side by side raise hands together to find what one cannot reach alone.

Kahlil Gibran 1883–1931: *Beloved Prophet: the love letters of Kahlil Gibran and Mary Haskell and her private journal* (1972)

4 Human beings have an inalienable right to invent themselves; when that right is pre-empted it is called brain-washing.

Germaine Greer 1939– : in *The Times* 1 February 1986

5 Each child hunts for a solution to the boredom of being no one but itself.

Candia McWilliam 1955– : *Debatable Land* (1994)

6 To be like everyone else. Isn't that what we all want in the end?

Carol Shields 1935– : *Larry's Party* (1997)

Information

see also **Knowledge**

1 Information can tell us everything. It has all the answers. But they are answers to questions we have not asked, and which doubtless don't even arise.

Jean Baudrillard 1929– : *Cool Memories* (1987)

2 Not many people know that.

Michael Caine 1933– : title of book (1984)

3 Now that I do know it, I shall do my best to forget it.

Arthur Conan Doyle 1859–1930: *A Study in Scarlet* (1887)

4 Where is the wisdom we have lost in knowledge?
Where is the knowledge we have lost in information?

T. S. Eliot 1888–1965: *The Rock* (1934)

5 Knowledge is of two kinds. We know a subject ourselves, or we know where we can find information upon it.

Samuel Johnson 1709–84: James Boswell *Life of Samuel Johnson* (1791) 18 April 1775

6 The motto of all the mongoose family is, 'Run and find out.'

Rudyard Kipling 1865–1936: *The Jungle Book* (1897)

7 You will find it a very good practice always to verify your references, sir!

Martin Joseph Routh 1755–1854: John William Burgon *Lives of Twelve Good Men* (1888 ed.)

8 That was a little bit more information than I needed to know.

Quentin Tarantino 1963– : *Pulp Fiction* (1994 film); spoken by Uma Thurman

Ingratitude

see also **Gratitude**

1 That's the way with these directors, they're always biting the hand that lays the golden egg.

Sam Goldwyn 1882–1974: Alva Johnston *The Great Goldwyn* (1937)

2 I have chosen such a good boy for Savita, and all everyone does is complain.

Vikram Seth 1952– : *A Suitable Boy* (1993)

3 How sharper than a serpent's tooth it is
To have a thankless child!

William Shakespeare 1564–1616: *King Lear* (1605–6)

4 There's plenty of boys that will come hankering and grovelling around you when you've got an apple, and beg the core off of you; but when they've got one, and you beg for the core and remind them how you give them a core one time, they say thank you 'most to death, but there ain't-a-going to be no core.

Mark Twain 1835–1910: *Tom Sawyer Abroad* (1894)

5 My children are ungrateful: they don't care. That is my great reward. They are free.

Fay Weldon 1931– : *Praxis* (1978)

In-Laws

see also **The Family**, **Marriage**

1 I should, many a good day, have blown my brains out, but for the recollection that it would have given pleasure to my mother-in-law; and,

even *then*, if I could have been certain
to haunt her . . .
  Lord Byron 1788–1824: letter 28 January 1817

2 The ideal is to marry an orphan.
  Jilly Cooper 1937– : *How to Stay Married*
  (1977)

3 The awe and dread with which the
untutored savage contemplates his
mother-in-law are amongst the most
familiar facts of anthropology.
  James George Frazer 1854–1941: *The Golden
  Bough* (2nd ed., 1900)

4 I was a post-war, utility son-in-law!
Not quite the Frog-Prince. Maybe the
Swineherd.
  Ted Hughes 1930–98: *Birthday Letters* (1998)
  'A Pink Wool Knitted Dress'

Innocence

see also **Guilt**

1 *Honi soit qui mal y pense.*
  Evil be to him who evil thinks.
  Anonymous: motto of the Order of the
  Garter, originated by Edward III, probably
  on 23 April of 1348 or 1349

2 Unto the pure all things are pure.
  Bible: Titus

3 It is not only our fate but our business
to lose innocence, and once we have
lost that, it is futile to attempt a picnic
in Eden.
  Elizabeth Bowen 1899–1973: 'Out of a Book'
  in *Orion III* (1946)

4 Innocence always calls mutely for
protection, when we would be so
much wiser to guard ourselves against
it: innocence is like a dumb leper who
has lost his bell, wandering the world
meaning no harm.
  Graham Greene 1904–91: *The Quiet American*
  (1955)

5 I love my work and my children. God
Is distant, difficult. Things happen.
Too near the ancient troughs of blood
Innocence is no earthly weapon.
  Geoffrey Hill 1932– : 'Ovid in the Third
  Reich' (1968)

6 Never such innocence,
Never before or since,

As changed itself to past
Without a word—the men
Leaving the gardens tidy,
The thousands of marriages
Lasting a little while longer:
Never such innocence again.
  Philip Larkin 1922–85: 'MCMXIV' (1964)

7 To the Puritan all things are impure,
as somebody says.
  D. H. Lawrence 1885–1930: *Etruscan Places*
  (1932)

8 We are stardust,
We are golden,
And we got to get ourselves
Back to the garden.
  Joni Mitchell 1945– : 'Woodstock' (1969
  song)

9 I'd the upbringing a nun would
envy . . . Until I was fifteen I was more
familiar with Africa than my own
body.
  Joe Orton 1933–67: *Entertaining Mr Sloane*
  (1964)

10 Innocence is a slippery substance. It
seems you can't possess it and at the
same time *know* you possess it.
  Carol Shields 1935– : *Larry's Party* (1997)

11 The innocent and the beautiful
Have no enemy but time.
  W. B. Yeats 1865–1939: 'In Memory of Eva
  Gore Booth and Con Markiewicz' (1933)

Insight

see also **Self-Knowledge**

1 The world is like a Mask dancing. If
you want to see it well you do not
stand in one place.
  Chinua Achebe 1930– : *Arrow of God* (1988)

2 If the doors of perception were
cleansed everything would appear to
man as it is, infinite.
  William Blake 1757–1827: *The Marriage of
  Heaven and Hell* (1790–3)

3 Know what I mean, Harry?
  Frank Bruno 1961– : supposed to have been
  said in interview with sports commentator
  Harry Carpenter, possibly apocryphal

4 One sees great things from the valley;
only small things from the peak.
G. K. Chesterton 1874–1936: *The Innocence of
Father Brown* (1911)

5 It is only with the heart that one can
see rightly; what is essential is
invisible to the eye.
Antoine de Saint-Exupéry 1900–44: *Le Petit
Prince* (1943)

6 If we had a keen vision and feeling of
all ordinary human life, it would be
like hearing the grass grow and the
squirrel's heart beat, and we should
die of that roar which lies on the other
side of silence.
George Eliot 1819–80: *Middlemarch* (1871–2)

7 Deprivation is for me what daffodils
were for Wordsworth.
Philip Larkin 1922–85: *Required Writing* (1983)

8 Come to the edge.
We might fall.
Come to the edge.
It's too high!
COME TO THE EDGE!
And they came
and he pushed
and they flew . . .
■ *on Apollinaire*
Christopher Logue 1926– : 'Come to the
edge' (1969)

9 The fact that for a long time Cubism
has not been understood and that
even today there are people who
cannot see anything in it, means
nothing. I do not read English, an
English book is a blank book to me.
This does not mean that the English
language does not exist.
Pablo Picasso 1881–1973: interview with
Marius de Zayas, 1923

10 I have striven not to laugh at human
actions, not to weep at them, nor to
hate them, but to understand them.
Baruch Spinoza 1632–77: *Tractatus Politicus*
(1677)

11 *Tout comprendre rend très indulgent.*
To be totally understanding makes
one very indulgent.
Mme de Staël 1766–1817: *Corinne* (1807)

12 The only people who remain
misunderstood are those who either
do not know what they want or are
not worth understanding.
Ivan Turgenev 1818–83: *Rudin* (1856)

Insults

....

1 I think I detect sarcasm. I can't be
doing with sarcasm. You know what
they say? Sarcasm is the greatest
weapon of the smallest mind.
Alan Ayckbourn 1939– : *Woman in Mind*
(1986)

2 An injury is much sooner forgotten
than an insult.
Lord Chesterfield 1694–1773: *Letters to his Son*
(1774) 9 October 1746

3 How easy it is to call rogue and villain,
and that wittily! But how hard to
make a man appear a fool, a
blockhead, or a knave, without using
any of those opprobrious terms! To
spare the grossness of the names, and
to do the thing yet more severely, is to
draw a full face, and to make the nose
and cheeks stand out, and yet not to
employ any depth of shadowing.
John Dryden 1631–1700: *Of Satire* (1693)

4 Like being savaged by a dead sheep.
■ *on being criticized by Geoffrey Howe*
Denis Healey 1917– : speech in the House of
Commons, 14 June 1978

5 I decided the worst thing you can call
Paul Keating, quite frankly, is Paul
Keating.
John Hewson 1946– : Michael Gordon *A
Question of Leadership* (1993)

6 This little flower, this delicate little
beauty, this cream puff, is supposed to
be beyond personal criticism . . . He is
simply a shiver looking for a spine to
run up.
■ *of John Hewson*
Paul Keating 1944– : attributed

7 Curse the blasted, jelly-boned swines,
the slimy, the belly-wriggling
invertebrates, the miserable sodding
rotters, the flaming sods, the

snivelling, dribbling, dithering, palsied, pulse-less lot that make up England today. They've got white of egg in their veins, and their spunk is that watery it's a marvel they can breed. They *can* nothing but frog-spawn—the gibberers! God, how I hate them!

D. H. Lawrence 1885–1930: letter to Edward Garnett, 3 July 1912

8 The devil damn thee black, thou cream-faced loon!
Where gott'st thou that goose look?
William Shakespeare 1564–1616: *Macbeth* (1606)

9 Silence is the most perfect expression of scorn.
George Bernard Shaw 1856–1950: *Back to Methuselah* (1921)

10 JUDGE: You are extremely offensive, young man.
SMITH: As a matter of fact, we both are, and the only difference between us is that I am trying to be, and you can't help it.
F. E. Smith 1872–1930: 2nd Earl of Birkenhead *Earl of Birkenhead* (1933)

11 Okie use' ta mean you was from Oklahoma. Now it means you're a dirty son-of-a-bitch. Okie means you're scum. Don't mean nothing itself, it's the way they say it.
John Steinbeck 1902–68: *The Grapes of Wrath* (1939)

Intellectuals

1 To the man-in-the-street, who, I'm sorry to say,
Is a keen observer of life,
The word 'Intellectual' suggests straight away
A man who's untrue to his wife.
W. H. Auden 1907–73: *New Year Letter* (1941)

2 *La trahison des clercs.*
The treachery of the intellectuals.
Julien Benda 1867–1956: title of book (1927)

3 An intellectual is someone whose mind watches itself.
Albert Camus 1913–60: *Carnets, 1935–42* (1962)

4 Throughout my career I've been described as 'cerebral'. But I had to look up that word in a dictionary.
Graeme Le Saux 1968– : in *Independent on Sunday* 14 March 1999; cf. **Football** 8

5 'Hullo! friend,' I call out, 'Won't you lend us a hand?' 'I am an intellectual and don't drag wood about,' came the answer. 'You're lucky,' I reply. 'I too wanted to become an intellectual, but I didn't succeed.'
Albert Schweitzer 1875–1965: *Mitteilungen aus Lambarene* (1928)

6 American anti-intellectualism will never again be the same because of Bill Gates. Gates embodies what was supposed to be impossible—the practical intellectual.
Randall E. Stross: *The Microsoft Way* (1996)

7 What is a highbrow? He is a man who has found something more interesting than women.
Edgar Wallace 1875–1932: in *New York Times* 24 January 1932

8 I know I've got a degree. Why does that mean I have to spend my life with intellectuals? I've got a life-saving certificate but I don't spend my evenings diving for a rubber brick with my pyjamas on.
Victoria Wood 1953– : *Mens Sana in Thingummy Doodah* (1990)

Intelligence

1 It takes little talent to see clearly what lies under one's nose, a good deal of it to know in which direction to point that organ.
W. H. Auden 1907–73: *The Dyer's Hand* (1963)

2 He [Hercule Poirot] tapped his forehead. 'These little grey cells. It is "up to them".'
Agatha Christie 1890–1976: *The Mysterious Affair at Styles* (1920)

3 'Excellent,' I cried. 'Elementary,' said he.

> **Arthur Conan Doyle** 1859–1930: *The Memoirs of Sherlock Holmes* (1894); 'Elementary, my dear Watson' is not found in any book by Conan Doyle, but is first found in P. G. Wodehouse *Psmith Journalist* (1915)

4 As a human being, one has been endowed with just enough intelligence to be able to see clearly how utterly inadequate that intelligence is when confronted with what exists.

> **Albert Einstein** 1879–1955: letter to Queen Elisabeth of Belgium, 19 September 1932

5 The test of a first-rate intelligence is the ability to hold two opposed ideas in the mind at the same time, and still retain the ability to function.

> **F. Scott Fitzgerald** 1896–1940: in *Esquire* February 1936, 'The Crack-Up'

6 The clever men at Oxford
Know all that there is to be knowed.
But they none of them know one half
  as much
As intelligent Mr Toad!

> **Kenneth Grahame** 1859–1932: *Wind in the Willows* (1908)

7 Sir, I have found you an argument; but I am not obliged to find you an understanding.

> **Samuel Johnson** 1709–84: James Boswell *Life of Samuel Johnson* (1791) June 1784

8 No one in this world, so far as I know—and I have searched the records for years, and employed agents to help me—has ever lost money by underestimating the intelligence of the great masses of the plain people.

> **H. L. Mencken** 1880–1956: in *Chicago Tribune* 19 September 1926

9 You beat your pate, and fancy wit will come:
Knock as you please, there's nobody at home.

> **Alexander Pope** 1688–1744: 'Epigram: You beat your pate' (1732)

10 Intelligence is quickness to apprehend as distinct from ability, which is

capacity to act wisely on the thing apprehended.

> **Alfred North Whitehead** 1861–1947: *Dialogues* (1954) 15 December 1939

International Relations

see also **Diplomacy**, **Government**, **Politics**

1 Nations touch at their summits.

> **Walter Bagehot** 1826–77: *The English Constitution* (1867)

2 Since the day of the air, the old frontiers are gone. When you think of the defence of England you no longer think of the chalk cliffs of Dover; you think of the Rhine. That is where our frontier lies.

> **Stanley Baldwin** 1867–1947: speech, House of Commons, 30 July 1934

3 [Winston Churchill] does not talk the language of the 20th century but that of the 18th. He is still fighting Blenheim all over again. His only answer to a difficult situation is send a gun-boat.

> **Aneurin Bevan** 1897–1960: speech at Labour Party Conference, Scarborough, 2 October 1951

4 If you carry this resolution you will send Britain's Foreign Secretary naked into the conference chamber.

> ■ *on a motion proposing unilateral nuclear disarmament by the UK*
> **Aneurin Bevan** 1897–1960: speech at Labour Party Conference in Brighton, 3 October 1957

5 My [foreign] policy is to be able to take a ticket at Victoria Station and go anywhere I damn well please.

> **Ernest Bevin** 1881–1951: in *Spectator* 20 April 1951

6 This policy cannot succeed through speeches, and shooting-matches, and songs; it can only be carried out through blood and iron.

> **Otto von Bismarck** 1815–98: speech in the Prussian House of Deputies, 28 January 1886

7 Red China is not the powerful nation seeking to dominate the world.

Frankly, in the opinion of the Joint Chiefs of Staff, this strategy would involve us in the wrong war, at the wrong place, at the wrong time, and with the wrong enemy.

Omar Bradley 1893–1981: *US Cong. Senate Comm. on Armed Services* (1951)

8 The day of small nations has long passed away. The day of Empires has come.

Joseph Chamberlain 1836–1914: speech at Birmingham, 12 May 1904

9 If Hitler invaded hell I would make at least a favourable reference to the devil in the House of Commons.

Winston Churchill 1874–1965: *The Second World War* (1950) vol. 3

10 Peace, commerce, and honest friendship with all nations— entangling alliances with none.

Thomas Jefferson 1743–1826: inaugural address, 4th of March 1801

11 We hope that the world will not narrow into a neighbourhood before it has broadened into a brotherhood.

Lyndon Baines Johnson 1908–73: speech at the lighting of the Nation's Christmas Tree, 22 December 1963

12 *Ich bin ein Berliner.*

I am a Berliner.

■ *expressing US commitment to the support and defence of West Berlin*

John F. Kennedy 1917–63: speech in West Berlin, 26 June 1963

13 The great nations have always acted like gangsters, and the small nations like prostitutes.

Stanley Kubrick 1928–99: in *Guardian* 5 June 1963

14 [The Commonwealth] is a largely meaningless relic of Empire—like the smile on the face of the Cheshire Cat which remains when the cat has disappeared.

Nigel Lawson 1932– : attributed, 1993

15 We face neither East nor West: we face forward.

Kwame Nkrumah 1900–72: conference speech, Accra, 7 April 1960

16 Whatever it is that the government does, sensible Americans would prefer that the government does it to somebody else. This is the idea behind foreign policy.

P. J. O'Rourke 1947– : *Parliament of Whores* (1991)

17 We have no eternal allies and we have no perpetual enemies. Our interests are eternal and perpetual, and those interests it is our duty to follow.

Lord Palmerston 1784–1865: speech, House of Commons, 1 March 1848

18 In the field of world policy I would dedicate this Nation to the policy of the good neighbour.

Franklin D. Roosevelt 1882–1945: inaugural address, 4 March 1933

19 Living next to you is in some ways like sleeping with an elephant. No matter how friendly and even-tempered the beast, one is affected by every twitch and grunt.

■ *on relations between Canada and the US*

Pierre Trudeau 1919–2000: speech at National Press Club, Washington DC, 25 March 1969

20 Armed neutrality is ineffectual enough at best.

Woodrow Wilson 1856–1924: speech to Congress, 2 April 1917

The Internet

see also **Computers**

1 The Web is a tremendous grassroots revolution. All these people coming from very different directions achieved a change. There's a tremendous message of hope for humanity in that.

Tim Berners-Lee 1955– : in *Independent* 17 May 1999

2 The Internet is an elite organisation; most of the population of the world has never even made a phone call.

Noam Chomsky 1928– : in *Observer* 18 February 1996

3 I am afraid it is a non-starter. I cannot even use a bicycle pump.

■ *when asked whether she uses e-mail*
Judi Dench 1934– : in *The Times* 13 February 1999

4 The important thing to remember is that this is not a new form of life. It is just a new activity.

Esther Dyson 1951– : in *New York Times* 7 July 1996

5 The symbol of the atomic age, which tended to centralise power, was a nucleus with electrons held in tight orbit; the symbol of the digital age is the Web, with countless centres of power all equally networked.

Walter Isaacson 1952– : in *Time* 29 December 1997

6 This Ken Starr report is now posted on the Internet. I'll bet Clinton's glad he put a computer in every classroom now.

Jay Leno 1950– : attributed, in *Sunday Times* 20 September 1998

7 We can scarcely calculate the mutations in our experience of texts, music and art in the new worlds of the CD-ROM, of virtual reality, of cyberspace and the Internet.

George Steiner 1926– : attributed, in *Time* 8 June 1998

8 We've all heard that a million monkeys banging on a million typewriters will eventually reproduce the entire works of Shakespeare. Now, thanks to the Internet, we know this is not true.

Robert Wilensky 1951– : in *Mail on Sunday* 16 February 1997 'Quotes of the Week'; cf. **Chance** 3

Inventions and Discoveries

see also **Science**, **Technology**

1 When man wanted to make a machine that would walk he created the wheel, which does not resemble a leg.

Guillaume Apollinaire 1880–1918: *Les Mamelles de Tirésias* (1918)

2 *Eureka!*
I've got it!

Archimedes *c.*287–212 BC: Vitruvius Pollio *De Architectura*

3 The discovery of a new dish does more for human happiness than the discovery of a star.

Anthelme Brillat-Savarin 1755–1826: *Physiologie du Goût* (1826)

4 LORD CARNARVON: Can you see anything?
CARTER: Yes, wonderful things.

■ *on first looking into the tomb of Tutankhamun, 26 November 1922*
Howard Carter 1874–1939: *The Tomb of Tutankh-Amen* (1923)

5 Thus first necessity invented stools,
Convenience next suggested elbow-chairs,
And luxury the accomplished sofa last.

William Cowper 1731–1800: *The Task* (1785) 'The Sofa'

6 The unleashed power of the atom has changed everything save our modes of thinking and we thus drift toward unparalleled catastrophe.

Albert Einstein 1879–1955: telegram to prominent Americans, 24 May 1946

7 Why sir, there is every possibility that you will soon be able to tax it!

■ *to Gladstone, when asked about the usefulness of electricity*
Michael Faraday 1791–1867: W. E. H. Lecky *Democracy and Liberty* (1899 ed.)

8 Whatever Nature has in store for mankind, unpleasant as it may be, men must accept, for ignorance is never better than knowledge.

Enrico Fermi 1901–54: Laura Fermi *Atoms in the Family* (1955)

9 What is the use of a new-born child?

■ *when asked what was the use of a new invention*
Benjamin Franklin 1706–90: J. Parton *Life and Times of Benjamin Franklin* (1864)

10 They all laughed at Christopher Columbus
When he said the world was round

They all laughed when Edison
  recorded sound
They all laughed at Wilbur and his
  brother
When they said that man could fly;
They told Marconi
Wireless was a phony—
It's the same old cry!

Ira Gershwin 1896–1983: 'They All Laughed'
(1937 song)

11 We will probably never know who the
clever chap was who thought up the
itemised phone bill. But it ranks up
there with suspender belts, Sky Sports
channels and Loaded magazine as
inventions women could do without.

Maeve Haran 1950– : in *Sunday Times*
25 April 1999

12 Nothing is more contrary to the
organization of the mind, of the
memory, and of the imagination . . .
It's just tormenting the people with
trivia!!!

■ *on the introduction of the metric system*

Napoleon I 1769–1821: *Mémoires . . . écrits à
Ste-Hélène* (1823–5)

13 praise without end the go-ahead zeal
of whoever it was invented the wheel;
but never a word for the poor soul's
  sake
that thought ahead, and invented the
  brake.

Howard Nemerov 1920–91: 'To the Congress
of the United States, Entering Its Third
Century' 26 February 1989

14 I don't know what I may seem to the
world, but as to myself, I seem to have
been only like a boy playing on the
sea-shore and diverting myself in now
and then finding a smoother pebble
or a prettier shell than ordinary,
whilst the great ocean of truth lay all
undiscovered before me.

Isaac Newton 1642–1727: Joseph Spence
Anecdotes (ed. J. Osborn, 1966)

15 The Patent Office is the gatekeeper to
the new age.

Tom Stoppard 1937– : *The Invention of Love*
(1997)

16 Discovery consists of seeing what
everybody has seen and thinking what
nobody has thought.

Albert von Szent-Györgyi 1893–1986: Irving
Good (ed.) *The Scientist Speculates* (1962)

17 Name the greatest of all the inventors.
Accident.

Mark Twain 1835–1910: *Notebook* (1935)

18 Unlike science, the product of
technology is measured not against
nature but in terms of its novelty and
the value that a particular culture puts
on it.

Lewis Wolpert 1929– : *The Unnatural Nature
of Science* (1995)

Ireland

see also **Northern Ireland**

1 Do you not feel that this island is
moored only lightly to the sea-bed,
and might be off for the Americas at
any moment?

Sebastian Barry 1955– : *Prayers of Sherkin*
(1991)

2 I could wish that the English kept
history in mind more, that the Irish
kept it in mind less.

Elizabeth Bowen 1899–1973: 'Notes on Eire'
9 November 1949

3 For the great Gaels of Ireland
Are the men that God made mad,
For all their wars are merry,
And all their songs are sad.

G. K. Chesterton 1874–1936: *The Ballad of the
White Horse* (1911)

4 Don't be surprised
If I demur, for, be advised
My passport's green.
No glass of ours was ever raised
To toast *The Queen.*

■ *rebuking the editors of* The Penguin Book of
Contemporary British Poetry *for including him
among its authors*

Seamus Heaney 1939– : *Open Letter* (1983)

5 Ireland is the old sow that eats her
farrow.

James Joyce 1882–1941: *A Portrait of the Artist
as a Young Man* (1916)

6 Ireland never was contented . . .
Say you so? You are demented.
Ireland was contented when
All could use the sword and pen,
And when Tara rose so high
That her turrets split the sky.
   Walter Savage Landor 1775–1864: 'Ireland
   never was contented' (1853)

7 In Ireland the inevitable never
happens and the unexpected
constantly occurs.
   John Pentland Mahaffy 1839–1919: W. B.
   Stanford and R. B. McDowell *Mahaffy* (1971)

8 I'm Irish. We think sideways.
   Spike Milligan 1918–2002: in *Independent on
   Sunday* 20 June 1999

9 Spenser's Ireland
has not altered;—
a place as kind as it is green,
the greenest place I've never seen.
   Marianne Moore 1887–1972: 'Spenser's
   Ireland' (1941)

10 The Irish are still the people the
English understand least. And we're
just not sure . . . if they will ever really
forgive us for the unspeakable sin of
not wanting to be like them.
   Joseph O'Connor 1963– : *The Secret World of
   the Irish Male* (1994)

11 God made the grass, the air and the
rain; and the grass, the air and the
rain made the Irish; and the Irish
turned the grass, the air and the rain
back into God.
   Sean O'Faolain 1900–91: in *Holiday* June 1958

12 The moment the very name of Ireland
is mentioned, the English seem to bid
adieu to common feeling, common
prudence, and common sense, and to
act with the barbarity of tyrants, and
the fatuity of idiots.
   Sydney Smith 1771–1845: *Letters of Peter
   Plymley* (1807)

13 Out of Ireland have we come.
Great hatred, little room,
Maimed us at the start.
   W. B. Yeats 1865–1939: 'Remorse for
   Intemperate Speech' (1933)

Italy

see also **Venice**

1 Rome's just a city like anywhere else.
A vastly overrated city, I'd say. It
trades on belief just as Stratford trades
on Shakespeare.
   Anthony Burgess 1917–93: *Inside Mr Enderby*
   (1963)

2 While stands the Coliseum, Rome
shall stand;
When falls the Coliseum, Rome shall
fall;
And when Rome falls—the World.
   Lord Byron 1788–1824: *Childe Harold's
   Pilgrimage* (1812–18)

3 The traveller who has gone to Italy to
study the tactile values of Giotto, or
the corruption of the Papacy, may
return remembering nothing but the
blue sky and the men and women
under it.
   E. M. Forster 1879–1970: *A Room with a View*
   (1908)

4 Italy is a geographical expression.
   ■ *discussing the Italian question with
   Palmerston in 1847*
   Prince Metternich 1773–1859: *Mémoires,
   Documents, etc. de Metternich publiés par son
   fils* (1883)

5 Lump the whole thing! say that the
Creator made Italy from designs by
Michael Angelo!
   Mark Twain 1835–1910: *The Innocents Abroad*
   (1869)

6 With every smell, I smell food. With
every sight, I see food. I can almost
hear food. I want to spade the whole
lot through my mouth.
   ■ *on holiday in Italy*
   Sarah, Duchess of York 1959– : in *Spectator*
   16 August 1997

Henry James 1843–1916

1 The work of Henry James has always
seemed divisible by a simple dynastic

arrangement into three reigns: James I, James II, and the Old Pretender.
Philip Guedalla 1889–1944: *Supers and Supermen* (1920)

2 Poor Henry, he's spending eternity wandering round and round a stately park and the fence is just too high for him to peep over and they're having tea just too far away for him to hear what the countess is saying.
W. Somerset Maugham 1874–1965: *Cakes and Ale* (1930)

3 It is leviathan retrieving pebbles. It is a magnificent but painful hippopotamus resolved at any cost, even at the cost of its dignity, upon picking up a pea which has got into a corner of its den.
H. G. Wells 1866–1946: *Boon* (1915)

Jazz

1 If you still have to ask . . . shame on you.
■ *when asked what jazz is; sometimes quoted as, 'Man, if you gotta ask you'll never know'*
Louis Armstrong 1901–71: Max Jones et al. *Salute to Satchmo* (1970)

2 Jazz is the only music in which the same note can be played night after night but differently each time.
Ornette Coleman 1930– : W. H. Mellers *Music in a New Found Land* (1964)

3 Playing 'Bop' is like scrabble with all the vowels missing.
Duke Ellington 1899–1974: in *Look* 10 August 1954

4 A jazz musician is a juggler who uses harmonies instead of oranges.
Benny Green 1927– : *The Reluctant Art* (1962)

5 If you're in jazz and more than ten people like you, you're labelled commercial.
Herbie Mann 1930– : Henry Pleasants *Serious Music and All That Jazz!* (1969)

6 It don't mean a thing
If it ain't got that swing.
Irving Mills 1894–1985: 'It Don't Mean a Thing' (1932 song; music by Duke Ellington)

7 Jazz music is to be played sweet, soft, plenty rhythm.
Jelly Roll Morton 1885–1941: *Mister Jelly Roll* (1950)

8 What a terrible revenge by the culture of the Negroes on that of the whites!
Ignacy Jan Paderewski 1860–1941: attributed

9 Jazz will endure, just as long as people hear it through their feet instead of their brains.
John Philip Sousa 1854–1932: attributed

Jealousy

see also **Envy**

1 Love is strong as death; jealousy is cruel as the grave.
Bible: Song of Solomon

2 Jealousy is no more than feeling alone against smiling enemies.
Elizabeth Bowen 1899–1973: *The House in Paris* (1935)

3 As we all know from witnessing the consuming jealousy of husbands who are never faithful, people do not confine themselves to the emotions to which they are entitled.
Quentin Crisp 1908–99: *The Naked Civil Servant* (1968)

4 Jealousy is all the fun you *think* they had.
Erica Jong 1942– : *How to Save Your Own Life* (1977)

5 Though jealousy be produced by love, as ashes are by fire, yet jealousy extinguishes love as ashes smother the flame.
Marguerite d'Angoulême 1492–1549: *The Heptameron* (1558)

6 To jealousy, nothing is more frightful than laughter.
Françoise Sagan 1935– : *La Chamade* (1965)

7 Trifles light as air
Are to the jealous confirmations strong
As proofs of holy writ.
William Shakespeare 1564–1616: *Othello* (1602–4)

Journalism

see also **News, Newspapers, Press Photographers**

1 Anyone here been raped and speaks English?

   ■ *shouted by a British TV reporter in a crowd of Belgian civilians waiting to be airlifted out of the Belgian Congo, c.1960*
   Anonymous: Edward Behr *Anyone Here been Raped and Speaks English?* (1981)

2 I had the necessary qualifications: inexhaustible stamina, insatiable curiosity and a thick skin.

   Nora Beloff 1919–97: in *Guardian* 15 February 1997; obituary

3 Journalists say a thing that they know isn't true, in the hope that if they keep on saying it long enough it *will* be true.

   Arnold Bennett 1867–1931: *The Title* (1918)

4 When seagulls follow a trawler, it is because they think sardines will be thrown into the sea.

   Eric Cantona 1966– : to the media at the end of a press conference, 31 March 1995

5 Journalism largely consists in saying 'Lord Jones Dead' to people who never knew that Lord Jones was alive.

   G. K. Chesterton 1874–1936: *Wisdom of Father Brown* (1914)

6 The press is ferocious. It forgives nothing, it only hunts for mistakes . . . In my position anyone sane would have left a long time ago.

   ■ *contrasting British and foreign press reporting*
   Diana, Princess of Wales 1961–97: in *Le Monde* 27 August 1997

7 I believed that all one did about a war was go to it, as a gesture of solidarity, and get killed, or survive if lucky until the war was over . . . I had no idea you could be what I became, an unscathed tourist of wars.

   Martha Gellhorn 1908–98: *The Face of War* (1959)

8 Go to where the silence is and say something.

   ■ *accepting an award from Columbia University for her coverage of the 1991 massacre in East Timor by Indonesian troops*
   Amy Goodman 1957– : in *Columbia Journalism Review* March/April 1994

9 Success in journalism can be a form of failure. Freedom comes from lack of possessions. The truth-divulging paper must imitate the tramp and sleep under a hedge.

   Graham Greene 1904–91: in *New Statesman* 31 May 1968

10 You furnish the pictures and I'll furnish the war.

   ■ *message to the artist Frederic Remington in Havana, Cuba, during the Spanish-American War of 1898*
   William Randolph Hearst 1863–1951: attributed

11 My motto is publish and be sued.

   Richard Ingrams 1937– : on BBC Radio 4, 4 May 1977

12 The journalists have constructed for themselves a little wooden chapel, which they also call the Temple of Fame, in which they put up and take down portraits all day long and make such a hammering you can't hear yourself speak.

   Georg Christoph Lichtenberg 1742–99: A. Leitzmann *Georg Christoph Lichtenberg Aphorismen* (1904)

13 Under the modern journalist's code of Olympian objectivity (and total purity of motive), I am absolved of responsibility. We journalists don't have to step on roaches. All we have to do is turn on the kitchen light and watch the critters scurry.

   P. J. O'Rourke 1947– : *Parliament of Whores* (1991)

14 No government in history has been as obsessed with public relations as this one . . . Speaking for myself, if there is a message I want to be off it.

   Jeremy Paxman 1950– : in *Daily Telegraph* 3 July 1998

15 Journalists belong in the gutter
because that is where the ruling
classes throw their guilty secrets.
  Gerald Priestland 1927–91: in *Observer* 22 May
  1988

16 A cynical, mercenary, demagogic,
corrupt press will produce in time a
people as base as itself.
  Joseph Pulitzer 1847–1911: inscribed on the
  gateway to the Columbia School of
  Journalism in New York

17 The men with the muck-rakes are
often indispensable to the well-being
of society; but only if they know when
to stop raking the muck.
  Theodore Roosevelt 1858–1919: speech in
  Washington, 14 April 1906

18 Comment is free, but facts are sacred.
  C. P. Scott 1846–1932: in *Manchester Guardian*
  5 May 1921; cf. 20 below

19 I have no problem with cheque-book
journalism, as long as some of the
cheque goes to me.
  Jon Snow 1947– : in *Independent* 6 March
  1999

20 Comment is free but facts are on
expenses.
  Tom Stoppard 1937– : *Night and Day* (1978);
  see 18 above

21 All newspaper and journalistic
activity is an intellectual brothel from
which there is no retreat.
  Leo Tolstoy 1828–1910: letter to Prince V. P.
  Meshchersky, 22 August 1871

22 There are laws to protect the freedom
of the press's speech, but none that
are worth anything to protect the
people from the press.
  Mark Twain 1835–1910: 'License of the Press'
  (1873)

23 Journalism—an ability to meet the
challenge of filling the space.
  Rebecca West 1892–1983: in *New York Herald
  Tribune* 22 April 1956

24 You cannot hope
to bribe or twist,
thank God! the
British journalist.
But, seeing what
the man will do
unbribed, there's
no occasion to.
  Humbert Wolfe 1886–1940: 'Over the Fire'
  (1930)

25 Rock journalism is people who can't
write interviewing people who can't
talk for people who can't read.
  Frank Zappa 1940–93: Linda Botts *Loose Talk*
  (1980)

James Joyce 1882–1941

1 A dogged attempt to cover the
universe with mud, an inverted
Victorianism, an attempt to make
crossness and dirt succeed where
sweetness and light failed.
  ■ *of Ulysses*
  E. M. Forster 1879–1970: *Aspects of the Novel*
  (1927)

2 When a young man came up to him
in Zurich and said, 'May I kiss the
hand that wrote *Ulysses*?' Joyce
replied, somewhat like King Lear, 'No,
it did lots of other things too.'
  James Joyce 1882–1941: Richard Ellmann
  James Joyce (1959)

3 The scratching of pimples on the
body of the bootboy at Claridges.
  ■ *of Ulysses*
  Virginia Woolf 1882–1941: letter to Lytton
  Strachey, 24 April 1922

Justice

see also **Laws**, **Lawyers**

1 If it falls to me to start a fight to cut
out the cancer of bent and twisted
journalism in our country with the
simple sword of truth and the trusty
shield of British fair play, so be it.
  Jonathan Aitken 1942– : statement, London,
  10 April 1995

2 *Jedem das Seine.*
To each his own.
  ■ *often quoted as 'Everyone gets what he
  deserves'*
  Anonymous: inscription on the gate of
  Buchenwald concentration camp, *c.*1937

3 Who breaks a butterfly on a wheel?
■ *defending Mick Jagger after his arrest for cannabis possession*
Anonymous: leader in *The Times* 1 June 1967, written by William Rees-Mogg; cf. **Futility** 11

4 Life for life,
Eye for eye, tooth for tooth.
Bible: Exodus

5 It is better that ten guilty persons escape than one innocent suffer.
William Blackstone 1723–80: *Commentaries on the Laws of England* (1765)

6 When I hear of an 'equity' in a case like this, I am reminded of a blind man in a dark room—looking for a black hat—which isn't there.
Lord Bowen 1835–94: John Alderson Foote *Pie-Powder* (1911)

7 The life sentence goes on. It's like a runaway train that you can't just get off.
■ *of life after his conviction was quashed by the Court of Appeal*
Gerry Conlon 1954– : in *Irish Post* 13 September 1997

8 We shouldn't have all these campaigns to get the Birmingham Six released if they'd been hanged. They'd have been forgotten and the whole community would be satisfied.
Lord Denning 1899–1999: in *Spectator* 18 August 1990

9 Justice is truth in action.
Benjamin Disraeli 1804–81: speech, House of Commons, 11 February 1851

10 *Fiat justitia et pereat mundus.*
Let justice be done, though the world perish.
Ferdinand I 1503–64: motto; Johannes Manlius *Locorum Communium Collectanea* (1563)

11   Once in a lifetime
The longed-for tidal wave
Of justice can rise up,
And hope and history rhyme.
Seamus Heaney 1939– : *The Cure at Troy* (1990)

12 A long line of cases shows that it is not merely of some importance, but is of fundamental importance that justice should not only be done, but should manifestly and undoubtedly be seen to be done.
Gordon Hewart 1870–1943: Rex v Sussex Justices, 9 November 1923

13 If this is justice, I am a banana.
■ *on the libel damages awarded against* Private Eye *to Sonia Sutcliffe*
Ian Hislop 1960– : comment, 24 May 1989

14 Injustice anywhere is a threat to justice everywhere.
Martin Luther King 1929–68: letter from Birmingham Jail, Alabama, 16 April 1963

15 To no man will we sell, or deny, or delay, right or justice.
Magna Carta 1215: clause 40

16 In England, justice is open to all—like the Ritz Hotel.
James Mathew 1830–1908: R. E. Megarry *Miscellany-at-Law* (1955)

17 Injustice is relatively easy to bear; what stings is justice.
H. L. Mencken 1880–1956: *Prejudices, Third Series* (1922)

18 Justice must not only be done, it must be seen to be believed.
J. B. Morton ('Beachcomber') 1893–1975: attributed; cf. 12 above

19 What I say is that 'just' or 'right' means nothing but what is in the interest of the stronger party.
■ *spoken by Thrasymachus*
Plato 429–347 BC: *The Republic*

20 What good is an ounce of justice in an ocean of shit?
Sony Labou Tansi 1947–95: *The Antipeople* (1983)

21 *J'accuse.*
I accuse.
■ *on the Dreyfus affair*
Émile Zola 1840–1902: title of an open letter to the President of the French Republic in *L'Aurore* 13 January 1898

Kissing

1 I still remember the chewing gum, tobacco, and beer taste of my first kiss, exactly 40 years ago, although I have completely forgotten the face of the American sailor who kissed me.

Isabel Allende 1942– : in *The Times* 25 April 1998

2 But indeed, dear, these kisses on paper are scarce worth keeping. You gave me one on my neck that night you were in such good-humour, and one on my lips on some forgotten occasion, that I would not part with for a hundred thousand paper ones.

Jane Carlyle 1801–66: letter to Thomas Carlyle, 3 October 1826

3 It's like kissing Hitler.
■ *when asked what it was like to kiss Marilyn Monroe*
Tony Curtis 1925– : A. Hunter *Tony Curtis* (1985)

4 A fine romance with no kisses.
A fine romance, my friend, this is.
Dorothy Fields 1905–74: 'A Fine Romance' (1936 song)

5 Oh, innocent victims of Cupid,
Remember this terse little verse;
To let a fool kiss you is stupid,
To let a kiss fool you is worse.
E. Y. Harburg 1898–1981: 'Inscriptions on a Lipstick' (1965)

6 Where do the noses go? I always wondered where the noses would go.
Ernest Hemingway 1899–1961: *For Whom the Bell Tolls* (1940)

7 You must remember this, a kiss is still a kiss,
A sigh is just a sigh;
The fundamental things apply,
As time goes by.
Herman Hupfeld 1894–1951: 'As Time Goes By' (1931 song)

8 If love is the best thing in life, then the best part of love is the kiss.
Thomas Mann 1875–1955: *Lotte in Weimar* (1939)

9 I wasn't kissing her, I was just whispering in her mouth.
■ *on being discovered by his wife with a chorus girl*
Chico Marx 1891–1961: Groucho Marx and Richard J. Anobile *Marx Brothers Scrapbook* (1973)

10 A kiss can be a comma, a question mark or an exclamation point. That's basic spelling that every woman ought to know.
Mistinguette 1875–1956: in *Theatre Arts* December 1955

11 Kissing girls is not like science, nor is it like sport. It is the third thing when you thought there were only two.
Tom Stoppard 1937– : *The Invention of Love* (1997)

12 O Love, O fire! once he drew
With one long kiss my whole soul through
My lips, as sunlight drinketh dew.
Alfred, Lord Tennyson 1809–92: 'Fatima' (1832)

Knowledge
····································
see also **Ignorance**, **Information**

1 Everyman, I will go with thee, and be thy guide,
In thy most need to go by thy side.
■ *spoken by 'Knowledge'*
Anonymous: *Everyman* (*c*.1509–19)

2 The fox knows many things—the hedgehog one *big* one.
Archilochus 7th century BC: fragment

3 Knowledge itself is power.
Francis Bacon 1561–1626: *Meditationes Sacrae* (1597) 'Of Heresies'

4 He that increaseth knowledge increaseth sorrow.
Bible: Ecclesiastes

5 The price of wisdom is above rubies.
Bible: Job

6 It is better to know nothing than to know what ain't so.
Josh Billings 1818–85: *Proverb* (1874)

7 Does the eagle know what is in the pit?
Or wilt thou go ask the mole:
Can wisdom be put in a silver rod?
Or love in a golden bowl?
William Blake 1757–1827: *The Book of Thel* (1789) 'Thel's Motto'

8 Knowledge may give weight, but accomplishments give lustre, and many more people see than weigh.
Lord Chesterfield 1694–1773: *Maxims* (1774)

9 There is no such thing on earth as an uninteresting subject; the only thing that can exist is an uninterested person.
G. K. Chesterton 1874–1936: *Heretics* (1905)

10 For lust of knowing what should not be known,
We take the Golden Road to Samarkand.
James Elroy Flecker 1884–1915: *The Golden Journey to Samarkand* (1913)

11 And still they gazed, and still the wonder grew,
That one small head could carry all he knew.
Oliver Goldsmith 1728–74: *The Deserted Village* (1770)

12 They say that Mitterrand has 100 lovers—one with Aids, but he doesn't know which one; Bush has 100 bodyguards—one a terrorist, but he doesn't know which one; Gorbachev has 100 economic advisers—one is smart, but he doesn't know which one.
Mikhail Sergeevich Gorbachev 1931– : in *New York Times* 25 February 1988

13 We must know,
We will know.
David Hilbert 1862–1943: epitaph on his tombstone

14 If a little knowledge is dangerous, where is the man who has so much as to be out of danger?
T. H. Huxley 1825–95: 'On Elementary Instruction in Physiology' (written 1877)

15 I keep six honest serving-men (They taught me all I knew);
Their names are What and Why and When
And How and Where and Who.
Rudyard Kipling 1865–1936: *Just So Stories* (1902) 'The Elephant's Child'

16 Owl hasn't exactly got Brain, but he Knows Things.
A. A. Milne 1882–1956: *Winnie-the-Pooh* (1926)

17 *Que sais-je?*
What do I know?
■ *on the position of the sceptic*
Montaigne 1533–92: *Essais* (1580)

18 A little learning is a dangerous thing;
Drink deep, or taste not the Pierian spring.
Alexander Pope 1688–1744: *An Essay on Criticism* (1711)

19 I know nothing except the fact of my ignorance.
Socrates 469–399 BC: Diogenes Laertius *Lives of the Philosophers*

20 Knowledge is good. It does not have to look good or sound good or even do good. It is good just by being knowledge. And the only thing that makes it knowledge is that it is true. You can't have too much of it and there is no little too little to be worth having.
Tom Stoppard 1937– : *The Invention of Love* (1997)

21 Knowledge comes, but wisdom lingers.
Alfred, Lord Tennyson 1809–92: 'Locksley Hall' (1842)

22 My advice to you is not to inquire why or whither, but just to enjoy your ice cream while it's on your plate—that's my philosophy.
Thornton Wilder 1897–1975: *The Skin of Our Teeth* (1942)

Language

see also **Grammar, Meaning, Swearing, Words**

1 A phrase is born into the world both good and bad at the same time. The secret lies in a slight, an almost invisible twist. The lever should rest in your hand, getting warm, and you can only turn it once, not twice.
Isaac Babel 1894–1940: *Guy de Maupassant* (1932)

2 One picture is worth ten thousand words.
Frederick R. Barnard: in *Printers' Ink* 10 March 1927

3 A definition is the enclosing a wilderness of idea within a wall of words.
Samuel Butler 1835–1902: *Notebooks* (1912)

4 He who understands baboon would do more towards metaphysics than Locke.
Charles Darwin 1809–82: Notebook M (16 August 1838)

5 In language, the ignorant have prescribed laws to the learned.
Richard Duppa 1770–1831: *Maxims* (1830)

6 Language is fossil poetry.
Ralph Waldo Emerson 1803–82: *Essays. Second Series* (1844) 'The Poet'

7 Where in this small-talking world can I find
A longitude with no platitude?
Christopher Fry 1907– : *The Lady's not for Burning* (1949)

8 There's a cool web of language winds us in,
Retreat from too much joy or too much fear.
Robert Graves 1895–1985: 'The Cool Web' (1927)

9 It is hard for a woman to define her feelings in language which is chiefly made by men to express theirs.
Thomas Hardy 1840–1928: *Far from the Madding Crowd* (1874)

10 I believe that political correctness can be a form of linguistic fascism, and it sends shivers down the spine of my generation who went to war against fascism.
P. D. James 1920– : in *Paris Review* 1995

11 The mystery of language was revealed to me. I knew then that 'w-a-t-e-r' meant the wonderful cool something that was flowing over my hand. That living word awakened my soul, gave it light, joy, set it free!
Helen Keller 1880–1968: *The Story of My Life* (1902)

12 The cure for mixed metaphors, I have always found, is for the patient to be obliged to draw a picture of the result.
Bernard Levin 1928– : *In These Times* (1986)

13 Good heavens! For more than forty years I have been speaking prose without knowing it.
Molière 1622–73: *Le Bourgeois Gentilhomme* (1671)

14 Soundbite and slogan, strapline and headline, at every turn we meet hyperbole. The soaring inflation of the English language is more urgently in need of control than the economic variety.
Trevor Nunn 1940– : in *Evening Standard* 3 June 1999

15 Different persons growing up in the same language are like different bushes trimmed and trained to take the shape of identical elephants. The anatomical details of twigs and branches will fulfill the elephantine shape differently from bush to bush, but the overall outward results are alike.
W. V. O. Quine 1908– : *Word and Object* (1960)

16 One of our defects as a nation is a tendency to use what have been called 'weasel words'. When a weasel sucks eggs the meat is sucked out of the egg. If you use a 'weasel word' after another, there is nothing left of the other.
Theodore Roosevelt 1858–1919: speech in St Louis, 31 May 1916

17 Slang is a language that rolls up its sleeves, spits on its hands and goes to work.
Carl Sandburg 1878–1967: in *New York Times* 13 February 1959

18 Calling a spade a spade never made the spade interesting yet. Take my advice, leave spades alone.
Edith Sitwell 1887–1964: letter to Charles Henri Ford, 23 August 1933

19 The limits of my language mean the limits of my world.
Ludwig Wittgenstein 1889–1951: *Tractatus Logico-Philosophicus* (1922)

Languages

see also **Translation**

1 The great breeding people had gone out and multiplied; colonies in every clime attest our success; French is the *patois* of Europe; English is the language of the world.
   Walter Bagehot 1826–77: in *National Review* January 1856 'Edward Gibbon'

2 *on speaking French fluently rather than correctly:*
   It's nerve and brass, *audace* and disrespect, and leaping-before-you-look and what-the-hellism, that must be developed.
   Diana Cooper 1892–1986: Philip Ziegler *Diana Cooper* (1981)

3 My English text is chaste, and all licentious passages are left in the obscurity of a learned language.
   ■ *parodied as 'decent obscurity' in the* Anti-Jacobin, *1797–8*
   Edward Gibbon 1737–94: *Memoirs of My Life* (1796)

4 Written English is now inert and inorganic: not stem and leaf and flower, not even trim and well-joined masonry, but a daub of untempered mortar.
   A. E. Housman 1859–1936: in *Cambridge Review* 1917

5 I am always sorry when any language is lost, because languages are the pedigree of nations.
   Samuel Johnson 1709–84: James Boswell *Journal of a Tour to the Hebrides* (1785) 18 September 1773

6 There even are places where English completely disappears.
   In America, they haven't used it for years!
   Why can't the English teach their children how to speak?
   Alan Jay Lerner 1918–86: 'Why Can't the English?' (1956 song)

7 We are walking lexicons. In a single sentence of idle chatter we preserve Latin, Anglo-Saxon, Norse; we carry a museum inside our heads, each day we commemorate peoples of whom we have never heard.
   Penelope Lively 1933– : *Moon Tiger* (1987)

8 　　　　　To grow
   a second tongue, as
   harsh a humiliation
   as twice to be born.
   John Montague 1929– : 'A Grafted Tongue' (1972)

9 Waiting for the German verb is surely the ultimate thrill.
   Flann O'Brien 1911–66: *The Hair of the Dogma* (1977)

10 What is not clear is not French.
   Antoine de Rivarol 1753–1801: *Discours sur l'Universalité de la Langue Française* (1784)

11 England and America are two countries divided by a common language.
   George Bernard Shaw 1856–1950: attributed in this and other forms, but not found in Shaw's published writings

12 I am not like a lady at the court of Versailles, who said: 'What a dreadful pity that the bother at the tower of Babel should have got language all mixed up; but for that, everyone would always have spoken French.'
   Voltaire 1694–1778: letter to Catherine the Great, 26 May 1767

Last Words

1 *Ave Caesar, morituri te salutant.*
   Hail Caesar, those who are about to die salute you.
   ■ *gladiators saluting the Roman Emperor*
   Anonymous: Suetonius *Lives of the Caesars* 'Claudius'

2 We are putting passengers off in small boats . . . Engine room getting flooded . . . CQ.
   ■ *CQD was the original SOS call for shipping*
   Anonymous: last signals sent from the *Titanic*, 15 April 1912

3 Love? What is it? Most natural painkiller. What there is . . . LOVE.
   William S. Burroughs 1914–97: final entry in journal, 1 August 1997, the day before he died

4 My design is to make what haste I can to be gone.
Oliver Cromwell 1599–1658: John Morley *Oliver Cromwell* (1900)

5 All my possessions for a moment of time.
Elizabeth I 1533–1603: attributed, but almost certainly apocryphal

6 More light!
Johann Wolfgang von Goethe 1749–1832: attributed; actually 'Open the second shutter, so that more light can come in'

7 Well, I've had a happy life.
William Hazlitt 1778–1830: W. C. Hazlitt *Memoirs of William Hazlitt* (1867)

8 I am about to take my last voyage, a great leap in the dark.
Thomas Hobbes 1588–1679: John Watkins *Anecdotes of Men of Learning* (1808)

9 Why not, why not, why not. Yeah.
Timothy Leary 1920–96: in *Independent* 1 June 1996

10 Kiss me, Hardy.
Horatio, Lord Nelson 1758–1805: Robert Southey *Life of Nelson* (1813)

11 I am just going outside and may be some time.
Captain Lawrence Oates 1880–1912: Scott's diary entry, 16–17 March 1912

12 Die, my dear Doctor, that's the last thing I shall do!
Lord Palmerston 1784–1865: E. Latham *Famous Sayings and their Authors* (1904)

13 I am going to seek a great perhaps . . . Bring down the curtain, the farce is played out.
François Rabelais c.1494–c.1553: attributed, though none of his contemporaries authenticated the remarks

14 So little done, so much to do.
■ *said on the day of his death*
Cecil Rhodes 1853–1902: Lewis Michell *Life of Rhodes* (1910)

15 Lord take my soul, but the struggle continues.
■ *last words before he was hanged*
Ken Saro-Wiwa 1941–95: in *Daily Telegraph* 13 November 1995

16 For God's sake look after our people.
Robert Falcon Scott 1868–1912: last diary entry, 29 March 1912

17 Just before she [Stein] died she asked, 'What *is* the answer?' No answer came. She laughed and said, 'In that case what is the question?' Then she died.
Gertrude Stein 1874–1946: Donald Sutherland *Gertrude Stein* (1951)

18 If this is dying, then I don't think much of it.
Lytton Strachey 1880–1932: Michael Holroyd *Lytton Strachey* vol. 2 (1968)

19 This is no time for making new enemies.
■ *on being asked to renounce the Devil on his deathbed*
Voltaire 1694–1778: attributed

20 Tell them I've had a wonderful life.
Ludwig Wittgenstein 1889–1951: Ray Monk *Ludwig Wittgenstein* (1990)

Laws

see also **Crime**, **Justice**, **Lawyers**, **Police**, **Trials**

1 Written laws are like spider's webs; they will catch, it is true, the weak and poor, but would be torn in pieces by the rich and powerful.
Anacharsis 6th century BC: Plutarch *Parallel Lives* 'Solon'

2 Bad laws are the worst sort of tyranny.
Edmund Burke 1729–97: *Speech at Bristol, previous to the Late Election* (1780)

3 *Salus populi suprema est lex.*
The good of the people is the chief law.
Cicero 106–43 BC: *De Legibus*

4 How long soever it hath continued, if it be against reason, it is of no force in law.
Edward Coke 1552–1634: *The First Part of the Institutes of the Laws of England* (1628)

5 You know my views about some regulations—they're written for the obedience of fools and the guidance of wise men.
Harry Day: to Douglas Bader, 1931; Paul Brickhill *Reach for the Sky* (1954)

6 'If the law supposes that,' said Mr Bumble . . . 'the law is a ass—an idiot.'
Charles Dickens 1812–70: *Oliver Twist* (1838)

7 The one great principle of the English law is, to make business for itself.
Charles Dickens 1812–70: *Bleak House* (1853)

8 Today, 15 years after 8 May 1945, I know . . . that a life of obedience, led by orders, instructions, decrees and directives, is a very comfortable one in which one's creative thinking is diminished.
Adolf Eichmann 1906–62: memoirs, in *Independent* 13 August 1999

9 A verbal contract isn't worth the paper it is written on.
Sam Goldwyn 1882–1974: Alva Johnston *The Great Goldwyn* (1937)

10 I know no method to secure the repeal of bad or obnoxious laws so effective as their stringent execution.
Ulysses S. Grant 1822–85: inaugural address, 4 March 1869

11 I have come to regard the Law Courts not as a cathedral, but as a casino.
Richard Ingrams 1937– : in *Guardian* 30 July 1977

12 Loopholes are not always of a fixed dimension. They tend to enlarge as the numbers that pass through wear them away.
Harold Lever 1914–95: speech to Finance Bill Committee, 22 May 1968

13 However harmless a thing is, if the law forbids it most people will think it wrong.
W. Somerset Maugham 1874–1965: *A Writer's Notebook* (1949) written in 1896

14 Laws were made to be broken.
Christopher North 1785–1854: in *Blackwood's Magazine* (May 1830)

15 Ignorance of the law excuses no man; not that all men know the law, but because 'tis an excuse every man will plead, and no man can tell how to confute him.
John Selden 1584–1654: *Table Talk* (1689) 'Law'

16 Everything not forbidden is compulsory.
T. H. White 1906–64: *The Sword in the Stone* (1938)

Lawyers

1 No poet ever interpreted nature as freely as a lawyer interprets the truth.
Jean Giraudoux 1882–1944: *La Guerrè de Troie n'aura pas lieu* (1935)

2 A lawyer has no business with the justice or injustice of the cause which he undertakes, unless his client asks his opinion, and then he is bound to give it honestly. The justice or injustice of the cause is to be decided by the judge.
Samuel Johnson 1709–84: James Boswell *Journal of a Tour to the Hebrides* (1785) 15 August 1773

3 I don't know as I want a lawyer to tell me what I cannot do. I hire him to tell me how to do what I want to do.
John Pierpont Morgan 1837–1913: Ida M. Tarbell *The Life of Elbert H. Gary* (1925)

4 No brilliance is needed in the law. Nothing but common sense, and relatively clean fingernails.
John Mortimer 1923– : *A Voyage Round My Father* (1971)

5 A lawyer with his briefcase can steal more than a hundred men with guns.
Mario Puzo 1920–99: *The Godfather* (1969)

6 The Law: It has honoured us, may we honour it.
Daniel Webster 1782–1852: speech at the Charleston Bar Dinner, 10 May 1847

7 Judges must follow their oaths and do their duty, heedless of editorials, letters, telegrams, threats, petitions, panellists and talk shows.
Hiller B. Zobel 1932– : judicial ruling reducing the conviction of Louise Woodward from murder to manslaughter, 10 November 1997

Leadership

1 I know that the right kind of leader for the Labour Party is a desiccated calculating machine who must not in any way permit himself to be swayed by indignation.
   Aneurin Bevan 1897–1960: Michael Foot *Aneurin Bevan* (1973)

2 They be blind leaders of the blind. And if the blind lead the blind, both shall fall into the ditch.
   Bible: St Matthew

3 The art of leadership is saying no, not yes. It is very easy to say yes.
   Tony Blair 1953– : in *Mail on Sunday* 2 October 1994

4 The loyalties which centre upon number one are enormous. If he trips he must be sustained. If he makes mistakes they must be covered. If he sleeps he must not be wantonly disturbed. If he is no good he must be pole-axed. But this last extreme process cannot be carried out every day; and certainly not in the days just after he has been chosen.
   Winston Churchill 1874–1965: *The Second World War* vol. 2 (1949)

5 Leaders should never, ever try to look cool—that's for dictators.
   Ben Elton 1959– : in *Radio Times* 18/24 April 1998

6 The art of leadership . . . consists in consolidating the attention of the people against a single adversary and taking care that nothing will split up that attention.
   Adolf Hitler 1889–1945: *Mein Kampf* (1925)

7 So long as men worship the Caesars and Napoleons, Caesars and Napoleons will duly arise and make them miserable.
   Aldous Huxley 1894–1963: *Ends and Means* (1937)

8 Leadership is not about being nice. It's about being right and being strong.
   Paul Keating 1944– : in *Time* 9 January 1995

9 The final test of a leader is that he leaves behind him in other men the conviction and the will to carry on.
   Walter Lippmann 1889–1974: in *New York Herald Tribune* 14 April 1945

10 No human society, from the hunter-gatherer to the postindustrial, has come to the attention of anthropologists that did not have its leaders and the led; and no emergency was ever dealt with effectively by democratic process.
   Ian McEwan 1948– : *Enduring Love* (1998)

11 To grasp and hold a vision, that is the very essence of successful leadership—not only on the movie set where I learned it, but everywhere.
   Ronald Reagan 1911– : in *Wilson Quarterly* Winter 1994; attributed

12 I don't mind how much my Ministers talk, so long as they do what I say.
   Margaret Thatcher 1925– : in *Observer* 27 January 1980

13 At the age of four with paper hats and wooden swords we're all Generals. Only some of us never grow out of it.
   Peter Ustinov 1921– : *Romanoff and Juliet* (1956)

14 I used to say of him that his presence on the field made the difference of forty thousand men.
   ■ *of Napoleon*
   Duke of Wellington 1769–1852: Philip Henry Stanhope *Notes of Conversations with the Duke of Wellington* (1888) 2 November 1831

Leisure

see also **Holidays, Work**

1 We combat obstacles in order to get repose, and, when got, the repose is insupportable.
   Henry Brooks Adams 1838–1918: *The Education of Henry Adams* (1907)

2 If I am doing nothing, I like to be doing nothing to some purpose. That is what leisure means.
   Alan Bennett 1934– : *A Question of Attribution* (1989)

3 We are closer to the ants than to the butterflies. Very few people can endure much leisure.
  Gerald Brenan 1894–1987: *Thoughts in a Dry Season* (1978)

4 What is this life if, full of care,
We have no time to stand and stare.
  W. H. Davies 1871–1940: 'Leisure' (1911)

5 *Recreations*: growling, prowling, scowling and owling.
  Nicholas Fairbairn 1933–95: entry in *Who's Who* 1990

6 It was Einstein who made the real trouble. He announced in 1905 that there was no such thing as absolute rest. After that there never was.
  Stephen Leacock 1869–1944: *The Boy I Left Behind Me* (1947)

7 Man's heart expands to tinker with his car
For this is Sunday morning, Fate's great bazaar.
  Louis MacNeice 1907–63: 'Sunday Morning' (1935)

8 To be able to fill leisure intelligently is the last product of civilization.
  Bertrand Russell 1872–1970: *The Conquest of Happiness* (1930)

9 The world is too much with us; late and soon,
Getting and spending, we lay waste our powers.
  William Wordsworth 1770–1850: 'The world is too much with us' (1807)

Lending

see also **Debt**

1 Never lend books, for no one ever returns them; the only books I have in my library are those that other people have lent me.
  Anatole France 1844–1924: *La Vie littéraire* (1888)

2 The human species, according to the best theory I can form of it, is composed of two distinct races, *the men who borrow*, and *the men who lend*.
  Charles Lamb 1775–1834: *Essays of Elia* (1823) 'The Two Races of Men'

3 Neither a borrower, nor a lender be;
For loan oft loses both itself and friend,
And borrowing dulls the edge of husbandry.
  William Shakespeare 1564–1616: *Hamlet* (1601)

4 Three things I never lends—my 'oss, my wife, and my name.
  R. S. Surtees 1805–64: *Hillingdon Hall* (1845)

Lesbianism

see also **Homosexuality**, **Sex**

1 You're neither unnatural, nor abominable, nor mad; you're as much a part of what people call nature as anyone else; only you're unexplained as yet—you've not got your niche in creation.
  Radclyffe Hall 1883–1943: *The Well of Loneliness* (1928)

2 While gays have Michelangelo, Tchaikovsky and Capote as icons, lesbians have to make do with ex-tennis players.
  Susan Harben: attributed, in *Guardian* 28 March 1996

3 I do
And then again
She does
And then sometimes
Neither of us
Wears any trousers at all.
  Maria Jastrzebska 1953– : 'Which of Us Wears the Trousers'

4 Many years ago I chased a woman for almost two years, only to discover that her tastes were exactly like mine: we both were crazy about girls.
  Groucho Marx 1895–1977: letter 28 March 1955

5 Gay men may seek sex without emotion; lesbians often end up in emotion without sex.
  Camille Paglia 1947– : in *Esquire* October 1991

Letters

1 You bid me burn your letters. But I must forget you first.
   John Adams 1735–1826: letter to Abigail Adams, 28 April 1776

2 Letters of thanks, letters from banks,
   Letters of joy from girl and boy,
   Receipted bills and invitations
   To inspect new stock or to visit relations,
   And applications for situations,
   And timid lovers' declarations,
   And gossip, gossip from all the nations.
   W. H. Auden 1907–73: 'Night Mail' (1936)

3 She'll vish there wos more, and that's the great art o' letter writin'.
   Charles Dickens 1812–70: *Pickwick Papers* (1837-8)

4 Sir, more than kisses, letters mingle souls.
   John Donne 1572–1631: 'To Sir Henry Wotton' (1597–8)

5 It is wonderful how much news there is when people write every other day; if they wait for a month, there is nothing that seems worth telling.
   O. Douglas 1877–1948: *Penny Plain* (1920)

6 Why it should be such an effort to write to the people one loves I can't imagine. It's none at all to write to those who don't really count.
   Katherine Mansfield 1888–1923: *Journal of Katherine Mansfield* (1930)

7 A man seldom puts his authentic self into a letter. He writes it to amuse a friend or to get rid of a social or business obligation, which is to say, a nuisance.
   H. L. Mencken 1880–1956: *Minority Report* (1956)

8 The very touch of the letter was as if you had taken me all into your arms.
   Anais Nin 1903–77: letter to Henry Miller, 6 August 1932

9 I have made this [letter] longer than usual, only because I have not had the time to make it shorter.
   Blaise Pascal 1623–62: *Lettres Provinciales* (1657)

10 Don't think that this is a letter. It is only a small eruption of a disease called friendship.
   Jean Renoir 1894–1979: letter to Janine Bazin, 12 June 1974

11 A woman seldom writes her mind but in her postscript.
   Richard Steele 1672–1729: in *The Spectator* 31 May 1711

12 Beware of writing to me. I always answer . . . My father spent the last 20 years of his life writing letters. If someone thanked him for a present, he thanked them for thanking him and there was no end to the exchange but death.
   Evelyn Waugh 1903–66: letter to Lady Mosley, 30 March 1966

13 It is not in my power to tell thee how I have been affected by this dearest of all letters—it was so unexpected—so new a thing to see the breathing of thy inmost heart upon paper.
   Mary Wordsworth 1782–1859: letter to William Wordsworth, 1 August 1810

Liberty

1 Liberty is always unfinished business.
   Anonymous: title of 36th Annual Report of the American Civil Liberties Union, 1 July 1955–30 June 1956

2 Liberty is liberty, not equality or fairness or justice or human happiness or a quiet conscience.
   Isaiah Berlin 1909–97: *Two Concepts of Liberty* (1958)

3 Liberty does not consist merely of denouncing Tyranny, any more than horticulture does of deploring and abusing weeds, or even pulling them out.
   Arthur Bryant 1899–1985: in *Illustrated London News* 24 June 1939

4 The condition upon which God hath given liberty to man is eternal

vigilance; which condition if he break, servitude is at once the consequence of his crime, and the punishment of his guilt.

John Philpot Curran 1750–1817: speech on the right of election of the Lord Mayor of Dublin, 10 July 1790

5 The moment the slave resolves that he will no longer be a slave, his fetters fall. He frees himself and shows the way to others. Freedom and slavery are mental states.

Mahatma Gandhi 1869–1948: *Non-Violence in Peace and War* (1949)

6 Freedom is about the willingness of every single human being to cede to lawful authority a great deal of discretion about what you do, and how you do it.

Rudy Giuliani 1944– : attributed, in *Independent* 10 July 1999

7 I know not what course others may take; but as for me, give me liberty, or give me death!

Patrick Henry 1736–99: speech in Virginia Convention, 23 March 1775

8 Only very slowly and late have men come to realize that unless freedom is universal it is only extended privilege.

Christopher Hill 1912– : *Century of Revolution* (1961)

9 The most stringent protection of free speech would not protect a man falsely shouting fire in a theatre and causing a panic.

■ *sometimes quoted as, 'shouting fire in a crowded theatre'*

Oliver Wendell Holmes Jr. 1841–1935: in *Schenck v. United States* (1919)

10 It is better to die on your feet than to live on your knees.

Dolores Ibarruri 1895–1989: speech in Paris, 3 September 1936; also attributed to Emiliano Zapata

11 The enemies of Freedom do not argue; they shout and they shoot.

William Ralph Inge 1860–1954: *End of an Age* (1948)

12 The tree of liberty must be refreshed from time to time with the blood of patriots and tyrants. It is its natural manure.

Thomas Jefferson 1743–1826: letter to W. S. Smith, 13 November 1787

13 Liberty is, to the lowest rank of every nation, little more than the choice of working or starving.

Samuel Johnson 1709–84: 'The Bravery of the English Common Soldier' (1760)

14 It's often better to be in chains than to be free.

Franz Kafka 1883–1924: *The Trial* (1925)

15 They took away my liberty, not my freedom.

■ *of his captivity in Lebanon*

Brian Keenan 1950– : news conference, Dublin, 30 August 1990

16 Let every nation know, whether it wishes us well or ill, that we shall pay any price, bear any burden, meet any hardship, support any friend, oppose any foe to assure the survival and the success of liberty.

John F. Kennedy 1917–63: inaugural address, 20 January 1961

17 Freedom's just another word for nothin' left to lose,
Nothin' ain't worth nothin', but it's free.

Kris Kristofferson 1936– : 'Me and Bobby McGee' (1969 song, with Fred Foster)

18 Liberty is precious—so precious that it must be rationed.

Lenin 1870–1924: Sidney and Beatrice Webb *Soviet Communism* (1936)

19 Freedom is always and exclusively freedom for the one who thinks differently.

Rosa Luxemburg 1871–1919: *Die Russische Revolution* (1918)

20 If men are to wait for liberty till they become wise and good in slavery, they may indeed wait for ever.

Lord Macaulay 1800–59: *Essays Contributed to the Edinburgh Review* (1843) 'Milton'

21 The word 'freedom' means for me not a point of departure but a genuine point of arrival. The point of departure is defined by the word

'order'. Freedom cannot exist without the concept of order.
Prince Metternich 1773–1859: *Mein Politisches Testament* (1880)

22 The liberty of the individual must be thus far limited; he must not make himself a nuisance to other people.
John Stuart Mill 1806–73: *On Liberty* (1859)

23 Ask the first man you meet what he means by defending freedom, and he'll tell you privately he means defending the standard of living.
Martin Niemöller 1892–1984: address at Augsburg, January 1958

24 Freedom is not something that one people can bestow on another as a gift. They claim it as their own and none can keep it from them.
Kwame Nkrumah 1900–72: speech in Accra, 10 July 1953

25 Freedom is the freedom to say that two plus two make four. If that is granted, all else follows.
George Orwell 1903–50: *Nineteen Eighty-Four* (1949)

26 Tyranny is always better organized than freedom.
Charles Péguy 1873–1914: *Basic Verities* (1943) 'War and Peace'

27 O liberty! O liberty! what crimes are committed in thy name!
Mme Roland 1754–93: A. de Lamartine *Histoire des Girondins* (1847)

28 Man was born free, and everywhere he is in chains.
Jean-Jacques Rousseau 1712–78: *Du Contrat social* (1762)

29 I am condemned to be free.
Jean-Paul Sartre 1905–80: *L'Être et le néant* (1943)

30 Of course liberty is not licence. Liberty in my view is conforming to majority opinion.
Hugh Scanlon 1913– : television interview, 9 August 1977

31 Liberty means responsibility. That is why most men dread it.
George Bernard Shaw 1856–1950: *Man and Superman* (1903) 'Maxims: Liberty and Equality'

Libraries
....
see also **Books**, **Lending**, **Reading**

1 If you file your waste-paper basket for 50 years, you have a public library.
Tony Benn 1925– : in *Daily Telegraph* 5 March 1994

2 Being a librarian doesn't help. I've always found them close relatives of the walking dead.
Alan Bennett 1934– : Anthony Thwaite *Larkin at Sixty* (1982)

3 Cultures of East and West, the entire atlas,
Encyclopedias, centuries, dynasties,
Symbols, the cosmos, and cosmogonies
Are offered from the walls.
Jorge Luis Borges 1899–1986: 'Poem of the Gifts' (1972)

4 With awe, around these silent walks I tread;
These are the lasting mansions of the dead.
George Crabbe 1754–1832: 'The Library' (1808)

5 A man should keep his little brain attic stocked with all the furniture that he is likely to use, and the rest he can put away in the lumber room of his library, where he can get it if he wants it.
Arthur Conan Doyle 1859–1930: *The Adventures of Sherlock Holmes* (1892)

6 No place affords a more striking conviction of the vanity of human hopes, than a public library.
Samuel Johnson 1709–84: in *The Rambler* 23 March 1751

7 What is more important in a library than anything else—than everything else—is the fact that it exists.
Archibald MacLeish 1892–1982: 'The Premise of Meaning' in *American Scholar* 5 June 1972

8 A library is thought in cold storage.
Lord Samuel 1870–1963: *A Book of Quotations* (1947)

9 Come, and take choice of all my library,

And so beguile thy sorrow.
William Shakespeare 1564–1616: *Titus Andronicus* (1590)

10 There is in the British Museum an enormous mind. Consider that Plato is there cheek by jowl with Aristotle; and Shakespeare with Marlowe. This great mind is hoarded beyond the power of any single mind to possess it.
Virginia Woolf 1882–1941: *Jacob's Room* (1922)

Lies
....
see also **Deception**, **Propaganda**, **Truth**

1 An abomination unto the Lord, but a very present help in time of trouble.
■ *definition of a lie, an amalgamation of Proverbs 12.22 and Psalms 46.1, often attributed to Adlai Stevenson*
Anonymous: Bill Adler *The Stevenson Wit* (1966)

2 She tells enough white lies to ice a wedding cake.
■ *of Lady Desborough*
Margot Asquith 1864–1945: in *Listener* 11 June 1953

3 One sometimes sees more clearly in the man who lies than in the man who tells the truth. Truth, like the light, blinds. Lying, on the other hand, is a beautiful twilight, which gives to each object its value.
Albert Camus 1913–60: attributed; Lord Trevelyan *Diplomatic Channels* (1973)

4 Without lies humanity would perish of despair and boredom.
Anatole France 1844–1924: *La Vie en fleur* (1922)

5 Whoever would lie usefully should lie seldom.
Lord Hervey 1696–1743: *Memoirs of the Reign of George II* (ed. J. W. Croker, 1848)

6 The broad mass of a nation . . . will more easily fall victim to a big lie than to a small one.
Adolf Hitler 1889–1945: *Mein Kampf* (1925)

7 A little inaccuracy sometimes saves tons of explanation.
Saki 1870–1916: *The Square Egg* (1924)

8 If you want truth to go round the world you must hire an express train to pull it; but if you want a lie to go round the world, it will fly: it is as light as a feather, and a breath will carry it. It is well said in the old proverb, 'a lie will go round the world while truth is pulling its boots on'.
C. H. Spurgeon 1834–92: *Gems from Spurgeon* (1859)

9 The cruellest lies are often told in silence.
Robert Louis Stevenson 1850–94: *Virginibus Puerisque* (1881)

10 He replied that I must needs be mistaken, or that I *said the thing which was not*. (For they have no word in their language to express lying or falsehood.)
Jonathan Swift 1667–1745: *Gulliver's Travels* (1726)

11 One of the most striking differences between a cat and a lie is that a cat has only nine lives.
Mark Twain 1835–1910: *Pudd'nhead Wilson* (1894)

12 I can't tell a lie, Pa; you know I can't tell a lie. I did cut it with my hatchet.
George Washington 1732–99: M. L. Weems *Life of George Washington* (10th ed., 1810)

Life
....
see also **Life Sciences**, **Lifestyles**

1 The Answer to the Great Question Of . . . Life, the Universe and Everything . . . [is] Forty-two.
Douglas Adams 1952–2001: *The Hitch Hiker's Guide to the Galaxy* (1979)

2 'Such,' he said, 'O King, seems to me the present life of men on earth, in comparison with that time which to us is uncertain, as if when on a winter's night you sit feasting with your ealdormen and thegns,—a single sparrow should fly swiftly into the hall, and coming in at one door, instantly fly out through another.'
The Venerable Bede AD 673–735: *Ecclesiastical History of the English People*

3 Life, you know, is rather like opening a tin of sardines. We are all of us looking for the key. And, I wonder, how many of you here tonight have wasted years of your lives looking behind the kitchen dressers of this life for that key.

Alan Bennett 1934– : *Beyond the Fringe* (1961 revue) 'Take a Pew'

4 Life is like playing a violin solo in public and learning the instrument as one goes on.

Samuel Butler 1835–1902: speech at the Somerville Club, 27 February 1895

5 Life is a horizontal fall.

Jean Cocteau 1889–1963: *Opium* (1930)

6 . . . There's no need to worry—Whatever you do, life is hell.

Wendy Cope 1945– : 'Advice to Young Women' (1992)

7 Life is an incurable disease.

Abraham Cowley 1618–67: 'To Dr Scarborough' (1656)

8 It's a funny old world—a man's lucky if he gets out of it alive.

Walter de Leon and **Paul M. Jones**: *You're Telling Me* (1934 film); spoken by W. C. Fields

9 I have measured out my life with coffee spoons.

T. S. Eliot 1888–1965: 'The Love Song of J. Alfred Prufrock' (1917)

10 Birth, and copulation, and death. That's all the facts when you come to brass tacks:
Birth, and copulation, and death. I've been born, and once is enough.

T. S. Eliot 1888–1965: *Sweeney Agonistes* (1932)

11 All that matters is love and work.

Sigmund Freud 1856–1939: attributed

12 Man wants but little here below, Nor wants that little long.

Oliver Goldsmith 1728–74: 'Edwin and Angelina, or the Hermit' (1766)

13 If we find the answer to that [why it is that we and the universe exist], it would be the ultimate triumph of human reason—for then we would know the mind of God.

Stephen Hawking 1942– : *A Brief History of Time* (1988)

14 No arts; no letters; no society; and which is worst of all, continual fear and danger of violent death; and the life of man, solitary, poor, nasty, brutish, and short.

Thomas Hobbes 1588–1679: *Leviathan* (1651)

15 Life is just one damned thing after another.

Elbert Hubbard 1859–1915: in *Philistine* December 1909; often attributed to Frank Ward O'Malley; cf. 24 below

16 Cats and monkeys—monkeys and cats—all human life is there!

Henry James 1843–1916: *The Madonna of the Future* (1879)

17 As far as we can discern, the sole purpose of human existence is to kindle a light in the darkness of mere being.

Carl Gustav Jung 1875–1961: *Erinnerungen, Träume, Gedanken* (1962)

18 Life must be understood backwards; but . . . it must be lived forwards.

Sören Kierkegaard 1813–55: *Journals and Papers* (1843)

19 Life is first boredom, then fear.

Philip Larkin 1922–85: 'Dockery & Son' (1964)

20 Life is like a sewer. What you get out of it depends on what you put into it.

Tom Lehrer 1928– : 'We Will All Go Together When We Go' (1953 song)

21 Life would be tolerable but for its amusements.

George Cornewall Lewis 1806–63: in *The Times* 18 September 1872

22 Life is real! Life is earnest! And the grave is not its goal;
Dust thou art, to dust returnest, Was not spoken of the soul.

Henry Wadsworth Longfellow 1807–82: 'A Psalm of Life' (1838)

23 What, knocked a tooth out? Never
mind, dear, laugh it off, laugh it off;
it's all part of life's rich pageant.
   Arthur Marshall 1910–89: *The Games Mistress*
   (recorded monologue, 1937)

24 It's not true that life is one damn
thing after another—it's one damn
thing over and over.
   Edna St Vincent Millay 1892–1950: letter to
   Arthur Davison Ficke, 24 October 1930; see
   15 above

25 The cradle rocks above an abyss, and
common sense tells us that our
existence is but a brief crack of light
between two eternities of darkness.
   Vladimir Nabokov 1899–1977: *Speak, Memory*
   (1951)

26 To live at all is miracle enough.
   Mervyn Peake 1911–68: *The Glassblower*
   (1950)

27 My momma always said life was like a
box of chocolates . . . you never know
what you're gonna get.
   Eric Roth: *Forrest Gump* (1994 film), based on
   the novel (1986) by Winston Groom; spoken
   by Tom Hanks

28 All the world's a stage,
   And all the men and women merely
      players:
   They have their exits and their
      entrances;
   And one man in his time plays many
      parts,
   His acts being seven ages.
   William Shakespeare 1564–1616: *As You Like It*
   (1599)

29 Life's but a walking shadow, a poor
      player,
   That struts and frets his hour upon
      the stage,
   And then is heard no more; it is a tale
   Told by an idiot, full of sound and
      fury,
   Signifying nothing.
   William Shakespeare 1564–1616: *Macbeth*
   (1606)

30 Life, like a dome of many-coloured
      glass,
   Stains the white radiance of Eternity,

Until Death tramples it to fragments.
   Percy Bysshe Shelley 1792–1822: *Adonais*
   (1821)

31 Not to be born is, past all prizing,
best.
   Sophocles *c*.496–406 BC: *Oedipus Coloneus*;
   cf. 38 below

32 Life is a gamble at terrible odds—if it
was a bet, you wouldn't take it.
   Tom Stoppard 1937– : *Rosencrantz and
   Guildenstern are Dead* (1967)

33 Oh, isn't life a terrible thing, thank
God?
   Dylan Thomas 1914–53: *Under Milk Wood*
   (1954)

34 The mass of men lead lives of quiet
desperation.
   Henry David Thoreau 1817–62: *Walden* (1854)

35 Expect nothing. Live frugally
on surprise.
   Alice Walker 1944– : 'Expect nothing' (1973)

36 This world is a comedy to those that
think, a tragedy to those that feel.
   Horace Walpole 1717–97: letter to Anne,
   Countess of Upper Ossory, 16 August 1776

37 Isn't life a series of images that change
as they repeat themselves?
   Andy Warhol 1927–87: Victor Bokris *Andy
   Warhol* (1989)

38 Never to have lived is best, ancient
      writers say;
   Never to have drawn the breath of life,
      never to have looked into the eye of
      day;
   The second best's a gay goodnight and
      quickly turn away.
   W. B. Yeats 1865–1939: 'From *Oedipus at
   Colonus*' (1928); see 31 above

39 Life is a rainbow which also includes
black.
   Yevgeny Yevtushenko 1933– : in *Guardian*
   11 August 1987

Life Sciences
....

see also **Genetic Engineering, Human
Race, Life, Nature, Science, Science and
Religion, Science and Society**

1 [The science of life] is a superb and
dazzlingly lighted hall which may be

reached only by passing through a long and ghastly kitchen.

Claude Bernard 1813–78: *An Introduction to the Study of Experimental Medicine* (1865)

2 It has, I believe, been often remarked that a hen is only an egg's way of making another egg.

Samuel Butler 1835–1902: *Life and Habit* (1877)

3 Almost all aspects of life are engineered at the molecular level, and without understanding molecules we can only have a very sketchy understanding of life itself.

Francis Crick 1916– : *What Mad Pursuit* (1988)

4 I have called this principle, by which each slight variation, if useful, is preserved, by the term of Natural Selection.

Charles Darwin 1809–82: *On the Origin of Species* (1859)

5 [Natural selection] has no vision, no foresight, no sight at all. If it can be said to play the role of watchmaker in nature, it is the *blind* watchmaker.

■ *referring to William Paley's conception of the world as a watch, made by God*
Richard Dawkins 1941– : *The Blind Watchmaker* (1986)

6 The essence of life is statistical improbability on a colossal scale.

Richard Dawkins 1941– : *The Blind Watchmaker* (1986)

7 Life is a copiously branching bush, continually pruned by the grim reaper of extinction, not a ladder of predictable progress.

Stephen Jay Gould 1941–2002: *Wonderful Life* (1989)

8 I'd lay down my life for two brothers or eight cousins.

J. B. S. Haldane 1892–1964: attributed; in *New Scientist* 8 August 1974

9 Life exists in the universe only because the carbon atom possesses certain exceptional properties.

James Jeans 1877–1946: *The Mysterious Universe* (1930)

10 Population, when unchecked, increases in a geometrical ratio. Subsistence only increases in an arithmetical ratio.

Thomas Robert Malthus 1766–1834: *Essay on the Principle of Population* (1798)

11 The biologist passes, the frog remains.

■ *sometimes quoted as 'Theories pass. The frog remains'*
Jean Rostand 1894–1977: *Inquiétudes d'un biologiste* (1967)

12 Genes are not like engineering blueprints; they are more like recipes in a cookbook. They tell us what ingredients to use, in what quantities, and in what order—but they do not provide a complete, accurate plan of the final result.

Ian Stewart 1945– : *Life's Other Secret* (1998) preface

13 Water is life's *mater* and *matrix*, mother and medium. There is no life without water.

Albert von Szent-Györgyi 1893–1986: in *Perspectives in Biology and Medicine* Winter 1971

14 The history of the living world can be summarised as the elaboration of ever more perfect eyes within a cosmos in which there is always something more to be seen.

Pierre Teilhard de Chardin 1881–1955: *The Phenomenon of Man* (1959)

15 Evolution advances, not by a priori design, but by the selection of what works best out of whatever choices offer. We are the products of editing, rather than of authorship.

George Wald 1904–97: in *Annals of the New York Academy of Sciences* vol. 69 1957

16 We cannot cheat on DNA. We cannot get round photosynthesis. We cannot say I am not going to give a damn about phytoplankton. All these tiny mechanisms provide the preconditions of our planetary life. To say we do not care is to say in the most literal sense that 'we choose death'.

Barbara Ward 1914–81: *Only One Earth* (1972)

17 Was it through his grandfather or his grandmother that he claimed his descent from a monkey?

■ *addressed to T. H. Huxley in the debate on Darwin's theory of evolution*

Samuel Wilberforce 1805–73: at a meeting of British Association in Oxford, 30 June 1860; see **Human Race** 7, **Science and Religion** 6

18 Biology is the search for the chemistry that works.

R. J. P. Williams 1926– : lecture in Oxford, June 1996

Lifestyles

see also **Life**

1 Never play cards with a man called Doc. Never eat at a place called Mom's. Never sleep with a woman whose troubles are worse than your own.

Nelson Algren 1909– : in *Newsweek* 2 July 1956

2 I've lived a life that's full, I've travelled each and ev'ry highway
And more, much more than this. I did it my way.

Paul Anka 1941– : 'My Way' (1969 song)

3 Love and do what you will.

St Augustine of Hippo AD 354–430: *In Epistolam Joannis ad Parthos* (AD 413)

4 Another person's life, observed from outside, always has a shape and definition that one's own life lacks.

Pat Barker 1943– : *The Ghost Road* (1995)

5 A man hath no better thing under the sun, than to eat, and to drink, and to be merry.

Bible: Ecclesiastes

6 Thou shalt love thy neighbour as thyself.

Bible: Leviticus; see also St Matthew

7 Life is a matter of passing the time enjoyably. There may be other things in life, but I've been too busy passing my time enjoyably to think very deeply about them.

Peter Cook 1937–95: in *Guardian* 10 January 1994

8 Do what thou wilt shall be the whole of the Law.

Aleister Crowley 1875–1947: *Book of the Law* (1909)

9 Where is the Life we have lost in living?

T. S. Eliot 1888–1965: *The Rock* (1934)

10 Live all you can; it's a mistake not to. It doesn't so much matter what you do in particular, so long as you have your life. If you haven't had that, what *have* you had?

Henry James 1843–1916: *The Ambassadors* (1903)

11 Turn on, tune in and drop out.

Timothy Leary 1920–96: lecture, June 1966; *The Politics of Ecstasy* (1968)

12 We live, not as we wish to, but as we can.

Menander 342–*c*.292 BC: *The Lady of Andros*

13 Make sure that your Life is a Rare Entertainment!
It doesn't take anything drastic.
You needn't be gorgeous or wealthy or smart
Just Very Enthusiastic!

Bette Midler 1945– : *The Saga of Baby Divine* (1983)

14 Believe me! The secret of reaping the greatest fruitfulness and the greatest enjoyment from life is *to live dangerously*!

Friedrich Nietzsche 1844–1900: *Die fröhliche Wissenschaft* (1882)

15 Man is born to live, not to prepare for life.

Boris Pasternak 1890–1960: *Doctor Zhivago* (1958)

16 *Fay ce que vouldras.*
Do what you like.

François Rabelais *c*.1494–*c*.1553: *Gargantua* (1534)

17 You only live once, and the way I live, once is enough.

Frank Sinatra 1915–98: attributed, in *The Times* 16 May 1998

18 [Take] short views of human life—not
further than dinner or tea.
Sydney Smith 1771–1845: letter to Lady
Georgiana Morpeth, 16 February 1820

19 Do you want to know the great drama
of my life? It's that I have put my
genius into my life; all I've put into
my works is my talent.
Oscar Wilde 1854–1900: André Gide *Oscar
Wilde* (1910)

Likes and Dislikes

see also **Critics, Taste**

1 I do not love thee, Dr Fell.
The reason why I cannot tell;
But this I know, and know full well,
I do not love thee, Dr Fell.
Thomas Brown 1663–1704: translation of an
epigram by Martial AD *c.*40–*c.*104

2 For I've read in many a novel that,
unless they've souls that grovel,
Folks *prefer* in fact a hovel to your
dreary marble halls.
C. S. Calverley 1831–84: 'In the Gloaming'
(1872)

3 You're going to like this . . . not a
lot . . . but you'll like it!
Paul Daniels 1938– : catch-phrase used in his
conjuring act, especially on television from
1981 onwards

4 I don't care anything about reasons,
but I know what I like.
Henry James 1843–1916: *Portrait of a Lady*
(1881)

5 A little of what you fancy does you
good.
Fred W. Leigh d. 1924 and **George Arthurs**: title
of song (1915)

6 People who like this sort of thing will
find this the sort of thing they like.
■ *judgement of a book*
Abraham Lincoln 1809–65: G. W. E. Russell
Collections and Recollections (1898)

7 Tiggers don't like honey.
A. A. Milne 1882–1956: *House at Pooh Corner*
(1928)

8 I bet you if I had met him [Trotsky]
and had a chat with him, I would have

found him a very interesting and
human fellow, for I never yet met a
man that I didn't like.
Will Rogers 1879–1935: in *Saturday Evening
Post* 6 November 1926

9 Take care to get what you like or you
will be forced to like what you get.
George Bernard Shaw 1856–1950: *Man and
Superman* (1903) 'Maxims: Stray Sayings'

10 Do not do unto others as you would
that they should do unto you. Their
tastes may not be the same.
George Bernard Shaw 1856–1950: *Man and
Superman* (1903) 'Maxims for
Revolutionists: The Golden Rule'

Literature

see also **Art, Books, Fiction, Literature
and Society, Poetry, Reading, Writing**

1 A losing trade, I assure you, sir:
literature is a drug.
George Borrow 1803–81: *Lavengro* (1851)

2 As a form of moral insurance, at least,
literature is much more dependable
than a system of beliefs or a
philosophical doctrine.
Joseph Brodsky 1940–96: 'Uncommon
Visage', Nobel lecture 1987

3 What literature can and should do is
change the people who teach the
people who don't read the books.
A. S. Byatt 1936– : interview in *Newsweek*
5 June 1995

4 Literature is the art of writing
something that will be read twice;
journalism what will be read once.
Cyril Connolly 1903–74: *Enemies of Promise*
(1938)

5 He knew everything about literature
except how to enjoy it.
Joseph Heller 1923–99: *Catch-22* (1961)

6 Literature is news that STAYS news.
Ezra Pound 1885–1972: *The ABC of Reading*
(1934)

7 Literature is the one place in any
society where, within the secrecy of
our own heads, we can hear *voices*

talking about everything in every possible way.

Salman Rushdie 1947– : lecture 'Is Nothing Sacred' 6 February 1990

8 The illusion of art is to make one believe that great literature is very close to life, but exactly the opposite is true. Life is amorphous, literature is formal.

Françoise Sagan 1935– : Malcolm Cowley (ed.) *Writers at Work* (1958) 1st series

9 Remarks are not literature.

Gertrude Stein 1874–1946: *Autobiography of Alice B. Toklas* (1933)

10 Any writer worth his salt knows that only a small proportion of literature does more than partly compensate people for the damage they have suffered in learning to read.

Rebecca West 1892–1983: Peter Vansittart *Path from a White Horse* (1985)

11 True literature can exist only where it is created not by diligent and trustworthy officials, but by madmen, heretics, dreamers, rebels and sceptics. But when a writer must be sensible . . . there can be no bronze literature, there can only be a newspaper literature, which is read today, and used for wrapping soap tomorrow.

Yevgeny Zamyatin 1884–1937: 'I am Afraid' (1921)

Literature and Society

1 Nothing I wrote in the thirties saved one Jew from Auschwitz.

W. H. Auden 1907–73: attributed

2 People are always surprised when writers receive money, as if they don't have mortgages to pay.

Helen Dunmore 1952– : in *Guardian* 16 May 1996

3 The writer's only responsibility is to his art. He will be completely ruthless if he is a good one. . . . If a writer has to rob his mother, he will not hesitate;

the *Ode on a Grecian Urn* is worth any number of old ladies.

William Faulkner 1897–1962: in *Paris Review* Spring 1956

4 I am convinced more and more day by day that fine writing is next to fine doing the top thing in the world.

John Keats 1795–1821: letter to J. H. Reynolds, 24 August 1819

5 This poem about ice cream has nothing to do with government, with riot, with any political scheme.

Andrew Motion 1952– : 'To Whom It May Concern' (1997)

6 Russian literature saved my soul. When I was a young girl in school and I asked what is good and what is evil, no one in that corrupt system could show me.

Irina Ratushinskaya 1954– : in *Observer* 15 October 1989

7 One of the things a writer is for is to say the unsayable, speak the unspeakable and ask difficult questions.

Salman Rushdie 1947– : in *Independent on Sunday* 10 September 1995

8 I've used my talents as a writer to enable the Ogoni people to confront their tormentors. I was not able to do it as a politician or a businessman. My writing did it . . . I think I have the moral victory.

Ken Saro-Wiwa 1941–95: letter, shortly before his execution in 1995, to William Boyd

9 A writer must refuse, therefore, to allow himself to be transformed into an institution.

Jean-Paul Sartre 1905–80: refusing the Nobel Prize at Stockholm, 22 October 1964

10 There are various forms of production: artillery, automobiles, lorries. You also produce 'commodities', 'works', 'products'. Such things are highly necessary. Engineering things. For people's souls. 'Products' are highly necessary too. 'Products' are very important for

people's souls. You are engineers of
human souls.

Joseph Stalin 1879–1953: speech to writers at
Gorky's house, 26 October 1932; cf. **Art and
Society** 1, 2

David Lloyd George
1863–1945
....

1 He can't see a belt without hitting
below it.

Margot Asquith 1864–1945: in *Listener* 11 June
1953

2 [Lloyd George] did not seem to care
which way he travelled providing he
was in the driver's seat.

Lord Beaverbrook 1879–1964: *The Decline and
Fall of Lloyd George* (1963)

3 Seventy minutes had passed before
Mr Lloyd George arrived at his proper
theme. He spoke for a hundred and
seventeen minutes, in which period
he was detected only once in the use
of an argument.

Arnold Bennett 1867–1931: *Things that have
Interested Me* (1921)

4 This extraordinary figure of our time,
this syren, this goat-footed bard, this
half-human visitor to our age from
the hag-ridden magic and enchanted
woods of Celtic antiquity.

John Maynard Keynes 1883–1946: *Essays in
Biography* (1933) 'Mr Lloyd George'

Logic and Reason
....

1 Only reason can convince us of those
three fundamental truths without a
recognition of which there can be no
effective liberty: that what we believe
is not necessarily true; that what we
like is not necessarily good; and that
all questions are open.

Clive Bell 1881–1964: *Civilization* (1928)

2 'Contrariwise,' continued
Tweedledee, 'if it was so, it might be;
and if it were so, it would be: but as it
isn't, it ain't. That's logic.'

Lewis Carroll 1832–98: *Through the Looking-
Glass* (1872)

3 when man determined to destroy
himself he picked the was
of shall and finding only why
smashed it into because.

e. e. cummings 1894–1962: *1 x 1* (1944) no. 26

4 My chief desire is to let you see that
there is that which is rational, that
which is irrational and that which is
non-rational—and to leave you
weltering in the morass thereafter.

Seamus Deane 1940– : *Reading in the Dark*
(1996)

5 'Is there any other point to which you
would wish to draw my attention?'
'To the curious incident of the dog in
the night-time.'
'The dog did nothing in the night-
time.'
'That was the curious incident,'
remarked Sherlock Holmes.

Arthur Conan Doyle 1859–1930: *The Memoirs
of Sherlock Holmes* (1894)

6 Reasons are not like garments, the
worse for wearing.

Robert Devereux, Earl of Essex 1566–1601:
letter to Lord Willoughby, 4 January 1599

7 I'll not listen to reason . . . Reason
always means what someone else has
got to say.

Elizabeth Gaskell 1810–65: *Cranford* (1853)

8 Irrationally held truths may be more
harmful than reasoned errors.

T. H. Huxley 1825–95: *Science and Culture and
Other Essays* (1881) 'The Coming of Age of
the Origin of Species'

9 Logical consequences are the
scarecrows of fools and the beacons of
wise men.

T. H. Huxley 1825–95: *Science and Culture and
Other Essays* (1881) 'On the Hypothesis that
Animals are Automata'

10 After all, what was a paradox but a
statement of the obvious so as to
make it sound untrue?

Ronald Knox 1888–1957: *A Spiritual Aeneid*
(1918)

11 Logic must take care of itself.

Ludwig Wittgenstein 1889–1951: *Tractatus
Logico-Philosophicus* (1922)

London

1 London, thou art the flower of cities all!
   Anonymous: 'London' (poem of unknown authorship, previously attributed to William Dunbar, c.1465–c.1530)

2 *Was für Plunder!*
   What rubbish!
   ■ *of London as seen from the Monument in June 1814; often misquoted as '*Was für plündern [*What a place to plunder*]*!'*
   Gebhard Lebrecht Blücher 1742–1819: Evelyn Princess Blücher *Memoirs of Prince Blücher* (1932)

3 London Pride has been handed down to us.
   London Pride is a flower that's free.
   London Pride means our own dear town to us,
   And our pride it for ever will be.
   Noël Coward 1899–1973: 'London Pride' (1941 song)

4 Maybe it's because I'm a Londoner
   That I love London so.
   Hubert Gregg 1914– : 'Maybe It's Because I'm a Londoner' (1947 song)

5 When a man is tired of London, he is tired of life; for there is in London all that life can afford.
   Samuel Johnson 1709–84: James Boswell *Life of Samuel Johnson* (1791) 20 September 1777

6 I thought of London spread out in the sun,
   Its postal districts packed like squares of wheat.
   Philip Larkin 1922–85: 'The Whitsun Weddings' (1964)

7 The parks are the lungs of London.
   William Pitt, Earl of Chatham 1708–78: speech by William Windham, House of Commons, 30 June 1808

8 Earth has not anything to show more fair:
   Dull would he be of soul who could pass by
   A sight so touching in its majesty:
   This City now doth like a garment wear
   The beauty of the morning.
   William Wordsworth 1770–1850: 'Composed upon Westminster Bridge' (1807)

Loneliness

see also **Solitude**

1 Please fence me in baby the world's too big out here and I don't like it without you.
   Humphrey Bogart 1899–1957: telegram to Lauren Bacall; Lauren Bacall *By Myself* (1978)

2 Many a housewife staring at the back of her husband's newspaper, or listening to his breathing in bed is lonelier than any spinster in a rented room.
   Germaine Greer 1939– : *The Female Eunuch* (1970)

3 All the lonely people, where do they all come from?
   John Lennon 1940–80 and **Paul McCartney** 1942– : 'Eleanor Rigby' (1966 song)

4 Only the lonely (know the way I feel).
   Roy Orbison 1936–88: title of song (1960, with Joe Melson)

5 Thirty years is a very long time to live alone and life doesn't get any nicer.
   ■ *on widowhood, at the age of 92*
   Frances Partridge 1900– : G. Kinnock and F. Miller *By Faith and Daring* (1993)

6 The loneliness of the long-distance runner.
   Alan Sillitoe 1928– : title of novel (1959)

7 Oh, no no no, it was too cold always
   (Still the dead one lay moaning)
   I was much too far out all my life
   And not waving but drowning.
   Stevie Smith 1902–71: 'Not Waving but Drowning' (1957)

8 God created man and, finding him not sufficiently alone, gave him a companion to make him feel his solitude more keenly.
   Paul Valéry 1871–1945: *Tel Quel 1* (1941)

Love

see also **Courtship**, **Faithfulness**, **Kissing**, **Marriage**, **Relationships**, **Romance**, **Sex**

1 You know very well that love is, above all, the gift of oneself!
   Jean Anouilh 1910–87: *Ardèle* (1949)

2 Is it prickly to touch as a hedge is,
Or soft as eiderdown fluff?
Is it sharp or quite smooth at the
edges?
O tell me the truth about love.
W. H. Auden 1907–73: 'Oh Tell Me the Truth
about Love' (1938)

3 How in hell can you handle love
without turning your life upside
down? That's what love does, it
changes everything.
Lauren Bacall 1924– : *By Myself* (1978)

4 Love is just a system for getting
someone to call you darling after sex.
Julian Barnes 1946– : *Talking It Over* (1991)

5 The fate of love is that it always seems
too little or too much.
Amelia E. Barr 1831–1919: *The Belle of Bolling
Green* (1904)

6 To love someone is to isolate him
from the world, wipe out every trace
of him, dispossess him of his shadow,
drag him into a murderous future. It
is to circle around the other like a
dead star and absorb him into a black
light.
Jean Baudrillard 1929– : *Fatal Strategies*
(1983)

7 Love is patient and kind; love is not
jealous or boastful; it is not arrogant
or rude.
Love does not insist on its own way; it
is not irritable or resentful;
It does not rejoice at wrong, but
rejoices in the right.
Love bears all things, believes all
things, hopes all things, endures all
things.
Bible: I Corinthians

8 Love seeketh not itself to please,
Nor for itself hath any care;
But for another gives its ease,
And builds a Heaven in Hell's despair.
William Blake 1757–1827: 'The Clod and the
Pebble' (1794)

9 My love for Linton is like the foliage in
the woods; time will change it, I'm
well aware, as winter changes the
trees—My love for Heathcliff
resembles the eternal rocks

beneath:—a source of little visible
delight, but necessary.
Emily Brontë 1818–48: *Wuthering Heights*
(1847)

10 Real love is a pilgrimage. It happens
when there is no strategy, but it is very
rare because most people are
strategists.
Anita Brookner 1928– : Olga Kenyon (ed.)
Women Writers Talk (1989)

11 If thou must love me, let it be for
nought
Except for love's sake only.
Elizabeth Barrett Browning 1806–61: *Sonnets
from the Portuguese* (1850) no. 14

12 How do I love thee? Let me count the
ways.
I love thee to the depth and breadth
and height
My soul can reach.
Elizabeth Barrett Browning 1806–61: *Sonnets
from the Portuguese* (1850) no. 43

13 O, my Luve's like a red, red rose
That's newly sprung in June;
O my Luve's like the melodie
That's sweetly play'd in tune.
Robert Burns 1759–96: 'A Red Red Rose'
(1796); derived from various folk-songs

14 In her first passion woman loves her
lover,
In all the others all she loves is love.
Lord Byron 1788–1824: *Don Juan* (1819–24)

15 *when asked if he was 'in love':*
Yes . . . whatever that may mean.
■ *after the announcement of his engagement*
Charles, Prince of Wales 1948– : interview,
24 February 1981; cf. **Diana** 5

16 If grass can grow through cement,
love can find you at every time in your
life.
Cher 1946– : in *The Times* 30 May 1998

17 Love itself is what is left over when
being in love has burned away.
Louis de Bernières 1954– : *Captain Corelli's
Mandolin* (1994)

18 Experience shows us that love does
not consist in gazing at each other but

in looking together in the same direction.

Antoine de Saint-Exupéry 1900–44: *Wind, Sand and Stars* (1939)

19 Love is anterior to life,
Posterior to death,
Initial of creation, and
The exponent of breath.

Emily Dickinson 1830–86: 'Love is anterior to life'

20 The magic of first love is our ignorance that it can ever end.

Benjamin Disraeli 1804–81: *Henrietta Temple* (1837)

21 For God's sake hold your tongue, and let me love.

John Donne 1572–1631: 'The Canonization'

22 Love is a universal migraine.
A bright stain on the vision
Blotting out reason.

Robert Graves 1895–1985: 'Symptoms of Love'

23 What love is, if thou wouldst be taught,
Thy heart must teach alone—
Two souls with but a single thought,
Two hearts that beat as one.

Friedrich Halm 1806–71: *Der Sohn der Wildnis* (1842)

24 The ones we choose to love become our anchor
when the hawser of the blood-tie's hacked, or frays.

Tony Harrison 1953– : *v* (1985)

25 When love congeals
It soon reveals
The faint aroma of performing seals,
The double crossing of a pair of heels.
I wish I were in love again!

Lorenz Hart 1895–1943: 'I Wish I Were in Love Again' (1937 song)

26 Love is mutually feeding each other, not one living on another like a ghoul.

Bessie Head 1937–86: *A Question of Power* (1973)

27 Passion makes the world go round. Love just makes it a safer place.

Ice-T 1958– : *The Ice Opinion* (1994)

28 Love's like the measles—all the worse when it comes late in life.

Douglas Jerrold 1803–57: *The Wit and Opinions of Douglas Jerrold* (1859)

29 Love. Of course, love. Flames for a year, ashes for thirty.

Giuseppe di Lampedusa 1896–1957: *The Leopard* (1957)

30 What will survive of us is love.

Philip Larkin 1922–85: 'An Arundel Tomb' (1964)

31 Love doesn't just sit there, like a stone, it has to be made, like bread; remade all the time, made new.

Ursula K. Le Guin 1929– : *The Lathe of Heaven* (1971)

32 All you need is love.

John Lennon 1940–80 and **Paul McCartney** 1942– : title of song (1967)

33 How alike are the groans of love to those of the dying.

Malcolm Lowry 1909–57: *Under the Volcano* (1947)

34 If I were young and handsome as I was, instead of old and faded as I am, and you could lay the empire of the world at my feet, you should never share the heart and hand that once belonged to John, Duke of Marlborough.

■ *refusing an offer of marriage from the Duke of Somerset*

Sarah, Duchess of Marlborough 1660–1744: W. S. Churchill *Marlborough: His Life and Times* vol. 4 (1938)

35 Where both deliberate, the love is slight;
Who ever loved that loved not at first sight?

Christopher Marlowe 1564–93: *Hero and Leander* (1598)

36 The love that lasts longest is the love that is never returned.

W. Somerset Maugham 1874–1965: *A Writer's Notebook* (1949) written in 1894

37 To us love says humming that the heart's stalled motor has begun working again.

Vladimir Mayakovsky 1893–1930: 'Letter from Paris to Comrade Kostorov on the Nature of Love' (1928)

38 No, there's nothing half so sweet in
life
As love's young dream.
Thomas Moore 1779–1852: 'Love's Young
Dream' (1807)

39 Love is the extremely difficult
realisation that something other than
oneself is real. Love, and so art and
morals, is the discovery of reality.
Iris Murdoch 1919–99: 'The Sublime and the
Good' in *Chicago Review* 13 (1959)

40 If I can't love Hitler, I can't love at all.
Rev. A. J. Muste 1885–1967: at a Quaker
meeting 1940; in *New York Times* 12 February
1967

41 By the time you say you're his,
Shivering and sighing
And he vows his passion is
Infinite, undying—
Lady, make a note of this:
One of you is lying.
Dorothy Parker 1893–1967: 'Unfortunate
Coincidence' (1937)

42 Most people experience love, without
noticing that there is anything
remarkable about it.
Boris Pasternak 1890–1960: *Doctor Zhivago*
(1958)

43 Love is one of the answers humankind
invented to stare death in the face:
time ceases to be a measure, and we
can briefly know paradise.
Octavio Paz 1914– : *The Double Flame* (1995)

44 Birds do it, bees do it,
Even educated fleas do it.
Let's do it, let's fall in love.
Cole Porter 1891–1964: 'Let's Do It' (1954
song; words added to the 1928 original)

45 It's no longer a burning within my
veins: it's Venus entire latched onto
her prey.
Jean Racine 1639–99: *Phèdre* (1677)

46 Love was a terrible thing. You
poisoned it and stabbed at it and
knocked it down into the mud—well
down—and it got up and staggered
on, bleeding and muddy and awful.
Like—like Rasputin.
Jean Rhys c.1890–1979: *Quartet* (1928)

47 Love means not ever having to say
you're sorry.
Erich Segal 1937– : *Love Story* (1970)

48 The course of true love never did run
smooth.
William Shakespeare 1564–1616: *A
Midsummer Night's Dream* (1595–6)

49   To be wise, and love,
Exceeds man's might.
William Shakespeare 1564–1616: *Troilus and
Cressida* (1602)

50 Let me not to the marriage of true
minds
Admit impediments. Love is not love
Which alters when it alteration finds.
William Shakespeare 1564–1616: sonnet 116

51 To say a man is fallen in love,—or that
he is deeply in love,—or up to the ears
in love,—and sometimes even over
head and ears in it,—carries an
idiomatical kind of implication, that
love is a thing below a man.
Laurence Sterne 1713–68: *Tristram Shandy*
(1759–67)

52 Love is the fart
Of every heart:
It pains a man when 'tis kept close,
And others doth offend, when 'tis let
loose.
John Suckling 1609–42: 'Love's Offence'
(1646)

53 In the spring a young man's fancy
lightly turns to thoughts of love.
Alfred, Lord Tennyson 1809–92: 'Locksley
Hall' (1842)

54 'Tis better to have loved and lost
Than never to have loved at all.
Alfred, Lord Tennyson 1809–92: *In Memoriam
A. H. H.* (1850)

55 *Omnia vincit Amor: et nos cedamus
Amori.*
Love conquers all things: let us too
give in to Love.
Virgil 70–19 BC: *Eclogues*

56 If somebody says 'I love you,' to me, I
feel as though I had a pistol pointed at

my head. What can anybody reply under such conditions but that which the pistol-holder requires? 'I love you, too.'

Kurt Vonnegut 1922– : *Wampeters, Fama and Granfallons* (1974)

57 Yet each man kills the thing he loves,
By each let this be heard,
Some do it with a bitter look,
Some with a flattering word.
The coward does it with a kiss,
The brave man with a sword!

Oscar Wilde 1854–1900: *The Ballad of Reading Gaol* (1898)

58 A woman can be proud and stiff
When on love intent;
But Love has pitched his mansion in
The place of excrement;
For nothing can be sole or whole
That has not been rent.

W. B. Yeats 1865–1939: 'Crazy Jane Talks with the Bishop' (1932)

Loyalty

1 I may be wrong, but I have never found deserting friends conciliates enemies.

Margot Asquith 1864–1945: *Lay Sermons* (1927)

2 I am not standing by my man, like Tammy Wynette. I am sitting here because I love him, I respect him, and I honour what he's been through and what we've been through together.

Hillary Rodham Clinton 1947– : interview on *60 Minutes*, CBS-TV, 27 January 1992; cf. 8 below

3 Nothing aged one like loyalty.

James Hamilton-Paterson 1941– : *Griefwork* (1993)

4 I don't want loyalty. I want *loyalty*. I want him to kiss my ass in Macy's window at high noon and tell me it smells like roses. I want his pecker in my pocket.

Lyndon Baines Johnson 1908–73: David Halberstam *The Best and the Brightest* (1972)

5 We are the President's men, and we must behave accordingly.

Henry Kissinger 1923– : M. and B. Kalb *Kissinger* (1974)

6 I respect fidelity to colleagues even though they are fit for the hangman.

Harold Laski 1893–1950: letter to Oliver Wendell Holmes Jr., 4 December 1926

7 [Grant] stood by me when I was crazy, and I stood by him when he was drunk; and now we stand by each other always.

William Sherman 1820–91: in 1864; Geoffrey C. Ward *The Civil War* (1991)

8 Stand by your man.

Tammy Wynette 1942– : title of song (1968, with Billy Sherrill)

Luck

see also **Chance**

1 What we call luck is the inner man externalized. We make things happen to us.

Robertson Davies 1913–95: *What's Bred in the Bone* (1985)

2 There is much good luck in the world, but it is luck. We are none of us safe. We are children, playing or quarrelling on the line.

E. M. Forster 1879–1970: *The Longest Journey* (1907)

3 Care and diligence bring luck.

Thomas Fuller 1654–1734: *Gnomologia* (1732)

4 Some folk want their luck buttered.

Thomas Hardy 1840–1928: *The Mayor of Casterbridge* (1886)

5 All you know about it [luck] for certain is that it's bound to change.

Bret Harte 1836–1902: *The Outcasts of Poker Flat* (1871)

6 now and then
there is a person born
who is so unlucky
that he runs into accidents
which started to happen
to somebody else.

Don Marquis 1878–1937: *archys life of mehitabel* (1933)

Luxury

see also **Wealth**

1 The saddest thing I can imagine is to get used to luxury.
Charlie Chaplin 1889–1977: *My Autobiography* (1964)

2 In the affluent society no useful distinction can be made between luxuries and necessaries.
J. K. Galbraith 1908– : *The Affluent Society* (1958)

3 I spend my life ministering to the swinish luxury of the rich.
William Morris 1834–96: attributed, *c.*1877; W. R. Lethaby *Philip Webb* (1935)

4 Give us the luxuries of life, and we will dispense with its necessities.
John Lothrop Motley 1814–77: Oliver Wendell Holmes *Autocrat of the Breakfast-Table* (1857–8)

5 Walk! Not bloody likely. I am going in a taxi.
George Bernard Shaw 1856–1950: *Pygmalion* (1916)

6 The necessities were going by default to save the luxuries until I hardly knew which were necessities and which luxuries.
Frank Lloyd Wright 1867–1959: *Autobiography* (1945)

Madness

see also **Mental Illness, The Mind**

1 Babylon in all its desolation is a sight not so awful as that of the human mind in ruins.
Scrope Davies *c.*1783–1852: letter to Thomas Raikes, May 1835

2 Mad, is he? Then I hope he will *bite* some of my other generals.
■ *replying to the Duke of Newcastle, who had complained that General Wolfe was a madman*
George II 1683–1760: Henry Beckles Willson *Life and Letters of James Wolfe* (1909)

3 Every one is more or less mad on one point.
Rudyard Kipling 1865–1936: *Plain Tales from the Hills* (1888)

4 Madness need not be all breakdown. It may also be break-through.
R. D. Laing 1927–89: *The Politics of Experience* (1967)

5 They called me mad, and I called them mad, and damn them, they outvoted me.
Nathaniel Lee *c.*1653–92: R. Porter *A Social History of Madness* (1987)

6 Though this be madness, yet there is method in't.
William Shakespeare 1564–1616: *Hamlet* (1601)

7 O! let me not be mad, not mad, sweet heaven;
Keep me in temper; I would not be mad!
William Shakespeare 1564–1616: *King Lear* (1605–6)

8 As an experience, madness is terrific . . . and in its lava I still find most of the things I write about.
Virginia Woolf 1882–1941: letter to Ethel Smyth, 22 June 1930

Majorities

see **Minorities and Majorities**

Management

see also **Administration, Careers, Organization**

1 An industrial worker would sooner have a £5 note but a countryman must have praise.
Ronald Blythe 1922– : *Akenfield* (1969)

2 Every organization of today has to build into its very structure the *management of change*.
Peter F. Drucker 1909– : *Post-Capitalist Society* (1993)

3 If management are using a word you don't understand, nine times out of ten they are making you redundant.
John Edwards: on BBC Radio Four *Today*, 10 June 1996

4 Every time I make an appointment, I create a hundred malcontents and one ingrate.

Louis XIV 1638–1715: Voltaire *Siècle de Louis XIV* (1768 ed.)

5 Perfection of planned layout is achieved only by institutions on the point of collapse.

C. Northcote Parkinson 1909–93: *Parkinson's Law* (1958)

6 A good plan violently executed *Now* is better than a perfect plan next week.

George S. Patton 1885–1945: *War As I Knew It* (1947)

7 In a hierarchy every employee tends to rise to his level of incompetence.

Laurence J. Peter 1919–90: *The Peter Principle* (1969)

8 Management that wants to change an institution must first show it loves that institution.

John Tusa 1936– : in *Observer* 27 February 1994

9 Safe and sane business management . . . reduces itself in the main to a sagacious use of sabotage.

Thorstein Veblen 1857–1929: *The Nature of Peace* (1917)

Manners

see also **Behaviour**

1 Phone for the fish-knives, Norman
As Cook is a little unnerved;
You kiddies have crumpled the serviettes
And I must have things daintily served.

John Betjeman 1906–84: 'How to get on in Society' (1954)

2 Curtsey while you're thinking what to say. It saves time.

Lewis Carroll 1832–98: *Through the Looking-Glass* (1872)

3 The art of pleasing consists in being pleased.

William Hazlitt 1778–1830: *The Round Table* (1817) 'On Manner'

4 To Americans, English manners are far more frightening than none at all.

Randall Jarrell 1914–65: *Pictures from an Institution* (1954)

5 When suave politeness, tempering bigot zeal,
Corrected *I believe* to *One does feel*.

Ronald Knox 1888–1957: 'Absolute and Abitofhell' (1913)

6 'Always be civil to the girls, you never know who they may marry' is an aphorism which has saved many an English spinster from being treated like an Indian widow.

Nancy Mitford 1904–73: *Love in a Cold Climate* (1949)

7 Good manners are a combination of intelligence, education, taste, and style mixed together so that you don't need any of those things.

P. J. O'Rourke 1947– : *Modern Manners* (1984)

8 He is the very pineapple of politeness!

Richard Brinsley Sheridan 1751–1816: *The Rivals* (1775)

9 Good breeding consists in concealing how much we think of ourselves and how little we think of the other person.

Mark Twain 1835–1910: *Notebooks* (1935)

10 Manners are especially the need of the plain. The pretty can get away with anything.

Evelyn Waugh 1903–66: in *Observer* 15 April 1962

Maps

1 Topography displays no favourites; North's as near as West.
More delicate than the historians' are the map-makers' colours.

Elizabeth Bishop 1911–79: 'The Map' (1946)

2 'What's the good of *Mercator's* North Poles and Equators,
Tropics, Zones and Meridian lines?'
So the Bellman would cry: and the crew would reply,

'They are merely conventional signs!'
Lewis Carroll 1832–98: *The Hunting of the Snark* (1876)

3 So geographers, in Afric-maps,
With savage-pictures fill their gaps;
And o'er unhabitable downs
Place elephants for want of towns.
Jonathan Swift 1667–1745: 'On Poetry' (1733)

Marriage

see also **Bachelors**, **Courtship**, **Husbands**, **Love**, **Sex**, **Weddings**, **Wives**

1 Like everything which is not the involuntary result of fleeting emotion but the creation of time and will, any marriage, happy or unhappy, is infinitely more interesting than any romance, however passionate.
W. H. Auden 1907–73: *A Certain World* (1970)

2 To have and to hold from this day forward, for better for worse, for richer for poorer, in sickness and in health, to love, cherish, and to obey, till death us do part.
The Book of Common Prayer 1662: *Solemnization of Matrimony* Betrothal

3 Still I can't contradict, what so oft has been said,
'Though women are angels, yet wedlock's the devil.'
Lord Byron 1788–1824: 'To Eliza' (1806)

4 Love and marriage, love and marriage,
Go together like a horse and carriage,
This I tell ya, brother,
Ya can't have one without the other.
Sammy Cahn 1913–93: 'Love and Marriage' (1955 song)

5 The deep, deep peace of the double-bed after the hurly-burly of the chaise-longue.
■ *on her recent marriage*
Mrs Patrick Campbell 1865–1940: Alexander Woollcott *While Rome Burns* (1934)

6 I learnt a long time ago that the only people who count in any marriage are the two that are in it.
Hillary Rodham Clinton 1947– : television interview with NBC, 27 January 1998

7 Marriage is a wonderful invention; but, then again, so is a bicycle repair kit.
Billy Connolly 1942– : Duncan Campbell *Billy Connolly* (1976)

8 The heart of marriage is memories.
Bill Cosby 1937– : *Love and Marriage* (1989)

9 The value of marriage is not that adults produce children but that children produce adults.
Peter De Vries 1910–93: *The Tunnel of Love* (1954)

10 There were three of us in this marriage, so it was a bit crowded.
Diana, Princess of Wales 1961–97: interview on *Panorama*, BBC1 TV, 20 November 1995

11 I have always thought that every woman should marry, and no man.
Benjamin Disraeli 1804–81: *Lothair* (1870)

12 The chains of marriage are so heavy that it takes two to bear them, and sometimes three.
Alexandre Dumas 1824–95: Léon Treich *L'Esprit d'Alexandre Dumas*

13 Having once embarked upon your marital voyage, it is impossible not to be aware that you make no way and that the sea is not within sight—that in fact, you are exploring a closed basin.
George Eliot 1819–80: *Middlemarch* (1871–2)

14 Most marriages don't add two people together. They subtract one from the other.
Ian Fleming 1908–64: *Diamonds are Forever* (1956)

15 Do you think your mother and I should have lived comfortably so long together, if ever we had been married?
John Gay 1685–1732: *The Beggar's Opera* (1728)

16 By god, D. H. Lawrence was right when he had said there must be a dumb, dark, dull, bitter belly-tension between a man and a woman, and how else could this be achieved save in the long monotony of marriage?
Stella Gibbons 1902–89: *Cold Comfort Farm* (1932)

17 You shall be together when the white
wings of death scatter your days.
Ay, you shall be together even in the
silent memory of God.
But let there be spaces in your
togetherness,
And let the winds of the heavens
dance between you.
Kahlil Gibran 1883–1931: *The Prophet* (1923)
'On Marriage'

18 Hogamus, higamous
Man is polygamous
Higamus, hogamous
Woman monogamous.
William James 1842–1910: attributed

19 The triumph of hope over experience.
■ *of a man who remarried immediately after the
death of a wife with whom he had been unhappy*
Samuel Johnson 1709–84: James Boswell *Life
of Samuel Johnson* (1791) 1770

20 Call me pathetic . . . but I'm being
honest here. I want a bloke, a partner,
a long-term commitment. I want the
M word.
Marian Keyes: 'Late Opening at the Last
Chance Saloon' (1997)

21 So they were married—to be the more
together—
And found they were never again so
much together,
Divided by the morning tea,
By the evening paper,
By children and tradesmen's bills.
Louis MacNeice 1907–63: 'Les Sylphides'
(1941)

22 The trouble with marriage is that it
ends every night after making love,
and it must be rebuilt every morning
before breakfast.
Gabriel García Márquez 1928– : *Love in the
Time of Cholera* (1985)

23 One doesn't have to get anywhere in a
marriage. It's not a public
conveyance.
Iris Murdoch 1919–99: *A Severed Head* (1961)

24 To keep your marriage brimming
With love in the loving cup,
Whenever you're wrong, admit it,

Whenever you're right, shut up.
Ogden Nash 1902–71: 'A Word to Husbands'
(1957)

25 The great secret of a successful
marriage is to treat all disasters as
incidents and none of the incidents as
disasters.
Harold Nicolson 1886–1968: attributed

26 It doesn't much signify whom one
marries, for one is sure to find next
morning that it was someone else.
Samuel Rogers 1763–1855: Alexander Dyce
(ed.) *Table Talk of Samuel Rogers* (1860)

27 A young man married is a man that's
marred.
William Shakespeare 1564–1616: *All's Well that
Ends Well* (1603–4)

28 Marriage is popular because it
combines the maximum of
temptation with the maximum of
opportunity.
George Bernard Shaw 1856–1950: *Man and
Superman* (1903) 'Maxims: Marriage'

29 Chains do not hold a marriage
together. It is threads, hundreds of
tiny threads which sew people
together through the years. That is
what makes a marriage last—more
than passion or even sex!
Simone Signoret 1921–85: in *Daily Mail* 4 July
1978

30 Marriage I think
For women
Is the best of opiates.
It kills the thoughts
That think about the thoughts,
It is the best of opiates.
Stevie Smith 1902–71: 'Marriage I Think'

31 My definition of marriage . . . it
resembles a pair of shears, so joined
that they cannot be separated; often
moving in opposite directions, yet
always punishing anyone who comes
between them.
Sydney Smith 1771–1845: Lady Holland
Memoir (1855)

32 Marriage is like life in this—that it is a
field of battle, and not a bed of roses.
Robert Louis Stevenson 1850–94: *Virginibus
Puerisque* (1881)

33 Marriage isn't a word . . . it's a
sentence!
King Vidor 1895–1982: *The Crowd* (1928 film)

34 Marriage is the waste-paper basket of
the emotions.
Sidney Webb 1859–1947: Bertrand Russell
Autobiography (1967)

35 In married life three is company and
two none.
Oscar Wilde 1854–1900: *The Importance of
Being Earnest* (1895)

36 Marriage is a bribe to make a
housekeeper think she's a
householder.
Thornton Wilder 1897–1975: *The Merchant of
Yonkers* (1939)

Masturbation

1 Don't knock masturbation. It's sex
with someone I love.
Woody Allen 1935– : *Annie Hall* (1977 film,
with Marshall Brickman)

2 Masturbation is the thinking man's
television.
Christopher Hampton 1946– : *Philanthropist*
(1970)

3 One of my boys defined masturbation
as the pale shadow of sex.
A. S. Neill 1883–1973: letter to Henry Miller;
Jonathan Croall *Neill of Summerhill: The
Permanent Rebel* (1983)

4 Masturbation: the primary sexual
activity of mankind. In the nineteenth
century, it was a disease; in the
twentieth, it's a cure.
Thomas Szasz 1920– : *The Second Sin* (1973)

Mathematics

see also **Statistics**

1 Let no one enter who does not know
geometry [mathematics].
■ *inscription on Plato's door, probably at the
Academy at Athens*
Anonymous: Elias Philosophus *In Aristotelis
Categorias Commentaria*

2 If in other sciences we should arrive at
certainty without doubt and truth

without error, it behoves us to place
the foundations of knowledge in
mathematics.
Roger Bacon *c.*1220–*c.*1292: *Opus Majus*

3 The jury eagerly wrote down all three
dates on their slates, and then added
them up, and reduced the answer to
shillings and pence.
Lewis Carroll 1832–98: *Alice's Adventures in
Wonderland* (1865)

4 I never could make out what those
damned dots meant.
■ *on decimal points*
Lord Randolph Churchill 1849–94: W. S.
Churchill *Lord Randolph Churchill* (1906)

5 It is more important to have beauty in
one's equations than to have them fit
experiment . . . The discrepancy may
well be due to minor features . . . that
will get cleared up with further
developments.
Paul Dirac 1902–84: in *Scientific American*
May 1963

6 There is no 'royal road' to geometry.
Euclid fl. *c.*300 BC: addressed to Ptolemy I;
Proclus *Commentary on the First Book of
Euclid's Elementa*

7 The most devilish thing is 8 times
8 and 7 times 7 it is what nature itselfe
cant endure.
Marjory Fleming 1803–11: *Journals, Letters and
Verses* (ed. A. Esdaile, 1934)

8 Someone told me that each equation I
included in the book would halve the
sales.
Stephen Hawking 1942– : *A Brief History of
Time* (1988)

9 God made the integers, all the rest is
the work of man.
Leopold Kronecker 1823–91: *Jahrsberichte der
Deutschen Mathematiker Vereinigung*

10 Points
Have no parts or joints
How then can they combine
To form a line?
J. A. Lindon: M. Gardner *Wheels, Life and
Other Mathematical Amusements* (1983)

11 In mathematics you don't understand things. You just get used to them.
John von Neumann 1903–57: Gary Zukav *The Dancing Wu Li Masters* (1979)

12 Mathematics, rightly viewed, possesses not only truth, but supreme beauty—a beauty cold and austere, like that of sculpture.
Bertrand Russell 1872–1970: *Philosophical Essays* (1910)

13 Mathematics may be defined as the subject in which we never know what we are talking about, nor whether what we are saying is true.
Bertrand Russell 1872–1970: *Mysticism and Logic* (1918)

14 What would life be like without arithmetic, but a scene of horrors?
Sydney Smith 1771–1845: letter to Miss [Lucie Austen], 22 July 1835

Maturity

see also **Experience**

1 I gave my beauty and my youth to men. I am going to give my wisdom and experience to animals.
Brigitte Bardot 1934– : attributed, June 1987

2 When I was young I hoped that one day I should be able to go into a post office to buy a stamp without feeling nervous and shy: now I realize that I never shall.
Edmund Blunden 1896–1974: Rupert Hart-Davis, letter to George Lyttelton, 5 August 1956

3 I had always thought that once you grew up you could do anything you wanted—stay up all night or eat ice-cream straight out of the container.
Bill Bryson 1951– : *The Lost Continent* (1989)

4 How many roads must a man walk down
Before you can call him a man? . . .
The answer, my friend, is blowin' in the wind,
The answer is blowin' in the wind.
Bob Dylan 1941– : 'Blowin' in the Wind' (1962 song)

5 At twenty years of age, the will reigns; at thirty, the wit; and at forty, the judgement.
Benjamin Franklin 1706–90: *Poor Richard's Almanac* (1741)

6 Immature love says: 'I love you because I need you.' Mature love says: 'I need you because I love you.'
Erich Fromm 1900–80: *The Art of Loving* (1956)

7 One of the most obvious facts about grown-ups, to a child, is that they have forgotten what it is like to be a child.
Randall Jarrell 1914–65: Christina Stead *The Man Who Loved Children* (1965)

8 If you can talk with crowds and keep your virtue,
Or walk with Kings—nor lose the common touch,
If neither foes nor loving friends can hurt you,
If all men count with you, but none too much;
If you can fill the unforgiving minute
With sixty seconds' worth of distance run,
Yours is the Earth and everything that's in it,
And—which is more—you'll be a Man, my son!
Rudyard Kipling 1865–1936: 'If—' (1910)

9 To be adult is to be alone.
Jean Rostand 1894–1977: *Pensées d'un biologiste* (1954)

10 One's prime is elusive. You little girls, when you grow up, must be on the alert to recognise your prime at whatever time of your life it may occur.
Muriel Spark 1918– : *The Prime of Miss Jean Brodie* (1961)

Meaning

see also **Words**

1 No one means all he says, and yet very few say all they mean, for words are slippery and thought is viscous.
Henry Brooks Adams 1838–1918: *The Education of Henry Adams* (1907)

2 'Then you should say what you mean,'
the March Hare went on. 'I do,' Alice
hastily replied; 'at least—at least I
mean what I say—that's the same
thing, you know.' 'Not the same thing
a bit!' said the Hatter. 'Why, you
might just as well say that "I see what
I eat" is the same thing as "I eat what I
see!"'

Lewis Carroll 1832–98: *Alice's Adventures in
Wonderland* (1865)

3 You see it's like a portmanteau—there
are two meanings packed up into one
word.

Lewis Carroll 1832–98: *Through the Looking-
Glass* (1872)

4 It depends on what the meaning of 'is'
is.

Bill Clinton 1946– : videotaped evidence to
the grand jury; tapes broadcast 21 September
1998

5 If a lady says No, she means Perhaps;
if she says Perhaps, she means Yes; if
she says Yes, she is no Lady.
If a diplomat says Yes, he means
Perhaps; if he says Perhaps, he means
No; if he says No, he is no Diplomat.

Lord Dawson of Penn 1864–1945: Francis
Watson *Dawson of Penn* (1950)

6 The meaning doesn't matter if it's
only idle chatter of a transcendental
kind.

W. S. Gilbert 1836–1911: *Patience* (1881)

7 It all depends what you mean by . . .

C. E. M. Joad 1891–1953: answering questions
on 'The Brains Trust' (formerly 'Any
Questions'), BBC radio (1941–8)

8 Any general statement is like a cheque
drawn on a bank. Its value depends on
what is there to meet it.

Ezra Pound 1885–1972: *The ABC of Reading*
(1934)

9 Egad I think the interpreter is the
hardest to be understood of the two!

Richard Brinsley Sheridan 1751–1816: *The
Critic* (1779)

10 The little girl had the making of a poet
in her who, being told to be sure of
her meaning before she spoke, said,

'How can I know what I think till I see
what I say?'

Graham Wallas 1858–1932: *The Art of Thought*
(1926)

Means

see **Ways and Means**

Medicine

see also **Health**, **Sickness**

1 Medicinal discovery,
It moves in mighty leaps,
It leapt straight past the common cold
And gave it us for keeps.

Pam Ayres 1947– : 'Oh no, I got a cold' (1976)

2 We all labour against our own cure,
for death is the cure of all diseases.

Thomas Browne 1605–82: *Religio Medici*
(1643)

3 If a lot of cures are suggested for a
disease, it means that the disease is
incurable.

Anton Chekhov 1860–1904: *The Cherry
Orchard* (1904)

4 Every day, in every way, I am getting
better and better.

■ *to be said 15 to 20 times, morning and evening*
Émile Coué 1857–1926: *De la suggestion et de
ses applications* (1915)

5 The wounded surgeon plies the steel
That questions the distempered part;
Beneath the bleeding hands we feel
The sharp compassion of the healer's
art
Resolving the enigma of the fever
chart.

T. S. Eliot 1888–1965: *Four Quartets* 'East
Coker' (1940)

6 We shall have to learn to refrain from
doing things merely because we know
how to do them.

Theodore Fox 1899–1989: speech to Royal
College of Physicians, 18 October 1965

7 A cousin of mine who was a casualty
surgeon in Manhattan tells me that he
and his colleagues had a one-word
nickname for bikers: Donors.

Stephen Fry 1957– : *Paperweight* (1992)

8 When our organs have been
transplanted
And the new ones made happy to
lodge in us,
Let us pray one wish be granted—
We retain our zones erogenous.
   E. Y. Harburg 1898–1981: 'Seated One Day at
   the Organ' (1965)

9 Life is short, the art long.
   Hippocrates c.460–357 BC: *Aphorisms*

10 It may seem a strange principle to
enunciate as the very first
requirement in a Hospital that it
should do the sick no harm.
   Florence Nightingale 1820–1910: *Notes on
   Hospitals* (1863 ed.) preface

11 One finger in the throat and one in
the rectum makes a good
diagnostician.
   William Osler 1849–1919: *Aphorisms from his
   Bedside Teachings* (1961)

12 Cured yesterday of my disease,
I died last night of my physician.
   Matthew Prior 1664–1721: 'The Remedy
   Worse than the Disease' (1727)

13 My sleeping pill is white.
It is a splendid pearl;
it floats me out of myself,
my stung skin as alien
as a loose bolt of cloth.
   Anne Sexton 1928–74: 'Lullaby' (1960)

14 Throw physic to the dogs; I'll none of
it.
   William Shakespeare 1564–1616: *Macbeth*
   (1606)

15 There is at bottom only one genuinely
scientific treatment for all diseases,
and that is to stimulate the
phagocytes.
   George Bernard Shaw 1856–1950: *The Doctor's
   Dilemma* (1911)

16 I can't stand whispering. Every time a
doctor whispers in the hospital, next
day there's a funeral.
   Neil Simon 1927– : *The Gingerbread Lady*
   (1970)

17 Formerly, when religion was strong
and science weak, men mistook magic
for medicine; now, when science is
strong and religion weak, men
mistake medicine for magic.
   Thomas Szasz 1920– : *The Second Sin* (1973)

18 I am here—trying to do science in
hell.
   ■ *working as a doctor in Belsen at the end of the
   war*
   Janet-Maria Vaughan 1899–1993: letter to a
   friend, 12 May 1945

19 Ah, well, then, I suppose that I shall
have to die beyond my means.
   ■ *at the mention of a huge fee for a surgical
   operation*
   Oscar Wilde 1854–1900: R. H. Sherard *Life of
   Oscar Wilde* (1906)

Mediocrity

1 Some men are born mediocre, some
men achieve mediocrity, and some
men have mediocrity thrust upon
them. With Major Major it had been
all three.
   Joseph Heller 1923–99: *Catch-22* (1961)

2 If Richard Nixon was second-rate,
what in the world *is* third-rate?
   Joseph Heller 1923–99: *Good as Gold* (1979)

3 Not gods, nor men, nor even
booksellers have put up with poets
being second-rate.
   Horace 65–8 BC: *Ars Poetica*

4 There's only one real sin, and that is
to persuade oneself that the second-
best is anything but the second-best.
   Doris Lessing 1919– : *Golden Notebook* (1962)

5 Women want mediocre men, and
men are working hard to be as
mediocre as possible.
   Margaret Mead 1901–78: in *Quote Magazine*
   15 June 1958

6 She has a Rolls body and a Balham
mind.
   J. B. Morton ('Beachcomber') 1893–1975:
   Morton's Folly (1933)

7 It is our national joy to mistake for the
first-rate, the fecund rate.
   Dorothy Parker 1893–1967: in *New Yorker*
   16 March 1929

Meeting

see also **Parting**

1 Gin a body meet a body
Comin thro' the rye,
Gin a body kiss a body
Need a body cry?
Robert Burns 1759–96: 'Comin thro' the rye'
(1796)

2 'Is there anybody there?' said the
Traveller,
Knocking on the moonlit door.
Walter de la Mare 1873–1956: 'The Listeners'
(1912)

3 Of all the gin joints in all the towns in
all the world, she walks into mine.
Julius J. Epstein 1909–2001 et al.: *Casablanca*
(1942 film); spoken by Humphrey Bogart

4 Some enchanted evening,
You may see a stranger,
You may see a stranger,
Across a crowded room.
Oscar Hammerstein II 1895–1960: 'Some
Enchanted Evening' (1949 song)

5 Not many sounds in life, and I include
all urban and all rural sounds, exceed
in interest a knock at the door.
Charles Lamb 1775–1834: *Essays of Elia* (1823)
'Valentine's Day'

6 How d'ye do, and how is the old
complaint?
■ *reputed to be his greeting to all those he did not
know*
Lord Palmerston 1784–1865: A. West
Recollections (1899)

7 We'll meet again, don't know where,
Don't know when,
But I know we'll meet again some
sunny day.
Ross Parker 1914–74 and **Hugh Charles**
1907– : 'We'll Meet Again' (1939 song)

8 I wish I could remember the first day,
First hour, first moment of your
meeting me,
If bright or dim the season, it might
be
Summer or winter for aught I can say.
So unrecorded did it slip away.
Christina Rossetti 1830–94: 'The First Day'

9 Ill met by moonlight, proud Titania.
William Shakespeare 1564–1616: *A
Midsummer Night's Dream* (1595–6)

10 When shall we three meet again
In thunder, lightning, or in rain?
William Shakespeare 1564–1616: *Macbeth*
(1606)

11 Dr Livingstone, I presume?
Henry Morton Stanley 1841–1904: *How I found
Livingstone* (1872)

12 Why don't you come up sometime,
and see me?
■ *usually quoted as 'Why don't you come up and
see me sometime?'*
Mae West 1892–1980: *She Done Him Wrong*
(1933 film)

Memory

1 Memories are hunting horns
Whose sound dies on the wind.
Guillaume Apollinaire 1880–1918: 'Cors de
Chasse' (1912)

2 And we forget because we must
And not because we will.
Matthew Arnold 1822–88: 'Absence' (1852)

3 Someone said that God gave us
memory so that we might have roses
in December.
J. M. Barrie 1860–1937: Rectorial Address at St
Andrew's, 3 May 1922

4 Memories are not shackles, Franklin,
they are garlands.
Alan Bennett 1934– : *Forty Years On* (1969)

5 We'll tak a cup o' kindness yet,
For auld lang syne.
Robert Burns 1759–96: 'Auld Lang Syne'
(1796)

6 Poor people's memory is less
nourished than that of the rich; it has
fewer landmarks in space because
they seldom leave the place where
they live, and fewer reference points
in time . . . Of course, there is the
memory of the heart that they say is
the surest kind, but the heart wears
out with sorrow and labour, it forgets
sooner under the weight of fatigue.
Albert Camus 1913–60: *The First Man* (1994)

7 Our memories are card-indexes consulted, and then put back in disorder by authorities whom we do not control.

Cyril Connolly 1903–74: *The Unquiet Grave* (1944)

8 I have forgot much, Cynara! gone with the wind,
Flung roses, roses, riotously, with the throng,
Dancing, to put thy pale, lost lilies out of mind.

Ernest Dowson 1867–1900: 'Non Sum Qualis Eram' (1896); also known as 'Cynara'

9 There should be an invention that bottles up a memory like a perfume, and it never faded, never got stale, and whenever I wanted to I could uncork the bottle, and live the memory all over again.

Daphne Du Maurier 1907–89: *Rebecca* (1938)

10 Footfalls echo in the memory
Down the passage which we did not take
Towards the door we never opened
Into the rose-garden.

T. S. Eliot 1888–1965: *Four Quartets* 'Burnt Norton' (1936)

11 Everyone seems to remember with great clarity what they were doing on November 22nd, 1963, at the precise moment they heard President Kennedy was dead.

Frederick Forsyth 1938– : *The Odessa File* (1972)

12 Your memory is a monster; *you* forget—*it* doesn't. It simply files things away. It keeps things for you, or hides things from you—and summons them to your recall with a will of its own. You think you have a memory; but it has you!

John Irving 1942– : *A Prayer for Owen Meany* (1989)

13 We met at nine.
We met at eight.
I was on time.
No, you were late.
Ah yes! I remember it well.

Alan Jay Lerner 1918–86: 'I Remember it Well' (1958 song)

14 In childhood, the moments of consciousness that we later recall occur precisely when we are not happy, but these high moments transform themselves by a miracle into a memory of happiness, as though stones had hatched.

Candia McWilliam 1955– : *Debatable Land* (1994)

15 A cigarette that bears a lipstick's traces,
An airline ticket to romantic places;
And still my heart has wings
These foolish things
Remind me of you.

Holt Marvell: 'These Foolish Things Remind Me of You' (1935 song)

16 And entering with relief some quiet place
Where never fell his foot or shone his face
I say, 'There is no memory of him here!'
And so stand stricken, so remembering him.

Edna St Vincent Millay 1892–1950: 'Time does not bring relief'

17 You may break, you may shatter the vase, if you will,
But the scent of the roses will hang round it still.

Thomas Moore 1779–1852: 'Farewell!—but whenever' (1807)

18 The memories of long love gather like drifting snow, poignant as the mandarin ducks who float side by side in sleep.

Murasaki Shikibu c.978–c.1031: *The Tale of Genji*

19 What beastly incidents our memories insist on cherishing! . . . the ugly and disgusting . . . the beautiful things we have to keep diaries to remember!

Eugene O'Neill 1888–1953: *Strange Interlude* (1928)

20 And suddenly the memory revealed itself. The taste was that of the little piece of madeleine which on Sunday mornings at Combray . . . my aunt

Léonie used to give me, dipping it first in her own cup of tea or tisane.

Marcel Proust 1871–1922: *Swann's Way* (1913, vol. 1 of *Remembrance of Things Past*)

21 Better by far you should forget and smile
Than that you should remember and be sad.

Christina Rossetti 1830–94: 'Remember' (1862)

22 I've a grand memory for forgetting, David.

Robert Louis Stevenson 1850–94: *Kidnapped* (1886)

23 My memory is certainly in my hands. I can remember things only if I have a pencil and I can write with it and play with it. I think your hand concentrates for you.

Rebecca West 1892–1983: George Plimpton (ed.) *The Writer's Chapbook* (1989)

Men

see also **Bachelors, Husbands, Men and Women**

1 Are all men in disguise except those crying?

Dannie Abse 1923– : 'Encounter at a greyhound bus station' (1986)

2 Men have had every advantage of us in telling their own story. Education has been theirs in so much higher a degree; the pen has been in their hands.

Jane Austen 1775–1817: *Persuasion* (1818)

3 Nobody ever, unless he is very wicked, deliberately tries to hurt anybody. It's just that men cannot help not loving you or behaving badly.

Beryl Bainbridge 1933– : interview in *Daily Telegraph* 10 September 1996

4 Women were brought up to believe that men were the answer. They weren't. They weren't even one of the questions.

Julian Barnes 1946– : *Staring at the Sun* (1986)

5 Every modern male has, lying at the bottom of his psyche, a large, primitive being covered with hair down to his feet. Making contact with this Wild Man is the step the Eighties male or the Nineties male has yet to take.

Robert Bly 1926– : *Iron John* (1990)

6 Men build bridges and throw railroads across deserts, and yet they contend successfully that the job of sewing on a button is beyond them. Accordingly, they don't have to sew buttons.

Heywood Broun 1888–1939: *Seeing Things at Night* (1921)

7 Bloody men are like bloody buses—
You wait for about a year
And as soon as one approaches your stop
Two or three others appear.

Wendy Cope 1945– : 'Bloody Men' (1992)

8 What makes men so tedious
Is the need to show off and compete.
They'll bore you to death for hours and hours
Before they'll admit defeat.

Wendy Cope 1945– : 'Men and their boring arguments' (1988)

9 Why would I talk about the men in my life? For me, life is not about men.

■ *on writing her autobiography*
Catherine Deneuve 1943– : in *Independent* 26 April 1997

10 Man is to be held only by the *slightest* chains, with the idea that he can break them at pleasure, he submits to them in sport.

Maria Edgeworth 1768–1849: *Letters for Literary Ladies* (1795)

11 Whatever they may be in public life, whatever their relations with men, in their relations with women, all men are rapists, and that's all they are. They rape us with their eyes, their laws, and their codes.

Marilyn French 1929– : *The Women's Room* (1977)

12 It was the promise of men, that around each corner there was yet another man, more wonderful than the last, that sustained me. You see, I

had men confused with life . . . You can't get what I wanted from a man, not in this life.

Nancy Friday 1937– : *My Mother, My Self* (1977)

13 Men would rather take their trousers off in public when they're drunk than open the shield of their hearts when they are sober.

Stephen Fry 1957– : comment on the work of the Samaritans, 17 May 1996

14 We are lads. We have burgled houses and nicked car stereos, and we like girls and swear and go to the football and take the piss.

Noel Gallagher 1967– : interview in *Melody Maker* 30 March 1996

15 A man . . . is *so* in the way in the house!

Elizabeth Gaskell 1810–65: *Cranford* (1853)

16 Years ago, manhood was an opportunity for achievement, and now it is a problem to be overcome.

Garrison Keillor 1942– : *The Book of Guys* (1994)

17 If you wish—
. . . I'll be irreproachably tender;
not a man, but—a cloud in trousers!

Vladimir Mayakovsky 1893–1930: 'The Cloud in Trousers' (1915)

18 Sigh no more, ladies, sigh no more, Men were deceivers ever.

William Shakespeare 1564–1616: *Much Ado About Nothing* (1598–9)

19 Every man over forty is a scoundrel.

George Bernard Shaw 1856–1950: *Man and Superman* (1903) 'Maxims: Stray Sayings'

20 It's not the men in my life that counts—it's the life in my men.

Mae West 1892–1980: *I'm No Angel* (1933 film)

21 A hard man is good to find.

Mae West 1892–1980: attributed

22 There is, of course, no reason for the existence of the male sex except that sometimes one needs help with moving the piano.

Rebecca West 1892–1983: in *Sunday Telegraph* 28 June 1970

23 No nice men are good at getting taxis.

Katharine Whitehorn 1928– : in *Observer* 1977

Men and Women

see also **Men, Relationships, Woman's Role, Women**

1 In societies where men are truly confident of their own worth, women are not merely tolerated but valued.

Aung San Suu Kyi 1945– : videotape speech at NGO Forum on Women, China, early September 1995

2 Women love scallywags, but some marry them and then try to make them wear a blazer.

David Bailey 1938– : in *Mail on Sunday* 16 February 1997

3 Women are programmed to love completely, and men are programmed to spread it around.

Beryl Bainbridge 1933– : interview in *Daily Telegraph* 10 September 1996

4 Man's love is of man's life a thing apart,
'Tis woman's whole existence.

Lord Byron 1788–1824: *Don Juan* (1819–24)

5 Women deprived of the company of men pine, men deprived of the company of women become stupid.

Anton Chekhov 1860–1904: *Notebooks* (1921)

6 The man's desire is for the woman; but the woman's desire is rarely other than for the desire of the man.

Samuel Taylor Coleridge 1772–1834: *Table Talk* (1835) 23 July 1827

7 There is more difference within the sexes than between them.

Ivy Compton-Burnett 1884–1969: *Mother and Son* (1955)

8 In the sex-war thoughtlessness is the weapon of the male, vindictiveness of the female.

Cyril Connolly 1903–74: *The Unquiet Grave* (1944)

9 It is not in giving life but in risking life that man is raised above the animal; that is why superiority has been

accorded in humanity not to the sex that brings forth but to that which kills.
Simone de Beauvoir 1908–86: *The Second Sex* (1949)

10 A man has every season, while a woman has only the right to spring.
Jane Fonda 1937– : in *Daily Mail* 13 September 1989

11 Women have very little idea of how much men hate them.
Germaine Greer 1939– : *The Female Eunuch* (1971)

12 My mother said it was simple to keep a man, you must be a maid in the living room, a cook in the kitchen and a whore in the bedroom. I said I'd hire the other two and take care of the bedroom bit.
Jerry Hall: in *Observer* 6 October 1985

13 A woman has to use her influence with a man. She must mould him, make him into a better person, or what's the point of a relationship?
Ruth Prawer Jhabvala 1927– : *In Search of Love and Beauty* (1983)

14 Take my word for it, the silliest woman can manage a clever man; but it takes a very clever woman to manage a fool.
Rudyard Kipling 1865–1936: *Plain Tales from the Hills* (1888)

15 Why can't a woman be more like a man?
Men are so honest, so thoroughly square;
Eternally noble, historically fair.
Alan Jay Lerner 1918–86: 'A Hymn to Him' (1956 song)

16 I think men talk to women so they can sleep with them and women sleep with men so they can talk to them.
Jay McInerney 1955– : *Brightness Falls* (1992)

17 A woman can forgive a man for the harm he does her, but she can never forgive him for the sacrifices he makes on her account.
W. Somerset Maugham 1874–1965: *The Moon and Sixpence* (1919)

18 Every woman adores a Fascist,
The boot in the face, the brute
Brute heart of a brute like you.
Sylvia Plath 1932–63: 'Daddy' (1963)

19 More and more it appears that, biologically, men are designed for short, brutal lives and women for long miserable ones.
Estelle Ramey 1917– : in *Observer* 7 April 1985

20 Of all human struggles there is none so treacherous and remorseless as the struggle between the artist man and the mother woman.
George Bernard Shaw 1856–1950: *Man and Superman* (1903)

21 A woman without a man is like a fish without a bicycle.
Gloria Steinem 1934– : attributed

22 Whereas nature turns girls into women, society has to make boys into men.
Anthony Stevens: *Archetype* (1982)

23 Man is the hunter; woman is his game.
Alfred, Lord Tennyson 1809–92: *The Princess* (1847)

24 Me Tarzan, you Jane.
■ *summing up his role in* Tarzan, the Ape Man (1932 film)
Johnny Weissmuller 1904–84: in *Photoplay Magazine* June 1932; the words occur neither in the film nor the original novel, by Edgar Rice Burroughs

25 When women go wrong, men go right after them.
Mae West 1892–1980: *She Done Him Wrong* (1933 film)

26 Whatever women do they must do twice as well as men to be thought half as good.
Charlotte Whitton 1896–1975: in *Canada Month* June 1963

27 All women become like their mothers. That is their tragedy. No man does. That's his.
Oscar Wilde 1854–1900: *The Importance of Being Earnest* (1895)

28 Women have served all these centuries as looking-glasses possessing the

magic and delicious power of reflecting the figure of a man at twice its natural size.

Virginia Woolf 1882–1941: *A Room of One's Own* (1929)

Mental Illness

see also **Madness**, **The Mind**

1 In psychoanalysis nothing is true except the exaggerations.

Theodor Adorno 1903–69: *Minima Moralia* (1951)

2 Any man who goes to a psychiatrist should have his head examined.

Sam Goldwyn 1882–1974: Norman Zierold *Moguls* (1969)

3 There was only one catch and that was Catch-22, which specified that a concern for one's own safety in the face of dangers that were real and immediate was the process of a rational mind . . . Orr would be crazy to fly more missions and sane if he didn't, but if he was sane he had to fly them. If he flew them he was crazy and didn't have to; but if he didn't want to he was sane and had to.

Joseph Heller 1923–99: *Catch-22* (1961)

4 Schizophrenia cannot be understood without understanding despair.

R. D. Laing 1927–89: *The Divided Self* (1960)

5 The experience and behaviour that gets labelled schizophrenic is a special strategy that a person invents in order to live in an unlivable situation.

R. D. Laing 1927–89: *Politics of Experience* (1967)

6 Is there no way out of the mind?

Sylvia Plath 1932–63: 'Apprehensions' (1971)

7 The psychopath is the furnace that gives no heat.

Derek Raymond 1931–94: *The Hidden Files* (1992)

8 If you talk to God, you are praying; if God talks to you, you have schizophrenia. If the dead talk to you, you are a spiritualist; if God talks to you, you are a schizophrenic.

Thomas Szasz 1920– : *The Second Sin* (1973)

9 People are very unwilling to spend money on the mentally ill, particularly schizophrenics who frighten them. That's why you have to be careful with the idea of a democratic checklist—because of the people who would fall to the bottom of it every time.

Polly Toynbee 1946– : *The Future of Care for Older People* (1996)

Mexico and South America

1 Poor Mexico, so far from God and so close to the United States.

Porfirio Díaz 1830–1915: attributed

2 Latins are tenderly enthusiastic. In Brazil they throw flowers at you. In Argentina they throw themselves.

Marlene Dietrich 1901–92: in *Newsweek* 24 August 1959

3 To be a gringo in Mexico . . . ah, that is euthanasia.

Carlos Fuentes 1928– : *The Old Gringo* (1985)

4 Night, snow, and sand make up the form
of my thin country,
all silence lies in its long line,
all foam flows from its marine beard,
all coal covers it with mysterious kisses.

Pablo Neruda 1904–73: 'Discoverers of Chile' (1950)

5 Mexicans are descended from the Aztecs, Peruvians from the Incas and Argentinians from the ships.

Octavio Paz 1914– : attributed, in *Observer* 16 June 1990

6 Brazil—where the nuts come from.

Brandon Thomas 1856–1914: *Charlie's Aunt* (1892)

Middle Age

1 Years ago we discovered the exact point, the dead centre of middle age. It occurs when you are too young to

take up golf and too old to rush up to the net.

Franklin P. Adams 1881–1960: *Nods and Becks* (1944)

2 You are living in a land you no longer recognize. You don't know the language.

■ *on his 'cataclysmic mid-life crisis'*
Martin Amis 1949– : in *Times* 21 August 1997

3 I am past thirty, and three parts iced over.

Matthew Arnold 1822–88: letter to Arthur Hugh Clough, 12 February 1853

4 Mr Salteena was an elderly man of 42.

Daisy Ashford 1881–1972: *The Young Visiters* (1919)

5 Women over thirty are at their best, but men over thirty are too old to recognize it.

Jean-Paul Belmondo 1933– : attributed

6 Fiftieth birthdays should be times of huge goodwill . . . Only people who put on fake tan and pretend to be younger than they are don't get to join the party.

Maeve Binchy 1940– : in *Irish Times* 25 April 1998

7 After forty a woman has to choose between losing her figure or her face. My advice is to keep your face, and stay sitting down.

Barbara Cartland 1901–2000: in *The Times* 6 October 1993

8 At eighteen our convictions are hills from which we look; at forty-five they are caves in which we hide.

F. Scott Fitzgerald 1896–1940: 'Bernice Bobs her Hair' (1920)

9 He who thinks to realize when he is older the hopes and desires of youth is always deceiving himself, for every decade of a man's life possesses its own kind of happiness, its own hopes and prospects.

Johann Wolfgang von Goethe 1749–1832: *Elective Affinities* (1809)

10 Nobody loves a fairy when she's forty.

Arthur W. D. Henley: title of song (1934)

11 The afternoon of human life must also have a significance of its own and cannot be merely a pitiful appendage to life's morning.

Carl Gustav Jung 1875–1961: *The Stages of Life* (1930)

12 Men at forty
Learn to close softly
The doors to rooms they will not be
Coming back to.

Donald Justice 1925– : 'Men at Forty' (1967)

13 My biological clock is ticking so loud I'm nearly deafened by it. They search me going into planes.

Marian Keyes: 'Late Opening at the Last Chance Saloon' (1997)

14 At forty-five,
What next, what next?
At every corner,
I meet my Father,
my age, still alive.

Robert Lowell 1917–77: 'Middle Age' (1964)

15 The lovely thing about being forty is that you can appreciate twenty-five-year-old men more.

Colleen McCullough 1937– : attributed

16 I have a bone to pick with Fate.
Come here and tell me, girlie,
Do you think my mind is maturing late,
Or simply rotted early?

Ogden Nash 1902–71: 'Lines on Facing Forty' (1942)

17 One of the pleasures of middle age is to *find out* that one WAS right, and that one was much righter than one knew at say 17 or 23.

Ezra Pound 1885–1972: *ABC of Reading* (1934)

The Mind

see also **Counselling, Ideas, Logic and Reason, Madness, Mental Illness, Thinking**

1 Consciousness *isn't* intolerable. It is beautiful: the eternal creation and dissolution of mental forms.

Martin Amis 1949– : *Time's Arrow* (1991)

2 Psychoanalysis pretends to investigate the Unconscious. The Unconscious by definition is what you are not conscious of. But the Analysts already know what's in it—they should, because they put it all in beforehand.

Saul Bellow 1915– : *The Dean's December* (1982)

3 Minds are like parachutes. They only function when they are open.

James Dewar 1842–1923: attributed

4 To be conscious is an illness—a real thorough-going illness.

Fedor Dostoevsky 1821–81: *Notes from Underground* (1864)

5 If my mental processes are determined wholly by the motions of atoms in my brain, I have no reason for supposing that my beliefs are true. They may be sound chemically, but that does not make them sound logically. And hence I have no reason for supposing my brain to be composed of atoms.

J. B. S. Haldane 1892–1964: *Possible Worlds* (1927)

6 On earth there is nothing great but man; in man there is nothing great but mind.

William Hamilton 1788–1856: *Lectures on Metaphysics and Logic* (1859)

7 Purple haze is in my brain
Lately things don't seem the same.

Jimi Hendrix 1942–70: 'Purple Haze' (1967 song)

8 O the mind, mind has mountains; cliffs of fall
Frightful, sheer, no-man-fathomed.
Hold them cheap
May who ne'er hung there.

Gerard Manley Hopkins 1844–89: 'No worst, there is none' (written 1885)

9 The only means of strengthening one's intellect is to make up one's mind about nothing—to let the mind be a thoroughfare for all thoughts. Not a select party.

John Keats 1795–1821: letter to George and Georgiana Keats, 24 September 1819

10 If the nineteenth century was the age of the editorial chair, ours is the century of the psychiatrist's couch.

Marshall McLuhan 1911–80: *Understanding Media* (1964)

11 The mind is its own place, and in itself Can make a heaven of hell, a hell of heaven.

John Milton 1608–74: *Paradise Lost* (1667)

12 Those who are caught in mental cages can often picture freedom, it just has no attractive power.

Iris Murdoch 1919–99: *The Sea, The Sea* (1978)

13 Consciousness . . . is the phenomenon whereby the universe's very existence is made known.

Roger Penrose 1931– : *The Emperor's New Mind* (1989)

14 That's the classical mind at work, runs fine inside but looks dingy on the surface.

Robert M. Pirsig 1928– : *Zen and the Art of Motorcycle Maintenance* (1974)

15 What is Matter?—Never mind.
What is Mind?—No matter.

Punch: 14 July 1855

16 What a waste it is to lose one's mind, or not to have a mind. How true that is.

Dan Quayle 1947– : speech to the United Negro College Fund, whose slogan is 'a mind is a terrible thing to waste'; in *The Times* 26 May 1989

17 When people will not weed their own minds, they are apt to be overrun with nettles.

Horace Walpole 1717–97: letter to Caroline, Countess of Ailesbury, 10 July 1779

18 Mind in its purest play is like some bat That beats about in caverns all alone, Contriving by a kind of senseless wit Not to conclude against a wall of stone.

Richard Wilbur 1921– : 'Mind' (1956)

19 Every human brain is born not as a blank tablet (a *tabula rasa*) waiting to be filled in by experience but as 'an

exposed negative waiting to be slipped into developer fluid'.

■ *on the nature v. nurture debate*
Edward O. Wilson 1929– : attributed

20 To give a sex to mind was not very consistent with the principles of a man [Rousseau] who argued so warmly, and so well, for the immortality of the soul.

■ *often quoted as, 'Mind has no sex'*
Mary Wollstonecraft 1759–97: *A Vindication of the Rights of Woman* (1792)

Minorities and Majorities

see also **Democracy**

1 As for our majority . . . one is enough.
Benjamin Disraeli 1804–81: *Endymion* (1880); now often associated with Churchill

2 Nor is the people's judgement always true:
The most may err as grossly as the few.
John Dryden 1631–1700: *Absalom and Achitophel* (1681)

3 The majority never has right on its side. Never I say! That is one of the social lies that a free, thinking man is bound to rebel against. Who makes up the majority in any given country? Is it the wise men or the fools? I think we must agree that the fools are in a terrible overwhelming majority, all the wide world over. But, damn it, it can surely never be right that the stupid should rule over the clever!
Henrik Ibsen 1828–1906: *An Enemy of the People* (1882)

4 All, too, will bear in mind this sacred principle, that though the will of the majority is in all cases to prevail, that will to be rightful must be reasonable; that the minority possess their equal rights, which equal law must protect, and to violate would be oppression.
Thomas Jefferson 1743–1826: inaugural address, 4 March, 1801

5 The majority may rule in Britain, but in America it can only negotiate.
Raymond Seitz 1940– : *Over Here* (1998)

6 Minorities . . . are almost always in the right.
Sydney Smith 1771–1845: H. Pearson *The Smith of Smiths* (1934)

Misfortunes

see also **Adversity**

1 People will take balls,
Balls will be lost always, little boy,
And no one buys a ball back.
John Berryman 1914–72: 'The Ball Poem' (1948)

2 Man is born unto trouble, as the sparks fly upward.
Bible: Job

3 If Gladstone fell into the Thames, that would be misfortune; and if anybody pulled him out, that, I suppose, would be a calamity.
Benjamin Disraeli 1804–81: Leon Harris *The Fine Art of Political Wit* (1965)

4 In the words of one of my more sympathetic correspondents, it has turned out to be an 'annus horribilis'.
Elizabeth II 1926– : speech at Guildhall, London, 24 November 1992

5 Never cry over spilt milk, because it may have been poisoned.
W. C. Fields 1880–1946: to Carlotta Monti; Carlotta Monti with Cy Rice *W. C. Fields and Me* (1971)

6 I left the room with silent dignity, but caught my foot in the mat.
George and **Weedon Grossmith** 1847–1912, 1854–1919: *The Diary of a Nobody* (1894)

7 In the misfortune of our best friends, we always find something which is not displeasing to us.
Duc de la Rochefoucauld 1613–80: *Réflexions ou Maximes Morales* (1665)

8 I've no sympathy with people to whom things happen. It may be that their luck was bad, but is that to count in their favour?
Cormac McCarthy 1933– : *All the Pretty Horses* (1993)

9 boss there is always
a comforting thought
in time of trouble when
it is not our trouble.
Don Marquis 1878–1937: *archy does his part*
(1935)

10 I had never had a piece of toast
Particularly long and wide,
But fell upon the sanded floor,
And always on the buttered side.
James Payn 1830–98: in *Chambers's Journal*
2 February 1884; cf. **Transience** 12

11 Misery acquaints a man with strange
bedfellows.
William Shakespeare 1564–1616: *The Tempest*
(1611)

12 The fatal law of gravity: when you are
down everything falls on you.
Sylvia Townsend Warner 1893–1978: attributed

13 One likes people much better when
they're battered down by a prodigious
siege of misfortune than when they
triumph.
Virginia Woolf 1882–1941: diary 13 August 1921

Mistakes

1 It is worse than a crime, it is a blunder.
■ *on hearing of the execution of the Duc
d'Enghien, 1804*
Antoine Boulay de la Meurthe 1761–1840:
C.-A. Sainte-Beuve *Nouveaux Lundis* (1870)

2 As she frequently remarked when she
made any such mistake, it would be all
the same a hundred years hence.
Charles Dickens 1812–70: *Nicholas Nickleby*
(1839)

3 If all else fails, immortality can always
be assured by a spectacular error.
J. K. Galbraith 1908– : attributed

4 Mistakes are a fact of life
It is the response to error that counts.
Nikki Giovanni 1943– : 'Of Liberation' (1970)

5 The road to wisdom?—Well, it's plain
and simple to express:
Err
and err
and err again
but less

and less
and less.
Piet Hein 1905– : 'The Road to Wisdom'
(1966)

6 Crooked things may be as stiff and
unflexible as straight: and men may
be as positive in error as in truth.
John Locke 1632–1704: *An Essay concerning
Human Understanding* (1690)

7 The man who makes no mistakes does
not usually make anything.
Edward John Phelps 1822–1900: speech at the
Mansion House, London, 24 January 1889

8 One Galileo in two thousand years is
enough.
■ *on being asked to proscribe the works of
Teilhard de Chardin*
Pope Pius XII 1876–1958: attributed; Stafford
Beer *Platform for Change* (1975)

9 'Forward, the Light Brigade!'
Was there a man dismayed?
Not though the soldier knew
Some one had blundered.
Alfred, Lord Tennyson 1809–92: 'The Charge
of the Light Brigade' (1854)

10 Well, if I called the wrong number,
why did you answer the phone?
James Thurber 1894–1961: cartoon caption in
New Yorker 5 June 1937

11 The report of my death was an
exaggeration.
■ *usually quoted as 'Reports of my death have
been greatly exaggerated'*
Mark Twain 1835–1910: in *New York Journal*
2 June 1897

12 To lose one parent, Mr Worthing, may
be regarded as a misfortune; to lose
both looks like carelessness.
Oscar Wilde 1854–1900: *The Importance of
Being Earnest* (1895)

Moderation

1 Nothing in excess.
Anonymous: inscribed on the temple of
Apollo at Delphi, and variously ascribed to
the Seven Wise Men

2 To many, total abstinence is easier
than perfect moderation.
St Augustine of Hippo AD 354–430: *On the
Good of Marriage* (AD 401)

3 We know what happens to people who stay in the middle of the road. They get run down.
Aneurin Bevan 1897–1960: in *Observer* 6 December 1953

4 There's nothing in the middle of the road but yellow stripes and dead armadillos.
Jim Hightower: attributed, 1984

5 You will go most safely by the middle way.
Ovid 43 BC–AD c.17: *Metamorphoses*

6 Americans believe that anything worth doing is worth overdoing.
Raymond Seitz 1940– : *Over Here* (1998)

7 Above all, gentlemen, not the slightest zeal.
Charles-Maurice de Talleyrand 1754–1838: P. Chasles *Voyages d'un critique à travers la vie et les livres* (1868)

8 Moderation is a fatal thing, Lady Hunstanton. Nothing succeeds like excess.
Oscar Wilde 1854–1900: *A Woman of No Importance* (1893)

Money

see also **Economics**, **Greed**, **Poverty**, **Wealth**

1 The almighty dollar is the only object of worship.
Anonymous: in *Philadelphia Public Ledger* 2 December 1836

2 Money is like muck, not good except it be spread.
Francis Bacon 1561–1626: *Essays* (1625) 'Of Seditions and Troubles'

3 Money, it turned out, was exactly like sex, you thought of nothing else if you didn't have it and thought of other things if you did.
James Baldwin 1924–87: in *Esquire* May 1961 'Black Boy looks at the White Boy'

4 We could have saved sixpence. We have saved fivepence. (*Pause*) But at what cost?
Samuel Beckett 1906–89: *All That Fall* (1957)

5 Money speaks sense in a language all nations understand.
Aphra Behn 1640–89: *The Rover* pt. 2 (1681)

6 I'm tired of Love: I'm still more tired of Rhyme.
But Money gives me pleasure all the time.
Hilaire Belloc 1870–1953: 'Fatigued' (1923)

7 The love of money is the root of all evil.
Bible: I Timothy

8 What is robbing a bank compared with founding a bank?
Bertolt Brecht 1898–1956: *Die Dreigroschenoper* (1928)

9 Those who have some means think that the most important thing in the world is love. The poor know that it is money.
Gerald Brenan 1894–1987: *Thoughts in a Dry Season* (1978)

10 Money doesn't talk, it swears.
Bob Dylan 1941– : 'It's Alright, Ma (I'm Only Bleeding)' (1965 song)

11 Money is the sinews of love, as of war.
George Farquhar 1678–1707: *Love and a Bottle* (1698); see **Warfare** 7

12 Economy is going without something you do want in case you should, some day, want something you probably won't want.
Anthony Hope 1863–1933: *The Dolly Dialogues* (1894)

13 A bank is a place that will lend you money if you can prove that you don't need it.
Bob Hope 1903– : Alan Harrington *Life in the Crystal Palace* (1959)

14 If possible honestly, if not, somehow, make money.
Horace 65–8 BC: *Epistles*

15 I listen to money singing. It's like looking down
From long french windows at a provincial town,
The slums, the canal, the churches ornate and mad
In the evening sun. It is intensely sad.
Philip Larkin 1922–85: 'Money' (1974)

16 For I don't care too much for money,
For money can't buy me love.
   John Lennon 1940–80 and **Paul McCartney**
   1942– : 'Can't Buy Me Love' (1964 song)

17 Take care of the pence, and the
pounds will take care of themselves.
   William Lowndes 1652–1724: Lord
   Chesterfield *Letters to his Son* (1774)
   5 February 1750

18 Money is like a sixth sense without
which you cannot make a complete
use of the other five.
   W. Somerset Maugham 1874–1965: *Of Human
   Bondage* (1915)

19 Money couldn't buy friends but you
got a better class of enemy.
   Spike Milligan 1918–2002: *Puckoon* (1963)

20 I want the whole of Europe to have
one currency; it will make trading
much easier.
   Napoleon I 1769–1821: letter to his brother
   Louis, 6 May 1807

21 'My boy,' he says, 'always try to rub up
against money, for if you rub up
against money long enough, some of
it may rub off on you.'
   Damon Runyon 1884–1946: in *Cosmopolitan*
   August 1929, 'A Very Honourable Guy'

22 Pennies don't fall from heaven. They
have to be earned on earth.
   Margaret Thatcher 1925– : in *Observer*
   18 November 1979; see **Optimism** 2

23 From now the pound abroad is worth
14 per cent or so less in terms of other
currencies. It does not mean, of
course, that the pound here in Britain,
in your pocket or purse or in your
bank, has been devalued.
   Harold Wilson 1916–95: ministerial broadcast,
   19 November 1967

Marilyn Monroe 1926–62

1 Egghead weds hourglass.
   ▪ *on the marriage of Arthur Miller and Marilyn
   Monroe*
   Anonymous: headline in *Variety* 1956;
   attributed

2 Goodbye Norma Jean . . .
And it seems to me you lived your life
Like a candle in the wind.

Never knowing who to cling to
When the rain set in . . .
   Elton John 1947– and **Bernie Taupin** 1950– :
   'Candle in the Wind' (song, 1973); cf. **Singing**
   10

3 So we think of Marilyn who was every
man's love affair with America,
Marilyn Monroe who was blonde and
beautiful and had a sweet little rinky-
dink of a voice and all the cleanliness
of all the clean American backyards.
   Norman Mailer 1923– : *Marilyn* (1973)

Morality

1 It is always easier to fight for one's
principles than to live up to them.
   Alfred Adler 1870–1937: Phyllis Bottome
   Alfred Adler (1939)

2 Morality's *not* practical. Morality's a
gesture. A complicated gesture
learned from books.
   Robert Bolt 1924–95: *A Man for All Seasons*
   (1960)

3 Food comes first, then morals.
   Bertolt Brecht 1898–1956: *Die
   Dreigroschenoper* (1928)

4 Finding in 'primitive' languages a
dearth of words for moral ideas, many
people assumed these ideas did not
exist. But the concepts of 'good' or
'beautiful', so essential to Western
thought, are meaningless unless they
are rooted to things.
   Bruce Chatwin 1940–89: *In Patagonia* (1977)

5 The highest possible stage in moral
culture is when we recognize that we
ought to control our thoughts.
   Charles Darwin 1809–82: *The Descent of Man*
   (1871)

6 The last temptation is the greatest
treason:
To do the right deed for the wrong
reason.
   T. S. Eliot 1888–1965: *Murder in the Cathedral*
   (1935)

7 That action is best, which procures
the greatest happiness for the greatest
numbers.

> **Francis Hutcheson** 1694–1746: *An Inquiry into
> the Original of our Ideas of Beauty and Virtue*
> (1725); see **Society** 3

8 The end cannot justify the means, for
the simple and obvious reason that
the means employed determine the
nature of the ends produced.

> **Aldous Huxley** 1894–1963: *Ends and Means*
> (1937)

9 State a moral case to a ploughman
and a professor. The former will
decide it as well, and often better than
the latter, because he has not been led
astray by artificial rules.

> **Thomas Jefferson** 1743–1826: letter to Peter
> Carr, 10 August 1787

10 If people want a sense of purpose,
they should get it from their
archbishops. They should not hope to
receive it from their politicians.

> **Harold Macmillan** 1894–1986: to Henry
> Fairlie, 1963; H. Fairlie *The Life of Politics*
> (1968)

11 You can't learn too soon that the most
useful thing about a principle is that it
can always be sacrificed to expediency.

> **W. Somerset Maugham** 1874–1965: *The Circle*
> (1921)

12 Morality is the herd-instinct in the
individual.

> **Friedrich Nietzsche** 1844–1900: *Die fröhliche
> Wissenschaft* (1882)

13 In olden days a glimpse of stocking
Was looked on as something shocking
Now, heaven knows,
Anything goes.

> **Cole Porter** 1891–1964: 'Anything Goes' (1934
> song)

14 Values are tapes we play on the
Walkman of the mind: any tune we
choose so long as it does not disturb
others.

> **Jonathan Sacks** 1948– : *The Persistence of
> Faith* (1991)

15 The nation's morals are like its teeth:
the more decayed they are the more it
hurts to touch them.

> **George Bernard Shaw** 1856–1950: *The
> Shewing-up of Blanco Posnet* (1911)

16 Moral indignation is jealousy with a
halo.

> **H. G. Wells** 1866–1946: *The Wife of Sir Isaac
> Harman* (1914)

Mothers

see also **Parents**

1 I have reached the age when a woman
begins to perceive that she is growing
into the person she least plans to
resemble: her mother.

> **Anita Brookner** 1928– : *Incidents in the Rue
> Laugier* (1995)

2 Who needs a mother once the milk
has gone?

> **Esther Dyson** 1951– : remark aged 5, in
> *Independent* 11 January 1999

3 The mother's yearning, that
completest type of the life in another
life which is the essence of real human
love, feels the presence of the
cherished child even in the debased,
degraded man.

> **George Eliot** 1819–80: *Adam Bede* (1859)

4 If I were damned of body and soul,
I know whose prayers would make me
whole,
Mother o' mine, O mother o' mine.

> **Rudyard Kipling** 1865–1936: *The Light That
> Failed* (1891)

5 Here's to the happiest years of our
lives
Spent in the arms of other men's
wives.
Gentlemen!—Our mothers!

> ■ *proposing a toast*
> **Edwin Lutyens** 1869–1944: Clough Williams-
> Ellis *Architect Errant* (1971)

6 It is only in our advanced and
synthetic civilization that mothers no

longer sing to the babies they are
carrying.

Yehudi Menuhin 1916–99: in *Observer*
4 January 1987

7 It is not that I half knew my mother. I
knew half of her: the lower half—her
lap, legs, feet, her hands and wrists as
she bent forward.

Flann O'Brien 1911–66: *The Hard Life* (1961)

8 It is a dead-end job. You've no sooner
learned the skills than you are
redundant.

▪ *on motherhood*

Claire Rayner 1931– : in *Guardian*
15 December 1960

9 No matter how old a mother is she
watches her middle-aged children for
signs of improvement.

Florida Scott-Maxwell: *Measure of my Days*
(1968)

10 Motherhood is like sex and death: you
can't imagine it until you do it. It's a
completely overwhelming, all-else
obliterating passion for a little blob!

Juliet Stevenson 1956– : in *Independent on
Sunday* 9 May 1999

11 For the hand that rocks the cradle
Is the hand that rules the world.

William Ross Wallace d. 1881: 'What rules the
world' (1865)

12 In our society mothers take the place
elsewhere occupied by the Fates, the
System, Negroes, Communism or
Reactionary Imperialist Plots;
mothers go on getting blamed until
they're eighty, but shouldn't take it
personally.

Katharine Whitehorn 1928– : *Observations*
(1970)

Mountains

1 The Alps, the Rockies and all other
mountains are related to the earth, the
Himalayas to the heavens.

J. K. Galbraith 1908– : *A Life in our Times*
(1981)

2 Well, we knocked the bastard off!

▪ *on conquering Mount Everest, 1953*

Edmund Hillary 1919– : *Nothing Venture,
Nothing Win* (1975)

3 It is a fine thing to be out on the hills
alone. A man can hardly be a beast or
a fool alone on a great mountain.

Francis Kilvert 1840–79: diary 29 May 1871

4 Because it's there.

▪ *on being asked why he wanted to climb Mount
Everest*

George Leigh Mallory 1886–1924: in *New York
Times* 18 March 1923

5 To me the only way you achieve a
summit is to come back alive. The job
is half done if you don't get down
again.

▪ *son of George Mallory, who died on Everest*

John Mallory: in *Independent* 4 May 1999

6 My mountain did not seem to me a
lifeless thing of rock and ice, but
warm and friendly and living. She was
a mother hen, and the other
mountains were chicks under her
wings.

▪ *on Everest*

Tenzing Norgay 1914–86: *Man of Everest*
(1975)

Wolfgang Amadeus Mozart 1756–91

1 It may be that when the angels go
about their task of praising God, they
play only Bach. I am sure, however,
that when they are together *en famille*,
they play Mozart.

Karl Barth 1886–1968: *Wolfgang Amadeus
Mozart* (1956)

2 Too beautiful for our ears, and much
too many notes, dear Mozart.

▪ *of* The Abduction from the Seraglio (*1782*)

Joseph II 1741–90: attributed; Franz Xaver
Niemetschek *Life of Mozart* (1798)

3 Children are given Mozart because of
the small *quantity* of the notes;

grown-ups avoid Mozart because of the great *quality* of the notes.
Artur Schnabel 1882–1951: *My Life and Music* (1961)

Murder
....
see also **Death**

1 It might or might not be right to kill, but sometimes it is necessary.
Gerry Adams 1948– : view of the protagonist in a short story; *Before the Dawn* (1996)

2 Mordre wol out; that se we day by day.
Geoffrey Chaucer c.1343–1400: *The Canterbury Tales* 'The Nun's Priest's Tale'

3 Thou shalt not kill; but need'st not strive
Officiously to keep alive.
Arthur Hugh Clough 1819–61: 'The Latest Decalogue' (1862)

4 Murder considered as one of the fine arts.
Thomas De Quincey 1785–1859: in *Blackwood's Magazine* February 1827; essay title

5 Assassination has never changed the history of the world.
Benjamin Disraeli 1804–81: speech, House of Commons, 1 May 1865

6 Any man has to, needs to, wants to Once in a lifetime, do a girl in.
T. S. Eliot 1888–1965: *Sweeney Agonistes* (1932)

7 Television has brought back murder into the home—where it belongs.
Alfred Hitchcock 1899–1980: in *Observer* 19 December 1965

8 In that case, if we are to abolish the death penalty, let the murderers take the first step.
Alphonse Karr 1808–90: in *Les Guêpes* January 1849

9 Roast beef and Yorkshire, or roast pork and apple sauce, followed up by suet pudding and driven home, as it were, by a cup of mahogany-brown tea, have put you in just the right mood. Your pipe is drawing sweetly, the sofa cushions are soft underneath you, the fire is well alight, the air is warm and stagnant. In these blissful circumstances, what is it that you want to read about?
Naturally, about a murder.
George Orwell 1903–50: 'Decline of the English Murder' (written 1946)

10 Kill a man, and you are an assassin. Kill millions of men, and you are a conqueror. Kill everyone, and you are a god.
Jean Rostand 1894–1977: *Pensées d'un biologiste* (1939)

11 Murder most foul, as in the best it is;
But this most foul, strange, and unnatural.
William Shakespeare 1564–1616: *Hamlet* (1601)

12 I don't think a man who has watched the sun going down could walk away and commit a murder.
Laurens van der Post 1906–96: in *Daily Telegraph* 17 December 1996; obituary

Museums
....

1 An ace caff with quite a nice museum attached.
Advertising slogan: the Victoria and Albert Museum, February 1989

2 Despite running an institution saddled with the most disliked words in the English language—imperial, war and museum—if I can get people through the door, I can get them interested in the subject.
Alan Borg 1942– : in *Sunday Telegraph* 1 October 1995

3 Yes
You have come upon the fabled lands where myths
Go when they die.
James Fenton 1949– : 'The Pitt-Rivers Museum' (1983)

4 You've got to have two out of death, sex and jewels.
■ *the ingredients for a successful exhibition*
Roy Strong 1935– : in *Sunday Times* 23 January 1994

Music

see also **Jazz**, **Musical Instruments**, **Musicians**, **Opera**, **Rock and Pop Music**, **Singing**

1 Good music is that which penetrates the ear with facility and quits the memory with difficulty.
   Thomas Beecham 1879–1961: speech, c.1950; in *New York Times* 9 March 1961

2 Icelandic peoples were the ones who memorized sagas . . . We were the first rappers of Europe.
   Björk 1965– : attributed, January 1996

3 Music has charms to soothe a savage breast.
   William Congreve 1670–1729: *The Mourning Bride* (1697)

4 The whole problem can be stated quite simply by asking, 'Is there a meaning to music?' My answer to that would be, 'Yes.' And 'Can you state in so many words what the meaning is?' My answer to that would be, 'No.'
   Aaron Copland 1900–90: *What to Listen for in Music* (1939)

5 Extraordinary how potent cheap music is.
   Noël Coward 1899–1973: *Private Lives* (1930)

6 It is only that which cannot be expressed otherwise that is worth expressing in music.
   Frederick Delius 1862–1934: in *Sackbut* September 1920 'At the Crossroads'

7 There is music in the air.
   Edward Elgar 1857–1934: R. J. Buckley *Sir Edward Elgar* (1905)

8 If she can stand it, I can. Play it!
   ▪ *usually misquoted as 'Play it again, Sam'*
   Julius J. Epstein 1909–2001 et al.: *Casablanca* (1942 film); spoken by Humphrey Bogart

9 The hills are alive with the sound of music,
   With songs they have sung for a thousand years.
   The hills fill my heart with the sound of music,

My heart wants to sing ev'ry song it hears.
   Oscar Hammerstein II 1895–1960: 'The Sound of Music' (1959 song)

10 Classic music is th'kind that we keep thinkin'll turn into a tune.
   Frank McKinney ('Kin') Hubbard 1868–1930: *Comments of Abe Martin and His Neighbors* (1923)

11 A carpenter's hammer, in a warm summer noon, will fret me into more than midsummer madness. But those unconnected, unset sounds are nothing to the measured malice of music.
   Charles Lamb 1775–1834: *Elia* (1823)

12 The whole trouble with a folk song is that once you have played it through there is nothing much you can do except play it over again and play it rather louder.
   Constant Lambert 1905–51: *Music Ho!* (1934)

13 The symphony must be like the world. It must embrace everything.
   Gustav Mahler 1860–1911: remark to Sibelius, Helsinki, 1907

14 Music is spiritual. The music business is not.
   Van Morrison 1945– : in *The Times* 6 July 1990

15 Melody is the essence of music. I compare a good melodist to a fine racer, and counterpoints to hack post-horses.
   Wolfgang Amadeus Mozart 1756–91: remark to Michael Kelly, 1786; Michael Kelly *Reminiscences* (1826)

16 Music is your own experience, your thoughts, your wisdom. If you don't live it, it won't come out of your horn.
   Charlie Parker 1920–55: Nat Shapiro and Nat Hentoff *Hear Me Talkin' to Ya* (1955)

17 Music begins to atrophy when it departs too far from the dance . . . poetry begins to atrophy when it gets too far from music.
   Ezra Pound 1885–1972: *The ABC of Reading* (1934)

18 I am delighted to add another unplayable work to the repertoire. I

want the Concerto to be difficult and I
want the little finger to become
longer. I can wait.

■ *of his Violin Concerto*
Arnold Schoenberg 1874–1951: Joseph Machlis
Introduction to Contemporary Music (1963)

19 If music be the food of love, play on.
William Shakespeare 1564–1616: *Twelfth Night*
(1601)

20 Hell is full of musical amateurs: music
is the brandy of the damned.
George Bernard Shaw 1856–1950: *Man and
Superman* (1903)

21 Improvisation is too good to leave to
chance.
Paul Simon 1942– : in *Observer* 30 December
1990

22 I don't know whether I like it, but it's
what I meant.

■ *on his 4th symphony*
Ralph Vaughan Williams 1872–1958:
Christopher Headington *Bodley Head
History of Western Music* (1974)

23 You just pick a chord, go twang, and
you've got music.
Sid Vicious 1957–79: attributed

24 All my life I was having trouble with
women . . . Then, after I quit having
trouble with them, I could feel in my
heart that somebody would always
have trouble with them, so I kept
writing those blues.
Muddy Waters 1915–83: Tony Palmer *All You
Need is Love* (1976)

Musical Instruments

1 There is nothing to it. You only have
to hit the right notes at the right time
and the instrument plays itself.

■ *the organ*
Johann Sebastian Bach 1685–1750: K.
Geiringer *The Bach Family* (1954)

2 Like two skeletons copulating on a
corrugated tin roof.

■ *the harpsichord*
Thomas Beecham 1879–1961: Harold Atkins
and Archie Newman *Beecham Stories* (1978)

3 It is like a beautiful woman who has
not grown older, but younger with

time, more slender, more supple,
more graceful.

■ *the cello*
Pablo Casals 1876–1973: in *Time* 29 April 1957

4 The tuba is certainly the most
intestinal of instruments—the very
lower bowel of music.
Peter De Vries 1910–93: *The Glory of the
Hummingbird* (1974)

5 The piano is the easiest instrument to
play in the beginning, and the hardest
to master in the end.
Vladimir Horowitz 1904–89: David Dubal
Evenings with Horowitz (1992)

6 Is it not strange, that sheeps' guts
should hale souls out of men's bodies?
William Shakespeare 1564–1616: *Much Ado
About Nothing* (1598–9)

Musicians

see also **Bach, Beethoven, Mozart, Music,
Rock and Pop Music**

1 Please do not shoot the pianist. He is
doing his best.

■ *printed notice in a dancing saloon*
Anonymous: Oscar Wilde *Impressions of
America* 'Leadville' (*c*.1882–3)

2 There are two golden rules for an
orchestra: start together and finish
together. The public doesn't give a
damn what goes on in between.
Thomas Beecham 1879–1961: Harold Atkins
and Archie Newman *Beecham Stories* (1978)

3 The good thing about them is that
you can look at them with the sound
turned down.

■ *of the Spice Girls*
George Harrison 1943–2001: in *Independent*
28 August 1997

4 A musician, if he's a messenger, is like
a child who hasn't been handled too
many times by man, hasn't had too
many fingerprints across his brain.
Jimi Hendrix 1942–70: in *Life Magazine* (1969)

5 If I play Tchaikovsky I play his
melodies and skip his spiritual
struggles . . . If there's any time left

over I fill in with a lot of runs up and
down the keyboard.
Liberace 1919–87: Stuart Hall and Paddy
Whannel (eds.) *The Popular Arts* (1964)

6 Down the road someone is practising
scales,
The notes like little fishes vanish with
a wink of tails,
Louis MacNeice 1907–63: 'Sunday Morning'
(1935)

7 Ballads and babies. That's what
happened to me.
■ *on reaching the age of fifty*
Paul McCartney 1942– : in *Time* 8 June 1992

8 Something touched me deep inside
The day the music died.
■ *on the death of Buddy Holly*
Don McLean 1945– : 'American Pie' (1972
song)

9 We are the music makers,
We are the dreamers of dreams . . .
We are the movers and shakers
Of the world for ever, it seems.
Arthur O'Shaughnessy 1844–81: 'Ode' (1874)

10 If anyone has conducted a Beethoven
performance, and then doesn't have
to go to an osteopath, then there's
something wrong.
Simon Rattle 1955– : in *Guardian* 31 May
1990

11 Wagner has lovely moments but awful
quarters of an hour.
Gioacchino Rossini 1792–1868: said to Emile
Naumann, April 1867; E. Naumann
Italienische Tondichter (1883)

12 Ravel refuses the Legion of Honour,
but all his music accepts it.
Erik Satie 1866–1925: Jean Cocteau *Le
Discours d'Oxford* (1956)

13 The notes I handle no better than
many pianists. But the pauses
between the notes—ah, that is where
the art resides!
Artur Schnabel 1882–1951: in *Chicago Daily
News* 11 June 1958

14 As for the slow movement, I thought
it would never end. It was like being in
such a slow train with so many stops

that one becomes convinced that one
has passed one's station.
■ *on the performance of a Bruckner symphony*
Sylvia Townsend Warner 1893–1978: diary
20 November 1929

Names

1 I have fallen in love with American
names,
The sharp, gaunt names that never get
fat,
The snakeskin-titles of mining-
claims,
The plumed war-bonnet of Medicine
Hat,
Tucson and Deadwood and Lost Mule
Flat.
Stephen Vincent Benét 1898–1943: 'American
Names' (1927)

2 Remember, they only name things
after you when you're dead or really
old.
■ *at the naming ceremony for the George Bush
Centre for Intelligence*
Barbara Bush 1925– : in *Independent* 28 April
1999

3 With a name like yours, you might be
any shape, almost.
Lewis Carroll 1832–98: *Through the Looking-
Glass* (1872)

4 Dear 338171 (May I call you 338?).
Noël Coward 1899–1973: letter to T. E.
Lawrence, 25 August 1930

5 Every Tom, Dick and Harry is called
Arthur.
■ *to Arthur Hornblow, who was planning to
name his son Arthur*
Sam Goldwyn 1882–1974: Michael Freedland
The Goldwyn Touch (1986)

6 A self-made man may prefer a self-
made name.
■ *on Samuel Goldfish changing his name to
Samuel Goldwyn*
Learned Hand 1872–1961: Bosley Crowther
Lion's Share (1957)

7 A nickname is the heaviest stone that
the devil can throw at a man.
William Hazlitt 1778–1830: *Sketches and Essays*
(1839) 'Nicknames'

8 The names of a land show the heart of
   the race;
   They move on the tongue like the lilt
   of a song.
   You say the name and I see the
   place—
   Drumbo, Dungannon, or Annalong.
   Barony, townland, we cannot go
   wrong.
   John Hewitt 1907–87: 'Ulster Names'

9 If you should have a boy do not
   christen him John . . . 'Tis a bad name
   and goes against a man. If my name
   had been Edmund I should have been
   more fortunate.
   John Keats 1795–1821: letter to his sister-in-
   law, 13 January 1820

10 No, I'm breaking it in for a friend.
   ■ *when asked if Groucho were his real name*
   Groucho Marx 1895–1977: attributed

11 The name of a man is a numbing blow
   from which he never recovers.
   Marshall McLuhan 1911–80: *Understanding
   Media* (1964)

12 Just as crystallization of surnames was
   one of the steps in human civilization,
   their relinquishment gradually
   increases as we revert to savagery.
   Anthony Powell 1905–2000: *Fisher King*
   (1986)

13 There may have been disillusionments
   in the lives of the medieval saints, but
   they would scarcely have been better
   pleased if they could have forseen that
   their names would be associated
   nowadays chiefly with racehorses and
   the cheaper clarets.
   Saki 1870–1916: *Reginald* (1904)

14 What's in a name? that which we call a
   rose
   By any other name would smell as
   sweet.
   William Shakespeare 1564–1616: *Romeo and
   Juliet* (1595)

15 We do have these extraordinary
   names . . . When you see the sign
   'African Primates Meeting' you expect
   someone to produce bananas.
   Desmond Tutu 1931– : at his retirement
   service as Archbishop of Cape Town, 23 June
   1996

Nationality

see also **Patriotism**

1 INTERVIEWER: You are English, Mr
   Beckett?
   BECKETT: *Au contraire.*
   Samuel Beckett 1906–89: attributed

2 Some people . . . may be Rooshans,
   and others may be Prooshans; they
   are born so, and will please
   themselves. Them which is of other
   naturs thinks different.
   Charles Dickens 1812–70: *Martin Chuzzlewit*
   (1844)

3 The more transnational the world
   becomes, the more tribal it will
   therefore also be. This increasingly
   undermines the very foundations of
   the nation state.
   Peter F. Drucker 1909– : *Post-Capitalist
   Society* (1993)

4 Why is politics making us unhappy,
   separating us, when we ourselves
   know who is good and who isn't? We
   mix with the good, not with the bad.
   And among the good there are Serbs
   and Croats and Muslims, just as there
   are among the bad. I simply don't
   understand it.
   Zlata Filipovic 1980– : *Zlata's Diary: A
   Child's Life in Sarajevo* (1993) 19 November
   1992

5 I may be uninspiring, but I'll be
   damned if I'm an alien!
   ■ *on H. G. Wells's comment on 'an alien and
   uninspiring court'*
   George V 1865–1936: Sarah Bradford *George
   VI* (1989); attributed, perhaps apocryphal

6 A country is a piece of land
   surrounded on all sides by
   boundaries, usually unnatural.
   Joseph Heller 1923–99: *Catch-22* (1961)

7 Grab this land! Take it, hold it, my
   brothers, make it, my brothers, shake
   it, squeeze it, turn it, twist it, beat it,
   kick it, whip it, stomp it, dig it, plough
   it, seed it, reap it, rent it, buy it, sell it,
   own it, build it, multiply it, and pass it
   on—Can you hear me? Pass it on!
   Toni Morrison 1931– : *Song of Solomon* 1977

8 By blood and origin I am Albanian.
My citizenship is Indian. I am a
Catholic nun. As to my calling, I
belong to the whole world. As to my
heart, I belong entirely to the heart of
Jesus.
Mother Teresa 1910–97: in *Independent*
6 September 1997; obituary

9 Because a man is born in a stable, that
does not make him a horse.
■ *rejecting the view that his Irish birthplace
determined his nationality*
Duke of Wellington 1769–1852: attributed

Nature

see also **The Earth**, **Life Sciences**

1 Nature, Mr Allnutt, is what we are put
into this world to rise above.
James Agee 1909–55: *The African Queen*
(1951 film); not in the novel by C. S. Forester

2 What a book a devil's chaplain might
write on the clumsy, wasteful,
blundering, low, and horridly cruel
works of nature!
Charles Darwin 1809–82: letter to J. D.
Hooker, 13 July 1856

3 People thought they could explain
and conquer nature—yet the outcome
is that they destroyed it and
disinherited themselves from it.
Václav Havel 1936– : Lewis Wolpert *The
Unnatural Nature of Science* (1993)

4 For nature, heartless, witless nature,
Will neither care nor know
What stranger's feet may find the
meadow
And trespass there and go.
A. E. Housman 1859–1936: *Last Poems* (1922)
no. 40

5 Christianity deposes Mother Nature
and begets, on her prostrate body,
Science, which proceeds to destroy
Nature.
Ted Hughes 1930–98: in *Your Environment*
Summer 1970

6 In nature there are neither rewards
nor punishments—there are
consequences.
Robert G. Ingersoll 1833–99: *Some Reasons
Why* (1881)

7 'I play for Seasons; not Eternities!'
Says Nature.
George Meredith 1828–1909: *Modern Love*
(1862)

8 Pile the bodies high at Austerlitz and
Waterloo.
Shovel them under and let me work—
I am the grass; I cover all.
Carl Sandburg 1878–1967: 'Grass' (1918)

9 And this our life, exempt from public
haunt,
Finds tongues in trees, books in the
running brooks,
Sermons in stones, and good in
everything.
William Shakespeare 1564–1616: *As You Like It*
(1599)

10 Who trusted God was love indeed
And love Creation's final law—
Though Nature, red in tooth and claw
With ravine, shrieked against his
creed.
Alfred, Lord Tennyson 1809–92: *In Memoriam
A. H. H.* (1850)

11 Nature is not a temple, but a
workshop, and man's the workman in
it.
Ivan Turgenev 1818–83: *Fathers and Sons*
(1862)

12 I believe a leaf of grass is no less than
the journey-work of the stars,
And the pismire is equally perfect,
and a grain of sand, and the egg of
the wren,
And the tree toad is a chef-d'oeuvre
for the highest,
And the running blackberry would
adorn the parlours of heaven.
Walt Whitman 1819–92: 'Song of Myself'
(written 1855)

13 BRICK: Well, they say nature hates a
vacuum, Big Daddy.
BIG DADDY: That's what they say, but
sometimes I think that a vacuum is a
hell of a lot better than some of the
stuff that nature replaces it with.
Tennessee Williams 1911–83: *Cat on a Hot Tin
Roof* (1955)

14 One impulse from a vernal wood
May teach you more of man,
Of moral evil and of good,

Than all the sages can.
William Wordsworth 1770–1850: 'The Tables Turned' (1798)

The Navy

1 A willing foe and sea room.
Anonymous: naval toast in the time of Nelson; W. N. T. Beckett *A Few Naval Customs, Expressions, Traditions, and Superstitions* (1931)

2 My only great qualification for being put at the head of the Navy is that I am very much at sea.
Edward Carson 1854–1935: Ian Colvin *Life of Lord Carson* (1936)

3 It is upon the navy under the good Providence of God that the safety, honour, and welfare of this realm do chiefly depend.
Charles II 1630–85: 'Articles of War' preamble; Sir Geoffrey Callender *The Naval Side of British History* (1952); probably a modern paraphrase

4 Naval tradition? Monstrous. Nothing but rum, sodomy, prayers, and the lash.
■ *often quoted as, 'rum, sodomy, and the lash'*
Winston Churchill 1874–1965: Harold Nicolson, diary 17 August 1950

5 Heart of oak are our ships,
Heart of oak are our men:
We always are ready;
Steady, boys, steady;
We'll fight and we'll conquer again and again.
David Garrick 1717–79: 'Heart of Oak' (1759 song)

6 The navy has got to go increasingly under the sea: a very good place for the Silent Service.
Lord Montgomery 1887–1976: in *Observer* 18 December 1966

7 Don't cheer, men; those poor devils are dying.
John Woodward ('Jack') Philip 1840–1900: at the battle of Santiago, 4 July 1898

8 Without a decisive naval force we can do nothing definitive. And with it, everything honorable and glorious.
George Washington 1732–99: to Lafayette, 15 November 1781

Necessity

see also **Fate**

1 Must! Is *must* a word to be addressed to princes? Little man, little man! thy father, if he had been alive, durst not have used that word.
■ *to Robert Cecil, on his saying she must go to bed*
Elizabeth I 1533–1603: J. R. Green *A Short History of the English People* (1874)

2 Nothing have I found stronger than Necessity.
Euripides c.485–c.406 BC: *Alcestis* l. 965

3 A desperate disease requires a dangerous remedy.
Guy Fawkes 1570–1606: remark, 6 November 1605

4 Necessity never made a good bargain.
Benjamin Franklin 1706–90: *Poor Richard's Almanac* (1735)

5 What throws a monkey wrench in
A fella's good intention?
That nasty old invention—
Necessity!
E. Y. Harburg 1898–1981: 'Necessity' (1947)

6 Necessity has the face of a dog.
Gabriel García Márquez 1928– : *In Evil Hour* (1968)

7 Necessity is the plea for every infringement of human freedom: it is the argument of tyrants; it is the creed of slaves.
William Pitt 1759–1806: speech, House of Commons, 18 November 1783

8 The superfluous, a very necessary thing.
Voltaire 1694–1778: *Le Mondain* (1736)

Neighbours

1 For what do we live, but to make sport for our neighbours, and laugh at them in our turn?
Jane Austen 1775–1817: *Pride and Prejudice* (1813)

2 We make our friends, we make our enemies; but God makes our next-door neighbour.

G. K. Chesterton 1874–1936: *Heretics* (1905)

3 Your next-door neighbour . . . is not a man; he is an environment. He is the barking of a dog; he is the noise of a pianola; he is a dispute about a party wall; he is drains that are worse than yours, or roses that are better than yours.

G. K. Chesterton 1874–1936: *The Uses of Diversity* (1920)

4 If you would be known, and not know, vegetate in a village; if you would know, and not be known, live in a city.

Charles Caleb Colton *c*.1780–1832: *Lacon* (1820)

5 My apple trees will never get across And eat the cones under his pines, I tell him.
He only says, 'Good fences make good neighbours.'

Robert Frost 1874–1963: 'Mending Wall' (1914)

6 Whose woods are whose everybody knows exactly, and everybody knows who got them rezoned for a shopping mall and who couldn't get the financing to begin construction and why it was he couldn't get it.

■ *on a traditional New England community*
P. J. O'Rourke 1947– : *Parliament of Whores* (1991); see **Snow 2**

News

see also **Journalism**, **Newspapers**

1 How beautiful upon the mountains are the feet of him that bringeth good tidings.

Bible: Isaiah

2 When a dog bites a man, that is not news, because it happens so often. But if a man bites a dog, that is news.

John B. Bogart 1848–1921: F. M. O'Brien *The Story of the* [New York] *Sun* (1918); often attributed to Charles A. Dana

3 What news on the Rialto?

William Shakespeare 1564–1616: *The Merchant of Venice* (1596–8)

4 You might get bigger audiences for 'Noble Rover, the labrador, who saved beautiful baby in fire', but that ain't news—just an insidious form of patronising propaganda.

■ *on the desirability of promoting 'good news' stories*
John Simpson 1944– : interview in *Radio Times* 9 August 1997

5 News is what a chap who doesn't care much about anything wants to read. And it's only news until he's read it. After that it's dead.

Evelyn Waugh 1903–66: *Scoop* (1938)

Newspapers

see also **Journalism**, **News**, **Press Photographers**

1 The purchaser [of a newspaper] desires an article which he can appreciate at sight; which he can lay down and say, 'An excellent article, very excellent; exactly *my own* sentiments.'

Walter Bagehot 1826–77: in *National Review* July 1856

2 *The Times* has made many ministries.

Walter Bagehot 1826–77: *The English Constitution* (1867)

3 I ran the paper purely for propaganda, and with no other purpose.

■ *of the* Daily Express
Lord Beaverbrook 1879–1964: evidence to Royal Commission on the Press, 18 March 1948

4 If I rescued a child from drowning, the Press would no doubt headline the story 'Benn grabs child.'

Tony Benn 1925– : in *Observer* 2 March 1975

5 I read the newspapers avidly. It is my one form of continuous fiction.

Aneurin Bevan 1897–1960: in *The Times* 29 March 1960

6 Reading someone else's newspaper is like sleeping with someone else's wife.

Nothing seems to be precisely in the right place, and when you find what you are looking for, it is not clear then how to respond to it.

Malcolm Bradbury 1932–2000: *Stepping Westward* (1975)

7 Small earthquake in Chile. Not many dead.

■ *the words with which Cockburn claimed to have won a competition at* The Times *for the dullest headline*

Claud Cockburn 1904–81: *In Time of Trouble* (1956)

8 It's like opening a piece of used lavatory paper, reading newspapers.

Stephen Fry 1957– : in *Independent on Sunday* 26 February 1995

9 Let us today drudge on about our inescapably impossible task of providing every week a first rough draft of a history that will never be completed about a world we can never really understand.

Philip Graham 1915–63: remarks to *Newsweek* correspondents, London, 29 April 1963

10 What sells a newspaper? is a question often asked me. The first answer is 'war' . . . a paper has only to be able to put on its placard 'A Great Battle' for its sales to mount up.

Kennedy Jones: *Fleet Street and Downing Street* (1920)

11 Whenever I see a newspaper I think of the poor trees. As trees they provide beauty, shade and shelter. But as paper all they provide is rubbish.

Yehudi Menuhin 1916–99: attributed, 1982

12 A good newspaper, I suppose, is a nation talking to itself.

Arthur Miller 1915– : in *Observer* 26 November 1961

13 Exclusives aren't what they used to be. We tend to put 'exclusive' on everything just to annoy other papers. I once put 'exclusive' on the weather by mistake.

Piers Morgan 1965– : in *Independent on Sunday* 14 March 1999

14 I don't know. The editor did it when I was away.

■ *when asked why he had allowed Page 3 of the* Sun *to develop*

Rupert Murdoch 1931– : in *Guardian* 25 February 1994

15 The power of the press is very great, but not so great as the power of suppress.

Lord Northcliffe 1865–1922: office message, *Daily Mail* 1918; Reginald Rose and Geoffrey Harmsworth *Northcliffe* (1959)

16 Well, all I know is what I read in the papers.

Will Rogers 1879–1935: in *New York Times* 30 September 1923

17 Freedom of the press in Britain means freedom to print such of the proprietor's prejudices as the advertisers don't object to.

Hannen Swaffer 1879–1962: Tom Driberg *Swaff* (1974)

Night

see also **Day**, **Evening**

1 Lighten our darkness, we beseech thee, O Lord; and by thy great mercy defend us from all perils and dangers of this night.

The Book of Common Prayer 1662: *Evening Prayer*

2 The Sun's rim dips; the stars rush out; At one stride comes the dark.

Samuel Taylor Coleridge 1772–1834: 'The Rime of the Ancient Mariner' (1798)

3 The cares that infest the day Shall fold their tents, like the Arabs, And as silently steal away.

Henry Wadsworth Longfellow 1807–82: 'The Day is Done' (1844)

4 'Tis now the very witching time of night, When churchyards yawn and hell itself breathes out Contagion to this world.

William Shakespeare 1564–1616: *Hamlet* (1601)

5 To begin at the beginning: It is spring,
moonless night in the small town,
starless and bible-black.
  Dylan Thomas 1914–53: *Under Milk Wood*
  (1954)

Northern Ireland

see also **Ireland**

1 Ulster is Scotland in Ireland.
  Gustave de Beaumont 1802–66: *L'Irlande
  sociale, politique et religieuse* (1839)

2 The great thing I have discovered
about Orangemen is that they have
feelings.
  Brendan Behan 1923–64: attributed

3 The whole map of Europe has been
changed . . . but as the deluge subsides
and the waters fall short we see the
dreary steeples of Fermanagh and
Tyrone emerging once again.
  Winston Churchill 1874–1965: speech, House
  of Commons, 16 February 1922

4 Ulster will fight; Ulster will be right.
  Lord Randolph Churchill 1849–94: public
  letter, 7 May 1886

5 People don't march as an alternative
to jogging. They do it to assert their
supremacy. It is pure tribalism, the
cause of troubles all over the world.
  Gerry Fitt 1926– : in *The Times* 5 August 1994

6 My heart besieged by anger, my mind
  a gap of danger,
I walked among their old haunts, the
  home ground where they bled;
And in the dirt lay justice like an
  acorn in the winter
Till its oak would sprout in Derry
  where the thirteen men lay dead.
  ■ *of Bloody Sunday, Londonderry, 30 January
  1972*
  Seamus Heaney 1939– : 'The Road to Derry'

7   The famous
Northern reticence, the tight gag of
  place
And times: yes, yes. Of the 'wee six' I
  sing.
  Seamus Heaney 1939– : 'Whatever You Say
  Say Nothing' (1975)

8 A disease in the family that is never
mentioned.
  ■ *of the troubles in Northern Ireland*
  William Trevor 1928– : in *Observer*
  18 November 1990

Old Age

see also **Ageing, Middle Age**

1 If you want to be adored by your peers
and have standing ovations wherever
you go—live to be over ninety.
  George Abbott 1887–1995: in *The Times*
  2 February 1995; obituary

2 To me old age is always fifteen years
older than I am.
  Bernard Baruch 1870–1965: in *Newsweek*
  29 August 1955

3 If I'd known I was gonna live this
long, I'd have taken better care of
myself.
  ■ *on reaching the age of 100*
  Eubie Blake 1883–1983: in *Observer*
  13 February 1983

4 What is called the serenity of age is
only perhaps a euphemism for the
fading power to feel the sudden shock
of joy or sorrow.
  Arthur Bliss 1891–1975: *As I Remember* (1970)

5 Although I am 92, my brain is 30 years
old.
  Alfred Eisenstaedt 1898–1995: to a reporter in
  1991; in *Life* 24 August 1995

6 There's a fascination frantic
In a ruin that's romantic;
Do you think you are sufficiently
decayed?
  W. S. Gilbert 1836–1911: *The Mikado* (1885)

7 Age does not make us childish, as men
tell,
It merely finds us children still at
heart.
  Johann Wolfgang von Goethe 1749–1832: *Faust*
  pt. 1 (1808)

8 How happy he who crowns in shades
like these,
A youth of labour with an age of ease.
  Oliver Goldsmith 1728–74: *The Deserted
  Village* (1770)

9 The First Age of 'formation' should be a time to grow an identity before the consuming busyness. Properly balanced, the Second Age is the time of one's major contribution, to work or home or community. The Third Age is the opportunity to be someone different, if we want to be.

Charles Handy 1932– : *The Empty Raincoat* (1994)

10 It is better to be seventy years young than forty years old!

Oliver Wendell Holmes 1809–94: reply to invitation from Julia Ward Howe to her seventieth birthday party, 27 May 1889

11 When I am an old woman I shall wear purple
With a red hat which doesn't go, and doesn't suit me.
And I shall spend my pension on brandy and summer gloves
And satin sandals, and say we've got no money for butter.

Jenny Joseph 1932– : 'Warning' (1974)

12 Will you still need me, will you still feed me,
When I'm sixty four?

John Lennon 1940–80 and **Paul McCartney** 1942– : 'When I'm Sixty Four' (1967 song)

13 Old people have one advantage compared with young ones. They have been young themselves, and young people haven't been old.

Lord Longford 1905–2001: attributed; in *Independent* 6 March 1999

14 From the earliest times the old have rubbed it into the young that they are wiser than they, and before the young had discovered what nonsense this was they were old too, and it profited them to carry on the imposture.

W. Somerset Maugham 1874–1965: *Cakes and Ale* (1930)

15 I woke up this morning and I was still alive, so I am pretty cheerful.

■ *on being 79*

Spike Milligan 1918–2002: in *Irish Times* 8 November 1997

16 I saw how hard it is for our own society ever to become wise while old people are ostracized.

George Monbiot: *No Man's Land* (1994)

17 One of the worst things about being old is eating. First you have to find something you can eat and second you have to try not to drop it all over yourself.

Toni Morrison 1931– : *Tar Baby* (1981)

18   Last scene of all,
That ends this strange eventful history,
Is second childishness, and mere oblivion,
Sans teeth, sans eyes, sans taste, sans everything.

William Shakespeare 1564–1616: *As You Like It* (1599)

19 The nineties is a good time to die.

Stephen Spender 1909–95: Joseph Brodsky *On Grief and Reason* (1996)

20 Old age is the most unexpected of all things that happen to a man.

Leon Trotsky 1879–1940: diary 8 May 1935

21 It is pleasanter to help the young than the old. The young need crutches for a time, and then throw them away . . . Give the old crutches, and they use them for ever, complaining of their poor quality the while.

Fay Weldon 1931– : *Praxis* (1978)

22 Those that desire to write or say anything to me have no time to lose; for time has shaken me by the hand and death is not far behind.

John Wesley 1703–91: letter to Ezekiel Cooper, 1 February 1791

23 When you are old and grey and full of sleep,
And nodding by the fire, take down this book,
And slowly read, and dream of the soft look
Your eyes had once, and of their shadows deep.

W. B. Yeats 1865–1939: 'When You Are Old' (1893)

24 An aged man is but a paltry thing,
A tattered coat upon a stick, unless

Soul clap its hands and sing, and
  louder sing
For every tatter in its mortal dress.
  W. B. Yeats 1865–1939: 'Sailing to Byzantium'
  (1928)

Opera
....

see also **Culture**, **Music**, **Singing**

1 No opera plot can be sensible, for in
  sensible situations people do not sing.
  An opera plot must be, in both senses
  of the word, a melodrama.
  W. H. Auden 1907–73: in *Times Literary
  Supplement* 2 November 1967

2 People are wrong when they say that
  the opera isn't what it used to be. It is
  what it used to be—that's what's
  wrong with it.
  Noël Coward 1899–1973: *Design for Living*
  (1933)

3 Opera is when a guy gets stabbed in
  the back and, instead of bleeding, he
  sings.
  Ed Gardner 1901–63: in *Duffy's Tavern* (US
  radio programme, 1940s)

4 We mustn't downgrade the opera
  house. I don't want to sit next to
  somebody in a singlet, a pair of shorts
  and a smelly pair of trainers.
  Colin Southgate 1938– : in *Guardian*
  6 February 1998

5 An unalterable and unquestioned law
  of the musical world required that the
  German text of French operas sung by
  Swedish artists should be translated
  into Italian for the clearer
  understanding of English-speaking
  audiences.
  Edith Wharton 1862–1937: *The Age of
  Innocence* (1920)

Opinion
....

see also **Argument**

1 Why should you mind being wrong if
  someone can show you that you are?
  A. J. Ayer 1910–89: attributed

2 The public buys its opinions as it buys
  its meat, or takes in its milk, on the
  principle that it is cheaper to do this
  than to keep a cow. So it is, but the
  milk is more likely to be watered.
  Samuel Butler 1835–1902: *Notebooks* (1912)

3 He that complies against his will,
  Is of his own opinion still.
  Samuel Butler 1612–80: *Hudibras* pt. 3 (1680)

4 You might very well think that. I
  couldn't possibly comment.
  ■ *the Chief Whip's habitual response to
  questioning*
  Michael Dobbs 1948– : *House of Cards*
  (televised 1990)

5 Every man has a right to utter what he
  thinks truth, and every other man has
  a right to knock him down for it.
  Martyrdom is the test.
  Samuel Johnson 1709–84: James Boswell *Life
  of Samuel Johnson* (1791) 1780

6 There are nine and sixty ways of
    constructing tribal lays,
  And—every—single—one—of—
    them—is—right!
  Rudyard Kipling 1865–1936: 'In the Neolithic
  Age' (1893)

7 Thank God, in these days of
  enlightenment and establishment,
  everyone has a right to his own
  opinions, and chiefly to the opinion
  that nobody else has a right to theirs.
  Ronald Knox 1888–1957: *Reunion All Round*
  (1914)

8 If all mankind minus one were of one
  opinion, and only one person were of
  the contrary opinion, mankind would
  be no more justified in silencing that
  one person, than he, if he had the
  power, would be justified in silencing
  mankind.
  John Stuart Mill 1806–73: *On Liberty* (1859)

9 Opinion in good men is but
  knowledge in the making.
  John Milton 1608–74: *Areopagitica* (1644)

10 Some praise at morning what they
     blame at night;
   But always think the last opinion
   right.
   Alexander Pope 1688–1744: *An Essay on
   Criticism* (1711)

11 The opinions that are held with passion are always those for which no good ground exists; indeed the passion is the measure of the holder's lack of rational conviction.
Bertrand Russell 1872–1970: *Sceptical Essays* (1928)

12 A man can brave opinion, a woman must submit to it.
Mme de Staël 1766–1817: *Delphine* (1802)

13 INTERVIEWER: I hear you have strong political views.
TAYLOR: No. Extreme views, weakly held.
A. J. P. Taylor 1906–90: letter to Eva Haraszti Taylor, 16 July 1970

14 It were not best that we should all think alike; it is difference of opinion that makes horse-races.
Mark Twain 1835–1910: *Pudd'nhead Wilson* (1894)

15 An intellectual hatred is the worst, So let her think opinions are accursed.
W. B. Yeats 1865–1939: 'A Prayer for My Daughter' (1920)

Opportunity

1 Never the time and the place And the loved one all together!
Robert Browning 1812–89: 'Never the Time and the Place' (1883)

2 We must beat the iron while it is hot, but we may polish it at leisure.
John Dryden 1631–1700: *Aeneis* (1697)

3 She's got a ticket to ride, but she don't care.
John Lennon 1940–80 and **Paul McCartney** 1942– : 'Ticket to Ride' (1965 song)

4 *La carrière ouverte aux talents.*
The career open to the talents.
Napoleon I 1769–1821: Barry E. O'Meara *Napoleon in Exile* (1822)

5 If only I could get down to Sidcup! I've been waiting for the weather to break. He's got my papers, this man I left them with, it's got it all down there, I could prove everything.
Harold Pinter 1930– : *The Caretaker* (1960)

6 I could have had class. I could have been a contender.
Budd Schulberg 1914– : *On the Waterfront* (1954 film); spoken by Marlon Brando

7 There is a tide in the affairs of men, Which, taken at the flood, leads on to fortune;
Omitted, all the voyage of their life Is bound in shallows and in miseries.
William Shakespeare 1564–1616: *Julius Caesar* (1599)

Optimism

see also **Hope**, **Pessimism**

1 The lark's on the wing; The snail's on the thorn: God's in his heaven— All's right with the world!
Robert Browning 1812–89: *Pippa Passes* (1841)

2 Every time it rains, it rains Pennies from heaven. Don't you know each cloud contains Pennies from heaven?
Johnny Burke 1908–64: 'Pennies from Heaven' (1936 song)

3 I have known him come home to supper with a flood of tears, and a declaration that nothing was now left but a jail; and go to bed making a calculation of the expense of putting bow-windows to the house, 'in case anything turned up,' which was his favourite expression.
■ *of Mr Micawber*
Charles Dickens 1812–70: *David Copperfield* (1850)

4 Grab your coat, and get your hat, Leave your worry on the doorstep, Just direct your feet To the sunny side of the street.
Dorothy Fields 1905–74: 'On the Sunny Side of the Street' (1930 song)

5 Cheer up! the worst is yet to come!
Philander Chase Johnson 1866–1939: in *Everybody's Magazine* May 1920

6 but wotthehell archy wotthehell jamais triste archy jamais triste that is my motto.
Don Marquis 1878–1937: *archy and mehitabel* (1927)

7 You've got to ac-cent-tchu-ate the
positive
Elim-my-nate the negative
Latch on to the affirmative
Don't mess with Mister In-between.
Johnny Mercer 1909–76: 'Ac-cent-tchu-ate
the Positive' (1944 song)

8 Everything's coming up roses.
Stephen Sondheim 1930– : title of song
(1959)

9 In this best of possible worlds . . . all is
for the best.
■ *usually quoted as 'All is for the best in the best
of all possible worlds'*
Voltaire 1694–1778: *Candide* (1759)

Organization

1 A place for everything and everything
in its place.
Mrs Beeton 1836–65: *The Book of Household
Management* (1861); often attributed to
Samuel Smiles

2 This island is made mainly of coal and
surrounded by fish. Only an
organizing genius could produce a
shortage of coal and fish at the same
time.
Aneurin Bevan 1897–1960: speech at
Blackpool 24 May 1945

3 Oh, the Germans classify, but the
French arrange!
Willa Cather 1873–1947: *Death Comes For the
Archbishop* (1927))

4 First things first, second things never.
Shirley Conran 1932– : *Superwoman* (1975)

5 In preparing for battle I have always
found that plans are useless, but
planning is indispensable.
Dwight D. Eisenhower 1890–1969: Richard
Nixon *Six Crises* (1962); attributed

6 All organization is and must be
grounded on the idea of exclusion and
prohibition just as two objects cannot
occupy the same space.
Arthur Miller 1915– : *The Crucible* (1953)

7 The shortest way to do many things is
to do only one thing at once.
Samuel Smiles 1812–1904: *Self-Help* (1859)

Originality

see also **Plagiarism**

1 The truth is that the propensity of
man to imitate what is before him is
one of the strongest parts of his
nature.
Walter Bagehot 1826–77: *Physics and Politics*
(1872)

2 It is sometimes necessary to repeat
what we all know. All mapmakers
should place the Mississippi in the
same location, and avoid originality.
Saul Bellow 1915– : *Mr Sammler's Planet*
(1969)

3 The original writer is not he who
refrains from imitating others, but he
who can be imitated by none.
François-René Chateaubriand 1768–1848: *Le
Génie du Christianisme* (1802)

4 Every public action, which is not
customary, either is wrong, or, if it is
right, is a dangerous precedent. It
follows that nothing should ever be
done for the first time.
Francis M. Cornford 1874–1943:
Microcosmographia Academica (1908)

5 Let's have some new clichés.
Sam Goldwyn 1882–1974: attributed, perhaps
apocryphal

6 When people are free to do as they
please, they usually imitate each other.
Originality is deliberate and forced,
and partakes of the nature of a
protest.
Eric Hoffer 1902–83: *Passionate State of Mind*
(1955)

7 Nothing has yet been said that's not
been said before.
Terence *c.*190–159 BC: *Eunuchus*

8 What a good thing Adam had. When
he said a good thing he knew nobody
had said it before.
Mark Twain 1835–1910: *Notebooks* (1935)

9 Never forget what I believe was
observed to you by Coleridge, that
every great and original writer, in
proportion as he is great and original,

must himself create the taste by which he is to be relished.
William Wordsworth 1770–1850: letter to Lady Beaumont, 21 May 1807

Oxford

1 Beautiful city! so venerable, so lovely, so unravaged by the fierce intellectual life of our century, so serene! . . . whispering from her towers the last enchantments of the Middle Age . . . Home of lost causes, and forsaken beliefs, and unpopular names, and impossible loyalties!
Matthew Arnold 1822–88: *Essays in Criticism* First Series (1865)

2 And that sweet City with her
    dreaming spires,
  She needs not June for beauty's
    heightening.
Matthew Arnold 1822–88: 'Thyrsis' (1866)

3 Towery city and branchy between
    towers;
  Cuckoo-echoing, bell-swarmèd, lark-
    charmèd, rook-racked, river-
    rounded.
Gerard Manley Hopkins 1844–89: 'Duns Scotus's Oxford' (written 1879)

Pacifism

see also **Peace**, **Violence**

1 I ain't got no quarrel with the Viet Cong.
  ■ *refusing to be drafted to fight in Vietnam*
Muhammad Ali 1942– : at a press conference in Miami, Florida, February 1966

2 Pale Ebenezer thought it wrong to
    fight,
  But Roaring Bill (who killed him)
    thought it right.
Hilaire Belloc 1870–1953: 'The Pacifist' (1938)

3 Resist not evil: but whosoever shall smite thee on thy right cheek, turn to him the other also.
Bible: St Matthew

4 I am not only a pacifist but a militant pacifist. I am willing to fight for peace.

Nothing will end war unless the people themselves refuse to go to war.
Albert Einstein 1879–1955: interview with G. S. Viereck, January 1931

5 Non-violence is the first article of my faith. It is also the last article of my creed.
Mahatma Gandhi 1869–1948: speech at Shahi Bag, 18 March 1922, on a charge of sedition

6 CHAIRMAN OF MILITARY TRIBUNAL:
    What would you do if you saw a
    German soldier trying to violate
    your sister?
  STRACHEY: I would try to get between
    them.
  ■ *otherwise rendered as, 'I should interpose my body'*
Lytton Strachey 1880–1932: Robert Graves *Good-bye to All That* (1929)

7 Not believing in force is the same thing as not believing in gravitation.
Leon Trotsky 1879–1940: G. Maximov *The Guillotine at Work* (1940)

8 The quietly pacifist peaceful
    always die
  to make room for men
  who shout.
Alice Walker 1944– : 'The QPP' (1973)

Painting

see also **Art**, **Artists**, **Colours**, **Drawing**

1 What I see is a marvellous painting. But how are you going to make it? And, of course, as I don't know how to make it, I rely then on chance and accident making it for me.
Francis Bacon 1909–92: David Sylvester (ed.) *Interviews with Francis Bacon: the brutality of fact* (ed. 3, 1987)

2 Painting became everything to me . . . Through it I made articulate all that I saw and felt, all that went on inside the mind that was housed within my useless body like a prisoner in a cell.
Christy Brown 1932–81: *My Left Foot* (1954)

3 A product of the untalented, sold by the unprincipled to the utterly bewildered.

■ *on abstract art*

Al Capp 1907–79: in *National Observer* 1 July 1963

4 Good painters imitate nature, bad ones spew it up.

Cervantes 1547–1616: *El Licenciado Vidriera* (1613)

5 Treat nature in terms of the cylinder, the sphere, the cone, all in perspective.

Paul Cézanne 1839–1906: letter to Emile Bernard, 1904; Emile Bernard *Paul Cézanne* (1925)

6 A remarkable example of modern art. It certainly combines force with candour.

■ *on the notorious 80th birthday portrait by Graham Sutherland, later destroyed by Lady Churchill*

Winston Churchill 1874–1965: Martin Gilbert *Churchill: A Life* (1991)

7 The sound of water escaping from mill-dams, etc., willows, old rotten planks, slimy posts, and brickwork . . . those scenes made me a painter and I am grateful.

John Constable 1776–1837: letter to John Fisher, 23 October 1821

8 There are only two styles of portrait painting; the serious and the smirk.

Charles Dickens 1812–70: *Nicholas Nickleby* (1839)

9 For my part the famous smile has always seemed to me to be the smile of a woman who has just dined off her husband.

■ *of the Mona Lisa*

Lawrence Durrell 1912–90: *Justine* (1957)

10 All painting, no matter what you're painting, is abstract in that it's got to be organized.

David Hockney 1937– : *David Hockney* (1976)

11 Art does not reproduce the visible; rather, it makes visible.

Paul Klee 1879–1940: *Inward Vision* (1958) 'Creative Credo' (1920)

12 What I dream of is an art of balance, of purity and serenity devoid of troubling or depressing subject matter . . . a soothing, calming influence on the mind, rather like a good armchair which provides relaxation from physical fatigue.

Henri Matisse 1869–1954: *Notes d'un peintre* (1908)

13 You should not paint the chair, but only what someone has felt about it.

Edvard Munch 1863–1944: written *c.*1891; R. Heller *Munch* (1984)

14 No, painting is not made to decorate apartments. It's an offensive and defensive weapon against the enemy.

Pablo Picasso 1881–1973: interview with Simone Téry, 24 March 1945

15 There was a reviewer a while back who wrote that my pictures didn't have any beginning or any end. He didn't mean it as a compliment, but it was. It was a fine compliment.

Jackson Pollock 1912–56: Francis V. O'Connor *Jackson Pollock* (1967)

16 An imitation in lines and colours on any surface of all that is to be found under the sun.

■ *of painting*

Nicolas Poussin 1594–1665: letter to M. de Chambray, 1665

17 Do not judge this movement kindly. It is not just another amusing stunt. It is defiant—the desperate act of men too profoundly convinced of the rottenness of our civilization to want to save a shred of its respectability.

Herbert Read 1893–1968: International Surrealist Exhibition Catalogue, London 1936

18 It's with my brush that I make love.

■ *often quoted as 'I paint with my prick'*

Pierre Auguste Renoir 1841–1919: A. André *Renoir* (1919)

19 A mere copier of nature can never produce anything great.

Joshua Reynolds 1723–92: *Discourses on Art* 14 December 1770

20 Every time I paint a portrait I lose a friend.

John Singer Sargent 1856–1925: N. Bentley and E. Esar *Treasury of Humorous Quotations* (1951)

21 I am a painter and I nail my pictures together.
Kurt Schwitters 1887–1948: R. Hausmann *Am Anfang war Dada* (1972)

22 Painting is saying 'Ta' to God.
Stanley Spencer 1891–1959: letter from Spencer's daughter Shirin to *Observer* 7 February 1988

Parents
....

see also **Children**, **The Family**, **Fathers**, **Mothers**

1 Children always assume the sexual lives of their parents come to a grinding halt at their conception.
Alan Bennett 1934– : *Getting On* (1972)

2 Diogenes struck the father when the son swore.
Robert Burton 1577–1640: *The Anatomy of Melancholy* (1621–51)

3 Having one child makes you a parent; having two you are a referee.
David Frost 1939– : in *Independent* 16 September 1989

4 My father was frightened of his mother; I was frightened of my father, and I am damned well going to see to it that my children are frightened of me.
George V 1865–1936: attributed, perhaps apocryphal; Randolph S. Churchill *Lord Derby* (1959)

5 Your children are not your children.
They are the sons and daughters of Life's longing for itself.
They came through you but not from you
And though they are with you yet they belong not to you.
Kahlil Gibran 1883–1931: *The Prophet* (1923) 'On Children'

6 Do they know they're old,
These two who are my father and my mother
Whose fire from which I came, has now grown cold?
Elizabeth Jennings 1926–2001: 'One Flesh.' (1967)

7 Nothing has a stronger influence on their children than the unlived lives of their parents.
Carl Gustav Jung 1875–1961: attributed; in *Boston Magazine* June 1978

8 Fathers don't curse, they disinherit. Mothers curse.
Irma Kurtz: *Malespeak* (1986)

9 They fuck you up, your mum and dad.
They may not mean to, but they do.
They fill you with the faults they had
And add some extra, just for you.
Philip Larkin 1922–85: 'This Be The Verse' (1974)

10 If she never learns how to be a daughter, she can never learn how to be a woman . . . a woman good enough for a child; good enough for a man—good enough for the respect of other women.
Toni Morrison 1931– : *Tar Baby* (1981)

11 Children aren't happy with nothing to ignore,
And that's what parents were created for.
Ogden Nash 1902–71: 'The Parent' (1933)

12 Oh, what a tangled web do parents weave
When they think that their children are naïve.
Ogden Nash 1902–71: 'Baby, What Makes the Sky Blue' (1940); see **Deception 7**

13 The affection you get back from children is sixpence given as change for a sovereign.
Edith Nesbit 1858–1924: J. Briggs *A Woman of Passion* (1987)

14 If you bungle raising your children I don't think whatever else you do well matters very much.
Jacqueline Kennedy Onassis 1929–94: Theodore C. Sorenson *Kennedy* (1965)

15 Parents—especially step-parents—are sometimes a bit of a disappointment to their children. They don't fulfil the promise of their early years.
Anthony Powell 1905–2000: *A Buyer's Market* (1952)

16 People who have three daughters try
once more
And then it's fifty-fifty they'll have
four.
Those with a son or sons will let
things be.
Hence all these surplus women.
Q.E.D.

Justin Richardson 1900–75: 'Note for the
Scientist' (1959)

17 A Jewish man with parents alive is a
fifteen-year-old boy, and will remain a
fifteen-year-old boy until *they die*!

Philip Roth 1933– : *Portnoy's Complaint*
(1967)

18 The natural term of the affection of
the human animal for its offspring is
six years.

George Bernard Shaw 1856–1950: *Heartbreak
House* (1919)

19 Parentage is a very important
profession, but no test of fitness for it
is ever imposed in the interest of the
children.

George Bernard Shaw 1856–1950: *Everybody's
Political What's What?* (1944)

20 In most families it is the children who
leave home. In mine it was the
parents.

■ *of her anti-apartheid activist parents, Joe
Slovo and Ruth First*

Gillian Slovo 1952– : *Every Secret Thing*
(1997)

21 It's funny the way a parent's raised
eyebrow can do more damage to your
psyche than, say, Chinese water
torture.

Arabella Weir: *Does My Bum Look Big in
This?* (1997)

22 Children begin by loving their
parents; after a time they judge them;
rarely, if ever, do they forgive them.

Oscar Wilde 1854–1900: *A Woman of No
Importance* (1893)

23 A slavish bondage to parents cramps
every faculty of the mind.

Mary Wollstonecraft 1759–97: *A Vindication of
the Rights of Woman* (1792)

Parliament

1 Being an MP is a good job, the sort of
job all working-class parents want for
their children—clean, indoors and no
heavy lifting.

Diane Abbott 1953– : in *Independent*
18 January 1994

2 There can be no place in a 21st-
century parliament for people with
15th-century titles upholding 19th-
century prejudices.

Paddy Ashdown 1941– : comment,
24 November 1998

3 The British House of Lords is the
British Outer Mongolia for retired
politicians.

Tony Benn 1925– : in *Observer* 4 February
1962

4 My desire to get here was like miners'
coal dust, it was under my fingers and
I couldn't scrub it out.

Betty Boothroyd 1929– : Glenys Kinnock and
Fiona Millar (eds.) *By Faith and Daring*
(1993)

5 Your representative owes you, not his
industry only, but his judgement; and
he betrays, instead of serving you, if
he sacrifices it to your opinion.

Edmund Burke 1729–97: speech, Bristol,
3 November 1774

6 The only safe pleasure for a
parliamentarian is a bag of boiled
sweets.

Julian Critchley 1930–2000: in *Listener* 10 June
1982

7 The duty of an Opposition [is] very
simple . . . to oppose everything, and
propose nothing.

Edward Stanley, 14th Earl of Derby 1799–1869:
quoting 'Mr Tierney, a great Whig
authority', in House of Commons, 4 June
1841

8 Think of it! A second Chamber
selected by the Whips. A seraglio of
eunuchs.

Michael Foot 1913– : speech, House of
Commons, 3 February 1969

9 When in that House MPs divide,
If they've a brain and cerebellum too,

They have to leave that brain outside,
And vote just as their leaders tell 'em
to.
W. S. Gilbert 1836–1911: *Iolanthe* (1882)

10 Your business is not to govern the
country but it is, if you think fit, to
call to account those who do govern
it.
W. E. Gladstone 1809–98: speech to the House
of Commons, 29 January 1855

11 Though we cannot out-vote them we
will out-argue them.
■ *on the practical value of speeches in the House
of Commons*
Samuel Johnson 1709–84: James Boswell *Life
of Samuel Johnson* (1791) 3 April 1778

12 In the last Parliament, the House of
Commons had more MPs called John
than all the women MPs put together.
Tessa Jowell 1947– : in *Independent on
Sunday* 14 March 1999

13 I have neither eye to see, nor tongue
to speak here, but as the House is
pleased to direct me.
■ *on being asked if he had seen any of the five
MPs whom the King had ordered to be arrested*
William Lenthall 1591–1662: to Charles I,
4 January 1642

14 Being an MP feeds your vanity and
starves your self-respect.
Matthew Parris 1949– : in *The Times*
9 February 1994

15 Parliament itself would not exist in its
present form had people not defied
the law.
Arthur Scargill 1938– : evidence to House of
Commons Select Committee on
Employment, 2 April 1980

16 The longest running farce in the West
End.
■ *of the House of Commons*
Cyril Smith 1928– : *Big Cyril* (1977)

17 It is, I think, good evidence of life
after death.
■ *on the quality of debate in the House of Lords*
Donald Soper 1903–98: in *Listener* 17 August
1978

18 The House of Lords, an illusion to
which I have never been able to
subscribe—responsibility without
power, the prerogative of the eunuch
throughout the ages.
Tom Stoppard 1937– : *Lord Malquist and Mr
Moon* (1966); see **Responsibility** 3

Parties

see also **Guests**

1 The sooner every party breaks up the
better.
Jane Austen 1775–1817: *Emma* (1816)

2 I won't be going to any New Year's Eve
parties because I think they're naff.
The millennium is going to be the
naffest of them all. No one over the
age of 15 should bother going to
parties.
Julie Burchill 1960– : in *Observer* 3 January
1999

3 Like other parties of the kind, it was
first silent, then talky, then
argumentative, then disputatious,
then unintelligible, then altogethery,
then inarticulate, and then drunk.
Lord Byron 1788–1824: letter to Thomas
Moore, 31 October 1815

4 The best number for a dinner party is
two—myself and a dam' good head
waiter.
Nubar Gulbenkian 1896–1972: in *Daily
Telegraph* 14 January 1965

5 The tumult and the shouting dies,
The captains and the kings depart,
And we are left with large supplies
Of cold blancmange and rhubarb tart.
Ronald Knox 1888–1957: 'After the Party'
(1959); cf. **Humility** 4

6 At a dinner party one should eat
wisely but not too well, and talk well
but not too wisely.
W. Somerset Maugham 1874–1965: *Writer's
Notebook* (1949); written in 1896

7 Candy
Is dandy
But liquor
Is quicker.
Ogden Nash 1902–71: 'Reflections on Ice-
breaking' (1931)

8 Bachelors know all about parties. In fact, a good bachelor is a living, breathing party all by himself.

P. J. O'Rourke 1947– : *The Bachelor Home Companion* (1987)

9 Unless your life is going well you don't dream of giving a party. Unless you can look in the mirror and see a benign and generous and healthy human being, you shrink from acts of hospitality.

Carol Shields 1935– : *Larry's Party* (1997)

10 An office party is not, as is sometimes supposed, the Managing Director's chance to kiss the tea-girl. It is the tea-girl's chance to kiss the Managing Director.

Katharine Whitehorn 1928– : *Roundabout* (1962) 'The Office Party'

11 If one plays good music, people don't listen and if one plays bad music people don't talk.

Oscar Wilde 1854–1900: *The Importance of Being Earnest* (1895)

Parting

·················

see also **Meeting**

1 Once I leave, I leave. I am not going to speak to the man on the bridge, and I am not going to spit on the deck.

■ *on resigning*

Stanley Baldwin 1867–1947: statement to the Cabinet, 28 May 1937

2 I leave before being left. I decide.

Brigitte Bardot 1934– : in *Newsweek* 5 March 1973

3 Friends part
forever—wild geese
lost in cloud.

Matsuo Basho 1644–94: translated by Lucien Stryk

4 I'll be back.

James Cameron 1954– : *The Terminator* (1984 film, with Gale Anne Hurd); spoken by Arnold Schwarzenegger

5 *Atque in perpetuum, frater, ave atque vale.*

And so, my brother, hail, and farewell evermore!

Catullus *c.*84–*c.*54 BC: *Carmina*

6 How long ago Hector took off his plume,
Not wanting that his little son should cry,
Then kissed his sad Andromache goodbye—
And now we three in Euston waiting-room.

Frances Cornford 1886–1960: 'Parting in Wartime' (1948)

7 Parting is all we know of heaven,
And all we need of hell.

Emily Dickinson 1830–86: 'My life closed twice before its close'

8 Since there's no help, come let us kiss and part,
Nay, I have done: you get no more of me.

Michael Drayton 1563–1631: *Idea* (1619) sonnet 61

9 You and I, when our days are done, must say
Without exactly saying it, good-bye.

John Fuller 1937– : 'Pyrosymphonie' (1996)

10 If you can't leave in a taxi you can leave in a huff. If that's too soon, you can leave in a minute and a huff.

Bert Kalmar 1884–1947 et al.: *Duck Soup* (1933 film); spoken by Groucho Marx

11 She said she always believed in the old addage, 'Leave them while you're looking good.'

Anita Loos 1893–1981: *Gentlemen Prefer Blondes* (1925)

12 We're drinking my friend,
To the end of a brief episode,
Make it one for my baby
And one more for the road.

Johnny Mercer 1909–76: 'One For My Baby' (1943 song)

13 Now this is the last day of our acquaintance
I will meet you later in somebody's office
I'll talk but you won't listen to me

I know your answer already.
Sinéad O'Connor 1966– : 'The Last Day of
Our Acquaintance' (1990)

14 But how strange the change from
major to minor
Every time we say goodbye.
Cole Porter 1891–1964: 'Every Time We Say
Goodbye' (1944 song)

15 Good-night, good-night! parting is
such sweet sorrow
That I shall say good-night till it be
morrow.
William Shakespeare 1564–1616: *Romeo and
Juliet* (1595)

The Past

see also **History, Memory, The Present,
Tradition**

1 Even a god cannot change the past.
■ *literally 'The one thing which even God cannot
do is to make undone what has been done'*
Agathon b. *c.*445: Aristotle *Nicomachaean
Ethics*

2 In every age 'the good old days' were a
myth. No one ever thought they were
good at the time. For every age has
consisted of crises that seemed
intolerable to the people who lived
through them.
Brooks Atkinson 1894–1984: *Once Around the
Sun* (1951)

3 Stands the Church clock at ten to
three?
And is there honey still for tea?
Rupert Brooke 1887–1915: 'The Old Vicarage,
Grantchester' (1915)

4 The past is never dead. It's not even
past.
William Faulkner 1897–1962: *Requiem for a
Nun* (1951)

5 The moving finger writes; and, having
writ,
Moves on: nor all thy piety nor wit
Shall lure it back to cancel half a line,
Nor all thy tears wash out a word of it.
Edward Fitzgerald 1809–83: *The Rubáiyát of
Omar Khayyám* (1859)

6 It is not the literal past, the 'facts' of
history, that shape us, but images of

the past embodied in language . . . we
must never cease renewing those
images; because once we do, we
fossilize.
Brian Friel 1929– : *Translations* (1980)

7 The past is a foreign country: they do
things differently there.
L. P. Hartley 1895–1972: *The Go-Between*
(1953)

8 What are those blue remembered
hills,
What spires, what farms are those?
That is the land of lost content,
I see it shining plain,
The happy highways where I went
And cannot come again.
A. E. Housman 1859–1936: *A Shropshire Lad*
(1896)

9 They shut the road through the woods
Seventy years ago.
Weather and rain have undone it
again,
And now you would never know
There was once a road through the
woods.
Rudyard Kipling 1865–1936: 'The Way through
the Woods' (1910)

10 Yesterday, all my troubles seemed so
far away,
Now it looks as though they're here to
stay.
Oh I believe in yesterday.
John Lennon 1940–80 and **Paul McCartney**
1942– : 'Yesterday' (1965 song)

11 So the years hang like old clothes,
forgotten in the wardrobe of our
minds. Did I wear that? Who was I
then?
Brian Moore 1921– : *No Other Life* (1993)

12 Think of it, soldiers; from the summit
of these pyramids, forty centuries
look down upon you.
Napoleon I 1769–1821: speech, 21 July 1798,
before the Battle of the Pyramids

13 Things ain't what they used to be.
Ted Persons: title of song (1941)

14 I tell you the past is a bucket of ashes.
Carl Sandburg 1878–1967: 'Prairie' (1918)

15 Those who cannot remember the past are condemned to repeat it.
George Santayana 1863–1952: *The Life of Reason* (1905)

16 O! call back yesterday, bid time return.
William Shakespeare 1564–1616: *Richard II* (1595)

17 People who are always praising the past
And especially the times of faith as best
Ought to go and live in the Middle Ages
And be burnt at the stake as witches and sages.
Stevie Smith 1902–71: 'The Past' (1957)

18 I think that today's youth have a tendency to live in the present and work for the future—and to be totally ignorant of the past.
Steven Spielberg 1947– : in *Independent on Sunday* 22 August 1999

19 The past is the only dead thing that smells sweet.
Edward Thomas 1878–1917: 'Early one morning in May I set out' (1917)

20 Thanks to modern technology . . . history now comes equipped with a fast-forward button.
Gore Vidal 1925– : *Screening History* (1992)

21 *Mais où sont les neiges d'antan?*
But where are the snows of yesteryear?
François Villon b. 1431: *Le Grand Testament* (1461) 'Ballade des dames du temps jadis'

22 An old teapot, used daily, can tell me more of my past than anything I recorded of it. Continuity . . . continuity . . . it is that which we cannot write down, it is that we cannot compass, record or control.
Sylvia Townsend Warner 1893–1978: letter to Alyse Gregory, 26 May 1953

23 Reading about sex in yesterday's novels is like watching people smoke in old films.
Fay Weldon 1931– : in *Guardian* 1 December 1989

24 Hindsight is always twenty-twenty.
Billy Wilder 1906–2002: J. R. Columbo *Wit and Wisdom of the Moviemakers* (1979)

Patience

see also **Delay**, **Persistence**, **Waiting**

1 We had better wait and see.
Herbert Asquith 1852–1928: phrase used repeatedly in speeches in 1910; Roy Jenkins *Asquith* (1964)

2 Our patience will achieve more than our force.
Edmund Burke 1729–97: *Reflections on the Revolution in France* (1790)

3 Beware the fury of a patient man.
John Dryden 1631–1700: *Absalom and Achitophel* (1681)

4 Patience, that blending of moral courage with physical timidity.
Thomas Hardy 1840–1928: *Tess of the d'Urbervilles* (1891)

5 They also serve who only stand and wait.
John Milton 1608–74: 'When I consider how my light is spent' (1673)

6 I am extraordinarily patient, provided I get my own way in the end.
Margaret Thatcher 1925– : in *Observer* 4 April 1989

Patriotism

see also **Nationality**

1 Patriotism is a lively sense of collective responsibility. Nationalism is a silly cock crowing on its own dunghill.
Richard Aldington 1892–1962: *The Colonel's Daughter* (1931)

2 The cardinal virtue was no longer to love one's country. It was to feel compassion for one's fellow men and women.
■ *writing of his own generation*
Noel Annan 1916–2000: *Our Age* (1990)

3 If I should die, think only this of me:
That there's some corner of a foreign field

That is for ever England.
Rupert Brooke 1887–1915: 'The Soldier' (1914)

4 Standing, as I do, in view of God and eternity, I realize that patriotism is not enough. I must have no hatred or bitterness towards anyone.

■ *on the eve of her execution for helping Allied soldiers to escape from occupied Belgium*

Edith Cavell 1865–1915: in *The Times* 23 October 1915

5 'My country, right or wrong', is a thing that no patriot would think of saying except in a desperate case. It is like saying, 'My mother, drunk or sober'.

G. K. Chesterton 1874–1936: *Defendant* (1901) 'Defence of Patriotism'

6 Our country! In her intercourse with foreign nations, may she always be in the right; but our country, right or wrong.

Stephen Decatur 1779–1820: toast at Norfolk, Virginia, April 1816; cf. 18 below

7 Never was patriot yet, but was a fool.

John Dryden 1631–1700: *Absalom and Achitophel* (1681)

8 If I had to choose between betraying my country and betraying my friend, I hope I should have the guts to betray my country.

E. M. Forster 1879–1970: *Two Cheers for Democracy* (1951)

9 You think you are dying for your country; you die for the industrialists.

Anatole France 1844–1924: in *L'Humanité* 18 July 1922

10 That this House will in no circumstances fight for its King and Country.

D. M. Graham 1911–99: motion worded by Graham for a debate at the Oxford Union, 9 February 1933 (passed by 275 votes to 153)

11 I only regret that I have but one life to lose for my country.

■ *prior to his execution by the British for spying*

Nathan Hale 1755–76: Henry Phelps Johnston *Nathan Hale, 1776* (1914)

12 *Dulce et decorum est pro patria mori.*
Lovely and honourable it is to die for one's country.

Horace 65–8 BC: *Odes*; cf. **Warfare** 29

13 Patriotism is the last refuge of a scoundrel.

Samuel Johnson 1709–84: James Boswell *Life of Samuel Johnson* (1791) 7 April 1775

14 And so, my fellow Americans: ask not what your country can do for you— ask what you can do for your country.

John F. Kennedy 1917–63: inaugural address, 20 January 1961

15 I would die for my country but I could never let my country die for me.

Neil Kinnock 1942– : speech at Labour Party Conference, 30 September 1986

16 Men have been dying for Ireland since the beginning of time and look at the state of the country.

Frank McCourt 1930– : *Angela's Ashes* (1996)

17 These are the times that try men's souls. The summer soldier and the sunshine patriot will, in this crisis, shrink from the service of their country; but he that stands it *now*, deserves the love and thanks of men and women.

Thomas Paine 1737–1809: *The Crisis* (December 1776)

18 My country, right or wrong; if right, to be kept right; and if wrong, to be set right!

Carl Schurz 1829–1906: speech, US Senate, 29 February 1872; see 6 above

19 Breathes there the man, with soul so dead,
Who never to himself hath said,
This is my own, my native land!

Sir Walter Scott 1771–1832: *The Lay of the Last Minstrel* (1805)

20 You'll never have a quiet world till you knock the patriotism out of the human race.

George Bernard Shaw 1856–1950: *O'Flaherty V.C.* (1919)

21 I vow to thee, my country—all earthly things above—

Entire and whole and perfect, the
service of my love.

Cecil Spring-Rice 1859–1918: 'I Vow to Thee,
My Country' (1918)

22 The cricket test—which side do they
cheer for? . . . Are you still looking
back to where you came from or
where you are?

■ *on the loyalties of Britain's immigrant
population*

Norman Tebbit 1931– : interview in *Los
Angeles Times*; in *Daily Telegraph* 20 April
1990

Peace

see also **Pacifism**, **Warfare**

1 Peace cannot be built on exclusion.
That has been the price of the past
30 years.

Gerry Adams 1948– : in *Daily Telegraph*
11 April 1998

2 The peace we seek in Iraq, as
everywhere, is one that reflects the
lessons of our terrible century: that
peace is not true or lasting if it is
bought at any cost; that only peace
with justice can honour the victims of
war and violence; and that, without
democracy, tolerance and human
rights for all, no peace is truly safe.

Kofi Annan 1938– : speech to the Council on
Foreign Relations, New York, January 1999

3 I am beginning to rub my eyes at the
prospect of peace . . . One will at last
fully recognize that the dead are not
only dead for the duration of the war.

Cynthia Asquith 1887–1960: diary 7 October
1918

4 They shall beat their swords into
plowshares, and their spears into
pruninghooks: nation shall not lift up
sword against nation, neither shall
they learn war any more.

Bible: Isaiah

5 The peace of God, which passeth all
understanding, shall keep your hearts
and minds through Christ Jesus.

Bible: Philippians

6 Give peace in our time, O Lord.

The Book of Common Prayer 1662: *Morning
Prayer*

7 One observes, they have gone too long
without a war here. Where is morality
to come from in such a case, I ask?
Peace is nothing but slovenliness, only
war creates order.

Bertolt Brecht 1898–1956: *Mother Courage*
(1939)

8 This is the second time in our history
that there has come back from
Germany to Downing Street peace
with honour. I believe it is peace for
our time.

Neville Chamberlain 1869–1940: speech from
10 Downing Street, 30 September 1938

9 Go placidly amid the noise and the
haste, and remember what peace
there may be in silence.

■ *often wrongly dated to 1692, the date of
foundation of a church in Baltimore whose vicar
circulated the poem in 1956*

Max Ehrmann 1872–1945: 'Desiderata' (1948)

10 I think that people want peace so
much that one of these days
governments had better get out of the
way and let them have it.

Dwight D. Eisenhower 1890–1969: broadcast
discussion, 31 August 1959

11 Lord, make me an instrument of Your
peace!
Where there is hatred let me sow love.

St Francis of Assisi 1181–1226: 'Prayer of St
Francis'; attributed

12 I have many times asked myself
whether there can be more potent
advocates of peace upon earth
through the years to come than this
massed multitude of silent witnesses
to the desolation of war.

George V 1865–1936: message read at
Terlincthun Cemetery, Boulogne, 13 May
1922

13 War makes rattling good history; but
Peace is poor reading.

Thomas Hardy 1840–1928: *The Dynasts* (1904)

14 'Peace upon earth!' was said. We sing
it,
And pay a million priests to bring it.

After two thousand years of mass
We've got as far as poison-gas.
Thomas Hardy 1840–1928: 'Christmas: 1924'
(1928)

15 Give peace a chance.
John Lennon 1940–80 and **Paul McCartney**
1942– : title of song (1969)

16 Peace is indivisible.
Maxim Litvinov 1876–1951: note to the Allies,
25 February 1920

17 You can't separate peace from
freedom because no one can be at
peace unless he has his freedom.
Malcolm X 1925–65: speech in New York,
7 January 1965

18 You can't switch on peace like a light.
Mo Mowlam 1949– : in *Independent*
6 September 1999

19 The grim fact is that we prepare for
war like precocious giants and for
peace like retarded pygmies.
Lester Pearson 1897–1972: speech in Toronto,
14 March 1955

20 Enough of blood and tears. Enough.
Yitzhak Rabin 1922–95: at the signing of the
Israel-Palestine Declaration, Washington,
13 September 1993

21 The work, my friend, is peace. More
than an end of this war—an end to
the beginnings of all wars.
Franklin D. Roosevelt 1882–1945: undelivered
address for Jefferson Day, 13 April 1945 (the
day after Roosevelt died)

22 They make a wilderness and call it
peace.
Tacitus AD *c.*56–after 117: *Agricola*

People on People
·······································
see also **Churchill, Diana, Lloyd George,
Monroe, Musicians, Poets, Reagan,
Thatcher, Writers**

1 He is gone, but his shadow still stands
over all of us. It still dictates to us and
we, very often, obey.
■ *of her father, Joseph Stalin*
Svetlana Alliluyeva 1925– : *Twenty Letters to
a Friend* (1967)

2 Few thought he was even a starter
There were many who thought
themselves smarter
But he ended PM
CH and OM
An earl and a knight of the garter.
■ *of himself*
Clement Attlee 1883–1967: letter to Tom
Attlee, 8 April 1956

3 To us he is no more a person
now but a whole climate of opinion.
W. H. Auden 1907–73: 'In Memory of
Sigmund Freud' (1940)

4 A lath of wood painted to look like
iron.
■ *of Lord Salisbury*
Otto von Bismarck 1815–98: attributed, but
vigorously denied by Sidney Whitman in
Personal Reminiscences of Prince Bismarck
(1902)

5 She's a gay man trapped in a woman's
body.
■ *of Madonna*
Boy George 1961– : *Take It Like a Man* (1995)

6 A modest man who has a good deal to
be modest about.
■ *of Clement Attlee*
Winston Churchill 1874–1965: in *Chicago
Sunday Tribune Magazine of Books* 27 June
1954

7 In defeat unbeatable: in victory
unbearable.
■ *of Lord Montgomery*
Winston Churchill 1874–1965: Edward Marsh
Ambrosia and Small Beer (1964)

8 It is not necessary that every time he
rises he should give his famous
imitation of a semi-house-trained
polecat.
■ *of Norman Tebbit*
Michael Foot 1913– : speech, House of
Commons, 2 March 1978

9 Comrades, this man has a nice smile,
but he's got iron teeth.
■ *of Mikhail Gorbachev*
Andrei Gromyko 1909–89: speech to Soviet
Communist Party Central Committee,
11 March 1985

10 A man who so much resembled a
Baked Alaska—sweet, warm and

gungy on the outside, hard and cold within.
■ *of C. P. Snow*
Francis King 1923– : *Yesterday Came Suddenly* (1993)

11 Mad, bad, and dangerous to know.
■ *of Byron, after their first meeting*
Lady Caroline Lamb 1785–1828: diary, March 1812

12 An Archangel a little damaged.
■ *of Coleridge*
Charles Lamb 1775–1834: letter to Wordsworth, 26 April 1816

13 A good man fallen among Fabians.
■ *of George Bernard Shaw*
Lenin 1870–1924: Arthur Ransome *Six Weeks in Russia in 1919* (1919) 'Notes of Conversations with Lenin'

14 He seemed at ease and to have the look of the last gentleman in Europe.
■ *of Oscar Wilde*
Ada Leverson 1865–1936: *Letters to the Sphinx* (1930)

15 The Stag at Bay with the mentality of a fox at large.
■ *of Harold Macmillan*
Bernard Levin 1928– : *The Pendulum Years* (1970)

16 Every word she writes is a lie, including 'and' and 'the'.
■ *of Lillian Hellman*
Mary McCarthy 1912–89: in *New York Times* 16 February 1980

17 The thinking man's crumpet.
■ *of Joan Bakewell*
Frank Muir 1920–98: attributed

18 If only Bapu knew the cost of setting him up in poverty!
■ *of Mahatma Gandhi*
Sarojini Naidu 1879–1949: A. Campbell-Johnson *Mission with Mountbatten* (1951)

19 An elderly fallen angel travelling incognito.
■ *of André Gide*
Peter Quennell 1905– : *The Sign of the Fish* (1960)

20 A doormat in a world of boots.
■ *of herself*
Jean Rhys c.1890–1979: in *Guardian* 6 December 1990

21 Too clever by half.
■ *of Iain Macleod*
Lord Salisbury 1893–1972: speech, House of Lords, 7 March 1961

22 She would rather light a candle than curse the darkness, and her glow has warmed the world.
■ *on learning of Eleanor Roosevelt's death*
Adlai Stevenson 1900–65: in *New York Times* 8 November 1962

23 In a world of voluble hates, he plotted to make men like, or at least tolerate one another.
■ *of Stanley Baldwin*
G. M. Trevelyan 1876–1962: in *Dictionary of National Biography 1941–50* (1959)

24 He snatched the lightning shaft from heaven, and the sceptre from tyrants.
■ *of Benjamin Franklin, inventor of the lightning conductor and American statesman*
A. R. J. Turgot 1727–81: inscription for a bust

25 What, when drunk, one sees in other women, one sees in Garbo sober.
■ *of Greta Garbo*
Kenneth Tynan 1927–80: *Curtains* (1961)

26 As time requireth, a man of marvellous mirth and pastimes, and sometime of as sad gravity, as who say: a man for all seasons.
■ *of Sir Thomas More*
Robert Whittington: *Vulgaria* (1521)

27 She is so odd a blend of Little Nell and Lady Macbeth. It is not so much the familiar phenomenon of a hand of steel in a velvet glove as a lacy sleeve with a bottle of vitriol concealed in its folds.
■ *of Dorothy Parker*
Alexander Woollcott 1887–1943: *While Rome Burns* (1934)

Perfection

see also **Excellence**

1 Pictures of perfection as you know make me sick and wicked.
Jane Austen 1775–1817: letter to Fanny Knight, 23 March 1817

2 Faultless to a fault.
> **Robert Browning** 1812–89: *The Ring and the Book* (1868–9)

3 It's a delightful thing to think of perfection; but it's vastly more amusing to talk of errors and absurdities.
> **Fanny Burney** 1752–1840: *Camilla* (1796)

4 Here we are perfect. Metaphysical greenbirds
Perch over sunlit leaves; our feet converse
With the refreshing grass.
> **Douglas Dunn** 1942– : 'The Garden' (1972)

5 Nothing is an unmixed blessing.
> **Horace** 65–8 BC: *Odes*

6 Finality is death. Perfection is finality. Nothing is perfect. There are lumps in it.
> **James Stephens** 1882–1950: *The Crock of Gold* (1912)

7 Faultily faultless, icily regular, splendidly null,
Dead perfection, no more.
> **Alfred, Lord Tennyson** 1809–92: *Maud* (1855)

8 The intellect of man is forced to choose
Perfection of the life, or of the work.
> **W. B. Yeats** 1865–1939: 'The Choice' (1933)

Persistence

see also **Defeat, Determination, Patience**

1 'If seven maids with seven mops
Swept it for half a year,
Do you suppose,' the Walrus said,
'That they could get it clear?'
'I doubt it,' said the Carpenter,
And shed a bitter tear.
> **Lewis Carroll** 1832–98: *Through the Looking-Glass* (1872)

2 The comeback kid!
> **Bill Clinton** 1946– : description of himself after coming second in the New Hampshire primary, 1992

3 Nothing in the world can take the place of persistence. Talent will not; nothing is more common than unsuccessful men with talent. Genius will not; unrewarded genius is almost a proverb. Education will not; the world is full of educated derelicts. Persistence and determination are omnipotent. The slogan 'press on' has solved and always will solve the problems of the human race.
> **Calvin Coolidge** 1872–1933: attributed in the programme of a memorial service for Coolidge in 1933

4 There must be a beginning of any great matter, but the continuing unto the end until it be thoroughly finished yields the true glory.
> **Francis Drake** c.1540–96: dispatch to Sir Francis Walsingham, 17 May 1587

5 Pick yourself up,
Dust yourself off,
Start all over again.
> **Dorothy Fields** 1905–74: 'Pick Yourself Up' (1936 song)

6 If at first you don't succeed, try, try again. Then quit. No use being a damn fool about it.
> **W. C. Fields** 1880–1946: attributed

7 But above all
we have
the ability
to sort peas,
to cup water in our hands,
to seek
the right screw
under the sofa
for hours.
> **Miroslav Holub** 1923– : 'Wings' (1967)

8 The drop of rain maketh a hole in the stone, not by violence, but by oft falling.
> **Hugh Latimer** c.1485–1555: *The Second Sermon preached before the King's Majesty*, 19 April 1549

9 Keep right on to the end of the road,
Keep right on to the end.
Tho' the way be long, let your heart be strong,
Keep right on round the bend.
> **Harry Lauder** 1870–1950: 'The End of the Road' (1924 song)

10 The capacity women have for just
hanging on is depressing to
contemplate.
  Stevie Smith 1902–71: in *Tribune* c.1945

11 What is the victory of a cat on a hot
tin roof?—I wish I knew . . . Just
staying on it, I guess, as long as she
can.
  Tennessee Williams 1911–83: *Cat on a Hot Tin
  Roof* (1955)

Pessimism

see also **Despair, Hope, Optimisim**

1 Pessimism, when you get used to it, is
just as agreeable as optimism. Indeed,
I think it must be more agreeable,
must have a more real savour, than
optimism—from the way in which
pessimists abandon themselves to it.
  Arnold Bennett 1867–1931: *Things that have
  Interested Me* (1921) 'Slump in Pessimism'

2 The optimist proclaims that we live in
the best of all possible worlds; and the
pessimist fears this is true.
  James Branch Cabell 1879–1958: *The Silver
  Stallion* (1926); see **Optimism** 9

3 I don't consider myself a pessimist. I
think of a pessimist as someone who
is waiting for it to rain. And I feel
soaked to the skin.
  Leonard Cohen 1934– : in *Observer* 2 May
  1993

4 There are bad times just around the
corner,
There are dark clouds travelling
through the sky
And it's no good whining
About a silver lining
For we know from experience that
they won't roll by.
  Noël Coward 1899–1973: 'There are Bad
  Times Just Around the Corner' (1953 song)

5 If way to the Better there be, it exacts a
full look at the worst.
  Thomas Hardy 1840–1928: 'De Profundis'
  (1902)

6 Nothing to do but work,
Nothing to eat but food,

Nothing to wear but clothes
To keep one from going nude.
  Benjamin Franklin King 1857–94: 'The
  Pessimist'

7 If we see light at the end of the tunnel,
It's the light of the oncoming train.
  Robert Lowell 1917–77: 'Since 1939' (1977)

8 Pessimism was dear to him in its
impersonation of profundity and its
implication of arcane knowledge.
  Candia McWilliam 1955– : *Debatable Land*
  (1994)

9 'Twixt the optimist and pessimist
The difference is droll:
The optimist sees the doughnut
But the pessimist sees the hole.
  McLandburgh Wilson b. 1892: *Optimist and
  Pessimist* (c.1915)

Philosophy

see also **Logic and Reason**

1 To ask the hard question is simple.
  W. H. Auden 1907–73: title of poem (1933)

2 The Socratic manner is not a game at
which two can play.
  Max Beerbohm 1872–1956: *Zuleika Dobson*
  (1911)

3 Metaphysics is the finding of bad
reasons for what we believe upon
instinct; but to find these reasons is
no less an instinct.
  F. H. Bradley 1846–1924: *Appearance and
  Reality* (1893)

4 There is nothing so absurd but some
philosopher has said it.
  Cicero 106–43 BC: *De Divinatione*

5 I have tried too in my time to be a
philosopher; but, I don't know how,
cheerfulness was always breaking in.
  Oliver Edwards 1711–91: James Boswell *Life of
  Samuel Johnson* (1791) 17 April 1778

6 When philosophy paints its grey on
grey, then has a shape of life grown
old. By philosophy's grey on grey it
cannot be rejuvenated but only
understood. The owl of Minerva

spreads its wings only with the falling of the dusk.

G. W. F. Hegel 1770–1831: *Philosophy of Right* (1821)

7 The philosophers have only interpreted the world in various ways; the point is to change it.

Karl Marx 1818–83: *Theses on Feuerbach* (written 1845, published 1888)

8 What I understand by 'philosopher': a terrible explosive in the presence of which everything is in danger.

Friedrich Nietzsche 1844–1900: *Ecce Homo* (1908)

9 No more things should be presumed to exist than are absolutely necessary.

William of Occam c.1285–1349: not found in this form in his writings, although he frequently used similar expressions, e.g. 'Plurality should not be assumed unnecessarily'; *Quodlibeta* (c.1324)

10 Students of the heavens are separable into astronomers and astrologers as readily as are the minor domestic ruminants into sheep and goats, but the separation of philosophers into sages and cranks seems to be more sensitive to frames of reference.

W. V. O. Quine 1908– : *Theories and Things* (1981)

11 The unexamined life is not worth living.

Socrates 469–399 BC: Plato *Apology*

12 Superstition sets the whole world in flames; philosophy quenches them.

Voltaire 1694–1778: *Dictionnaire philosophique* (1764) 'Superstition'

13 The safest general characterization of the European philosophical tradition is that it consists of a series of footnotes to Plato.

Alfred North Whitehead 1861–1947: *Process and Reality* (1929)

14 What is your aim in philosophy?—To show the fly the way out of the fly-bottle.

Ludwig Wittgenstein 1889–1951: *Philosophische Untersuchungen* (1953)

Photography

see also **Art**, **Press Photographers**

1 A photograph is a secret about a secret. The more it tells you the less you know.

Diane Arbus 1923–71: Patricia Bosworth *Diane Arbus: a Biography* (1985)

2 It takes a lot of imagination to be a good photographer. You need less imagination to be a painter, because you can invent things. But in photography everything is so ordinary; it takes a lot of looking before you learn to see the ordinary.

David Bailey 1938– : interview in *The Face* December 1984

3 Most things in life are moments of pleasure and a lifetime of embarrassment; photography is a moment of embarrassment and a lifetime of pleasure.

Tony Benn 1925– : in *Independent* 21 October 1989

4 To me, photography is the simultaneous recognition, in a fraction of a second, of the significance of an event as well as of a precise organization of forms which give that event its proper expression.

Henri Cartier-Bresson 1908– : *The Decisive Moment* (1952)

5 It's more important to click with people than to click the shutter.

Alfred Eisenstaedt 1898–1995: in *Life* 24 August 1995

6 All you can do with most ordinary photographs is stare at them—they stare back, blankly—and presently your concentration begins to fade. They stare you down. I mean, photography is all right if you don't mind looking at the world from the point of view of a paralysed cyclops—*for a split second*.

David Hockney 1937– : as told to Lawrence Weschler, *Cameraworks* (1984)

7 The photographer is like the cod which produces a million eggs in order that one may reach maturity.
George Bernard Shaw 1856–1950: introduction to the catalogue for an exhibition at the Royal Photographic Society, 1906

8 A photograph is not only an image (as a painting is an image), an interpretation of the real; it is also a trace, something directly stencilled off the real, like a footprint or a death mask.
Susan Sontag 1933– : in *New York Review of Books* 23 June 1977

Physics

see also **Science**

1 All I know about the becquerel is that, like the Italian lira, you need an awful lot to amount to very much.
Arnold Allen 1924– : in *Financial Times* 19 September 1986

2 There is no democracy in physics. We can't say that some second-rate guy has as much right to opinion as Fermi.
Luis Walter Alvarez 1911–88: D. S. Greenberg *The Politics of Pure Science* (1969)

3 Anybody who is not shocked by this subject has failed to understand it.
■ *of quantum mechanics*
Niels Bohr 1885–1962: attributed

4 There was a young lady named Bright, Whose speed was far faster than light; She set out one day In a relative way And returned on the previous night.
Arthur Buller 1874–1944: 'Relativity' (1923)

5 If someone points out to you that your pet theory of the universe is in disagreement with Maxwell's equations—then so much the worse for Maxwell's equations. If it is found to be contradicted by observation— well, these experimentalists do bungle things sometimes. But if your theory is found to be against the second law of thermodynamics I can give you no

hope; there is nothing for it but to collapse in deepest humiliation.
Arthur Eddington 1882–1944: *The Nature of the Physical World* (1928)

6 If I could remember the names of all these particles I'd be a botanist.
Enrico Fermi 1901–54: R. L. Weber *More Random Walks in Science* (1973)

7 We do not know why they have the masses they do; we do not know why they transform into another the way they do; we do not know anything! The one concept that stands like the Rock of Gibraltar in our sea of confusion is the Pauli [exclusion] principle.
■ *of elementary particles*
George Gamow 1904–68: in *Scientific American* July 1959

8 If we assume that the last breath of, say, Julius Caesar has by now become thoroughly scattered through the atmosphere, then the chances are that each of us inhales one molecule of it with every breath we take.
■ *now usually quoted as the 'dying breath of Socrates'*
James Jeans 1877–1946: *An Introduction to the Kinetic Theory of Gases* (1940)

9 I remembered the line from the Hindu scripture, the *Bhagavad Gita* . . . 'I am become death, the destroyer of worlds.'
■ *on the explosion of the first atomic bomb near Alamogordo, New Mexico, 16 July 1945*
J. Robert Oppenheimer 1904–67: Len Giovannitti and Fred Freed *The Decision to Drop the Bomb* (1965)

10 In some sort of crude sense which no vulgarity, no humour, no overstatement can quite extinguish, the physicists have known sin; and this is a knowledge which they cannot lose.
J. Robert Oppenheimer 1904–67: lecture at Massachusetts Institute of Technology, 25 November 1947

11 Neutrinos, they are very small They have no charge and have no mass And do not interact at all.
John Updike 1932– : 'Cosmic Gall' (1964)

12 It would be a poor thing to be an
atom in a world without physicists.
And physicists are made of atoms. A
physicist is an atom's way of knowing
about atoms.
George Wald 1904–97: foreword to L. J.
Henderson *The Fitness of the Environment*
(1958)

Plagiarism

see also **Originality**

1 They lard their lean books with the fat
of others' works.
Robert Burton 1577–1640: *The Anatomy of
Melancholy* (1621–51)

2 Immature poets imitate; mature poets
steal.
T. S. Eliot 1888–1965: *The Sacred Wood* (1920)
'Philip Massinger'

3 No plagiarist can excuse the wrong by
showing how much of his work he did
not pirate.
Learned Hand 1872–1961: *Sheldon v. Metro-
Goldwyn Pictures Corp.* 1936

4 When 'Omer smote 'is bloomin' lyre,
He'd 'eard men sing by land an' sea;
An' what he thought 'e might require,
'E went an' took—the same as me!
Rudyard Kipling 1865–1936: 'When 'Omer
smote 'is bloomin' lyre' (1896)

5 If you steal from one author, it's
plagiarism; if you steal from many, it's
research.
Wilson Mizner 1876–1933: Alva Johnston *The
Legendary Mizners* (1953)

6 It could be said of me that in this book
I have only made up a bunch of other
men's flowers, providing of my own
only the string that ties them together.
Montaigne 1533–92: *Essais* (1580)

7 So, naturalists observe, a flea
Hath smaller fleas that on him prey;
And these have smaller fleas to bite
'em,
And so proceed *ad infinitum*.
Jonathan Swift 1667–1745: 'On Poetry' (1733)

Pleasure

see also **Happiness**

1 No pleasure is worth giving up for the
sake of two more years in a geriatric
home in Weston-super-Mare.
Kingsley Amis 1922–95: in *The Times* 21 June
1994; attributed

2 A fool bolts pleasure, then complains
of moral indigestion.
Minna Antrim 1861–1950: *Naked Truth and
Veiled Allusions* (1902)

3 One half of the world cannot
understand the pleasures of the other.
Jane Austen 1775–1817: *Emma* (1816)

4 The great pleasure in life is doing
what people say you cannot do.
Walter Bagehot 1826–77: in *Prospective
Review* 1853 'Shakespeare'

5 Let us have wine and women, mirth
and laughter,
Sermons and soda-water the day after.
Lord Byron 1788–1824: *Don Juan* (1819–24)

6 In love, as in gluttony, pleasure is a
matter of the utmost precision.
Italo Calvino 1923–85: Charles Fourier *Theory
of the Four Movements* (1971)

7 Lying in bed would be an altogether
perfect and supreme experience if
only one had a coloured pencil long
enough to draw on the ceiling.
G. K. Chesterton 1874–1936: *Tremendous
Trifles* (1909) 'On Lying in Bed'

8 There's no greater bliss in life than
when the plumber eventually comes
to unblock your drains. No writer can
give that sort of pleasure.
Victoria Glendinning 1937– : in *Observer*
3 January 1993

9 People must not do things for fun. We
are not here for fun. There is no
reference to fun in any Act of
Parliament.
A. P. Herbert 1890–1971: *Uncommon Law*
(1935)

10 A man enjoys the happiness he feels, a
woman the happiness she gives.
Pierre Choderlos de Laclos 1741–1803: *Les
Liaisons dangereuses* (1782)

11 The greatest pleasure I know, is to do a good action by stealth, and to have it found out by accident.
Charles Lamb 1775–1834: 'Table Talk by the late Elia' in *The Athenaeum* 4 January 1834

12 Who loves not woman, wine, and song
Remains a fool his whole life long.
Martin Luther 1483–1546: attributed; later inscribed in the Luther room in the Wartburg, but with no proof of authorship

13 The Puritan hated bear-baiting, not because it gave pain to the bear, but because it gave pleasure to the spectators.
Lord Macaulay 1800–59: *History of England* vol. 1 (1849)

14 It is a curious thing that people only ask if you are enjoying yourself when you aren't.
Edith Nesbit 1858–1924: *Five of Us, and Madeline* (1925)

15 I admit it is better fun to punt than to be punted, and that a desire to have all the fun is nine-tenths of the law of chivalry.
Dorothy L. Sayers 1893–1957: *Gaudy Night* (1935)

16 Pleasure is nothing else but the intermission of pain.
John Selden 1584–1654: *Table Talk* (1689) 'Pleasure'

17 All the things I really like to do are either illegal, immoral, or fattening.
Alexander Woollcott 1887–1943: R. E. Drennan *Wit's End* (1973)

18 It's always the good feel rotten. Pleasure's for those who are bad.
Sergei Yesenin 1895–1925: 'Pleasure's for the Bad' (1923)

Poetry

see also **Writing**

1 It is barbarous to write a poem after Auschwitz.
Theodor Adorno 1903–69: I. Buruma *Wages of Guilt* (1994)

2 A poet's hope: to be,
like some valley cheese,
local, but prized elsewhere.
W. H. Auden 1907–73: 'Shorts II' (1976)

3 Prose is when all the lines except the last go on to the end. Poetry is when some of them fall short of it.
Jeremy Bentham 1748–1832: M. St J. Packe *The Life of John Stuart Mill* (1954)

4 Some rhyme a neebor's name to lash;
Some rhyme (vain thought!) for needfu' cash;
Some rhyme to court the countra clash,
An' raise a din;
For me, an aim I never fash;
I rhyme for fun.
Robert Burns 1759–96: 'To J. S[mith]' (1786)

5 All poets are mad.
Robert Burton 1577–1640: *The Anatomy of Melancholy* (1621–51)

6 There's nothing in the world for which a poet will give up writing, not even when he is a Jew and the language of his poems is German.
Paul Celan 1920–70: letter to relatives, 2 August 1948

7 The worst tragedy for a poet is to be admired through being misunderstood.
Jean Cocteau 1889–1963: *Le Rappel à l'ordre* (1926)

8 That willing suspension of disbelief for the moment, which constitutes poetic faith.
Samuel Taylor Coleridge 1772–1834: *Biographia Literaria* (1817)

9 Prose = words in their best order;— poetry = the *best* words in the best order.
Samuel Taylor Coleridge 1772–1834: *Table Talk* (1835) 12 July 1827

10 Sometimes poetry is emotion recollected in a highly emotional state.
Wendy Cope 1945– : 'An Argument with Wordsworth' (1992); see 32 below

11 I am two fools, I know,
For loving, and for saying so
In whining poetry.
John Donne 1572–1631: 'The Triple Fool'

12 The beginning of a poem is always a moment of tiny revelation, a new way of seeing something, which almost simultaneously attracts language to it.
Carol Ann Duffy 1965– : in *Independent* 2 October 1999

13 As well as between tongue and teeth, poetry happens between the ears and behind the left nipple.
Douglas Dunn 1942– : in *Observer* 23 March 1997

14 Poetry is not a turning loose of emotion, but an escape from emotion; it is not the expression of personality but an escape from personality.
T. S. Eliot 1888–1965: *The Sacred Wood* (1920)

15 Poetry's a mere drug, Sir.
George Farquhar 1678–1707: *Love and a Bottle* (1698)

16 I'd as soon write free verse as play tennis with the net down.
Robert Frost 1874–1963: Edward Lathem *Interviews with Robert Frost* (1966)

17 As soon as war is declared it will be impossible to hold the poets back. Rhyme is still the most effective drum.
Jean Giraudoux 1882–1944: *La Guerre de Troie n'aura pas lieu* (1935)

18 What are poems for? They are to console us
with their own gift, which is like perfect pitch.
Let us commit that to our dust. What ought a poem be? Answer, *a sad and angry consolation.*
Geoffrey Hill 1932– : *The Triumph of Love* (1999)

19 Experience has taught me, when I am shaving of a morning, to keep watch over my thoughts, because, if a line of poetry strays into my memory, my skin bristles so that the razor ceases to act . . . The seat of this sensation is the pit of the stomach.
A. E. Housman 1859–1936: lecture at Cambridge, 9 May 1933

20 If poetry comes not as naturally as the leaves to a tree it had better not come at all.
John Keats 1795–1821: letter to John Taylor, 27 February 1818

21 The notion of expressing sentiments in short lines having similar sounds at their ends seems as remote as mangoes on the moon.
Philip Larkin 1922–85: letter to Barbara Pym, 22 January 1975

22 For twenty years I've stared my level best
To see if evening—any evening—would suggest
A patient etherized upon a table;
In vain. I simply wasn't able.
■ *on contemporary poetry*
C. S. Lewis 1898–1963: 'A Confession' (1964); see **Evening** 1

23 A poem should not mean
But be.
Archibald MacLeish 1892–1982: 'Ars Poetica' (1926)

24 In our language rhyme is a barrel. A barrel of dynamite. The line is a fuse. The line smoulders to the end and explodes; and the town is blown sky-high in a stanza.
Vladimir Mayakovsky 1893–1930: 'Conversation with an Inspector of Taxes about Poetry' (1926)

25 Most people ignore most poetry because
most poetry ignores most people.
Adrian Mitchell 1932– : *Poems* (1964)

26 All that is not prose is verse; and all that is not verse is prose.
Molière 1622–73: *Le Bourgeois Gentilhomme* (1671)

27 All a poet can do today is warn.
Wilfred Owen 1893–1918: preface (written 1918) in *Poems* (1963)

28 Poetry is the achievement of the synthesis of hyacinths and biscuits.

Carl Sandburg 1878–1967: in *Atlantic Monthly* March 1923

29 Poets are the unacknowledged legislators of the world.

Percy Bysshe Shelley 1792–1822: *A Defence of Poetry* (written 1821)

30 Poetry is not the most important thing in life . . . I'd much rather lie in a hot bath reading Agatha Christie and sucking sweets.

Dylan Thomas 1914–53: Joan Wyndham *Love is Blue* (1986) 6 July 1943

31 In this
most Christian of worlds all poets are Jews.

Marina Tsvetaeva 1892–1941: 'Poem of the End' (1924)

32 Poetry is the spontaneous overflow of powerful feelings: it takes its origin from emotion recollected in tranquillity.

William Wordsworth 1770–1850: *Lyrical Ballads* (2nd ed., 1802)

33 I said 'a line will take us hours maybe;
Yet if it does not seem a moment's thought,
Our stitching and unstitching has been naught.'

W. B. Yeats 1865–1939: 'Adam's Curse' (1904)

34 We make out of the quarrel with others, rhetoric, but of the quarrel with ourselves, poetry.

W. B. Yeats 1865–1939: *Essays* (1924) 'Anima Hominis'

35 I think poetry should be alive. You should be able to dance it.

Benjamin Zephaniah 1958– : in *Sunday Times* 23 August 1987

Poets

....

1 He spoke, and loosed our heart in tears.
He laid us as we lay at birth
On the cool flowery lap of earth.
▪ *of Wordsworth*

Matthew Arnold 1822–88: 'Memorial Verses, April 1850' (1852)

2 In poetry, no less than in life, he is 'a beautiful and ineffectual angel, beating in the void his luminous wings in vain'.

Matthew Arnold 1822–88: *Essays in Criticism* Second Series (1888) 'Shelley'

3 You were silly like us; your gift survived it all:
The parish of rich women, physical decay,
Yourself. Mad Ireland hurt you into poetry.

W. H. Auden 1907–73: 'In Memory of W. B. Yeats' (1940)

4 The reason Milton wrote in fetters when he wrote of Angels and God, and at liberty when of Devils and Hell, is because he was a true Poet, and of the Devil's party without knowing it.

William Blake 1757–1827: *The Marriage of Heaven and Hell* (1790–3)

5 How thankful we ought to be that Wordsworth was only a poet and not a musician. Fancy a symphony by Wordsworth! Fancy having to sit it out! And fancy what it would have been if he had written fugues!

Samuel Butler 1835–1902: *Notebooks* (1912)

6 He could not think up to the height of his own towering style.
▪ *of Tennyson*

G. K. Chesterton 1874–1936: *The Victorian Age in Literature* (1912)

7 With Donne, whose muse on dromedary trots,
Wreathe iron pokers into true-love knots.

Samuel Taylor Coleridge 1772–1834: 'On Donne's Poetry' (1818)

8 You who desired so much—in vain to ask—
Yet fed your hunger like an endless task,
Dared dignify the labor, bless the quest—
Achieved that stillness ultimately best,

Being, of all, least sought for: Emily, hear!
Hart Crane 1899–1932: 'To Emily Dickinson' (1927)

9 'Tis sufficient to say, according to the proverb, that here is God's plenty.
■ *of Chaucer*
John Dryden 1631–1700: *Fables Ancient and Modern* (1700)

10 How unpleasant to meet Mr Eliot!
With his features of clerical cut,
And his brow so grim
And his mouth so prim
And his conversation, so nicely
Restricted to What Precisely
And If and Perhaps and But.
T. S. Eliot 1888–1965: 'Five-Finger Exercises' (1936)

11 *Hugo—hélas!*
Hugo—alas!
■ *when asked who was the greatest 19th-century poet*
André Gide 1869–1951: Claude Martin *La Maturité d'André Gide* (1977)

12 Dr Donne's verses are like the peace of God; they pass all understanding.
James I 1566–1625: remark recorded by Archdeacon Plume (1630–1704)

13 Milton, Madam, was a genius that could cut a Colossus from a rock; but could not carve heads upon cherry-stones.
■ *to Hannah More, who had expressed a wonder that the poet who had written* Paradise Lost *should write such poor sonnets*
Samuel Johnson 1709–84: James Boswell *Life of Samuel Johnson* (1791) 13 June 1784

14 Self-contempt, well-grounded.
■ *on the foundation of T. S. Eliot's work*
F. R. Leavis 1895–1978: in *Times Literary Supplement* 21 October 1988

15 The high-water mark, so to speak, of Socialist literature is W. H. Auden, a sort of gutless Kipling.
George Orwell 1903–50: *The Road to Wigan Pier* (1937)

16 A cloud-encircled meteor of the air,
A hooded eagle among blinking owls.
■ *of Coleridge*
Percy Bysshe Shelley 1792–1822: 'Letter to Maria Gisborne' (1820)

17 Life's a curse, love's a blight, God's a blaggard, cherry blossom is quite nice.
■ *on A. E. Housman*
Tom Stoppard 1937– : *The Invention of Love* (1997)

18 To see him fumbling with our rich and delicate language is to experience all the horror of seeing a Sèvres vase in the hands of a chimpanzee.
■ *of Stephen Spender*
Evelyn Waugh 1903–66: in *The Tablet* 5 May 1951

19 Chaos, illumined by flashes of lightning.
■ *on Robert Browning's 'style'*
Oscar Wilde 1854–1900: Ada Leverson *Letters to the Sphinx* (1930)

20 I thought of Chatterton, the marvellous boy,
The sleepless soul that perished in its pride.
William Wordsworth 1770–1850: 'Resolution and Independence' (1807)

Police
....
see also **Laws**

1 When constabulary duty's to be done,
A policeman's lot is not a happy one.
W. S. Gilbert 1836–1911: *The Pirates of Penzance* (1879)

2 There is no class of person more moved by hatred than the motorist and the policeman is a convenient receptacle for his feeling.
C. W. Hewitt: speech to the Lawyers' Club of the London School of Economics, 22 October 1959

3 Every society gets the kind of criminal it deserves. What is equally true is that every community gets the kind of law enforcement it insists on.
Robert Kennedy 1925–68: *The Pursuit of Justice* (1964)

4 The South African police would leave no stone unturned to see that nothing disturbed the even terror of their lives.
Tom Sharpe 1928– : *Indecent Exposure* (1973)

5 A liberal is a conservative who has been arrested.

Tom Wolfe 1931– : *The Bonfire of the Vanities* (1987)

Political Parties

see also **Communism, Politicians, Politics**

1 The language of priorities is the religion of Socialism.

Aneurin Bevan 1897–1960: speech at Labour Party Conference in Blackpool, 8 June 1949

2 Fascism is not in itself a new order of society. It is the future refusing to be born.

Aneurin Bevan 1897–1960: Leon Harris *The Fine Art of Political Wit* (1965)

3 God will not always be a Tory.

Lord Byron 1788–1824: letter 2 February 1821

4 Then raise the scarlet standard high!
Within its shade we'll live or die.
Tho' cowards flinch and traitors sneer,
We'll keep the red flag flying here.

James M. Connell 1852–1929: 'The Red Flag' (1889 song)

5 Damn your principles! Stick to your party.

Benjamin Disraeli 1804–81: attributed to Disraeli and believed to have been said to Edward Bulwer-Lytton; E. Latham *Famous Sayings and their Authors* (1904)

6 I did not vote Labour because they've heard of Oasis and nobody is going to vote Tory because William Hague has got a baseball cap.

Ben Elton 1959– : in *Radio Times* 18 April 1998

7 The Provisional IRA is no more a left-wing movement than Hitler's National Socialist Party was.

Garret Fitzgerald 1926– : comment, 1973

8 There are some of us . . . who will fight and fight and fight again to save the Party we love.

Hugh Gaitskell 1906–63: speech at Labour Party Conference, 5 October 1960

9 I always voted at my party's call,
And I never thought of thinking for myself at all.

W. S. Gilbert 1836–1911: *HMS Pinafore* (1878)

10 Conservatives do not believe that the political struggle is the most important thing in life . . . The simplest of them prefer fox-hunting—the wisest religion.

Lord Hailsham 1907–2001: *The Case for Conservatism* (1947)

11 We are all socialists now.

■ *during the passage of the 1888 budget, noted for the reduction of the National Debt*

William Harcourt 1827–1904: attributed; Hubert Bland 'The Outlook' in G. B. Shaw (ed.) *Fabian Essays in Socialism* (1889)

12 A dead or dying beast lying across a railway line and preventing other trains from getting through.

■ *of the Labour Party*

Roy Jenkins 1920–2003: in *Guardian* 16 May 1987

13 I am a free man, an American, a United States Senator, and a Democrat, in that order.

Lyndon Baines Johnson 1908–73: in *Texas Quarterly* Winter 1958

14 The longest suicide note in history.

■ *on the Labour Party's election manifesto* New Hope for Britain *(1983)*

Gerald Kaufman 1930– : Denis Healey *The Time of My Life* (1989)

15 When in office, the Liberals forget their principles and the Tories remember their friends.

Thomas Kettle 1880–1916: Nicholas Mansergh *The Irish Question* (ed. 3, 1975)

16 Loyalty is the Tory's secret weapon.

Lord Kilmuir 1900–67: Anthony Sampson *Anatomy of Britain* (1962)

17 What is conservatism? Is it not adherence to the old and tried, against the new and untried?

Abraham Lincoln 1809–65: speech, 27 February 1860

18 As usual the Liberals offer a mixture of sound and original ideas. Unfortunately none of the sound ideas is original and none of the original ideas is sound.

Harold Macmillan 1894–1986: speech to London Conservatives, 7 March 1961

19 Under democracy one party always devotes its energies to trying to prove that the other party is unfit to rule— and both commonly succeed and are right.

H. L. Mencken 1880–1956: *Minority Report* (1956)

20 I fear my Socialism is purely cerebral; I do not like the masses in the flesh.

Harold Nicolson 1886–1968: letter to Vita Sackville-West, 7 May 1948

21 I have only one firm belief about the American political system, and that is this: God is a Republican and Santa Claus is a Democrat.

P. J. O'Rourke 1947– : *Parliament of Whores* (1991)

22 To the ordinary working man, the sort you would meet in any pub on Saturday night, Socialism does not mean much more than better wages and shorter hours and nobody bossing you about.

George Orwell 1903–50: *The Road to Wigan Pier* (1937)

23 The Labour Party owes more to Methodism than to Marxism.

Morgan Phillips 1902–63: James Callaghan *Time and Chance* (1987)

24 I am reminded of four definitions: A Radical is a man with both feet firmly planted—in the air. A Conservative is a man with two perfectly good legs who, however, has never learned to walk forward. A Reactionary is a somnambulist walking backwards. A Liberal is a man who uses his legs and his hands at the behest—at the command—of his head.

Franklin D. Roosevelt 1882–1945: radio address, 26 October 1939

25 If they [the Republicans] will stop telling lies about the Democrats, we will stop telling the truth about them.

Adlai Stevenson 1900–65: speech during 1952 Presidential campaign; J. B. Martin *Adlai Stevenson and Illinois* (1976)

26 An independent is a guy who wants to take the politics out of politics.

Adlai Stevenson 1900–65: Bill Adler *The Stevenson Wit* (1966)

27 Socialism can only arrive by bicycle.

José Antonio Viera Gallo 1943– : Ivan Illich *Energy and Equity* (1974) epigraph

28 This party is a moral crusade or it is nothing.

Harold Wilson 1916–95: speech at the Labour Party Conference, 1 October 1962

29 This party is a bit like an old stage-coach. If you drive along at a rapid rate, everyone aboard is either so exhilarated or so seasick that you don't have a lot of difficulty.

■ *of the Labour Party*

Harold Wilson 1916–95: Anthony Sampson *The Changing Anatomy of Britain* (1982)

Politicians

see also **People**, **Political Parties**, **Politics**, **The Presidency**, **Prime Ministers**, **Speeches**

1 A political leader must keep looking over his shoulder all the time to see if the boys are still there. If they aren't still there, he's no longer a political leader.

Bernard Baruch 1870–1965: in *New York Times* 21 June 1965

2 I am not going to spend any time whatsoever in attacking the Foreign Secretary . . . If we complain about the tune, there is no reason to attack the monkey when the organ grinder is present.

■ *during a debate on the Suez crisis*

Aneurin Bevan 1897–1960: speech, House of Commons, 16 May 1957

3 An honest politician is one who when he's bought stays bought.

Simon Cameron 1799–1889: attributed

4 A minister who moves about in society is in a position to read the signs of the times even in a festive gathering, but one who remains shut up in his office learns nothing.

Duc de Choiseul 1719–85: Jack F. Bernard *Talleyrand* (1973)

5 The ability to foretell what is going to happen tomorrow, next week, next month, and next year. And to have the ability afterwards to explain why it didn't happen.

■ *describing the qualifications desirable in a prospective politician*

Winston Churchill 1874–1965: B. Adler *Churchill Wit* (1965)

6 I do not wear a bleeper. I can't speak in soundbites. I refuse to repeat slogans. . . . I hate focus groups. I absolutely hate image consultants.

Kenneth Clarke 1940– : in *New Statesman* 12 February 1999

7 a politician is an arse upon which everyone has sat except a man.

e. e. cummings 1894–1962: *1 x 1* (1944) no. 10

8 'Do you pray for the senators, Dr Hale?' 'No, I look at the senators and I pray for the country.'

Edward Everett Hale 1822–1909: Van Wyck Brooks *New England Indian Summer* (1940)

9 Politicians are entitled to change their minds. But when they adjust their principles some explanation is necessary.

Roy Hattersley 1932– : in *Observer* 21 March 1999

10 If you want to succeed in politics, you must keep your conscience well under control.

David Lloyd George 1863–1945: Lord Riddell, diary, 23 April 1919

11 Forever poised between a cliché and an indiscretion.

■ *on the life of a Foreign Secretary*

Harold Macmillan 1894–1986: in *Newsweek* 30 April 1956

12 did you ever
notice that when
a politician
does get an idea
he usually

gets it all wrong.

Don Marquis 1878–1937: *archys life of mehitabel* (1933)

13 What I want is men who will support me when I am in the wrong.

■ *replying to a politician who said 'I will support you as long as you are in the right'*

Lord Melbourne 1779–1848: Lord David Cecil *Lord M* (1954)

14 The greatest gift of any statesman rests not in knowing what concessions to make, but recognising when to make them.

Prince Metternich 1773–1859: *Concessionen und Nichtconcessionen* (1852)

15 If I saw Mr Haughey buried at midnight at a crossroads, with a stake driven through his heart—politically speaking—I should continue to wear a clove of garlic round my neck, just in case.

Conor Cruise O'Brien 1917– : in *Observer* 10 October 1982

16 Why waste it on some vanilla-flavoured pixie. Bring on the fruitcakes, we want a fruitcake for an unlosable seat. They enliven the Commons.

■ *the day before the Kensington and Chelsea association chose Alan Clark as their parliamentary candidate*

Matthew Parris 1949– : in *Mail on Sunday* 26 January 1997; cf. **Politics** 13

17 A statesman is a politician who places himself at the service of the nation. A politician is a statesman who places the nation at his service.

Georges Pompidou 1911–74: in *Observer* 30 December 1973

18 All political lives, unless they are cut off in midstream at a happy juncture, end in failure, because that is the nature of politics and of human affairs.

Enoch Powell 1912–98: *Joseph Chamberlain* (1977)

19 He may be a son of a bitch, but he's our son of a bitch.

■ *on President Somoza of Nicaragua, 1938*

Franklin D. Roosevelt 1882–1945: attributed

20 He knows nothing; and he thinks he knows everything. That points clearly to a political career.
> **George Bernard Shaw** 1856–1950: *Major Barbara* (1907)

21 Someone must fill the gap between platitudes and bayonets.
> **Adlai Stevenson** 1900–65: Leon Harris *The Fine Art of Political Wit* (1965)

22 In politics, if you want anything said, ask a man. If you want anything done, ask a woman.
> **Margaret Thatcher** 1925– : in 1970; in *People* (New York) 15 September 1975

23 A politician is a man who understands government, and it takes a politician to run a government. A statesman is a politician who's been dead 10 or 15 years.
> **Harry S. Truman** 1884–1972: in *New York World Telegram and Sun* 12 April 1958

24 I don't always admit to being an MP. If I'm in a bar with people I don't know, to say you're a Labour MP isn't always a good move. I have said I'm a solicitor.
> **Claire Ward** 1972– : in *Independent on Sunday* 14 March 1999

25 The best time to listen to a politician is when he's on the stump on a street corner in the rain late at night when he's exhausted. Then he doesn't lie.
> **Theodore H. White** 1915–86: in *New York Times* 5 January 1969

26 The average footslogger in the New South Wales Right . . . generally speaking carries a dagger in one hand and a Bible in the other and doesn't put either to really elegant use.
> **Neville Wran** 1926– : in 1973; Michael Gordon *A Question of Leadership* (1993)

27 We enjoyed . . . his slyness. He mastered the art of walking backward into the future. He would say 'After me'. And some people went ahead, and some went behind, and he would go backward.
> ■ *of Mikhail Gorbachev*
> **Mikhail Zhvanetsky** 1934– : in *Time* 12 September 1994; attributed

Politics
. . . .
see also **Democracy, Elections, Government, International Relations, Parliament, Political Parties, Politicians, Power, Protest, Revolution, Terrorism**

1 The trouble with this country is that there are too many politicians who believe, with a conviction based on experience, that you can fool all of the people all of the time.
> **Franklin P. Adams** 1881–1960: *Nods and Becks* (1944); see **Deception** 5

2 Politics, as a practice, whatever its professions, has always been the systematic organization of hatreds.
> **Henry Brooks Adams** 1838–1918: *The Education of Henry Adams* (1907)

3 I agree with you that in politics the middle way is none at all.
> **John Adams** 1735–1826: letter to Horatio Gates, 23 March 1776

4 Man is by nature a political animal.
> **Aristotle** 384–322 BC: *Politics*

5 We should put the spin-doctors in spin clinics, where they can meet other spin patients and be treated by spin consultants. The rest of us can get on with the proper democratic process.
> **Tony Benn** 1925– : in *Independent* 25 October 1997

6 A statesman . . . must wait until he hears the steps of God sounding through events; then leap up and grasp the hem of his garment.
> **Otto von Bismarck** 1815–98: A. J. P. Taylor *Bismarck* (1955)

7 Politics is the art of the possible.
> **Otto von Bismarck** 1815–98: in conversation with Meyer von Waldeck, 11 August 1867

8 The liberals can understand everything but people who don't understand them.
> **Lenny Bruce** 1925–66: John Cohen (ed.) *The Essential Lenny Bruce* (1967)

9 In politics you must always keep running with the pack. The moment that you falter and they sense that you

are injured, the rest will turn on you like wolves.
R. A. Butler 1902–82: Dennis Walters *Not Always with the Pack* (1989)

10 In politics, there is no use looking beyond the next fortnight.
Joseph Chamberlain 1836–1914: letter from A. J. Balfour to 3rd Marquess of Salisbury, 24 March 1886

11 Politics are almost as exciting as war and quite as dangerous. In war you can only be killed once, but in politics—many times.
Winston Churchill 1874–1965: attributed

12 There are no true friends in politics. We are all sharks circling, and waiting, for traces of blood to appear in the water.
Alan Clark 1928–99: diary 30 November 1990

13 Safe is spelled D-U-L-L. Politics has got to be a fun activity, otherwise people turn their back on it.
Alan Clark 1928–99: on being selected as parliamentary candidate for Kensington and Chelsea, 24 January 1997; cf. **Politicians** 16

14 If something makes you cry, you have to do something about it. That's the difference between politics and guilt.
Bill Clinton 1946– : *On the Make* (1994)

15 International life is right-wing, like nature. The social contract is left-wing, like humanity.
Régis Debray 1940– : *Charles de Gaulle* (1994)

16 Politics are too serious a matter to be left to the politicians.
■ *replying to Attlee's remark that 'De Gaulle is a very good soldier and a very bad politician'*
Charles de Gaulle 1890–1970: Clement Attlee *A Prime Minister Remembers* (1961)

17 Finality is not the language of politics.
Benjamin Disraeli 1804–81: speech, House of Commons, 28 February 1859

18 I never dared be radical when young For fear it would make me conservative when old.
Robert Frost 1874–1963: 'Precaution' (1936)

19 Politics is not the art of the possible. It consists in choosing between the disastrous and the unpalatable.
J. K. Galbraith 1908– : letter to President Kennedy, 2 March 1962; see 7 above

20 In politics, being ridiculous is more damaging than being extreme.
Roy Hattersley 1932– : in *Evening Standard* 9 May 1989

21 Let us teach ourselves and others that politics can be not only the art of the possible, especially if this means the art of speculation, calculation, intrigue, secret deals, and pragmatic manoeuvring, but that it can even be the art of the impossible, namely, the art of improving ourselves and the world.
Václav Havel 1936– : speech, Prague, 1 January 1990; cf. 7 above

22 Healey's first law of politics: when you're in a hole, stop digging.
Denis Healey 1917– : attributed

23 Politics is a marathon, not a sprint.
Ken Livingstone 1945– : in *New Statesman* 10 October 1997

24 Events, dear boy. Events.
■ *when asked what his biggest problem was*
Harold Macmillan 1894–1986: attributed

25 Politics is war without bloodshed while war is politics with bloodshed.
Mao Zedong 1893–1976: lecture, 1938

26 All reactionaries are paper tigers. In appearance, the reactionaries are terrifying, but in reality they are not so powerful. From a long-term point of view, it is not the reactionaries but the people who are really powerful.
Mao Zedong 1893–1976: interview with Anne Louise Strong, August 1946

27 Political language . . . is designed to make lies sound truthful and murder respectable, and to give an appearance of solidity to pure wind.
George Orwell 1903–50: *Shooting an Elephant* (1950) 'Politics and the English Language'

28 Men enter local politics solely as a
result of being unhappily married.
C. Northcote Parkinson 1909–93: *Parkinson's
Law* (1958)

29 Politics is supposed to be the second
oldest profession. I have come to
realize that it bears a very close
resemblance to the first.
Ronald Reagan 1911– : at a conference in Los
Angeles, 2 March 1977

30 What is morally wrong cannot be
politically right.
Donald Soper 1903–98: speech, House of
Lords, 1966

31 A week is a long time in politics.
■ *probably first said at the time of the
1964 sterling crisis*
Harold Wilson 1916–95: Nigel Rees *Sayings of
the Century* (1984)

Pollution

see also **The Earth**, **The Environment**,
Nature

1 And did the Countenance Divine
Shine forth upon our clouded hills?
And was Jerusalem builded here
Among these dark Satanic mills?
William Blake 1757–1827: *Milton* (1804–10)
'And did those feet in ancient time'

2 Over increasingly large areas of the
United States, spring now comes
unheralded by the return of the birds,
and the early mornings are strangely
silent where once they were filled with
the beauty of bird song.
Rachel Carson 1907–64: *The Silent Spring*
(1962)

3 The river Rhine, it is well known,
Doth wash your city of Cologne;
But tell me, Nymphs, what power
divine
Shall henceforth wash the river
Rhine?
Samuel Taylor Coleridge 1772–1834: 'Cologne'
(1834)

4 The sea is the universal sewer.
Jacques Cousteau 1910–97: testimony before
the House Committee on Science and
Astronautics, 28 January 1971

5 Pollution knows no boundaries any
more than do money or information.
Peter F. Drucker 1909– : *Post-Capitalist
Society* (1993)

6 Clear the air! clean the sky! wash the
wind!
T. S. Eliot 1888–1965: *Murder in the Cathedral*
(1935)

7 The sanitary and mechanical age we
are now entering makes up for the
mercy it grants to our sense of smell
by the ferocity with which it assails
our sense of hearing. As usual, what
we call 'progress' is the exchange of
one nuisance for another nuisance.
Havelock Ellis 1859–1939: *Impressions and
Comments* (1914)

8 We live in a world where emissions
from our refrigerators have caused the
ozone layer to evaporate and we'll get
skin cancer if we sunbathe. If that's
not a science fiction scenario, I don't
know what is.
William Gibson 1948– : in *Newsweek* 5 June
1995

9 Dirt is only matter out of place.
John Chipman Gray 1839–1915: *Restraints on
the Alienation of Property* (2nd ed., 1895)

10 And all is seared with trade; bleared,
smeared with toil;
And wears man's smudge and shares
man's smell.
Gerard Manley Hopkins 1844–89: 'God's
Grandeur' (written 1877)

11 Forget six counties overhung with
smoke,
Forget the snorting steam and piston
stroke,
Forget the spreading of the hideous
town;
Think rather of the pack-horse on the
down,
And dream of London, small and
white and clean,
The clear Thames bordered by its
gardens green.
William Morris 1834–96: *The Earthly Paradise*
(1868–70)

12 It goes so heavily with my disposition
that this goodly frame, the earth,

seems to me a sterile promontory; this most excellent canopy, the air, look you, this brave o'erhanging firmament, this majestical roof fretted with golden fire, why, it appears no other thing to me but a foul and pestilent congregation of vapours.

William Shakespeare 1564–1616: *Hamlet* (1601)

13 I do wonder whether there will come a time when we can no longer afford our wastefulness—chemical wastes in the rivers, metal wastes everywhere, and atomic wastes buried deep in the earth or sunk in the sea. When an Indian village became too deep in its own filth, the inhabitants moved. And we have no place to which to move.

John Steinbeck 1902–68: *Travels With Charley* (1962)

14 There should be supermarkets that sell things and supermarkets that buy things back, and until that equalizes, there'll be more waste than there should be.

Andy Warhol 1927–87: *Philosophy of Andy Warhol* (*From A to B and Back Again*) (1975)

15 The packet of biscuits I opened for my elevenses this morning was wrapped up in more layers than a pensioner going out into the snow.

Keith Waterhouse 1929– : in *Daily Mail* 11 June 1998

Pop Music

see **Rock and Pop Music**

Pornography

1 A widespread taste for pornography means that nature is alerting us to some threat of extinction.

J. G. Ballard 1930– : *Myths of the Near Future* (1982)

2 Pornography is rather like trying to find out about a Beethoven symphony by having somebody tell you about it and perhaps hum a few bars.

Robertson Davies 1913–95: in 1972; *The Enthusiasms of Robertson Davies* (1990)

3 Porn is altogether pragmatic. It exists to stimulate and satisfy an appetite just the way cookery books do, except the porn reader always has his ingredients to hand.

Irma Kurtz: *Malespeak* (1986)

4 Pornography is the attempt to insult sex, to do dirt on it.

D. H. Lawrence 1885–1930: *Phoenix* (1936) 'Pornography and Obscenity'

5 It is obvious that 'obscenity' is not a term capable of exact legal definition; in the practice of the Courts, it means 'anything that shocks the magistrate'.

Bertrand Russell 1872–1970: *Sceptical Essays* (1928) 'The Recrudescence of Puritanism'

6 What pornography is really about, ultimately, isn't sex but death.

Susan Sontag 1933– : in *Partisan Review* Spring 1967

Possessions

1 The goal of all inanimate objects is to resist man and ultimately to defeat him.

Russell Baker 1925– : in *New York Times* 18 June 1968

2 For we brought nothing into this world, and it is certain we can carry nothing out.

Bible: I Timothy

3 There are only two families in the world, as a grandmother of mine used to say: the haves and the have-nots.

Cervantes 1547–1616: *Don Quixote* (1605)

4 People don't resent having nothing nearly as much as too little.

Ivy Compton-Burnett 1884–1969: *A Family and a Fortune* (1939)

5 The moon belongs to everyone, The best things in life are free.

Buddy De Sylva 1895–1950 and **Lew Brown** 1893–1958: 'The Best Things in Life are Free' (1927 song)

6 Property has its duties as well as its rights.
   Thomas Drummond 1797–1840: letter to the Earl of Donoughmore, 22 May 1838

7 Well! some people talk of morality, and some of religion, but give me a little snug property.
   Maria Edgeworth 1768–1849: *The Absentee* (1812)

8 People who get through life dependent on other people's possessions are always the first to lecture you on how little possessions count.
   Ben Elton 1959– : *Stark* (1989)

9 Things are in the saddle, And ride mankind.
   Ralph Waldo Emerson 1803–82: 'Ode' Inscribed to W. H. Channing (1847)

10 Man must choose whether to be rich in things or in the freedom to use them.
   Ivan Illich 1926– : *Deschooling Society* (1971)

11 Have nothing in your houses that you do not know to be useful, or believe to be beautiful.
   William Morris 1834–96: *Hopes and Fears for Art* (1882)

12 Property is theft.
   Pierre-Joseph Proudhon 1809–65: *Qu'est-ce que la propriété?* (1840)

13 How many things I can do without!
   ■ *on looking at a multitude of wares exposed for sale*
   Socrates 469–399 BC: Diogenes Laertius *Lives of the Philosophers*

14 The constant desire to have more things and a still better life, and the struggle to this end imprints many Western faces with worry and even depression, though it is customary to carefully conceal such feelings.
   Alexander Solzhenitsyn 1918– : speech in Cambridge, Massachusetts, 8 June 1978

15 Never be afraid of throwing away what you have, if you *can* throw it away, it is not really yours.
   R. H. Tawney 1880–1962: diary 1912

16 If men are to respect each other for what they are, they must cease to respect each other for what they own.
   A. J. P. Taylor 1906–90: *Politicians, Socialism and Historians* (1980)

Poverty

see also **Money**, **Wealth**

1 She was poor but she was honest
   Victim of a rich man's game.
   First he loved her, then he left her,
   And she lost her maiden name . . .
   It's the same the whole world over,
   It's the poor wot gets the blame,
   It's the rich wot gets the gravy.
   Ain't it all a bleedin' shame?
   Anonymous: 'She was Poor but she was Honest'; sung by British soldiers in the First World War

2 Anyone who has ever struggled with poverty knows how extremely expensive it is to be poor.
   James Baldwin 1924–87: *Nobody Knows My Name* (1961)

3 Come away; poverty's catching.
   Aphra Behn 1640–89: *The Rover* pt. 2 (1681)

4 The poor always ye have with you.
   Bible: St John

5 In future, welfare will be a hand-up not a hand-out.
   Tony Blair 1953– : lecture, London, 18 March 1999

6 When I give food to the poor they call me a saint. When I ask why the poor have no food they call me a communist.
   Helder Camara 1909– : attributed

7 The poor are Europe's blacks.
   Nicolas-Sébastien Chamfort 1741–94: *Maximes et Pensées* (1796)

8 The poor cannot always reach those whom they want to love, and they can hardly ever escape from those whom they no longer love.
   E. M. Forster 1879–1970: *Howards End* (1910)

9 They [the poor] have to labour in the face of the majestic equality of the law,

which forbids the rich as well as the poor to sleep under bridges, to beg in the streets, and to steal bread.

Anatole France 1844–1924: *Le Lys rouge* (1894)

10 Laws grind the poor, and rich men rule the law.

Oliver Goldsmith 1728–74: *The Traveller* (1764)

11 Let not ambition mock their useful toil,
Their homely joys, and destiny obscure;
Nor grandeur hear with a disdainful smile,
The short and simple annals of the poor.

Thomas Gray 1716–71: *Elegy Written in a Country Churchyard* (1751)

12 Brother can you spare a dime?

E. Y. Harburg 1898–1981: title of song (1932)

13 I want there to be no peasant in my kingdom so poor that he is unable to have a chicken in his pot every Sunday.

Henri IV 1553–1610: Hardouin de Péréfixe *Histoire de Henry le Grand* (1681); cf. **Progress** 11

14 Oh! God! that bread should be so dear,
And flesh and blood so cheap!

Thomas Hood 1799–1845: 'The Song of the Shirt' (1843)

15 Resolve not to be poor: whatever you have, spend less. Poverty is a great enemy to human happiness; it certainly destroys liberty, and it makes some virtues impracticable, and others extremely difficult.

Samuel Johnson 1709–84: letter to Boswell, 7 December 1782

16 The misfortunes of poverty carry with them nothing harder to bear than that it makes men ridiculous.

Juvenal AD *c.*60–*c.*130: *Satires*

17 There's nothing surer,
The rich get rich and the poor get children.

Gus Kahn 1886–1941 and **Raymond B. Egan** 1890–1952: 'Ain't We Got Fun' (1921 song)

18 I never saw a beggar yet who would recognise guilt if it bit him on his unwashed ass.

Tony Parsons 1953– : *Dispatches from the Front Line of Popular Culture* (1994)

19 The greatest of evils and the worst of crimes is poverty.

George Bernard Shaw 1856–1950: *Major Barbara* (1907)

20 Born down in a dead man's town
The first kick I took was when I hit the ground.

Bruce Springsteen 1949– : 'Born in the USA' (1984 song)

21 She was not so much a person as an implication of dreary poverty, like an open door in a mean house that lets out the smell of cooking cabbage and the screams of children.

Rebecca West 1892–1983: *The Return of the Soldier* (1918)

Power

see also **Politics**, **Strength and Weakness**

1 Power tends to corrupt and absolute power corrupts absolutely.

Lord Acton 1834–1902: letter to Bishop Mandell Creighton, 3 April 1887

2 When he laughed, respectable senators burst with laughter,
And when he cried the little children died in the streets.

W. H. Auden 1907–73: 'Epitaph on a Tyrant' (1940)

3 Whatever happens we have got
The Maxim Gun, and they have not.

Hilaire Belloc 1870–1953: *The Modern Traveller* (1898)

4 Every dictator uses religion as a prop to keep himself in power.

Benazir Bhutto 1953– : interview on *60 Minutes*, CBS-TV, 8 August 1986

5 The finest plans are always ruined by the littleness of those who ought to carry them out, for the Emperors can actually do nothing.

Bertolt Brecht 1898–1956: *Mother Courage* (1939)

6 'The question is,' said Humpty
Dumpty, 'which is to be master—
that's all.'
Lewis Carroll 1832–98: *Through the Looking-Glass* (1872); cf. 19 below

7 I shall be an autocrat: that's my trade.
And the good Lord will forgive me:
that's his.
Catherine the Great 1729–96: attributed

8 Nature has left this tincture in the
blood,
That all men would be tyrants if they
could.
Daniel Defoe 1660–1731: *The History of the
Kentish Petition* (1712–13)

9 Power concedes nothing without a
demand. It never did, and it never
will.
Frederick Douglass *c.*1818–95: letter to Gerrit
Smith, 30 March 1849

10 The closer I came to the centre of
power, the less fulfilling and pleasant I
found it to be.
Derek Draper: in *Daily Telegraph* 3 March
1999

11 A fly, Sir, may sting a stately horse and
make him wince; but one is but an
insect, and the other is a horse still.
Samuel Johnson 1709–84: James Boswell *Life
of Samuel Johnson* (1791) 1754

12 Power is the great aphrodisiac.
Henry Kissinger 1923– : in *New York Times*
19 January 1971

13 I claim not to have controlled events,
but confess plainly that events have
controlled me.
Abraham Lincoln 1809–65: letter to A. G.
Hodges, 4 April 1864

14 Power? It's like a Dead Sea fruit.
When you achieve it, there is nothing
there.
Harold Macmillan 1894–1986: Anthony
Sampson *The New Anatomy of Britain* (1971)

15 Every Communist must grasp the
truth, 'Political power grows out of
the barrel of a gun'.
Mao Zedong 1893–1976: speech, 6 November
1938

16 When you make your peace with
authority, you become an authority.
Jim Morrison 1943–71: Andrew Doe and John
Tobler *In Their Own Words: The Doors* (1988)

17 Who controls the past controls the
future: who controls the present
controls the past.
George Orwell 1903–50: *Nineteen Eighty-Four*
(1949)

18 Seven months ago I could give a single
command and 541,000 people would
immediately obey it. Today I can't get
a plumber to come to my house.
H. Norman Schwarzkopf III 1934– : in
Newsweek 11 November 1991

19 'But,' said Alice, 'the question is
whether you can make a word mean
different things.' 'Not so,' said
Humpty-Dumpty, 'the question is
which is to be the master. That's all.'
We are the masters at the moment,
and not only at the moment, but for a
very long time to come.
■ *often quoted as 'We are the masters now'*
Hartley Shawcross 1902– : speech, House of
Commons, 2 April 1946; see 6 above

20 You only have power over people as
long as you don't take *everything* away
from them. But when you've robbed a
man of *everything* he's no longer in
your power—he's free again.
Alexander Solzhenitsyn 1918– : *The First
Circle* (1968)

21 The hand that signed the paper felled
a city;
Five sovereign fingers taxed the
breath,
Doubled the globe of dead and halved
a country;
These five kings did a king to death.
Dylan Thomas 1914–53: 'The hand that signed
the paper felled a city' (1936)

Practicality

1 It's grand, and you canna expect to be
baith grand and comfortable.
J. M. Barrie 1860–1937: *The Little Minister*
(1891)

2 Put your trust in God, my boys, and keep your powder dry.
Valentine Blacker 1728–1823: 'Oliver's Advice'; often attributed to Oliver Cromwell himself

3 Whenever our neighbour's house is on fire, it cannot be amiss for the engines to play a little on our own.
Edmund Burke 1729–97: *Reflections on the Revolution in France* (1790)

4 Life is too short to stuff a mushroom.
Shirley Conran 1932– : *Superwoman* (1975)

5 Common sense is the best distributed commodity in the world, for every man is convinced that he is well supplied with it.
René Descartes 1596–1650: *Le Discours de la méthode* (1637)

6 Common sense is nothing more than a deposit of prejudices laid down in the mind before you reach eighteen.
Albert Einstein 1879–1955: Lincoln Barnett *The Universe and Dr Einstein* (1950 ed.)

7 Praise the Lord and pass the ammunition.
■ *moving along a line of sailors passing ammunition by hand to the deck*
Howell Forgy 1908–83: at Pearl Harbor, 7 December 1941; later the title of a song by Frank Loesser, 1942

8 A dead woman bites not.
■ *pressing for the execution of Mary Queen of Scots in 1587*
Patrick, Lord Gray d. 1612: oral tradition; William Camden *Annals of the Reign of Queen Elizabeth* (1615)

9 So I really think that American gentlemen are the best after all, because kissing your hand may make you feel very very good but a diamond and safire bracelet lasts forever.
Anita Loos 1893–1981: *Gentlemen Prefer Blondes* (1925)

10 Be nice to people on your way up because you'll meet 'em on your way down.
Wilson Mizner 1876–1933: Alva Johnston *The Legendary Mizners* (1953)

11 And he gave it for his opinion, that whoever could make two ears of corn or two blades of grass to grow upon a spot of ground where only one grew before, would deserve better of mankind, and do more essential service to his country than the whole race of politicians put together.
Jonathan Swift 1667–1745: *Gulliver's Travels* (1726) 'A Voyage to Brobdingnag'

12 Common sense is not so common.
Voltaire 1694–1778: *Dictionnaire philosophique* (1765) 'Sens Commun'

Praise

see also **Flattery**

1 The advantage of doing one's praising for oneself is that one can lay it on so thick and exactly in the right places.
Samuel Butler 1835–1902: *The Way of All Flesh* (1903)

2 It would be nice if sometimes the kind things I say were considered worthy of quotation. It isn't difficult, you know, to be witty or amusing when one has something to say that is destructive, but damned hard to be clever and quotable when you are singing someone's praises.
Noël Coward 1899–1973: William Marchant *The Pleasure of His Company* (1981)

3 Nothing so soon the drooping spirits can raise
As praises from the men, whom all men praise.
Abraham Cowley 1618–67: 'Ode upon a Copy of Verses of My Lord Broghill's' (1663)

4 And even the ranks of Tuscany
Could scarce forbear to cheer.
Lord Macaulay 1800–59: *Lays of Ancient Rome* (1842) 'Horatius'

5 Of whom to be dispraised were no small praise.
John Milton 1608–74: *Paradise Regained* (1671)

6 Damn with faint praise, assent with civil leer,

And without sneering, teach the rest to sneer.

■ *of Addison*

Alexander Pope 1688–1744: 'An Epistle to Dr Arbuthnot' (1735)

Prayer

1 O God, if there be a God, save my soul, if I have a soul!

■ *prayer of a common soldier before the battle of Blenheim, 1704*

Anonymous: in *Notes and Queries* 9 October 1937

2 O Lord! thou knowest how busy I must be this day: if I forget thee, do not thou forget me.

■ *prayer before the Battle of Edgehill, 1642*

Jacob Astley 1579–1652: Sir Philip Warwick *Memoires* (1701)

3 The wish for prayer is a prayer in itself.

Georges Bernanos 1888–1948: *Journal d'un curé de campagne* (1936)

4 Ask, and it shall be given you; seek, and ye shall find; knock, and it shall be opened unto you.

Bible: St Matthew

5 And lips say, 'God be pitiful,'
Who ne'er said, 'God be praised.'

Elizabeth Barrett Browning 1806–61: 'The Cry of the Human' (1844)

6 He prayeth well, who loveth well
Both man and bird and beast.

He prayeth best, who loveth best
All things both great and small.

Samuel Taylor Coleridge 1772–1834: 'The Rime of the Ancient Mariner' (1798)

7 I throw myself down in my Chamber, and I call in, and invite God, and his Angels thither, and when they are there, I neglect God and his Angels, for the noise of a fly, for the rattling of a coach, for the whining of a door.

John Donne 1572–1631: *LXXX Sermons* (1640) 12 December 1626

8 The prayers of the dying are especially precious to God, because they will soon be in His presence.

Basil Hume 1923–99: in *Independent* 18 June 1999

9 To lift up the hands in prayer gives God glory, but a man with a dungfork in his hand, a woman with a slop-pail, give him glory too. He is so great that all things give him glory if you mean they should.

Gerard Manley Hopkins 1844–89: 'The Principle or Foundation' (1882)

10 Often when I pray I wonder if I am not posting letters to a non-existent address.

C. S. Lewis 1898–1963: letter to Arthur Greeves, 24 December 1930

11 Hush! Hush! Whisper who dares! Christopher Robin is saying his prayers.

A. A. Milne 1882–1956: 'Vespers' (1924)

12 Christ beside me,
Christ before me,
Christ behind me,
Christ within me,
Christ beneath me,
Christ above me.

St Patrick fl. 5th cent.: 'St Patrick's Breastplate'

13 School prayer . . . bears about as much resemblance to real spiritual experience as that freeze-dried astronaut food bears to a nice standing rib roast.

Anna Quindlen 1953– : in *New York Times* 7 December 1994

14 I am just going to pray for you at St Paul's, but with no very lively hope of success.

Sydney Smith 1771–1845: H. Pearson *The Smith of Smiths* (1934)

15 More things are wrought by prayer
Than this world dreams of.

Alfred, Lord Tennyson 1809–92: *Idylls of the King* 'The Passing of Arthur' (1869)

16 Whatever a man prays for, he prays for a miracle. Every prayer reduces

itself to this: Great God, grant that
twice two be not four.

Ivan Turgenev 1818–83: *Poems in Prose* (1881)
'Prayer'

17 You can't pray a lie.

Mark Twain 1835–1910: *Adventures of
Huckleberry Finn* (1885)

Pregnancy

see also **Birth, Birth Control**

1 Abortions will not let you forget.
You remember the children you got
that you did not get . . .

Gwendolyn Brooks 1917–2000: 'The Mother'
(1945)

2 If men had to have babies, they would
only ever have one each.

Diana, Princess of Wales 1961–97: in *Observer*
29 July 1984

3 If men could get pregnant, abortion
would be a sacrament.

Florynce Kennedy 1916–2001: in *Ms.* March
1973

4 I am not yet born; O fill me
With strength against those who
would freeze my
humanity, would dragoon me into a
lethal automaton,
would make me a cog in a machine, a
thing with
one face, a thing.

Louis MacNeice 1907–63: 'Prayer Before Birth'
(1944)

5 Let them not make me a stone and let
them not spill me,
Otherwise kill me.

Louis MacNeice 1907–63: 'Prayer Before Birth'
(1944)

6 In the dark womb where I began
My mother's life made me a man.
Through all the months of human
birth
Her beauty fed my common earth.
I cannot see, nor breathe, nor stir,
But through the death of some of her.

John Masefield 1878–1967: 'C. L. M.' (1910)

7 I wish either my father or my mother,
or indeed both of them, as they were

in duty both equally bound to it, had
minded what they were about when
they begot me.

Laurence Sterne 1713–68: *Tristram Shandy*
(1759–67)

Prejudice

see also **Impartiality, Racism, Tolerance**

1 Bigotry may be roughly defined as the
anger of men who have no opinions.

G. K. Chesterton 1874–1936: *Heretics* (1905)

2 If my theory of relativity is proven
correct, Germany will claim me as a
German and France will declare that I
am a citizen of the world. Should my
theory prove untrue, France will say
that I am a German and Germany will
declare that I am a Jew.

Albert Einstein 1879–1955: address at the
Sorbonne, Paris, possibly early December
1929; in *New York Times* 16 February 1930

3 Drive out prejudices through the
door, and they will return through the
window.

Frederick the Great 1712–86: letter to Voltaire,
19 March 1771

4 Intolerance of groups is often,
strangely enough, exhibited more
strongly against small differences than
against fundamental ones.

Sigmund Freud 1856–1939: *Moses and
Monotheism* (1938)

5 Prejudice is the child of ignorance.

William Hazlitt 1778–1830: 'On Prejudice'
(1830)

6 Oh who is that young sinner with the
handcuffs on his wrists?
And what has he been after that they
groan and shake their fists?
And wherefore is he wearing such a
conscience-stricken air?
Oh they're taking him to prison for
the colour of his hair.

A. E. Housman 1859–1936: *Collected Poems*
(1939) 'Additional Poems' no. 18

7 PLEASE ACCEPT MY RESIGNATION. I
DON'T WANT TO BELONG TO ANY CLUB
THAT WILL ACCEPT ME AS A MEMBER.
Groucho Marx 1895–1977: *Groucho and Me*
(1959)

8 Four legs good, two legs bad.
George Orwell 1903–50: *Animal Farm* (1945)

9 Who's 'im, Bill?
A stranger!
'Eave 'arf a brick at 'im.
Punch: 25 February 1854

10 Bigotry tries to keep truth safe in its
hand
With a grip that kills it.
Rabindranath Tagore 1861–1941: *Fireflies*
(1928)

The Present

see also **The Past**

1 To-morrow for the young the poets
exploding like bombs,
The walks by the lake, the weeks of
perfect communion;
To-morrow the bicycle races
Through the suburbs on summer
evenings: but to-day the struggle.
W. H. Auden 1907–73: 'Spain 1937' (1937)

2 Take therefore no thought for the
morrow: for the morrow shall take
thought for the things of itself.
Sufficient unto the day is the evil
thereof.
Bible: St Matthew

3 It's not perfect, but to me on balance
Right Now is a lot better than the
Good Old Days.
Maeve Binchy 1940– : in *Irish Times*
15 November 1997

4 Exhaust the little moment. Soon it
dies.
And be it gash or gold it will not come
Again in this identical disguise.
Gwendolyn Brooks 1917–2000: 'Exhaust the
little moment' (1949)

5 The rule is, jam to-morrow and jam
yesterday—but never jam today.
Lewis Carroll 1832–98: *Through the Looking-
Glass* (1872)

6 The present is the funeral of the past,
And man the living sepulchre of life.
John Clare 1793–1864: 'The present is the
funeral of the past' (written 1845)

7 Ah, fill the cup:—what boots it to
repeat
How time is slipping underneath our
feet:
Unborn TO-MORROW, and dead
YESTERDAY,
Why fret about them if TO-DAY be
sweet!
Edward Fitzgerald 1809–83: *The Rubáiyát of
Omar Khayyám* (1859)

8 Ah, *now*! That odd time—the oddest
time of all times; the time it always
is . . . by the time we've reached the
'w' of 'now' the 'n' is ancient history.
Michael Frayn 1933– : *Constructions* (1974)

9 *Carpe diem, quam minimum credula
postero.*
Seize the day, put no trust in the
future.
Horace 65–8 BC: *Odes*

10 When it's three o'clock in New York,
it's still 1938 in London.
Bette Midler 1945– : attributed

11 Below my window . . . the blossom is
out in full now . . . I *see* it is the
whitest, frothiest, blossomiest
blossom that there ever could be, and
I can see it. Things are both more
trivial than they ever were, and more
important than they ever were, and
the difference between the trivial and
the important doesn't seem to matter.
But the nowness of everything is
absolutely wondrous.
■ *on his heightened awareness of things, in the
face of his imminent death*
Dennis Potter 1935–94: *Seeing the Blossom*
(1994)

12 The New Age? It's just the old age
stuck in a microwave oven for fifteen
seconds.
James Randi 1928– : in *Observer* 14 April 1991

13 Life is one tenth Here and Now, nine-
tenths a history lesson. For most of

the time the Here and Now is neither now nor here.
Graham Swift 1949– : *Waterland* (1984)

14 Like a monkey scratching for the wrong fleas, every age assiduously seeks out in itself those vices which it does not in fact have, while ignoring the large, red, beady-eyed crawlers who scuttle around unimpeded.
Katharine Whitehorn 1928– : *Observations* (1970)

The Presidency

see also **Politicians, Reagan, United States**

1 Richard Nixon impeached himself. He gave us Gerald Ford as his revenge.
Bella Abzug 1920–98: in *Rolling Stone*; Linda Botts *Loose Talk* (1980)

2 Anybody that wants the presidency so much that he'll spend two years organizing and campaigning for it is not to be trusted with the office.
David Broder 1929– : in *Washington Post* 18 July 1973

3 The US presidency is a Tudor monarchy plus telephones.
Anthony Burgess 1917–93: George Plimpton (ed.) *Writers at Work* 4th Series (1977)

4 Somewhere out in this audience may even be someone who will one day follow in my footsteps, and preside over the White House as the President's spouse. I wish him well!
Barbara Bush 1925– : remarks at Wellesley College Commencement, 1 June 1990

5 When I was a boy I was told that anybody could become President. I'm beginning to believe it.
Clarence Darrow 1857–1938: Irving Stone *Clarence Darrow for the Defence* (1941)

6 From what I've seen, the answer is yes.
■ *on being asked if the country is ready for its first woman President*
Elizabeth Dole 1936– : in *Sunday Telegraph* 14 March 1999

7 No easy problems ever come to the President of the United States. If they

are easy to solve, somebody else has solved them.
Dwight D. Eisenhower 1890–1969: in *Parade Magazine* 8 April 1962

8 The vice-presidency isn't worth a pitcher of warm piss.
John Nance Garner 1868–1967: O. C. Fisher *Cactus Jack* (1978)

9 There can be no whitewash at the White House.
■ *on Watergate*
Richard Nixon 1913–94: television speech, 30 April 1973

10 When the President does it, that means that it is not illegal.
Richard Nixon 1913–94: David Frost *I Gave Them a Sword* (1978)

11 The one thing I do not want to be called is First Lady. It sounds like a saddle horse.
Jacqueline Kennedy Onassis 1929–94: Peter Collier and David Horowitz *The Kennedys* (1984)

12 If the President has a bully pulpit, then the First Lady has a white glove pulpit . . . more refined, restricted, ceremonial, but it's a pulpit all the same.
Nancy Reagan 1923– : in *New York Times* 10 March 1988; cf. 13 below

13 I have got such a bully pulpit!
Theodore Roosevelt 1858–1919: in *Outlook* (New York) 27 February 1909

14 The answer to the runaway Presidency is not the messenger-boy Presidency. The American democracy must discover a middle way between making the President a tsar and making him a puppet.
Arthur M. Schlesinger Jr. 1917– : *The Imperial Presidency* (1973); preface

15 Log-cabin to White House.
William Roscoe Thayer 1859–1923: title of biography (1910) of James Garfield (1831–81)

16 He'll sit right here and he'll say do this, do that! And nothing will

happen. Poor Ike—it won't be a bit like the Army.

Harry S. Truman 1884–1972: *Harry S. Truman* (1973)

Press Photographers

see also **Journalism, Newspapers**

1 If your pictures aren't good enough, you aren't close enough.

Robert Capa 1913–54: Russell Miller *Magnum: Fifty years at the Front Line of History* (1997)

2 The paparazzi are nothing but dogs of war.

■ *after the death in a car crash of Diana, Princess of Wales*

Catherine Deneuve 1943– : in *Daily Telegraph* 3 September 1997

3 There are very few professions where even when you are at the top, a household name, you might still be standing on a draughty street corner with your feet getting wet and cold, waiting for something to happen.

■ *of working as a photojournalist*

Philip Jones Griffiths: Russell Miller *Magnum: Fifty Years at the Front Line of History* (1997)

4 I don't trust photographers. I'm now a relaxed, contented 60-year-old, but look at my pictures and you see a crazy, bug-eyed serial killer.

Richard Ingrams 1937– : in *Observer* 24 August 1997

5 I'd say our newspapers paid far too much for them.

■ *of buying paparazzi pictures*

Rupert Murdoch 1931– : in *Daily Telegraph* 8 October 1997

6 I always believed the press would kill her in the end. But not even I could believe they would take such a direct hand in her death as seems to be the case . . . Every proprietor and editor of every publication that has paid for intrusive and exploitative photographs of her . . . has blood on their hands today.

■ *on the death of his sister, Diana, Princess of Wales, in a car crash while being pursued by photographers*

Lord Spencer 1964– : in *Daily Telegraph* 1 September 1997

Prime Ministers

1 If the King asks you to form a Government you say 'Yes' or 'No', not 'I'll let you know later!'

Clement Attlee 1883–1967: Kenneth Harris *Attlee* (1982)

2 There are three classes which need sanctuary more than others—birds, wild flowers, and Prime Ministers.

Stanley Baldwin 1867–1947: in *Observer* 24 May 1925

3 I am from the Disraeli school of Prime Ministers in their relations with the Monarch.

Tony Blair 1953– : at the Queen's golden wedding celebration, 20 November 1997; cf. **Flattery** 3, 4

4 I think a Prime Minister has to be a butcher and know the joints. That is perhaps where I have not been quite competent, in knowing all the ways that you can cut up a carcass.

R. A. Butler 1902–82: in *Listener* 28 June 1966

5 I've known every Prime Minister to a greater or lesser extent since Balfour, and most of them have died unhappy.

Lord Hailsham 1907–2001: attributed

6 INTERVIEWER: What three skills should every great Prime Minister have? Did you have them?
HEATH: Patience, stamina and good luck. Two out of three isn't bad!

Edward Heath 1916– : in *Independent* 25 November 1998

7 Nearly all Prime Ministers are dissatisfied with their successors, perhaps even more so if they come from their own party.

Roy Jenkins 1920–2003: *Gladstone* (1995)

8 We all know that Prime Ministers are wedded to the truth, but like other married couples they sometimes live apart.

Saki 1870–1916: *The Unbearable Bassington* (1912)

9 Senior position in government involving long hours, short holidays and tall orders. Expertise required in

the whole range of government policy and especially in carrying cans. Tied cottage—makes job ideal for someone used to living above the shop . . . Current status: 650 applicants and no vacancy.

Margaret Thatcher 1925– : speech, Cheltenham, 31 March 1990

10 Every Prime Minister needs a Willie.

■ *at the farewell dinner to Lord Whitelaw*
Margaret Thatcher 1925– : in *Guardian* 7 August 1991

Prison
....
see also **Laws**

1 *reply to a prison visitor who asked if he were sewing:*
No, reaping.

Horatio Bottomley 1860–1933: S. T. Felstead *Horatio Bottomley* (1936)

2 Jails and prisons are designed to break human beings, to convert the population into specimens in a zoo— obedient to our keepers, but dangerous to each other.

Angela Davis 1944– : *An Autobiography* (1974)

3 Your mind stays alive all the time you're locked up—you might be shut away, but you don't shut down.

Brian Keenan 1950– : in *Observer* 22 August 1999

4 Stone walls do not a prison make, Nor iron bars a cage.

Richard Lovelace 1618–58: 'To Althea, From Prison' (1649)

5 The thoughts of a prisoner—they're not free either. They keep returning to the same things.

Alexander Solzhenitsyn 1918– : *One Day in the Life of Ivan Denisovich* (1962)

6 You have to pray daily, light a candle—get down on your knees—as far as the prisons are concerned.

Jack Straw 1946– : in *Independent* 22 January 1999

7 Any one who has been to an English public school will always feel comparatively at home in prison. It is

the people brought up in the gay intimacy of the slums, Paul learned, who find prison so soul-destroying.

Evelyn Waugh 1903–66: *Decline and Fall* (1928)

8 I want to see the word laogai in every dictionary in every language in the world. I want to see the laogai ended. Before 1974, the word 'gulag' did not appear in any dictionary. Today, this single word conveys the meaning of Soviet political violence and its labour camp system. 'Laogai' also deserves a place in our dictionaries.

■ *the* laogai *are Chinese labour camps*
Harry Wu 1937– : in *Washington Post* 26 May 1996

Problems and Solutions
....
see also **Ways and Means**

1 If a problem is too difficult to solve, one cannot claim that it is solved by pointing at all the efforts made to solve it.

Hannes Alfven 1908–95: A. Sampson *The Changing Anatomy of Britain* (1982)

2 Probable impossibilities are to be preferred to improbable possibilities.

Aristotle 384–322 BC: *Poetics*

3 Rutherford was a disaster. He started the 'something for nothing' tradition . . . the notion that research can always be done on the cheap . . . The war taught us differently. If you want quick and effective results you must put the money in.

Edward Bullard 1907–80: P. Grosvenor and J. McMillan *The British Genius* (1973); see 12 below

4 It isn't that they can't see the solution. It is that they can't see the problem.

G. K. Chesterton 1874–1936: *Scandal of Father Brown* (1935)

5 Let me have the best solution worked out. Don't argue the matter. The difficulties will argue for themselves.

■ *on the Mulberry floating harbours*
Winston Churchill 1874–1965: minute to Lord Mountbatten, 30 May 1942

6 What we're saying today is that you're either part of the solution or you're part of the problem.
Eldridge Cleaver 1935–98: speech in San Francisco, 1968

7 How often have I said to you that when you have eliminated the impossible, whatever remains, *however improbable*, must be the truth?
Arthur Conan Doyle 1859–1930: *The Sign of Four* (1890)

8 Problems worthy
of attack
prove their worth
by hitting back.
Piet Hein 1905– : 'Problems' (1969)

9 Another nice mess you've gotten me into.
Stan Laurel 1890–1965: *Another Fine Mess* (1930 film) and many other Laurel and Hardy films; spoken by Oliver Hardy

10 Houston, we've had a problem.
James Lovell 1928– : on Apollo 13 space mission, 14 April 1970

11 One hears only those questions for which one is able to find answers.
Friedrich Nietzsche 1844–1900: *The Gay Science* (1882)

12 We haven't got the money, so we've got to think!
Ernest Rutherford 1871–1937: in *Bulletin of the Institute of Physics* (1962)

13 American history promotes the idea of solving problems while British history suggests problems are to be managed. Americans are therefore given to reinventing the wheel whereas the British believe they invented the wheel in the first place.
Raymond Seitz 1940– : *Over Here* (1998)

14 The fascination of what's difficult
Has dried the sap of my veins, and rent
Spontaneous joy and natural content
Out of my heart.
W. B. Yeats 1865–1939: 'The Fascination of What's Difficult' (1910)

Progress

....

see also **Change**

1 The new growth in the plant swelling against the sheath, which at the same time imprisons and protects it, must still be the truest type of progress.
Jane Addams 1860–1935: *Democracy and Social Ethics* (1907)

2 We are like dwarfs on the shoulders of giants, so that we can see more than they, and things at a greater distance, not by virtue of any sharpness of sight on our part, or any physical distinction, but because we are carried high and raised up by their giant size.
Bernard of Chartres d. *c*.1130: John of Salisbury *The Metalogicon* (1159); cf. 15 below

3 Want is one only of five giants on the road of reconstruction . . . the others are Disease, Ignorance, Squalor and Idleness.
William Henry Beveridge 1879–1963: *Social Insurance and Allied Services* (1942)

4 The thing that hath been, it is that which shall be; and that which is done is that which shall be done: and there is no new thing under the sun.
Bible: Ecclesiastes

5 Man aspires to the stars. But if he can get his sewage and refuse distributed and utilised in orderly fashion he will be doing very well.
Roy Bridger: in *The Times* 13 July 1959

6 Nothing in progression can rest on its original plan. We may as well think of rocking a grown man in the cradle of an infant.
Edmund Burke 1729–97: *Letter to the Sheriffs of Bristol* (1777)

7 pity this busy monster, manunkind, not. Progress is a comfortable disease.
e. e. cummings 1894–1962: *1 x 1* (1944) no. 14

8 The European talks of progress because by an ingenious application of some scientific acquirements he has

established a society which has mistaken comfort for civilization.
Benjamin Disraeli 1804–81: *Tancred* (1847)

9 Think what we would have missed if we had never . . . used a mobile phone or surfed the Net—or, to be honest, listened to other people talking about surfing the Net.
■ *reflecting on developments in the past 50 years*
Elizabeth II 1926– : in *Daily Telegraph* 21 November 1997

10 From time to time, in the towns, I open a newspaper. Things seem to be going at a dizzy rate. We are dancing not on a volcano, but on the rotten seat of a latrine.
Gustave Flaubert 1821–80: letter to Louis Bouilhet, 14 November 1850

11 The slogan of progress is changing from the full dinner pail to the full garage.
■ *sometimes paraphrased as, 'a car in every garage and a chicken in every pot'*
Herbert Hoover 1874–1964: speech in New York, 22 October 1928; cf. **Poverty** 13

12 Is it progress if a cannibal uses knife and fork?
Stanislaw Lec 1909–66: *Unkempt Thoughts* (1962)

13 One step forward two steps back.
Lenin 1870–1924: title of book (1904)

14 Let us be frank about it: most of our people have never had it so good.
Harold Macmillan 1894–1986: speech at Bedford, 20 July 1957; 'You Never Had It So Good' was the Democratic Party slogan during the 1952 US election campaign

15 If I have seen further it is by standing on the shoulders of giants.
Isaac Newton 1642–1727: letter to Robert Hooke, 5 February 1676; cf. 2 above

16 In time to come, I tell them, we'll be equal
to 'any living now. If cripples, then no matter; we shall just have been run over
by 'New Man' in the wagon of his 'Plan'.
Boris Pasternak 1890–1960: 'When I Grow Weary' (1932)

17 'Change' is scientific, 'progress' is ethical; change is indubitable, whereas progress is a matter of controversy.
Bertrand Russell 1872–1970: *Unpopular Essays* (1950) 'Philosophy and Politics'

18 The reasonable man adapts himself to the world: the unreasonable one persists in trying to adapt the world to himself. Therefore all progress depends on the unreasonable man.
George Bernard Shaw 1856–1950: *Man and Superman* (1903)

Propaganda

1 When war is declared, Truth is the first casualty.
Anonymous: epigraph to Arthur Ponsonby's *Falsehood in Wartime* (1928); attributed also to Hiram Johnson, speaking in the US Senate, 1918, but not recorded in his speech; possibly based on a passage by Samuel Johnson in *The Idler* 11 November 1758

2 Propaganda is a soft weapon: hold it in your hands too long, and it will move about like a snake, and strike the other way.
Jean Anouilh 1910–87: *The Lark* (adapted by Lillian Hellman, 1955)

3 In wartime . . . truth is so precious that she should always be attended by a bodyguard of lies.
Winston Churchill 1874–1965: *The Second World War* vol. 5 (1951)

4 That branch of the art of lying which consists in very nearly deceiving your friends without quite deceiving your enemies.
Francis M. Cornford 1874–1943: *Microcosmographia Academica* (1922 ed.)

5 Propaganda can be defined as the art of managing one's legend.
Régis Debray 1940– : Régis Debray *Charles de Gaulle: Futurist of the Nation* (1994)

6 Anything that sounds like propaganda is not good propaganda.
David Hare 1947– : *Licking Hitler* (1978)

7 Today words have become battles. The right words, battles won; the wrong words, battles lost.

> **Erich von Ludendorff** 1865–1937: George C. Bruntz *Allied Propaganda and the Collapse of the German Empire in 1918* (1938)

8 A false report, if believed during three days, may be of great service to a government.

> **Catherine de' Medici** 1518–89: Isaac D'Israeli *Curiosities of Literature* Second Series vol. 2 (1849)

9 In our country the lie has become not just a moral category but a pillar of the State.

> **Alexander Solzhenitsyn** 1918– : 1974 interview, in *The Oak and the Calf* (1975)

Protest

see also **Politics**, **Revolution**

1 When cult is added to power
even the chairman makes mistakes
Xiaoping suffered criticism (in the Cultural Revolution)
and the people raised him up.
Now he represents bureaucracy
and official corruption.
The country does not want him,
the people do not want him.

> **Anonymous**: poem put up in the Forbidden City in 1989, shortly before the tanks moved into Tiananmen Square

2 Even a purely moral act that has no hope of any immediate and visible political effect can gradually and indirectly, over time, gain in political significance.

> **Václav Havel** 1936– : letter to Alexander Dubček, August 1969

3 Ev'rywhere I hear the sound of marching, charging feet, boy,
'Cause summer's here and the time is right for fighting in the street, boy.

> **Mick Jagger** 1943– and **Keith Richards** 1943– : 'Street Fighting Man' (1968 song)

4 One-fifth of the people are against everything all the time.

> **Robert Kennedy** 1925–68: speech, University of Pennsylvania, 6 May 1964

5 I'm interested in anything about revolt, disorder, chaos, especially activity that appears to have no meaning. It seems to me to be the road toward freedom.

> **Jim Morrison** 1943–71: in *Time* 24 January 1968

6 There are now two classes of student—those who have enough money not to bother about the issues and those who are so skint they have to work in Tesco every afternoon, so haven't the time.

> ■ *on student protest*
> **Sarah-Louise Puntan-Galeo**: in *Daily Telegraph* 21 January 1997

7 I've always had the impression that real militants are like cleaning women, doing a thankless, daily but necessary job.

> **François Truffaut** 1932–84: letter to Jean-Luc Godard, May–June 1973

Publishing

see also **Books**

1 If I had been someone not very clever, I would have done an easier job like publishing. That's the easiest job I can think of.

> **A. J. Ayer** 1910–89: attributed

2 The poem will please if it is lively—if it is stupid it will fail—but I will have none of your damned cutting and slashing.

> **Lord Byron** 1788–1824: letter to his publisher John Murray, 6 April 1819

3 Now Barabbas was a publisher.

> ■ *alteration in a Bible of the verse 'Now Barabbas was a robber'*
> **Thomas Campbell** 1777–1844: attributed, in Samuel Smiles *A Publisher and his Friends* (1891); also attributed, wrongly, to Byron

4 The whole world of publishing has changed. The accountants have moved in. It's now the bottom line, not is it a good book?

> **Hammond Innes** 1913– : interview in *Daily Telegraph* 3 August 1996

5 Of all the literary scenes
Saddest this sight to me:

The graves of little magazines
Who died to make verse free.
Keith Preston 1884–1927: 'The Liberators'

6 Publish and be damned.
■ *replying to Harriette Wilson's blackmail threat, c.1825*
Duke of Wellington 1769–1852: attributed

7 Being published by the Oxford University Press is rather like being married to a duchess: the honour is almost greater than the pleasure.
G. M. Young 1882–1959: Rupert Hart-Davis, letter to George Lyttelton, 29 April 1956

Punctuality
....
see also **Waiting**

1 I will surprise God because I'm late. I was always very punctual with the Devil.
■ *on his imminent death*
Jeffrey Bernard 1932–97: in *Guardian* 6 September 1997

2 The only way of catching a train I have ever discovered is to miss the train before.
G. K. Chesterton 1874–1936: *Tremendous Trifles* (1909)

3 We've been waiting 700 years, you can have the seven minutes.
■ *on arriving at Dublin Castle for the handover by British forces on 16 January 1922, and being told that he was seven minutes late*
Michael Collins 1880–1922: Tim Pat Coogan *Michael Collins* (1990); attributed, perhaps apocryphal

4 Recollect that painting and punctuality mix like oil and vinegar, and that genius and regularity are utter enemies, and must be to the end of time.
Thomas Gainsborough 1727–88: letter to Edward Stratford, 1 May 1772

5 Punctuality is the politeness of kings.
Louis XVIII 1755–1824: *Souvenirs de J. Lafitte* (1844); attributed

6 I have noticed that the people who are late are often so much jollier than the people who have to wait for them.
E. V. Lucas 1868–1938: *365 Days and One More* (1926)

7 We must leave exactly on time . . . From now on everything must function to perfection.
■ *to a station-master*
Benito Mussolini 1883–1945: Giorgio Pini *Mussolini* (1939)

8 You come most carefully upon your hour.
William Shakespeare 1564–1616: *Hamlet* (1601)

9 Punctuality is the virtue of the bored.
Evelyn Waugh 1903–66: diary 26 March 1962

10 My Aunt Minnie would always be punctual and never hold up production, but who would pay to see my Aunt Minnie?
■ *on Marilyn Monroe's unpunctuality*
Billy Wilder 1906–2002: P. F. Boller and R. L. Davis *Hollywood Anecdotes* (1988)

Punishment
....
see also **Crime, Laws, Prison**

1 All punishment is mischief: all punishment in itself is evil.
Jeremy Bentham 1748–1832: *Principles of Morals and Legislation* (1789)

2 He that spareth his rod hateth his son.
Bible: Proverbs

3 Hanging is too good for him, said Mr Cruelty.
John Bunyan 1628–88: *The Pilgrim's Progress* (1678)

4 Excessive bail shall not be required, nor excessive fines imposed, nor cruel and unusual punishment inflicted.
Constitution of the United States 1787: *Eighth Amendment* (1791)

5 Better build schoolrooms for 'the boy',
Than cells and gibbets for 'the man'.
Eliza Cook 1818–89: 'A Song for the Ragged Schools' (1853)

6 To crush, to annihilate a man utterly, to inflict on him the most terrible punishment so that the most ferocious murderer would shudder at

it beforehand, one need only give him work of an absolutely, completely useless and irrational character.

Fedor Dostoevsky 1821–81: *House of the Dead* (1862)

7 Punishment is not for revenge, but to lessen crime and reform the criminal.

Elizabeth Fry 1780–1845: Rachel E. Cresswell and Katharine Fry *Memoir of the Life of Elizabeth Fry* (1848)

8 Whenever the offence inspires less horror than the punishment, the rigour of penal law is obliged to give way to the common feelings of mankind.

Edward Gibbon 1737–94: attributed

9 My object all sublime
I shall achieve in time—
To let the punishment fit the crime—
The punishment fit the crime.

W. S. Gilbert 1836–1911: *The Mikado* (1885)

10 Men are not hanged for stealing horses, but that horses may not be stolen.

Lord Halifax 1633–95: *Political, Moral, and Miscellaneous Thoughts and Reflections* (1750) 'Of Punishment'

11 This is the first of punishments, that no guilty man is acquitted if judged by himself.

Juvenal AD c.60–c.130: *Satires*

12 If you import cannabis you get 25 years—is importation of cannabis four times as bad as rape?

Lord McCluskey 1914– : speech, Edinburgh, 12 July 1999

13 Society needs to condemn a little more and understand a little less.

John Major 1943– : interview with *Mail on Sunday* 21 February 1993

14 For de little stealin' dey gits you in jail soon or late. For de big stealin' dey makes you Emperor and puts you in de Hall o' Fame when you croaks.

Eugene O'Neill 1888–1953: *The Emperor Jones* (1921)

15 Lay then the axe to the root, and teach governments humanity. It is their sanguinary punishments which corrupt mankind.

Thomas Paine 1737–1809: *The Rights of Man* (1791)

16 Between the possibility of being hanged in all innocence, and the certainty of a public and merited disgrace, no gentleman of spirit could long hesitate.

Robert Louis Stevenson 1850–94: *The Wrong Box* (with Lloyd Osbourne, 1889)

17 A child, punished by selfish parents, does not feel anger. It goes to its little private corner to weep.

Rose Tremain 1943– : *Restoration* (1989)

18 I'm all for bringing back the birch, but only between consenting adults.

Gore Vidal 1925– : in *Sunday Times Magazine* 16 September 1973

Quotations

1 The surest way to make a monkey of a man is to quote him.

Robert Benchley 1889–1945: *My Ten Years in a Quandary* (1936)

2 A quotation is what a speaker wants to say—unlike a soundbite which is all that an interviewer allows you to say.

Tony Benn 1925– : letter to Antony Jay, August 1996

3 It is a good thing for an uneducated man to read books of quotations.

Winston Churchill 1874–1965: *My Early Life* (1930)

4 I know heaps of quotations, so I can always make quite a fair show of knowledge.

O. Douglas 1877–1948: *The Setons* (1917)

5 I hate quotation. Tell me what you know.

Ralph Waldo Emerson 1803–82: diary May 1849

6 Next to the originator of a good sentence is the first quoter of it.

Ralph Waldo Emerson 1803–82: *Letters and Social Aims* (1876)

7 Windbags can be right. Aphorists can be wrong. It is a tough world.

James Fenton 1949– : in *Times* 21 February 1985

8 You must not treat my immortal works as quarries to be used at will by the various hacks whom you may employ to compile anthologies.

A. E. Housman 1859–1936: letter to his publisher Grant Richards, 29 June 1907

9 He wrapped himself in quotations— as a beggar would enfold himself in the purple of emperors.

Rudyard Kipling 1865–1936: *Many Inventions* (1893)

10 Misquotation is, in fact, the pride and privilege of the learned. A widely-read man never quotes accurately, for the rather obvious reason that he has read too widely.

Hesketh Pearson 1887–1964: *Common Misquotations* (1934)

11 An anthology is like all the plums and orange peel picked out of a cake.

Walter Raleigh 1861–1922: letter to Mrs Robert Bridges, 15 January 1915

12 A proverb is one man's wit and all men's wisdom.

Lord John Russell 1792–1878: R. J. Mackintosh *Sir James Mackintosh* (1835)

13 I always have a quotation for everything—it saves original thinking.

Dorothy L. Sayers 1893–1957: *Have His Carcase* (1932)

14 OSCAR WILDE: How I wish I had said that.

WHISTLER: You will, Oscar, you will.

James McNeill Whistler 1834–1903: R. Ellman *Oscar Wilde* (1987)

15 The nice thing about quotes is that they give us a nodding acquaintance with the originator which is often socially impressive.

Kenneth Williams 1926–88: *Acid Drops* (1980)

Race

see also **Racism**

1 When I recovered a little I found some black people about me . . . I asked them if we were not to be eaten by those white men with horrible looks, red faces, and loose hair.

Olaudah Equiano c.1745–c.1797: *Narrative of the Life of Olaudah Equiano* (1789)

2 The so-called white races are really pinko-grey.

E. M. Forster 1879–1970: *A Passage to India* (1924)

3 Irish Americans are about as Irish as black Americans are African.

Bob Geldof 1954– : in *Observer* 22 June 1986

4 Though it be a thrilling and marvellous thing to be merely young and gifted in such times, it is doubly so, doubly dynamic—to be young, gifted and *black*.

Lorraine Hansberry 1930–65: *To be young, gifted and black: Lorraine Hansberry in her own words* (1969) adapted by Robert Nemiroff

5 When I look out at this convention, I see the face of America, red, yellow, brown, black, and white. We are all precious in God's sight—the real rainbow coalition.

Jesse Jackson 1941– : speech at Democratic National Convention, Atlanta, 19 July 1988

6 There are no 'white' or 'coloured' signs on the foxholes or graveyards of battle.

John F. Kennedy 1917–63: message to Congress on proposed Civil Rights Bill, 19 June 1963

7 The ultimate human mystery may not be anything more than the claims on us of clan and race, which may yet turn out to have the power, because they defy the rational mind, to kill the world.

Arthur Miller 1915– : *Timebends* (1987)

8 There are no 'mixed' marriages. It just looks that way. People don't mix races; they abandon them or pick them.

Toni Morrison 1931– : *Tar Baby* (1981)

9 Growing up, I came up with this name: I'm a Cablinasian.

  ■ *explaining his rejection of 'African-American' as the term to describe his Caucasian, Afro-American, Native American, Thai, and Chinese ancestry*

  Tiger Woods 1975– : interviewed by Oprah Winfrey, 21 April 1997

Racism

....

see also **Equality**, **Genocide**, **Prejudice**, **Race**, **Tolerance**

1 It comes as a great shock around the age of 5, 6 or 7 to discover that the flag to which you have pledged allegiance, along with everybody else, has not pledged allegiance to you. It comes as a great shock to see Gary Cooper killing off the Indians and, although you are rooting for Gary Cooper, that the Indians are you.

  ■ *speaking for the proposition that 'The American Dream is at the expense of the American Negro'*

  James Baldwin 1924–87: Cambridge Union, England, 17 February 1965

2 The basic tenet of Black consciousness is that the Black man must reject all value systems that seek to make him a foreigner in the country of his birth and reduce his basic human dignity.

  Steve Biko 1946–77: statement as witness, 3 May 1976

3 Being a star has made it possible for me to get insulted in places where the average Negro could never *hope* to go and get insulted.

  Sammy Davis Jnr. 1925–90: *Yes I Can* (1965)

4 You have seen how a man was made a slave; you shall see how a slave was made a man.

  Frederick Douglass c.1818–95: *Narrative of the Life of Frederick Douglass* (1845)

5 Some of my best friends are white boys.
  when I meet 'em
  I treat 'em
  just the same as if they was people.

  Ray Durem 1915–63: 'Broadminded' (written 1951)

6 Because a man has a black face and a different religion from our own, there is no reason why he should be treated as a brute.

  Edward VII 1841–1910: letter to Lord Granville, 30 November 1875

7 How odd
  Of God
  To choose
  The Jews.

  ■ *to which Cecil Browne replied: 'But not so odd/As those who choose/A Jewish God/But spurn the Jews.'*

  William Norman Ewer 1885–1976: *Week-End Book* (1924)

8 You've got to be taught to be afraid
  Of people whose eyes are oddly made,
  Of people whose skin is a different shade.
  You've got to be carefully taught.

  Oscar Hammerstein II 1895–1960: 'You've Got to be Carefully Taught' (1949)

9 The Gypsies are a litmus test not of democracy but of civil society.

  Václav Havel 1936– : attributed

10 And if the white man thought that Asians were a low, filthy nation, Asians could still smile with relief—at least, they were not Africans. And if the white man thought that Africans were a low, filthy nation, Africans in southern Africa could still smile—at least, they were not bushmen. They all have their monsters.

  Bessie Head 1937–86: *Maru* (1971)

11 Southern trees bear strange fruit,
  Blood on the leaves and blood at the root,
  Black bodies swinging in the Southern breeze,
  Strange fruit hanging from the poplar trees.

  Billie Holiday 1915–59: 'Strange Fruit' (1939)

12 You can be up to your boobies in white satin, with gardenias in your hair and no sugar cane for miles, but you can still be working on a plantation.

  Billie Holiday 1915–59: *Lady Sings the Blues* (1956, with William Duffy)

13 I, too, sing America.
I am the darker brother.
They send me to eat in the kitchen
When company comes.
Langston Hughes 1902–67: 'I, Too' (1925)

14 When they call you articulate, that's
another way of saying 'He talks good
for a black guy'.
Ice-T 1958– : in *Independent* 30 December
1995

15 I want to be the white man's brother,
not his brother-in-law.
Martin Luther King 1929–68: in *New York
Journal-American* 10 September 1962

16 As I look ahead, I am filled with
foreboding. Like the Roman, I seem to
see 'the River Tiber foaming with
much blood'.
■ *on the probable consequences of immigration*
Enoch Powell 1912–98: speech, Birmingham,
20 April 1968

17 First for a few blocks the Irish kids
threw rocks at me. Then the German
kids threw rocks at me. Then the Eye-
talian, then the coloured, then the
Mohawk kids . . . hell, even the Jew
kids threw rocks at me, while they was
runnin' away from the kids throwin'
rocks at them.
Philip Roth 1933– : *The Great American Novel*
(1973)

18 The only good Indian is a dead
Indian.
■ *at Fort Cobb, January 1869*
Philip Henry Sheridan 1831–88: attributed

19 Segregation now, segregation
tomorrow and segregation forever!
George Wallace 1919– : inaugural speech as
Governor of Alabama, 14 January 1963

20 Am I not a man and a brother.
■ *legend on Wedgwood cameo, depicting a
kneeling Negro slave in chains*
Josiah Wedgwood 1730–95: E. Darwin *The
Botanic Garden* pt. 1 (1791)

Railways

1 This is the Night Mail crossing the
Border,
Bringing the cheque and the postal
order,
Letters for the rich, letters for the
poor,
The shop at the corner, the girl next
door.
Pulling up Beattock, a steady climb:
The gradient's against her, but she's
on time.
W. H. Auden 1907–73: 'Night Mail' (1936)

2 You've a lot to learn about trucks,
little Thomas. They are silly things
and must be kept in their place . . .
Then you'll be a Really Useful Engine.
Revd W. Awdry 1911–97: *Thomas the Tank
Engine* (1946)

3 Railways and the Church have their
critics, but both are the best ways of
getting a man to his ultimate
destination.
Revd W. Awdry 1911–97: in *Daily Telegraph*
22 March 1997; obituary

4 Railway termini. They are our gates to
the glorious and the unknown.
Through them we pass out into
adventure and sunshine, to them,
alas! we return.
E. M. Forster 1879–1970: *Howards End* (1910)

5 Sir, Saturday morning, although
recurring at regular and well-foreseen
intervals, always seems to take this
railway by surprise.
W. S. Gilbert 1836–1911: letter to the station-
master at Baker Street, on the Metropolitan
line; John Julius Norwich *Christmas Crackers*
(1980)

6 May his anorak grow big with jotters,
Noting the numbers of trains he saw.
Glyn Maxwell 1962– : 'Curse on a Child'
(1995)

7 That life-quickening atmosphere of a
big railway station where everything is
something trembling on the brink of
something else.
Vladimir Nabokov 1899–1977: *Spring in Fialta
and other stories* (1956)

8 Do engine-drivers, I wonder, eternally
wish they were small boys?
Flann O'Brien 1911–66: *The Best of Myles*
(1968)

9 After the first powerful plain
  manifesto
  The black statement of pistons,
  without more fuss
  But gliding like a queen, she leaves the
  station.
  Stephen Spender 1909–95: 'The Express'
  (1933)

Rain

1 Rainy days—
  silkworms droop
  on mulberries.
  Matsuo Basho 1644–94: translated by Lucien
  Stryk

2 The rain fell in a uniform untroubled
  manner. It fell upon the bay, the
  littoral, the mountains and the plains,
  and notably upon the Central Bog it
  fell with a rather desolate uniformity.
  Samuel Beckett 1906–89: 'A Wet Night'
  (1934)

3 You can call this rain bad weather, but
  it is not. It is simply weather, and
  weather means rough weather. It
  reminds us forcibly that its element is
  water, falling water. And water is hard.
  Heinrich Böll 1917–85: *Irish Journal* (1957,
  translated Leila Vennewitz)

4 The rain, it raineth on the just
  And also on the unjust fella:
  But chiefly on the just, because
  The unjust steals the just's umbrella.
  Lord Bowen 1835–94: Walter Sichel *Sands of
  Time* (1923); see **Equality 2**

5 It is impossible to live in a country
  which is continually under
  hatches . . . Rain! Rain! Rain!
  John Keats 1795–1821: letter to J. H. Reynolds
  from Devon, 10 April 1818

6 I liked rain. The hiss of the water and
  the earth so soft bright green plants
  would nearly sprout beside you.
  Patrick McCabe 1955– : *The Butcher Boy*
  (1992)

Readiness

1 The scouts' motto is founded on my
  initials, it is: BE PREPARED, which

means, you are always to be in a state
of readiness in mind and body to do
your duty.
  Robert Baden-Powell 1857–1941: *Scouting for
  Boys* (1908)

2 Barkis is willin'.
  Charles Dickens 1812–70: *David Copperfield*
  (1850)

3 I think the necessity of being *ready*
  increases. Look to it.
  Abraham Lincoln 1809–65: the whole of a
  letter to Governor Andrew Curtin of
  Pennsylvania, 8 April 1861

4 No time like the present.
  Mrs Manley 1663–1724: *The Lost Lover* (1696)

5 Go ahead, make my day.
  Joseph C. Stinson 1947– : *Sudden Impact*
  (1983 film); spoken by Clint Eastwood

Reading

see also **Books**, **Literature**

1 The world may be full of fourth-rate
  writers but it's also full of fourth-rate
  readers.
  Stan Barstow 1928– : in *Daily Mail* 15 August
  1989

2 Choose an author as you choose a
  friend.
  Wentworth Dillon, Lord Roscommon
  c.1633–85: *Essay on Translated Verse* (1684)

3 When I want to read a novel, I write
  one.
  Benjamin Disraeli 1804–81: W. Monypenny
  and G. Buckle *Life of Benjamin Disraeli* vol. 6
  (1920)

4 Reading one book is like eating one
  crisp.
  Diane Duane 1952– : *So You Want to Be a
  Wizard* (1983)

5 What do we ever get nowadays from
  reading to equal the excitement and
  the revelation in those first fourteen
  years?
  Graham Greene 1904–91: *The Lost Childhood
  and Other Essays* (1951)

6 A man ought to read just as
inclination leads him; for what he
reads as a task will do him little good.
Samuel Johnson 1709–84: James Boswell *Life
of Samuel Johnson* (1791) 14 July 1763

7 Don't read too much now: the dude
Who lets the girl down before
The hero arrives, the chap
Who's yellow and keeps the store,
Seem far too familiar. Get stewed:
Books are a load of crap.
Philip Larkin 1922–85: 'Study of Reading
Habits' (1964)

8 [*The Compleat Angler*] is
acknowledged to be one of the world's
books. Only the trouble is that the
world doesn't read its books, it
borrows a detective story instead.
Stephen Leacock 1869–1944: *The Boy I Left
Behind Me* (1947)

9 Curiously enough, one cannot *read* a
book: one can only reread it. A good
reader, a major reader, an active and
creative reader is a rereader.
Vladimir Nabokov 1899–1977: *Lectures on
Literature* (1980)

10 What really knocks me out is a book
that, when you're all done reading it,
you wish the author that wrote it was
a terrific friend of yours and you
could call him up on the phone
whenever you felt like it.
J. D. Salinger 1919– : *Catcher in the Rye* (1951)

11 POLONIUS: What do you read, my
lord?
HAMLET: Words, words, words.
William Shakespeare 1564–1616: *Hamlet*
(1601)

12 People say that life is the thing, but I
prefer reading.
Logan Pearsall Smith 1865–1946:
Afterthoughts (1931)

13 Reading is to the mind what exercise
is to the body.
Richard Steele 1672–1729: in *The Tatler*
18 March 1710

14 Digressions, incontestably, are the
sunshine;—they are the life, the soul
of reading;—take them out of this

book for instance,—you might as well
take the book along with them.
Laurence Sterne 1713–68: *Tristram Shandy*
(1759–67)

Ronald Reagan 1911–

1 Ronald Reagan, the President who
never told bad news to the American
people.
Garrison Keillor 1942– : *We Are Still Married*
(1989)

2 The battle for the mind of Ronald
Reagan was like the trench warfare of
World War I. Never have so many
fought so hard for such barren
terrain.
Peggy Noonan 1950– : *What I Saw at the
Revolution* (1990)

3 Ronald Reagan . . . is attempting a
great breakthrough in political
technology—he has been perfecting
the Teflon-coated Presidency. He sees
to it that nothing sticks to him.
Patricia Schroeder 1940– : speech in the US
House of Representatives, 2 August 1983

4 A triumph of the embalmer's art.
Gore Vidal 1925– : in *Observer* 26 April 1981

5 No, *no. Jimmy Stewart* for governor—
Reagan for his best friend.
■ *on hearing that Reagan was seeking
nomination as Governor of California, 1966*
Jack Warner 1892–1978: Max Wilk *The Wit
and Wisdom of Hollywood* (1972)

Reality

see also **Appearance, Facts**

1 Reality goes bounding past the satirist
like a cheetah laughing as it lopes
ahead of the greyhound.
Claud Cockburn 1904–81: *Crossing the Line*
(1958)

2 Perhaps the rare and simple pleasure
of being seen for what one is
compensates for the misery of being
it.
Margaret Drabble 1939– : *A Summer Bird-
Cage* (1963)

3 Between the idea
And the reality
Between the motion
And the act
Falls the Shadow.

T. S. Eliot 1888–1965: 'The Hollow Men' (1925)

4 All theory, dear friend, is grey, but the golden tree of actual life springs ever green.

Johann Wolfgang von Goethe 1749–1832: *Faust* pt. 1 (1808)

5 I refute it *thus*.

■ *kicking a large stone by way of refuting Bishop Berkeley's theory of the non-existence of matter*

Samuel Johnson 1709–84: James Boswell *Life of Samuel Johnson* (1791) 6 August 1763

6 Do you think that the things people make fools of themselves about are any less real and true than the things they behave sensibly about? They are more true: they are the only things that are true.

George Bernard Shaw 1856–1950: *Candida* (1898)

7 The camera makes everyone a tourist in other people's reality, and eventually in one's own.

Susan Sontag 1933– : in *New York Review of Books* 18 April 1974

8 They said, 'You have a blue guitar,
You do not play things as they are.'
The man replied, 'Things as they are
Are changed upon the blue guitar.'

Wallace Stevens 1879–1955: 'The Man with the Blue Guitar' (1937)

9 Reality's not strange, not unexpected. Reality doesn't reside in the sudden hallucination of events. Reality is uneventfulness, vacancy, flatness. Reality is that nothing happens. How many of the events of history have occurred . . . for no other reason, fundamentally, than the desire to make things happen?

Graham Swift 1949– : *Waterland* (1984)

10 It is the spirit of the age to believe that any fact, no matter how suspect, is superior to any imaginative exercise, no matter how true.

Gore Vidal 1925– : in *Encounter* December 1967

11 The nineteenth century dislike of Realism is the rage of Caliban seeing his own face in the glass.

Oscar Wilde 1854–1900: *The Picture of Dorian Gray* (1891)

12 BLANCHE: I don't want realism.
MITCH: Naw, I guess not.
BLANCHE: I'll tell you what I want. Magic!

Tennessee Williams 1911–83: *A Streetcar Named Desire* (1947)

Reason

see **Logic and Reason**

Relationships

see also **Friendship**, **Hatred**, **Love**, **Sex**

1 He who has a thousand friends has not a friend to spare,
And he who has one enemy will meet him everywhere.

Ali ibn-Abi-Talib c.602–661: *A Hundred Sayings*

2 Almost all of our relationships begin and most of them continue as forms of mutual exploitation, a mental or physical barter, to be terminated when one or both parties run out of goods.

W. H. Auden 1907–73: *The Dyer's Hand* (1963)

3 In necessary things, unity; in doubtful things, liberty; in all things, charity.

Richard Baxter 1615–91: motto

4 Am I my brother's keeper?

Bible: Genesis

5 Love, friendship, respect do not unite people as much as common hatred for something.

Anton Chekhov 1860–1904: *Notebooks* (1921)

6 In the beginning of all relationships you are out there bungee jumping every weekend but after six months you are renting videos and buying

corn chips just like everyone else—
and the next day you can't even
remember what video you rented.
Douglas Coupland 1961– : *Life After God*
(1994)

7 I know a lot of people didn't expect
our relationship to last—but we've
just celebrated our two months
anniversary.
Britt Ekland 1942– : attributed

8 Here's how men think. Sex, work—
and those are reversible, depending
on age—sex, work, food, sports and
lastly, begrudgingly, relationships.
And here's how women think.
Relationships, relationships,
relationships, work, sex, shopping,
weight, food.
Carrie Fisher 1956– : *Surrender the Pink*
(1990)

9 Personal relations are the important
thing for ever and ever, and not this
outer life of telegrams and anger.
E. M. Forster 1879–1970: *Howards End* (1910)

10 The number one complaint women
have in relationships is: 'I don't feel
heard.'
John Gray 1951– : *Men are from Mars, Women
are from Venus* (1992)

11 Their relationship consisted
In discussing if it existed.
Thom Gunn 1929– : 'Jamesian' (1992)

12 There are those who never stretch out
the hand for fear it will be bitten. But
those who never stretch out the hand
will never feel it clasped in friendship.
Michael Heseltine 1933– : *Where There's a
Will* (1987)

13 The meeting of two personalities is
like the contact of two chemical
substances: if there is any reaction,
both are transformed.
Carl Gustav Jung 1875–1961: *Modern Man in
Search of a Soul* (1933)

14 We've got this gift of love, but love is
like a precious plant. You can't just
accept it and leave it in the cupboard
or just think it's going to get on by
itself. You've got to keep watering it.

You've got to really look after it and
nurture it.
John Lennon 1940–80: television interview,
30 December 1969

15 Ships that pass in the night, and speak
each other in passing;
Only a signal shown and a distant
voice in the darkness;
So on the ocean of life we pass and
speak one another,
Only a look and a voice; then darkness
again and a silence.
Henry Wadsworth Longfellow 1807–82: *Tales
of a Wayside Inn* pt. 3 (1874)

16 If we were actually to comprehend
other people we would not be able to
use them for our own ends.
Candia McWilliam 1955– : *Debatable Land*
(1994)

17 Difficult or easy, pleasant or bitter,
you are the same you: I cannot live
with you—or without you.
Martial AD *c.*40–*c.*104: *Epigrammata*

18 I love her too, but our neuroses just
don't match.
Arthur Miller 1915– : *The Ride Down Mount
Morgan* (1991)

19 I believe a little incompatibility is the
spice of life, particularly if he has
income and she is pattable.
Ogden Nash 1902–71: 'I Do, I Will, I Have'
(1949)

20 Ah, the relationships we get into just
to get out of the ones we are not brave
enough to say are over.
Julia Phillips 1944– : *You'll Never Eat Lunch
in This Town Again* (1991)

21 She experienced all the cosiness and
irritation which can come from living
with thoroughly nice people with
whom one has nothing in common.
Barbara Pym 1913–80: *Less than Angels* (1955)

22 I hold this to be the highest task for a
bond between two people: that each
protects the solitude of the other.
Rainer Maria Rilke 1875–1926: letter to Paula
Modersohn-Becker, 12 February 1902

23 We would never love anybody if we
could see past our invention.
Tom Stoppard 1937– : *The Invention of Love*
(1997)

24 Love and sex can go together and sex
and unlove can go together and love
and unsex can go together. But
personal love and personal sex is bad.
Andy Warhol 1927–87: *Philosophy of Andy
Warhol (From A to B and Back Again)* (1975)

Religion

see also **The Bible, Christianity, The
Church, Clergy, Faith, God, Prayer,
Science and Religion**

1 Render therefore unto Caesar the
things which are Caesar's; and unto
God the things that are God's.
Bible: St Matthew

2 Religions are kept alive by heresies,
which are really sudden explosions of
faith. Dead religions do not produce
them.
Gerald Brenan 1894–1987: *Thoughts in a Dry
Season* (1978)

3 One religion is as true as another.
Robert Burton 1577–1640: *The Anatomy of
Melancholy* (1621–51)

4 'Sensible men are all of the same
religion.' 'And pray what is that?' . . .
'Sensible men never tell.'
Benjamin Disraeli 1804–81: *Endymion* (1880)

5 So long as man remains free he strives
for nothing so incessantly and so
painfully as to find someone to
worship.
Fedor Dostoevsky 1821–81: *The Brothers
Karamazov* (1879–80)

6 It [religion] can trap us in language
about mysteries rather than open us to
the mysteries themselves.
Richard Holloway 1933– : introduction to
The Gospel According to Luke (1998)

7 To become a popular religion, it is
only necessary for a superstition to
enslave a philosophy.
William Ralph Inge 1860–1954: *Idea of Progress*
(1920)

8 Religion's in the heart, not in the
knees.
Douglas Jerrold 1803–57: *The Devil's Ducat*
(1830)

9 It is our first duty to serve society,
and, after we have done that, we may
attend wholly to the salvation of our
own souls. A youthful passion for
abstracted devotion should not be
encouraged.
Samuel Johnson 1709–84: James Boswell *Life
of Samuel Johnson* (1791) February 1766

10 Religion is the frozen thought of men
out of which they build temples.
Jiddu Krishnamurti 1895–1986: in *Observer*
22 April 1928

11 These damned mystics with a private
line to God ought to be compelled to
disconnect. I cannot see that they
have done anything save prevent
necessary change.
Harold Laski 1893–1950: letter to Oliver
Wendell Holmes, 29 January 1919

12 I count religion but a childish toy,
And hold there is no sin but
ignorance.
Christopher Marlowe 1564–93: *The Jew of
Malta* (c.1592)

13 Religion . . . is the opium of the
people.
Karl Marx 1818–83: *A Contribution to the
Critique of Hegel's Philosophy of Right*
(1843–4)

14 Things have come to a pretty pass
when religion is allowed to invade the
sphere of private life.
■ *on hearing an evangelical sermon*
Lord Melbourne 1779–1848: G. W. E. Russell
Collections and Recollections (1898)

15 If even a dog's tooth is truly
worshipped it glows with light. The
venerated object is endowed with
power, that is the simple sense of the
ontological proof.
Iris Murdoch 1919–99: *The Sea, The Sea* (1978)

16 There's no reason to bring religion
into it. I think we ought to have as
great a regard for religion as we can,

so as to keep it out of as many things as possible.

Sean O'Casey 1880–1964: *The Plough and the Stars* (1926)

17 My country is the world, and my religion is to do good.

Thomas Paine 1737–1809: *The Rights of Man* pt. 2 (1792)

18 Any system of religion that has any thing in it that shocks the mind of a child cannot be a true system.

Thomas Paine 1737–1809: *The Age of Reason* pt. 1 (1794)

19 Religion to me has always been the wound, not the bandage.

Dennis Potter 1935–94: *Seeing the Blossom* (1994)

20 Religion may in most of its forms be defined as the belief that the gods are on the side of the Government.

Bertrand Russell 1872–1970: attributed

21 Had I but served my God with half the zeal
I served my king, he would not in mine age
Have left me naked to mine enemies.

William Shakespeare 1564–1616: *Henry VIII* (1613)

22 We have just enough religion to make us hate, but not enough to make us love one another.

Jonathan Swift 1667–1745: *Thoughts on Various Subjects* (1711)

23 Orthodoxy is my doxy; heterodoxy is another man's doxy.

William Warburton 1698–1779: to Lord Sandwich; Joseph Priestley *Memoirs* (1807)

24 Zen . . . does not confuse spirituality with thinking about God while one is peeling potatoes. Zen spirituality is just to peel the potatoes.

Alan Watts 1915–73: *The Way of Zen* (1957)

25 I went to America to convert the Indians; but oh, who shall convert me?

John Wesley 1703–91: diary 24 January 1738

26 So many gods, so many creeds,
So many paths that wind and wind,

While just the art of being kind
Is all the sad world needs.

Ella Wheeler Wilcox 1855–1919: 'The World's Need'

Reputation

see also **Fame**

1 Woe unto you, when all men shall speak well of you!

Bible: St Luke

2 The devil's most devilish when respectable.

Elizabeth Barrett Browning 1806–61: *Aurora Leigh* (1857)

3 Caesar's wife must be above suspicion.

Julius Caesar 100–44 BC: oral tradition, based on Plutarch *Parallel Lives* 'Julius Caesar'

4 The reputation which the world bestows
is like the wind, that shifts now here now there,
its name changed with the quarter whence it blows.

Dante Alighieri 1265–1321: *Divina Commedia* 'Purgatorio'

5 I think that's just another word for a washed-up has-been.

■ *on being an 'icon'*
Bob Dylan 1941– : in *Mail on Sunday* 18 January 1998

6 Always providing you have enough courage—or money—you can do without a reputation.

Margaret Mitchell 1900–49: *Gone with the Wind* (1936)

7 You can't shame or humiliate modern celebrities. What used to be called shame and humiliation is now called publicity.

P. J. O'Rourke 1947– : *Give War a Chance* (1992)

8 Honour is like a match, you can only use it once.

Marcel Pagnol 1895–1974: *Marius* (1946)

9 What is merit? The opinion one man entertains of another.

> **Lord Palmerston** 1784–1865: Thomas Carlyle *Shooting Niagara: and After?* (1867)

10   He that filches from me my good name
Robs me of that which not enriches him,
And makes me poor indeed.

> **William Shakespeare** 1564–1616: *Othello* (1602–4)

11 We owe respect to the living; to the dead we owe only truth.

> **Voltaire** 1694–1778: 'Première Lettre sur Oedipe' in *Oeuvres* (1785)

12 I'm the girl who lost her reputation and never missed it.

> **Mae West** 1892–1980: P. F. Boller and R. L. Davis *Hollywood Anecdotes* (1988)

Research

see also **Experiment**, **Science**, **Theory**

1 In the culture I grew up in you did your work and you did not put your arm around it to stop other people from looking—you took the earliest possible opportunity to make knowledge available.

> ■ *on modern medical research*
> **James Black** 1924– : in *Daily Telegraph* 11 December 1995

2 Basic research is what I am doing when I don't know what I am doing.

> **Wernher von Braun** 1912–77: R. L. Weber *A Random Walk in Science* (1973)

3 If politics is the art of the possible, research is surely the art of the soluble. Both are immensely practical-minded affairs.

> **Peter Medawar** 1915–87: in *New Statesman* 19 June 1964; cf. **Politics** 7

4 In research the horizon recedes as we advance, and is no nearer at sixty than it was at twenty. As the power of endurance weakens with age, the urgency of the pursuit grows more intense . . . And research is always incomplete.

> **Mark Pattison** 1813–84: *Isaac Casaubon* (1875)

5 He had been eight years upon a project for extracting sun-beams out of cucumbers, which were to be put into vials hermetically sealed, and let out to warm the air in raw inclement summers.

> **Jonathan Swift** 1667–1745: *Gulliver's Travels* (1726)

6 The outcome of any serious research can only be to make two questions grow where one question grew before.

> **Thorstein Veblen** 1857–1929: *University of California Chronicle* (1908)

7 No more impressive warning can be given to those who would confine knowledge and research to what is apparently useful, than the reflection that conic sections were studied for eighteen hundred years merely as an abstract science, without regard to any utility other than to satisfy the craving for knowledge on the part of mathematicians, and that then at the end of this long period of abstract study, they were found to be the necessary key with which to attain the knowledge of the most important laws of nature.

> **Alfred North Whitehead** 1861–1947: *Introduction to Mathematics* (1911)

8 As one explores phenomena or ideas at the frontiers of scientific knowledge it is the unexpected that provides the clues to guide further work.

> **Lewis Wolpert** 1929– : *The Unnatural Nature of Science* (1995)

Responsibility

see also **Duty**

1 When a man assumes a public trust, he should consider himself as public property.

> **Thomas Jefferson** 1743–1826: to Baron von Humboldt, 1807; B. L. Rayner *Life of Jefferson* (1834)

2 But how can you bear the responsibility of telling people what to *think*?

■ *to a newspaper editor*
Keith Joseph 1918–94: in *Observer* 14 October 1990

3 Power without responsibility: the prerogative of the harlot throughout the ages.

■ *summing up Lord Beaverbrook's political standpoint as a newspaper editor; Stanley Baldwin, Kipling's cousin, subsequently obtained permission to use the phrase in a speech*
Rudyard Kipling 1865–1936: in *Kipling Journal* December 1971

4 The buck stops here.

Harry S. Truman 1884–1972: unattributed motto on Truman's desk

Revenge

1 Revenge is a kind of wild justice, which the more man's nature runs to, the more ought law to weed it out.

Francis Bacon 1561–1626: *Essays* (1625) 'Of Revenge'

2 Vengeance is mine; I will repay, saith the Lord.

Bible: Romans

3 You can't be fuelled by bitterness. It can eat you up, but it cannot drive you.

Benazir Bhutto 1953– : *Daughter of Destiny* (1989)

4 Sweet is revenge—especially to women.

Lord Byron 1788–1824: *Don Juan* (1819–24)

5 It may be that vengeance is sweet, and that the gods forbade vengeance to men because they reserved for themselves so delicious and intoxicating a drink. But no one should drain the cup to the bottom. The dregs are often filthy-tasting.

Winston Churchill 1874–1965: *The River War* (1899)

6 Heaven has no rage, like love to hatred turned,

Nor Hell a fury, like a woman scorned.

William Congreve 1670–1729: *The Mourning Bride* (1697)

7 Cancel the kitchen scraps for lepers and orphans. No more merciful beheadings. And call off Christmas!

Pen Densham and **John Watson**: *Robin Hood, Prince of Thieves* (1991 film); spoken by Alan Rickman

8 The Germans, if this Government is returned, are going to pay every penny; they are going to be squeezed as a lemon is squeezed—until the pips squeak.

Eric Geddes 1875–1937: speech at Cambridge, 10 December 1918

9 Nobody ever forgets where he buried a hatchet.

Frank McKinney ('Kin') Hubbard 1868–1930: *Abe Martin's Broadcast* (1930)

10 Get your retaliation in first.

Carwyn James 1929–83: attributed, 1971

11 Indeed, revenge is always the pleasure of a paltry, feeble, tiny mind.

Juvenal AD *c*.60–*c*.130: *Satires*

12 Men should be either treated generously or destroyed, because they take revenge for slight injuries—for heavy ones they cannot.

Niccolò Machiavelli 1469–1527: *The Prince* (written 1513)

13 Beware of the man who does not return your blow: he neither forgives you nor allows you to forgive yourself.

George Bernard Shaw 1856–1950: *Man and Superman* (1903)

14 Two wrongs don't make a right, but they make a good excuse.

Thomas Szasz 1920– : *The Second Sin* (1973)

Reviews

see also **Critics**

1 A bad review may spoil your breakfast but you shouldn't allow it to spoil your lunch.

Kingsley Amis 1922–95: attributed; Giles Gordon *Aren't We Due a Royalty Statement?* (1993)

2 One cannot review a bad book
without showing off.

W. H. Auden 1907–73: *The Dyer's Hand* (1963)
'Reading'

3 I have spent years as a professional
writer and what I know now is that
the only review that is no use to me is
a review that lies.

Kazuo Ishiguro 1954– : in *Guardian* 15 May
1996

4 When the reviews are bad I tell my
staff that they can join me as I cry all
the way to the bank.

Liberace 1919–87: *Autobiography* (1973);
coined in the mid-1950s

5 From the moment I picked up your
book until I laid it down, I was
convulsed with laughter. Some day I
intend reading it.

■ *blurb written for S. J. Perelman's book* Dawn
Ginsberg's Revenge (*1928*)

Groucho Marx 1895–1977: Hector Arce
Groucho (1979)

6 I am sitting in the smallest room of
my house. I have your review before
me. In a moment it will be behind me.

■ *responding to a savage review by Rudolph
Louis in* Münchener Neueste Nachrichten,
7 *February 1906*

Max Reger 1873–1916: Nicolas Slonimsky
Lexicon of Musical Invective (1953)

7 While the critic caused me a
somewhat uneasy breakfast, I
contented myself with the knowledge
that I had given him a perfectly
ghastly evening.

Jeremy Sinden 1950–96: in *The Times* 31 May
1996

8 I never read a book before reviewing
it; it prejudices a man so.

Sydney Smith 1771–1845: H. Pearson *The
Smith of Smiths* (1934)

Revolution

see also **Politics, Protest**

1 The most radical revolutionary will
become a conservative on the day
after the revolution.

Hannah Arendt 1906–75: in *New Yorker*
12 September 1970

2 Those who have served the cause of
the revolution have ploughed the sea.

Simón Bolívar 1783–1830: attributed

3 Revolutions are celebrated when they
are no longer dangerous.

Pierre Boulez 1925– : in *Guardian* 13 January
1989

4 Would it not be easier
In that case for the government
To dissolve the people
And elect another?

■ *on the 1953 uprising in East Germany*

Bertolt Brecht 1898–1956: 'The Solution'
(1953)

5 All modern revolutions have ended in
a reinforcement of the State.

Albert Camus 1913–60: *L'Homme révolté*
(1951)

6 What is a rebel? A man who says no.

Albert Camus 1913–60: *L'Homme révolté*
(1951)

7 History will absolve me.

Fidel Castro 1927– : title of pamphlet (1953)

8 The Revolution is made by man, but
man must forge his revolutionary
spirit from day to day.

Ernesto ('Che') Guevara 1928–67: *Socialism
and Man in Cuba* (1968)

9 When the people contend for their
liberty, they seldom get anything by
their victory but new masters.

Lord Halifax 1633–95: *Political, Moral, and
Miscellaneous Thoughts and Reflections* (1750)
'Of Prerogative, Power and Liberty'

10 That special time caught me up in its
wild vortex and—in the absence of
leisure to reflect on the matter—
compelled me to do what had to be
done.

■ *on his election to the Presidency*

Václav Havel 1936– : *Summer Meditations*
(1992)

11 Maximilien Robespierre was nothing
but the hand of Jean Jacques
Rousseau, the bloody hand that drew

from the womb of time the body whose soul Rousseau had created.
Heinrich Heine 1797–1856: *Zur Geschichte der Religion und Philosophie in Deutschland* (1834)

12 I will die like a true-blue rebel. Don't waste any time in mourning— organize.
■ *prior to his death by firing squad*
Joe Hill 1879–1915: farewell telegram to Bill Haywood, 18 November 1915

13 A little rebellion now and then is a good thing.
Thomas Jefferson 1743–1826: letter to James Madison, 30 January 1787

14 Those who make peaceful revolution impossible will make violent revolution inevitable.
John F. Kennedy 1917–63: speech at the White House, 13 March 1962

15 A share in two revolutions is living to some purpose.
Thomas Paine 1737–1809: Eric Foner *Tom Paine and Revolutionary America* (1976)

16 Revolutions are not made; they come. A revolution is as natural a growth as an oak. It comes out of the past. Its foundations are laid far back.
Wendell Phillips 1811–84: speech 8 January 1852

17 *Après nous le déluge.*
After us the deluge.
Madame de Pompadour 1721–64: Madame du Hausset *Mémoires* (1824)

18 Ten days that shook the world.
■ *of the Russian revolution*
John Reed 1887–1920: title of book (1919)

19 I know, and all the world knows, that revolutions never go backward.
William Seward 1801–72: speech at Rochester, 25 October 1858

20 Revolutions have never lightened the burden of tyranny: they have only shifted it to another shoulder.
George Bernard Shaw 1856–1950: *Man and Superman* (1903) 'The Revolutionist's Handbook' foreword

21 The social order destroyed by a revolution is almost always better than that which immediately preceded it, and experience shows that the most dangerous moment for a bad government is generally that in which it sets about reform.
Alexis de Tocqueville 1805–59: *L'Ancien régime* (1856)

22 Bliss was it in that dawn to be alive, But to be young was very heaven!
William Wordsworth 1770–1850: 'The French Revolution, as it Appeared to Enthusiasts' (1809)

Risk
see also **Danger**, **Security**

1 My only solution for the problem of habitual accidents . . . is to stay in bed all day. Even then, there is always the chance that you will fall out.
Robert Benchley 1889–1945: *Chips off the old Benchley* (1949)

2 The girls in Canadian lap dancing bars are allowed to remove all their clothes and touch the customers, but while this is undoubtedly a Good Thing, we should remember that Canada is home to 87% of all the world's mosquitoes.
Jeremy Clarkson 1960– : in *Sunday Times* 18 July 1999

3 He either fears his fate too much, Or his deserts are small, That puts it not unto the touch To win or lose it all.
James Graham, Marquess of Montrose 1612–50: 'My Dear and Only Love' (written *c*.1642)

4 My inclination to go by Air Express is confirmed by the crash they had yesterday, which will make them careful in the immediate future.
A. E. Housman 1859–1936: letter 17 August 1920

5 Where there is no risk there can be no pride in achievement and consequently no happiness.
Ray Kroc 1902–84: *Grinding It Out* (1977)

6 BETTER DROWNED THAN DUFFERS IF
NOT DUFFERS WONT DROWN.
Arthur Ransome 1884–1967: *Swallows and
Amazons* (1930)

7 We took risks, we knew we took them;
things have come out against us, and
therefore we have no cause for
complaint.
Robert Falcon Scott 1868–1912: 'The Last
Message' in *Scott's Last Expedition* (1913)

8 The nanny state has decreed that
tobacco is so dangerous it can only be
advertised on vehicles travelling at
over 150 mph.
■ *on the exemption of Formula One from a ban
on cigarette advertising*
Ann Widdecombe 1947– : at the Conservative
Party Conference, Bournemouth, 6 October
1998

Rivers

1 Says Tweed to Till—
'What gars ye rin sae still?'
Says Till to Tweed—
'Though ye rin with speed
And I rin slaw,
For ae man that ye droon
I droon twa.'
Anonymous: traditional rhyme

2 The Thames is liquid history.
■ *to an American who had compared the
Thames disparagingly with the Mississippi*
John Burns 1858–1943: in *Daily Mail*
25 January 1943

3 I do not know much about gods; but I
think that the river
Is a strong brown god—sullen,
untamed and intractable.
T. S. Eliot 1888–1965: *Four Quartets* 'The Dry
Salvages' (1941)

4 Ol' man river, dat ol' man river,
He must know sumpin', but don't say
nothin',
He jus' keeps rollin',
He jus' keeps rollin' along.
Oscar Hammerstein II 1895–1960: 'Ol' Man
River' (1927 song)

5 I've known rivers:
I've known rivers ancient as the world

and older than the flow of human
blood in human veins.
Langston Hughes 1902–67: 'The Negro Speaks
of Rivers' (1921)

6 I bathed in the Euphrates when dawns
were young.
I built my hut near the Congo and it
lulled me to sleep.
I looked upon the Nile and raised the
pyramids above it.
I heard the singing of the Mississippi
when Abe Lincoln went down to
New Orleans, and I've seen its
muddy bosom turn all golden in the
sunset.
Langston Hughes 1902–67: 'The Negro Speaks
of Rivers' (1921)

7 Then I saw the Congo, creeping
through the black,
Cutting through the forest with a
golden track.
Vachel Lindsay 1879–1931: 'The Congo' (1914)

8 Sabrina fair,
Listen where thou art sitting
Under the glassy, cool, translucent
wave,
In twisted braids of lilies knitting
The loose train of thy amber-
dropping hair.
■ *Sabrina, the nymph of the River Severn*
John Milton 1608–74: *Comus* (1637)

9 Sweet Thames, run softly, till I end my
song.
Edmund Spenser c.1552–99: *Prothalamion*
(1596)

10 I come from haunts of coot and hern,
I make a sudden sally
And sparkle out among the fern,
To bicker down a valley.
Alfred, Lord Tennyson 1809–92: 'The Brook'
(1855)

Rock and Pop Music

see also **Musicians**

1 They didn't have Kalashnikovs but
U2 tickets in their hands.
■ *of the audience*
Bono 1960– : at the U2 concert, Sarajevo,
24 September 1997

2 I would hope we mean more to people than putting money in a church basket and saying ten Hail Marys on a Sunday. Has God played Knebworth recently?

■ *on the drawing power of Oasis*
Noel Gallagher 1967– : in *New Musical Express* 12 July 1997

3 We will not be a footnote—we'll be a footprint in the history of rock music.
Noel Gallagher 1967– : in *Independent* 16 August 1997

4 Pop music should be treated with the disrespect it deserves.
Bob Geldof 1954– : *Is That It?* (1986)

5 Most people get into bands for three very simple rock and roll reasons: to get laid, to get fame, and to get rich.
Bob Geldof 1954– : in *Melody Maker* 27 August 1977

6 The more you jump around, the bigger your hat is, the more people listen to your music . . . The only important thing is to sell, and make money. It's nothing to do with talent.

■ *of modern music as exemplified by Oasis and U2*
George Harrison 1943–2001: in *Independent* 28 August 1997

7 I'm rock-'n'-roll anyway. My definition of rock-'n'-roll is if you're dealing with the system and dealing with milk shakes and home work, you're pop. When you decide to take the system and rock it, you're rock-'n'-roll.
Ice-T 1958– : interview in *Bill Board* 8 June 1991

8 The rhythm hammers us, hits us and possesses us, making us prisoners of noise. It's like a drug.

■ *of popular music*
Jeanne Moreau 1928– : in *Guardian* 13 August 1997

9 I'm dealing in rock'n'roll. I'm, like, I'm not a bona fide human being.
Phil Spector 1940– : attributed

Romance

1 One is never too old for romance.
Ingrid Bergman 1915–82: in *Sunday Mirror* 5 May 1974

2 The essence of romantic love is that wonderful beginning, after which sadness and impossibility may become the rule.
Anita Brookner 1928– : *A Friend From England* (1987)

3 Personally, I can't see why it would be any less romantic to find a husband in a nice four-colour catalogue than in the average downtown bar at happy hour.
Barbara Ehrenreich 1941– : *The Worst Years of Our Lives* (1991)

4 Oh God. Valentine's Day tomorrow. Why? Why? Why is entire world geared to make people not involved in romance feel stupid when everyone knows romance does not work anyway.
Helen Fielding 1958– : *Bridget Jones's Diary* (1996)

5 I have met with women whom I really think would like to be married to a poem and to be given away by a novel.
John Keats 1795–1821: letter to Fanny Brawne, 8 July 1819

6 For a man, romantic love is worship. He doesn't want to do great things with a woman, he wants to do them for her.
Irma Kurtz: *Malespeak* (1986)

7 'Our couch shall be roses all spangled with dew'
It would give me rheumatics, and so it would you.
Walter Savage Landor 1775–1864: 'A Sensible Girl's Reply to Moore'; an original has not been found in Moore's works

8 Love is not the dying moan of a distant violin—it's the triumphant twang of the bedspring.
S. J. Perelman 1904–79: attributed

9 It's our *own* story *exactly*! He bold as a hawk, she soft as the dawn.

> **James Thurber** 1894–1961: cartoon caption in *New Yorker* 25 February 1939

10 Men are so romantic, don't you think? They look for a perfect partner when what they should be looking for is perfect love.

> **Fay Weldon** 1931– : in *Sunday Times* 6 September 1987

The Royal Family

see also **Diana**

1 She is only 5ft 4in, and to make someone that height look regal is difficult. Fortunately she holds herself very well.

> ■ *of Queen Elizabeth II*
> **Hardy Amies** 1909– : interview in *Sunday Telegraph* 9 February 1997

2 When I appear in public people expect me to neigh, grind my teeth, paw the ground and swish my tail—none of which is easy.

> **Anne, Princess Royal** 1950– : in *Observer* 22 May 1977

3 I declare before you all that my whole life, whether it be long or short, shall be devoted to your service and the service of our great Imperial family to which we all belong.

> **Elizabeth II** 1926– : broadcast speech to the Commonwealth from Cape Town, 21 April 1947

4 The family firm.

> ■ *description of the British monarchy*
> **George VI** 1895–1952: attributed

5 The personality conveyed by the utterances which are put into her mouth is that of a priggish schoolgirl, captain of the hockey team, a prefect, and a recent candidate for confirmation. It is not thus that she will be able to come into her own as an independent and distinctive character.

> ■ *of Queen Elizabeth II*
> **John Grigg** 1924– : in *National and English Review* August 1958

6 The House of Hanover, like ducks, produce bad parents—they trample on their young.

> **Owen Morshead** 1893–1977: Harold Nicolson, letter to Vita Sackville-West, 7 January 1949

7 For seventeen years he did nothing at all but kill animals and stick in stamps.

> ■ *of King George V*
> **Harold Nicolson** 1886–1968: diary 17 August 1949

8 She's head of a dysfunctional family—if she lived on a council estate in Sheffield, she'd probably be in council care.

> ■ *of Queen Elizabeth II*
> **Michael Parkinson** 1935– : in *Mail on Sunday* 17 January 1999

9 Tolerance is the one essential ingredient . . . You can take it from me that the Queen has the quality of tolerance in abundance.

> ■ *his recipe for a successful marriage*
> **Prince Philip, Duke of Edinburgh** 1921– : in *The Times* 20 November 1997

10 If you have a Royal Family you have to make the best of whatever personalities the genetic lottery comes up with.

> **Ben Pimlott** 1945– : in *Independent* 13 September 1997

11 The *éminence cerise*, the bolster behind the throne.

> ■ *of Queen Elizabeth the Queen Mother*
> **Will Self** 1961– : in *Independent on Sunday* 8 August 1999

Royalty

see also **The Royal Family**

1 Above all things our royalty is to be reverenced, and if you begin to poke about it you cannot reverence it . . . Its mystery is its life. We must not let in daylight upon magic.

> **Walter Bagehot** 1826–77: *The English Constitution* (1867)

2 The Sovereign has, under a constitutional monarchy such as ours,

three rights—the right to be consulted, the right to encourage, the right to warn.
Walter Bagehot 1826–77: *The English Constitution* (1867)

3 To be Prince of Wales is not a position. It is a predicament.
Alan Bennett 1934– : *The Madness of King George* (1995 film)

4 A subject and a sovereign are clean different things.
Charles I 1600–49: speech on the scaffold, 30 January 1649

5 The influence of the Crown has increased, is increasing, and ought to be diminished.
John Dunning 1731–83: resolution passed in the House of Commons, 6 April 1780

6 At long last I am able to say a few words of my own . . . you must believe me when I tell you that I have found it impossible to carry the heavy burden of responsibility and to discharge my duties as King as I would wish to do without the help and support of the woman I love.
Edward VIII 1894–1972: radio broadcast following his abdication, 11 December 1936

7 I know I have the body of a weak and feeble woman, but I have the heart and stomach of a king, and of a king of England too.
Elizabeth I 1533–1603: speech to the troops at Tilbury on the approach of the Armada, 1588

8 It is a very curious thing that no matter where I go, in whatever country, the children always think I should be wearing a silver dress and a golden crown. They must all be bitterly disappointed. Maybe I should.
Elizabeth II 1926– : remark on tour of China, 1985

9 We could not go anywhere without sending word ahead so that life might be put on parade for us.
Infanta Eulalia of Spain 1864–1958: *Court Life from Within* (1915)

10 For I've danced with a man.
I've danced with a man
Who—well, you'll never guess.

I've danced with a man who's danced with a girl
Who's danced with the Prince of Wales!
Herbert Farjeon 1887–1945: 'I've danced with a man who's danced with a girl'; first written for Elsa Lanchester and sung at private parties; later sung on stage by Mimi Crawford (1928)

11 The whole world is in revolt. Soon there will be only five Kings left—the King of England, the King of Spades, the King of Clubs, the King of Hearts and the King of Diamonds.
King Farouk 1920–65: addressed to the author at a conference in Cairo, 1948; Lord Boyd-Orr *As I Recall* (1966)

12 I don't enjoy my public obligations. I was not made to cut ribbons and kiss babies.
Princess Michael of Kent 1945– : in *Life* November 1986

13 Whoso pulleth out this sword of this stone and anvil is rightwise King born of all England.
Thomas Malory d. 1471: *Le Morte D'Arthur* (1470)

14 Royalty is the gold filling in a mouthful of decay.
John Osborne 1929–94: 'They call it cricket' in T. Maschler (ed.) *Declaration* (1957)

15 I see it is impossible for the King to have things done as cheap as other men.
Samuel Pepys 1633–1703: diary 21 July 1662

16 For the past 40 years I had never folded my own quilt, made my own bed, or poured out my own washing. I had never even washed my own feet or tied my shoes.
■ *having been Emperor of China 1908–12 and Japan's puppet emperor of Manchuria 1934–45*
Pu Yi 1906–67: *From Emperor to Citizen* (1964)

17 Uneasy lies the head that wears a crown.
William Shakespeare 1564–1616: *Henry IV, Part 2* (1597)

18 Monarchy is only the string that ties
the robber's bundle.
Percy Bysshe Shelley 1792–1822: *A
Philosophical View of Reform* (written
1819–20)

19 I will be good.
■ *on being shown a chart of the line of
succession, 11 March 1830*
Queen Victoria 1819–1901: Theodore Martin
The Prince Consort (1875)

Russia

see also **Communism**

1 Every country has its own
constitution; ours is absolutism
moderated by assassination.
Anonymous: Ernst Friedrich Herbert, Count
Münster, quoting 'an intelligent Russian', in
*Political Sketches of the State of Europe,
1814–1867* (1868)

2 [Russian Communism is] the
illegitimate child of Karl Marx and
Catherine the Great.
Clement Attlee 1883–1967: speech at Aarhus
University, 11 April 1956

3 Russia can be an empire or a
democracy, but it cannot be both.
Zbigniew Brzezinski 1928– : in *Foreign Affairs*
March/April 1994

4 The Lord God has given us vast
forests, immense fields, wide
horizons; surely we ought to be giants,
living in such a country as this.
Anton Chekhov 1860–1904: *The Cherry
Orchard* (1904)

5 I cannot forecast to you the action of
Russia. It is a riddle wrapped in a
mystery inside an enigma.
Winston Churchill 1874–1965: radio broadcast,
1 October 1939

6 Petersburg, the most abstract and
premeditated city on earth.
Fedor Dostoevsky 1821–81: *Notes from
Underground* (1864)

7 The idea of restructuring
[perestroika] . . . combines continuity
and innovation, the historical
experience of Bolshevism and the
contemporaneity of socialism.
Mikhail Sergeevich Gorbachev 1931– : speech
on the seventieth anniversary of the Russian
Revolution, 2 November 1987

8 They are strangely primitive in the
completeness with which they
surrender themselves to emotion . . .
like Aeolian harps upon which a
hundred winds play a hundred
melodies, and so it seems as though
the instrument were of unimaginable
complexity.
■ *on the Russians*
W. Somerset Maugham 1874–1965: *A Writers
Notebook* (1949) written in 1917

9 Russia has two generals in whom she
can confide—Generals Janvier
[January] and Février [February].
Nicholas I 1796–1855: attributed; *Punch*
10 March 1855

10 Moscow: those syllables can start
A tumult in the Russian heart.
Alexander Pushkin 1799–1837: *Eugene Onegin*
(1833)

11 Through reason Russia can't be
known,
No common yardstick can avail you:
She has a nature all her own—
Have faith in her, all else will fail you.
F. I. Tyutchev 1803–73: 'Through reason
Russia can't be known' (1866)

12 God of frostbite, God of famine,
beggars, cripples by the yard,
farms with no crops to examine—
that's him, that's your Russian God.
Prince Peter Vyazemsky 1792–1878: 'The
Russian God' (1828)

13 Today is the last day of an era past.
■ *at a Berlin ceremony to end the Soviet military
presence in Germany*
Boris Yeltsin 1931– : in *Guardian* 1 September
1994

Sacrifice

see also **Self-Interest**, **Suffering**

1 Greater love hath no man than this,
that a man lay down his life for his
friends.
Bible: St John

2 Any great love involves sacrifice. You feel that as a father, as a husband. You give up all your freedom. But the love is so much greater than the freedom.
Nicolas Cage 1964– : in *The Times* 17 June 1998

3 I have nothing to offer but blood, toil, tears and sweat.
Winston Churchill 1874–1965: speech, House of Commons, 13 May 1940

4 Am I prepared to lay down my life for the British female?
Really, who knows? . . .
Ah, for a child in the street I could strike; for the full-blown lady—
Somehow, Eustace, alas! I have not felt the vocation.
Arthur Hugh Clough 1819–61: *Amours de Voyage* (1858)

5 It is a far, far better thing that I do, than I have ever done; it is a far, far better rest that I go to, than I have ever known.
■ *Sydney Carton's thoughts on the steps of the guillotine, taking the place of Charles Darnay whom he has smuggled out of prison*
Charles Dickens 1812–70: *A Tale of Two Cities* (1859)

6 I gave my life for freedom—This I know:
For those who bade me fight had told me so.
William Norman Ewer 1885–1976: 'Five Souls' (1917)

7 She's the sort of woman who lives for others—you can always tell the others by their hunted expression.
C. S. Lewis 1898–1963: *The Screwtape Letters* (1942)

8 To gain that which is worth having, it may be necessary to lose everything else.
Bernadette Devlin McAliskey 1947– : preface to *The Price of My Soul* (1969)

9 I do not think you have ever realised the shock, which the attitude you took up caused your family and the whole nation. It seemed inconceivable to those who had made such sacrifices during the war that you, as their King, refused a lesser sacrifice.
Queen Mary 1867–1953: letter to the Duke of Windsor, July 1938

10 From the standpoint of pure reason, there are no good grounds to support the claim that one should sacrifice one's own happiness to that of others.
W. Somerset Maugham 1874–1965: *A Writer's Notebook* (1949) written in 1896

11 A woman will always sacrifice herself if you give her the opportunity. It is her favourite form of self-indulgence.
W. Somerset Maugham 1874–1965: *The Circle* (1921)

12 Self-sacrifice enables us to sacrifice other people without blushing.
George Bernard Shaw 1856–1950: *Man and Superman* (1903) 'Maxims: Self-Sacrifice'

Saints

1 SAINT, *n.* A dead sinner revised and edited.
Ambrose Bierce 1842–c.1914: *The Devil's Dictionary* (1911)

2 Saints should always be judged guilty until they are proved innocent.
George Orwell 1903–50: *Shooting an Elephant* (1950) 'Reflections on Gandhi'

3 If you can't bear the thought of messing up your nice clean soul, you'd better give up the whole idea of life and become a saint. Because you'll never make it as a human being. It's either this world or the next.
John Osborne 1929–94: *Look Back in Anger* (1956)

4 It is easier to make a saint out of a libertine than out of a prig.
George Santayana 1863–1952: *The Life of Reason* (1905)

5 The only difference between the saint and the sinner is that every saint has a past, and every sinner has a future.
Oscar Wilde 1854–1900: *A Woman of No Importance* (1893)

Satire

....
see **Wit and Satire**

Schools

....
see also **Children, Education, Teaching**

1 The dread of beatings! Dread of being late!
And, greatest dread of all, the dread of games!
John Betjeman 1906–84: *Summoned by Bells* (1960)

2 Forty years on, when afar and asunder Parted are those who are singing to-day.
E. E. Bowen 1836–1901: 'Forty Years On' (Harrow School Song, published 1886)

3 Headmasters have powers at their disposal with which Prime Ministers have never yet been invested.
Winston Churchill 1874–1965: *My Early Life* (1930)

4 Schools are for schooling, not social engineering.
Brian Cox 1928– and **Rhodes Boyson** 1925– : *Black Paper 1975* (1975)

5 You send your child to the schoolmaster, but 'tis the schoolboys who educate him.
Ralph Waldo Emerson 1803–82: *Conduct of Life* (1860)

6 Our schools are improving. It's childhoods that are not.
Keith Geiger 1941– : in *New York Times* 5 July 1991

7 The dawn of legibility in his handwriting has revealed his utter inability to spell.
Ian Hay 1876–1952: attributed; perhaps used in a dramatization of *The Housemaster* (1938)

8 I say to parents they must observe what I call the three Hs—haircuts, holidays and homework.
John McIntosh 1946– : in *Independent* 4 January 1999

9 As we read the school reports on our children we realize a sense of relief that . . . nobody is reporting in this fashion on us!
J. B. Priestley 1894–1984: in *Reader's Digest* June 1964

10 Dear Parents
If you don't believe everything your child tells you about school, I will not believe everything your child tells me about home.
John Rae 1931– : *Letters from School* (1987)

11 Reports always tell the truth. The problem for parents is to know whether it is the truth about the pupil or the truth about the teacher—or both.
John Rae 1931– : *Letters from School* (1987)

12 Make the boy interested in natural history if you can; it is better than games.
Robert Falcon Scott 1868–1912: last letter to his wife, in *Scott's Last Expedition* (1913)

13 For every person who wants to teach there are approximately thirty who don't want to learn—much.
W. C. Sellar 1898–1951 and **R. J. Yeatman** 1898–1968: *And Now All This* (1932)

14 I am putting old heads on your young shoulders . . . all my pupils are the crème de la crème.
Muriel Spark 1918– : *The Prime of Miss Jean Brodie* (1961)

15 The only good things about skool are the BOYS wizz who are noble brave fearless etc. although you hav various swots, bulies, cissies, milksops, greedy guts and oiks with whom i am forced to mingle hem-hem.
Geoffrey Willans 1911–58 and **Ronald Searle** 1920– : *Down With Skool!* (1953)

Science

....
see also **Arts and Sciences, Experiment, Facts, Genetic Engineering, Inventions and Discoveries, Life Sciences, Physics, Research, Science and Religion, Science and Society, Technology, Theory**

1 The joke definition according to which 'Science is the best way of

satisfying the curiosity of individuals at government expense' is more or less correct.

L. A. Artsimovich 1909–73: in *Novy Mir* January 1967

2 The aim of science is not to open the door to infinite wisdom, but to set a limit to infinite error.

Bertolt Brecht 1898–1956: *Life of Galileo* (1939)

3 The essence of science: ask an impertinent question, and you are on the way to a pertinent answer.

Jacob Bronowski 1908–74: *The Ascent of Man* (1973)

4 In science the credit goes to the man who convinces the world, not to the man to whom the idea first occurs.

Francis Darwin 1848–1925: in *Eugenics Review* April 1914 'Francis Galton'

5 I ask you to look both ways. For the road to a knowledge of the stars leads through the atom; and important knowledge of the atom has been reached through the stars.

Arthur Eddington 1882–1944: *Stars and Atoms* (1928)

6 Science has lost its virgin purity, has become dogmatic instead of seeking for enlightenment and has gradually fallen into the hands of the traders.

Robert Graves 1895–1985: Bruno Friedman *Flawed science, damaged human life* (1969)

7 In effect, we have redefined the task of science to be the discovery of laws that will enable us to predict events up to the limits set by the uncertainty principle.

Stephen Hawking 1942– : *A Brief History of Time* (1988)

8 The importance of a scientific work can be measured by the number of previous publications it makes it superfluous to read.

David Hilbert 1862–1943: attributed; Lewis Wolpert *The Unnatural Nature of Science* (1993)

9 Science is nothing but trained and organized common sense, differing from the latter only as a veteran may differ from a raw recruit: and its methods differ from those of common sense only as far as the guardsman's cut and thrust differ from the manner in which a savage wields his club.

T. H. Huxley 1825–95: *Collected Essays* (1893–4) 'The Method of Zadig'

10 When you can measure what you are speaking about, and express it in numbers, you know something about it; but when you cannot measure it, when you cannot express it in numbers, your knowledge is of a meagre and unsatisfactory kind: it may be the beginning of knowledge, but you have scarcely, in your thoughts, advanced to the stage of *science*, whatever the matter may be.

■ *often quoted as 'If you cannot measure it, then it is not science'*

Lord Kelvin 1824–1907: 'Electrical Units of Measurement', lecture delivered 3 May 1883

11 Modern science was largely conceived of as an answer to the servant problem.

Fran Lebowitz 1946– : *Metropolitan Life* (1978)

12 Scientific truth should be presented in different forms, and should be regarded as equally scientific whether it appears in the robust form and the vivid colouring of a physical illustration, or in the tenuity and paleness of a symbolic expression.

James Clerk Maxwell 1831–79: attributed

13 To mistrust science and deny the validity of the scientific method is to resign your job as a human. You'd better go look for work as a plant or wild animal.

P. J. O'Rourke 1947– : *Parliament of Whores* (1991)

14 There are no such things as applied sciences, only applications of science.

Louis Pasteur 1822–95: address, Lyons, 11 September 1872

15 A new scientific truth does not triumph by convincing its opponents and making them see the light, but rather because its opponents

eventually die, and a new generation grows up that is familiar with it.

Max Planck 1858–1947: *A Scientific Autobiography* (1949)

16 Science is built up of facts, as a house is built of stones; but an accumulation of facts is no more a science than a heap of stones is a house.

Henri Poincaré 1854–1912: *Science and Hypothesis* (1905)

17 Nature, and Nature's laws lay hid in night.
God said, *Let Newton be!* and all was light.

Alexander Pope 1688–1744: 'Epitaph: Intended for Sir Isaac Newton' (1730); cf. 19 below

18 All science is either physics or stamp collecting.

Ernest Rutherford 1871–1937: J. B. Birks *Rutherford at Manchester* (1962)

19 It did not last: the Devil howling 'Ho! Let Einstein be!' restored the status quo.

J. C. Squire 1884–1958: 'In continuation of Pope on Newton' (1926); see 17 above

20 There is something fascinating about science. One gets such wholesale returns of conjecture out of such a trifling investment of fact.

Mark Twain 1835–1910: *Life on the Mississippi* (1883)

Science and Religion

1 The atoms of Democritus
And Newton's particles of light
Are sands upon the Red sea shore
Where Israel's tents do shine so bright.

William Blake 1757–1827: *MS Note-Book*

2 We have grasped the mystery of the atom and rejected the Sermon on the Mount.

Omar Bradley 1893–1981: speech on Armistice Day, 1948

3 Science offers the best answers to the meaning of life. Science offers you the privilege before you die of

understanding why you were ever born in the first place.

Richard Dawkins 1941– : in *Break the Science Barrier with Richard Dawkins* (Channel 4) 1 September 1996

4 Science without religion is lame, religion without science is blind.

Albert Einstein 1879–1955: *Science, Philosophy and Religion: a Symposium* (1941)

5 If ignorance of nature gave birth to the Gods, knowledge of nature is destined to destroy them.

Paul Henri, Baron d'Holbach 1723–89: *Système de la Nature* (1770)

6 I asserted—and I repeat—that a man has no reason to be ashamed of having an ape for his grandfather. If there were an ancestor whom I should feel shame in recalling it would rather be a *man*—a man of restless and versatile intellect—who, not content with an equivocal success in his own sphere of activity, plunges into scientific questions with which he has no real acquaintance, only to obscure them by an aimless rhetoric, and distract the attention of his hearers from the real point at issue by eloquent digressions and skilled appeals to religious prejudice.

■ *replying to Bishop Samuel Wilberforce in the debate on Darwin's theory of evolution*

T. H. Huxley 1825–95: at a meeting of the British Association in Oxford, 30 June 1860; see **Life Sciences** 17

7 The means by which we live have outdistanced the ends for which we live. Our scientific power has outrun our spiritual power. We have guided missiles and misguided men.

Martin Luther King 1929–68: *Strength to Love* (1963)

8 The scientist who yields anything to theology, however slight, is yielding to ignorance and false pretences, and as certainly as if he granted that a horse-hair put into a bottle of water will turn into a snake.

H. L. Mencken 1880–1956: *Minority Report* (1956)

9 The Buddha, the Godhead, resides quite as comfortably in the circuits of

a digital computer or the gears of a cycle transmission as he does at the top of a mountain or in the petals of a flower.

Robert M. Pirsig 1928– : *Zen and the Art of Motorcycle Maintenance* (1974)

10 How is it that hardly any major religion has looked at science and concluded, 'This is better than we thought! The Universe is much bigger than our prophets said, grander, more subtle, more elegant'?

Carl Sagan 1934–96: *Pale Blue Dot* (1995)

11 There is no evil in the atom; only in men's souls.

Adlai Stevenson 1900–65: speech at Hartford, Connecticut, 18 September 1952

Science and Society

see also **Genetic Engineering**

1 A public that does not understand how science works can all too easily fall prey to those ignoramuses like Senator Proxmire who make fun of what they do not understand, or to the sloganeers who proclaim scientists to be the mercenary warriors of today, and the tools of the military.

Isaac Asimov 1920–92: in *Nature* 10 November 1963

2 In science, we must be interested in things, not in persons.

Marie Curie 1867–1934: to an American journalist, c.1904; Eve Curie *Madame Curie* (1937)

3 One must divide one's time between politics and equations. But our equations are much more important to me.

Albert Einstein 1879–1955: C. P. Snow 'Einstein' in M. Goldsmith et al. (eds.) *Einstein* (1980)

4 Science is an integral part of culture. It's not this foreign thing, done by an arcane priesthood. It's one of the glories of human intellectual tradition.

Stephen Jay Gould 1941–2002: in *Independent* 24 January 1990

5 Realistically, the argument saying that you won't find a good scientist without industry connections is almost certainly right.

Doug Parr: in *Independent* 12 June 1999

6 The priest persuades humble people to endure their hard lot; the politician urges them to rebel against it; and the scientist thinks of a method that does away with the hard lot altogether.

Max Perutz 1914– : *Is Science Necessary* (1989)

7 Every day I saw the huge material, intellectual and nervous resources of thousands of people being poured into the creation of a means of total destruction, something capable of annihilating all human civilization. I noticed that the control levers were in the hands of people who, though talented in their own ways, were cynical.

Andrei Sakharov 1921–89: *Sakharov Speaks* (1974)

Science Fiction

see also **Fantasy**

1 Science Fiction is no more written for scientists than ghost stories are written for ghosts.

Brian Aldiss 1925– : introduction to *Penguin Science Fiction* (1962)

2 The only genuine consciousness-expanding drug.

■ *on science fiction*

Arthur C. Clarke 1917– : letter claiming coinage in *New Scientist* 2 April 1994

3 Science fiction is a kind of archaeology of the future.

Clifton Fadiman 1904– : *Selected Writings* (1955)

4 If science fiction is the myth of modern technology, then its myth is tragic.

Ursula K. Le Guin 1929– : 'The Carrier Bag Theory of Fiction' (written 1986); *Dancing at the Edge of the World* (1989)

5 What you get in science fiction is what someone once called 'the view from a

distant star'. It helps us to see our
world from outside.

Frederik Pohl 1919– : Stan Nicholls (ed.)
Wordsmiths of Wonder (1993)

Scotland

1 O ye'll tak' the high road, and I'll tak'
the low road,
And I'll be in Scotland afore ye,
But me and my true love will never
meet again,
On the bonnie, bonnie banks o' Loch
Lomon'.

Anonymous: 'The Bonnie Banks o' Loch
Lomon' (traditional song)

2 There are few more impressive sights
in the world than a Scotsman on the
make.

J. M. Barrie 1860–1937: *What Every Woman
Knows* (1918)

3 Scotland, land of the omnipotent No.

Alan Bold 1943– : 'A Memory of Death'
(1969)

4 My heart's in the Highlands, my heart
is not here;
My heart's in the Highlands a-chasing
the deer.

Robert Burns 1759–96: 'My Heart's in the
Highlands' (1790)

5 Scots, wha hae wi' Wallace bled,
Scots, wham Bruce has aften led,
Welcome to your gory bed,—
Or to victorie.

Robert Burns 1759–96: 'Robert Bruce's March
to Bannockburn' (1799) (also known as
'Scots, Wha Hae')

6 My poems should be Clyde-built,
crude and sure,
With images of those dole-deployed
To honour the indomitable Reds,
Clydesiders of slant steel and angled
cranes;
A poetry of nuts and bolts, born,
bred,
Embattled by the Clyde, tight and
impure.

Douglas Dunn 1942– : 'Clydesiders' (1974)

7 From the lone shieling of the misty
island

Mountains divide us, and the waste of
seas—
Yet still the blood is strong, the heart
is Highland,
And we in dreams behold the
Hebrides!

John Galt 1779–1839: 'Canadian Boat Song'
(1829); translated from the Gaelic; attributed

8 The noblest prospect which a
Scotchman ever sees, is the high road
that leads him to England!

Samuel Johnson 1709–84: James Boswell *Life
of Samuel Johnson* (1791) 6 July 1763

9 Who owns this landscape?
The millionaire who bought it or
the poacher staggering downhill in
the early morning
with a deer on his back?

Norman McCaig 1910–96: 'A Man in Assynt'
(1969)

10 Scotland small? Our multiform, our
infinite Scotland *small*?
Only as a patch of hillside may be a
cliché corner
To a fool who cries 'Nothing but
heather!' . . .

Hugh MacDiarmid 1892–1978: *Direadh* 1 (1974)

11 Minds like ours, my dear James, must
always be above national prejudices,
and in all companies it gives me true
pleasure to declare, that, as a people,
the English are very little indeed
inferior to the Scotch.

Christopher North 1785–1854: in *Blackwood's
Magazine* October 1826

12 O Caledonia! stern and wild,
Meet nurse for a poetic child!

Sir Walter Scott 1771–1832: *The Lay of the Last
Minstrel* (1805)

13 It's ill taking the breeks aff a wild
Highlandman.

Sir Walter Scott 1771–1832: *The Fortunes of
Nigel* (1822)

14 Stands Scotland where it did?

William Shakespeare 1564–1616: *Macbeth*
(1606)

15 It's nae good blamin' it oan the
English fir colonising us. Ah don't
hate the English. They're just

wankers. We can't even pick a decent vibrant, healthy culture to be colonised by.

Irvine Welsh 1957– : *Trainspotting* (1994)

16 O flower of Scotland, when will we see
your like again,
that fought and died for your bit hill
and glen
and stood against him, proud
Edward's army,
and sent him homeward tae think
again.

■ *unofficial Scottish Nationalist anthem*
Roy Williamson 1936–90: 'O Flower of
Scotland' (1968)

17 It is never difficult to distinguish
between a Scotsman with a grievance
and a ray of sunshine.

P. G. Wodehouse 1881–1975: *Blandings Castle
and Elsewhere* (1935)

Sculpture

see also **Art**

1 Most statues seem sad and
introspective,
they hold their breath between
coming and going,
They lament their devoured, once
shuddering stone.

Dannie Abse 1923– : 'At the Tate'

2 Why don't they stick to murder and
leave art to us?

■ *on hearing that his statue of Lazarus in New
College chapel, Oxford, kept Khrushchev awake
at night*
Jacob Epstein 1880–1959: attributed

3 The old ideas of nobility and sacrifice
have become a howitzer squatting at
Hyde Park like a petrified toad, and
the hero has become a cabinet
minister on a pedestal in bronze
boots.

■ *on modern sculpture*
Geoffrey Grigson 1905–85: *Henry Moore*
(1944)

4 Carving is interrelated masses
conveying an emotion: a perfect
relationship between the mind and
the colour, light and weight which is

the stone, made by the hand which
feels.

Barbara Hepworth 1903–75: Herbert Read
(ed.) *Unit One* (1934)

5 Sculpture to me is primitive, religious,
passionate, and magical—always,
always affirmative.

Barbara Hepworth 1903–75: A. M.
Hammacher *Barbara Hepworth* (1968)

6 The marble not yet carved can hold
the form
Of every thought the greatest artist
has.

Michelangelo 1475–1564: Sonnet 15

7 The first hole made through a piece of
stone is a revelation.

Henry Moore 1898–1986: in *Listener* 18 August
1937

The Sea

see also **Boats, The Navy**

1 They that go down to the sea in ships:
and occupy their business in great
waters;
These men see the works of the Lord:
and his wonders in the deep.

Bible: Psalm 107

2 Roll on, thou deep and dark blue
Ocean—roll!
Ten thousand fleets sweep over thee in
vain;
Man marks the earth with ruin—his
control
Stops with the shore.

Lord Byron 1788–1824: *Childe Harold's
Pilgrimage* (1812–18)

3 Water, water, everywhere,
And all the boards did shrink;
Water, water, everywhere,
Nor any drop to drink.

Samuel Taylor Coleridge 1772–1834: 'The
Rime of the Ancient Mariner' (1798)

4 I can't bear iced drinks . . . the
iceberg, you know. Perhaps some
champagne, though.

■ *the youngest survivor of the Titanic disaster,
while visiting the house in Kansas City,
Missouri, in which her family would have lived*
Millvina Dean 1911– : in *The Times* 20 August
1997

5 They didn't think much to the Ocean:
  The waves, they were fiddlin' and
    small,
  There was no wrecks and nobody
    drowned,
  Fact, nothing to laugh at at all.
  Marriott Edgar 1880–1951: 'The Lion and
  Albert' (1932)

6 The dragon-green, the luminous, the
  dark, the serpent-haunted sea.
  James Elroy Flecker 1884–1915: 'The Gates of
  Damascus' (1913)

7 The snotgreen sea. The
  scrotumtightening sea.
  James Joyce 1882–1941: *Ulysses* (1922)

8 It is an interesting biological fact that
  all of us have in our veins the exact
  same percentage of salt in our blood
  that exists in the ocean, and therefore,
  we have salt in our blood, in our
  sweat, in our tears. We are tied to the
  ocean. And when we go back to the
  sea—whether it is to sail or to watch
  it—we are going back from whence
  we came.
  John F. Kennedy 1917–63: speech, Newport,
  Rhode Island, 14 September 1962

9 I must go down to the sea again, to the
  lonely sea and the sky,
  And all I ask is a tall ship and a star to
    steer her by,
  And the wheel's kick and the wind's
    song and the white sail's shaking,
  And a grey mist on the sea's face and a
    grey dawn breaking.
  John Masefield 1878–1967: 'Sea Fever'; 'I must
  down to the seas' in the original of 1902,
  possibly a misprint

10 It [the Channel] is a mere ditch, and
   will be crossed as soon as someone
   has the courage to attempt it.
   Napoleon I 1769–1821: letter to Consul
   Cambacérès, 16 November 1803

11 The sea hates a coward!
   Eugene O'Neill 1888–1953: *Mourning becomes
   Electra* (1931)

12 The sea has such extraordinary
   moods that sometimes you feel this is

the only sort of life—and 10 minutes
later you're praying for death.
Prince Philip, Duke of Edinburgh 1921– : in
Independent 31 December 1998

13 'A man who is not afraid of the sea
   will soon be drowned,' he said 'for
   he will be going out on a day he
   shouldn't. But we do be afraid of the
   sea, and we do only be drowned now
   and again.'
   John Millington Synge 1871–1909: *The Aran
   Islands* (1907)

14 Break, break, break,
   On thy cold grey stones, O Sea!
   And I would that my tongue could
     utter
   The thoughts that arise in me.
   Alfred, Lord Tennyson 1809–92: 'Break, Break,
   Break' (1842)

15 Rocked in the cradle of the deep.
   Emma Hart Willard 1787–1870: title of song
   (1840), inspired by a prospect of the Bristol
   Channel

Secrecy

1 A Company for carrying on an
  undertaking of Great Advantage, but
  no one to know what it is.
  Anonymous: Company Prospectus at the
  time of the South Sea Bubble (1711)

2 I shall be but a short time tonight. I
  have seldom spoken with greater
  regret, for my lips are not yet
  unsealed. Were these troubles over I
  would make a case, and I guarantee
  that not a man would go into the
  lobby against us.
  ■ *on the Abyssinian crisis; usually quoted as 'My
  lips are sealed'*
  Stanley Baldwin 1867–1947: speech, House of
  Commons, 10 December 1935

3 Let not thy left hand know what thy
  right hand doeth.
  Bible: St Matthew

4 The truth is out there.
  Chris Carter 1957– : catchphrase; *The X Files*
  (American television series, 1993–)

5 After the first silence the small man
  said to the other: 'Where does a wise
  man hide a pebble?' And the tall man

answered in a low voice: 'On the beach.' The small man nodded, and after a short silence said: 'Where does a wise man hide a leaf?' And the other answered: 'In the forest.'

G. K. Chesterton 1874–1936: *The Innocence of Father Brown* (1911)

6 The best leaks always take place in the urinal.

John Cole 1927– : in *Independent* 3 June 1996

7 I know that's a secret, for it's whispered every where.

William Congreve 1670–1729: *Love for Love* (1695)

8 Secrets with girls, like loaded guns with boys,
Are never valued till they make a noise.

George Crabbe 1754–1832: *Tales of the Hall* (1819) 'The Maid's Story'

9 We never knows wot's hidden in each other's hearts; and if we had glass winders there, we'd need keep the shutters up, some on us, I do assure you!

Charles Dickens 1812–70: *Martin Chuzzlewit* (1844)

10 I would not open windows into men's souls.

Elizabeth I 1533–1603: oral tradition, the words very possibly originating in a letter drafted by Bacon; J. B. Black *Reign of Elizabeth 1558–1603* (1936)

11 If a man cannot keep a measly affair secret, what is he doing in charge of the Intelligence Service?

■ *on the break-up of the marriage of Foreign Secretary Robin Cook*

Frederick Forsyth 1938– : in *Guardian* 14 January 1998

12 We dance round in a ring and suppose,
But the Secret sits in the middle and knows.

Robert Frost 1874–1963: 'The Secret Sits' (1942)

13 Once the toothpaste is out of the tube, it is awfully hard to get it back in.

■ *on the Watergate affair*

H. R. Haldeman 1929– : to John Dean, 8 April 1973

14 Anonymous, unseen—
You're dealing with the all-time king or queen
Of undercover loves.
The author of this valentine wore gloves.

Sophie Hannah 1971– : 'Poem for a Valentine Card' (1995)

15 Truth is suppressed, not to protect the country from enemy agents but to protect the Government of the day against the people.

Roy Hattersley 1932– : in *Independent* 18 February 1995

16 Stolen sweets are always sweeter,
Stolen kisses much completer,
Stolen looks are nice in chapels,
Stolen, stolen, be your apples.

Leigh Hunt 1784–1859: 'Song of Fairies Robbing an Orchard' (1830)

17 That's another of those irregular verbs, isn't it? I give confidential briefings; you leak; he has been charged under Section 2a of the Official Secrets Act.

Jonathan Lynn 1943– and **Antony Jay** 1930– : *Yes Prime Minister* (1987) vol. 2 'Man Overboard'

18 I sometimes call them the people who live in the dark. Everything they do is in hiding . . . Everything we do is in the light. They live in the dark.

■ *contrasting political advisers with elected politicians*

Clare Short 1946– : in *New Statesman* 9 August 1996

Security

see also **Risk**

1 But I loathe Classic FM more and more for its cosiness, its safety and its wholehearted endorsement of the post-Thatcher world, with medical insurance and Saga holidays rammed down your throat between every item.

Alan Bennett 1934– : diary, 3 July 1996

2 In my view, stability is a sexy thing.

Tony Blair 1953– : in *The Week* 28 November 1998

3 Security is when everything is settled, when nothing can happen to you; security is the denial of life.
   Germaine Greer 1939– : *The Female Eunuch* (1970)

4 Security is mostly a superstition. It does not exist in nature, nor do the children of men as a whole experience it. Avoiding danger is no safer in the long run than outright exposure. Life is either a daring adventure, or nothing.
   Helen Keller 1880–1968: *The Open Door* (1957)

5 He had grown up in a country run by politicians who sent the pilots to man the bombers to kill the babies to make the world safer for children to grow up in.
   Ursula K. Le Guin 1929– : *The Lathe of Heaven* (1971)

Seduction

see also **Sex**

1 He said it was artificial respiration, but now I find I am to have his child.
   Anthony Burgess 1917–93: *Inside Mr Enderby* (1963)

2 A little still she strove, and much repented,
   And whispering 'I will ne'er consent'—consented.
   Lord Byron 1788–1824: *Don Juan* (1819–24)

3 Seduction is often difficult to distinguish from rape. In seduction, the rapist bothers to buy a bottle of wine.
   Andrea Dworkin 1946– : speech to women at *Harper & Row*, 1976; in *Letters from a War Zone* (1988)

4 He in a few minutes ravished this fair creature, or at least would have ravished her, if she had not, by a timely compliance, prevented him.
   Henry Fielding 1707–54: *Jonathan Wild* (1743)

5 Pursuit and seduction are the essence of sexuality. It's part of the sizzle.
   Camille Paglia 1947– : in *Playboy* October 1991

The Self

see also **Individuality**, **Self-Knowledge**

1 My one regret in life is that I am not someone else.
   Woody Allen 1935– : Eric Lax *Woody Allen and his Comedy* (1975)

2 The image of myself which I try to create in my own mind in order that I may love myself is very different from the image which I try to create in the minds of others in order that they may love me.
   W. H. Auden 1907–73: *The Dyer's Hand* (1963) 'Hic et Ille'

3 Some thirty inches from my nose
   The frontier of my Person goes,
   And all the untilled air between
   Is private *pagus* or demesne.
   Stranger, unless with bedroom eyes
   I beckon you to fraternize,
   Beware of rudely crossing it:
   I have no gun, but I can spit.
   W. H. Auden 1907–73: 'Prologue: the Birth of Architecture' (1966)

4 In the greatest confusion there is still an open channel to the soul. It may be difficult to find because by midlife it is overgrown, and some of the wildest thickets that surround it grow out of what we describe as our education. But the channel is always there, and it is our business to keep it open, to have access to the deepest part of ourselves.
   Saul Bellow 1915– : Allan Bloom *The Closing of the American Mind* (1987)

5 Through the Thou a person becomes I.
   Martin Buber 1878–1965: *Ich und Du* (1923)

6 The men who really believe in themselves are all in lunatic asylums.
   G. K. Chesterton 1874–1936: *Orthodoxy* (1908)

7 I am—yet what I am, none cares or knows;
   My friends forsake me like a memory lost:
   I am the self-consumer of my woes.
   John Clare 1793–1864: 'I Am' (1848)

8 We are all serving a life-sentence in the dungeon of self.
   Cyril Connolly 1903–74: *The Unquiet Grave* (1944)

9 'You' your joys and your sorrows, your memories and ambitions, your sense of personal identity and free will, are in fact no more than the behaviour of a vast assembly of nerve cells and their associated molecules.
   Francis Crick 1916– : *The Astonishing Hypothesis: The Scientific Search for the Soul* (1994)

10 But I do nothing upon my self, and yet I am mine own *Executioner*.
   John Donne 1572–1631: *Devotions upon Emergent Occasions* (1624)

11 I think of who I am as what I've done.
   Esther Dyson 1951– : in *Independent* 11 January 1999

12 Every man contains within himself a ghost continent—a place circled as warily as Antarctica was circled two hundred years ago by Captain James Cook.
   Loren Eiseley 1907–77: *The Unexpected Universe* (1969)

13 It matters not how strait the gate, How charged with punishments the scroll, I am the master of my fate: I am the captain of my soul.
   W. E. Henley 1849–1903: 'Invictus. In Memoriam R.T.H.B.' (1888)

14 If I am not for myself who is for me; and being for my own self what am I? If not now when?
   Hillel 'The Elder' c.60 BC–AD c.9: *Pirqe Aboth*

15 It is not contrary to reason to prefer the destruction of the whole world to the scratching of my finger.
   David Hume 1711–76: *A Treatise upon Human Nature* (1739)

16 I will not serve that in which I no longer believe whether it call itself my home, my fatherland or my church: and I will try to express myself in some mode of life or art as freely as I can and as wholly as I can, using for my defence the only arms I allow myself to use, silence, exile, and cunning.
   James Joyce 1882–1941: *A Portrait of the Artist as a Young Man* (1916)

17 I am not a number, I am a free man!
   Patrick McGoohan 1928– et al.: Number Six, in *The Prisoner* (TV series 1967–68)

18 A man should keep for himself a little back shop, all his own, quite unadulterated, in which he establishes his true freedom and chief place of seclusion and solitude.
   Montaigne 1533–92: *Essais* (1580)

19 I am I plus my surroundings, and if I do not preserve the latter I do not preserve myself.
   José Ortega y Gasset 1883–1955: *Meditaciones del Quijote* (1914)

20 The self is hateful.
   Blaise Pascal 1623–62: *Pensées* (1670)

21 The whole human way of life has been destroyed and ruined. All that's left is the bare, shivering human soul, stripped to the last shred, the naked force of the human psyche for which nothing has changed because it was always cold and shivering and reaching out to its nearest neighbour, as cold and lonely as itself.
   Boris Pasternak 1890–1960: *Doctor Zhivago* (1958)

22 Personal isn't the same as important.
   Terry Pratchett 1948– : *Men at Arms* (1993)

23 This above all: to thine own self be true, And it must follow, as the night the day, Thou canst not then be false to any man.
   William Shakespeare 1564–1616: *Hamlet* (1601)

24 Rose is a rose is a rose is a rose, is a rose.
   Gertrude Stein 1874–1946: *Sacred Emily* (1913)

25 I am a writer who came of a sheltered life. A sheltered life can be a daring life as well. For all serious daring starts from within.

Eudora Welty 1909–2001: *One Writer's Beginnings* (1984)

26 Each had his past shut in him like the leaves of a book known to him by heart; and his friends could only read the title.

Virginia Woolf 1882–1941: *Jacob's Room* (1922)

Self-Esteem and Assertiveness

see also **Humility**

1 I'm the greatest.

Muhammad Ali 1942– : catch-phrase used from 1962, in *Louisville Times* 16 November 1962

2 His opinion of himself, having once risen, remained at 'set fair'.

Arnold Bennett 1867–1931: *The Card* (1911)

3 Anything you can do, I can do better, I can do anything better than you.

Irving Berlin 1888–1989: 'Anything You Can Do' (1946 song)

4 Pride goeth before destruction, and an haughty spirit before a fall.

Bible: Proverbs

5 That's it baby, when you got it, flaunt it.

Mel Brooks 1927– : *The Producers* (1968 film)

6 I know of no case where a man added to his dignity by standing on it.

Winston Churchill 1874–1965: attributed

7 Pretentious? *Moi*?

John Cleese 1939– and **Connie Booth**: *Fawlty Towers* 'The Psychiatrist' (BBC TV programme, 1979)

8 If I'm ever feeling a bit uppity, whenever I get on my high horse, I go and take another look at my dear Mam's mangle that has pride of place in the dining-room.

Brian Clough 1935– : *Clough: The Autobiography* (1994)

9 In the company of those she found unimportant, her spirits sank: she felt insignificant, plain and ordinary as though ordinariness was contagious.

Alice Thomas Ellis 1932– : *The Inn at the Edge of the World* (1990)

10 You must stir it and stump it, And blow your own trumpet, Or trust me, you haven't a chance.

W. S. Gilbert 1836–1911: *Ruddigore* (1887)

11 It's easy to be independent when you've got money. But to be independent when you haven't got a thing—that's the Lord's test.

Mahalia Jackson 1911–72: *Movin' On Up* (with Evan McLoud Wylie 1966)

12 Shyness is egotism out of its depth.

Penelope Keith 1940– : in *Daily Mail* 27 June 1988

13 Our mistreatment was just not right, and I was tired of it.

■ *of her refusal, on 1 December 1955, to surrender her seat on a segregated bus in Alabama to a white man*

Rosa Parks 1913– : *Quiet Strength* (1994)

14 He fell in love with himself at first sight and it is a passion to which he has always remained faithful.

Anthony Powell 1905–2000: *The Acceptance World* (1955)

15 No one can make you feel inferior without your consent.

Eleanor Roosevelt 1884–1962: in *Catholic Digest* August 1960

16 It is easy—terribly easy—to shake a man's faith in himself. To take advantage of that to break a man's spirit is devil's work.

George Bernard Shaw 1856–1950: *Candida* (1898)

17 I have often wished I had time to cultivate modesty . . . But I am too busy thinking about myself.

Edith Sitwell 1887–1964: in *Observer* 30 April 1950

18 As for conceit, what man will do any good who is not conceited? Nobody

holds a good opinion of a man who
has a low opinion of himself.

Anthony Trollope 1815–82: *Orley Farm* (1862)

19 Pavarotti is not vain, but conscious of
being unique.

Peter Ustinov 1921– : in *Independent on
Sunday* 12 September 1993

20 Our deepest fear is not that we are
inadequate. Our deepest fear is that
we are powerful beyond measure. It is
our light, not our darkness, that most
frightens us.

Marianne Williamson 1953– : *A Return to Love*
(1992)

Self-Interest

see also **Sacrifice**

1 And this is law, I will maintain,
Unto my dying day, Sir,
That whatsoever King shall reign,
I will be the Vicar of Bray, sir!

Anonymous: 'The Vicar of Bray' (1734 song)

2 Men are nearly always willing to
believe what they wish.

Julius Caesar 100–44 BC: *De Bello Gallico*

3 It's the first time in recorded history
that turkeys have been known to vote
for an early Christmas.

■ *on the collapse of the pact between Labour and
the Liberals*

James Callaghan 1912– : in the House of
Commons, 28 March 1979

4 We are all special cases. We all want to
appeal against something! Everyone
insists on his innocence, at all costs,
even if it means accusing the rest of
the human race and heaven.

Albert Camus 1913–60: *La Chute* (1956)

5 *Cui bono?*
To whose profit?

Cicero 106–43 BC: *Pro Roscio Amerino*;
quoting L. Cassius Longinus Ravilla

6 All sensible people are selfish, and
nature is tugging at every contract to
make the terms of it fair.

Ralph Waldo Emerson 1803–82: *The Conduct
of Life* (1860)

7 Fourteen heart attacks and he had to
die in my week. In MY week.

■ *when ex-President Eisenhower's death
prevented her photograph appearing on the
cover of* Newsweek

Janis Joplin 1943–70: in *New Musical Express*
12 April 1969

8 Selflessness . . . is always the greatest
insult to the ghetto, for selflessness is a
luxury to the poor, it beckons to the
spineless, the undifferentiated, the
inept, the derelict, the drowning—a
poor man is nothing without the
fierce thorns of his ego.

Norman Mailer 1923– : *Miami and the Siege
of Chicago* (1968)

9 He would, wouldn't he?

■ *on being told that Lord Astor claimed that her
allegations, concerning himself and his house
parties at Cliveden, were untrue*

Mandy Rice-Davies 1944– : at the trial of
Stephen Ward, 29 June 1963

10 We are now in the Me Decade—
seeing the upward roll of . . . the third
great religious wave in American
history . . . and this one has the
mightiest, holiest roll of all, the beat
that goes . . . Me . . . Me . . . Me . . .
Me.

Tom Wolfe 1931– : *Mauve Gloves and
Madmen* (1976)

Self-Knowledge

see also **The Self**

1 Know thyself.

Anonymous: inscribed on the temple of
Apollo at Delphi; Plato ascribes the saying to
the Seven Wise Men

2 Between the ages of twenty and forty
we are engaged in the process of
discovering who we are, which
involves learning the difference
between accidental limitations which
it is our duty to outgrow and the
necessary limitations of our nature
beyond which we cannot trespass
with impunity.

W. H. Auden 1907–73: *The Dyer's Hand* (1963)
'Reading'

3 The tragedy of a man who has found himself out.

J. M. Barrie 1860–1937: *What Every Woman Knows* (1918)

4 No, when the fight begins within himself,
A man's worth something.

Robert Browning 1812–89: 'Bishop Blougram's Apology' (1855)

5 O wad some Pow'r the giftie gie us
To see oursels as others see us!
It wad frae mony a blunder free us,
And foolish notion.

Robert Burns 1759–96: 'To a Louse' (1786)

6 How little do we know that which we are!
How less what we may be!

Lord Byron 1788–1824: *Don Juan* (1819–24)

7 I do not know myself, and God forbid that I should.

Johann Wolfgang von Goethe 1749–1832: J. P. Eckermann *Gespräche mit Goethe* (1836–48) 10 April 1829

8 [Alfred Hitchcock] thought of himself as looking like Cary Grant. That's tough, to think of yourself one way and look another.

Tippi Hedren 1935– : interview in California, 1982

9 The chief requirement of the good life, is to live without any image of oneself.

Iris Murdoch 1919–99: *The Bell* (1958)

10 Satire is a sort of glass, wherein beholders do generally discover everybody's face but their own.

Jonathan Swift 1667–1745: *The Battle of the Books* (1704)

11 There are few things more painful than to recognise one's own faults in others.

John Wells 1936– : in *Observer* 23 May 1982

12 At thirty a man suspects himself a fool;
Knows it at forty, and reforms his plan;
At fifty chides his infamous delay,
Pushes his prudent purpose to resolve;

In all the magnanimity of thought
Resolves; and re-resolves; then dies the same.

Edward Young 1683–1765: *Night Thoughts* (1742–5)

13 I do not know whether I was then a man dreaming I was a butterfly, or whether I am now a butterfly dreaming I am a man.

Zhuangzi *c.*369–286 BC: *Chuang Tzu* (1889)

The Senses

see also **The Body**

1 Any nose
May ravage with impunity a rose.

Robert Browning 1812–89: *Sordello* (1840)

2 By convention there is colour, by convention sweetness, by convention bitterness, but in reality there are atoms and space.

Democritus *c.*460–*c.*370 BC: fragment 125

3 Friday I tasted life. It was a vast morsel. A Circus passed the house—still I feel the red in my mind though the drums are out. The Lawn is full of south and the odours tangle, and I hear to-day for the first time the river in the tree.

Emily Dickinson 1830–86: letter to Mrs J. G. Holland, May 1866

4 You see, but you do not observe.

Arthur Conan Doyle 1859–1930: *The Adventures of Sherlock Holmes* (1892)

5 The important thing is not the camera but the eye.

Alfred Eisenstaedt 1898–1995: in *New York Times* 26 September 1994

6 Man is only six foot tall and our whole vision changes according to height and perhaps in depth, and it is a physical reaction which tells on all our spiritual perceptions.

Barbara Hepworth 1903–75: A. M. Hammacher *Barbara Hepworth* (1968)

7 Whatever withdraws us from the power of our senses; whatever makes the past, the distant, or the future predominate over the present, advances us in the dignity of thinking beings.

Samuel Johnson 1709–84: *A Journey to the Western Islands of Scotland* (1775)

8 O for a life of sensations rather than of thoughts!

John Keats 1795–1821: letter to Benjamin Bailey, 22 November 1817

9 Fortissimo at last!

■ *on seeing Niagara Falls*

Gustav Mahler 1860–1911: K. Blaukopf *Gustav Mahler* (1973)

10 I test my bath before I sit,
And I'm always moved to wonderment
That what chills the finger not a bit
Is so frigid upon the fundament.

Ogden Nash 1902–71: 'Samson Agonistes' (1942)

11 Each day I live in a glass room
Unless I break it with the thrusting
Of my senses and pass through
The splintered walls to the great landscape.

Mervyn Peake 1911–68: 'Each day I live in a glass room' (1967)

12 Is this a dagger which I see before me,
The handle toward my hand? Come, let me clutch thee:
I have thee not, and yet I see thee still.

William Shakespeare 1564–1616: *Macbeth* (1606)

Sex
....

see also **Bisexuality**, **Celibacy**, **Homosexuality**, **Lesbianism**, **Love**, **Marriage**, **Masturbation**, **Pornography**, **Relationships**, **Seduction**

1 Is sex dirty? Only if it's done right.

Woody Allen 1935– : *Everything You Always Want to Know about Sex* (1972 film)

2 That [sex] was the most fun I ever had without laughing.

Woody Allen 1935– : *Annie Hall* (1977 film, with Marshall Brickman)

3 In the old days a lot of people, men as well as women, didn't quite know

what to expect from sex so they didn't worry when it didn't work too well.

Kingsley Amis 1922–95: *Jake's Thing* (1979)

4 Give me chastity and continency—but not yet!

St Augustine of Hippo AD 354–430: *Confessions* (AD 397–8)

5 When I look back on the paint of sex, the love like a wild fox so ready to bite, the antagonism that sits like a twin beside love, and contrast it with affection, so deeply unrepeatable, of two people who have lived a life together (and of whom one must die), it's the affection I find richer. It's that I would have again. Not all those doubtful rainbow colours. (But then she's old, one must say.)

Enid Bagnold 1889–1981: *Autobiography* (1969)

6 I don't know what I am, darling. I've tried several varieties of sex. The conventional position makes me claustrophobic. And the others give me either stiff neck or lockjaw.

Tallulah Bankhead 1903–68: Lee Israel *Miss Tallulah Bankhead* (1972)

7 *at the age of ninety-seven, Blake was asked at what age the sex drive goes:*
You'll have to ask somebody older than me.

Eubie Blake 1883–1983: in *Ned Sherrin in his Anecdotage* (1993)

8 Sex has never been an obsession with me. It's just like eating a bag of crisps. Quite nice, but nothing marvellous. Sex is not simply black and white. There's a lot of grey.

Boy George 1961– : in *Sun* 21 October 1982

9 Now the whole dizzying and delirious range of sexual possibilities has been boiled down to that one big, boring, bulimic word. RELATIONSHIP.

Julie Burchill 1960– : *Sex and Sensibility* (1992)

10 It doesn't matter what you do in the bedroom as long as you don't do it in the street and frighten the horses.

Mrs Patrick Campbell 1865–1940: Daphne Fielding *The Duchess of Jermyn Street* (1964)

11 The pleasure is momentary, the position ridiculous, and the expense damnable.
   Lord Chesterfield 1694–1773: attributed

12 I have never yet seen anyone whose desire to build up his moral power was as strong as sexual desire.
   Confucius 551–479 BC: *Analects*

13 i like my body when it is with your body. It is so quite new a thing. Muscles better and nerves more. i like your body. i like what it does, i like its hows.
   e. e. cummings 1894–1962: 'Sonnets–Actualities' no. 8 (1925)

14 License my roving hands, and let them go,
   Behind, before, above, between, below.
   O my America, my new found land, My kingdom, safeliest when with one man manned.
   John Donne 1572–1631: 'To His Mistress Going to Bed' (*c*.1595)

15 I'll have what she's having.
   ■ *woman to waiter, seeing Sally acting an orgasm*
   Nora Ephron 1941– : *When Harry Met Sally* (1989 film)

16 Personally I know nothing about sex because I've always been married.
   Zsa Zsa Gabor 1919– : in *Observer* 16 August 1987

17 But did thee feel the earth move?
   Ernest Hemingway 1899–1961: *For Whom the Bell Tolls* (1940)

18 When I hear his steps outside my door I lie down on my bed, close my eyes, open my legs, and think of England.
   Lady Hillingdon 1857–1940: diary 1912 (original untraced, perhaps apocryphal); J. Gathorne-Hardy *The Rise and Fall of the British Nanny* (1972)

19 I was mistaken for a prostitute once in the last war. When a GI asked me what I charged, I said, 'Well, dear, what do your mother and sisters normally ask for?'
   Thora Hird 1911– : in *Independent* 27 February 1999

20 I'll come no more behind your scenes, David; for the silk stockings and white bosoms of your actresses excite my amorous propensities.
   Samuel Johnson 1709–84: James Boswell *Life of Samuel Johnson* (1791) 1750

21 Sex and taxes are in many ways the same. Tax does to cash what males do to genes. It dispenses assets among the population as a whole. Sex, not death, is the great leveller.
   Steve Jones 1944– : speech to the Royal Society; in *Independent* 25 January 1997

22 The only unnatural sex act is that which you cannot perform.
   Alfred Kinsey 1894–1956: attributed; in *Time* 21 January 1966

23 'Tisn't beauty, so to speak, nor good talk necessarily. It's just It. Some women'll stay in a man's memory if they once walked down a street.
   Rudyard Kipling 1865–1936: *Traffics and Discoveries* (1904)

24 There is no unhappier creature on earth than a fetishist who yearns to embrace a woman's shoe and has to embrace the whole woman.
   Karl Kraus 1874–1936: *Aphorisms and More Aphorisms* (1909)

25 Sexual intercourse began
   In nineteen sixty-three
   (Which was rather late for me)—
   Between the end of the *Chatterley* ban
   And the Beatles' first LP.
   Philip Larkin 1922–85: 'Annus Mirabilis' (1974)

26   While we think of it, and talk of it Let us leave it alone, physically, keep apart.
   For while we have sex in the mind, we truly have none in the body.
   D. H. Lawrence 1885–1930: 'Leave Sex Alone' (1929)

27 There is nothing safe about sex. There never will be.
   Norman Mailer 1923– : in *International Herald Tribune* 24 January 1992

28 The Duke returned from the wars today and did pleasure me in his top-boots.
Sarah, Duchess of Marlborough 1660–1744: oral tradition, attributed in various forms

29 Continental people have sex life; the English have hot-water bottles.
George Mikes 1912– : *How to be an Alien* (1946)

30 The orgasm has replaced the Cross as the focus of longing and the image of fulfilment.
Malcolm Muggeridge 1903–90: *Tread Softly* (1966)

31 Lolita, light of my life, fire of my loins. My sin, my soul.
Vladimir Nabokov 1899–1977: *Lolita* (1955)

32 Not tonight, Josephine.
Napoleon I 1769–1821: attributed, but probably apocryphal

33 Modest? My word, no . . . He was an all-the-lights-on man.
Henry Reed 1914–86: *A Very Great Man Indeed* (1953 radio play)

34 Love is two minutes fifty-two seconds of squishing noises.
Johnny Rotten 1957– : in *Daily Mirror*, 1983

35 Is it not strange that desire should so many years outlive performance?
William Shakespeare 1564–1616: *Henry IV, Part 2* (1597)

36 Someone asked Sophocles, 'How is your sex-life now? Are you still able to have a woman?' He replied, 'Hush, man; most gladly indeed am I rid of it all, as though I had escaped from a mad and savage master.'
Sophocles c.496–406 BC: Plato *Republic*

37 Traditionally, sex has been a very private, secretive activity. Herein perhaps lies its powerful force for uniting people in a strong bond. As we make sex less secretive, we may rob it of its power to hold men and women together.
Thomas Szasz 1920– : *The Second Sin* (1973)

38 In my day, I would only have sex with a man if I found him extremely attractive. These days, girls seem to choose them in much the same way as they might choose to suck on a boiled sweet.
Mary Wesley 1912– : in *Independent* 18 October 1997

39 Give a man a free hand and he'll try to put it all over you.
Mae West 1892–1980: *Klondike Annie* (1936 film)

40 Is that a gun in your pocket, or are you just glad to see me?
■ *usually quoted as 'Is that a pistol in your pocket . . .'*
Mae West 1892–1980: Joseph Weintraub *Peel Me a Grape* (1975)

41 Sex has never been an act of freedom for me. Robert and I climb into the bath together, but we tend to talk about quantum physics.
Toyah Wilcox: in *Independent on Sunday* 29 December 1996

William Shakespeare
1564–1616

1 Others abide our question. Thou art free.
We ask and ask: Thou smilest and art still,
Out-topping knowledge.
Matthew Arnold 1822–88: 'Shakespeare' (1849)

2 Shakespeare is so tiring. You never get a chance to sit down unless you're a king.
Josephine Hull ?1886–1957: in *Time* 16 November 1953

3 He was not of an age, but for all time!
Ben Jonson c.1573–1637: 'To the Memory of My Beloved, the Author, Mr William Shakespeare' (1623)

4 Thou hadst small Latin, and less Greek.
Ben Jonson c.1573–1637: 'To the Memory of My Beloved, the Author, Mr William Shakespeare' (1623)

5 When I read Shakespeare I am struck with wonder

That such trivial people should muse
and thunder
In such lovely language.
D. H. Lawrence 1885–1930: 'When I Read
Shakespeare' (1929)

6 Shakespeare—the nearest thing in
incarnation to the eye of God.
Laurence Olivier 1907–89: in *Kenneth Harris
Talking To* (1971) 'Sir Laurence Olivier'

7 Brush up your Shakespeare,
Start quoting him now.
Brush up your Shakespeare
And the women you will wow.
Cole Porter 1891–1964: 'Brush Up your
Shakespeare' (1948 song)

8 With the single exception of Homer,
there is no eminent writer, not even
Sir Walter Scott, whom I can despise
so entirely as I despise Shakespeare
when I measure my mind against his.
George Bernard Shaw 1856–1950: in *Saturday
Review* 26 September 1896

9 Scorn not the Sonnet; Critic, you have
frowned,
Mindless of its just honours; with this
key
Shakespeare unlocked his heart.
William Wordsworth 1770–1850: 'Scorn not
the Sonnet' (1827)

Shopping

see also **Consumer Society**

1 We used to build civilizations. Now
we build shopping malls.
Bill Bryson 1951– : *Neither Here Nor There*
(1991)

2 Pile it high, sell it cheap.
John Cohen 1898–1979: slogan associated with
his company Tesco

3 What peaches and what penumbras!
Whole families shopping at night!
Aisles full of husbands! Wives in the
avocados, babies in the tomatoes!—
and you, Garcia Lorca what were you
doing down by the watermelons?
Allen Ginsberg 1926–97: 'A Supermarket in
California' (1956)

4 The thrill was in the trying on, in the
buying. The moment after she had

acquired something new it became
meaningless to her.
Judith Krantz 1932– : *Scruples* (1978)

5 The car, the furniture, the wife, the
children—everything has to be
disposable. Because you see the main
thing today is—shopping.
Arthur Miller 1915– : *The Price* (1968)

6 Buying is much more American than
thinking and I'm as American as they
come.
Andy Warhol 1927–87: *Philosophy of Andy
Warhol* (*From A to B and Back Again*) (1975)

7 Those women who spend their
mornings hovering round drapery
shops . . . remind one, in their
obvious ignorance of what they want
and their occasional bursts of
predatory enthusiasm, of a hen
picking at random round a rubbish
heap.
Rebecca West 1892–1983: *The Young Rebecca*
(1982)

Sickness

see also **Aids**, **Alzheimer's Disease**,
Cancer, **Health**, **Medicine**, **Mental Illness**

1 I know the colour rose, and it is lovely,
But not when it ripens in a tumour;
And healing greens, leaves and grass,
so springlike,
In limbs that fester are not springlike.
Dannie Abse 1923– : 'Pathology of Colours'
(1968)

2 A man's illness is his private territory
and, no matter how much he loves
you and how close you are, you stay
an outsider. You are healthy.
Lauren Bacall 1924– : *By Myself* (1978)

3 'Ye can call it influenza if ye like,' said
Mrs Machin. 'There was no influenza
in my young days. We called a cold a
cold.'
Arnold Bennett 1867–1931: *The Card* (1911)

4 Meningitis. It was a word you had to
bite on to say it. It had a fright and a
hiss in it.
Seamus Deane 1940– : *Reading in the Dark*
(1996)

5 People mean well and do not see how
distancing insistent cheeriness is, how
it denies another's reality, denies a
sick person the space or right to be
sick and in pain.
   Marilyn French 1929– : *A Season in Hell*
   (1998)

6 Did God who gave us flowers and
trees,
Also provide the allergies?
   E. Y. Harburg 1898–1981: 'A Nose is a Nose is a
   Nose' (1965)

7 Venerable Mother Toothache
Climb down from the white
battlements,
Stop twisting in your yellow fingers
The fourfold rope of nerves.
   John Heath-Stubbs 1918– : 'A Charm Against
   the Toothache' (1954)

8 It is a most extraordinary thing, but I
never read a patent medicine
advertisement without being impelled
to the conclusion that I am suffering
from the particular disease therein
dealt with in its most virulent form.
   Jerome K. Jerome 1859–1927: *Three Men in a
   Boat* (1889)

9 Besides death, constipation is the big
fear in hospitals.
   Robert McCrum 1953– : *My Year Off* (1998)

10 Illness is not something a person *has*;
it's another way of *being*.
   Jonathan Miller 1934– : *The Body in Question*
   (1978)

11 I enjoy convalescence. It is the part
that makes illness worth while.
   George Bernard Shaw 1856–1950: *Back to
   Methuselah* (1921)

12 Illness is the night-side of life, a more
onerous citizenship. Everyone who is
born holds dual citizenship, in the
kingdom of the well and in the
kingdom of the sick.
   Susan Sontag 1933– : in *New York Review of
   Books* 26 January 1978

13 The biggest disease today is not
leprosy or tuberculosis, but rather the
feeling of being unwanted, uncared
for and deserted by everybody.
   Mother Teresa 1910–97: in *The Observer*
   3 October 1971

Silence

1 Under all speech that is good for
anything there lies a silence that is
better. Silence is deep as Eternity;
speech is shallow as Time.
   Thomas Carlyle 1795–1881: *Critical and
   Miscellaneous Essays* (1838) 'Sir Walter Scott'

2 No voice; but oh! the silence sank
Like music on my heart.
   Samuel Taylor Coleridge 1772–1834: 'The
   Rime of the Ancient Mariner' (1798)

3 Speech is often barren; but silence also
does not necessarily brood over a full
nest. Your still fowl, blinking at you
without remark, may all the while be
sitting on one addled egg; and when it
takes to cackling will have nothing to
announce but that addled delusion.
   George Eliot 1819–80: *Felix Holt* (1866)

4 Elected Silence, sing to me
And beat upon my whorlèd ear.
   Gerard Manley Hopkins 1844–89: 'The Habit
   of Perfection' (written 1866)

5 Thou still unravished bride of
quietness,
Thou foster-child of silence and slow
time.
   John Keats 1795–1821: 'Ode on a Grecian Urn'
   (1820)

6 Shallow brooks murmur most, deep
silent slide away.
   Philip Sidney 1554–86: *Arcadia* (1581)

7 People talking without speaking
People hearing without listening . . .
'Fools,' said I, 'You do not know
Silence like a cancer grows.'
   Paul Simon 1942– : 'Sound of Silence' (1964
   song)

Similarity and Difference

1 One of the most common defects of
half-instructed minds is to think
much of that in which they differ

from others, and little of that in which
they agree with others.

> **Walter Bagehot** 1826–77: in *Economist* 11 June
> 1870

2   Near all the birds
Will sing at dawn,—and yet we do not
take
The chaffering swallow for the holy
lark.

> **Elizabeth Barrett Browning** 1806–61: *Aurora
> Leigh* (1857)

3 Not merely a chip of the old 'block',
but the old block itself.

> ■ *on the younger Pitt's maiden speech, February
> 1781*
> **Edmund Burke** 1729–97: N. W. Wraxall
> *Historical Memoirs of My Own Time* (1904
> ed.)

4 The road up and the road down are
one and the same.

> **Heraclitus** *c.*540–*c.*480 BC: fragment 60

5 If we cannot end now our differences,
at least we can help make the world
safe for diversity.

> **John F. Kennedy** 1917–63: address at American
> University, Washington, DC, 10 June 1963

6 When Greeks joined Greeks, then was
the tug of war!

> **Nathaniel Lee** *c.*1653–92: *The Rival Queens*
> (1677)

7 World is crazier and more of it than
we think,
Incorrigibly plural. I peel and portion
A tangerine and spit the pips and feel
The drunkenness of things being
various.

> **Louis MacNeice** 1907–63: 'Snow' (1935)

8 Comparisons are odorous.

> **William Shakespeare** 1564–1616: *Much Ado
> About Nothing* (1598–9)

9 No caparisons, Miss, if you please!—
Caparisons don't become a young
woman.

> **Richard Brinsley Sheridan** 1751–1816: *The
> Rivals* (1775)

Simplicity

1 Simplicity is not a goal, but one
arrives at simplicity in spite of oneself,
as one approaches the real meaning of
things.

> **Constantin Brancusi** 1876–1957: Ionel Jianou
> *Brancusi* (1963)

2 Out of intense complexities intense
simplicities emerge.

> **Winston Churchill** 1874–1965: *The World Crisis*
> (1923–9)

3 Less is more.

> **Mies van der Rohe** 1886–1969: P. Johnson
> *Mies van der Rohe* (1947); cf. **Architecture** 15

4 Simplicity is light, carefree, neat, and
loving—not a self-punishing ascetic
trip.

> **Gary Snyder** 1930– : *A Place in Space* (1995)

5 Our life is frittered away by detail . . .
Simplify, simplify.

> **Henry David Thoreau** 1817–62: *Walden* (1854)

Sin

see also **Evil**, **Temptation**, **Virtue**

1 All sin tends to be addictive, and the
terminal point of addiction is what is
called damnation.

> **W. H. Auden** 1907–73: *A Certain World* (1970)
> 'Hell'

2 With love for mankind and hatred of
sins.

> ■ *often quoted as 'Love the sinner but hate the
> sin'*
> **St Augustine of Hippo** AD 354–430: letter 211;
> J.-P. Migne (ed.) *Patrologiae Latinae* (1845)

3 Be sure your sin will find you out.

> **Bible**: Numbers

4 The wages of sin is death.

> **Bible**: Romans

5 We have left undone those things
which we ought to have done; And we
have done those things which we
ought not to have done; And there is
no health in us.

> **The Book of Common Prayer** 1662: *Morning
> Prayer* General Confession

6 We have erred, and strayed from thy
ways like lost sheep. We have followed

too much the devices and desires of
our own hearts.
The Book of Common Prayer 1662: *Morning
Prayer* General Confession

7 I waive the quantum o' the sin;
The hazard of concealing;
But och! it hardens a' within,
And petrifies the feeling!
Robert Burns 1759–96: 'Epistle to a Young
Friend' (1786)

8 There are different kinds of wrong.
The people sinned against are not
always the best.
Ivy Compton-Burnett 1884–1969: *The Mighty
and their Fall* (1961)

9 *when asked by Mrs Coolidge what a sermon had
been about:*
'Sins,' he said. 'Well, what did he say
about sin?' 'He was against it.'
Calvin Coolidge 1872–1933: John H. McKee
Coolidge: Wit and Wisdom (1933); perhaps
apocryphal

10 For the sin ye do by two and two ye
must pay for one by one!
Rudyard Kipling 1865–1936: 'Tomlinson'
(1892)

11 Shoot all the bluejays you want, if you
can hit 'em, but remember it's a sin to
kill a mockingbird.
Harper Lee 1926– : *To Kill a Mockingbird*
(1960)

12 It is public scandal that constitutes
offence, and to sin in secret is not to
sin at all.
Molière 1622–73: *Le Tartuffe* (1669)

13 She [the Catholic Church] holds that
it were better for sun and moon to
drop from heaven, for the earth to fail,
and for all the many millions who are
upon it to die of starvation in
extremest agony, as far as temporal
affliction goes, than that one soul, I
will not say, should be lost, but should
commit one single venial sin, should
tell one wilful untruth . . . or steal one
poor farthing without excuse.
John Henry Newman 1801–90: *Lectures on
Anglican Difficulties* (1852)

14 Sins become more subtle as you grow
older. You commit sins of despair
rather than lust.
Piers Paul Read 1941– : in *Daily Telegraph*
3 October 1990

15 Commit
The oldest sins the newest kind of
ways.
William Shakespeare 1564–1616: *Henry IV,
Part 2* (1597)

16 All sins are attempts to fill voids.
Simone Weil 1909–43: *La Pesanteur et la grâce*
(1948)

17 When I'm good, I'm very, very good,
but when I'm bad, I'm better.
Mae West 1892–1980: *I'm No Angel* (1933 film)

Singing

see also **Music**, **Opera**

1 We all fell in love, fell out of love, and
fell in love again to the sound of his
voice.
■ *of Frank Sinatra*
Tony Bennett 1926– : at Sinatra's funeral,
Beverley Hills, 20 May 1998

2 The exercise of singing is delightful to
Nature, and good to preserve the
health of man. It doth strengthen all
parts of the breast, and doth open the
pipes.
William Byrd 1543–1623: *Psalms, Sonnets and
Songs* (1588)

3 He was an average guy who could
carry a tune.
■ *Crosby's own suggestion for his epitaph*
Bing Crosby 1903–77: in *Newsweek* 24 October
1977

4 Every tone [of the songs of the slaves]
was a testimony against slavery, and a
prayer to God for deliverance from
chains.
Frederick Douglass c.1818–95: *Narrative of the
Life of Frederick Douglass* (1845)

5 In writing songs I've learned as much
from Cézanne as I have from Woody
Guthrie.
Bob Dylan 1941– : Clinton Heylin *Dylan:
Behind the Shades* (1991)

6 Maybe the most that you can expect from a relationship that goes bad is to come out of it with a few good songs.

Marianne Faithfull 1946– : *Faithfull* (1994)

7 A good lyric should be rhymed conversation.

Ira Gershwin 1896–1983: Philip Furia *Ira Gershwin* (1966)

8 I only know two tunes. One of them is 'Yankee Doodle' and the other isn't.

Ulysses S. Grant 1822–85: attributed

9 Words make you think a thought. Music makes you feel a feeling. A song makes you feel a thought.

E. Y. Harburg 1898–1981: lecture given at the New York YMCA in 1970

10 It's the only song I've ever written where I get goose bumps every time I play it.

■ *of 'Candle in the Wind'*
Elton John 1947– : in *Daily Telegraph* 9 September 1997; cf. **Diana 6, Monroe 2**

11 You think that's noise—you ain't heard nuttin' yet!

■ *first said in a café, competing with the din from a neighbouring building site, in 1906; subsequently an aside in the 1927 film* The Jazz Singer
Al Jolson 1886–1950: Martin Abramson *The Real Story of Al Jolson* (1950); also the title of a Jolson song, 1919, in the form 'You Ain't Heard Nothing Yet'

12 Tenors get women by the score.

James Joyce 1882–1941: *Ulysses* (1922)

13 Sentimentally I am disposed to harmony. But organically I am incapable of a tune.

Charles Lamb 1775–1834: *Essays of Elia* (1823) 'A Chapter on Ears'

14 Clichés make the best songs. I put down every one I can find.

Bob Merrill 1921–98: in *New York Times* 19 February 1998

15 Everyone suddenly burst out singing; And I was filled with such delight As prisoned birds must find in freedom.

Siegfried Sassoon 1886–1967: 'Everyone Sang' (1919)

16 Nothing can be more disgusting than an oratorio. How absurd to see 500 people fiddling like madmen about Israelites in the Red Sea!

Sydney Smith 1771–1845: Hesketh Pearson *The Smith of Smiths* (1934)

17 I love it for all its magnificent foolishness, its grand illusion that it brings together the diverse peoples and cultures of Europe on one great wing of song, when all it makes manifest is how far apart everybody is.

■ *of the Eurovision Song Contest*
Terry Wogan 1938– : in *Irish Times* 9 May 1998

Situation

see **Circumstance and Situation**

The Skies

see also **Space**, **The Universe**

1 Our windy, untidy loft
where old people had flung up old junk
they'd thought might come in handy
ploughs, ladles, bears, lions, a clatter of heroes.

Moya Cannon 1956– : 'The Stars' (1997)

2 We have seen
The moon in lonely alleys make
A grail of laughter of an empty ash can.

Hart Crane 1899–1932: 'Chaplinesque' (1926)

3 Slowly, silently, now the moon
Walks the night in her silver shoon.

Walter de la Mare 1873–1956: 'Silver' (1913)

4 Busy old fool, unruly sun,
Why dost thou thus,
Through windows, and through curtains call on us?
Must to thy motions lovers' seasons run?

John Donne 1572–1631: 'The Sun Rising'

5 The moon is nothing
But a circumambulating aphrodisiac

Divinely subsidized to provoke the
world
Into a rising birth-rate.
Christopher Fry 1907– : *The Lady's not for
Burning* (1949)

6 But it does move.
■ *after his recantation, that the earth moves
around the sun, in 1632*
Galileo Galilei 1564–1642: attributed

7 Look at the stars! look, look up at the
skies!
O look at all the fire-folk sitting in the
air!
The bright boroughs, the circle-
citadels there!
Gerard Manley Hopkins 1844–89: 'The
Starlight Night' (written 1877)

8 The heaventree of stars hung with
humid nightblue fruit.
James Joyce 1882–1941: *Ulysses* (1922)

9   The evening star,
Love's harbinger.
John Milton 1608–74: *Paradise Lost* (1667)

10   The moon's an arrant thief,
And her pale fire she snatches from
the sun.
William Shakespeare 1564–1616: *Timon of
Athens* (c.1607)

11 I am the daughter of Earth and Water,
And the nursling of the Sky;
I pass through the pores of the ocean
and shores;
I change, but I cannot die.
Percy Bysshe Shelley 1792–1822: 'The Cloud'
(1819)

Sleep
....

see also **Dreams**

1   The cool kindliness of sheets,
that soon
Smooth away trouble; and the rough
male kiss
Of blankets.
Rupert Brooke 1887–1915: 'The Great Lover'
(1914)

2 Care-charmer Sleep, son of the sable
Night,

Brother to Death, in silent darkness
born.
Samuel Daniel 1563–1619: *Delia* (1592) sonnet
54

3 Sleep is when all the unsorted stuff
comes flying out as from a dustbin
upset in a high wind.
William Golding 1911–93: *Pincher Martin*
(1956)

4 I love sleep because it is both pleasant
and safe to use.
Fran Lebowitz 1946– : *Metropolitan Life*
(1978)

5 What hath night to do with sleep?
John Milton 1608–74: *Comus* (1637)

6 And so to bed.
Samuel Pepys 1633–1703: diary 20 April 1660

7 Not to be a-bed after midnight is to be
up betimes.
William Shakespeare 1564–1616: *Twelfth Night*
(1601)

8 Methought I heard a voice cry, 'Sleep
no more!
Macbeth does murder sleep,' the
innocent sleep,
Sleep that knits up the ravelled sleave
of care.
William Shakespeare 1564–1616: *Macbeth*
(1606)

9 In winter I get up at night
And dress by yellow candle-light.
In summer, quite the other way,—
I have to go to bed by day.
Robert Louis Stevenson 1850–94: 'Bed in
Summer' (1885)

10 Must we to bed indeed? Well then,
Let us arise and go like men,
And face with an undaunted tread
The long black passage up to bed.
Robert Louis Stevenson 1850–94: 'North-
West Passage. Good-Night' (1885)

11 Early to rise and early to bed makes a
male healthy and wealthy and dead.
James Thurber 1894–1961: 'The Shrike and the
Chipmunks' in *New Yorker* 18 February 1939

12 'Tis the voice of the sluggard; I heard
him complain,
'You have waked me too soon, I must
slumber again'.

As the door on its hinges, so he on his
bed,
Turns his sides and his shoulders and
his heavy head.
Isaac Watts 1674–1748: 'The Sluggard' (1715)

13 Tired Nature's sweet restorer, balmy
sleep!
Edward Young 1683–1765: *Night Thoughts*
(1742–5)

Smoking

1 I have to smoke more [cigarettes]
than most people—because the ones I
smoke are very small and full of holes.
Beryl Bainbridge 1933– : in *Daily Telegraph*
28 February 1998

2 It has been said that cigarettes are the
only product that, if used according to
the manufacturer's instructions, have
a very high chance of killing you.
Michael Buerk 1946– : in *Sunday Times*
11 July 1999

3 The pipe with solemn interposing
puff,
Makes half a sentence at a time
enough;
The dozing sages drop the drowsy
strain,
Then pause, and puff—and speak,
and pause again.
William Cowper 1731–1800: 'Conversation'
(1782)

4 The wretcheder one is, the more one
smokes; and the more one smokes,
the wretcheder one gets—a vicious
circle!
George du Maurier 1834–96: *Peter Ibbetson*
(1892)

5 The roots of tobacco plants must go
clear through to hell.
Thomas Alva Edison 1847–1931: in *American
Heritage* 12 July 1885

6 A custom loathsome to the eye,
hateful to the nose, harmful to the
brain, dangerous to the lungs, and in
the black, stinking fume thereof,
nearest resembling the horrible

Stygian smoke of the pit that is
bottomless.
James I 1566–1625: *A Counterblast to Tobacco*
(1604)

7 This very night I am going to leave off
tobacco! Surely there must be some
other world in which this
unconquerable purpose shall be
realized.
Charles Lamb 1775–1834: letter to Thomas
Manning, 26 December 1815

8 He who lives without tobacco is not
worthy to live.
Molière 1622–73: *Don Juan* (performed 1665)

9 But the cigarette, well, I love stroking
this lovely tube of delight.
Dennis Potter 1935–94: *Seeing the Blossom*
(1994)

10 I smoked my first cigarette and kissed
my first woman on the same day. I
have never had time for tobacco since.
Arturo Toscanini 1867–1957: in *Observer*
30 June 1946

11 A cigarette is the perfect type of a
perfect pleasure. It is exquisite, and it
leaves one unsatisfied. What more can
one want?
Oscar Wilde 1854–1900: *The Picture of Dorian
Gray* (1891)

Snow

1 When men were all asleep the snow
came flying,
In large white flakes falling on the city
brown,
Stealthily and perpetually settling and
loosely lying,
Hushing the latest traffic of the
drowsy town.
Robert Bridges 1844–1930: 'London Snow'
(1890)

2 Whose woods these are I think I
know.
His house is in the village though;
He will not see me stopping here
To watch his woods fill up with snow.
Robert Frost 1874–1963: 'Stopping by Woods
on a Snowy Evening' (1923)

3 The first fall of snow is not only an event, but it is a magical event. You go to bed in one kind of world and wake up to find yourself in another quite different, and if this is not enchantment, then where is it to be found?
J. B. Priestley 1894–1984: *Apes and Angels* (1928) 'First Snow'

4 It was the wrong kind of snow.
■ *explaining disruption on British Rail*
Terry Worrall: in *The Independent* 16 February 1991

Society
see also **Art and Society**, **Government**, **The Human Race**, **Literature and Society**, **Science and Society**

1 There is no such thing as the State
And no one exists alone;
Hunger allows no choice
To the citizen or the police;
We must love one another or die.
W. H. Auden 1907–73: 'September 1, 1939' (1940)

2 We started off trying to set up a small anarchist community, but people wouldn't obey the rules.
Alan Bennett 1934– : *Getting On* (1972)

3 The greatest happiness of the greatest number is the foundation of morals and legislation.
Jeremy Bentham 1748–1832: *The Commonplace Book*; Bentham claimed that either Joseph Priestley (1733–1804) or Cesare Beccaria (1738–94) passed on the 'sacred truth'

4 No man is an Island, entire of it self; every man is a piece of the Continent, a part of the main; if a clod be washed away by the sea, Europe is the less, as well as if a promontory were.
John Donne 1572–1631: *Devotions upon Emergent Occasions* (1624)

5 You gotta say this for the white race— its self-confidence knows no bounds. Who else could go to a small island in the South Pacific where there's no poverty, no crime, no unemployment, no war and no worry—and call it a 'primitive society'?
Dick Gregory 1932– : *From the Back of the Bus* (1962)

6 Only in the state does man have a rational existence . . . Man owes his entire existence to the state, and has his being within it alone. Whatever worth and spiritual reality he possesses are his solely by virtue of the state.
G. W. F. Hegel 1770–1831: *Lectures on the Philosophy of World History: Introduction* (1830)

7 Polluted rivers, filthy streets, bodies bedded down in doorways are no advertisement for a prosperous or caring society.
Michael Heseltine 1933– : speech at Conservative Party Conference 10 October 1989

8 In your time we have the opportunity to move not only toward the rich society and the powerful society, but upward to the Great Society.
Lyndon Baines Johnson 1908–73: speech at University of Michigan, 22 May 1964

9 If a free society cannot help the many who are poor, it cannot save the few who are rich.
John F. Kennedy 1917–63: inaugural address, 20 January 1961

10 From each according to his abilities, to each according to his needs.
Karl Marx 1818–83: *Critique of the Gotha Programme* (written 1875, but of earlier origin)

11 When society requires to be rebuilt, there is no use in attempting to rebuild it on the old plan.
John Stuart Mill 1806–73: *Dissertations and Discussions* vol. 1 (1859) 'Essay on Coleridge'

12 Peace, political stability and reconciliation are not too much to ask for. They are the minimum that a decent society provides.
George Mitchell 1933– : in *Irish Post* 18 April 1998

13 There is no such thing as Society.
There are individual men and women,
and there are families.
   Margaret Thatcher 1925– : in *Woman's Own*
   31 October 1987

14 Wherever a man goes, men will
pursue him and paw him with their
dirty institutions, and, if they can,
constrain him to belong to their
desperate oddfellow society.
   Henry David Thoreau 1817–62: *Walden* (1854)
   'The Village'

15 The Social Contract is nothing more
or less than a vast conspiracy of
human beings to lie to and humbug
themselves and one another for the
general Good. Lies are the mortar that
bind the savage individual man into
the social masonry.
   H. G. Wells 1866–1946: *Love and Mr Lewisham*
   (1900)

Solitude

see also **Loneliness**

1 In human intimacy there is a secret
boundary; neither the experience of
being in love nor passion can cross it,
though lips be joined together in
awful silence, and the heart break
asunder with love.
   Anna Akhmatova 1889–1966: 'In Human
   Intimacy' (1915)

2 He who is unable to live in society, or
who has no need because he is
sufficient for himself, must be either a
beast or a god.
   Aristotle 384–322 BC: *Politics*

3 [Barrymore] would quote from
Genesis the text which says, 'It is not
good for man to be alone,' and then
add, 'But O my God, what a relief.'
   John Barrymore 1882–1942: Alma Power-
   Waters *John Barrymore* (1941)

4 To fly from, need not be to hate,
mankind.
   Lord Byron 1788–1824: *Childe Harold's
   Pilgrimage* (1812–18)

5 You come into the world alone and
you go out of the world alone yet it

seems to me you are more alone while
living than even going and coming.
   Emily Carr 1871–1945: *Hundreds and
   Thousands: The Journals of Emily Carr* (1966)
   16 July 1933

6 We live, as we dream—alone.
   Joseph Conrad 1857–1924: *Heart of Darkness*
   (1902)

7 Anythin' for a quiet life, as the man
said wen he took the sitivation at the
lighthouse.
   Charles Dickens 1812–70: *Pickwick Papers*
   (1837)

8 I am light with meditation, religiose
And mystic with a day of solitude.
   Douglas Dunn 1942– : 'Reading Pascal in the
   Lowlands' (1985)

9 How does it feel
To be on your own
With no direction home
Like a complete unknown
Like a rolling stone?
   Bob Dylan 1941– : *Like a Rolling Stone* (1965
   song)

10 I want to be alone.
   Greta Garbo 1905–90: *Grand Hotel* (1932
   film), the phrase already being associated
   with Garbo

11 Down to Gehenna or up to the
Throne,
He travels the fastest who travels
alone.
   Rudyard Kipling 1865–1936: 'The Winners'
   (*The Story of the Gadsbys*, 1890)

12 My heart is a lonely hunter that hunts
on a lonely hill.
   Fiona McLeod 1855–1905: 'The Lonely Hunter'
   (1896); reworked by Carson McCullers as
   'The heart is a lonely hunter' for the title of a
   novel, 1940

13 You come into the world alone, you
go out alone. In between it's nice to
know a few people, but being alone is
a fundamental quality of human life,
depressing as that is.
   Helen Mirren 1945– : in *Observer* 29 January
   1989

14 What Chekhov saw in our failure to
communicate was something positive
and precious: the private silence in

which we live, and which enables us to endure our own solitude.
  V. S. Pritchett 1900–97: *Myth Makers* (1979)

15 Man goes into the noisy crowd to drown his own clamour of silence.
  Rabindranath Tagore 1861–1941: 'Stray Birds' (1916)

16 We're all of us sentenced to solitary confinement inside our own skins, for life!
  Tennessee Williams 1911–83: *Orpheus Descending* (1958)

17 I will arise and go now, and go to Innisfree,
And a small cabin build there, of clay and wattles made;
Nine bean rows will I have there, a hive for the honey bee,
And live alone in the bee-loud glade.
  W. B. Yeats 1865–1939: 'The Lake Isle of Innisfree' (1893)

Solutions
see **Problems and Solutions**

Sorrow
see also **Bereavement**, **Depression**, **Suffering**

1 Sob, heavy world,
Sob as you spin
Mantled in mist, remote from the happy.
  W. H. Auden 1907–73: *The Age of Anxiety* (1947)

2 By the waters of Babylon we sat down and wept: when we remembered thee, O Sion.
  Bible: Psalm 137

3 I tell you, hopeless grief is passionless.
  Elizabeth Barrett Browning 1806–61: 'Grief' (1844)

4 All my joys to this are folly,
Naught so sweet as Melancholy.
  Robert Burton 1577–1640: *The Anatomy of Melancholy* (1621–51)

5 MEDVEDENKO: Why do you wear black all the time?

MASHA: I'm in mourning for my life, I'm unhappy.
  Anton Chekhov 1860–1904: *The Seagull* (1896)

6 . . . Nessun maggior dolore,
Che ricordarsi del tempo felice
Nella miseria.

There is no greater pain than to remember a happy time when one is in misery.
  Dante Alighieri 1265–1321: *Divina Commedia* 'Inferno'

7 Adieu tristesse
Bonjour tristesse
Tu es inscrite dans les lignes du plafond.

Farewell sadness
Good-day sadness
You are inscribed in the lines of the ceiling.
  Paul Éluard 1895–1952: 'À peine défigurée' (1932)

8 He felt the loyalty we all feel to unhappiness—the sense that that is where we really belong.
  Graham Greene 1904–91: *The Heart of the Matter* (1948)

9 Now laughing friends deride tears I cannot hide,
So I smile and say 'When a lovely flame dies,
Smoke gets in your eyes.'
  Otto Harbach 1873–1963: 'Smoke Gets in your Eyes' (1933 song)

10 Áh! ás the heart grows older
It will come to such sights colder
By and by, nor spare a sigh
Though worlds of wanwood leafmeal lie;
And yet you *will* weep and know why.
  Gerard Manley Hopkins 1844–89: 'Spring and Fall: to a young child' (written 1880)

11 Grief is a species of idleness.
  Samuel Johnson 1709–84: letter to Mrs Thrale, 17 March 1773

12 No one ever told me that grief felt so like fear.
  C. S. Lewis 1898–1963: *A Grief Observed* (1961)

13 Nothing is here for tears.
  John Milton 1608–74: *Samson Agonistes* (1671)

14 All the old statues of Victory have
wings: but Grief has no wings. She is
the unwelcome lodger that squats on
the hearth-stone between us and the
fire and will not move or be
dislodged.
Arthur Quiller-Couch 1863–1944: Armistice
Day anniversary sermon, Cambridge,
November 1923

15 Men who are unhappy, like men who
sleep badly, are always proud of the
fact.
Bertrand Russell 1872–1970: *The Conquest of
Happiness* (1930)

16 If you have tears, prepare to shed
them now.
William Shakespeare 1564–1616: *Julius Caesar*
(1599)

17 When sorrows come, they come not
single spies,
But in battalions.
William Shakespeare 1564–1616: *Hamlet*
(1601)

18 Tears, idle tears, I know not what they
mean,
Tears from the depth of some divine
despair.
Alfred, Lord Tennyson 1809–92: *The Princess*
(1850 ed.)

19 *Sunt lacrimae rerum et mentem
mortalia tangunt.*

There are tears shed for things even
here and mortality touches the heart.
Virgil 70–19 BC: *Aeneid*

20 Total grief is like a minefield. No
knowing when one will touch the
tripwire.
Sylvia Townsend Warner 1893–1978: diary
11 December 1969

21 We think caged birds sing, when
indeed they cry.
John Webster c.1580–c.1625: *The White Devil*
(1612)

22 Laugh and the world laughs with you;
Weep, and you weep alone;
For the sad old earth must borrow its
mirth,

But has trouble enough of its own.
Ella Wheeler Wilcox 1855–1919: 'Solitude'

South America

see **Mexico and South America**

Space

see also **The Skies**, **The Universe**

1 Houston, Tranquillity Base here. The
Eagle has landed.
Neil Armstrong 1930– : landing on the moon,
20 July 1969

2 Don't tell me that man doesn't belong
out there. Man belongs wherever he
wants to go—and he'll do plenty well
when he gets there.
Wernher von Braun 1912–77: in *Time*
17 February 1958

3 I think it is likely that there is life out
there. I fear we shall never know
about it.
Richard Dawkins 1941– : *Seven Wonders of the
World* (BBC TV) 9 April 1997

4 *on Felix Bloch's stating that space was the field of
linear operations:*
Nonsense. Space is blue and birds fly
through it.
Werner Heisenberg 1901–76: Felix Bloch
'Heisenberg and the early days of quantum
mechanics', in *Physics Today* December 1976

5 Space isn't remote at all. It's only an
hour's drive away if your car could go
straight upwards.
Fred Hoyle 1915–2001: in *Observer*
9 September 1979

6 The pursuit of the good and evil are
now linked in astronomy as in almost
all science . . . The fate of human
civilization will depend on whether
the rockets of the future carry the
astronomer's telescope or a hydrogen
bomb.
Bernard Lovell 1913– : *The Individual and the
Universe* (1959)

7 The eternal silence of these infinite
spaces [the heavens] terrifies me.
Blaise Pascal 1623–62: *Pensées* (1670)

8 Space is almost infinite. As a matter of fact, we think it is infinite.

Dan Quayle 1947– : in *Daily Telegraph* 8 March 1989

9 We will never forget them, nor the last time we saw them this morning, as they prepared for the journey and waved goodbye and 'slipped the surly bonds of earth' to 'touch the face of God.'

■ *after the loss of the space shuttle* Challenger *with all its crew*

Ronald Reagan 1911– : broadcast from the Oval Office, 28 January 1986; cf. **Air Travel** 3

10 Nothing is more symptomatic of the enervation, of the decompression of the Western imagination, than our incapacity to respond to the landings on the Moon. Not a single great poem, picture, metaphor has come of this breathtaking act, of Prometheus' rescue of Icarus or of Phaeton in flight towards the stars.

George Steiner 1926– : 'Modernity, Mythology and Magic', lecture at the 1994 Salzburg Festival

Speech

see also **Conversation**, **Grammar**, **Language**, **Silence**

1 Sentence structure is innate but whining is acquired.

Woody Allen 1935– : 'Remembering Needleman' (1976)

2 Never express yourself more clearly than you think.

Niels Bohr 1885–1962: Abraham Pais *Einstein Lived Here* (1994)

3 Take care of the sense, and the sounds will take care of themselves.

Lewis Carroll 1832–98: *Alice's Adventures in Wonderland* (1865)

4 Somwhat he lipsed, for his wantownesse,
  To make his Englissh sweete upon his tonge.

Geoffrey Chaucer c.1343–1400: *The Canterbury Tales* 'The General Prologue'

5 No, Sir, because I have time to think before I speak, and don't ask impertinent questions.

■ *when asked if he found his stammering very inconvenient*

Erasmus Darwin 1731–1802: Francis Darwin 'Reminiscences of My Father's Everyday Life', in Charles Darwin *Autobiography* (1877 ed.)

6 Half the sorrows of women would be averted if they could repress the speech they know to be useless; nay, the speech they have resolved not to make.

George Eliot 1819–80: *Felix Holt* (1866)

7   Speech impelled us
To purify the dialect of the tribe
And urge the mind to aftersight and foresight.

T. S. Eliot 1888–1965: *Four Quartets* 'Little Gidding' (1942)

8 Human speech is like a cracked kettle on which we tap crude rhythms for bears to dance to, while we long to make music that will melt the stars.

Gustave Flaubert 1821–80: *Madame Bovary* (1857)

9 It has been well said, that heart speaks to heart, whereas language only speaks to the ears.

St Francis de Sales 1567–1622: letter to the Archbishop of Bourges, 5 October 1604, paraphrased by John Henry Newman as '*cor ad cor loquitur* [heart speaks to heart]'

10 You like potato and I like po-tah-to,
You like tomato and I like to-mah-to;
Potato, po-tah-to, tomato, to-mah-to—
  Let's call the whole thing off!

Ira Gershwin 1896–1983: 'Let's Call the Whole Thing Off' (1937 song)

11 Most men make little other use of their speech than to give evidence against their own understanding.

Lord Halifax 1633–95: *Political, Moral, and Miscellaneous Thoughts and Reflections* (1750)

12 If, sir, I possessed, as you suggest, the power of conveying unlimited sexual attraction through the potency of my voice, I would not be reduced to accepting a miserable pittance from

the BBC for interviewing a faded female in a damp basement.

■ *reply to Mae West's manager who asked 'Can't you sound a bit more sexy when you interview her?'*

Gilbert Harding 1907–60: S. Grenfell *Gilbert Harding by his Friends* (1961)

13 To Trinity Church, Dorchester. The rector in his sermon delivers himself of mean images in a very sublime voice, and the effect is that of a glowing landscape in which clothes are hung up to dry.

Thomas Hardy 1840–1928: *Notebooks* 1 February 1874

14   HERE IS THE NEWS,
Said the absolute speaker. Between him and us
A great gulf was fixed where pronunciation
Reigned tyrannically

Seamus Heaney 1939– : 'A Sofa in the Forties' (1996)

15 A tart temper never mellows with age, and a sharp tongue is the only edged tool that grows keener with constant use.

Washington Irving 1783–1859: *The Sketch Book* (1820)

16 Speech is civilisation itself. The word, even the most contradictory word, preserves contact—it is silence which isolates.

Thomas Mann 1875–1955: *The Magic Mountain* (1924)

17 Continual eloquence is tedious.

Blaise Pascal 1623–62: *Pensées* (1670)

18 I do not much dislike the matter, but The manner of his speech.

William Shakespeare 1564–1616: *Antony and Cleopatra* (1606–7)

19 Nagging is the repetition of unpalatable truths.

Edith Summerskill 1901–80: speech to the Married Women's Association, House of Commons, 14 July 1960

20 Faith, that's as well said, as if I had said it myself.

Jonathan Swift 1667–1745: *Polite Conversation* (1738)

21 What can be said at all can be said clearly; and whereof one cannot speak thereof one must be silent.

Ludwig Wittgenstein 1889–1951: *Tractatus Logico-Philosophicus* (1922)

22 The reason why we have two ears and only one mouth is that we may listen the more and talk the less.

Zeno 333–261 BC: Diogenes Laertius *Lives of the Philosophers*

Speeches

1 I do not object to people looking at their watches when I am speaking. But I strongly object when they start shaking them to make certain they are still going.

Lord Birkett 1883–1962: in *Observer* 30 October 1960

2 I take the view, and always have, that if you cannot say what you are going to say in twenty minutes you ought to go away and write a book about it.

Lord Brabazon 1884–1964: speech, House of Lords, 21 June 1955

3 Grasp the subject, the words will follow.

Cato the Elder 234–149 BC: Caius Julius Victor *Ars Rhetorica*

4 And adepts in the speaking trade Keep a cough by them ready made.

Charles Churchill 1731–64: *The Ghost* (1763)

5 He is one of those orators of whom it was well said, 'Before they get up, they do not know what they are going to say; when they are speaking, they do not know what they are saying; and when they have sat down, they do not know what they have said.'

■ *of Lord Charles Beresford*

Winston Churchill 1874–1965: speech, House of Commons, 20 December 1912

6 It was the nation and the race dwelling all round the globe that had the lion's heart. I had the luck to be called upon to give the roar. I also

hope that I sometimes suggested to the lion the right place to use his claws.

Winston Churchill 1874–1965: speech at Westminster Hall, 30 November 1954

7 If you don't say anything, you won't be called on to repeat it.

Calvin Coolidge 1872–1933: attributed

8 Humming, Hawing and Hesitation are the three Graces of contemporary Parliamentary oratory.

Julian Critchley 1930–2000: *Westminster Blues* (1985)

9 When asked what was first in oratory, [he] replied to his questioner, 'action,' what second, 'action,' and again third, 'action'.

Demosthenes c.384—c.322 BC: Cicero *Brutus*

10 Public speaking is like the winds of the desert: it blows constantly without doing any good.

■ *when asked, at the inception of the UN in 1945, why he (as Saudi Arabian minister) was the only delegate not to have delivered a speech*

Faisal: Y. Karsh *Karsh: A 50-Year Retrospective* (1983)

11 The finest eloquence is that which gets things done and the worst is that which delays them.

David Lloyd George 1863–1945: speech at Paris Peace Conference, 18 January 1919

12 But all was false and hollow; though his tongue
Dropped manna, and could make the worse appear
The better reason.

John Milton 1608–74: *Paradise Lost* (1667)

13 Poor George, he can't help it—he was born with a silver foot in his mouth.

■ *of George Bush*

Ann Richards 1933– : keynote speech at the Democratic convention, in *Independent* 20 July 1988

14 Friends, Romans, countrymen, lend me your ears.

William Shakespeare 1564–1616: *Julius Caesar* (1599)

15 The Right Honourable gentleman is indebted to his memory for his jests, and to his imagination for his facts.

Richard Brinsley Sheridan 1751–1816: T. Moore *Life of Sheridan* (1825)

16 When someone asks a question about sex in Hyde Park you double the crowd and halve the argument.

Donald Soper 1903–98: attributed, in *The Times* 23 December 1998

17 Do you remember that in classical times when Cicero had finished speaking, the people said, 'How well he spoke', but when Demosthenes had finished speaking, they said, 'Let us march.'

Adlai Stevenson 1900–65: introducing John F. Kennedy in 1960; Bert Cochran *Adlai Stevenson* (1969)

18 Preach not because you have to say something, but because you have something to say.

Richard Whately 1787–1863: *Apophthegms* (1854)

19 If I am to speak for ten minutes, I need a week for preparation; if fifteen minutes, three days; if half an hour, two days; if an hour, I am ready now.

Woodrow Wilson 1856–1924: Josephus Daniels *The Wilson Era* (1946)

Speed

see also **Delay**

1 *Festina lente.*
Make haste slowly.

Augustus 63 BC–AD 14: Suetonius *Lives of the Caesars* 'Divus Augustus'

2 Men travel faster now, but I do not know if they go to better things.

Willa Cather 1873–1947: *Death Comes for the Archbishop* (1927)

3 I never run for the bus.

Linford Christie 1960– : in *Independent* 19 May 1999

4 [There are] only two classes of pedestrians in these days of reckless

motor traffic—the quick, and the
dead.
   Lord Dewar 1864–1930: George Robey
   Looking Back on Life (1933)

5 Home James, and don't spare the
horses.
   Fred Hillebrand 1893– : title of song (1934)

6 What good is speed if the brain has
oozed out on the way?
   Karl Kraus 1874–1936: in *Die Fackel*
   September 1909

7 I'll put a girdle round about the earth
In forty minutes.
   William Shakespeare 1564–1616: *A
   Midsummer Night's Dream* (1595–6)

8 Though I am always in haste, I am
never in a hurry.
   John Wesley 1703–91: letter to Miss March,
   10 December 1777

Sports and Games

see also **Baseball**, **Boxing**, **Cricket**,
Football, **Field Sports**, **Fishing**, **Golf**,
Hunting, **Tennis**, **Winning**

1 In America, it is sport that is the
opiate of the masses.
   Russell Baker 1925– : in *New York Times*
   3 October 1967

2 If people don't want to come out to
the ball park, nobody's going to stop
'em.
   Yogi Berra 1925– : attributed

3 What I know most surely about
morality and the duty of man I owe to
sport.
   ■ *often quoted as, '. . . I owe to football'*
   Albert Camus 1913–60: Herbert R. Lottman
   Albert Camus (1979)

4 There is plenty of time to win this
game, and to thrash the Spaniards
too.
   ■ *receiving news of the Armada while playing
   bowls on Plymouth Hoe*
   Francis Drake c.1540–96: attributed

5 I called off his players' names as they
came marching up the steps behind

him . . . All nice guys. They'll finish
last. Nice guys. Finish last.
   ■ *usually quoted as 'Nice guys finish last'*
   Leo Durocher 1906–91: casual remark at a
   practice ground, July 1946

6 There is this idea that if you like
football you also like beer and
grabbing women's breasts. If you like
rugby you also like Dire Straits and
wine. And if you don't like either you
must be a pacifist vegetarian.
   Colin Firth 1960– : in *Independent* 29 March
   1997

7 The thing about sport, any sport, is
that swearing is very much part of it.
   Jimmy Greaves 1940– : in *Observer* 1 January
   1989

8 The only athletic sport I ever
mastered was backgammon.
   Douglas Jerrold 1803–57: Walter Jerrold
   Douglas Jerrold (1914)

9 I am sorry I have not learned to play
at cards. It is very useful in life: it
generates kindness and consolidates
society.
   Samuel Johnson 1709–84: James Boswell
   Journal of a Tour to the Hebrides (1785)
   21 November 1773

10 Then ye returned to your trinkets;
then ye contented your souls
With the flannelled fools at the wicket
or the muddied oafs at the goals.
   Rudyard Kipling 1865–1936: 'The Islanders'
   (1903)

11   Chaos umpire sits,
And by decision more embroils the
fray.
   John Milton 1608–74: *Paradise Lost* (1667)

12 Everything about sport is derived
from the hunt: there is no sport in
existence that does not base itself
either on the chase or on aiming, the
two key elements of primeval
hunting.
   Desmond Morris 1928– : *The Animal
   Contract* (1990)

13 I don't really see the hurdles. I sense
them like a memory.
   Edwin Moses 1955– : attributed

14 And it's not for the sake of a ribboned coat,
Or the selfish hope of a season's fame,
But his Captain's hand on his shoulder smote—
'Play up! play up! and play the game!'
Henry Newbolt 1862–1938: 'Vitaï Lampada' (1897)

15 Serious sport has nothing to do with fair play. It is bound up with hatred, jealousy, boastfulness, and disregard of all the rules.
George Orwell 1903–50: *Shooting an Elephant* (1950) 'I Write as I Please'

16 Don't look back. Something may be gaining on you.
■ *a baseball pitcher's advice*
Satchel Paige 1906–82: in *Collier's* 13 June 1953

17 The theory and practice of gamesmanship or The art of winning games without actually cheating.
Stephen Potter 1900–69: title of book (1947)

18 To play billiards well is a sign of an ill-spent youth.
Charles Roupell: attributed; D. Duncan *Life of Herbert Spencer* (1908)

19 I can't see who's in the lead but it's either Oxford or Cambridge.
John Snagge 1904–96: commentary on the 1949 Boat Race

20 The harmless art of knucklebones has seen the fall of the Roman empire and the rise of the United States.
Robert Louis Stevenson 1850–94: *Across the Plains* (1892) 'The Lantern-Bearers'

21 What a sad old age you are preparing for yourself.
■ *to a young diplomat who boasted of his ignorance of whist*
Charles-Maurice de Talleyrand 1754–1838: J. Amédée Pichot *Souvenirs Intimes sur M. de Talleyrand* (1870)

22 I used to think the only use for it was to give small boys something else to kick besides me.
■ *of sport*
Katharine Whitehorn 1928– : *Observations* (1970)

23 Jogging is for people who aren't intelligent enough to watch television.
Victoria Wood 1953– : *Mens Sana in Thingummy Doodah* (1990)

Spring

1 It is about five o'clock in an evening that the first hour of spring strikes—autumn arrives in the early morning, but spring at the close of a winter day.
Elizabeth Bowen 1899–1973: *The Death of the Heart* (1938)

2 Oh, to be in England
Now that April's there,
And whoever wakes in England
Sees, some morning, unaware,
That the lowest boughs and the brushwood sheaf
Round the elm-tree bole are in tiny leaf,
While the chaffinch sings on the orchard bough
In England—now!
Robert Browning 1812–89: 'Home-Thoughts, from Abroad' (1845)

3 April is the cruellest month, breeding
Lilacs out of the dead land, mixing
Memory and desire, stirring
Dull roots with spring rain.
T. S. Eliot 1888–1965: *The Waste Land* (1922)

4 And since to look at things in bloom
Fifty springs are little room,
About the woodlands I will go
To see the cherry hung with snow.
A. E. Housman 1859–1936: *A Shropshire Lad* (1896)

5 Work seethes in the hands of spring,
That strapping dairymaid.
Boris Pasternak 1890–1960: *Doctor Zhivago* (1958) 'Zhivago's Poems: March'

Statistics

see also **Mathematics**

1 [The War Office kept three sets of figures:] one to mislead the public, another to mislead the Cabinet, and the third to mislead itself.
Herbert Asquith 1852–1928: Alistair Horne *Price of Glory* (1962)

2 Every moment dies a man,
Every moment 1¹⁄₁₆ is born.

Charles Babbage 1792–1871: parody of
Tennyson's 'Vision of Sin' in an unpublished
letter to the poet; in *New Scientist*
4 December 1958; see 11 below

3 One of the thieves was saved. (*Pause*)
It's a reasonable percentage.

Samuel Beckett 1906–89: *Waiting for Godot*
(1955)

4 A witty statesman said, you might
prove anything by figures.

Thomas Carlyle 1795–1881: *Chartism* (1839)

5 There are three kinds of lies: lies,
damned lies and statistics.

Benjamin Disraeli 1804–81: attributed; Mark
Twain *Autobiography* (1924)

6 From the fact that there are
400,000 species of beetles on this
planet, but only 8,000 species of
mammals, he [Haldane] concluded
that the Creator, if He exists, has a
special preference for beetles.

J. B. S. Haldane 1892–1964: report of lecture,
7 April 1951

7 We are just statistics, born to consume
resources.

Horace 65–8 BC: *Epistles*

8 He uses statistics as a drunken man
uses lampposts—for support rather
than for illumination.

Andrew Lang 1844–1912: attributed

9 You mean, your statistics are facts, but
my facts are just statistics.

Jonathan Lynn 1943– and **Antony Jay** 1930– :
Yes Prime Minister (1986) vol. 1

10 If your experiment needs statistics,
you ought to have done a better
experiment.

Ernest Rutherford 1871–1937: Norman T. J.
Bailey *The Mathematical Approach to Biology
and Medicine* (1967)

11 Every moment dies a man,
Every moment one is born.

Alfred, Lord Tennyson 1809–92: 'The Vision of
Sin' (1842); cf. 2 above

12 The so-called science of poll-taking is
not a science at all but a mere
necromancy. People are unpredictable

by nature, and although you can take
a nation's pulse, you can't be sure that
the nation hasn't just run up a flight
of stairs.

E. B. White 1899–1985: in *New Yorker*
13 November 1948

Strength and Weakness

see also **Determination**

1 Our cock won't fight.

■ *of Edward VIII, said to Winston Churchill
during the abdication crisis of 1936*

Lord Beaverbrook 1879–1964: Frances
Donaldson *Edward VIII* (1974)

2 For the good that I would I do not:
but the evil which I would not, that I
do.

Bible: Romans

3 If God be for us, who can be against
us?

Bible: Romans

4 The weak have one weapon: the errors
of those who think they are strong.

Georges Bidault 1899–1983: in *Observer*
15 July 1962

5 The most potent weapon in the hands
of the oppressor is the mind of the
oppressed.

Steve Biko 1946–77: statement as witness,
3 May 1976

6 The weak are strong because they are
reckless. The strong are weak because
they have scruples.

Otto von Bismarck 1815–98: quoted by Henry
Kissinger to James Callaghan, 1975; James
Callaghan *Time and Chance* (1987)

7 It is the nature, and the advantage, of
strong people that they can bring out
the crucial questions and form a clear
opinion about them. The weak always
have to decide between alternatives
that are not their own.

Dietrich Bonhoeffer 1906–45: *Resistance and
Submission* (1951)

8 The concessions of the weak are the
concessions of fear.

Edmund Burke 1729–97: *On Conciliation with
America* (1775)

9 As you know, God is usually on the side of the big squadrons against the small.

  ■ *often quoted as 'Providence is always on the side of the big battalions'*
  Comte de Bussy-Rabutin 1618–93: letter to the Comte de Limoges, 18 October 1677

10 Toughness doesn't have to come in a pinstripe suit.
  Dianne Feinstein 1933– : in *Time* 4 June 1984

11 Nothing is wasted, nothing is in vain: The seas roll over but the rocks remain.
  A. P. Herbert 1890–1971: *Tough at the Top* (operetta *c.*1949)

12 The thing is, you see, that the strongest man in the world is the man who stands most alone.
  Henrik Ibsen 1828–1906: *An Enemy of the People* (1882)

13 All the world knows that the weak overcomes the strong and the soft overcomes the hard.
  But none can practice it.
  Lao Tzu *c.*604–*c.*531 BC: *Tao-te Ching*

14 Strength through joy.
  Robert Ley 1890–1945: German Labour Front slogan from 1933

15 People assumed I was a lot stronger than I was because I had a big mouth and a shaved head. I acted tough to cover the vulnerability.
  Sinéad O'Connor 1966– : in *Irish Times* 22 November 1997

16 This is the law of the Yukon, that only the Strong shall thrive;
  That surely the Weak shall perish, and only the Fit survive.
  Robert W. Service 1874–1958: 'The Law of the Yukon' (1907)

17 The gods are on the side of the stronger.
  Tacitus AD *c.*56–after 117: *Histories*

18 If you can't stand the heat, get out of the kitchen.
  Harry S. Truman 1884–1972: in *Time* 28 April 1952; associated with Truman, but attributed by him to Harry Vaughan, his 'military jester'

Style

see also **Language**

1 People think that I can teach them style. What stuff it all is! Have something to say, and say it as clearly as you can. That is the only secret of style.
  Matthew Arnold 1822–88: G. W. E. Russell *Collections and Recollections* (1898)

2 No iron can stab the heart with such force as a full stop put just at the right place.
  Isaac Babel 1894–1940: *Guy de Maupassant* (1932)

3 These things [subject matter] are external to the man; style is the man.
  Comte de Buffon 1707–88: *Discours sur le style*; address given to the Académie Française, 25 August 1753

4 The Mandarin style . . . is beloved by literary pundits, by those who would make the written word as unlike as possible to the spoken one.
  Cyril Connolly 1903–74: *Enemies of Promise* (1938)

5 Style is life! It is the very life-blood of thought!
  Gustave Flaubert 1821–80: letter to Louise Colet, 7 September 1853

6 I strive to be brief, and I become obscure.
  Horace 65–8 BC: *Ars Poetica*

7 When we see a natural style, we are quite surprised and delighted, for we expected to see an author and we find a man.
  Blaise Pascal 1623–62: *Pensées* (1670)

8 True wit is Nature to advantage dressed,
  What oft was thought, but ne'er so well expressed.
  Alexander Pope 1688–1744: *An Essay on Criticism* (1711)

9 More matter with less art.
  William Shakespeare 1564–1616: *Hamlet* (1601)

10 Proper words in proper places, make the true definition of a style.

Jonathan Swift 1667–1745: *Letter to a Young Gentleman lately entered into Holy Orders* 9 January 1720

11 As to the Adjective: when in doubt, strike it out.

Mark Twain 1835–1910: *Pudd'nhead Wilson* (1894)

12 'Feather-footed through the plashy fen passes the questing vole' . . . 'Yes,' said the Managing Editor. 'That must be good style.'

Evelyn Waugh 1903–66: *Scoop* (1938)

13 Style is the dress of thought; a modest dress,
Neat, but not gaudy, will true critics please.

Samuel Wesley 1662–1735: 'An Epistle to a Friend concerning Poetry' (1700)

14 It's not what I do, but the way I do it.
It's not what I say, but the way I say it.

Mae West 1892–1980: G. Eells and S. Musgrove *Mae West* (1989)

15 I don't wish to sign my name, though I am afraid everybody will know who the writer is: one's style is one's signature always.

Oscar Wilde 1854–1900: letter to the *Daily Telegraph*, 2 February 1891

Success

see also **Defeat**, **Failure**, **Winning**

1 'Tis not in mortals to command success,
But we'll do more, Sempronius; we'll deserve it.

Joseph Addison 1672–1719: *Cato* (1713)

2 For what shall it profit a man, if he shall gain the whole world, and lose his own soul?

Bible: St Mark

3 It was roses, roses, all the way.

Robert Browning 1812–89: 'The Patriot' (1855)

4 At the end of your life you will never regret not having passed one more test, winning one more verdict or not closing one more deal. You will regret time not spent with a husband, a child, a friend or a parent.

Barbara Bush 1925– : in *Washington Post* 2 June 1990

5 *Veni, vidi, vici.*
I came, I saw, I conquered.

Julius Caesar 100–44 BC: inscription displayed in Caesar's Pontic triumph, according to Suetonius *Lives of the Caesars* 'Divus Julius'; or, according to Plutarch *Parallel Lives* 'Julius Caesar', written in a letter by Caesar, announcing the victory of Zela which concluded the Pontic campaign

6 My career must be slipping. This is the first time I've been available to pick up an award.

Michael Caine 1933– : at the Golden Globe awards, Beverly Hills, California, 24 January 1999

7 How to win friends and influence people.

Dale Carnegie 1888–1955: title of book (1936)

8 Success took me to her bosom like a maternal boa constrictor.

Noël Coward 1899–1973: Sheridan Morley *A Talent to Amuse* (1969)

9 Success is counted sweetest
By those who ne'er succeed.
To comprehend a nectar
Requires sorest need.

Emily Dickinson 1830–86: 'Success is counted sweetest' (1859)

10 In the United States there's a Puritan ethic and a mythology of success. He who is successful is good. In Latin countries, in Catholic countries, a successful person is a sinner.

Umberto Eco 1932– : in *International Herald Tribune* 14 December 1988

11 If *A* is a success in life, then *A* equals *x* plus *y* plus *z*. Work is *x*; *y* is play; and *z* is keeping your mouth shut.

Albert Einstein 1879–1955: in *Observer* 15 January 1950

12 Success is relative:
It is what we can make of the mess we
have made of things.
T. S. Eliot 1888–1965: *The Family Reunion*
(1939)

13 The moral flabbiness born of the
exclusive worship of the bitch-
goddess *success*.
William James 1842–1910: letter to H. G.
Wells, 11 September 1906

14 Sweet smell of success.
Ernest Lehman 1920– : title of book and film
(1957)

15 I am a West Indian peasant who has
drifted into this business and who has
survived. If I knew the secret, I would
bottle it and sell it.
Trevor McDonald 1939– : in *Independent*
20 April 1996

16 You cannot ditch policies that
succeeded so convincingly that they
were adopted by our opponents.
Michael Portillo 1953– : in *Independent*
27 April 1999

17 Is it possible to succeed without any
act of betrayal?
Jean Renoir 1894–1979: *My Life and My Films*
(1974)

18 The world continues to offer glittering
prizes to those who have stout hearts
and sharp swords.
F. E. Smith 1872–1930: Rectorial Address,
Glasgow University, 7 November 1923

19 Success makes life easier. It doesn't
make *living* easier.
Bruce Springsteen 1949– : in *Q Magazine*
August 1992

20 Success to me is having ten honeydew
melons and eating only the top half of
each one.
Barbra Streisand 1942– : in *Life*
20 September 1963

21 All you need in this life is ignorance
and confidence; then success is sure.
Mark Twain 1835–1910: letter to Mrs Foote,
2 December 1887

22 Whenever a friend succeeds, a little
something in me dies.
Gore Vidal 1925– : in *Sunday Times Magazine*
16 September 1973

Suffering

see also **Compassion**, **Sacrifice**, **Sorrow**,
Tragedy

1 Children's talent to endure stems
from their ignorance of alternatives.
Maya Angelou 1928– : *I Know Why The
Caged Bird Sings* (1969)

2 About suffering they were never
wrong,
The Old Masters: how well they
understood
Its human position; how it takes place
While someone else is eating or
opening a window or just walking
dully along.
W. H. Auden 1907–73: 'Musée des Beaux Arts'
(1940)

3 Nothing happens to anybody which
he is not fitted by nature to bear.
Marcus Aurelius AD 121–80: *Meditations*

4 Misery such as mine has no pride. I
care not who knows that I am
wretched.
Jane Austen 1775–1817: *Sense and Sensibility*
(1811)

5 Some people like being burdened. It
gives them an interest.
Beryl Bainbridge 1933– : *An Awfully Big
Adventure* (1989)

6 The most extreme agony is to feel that
one has been utterly forsaken.
Bruno Bettelheim 1903–90: *Surviving and
other essays* (1979)

7   For frequent tears have run
The colours from my life.
Elizabeth Barrett Browning 1806–61: *Sonnets
from the Portuguese* (1850)

8 After great pain, a formal feeling
comes—
The Nerves sit ceremonious, like
Tombs—
The stiff Heart questions was it He,
that bore,
And Yesterday, or Centuries before?
Emily Dickinson 1830–86: 'After great pain, a
formal feeling comes' (1862)

9 To each his suff'rings, all are men,
Condemned alike to groan;

The tender for another's pain,
Th' unfeeling for his own.
Thomas Gray 1716–71: *Ode on a Distant Prospect of Eton College* (1747)

10 Pity is the feeling which arrests the mind in the presence of whatsoever is grave and constant in human sufferings and unites it with the human sufferer. Terror is the feeling which arrests the mind in the presence of whatsoever is grave and constant in human sufferings and unites it with the secret cause.
James Joyce 1882–1941: *A Portrait of the Artist as a Young Man* (1916)

11 Fade far away, dissolve, and quite forget
What thou among the leaves hast never known,
The weariness, the fever, and the fret
Here, where men sit and hear each other groan;
Where palsy shakes a few, sad, last grey hairs,
Where youth grows pale, and spectre-thin, and dies;
Where but to think is to be full of sorrow
And leaden-eyed despairs.
John Keats 1795–1821: 'Ode to a Nightingale' (1820)

12 The toad beneath the harrow knows
Exactly where each tooth-point goes;
The butterfly upon the road
Preaches contentment to that toad.
Rudyard Kipling 1865–1936: 'Pagett, MP' (1886)

13 Sorrow and silence are strong, and patient endurance is godlike.
Henry Wadsworth Longfellow 1807–82: *Evangeline* (1847)

14 Scars have the strange power to remind us that our past is real.
Cormac McCarthy 1933– : *All the Pretty Horses* (1993)

15 It is not true that suffering ennobles the character; happiness does that sometimes, but suffering, for the most part, makes men petty and vindictive.
W. Somerset Maugham 1874–1965: *The Moon and Sixpence* (1919)

16 Willy Loman never made a lot of money. His name was never in the paper. He's not the finest character that ever lived. But he's a human being, and a terrible thing is happening to him. So attention must be paid.
Arthur Miller 1915– : *Death of a Salesman* (1949)

17 I successfully don't think about it for most of my life because I'm in that sunlit part of the landscape where I don't hear the cries of the tormented. It's the way things are.
■ *when asked how he dealt with the atrocities of this century*
Jonathan Miller 1934– : in *Observer* 10 March 1996

18 What does not kill me makes me stronger.
Friedrich Nietzsche 1844–1900: *Twilight of the Idols* (1889)

19 We can't all be happy, we can't all be rich, we can't all be lucky . . . Some must cry so that others may be able to laugh the more heartily.
Jean Rhys c.1890–1979: *Good Morning, Midnight* (1939)

20 He jests at scars, that never felt a wound.
William Shakespeare 1564–1616: *Romeo and Juliet* (1595)

21   The worst is not,
So long as we can say, 'This is the worst.'
William Shakespeare 1564–1616: *King Lear* (1605–6)

22 How can you expect a man who's warm to understand one who's cold?
Alexander Solzhenitsyn 1918– : *One Day in the Life of Ivan Denisovich* (1962)

23 Nothing begins, and nothing ends,
That is not paid with moan;
For we are born in other's pain,
And perish in our own.
Francis Thompson 1859–1907: 'Daisy' (1913)

24 Suffering is permanent, obscure and dark,

And shares the nature of infinity.
William Wordsworth 1770–1850: *The Borderers*
(1842)

25 Too long a sacrifice
Can make a stone of the heart.
W. B. Yeats 1865–1939: 'Easter, 1916' (1921)

Suicide

1 Without the possibility of suicide, I
would have killed myself long ago.
E. M. Cioran 1911–95: in *Independent*
2 December 1989

2 A suicide kills two people, Maggie,
that's what it's for!
Arthur Miller 1915– : *After the Fall* (1964)

3 The thought of suicide is a great
source of comfort: with it a calm
passage is to be made across many a
bad night.
Friedrich Nietzsche 1844–1900: *Jenseits von
Gut und Böse* (1886)

4 Guns aren't lawful;
Nooses give;
Gas smells awful;
You might as well live.
Dorothy Parker 1893–1967: 'Résumé' (1937)

5 If I cannot give consent to my own
death, then whose body is this? Who
owns my life?
Sue Rodriguez 1951–94: appealing to a
subcomittee of the Canadian Commons,
November 1992

6 But suicides have a special language.
Like carpenters they want to know
which tools.
They never ask *why build.*
Anne Sexton 1928–74: 'Wanting to Die'
(1966)

7 For who would bear the whips and
scorns of time,
The oppressor's wrong, the proud
man's contumely,
The pangs of disprized love, the law's
delay,
The insolence of office, and the
spurns
That patient merit of the unworthy
takes,

When he himself might his quietus
make
With a bare bodkin?
William Shakespeare 1564–1616: *Hamlet*
(1601)

8 Suicide is no more than a trick played
on the calendar.
Tom Stoppard 1937– : *The Dog It Was That
Died* (1983)

9   Nor at all can tell
Whether I mean this day to end
myself,
Or lend an ear to Plato where he says,
That men like soldiers may not quit
the post
Allotted by the Gods.
Alfred, Lord Tennyson 1809–92: 'Lucretius'
(1868)

10 In this life there's nothing new in
dying,
But nor, of course, is living any newer.
■ *his final poem, written in his own blood the
day before he hanged himself in his Leningrad
hotel room*
Sergei Yesenin 1895–1925: 'Goodbye, my
Friend, Goodbye' (1925)

11 It's better to burn out
Than to fade away.
■ *quoted by Kurt Cobain in his suicide note,
8 April 1994*
Neil Young 1945– : 'My My, Hey Hey (Out of
the Blue)' (1978 song, with Jeff Blackburn)

Summer

1 Sumer is icumen in,
Lhude sing cuccu!
Groweth sed, and bloweth med,
And springth the wude nu.
Anonymous: 'Cuckoo Song' (*c*.1250)

2 Summer has set in with its usual
severity.
Samuel Taylor Coleridge 1772–1834: letter
from Charles Lamb to Vincent Novello,
9 May 1826

3 June is bustin' out all over.
Oscar Hammerstein II 1895–1960: title of song
(1945)

4 Summer time an' the livin' is easy,
  Fish are jumpin' an' the cotton is
  high.
  Du Bose Heyward 1885–1940 and **Ira Gershwin**
  1896–1983: 'Summertime' (1935 song)

5 August creates as she slumbers,
  replete and satisfied.
  Joseph Wood Krutch 1893–1970: *Twelve Seasons* (1949)

6 August is a wicked month.
  Edna O'Brien 1936– : title of novel (1965)

7 The way to ensure summer in
  England is to have it framed and
  glazed in a comfortable room.
  Horace Walpole 1717–97: letter to Revd
  William Cole, 28 May 1774

The Supernatural

1 Up the airy mountain,
  Down the rushy glen,
  We daren't go a-hunting,
  For fear of little men.
  William Allingham 1824–89: 'The Fairies'
  (1850)

2 From ghoulies and ghosties and long-
    leggety beasties
  And things that go bump in the night,
  Good Lord, deliver us!
  Anonymous: 'The Cornish or West Country
  Litany'; Francis T. Nettleinghame *Polperro
  Proverbs and Others* (1926)

3 I always knew the living talked rot, but
  it's nothing to the rot the dead talk.
  ■ *on spiritualism*
  Margot Asquith 1864–1945: Chips Channon,
  diary, 20 December 1937

4 There is a superstition in avoiding
  superstition.
  Francis Bacon 1561–1626: *Essays* (1625) 'Of
  Superstition'

5 Every time a child says 'I don't believe
  in fairies' there is a little fairy
  somewhere that falls down dead.
  J. M. Barrie 1860–1937: *Peter Pan* (1928)

6 For we wrestle not against flesh and
  blood, but against principalities,
  against powers, against the rulers of
  the darkness of this world, against
  spiritual wickedness in high places.
  Bible: Ephesians

7 Superstition is the religion of feeble
  minds.
  Edmund Burke 1729–97: *Reflections on the
  Revolution in France* (1790)

8 Go, and catch a falling star,
  Get with child a mandrake root,
  Tell me, where all past years are,
  Or who cleft the Devil's foot.
  John Donne 1572–1631: 'Song: Go and catch a
  falling star'

9 There are fairies at the bottom of our
  garden!
  Rose Fyleman 1877–1957: 'The Fairies' (1918)

10 Superstition is the poetry of life.
   Johann Wolfgang von Goethe 1749–1832:
   Maximen und Reflexionen (1819)

11 All argument is against it; but all
   belief is for it.
   ■ *of the existence of ghosts*
   Samuel Johnson 1709–84: James Boswell *Life
   of Samuel Johnson* (1791) 31 March 1778

12 There are more things in heaven and
     earth, Horatio,
   Than are dreamt of in your
     philosophy.
   William Shakespeare 1564–1616: *Hamlet*
   (1601)

13 GLENDOWER: I can call spirits from
     the vasty deep.
   HOTSPUR: Why, so can I, or so can any
     man;
   But will they come when you do call
     for them?
   William Shakespeare 1564–1616: *Henry IV,
   Part 1* (1597)

14 Double, double toil and trouble;
   Fire burn and cauldron bubble.
   William Shakespeare 1564–1616: *Macbeth*
   (1606)

15 Out flew the web and floated wide;
   The mirror cracked from side to side;
   'The curse is come upon me,' cried
   The Lady of Shalott.
   Alfred, Lord Tennyson 1809–92: 'The Lady of
   Shalott' (1832, revised 1842)

Surprise

1 Surprises are foolish things. The
pleasure is not enhanced, and the
inconvenience is often considerable.
Jane Austen 1775–1817: *Emma* (1816)

2 'Curiouser and curiouser!' cried Alice.
Lewis Carroll 1832–98: *Alice's Adventures in
Wonderland* (1865)

3 Nobody expects the Spanish
Inquisition!
Graham Chapman 1941–89, **John Cleese**
1939– , et al.: *Monty Python's Flying Circus*
(BBC TV programme, 1970)

4 It was quite the most incredible event
that has ever happened to me in my
life. It was almost as incredible as if
you fired a 15-inch shell at a piece of
tissue paper and it came back and hit
you.
■ *on the back-scattering effect of metal foil on
alpha-particles*
Ernest Rutherford 1871–1937: E. N. da C.
Andrade *Rutherford and the Nature of the
Atom* (1964)

5 O wonderful, wonderful, and most
wonderful wonderful! and yet again
wonderful, and after that, out of all
whooping!
William Shakespeare 1564–1616: *As You Like It*
(1599)

6 I turned to Aunt Agatha, whose
demeanour was now rather like that
of one who, picking daisies on the
railway, has just caught the down
express in the small of the back.
P. G. Wodehouse 1881–1975: *The Inimitable
Jeeves* (1923)

Swearing

1 Expletive deleted.
Anonymous: *Submission of Recorded
Presidential Conversations to the Committee
on the Judiciary of the House of
Representatives by President Richard M.
Nixon* 30 April 1974

2 Don't swear, boy. It shows a lack of
vocabulary.
Alan Bennett 1934– : *Forty Years On* (1969)

3 The man who first abused his fellows
with swear-words instead of bashing
their brains out with a club should be
counted among those who laid the
foundations of civilization.
John Cohen 1911– : in *Observer* 21 November
1965

4 Though 'Bother it' I may
Occasionally say,
I never use a big, big D—
W. S. Gilbert 1836–1911: *HMS Pinafore* (1878)

5 The word I used was 'bloody', which,
where I come from in Yorkshire, is
practically the only surviving
adjective.
Maureen Lipman 1946– : in *The Times*
13 February 1999

6 Swear-words are neutral; they only
become objectionable when someone
is offended by them. The art of good
manners (as well as bad manners) is
knowing who will be offended by
what.
John Rae 1931– : *Letters from School* (1987)

7 You taught me language; and my
profit on't
Is, I know how to curse: the red plague
rid you,
For learning me your language!
William Shakespeare 1564–1616: *The Tempest*
(1611)

8 If ever I utter an oath again may my
soul be blasted to eternal damnation!
George Bernard Shaw 1856–1950: *Saint Joan*
(1924)

Tact

1 The tribute which intelligence pays to
humbug.
St John Brodrick 1856–1942: Lady Ribblesdale
to Lord Curzon 3 April 1891; Kenneth Rose
Superior Person (1969)

2 'Not to put too fine a point upon
it'—a favourite apology for plain-
speaking with Mr Snagsby.
Charles Dickens 1812–70: *Bleak House* (1853)

3 BISHOP: I'm afraid you've got a bad
egg, Mr Jones.

CURATE: Oh no, my Lord, I assure you! Parts of it are excellent!
Punch: 11 May 1895

4 Up to a point, Lord Copper.
■ *meaning no*
Evelyn Waugh 1903–66: *Scoop* (1938)

Taste

....

see also **Vulgarity**

1 Good taste is better than bad taste, but bad taste is better than no taste, and men without individuality have no taste—at any rate no taste that they can impose on their publics.
Arnold Bennett 1867–1931: in *Evening Standard* 21 August 1930

2 A difference of taste in jokes is a great strain on the affections.
George Eliot 1819–80: *Daniel Deronda* (1876)

3 Taste is the feminine of genius.
Edward Fitzgerald 1809–83: letter to J. R. Lowell, October 1877

4 Our tastes greatly alter. The lad does not care for the child's rattle, and the old man does not care for the young man's whore.
Samuel Johnson 1709–84: James Boswell *Life of Samuel Johnson* (1791) Spring 1766

5 Nowhere probably is there more true feeling, and nowhere worse taste, than in a churchyard.
Benjamin Jowett 1817–93: Evelyn Abbott and Lewis Campbell (eds.) *Letters of Benjamin Jowett* (1899)

6 The kind of people who always go on about whether a thing is in good taste invariably have very bad taste.
Joe Orton 1933–67: in *Transatlantic Review* Spring 1967

7 Could we teach taste or genius by rules, they would be no longer taste and genius.
Joshua Reynolds 1723–92: *Discourses on Art* 14 December 1770

8 The play, I remember, pleased not the million; 'twas caviare to the general.
William Shakespeare 1564–1616: *Hamlet* (1601)

9 *of the wallpaper in the room where he was dying:*
One of us must go.
Oscar Wilde 1854–1900: attributed, probably apocryphal

Taxes

....

1 Can't pay, won't pay.
Anonymous: anti-Poll Tax slogan, *c.*1990

2 To tax and to please, no more than to love and to be wise, is not given to men.
Edmund Burke 1729–97: *On American Taxation* (1775)

3 Read my lips: no new taxes.
George Bush 1924– : campaign pledge on taxation, in *New York Times* 19 August 1988

4 In this world nothing can be said to be certain, except death and taxes.
Benjamin Franklin 1706–90: letter to Jean Baptiste Le Roy, 13 November 1789

5 Only the little people pay taxes.
Leona Helmsley *c.*1920– : addressed to her housekeeper in 1983, and reported at her trial for tax evasion; in *New York Times* 12 July 1989

6 *Excise.* A hateful tax levied upon commodities.
Samuel Johnson 1709–84: *A Dictionary of the English Language* (1755)

7 Death is the most convenient time to tax rich people.
David Lloyd George 1863–1945: in *Lord Riddell's Intimate Diary of the Peace Conference and After, 1918–23* (1933)

8 The Chancellor of the Exchequer is a man whose duties make him more or less of a taxing machine. He is intrusted with a certain amount of misery which it is his duty to distribute as fairly as he can.
Robert Lowe 1811–92: speech, House of Commons, 11 April 1870

9 Taxation without representation is tyranny.
James Otis 1725–83: watchword (*c.*1761) of the American Revolution; in *Dictionary of American Biography*

10 Income Tax has made more Liars out of the American people than Golf.
Will Rogers 1879–1935: *The Illiterate Digest* (1924) 'Helping the Girls with their Income Taxes'

11 There is no art which one government sooner learns of another than that of draining money from the pockets of the people.
Adam Smith 1723–90: *Wealth of Nations* (1776)

12 Money has no smell.
■ *quashing an objection to a tax on public lavatories*
Vespasian AD 9–79: traditional summary; Suetonius *Lives of the Caesars* 'Vespasian'

Teaching

see also **Education**, **Schools**

1 A teacher affects eternity; he can never tell where his influence stops.
Henry Brooks Adams 1838–1918: *The Education of Henry Adams* (1907)

2 There is no such whetstone, to sharpen a good wit and encourage a will to learning, as is praise.
Roger Ascham 1515–68: *The Schoolmaster* (1570)

3 That is the difference between good teachers and great teachers: good teachers make the best of a pupil's means: great teachers foresee a pupil's ends.
Maria Callas 1923–77: *Kenneth Harris Talking To* (1971) 'Maria Callas'

4 A man who reviews the old so as to find out the new is qualified to teach others.
Confucius 551–479 BC: *Analects*

5 C-l-e-a-n, clean, verb active, to make bright, to scour. W-i-n, win, d-e-r, der, winder, a casement. When the boy knows this out of the book, he goes and does it.
Charles Dickens 1812–70: *Nicholas Nickleby* (1839)

6 Technology is just a tool. In terms of getting the kids working together and

motivating them, the teacher is the most important.
Bill Gates 1955– : in *Independent on Sunday* 12 October 1997

7 It is no matter what you teach them [children] first, any more than what leg you shall put into your breeches first.
Samuel Johnson 1709–84: James Boswell *Life of Samuel Johnson* (1791) 26 July 1763

8 We teachers can only help the work going on, as servants wait upon a master.
Maria Montessori 1870–1952: *The Absorbent Mind* (1949)

9 Discussion in class, which means letting twenty young blockheads and two cocky neurotics discuss something that neither their teacher nor they know.
Vladimir Nabokov 1899–1977: *Pnin* (1957)

10 Men must be taught as if you taught them not,
And things unknown proposed as things forgot.
Alexander Pope 1688–1744: *An Essay on Criticism* (1711)

11 Few have been taught to any purpose who have not been their own teachers.
Joshua Reynolds 1723–92: *Discourses on Art* 11 December 1769

12 Even while they teach, men learn.
Seneca c.4 BC–AD 65: *Epistulae Morales*

13 He who can, does. He who cannot, teaches.
George Bernard Shaw 1856–1950: *Man and Superman* (1903)

14 A teacher should have maximal authority and minimal power.
Thomas Szasz 1920– : *The Second Sin* (1973) 'Education'

15 Delightful task! to rear the tender thought,
To teach the young idea how to shoot.
James Thomson 1700–48: *The Seasons* (1746) 'Spring'

16 I expect you'll be becoming a schoolmaster, sir. That's what most of

the gentlemen does, sir, that gets sent
down for indecent behaviour.
Evelyn Waugh 1903–66: *Decline and Fall*
(1928)

17 To reject didactic teaching is to reject
teaching itself.
Chris Woodhead 1946– : Melanie Phillips *All
Must Have Prizes* (1996)

Technology
....
see also **Inventions and Discoveries**,
Science

1 Science finds, industry applies, man
conforms.
Anonymous: subtitle of guidebook to
1933 Chicago World's Fair

2 The three fundamental Rules of
Robotics . . . One, a robot may not
injure a human being, or, through
inaction, allow a human being to
come to harm . . . Two . . . a robot
must obey the orders given it by
human beings except where such
orders would conflict with the First
Law . . . three, a robot must protect its
own existence as long as such
protection does not conflict with the
First or Second Laws.
Isaac Asimov 1920–92: *I, Robot* (1950)
'Runaround'

3 Inanimate objects are classified
scientifically into three major
categories—those that don't work,
those that break down, and those that
get lost.
Russell Baker 1925– : in *New York Times*
18 June 1968

4 I am a sundial, and I make a botch
Of what is done much better by a
watch.
Hilaire Belloc 1870–1953: 'On a Sundial' (1938)

5 The biggest obstacle to professional
writing is the necessity for changing a
typewriter ribbon.
Robert Benchley 1889–1945: *Chips off the old
Benchley* (1949) 'Learn to Write'

6 Your worship is your furnaces,
Which, like old idols, lost obscenes,
Have molten bowels; your vision is
Machines for making more machines.
Gordon Bottomley 1874–1948: 'To
Ironfounders and Others' (1912)

7 I sell here, Sir, what all the world
desires to have—POWER.
■ *of his engineering works*
Matthew Boulton 1728–1809: James Boswell
Life of Samuel Johnson (1791) 22 March 1776

8 Electric typewriters keep going
'mmmmmmm—what are you
waiting for?'
Anthony Burgess 1917–93: Clare Boylan (ed.)
The Agony and the Ego (1993)

9 Man is a tool-using animal . . .
Without tools he is nothing, with
tools he is all.
Thomas Carlyle 1795–1881: *Sartor Resartus*
(1834)

10 Any sufficiently advanced technology
is indistinguishable from magic.
Arthur C. Clarke 1917– : *Profiles of the Future*
(1962)

11 The first rule of intelligent tinkering is
to save all the parts.
Paul Ralph Ehrlich 1932– : in *Saturday Review*
5 June 1971

12 For a successful technology, reality
must take precedence over public
relations, for nature cannot be fooled.
Richard Phillips Feynman 1918–88: Appendix
to the *Rogers Commission Report on the Space
Shuttle Challenger Accident* 6 June 1986

13 Technology . . . the knack of so
arranging the world that we need not
experience it.
Max Frisch 1911–91: *Homo Faber* (1957)

14 Technology happens. It's not good,
it's not bad. Is steel good or bad?
Andrew Grove 1936– : in *Time* 29 December
1997

15 The thing with high-tech is that you
always end up using scissors.
David Hockney 1937– : in *Observer* 10 July
1994

16 This is not the age of pamphleteers. It
is the age of the engineers. The spark-
gap is mightier than the pen.
Lancelot Hogben 1895–1975: *Science for the
Citizen* (1938)

17 One machine can do the work of fifty ordinary men. No machine can do the work of one extraordinary man.
Elbert Hubbard 1859–1915: *Thousand and One Epigrams* (1911)

18 How very bold of you to buy an electric typewriter; the only time I tried one I was scared to death, as it seemed to be running away with me. I felt as if I had been put at the controls of Concorde after five minutes' tuition.
Philip Larkin 1922–85: letter to Anthony Powell, 7 August 1985

19 When this circuit learns your job, what are you going to do?
Marshall McLuhan 1911–80: *The Medium is the Massage* (1967)

20 The medium is the message.
Marshall McLuhan 1911–80: *Understanding Media* (1964)

21 Gutenberg made everybody a reader. Xerox makes everybody a publisher.
Marshall McLuhan 1911–80: in *Guardian Weekly* 12 June 1977

22 When you see something that is technically sweet, you go ahead and do it and you argue about what to do about it only after you have had your technical success. That is the way it was with the atomic bomb.
J. Robert Oppenheimer 1904–67: in *In the Matter of J. Robert Oppenheimer, USAEC Transcript of Hearing Before Personnel Security Board* (1954)

23 Machines are worshipped because they are beautiful, and valued because they confer power; they are hated because they are hideous, and loathed because they impose slavery.
Bertrand Russell 1872–1970: *Sceptical Essays* (1928) 'Machines and Emotions'

24 One servant is worth a thousand gadgets.
Joseph Alois Schumpeter 1883–1950: J. K. Galbraith *A Life in our Times* (1981)

25 But far above and far as sight endures
Like whips of anger
With lightning's danger

There runs the quick perspective of the future.
Stephen Spender 1909–95: 'The Pylons' (1933)

26 The things I want to show are mechanical. Machines have less problems.
Andy Warhol 1927–87: Mike Wrenn *Andy Warhol: In His Own Words* (1991)

27 The Britain that is going to be forged in the white heat of this revolution will be no place for restrictive practices or for outdated methods on either side of industry.
■ *usually quoted as 'the white heat of the technological revolution'*
Harold Wilson 1916–95: speech at the Labour Party Conference, 1 October 1963

28 JACKIE: (*very slowly*) Take Tube A and apply to Bracket D.
VICTORIA: Reading it slower does not make it any easier to do.
Victoria Wood 1953– : *Mens Sana in Thingummy Doodah* (1990)

Teetotalism

1 One reason why I don't drink is because I wish to know when I am having a good time.
Nancy Astor 1879–1964: in *Christian Herald* June 1960

2 Our country has deliberately undertaken a great social and economic experiment, noble in motive and far-reaching in purpose.
■ *on the Eighteenth Amendment enacting Prohibition*
Herbert Hoover 1874–1964: letter to Senator W. H. Borah, 23 February 1928

3 No verse can give pleasure for long, nor last, that is written by drinkers of water.
Horace 65–8 BC: *Epistles*

4 Prohibition makes you want to cry into your beer and denies you the beer to cry into.
Don Marquis 1878–1937: *Sun Dial Time* (1936)

5 I'd hate to be a teetotaller. Imagine getting up in the morning and knowing that's as good as you're going to feel all day.

Dean Martin 1917– : attributed; also attributed to Jimmy Durante

6 I'm only a beer teetotaller, not a champagne teetotaller.

George Bernard Shaw 1856–1950: *Candida* (1898)

7 Your lips, on my own, when they printed 'Farewell',
Had never been soiled by the 'beverage of hell';
But they come to me now with the bacchanal sign,
And the lips that touch liquor must never touch mine.

George W. Young 1846–1919: 'The Lips That Touch Liquor Must Never Touch Mine' (*c.*1870); also attributed, in a different form, to Harriet A. Glazebrook, 1874

Television
....

1 TV—a clever contraction derived from the words Terrible Vaudeville . . . we call it a medium because nothing's well done.

Goodman Ace 1899–1982: letter to Groucho Marx, *c.*1953

2 So much chewing gum for the eyes.

■ *small boy's definition of certain television programmes*

Anonymous: James Beasley Simpson *Best Quotes of '50, '55, '56* (1957)

3 Television . . . thrives on unreason, and unreason thrives on television . . . [It] strikes at the emotions rather than the intellect.

Robin Day 1923– : *Grand Inquisitor* (1989)

4 We exercise the ultimate sanction of switching off only in an extreme case, like a heroin addict rejecting the needle in the face of death.

■ *on television as an agent of cultural destruction*

Richard Eyre 1943– : attributed, 1995

5 Let's face it, there are no plain women on television.

Anna Ford 1943– : in *Observer* 23 September 1979

6 It's television, you see. If you are not on the thing every week, the public think you are either dead or deported.

Frankie Howerd 1922–92: attributed

7 Television is simultaneously blamed, often by the same people, for worsening the world and for being powerless to change it.

Clive James 1939– : *Glued to the Box* (1981)

8 For all its flexibility, television is more a mirror of taste than a shaper of it.

Russell Lynes 1910–91: *The Phenomenon of Change* (1984)

9 We are surfing food.

■ *of cable television*

Kelvin Mackenzie 1946– : in *Trouble at the Top* (BBC2) 12 February 1997

10 Television brought the brutality of war into the comfort of the living room. Vietnam was lost in the living rooms of America—not the battlefields of Vietnam.

Marshall McLuhan 1911–80: in *Montreal Gazette* 16 May 1975

11 When the politicians complain that TV turns their proceedings into a circus, it should be made plain that the circus was already there, and that TV has merely demonstrated that not all the performers are well trained.

Ed Murrow 1908–65: attributed, 1959

12 Television is actually closer to reality than anything in books. The madness of TV is the madness of human life.

Camille Paglia 1947– : in *Harper's Magazine* March 1991

13 Television has made dictatorship impossible, but democracy unbearable.

Shimon Peres 1923– : at a Davos meeting, in *Financial Times* 31 January 1995

14 If we may say that the Age of Andrew Jackson took political life out of the hands of aristocrats and turned it over to the masses, then we may say, with equal justification, that the Age of Television has taken politics away from the adult mind altogether.

Neil Postman 1931– : *The Disappearance of Childhood* (1982)

15 Nation shall speak peace unto nation.
Montague John Rendall 1862–1950: motto of the BBC; see **Peace** 4

16 Radio and television . . . have succeeded in lifting the manufacture of banality out of the sphere of handicraft and placed it in that of a major industry.
Nathalie Sarraute 1902– : in *Times Literary Supplement* 10 June 1960

17 *Television*? The word is half Greek, half Latin. No good can come of it.
C. P. Scott 1846–1932: Asa Briggs *The BBC: the First Fifty Years* (1985)

18 My show is the stupidest show on TV. If you are watching it, get a life. I would not watch my show. My show is a circus. That's all it is.
Jerry Springer 1944– : in *Independent on Sunday* 7 March 1999

19 A terminal blight has hit the TV industry nipping fun in the bud and stunting our growth. This blight is management—the dreaded Four M's: male, middle class, middle-aged and mediocre.
Janet Street-Porter 1946– : MacTaggart Lecture, Edinburgh Television Festival, 25 August 1995

20 Like having your own licence to print money.
■ *on the profitability of commercial television in Britain*
Roy Thomson 1894–1976: R. Braddon *Roy Thomson* (1965)

21 It is stupidvision—where most of the presenters look like they have to pretend to be stupid because they think their audience is . . . It patronises. It talks to the vacuum cleaner and the washing machine without much contact with the human brain.
■ *of daytime television*
Polly Toynbee 1946– : in *Daily Telegraph* 7 May 1996

22 It always makes me laugh when people ask why anyone would want to do a sitcom in America. If it runs five years, you never have to work again.
Twiggy 1949– : in *Independent* 4 October 1997

23 I hate television. I hate it as much as peanuts. But I can't stop eating peanuts.
Orson Welles 1915–85: in *New York Herald Tribune* 12 October 1956

24 It used to be that we in films were the lowest form of art. Now we have something to look down on.
■ *of television*
Billy Wilder 1906–2002: A. Madsen *Billy Wilder* (1968)

25 Television contracts the imagination and radio expands it.
Terry Wogan 1938– : attributed, 1984

Temptation

1 Watch and pray, that ye enter not into temptation: the spirit indeed is willing but the flesh is weak.
Bible: St Matthew

2 What's done we partly may compute, But know not what's resisted.
Robert Burns 1759–96: 'Address to the Unco Guid' (1787)

3 I've looked on a lot of women with lust. I've committed adultery in my heart many times. This is something that God recognizes I will do—and I have done it—and God forgives me for it.
Jimmy Carter 1924– : in *Playboy* November 1976

4 Who was it said a temptation resisted is a true measure of character? Certainly no one in Beverly Hills.
Joan Collins 1933– : in *Independent* 18 July 1998

5 The Lord above made liquor for temptation
To see if man could turn away from sin.
The Lord above made liquor for temptation—but
With a little bit of luck,

With a little bit of luck,
When temptation comes you'll give
right in!
Alan Jay Lerner 1918–86: 'With a Little Bit of
Luck' (1956 song)

6 He that but looketh on a plate of ham
and eggs to lust after it, hath already
committed breakfast with it in his
heart.
C. S. Lewis 1898–1963: letter 10 March 1954

7 This extraordinary pride in being
exempt from temptation that you
have not yet risen to the level of!
Eunuchs boasting of their chastity!
C. S. Lewis 1898–1963: 'Unreal Estates' in
Kingsley Amis and Robert Conquest (eds.)
Spectrum IV (1965)

8 If we are to be punished for the sins
we have committed, at least we should
be praised for our yearning for the
sins we have not committed.
■ *paraphrasing the poet Mirza Ghalib*
(1797–1849)
Jawaharlal Nehru 1889–1964: letter to Indira
Gandhi, 7 May 1943

9 Temptations came to him, in middle
age, tentatively and without
insistence, like a neglected butcher-
boy who asks for a Christmas box in
February for no more hopeful reason
than that he didn't get one in
December.
Saki 1870–1916: *The Chronicles of Clovis* (1911)

10   Is this her fault or mine?
The tempter or the tempted, who sins
most?
William Shakespeare 1564–1616: *Measure for
Measure* (1604)

11 It may almost be a question whether
such wisdom as many of us have in
our mature years has not come from
the dying out of the power of
temptation, rather than as the results
of thought and resolution.
Anthony Trollope 1815–82: *The Small House at
Allington* (1864)

12 There are several good protections
against temptations, but the surest is
cowardice.
Mark Twain 1835–1910: *Following the Equator*
(1897)

13 I can resist everything except
temptation.
Oscar Wilde 1854–1900: *Lady Windermere's
Fan* (1892)

Tennis

1 Love-thirty, love-forty, oh! weakness
of joy,
The speed of a swallow, the grace of a
boy,
With carefullest carelessness, gaily you
won,
I am weak from your loveliness, Joan
Hunter Dunn.
John Betjeman 1906–84: 'A Subaltern's Love-
Song' (1945)

2 I call tennis the McDonald's of
sport—you go in, they make a quick
buck out of you, and you're out.
Pat Cash 1965– : in *Independent on Sunday*
4 July 1999

3 New Yorkers love it when you spill
your guts out there. Spill your guts at
Wimbledon and they make you stop
and clean it up.
Jimmy Connors 1952– : at Flushing Meadow,
1984

4 You cannot be serious!
John McEnroe 1959– : said to tennis umpire
at Wimbledon, early 1980s

Terrorism

see also **Violence**

1 The Volkswagen parked in the gap,
But gently ticking over.
You wonder if it's lovers
And not men hurrying back
Across two fields and a river.
Paul Muldoon 1951– : 'Ireland' (1980)

2 We are especially not going to tolerate
these attacks from outlaw states run
by the strangest collection of misfits,
Looney Tunes, and squalid criminals
since the advent of the Third Reich.
Ronald Reagan 1911– : speech following the
hijack of a US plane, 8 July 1985

3 It is of little use trying to suppress
terrorism if the production of deadly

devices continues to be deemed a legitimate employment of man's creative powers.

E. F. Schumacher 1911–77: *Small is Beautiful* (1973)

4 We must try to find ways to starve the terrorist and the hijacker of the oxygen of publicity on which they depend.

Margaret Thatcher 1925– : speech, 15 July 1985

5 The terrible thing about terrorism is that ultimately it destroys those who practise it. Slowly but surely, as they try to extinguish life in others, the light within them dies.

Terry Waite 1939– : in *Guardian* 20 February 1992

Margaret Thatcher
1925–

1 The iron lady.

■ *in Soviet defence ministry newspaper* Red Star, *which accused her of trying to revive the cold war*

Anonymous: in *Sunday Times* 25 January 1976

2 Q: If Mrs Thatcher were run over by a bus . . . ?

LORD CARRINGTON: It wouldn't dare.

Lord Carrington 1919– : Russell Lewis *Margaret Thatcher* (1984)

3 She is so clearly the best man among them.

Barbara Castle 1910–2002: diary, 11 February 1975

4 She cannot see an institution without hitting it with her handbag.

Julian Critchley 1930–2000: in *The Times* 21 June 1982

5 She has no hinterland; in particular she has no sense of history.

Edna Healey 1918– : Denis Healey *The Time of My Life* (1989)

6 She has the eyes of Caligula, but the mouth of Marilyn Monroe.

François Mitterrand 1916–96: comment to his new European Minister Roland Dumas; in *Observer* 25 November 1990

7 A big cat detained briefly in a poodle parlour, sharpening her claws on the velvet.

■ *of Lady Thatcher in the House of Lords*

Matthew Parris 1949– : *Look Behind You!* (1993)

The Theatre

see also **Acting, Actors, Shakespeare**

1 I go to the theatre to be entertained, I want to be taken out of myself, I don't want to see lust and rape and incest and sodomy and so on, I can get all that at home.

Alan Bennett 1934– : Alan Bennett et al. *Beyond the Fringe* (1963) 'Man of Principles'

2 There's no business like show business.

Irving Berlin 1888–1989: title of song (1946)

3 The theatre exists in movement.

Peter Brook 1925– : *Threads of Time* (1998)

4 NINA: Your play's hard to act, there are no living people in it.

TREPLEV: Living people! We should show life neither as it is nor as it ought to be, but as we see it in our dreams.

Anton Chekhov 1860–1904: *The Seagull* (1896)

5 Things on stage should be as complicated and as simple as in life. People dine, just dine, while their happiness is made and their lives are smashed. If in Act 1 you have a pistol hanging on the wall, then it must fire in the last act.

Anton Chekhov 1860–1904: attributed; Donald Rayfield *Anton Chekhov* (1997)

6 *Étonne-moi.*

Astonish me.

■ *to Jean Cocteau*

Sergei Diaghilev 1872–1929: Wallace Fowlie (ed.) *Journals of Jean Cocteau* (1956)

7 Shaw is like a train. One just speaks the words and sits in one's place. But Shakespeare is like bathing in the sea—one swims where one wants.

Vivien Leigh 1913–67: letter from Harold Nicolson to Vita Sackville-West, 1 February 1956

8 Don't clap too hard—it's a very old building.
   John Osborne 1929–94: *The Entertainer* (1957)

9 The weasel under the cocktail cabinet.
   ■ *on being asked what his plays were about*
   Harold Pinter 1930– : J. Russell Taylor *Anger and After* (1962)

10 You've got to perform in a role hundreds of times. In keeping it fresh one can become a large, madly humming, demented refrigerator.
   Ralph Richardson 1902–83: in *Time* 21 August 1978

11 The play-bill, which is said to have announced the tragedy of Hamlet, the character of the Prince of Denmark being left out.
   ■ *commonly alluded to as 'Hamlet without the Prince'*
   Sir Walter Scott 1771–1832: *The Talisman* (1825)

12   Can this cockpit hold
   The vasty fields of France? or may we cram
   Within this wooden O the very casques
   That did affright the air at Agincourt?
   William Shakespeare 1564–1616: *Henry V* (1599)

13 The theatre is the only institution in the world which has been dying for four thousand years and has never succumbed.
   John Steinbeck 1902–68: *Once There Was a War* (1958)

14 I can do you blood and love without the rhetoric, and I can do you blood and rhetoric without the love, and I can do you all three concurrent or consecutive, but I can't do you love and rhetoric without the blood. Blood is compulsory—they're all blood, you see.
   Tom Stoppard 1937– : *Rosencrantz and Guildenstern are Dead* (1967)

15 I've never much enjoyed going to plays . . . The unreality of painted people standing on a platform saying things they've said to each other for months is more than I can overlook.
   John Updike 1932– : George Plimpton (ed.) *Writers at Work* 4th Series (1977)

16 We never closed.
   ■ *of the Windmill Theatre, London, during the Second World War*
   Vivian van Damm c.1889–1960: *Tonight and Every Night* (1952)

17 The soporific content of the majority of West End plays and the Cricket Test ambience of the theatre seems designed to keep a younger, hipper crew away.
   Irvine Welsh 1957– : in *The Times* 10 February 1999

18 It's a sound you can't get in the movies or television . . . the sound of a wonderful, deep silence that means you've hit them where they live.
   Shelley Winters 1922– : in *Theatre Arts* June 1956

Theory

see also **Experiment**, **Facts**, **Ideas**, **Science**

1 When, however, the lay public rallies around an idea that is denounced by distinguished but elderly scientists and supports that idea with great fervour and emotion—the distinguished but elderly scientists are then, after all, probably right.
   ■ *corollary to Arthur C. Clarke's law; see 2 below*
   Isaac Asimov 1920–92: Arthur C. Clarke 'Asimov's Corollary' in K. Frazier (ed.) *Paranormal Borderlands of Science* (1981)

2 If an elderly but distinguished scientist says that something is possible he is almost certainly right, but if he says that it is impossible he is very probably wrong.
   Arthur C. Clarke 1917– : in *New Yorker* 9 August 1969; cf. 1 above

3 False views, if supported by some evidence, do little harm, for everyone takes a salutary pleasure in proving their falseness.
   Charles Darwin 1809–82: *The Descent of Man* (1871)

4 It is a capital mistake to theorize before you have all the evidence. It biases the judgement.
Arthur Conan Doyle 1859–1930: *A Study in Scarlet* (1888)

5 The grand aim of all science [is] to cover the greatest number of empirical facts by logical deduction from the smallest possible number of hypotheses or axioms.
Albert Einstein 1879–1955: Lincoln Barnett *The Universe and Dr Einstein* (1950 ed.)

6 With five free parameters, a theorist could fit the profile of an elephant.
George Gamow 1904–68: attributed; in *Nature* 21 June 1990

7 The great tragedy of Science—the slaying of a beautiful hypothesis by an ugly fact.
T. H. Huxley 1825–95: *Collected Essays* (1893–4) 'Biogenesis and Abiogenesis'

8 It is a good morning exercise for a research scientist to discard a pet hypothesis every day before breakfast. It keeps him young.
Konrad Lorenz 1903–89: *Das Sogenannte Böse* (1963; translated by Marjorie Latzke as *On Aggression*, 1966)

9 How seldom is it that theories stand the wear and tear of practice!
Anthony Trollope 1815–82: *Thackeray* (1879)

10 No *good* model ever accounted for *all* the facts since some data was bound to be misleading if not plain wrong.
James D. Watson 1928– : Francis Crick *Some Mad Pursuit* (1988)

Thinking

see also **Ideas**, **The Mind**

1 To change your mind and to follow him who sets you right is to be nonetheless the free agent that you were before.
Marcus Aurelius AD 121–80: *Meditations*

2 He can't think without his hat.
Samuel Beckett 1906–89: *Waiting for Godot* (1955)

3 Stung by the splendour of a sudden thought.
Robert Browning 1812–89: 'A Death in the Desert' (1864)

4 What was once thought can never be unthought.
Friedrich Dürrenmatt 1921– : *The Physicists* (1962)

5 *Je pense, donc je suis.*
I think, therefore I am.
■ *usually quoted as, 'Cogito, ergo sum', from the 1641 Latin edition*
René Descartes 1596–1650: *Le Discours de la méthode* (1637)

6 It is quite a three-pipe problem, and I beg that you won't speak to me for fifty minutes.
Arthur Conan Doyle 1859–1930: *The Adventures of Sherlock Holmes* (1892)

7 How can I tell what I think till I see what I say?
E. M. Forster 1879–1970: *Aspects of the Novel* (1927)

8 It is a far, far better thing to have a firm anchor in nonsense than to put out on the troubled seas of thought.
J. K. Galbraith 1908– : *The Affluent Society* (1958)

9 A man of action forced into a state of thought is unhappy until he can get out of it.
John Galsworthy 1867–1933: *Maid in Waiting* (1931)

10 To daze with little bells the spirit that would think.
Victor Hugo 1802–85: *Le Roi s'amuse* (1833)

11 Two things fill the mind with ever new and increasing wonder and awe, the more often and the more seriously reflection concentrates upon them: the starry heaven above me and the moral law within me.
Immanuel Kant 1724–1804: *Critique of Practical Reason* (1788)

12 *I think, therefore I am* is the statement of an intellectual who underrates toothaches.
Milan Kundera 1929– : *Immortality* (1991)

13 She did her work with the thoroughness of a mind which reveres

details and never quite understands them.
Sinclair Lewis 1885–1951: *Babbitt* (1922)

14 Pooh began to feel a little more comfortable, because when you are a Bear of Very Little Brain, and you Think of Things, you find sometimes that a Thing which seemed very Thingish inside you is quite different when it gets out into the open and has other people looking at it.
A. A. Milne 1882–1956: *The House at Pooh Corner* (1928)

15 *Doublethink* means the power of holding two contradictory beliefs in one's mind simultaneously, and accepting both of them.
George Orwell 1903–50: *Nineteen Eighty-Four* (1949)

16 I don't mind your thinking slowly: I mind your publishing faster than you think.
Wolfgang Pauli 1900–58: attributed

17 The question of whether a mechanical device could ever be said to think— perhaps even to experience feelings, or to have a mind—is not really a new one. But it has been given a new impetus, even an urgency, by the advent of modern computer technology.
Roger Penrose 1931– : *The Emperor's New Mind* (1989)

18 Sometimes I sits and thinks, and then again I just sits.
Punch: 24 October 1906

19 The real question is not whether machines think but whether men do.
B. F. Skinner 1904–90: *Contingencies of Reinforcement* (1969)

20 How often misused words generate misleading thoughts.
Herbert Spencer 1820–1903: *Principles of Ethics* (1879)

21 Heretics are the only bitter remedy against the entropy of human thought.
Yevgeny Zamyatin 1884–1937: 'Literature, Revolution and Entropy' quoted in *The Dragon and other Stories* (1967) introduction

Time
....
see also **The Future, The Past, The Present, Transience**

1 Every instant of time is a pinprick of eternity.
Marcus Aurelius AD 121–80: *Meditations*

2 VLADIMIR: That passed the time.
ESTRAGON: It would have passed in any case.
VLADIMIR: Yes, but not so rapidly.
Samuel Beckett 1906–89: *Waiting for Godot* (1955)

3 I am Time grown old to destroy the world,
Embarked on the course of world annihilation.
Bhagavad Gita 250 BC–AD 250: ch. 11

4 Men talk of killing time, while time quietly kills them.
Dion Boucicault 1820–90: *London Assurance* (1841)

5 He said, 'What's time? Leave Now for dogs and apes!
Man has Forever.'
Robert Browning 1812–89: 'A Grammarian's Funeral' (1855)

6 I recommend to you to take care of minutes: for hours will take care of themselves.
Lord Chesterfield 1694–1773: *Letters to his Son* (1774) 6 November 1747

7 Time has too much credit . . . It is not a great healer. It is an indifferent and perfunctory one. Sometimes it does not heal at all. And sometimes when it seems to, no healing has been necessary.
Ivy Compton-Burnett 1884–1969: *Darkness and Day* (1951)

8 Time is the great physician.
Benjamin Disraeli 1804–81: *Henrietta Temple* (1837)

9 The distinction between past, present and future is only an illusion, however persistent.
Albert Einstein 1879–1955: letter to Michelangelo Besso, 21 March 1955

10 Time present and time past
Are both perhaps present in time future,
And time future contained in time past.
T. S. Eliot 1888–1965: *Four Quartets* 'Burnt Norton' (1936)

11 Remember that time is money.
Benjamin Franklin 1706–90: *Advice to a Young Tradesman* (1748)

12 Time is . . . Time was . . . Time is past.
Robert Greene c.1560–92: *Friar Bacon and Friar Bungay* (1594)

13 Time, you old gipsy man,
Will you not stay,
Put up your caravan
Just for one day?
Ralph Hodgson 1871–1962: 'Time, You Old Gipsy Man' (1917)

14 But at my back I always hear
Time's wingèd chariot hurrying near:
And yonder all before us lie
Deserts of vast eternity.
Andrew Marvell 1621–78: 'To His Coy Mistress' (1681)

15 *Tempus edax rerum.*
Time the devourer of everything.
Ovid 43 BC–AD c.17: *Metamorphoses*

16 Even such is Time, which takes in trust
Our youth, our joys, and all we have,
And pays us but with age and dust.
Walter Ralegh c.1552–1618: written the night before his death, and found in his Bible in the Gate-house at Westminster

17 Half our life is spent trying to find something to do with the time we have rushed through life trying to save.
Will Rogers 1879–1935: letter in *New York Times* 29 April 1930

18 Three o'clock is always too late or too early for anything you want to do.
Jean-Paul Sartre 1905–80: *La Nausée* (1938)

19 Ah! the clock is always slow;
It is later than you think.
Robert W. Service 1874–1958: 'It Is Later Than You Think' (1921)

20 To-morrow, and to-morrow, and to-morrow,
Creeps in this petty pace from day to day,
To the last syllable of recorded time;
And all our yesterdays have lighted fools
The way to dusty death.
William Shakespeare 1564–1616: *Macbeth* (1606)

21 Eternity's a terrible thought. I mean, where's it all going to end?
Tom Stoppard 1937– : *Rosencrantz and Guildenstern are Dead* (1967)

22 As if you could kill time without injuring eternity.
Henry David Thoreau 1817–62: *Walden* (1854) 'Economy'

23 Time is
Too slow for those who wait,
Too swift for those who fear,
Too long for those who grieve,
Too short for those who rejoice;
But for those who love,
Time is eternity.
Henry Van Dyke 1852–1933: 'Time is too slow for those who wait' (1905), read at the funeral of Diana, Princess of Wales; the original form of the last line is 'Time is not'

24 *Sed fugit interea, fugit inreparabile tempus.*
But meanwhile it is flying, irretrievable time is flying.
■ *usually quoted as* 'tempus fugit [time flies]'
Virgil 70–19 BC: *Georgics*

25 The years like great black oxen tread the world,
And God the herdsman goads them on behind,
And I am broken by their passing feet.
W. B. Yeats 1865–1939: *The Countess Cathleen* (1895)

Titles

see also **Aristocracy**, **Class**

1 Not a reluctant peer but a persistent commoner.
■ *of his ultimately successful fight to disclaim his inherited title of Viscount Stansgate*
Tony Benn 1925– : at a press conference, 23 November 1960

2 Tyndall, I must remain plain Michael Faraday to the last; and let me now tell you, that if I accepted the honour which the Royal Society desires to confer upon me, I would not answer for the integrity of my intellect for a single year.

■ *on being offered the Presidency of the Royal Society*
Michael Faraday 1791–1867: J. Tyndall *Faraday as a Discoverer* (1868)

3 When I want a peerage, I shall buy it like an honest man.
Lord Northcliffe 1865–1922: Tom Driberg *Swaff* (1974)

4 There is no stronger craving in the world than that of the rich for titles, except perhaps that of the titled for riches.
Hesketh Pearson 1887–1964: *The Pilgrim Daughters* (1961)

5 Titles distinguish the mediocre, embarrass the superior, and are disgraced by the inferior.
George Bernard Shaw 1856–1950: *Man and Superman* (1903)

6 She needed no royal title to continue to generate her particular brand of magic.
■ *of his sister, Diana, Princess of Wales*
Lord Spencer 1964– : tribute at her funeral, 7 September 1997

7 What harm have I ever done to the Labour Party?
■ *declining the offer of a peerage*
R. H. Tawney 1880–1962: in *Evening Standard* 18 January 1962

Tolerance

see also **Compromise**, **Impartiality**, **Prejudice**

1 Hear the other side.
St Augustine of Hippo AD 354–430: *De Duabus Animabus contra Manicheos*

2 Judge not, that ye be not judged.
Bible: St Matthew

3 There is, however, a limit at which forbearance ceases to be a virtue.
Edmund Burke 1729–97: *Observations on a late Publication on the Present State of the Nation* (2nd ed., 1769)

4 Make hatred hated!
Anatole France 1844–1924: speech to public school teachers in Tours, August 1919

5 Tolerance is only another name for indifference.
W. Somerset Maugham 1874–1965: *A Writer's Notebook* (1949) written in 1896

6 We should therefore claim, in the name of tolerance, the right not to tolerate the intolerant.
Karl Popper 1902–94: *The Open Society and Its Enemies* (1945)

7 You might as well fall flat on your face as lean over too far backward.
James Thurber 1894–1961: 'The Bear Who Let It Alone' in *New Yorker* 29 April 1939

Trade Unions

see also **Employment**, **Work**

1 Had the employers of past generations all of them dealt fairly with their men there would have been no unions.
Stanley Baldwin 1867–1947: speech in Birmingham, 14 January 1931

2 The most conservative man in this world is the British Trade Unionist when you want to change him.
Ernest Bevin 1881–1951: speech, Trades Union Congress, 8 September 1927

3 I had known it was going to be a 'winter of discontent'.
■ *echoing Shakespeare's* Richard III
James Callaghan 1912– : television interview, 8 February 1979

4 Not a penny off the pay, not a second on the day.
■ *often quoted with 'minute' substituted for 'second'*
A. J. Cook 1885–1931: speech at York, 3 April 1926

5 Industrial relations are like sexual relations. It's better between two consenting parties.
Vic Feather 1908–76: in *Guardian Weekly* 8 August 1976

6 Class v. class, bitter as before,
The unending violence of US and
THEM,
personified in 1984
by Coal Board MacGregor and the
NUM.
  Tony Harrison 1953– : *v* (1985)

7 You cannot argue for democracy in
the workplace unless you have the
mechanisms for democracy in your
internal organization.
  Bill Morris 1938– : speech to trade unionists,
London, February 1994

8 Worker's control means the castration
of the trade union.
  Arthur Scargill 1938– : in *Observer*
31 December 1978

9 'Solidarity' means taking care of the
person standing next to you.
  Lech Wałęsa 1943– : speech, Gdansk, Poland,
May 1988

Tradition

1 One can't carry one's father's corpse
about everywhere.
  Guillaume Apollinaire 1880–1918: *Les peintres
cubistes* (1965)

2 Tradition means giving votes to the
most obscure of all classes, our
ancestors. It is the democracy of the
dead.
  G. K. Chesterton 1874–1936: *Orthodoxy* (1908)

3 The tradition of all the dead
generations weighs like a nightmare
on the brain of the living.
  Karl Marx 1818–83: *The Eighteenth Brumaire
of Louis Bonaparte* (1852)

4 But to my mind,—though I am native
here,
And to the manner born,—it is a
custom
More honoured in the breach than the
observance.
  William Shakespeare 1564–1616: *Hamlet*
(1601)

5 Tradition is entirely different from
habit, even from an excellent habit,
since habit is by definition an
unconscious acquisition and tends to
become mechanical, whereas
tradition results from a conscious and
deliberate acceptance . . . Tradition
presupposes the reality of what
endures.
  Igor Stravinsky 1882–1971: *Poetics of Music*
(1947)

Tragedy

see also **Suffering**

1 Tragedy is clean, it is restful, it is
flawless.
  Jean Anouilh 1910–87: *Antigone* (1944)

2 Tragedy is thus a representation of an
action that is worth serious attention,
complete in itself and of some
amplitude . . . by means of pity and
fear bringing about the purgation of
such emotions.
  Aristotle 384–322 BC: *Poetics*

3 What the American public always
wants is a tragedy with a happy
ending.
  William Dean Howells 1837–1920: to Edith
Wharton in October 1906

4 That was how his life happened.
No mad hooves galloping in the sky,
But the weak, washy way of true
tragedy—
A sick horse nosing around the
meadow for a clean place to die.
  Patrick Kavanagh 1904–67: 'The Great
Hunger' (1947)

5 Tragedy ought really to be a great kick
at misery.
  D. H. Lawrence 1885–1930: letter to A. W.
McLeod, 6 October 1912

6 The bad end unhappily, the good
unluckily. That is what tragedy
means.
  Tom Stoppard 1937– : *Rosencrantz and
Guildenstern are Dead* (1967)

7 The composition of a tragedy requires
testicles.
  ■ *on being asked why no woman had ever
written 'a tolerable tragedy'*
  Voltaire 1694–1778: letter from Byron to John
Murray, 2 April 1817

Transience

see also **Opportunity**, **Time**

1 All flesh is as grass, and all the glory of man as the flower of grass. The grass withereth, and the flower thereof falleth away.
Bible: I Peter

2 He who binds to himself a joy
Doth the winged life destroy
But he who kisses the joy as it flies
Lives in Eternity's sunrise.
William Blake 1757–1827: *MS Note-Book*

3 We are all of us balloons dancing in a world of pins.
Anthony Montague Browne 1923– : *Long Sunset* (1995)

4 A rainbow and a cuckoo's song
May never come together again;
May never come
This side the tomb.
W. H. Davies 1871–1940: 'A Great Time' (1914)

5 Treaties, you see, are like girls and roses: they last while they last.
Charles de Gaulle 1890–1970: speech at Elysée Palace, 2 July 1963

6 Look thy last on all things lovely,
Every hour.
Walter de la Mare 1873–1956: 'Fare Well' (1918)

7 They are not long, the days of wine and roses:
Out of a misty dream
Our path emerges for a while, then closes
Within a dream.
Ernest Dowson 1867–1900: 'Vitae Summa Brevis' (1896)

8 Gather ye rosebuds while ye may,
Old Time is still a-flying:
And this same flower that smiles to-day,
To-morrow will be dying.
Robert Herrick 1591–1674: 'To the Virgins, to Make Much of Time' (1648)

9 Like that of leaves is a generation of men.
Homer 8th century BC: *The Iliad*

10 He will be just like the scent on a pocket handkerchief.
■ *on being asked what place Arthur Balfour would have in history*
David Lloyd George 1863–1945: Thomas Jones diary 9 June 1922

11 The sunlight on the garden
Hardens and grows cold,
We cannot cage the minute
Within its net of gold.
Louis MacNeice 1907–63: 'Sunlight on the Garden' (1938)

12 I never nursed a dear gazelle,
To glad me with its soft black eye,
But when it came to know me well,
And love me, it was sure to die!
Thomas Moore 1779–1852: *Lalla Rookh* (1817) 'The Fire-Worshippers'; cf. **Disillusion** 2, **Value** 4

13 Ev'ry day a little death
On the lips and in the eyes,
In the murmurs, in the pauses,
In the gestures, in the sighs.
Ev'ry day a little dies.
Stephen Sondheim 1930– : 'Every Day a Little Death' (1973 song)

14 The rainbow comes and goes,
And lovely is the rose.
William Wordsworth 1770–1850: 'Ode. Intimations of Immortality' (1807)

Translation

1 The original is unfaithful to the translation.
■ *on Henley's translation of Beckford's* Vathek
Jorge Luis Borges 1899–1986: *Sobre el 'Vathek' de William Beckford* (1974)

2 Translations (like wives) are seldom strictly faithful if they are in the least attractive.
Roy Campbell 1901–57: in *Poetry Review* June-July 1949

3 The vanity of translation; it were as wise to cast a violet into a crucible that you might discover the formal principle of its colour and odour, as seek to transfuse from one language to another the creations of a poet. The

plant must spring again from its seed,
or it will bear no flower.
Percy Bysshe Shelley 1792–1822: *A Defence of Poetry* (written 1821)

4 It has never occurred to Anderson
that one foreign language can be
translated into another. He assumes
that every strange tongue exists only
by virtue of its not being English.
Tom Stoppard 1937– : *Where Are They Now?* (1973)

5 A translation is no translation unless
it will give you the music of a poem
along with the words of it.
John Millington Synge 1871–1909: *The Aran Islands* (1907)

Travel

·················
see also **Exploration, Holidays, Maps**

1 Travel, in the younger sort, is a part of
education; in the elder, a part of
experience. He that travelleth into a
country before he hath some entrance
into the language, goeth to school,
and not to travel.
Francis Bacon 1561–1626: *Essays* (1625) 'Of Travel'

2 In America there are two classes of
travel—first class, and with children.
Robert Benchley 1889–1945: *Pluck and Luck* (1925)

3 What an odd thing tourism is. You fly
off to a strange land, eagerly
abandoning all the comforts of home,
and then expend vast quantities of
time and money in a largely futile
attempt to recapture the comforts
that you wouldn't have lost if you
hadn't left home in the first place.
Bill Bryson 1951– : *Neither Here Nor There* (1991)

4 See one promontory (said Socrates of
old), one mountain, one sea, one
river, and see all.
Robert Burton 1577–1640: *The Anatomy of Melancholy* (1621–51)

5 When you set out for Ithaka
ask that your way be long.
Constantine Cavafy 1863–1933: 'Ithaka' (1911)

6 I like my 'abroad' to be Catholic and
sensual.
Henry ('Chips') Channon 1897–1958: diary
18 January 1924

7 Why do the wrong people travel,
travel, travel,
When the right people stay back
home?
Noël Coward 1899–1973: 'Why do the Wrong People Travel?' (1961 song)

8 São Paulo is like Reading, only much
farther away.
Peter Fleming 1907–71: *Brazilian Adventure* (1933)

9 Worth seeing, yes; but not worth
going to see.
■ *on the Giant's Causeway*
Samuel Johnson 1709–84: James Boswell *Life of Samuel Johnson* (1791) 12 October 1779

10 Of all noxious animals, too, the most
noxious is a tourist. And of all tourists
the most vulgar, ill-bred, offensive
and loathsome is the British tourist.
Francis Kilvert 1840–79: diary 5 April 1870

11 Thanks to the interstate highway
system, it is now possible to travel
from coast to coast without seeing
anything.
Charles Kuralt 1934–97: *On the Road* (1980)

12 A good traveller is one who does not
know where he is going to, and a
perfect traveller does not know where
he came from.
Lin Yutang 1895–1976: *The Importance of Living* (1938)

13 Frogs . . . are slightly better than Huns
or Wops, but abroad is unutterably
bloody and foreigners are fiends.
Nancy Mitford 1904–73: *The Pursuit of Love* (1945)

14 A man travels the world in search of
what he needs and returns home to
find it.
George Moore 1852–1933: *The Brook Kerith* (1916)

15 It is very much better to go out in a
bowler and speaking Spanish than in
a sombrero and speaking English.
Prince Philip, Duke of Edinburgh 1921– : in
Observer 15 April 1962

16 In the middle ages people were tourists because of their religion, whereas now they are tourists because tourism is their religion.
   Robert Runcie 1921–99: speech in London, 6 December 1988

17 In these days of rapid and convenient travel . . . to come from Leighton Buzzard does not necessarily denote any great strength of character. It might only mean mere restlessness.
   Saki 1870–1916: *The Chronicles of Clovis* (1911)

18 For my part, I travel not to go anywhere, but to go. I travel for travel's sake. The great affair is to move.
   Robert Louis Stevenson 1850–94: *Travels with a Donkey* (1879)

19 To travel hopefully is a better thing than to arrive, and the true success is to labour.
   Robert Louis Stevenson 1850–94: *Virginibus Puerisque* (1881)

20 In Turkey it was always 1952, in Malaysia 1937; Afghanistan was 1910 and Bolivia 1949. It is twenty years ago in the Soviet Union, ten in Norway, five in France. It is always last year in Australia and next week in Japan.
   Paul Theroux 1941– : *The Kingdom by the Sea* (1983)

21 It is not worthwhile to go around the world to count the cats in Zanzibar.
   Henry David Thoreau 1817–62: *Walden* (1854) 'Conclusion'

22 Commuter—one who spends his life In riding to and from his wife; A man who shaves and takes a train, And then rides back to shave again.
   E. B. White 1899–1985: 'The Commuter' (1982)

Trees

1 Under the cherry— blossom soup, blossom salad.
   Matsuo Basho 1644–94: translated by Lucien Stryk

2 I am for the woods against the world, But are the woods for me?
   Edmund Blunden 1896–1974: 'The Kiss' (1931)

3 Generations pass while some trees stand, and old families last not three oaks.
   Thomas Browne 1605–82: *Hydriotaphia* (Urn Burial, 1658)

4 I like trees because they seem more resigned to the way they have to live than other things do.
   Willa Cather 1873–1947: *O Pioneers!* (1913)

5 For pines are gossip pines the wide world through And full of runic tales to sigh or sing.
   James Elroy Flecker 1884–1915: *Golden Journey to Samarkand* (1913) 'Brumana'

6 The woods are lovely, dark and deep. But I have promises to keep, And miles to go before I sleep, And miles to go before I sleep.
   Robert Frost 1874–1963: 'Stopping by Woods on a Snowy Evening' (1923)

7 He that plants trees loves others beside himself.
   Thomas Fuller 1654–1734: *Gnomologia* (1732)

8 Loveliest of trees, the cherry now Is hung with bloom along the bough, And stands about the woodland ride Wearing white for Eastertide.
   A. E. Housman 1859–1936: *A Shropshire Lad* (1896)

9 I think that I shall never see A poem lovely as a tree.
   Joyce Kilmer 1886–1918: 'Trees' (1914); cf. **Environment** 15

10 Of all the trees that grow so fair, Old England to adorn, Greater are none beneath the Sun, Than Oak, and Ash, and Thorn.
   Rudyard Kipling 1865–1936: *Puck of Pook's Hill* (1906) 'A Tree Song'

11 Woodman, spare that tree! Touch not a single bough! In youth it sheltered me, And I'll protect it now.
   George Pope Morris 1802–64: 'Woodman, Spare That Tree' (1830)

12 Now dream
of that sweet
equal republic
where the juniper
talks to the oak,
the thistle,
the bandaged elm,
and the jolly jolly chestnut.

    Tom Paulin 1949– : 'The Book of Juniper'
    (1983)

13 Willows whiten, aspens quiver,
Little breezes dusk and shiver.

    Alfred, Lord Tennyson 1809–92: 'The Lady of
    Shalott' (1832, revised 1842)

14 Laburnums, dropping-wells of fire.

    Alfred, Lord Tennyson 1809–92: *In Memoriam
    A. H. H.* (1850)

Trials

see also **Justice, Laws**

1 If ever there was a case of clearer
evidence than this of persons acting
together, this case is that case.

    William Arabin 1773–1841: H. B. Churchill
    Arabiniana (1843)

2 That four great nations, flushed with
victory and stung with injury, stay the
hands of vengeance and voluntarily
submit their captive enemies to the
judgement of the law, is one of the
most significant tributes that Power
has ever paid to Reason.

    Robert H. Jackson 1892–1954: opening
    statement for the prosecution, International
    Military Tribunal in Nuremberg,
    21 November 1945

3 You may object that it is not a trial at
all; you are quite right, for it is only a
trial if I recognize it as such.

    Franz Kafka 1883–1924: *The Trial* (1925)

4 The art of cross-examination is not
the art of examining crossly. It's the
art of leading the witness through a
line of propositions he agrees to until
he's forced to agree to the *one fatal
question.*

    Clifford Mortimer d. 1960: John Mortimer
    Clinging to the Wreckage (1982)

5 Not only did we play the race card, we
played it from the bottom of the deck.

    ■ *on the defence's conduct of the O. J. Simpson
    trial*

    Robert Shapiro 1942– : interview, 3 October
    1995

6 Asking the ignorant to use the
incomprehensible to decide the
unknowable.

    ■ *on the jury system*

    Hiller B. Zobel 1932– : 'The Jury on Trial' in
    American Heritage July–August 1995

Trust

see also **Betrayal, Faithfulness**

1 Would you buy a used car from this
man?

    Anonymous: campaign slogan directed
    against Richard Nixon, 1968

2 Suspicions amongst thoughts are like
bats amongst birds, they ever fly by
twilight.

    Francis Bacon 1561–1626: *Essays* (1625) 'Of
    Suspicion'

3 The thing on the blind side of the
heart,
On the wrong side of the door,
The green plant groweth, menacing
Almighty lovers in the Spring;
There is always a forgotten thing,
And love is not secure.

    G. K. Chesterton 1874–1936: *The Ballad of the
    White Horse* (1911)

4 Frankly speaking it is difficult to trust
the Chinese. Once bitten by a snake
you feel suspicious even when you see
a piece of rope.

    Dalai Lama 1935– : attributed, 1981

5 To trust people is a luxury in which
only the wealthy can indulge; the poor
cannot afford it.

    E. M. Forster 1879–1970: *Howards End* (1910)

6 It is better to suffer wrong than to do
it, and happier to be sometimes
cheated than not to trust.

    Samuel Johnson 1709–84: in *Rambler*
    18 December 1750

7 *Quis custodiet ipsos custodes?*
Who is to guard the guards
themselves?
Juvenal AD c.60–c.130: *Satires*

8 It is more shameful to doubt one's
friends than to be duped by them.
Duc de la Rochefoucauld 1613–80: *Maximes*
(1678)

9 After first confidences between people
moving towards friendship, a rest
between exchanges of information
somehow hastens, not impedes, the
growing trust.
Candia McWilliam 1955– : *Debatable Land*
(1994)

10 A promise made is a debt unpaid, and
the trail has its own stern code.
Robert W. Service 1874–1958: 'The Cremation
of Sam McGee' (1907)

11 And trust me not at all or all in all.
Alfred, Lord Tennyson 1809–92: *Idylls of the
King* 'Merlin and Vivien' (1859)

12 We have to distrust each other. It's our
only defence against betrayal.
Tennessee Williams 1911–83: *Camino Real*
(1953)

13 He trusted neither of them as far as he
could spit, and he was a poor spitter,
lacking both distance and control.
P. G. Wodehouse 1881–1975: *Money in the
Bank* (1946)

Truth

. . . .
see also **Honesty, Lies**

1 The truth is often a terrible weapon of
aggression. It is possible to lie, and
even to murder, for the truth.
Alfred Adler 1870–1937: *The Problems of
Neurosis* (1929)

2 The truth which makes men free is for
the most part the truth which men
prefer not to hear.
Herbert Agar 1897–1980: *A Time for Greatness*
(1942)

3 It contains a misleading impression,
not a lie. It was being economical with
the truth.
■ *the phrase 'economy of truth' was earlier used
by Edmund Burke (1729–97)*
Robert Armstrong 1927– : referring to a letter
during the 'Spycatcher' trial, Supreme
Court, New South Wales, in *Daily Telegraph*
19 November 1986

4 What is truth? said jesting Pilate; and
would not stay for an answer.
Francis Bacon 1561–1626: *Essays* (1625) 'Of
Truth'

5 A platitude is simply a truth repeated
until people get tired of hearing it.
Stanley Baldwin 1867–1947: speech, House of
Commons, 29 May 1924

6 And ye shall know the truth, and the
truth shall make you free.
Bible: St John

7 A truth that's told with bad intent
Beats all the lies you can invent.
William Blake 1757–1827: 'Auguries of
Innocence' (c.1803)

8 One of the favourite maxims of my
father was the distinction between the
two sorts of truths, profound truths
recognized by the fact that the
opposite is also a profound truth, in
contrast to trivialities where opposites
are obviously absurd.
Niels Bohr 1885–1962: S. Rozental *Niels Bohr*
(1967)

9 Many from . . . an inconsiderate zeal
unto truth, have too rashly charged
the troops of error, and remain as
trophies unto the enemies of truth.
Thomas Browne 1605–82: *Religio Medici*
(1643)

10 'Tis strange—but true; for truth is
always strange;
Stranger than fiction.
Lord Byron 1788–1824: *Don Juan* (1819–24)

11 What I tell you three times is true.
Lewis Carroll 1832–98: *The Hunting of the
Snark* (1876)

12 An exaggeration is a truth that has lost
its temper.
Kahlil Gibran 1883–1931: *Sand and Foam*
(1926)

13 Truth, like a torch, the more it's shook it shines.

William Hamilton 1788–1856: *Discussions on Philosophy* (1852)

14 Truth is not merely what we are thinking, but also why, to whom and under what circumstances we say it.

Václav Havel 1936– : *Temptation* (1985)

15 It ain't necessarily so,
It ain't necessarily so,
De t'ings dat yo' li'ble
To read in de Bible
It ain't necessarily so.

Du Bose Heyward 1885–1940 and **Ira Gershwin** 1896–1983: 'It ain't necessarily so' (1935)

16 It is the customary fate of new truths to begin as heresies and to end as superstitions.

T. H. Huxley 1825–95: *Science and Culture and Other Essays* (1881) 'The Coming of Age of the Origin of Species'

17 Truth is a pathless land, and you cannot approach it by any path whatsoever, by any religion, by any sect.

Jiddu Krishnamurti 1895–1986: speech in Holland, 3 August 1929

18 It is one thing to show a man that he is in error, and another to put him in possession of truth.

John Locke 1632–1704: *An Essay concerning Human Understanding* (1690)

19 He who does not bellow the truth when he knows the truth makes himself the accomplice of liars and forgers.

Charles Péguy 1873–1914: *Basic Verities* (1943) 'Lettre du Provincial' 21 December 1899

20 But, my dearest Agathon, it is truth which you cannot contradict; you can without any difficulty contradict Socrates.

Socrates 469–399 BC: Plato *Symposium*

21 In exceptional circumstances it is necessary to say something that is untrue in the House of Commons.

William Waldegrave 1946– : in *Guardian* 9 March 1994

22 There are no whole truths; all truths are half-truths. It is trying to treat them as whole truths that plays the devil.

Alfred North Whitehead 1861–1947: *Dialogues* (1954)

23 The truth is rarely pure, and never simple.

Oscar Wilde 1854–1900: *The Importance of Being Earnest* (1895)

Twentieth Century

1 Will the last generation of the twentieth century differ very much from the first? Will they be healthier and longer-lived, wiser, better, and more intelligent, or will they remain substantially the same as the people we have known and the people whom history has portrayed to us?

Anonymous: in *The Times* 1 January 1901

2 Everything is becoming science fiction. From the margins of an almost invisible literature has sprung the intact reality of the 20th century.

J. G. Ballard 1930– : 'Fictions of Every Kind' in *Books and Bookmen* February 1971

3 What we may be witnessing is not just the end of the Cold War but the end of history as such: that is, the end point of man's ideological evolution and the universalism of Western liberal democracy.

Francis Fukuyama 1952– : in *Independent* 20 September 1989

4 For 80 per cent of humanity the Middle Ages ended suddenly in the 1950s; or perhaps better still, they were *felt* to end in the 1960s.

Eric Hobsbawm 1917– : *Age of Extremes* (1994)

5 Momentum was part of the exhilaration and the exhaustion of the twentieth century which Coward decoded for the British but borrowed wholesale from the Americans.

John Lahr 1941– : in *New Yorker* 9 September 1996

6 The Nineteenth Century. The
Twentieth Century.
There were never any others. No
centuries before these.
Dante was not hailed in his time as an
Authentic
Fourteenth Century Voice. Nor did
Cromwell thunder.
After all, in the bowels of Christ, this
is the Seventeenth Century.
  Les A. Murray 1938– : 'The C19-20'

7 It was in 1915 the old world ended.
  D. H. Lawrence 1885–1930: *Kangaroo* (1923)

8 Our gadget-filled paradise suspended
in a hell of international insecurity.
  Reinhold Niebuhr 1892–1971: *Pious and
  Secular America* (1957)

9 It was she who established the fact
that this latter half of the twentieth
century belongs to Youth.
  ■ *of her invention, the Chelsea Girl*
  Mary Quant 1934– : *Quant by Quant* (1966)

10 Suppose . . . that Lenin had died of
typhus in Siberia in 1895 and Hitler
had been killed on the western front
in 1916. What would the twentieth
century have looked like now?
  Arthur M. Schlesinger Jr. 1917– : *The Cycles of
  American History* (1986)

11 After the suffering of decades of
violence and oppression, the human
soul longs for higher things, warmer
and purer than those offered by
today's mass living habits, introduced
as by a calling card by the revolting
invasion of commercial advertising,
by TV stupor and by intolerable
music.
  Alexander Solzhenitsyn 1918– : speech in
  Cambridge, Massachusetts, 8 June 1978

12 The twentieth century decorates life
like a Christmas cake, but it still
cannot do anything about the basic
ingredients.
  Derek Tangye 1912–96: *A Gull on the Roof*
  (1961)

13 The twentieth century will be
remembered chiefly, not as an age of
political conflicts and technical
inventions, but as an age in which
human society dared to think of the
health of the whole human race as a
practical objective.
  Arnold Toynbee 1889–1975: attributed

14 The twentieth century really belongs
to those who will build it. The future
can be promised to no one.
  Pierre Trudeau 1919–2000: in 1968; cf. **Canada**
  8

15 Never before has a civilization
reached such a degree of a contempt
for life; never before has a generation,
drowned in mortification, felt such a
rage to live.
  ■ *of the 1960s*
  Raoul Vaneigem 1934– : *The Revolution of
  Everyday Life* (1967)

Twenty-first Century

1 The 1970s for me started the 21st
century—it was the beginning of a
true pluralism in social attitudes.
  David Bowie 1947– : *An Earthling at 50* ITV
  programme; in *Sunday Times* 12 January 1997

2 High on the agenda for the 21st
century will be the need to restore
some kind of tragic consciousness.
  Carlos Fuentes 1928– : Rushworth M. Kidder
  An Agenda for the 21st Century (1987)

3 The turn of the century raises
expectations. The end of a
millennium promises apocalypse and
revelation. But at the close of the
twentieth century the golden age
seems behind us, not ahead. The end
game of the 1990s promises neither
nirvana nor Armageddon, but
entropy.
  Robert Hewison 1943– : *Future Tense* (1990)

4 The American century—and the
European half millennium—is
coming to an end. The world century
is beginning.
  Rosabeth Moss Kanter 1943– : *World Class*
  (1995)

Unemployment

1 Machines are the new proletariat. The
 working class is being given its
 walking papers.
   Jacques Attali 1943– : *Millenium: Winners
   and Losers in the Coming World Order* (1991)

2 Naturally, the workers are perfectly
 free; the manufacturer does not force
 them to take his materials and his
 cards, but he says to them . . . 'If you
 don't like to be frizzled in my frying-
 pan, you can take a walk into the fire'.
   Friedrich Engels 1820–95: *The Condition of the
   Working Class in England in 1844* (1892)

3 If security no longer comes from
 being employed, it must come from
 being employable.
   Rosabeth Moss Kanter 1943– : attributed,
   1994

4 Recession is when you have to tighten
 the belt. Depression is when there is
 no belt to tighten. We are probably in
 the next degree of collapse when there
 are no trousers as such.
   Boris Pankin 1931– : in *Independent* 25 July
   1992

5 I grew up in the Thirties with our
 unemployed father. He did not riot,
 he got on his bike and looked for
 work.
   Norman Tebbit 1931– : speech at
   Conservative Party Conference, 15 October
   1981

6 It's a recession when your neighbour
 loses his job; it's a depression when
 you lose yours.
   Harry S. Truman 1884–1972: in *Observer*
   13 April 1958

United States

see also **American Cities and States**

1 America! America!
 God shed His grace on thee
 And crown thy good with
   brotherhood
 From sea to shining sea!
   Katherine Lee Bates 1859–1929: 'America the
   Beautiful' (1893)

2 The microwave, the waste disposal,
 the orgasmic elasticity of the carpets,
 this soft resort-style civilization
 irresistibly evokes the end of the
 world.
   Jean Baudrillard 1929– : *America* (1986)

3 God bless America,
 Land that I love,
 Stand beside her and guide her
 Thru the night with a light from
   above.
 From the mountains to the prairies,
 To the oceans white with foam,
 God bless America,
 My home sweet home.
   Irving Berlin 1888–1989: 'God Bless America'
   (1939 song)

4 We are a nation of communities, of
 tens and tens of thousands of ethnic,
 religious, social, business, labour
 union, neighbourhood, regional and
 other organizations, all of them
 varied, voluntary, and unique . . . a
 brilliant diversity spread like stars, like
 a thousand points of light in a broad
 and peaceful sky.
   George Bush 1924– : acceptance speech at the
   Republican National Convention in New
   Orleans, 18 August 1988

5 I'm a Yankee Doodle Dandy,
 A Yankee Doodle, do or die;
 A real live nephew of my Uncle Sam's,
 Born on the fourth of July.
   George M. Cohan 1878–1942: 'Yankee Doodle
   Boy' (1904 song)

6 The chief business of the American
 people is business.
   Calvin Coolidge 1872–1933: speech in
   Washington, 17 January 1925

7 'next to of course god america i
 love you land of the pilgrims' and so
   forth oh
 say can you see by the dawn's early my
 country 'tis of centuries come and go
   e. e. cummings 1894–1962: *is 5* (1926)

8 The thing that impresses me most
 about America is the way parents obey
 their children.
   Edward VIII 1894–1972: in *Look* 5 March 1957

9 Isn't this a billion dollar country?
   ■ *responding to a Democratic gibe about a 'million dollar Congress'*
   Charles Foster 1828–1904: at the 51st Congress, in *North American Review* March 1892; also attributed to Thomas B. Reed

10 Yes, America is gigantic, but a gigantic mistake.
   Sigmund Freud 1856–1939: Peter Gay *Freud: A Life for Our Time* (1988)

11 Go West, young man, and grow up with the country.
   Horace Greeley 1811–72: *Hints toward Reforms* (1850)

12 This land is your land, this land is my land,
   From California to the New York Island.
   From the redwood forest to the Gulf Stream waters
   This land was made for you and me.
   Woody Guthrie 1912–67: 'This Land is Your Land' (1956 song)

13 The American system of rugged individualism.
   Herbert Hoover 1874–1964: speech in New York City, 22 October 1928

14 'Tis the star-spangled banner; O long may it wave
   O'er the land of the free, and the home of the brave!
   Francis Scott Key 1779–1843: 'The Star-Spangled Banner' (1814)

15 Give me your tired, your poor,
   Your huddled masses yearning to breathe free.
   ■ *inscription on the Statue of Liberty, New York*
   Emma Lazarus 1849–87: 'The New Colossus' (1883)

16 The immense popularity of American movies abroad demonstrates that Europe is the unfinished negative of which America is the proof.
   Mary McCarthy 1912–89: *On the Contrary* (1961)

17 Our national flower is the concrete cloverleaf.
   Lewis Mumford 1895–1990: in *Quote Magazine* 8 October 1961

18 The weakness of American civilization, and perhaps the chief reason why it creates so much discontent, is that it is so curiously abstract. It is a bloodless extrapolation of a satisfying life . . . You dine off the advertisers 'sizzling' and not the meat of the steak.
   J. B. Priestley 1894–1984: in *New Statesman* 10 December 1971

19 I pledge you, I pledge myself, to a new deal for the American people.
   Franklin D. Roosevelt 1882–1945: speech to the Democratic Convention in Chicago, 2 July 1932, accepting the presidential nomination

20 There is no room in this country for hyphenated Americanism . . . The one absolutely certain way of bringing this nation to ruin, of preventing all possibility of its continuing to be a nation at all, would be to permit it to become a tangle of squabbling nationalities.
   Theodore Roosevelt 1858–1919: speech in New York, 12 October 1915

21 What law have I broken? Is it wrong for me to love my own? Is it wicked for me because my skin is red? Because I am Sioux; because I was born where my fathers lived; because I would die for my people and my country?
   Sitting Bull (Tatanka Iyotake) *c.*1831–90: to Major Brotherton, recorded July 1881; Gary C. Anderson *Sitting Bull* (1996)

22 I like to be in America!
   O.K. by me in America!
   Ev'rything free in America
   For a small fee in America!
   Stephen Sondheim 1930– : 'America' (1957 song)

23 In the United States there is more space where nobody is than where anybody is. That is what makes America what it is.
   Gertrude Stein 1874–1946: *The Geographical History of America* (1936)

24 Where today are the Pequot? Where are the Narragansett, the Mohican, the Pokanoket, and many other once powerful tribes of our people? They have vanished before the avarice and

oppression of the white man, as snow before the summer sun.

Tecumseh 1768–1813: Dee Brown *Bury My Heart at Wounded Knee* (1970)

25 America is a vast conspiracy to make you happy.

John Updike 1932– : *Problems* (1980)

26 America is a nation created by all the hopeful wanderers of Europe, not out of geography and genetics, but out of purpose.

Theodore H. White 1915–86: *Making of the President* (1960)

27 The United States themselves are essentially the greatest poem.

Walt Whitman 1819–92: *Leaves of Grass* (1855)

28 America is God's Crucible, the great Melting-Pot where all the races of Europe are melting and re-forming!

Israel Zangwill 1864–1926: *The Melting Pot* (1908)

The Universe

see also **The Earth**, **The Skies**, **Space**

1 Had I been present at the Creation, I would have given some useful hints for the better ordering of the universe.

■ *on studying the Ptolemaic system*
Alfonso 'the Wise' of Castile 1221–84: attributed

2 We are the children of chaos, and the deep structure of change is decay. At root, there is only corruption, and the unstemmable tide of chaos. Gone is purpose; all that is left is direction. This is the bleakness we have to accept as we peer deeply and dispassionately into the heart of the Universe.

Peter Atkins 1940– : *The Second Law* (1984)

3 For one of those gnostics, the visible universe was an illusion or, more precisely, a sophism. Mirrors and fatherhood are abominable because they multiply it and extend it.

Jorge Luis Borges 1899–1986: *Tlön, Uqbar, Orbis Tertius* (1941)

4 *on hearing that Margaret Fuller 'accepted the universe':*
Gad! she'd better!

Thomas Carlyle 1795–1881: William James *Varieties of Religious Experience* (1902)

5 The eternal mystery of the world is its comprehensibility . . . The fact that it is comprehensible is a miracle.

■ *usually quoted as 'The most incomprehensible fact about the universe is that it is comprehensible'*
Albert Einstein 1879–1955: in *Franklin Institute Journal* March 1936 'Physics and Reality'

6 The world is disgracefully managed, one hardly knows to whom to complain.

Ronald Firbank 1886–1926: *Vainglory* (1915)

7 It is often said that there is no such thing as a free lunch. The Universe, however, is a free lunch.

Alan Guth 1947– : in *Harpers* November 1994

8 Now, my own suspicion is that the universe is not only queerer than we suppose, but queerer than we *can* suppose . . . I suspect that there are more things in heaven and earth than are dreamed of, or can be dreamed of, in any philosophy.

J. B. S. Haldane 1892–1964: *Possible Worlds and Other Essays* (1927) 'Possible Worlds'; see **The Supernatural** 12

9 What is it that breathes fire into the equations and makes a universe for them to describe . . . Why does the universe go to all the bother of existing?

Stephen Hawking 1942– : *A Brief History of Time* (1988)

10 This, now, is the judgement of our scientific age—the third reaction of man upon the universe! This universe is not hostile, nor yet is it friendly. It is simply indifferent.

John H. Holmes 1879–1964: *The Sensible Man's View of Religion* (1932)

11 There is a coherent plan to the universe, though I don't know what it's a plan for.

Fred Hoyle 1915–2001: attributed

12 From the intrinsic evidence of his creation, the Great Architect of the Universe now begins to appear as a pure mathematician.

James Jeans 1877–1946: *The Mysterious Universe* (1930)

13 Not a sound. The universe sleeps, resting a huge ear on its paw with mites of stars.

Vladimir Mayakovsky 1893–1930: 'The Cloud in Trousers' (1915)

14 The Greeks said God was always doing geometry, modern physicists say he's playing roulette, everything depends on the observer, the universe is a totality of observations, it's a work of art created by us.

Iris Murdoch 1919–99: *The Good Apprentice* (1985)

15 The world is everything that is the case.

Ludwig Wittgenstein 1889–1951: *Tractatus Logico-Philosophicus* (1922)

Universities

see also **Education**, **Teaching**

1 The delusion that there are thousands of young people about who are capable of benefiting from university training, but have somehow failed to find their way there, is . . . a necessary component of the expansionist case . . . More will mean worse.

Kingsley Amis 1922–95: in *Encounter* July 1960

2 There is one thing that a professor can be absolutely certain of: almost every student entering the university believes, or says he believes, that truth is relative.

Allan Bloom 1930–92: *The Closing of the American Mind* (1987)

3 Gentlemen: I have not had your advantages. What poor education I have received has been gained in the University of Life.

Horatio Bottomley 1860–1933: speech at the Oxford Union, 2 December 1920

4 The true University of these days is a collection of books.

Thomas Carlyle 1795–1881: *On Heroes, Hero-Worship, and the Heroic* (1841)

5 A University should be a place of light, of liberty, and of learning.

Benjamin Disraeli 1804–81: speech, House of Commons, 11 March 1873

6 Princeton is a wonderful little spot. A quaint and ceremonious village of puny demigods on stilts.

Albert Einstein 1879–1955: letter to Queen Elisabeth of Belgium, 20 November 1933

7 The most prominent requisite to a lecturer, though perhaps not really the most important, is a good delivery; for though to all true philosophers science and nature will have charms innumerable in every dress, yet I am sorry to say that the generality of mankind cannot accompany us one short hour unless the path is strewed with flowers.

Michael Faraday 1791–1867: *Advice to a Lecturer* (1960); from his letters and notebook written at age 21

8 Why am I the first Kinnock in a thousand generations to be able to get to a university?

■ *later plagiarized by the American politician Joe Biden*

Neil Kinnock 1942– : speech in party political broadcast, 21 May 1987

9 Our American professors like their literature clear and cold and pure and very dead.

Sinclair Lewis 1885–1951: Nobel Prize Address, 12 December 1930

10 As to our universities, I've come to the conclusion that they are élitist where they should be egalitarian and egalitarian where they should be élitist.

David Lodge 1935– : *Nice Work* (1989)

11 I am told that today rather more than 60 per cent of the men who go to the universities go on a Government grant. This is a new class that has entered upon the scene . . . They are scum.

W. Somerset Maugham 1874–1965: in *Sunday Times* 25 December 1955

12 A whaleship was my Yale College and my Harvard.

Herman Melville 1819–91: *Moby Dick* (1851)

13 I don't think one 'comes down' from Jimmy's university. According to him, it's not even red brick, but white tile.

John Osborne 1929–94: *Look Back in Anger* (1956)

14 The discipline of colleges and universities is in general contrived, not for the benefit of the students, but for the interest, or more properly speaking, for the ease of the masters.

Adam Smith 1723–90: *Wealth of Nations* (1776)

15 A classic lecture, rich in sentiment,
With scraps of thundrous epic lilted out
By violet-hooded Doctors, elegies
And quoted odes, and jewels five-words-long,
That on the stretched forefinger of all Time
Sparkle for ever.

Alfred, Lord Tennyson 1809–92: *The Princess* (1847)

Value

1 Nothing that costs only a dollar is worth having.

Elizabeth Arden 1876–1966: attributed; in *Fortune* October 1973

2 There is less in this than meets the eye.

■ *on a revival of Maeterlinck's play 'Aglavaine and Selysette'*

Tallulah Bankhead 1903–68: Alexander Woollcott *Shouts and Murmurs* (1922)

3 A living dog is better than a dead lion.

Bible: Ecclesiastes

4 I never loved a dear Gazelle—
*Nor anything that cost me much:
High prices profit those who sell,
But why should I be fond of such?*

Lewis Carroll 1832–98: *Phantasmagoria* (1869) 'Theme with Variations'; see **Transience** 12

5 Men do not weigh the stalk for that it was,
When once they find her flower, her glory, pass.

Samuel Daniel 1563–1619: *Delia* (1592) sonnet 32

6 It has long been an axiom of mine that the little things are infinitely the most important.

Arthur Conan Doyle 1859–1930: *Adventures of Sherlock Holmes* (1892)

7 Every man is wanted, and no man is wanted much.

Ralph Waldo Emerson 1803–82: *Essays. Second Series* (1844) 'Nominalist and Realist'

8 You can calculate the worth of a man by the number of his enemies, and the importance of a work of art by the harm that is spoken of it.

Gustave Flaubert 1821–80: letter to Louise Colet, 14 June 1853

9   Then on the shore
Of the wide world I stand alone and think
Till love and fame to nothingness do sink.

John Keats 1795–1821: 'When I have fears that I may cease to be' (written 1818)

10 Thirty spokes share the wheel's hub;
It is the centre hole that makes it useful.
Shape clay into a vessel;
It is the space within that makes it useful.
Cut doors and windows for a room;
It is the holes which make it useful.
Therefore profit comes from what is there;
Usefulness from what is not there.

Lao Tzu c.604–c.531 BC: *Tao-Tê-Ching*

11 An acre in Middlesex is better than a principality in Utopia.

Lord Macaulay 1800–59: *Essays Contributed to the Edinburgh Review* (1843) 'Lord Bacon'

12 O monstrous! but one half-pennyworth of bread to this intolerable deal of sack!

William Shakespeare 1564–1616: *Henry IV, Part 1* (1597)

13 I cannot help it that my pictures do not sell. Nevertheless the time will come when people will see that they are worth more than the price of the paint.

Vincent Van Gogh 1853–90: letter to his brother Theo, 20 October 1888

14 It is not that pearls fetch a high price *because* men have dived for them; but on the contrary, men dive for them because they fetch a high price.

Richard Whately 1787–1863: *Introductory Lectures on Political Economy* (1832)

Venice

1 STREETS FLOODED. PLEASE ADVISE.

■ *telegraph message on arriving in Venice*
Robert Benchley 1889–1945: R. E. Drennan (ed.) *Wits End* (1973)

2 Venice is like eating an entire box of chocolate liqueurs in one go.

Truman Capote 1924–84: in *Observer* 26 November 1961

3 Sun-girt city, thou hast been
Ocean's child, and then his queen;
Now is come a darker day,
And thou soon must be his prey.

Percy Bysshe Shelley 1792–1822: 'Lines written amongst the Euganean Hills' (1818)

Vietnam War

1 It became necessary to destroy the town to save it.

■ *statement by unidentified US Army Major, referring to Ben Tre in Vietnam*
Anonymous: Associated Press Report, *New York Times* 8 February 1968

2 Kissinger brought peace to Vietnam the same way Napoleon brought peace to Europe: by losing.

Joseph Heller 1923–99: *Good as Gold* (1979)

3 We are not about to send American boys 9 or 10,000 miles away from home to do what Asian boys ought to be doing for themselves.

Lyndon Baines Johnson 1908–73: speech at Akron University, 21 October 1964

4 They've got to draw in their horns and stop their aggression, or we're going to bomb them back into the Stone Age.

■ *on the North Vietnamese*
Curtis E. LeMay 1906–90: *Mission with LeMay* (1965)

5 I don't object to it's being called 'McNamara's War' . . . It is a very important war and I am pleased to be identified with it and do whatever I can to win it.

Robert McNamara 1916– : in *New York Times* 25 April 1964

6 We . . . acted according to what we thought were the principles and traditions of this nation. We were wrong. We were terribly wrong.

■ *of the conduct of the Vietnam War by the Kennedy and Johnson administrations*
Robert McNamara 1916– : speaking in Washington, just before the twentieth anniversary of the American withdrawal from Vietnam, April 1995

7 I love the smell of napalm in the morning. It smells like victory.

Francis Ford Coppola 1939– : *Apocalypse Now* (1979 film, with John Milius)

8 Let us understand: North Vietnam cannot defeat or humiliate the United States. Only Americans can do that.

Richard Nixon 1913–94: broadcast, 3 November 1969

Violence

see also **Pacifism**, **Terrorism**

1 Keep violence in the mind
Where it belongs.

Brian Aldiss 1925– : *Barefoot in the Head* (1969) 'Charteris'

2 Some women . . . enjoy tremendously being told they look a mess—and they actually thrill to the threat of physical violence. I've never met one that does, mind you, but they probably do exist. In books. By men.

Alan Ayckbourn 1939– : *Round and Round the Garden* (1975)

3 The only thing that's been a worse flop than the organization of non-violence has been the organization of violence.

Joan Baez 1941– : *Daybreak* (1970)

4 All they that take the sword shall perish with the sword.

Bible: St Matthew

5 I say violence is necessary. It is as American as cherry pie.

H. Rap Brown 1943– : speech at Washington, 27 July 1967

6 Certain women should be struck regularly, like gongs.

Noël Coward 1899–1973: *Private Lives* (1930)

7 Not hard enough.

■ *when asked how hard she had slapped a policeman*

Zsa Zsa Gabor 1919– : in *Independent* 21 September 1989

8 Wisdom has taught us to be calm and meek,
To take one blow, and turn the other cheek;
It is not written what a man shall do
If the rude caitiff smite the other too!

Oliver Wendell Holmes 1809–94: 'Non-Resistance' (1861)

9 Force, unaided by judgement, collapses through its own weight.

Horace 65–8 BC: *Odes*

10 A man may build himself a throne of bayonets, but he cannot sit on it.

■ *quoted by Boris Yeltsin at the time of the failed military coup in Russia, August 1991*

William Ralph Inge 1860–1954: *Philosophy of Plotinus* (1923)

11 A riot is at bottom the language of the unheard.

Martin Luther King 1929–68: *Where Do We Go From Here?* (1967)

12 Violence is not a knife in the hand. It grows like a poison tree inside other people who have not learned to value other human beings.

Frances Lawrence: in *Observer* 17 December 1995

13 In violence, we forget who we are.

Mary McCarthy 1912–89: *On the Contrary* (1961) 'Characters in Fiction'

14 If you strike a child take care that you strike it in anger, even at the risk of maiming it for life. A blow in cold blood neither can nor should be forgiven.

George Bernard Shaw 1856–1950: *Man and Superman* (1903) 'Maxims: How to Beat Children'

15 Where force is necessary, there it must be applied boldly, decisively and completely. But one must know the limitations of force; one must know when to blend force with a manoeuvre, a blow with an agreement.

Leon Trotsky 1879–1940: *What Next?* (1932)

16 It's very unfashionable to say this, but rape actually isn't the worst thing that can happen to a woman if you're safe, alive and unmarked after the event.

Fay Weldon 1931– : in *Radio Times* 4 July 1998

Vulgarity

1 Vulgarity has its uses. Vulgarity often cuts ice which refinement scrapes at vainly.

Max Beerbohm 1872–1956: letter, 21 May 1921

2 There is no other antidote to the vulgarity of the human heart than doubt and good taste, which one finds fused in works of great literature.

Joseph Brodsky 1940–96: 'Letter to a President [Václav Havel]' (1993), in *On Grief and Reason* (1996)

3 The Duchess of York is a vulgarian. She is vulgar, vulgar, vulgar, and that is that.

Lord Charteris 1913–99: in *Spectator* 5 January 1995

4 Very notable was his distinction between coarseness and vulgarity (coarseness, revealing something; vulgarity, concealing something).

E. M. Forster 1879–1970: *The Longest Journey* (1907)

5 It's worse than wicked, my dear, it's vulgar.

Punch: Almanac (1876)

Waiting

....

see also **Delay**, **Punctuality**

1 ESTRAGON: Charming spot. Inspiring prospects. Let's go.
VLADIMIR: We can't.
ESTRAGON: Why not?
VLADIMIR: We're waiting for Godot.
Samuel Beckett 1906–89: *Waiting for Godot* (1955)

2 I think we ought to let him hang there. Let him twist slowly, slowly in the wind.
■ *opposing the nomination of Patrick Gray as director of the FBI*
John Ehrlichman 1925–99: telephone conversation with John Dean, in *Washington Post* 27 July 1973

3 There was a pause—just long enough for an angel to pass, flying slowly.
Ronald Firbank 1886–1926: *Vainglory* (1915)

4 If anyone believes that our smiles involve abandonment of the teaching of Marx, Engels and Lenin he deceives himself. Those who wait for that must wait until a shrimp learns to whistle.
Nikita Khrushchev 1894–1971: speech in Moscow, 17 September 1955

5 How men hate waiting while their wives shop for clothes and trinkets; how women hate waiting, often for much of their lives, while their husbands shop for fame and glory.
Thomas Szasz 1920– : *The Second Sin* (1973)

Wales

....

1 It profits a man nothing to give his soul for the whole world . . . But for Wales—!
Robert Bolt 1924–95: *A Man for All Seasons* (1960)

2 Who dare compare the English, the most degraded of all the races under heaven, with the Welsh?
Giraldus Cambrensis 1146?–1220?: attributed

3 Wales, Wales, sweet are thy hills and vales,

Thy speech, thy song,
To thee belong,
O may they live ever in Wales.
Evan James: 'Land of My Fathers' (1856)

4 Among our ancient mountains,
And from our lovely vales,
Oh, let the prayer re-echo:
'God bless the Prince of Wales!'
George Linley 1798–1865: 'God Bless the Prince of Wales' (1862 song); translated from the Welsh original by J. C. Hughes (1837–87)

5 The land of my fathers. My fathers can have it.
Dylan Thomas 1914–53: in *Adam* December 1953

6 I wanted a play that would paint the full face of sensuality, rebellion and revivalism. In South Wales these three phenomena have played second fiddle only to Rugby Union which is a distillation of all three.
Gwyn Thomas 1913–81: introduction to *Jackie the Jumper* (1962)

7 There is no present in Wales,
And no future;
There is only the past,
Brittle with relics . . .
And an impotent people,
Sick with inbreeding,
Worrying the carcase of an old song.
R. S. Thomas 1913–2000: 'Welsh Landscape' (1955)

8 'I often think,' he continued, 'that we can trace almost all the disasters of English history to the influence of Wales!'
Evelyn Waugh 1903–66: *Decline and Fall* (1928)

Warfare

....

see also **The Air Force**, **American Civil War**, **American War of Independence**, **The Army**, **Falklands War**, **Gulf War**, **The Navy**, **Peace**, **Vietnam War**, **Wars**, **Waterloo**, **Weapons**, **World War I**, **World War II**

1 We make war that we may live in peace.
Aristotle 384–322 BC: *Nicomachean Ethics*

2 In war there is no second prize for the runner-up.
  Omar Bradley 1893–1981: in *Military Review* February 1950

3 War always finds a way.
  Bertolt Brecht 1898–1956: *Mother Courage* (1939)

4 In war, whichever side may call itself the victor, there are no winners, but all are losers.
  Neville Chamberlain 1869–1940: speech at Kettering, 3 July 1938

5 In war: resolution. In defeat: defiance. In victory: magnanimity. In peace: goodwill.
  Winston Churchill 1874–1965: *The Second World War* vol. 1 (1948)

6 Laws are silent in time of war.
  Cicero 106–43 BC: *Pro Milone*

7 The sinews of war, unlimited money.
  Cicero 106–43 BC: *Fifth Philippic*

8 Everything is very simple in war, but the simplest thing is difficult. These difficulties accumulate and produce a friction which no man can imagine exactly who has not seen war.
  Karl von Clausewitz 1780–1831: *On War* (1832–4)

9 War is nothing but a continuation of politics with the admixture of other means.
  ■ *commonly rendered as 'War is the continuation of politics by other means'*
  Karl von Clausewitz 1780–1831: *On War* (1832–4)

10 War is too serious a matter to entrust to military men.
  Georges Clemenceau 1841–1929: attributed to Clemenceau, but also to Briand and Talleyrand

11 War is the most exciting and dramatic thing in life. In fighting to the death you feel terribly relaxed when you manage to come through.
  Moshe Dayan 1915–81: in *Observer* 13 February 1972

12 There never was a good war, or a bad peace.
  Benjamin Franklin 1706–90: letter to Josiah Quincy, 11 September 1783

13 When you're in the battlefield, survival is all there is. Death is the only great emotion.
  Sam Fuller 1912– : in *Guardian* 26 February 1991

14 What difference does it make to the dead, the orphans and the homeless, whether the mad destruction is wrought under the name of totalitarianism or the holy name of liberty or democracy?
  Mahatma Gandhi 1869–1948: *Non-Violence in Peace and War* (1942)

15 War is hell, and all that, but it has a good deal to recommend it. It wipes out all the small nuisances of peace-time.
  Ian Hay 1876–1952: *The First Hundred Thousand* (1915)

16 Older men declare war. But it is youth who must fight and die.
  Herbert Hoover 1874–1964: speech at the Republican National Convention, Chicago, 27 June 1944

17 Mankind must put an end to war or war will put an end to mankind.
  John F. Kennedy 1917–63: speech to United Nations General Assembly, 25 September 1961

18 The conventional army loses if it does not win. The guerrilla wins if he does not lose.
  Henry Kissinger 1923– : in *Foreign Affairs* January 1969

19 It is well that war is so terrible. We should grow too fond of it.
  Robert E. Lee 1807–70: after the battle of Fredericksburg, December 1862; attributed

20 I have never met anyone who wasn't against war. Even Hitler and Mussolini were, according to themselves.
  David Low 1891–1963: in *New York Times Magazine* 10 February 1946

21 He knew that the essence of war is violence, and that moderation in war is imbecility.

Lord Macaulay 1800–59: *Essays Contributed to the Edinburgh Review* (1843) 'John Hampden'

22 Wars begin when you will, but they do not end when you please.

Niccolò Machiavelli 1469–1527: *History of Florence* (1521–4)

23 There are not fifty ways of fighting, there's only one, and that's to win. Neither revolution nor war consists in doing what one pleases.

André Malraux 1901–76: *L'Espoir* (1937)

24 Everlasting peace is a dream, and not even a pleasant one; and war is a necessary part of God's arrangement of the world . . . Without war the world would deteriorate into materialism.

Helmuth von Moltke 1800–91: letter to Dr J. K. Bluntschli, 11 December 1880

25 Rule 1, on page 1 of the book of war, is: 'Do not march on Moscow' . . . [Rule 2] is: 'Do not go fighting with your land armies in China.'

Lord Montgomery 1887–1976: speech, House of Lords, 30 May 1962

26 In war, three-quarters turns on personal character and relations; the balance of manpower and materials counts only for the remaining quarter.

Napoleon I 1769–1821: 'Observations sur les affaires d'Espagne, Saint-Cloud, 27 août 1808'

27 The quickest way of ending a war is to lose it.

George Orwell 1903–50: in *Polemic* May 1946

28 My subject is War, and the pity of War. The Poetry is in the pity.

Wilfred Owen 1893–1918: preface (written 1918) in *Poems* (1963)

29 If you could hear, at every jolt, the blood
Come gargling from the froth-corrupted lungs,
Obscene as cancer, bitter as the cud
Of vile, incurable sores on innocent tongues,—
My friend, you would not tell with such high zest
To children ardent for some desperate glory,
The old Lie: Dulce et decorum est
Pro patria mori.

Wilfred Owen 1893–1918: 'Dulce et Decorum Est'; see **Patriotism** 12

30 History is littered with the wars which everybody knew would never happen.

Enoch Powell 1912–98: speech to the Conservative Party Conference, 19 October 1967

31 I have seen war. I have seen war on land and sea. I have seen blood running from the wounded. I have seen men coughing out their gassed lungs. I have seen the dead in the mud. I have seen cities destroyed. I have seen 200 limping, exhausted men come out of line—the survivors of a regiment of 1,000 that went forward 48 hours before. I have seen children starving. I have seen the agony of mothers and wives. I hate war.

Franklin D. Roosevelt 1882–1945: speech at Chautauqua, NY, 14 August 1936

32 Little girl . . . Sometime they'll give a war and nobody will come.

Carl Sandburg 1878–1967: *The People, Yes* (1936); 'Suppose They Gave a War and Nobody Came?' was the title of a 1970 film

33 Once you're committed to war, then be ferocious enough to do whatever is necessary to get it over with as quickly as possible in victory.

H. Norman Schwarzkopf III 1934– : in *New York Times* 28 January 1991

34 When we, the Workers, all demand: 'What are WE fighting for?' . . . Then, then we'll end that stupid crime, that devil's madness—War.

Robert W. Service 1874–1958: 'Michael' (1921)

35 Once more unto the breach, dear friends, once more;

Or close the wall up with our English
dead!
In peace there's nothing so becomes a
man
As modest stillness and humility:
But when the blast of war blows in our
ears,
Then imitate the action of the tiger;
Stiffen the sinews, summon up the
blood,
Disguise fair nature with hard-
favoured rage.
William Shakespeare 1564–1616: *Henry V*
(1599)

36 There is many a boy here to-day who
looks on war as all glory, but, boys, it
is all hell.
William Sherman 1820–91: speech at
Columbus, Ohio, 11 August 1880

37 I do wish people would not deceive
themselves by talk of a just war. There
is no such thing as a just war. What we
are doing is casting out Satan by
Satan.
Charles Hamilton Sorley 1895–1915: letter to
his mother from Aldershot, March 1915

38 War is capitalism with the gloves off
and many who go to war know it but
they go to war because they don't
want to be a hero.
Tom Stoppard 1937– : *Travesties* (1975)

39 Waste of Blood, and waste of Tears,
Waste of youth's most precious years,
Waste of ways the saints have trod,
Waste of Glory, waste of God,
War!
G. A. Studdert Kennedy 1883–1929: 'Waste'
(1919)

40 Dead battles, like dead generals, hold
the military mind in their dead grip
and Germans, no less than other
peoples, prepare for the last war.
Barbara W. Tuchman 1912–89: *August 1914*
(1962)

41 God is on the side not of the heavy
battalions, but of the best shots.
Voltaire 1694–1778: 'The Piccini Notebooks'
(*c*.1735–50); cf. **Strength 9**

42 I am Goya
of the bare field, by the enemy's beak
gouged
till the craters of my eyes gape,
I am grief,
I am the tongue
of war, the embers of cities
on the snows of the year 1941
I am hunger.
Andrei Voznesensky 1933– : 'Goya' (1960)

43 Next to a battle lost, the greatest
misery is a battle gained.
Duke of Wellington 1769–1852: in *Diary of
Frances, Lady Shelley 1787–1817* (ed. R.
Edgcumbe)

44 All the business of war, and indeed all
the business of life, is to endeavour to
find out what you don't know by what
you do; that's what I called 'guessing
what was at the other side of the hill'.
Duke of Wellington 1769–1852: in *The Croker
Papers* (1885)

45 Once lead this people into war and
they will forget there ever was such a
thing as tolerance.
Woodrow Wilson 1856–1924: John Dos Passos
Mr Wilson's War (1917)

46 One to destroy, is murder by the law;
And gibbets keep the lifted hand in
awe;
To murder thousands, takes a
specious name,
'War's glorious art', and gives
immortal fame.
Edward Young 1683–1765: *The Love of Fame*
(1725–8)

Waterloo 1815

1 *La Garde meurt, mais ne se rend pas.*
The Guards die but do not surrender.
■ *when called upon to surrender at Waterloo,
1815*
Pierre, Baron de Cambronne 1770–1842:
attributed to Cambronne, but later denied
by him

2 Probably the battle of Waterloo *was*
won on the playing-fields of Eton, but

the opening battles of all subsequent wars have been lost there.

George Orwell 1903–50: *The Lion and the Unicorn* (1941) 'England Your England'; see 5 below

3 Up Guards and at them!

Duke of Wellington 1769–1852: in *The Battle of Waterloo* by a Near Observer [J. Booth] (1815); later denied by Wellington

4 Hard pounding this, gentlemen; let's see who will pound longest.

Duke of Wellington 1769–1852: Sir Walter Scott *Paul's Letters* (1816)

5 The battle of Waterloo was won on the playing fields of Eton.

Duke of Wellington 1769–1852: oral tradition, but not found in this form of words; C. F. R. Montalembert *De l'avenir politique de l'Angleterre* (1856); cf. 2 above

Ways and Means

1 It is in life as it is in ways, the shortest way is commonly the foulest, and surely the fairer way is not much about.

Francis Bacon 1561–1626: *The Advancement of Learning* (1605)

2 A servant's too often a negligent elf;
—If it's business of consequence, DO IT YOURSELF!

R. H. Barham 1788–1845: 'The Ingoldsby Penance!—Moral' (1842)

3 They sought it with thimbles, they sought it with care;
They pursued it with forks and hope;
They threatened its life with a railway-share;
They charmed it with smiles and soap.

Lewis Carroll 1832–98: *The Hunting of the Snark* (1876)

4 The colour of the cat doesn't matter as long as it catches the mice.

■ *quoting a Chinese proverb*
Deng Xiaoping 1904–97: in *Financial Times* 18 December 1986

5 *Dans ce pays-ci il est bon de tuer de temps en temps un amiral pour encourager les autres.*

In this country [England] it is thought well to kill an admiral from time to time to encourage the others.

■ *referring to the controversial execution of Admiral John Byng, 1757*
Voltaire 1694–1778: *Candide* (1759)

Weakness

see **Strength and Weakness**

Wealth

see also **Luxury**, **Money**

1 If you really want to make a million . . . the quickest way is to start your own religion.

Anonymous: previously attributed to L. Ron Hubbard 1911–86 in B. Corydon and L. Ron Hubbard Jr. *L. Ron Hubbard* (1987), but attribution subsequently rejected by L. Ron Hubbard Jr., who also dissociated himself from the book

2 Riches are for spending.

Francis Bacon 1561–1626: *Essays* (1625) 'Of Expense'

3 People say I wasted my money. I say 90 per cent went on women, fast cars and booze. The rest I wasted.

George Best 1946– : in *Daily Telegraph* 29 December 1990

4 It is easier for a camel to go through the eye of a needle, than for a rich man to enter into the kingdom of God.

Bible: St Matthew

5 The man who dies . . . rich dies disgraced.

Andrew Carnegie 1835–1919: in *North American Review* June 1889 'Wealth'

6 To be clever enough to get all that money, one must be stupid enough to want it.

G. K. Chesterton 1874–1936: *Wisdom of Father Brown* (1914)

7 The minute you walked in the joint, I could see you were a man of distinction,
A real big spender . . .

Hey! big spender, spend a little time
with me.
Dorothy Fields 1905–74: 'Big Spender' (1966
song)

8 Let me tell you about the very rich.
They are different from you and me.
F. Scott Fitzgerald 1896–1940: *All the Sad
Young Men* (1926); to which Ernest
Hemingway replied, 'Yes, they have more
money', in *Esquire* August 1936

9 In every well-governed state, wealth is
a sacred thing; in democracies it is the
only sacred thing.
Anatole France 1844–1924: *L'Île des pingouins*
(1908)

10 The greater the wealth, the thicker will
be the dirt.
J. K. Galbraith 1908– : *The Affluent Society*
(1958)

11 If you can actually count your money,
then you are not really a rich man.
J. Paul Getty 1892–1976: in *Observer*
3 November 1957

12 We are not here to sell a parcel of
boilers and vats, but the potentiality
of growing rich, beyond the dreams of
avarice.
■ *at the sale of Thrale's brewery*
Samuel Johnson 1709–84: James Boswell *Life
of Samuel Johnson* (1791) 6 April 1781

13　　　　　　　　I glory
More in the cunning purchase of my
wealth
Than in the glad possession.
Ben Jonson c.1573–1637: *Volpone* (1606)

14 Will the people in the cheaper seats
clap your hands? All the rest of you, if
you'll just rattle your jewellery.
John Lennon 1940–80: at the Royal Variety
Performance, 4 November 1963

15 I want to spend, and spend, and
spend.
■ *said to reporters on arriving to collect her
husband's football pools winnings of £152,000*
Vivian Nicholson 1936– : in *Daily Herald*
28 September 1961

16 Get place and wealth, if possible, with
grace;

If not, by any means get wealth and
place.
Alexander Pope 1688–1744: *Imitations of
Horace* (1738)

17 Having money is rather like being a
blonde. It is more fun but not vital.
Mary Quant 1934– : in *Observer* 2 November
1986

18 A kiss on the hand may be quite
continental,
But diamonds are a girl's best friend.
Leo Robin 1900–84: 'Diamonds are a Girl's
Best Friend' (1949 song)

19 The chief enjoyment of riches consists
in the parade of riches.
Adam Smith 1723–90: *Wealth of Nations*
(1776)

20 To suppose, as we all suppose, that we
could be rich and not behave as the
rich behave, is like supposing that we
could drink all day and keep
absolutely sober.
Logan Pearsall Smith 1865–1946:
Afterthoughts (1931)

21 I've been rich and I've been poor: rich
is better.
Sophie Tucker c.1884–1966: attributed

Weapons

1 Weapons are like money; no one
knows the meaning of *enough*.
Martin Amis 1949– : *Einstein's Monsters*
(1987)

2 A bigger bang for a buck.
Anonymous: Charles E. Wilson's defence
policy, in *Newsweek* 22 March 1954

3 The pike in the thatch is not quite the
same as the surface-to-air missile in
the thatch.
■ *on decommissioning in Northern Ireland*
John de Chastelain: interview in *Daily
Telegraph* 11 June 1999

4 Every gun that is made, every warship
launched, every rocket fired signifies,
in the final sense, a theft from those
who hunger and are not fed, those

who are cold and are not clothed. This world in arms is not spending money alone. It is spending the sweat of its labourers, the genius of its scientists, the hopes of its children.
Dwight D. Eisenhower 1890–1969: speech in Washington, 16 April 1953

5 We can manage without butter but not, for example, without guns. If we are attacked we can only defend ourselves with guns not with butter.
Joseph Goebbels 1897–1945: speech in Berlin, 17 January 1936

6 We have no butter . . . but I ask you— would you rather have butter or guns? . . . preparedness makes us powerful. Butter merely makes us fat.
Hermann Goering 1893–1946: speech at Hamburg, 1936; W. Frischauer *Goering* (1951)

7 History could hang in the balance tonight. Give us bombs for peace.
■ *on the need to maintain military pressure on Serbia*
Richard Holbrooke 1941– : telegram to State Department, summer 1995

8 If the Third World War is fought with nuclear weapons, the fourth will be fought with bows and arrows.
Lord Mountbatten 1900–79: in *Maclean's* 17 November 1975

9 Wars may be fought with weapons, but they are won by men.
George S. Patton 1885–1945: in *Cavalry Journal* September 1933

10 You can't say civilization don't advance, however, for in every war they kill you in a new way.
Will Rogers 1879–1935: in *New York Times* 23 December 1929

11 Cannon to right of them,
Cannon to left of them,
Cannon in front of them
Volleyed and thundered.
Alfred, Lord Tennyson 1809–92: 'The Charge of the Light Brigade' (1854)

12 Spare us all word of the weapons, their force and range,

The long numbers that rocket the mind.
Richard Wilbur 1921– : 'Advice to a Prophet' (1961)

Weather

see also **Fog**, **Rain**, **Snow**, **Wind**

1 How pleasant—
just once *not* to see
Fuji through mist.
Matsuo Basho 1644–94: translated by Lucien Stryk

2 Wet spring had merged imperceptibly into bleak autumn. For months the sky had remained a depthless grey. Sometimes it rained, but mostly it was just dull . . . It was like living inside Tupperware.
Bill Bryson 1951– : *The Lost Continent* (1989)

3 The frost performs its secret ministry, Unhelped by any wind.
Samuel Taylor Coleridge 1772–1834: 'Frost at Midnight' (1798)

4 I believe we should all behave quite differently if we lived in a warm, sunny climate all the time.
Noël Coward 1899–1973: *Brief Encounter* (1945)

5 It ain't a fit night out for man or beast.
W. C. Fields 1880–1946: adopted by Fields but claimed by him not to be original; letter, 8 February 1944

6 A woman rang to say she heard there was a hurricane on the way. Well don't worry, there isn't.
■ *weather forecast on the night before serious gales in southern England*
Michael Fish 1944– : BBC TV, 15 October 1987

7 This is the weather the cuckoo likes, And so do I;
When showers betumble the chestnut spikes,
And nestlings fly.
Thomas Hardy 1840–1928: 'Weathers' (1922)

8 When two Englishmen meet, their first talk is of the weather.
Samuel Johnson 1709–84: in *The Idler* 24 June 1758

9 Thank heavens, the sun has gone in, and I don't have to go out and enjoy it.

Logan Pearsall Smith 1865–1946: *Afterthoughts* (1931)

10 There is a sumptuous variety about the New England weather that compels the stranger's admiration— and regret. The weather is always doing something there; always attending strictly to business; always getting up new designs and trying them on the people to see how they will go.

Mark Twain 1835–1910: speech to New England Society, 22 December 1876

11 The best sun we have is made of Newcastle coal.

Horace Walpole 1717–97: letter to George Montagu, 15 June 1768

Weddings
....
see also **Marriage**

1 If it were not for the presents, an elopement would be preferable.

George Ade 1866–1944: *Forty Modern Fables* (1901)

2 I think weddings is sadder than funerals, because they remind you of your own wedding. You can't be reminded of your own funeral because it hasn't happened. But weddings always make me cry.

Brendan Behan 1923–64: *Richard's Cork Leg*

3 All weddings are similar but every marriage is different. Death comes to everyone but one mourns alone.

John Berger 1926– : *The White Bird* (1985)

4 Oh! how many torments lie in the small circle of a wedding-ring!

Colley Cibber 1671–1757: *The Double Gallant* (1707)

5 O God, and the wedding! All her family and her friends and only a handful of mine all scroungy and bearded just wait to get at the drinks and food.

Gregory Corso 1930– : 'Marriage' (1960)

6 It's pretty easy. Just say 'I do' whenever anyone asks you a question.

Richard Curtis 1956– : *Four Weddings and a Funeral* (1994 film)

7 In your pink wool knitted dress Before anything had smudged anything You stood at the altar.

Ted Hughes 1930–98: *Birthday Letters* (1998) 'A Pink Wool Knitted Dress'

8 I'm getting married in the morning, Ding dong! The bells are gonna chime. Pull out the stopper; Let's have a whopper; But get me to the church on time!

Alan Jay Lerner 1918–86: 'Get Me to the Church on Time' (1956 song)

9   The trouble with being best man is, you don't get a chance to prove it.

Les A. Murray 1938– : *The Boys Who Stole the Funeral* (1989)

10 I said 'Yes'. Isn't that enough?

■ *asked for a comment on her wedding*
Françoise Sagan 1935– : in *New York Mirror* 16 March 1958

11 You can't imagine how many clothes you have to put on a girl when the sole purpose is to get them off.

John Steinbeck 1902–68: letter to Graham Watson, 2 July 1956

12 It was one of those weddings where the bride's and groom's families stand out like opposing football teams, wearing their colours. All the decent hats were, thank God, on our side.

Barbara Trapido 1941– : *Brother of the More Famous Jack* (1982)

13 What a holler there would be if people had to pay the minister as much to marry them as they have to pay a lawyer to get them a divorce.

Claire Trevor: in *New York Journal-American* 12 October 1960

14 Her veil blows across my face as we cling together in the porch. Propped on the mantelpiece, The photograph distils our ecstasy.

Hugo Williams 1942– : 'Love-Life'

Wind

1   We just sit tight while wind dives
And strafes invisibly. Space is a salvo,
We are bombarded by the empty air.
Strange, it is a huge nothing that we
fear.
Seamus Heaney 1939– : 'Storm on the Island'
(1966)

2 On Wenlock Edge the wood's in
trouble;
His forest fleece the Wrekin heaves;
The gale, it plies the saplings double,
And thick on Severn snow the leaves.
A. E. Housman 1859–1936: *A Shropshire Lad*
(1896)

3 Welcome, wild North-easter!
Shame it is to see
Odes to every zephyr;
Ne'er a verse to thee.
Charles Kingsley 1819–75: 'Ode to the North-
East Wind' (1858)

4 No one can tell me,
Nobody knows,
Where the wind comes from,
Where the wind goes.
A. A. Milne 1882–1956: 'Wind on the Hill'
(1927)

5 O wild West Wind, thou breath of
Autumn's being,
Thou, from whose unseen presence
the leaves dead
Are driven, like ghosts from an
enchanter fleeing,
Yellow, and black, and pale, and hectic
red,
Pestilence-stricken multitudes.
Percy Bysshe Shelley 1792–1822: 'Ode to the
West Wind' (1819)

Winning

....

see also **Awards, Defeat, Failure, Success**

1 Anybody can Win, unless there
happens to be a Second Entry.
George Ade 1866–1944: *Fables in Slang* (1900)

2 EVERYBODY has won, and all must
have prizes.
Lewis Carroll 1832–98: *Alice's Adventures in
Wonderland* (1865)

3 What's lost upon the roundabouts we
pulls up on the swings!
Patrick Reginald Chalmers 1872–1942:
'Roundabouts and Swings' (1912)

4 What is our aim? . . . Victory, victory
at all costs, victory in spite of all
terror; victory, however long and hard
the road may be; for without victory,
there is no survival.
Winston Churchill 1874–1965: speech, House
of Commons, 13 May 1940

5 The important thing in life is not the
victory but the contest; the essential
thing is not to have won but to have
fought well.
Baron Pierre de Coubertin 1863–1937: speech
on the Olympic Games, London, 24 July 1908

6 Of course I want to win it . . . I'm not
here to have a good time, nor to keep
warm and dry.
■ *while leading the field, in wet weather, during
the PGA golf championship*
Nick Faldo 1957– : in *Guardian* 25 May 1996

7 Winning is everything. The only ones
who remember you when you come
second are your wife and your dog.
Damon Hill 1960– : in *Sunday Times*
18 December 1994

8 When in doubt, win the trick.
Edmond Hoyle 1672–1769: *Hoyle's Games
Improved* (ed. Charles Jones, 1790) 'Twenty-
four Short Rules for Learners' (though
attributed to Hoyle, this may well have been
an editorial addition by Jones, since it is not
found in earlier editions)

9 The politicians of New York . . . see
nothing wrong in the rule, that to the
victor belong the spoils of the enemy.
William Learned Marcy 1786–1857: speech to
the Senate, 25 January 1832

10 The moment of victory is much too
short to live for that and nothing else.
Martina Navratilova 1956– : in *Independent*
21 June 1989

11 Eclipse first, the rest nowhere.
■ *comment on a horse-race at Epsom, 3 May
1769*
Dennis O'Kelly c.1720–87: in *Annals of
Sporting* (1822); *Dictionary of National
Biography* gives the occasion as the Queen's
Plate at Winchester, 1769

12 One more such victory and we are lost.

■ *on defeating the Romans at Asculum,* 279 BC

Pyrrhus 319–272 BC: Plutarch *Parallel Lives* 'Pyrrhus'

13 Sure, winning isn't everything. It's the only thing.

Henry 'Red' Sanders: in *Sports Illustrated* 26 December 1955; often attributed to Vince Lombardi

Winter

1 The English winter—ending in July, To recommence in August.
Lord Byron 1788–1824: *Don Juan* (1819–24)

2 There is something about winter which pares things down to their essentials
a bare tree
a black hedge
hold their own stark throne in our hearts.
Moya Cannon 1956– : 'Winter Paths' (1997)

3 No warmth, no cheerfulness, no healthful ease,
No comfortable feel in any member—
No shade, no shine, no butterflies, no bees,
No fruits, no flowers, no leaves, no birds,—
November!
Thomas Hood 1799–1845: 'No!' (1844)

4 Winter is icummen in,
Lhude sing Goddamm,
Raineth drop and staineth slop,
And how the wind doth ramm!
Sing: Goddamm.
Ezra Pound 1885–1972: 'Ancient Music' (1917); see **Summer** 1

5 A tedious season they await
Who hear November at the gate.
Alexander Pushkin 1799–1837: *Eugene Onegin* (1833)

6 O, Wind,
If Winter comes, can Spring be far behind?
Percy Bysshe Shelley 1792–1822: 'Ode to the West Wind' (1819)

7 She has made me in love with a cold climate, and frost and snow, with a northern moonlight.

■ *on Mary Wollstonecraft's letters from Sweden and Norway*

Robert Southey 1774–1843: letter to his brother Thomas, 28 April 1797

Wit and Satire

see also **Humour**, **Wordplay**

1 Satire is dependent on strong beliefs, and on strong beliefs wounded.
Anita Brookner 1928– : in *Spectator* 23 March 1989

2 A thing well said will be wit in all languages.
John Dryden 1631–1700: *An Essay of Dramatic Poesy* (1668)

3 I shouldn't call myself a satirist. To be a satirist, you have to know better than everyone else, and I've never done that.
Philip Larkin 1922–85: A. N. Wilson *Penfriends from Porlock* (1988)

4 Epigram: a wisecrack that played Carnegie Hall.
Oscar Levant 1906–72: in *Coronet* September 1958

5 Impropriety is the soul of wit.
W. Somerset Maugham 1874–1965: *The Moon and Sixpence* (1919)

6 Satire is a lesson, parody is a game.
Vladimir Nabokov 1899–1977: *Strong Opinions* (1974)

7 Wit is the epitaph of an emotion.
Friedrich Nietzsche 1844–1900: *Menschliches, Allzumenschliches* (1867–80)

8 There is parody, when you make fun of people who are smarter than you; satire, when you make fun of people who are richer than you; and burlesque, when you make fun of both while taking off your clothes.
P. J. O'Rourke 1947– : in 1980; *Age and Guile* (1995)

9 There's a hell of a distance between wise-cracking and wit. Wit has truth

in it; wise-cracking is simply callisthenics with words.
Dorothy Parker 1893–1967: in *Paris Review* Summer 1956

10 I am not only witty in myself, but the cause that wit is in other men.
William Shakespeare 1564–1616: *Henry IV, Part 2* (1597)

11 Brevity is the soul of wit.
William Shakespeare 1564–1616: *Hamlet* (1601)

12 There's no possibility of being witty without a little ill-nature; the malice of a good thing is the barb that makes it stick.
Richard Brinsley Sheridan 1751–1816: *The School for Scandal* (1777)

Wives

see also **Marriage, Women**

1 Wives are young men's mistresses, companions for middle age, and old men's nurses.
Francis Bacon 1561–1626: *Essays* (1625) 'Of Marriage and the Single Life'

2 A man's mother is his misfortune, but his wife is his fault.
■ *on being urged to marry by his mother*
Walter Bagehot 1826–77: in Norman St John Stevas *Works of Walter Bagehot* (1986) vol. 15 'Walter Bagehot's Conversation'

3 Meek wifehood is no part of my profession;
I am your friend, but never your possession.
Vera Brittain 1893–1970: 'Married Love'

4 If you want to know about a man you can find out an awful lot by looking at who he married.
Kirk Douglas 1916– : in *Daily Mail* 9 September 1988

5 May she have children of her own And as many husbands as will praise her—
For what are husbands for, but to praise their wives?
Paul Durcan 1944– : 'Divorce Referendum, Ireland' (1986)

6 I think everybody really will concede that on this, of all days, I should begin my speech with the words 'My husband and I'.
Elizabeth II 1926– : speech at Guildhall, London, on her 25th wedding anniversary, 20 November 1972

7 We were married.
'A wife is a wife,'
Some husband said. If only it were true!
My wife is a girl playing house With the girl next door.
Randall Jarrell 1914–65: 'Hope' (1966)

8 I am a source of satisfaction to him, a nurse, a piece of furniture, a *woman*—nothing more.
Sonya Tolstoy 1844–1919: diary, 13 November 1893

9 What man thinks of changing himself so as to suit his wife? And yet men expect that women shall put on altogether new characters when they are married, and girls think that they can do so.
Anthony Trollope 1815–82: *Phineas Redux* (1874)

10 After my marriage, she edited everything I wrote. And what is more—she not only edited my works—she edited me!
■ *of his wife, Livy*
Mark Twain 1835–1910: Van Wyck Brooks *The Ordeal of Mark Twain* (1920)

11 She was the kind of wife, who looks out of her front door in the morning and, if it's raining, apologizes.
Fay Weldon 1931– : *Heart of the Country* (1987)

Woman's Role

see also **Men and Women**

1 In the new code of laws which I suppose it will be necessary for you to make I desire you would remember the ladies, and be more generous and favourable to them than your ancestors. Do not put such unlimited power into the hands of the husbands.

Remember all men would be tyrants if they could.
   Abigail Adams 1744–1818: letter to John Adams, 31 March 1776

2 The sadness of the women's movement is that they don't allow the necessity of love. See, I don't personally trust any revolution where love is not allowed.
   Maya Angelou 1928– : in *California Living* 14 May 1975

3 If all men are born free, how is it that all women are born slaves?
   Mary Astell 1668–1731: *Some Reflections upon Marriage* (1706 ed.)

4 The only position for women in SNCC is prone.
   Stokely Carmichael 1941–98: response to a question about the position of women at a Student Nonviolent Coordinating Committee conference, November 1964

5 Woman stock is rising in the market. I shall not live to see women vote, but I'll come and rap at the ballot box.
   Lydia Maria Child 1802–80: letter to Sarah Shaw, 3 August 1856

6 I could have stayed home and baked cookies and had teas. But what I decided was to fulfil my profession, which I entered before my husband was in public life.
   Hillary Rodham Clinton 1947– : comment on questions raised by rival Democratic contender Edmund G. Brown Jr.; in *Albany Times-Union* 17 March 1992

7 I want to be something so much worthier than the doll in the doll's house.
   Charles Dickens 1812–70: *Our Mutual Friend* (1865)

8 Today the problem that has no name is how to juggle work, love, home and children.
   Betty Friedan 1921– : *The Second Stage* (1987)

9 I didn't fight to get women out from behind the vacuum cleaner to get them onto the board of Hoover.
   Germaine Greer 1939– : in *Guardian* 27 October 1986

10 When Grandma was a lassie
That tyrant known as man
Thought a woman's place
Was just the space
Around a fryin' pan.
It was good enough for Grandma
But it ain't good enough for us!
   E. Y. Harburg 1898–1981: 'It was Good Enough for Grandma' (1944)

11 A woman's preaching is like a dog's walking on his hinder legs. It is not done well; but you are surprised to find it done at all.
   Samuel Johnson 1709–84: James Boswell *Life of Samuel Johnson* (1791) 31 July 1763

12 A man is in general better pleased when he has a good dinner upon his table, than when his wife talks Greek.
   Samuel Johnson 1709–84: John Hawkins (ed.) *The Works of Samuel Johnson* (1787) 'Apophthegms, Sentiments, Opinions, etc.'

13 I'm furious about the women's liberationists. They keep getting up on soap boxes and proclaiming that women are brighter than men. That's true, but it should be kept very quiet or it ruins the whole racket.
   Anita Loos 1893–1981: attributed

14 But if God had wanted us to think just with our wombs, why did He give us a brain?
   Clare Booth Luce 1903–87: in *Life* 16 October 1970

15 Women's Liberation is just a lot of foolishness. It's the men who are discriminated against. They can't bear children. And no-one's likely to do anything about that.
   Golda Meir 1898–1978: in *Newsweek* 23 October 1972

16 Religion is an all-important matter in a public school for girls. Whatever people say, it is the mother's safeguard, and the husband's. What we ask of education is not that girls should think, but that they should believe.
   Napoleon I 1769–1821: 'Note sur L'Établissement D'Écouen' 15 May 1807

17 Woman is the nigger of the world.
   Yoko Ono 1933– : remark made in a 1968 interview for *Nova* magazine and adopted by John Lennon as the title of a song (1972)

18 We are here to claim our right as women, not only to be free, but to fight for freedom. That it is our right as well as our duty.
   Christabel Pankhurst 1880–1958: in *Votes for Women* 31 March 1911

19 The one point on which all women are in furious secret rebellion against the existing law is the saddling of the right to a child with the obligation to become the servant of a man.
   George Bernard Shaw 1856–1950: *Getting Married* (1911)

20 We are becoming the men we wanted to marry.
   Gloria Steinem 1934– : in *Ms* July/August 1982

21 Feminism is the most revolutionary idea there has ever been. Equality for women demands a change in the human psyche more profound than anything Marx dreamed of. It means valuing parenthood as much as we value banking.
   Polly Toynbee 1946– : in *Guardian* 19 January 1987

22 That little man . . . he says women can't have as much rights as men, cause Christ wasn't a woman. Where did your Christ come from? From God and a woman. Man had nothing to do with Him.
   Sojourner Truth c.1797–1883: speech at Women's Rights Convention, Akron, Ohio, 1851

23 Always suspect any job men willingly vacate for women.
   Jill Tweedie 1936–93: *It's Only Me* (1980)

24 The Queen is most anxious to enlist every one who can speak or write to join in checking this mad, wicked folly of 'Woman's Rights', with all its attendant horrors, on which her poor feeble sex is bent, forgetting every sense of womanly feeling and propriety.
   Queen Victoria 1819–1901: letter to Theodore Martin, 29 May 1870

25 I myself have never been able to find out precisely what feminism is: I only know that people call me a feminist whenever I express sentiments that differentiate me from a doormat or a prostitute.
   Rebecca West 1892–1983: in *The Clarion* 14 November 1913

26 I do not wish them [women] to have power over men; but over themselves.
   Mary Wollstonecraft 1759–97: *A Vindication of the Rights of Woman* (1792)

Women

see also **Men and Women, Wives, Woman's Role**

1 All the privilege I claim for my own sex . . . is that of loving longest, when existence or when hope is gone.
   Jane Austen 1775–1817: *Persuasion* (1818)

2 Women—one half the human race at least—care fifty times more for a marriage than a ministry.
   Walter Bagehot 1826–77: *The English Constitution* (1867) 'The Monarchy'

3 Who can find a virtuous woman? for her price is far above rubies.
   Bible: Proverbs

4 Women have no wilderness in them,
   They are provident instead,
   Content in the tight hot cell of their hearts
   To eat dusty bread.
   Louise Bogan 1897–1970: 'Women' (1923)

5 The freedom women were supposed to have found in the Sixties largely boiled down to easy contraception and abortion: things to make life easier for men, in fact.
   Julie Burchill 1960– : *Damaged Goods* (1986) 'Born Again Cows'

6 Auld nature swears, the lovely dears
   Her noblest work she classes, O;
   Her prentice han' she tried on man,
   An' then she made the lasses, O.
   Robert Burns 1759–96: 'Green Grow the Rashes' (1787)

7 If *Miss* means respectably unmarried, and *Mrs* respectably married, then *Ms* means nudge, nudge, wink, wink.

> **Angela Carter** 1940–92: 'The Language of Sisterhood' in Christopher Ricks (ed.) *The State of the Language* (1980)

8 The prime truth of woman, the universal mother . . . that if a thing is worth doing, it is worth doing badly.

> **G. K. Chesterton** 1874–1936: *What's Wrong with the World* (1910) 'Folly and Female Education'

9 One is not born a woman: one becomes one.

> **Simone de Beauvoir** 1908–86: *Le deuxième sexe* (1949)

10 Women never have young minds. They are born three thousand years old.

> **Shelagh Delaney** 1939– : *A Taste of Honey* (1959)

11 She knows her man, and when you rant and swear,
Can draw you to her *with a single hair.*

> **John Dryden** 1631–1700: translation of Persius *Satires*

12 She takes just like a woman, yes, she does
She makes love just like a woman, yes, she does
And she aches just like a woman
But she breaks like a little girl.

> **Bob Dylan** 1941– : 'Just Like a Woman' (1966 song)

13 The great question that has never been answered and which I have not yet been able to answer, despite my thirty years of research into the feminine soul, is 'What does a woman want?'

> **Sigmund Freud** 1856–1939: to Marie Bonaparte; Ernest Jones *Sigmund Freud: Life and Work* (1955)

14 Eternal Woman draws us upward.

> **Johann Wolfgang von Goethe** 1749–1832: *Faust* pt. 2 (1832) 'Hochgebirg'

15 You can now see the Female Eunuch the world over . . . spreading herself wherever blue jeans and Coca-Cola may go. Wherever you see nail varnish, lipstick, brassieres, and high heels, the Eunuch has set up her camp.

> **Germaine Greer** 1939– : *The Female Eunuch* (20th anniversary ed., 1991)

16 There is nothin' like a dame.

> **Oscar Hammerstein II** 1895–1960: title of song (1949)

17 Woman may born you, love you, an' mourn you,
But a woman is a sometime thing.

> **Du Bose Heyward** 1885–1940 and **Ira Gershwin** 1896–1983: 'A Woman is a Sometime Thing' (1935 song)

18 When you get to a man in the case,
They're like as a row of pins—
For the Colonel's Lady an' Judy O'Grady
Are sisters under their skins!

> **Rudyard Kipling** 1865–1936: 'The Ladies' (1896)

19 The female of the species is more deadly than the male.

> **Rudyard Kipling** 1865–1936: 'The Female of the Species' (1919)

20 Being a woman is of special interest only to aspiring male transsexuals. To actual women, it is merely a good excuse not to play football.

> **Fran Lebowitz** 1946– : *Metropolitan Life* (1978)

21 I got a twenty dollar piece says
There ain't nothin' I can't do.
I can make a dress out of a feed bag an' I can make a man out of you.
'Cause I'm a woman
W-O-M-A-N
I'll say it again.

> **Jerry Leiber** 1933– : 'I'm a Woman' (1962 song)

22 Thank heaven for little girls!
For little girls get bigger every day.

> **Alan Jay Lerner** 1918–86: 'Thank Heaven for Little Girls' (1958 song)

23 I have never had any great esteem for the generality of the fair sex, and my only consolation for being of that gender has been the assurance it gave

me of never being married to anyone
amongst them.
  Lady Mary Wortley Montagu 1689–1762: letter
  to Mrs Calthorpe, 7 December 1723

24 Sisterhood is powerful.
  Robin Morgan 1941– : title of book (1970)

25 Women would rather be right than be
reasonable.
  Ogden Nash 1902–71: 'Frailty, Thy Name is a
  Misnomer' (1942)

26 Woman was God's second blunder.
  Friedrich Nietzsche 1844–1900: *Der Antichrist*
  (1888)

27 Slamming their doors, stamping their
high heels, banging their irons and
saucepans—the eternal flaming racket
of the female.
  John Osborne 1929–94: *Look Back in Anger*
  (1956)

28 There is no female Mozart because
there is no female Jack the Ripper.
  Camille Paglia 1947– : in *International
  Herald Tribune* 26 April 1991

29 You can have it all, but you can't do it
all.
  Michelle Pfeiffer 1959– : attributed; in
  Guardian 4 January 1996

30 The perpetual hunger to be beautiful
and that thirst to be loved which is the
real curse of Eve.
  Jean Rhys c.1890–1979: *The Left Bank* (1927)
  'Illusion'

31 Only the male intellect, clouded by
sexual impulse, could call the
undersized, narrow-shouldered,
broad-hipped, and short-legged sex
the fair sex.
  Arthur Schopenhauer 1788–1860: 'On
  Women' (1851)

32 O Woman! in our hours of ease,
Uncertain, coy, and hard to please,
And variable as the shade
By the light quivering aspen made;
When pain and anguish wring the
brow,

A ministering angel thou!
  Sir Walter Scott 1771–1832: *Marmion* (1808)

33 Frailty, thy name is woman!
  William Shakespeare 1564–1616: *Hamlet*
  (1601)

34 Here's to the maiden of bashful fifteen
Here's to the widow of fifty
Here's to the flaunting, extravagant
  quean;
And here's to the housewife that's
  thrifty.
  Richard Brinsley Sheridan 1751–1816: *The
  School for Scandal* (1777)

35 The great and almost only comfort
about being a woman is that one can
always pretend to be more stupid than
one is and no one is surprised.
  Freya Stark 1893–1993: *The Valleys of the
  Assassins* (1934)

36   The woman is so hard
Upon the woman.
  Alfred, Lord Tennyson 1809–92: *The Princess*
  (1847)

37 From birth to 18 a girl needs good
parents. From 18 to 35, she needs good
looks. From 35 to 55, good personality.
From 55 on, she needs good cash.
  Sophie Tucker 1884–1966: Michael Freedland
  Sophie (1978)

38 When once a woman has given you
her heart, you can never get rid of the
rest of her body.
  John Vanbrugh 1664–1726: *The Relapse* (1696)

39 a woman is not
a potted plant
her leaves trimmed
to the contours
of her sex.
  Alice Walker 1944– : 'A woman is not a
  potted plant'

40 One should never trust a woman who
tells one her real age. A woman who
would tell one that, would tell one
anything.
  Oscar Wilde 1854–1900: *A Woman of No
  Importance* (1893)

Wordplay

see also **Wit and Satire**

1 The *t* is silent, as in *Harlow*.
   ■ *to Jean Harlow, who had been mispronouncing 'Margot'*
   Margot Asquith 1864–1945: T. S. Matthews *Great Tom* (1973)

2 Apt Alliteration's artful aid.
   Charles Churchill 1731–64: *The Prophecy of Famine* (1763)

3 What is an Epigram? a dwarfish whole,
   Its body brevity, and wit its soul.
   Samuel Taylor Coleridge 1772–1834: 'Epigram' (1809)

4 A man who could make so vile a pun would not scruple to pick a pocket.
   John Dennis 1657–1734: editorial note in *The Gentleman's Magazine* (1781)

5 Those who cannot miss an opportunity of saying a good thing . . . are not to be trusted with the management of any great question.
   William Hazlitt 1778–1830: *Characteristics* (1823)

6 [A pun] is a pistol let off at the ear; not a feather to tickle the intellect.
   Charles Lamb 1775–1834: *Last Essays of Elia* (1833) 'Popular Fallacies'

7 Many of us can still remember the social nuisance of the inveterate punster. This man followed conversation as a shark follows a ship.
   Stephen Leacock 1869–1944: *The Boy I Left Behind Me* (1947)

8 You merely loop the loop on a commonplace and come down between the lines.
   ■ *when asked how to make an epigram by a young man in the flying corps*
   W. Somerset Maugham 1874–1965: *A Writer's Notebook* (1949) written in 1933

9 The conclusion of your syllogism, I said lightly, is fallacious, being based upon licensed premises.
   Flann O'Brien 1911–66: *At Swim-Two-Birds* (1939)

10 If, with the literate, I am
   Impelled to try an epigram,
   I never seek to take the credit;
   We all assume that Oscar said it.
   Dorothy Parker 1893–1967: 'A Pig's-Eye View of Literature' (1937)

11 If I reprehend any thing in this world, it is the use of my oracular tongue, and a nice derangement of epitaphs!
   Richard Brinsley Sheridan 1751–1816: *The Rivals* (1775)

12 I summed up all systems in a phrase, and all existence in an epigram.
   Oscar Wilde 1854–1900: letter, from Reading Prison, to Lord Alfred Douglas, January–March 1897

Words

see also **Dictionaries**, **Grammar**, **Language**, **Meaning**, **Names**, **Words and Deeds**

1 The Greeks had a word for it.
   Zoë Akins 1886–1958: title of play (1930)

2 The day of the jewelled epigram is passed and, whether one likes it or not, one is moving into the stern puritanical era of the four-letter word.
   Noel Annan 1916–2000: in the House of Lords, 1966; George Greenfield *Scribblers for Bread* (1989)

3 There is no use indicting words, they are no shoddier than what they peddle.
   Samuel Beckett 1906–89: *Malone Dies* (1958)

4 'When *I* use a word,' Humpty Dumpty said in a rather scornful tone, 'it means just what I choose it to mean—neither more nor less.'
   Lewis Carroll 1832–98: *Through the Looking-Glass* (1872)

5 'Do you spell it with a ''V'' or a ''W''?' inquired the judge. 'That depends upon the taste and fancy of the speller, my Lord,' replied Sam [Weller].
   Charles Dickens 1812–70: *Pickwick Papers* (1837)

6 I gotta use words when I talk to you.
T. S. Eliot 1888–1965: *Sweeney Agonistes* (1932)

7   Words strain,
Crack and sometimes break, under
    the burden,
Under the tension, slip, slide, perish,
Decay with imprecision, will not stay
    in place,
Will not stay still.
T. S. Eliot 1888–1965: *Four Quartets* 'Burnt
Norton' (1936)

8 Some word that teems with hidden
meaning—like Basingstoke.
W. S. Gilbert 1836–1911: *Ruddigore* (1887)

9 It's exactly where a thought is lacking
That, just in time, a word shows up
instead.
Johann Wolfgang von Goethe 1749–1832: *Faust*
(1808)

10 Words are chameleons, which reflect
the colour of their environment.
Learned Hand 1872–1961: in *Commissioner v.
National Carbide Corp.* (1948)

11 And once sent out a word takes wing
beyond recall.
Horace 65–8 BC: *Epistles*

12 Summer afternoon—summer
afternoon . . . the two most beautiful
words in the English language.
Henry James 1843–1916: Edith Wharton *A
Backward Glance* (1934)

13 He never used one syllable where
none would do.
■ *of Attlee*
Douglas Jay 1907–96: Peter Hennessy
Muddling Through (1996)

14 I am not yet so lost in lexicography as
to forget that words are the daughters
of earth, and that things are the sons
of heaven. Language is only the
instrument of science, and words are
but the signs of ideas: I wish, however,
that the instrument might be less apt
to decay, and that signs might be
permanent, like the things which they
denote.
Samuel Johnson 1709–84: *A Dictionary of the
English Language* (1755)

15 I fear those big words, Stephen said,
which make us so unhappy.
James Joyce 1882–1941: *Ulysses* (1922)

16 Words are, of course, the most
powerful drug used by mankind.
Rudyard Kipling 1865–1936: speech,
14 February 1923

17 In my youth there were words you
couldn't say in front of a girl; now you
can't say 'girl'.
Tom Lehrer 1928– : interview in *The Oldie*,
1996

18 My spelling is Wobbly. It's good
spelling but it Wobbles, and the letters
get in the wrong places.
A. A. Milne 1882–1956: *Winnie-the-Pooh*
(1926)

19 MIKE: There's no word in the Irish
language for what you were doing.
WILSON: In Lapland they have no
word for snow.
Joe Orton 1933–67: *The Ruffian on the Stair*
(rev. ed. 1967)

20 Words are like leaves; and where they
most abound,
Much fruit of sense beneath is rarely
found.
Alexander Pope 1688–1744: *An Essay on
Criticism* (1711)

21 In a world full of audio visual marvels,
may words matter to you and be full
of magic.
Godfrey Smith 1926– : letter to a new
grandchild, in *Sunday Times* 5 July 1987

22 Man does not live by words alone,
despite the fact that he sometimes has
to eat them.
Adlai Stevenson 1900–65: *The Wit and
Wisdom of Adlai Stevenson* (1965)

Words and Deeds

1 Because half a dozen grasshoppers
under a fern make the field ring with
their importunate chink, whilst
thousands of great cattle, reposed
beneath the shadow of the British oak,
chew the cud and are silent, pray do

not imagine that those who make the noise are the only inhabitants of the field.

Edmund Burke 1729–97: *Reflections on the Revolution in France* (1790)

2 The end of man is an action and not a thought, though it were the noblest.
Thomas Carlyle 1795–1881: *Sartor Resartus* (1834)

3 This is very true: for my words are my own, and my actions are my ministers'.

■ *reply to Lord Rochester's epitaph*

Charles II 1630–85: in *Thomas Hearne: Remarks and Collections* (1885–1921) 17 November 1706; see 6 below

4 People who could not tell a lathe from a lawn mower and have never carried the responsibilities of management never tire of telling British management off for its alleged inefficiency.
Keith Joseph 1918–94: in *The Times* 9 August 1974

5 Considering how foolishly people act and how pleasantly they prattle, perhaps it would be better for the world if they talked more and did less.
W. Somerset Maugham 1874–1965: *A Writer's Notebook* (1949) written in 1892

6 Here lies a great and mighty king Whose promise none relies on; He never said a foolish thing, Nor ever did a wise one.

■ *on Charles II*

Lord Rochester 1647–80: 'The King's Epitaph' (alternatively 'Here lies our sovereign lord the King'); see 3 above

7 Do not, as some ungracious pastors do,
Show me the steep and thorny way to heaven,
Whiles, like a puffed and reckless libertine,
Himself the primrose path of dalliance treads,
And recks not his own rede.
William Shakespeare 1564–1616: *Hamlet* (1601)

Work
....
see also **Careers, Employment, Idleness, Leisure, Trade Unions, Unemployment**

1 *Arbeit macht frei.*
Work liberates.
Anonymous: words inscribed on the gates of Dachau concentration camp, 1933, and subsequently on those of Auschwitz

2 If any would not work, neither should he eat.
Bible: II Thessalonians

3 Who built Thebes of the seven gates?
In the books you will find the names of kings.
Did the kings haul up the lumps of rock? . . .
Where, the evening that the wall of China was finished
Did the masons go?
Bertolt Brecht 1898–1956: 'Questions From A Worker Who Reads' (1935)

4 Without work, all life goes rotten, but when work is soulless, life stifles and dies.
Albert Camus 1913–60: attributed; E. F. Schumacher *Good Work* (1979)

5 It has been my experience that one cannot, in any shape or form, depend on human relations for lasting reward. It is only work that truly satisfies.
Bette Davis 1908–89: *The Lonely Life* (1962)

6 My life is one demd horrid grind!
Charles Dickens 1812–70: *Nicholas Nickleby* (1839)

7 Work is love made visible.
Kahlil Gibran 1883–1931: *The Prophet* (1923)

8 I have long been of the opinion that if work were such a splendid thing the rich would have kept more of it for themselves.
Bruce Grocott 1940– : in *Observer* 22 May 1988

9 Generations have trod, have trod, have trod;

And all is seared with trade; bleared,
smeared with toil.
Gerard Manley Hopkins 1844–89: 'God's
Grandeur' (written 1877)

10 I like work: it fascinates me. I can sit
and look at it for hours. I love to keep
it by me: the idea of getting rid of it
nearly breaks my heart.
Jerome K. Jerome 1859–1927: *Three Men in a
Boat* (1889)

11 For men must work, and women
must weep,
And there's little to earn, and many to
keep,
Though the harbour bar be moaning.
Charles Kingsley 1819–75: 'The Three Fishers'
(1858)

12 Who first invented work—and tied
the free
And holy-day rejoicing spirit down
To the ever-haunting importunity
Of business?
Charles Lamb 1775–1834: letter to Bernard
Barton, 11 September 1822

13 Why should I let the toad *work*
Squat on my life?
Can't I use my wit as a pitchfork
And drive the brute off?
Philip Larkin 1922–85: 'Toads' (1955)

14 Blessèd are the horny hands of toil!
James Russell Lowell 1819–91: 'A Glance
Behind the Curtain' (1844)

15 Work expands so as to fill the time
available for its completion.
C. Northcote Parkinson 1909–93: *Parkinson's
Law* (1958)

16 We spend our midday sweat, our
midnight oil;
We tire the night in thought, the day
in toil.
Francis Quarles 1592–1644: *Emblems* (1635)

17 It's true hard work never killed
anybody, but I figure why take the
chance?
Ronald Reagan 1911– : interview, *Guardian*
31 March 1987

18 If you have great talents, industry will
improve them: if you have but

moderate abilities, industry will
supply their deficiency.
Joshua Reynolds 1723–92: *Discourses on Art*
11 December 1769

19 Finding an alternative to formal work
in the marketplace is the critical task
ahead for every nation on earth.
Jeremy Rifkin 1945– : *The End of Work* (1995)

20 Labour without joy is base. Labour
without sorrow is base. Sorrow
without labour is base. Joy without
labour is base.
John Ruskin 1819–1900: *Time and Tide* (1867)

21 The labour we delight in physics pain.
William Shakespeare 1564–1616: *Macbeth*
(1606)

22 Work was like a stick. It had two ends.
When you worked for the knowing
you gave them quality; when you
worked for a fool you simply gave him
eye-wash.
Alexander Solzhenitsyn 1918– : *One Day in
the Life of Ivan Denisovich* (1962)

23 Work to survive, survive by
consuming, survive to consume: the
hellish cycle is complete.
Raoul Vaneigem 1934– : *The Revolution of
Everyday Life* (1967)

24 Work is the curse of the drinking
classes.
Oscar Wilde 1854–1900: H. Pearson *Life of
Oscar Wilde* (1946)

World War I

see also **The Army**, **Warfare**

1 *Ils ne passeront pas.*
They shall not pass.
Anonymous: slogan used by the French army
at the defence of Verdun in 1916; variously
attributed to Marshal Pétain and to General
Robert Nivelle

2 The Somme is like the Holocaust. It
revealed things about mankind that
we cannot come to terms with and
cannot forget. It can never become
the past.
Pat Barker 1943– : on winning the Booker
Prize, November 1995

3 Now, God be thanked Who has
matched us with His hour,
And caught our youth, and wakened
us from sleeping,
With hand made sure, clear eye, and
sharpened power,
To turn, as swimmers into cleanness
leaping.

Rupert Brooke 1887–1915: 'Peace' (1914)

4 My home policy: I wage war; my
foreign policy: I wage war. All the
time I wage war.

Georges Clemenceau 1841–1929: speech to
French Chamber of Deputies, 8 March 1918

5 Over there, over there,
Send the word, send the word over
there
That the Yanks are coming, the Yanks
are coming . . .
We'll be over, we're coming over
And we won't come back till it's over,
over there.

George M. Cohan 1878–1942: 'Over There'
(1917 song)

6 See that little stream—we could walk
to it in two minutes. It took the
British a month to walk it—a whole
empire walking very slowly, dying in
front and pushing forward behind.
And another empire walked very
slowly backward a few inches a day,
leaving the dead like a million bloody
rugs.

F. Scott Fitzgerald 1896–1940: *Tender is the
Night* (1934)

7 This is not a peace treaty, it is an
armistice for twenty years.

Ferdinand Foch 1851–1929: at the signing of
the Treaty of Versailles, 1919; Paul Reynaud
Mémoires (1963)

8 My centre is giving way, my right is
retreating, situation excellent, I am
attacking.

Ferdinand Foch 1851–1929: message sent
during the first Battle of the Marne,
September 1914; R. Recouly *Foch* (1919)

9 *Gott strafe England!*
God punish England!

Alfred Funke b. 1869: *Schwert und Myrte*
(1914)

10 The lamps are going out all over
Europe; we shall not see them lit again
in our lifetime.

Edward Grey 1862–1933: remark on the eve of
the First World War, *25 Years* (1925)

11 The war has used up words.

Henry James 1843–1916: in *New York Times*
21 March 1915

12 Do your duty bravely. Fear God.
Honour the King.

Lord Kitchener 1850–1916: message to soldiers
of the British Expeditionary Force, August
1914

13 At eleven o'clock this morning came
to an end the cruellest and most
terrible war that has ever scourged
mankind. I hope we may say that
thus, this fateful morning, came to an
end all wars.

David Lloyd George 1863–1945: speech, House
of Commons, 11 November 1918

14 In Flanders fields the poppies blow
Between the crosses, row on row.

John McCrae 1872–1918: 'In Flanders Fields'
(1915)

15 I remember an officer saying to me,
'Paint the Somme? I could do it from
memory—just a flat horizon-line and
mud-holes and water, with the
stumps of a few battered trees,' but
one could not paint the smell.

■ *as an official war artist in the First World War*
William Orpen 1878–1931: *An Onlooker in
France* (1921)

16 All quiet on the western front.

Erich Maria Remarque 1898–1970: English title
of *Im Westen nichts Neues* (1929 novel)

17 Oh! we don't want to lose you but we
think you ought to go
For your King and your Country both
need you so.

Paul Alfred Rubens 1875–1917: 'Your King and
Country Want You' (1914 song)

18 You are all a lost generation.

■ *of the young who served in the First World War*
Gertrude Stein 1874–1946: phrase borrowed
(in translation) from a French garage
mechanic, whom Stein heard address it
disparagingly to an incompetent apprentice;
epigraph to Ernest Hemingway *The Sun Also
Rises* (1926)

19 The First World War had begun—
imposed on the statesmen of Europe
by railway timetables.
A. J. P. Taylor 1906–90: *The First World War*
(1963)

World War II
....
see also **Genocide**, **Warfare**

1 I think we might be going a bridge too
far.
■ *expressing reservations about the Arnhem*
'Market Garden' operation
Frederick ('Boy') Browning 1896–1965: to Field
Marshal Montgomery on 10 September 1944

2 How horrible, fantastic, incredible it
is that we should be digging trenches
and trying on gas-masks here because
of a quarrel in a far away country
between people of whom we know
nothing.
■ *on Germany's annexation of the Sudetenland*
Neville Chamberlain 1869–1940: radio
broadcast, 27 September 1938

3 It may almost be said, 'Before
Alamein we never had a victory. After
Alamein we never had a defeat.'
Winston Churchill 1874–1965: *Second World*
War (1951)

4 We shall not flag or fail. We shall go
on to the end. We shall fight in France,
we shall fight on the seas and oceans,
we shall fight with growing
confidence and growing strength in
the air, we shall defend our island,
whatever the cost may be. We shall
fight on the beaches, we shall fight on
the landing grounds, we shall fight in
the fields and in the streets, we shall
fight in the hills; we shall never
surrender.
Winston Churchill 1874–1965: speech, House
of Commons, 4 June 1940

5 Let us therefore brace ourselves to our
duty, and so bear ourselves that, if the
British Empire and its
Commonwealth lasts for a thousand
years, men will still say, 'This was their
finest hour.'
Winston Churchill 1874–1965: speech, House
of Commons, 18 June 1940

6 Don't let's be beastly to the Germans
When our Victory is ultimately won.
Noël Coward 1899–1973: 'Don't Let's Be
Beastly to the Germans' (1943 song)

7 France has lost a battle. But France
has not lost the war!
Charles de Gaulle 1890–1970: proclamation,
18 June 1940

8 I'm glad we've been bombed. It makes
me feel I can look the East End in the
face.
Queen Elizabeth, the Queen Mother
1900–2002: to a London policeman,
13 September 1940

9 I would not regard the whole of the
remaining cities of Germany as worth
the bones of one British Grenadier.
■ *supporting the continued strategic bombing of*
German cities
Arthur Harris 1892–1984: letter to Norman
Bottomley, deputy Chief of Air Staff,
29 March 1945; Max Hastings *Bomber*
Command (1979)

10 We're gonna hang out the washing on
the Siegfried Line.
Jimmy Kennedy and **Michael Carr**: title of
song (1939)

11 I came through and I shall return.
■ *on reaching Australia, having broken through*
Japanese lines en route from Corregidor
Douglas MacArthur 1880–1964: statement in
Adelaide, 20 March 1942

12 Götterdämmerung without the gods.
■ *of the use of atomic bombs against the*
Japanese
Dwight Macdonald 1906–82: in *Politics*
September 1945 'The Bomb'

13 Who do you think you are kidding,
Mister Hitler?
If you think we're on the run?
We are the boys who will stop your
little game
We are the boys who will make you
think again.
Jimmy Perry: 'Who do you think you are
kidding, Mister Hitler' (theme song of *Dad's*
Army, BBC television, 1968–77)

14 This little steamer, like all her brave
and battered sisters, is immortal.
She'll go sailing proudly down the
years in the epic of Dunkirk. And our
great-grand-children, when they learn

how we began this war by snatching glory out of defeat, and then swept on to victory, may also learn how the little holiday steamers made an excursion to hell and came back glorious.

J. B. Priestley 1894–1984: radio broadcast, 5 June 1940

15 We have the men—the skill—the wealth—and above all, the will . . . We must be the great arsenal of democracy.

Franklin D. Roosevelt 1882–1945: 'Fireside Chat' radio broadcast, 29 December 1940

16 Yesterday, December 7, 1941—a date which will live in infamy—the United States of America was suddenly and deliberately attacked by naval and air forces of the Empire of Japan.

Franklin D. Roosevelt 1882–1945: address to Congress, 8 December 1941

17 So on and on
we walked without thinking of rest
passing craters, passing fire,
under the rocking sky of '41
tottering crazy on its smoking
columns.

Yevgeny Yevtushenko 1933– : 'The Companion' (1954)

Worry

1 What's the use of worrying?
It never was worth while,
So, pack up your troubles in your old kit-bag,
And smile, smile, smile.

George Asaf 1880–1951: 'Pack up your Troubles' (1915 song)

2 In trouble to be troubled
Is to have your trouble doubled.

Daniel Defoe 1660–1731: *The Farther Adventures of Robinson Crusoe* (1719)

3 Men show their love by not worrying. A man questions 'How can you worry about someone whom you admire and trust?'

John Gray 1951– : *Men are from Mars, Women are from Venus* (1992)

4 Nothing puzzles me more than time and space; and yet nothing troubles me less, as I never think about them.

Charles Lamb 1775–1834: letter to Thomas Manning, 2 January 1810

5 Paul Getty . . . had always been vastly, immeasurably wealthy, and yet went about looking like a man who cannot quite remember whether he remembered to turn the gas off before leaving home.

Bernard Levin 1928– : *The Pendulum Years* (1970)

6 I'm not [biting my fingernails]. I'm biting my knuckles. I finished the fingernails months ago.

■ *while directing* Cleopatra (1963)
Joseph L. Mankiewicz 1909– : Dick Sheppard *Elizabeth* (1975)

7 O polished perturbation! golden care!
That keep'st the ports of slumber open wide
To many a watchful night!

William Shakespeare 1564–1616: *Henry IV, Part 2* (1597)

8 Neurosis is the way of avoiding non-being by avoiding being.

Paul Tillich 1886–1965: *The Courage To Be* (1952)

9 A neurosis is a secret you don't know you're keeping.

Kenneth Tynan 1927–80: Kathleen Tynan *Life of Kenneth Tynan* (1987)

Writers

see also **Austen**, **James**, **Joyce**, **Poets**, **Shakespeare**

1 Shaw's plays are the price we pay for Shaw's prefaces.

James Agate 1877–1947: diary 10 March 1933

2 He describes London like a special correspondent for posterity.

Walter Bagehot 1826–77: *National Review* 7 October 1858 'Charles Dickens'

3 We were put to Dickens as children but it never quite took. That unremitting humanity soon had me cheesed off.

Alan Bennett 1934– : *The Old Country* (1978)

4 Thou large-brained woman and large-hearted man.
Elizabeth Barrett Browning 1806–61: 'To George Sand—A Desire' (1844)

5 Coleridge was a drug addict. Poe was an alcoholic. Marlowe was stabbed by a man whom he was treacherously trying to stab. Pope took money to keep a woman's name out of a satire; then wrote a piece so that she could still be recognized anyhow. Chatterton killed himself. Byron was accused of incest. *Do you still want to be a writer—and if so, why?*
Bennett Cerf 1898–1971: *Shake Well Before Using* (1948)

6 Hardy went down to botanize in the swamp, while Meredith climbed towards the sun. Meredith became, at his best, a sort of daintily dressed Walt Whitman: Hardy became a sort of village atheist brooding and blaspheming over the village idiot.
G. K. Chesterton 1874–1936: *The Victorian Age in Literature* (1912)

7 Swift was *anima Rabelaisii habitans in sicco*—the soul of Rabelais dwelling in a dry place.
Samuel Taylor Coleridge 1772–1834: *Table Talk* (1835) 15 June 1830

8 He could not blow his nose without moralising on the state of the handkerchief industry.
■ *of George Orwell*
Cyril Connolly 1903–74: in *Sunday Times* 29 September 1968

9 The mama of dada.
■ *of Gertrude Stein*
Clifton Fadiman 1904– : *Party of One* (1955)

10 It was like watching someone organize her own immortality. Every phrase and gesture was studied. Now and again, when she said something a little out of the ordinary, she wrote it down herself in a notebook.
■ *of Virginia Woolf*
Harold Laski 1893–1950: letter to Oliver Wendell Holmes, 30 November 1930

11 E. M. Forster never gets any further than warming the teapot. He's a rare fine hand at that. Feel this teapot. Is it not beautifully warm? Yes, but there ain't going to be no tea.
Katherine Mansfield 1888–1923: diary, May 1917

12 The humour of Dostoievsky is the humour of a bar-loafer who ties a kettle to a dog's tail.
W. Somerset Maugham 1874–1965: *A Writer's Notebook* (1949) written in 1917

13 English literature's performing flea.
■ *of P. G. Wodehouse*
Sean O'Casey 1880–1964: P. G. Wodehouse *Performing Flea* (1953)

14 For years a secret shame destroyed my peace—
I'd not read Eliot, Auden or MacNeice.
But then I had a thought that brought me hope—
Neither had Chaucer, Shakespeare, Milton, Pope.
Justin Richardson 1900–75: 'Take Heart, Illiterates' (1966)

15 I enjoyed talking to her, but thought *nothing* of her writing. I considered her 'a beautiful little knitter'.
■ *of Virginia Woolf*
Edith Sitwell 1887–1964: letter to Geoffrey Singleton, 11 July 1955

16 The magic of Shaw's words may still bewitch posterity . . . but it will find that he has nothing to say.
A. J. P. Taylor 1906–90: in *Observer* 22 July 1956

17 Meredith's a prose Browning, and so is Browning.
Oscar Wilde 1854–1900: *Intentions* (1891) 'The Critic as Artist'

Writing

see also **Books**, **Fiction**, **Literature**, **Originality**, **Poetry**, **Style**, **Words**

1 If you can't annoy somebody with what you write, I think there's little point in writing.
Kingsley Amis 1922–95: in *Radio Times* 1 May 1971

2 Let other pens dwell on guilt and misery. I quit such odious subjects as soon as I can.

Jane Austen 1775–1817: *Mansfield Park* (1814)

3 Writers, like teeth, are divided into incisors and grinders.

Walter Bagehot 1826–77: *Estimates of some Englishmen and Scotchmen* (1858) 'The First Edinburgh Reviewers'

4 The writer must be universal in sympathy and an outcast by nature: only then can he see clearly.

Julian Barnes 1946– : *Flaubert's Parrot* (1984)

5 It is a foolish thing to make a long prologue, and to be short in the story itself.

Bible: II Maccabees

6 Of every four words I write, I strike out three.

Nicolas Boileau 1636–1711: *Satire* (2). *A M. Molière* (1665)

7 Beneath the rule of men entirely great The pen is mightier than the sword.

Edward Bulwer-Lytton 1803–73: *Richelieu* (1839)

8 Go, litel bok, go, litel myn tragedye, Ther God thi makere yet, er that he dye,
So sende myght to make in som comedye!

Geoffrey Chaucer c.1343–1400: *Troilus and Criseyde*

9 A writer must be as objective as a chemist: he must abandon the subjective line; he must know that dung-heaps play a very reasonable part in a landscape, and that evil passions are as inherent in life as good ones.

Anton Chekhov 1860–1904: letter to M. V. Kiselev, 14 January 1887

10 Until you understand a writer's ignorance, presume yourself ignorant of his understanding.

Samuel Taylor Coleridge 1772–1834: *Biographia Literaria* (1817)

11 Write to amuse? What an appalling suggestion!
I write to make people anxious and miserable and to worsen their indigestion.

Wendy Cope 1945– : 'Serious Concerns' (1992)

12 They shut me up in prose—
As when a little girl
They put me in the closet—
Because they liked me 'still'.

Emily Dickinson 1830–86: 'They shut me up in prose' (c.1862)

13 My theory of writing I can sum up in one sentence. An author ought to write for the youth of his own generation, the critics of the next, and the schoolmasters of ever after.

F. Scott Fitzgerald 1896–1940: letter to the Booksellers' Convention, April 1920

14 Only connect! . . . Only connect the prose and the passion, and both will be exalted, and human love will be seen at its height.

E. M. Forster 1879–1970: *Howards End* (1910)

15 Another damned, thick, square book! Always scribble, scribble, scribble! Eh! Mr Gibbon?

William Henry, Duke of Gloucester 1743–1805: Henry Best *Personal and Literary Memorials* (1829); also attributed to the Duke of Cumberland and King George III

16 Any fool may write a most valuable book by chance, if he will only tell us what he heard and saw with veracity.

Thomas Gray 1716–71: letter to Horace Walpole, 25 February 1768

17 The business of the poet and novelist is to show the sorriness underlying the grandest things, and the grandeur underlying the sorriest things.

Thomas Hardy 1840–1928: notebook entry for 19 April 1885

18 The most essential gift for a good writer is a built-in, shock-proof shit detector. This is the writer's radar and all great writers had it.

Ernest Hemingway 1899–1961: in *Paris Review* Spring 1958

19 I am a camera with its shutter open, quite passive, recording, not thinking.

Christopher Isherwood 1904–86: *Goodbye to Berlin* (1939) 'Berlin Diary' Autumn 1930

20 Journalism is about working yourself up into a lather over things you previously felt nothing about. It is diametrically opposed to what you do as a novelist, which is very slowly to discover what it is you really think about things.

Kazuo Ishiguro 1954– : in *Guardian* 15 May 1996

21 Read over your compositions, and where ever you meet with a passage which you think is particularly fine, strike it out.

Samuel Johnson 1709–84: quoting a college tutor; James Boswell *Life of Samuel Johnson* (1791) 30 April 1773

22 No man but a blockhead ever wrote, except for money.

Samuel Johnson 1709–84: James Boswell *Life of Samuel Johnson* (1791) 5 April 1776

23 A writer's ambition should be . . . to trade a hundred contemporary readers for ten readers in ten years' time and for one reader in a hundred years.

Arthur Koestler 1905–83: in *New York Times Book Review* 1 April 1951

24 When my sonnet was rejected, I exclaimed, 'Damn the age; I will write for Antiquity!'

Charles Lamb 1775–1834: letter to B. W. Proctor 22 January 1829

25 There is no need for the writer to eat a whole sheep to be able to tell you what mutton tastes like. It is enough if he eats a cutlet. But he should do that.

W. Somerset Maugham 1874–1965: *A Writer's Notebook* (1949) written in 1941

26   What in me is dark
Illumine, what is low raise and support;
That to the height of this great argument
I may assert eternal providence,
And justify the ways of God to men.

John Milton 1608–74: *Paradise Lost* (1667)

27 Good prose is like a window-pane.

George Orwell 1903–50: *Collected Essays* (1968) vol. 1 'Why I Write'

28 The last thing one knows in constructing a work is what to put first.

Blaise Pascal 1623–62: *Pensées* (1670)

29 The tip's a good one, as for literature
It gives no man a sinecure.
And no one knows, at sight, a masterpiece.
And give up verse, my boy,
There's nothing in it.

Ezra Pound 1885–1972: *Hugh Selwyn Mauberley* (1920) 'Mr Nixon'

30 If writing did not exist, what terrible depressions we should suffer from.

Sei Shōnagon c.966–c.1013: *The Pillow Book of Sei Shōnagon*

31 And, as imagination bodies forth
The forms of things unknown, the poet's pen
Turns them to shapes, and gives to airy nothing
A local habitation and a name.

William Shakespeare 1564–1616: *A Midsummer Night's Dream* (1595–6)

32 You write with ease, to show your breeding,
But easy writing's vile hard reading.

Richard Brinsley Sheridan 1751–1816: 'Clio's Protest' (written 1771, published 1819)

33 Writing is not a profession but a vocation of unhappiness.

Georges Simenon 1903–89: interview in *Paris Review* Summer 1955

34 Writing, when properly managed (as you may be sure I think mine is) is but a different name for conversation.

Laurence Sterne 1713–68: *Tristram Shandy* (1759–67)

35 The shelf life of the modern hardback writer is somewhere between the milk and the yoghurt.

Calvin Trillin 1935– : in *Sunday Times* 9 June 1991; attributed

36 Three hours a day will produce as much as a man ought to write.

Anthony Trollope 1815–82: *Autobiography* (1883)

37 I come from a backward place: your duty is supplied by life around you.

One guy plants bananas; another plants cocoa; I'm a writer, I plant lines. There's the same clarity of occupation, and the sense of devotion.

Derek Walcott 1930– : in *Guardian* 12 July 1997

38 A woman must have money and a room of her own if she is to write fiction.

Virginia Woolf 1882–1941: *A Room of One's Own* (1929)

Youth

see also **Children**, **The Generation Gap**

1 Youth would be an ideal state if it came a little later in life.

Herbert Asquith 1852–1928: in *Observer* 15 April 1923

2 I'm not young enough to know everything.

J. M. Barrie 1860–1937: *The Admirable Crichton* (performed 1902, published 1914)

3 Are you there God? It's me, Margaret. I just told my mother I want a bra. Please help me grow God. You know where.
I want to be like everyone else.

Judy Blume 1938– : *Are You There God? It's Me, Margaret* (1970)

4 We have created a child who will be so exposed to the media that he will be lost to his parents by the time he is 12.

David Bowie 1947– : in *Melody Maker* 22 January 1972

5 It's that second time you hear your love song sung,
Makes you think perhaps, that
Love like youth is wasted on the young.

Sammy Cahn 1913–93: 'The Second Time Around' (1960 song)

6 Youth is something very new: twenty years ago no one mentioned it.

Coco Chanel 1883–1971: Marcel Haedrich *Coco Chanel, Her Life, Her Secrets* (1971)

7 To find a young fellow that is neither a wit in his own eye, nor a fool in the eye of the world, is a very hard task.

William Congreve 1670–1729: *Love for Love* (1695)

8 I remember my youth and the feeling that will never come back any more— the feeling that I could last for ever, outlast the sea, the earth, and all men; the deceitful feeling that lures us on to joys, to perils, to love, to vain effort— to death; the triumphant conviction of strength, the heat of life in the handful of dust, the glow in the heart that with every year grows dim, grows cold, grows small, and expires—and expires, too soon, too soon—before life itself.

Joseph Conrad 1857–1924: *Youth* (1902)

9 It is better to waste one's youth than to do nothing with it at all.

Georges Courteline 1858–1929: *La Philosophie de Georges Courteline* (1948)

10 The Youth of a Nation are the trustees of Posterity.

Benjamin Disraeli 1804–81: *Sybil* (1845)

11 Remember that as a teenager you are at the last stage in your life when you will be happy to hear that the phone is for you.

Fran Lebowitz 1946– : *Social Studies* (1981)

12 Youth is vivid rather than happy, but memory always remembers the happy things.

Bernard Lovell 1913– : in *The Times* 20 August 1993

13 It is thinking about themselves that is really the curse of the younger generation—they appear to have no other subject which interests them at all.

Harold Macmillan 1894–1986: the 'Tuesday memorandum', a draft of a letter to the Queen, advising on his successor but not sent, 1963; D. R. Thorpe *Alec Douglas-Home* (1996)

14 Whom the gods love dies young.

Menander 342–*c*.292 BC: *Dis Exapaton*

15 The atrocious crime of being a young
man . . . I shall neither attempt to
palliate nor deny.

William Pitt, Earl of Chatham 1708–78: speech,
House of Commons, 2 March 1741

16 Being young is greatly
overestimated . . . Any failure seems
so total. Later on you realize you can
have another go.

Mary Quant 1934– : interview in *Observer*
5 May 1996

17 In delay there lies no plenty;
Then come kiss me, sweet and twenty,
Youth's a stuff will not endure.

William Shakespeare 1564–1616: *Twelfth Night*
(1601)

18 What music is more enchanting than
the voices of young people, when you
can't hear what they say?

Logan Pearsall Smith 1865–1946:
Afterthoughts (1931) 'Age and Death'

19 Live as long as you may, the first
twenty years are the longest half of
your life.

Robert Southey 1774–1843: *The Doctor* (1812)

20 The force that through the green fuse
drives the flower
Drives my green age.

Dylan Thomas 1914–53: 'The force that
through the green fuse drives the flower'
(1934)

21 Being young is not having any money;
being young is not minding not
having any money.

Katharine Whitehorn 1928– : *Observations*
(1970)

22 Heaven lies about us in our infancy!
Shades of the prison-house begin to
close
Upon the growing boy,

William Wordsworth 1770–1850: 'Ode.
Intimations of Immortality' (1807)

Author Index

Abbott, Diane (1953–)
British Labour politician

indoors and no heavy lifting — PARLIAMENT 1

Abbott, George (1887–1995)
American director, producer, and dramatist

be adored by your peers — OLD AGE 1

Abse, Dannie (1923–)
Welsh-born doctor and poet

Are all men in disguise — MEN 1
ripens in a tumour — SICKNESS 1
sad and introspective — SCULPTURE 1

Abzug, Bella (1920–98)
American politician

Nixon impeached himself — PRESIDENCY 1
trained to speak softly — COSMETICS 1

Accius (170–*c*.86 BC)
Latin poet and dramatist

Let them hate — GOVERNMENT 1

Ace, Goodman (1899–1982)
American humorist

Terrible Vaudeville — TELEVISION 1

Achebe, Chinua (1930–)
Nigerian novelist

jealous of another's position — ENVY 1
like a Mask dancing — INSIGHT 1
shoot your murderer — HEROES 1

Acheson, Dean (1893–1971)
American politician

lost an empire — BRITAIN 1
memorandum is written — ADMIN 1

Acton, Harold (1904–94)
English historian

Japanese are full of surprises — ASIA 1

Acton, Lord (1834–1902)
British historian

Power tends to corrupt — POWER 1

Adams, Abigail (1744–1818)
American letter writer

all men would be tyrants — WOMAN'S R 1
great characters are formed — CHARACTER 1

Adams, Douglas (1952–2001)
English science fiction writer

Don't panic — ADVICE 1
Life, the Universe — LIFE 1

Adams, Franklin P. (1881–1960)
American journalist and humorist

dead centre of middle age — MIDDLE AGE 1
fool all of the people — POLITICS 1

Adams, Gerry (1948–)
Northern Irish politician

built on exclusion — PEACE 1
sometimes it is necessary — MURDER 1

Adams, Henry Brooks (1838–1918)
American man of letters

arch to build upon — EXPERIENCE 1
Chaos often breeds life — CHAOS 1
One friend in a lifetime — FRIENDSHIP 1
organization of hatreds — POLITICS 2
repose is insupportable — LEISURE 1
teacher affects eternity — TEACHING 1
thought is viscous — MEANING 1

Adams, John (1735–1826)
American statesman, President 1797–1801

government of laws — GOVERNMENT 2
happiness of society — GOVERNMENT 3
middle way is none at all — POLITICS 3
right to study painting — CULTURE 1
You bid me burn your letters — LETTERS 1

Adams, Samuel (1722–1803)
American revolutionary leader

glorious morning — AMERICAN WAR 1

Adamson, Harold (1906–80)
American songwriter
on a wing and a pray'r — CRISES 1

Addams, Jane (1860–1935)
American social worker
enlarged housekeeping — CITIES 1
new growth in the plant — PROGRESS 1

Addison, Joseph (1672–1719)
English poet, dramatist, and essayist
more requisite in business — BUSINESS 1
Our disputants put me in mind — ARGUMENT 1
something for Posterity — FUTURE 1
'Tis not in mortals — SUCCESS 1
works of a great genius — GENIUS 1
works of humour — HUMOUR 1

Ade, George (1866–1944)
American humorist and dramatist
Anybody can Win — WINNING 1
elopement would be preferable — WEDDINGS 1

Adenauer, Konrad (1876–1967)
German statesman
thick skin is a gift — CHARACTER 2

Adler, Alfred (1870–1937)
Austrian psychologist and psychiatrist
fight for one's principles — MORALITY 1
terrible weapon of aggression — TRUTH 1

Adorno, Theodor (1903–69)
German philosopher and musicologist
except the exaggerations — MENTAL 1
write a poem after Auschwitz — POETRY 1

Advertising slogan
ace caff with a museum — MUSEUMS 1
drama out of a crisis — CRISES 2
safe to go back in the water — FILMS 1

Agar, Herbert (1897–1980)
American poet and writer
men prefer not to hear — TRUTH 2

Agate, James (1877–1947)
British drama critic and novelist
finishing the damned thing — DIARIES 1
My mind is not a bed — CERTAINTY 1
pay for Shaw's prefaces — WRITERS 1
professional is a man who can — EMPLOYMENT 1

Agathon (b. c.445)
Greek tragic poet
Even a god cannot change — PAST 1

Agee, James (1909–55)
American writer
Nature, Mr Allnutt — NATURE 1

Aitken, Jonathan (1942–)
British Conservative politician
bent and twisted journalism — JUSTICE 1

Akhmatova, Anna (1889–1966)
Russian poet
not recognize my shores — CIRCUMSTANCE 1
there is a secret boundary — SOLITUDE 1

Akins, Zoë (1886–1958)
American poet and dramatist
Greeks had a word for it — WORDS 1

Alain (1868–1951)
French poet and philosopher
more dangerous than an idea — IDEAS 1

Aldington, Richard (1892–1962)
English poet, novelist, and biographer
collective responsibility — PATRIOTISM 1

Aldiss, Brian (1925–)
English science fiction writer
Keep violence in the mind — VIOLENCE 1
no more written for scientists — SCIENCE FICT 1

Alexander, Cecil Frances (1818–95)
Irish poet and hymn writer
rich man in his castle — CLASS 1

Alfonso 'the Wise' of Castile (1221–84)
King of Castile and León from 1252
hints for the better ordering — UNIVERSE 1

Alfven, Hannes (1908–95)
efforts made to solve it — PROBLEMS 1

Algren, Nelson (1909–)
American novelist
cards with a man called Doc — LIFESTYLES 1

Ali ibn-Abi-Talib (*c.*602–661) *fourth Islamic caliph*	he who has one enemy	RELATIONSHIPS 1
Ali, Muhammad (1942–) *American boxer*	Float like a butterfly I'm the greatest quarrel with the Viet Cong	BOXING 1 SELF-ESTEEM 1 PACIFISM 1
Allen, Arnold (1924–) *British civil servant*	know about the becquerel	PHYSICS 1
Allen, Fred (1894–1956) *American humorist*	happen to be an orange individually can do nothing	AMERICAN CITIES 1 COMMITTEES 1
Allen, Woody (1935–) *American film director, writer, and actor*	asked a girl to go to bed calf won't get much sleep doubles your chances give me some clear sign It's benign just don't want to be there mankind faces a crossroads most fun I ever had My one regret in life Only if it's done right second favourite organ sex with someone I love third of my life is over whining is acquired	BIRTH CONT 1 COOPERATION 1 BISEXUAL 1 GOD 1 CANCER 1 DYING 1 FUTURE 2 SEX 2 SELF 1 SEX 1 BODY 1 MASTURBATION 1 AGEING 1 SPEECH 1
Allende, Isabel (1942–) *Chilean novelist*	chewing gum, tobacco, and beer repent of my diets watching him prepare dinner	KISSING 1 DIETS 1 COOKING 1
Alliluyeva, Svetlana (1925–) *daughter of Joseph Stalin*	his shadow still stands	PEOPLE 1
Allingham, William (1824–89) *Irish poet*	Up the airy mountain	SUPERNATURAL 1
Alvarez, Alfred (1929–) *English poet and writer*	divorce, unlike suicide	DIVORCE 1
Alvarez, Luis Walter (1911–88) *American physicist*	no democracy in physics	PHYSICS 2
Ambrose, St (*c.*339–97) *French-born bishop of Milan*	When I go to Rome	BEHAVIOUR 1
Amery, Leo (1873–1955) *British Conservative politician*	line of least resistance	EFFORT 1
Amies, Hardy (1909–) *English couturier*	holds herself very well not a dirt gardener well dressed in cheap shoes	ROYAL F 1 GARDENS 1 CLOTHES 1
Amis, Kingsley (1922–95) *English novelist and poet*	allow it to spoil your lunch didn't know what to expect If you can't annoy somebody light did him harm More will mean worse Outside every fat man They bring it to you, free years in a geriatric home	REVIEWS 1 SEX 3 WRITING 1 ALCOHOL 1 UNIVERSITIES 1 FAT 1 DEATH 1 PLEASURE 1
Amis, Martin (1949–) *English novelist*	Consciousness *isn't* intolerable eternal human vulgarity knows the meaning of *enough* Prizes are like sashes You don't know the language	MIND 1 BIOGRAPHY 1 WEAPONS 1 AWARDS 1 MIDDLE AGE 2

Anacharsis (6th century BC)	laws are like spider's webs	LAWS 1
Scythian prince		
Anderson, Donald (1939–)	being a Rolls-Royce	CIVIL SERV 1
British Labour politician		
Anderson, Maxwell (1888–1959)	days grow short	AUTUMN 1
American dramatist	What price glory	FAME 1
Angelou, Maya (1928–)	Children's talent to endure	SUFFERING 1
American writer	of the women's movement	WOMAN'S R 2
	we are more alike	HUMAN RACE 1
Anka, Paul (1941–)	I did it my way	LIFESTYLES 2
Canadian singer and composer		
Annan, Kofi (1938–)	lessons of our terrible century	PEACE 2
Ghanaian diplomat		
Annan, Noel (1916–2000)	cardinal virtue	PATRIOTISM 2
English historian and writer	era of the four-letter word	WORDS 2
Anne, Princess Royal (1950–)	cuddled by a complete stranger	CHILDREN 1
British princess	expect me to neigh	ROYAL F 2
Anonymous	abomination unto the Lord	LIES 1
	all men are created equal	HUMAN RIGHTS 1
	almost meaningless	CENSORSHIP 1
	always unfinished business	LIBERTY 1
	banks o' Loch Lomon'	SCOTLAND 1
	be the Vicar of Bray, sir	SELF-INTEREST 1
	bigger bang for a buck	WEAPONS 2
	breaks a butterfly on a wheel	JUSTICE 3
	Can't act. Slightly bald	DANCE 1
	Can't pay, won't pay	TAXES 1
	centre is everywhere	GOD 2
	chewing gum for the eyes	TELEVISION 2
	comfort of feeling safe	FRIENDSHIP 2
	Crisis? What Crisis	CRISES 3
	cult is added to power	PROTEST 1
	denies the first principles	ARGUMENT 2
	destroy the town to save it	VIETNAM 1
	Died at The Oval	CRICKET 1
	do not shoot the pianist	MUSICIANS 1
	Does he take sugar	DISABILITY 1
	Egghead weds hourglass	MONROE 1
	Everyman, I will go with thee	KNOWLEDGE 1
	Evil be to him	INNOCENCE 1
	Expletive deleted	SWEARING 1
	free and equal in dignity	HUMAN RIGHTS 3
	Free at last	EPITAPHS 2
	free lunch	ECONOMICS 1
	Freedom! Equality	HUMAN RIGHTS 2
	go bump in the night	SUPERNATURAL 2
	God Calls Me God	AWARDS 2
	Gotcha	FALKLANDS 1
	home life of our own Queen	ACTORS 1
	I will be millions	EPITAPHS 3
	in time of peace thinks of war	CAUTION 1
	incest and folk-dancing	EXPERIENCE 2
	industry applies	TECHNOLOGY 1
	into a dry Martini	ALCOHOL 2
	iron lady	THATCHER 1
	It takes 40 dumb animals	ANIMAL RIGHTS 1
	It's a plane! It's Superman	HEROES 2
	known unto God	EPITAPHS 5
	Know thyself	SELF-KNOW 1

Anonymous (*cont.*)

Lions led by donkeys	ARMY 1
loved her, then he left her	POVERTY 1
mistake shall not be repeated	EPITAPHS 4
moderated by assassination	RUSSIA 1
No surrender	DEFIANCE 1
Nothing in excess	MODERATION 1
only object of worship	MONEY 1
paid to see Dr Grace bat	CRICKET 2
rabbit has a charming face	ANIMALS 1
raped and speaks English	JOURNALISM 1
really foul things up	COMPUTERS 1
rejoined the world of silence	EPITAPHS 1
replace lawned areas	GARDENS 2
save my soul, if I have a soul	PRAYER 1
Says Tweed to Till	RIVERS 1
Sumer is icumen in	SUMMER 1
Sun Wot Won It	ELECTIONS 1
They shall not pass	WORLD W I 1
Think globally, act locally	ENVIRONMENT 1
those who are about to die	LAST WORDS 1
thou art the flower of cities	LONDON 1
Thought shall be the harder	DETERMINATION 1
thousand winds that blow	BEREAVEMENT 1
thy sting-a-ling-a-ling	ARMY 2
Timothy has passed	EPITAPHS 6
To each his own	JUSTICE 2
Truth is the first casualty	PROPAGANDA 1
undertaking of Great Advantage	SECRECY 1
want to make a million	WEALTH 1
We are putting passengers off	LAST WORDS 2
weaned on a pickle	APPEARANCE 1
what is considered natural	GENETIC 1
who does not know geometry	MATHS 1
Whose finger do you want	CHOICE 1
will they remain the same	TWENTIETH 1
willing foe and sea room	NAVY 1
Winston is back	CHURCHILL 1
Work liberates	WORK 1
world is full of fools	FOOLS 1
Would you buy a used car	TRUST 1

Anouilh, Jean (1910–87)
French dramatist

gift of oneself	LOVE 1
spring is wound up tight	FATE 1
strike the other way	PROPAGANDA 2
Tragedy is clean	TRAGEDY 1

Antrim, Minna (1861–1950)
American writer

fool bolts pleasure	PLEASURE 2

Apollinaire, Guillaume (1880–1918)
French poet

carry one's father's corpse	TRADITION 1
machine that would walk	INVENTIONS 1
Memories are hunting horns	MEMORY 1

Appleton, Thomas Gold (1812–84)
American epigrammatist

Boston man	AMERICAN CITIES 2

Arabin, William (1773–1841)
English judge

go about stealing ducks	ABILITY 1
this case is that case	TRIALS 1

Arbus, Diane (1923–71)
American photographer

born with their trauma	FEAR 1
secret about a secret	PHOTOGRAPHY 1

Archilochus (7th century BC)
Greek poet

fox knows many things	KNOWLEDGE 2

Archimedes (*c.*287–212 BC)
Greek mathematician and inventor

I've got it	INVENTIONS 2

Arden, Elizabeth (1876–1966) *Canadian-born American businesswoman*	costs only a dollar	VALUE 1
Arendt, Hannah (1906–75) *American political philosopher*	banality of evil easier to act than to think most radical revolutionary	EVIL 1 ACTION 1 REVOLUTION 1
Aristotle (384–322 BC) *Greek philosopher*	by means of pity and fear by nature a political animal either a beast or a god Probable impossibilities soul inhabiting two bodies that we may live in peace	TRAGEDY 2 POLITICS 4 SOLITUDE 2 PROBLEMS 2 FRIENDSHIP 3 WARFARE 1
Armistead, Lewis Addison (1817–63) *American army officer*	Give them the cold steel	AMERICAN CIVIL 1
Armour, Richard (1906–89)	shake The catsup bottle	FOOD 1
Armstrong, Louis (1901–71) *American singer and jazz musician*	shame on you	JAZZ 1
Armstrong, Neil (1930–) *American astronaut*	Eagle has landed one small step for man	SPACE 1 ACHIEVEMENT 1
Armstrong, Robert (1927–) *British civil servant*	economical with the truth	TRUTH 3
Arnald-Amaury (d. 1225) *French abbot*	Kill them all	CYNICISM 1
Arnold, George (1834–65) *American humorist*	living need charity	CHARITY 1
Arnold, Matthew (1822–88) *English poet and essayist*	cool flowery lap of earth enchantments of the Middle Age Have something to say ineffectual angel long, withdrawing roar Thou smilest and art still three parts iced over we forget because we must with her dreaming spires	POETS 1 OXFORD 1 STYLE 1 POETS 2 FAITH 1 SHAKESPEARE 1 MIDDLE AGE 3 MEMORY 2 OXFORD 2
Arthurs, George see **Leigh, Fred W. and Arthurs, George**		
Artsimovich, L. A. (1909–73)	curiosity of individuals	SCIENCE 1
Asaf, George (1880–1951) *British songwriter*	troubles in your old kit-bag	WORRY 1
Ascham, Roger (1515–68) *English scholar, writer, and courtier*	encourage a will to learning	TEACHING 2
Ashdown, Paddy (1941–) *British Liberal Democrat politician*	with 15th-century titles	PARLIAMENT 2
Ashford, Daisy (1881–1972) *English child author*	elderly man of 42 You look rather rash my dear	MIDDLE AGE 4 COSMETICS 2
Asimov, Isaac (1920–92) *Russian-born biochemist and science fiction writer*	foresee the inevitable it's bad for you lay public rallies mercenary warriors of today Rules of Robotics	FORESIGHT 1 DIETS 2 THEORY 1 SCIENCE & SOC 1 TECHNOLOGY 2
Asquith, Cynthia (1887–1960) *English writer*	not only dead for the duration	PEACE 3

Asquith, Herbert (1852–1928)
British Liberal statesman, Prime Minister
1908–16

kept three sets of figures — STATISTICS 1
little later in life — YOUTH 1
We had better wait and see — PATIENCE 1

Asquith, Margot (1864–1945)
British political hostess

conciliates enemies — LOYALTY 1
He can't see a belt — LLOYD 1
rot the dead talk — SUPERNATURAL 3
t is silent, as in *Harlow* — WORDPLAY 1
tells enough white lies — LIES 2

Astell, Mary (1668–1731)
English poet and feminist

all women are born slaves — WOMAN'S R 3

Astley, Jacob (1579–1652)
English soldier and Royalist

do not thou forget me — PRAYER 2

Astor, Nancy (1879–1964)
American-born British Conservative
politician

reason why I don't drink — TEETOTALISM 1

Atkins, Peter (1940–)
British chemist

We are the children of chaos — UNIVERSE 2

Atkinson, Brooks (1894–1984)
American journalist and critic

'good old days' were a myth — PAST 2
little less democracy — DEMOCRACY 1
only common interest — CAPITALISM 1

Atkinson, E. L. (1882–1929) **and Cherry-**
Garrard, Apsley (1882–1959)
British polar explorers

walked willingly to his death — EPITAPHS 7

Atkinson, Rowan (1955–)
British actor and comedian

beautiful and emotive object — CARS 1

Attali, Jacques (1943–)
French economist and writer

new proletariat — UNEMPLOYMENT 1

Attenborough, David (1926–)
English naturalist and broadcaster

not over-fond of animals — ANIMALS 2

Attlee, Clement (1883–1967)
British Labour statesman, Prime Minister
1945–51

child of Karl Marx — RUSSIA 2
government by discussion — DEMOCRACY 2
he ended PM CH and OM — PEOPLE 2
If the King asks you — PRIME 1

Atwood, Margaret (1939–)
Canadian novelist

lack of love we die from — CELIBACY 1
like an amputation — DIVORCE 2

Auden, W. H. (1907–73)
English poet

as crooked as corkscrews — EMOTIONS 1
ask the hard question — PHILOSOPHY 1
asked this man to die — ARMY 3
at 4.15 p.m. next Tuesday — COMMITMENT 1
Behaviourism 'works' — BELIEF 1
born of humiliation — ART 1
creation of time and will — MARRIAGE 1
discovering who we are — SELF-KNOW 2
face looks like a wedding-cake — FACE 1
feel like a shabby curate — ARTS AND SCI 1
gossip from all the nations — LETTERS 2
Happy the hare at morning — IGNORANCE 1
He was my North, my South — BEREAVEMENT 2
in a homosexual relationship — FAITHFULNESS 2
Intellectual disgrace — COMPASSION 1
Is it prickly to touch — LOVE 2
lane to the land of the dead — FUTILITY 1
local, but prized elsewhere — POETRY 2
love one another or die — SOCIETY 1
luckiest of mortals — GENIUS 2
Mad Ireland hurt you — POETS 3

Auden, W. H. (*cont.*)	man who's untrue to his wife	INTELLECTUALS 1
	mental or physical barter	RELATIONSHIPS 2
	mis-fits, forced by failure	CHANGE 1
	never wrong, the Old Masters	SUFFERING 2
	Night Mail crossing the Border	RAILWAYS 1
	No opera plot can be sensible	OPERA 1
	Nothing much happened	DRUGS 1
	Once we had a country	EXILE 1
	Private faces	BEHAVIOUR 2
	review a bad book	REVIEWS 2
	saved one Jew from Auschwitz	LITERATURE/SOC 1
	say Alas but cannot help	DEFEAT 1
	senators burst with laughter	POWER 2
	sign of ambition	HABIT 1
	sin tends to be addictive	SIN 1
	Sob, heavy world	SORROW 1
	that I may love myself	SELF 2
	thirty inches from my nose	SELF 3
	Till China and Africa meet	FAITHFULNESS 1
	to whom evil is done	EVIL 2
	to-day the struggle	PRESENT 1
	tried to vex my elders	GENERATION 1
	undeservedly forgotten	BOOKS 1
	what lies under one's nose	INTELLIGENCE 1
	whole climate of opinion	PEOPLE 3
Augarten, Stan	numerical irrigation system	COMPUTERS 2
Augustine, St of Hippo (AD 354–430) *Early Christian theologian*	continency—but not yet	SEX 4
	Hear the other side	TOLERANCE 1
	Love and do what you will	LIFESTYLES 3
	total abstinence is easier	MODERATION 1
	With love for mankind	SIN 2
Augustus (63 BC–AD 14) *Roman emperor*	Make haste slowly	SPEED 1
Aung San Suu Kyi (1945–) *Burmese political leader*	didn't know what vicious was	EVIL 3
	men are truly confident	MEN/WOMEN 1
Aurelius, Marcus (AD 121–80) *Roman emperor from AD 161*	fitted by nature to bear	SUFFERING 3
	him who sets you right	THINKING 1
	pinprick of eternity	TIME 1
Austen, Jane (1775–1817) *English novelist*	All the privilege I claim	WOMEN 1
	as the event decides	ADVICE 2
	child ought to be of the party	CONVERSATION 1
	egg boiled very soft	FOOD 2
	every advantage of us	MEN 2
	every party breaks up	PARTIES 1
	forgive them as a Christian	FORGIVENESS 1
	hopes from Birmingham	BRITISH CIT 2
	I care not who knows	SUFFERING 4
	I quit such odious subjects	WRITING 2
	impulse of the moment	IMPULSIVE 1
	little bit of ivory	AUSTEN 1
	make me sick and wicked	PERFECTION 1
	make sport for our neighbours	NEIGHBOURS 1
	man who has nothing to do	IDLENESS 1
	marry Mr Collins	CHOICE 2
	myrtle and turkey part of it	HAPPINESS 1
	One half of the world	PLEASURE 3
	pleasure is not enhanced	SURPRISE 1
	ruinous depredations of time	COUNTRY 1
	should always be ignorant	IGNORANCE 2
	Those who do not complain	COMPASSION 2

Austen, Jane (*cont.*)	tired of Bath	BRITISH CIT 1
	truth universally acknowledged	BACHELORS 1
	voluntary spies	GOSSIP 1
Austin, George (1931–)	effete, liberal elitism	FAITH 2
British Anglican clergyman		
Awdry, Revd W. (1911–97)	He helped people see God	EPITAPHS 8
English writer of children's books	Railways and the Church	RAILWAYS 3
	Really Useful Engine	RAILWAYS 1
Ayckbourn, Alan (1939–)	actually thrill to the threat	VIOLENCE 2
English dramatist	be a little more subtle	FLATTERY 1
	I can't bear salad	FOOD 3
	pay a woman a compliment	COURTSHIP 1
	weapon of the smallest mind	INSULTS 1
Ayer, A. J. (1910–89)	easier job like publishing	PUBLISHING 1
English philosopher	make life more rational	FUTILITY 2
	mind being wrong	OPINION 1
Ayres, Pam (1947–)	straight past the common cold	MEDICINE 1
English writer of humorous verse		
Babbage, Charles (1792–1871)	Every moment dies a man	STATISTICS 2
English mathematician and inventor		
Babel, Isaac (1894–1940)	blanket over his head	FEAR 2
Russian short-story writer	phrase is born into the world	LANGUAGE 1
	stab the heart	STYLE 2
Bacall, Lauren (1924–)	his private territory	SICKNESS 2
American actress	life shows in your face	FACE 2
	turning your life upside down	LOVE 3
Bach, Johann Sebastian (1685–1750)	instrument plays itself	MUSICAL INST 1
German composer		
Bacon, Francis (1561–1626)	agree in the dark	INDIFFERENCE 1
English lawyer, courtier, philosopher, and	avoiding superstition	SUPERNATURAL 4
essayist	Books will speak plain	ADVICE 3
	chewed and digested	BOOKS 2
	content to begin with doubts	DOUBT 1
	God and angels	ACTION 2
	greatest innovator	CHANGE 2
	green grass kept finely shorn	GARDENS 4
	hostages to fortune	FAMILY 1
	in life as it is in ways	WAYS 1
	jesting Pilate	TRUTH 4
	kind of wild justice	REVENGE 1
	Knowledge itself is power	KNOWLEDGE 3
	make misfortunes more bitter	CHILDREN 2
	Money is like muck	MONEY 2
	part of education	TRAVEL 1
	pencil of the Holy Ghost	BIBLE 1
	purest of human pleasures	GARDENS 3
	Riches are for spending	WEALTH 2
	Suspicions amongst thoughts	TRUST 2
	would like to be true	BELIEF 2
	young men's mistresses	WIVES 1
Bacon, Francis (1909–92)	marvellous painting	PAINTING 1
Irish painter	Who can I tear to pieces	FRIENDSHIP 4
Bacon, Roger (*c.*1220–*c.*1292)	foundations of knowledge	MATHS 2
English philosopher and Franciscan monk		
Baden-Powell, Robert (1857–1941)	it is: BE PREPARED	READINESS 1
English soldier; founder of the Boy Scouts		

Baez, Joan (1941–)
American singer and songwriter

organization of non-violence	VIOLENCE 3

Bagehot, Walter (1826–77)
English economist and essayist

both free and equal	EQUALITY 1
care more for routine	BUREAUCRACY 1
colonies in every clime	LANGUAGES 1
correspondent for posterity	WRITERS 2
exactly *my own* sentiments	NEWSPAPERS 1
half-instructed minds	SIMILARITY 1
his wife is his fault	WIVES 2
imitate what is before him	ORIGINALITY 1
Its mystery is its life	ROYALTY 1
made many ministries	NEWSPAPERS 2
marriage than a ministry	WOMEN 2
Sovereign has three rights	ROYALTY 2
suppressed ill-feeling	FAMILY 2
touch at their summits	INTERNATIONAL 1
victorious in barbarous ages	HUMAN NATURE 1
what people say you cannot do	PLEASURE 4
Writers, like teeth	WRITING 3

Bagnold, Enid (1889–1981)
English novelist and dramatist

affection I find richer	SEX 5

Bailey, David (1938–)
English photographer

Amusing little seams	FASHION 1
takes a lot of imagination	PHOTOGRAPHY 2
Women love scallywags	MEN/WOMEN 2

Bainbridge, Beryl (1933–)
English novelist

men cannot help not loving you	MEN 3
ones I smoke are very small	SMOKING 1
people like being burdened	SUFFERING 5
programmed to love completely	MEN/WOMEN 3

Bairnsfather, Bruce (1888–1959)
British cartoonist

knows of a better 'ole	ADVICE 4

Baker, Russell (1925–)
American journalist and columnist

beauty of the written word	ADVERTISING 1
goal of all inanimate objects	POSSESSIONS 1
opiate of the masses	SPORTS 1
those that don't work	TECHNOLOGY 3

Bakunin, Michael (1814–76)
Russian revolutionary and anarchist

urge for destruction	CREATIVITY 1
world will perish	BEETHOVEN 1

Baldwin, James (1924–87)
American novelist and essayist

exactly like sex	MONEY 3
Indians are you	RACISM 1
struggled with poverty	POVERTY 2

Baldwin, Stanley (1867–1947)
British Conservative statesman, Prime Minister 1923–4, 1924–9, 1935–7

classes which need sanctuary	PRIME 2
day of the air	INTERNATIONAL 2
dealt fairly with their men	TRADE 1
man on the bridge	PARTING 1
my lips are not yet unsealed	SECRECY 2
only defence is in offence	AIR FORCE 1
platitude is simply a truth	TRUTH 5

Balfour, Arthur James (1848–1930)
British Conservative statesman, Prime Minister 1902–5

I always forget	FORGIVENESS 2
why I should break my neck	HUNTING 1
young man of promises	CHURCHILL 2

Ballard, J. G. (1930–)
British writer

becoming science fiction	TWENTIETH 2
cultural Stalingrad	CULTURE 2
threat of extinction	PORNOGRAPHY 1
tremendous sexual event	CARS 2

Balliett, Whitney (1926–)
American writer

bundle of biases	CRITICS 1

Balmain, Pierre (1914–82) *French couturier*	trick of wearing mink	CLOTHES 2
Balzac, Honoré de (1799–1850) *French novelist*	Hatred is a tonic when there has been no love	COMPASSION 3 FAITHFULNESS 3
Bankhead, Tallulah (1903–68) *American actress*	Cocaine habit-forming pure as the driven slush Shakespeare and the Bible stiff neck or lockjaw There is less in this	DRUGS 2 GOODNESS 1 EDUCATION 1 SEX 6 VALUE 2
Banks-Smith, Nancy	modern architecture	ARCHITECT 1
Baraka, Imamu Amiri (1934–) *American poet and dramatist*	God has been replaced	GOD 3
Baratynsky, Yevgeny (1800–44) *Russian poet*	hopelessness and calm	HOPE 1
Bardot, Brigitte (1934–) *French actress*	better to be unfaithful I gave my beauty and my youth leave before being left	FAITHFULNESS 4 MATURITY 1 PARTING 2
Barham, R. H. (1788–1845) *English clergyman*	business of consequence	WAYS 2
Barker, Pat (1943–) *English novelist*	shape and definition Somme is like the Holocaust	LIFESTYLES 4 WORLD W I 2
Barker, Ronnie (1929–) *English comedian*	joke with a double meaning	HUMOUR 2
Barnard, Frederick R.	worth ten thousand words	LANGUAGE 2
Barnes, Julian (1946–) *English novelist*	Art is not a *brassière* call you darling after sex History just burps make sense of life men were the answer outcast by nature	ART 2 LOVE 4 HISTORY 1 BOOKS 3 MEN 4 WRITING 4
Barnum, Phineas T. (1810–91) *American showman*	sucker born every minute	FOOLS 2
Barr, Amelia E. (1831–1919) *American author and journalist*	seems too little or too much	LOVE 5
Barr, Roseanne (1953–) *American comedian*	about thirty-five pages get My gender right married to a couch	AUTOBIOG 1 GOD 4 HUSBANDS 1
Barrie, J. M. (1860–1937) *Scottish writer and dramatist*	All goes if courage goes awfully big adventure baith grand and comfortable bloom on a woman I don't believe in fairies I'm not young enough incredibly fat jealousy to the bride man who has found himself out roses in December Scotsman on the make	COURAGE 1 DYING 2 PRACTICAL 1 CHARM 1 SUPERNATURAL 5 YOUTH 2 APPEARANCE 2 HUMAN NATURE 2 SELF-KNOW 3 MEMORY 3 SCOTLAND 2
Barry, Sebastian (1955–) *Irish writer and dramatist*	island is moored only lightly	IRELAND 1
Barrymore, Ethel (1879–1959) *American actress*	actress to be a success	ACTORS 2

Barrymore, John (1882–1942) *American actor*	O my God, what a relief	SOLITUDE 3
Barstow, Stan (1928–) *English novelist*	fourth-rate writers	READING 1
Barth, Karl (1886–1968) *Swiss Protestant theologian*	angels play only Bach	MOZART 1
Barthes, Roland (1915–80) *French writer and critic*	great Gothic cathedrals	CARS 3
Bartlett, Vernon (1894–1983) *British journalist and writer*	destined to rule the world	HITLER 1
Baruch, Bernard (1870–1965) *American financier*	always fifteen years older if the boys are still there man who promises least	OLD AGE 2 POLITICIANS 1 ELECTIONS 2
Baryshnikov, Mikhail (1948–) *American ballet dancer*	arrogance of the gods	DANCE 2
Basho, Matsuo (1644–94) *Japanese poet*	blossom soup, blossom salad leap-splash—a frog one green see Fuji through mist silkworms droop on mulberries wild geese lost in cloud	TREES 1 ANIMALS 3 AUTUMN 2 WEATHER 1 RAIN 1 PARTING 3
Bates, Katherine Lee (1859–1929) *American writer and educationist*	From sea to shining sea	UNITED S 1
Baudelaire, Charles (1821–67) *French poet and critic*	at once sordid and agreeable *épater le bourgeois*	CHANGE 3 CLASS 2
Baudrillard, Jean (1929–) *French sociologist and cultural critic*	absorb him into a black light questions we have not asked soft resort-style civilization	LOVE 6 INFORMATION 1 UNITED S 2
Bauer, Lord (1915–) *British economist*	poor people in rich countries	AID 1
Baxter, Richard (1615–91) *English divine*	In necessary things, unity	RELATIONSHIPS 3
Bayley, John (1925–) *English academic*	dark escort of Alzheimer's falling from stair to stair	ALZHEIMER'S 2 ALZHEIMER'S 1
Beaton, Alistair and Sherrin, Ned (1931–)	gender bender	BISEXUAL 2
Beatty, Warren (1937–) *American actor, film director, and screenwriter*	level of sexual excitement	FAITHFULNESS 5
Beaumarchais, Pierre-Augustin Caron de (1732–99) *French dramatist*	fear of having to weep making love all year round	HUMOUR 3 HUMAN RACE 2
Beaumont, Gustave de (1802–66)	Scotland in Ireland	NORTHERN 1
Beaverbrook, Lord (1879–1964) *Canadian-born British newspaper proprietor and Conservative politician*	boys in the back rooms care which way he travelled Mr Baldwin denouncing sanctions Our cock won't fight purely for propaganda sit on the wharf	FAME 2 LLOYD 2 INDECISION 1 STRENGTH 1 NEWSPAPERS 3 INDECISION 2
Beckett, Samuel (1906–89) *Irish dramatist, novelist, and poet*	air is full of our cries blaming on his boots can't think without his hat	HABIT 2 HUMAN NATURE 3 THINKING 2

Beckett, Samuel (*cont.*)

could have saved sixpence	MONEY 4
Fail again. Fail better	FAILURE 1
I would like my love to die	DEATH 2
It's a reasonable percentage	STATISTICS 3
no use indicting words	WORDS 3
Nothing happens	BOREDOM 1
Nothing to be done	FUTILITY 3
rather desolate uniformity	RAIN 2
some ghastly hallucination	DEATH 3
That passed the time	TIME 2
We're waiting for Godot	WAITING 1
You are English, Mr Beckett	NATIONALITY 1

Bede, The Venerable (AD 673–735)
English historian and scholar

single sparrow should fly	LIFE 2

Bee, Barnard Elliott (1823–61)
American Confederate general

standing like a stone wall	AMERICAN CIVIL 2

Beecham, Thomas (1879–1961)
English conductor

golden rules for an orchestra	MUSICIANS 2
Like two skeletons copulating	MUSICAL INST 2
penetrates the ear	MUSIC 1
Protestant counterpoint	BACH 1

Beerbohm, Max (1872–1956)
English critic, essayist, and caricaturist

envy of brilliant men	EXCELLENCE 1
game at which two can play	PHILOSOPHY 2
I know what I like	CRITICS 2
sheep on its hind-legs	CONFORMITY 1
solid base in reality	FANTASY 1
third act in a nightmare	DREAMS 1
two great classes	GUESTS 1
Vulgarity often cuts ice	VULGARITY 1
young as they are painted	COSMETICS 3

Beers, Ethel Lynn (1827–79)
American poet

All quiet along the Potomac	AMERICAN CIVIL 3

Beethoven, Ludwig van (1770–1827)
German composer

cannot make a good soup	COOKING 2
immortal god of harmony	BACH 2
It must be	FATE 2

Beeton, Mrs (1836–65)
English writer

place for everything	ORGANIZATION 1

Behan, Brendan (1923–64)
Irish dramatist

bad publicity	FAME 3
discovered about Orangemen	NORTHERN 2
sadder than funerals	WEDDINGS 2
shoot me in my absence	ABSENCE 1

Behn, Aphra (1640–89)
English dramatist, poet, and novelist

Come away; poverty's catching	POVERTY 3
language all nations understand	MONEY 5

Bell, Clive (1881–1964)
English art critic

all questions are open	LOGIC 1

Bell, Daniel (1919–)
American journalist and sociologist

wherein man exploits man	COMMUNISM 1

Belloc, Hilaire (1870–1953)
*British poet, essayist, historian, novelist, and
Liberal politician*

always keep a-hold of Nurse	CAUTION 2
employment to the artisan	EMPLOYMENT 2
fleecy hairy goat	ANIMALS 5
goes with Women, and Champagne	ELECTIONS 3
his books were read	EPITAPHS 9
I am a sundial	TECHNOLOGY 4
make omelettes properly	COOKING 3
pleasure all the time	MONEY 6
So large a trunk before	ANIMALS 4
thought it wrong to fight	PACIFISM 2

Belloc, Hilaire (*cont.*)	we have got The Maxim Gun	POWER 3
	What nobody is sure about	DOUBT 2
Bellow, Saul (1915–)	collapse of civilization	AMERICAN CITIES 3
American novelist	FBI and the CIA	BIOGRAPHY 2
	investigate the Unconscious	MIND 2
	open channel to the soul	SELF 4
	repeat what we all know	ORIGINALITY 2
Belmondo, Jean-Paul (1933–)	Women over thirty	MIDDLE AGE 5
French film actor		
Beloff, Nora (1919–97)	curiosity and a thick skin	JOURNALISM 2
British journalist		
Benchley, Robert (1889–1945)	changing a typewriter ribbon	TECHNOLOGY 5
American humorist	first class, and with children	TRAVEL 2
	make a monkey of a man	QUOTATIONS 1
	stay in bed all day	RISK 1
	streets flooded. please advise	VENICE 1
Benda, Julien (1867–1956)	treachery of the intellectuals	INTELLECTUALS 2
French philosopher and novelist		
Benét, Stephen Vincent (1898–1943)	in love with American names	NAMES 1
American poet and novelist	kept his heart a secret	BIOGRAPHY 3
Benigni, Roberto (1952–)	organize your body	BODY 2
Italian actor and film director		
Benn, Tony (1925–)	British Outer Mongolia	PARLIAMENT 3
British Labour politician	Cool Britannia	BRITAIN 2
	file your waste-paper basket	LIBRARIES 1
	moment of embarrassment	PHOTOGRAPHY 3
	Not a reluctant peer	TITLES 1
	rescued a child from drowning	NEWSPAPERS 4
	something you die for	FAITH 3
	spin-doctors in spin clinics	POLITICS 5
	unlike a soundbite	QUOTATIONS 2
	we thought was for tomorrow	FORESIGHT 2
	wrong to blame Marx	COMMUNISM 2
Bennett, Alan (1934–)	at their best	BEHAVIOUR 3
English actor and dramatist	avenues open up all round	DIVORCE 3
	be taken out of myself	THEATRE 1
	carrying celibacy to extremes	COURTSHIP 2
	doing nothing to some purpose	LEISURE 2
	It is a predicament	ROYALTY 3
	its cosiness, its safety	SECURITY 1
	kitchen dressers of this life	LIFE 3
	Leave us our villains	HEROES 3
	liking for war	FAMILY 3
	Memories are not shackles	MEMORY 4
	One mad magenta moment	EMOTIONS 2
	proper measure of self-esteem	CLASS 3
	put to Dickens as children	WRITERS 3
	relatives of the walking dead	LIBRARIES 2
	resort to the lavatory	HUMOUR 4
	sexual lives of their parents	PARENTS 1
	shows a lack of vocabulary	SWEARING 2
	small anarchist community	SOCIETY 2
	Snobbery with Violence	CRIME FICT 1
	where they commit suicide	EUROPE 1
Bennett, Arnold (1867–1931)	His opinion of himself	SELF-ESTEEM 2
English novelist	just as agreeable as optimism	PESSIMISM 1
	keep on saying it long enough	JOURNALISM 3
	like champagne or high heels	IDEALISM 1

Bennett, Arnold (*cont.*)

men without individuality	TASTE 1
Seventy minutes had passed	LLOYD 3
we called a cold a cold	SICKNESS 3
why so many husbands fail	HUSBANDS 2

Bennett, Brian
see **Welch, Bruce and Bennett, Brian**

Bennett, Jill (1931–90)
English actress

man who hates his mother	HUSBANDS 3

Bennett, Tony (1926–)
American singer

to the sound of his voice	SINGING 1

Bensley, Connie (1929–)

outside, they make a mess	BODY 3

Bentham, Jeremy (1748–1832)
English philosopher

All punishment is mischief	PUNISHMENT 1
Can they suffer	ANIMAL RIGHTS 2
greatest happiness	SOCIETY 3
Prose is when all the lines	POETRY 3
rights is simple nonsense	HUMAN RIGHTS 4

Bentley, Edmund Clerihew (1875–1956)
English writer

Biography is about Chaps	BIOGRAPHY 4
red in the face	CORRUPTION 1

Beresford, Lord Charles (1846–1919)
British politician

Lie follows by post	APOLOGY 1

Berger, John (1926–)
British writer and art critic

every marriage is different	WEDDINGS 3

Bergman, Ingmar (1918–)
Swedish film director

images of life and death	CINEMA 2
light on the human soul	CINEMA 1

Bergman, Ingrid (1915–82)
Swedish actress

never too old for romance	ROMANCE 1

Bergson, Henri (1859–1941)
French philosopher

found in the effect	CAUSES 1

Berlin, Irving (1888–1989)
American songwriter

Anything you can do	SELF-ESTEEM 3
business like show business	THEATRE 2
dancing cheek-to-cheek	DANCE 4
dreaming of a white Christmas	CHRISTMAS 1
girl is like a melody	BEAUTY 1
God bless America	UNITED S 3
hate to get up in the morning	IDLENESS 2
Let's face the music and dance	DANCE 3

Berlin, Isaiah (1909–97)
British philosopher

first militant lowbrow	CULTURE 3
Liberty is liberty	LIBERTY 2
single central vision	CHARACTER 3

Bernal, J. D. (1901–71)
Irish-born physicist

manufacture life	GENETIC 2

Bernall, Cassie (1981–99)
American student

Yes, I believe in God	FAITH 4

Bernanos, Georges (1888–1948)
French novelist and essayist

love no more	HELL 1
wish for prayer	PRAYER 3

Bernard of Chartres (d. *c.*1130)
French philosopher

on the shoulders of giants	PROGRESS 2

Bernard, Claude (1813–78)
French physiologist

change a blunt lancet	IDEAS 2
dazzlingly lighted hall	LIFE SCI 1
science is ourselves	ARTS AND SCI 2

Bernard, Jeffrey (1932–97)
English journalist

punctual with the Devil	PUNCTUALITY 1
they will be black holes	FAME 4

Berners, Lord (1883–1950)
English composer, artist, and writer

backing into the limelight — FAME 5

Berners-Lee, Tim (1955–)
English computer scientist

message of hope for humanity — INTERNET 1

Berra, Yogi (1925–)
American baseball player

ain't over till it's over	ENDING 1
ain't what it used to be	FUTURE 3
come out to the ball park	SPORTS 2
déjà vu all over again	FORESIGHT 3
think and hit	BASEBALL 1

Berryman, John (1914–72)
American poet

Balls will be lost always	MISFORTUNES 1
in the direction of our fear	FEAR 3
you have no Inner Resources	BOREDOM 2

Berton, Pierre (1920–)
Canadian writer

make love in a canoe — CANADA 1

Best, George (1946–)
Northern Irish footballer

women, fast cars and booze — WEALTH 3

Betjeman, John (1906–84)
English poet

aggressively neuter	ARCHITECT 2
Come, friendly bombs	BRITISH CIT 3
Democracy and proper drains	ENGLAND 1
dread of beatings	SCHOOLS 1
girls in slacks	CHRISTMAS 2
have things daintily served	MANNERS 1
sights before the dark	CHILDHOOD 1
weak from your loveliness	TENNIS 1

Bettelheim, Bruno (1903–90)
Austrian-born American psychologist

one has been utterly forsaken — SUFFERING 6

Bevan, Aneurin (1897–1960)
British Labour politician

form of continuous fiction	NEWSPAPERS 5
future refusing to be born	POLITICAL P 2
in the middle of the road	MODERATION 3
language of priorities	POLITICAL P 1
leader for the Labour Party	LEADERSHIP 1
naked into the conference	INTERNATIONAL 4
organ grinder is present	POLITICIANS 2
shortage of coal and fish	ORGANIZATION 2
still fighting Blenheim	INTERNATIONAL 3
stuffed their mouths with gold	CORRUPTION 2

Beveridge, William Henry (1879–1963)
British economist

Disease, Ignorance, Squalor	PROGRESS 3
Ignorance is an evil weed	IGNORANCE 3

Bevin, Ernest (1881–1951)
British Labour politician and trade unionist

anywhere I damn well please	INTERNATIONAL 5
most conservative man	TRADE 2
Not while I'm alive	ENEMIES 1
what Trojan 'orses	EUROPE 2

Bhagavad Gita (*c.*150 BC– AD 150)
Hindu poem

destroy the world — TIME 3

Bhutto, Benazir (1953–)
Pakistani stateswoman

fuelled by bitterness	REVENGE 3
religion as a prop	POWER 4

Bible

all is vanity	FUTILITY 4
all men shall speak well	REPUTATION 1
All they that take the sword	VIOLENCE 4
all things are possible	GOD 5
all things are pure	INNOCENCE 2
Am I my brother's keeper	RELATIONSHIPS 4
beautiful upon the mountains	NEWS 1
Better is the end	ENDING 2
better than a dead lion	VALUE 3
blind lead the blind	LEADERSHIP 2

Bible (*cont.*)

brought nothing into this world	POSSESSIONS 2
By the waters of Babylon	SORROW 2
cheerful countenance	FACE 3
Consider the lilies	BEAUTY 2
desert shall rejoice	ENVIRONMENT 2
desire accomplished is sweet	ACHIEVEMENT 2
Ethiopian change his skin	CHANGE 4
Eye for eye, tooth for tooth	JUSTICE 4
Faith without works	FAITH 5
friend that sticketh closer	FRIENDSHIP 5
go down to the sea in ships	SEA 1
God is love	GOD 6
God said, Let there be light	BEGINNING 1
good that I would I do not	STRENGTH 2
grass withereth	TRANSIENCE 1
Greater love hath no man	SACRIFICE 1
halt ye between two opinions	DOUBT 3
haughty spirit before a fall	SELF-ESTEEM 4
He that increaseth knowledge	KNOWLEDGE 4
He that is without sin	GUILT 1
He that spareth his rod	PUNISHMENT 2
help thou mine unbelief	BELIEF 3
house cannot stand	COOPERATION 2
If God be for us	STRENGTH 3
jealousy is cruel as the grave	JEALOUSY 1
join house to house	CITIES 2
keep himself from doing wrong	BUSINESS 2
laid him in a manger	CHRISTMAS 3
Let not thy left hand know	SECRECY 3
loose the bands of Orion	FATE 3
Love is patient and kind	LOVE 7
love thy neighbour as thyself	LIFESTYLES 6
Love your enemies	ENEMIES 3
make a long prologue	WRITING 5
Man is born unto trouble	MISFORTUNES 2
many are called	CHOICE 3
more blessed to give	GIVING 1
name liveth for evermore	EPITAPHS 10
neither should he eat	WORK 2
no new thing under the sun	PROGRESS 4
not with me is against me	ENEMIES 2
O death, where is thy sting	DEATH 4
on the just and on the unjust	EQUALITY 2
passeth all understanding	PEACE 5
poor always ye have with you	POVERTY 4
price of wisdom	KNOWLEDGE 5
price is far above rubies	WOMEN 3
promotion cometh neither	CAREERS 1
prophet is not without honour	FAMILIAR 1
Render therefore unto Caesar	RELIGION 1
root of all evil	MONEY 7
rulers of the darkness	SUPERNATURAL 6
seek, and ye shall find	PRAYER 4
smite thee on thy right cheek	PACIFISM 3
soft answer turneth away wrath	ANGER 1
spirit indeed is willing	TEMPTATION 1
Sufficient unto the day	PRESENT 2
swords into plowshares	PEACE 4
tender mercies of the wicked	ANIMAL RIGHTS 3
that ye be not judged	TOLERANCE 2
they shall be comforted	BEREAVEMENT 3
they shall inherit the earth	HUMILITY 1
through the eye of a needle	WEALTH 4
time to every purpose	CIRCUMSTANCE 2

Bible (*cont.*)

to drink, and to be merry	LIFESTYLES 5
truth shall make you free	TRUTH 6
Vengeance is mine	REVENGE 2
wages of sin is death	SIN 4
weariness of the flesh	BOOKS 4
what shall it profit a man	SUCCESS 2
Whatsoever a man soweth	CAUSES 2
Where there is no vision	IDEALISM 2
why hast thou forsaken me	DESPAIR 1
your sin will find you out	SIN 3

Bidault, Georges (1899–1983)
French politician

weak have one weapon	STRENGTH 4

Bierce, Ambrose (1842–*c.*1914)
American writer

dead sinner revised and edited	SAINTS 1
sees things as they are	CYNICISM 2

Biko, Steve (1946–77)
South African anti-apartheid campaigner

mind of the oppressed	STRENGTH 5
tenet of Black consciousness	RACISM 2

Billings, Josh (1818–85)
American humorist

better to know nothing	KNOWLEDGE 6

Binchy, Maeve (1940–)
Irish novelist

meant to be a festival	CELEBRATIONS 1
Right Now is a lot better	PRESENT 3
times of huge goodwill	MIDDLE AGE 6

Binyon, Laurence (1869–1943)
English poet

Age shall not weary them	EPITAPHS 11
burning of the leaves	AUTUMN 3

Bion (*c.*325–*c.*255 BC)
Greek popular philosopher

frogs don't die for 'fun'	CRUELTY 1

Birkett, Lord (1883–1962)
English barrister and judge

looking at their watches	SPEECHES 1

Birney, Earle (1904–)
Canadian poet

bloodless civil bore	CANADA 2

Birrell, Augustine (1850–1933)
British essayist

That great dust-heap	HISTORY 2

Birtwistle, Harrison (1934–)
English composer and clarinettist

Composing's not voluntary	IDEAS 3

Birtwistle, Sue (1945–)

plot works like a Swiss clock	FICTION 1

Bishop, Elizabeth (1911–79)
American poet

armoured cars of dreams	DREAMS 2
North's as near as West	MAPS 1
state with the prettiest name	AMERICAN CITIES 4

Bismarck, Otto von (1815–98)
German statesman

art of the possible	POLITICS 7
damned silly thing	BALKANS 2
geographical concept	EUROPE 3
hears the steps of God	POLITICS 6
honest broker	DIPLOMACY 1
painted to look like iron	PEOPLE 4
single Pomeranian grenadier	BALKANS 1
through blood and iron	INTERNATIONAL 6
weak are strong	STRENGTH 6

Björk (1965–)
Icelandic pop star

first rappers of Europe	MUSIC 2

Black, James (1924–)
British analytical pharmacologist

make knowledge available	RESEARCH 1

Blacker, Valentine (1728–1823)
Anglo-Indian soldier

keep your powder dry	PRACTICAL 2

Blackstone, William (1723–80)
English jurist

ten guilty persons escape — JUSTICE 5

Blair, Tony (1953–)
British Labour statesman, Prime Minister since 1997

education and education — EDUCATION 2
hand-up not a hand-out — POVERTY 5
it is time now to do — ACTION 3
People's Princess — DIANA 1
relations with the Monarch — PRIME 3
saying no, not yes — LEADERSHIP 3
sex and sleaze — CORRUPTION 3
stability is a sexy thing — SECURITY 2
tough on the causes of crime — CRIME 1

Blake, Eubie (1883–1983)
American ragtime pianist

ask somebody older than me — SEX 7
I was gonna live this long — OLD AGE 3

Blake, William (1757–1827)
English poet

binds to himself a joy — TRANSIENCE 2
dark Satanic mills — POLLUTION 1
Does the eagle know — KNOWLEDGE 7
doors of perception — INSIGHT 2
drive an angel from your door — COMPASSION 4
fool sees not the same tree — FOOLS 3
green and pleasant land — ENGLAND 2
of the Devil's party — POETS 4
rich, ugly, old maid — CAUTION 3
robin red breast in a cage — ANIMAL RIGHTS 4
seeketh not itself to please — LOVE 8
told with bad intent — TRUTH 7
Tyger Tyger, burning bright — ANIMALS 6
tygers of wrath are wiser — ANGER 2
Where Israel's tents do shine — SCIENCE & REL 1
world in a grain of sand — IMAGINATION 1

Blanchflower, Danny (1926–93)
English footballer

doing things in style — FOOTBALL 1

Bliss, Arthur (1891–1975)
English composer

called the serenity of age — OLD AGE 4

Bloom, Allan (1930–92)
American writer and educator

resist the easy answers — EDUCATION 3
truth is relative — UNIVERSITIES 2

Blücher, Gebhard Lebrecht (1742–1819)
Prussian field marshal

What rubbish — LONDON 2

Blume, Judy (1938–)
American writer

Please help me grow God — YOUTH 3

Blunden, Edmund (1896–1974)
English poet

feeling nervous and shy — MATURITY 2
I am for the woods — TREES 2

Blunkett, David (1947–)
British Labour politician

almost a badge of pride — IGNORANCE 4
failed football coach — DISABILITY 2

Bly, Robert (1926–)
American writer

contact with this Wild Man — MEN 5

Blythe, Ronald (1922–)
English writer

countryman must have praise — MANAGEMENT 1
learn how to be aged — AGEING 2

Boaz, David (1953–)
American lawyer

high crime rates — DRUGS 3

Boesky, Ivan F. (1937–)
American businessman

Greed is all right — GREED 1

Bogan, Louise (1897–1970)
American poet

no wilderness in them — WOMEN 4

Bogart, Humphrey (1899–1957) *American actor*	Please fence me in baby	LONELINESS 1
Bogart, John B. (1848–1921) *American journalist*	dog bites a man	NEWS 2
Bohr, Niels (1885–1962) *Danish physicist*	express yourself more clearly I am told it works shocked by this subject two sorts of truths	SPEECH 2 BELIEF 4 PHYSICS 3 TRUTH 8
Boileau, Nicolas (1636–1711) *French critic and poet*	always find a greater fool Of every four words I write	FOOLS 4 WRITING 6
Bold, Alan (1943–) *Scottish poet*	core Of a world's culture land of the omnipotent No	GENOCIDE 1 SCOTLAND 3
Bolívar, Simón (1783–1830) *Venezuelan patriot and statesman*	ploughed the sea	REVOLUTION 2
Böll, Heinrich (1917–85) *German novelist and short-story writer*	its element is water	RAIN 3
Bolt, Robert (1924–95) *English dramatist*	give his soul Morality's a gesture	WALES 1 MORALITY 2
Bonaparte, Elizabeth Patterson (1785–1879) *American-born wife of Jérôme Bonaparte*	ennui of a solitary existence	HUSBANDS 4
Bonhoeffer, Dietrich (1906–45) *German Lutheran theologian*	decide between alternatives	STRENGTH 7
Bono (1960–) *Irish rock star*	make some sense out of U2 tickets in their hands	AID 2 ROCK 1
Book of Common Prayer, The (1662)	earth to earth, ashes to ashes In the midst of life Lighten our darkness peace in our time, O Lord there is no health in us till death us do part We have erred	DEATH 6 DEATH 5 NIGHT 1 PEACE 6 SIN 5 MARRIAGE 2 SIN 6
Boorstin, Daniel J. (1914–) *American historian*	known for his well-knownness	FAME 6
Booth, Connie see **Cleese, John and Booth, Connie**		
Boothroyd, Betty (1929–) *British Labour politician*	like miners' coal dust toadies that have prospered	PARLIAMENT 4 FLATTERY 2
Boren, James H. (1925–) *American bureaucrat*	When in charge, ponder	BUREAUCRACY 2
Borg, Alan (1942–) *British museum director*	get people through the door	MUSEUMS 2
Borges, Jorge Luis (1899–1986) *Argentinian writer*	Cultures of East and West from a vertiginous country Mirrors and fatherhood two bald men over a comb unfaithful to the translation	LIBRARIES 3 CHANCE 1 UNIVERSE 3 FALKLANDS 2 TRANSLATION 1
Borgia, Cesare (1476–1507) *Italian statesman*	Caesar or nothing	AMBITION 1
Borrow, George (1803–81) *English writer*	literature is a drug	LITERATURE 1

Bosquet, Pierre (1810–61)
French general
ce n'est pas la guerre — ARMY 4

Bossidy, John Collins (1860–1928)
American oculist
Cabots talk only to God — AMERICAN CITIES 5

Boswell, James (1740–95)
Scottish lawyer and biographer
you tossed and gored — CONVERSATION 2

Bottomley, Gordon (1874–1948)
English poet and dramatist
your vision is machines — TECHNOLOGY 6

Bottomley, Horatio (1860–1933)
British newspaper proprietor and financier
No, reaping — PRISON 1
University of Life — UNIVERSITIES 3

Boucicault, Dion (1820–90)
Irish dramatist
Men talk of killing time — TIME 4

Boulay de la Meurthe, Antoine (1761–1840)
French statesman
worse than a crime — MISTAKES 1

Boulez, Pierre (1925–)
French conductor and composer
Revolutions are celebrated — REVOLUTION 3

Boulton, Matthew (1728–1809)
British engineer
world desires to have — TECHNOLOGY 7

Bowen, E. E. (1836–1901)
English schoolmaster
those who are singing to-day — SCHOOLS 2

Bowen, Elizabeth (1899–1973)
Anglo-Irish novelist
absence blots people out — ABSENCE 2
alone against smiling enemies — JEALOUSY 2
attempt a picnic in Eden — INNOCENCE 3
begins to repeat itself — EXPERIENCE 3
can go on mattering — ART 3
English kept history in mind — IRELAND 2
Fate is not an eagle — FATE 4
five o'clock in an evening — SPRING 1
no end to the violations — CHILDREN 3

Bowen, Lord (1835–94)
English judge
blind man in a dark room — JUSTICE 6
rain, it raineth on the just — RAIN 4

Bowie, David (1947–)
English rock musician
next best thing to Chekhov — CULTURE 4
pluralism in social attitudes — TWENTY-FIRST 1
so exposed to the media — YOUTH 4

Bowra, Maurice (1898–1971)
English scholar and literary critic
buggers can't be choosers — HOMOSEXUAL 1
Don't like bishops. Fishy lot — CLERGY 1

Boy George (1961–)
English pop singer and songwriter
gays have sex — HOMOSEXUAL 2
like eating a bag of crisps — SEX 8
She's a gay man trapped — PEOPLE 5
still an A1 freak — CONFORMITY 2

Boyson, Rhodes (1925–)
see **Cox, Brian and Boyson, Rhodes**

Brabazon, Lord (1884–1964)
British aviator and politician
say in twenty minutes — SPEECHES 2

Brackett, Charles (1892–1969) and Wilder, Billy (1906–2002)
American screenwriters
pictures that got small — CINEMA 3
That depends on the tip — BUSINESS 3

Bradbury, Malcolm (1932–2000)
English novelist, critic, and academic
someone else's newspaper — NEWSPAPERS 6

Bradford, John (c.1510–55)
English Protestant martyr
But for the grace of God — CIRCUMSTANCE 3

Bradley, F. H. (1846–1924) *English philosopher*	finding of bad reasons	PHILOSOPHY 3
Bradley, Omar (1893–1981) *American general*	involve us in the wrong war	INTERNATIONAL 7
	second prize for the runner-up	WARFARE 2
	Sermon on the Mount	SCIENCE & REL 2
Bramah, Ernest (1868–1942) *English writer*	cannot meet a cripple	CONVERSATION 3
Brancusi, Constantin (1876–1957) *Romanian sculptor*	real meaning of things	SIMPLICITY 1
Brandreth, Gyles (1948–) *British writer and broadcaster*	I am going bald	COMMITMENT 2
Branson, Richard (1950–) *English businessman*	above what they would expect	ACHIEVEMENT 3
	possibility of good times	EMPLOYMENT 3
	you must *do* things	ACTION 4
Braque, Georges (1882–1963) *French painter*	Art is meant to disturb	ARTS AND SCI 3
Braun, Wernher von (1912–77) *German-born American rocket engineer*	don't know what I am doing	RESEARCH 2
	Man belongs wherever he wants	SPACE 2
Braverman, Harry *American industrial historian*	source of status	CONSUMER 1
Brecht, Bertolt (1898–1956) *German dramatist*	compared with founding a bank	MONEY 8
	dissolve the people	REVOLUTION 4
	Food comes first	MORALITY 3
	Hesitating doesn't matter	DELAY 1
	land that needs heroes	HEROES 4
	plans are always ruined	POWER 5
	set a limit to infinite error	SCIENCE 2
	temptation to be good	GOODNESS 2
	too long without a war here	PEACE 7
	trampling down twelve others	CHARITY 2
	underwear first, last	CLOTHES 3
	War always finds a way	WARFARE 3
	Who built Thebes	WORK 3
Brenan, Gerald (1894–1987) *British travel writer and novelist*	kept alive by heresies	RELIGION 2
	poor know that it is money	MONEY 9
	We are closer to the ants	LEISURE 3
Brenner, Sydney (1927–) *British scientist*	modern computer hovers	COMPUTERS 3
Bridger, Roy	sewage and refuse distributed	PROGRESS 5
Bridges, Robert (1844–1930) *English poet*	When men were all asleep	SNOW 1
Brillat-Savarin, Anthelme (1755–1826) *French jurist and gourmet*	Adam was born hungry	COOKING 4
	does more for human happiness	INVENTIONS 3
	tell you what you are	EATING 1
Brittain, Vera (1893–1970) *English writer*	never your possession	WIVES 3
Britten, Philip (1957–) *British chef*	restaurant is like a theatre	FOOD 4
Brockbank, Russell (1913–) *British cartoonist*	Continent isolated	EUROPE 4
Broder, David (1929–) *American columnist*	wants the presidency so much	PRESIDENCY 2

Brodkey, Harold (1930–96)
American writer

optimistic for the moment — DYING 3

Brodrick, St John (1856–1942)
British Conservative politician

intelligence pays to humbug — TACT 1

Brodsky, Joseph (1940–96)
Russian-born American poet

antidote to the vulgarity — VULGARITY 2
form of moral insurance — LITERATURE 2

Bronowski, Jacob (1908–74)
Polish-born mathematician and humanist

cutting edge of the mind — ACTION 5
get into the first team — FAILURE 2
intoxication with pain — CRUELTY 2
tenth American muse — COUNSELLING 1
way to a pertinent answer — SCIENCE 3

Brontë, Charlotte (1816–55)
English novelist

face of the Pharisee — HYPOCRISY 1
satisfied with tranquillity — ACTION 6

Brontë, Emily (1818–48)
English novelist and poet

My love for Heathcliff — LOVE 9
No coward soul is mine — COURAGE 2

Brook, Peter (1925–)
English producer and director

theatre exists in movement — THEATRE 3

Brooke, Rupert (1887–1915)
English poet

cool kindliness of sheets — SLEEP 1
corner of a foreign field — PATRIOTISM 3
English unofficial rose — FLOWERS 1
honey still for tea — PAST 3
matched us with His hour — WORLD W I 3
men with Splendid Hearts — ENGLAND 3

Brookner, Anita (1928–)
British novelist and art historian

award just for women — AWARDS 3
dependent on strong beliefs — WIT 1
never take the blame — GUILT 2
Real love is a pilgrimage — LOVE 10
sadness and impossibility — ROMANCE 2
woman begins to perceive — MOTHERS 1

Brooks, Gwendolyn (1917–2000)
American poet

Abortions will not let you — PREGNANCY 1
Exhaust the little moment — PRESENT 4

Brooks, J.

four-legged friend — ANIMALS 7

Brooks, Mel (1927–)
American film director and actor

when you got it, flaunt it — SELF-ESTEEM 5

Brougham, Lord (1778–1868)
Scottish lawyer and politician

impossible to enslave — EDUCATION 4

Broun, Heywood (1888–1939)
American journalist

conviction begins as a whim — FANATICISM 1
job of sewing on a button — MEN 6
no axes are being ground — CENSORSHIP 2

Brown, Christy (1932–81)
Irish writer

Painting became everything — PAINTING 2

Brown, Frederic (1906–72)
American science fiction writer

some day may be — FANTASY 2

Brown, H. Rap (1943–)
American Black Power leader

American as cherry pie — VIOLENCE 5

Brown, Lew (1893–1958)
see De Sylva, Buddy and Brown, Lew

Brown, Thomas (1663–1704)
English satirist

I do not love thee, Dr Fell — LIKES 1

Browne, Anthony Montague (1923–)
British civil servant

dancing in a world of pins — TRANSIENCE 3

Browne, Thomas (1605–82)	all Africa and her prodigies	HUMAN RACE 3
English writer and physician	charged the troops of error	TRUTH 9
	death is the cure of all	MEDICINE 2
	families last not three oaks	TREES 3
Browning, Elizabeth Barrett (1806–61)	birds will sing at dawn	SIMILARITY 2
English poet	Colours seen by candle-light	CHANGE 5
	devilish when respectable	REPUTATION 2
	for love's sake only	LOVE 11
	genius found respectable	GENIUS 3
	hopeless grief is passionless	SORROW 3
	large-brained woman	WRITERS 4
	Let me count the ways	LOVE 12
	lips say, 'God be pitiful'	PRAYER 5
	run the colours from my life	SUFFERING 7
Browning, Frederick ('Boy') (1896–1965)	going a bridge too far	WORLD W II 1
British soldier		
Browning, Robert (1812–89)	All's right with the world	OPTIMISM 1
English poet	distinct damnations	BIBLE 2
	Faultless to a fault	PERFECTION 2
	fifty hopes and fears	BELIEF 5
	fight begins within himself	SELF-KNOW 4
	first fine careless rapture	BIRDS 1
	forgotten even by God	DESPAIR 2
	high man, aiming at a million	ACHIEVEMENT 4
	I was ever a fighter	DEFIANCE 2
	Ignorance is not innocence	IGNORANCE 5
	Just for a riband	BETRAYAL 1
	leave a child alone	CHILDREN 4
	Leave Now for dogs and apes	TIME 5
	Never glad confident morning	DISILLUSION 1
	Never the time and the place	OPPORTUNITY 1
	Oh, to be in England	SPRING 2
	ravage with impunity a rose	SENSES 1
	reach should exceed his grasp	AMBITION 2
	roses, roses, all the way	SUCCESS 3
	splendour of a sudden thought	THINKING 3
	terrible choice	CHOICE 4
Bruce, Lenny (1925–66)	liberals can understand everything	POLITICS 8
American comedian	like kissing God	DRUGS 4
	what is, not what should be	CIRCUMSTANCE 4
Brundtland, Gro Harlem (1939–)	government as an adversary	ENVIRONMENT 3
Norwegian stateswoman		
Bruno, Frank (1961–)	Know what I mean, Harry	INSIGHT 3
English boxer	show business with blood	BOXING 2
Bryan, William Jennings (1860–1925)	upon a cross of gold	GREED 2
American Democratic politician		
Bryant, Anita (1940–)	made Adam and Bruce	HOMOSEXUAL 3
Bryant, Arthur (1899–1985)	denouncing Tyranny	LIBERTY 3
British historian and biographer		
Bryson, Bill (1951–)	how flat and empty	AMERICAN CITIES 6
American travel writer	like living inside Tupperware	WEATHER 2
	Now we build shopping malls	SHOPPING 1
	only possible pet is a cow	ANIMALS 8
	out of the container	MATURITY 3
	recapture the comforts	TRAVEL 3
Brzezinski, Zbigniew (1928–)	empire or a democracy	RUSSIA 3
American politician		

Buber, Martin (1878–1965) *Austrian-born religious philosopher*	Through the Thou	SELF 5
Buchan, John (1875–1940) *Scottish novelist; Governor-General of* *Canada, 1935–40*	close to great minds if you don't weaken no invisible means of support	EDUCATION 5 DETERMINATION 2 ATHEISM 1
Buchman, Frank (1878–1961) *American evangelist*	anti-Christ of Communism for everyone's need	HITLER 2 GREED 3
Buck, Pearl S. (1892–1973) *American writer*	relentless survivors	ASIA 2
Buerk, Michael (1946–) *British broadcaster and journalist*	manufacturer's instructions	SMOKING 2
Buffon, Comte de (1707–88) *French naturalist*	style is the man	STYLE 3
Bullard, Edward (1907–80) *English geophysicist*	Rutherford was a disaster	PROBLEMS 3
Buller, Arthur (1874–1944) *British botanist and mycologist*	returned on the previous night	PHYSICS 4
Bulwer-Lytton, Edward (1803–73) *British novelist and politician*	In science, read the newest mightier than the sword	ARTS AND SCI 4 WRITING 7
Bunting, Basil (1900–85) *English poet*	workshop, larder, middenpit	EARTH 1
Buñuel, Luis (1900–83) *Spanish film director*	Thanks to God	ATHEISM 2
Bunyan, John (1628–88) *English writer and Nonconformist preacher*	from the gates of heaven Hanging is too good for him He that is down One leak will sink a ship	HELL 2 PUNISHMENT 3 HUMILITY 2 CAUSES 3
Burchill, Julie (1960–) *English journalist and writer*	dizzying and delirious range make life easier for men No one over the age of 15 silly Sloane	SEX 9 WOMEN 5 PARTIES 2 DIANA 2
Burgess, Anthony (1917–93) *English novelist and critic*	artificial respiration substitute for reading trades on belief Tudor monarchy plus telephones typewriters keep going	SEDUCTION 1 BOOKS 5 ITALY 1 PRESIDENCY 3 TECHNOLOGY 8
Burgon, John William (1813–88) *English clergyman*	rose-red city	ASIA 3
Burke, Edmund (1729–97) *Irish-born Whig politician and man of letters*	ambition can creep antagonist is our helper begin our public affections being despised grow great ceases to be a virtue chip of the old 'block' concessions of fear conduct of a losing party Custom reconciles us effectually robs the mind good man to do nothing grown man in the cradle look forward to posterity neighbour's house is on fire not given to men Our patience will achieve more	AMBITION 3 ENEMIES 4 FAMILY 4 DANGER 1 TOLERANCE 3 SIMILARITY 3 STRENGTH 8 FAILURE 3 HABIT 3 FEAR 4 EVIL 4 PROGRESS 6 FUTURE 4 PRACTICAL 3 TAXES 2 PATIENCE 2

Burke, Edmund (*cont.*)

plan the future by the past	FORESIGHT 4
religion of feeble minds	SUPERNATURAL 7
those who make the noise	WORDS/DEED 1
virtue of paper government	ADMIN 2
When bad men combine	COOPERATION 3
worst sort of tyranny	LAWS 2
Your representative owes you	PARLIAMENT 5

Burke, Johnny (1908–64)
American songwriter

Pennies from heaven	OPTIMISM 2

Burney, Fanny (1752–1840)
English novelist and diarist

errors and absurdities	PERFECTION 3
so insipid as a medium	INDIFFERENCE 2

Burns, George (1896–1996)
American comedian

busy driving taxicabs	EXPERTS 1

Burns, John (1858–1943)
British Liberal politician

Thames is liquid history	RIVERS 2

Burns, Robert (1759–96)
Scottish poet

auld acquaintance be forgot	FRIENDSHIP 6
chieftain o' the puddin'-race	FOOD 5
Comin thro' the rye	MEETING 1
cow'rin', tim'rous beastie	FEAR 5
For auld lang syne	MEMORY 5
Freedom and Whisky	ALCOHOL 3
heart's in the Highlands	SCOTLAND 4
I rhyme for fun	POETRY 4
know not what's resisted	TEMPTATION 2
let the Lord be thankit	EATING 2
Luve's like a red, red rose	LOVE 13
man's a man for a' that	EQUALITY 3
Man's inhumanity to man	CRUELTY 3
petrifies the feeling	SIN 7
rank is but the guinea's stamp	ARISTOCRACY 1
schemes o' mice an' men	FORESIGHT 5
see oursels as others see us	SELF-KNOW 5
spark o' Nature's fire	EDUCATION 6
then she made the lasses, O	WOMEN 6
Welcome to your gory bed	SCOTLAND 5

Burnum, Burnum (1936–97)
Australian political activist

England's native people	AUSTRALIA 1

Burroughs, William S. (1914–97)
American novelist

face of total need	EVIL 5
In homosexual sex you know	HOMOSEXUAL 4
Most natural painkiller	LAST WORDS 3
ultimate merchandise	DRUGS 5

Burton, Robert (1577–1640)
English clergyman and scholar

All poets are mad	POETRY 5
as true as another	RELIGION 3
Diogenes struck the father	PARENTS 2
lard their lean books	PLAGIARISM 1
See one promontory	TRAVEL 4
so sweet as Melancholy	SORROW 4

Bush, Barbara (1925–)
wife of George Bush

I wish him well	PRESIDENCY 4
name things after you	NAMES 2
spent with a husband, a child	SUCCESS 4

Bush, George (1924–)
*American Republican statesman, President
1989–93*

boring kind of guy	BOREDOM 3
eat any more broccoli	FOOD 6
new world order	FUTURE 5
Oh, the vision thing	IDEALISM 3
Read my lips: no new taxes	TAXES 3
thousand points of light	UNITED S 4

Bussy-Rabutin, Comte de (1618–93) *French soldier and poet*	side of the big squadrons	STRENGTH 9
Butler, Nicholas Murray (1862–1947) *President of Columbia University*	knows more and more	EXPERTS 2
Butler, R. A. (1902–82) *British Conservative politician*	bit like a Rolls-Royce greatest adventurer has to be a butcher keep running with the pack	CIVIL SERV 2 CHURCHILL 3 PRIME 4 POLITICS 9
Butler, Samuel (1612–80) *English poet*	complies against his will perceive a juggler's sleight two hundred pounds a year	OPINION 1 DECEPTION 1 CYNICISM 3
Butler, Samuel (1835–1902) *English novelist*	apology for the Devil business of life is to enjoy enclosing a wilderness of idea God cannot alter the past good digestions history of revivals like playing a violin solo make a fool of yourself making another egg O God! O Montreal one can lay it on so thick public buys its opinions soon leaves off talking symphony by Wordsworth	BIBLE 3 ANIMALS 9 LANGUAGE 3 HISTORY 3 EATING 3 ART 4 LIFE 4 DOGS 1 LIFE SCI 2 CANADA 3 PRAISE 1 OPINION 2 CONSCIENCE 1 POETS 5
Butler, William (1535–1618) *English physician*	made a better berry	FOOD 7
Byatt, A. S. (1936–) *English novelist*	change the people who teach	LITERATURE 3
Byrd, William (1543–1623) *English composer*	delightful to Nature	SINGING 2
Byron, Lord (1788–1824) *English poet*	all the virtues of Man blown my brains out burnt each other chase the glowing Hours climax of all human ills critics all are ready made damned cutting and slashing detest at leisure finished by a death first silent, then talky fly from, need not be to hate found myself famous Friendship is Love 'I told you so.' In her first passion keep down a single petticoat know that which we are little still she strove not always be a Tory paint on the face of Existence Petrarch's wife Roll on, thou deep scream in a low voice She walks in beauty Stranger than fiction Sweet is revenge talent of a liar wedlock's the devil	DOGS 2 IN-LAWS 1 CHRISTIAN 1 DANCE 5 DEBT 1 CRITICS 3 PUBLISHING 2 HATRED 1 ENDING 3 PARTIES 3 SOLITUDE 4 FAME 7 FRIENDSHIP 7 ADVICE 5 LOVE 14 CENSORSHIP 3 SELF-KNOW 6 SEDUCTION 2 POLITICAL P 3 HOPE 2 FAMILIAR 2 SEA 2 CHILDREN 5 BEAUTY 3 TRUTH 10 REVENGE 4 FICTION 2 MARRIAGE 3

Byron, Lord (*cont.*)	when Rome falls	ITALY 2
	Where burning Sappho loved	GREECE 1
	wine and women, mirth	PLEASURE 5
	winter—ending in July	WINTER 1
	woman's whole existence	MEN/WOMEN 4
	young barbarians all at play	CRUELTY 4
Byron, Robert (1905–41) *English traveller, art critic, and historian*	St Peter's is vilely small	BUILDINGS 1
Bywater, Michael	Queen drops in for tea	BRITAIN 3
Cabell, James Branch (1879–1958) *American novelist and essayist*	best of all possible worlds	PESSIMISM 2
Caesar, Julius (100–44 BC) *Roman general and statesman*	believe what they wish	SELF-INTEREST 2
	die is cast	CRISES 4
	Et tu, Brute?	BETRAYAL 2
	first in a village	AMBITION 4
	I came, I saw, I conquered	SUCCESS 5
	must be above suspicion	REPUTATION 3
Cage, Nicolas (1964–) *American actor*	asked her to put me on a quest	COURTSHIP 3
	You give up all your freedom	SACRIFICE 2
Cahn, Sammy (1913–93) *American songwriter*	love and marriage	MARRIAGE 4
	wasted on the young	YOUTH 5
Caine, Michael (1933–) *English film actor*	My career must be slipping	SUCCESS 6
	Not many people know	INFORMATION 2
Caligula (AD 12–41) *Roman emperor from AD 37*	feel that he is dying	CRUELTY 5
Callaghan, James (1912–) *British Labour statesman, Prime Minister 1976–9*	didn't go down on one knee	COURTSHIP 4
	never reach the promised land	IDEALISM 4
	vote for an early Christmas	SELF-INTEREST 3
	winter of discontent	TRADE 3
Callas, Maria (1923–77) *American-born operatic soprano*	great teachers foresee	TEACHING 3
Calverley, C. S. (1831–84) *English writer*	Folks *prefer* in fact a hovel	LIKES 2
Calvino, Italo (1923–85) *Italian novelist and short-story writer*	already begun before	BEGINNING 2
	In love, as in gluttony	PLEASURE 6
Camara, Helder (1909–99) *Brazilian priest*	why the poor have no food	POVERTY 6
Cambronne, Pierre, Baron de (1770–1842) *French general*	*La Garde meurt*	WATERLOO 1
Cameron, James (1954–) *Canadian-born American film director*	I'll be back	PARTING 4
Cameron, Simon (1799–1889) *American politician*	when he's bought stays bought	POLITICIANS 3
Campbell, Jane Montgomery (1817–78) *English hymn-writer*	We plough the fields	FARMING 1
Campbell, Mrs Patrick (1865–1940) *English actress*	deep peace of the double-bed	MARRIAGE 5
	don't do it in the street	SEX 10
Campbell, Naomi (1970–) *British fashion model*	make my boyfriends famous	GOSSIP 2
Campbell, Roy (1901–57) *South African poet*	I hate 'Humanity'	HUMAN RACE 4
	Keeping a light-house	ANIMALS 10

Campbell, Roy (*cont.*)	seldom strictly faithful	TRANSLATION 2
Campbell, Thomas (1777–1844)	Barabbas was a publisher	PUBLISHING 3
Scottish poet	distance lends enchantment	COUNTRY 2
Camus, Albert (1913–60)	all life goes rotten	WORK 4
French novelist, dramatist, and essayist	beautiful twilight	LIES 3
	man who says no	REVOLUTION 6
	mind watches itself	INTELLECTUALS 3
	morality and the duty of man	SPORTS 3
	Poor people's memory	MEMORY 6
	reinforcement of the State	REVOLUTION 5
	way of getting the answer yes	CHARM 2
	We are all special cases	SELF-INTEREST 4
	When the imagination sleeps	IMAGINATION 2
Canetti, Elias (1905–94)	clutch out of the darkness	CRIME 2
Bulgarian-born writer and novelist	scream for help	DREAMS 3
Canning, George (1770–1827)	from the candid friend	FRIENDSHIP 8
British Tory statesman, Prime Minister 1827		
Cannon, Moya (1956–)	Our windy, untidy loft	SKIES 1
Irish poet	something about winter	WINTER 2
Cantona, Eric (1966–)	seagulls follow a trawler	JOURNALISM 4
French footballer		
Capa, Robert (1913–54)	you aren't close enough	PRESS 1
Hungarian-born American photojournalist		
Capone, Al (1899–1947)	Once in the racket	CRIME 3
Italian-born American gangster		
Capote, Truman (1924–84)	box of chocolate liqueurs	VENICE 2
American writer and novelist		
Capp, Al (1907–79)	product of the untalented	PAINTING 3
American cartoonist		
Capra, Frank (1897–1991)	no rules in filmmaking	CINEMA 4
Italian-born American film director		
Caracciolo, Francesco (1752–99)	only one sauce	ENGLAND 4
Neapolitan diplomat		
Cardus, Neville (1889–1975)	eternal Englishness	CRICKET 3
English critic and writer		
Carey, George (1935–)	elderly lady, who mutters	CHURCH 1
Archbishop of Canterbury from 1991	one generation away	CHURCH 2
Carey, John (1934–)	contempt for ordinary citizens	CAREERS 2
British literary scholar		
Carlyle, Jane (1801–66)	person you and I took me for	CHARACTER 4
wife of Thomas Carlyle	these kisses on paper	KISSING 2
Carlyle, Thomas (1795–1881)	collection of books	UNIVERSITIES 4
Scottish historian and political philosopher	despotism tempered by epigrams	FRANCE 1
	end of man is an action	WORDS/DEED 2
	foul sluggard's comfort	IDLENESS 3
	Gad! she'd better	UNIVERSE 4
	man who can stand prosperity	ADVERSITY 4
	prove anything by figures	STATISTICS 4
	speech is shallow as Time	SILENCE 1
	three great elements	CIVILIZATION 1
	tool-using animal	TECHNOLOGY 9
	well-written Life	BIOGRAPHY 5

Carmichael, Stokely (1941–98) *American Black Power leader*	only position for women	WOMAN'S R 4
Carnegie, Andrew (1835–1919) *American industrialist and philanthropist*	man who dies . . . rich	WEALTH 5
Carnegie, Dale (1888–1955) *American writer and lecturer*	How to win friends	SUCCESS 7
Carr, Emily (1871–1945) *Canadian artist*	more alone while living	SOLITUDE 5
Carr, Michael see **Kennedy, Jimmy and Carr, Michael**		
Carrington, Lord (1919–) *British Conservative politician*	run over by a bus	THATCHER 2
Carroll, Lewis (1832–98) *English writer and logician*	all must have prizes	WINNING 2
	Begin at the beginning	BEGINNING 3
	but as it isn't, it ain't	LOGIC 2
	cabbages—and kings—	CONVERSATION 4
	Curiouser and curiouser	SURPRISE 2
	Curtsey while you're thinking	MANNERS 2
	I never loved a dear Gazelle	VALUE 4
	jam to-morrow	PRESENT 5
	jury eagerly wrote down	MATHS 3
	like a portmanteau	MEANING 3
	merely conventional signs	MAPS 2
	only does it to annoy	BEHAVIOUR 4
	pictures or conversations	BOOKS 6
	run at least twice as fast	EFFORT 2
	seven maids with seven mops	PERSISTENCE 1
	six impossible things	BELIEF 6
	sought it with thimbles	WAYS 3
	Take care of the sense	SPEECH 3
	till the week after next	DELAY 2
	twice as natural	APPEARANCE 3
	un-birthday present	GIVING 2
	what I choose it to mean	WORDS 4
	What I tell you three times	TRUTH 11
	which is to be master	POWER 6
	you might be any shape	NAMES 3
	you should say what you mean	MEANING 2
Carson, Edward (1854–1935) *British lawyer and politician*	I am very much at sea	NAVY 2
Carson, Rachel (1907–64) *American zoologist*	mornings are strangely silent	POLLUTION 2
Carter, Angela (1940–92) *English novelist*	Clothes are our weapons	CLOTHES 4
	happens to *other* people	COMEDY 1
	Ms means nudge, nudge	WOMEN 7
Carter, Chris (1957–) *American producer and director*	truth is out there	SECRECY 4
Carter, Henry (d. 1806)	True patriots we	AUSTRALIA 2
Carter, Howard (1874–1939) *English archaeologist*	Yes, wonderful things	INVENTIONS 4
Carter, Jimmy (1924–) *American Democratic statesman, President 1977–81*	adultery in my heart	TEMPTATION 3
	never won an argument with her	ARGUMENT 3
Cartier-Bresson, Henri (1908–) *French photographer and artist*	precise organization of forms	PHOTOGRAPHY 4

Cartland, Barbara (1901–2000)
English writer

diet directs sexual energy	DIETS 3
her figure or her face	MIDDLE AGE 7
make love in the afternoon	FRANCE 2
pink on the walls	COLOURS 1

Casals, Pablo (1876–1973)
Spanish cellist, conductor, and composer

like a beautiful woman	MUSICAL INST 3
works and is not bored	AGEING 3

Cash, Pat (1965–)
Australian tennis player

McDonald's of sport	TENNIS 2

Cassandre, A. M. (1901–68)
French illustrator

visual telegram	ADVERTISING 2

Cassatt, Mary (1844–1926)
American artist

people so love to wander	EXPLORATION 1

Casson, Hugh (1910–99)
English architect

hard steel canisters	CARS 4

Castle, Barbara (1910–2002)
British Labour politician

best man among them	THATCHER 3
fight for what I believe in	DETERMINATION 3

Castro, Fidel (1927–)
Cuban statesman

Capitalism is using its money	COMMUNISM 3
History will absolve me	REVOLUTION 7

Cather, Willa (1873–1947)
American novelist

Germans classify	ORGANIZATION 3
go to better things	SPEED 2
such a thing as creative hate	HATRED 2
they seem more resigned	TREES 4

Catherine the Great (1729–96)
Empress of Russia from 1762

I shall be an autocrat	POWER 7

Cato the Elder (234–149 BC)
Roman statesman, orator, and writer

Grasp the subject	SPEECHES 3

Catullus (c.84–c.54 BC)
Roman poet

hail, and farewell evermore	PARTING 5

Cavafy, Constantine (1863–1933)
Greek poet

barbarians are to arrive	CULTURE 5
When you set out for Ithaka	TRAVEL 5

Cave, A. J. E.
see **Strauss, William L. and Cave, A. J. E.**

Cavell, Edith (1865–1915)
English nurse

patriotism is not enough	PATRIOTISM 4

Ceaușescu, Nicolae (1918–89)
Romanian Communist statesman

Fidel Castro is right	ENEMIES 5

Cecil, Lord Edward (1867–1918)
British soldier and civil servant

agreement between two men	COMPROMISE 1

Cecil, Lord Hugh (1869–1956)
British politician

good music and bad preaching	CHURCH 3

Celan, Paul (1920–70)
German poet

play death more sweetly	DEATH 7
There's nothing in the world	POETRY 6

Centlivre, Susannah (c.1669–1723)
English actress and dramatist

in love as well as law	CORRUPTION 4

Cerf, Bennett (1898–1971)
American humorist

Coleridge was a drug addict	WRITERS 5

Cervantes (1547–1616)
Spanish novelist

Good painters imitate nature	PAINTING 4
haves and the have-nots	POSSESSIONS 3

Cézanne, Paul (1839–1906)
French painter

in terms of the cylinder	PAINTING 5
Monet is only an eye	ARTISTS 1

Chalmers, Patrick Reginald (1872–1942) *British banker and writer*	lost upon the roundabouts	WINNING 3
Chamberlain, Joseph (1836–1914) *British Liberal politician*	beyond the next fortnight day of small nations	POLITICS 10 INTERNATIONAL 8
Chamberlain, Neville (1869–1940) *British Conservative statesman, Prime Minister 1937–40*	all are losers it is peace for our time quarrel in a far away country	WARFARE 4 PEACE 8 WORLD W II 2
Chamfort, Nicolas-Sébastien (1741–94) *French writer*	poor are Europe's blacks Qualities too elevated	POVERTY 7 CHARACTER 5
Chandler, Raymond (1888–1959) *American writer of detective fiction*	Alcohol is like love aspirin for a brain tumour big hard-boiled city Down these mean streets gun in his hand invited to Hollywood It was a blonde purist who reads your proofs	ALCOHOL 4 CRIME 4 AMERICAN CITIES 7 HEROES 5 CRIME FICT 2 CINEMA 5 HAIR 1 GRAMMAR 1
Chanel, Coco (1883–1971) *French couturière*	dress to astonish one another Passion always goes that's for the cows Youth is something very new	CLOTHES 5 EMOTIONS 3 HAPPINESS 7 YOUTH 6
Channon, Henry ('Chips') (1897–1958) *American-born British Conservative politician and diarist*	Catholic and sensual have a discreet soul memoirs of the frivolous	TRAVEL 6 DIARIES 2 BIOGRAPHY 6
Chaplin, Charlie (1889–1977) *English film actor and director*	policeman and a pretty girl saddest thing I can imagine Words are cheap	COMEDY 2 LUXURY 1 CINEMA 6
Chapman, Graham (1941–89), **Cleese, John** (1939–), et al. *British comedy writers and actors*	something completely different Spanish Inquisition This is an ex-parrot	CHANGE 6 SURPRISE 3 DEATH 8
Charles I (1600–49) *King from 1625*	before you be accused subject and a sovereign	APOLOGY 2 ROYALTY 3
Charles II (1630–85) *King from 1660*	my actions are my ministers' welfare of this realm	WORDS/DEED 3 NAVY 3
Charles, Prince of Wales (1948–) *Heir apparent to the British throne*	come and talk to the plants monstrous carbuncle whatever that may mean	GARDENS 5 BUILDINGS 2 LOVE 15
Charles, Hugh (1907–) see **Parker, Ross and Charles, Hugh**		
Charteris, Lord (1913–99) *the Queen's former private secretary*	Duchess of York is a vulgarian	VULGARITY 3
Chateaubriand, François-René (1768–1848) *French writer and diplomat*	can be imitated by none	ORIGINALITY 3
Chatwin, Bruce (1940–89) *English writer and traveller*	If you walk hard enough words for moral ideas	EXERCISE 1 MORALITY 4
Chaucer, Geoffrey (c.1343–1400) *English poet*	Go, litel bok make his Englissh sweete Mordre wol out rose in May	WRITING 8 SPEECH 4 MURDER 4 BEAUTY 4
Chekhov, Anton (1860–1904) *Russian dramatist and short-story writer*	as simple as in life as we see it in our dreams become a man's friend	THEATRE 5 THEATRE 4 FRIENDSHIP 9

Chekhov, Anton (*cont.*)	common hatred for something	RELATIONSHIPS 5
	deprived of the company	MEN/WOMEN 5
	disease is incurable	MEDICINE 3
	God has given us vast forests	RUSSIA 4
	in mourning for my life	SORROW 5
	land grows poorer and uglier	ENVIRONMENT 4
	objective as a chemist	WRITING 9
	You have lovely eyes	BEAUTY 5
Cher (1946–) *American singer and actress*	at every time in your life	LOVE 16
	counterfeit $20 bill	BODY 4
Cherry-Garrard, Apsley (1882–1959) *British polar explorer*	way of having a bad time	EXPLORATION 2
Cherry-Garrard, Apsley (1882–1959) see **Atkinson, E. L. and Cherry-Garrard, Apsley**		
Chesterfield, Lord (1694–1773) *English writer and politician*	accomplishments give lustre	KNOWLEDGE 8
	chapter of accidents	CHANCE 2
	injury is sooner forgotten	INSULTS 2
	pleasure is momentary	SEX 11
	proper subject of conversation	CONVERSATION 5
	refuge of weak minds	IDLENESS 4
	religion and matrimony	ADVICE 6
	take care of minutes	TIME 6
	tone of the company	BEHAVIOUR 5
Chesterton, G. K. (1874–1936) *English essayist, novelist, and poet*	adventure is an inconvenience	IMAGINATION 3
	all four-footed things	ANIMALS 11
	all in lunatic asylums	SELF 6
	all their songs are sad	IRELAND 3
	blind side of the heart	TRUST 3
	can't see the solution	PROBLEMS 4
	Cocoa is a vulgar beast	FOOD 8
	danger does lie in logic	ARTS AND SCI 5
	democracy of the dead	TRADITION 2
	don't believe in nothing	ATHEISM 3
	drains that are worse	NEIGHBOURS 3
	draw on the ceiling	PLEASURE 7
	great things from the valley	INSIGHT 4
	Hardy went down to botanize	WRITERS 6
	his own towering style	POETS 6
	leave a thing alone	CHANGE 7
	Literature is a luxury	FICTION 3
	men who have no opinions	PREJUDICE 1
	miss the train before	PUNCTUALITY 2
	My mother, drunk or sober	PATRIOTISM 5
	saying 'Lord Jones Dead'	JOURNALISM 5
	stupid enough to want it	WEALTH 6
	Thieves respect property	CRIME 5
	tried and found wanting	CHRISTIAN 2
	uninteresting subject	KNOWLEDGE 9
	We make our friends	NEIGHBOURS 2
	wise man hide a pebble	SECRECY 5
	woman, the universal mother	WOMEN 8
Chevalier, Maurice (1888–1972) *French singer and actor*	Considering the alternative	AGEING 4
Child, Lydia Maria (1802–80) *American abolitionist and suffragist*	live to see women vote	WOMAN'S R 5
Chisholm, Melanie ('Mel C.') (1974–) *English pop singer*	Bigger than Buddha	FAME 8

Choiseul, Duc de (1719–85)
French politician
read the signs of the times — POLITICIANS 4

Chomsky, Noam (1928–)
American linguistics scholar
Colourless green ideas — GRAMMAR 2
never even made a phone call — INTERNET 2

Christie, Agatha (1890–1976)
English writer of detective fiction
marry an archaeologist — ARCHAEOLOGY 1
One Way Street — EXPERIENCE 4
These little grey cells — INTELLIGENCE 2

Christie, Linford (1960–)
Jamaican-born British sprinter
never run for the bus — SPEED 3

Chuo Wen-chun (*c.*179–117 BC)
Chinese poet
man With a single heart — HUSBANDS 5

Church, Francis Pharcellus (1839–1906)
American journalist
there is a Santa Claus — CHRISTMAS 4

Churchill, Charles (1731–64)
English poet
adepts in the speaking trade — SPEECHES 4
Apt Alliteration's artful aid — WORDPLAY 2
daring to excel — EXCELLENCE 2
Keep up appearances — HYPOCRISY 2

Churchill, Lord Randolph (1849–94)
British Conservative politician
Ulster will fight — NORTHERN 4
what those damned dots meant — MATHS 4

Churchill, Winston (1874–1965)
British Conservative statesman, Prime Minister 1940–5, 1951–5
ability to foretell — POLITICIANS 5
After Alamein — WORLD W II 3
almost as exciting as war — POLITICS 11
Bessie, you're ugly — DRUNKEN 1
bloodthirsty guttersnipe — HITLER 3
blood, toil, tears and sweat — SACRIFICE 3
bodyguard of lies — PROPAGANDA 3
British nation is unique — BRITAIN 4
called upon to give the roar — SPEECHES 6
can't change his mind — FANATICISM 2
casts a shadow — AWARDS 4
centre upon number one — LEADERSHIP 4
combines force with candour — PAINTING 6
delicious and intoxicating — REVENGE 5
Don't argue the matter — PROBLEMS 5
dreary steeples of Fermanagh — NORTHERN 3
empires of the mind — EDUCATION 7
end of the beginning — ENDING 4
fire brigade and the fire — IMPARTIAL 1
Give us the tools — ACHIEVEMENT 5
good deal to be modest about — PEOPLE 6
I am a glow-worm — CHARACTER 6
If Hitler invaded hell — INTERNATIONAL 9
In defeat unbeatable — PEOPLE 7
In war: resolution — WARFARE 5
ingenuity to re-rat — BETRAYAL 3
iron curtain has descended — COMMUNISM 4
jaw-jaw is always better — DIPLOMACY 3
man added to his dignity — SELF-ESTEEM 6
merely the glittering scum — CULTURE 6
Nothing but rum, sodomy — NAVY 4
one who feeds a crocodile — DIPLOMACY 2
Out of intense complexities — SIMPLICITY 2
Pigs treat us as equals — ANIMALS 12
powers at their disposal — SCHOOLS 3
putting milk into babies — CHILDREN 6
read books of quotations — QUOTATIONS 3
riddle wrapped in a mystery — RUSSIA 5
so much owed by so many — AIR FORCE 2
sorry for the poor browns — COLOURS 2

Churchill, Winston (*cont.*)	Take away that pudding	FOOD 9
	taken more out of alcohol	ALCOHOL 5
	This was their finest hour	WORLD W II 5
	up with which I will not put	GRAMMAR 3
	victory at all costs	WINNING 4
	walking with destiny	CRISES 5
	we shall never surrender	WORLD W II 4
	what they have said	SPEECHES 5
	worst form of Government	DEMOCRACY 3
	worthy to pass into Harrow	EXAMINATIONS 1
Ciano, Count Galeazzo (1903–44) *Italian fascist politician*	Victory has a hundred fathers	DEFEAT 2
Cibber, Colley (1671–1757) *English dramatist*	Oh! how many torments	WEDDINGS 4
Cicero (106–43 BC) *Roman orator and statesman*	good of the people	LAWS 3
	Laws are silent	WARFARE 6
	O tempora, O mores	BEHAVIOUR 6
	some philosopher has said it	PHILOSOPHY 4
	To whose profit	SELF-INTEREST 5
	unlimited money	WARFARE 7
Cioran, E. M. (1911–95) *Romanian-born French philosopher*	killed myself long ago	SUICIDE 1
	see the hours pass	IDLENESS 5
Clare, John (1793–1864) *English poet*	living sepulchre of life	PRESENT 6
	self-consumer of my woes	SELF 7
Clark, Alan (1928–99) *British Conservative politician*	If you have bright plumage	CHARACTER 7
	join Tom and the other dogs	EPITAPHS 12
	Safe is spelled D-U-L-L	POLITICS 13
	We are all sharks circling	POLITICS 12
	wreck it with clichés	CIVIL SERV 3
Clarke, Arthur C. (1917–) *English science fiction writer*	consciousness-expanding drug	SCIENCE FICT 2
	indistinguishable from magic	TECHNOLOGY 10
	it is clearly Ocean	EARTH 2
	something is possible	THEORY 2
Clarke, Kenneth (1940–) *British Conservative politician*	I do not wear a bleeper	POLITICIANS 6
Clarkson, Jeremy (1960–) *British journalist and broadcaster*	87% of all mosquitoes	RISK 2
	wonderful quality of death	EUROPE 5
Clausewitz, Karl von (1780–1831) *Prussian soldier and military theorist*	continuation of politics	WARFARE 9
	simplest thing is difficult	WARFARE 8
Clay, Henry (1777–1852) *American politician*	forcibly if we must	DIPLOMACY 4
	rather be right	AMBITION 5
Clayton, Tubby (1885–1972) *Australian-born British clergyman*	What is service	GIVING 3
Cleaver, Eldridge (1935–98) *American political activist*	part of the solution	PROBLEMS 6
Cleese, John (1939–) **and Booth, Connie**	Don't mention the war	EUROPE 6
	Pretentious? *Moi*	SELF-ESTEEM 7
	Torquay bedroom window	HOLIDAYS 1
Cleese, John (1939–) see **Chapman, Graham , Cleese, John , et al.**		
Cleese, John (1939–) see **Skynner, Robin and Cleese, John**		

Clemenceau, Georges (1841–1929)	All the time I wage war	WORLD W I 4
French statesman	entrust to military men	WARFARE 10
	Oh, to be seventy again	AGEING 5
Clinton, Bill (1946–)	asks for forgiveness	FORGIVENESS 3
American Democratic statesman, President	comeback kid	PERSISTENCE 2
from 1993	full of the broken promises	BALKANS 3
	I didn't inhale	DRUGS 6
	If something makes you cry	POLITICS 14
	what the meaning of 'is' is	MEANING 4
Clinton, Hillary Rodham (1947–)	I am not standing by my man	LOYALTY 2
American lawyer	only people who count	MARRIAGE 6
	other people's children	CHILDREN 7
	stayed home and baked cookies	WOMAN'S R 6
Clough, Arthur Hugh (1819–61)	Ah, for a child in the street	SACRIFICE 4
English poet	all forms of competition	ENVY 2
	Disease, or sorrows strike	GOD 7
	fears may be liars	HOPE 3
	fought and lost	FAILURE 4
	lucrative to cheat	CRIME 5
	Officiously to keep alive	MURDER 3
	struggle naught availeth	EFFORT 3
Clough, Brian (1935–)	my dear Mam's mangle	SELF-ESTEEM 8
English football player and manager		
Cockburn, Claud (1904–81)	bounding past the satirist	REALITY 1
British writer and journalist	Small earthquake in Chile	NEWSPAPERS 7
Cocteau, Jean (1889–1963)	greatest masterpiece	DICTIONARIES 1
French dramatist and film director	Life is a horizontal fall	LIFE 5
	tactful in audacity	BEHAVIOUR 7
	who is to be crucified	CHOICE 5
	worst tragedy for a poet	POETRY 7
Coetzee, J. M. (1940–)	essence of servanthood	CLASS 4
South African novelist	moment of awakening	DREAMS 4
	sex as demonic	AUSTEN 2
Coffey, Denise	twentieth-century failure	CELIBACY 2
British actress		
Cohan, George M. (1878–1942)	spell my name right	FAME 9
American songwriter, dramatist, and	Yankee Doodle Dandy	UNITED S 5
producer	Yanks are coming	WORLD W I 5
Cohen, John (1898–1979)	Pile it high	SHOPPING 2
British businessman		
Cohen, John (1911–)	foundations of civilization	SWEARING 3
Cohen, Leonard (1934–)	unreliable ally	BODY 5
Canadian singer and writer	waiting for it to rain	PESSIMISM 3
Coke, Edward (1552–1634)	if it be against reason	LAWS 4
English jurist		
Cole, John (1927–)	best leaks always take place	SECRECY 6
Northern Irish journalist and broadcaster		
Coleman, Ornette (1930–)	differently each time	JAZZ 2
American jazz musician		
Coleridge, Samuel Taylor (1772–1834)	At one stride comes the dark	NIGHT 2
English poet, critic, and philosopher	*best* words in the best order	POETRY 9
	lantern on the stern	EXPERIENCE 5
	Like music on my heart	SILENCE 2
	loving Christianity better	CHRISTIAN 3

Coleridge, Samuel Taylor (*cont.*)	man's desire is for the woman	MEN/WOMEN 6
	muse on dromedary trots	POETS 7
	performs its secret ministry	WEATHER 3
	prayeth well, who loveth well	PRAYER 6
	soul of Rabelais	WRITERS 7
	understand a writer's ignorance	WRITING 10
	wash the river Rhine	POLLUTION 3
	Water, water, everywhere	SEA 3
	What is an Epigram	WORDPLAY 3
	willing suspension of disbelief	POETRY 8
	with its usual severity	SUMMER 2

| **Colette** (1873–1954) | dozen heart-breaks | DIETS 4 |
| *French novelist* | so lightly called physical | EMOTIONS 4 |

Collins, Joan (1933–)	no one in Beverly Hills	TEMPTATION 4
British actress	on a life-support machine	APPEARANCE 4
	What I need is a wife	HUSBANDS 6

| **Collins, Michael** (1880–1922) | We've been waiting 700 years | PUNCTUALITY 3 |
| *Irish revolutionary* | | |

| **Colombo, John Robert** (1936–) | American know-how | CANADA 4 |
| *Canadian writer* | | |

| **Colton, Charles Caleb** (*c.*1780–1832) | greatest fool may ask | EXAMINATIONS 2 |
| *English clergyman and writer* | vegetate in a village | NEIGHBOURS 4 |

| **Comden, Betty** (1919–) **and Green, Adolph** (1915–) | New York, New York | AMERICAN CITIES 8 |
| | time to call it a day | ENDING 5 |

| **Compton, Denis** (1918–) | get bored and fall over | CRICKET 4 |
| *British cricketer* | | |

Compton-Burnett, Ivy (1884–1969)	Being cruel to be kind	CRUELTY 6
English novelist	difference within the sexes	MEN/WOMEN 7
	different kinds of wrong	SIN 8
	does not change his spots	HABIT 4
	It is not a great healer	TIME 7
	resent having nothing	POSSESSIONS 4

Confucius (551–479 BC)	build up his moral power	SEX 12
Chinese philosopher	By nature men are alike	HUMAN NATURE 4
	man who reviews the old	TEACHING 4
	no class distinction	EDUCATION 8

Congreve, William (1670–1729)	fury, like a woman scorned	REVENGE 6
English dramatist	it's whispered every where	SECRECY 7
	seem unaffected	BEHAVIOUR 8
	soothe a savage breast	MUSIC 3
	very witty prologue	COURTSHIP 5
	wit in his own eye	YOUTH 7

| **Conlon, Gerry** (1954–) | like a runaway train | JUSTICE 7 |
| *Irish member of the Guildford Four* | | |

| **Connell, James M.** (1852–1929) | keep the red flag flying | POLITICAL P 4 |
| *Irish socialist songwriter* | | |

| **Connolly, Billy** (1942–) | bicycle repair kit | MARRIAGE 7 |
| *Scottish comedian* | don't get caught acting | ACTING 1 |

Connolly, Cyril (1903–74)	all serving a life-sentence	SELF 8
English writer	bourgeois always bounces up	CLASS 5
	could not blow his nose	WRITERS 8
	everyone changes sides	GENERATION 2
	gods wish to destroy	CRITICS 4
	Imprisoned in every fat man	FAT 2
	incubators of apathy	CITIES 3

Connolly, Cyril (*cont.*)

Mandarin style . . . is beloved	STYLE 4
memories are card-indexes	MEMORY 7
M is for Marx	COMMUNISM 5
weapon of the male	MEN/WOMEN 8
what will be read once	LITERATURE 4

Connolly, James (1868–1916)
Irish labour leader and nationalist

slave of that slave	CAPITALISM 2

Connors, Jimmy (1952–)
American tennis player

Spill your guts at Wimbledon	TENNIS 3

Conrad, Joseph (1857–1924)
Polish-born English novelist

Action is consolatory	ACTION 7
All ambitions are lawful	AMBITION 6
horror! The horror	FEAR 6
I could last for ever	YOUTH 8
judge of a man by his foes	ENEMIES 6
Never confess! Never, never	APOLOGY 3
terrorist and the policeman	HUMAN NATURE 5
We live, as we dream	SOLITUDE 6

Conran, Shirley (1932–)
English writer

Conran's Law of Housework	HOUSEWORK 1
second things never	ORGANIZATION 4
stuff a mushroom	PRACTICAL 4

Conran, Terence (1931–)
British designer and businessman

cooked a few meals	DIVORCE 4

Constable, John (1776–1837)
English painter

calm sunshine of the heart	ARTISTS 2
nothing ugly	BEAUTY 6
sound of water escaping	PAINTING 7

Constant, Benjamin (1767–1834)
French novelist, political philosopher, and politician

Art for art's sake	ART 5

Constitution of the United States (1787)

cruel and unusual punishment	PUNISHMENT 4

Cook, A. J. (1885–1931)
English labour leader

Not a penny off the pay	TRADE 4

Cook, Eliza (1818–89)
English poet

Better build schoolrooms	PUNISHMENT 5

Cook, Peter (1937–95)
English satirist and actor

passing the time enjoyably	LIFESTYLES 7

Coolidge, Calvin (1872–1933)
American Republican statesman, President 1923–9

business of the American	UNITED S 6
If you don't say anything	SPEECHES 7
slogan 'press on'	PERSISTENCE 3
They hired the money	DEBT 2
what did he say about sin	SIN 9

Cooper, Diana (1892–1986)
wife of Duff Cooper

nerve and brass	LANGUAGES 2

Cooper, Henry (1934–)
English boxer

made for loving	BOXING 3

Cooper, Jilly (1937–)
British writer

marry an orphan	IN-LAWS 2

Cope, Wendy (1945–)
English poet

highly emotional state	POETRY 10
like bloody buses	MEN 7
What makes men so tedious	MEN 8
Whatever you do, life is hell	LIFE 6
write to make people anxious	WRITING 11
You're almost human	HUMAN RACE 5

Copland, Aaron (1900–90) *American composer and musician*	meaning to music	MUSIC 4
Coppola, Francis Ford (1939–) *American film director, writer, and producer*	I love the smell of napalm water's the same shape	VIETNAM 7 CAREERS 3
Corelli, Marie (1855–1924) *English writer of romantic fiction*	I have three pets at home	HUSBANDS 7
Corneille, Pierre (1606–84) *French dramatist*	impulse was never a crime leave the outcome to the Gods no glory in the triumph	IMPULSIVE 2 DUTY 1 DANGER 2
Cornes, Ralph	anti-Faraday machines	COMPUTERS 4
Cornfeld, Bernard (1927–) *American businessman*	sincerely want to be rich	AMBITION 7
Cornford, Frances (1886–1960) *English poet*	Hector took off his plume Missing so much	PARTING 6 COUNTRY 3
Cornford, Francis M. (1874–1943) *English academic*	dangerous precedent nearly deceiving your friends voted into the chair	ORIGINALITY 4 PROPAGANDA 4 COMMITTEES 2
Cornuel, Mme (1605–94) *French society hostess*	hero to his valet	HEROES 6
Corso, Gregory (1930–) *American poet*	All her family and her friends	WEDDINGS 5
Cory, William (1823–92) *English poet*	Jolly boating weather	BOATS 1
Cosby, Bill (1937–) *American comedian, actor, and producer*	heart of marriage is memories	MARRIAGE 8
Coubertin, Baron Pierre de (1863–1937) *French sportsman and educationist*	not the victory	WINNING 5
Coué, Émile (1857–1926) *French psychologist*	Every day, in every way	MEDICINE 4
Coupland, Douglas (1961–) *Canadian author*	no-future job out there bungee jumping paid for becoming a couple	CAREERS 4 RELATIONSHIPS 6 INDIVIDUAL 1
Courteline, Georges (1858–1929) *French writer and dramatist*	better to waste one's youth	YOUTH 9
Cousteau, Jacques (1910–97) *French underwater explorer*	more damage to the earth sea is the universal sewer	ENVIRONMENT 5 POLLUTION 4
Coward, Noël (1899–1973) *English dramatist, actor, and composer*	apocryphal jokes I never made clever and quotable Don't let's be beastly how potent cheap music is in a warm, sunny climate It is what it used to be just around the corner Just say the lines London Pride is a flower Mad dogs and Englishmen maternal boa constrictor May I call you 338 put your daughter on the stage right people stay back home sand in the porridge Stately Homes of England struck regularly, like gongs	EPITAPHS 13 PRAISE 2 WORLD W II 6 MUSIC 5 WEATHER 4 OPERA 2 PESSIMISM 4 ACTING 2 LONDON 3 ENGLAND 5 SUCCESS 8 NAMES 4 ACTORS 3 TRAVEL 7 HOLIDAYS 2 ARISTOCRACY 2 VIOLENCE 6

Cowley, Abraham (1618–67)
English poet and essayist

| drooping spirits can raise | PRAISE 3 |
| Life is an incurable disease | LIFE 7 |

Cowper, William (1731–1800)
English poet

Beware of desperate steps	CAUTION 4
man made the town	CITIES 4
moves in a mysterious way	GOD 8
necessity invented stools	INVENTIONS 5
now and then be right	FOOLS 5
pardon or to bear it	FRIENDSHIP 10
solemn interposing puff	SMOKING 3
very spice of life	CHANGE 8

Cox, Brian (1928–) **and Boyson, Rhodes** (1925–)
British academic; British politician

| equality of opportunity | EQUALITY 4 |
| Schools are for schooling | SCHOOLS 4 |

Crabbe, George (1754–1832)
English poet

all the test of truth	HABIT 5
mansions of the dead	LIBRARIES 4
never lost till won	DEFEAT 3
Secrets with girls	SECRECY 8

Craig, Maurice James (1919–)

| damp Lagan fog | BRITISH CIT 4 |

Crane, Hart (1899–1932)
American poet

| moon in lonely alleys | SKIES 2 |
| You who desired so much | POETS 8 |

Creighton, Mandell (1843–1901)
English prelate

| go about doing good | GOODNESS 3 |

Crick, Francis (1916–)
English biophysicist

| understanding molecules | LIFE SCI 3 |
| vast assembly of nerve cells | SELF 9 |

Crisp, Quentin (1908–99)
English writer

After the first four years	HOUSEWORK 2
all that damn disco music	HOMOSEXUAL 5
consuming jealousy of husbands	JEALOUSY 3
obituary in serial form	AUTOBIOG 2

Critchley, Julian (1930–2000)
British Conservative politician and journalist

bag of boiled sweets	PARLIAMENT 6
hitting it with her handbag	THATCHER 4
Parliamentary oratory	SPEECHES 8

Crompton, Richmal (1890–1969)
English author of books for children

| thcream till I'm thick | ARGUMENT 4 |

Cromwell, Oliver (1599–1658)
English soldier and statesman, Lord Protector from 1653

bowels of Christ	CERTAINTY 2
In the name of God, go	ACTION 8
make what haste I can	LAST WORDS 4
None climbs so high as he	ACHIEVEMENT 6
pimples, warts, and everything	HONESTY 1

Crosby, Bing (1903–77)
American singer and film actor

| He was an average guy | SINGING 3 |

Cross, Amanda (1926–)
American crime writer and academic

| assumption of innocence | GUILT 3 |

Cross, Douglas
American songwriter

| left my heart in San Francisco | AMERICAN CITIES 9 |

Crossman, Richard (1907–74)
British Labour politician

| profoundly deferential | CIVIL SERV 4 |

Crowley, Aleister (1875–1947)
English diabolist

| Do what thou wilt | LIFESTYLES 8 |

cummings, e. e. (1894–1962)
American poet

god decided to invent	BEGINNING 4
i like what it does	SEX 13
jesus told him	BELIEF 7
next to of course god	UNITED S 7
pity this busy monster	PROGRESS 7

cummings, e. e. (*cont.*)

politician is an arse	POLITICIANS 7
smashed it into because	LOGIC 3

Cunningham, Allan (1784–1842)
Scottish poet

gallant mast	BOATS 2

Cuomo, Mario (1932–)
American Democratic politician

campaign in poetry	ELECTIONS 4

Cupitt, Don (1934–)
British theologian

Disneyfication of Christianity	CHRISTMAS 5

Curie, Marie (1867–1934)
Polish-born French physicist

must be interested in things	SCIENCE & SOC 2

Curran, John Philpot (1750–1817)
Irish judge

eternal vigilance	LIBERTY 4
silver plate on a coffin	APPEARANCE 5

Curtis, Richard (1956–)
New Zealand-born writer

It's pretty easy	WEDDINGS 6
serial monogamist	FAITHFULNESS 6

Curtis, Tony (1925–)
American actor

It's like kissing Hitler	KISSING 3

Curtiz, Michael (1888–1962)
Hungarian-born American film director

Bring on the empty horses	CINEMA 7

Curzon, Lord (1859–1925)
British Conservative politician

such white skins	CLASS 6

Cyprian, St (*c.*AD 200–258)
Latin Christian writer and martyr

have God for his father	CHURCH 4

Dalai Lama (1935–)
Spiritual head of Tibetan Buddhism

difficult to trust the Chinese	TRUST 4

Dali, Salvador (1904–89)
Spanish painter

Picasso is Spanish, I am too	ARTISTS 3
wanted to be a cook	AMBITION 8

Dalton, Hugh (1887–1962)
British Labour politician

colleague-free day	EMPLOYMENT 4
loyal to his own career	AMBITION 9

Daniel, Samuel (1563–1619)
English poet and dramatist

Men do not weigh the stalk	VALUE 5
son of the sable Night	SLEEP 2

Daniels, Paul (1938–)
British conjuror

You're going to like this	LIKES 3

Dante Alighieri (1265–1321)
Italian poet

Abandon all hope	HELL 3
remember a happy time	SORROW 6
shifts now here now there	REPUTATION 4

Danton, Georges Jacques (1759–94)
French revolutionary

always boldness	COURAGE 3

Darion, Joe (1917–2001)
American songwriter

dream the impossible dream	IDEALISM 5

Darnell, Bill
Canadian environmentalist

Make it a *green* peace	ENVIRONMENT 6

Darrow, Clarence (1857–1938)
American lawyer

anybody could become President	PRESIDENCY 5
colour or his creed	HUMAN RIGHTS 5
many ignorant men are sure	BELIEF 8

Darwin, Charles (1809–82)
English natural historian

cruel works of nature	NATURE 2
He who understands baboon	LANGUAGE 4
ought to control our thoughts	MORALITY 5
proving their falseness	THEORY 3
term of Natural Selection	LIFE SCI 4
we have made our slaves	ANIMAL RIGHTS 5

Darwin, Erasmus (1731–1802) *English physician*	time to think before I speak	SPEECH 5
Darwin, Francis (1848–1925) *English botanist*	man who convinces the world	SCIENCE 4
Davies, Robertson (1913–95) *Canadian novelist*	life of somebody else	BIOGRAPHY 7
	mystical spirit	CANADA 5
	perhaps hum a few bars	PORNOGRAPHY 2
	We make things happen	LUCK 1
Davies, Scrope (c.1783–1852) *English conversationalist*	human mind in ruins	MADNESS 1
Davies, W. H. (1871–1940) *Welsh poet*	rainbow and a cuckoo's song	TRANSIENCE 4
	Rainbow gave thee birth	BIRDS 2
	What is this life	LEISURE 4
Davis, Angela (1944–) *American political activist*	obedient to our keepers	PRISON 2
Davis, Bette (1908–89) *American actress*	only work that truly satisfies	WORK 5
	Playing our parts	ACTING 3
Davis, Sammy Jnr. (1925–90) *American entertainer*	Being a star	RACISM 3
Dawkins, Richard (1941–) *English biologist*	answers to the meaning of life	SCIENCE & REL 3
	blind watchmaker	LIFE SCI 5
	likely that there is life	SPACE 3
	statistical improbability	LIFE SCI 6
Dawson, Christopher (1889–1970) *English historian*	good becomes indistinguishable	EVIL 6
Dawson of Penn, Lord (1864–1945) *Physician to King George V*	If a lady says No	MEANING 5
Day, Harry *British pilot*	for the obedience of fools	LAWS 5
Day, Robin (1923–) *British broadcaster*	unreason thrives on television	TELEVISION 3
Dayan, Moshe (1915–81) *Israeli statesman and general*	most exciting and dramatic	WARFARE 11
Dean, Millvina (1911–)	can't bear iced drinks	SEA 4
Deane, Seamus (1940–) *Irish poet and novelist*	that which is irrational	LOGIC 4
	word you had to bite on	SICKNESS 4
de Beauvoir, Simone (1908–86) *French novelist and feminist*	Garbo's visage	ACTORS 4
	like the torture of Sisyphus	HOUSEWORK 3
	not in giving life	MEN/WOMEN 9
	One is not born a woman	WOMEN 9
de Bernières, Louis (1954–) *British novelist and short-story writer*	disorder in its geometry	EMOTIONS 5
	transformed into archangel	ACHIEVEMENT 7
	what is left over	LOVE 17
Debord, Guy (1931–94) *French philosopher*	global spectacle's vulgarity	EARTH 3
Debray, Régis (1940–) *French Marxist theorist*	managing one's legend	PROPAGANDA 5
	right-wing, like nature	POLITICS 15
Debs, Eugene Victor (1855–1926) *founder of the Socialist party of America*	While there is a lower class	EQUALITY 5

Decatur, Stephen (1779–1820)
American naval officer

our country, right or wrong — PATRIOTISM 6

de Chastelain, John
Canadian soldier and diplomat

pike in the thatch — WEAPONS 3

Defoe, Daniel (1660–1731)
English novelist and journalist

all men would be tyrants — POWER 8
Fools out of favour — ENVY 3
have your trouble doubled — WORRY 2

Degas, Edgar (1834–1917)
French artist

Art is vice — ART 6

de Gaulle, Charles (1890–1970)
French soldier and statesman, President 1959–69

246 varieties of cheese — FRANCE 3
decide the fate of the world — EUROPE 7
EEC is a horse and carriage — EUROPEAN C 1
France has lost a battle — WORLD W II 7
Free Quebec — CANADA 6
girls and roses — TRANSIENCE 5
like everyone else — DISABILITY 3
Politics are too serious — POLITICS 16
put Voltaire in the Bastille — CENSORSHIP 4

Delafield, E. M. (1890–1943)
English journalist and magistrate

rapid flight of time — HOLIDAYS 3

de la Mare, Walter (1873–1956)
English poet and novelist

in her silver shoon — SKIES 3
Is there anybody there? — MEETING 2
Look thy last — TRANSIENCE 6
Through what wild centuries — FLOWERS 2
whatever Miss T eats — EATING 4

Delaney, Shelagh (1939–)
English dramatist

never have young minds — WOMEN 10

de Leon, Walter and Jones, Paul M.

It's a funny old world — LIFE 8

Delius, Frederick (1862–1934)
English composer

cannot be expressed otherwise — MUSIC 6

de Mille, Agnes (1908–93)
American dancer and choreographer

Bodies never lie — DANCE 6

Democritus (*c.*460–*c.*370 BC)
Greek philosopher

By convention there is colour — SENSES 2

Demosthenes (*c.*384—*c.*322 BC)
Athenian orator and statesman

what was first in oratory — SPEECHES 9

Dempsey, Jack (1895–1983)
American boxer

forgot to duck — BOXING 4

Dench, Judi (1934–)
British actress

get a little bit of him — ACHIEVEMENT 8
public didn't know so much — ACTORS 5
use a bicycle pump — INTERNET 3

Deneuve, Catherine (1943–)
French actress

life is not about men — MEN 9
nothing but dogs of war — PRESS 2
sexuality in the movies — CINEMA 8

Deng Xiaoping (1904–97)
Chinese Communist statesman

colour of the cat — WAYS 4

Denning, Lord (1899–1999)
British judge

Birmingham Six released — JUSTICE 8

Dennis, John (1657–1734)
English critic, poet, and dramatist

make so vile a pun — WORDPLAY 4

Densham, Pen and Watson, John	call off Christmas	REVENGE 7
De Quincey, Thomas (1785–1859) *English essayist and critic*	keys of Paradise one of the fine arts	DRUGS 7 MURDER 4
Derby, Edward Stanley, 14th Earl of (1799–1869) *British Conservative statesman*	duty of an Opposition	PARLIAMENT 7
Derrida, Jacques (1930–) *French philosopher and critic*	nothing outside of the text	CRITICS 5
de Saint-Exupéry, Antoine (1900–44) *French novelist*	in the same direction only with the heart tiresome for children	LOVE 18 INSIGHT 5 GENERATION 3
Descartes, René (1596–1650) *French philosopher and mathematician*	best distributed commodity I think, therefore I am	PRACTICAL 5 THINKING 5
De Sylva, Buddy (1895–1950) **and Brown,** **Lew** (1893–1958)	best things in life are free	POSSESSIONS 5
de Valera, Eamon (1882–1975) *American-born Irish statesman*	brought up for export	EXILE 2
De Vries, Peter (1910–93) *American novelist and humorist*	children produce adults most intestinal of instruments proof of God's omnipotence something is eating us	MARRIAGE 9 MUSICAL INST 4 GOD 9 EATING 5
Dewar, James (1842–1923) *Scottish physicist*	Minds are like parachutes	MIND 3
Dewar, Lord (1864–1930) *British industrialist*	quick, and the dead	SPEED 4
Diaghilev, Sergei (1872–1929) *Russian ballet impresario*	Astonish me	THEATRE 6
Diamond, John	only rational position to take	HEALTH 1
Diana, Princess of Wales (1961–97) *former wife of Charles, Prince of Wales*	anyone sane would have left bloatedness of your stomach If men had to have babies queen in people's hearts She won't go quietly three of us in this marriage	JOURNALISM 6 EATING 6 PREGNANCY 2 DIANA 3 DEFIANCE 3 MARRIAGE 10
Diaz, Porfirio (1830–1915) *Mexican revolutionary and statesman*	Mexico, so far from God	MEXICO 1
Dickens, Charles (1812–70) *English novelist*	Annual income twenty pounds Anythin' for a quiet life 'Bah,' said Scrooge Barkis is willin' Circumlocution Office conquered human natur doll in the doll's house faith in the people governing feel ashamed of home hundred years hence I want some more in case anything turned up It is a far, far better thing law is a ass—a idiot let us love our occupations make business for itself Not to put too fine a point nursed a dear Gazelle	DEBT 3 SOLITUDE 7 CHRISTMAS 6 READINESS 2 BUREAUCRACY 3 HUMAN NATURE 6 WOMAN'S R 7 GOVERNMENT 4 HOME 1 MISTAKES 2 GREED 4 OPTIMISM 3 SACRIFICE 5 LAWS 6 CLASS 7 LAWS 7 TACT 2 DISILLUSION 2

Dickens, Charles (*cont.*)	one demd horrid grind	WORK 6
	others may be Prooshans	NATIONALITY 2
	She'll vish there wos more	LETTERS 3
	Shout with the largest	CONFORMITY 3
	styles of portrait painting	PAINTING 8
	taste and fancy of the speller	WORDS 5
	This is a London particular	FOG 1
	true business precept	BUSINESS 4
	We are so very 'umble	HUMILITY 3
	We never knows wot's hidden	SECRECY 9
	what I want is, Facts	FACTS 1
	winder, a casement	TEACHING 5
	work its way with the women	CLOTHES 6
Dickinson, Emily (1830–86) *American poet*	all we need of hell	PARTING 7
	feel the red in my mind	SENSES 3
	Love is anterior to life	LOVE 19
	Nerves sit ceremonious	SUFFERING 8
	Sweeping up the Heart	BEREAVEMENT 4
	They shut me up in prose	WRITING 12
	those who ne'er succeed	SUCCESS 9
Dickinson, John (1732–1808) *American politician*	By uniting we stand	COOPERATION 4
Didion, Joan (1934–) *American writer*	point free in time	CHOICE 6
Dietrich, Marlene (1901–92) *German-born American actress and singer*	In Brazil they throw flowers	MEXICO 2
Dillon, Wentworth , Lord Roscommon (*c.*1633–85) *Irish poet and critic*	as you choose a friend	READING 2
DiMaggio, Joe (1914–99) *American baseball player*	got to be kept hungry	BASEBALL 2
Dinesen, Isak (1885–1962) *Danish novelist and short-story writer*	ingenious machine	HUMAN RACE 6
	vegetative gracefulness	ANIMALS 13
Diogenes (404–323 BC) *Greek Cynic philosopher*	practice in being refused	CYNICISM 4
Dirac, Paul (1902–84) *British theoretical physicist*	beauty in one's equations	MATHS 5
Disney, Walt (1901–66) *American animator and film producer*	invention of a mouse	FAME 10
Disraeli, Benjamin (1804–81) *British Tory statesman and novelist, Prime Minister 1868, 1874–80*	Change is inevitable	CHANGE 9
	Christianity was muscular	CHRISTIAN 4
	Damn your principles	POLITICAL P 5
	damned lies and statistics	STATISTICS 5
	do nothing and get something	CAREERS 5
	every woman should marry	MARRIAGE 11
	Everyone likes flattery	FLATTERY 3
	Finality is not the language	POLITICS 17
	formidable Opposition	GOVERNMENT 5
	go down to posterity	GRAMMAR 4
	great physician	TIME 8
	history of the world	MURDER 5
	If Gladstone fell	MISFORTUNES 3
	illimitable was annihilated	EXPLORATION 3
	Justice is truth in action	JUSTICE 9
	magic of first love	LOVE 20
	men who have failed	CRITICS 6
	mistaken comfort for civilization	PROGRESS 8

Disraeli, Benjamin (*cont.*)	Never complain and never explain	APOLOGY 4
	no dogma, no Dean	CLERGY 2
	on the side of the angels	HUMAN RACE 7
	one is enough	MINORITIES 1
	place of light, of liberty	UNIVERSITIES 5
	posterity is a pack-horse	FUTURE 6
	Sensible men never tell	RELIGION 4
	trustees of Posterity	YOUTH 10
	When I want to read a novel	READING 3
Djilas, Milovan (1911–)	there is no Party line	CONFORMITY 4
Yugoslav politician and writer		
Dobbs, Michael (1948–)	I couldn't possibly comment	OPINION 4
British novelist and broadcaster		
Dodd, Ken (1931–)	play the old Glasgow Empire	HUMOUR 5
British comedian		
Dole, Elizabeth (1936–)	answer is yes	PRESIDENCY 6
American administrator and politician		
Donaldson, Stephen (1947–)	metaphors of magic	FANTASY 3
American writer		
Donleavy, J. P. (1926–)	When you don't have any money	DISCONTENT 1
Irish-American novelist		
Donne, John (1572–1631)	Busy old fool, unruly sun	SKIES 4
English poet and divine	Death be not proud	DEATH 9
	for whom the bell tolls	DEATH 10
	Go, and catch a falling star	SUPERNATURAL 8
	hold your tongue	LOVE 21
	I am mine own *Executioner*	SELF 10
	I neglect God and his Angels	PRAYER 7
	if it were done but once	FAMILIAR 3
	letters mingle souls	LETTERS 4
	License my roving hands	SEX 14
	Love built on beauty	BEAUTY 7
	loving, and for saying so	POETRY 11
	No man is an Island	SOCIETY 4
	world's last night	ENDING 6
Dostoevsky, Fedor (1821–81)	abstract and premeditated city	RUSSIA 6
Russian novelist	annihilate a man utterly	PUNISHMENT 6
	devil doesn't exist	CREATIVITY 2
	find someone to worship	RELIGION 5
	God and devil	BEAUTY 8
	Men reject their prophets	HEROES 7
	most intense enjoyments	DESPAIR 3
	one tiny creature	EVIL 7
	thorough-going illness	MIND 4
Doty, Mark (1953–)	hear the virus humming	AIDS 1
American poet		
Douglas, Keith (1920–44)	lover and killer are mingled	ARMY 5
English poet	unlucky explorers	FAILURE 5
Douglas, Kirk (1916–)	want to know about a man	WIVES 4
American film actor and producer		
Douglas, Lord Alfred (1870–1945)	dare not speak its name	HOMOSEXUAL 6
English poet		
Douglas, Norman (1868–1952)	one must close one eye	FRIENDSHIP 11
Scottish-born novelist and essayist	tell the ideals of a nation	ADVERTISING 3

Douglas, O. (1877–1948)
Scottish writer

fair show of knowledge	QUOTATIONS 4
write every other day	LETTERS 5

Douglass, Frederick (*c.*1818–95)
American former slave and civil rights campaigner

chain about the ankle	HUMAN RIGHTS 6
Power concedes nothing	POWER 9
slave was made a man	RACISM 4
testimony against slavery	SINGING 4

Dowd, Maureen (1952–)
American journalist

queen of surfaces	DIANA 4

Dowson, Ernest (1867–1900)
English poet

days of wine and roses	TRANSIENCE 7
gone with the wind	MEMORY 8
sick of an old passion	FAITHFULNESS 7

Doyle, Arthur Conan (1859–1930)
Scottish-born writer of detective fiction

do my best to forget it	INFORMATION 3
dreadful record of sin	COUNTRY 4
'Elementary,' said he	INTELLIGENCE 3
eliminated the impossible	PROBLEMS 7
featureless and commonplace	CRIME 7
fifth proposition of Euclid	CRIME FICT 3
his little brain attic stocked	LIBRARIES 5
It biases the judgement	THEORY 4
long been an axiom of mine	VALUE 6
That was the curious incident	LOGIC 5
there is no horror	IMAGINATION 4
three-pipe problem	THINKING 6
you do not observe	SENSES 4

Doyle, Roddy (1958–)
Irish novelist

people are their talk	CONVERSATION 6

Drabble, Margaret (1939–)
English novelist

incommunicable small terrors	CHILDHOOD 2
post-industrial slag-heap	ENGLAND 6
seen for what one is	REALITY 2

Drake, Francis (*c.*1540–96)
English sailor and explorer

thrash the Spaniards too	SPORTS 4
yields the true glory	PERSISTENCE 4

Draper, Derek
British political adviser

closer I came to the centre	POWER 10
sort of 'gunpowder'	DEPRESSION 1

Drayton, Michael (1563–1631)
English poet

come let us kiss	PARTING 8

Drucker, Peter F. (1909–)
Austrian-born American management consultant, educator, and author

Knowledge employees	EMPLOYMENT 5
management of change	MANAGEMENT 2
more transnational the world	NATIONALITY 3
only meaningful resource	BUSINESS 5
Pollution knows no boundaries	POLLUTION 5
totalitarian controls	CENSORSHIP 5

Drummond, Thomas (1797–1840)
British government official

Property has its duties	POSSESSIONS 6

Dryden, John (1631–1700)
English poet, critic, and dramatist

beat the iron while it is hot	OPPORTUNITY 2
fury of a patient man	PATIENCE 3
here is God's plenty	POETS 9
make a man appear a fool	INSULTS 3
most may err as grossly	MINORITIES 2
Never was patriot yet	PATRIOTISM 7
None but the brave	COURAGE 4
rest from pain	HAPPINESS 3
to madness near allied	GENIUS 4
when you rant and swear	WOMEN 11
wit in all languages	WIT 2

Duane, Diane (1952–)
American writer

like eating one crisp	READING 4

Dubček, Alexander (1921–92) *Czechoslovak statesman*	lose its human face	COMMUNISM 6
Du Deffand, Mme (1697–1780) *French literary hostess*	first step that is difficult	ACHIEVEMENT 9
Duffy, Carol Ann (1965–) *English poet*	childhood is an emigration moment of tiny revelation vividly gifted in love	CHILDHOOD 3 POETRY 12 DIANA 5
Dumas, Alexandre (1802–70) *French novelist and dramatist*	All for one, one for all	COOPERATION 5
Dumas, Alexandre (1824–95) *French writer*	it takes two to bear them	MARRIAGE 12
Du Maurier, Daphne (1907–89) *English novelist*	bottles up a memory	MEMORY 9
du Maurier, George (1834–96) *French-born cartoonist and novelist*	wretcheder one gets	SMOKING 4
Dumouriez, Charles François du Périer (1739–1823) *French general*	courtiers who surround him	EXPERIENCE 6
Dunant, Sarah (1950–) *British writer and broadcaster*	about money and power	AWARDS 5
Duncan, Ronald (1914–82) *English dramatist*	nobility without pride	HORSES 1
Dunmore, Helen (1952–) *British poet and novelist*	That killed head when writers receive money	GULF 1 LITERATURE/SOC 2
Dunn, Douglas (1942–) *Scottish poet*	behind the left nipple Here we are perfect I am light with meditation poems should be Clyde-built	POETRY 13 PERFECTION 4 SOLITUDE 8 SCOTLAND 6
Dunne, Sean (1956–97) *Irish poet*	wears their going like a scar	EXILE 3
Dunning, John (1731–83) *English lawyer and politician*	influence of the Crown	ROYALTY 5
Duppa, Richard (1770–1831) *English artist and writer*	ignorant have prescribed laws	LANGUAGE 5
Duras, Marguerite (1914–96) *French writer*	men I deceived the most passion is homosexuality itself	DECEPTION 2 HOMOSEXUAL 7
Durcan, Paul (1944–) *Irish poet*	what are husbands for	WIVES 5
Durem, Ray (1915–63) *American poet*	best friends are white boys	RACISM 5
Durocher, Leo (1906–91) *American baseball coach*	Nice guys finish last	SPORTS 5
Durrell, Lawrence (1912–90) *English novelist, poet, and travel writer*	echo of a pistol-shot just dined off her husband like abandoned computers wet crabs in a basket	BALKANS 4 PAINTING 9 BUILDINGS 3 CIRCUMSTANCE 5
Dürrenmatt, Friedrich (1921–) *Swiss writer*	What was once thought	THINKING 4
Dworkin, Andrea (1946–) *American feminist and writer*	distinguish from rape solitary, existential courage	SEDUCTION 3 BIRTH 1

Dylan, Bob (1941–)
American singer and songwriter

answer is blowin' in the wind	MATURITY 4
as much from Cézanne	SINGING 5
Like a rolling stone	SOLITUDE 9
Money doesn't talk, it swears	MONEY 10
She takes just like a woman	WOMEN 12
times they are a-changin'	GENERATION 4
washed-up has-been	REPUTATION 5
Whether Judas Iscariot Had God	GOD 10
you treated me unkind	FORGIVENESS 4

Dyson, Esther (1951–)
American businesswoman

not a new form of life	INTERNET 4
think of who I am	SELF 11
Who needs a mother	MOTHERS 2

Early, Stephen T. (1889–1951)

on 4 ulcer pay	CAREERS 6

Eco, Umberto (1932–)
Italian novelist and semiotician

good of a book	BOOKS 7
He who is successful is good	SUCCESS 10

Eddington, Arthur (1882–1944)
British astrophysicist

army of monkeys	CHANCE 3
knowledge of the stars	SCIENCE 5
second law of thermodynamics	PHYSICS 5

Eden, Anthony (1897–1977)
British Conservative statesman

in favour of general economy	ECONOMICS 2
not always to be wrong	CRITICS 7

Edgar, Marriott (1880–1951)

didn't think much to the Ocean	SEA 5

Edgeworth, Maria (1768–1849)
Anglo-Irish novelist

little snug property	POSSESSIONS 7
only by the *slightest* chains	MEN 10

Edison, Thomas Alva (1847–1931)
American inventor

one per cent inspiration	GENIUS 5
roots of tobacco plants	SMOKING 5

Edmonds, John Maxwell (1875–1958)
English classicist

these gave their today	EPITAPHS 14

Edward III (1312–77)
King of England from 1327

this day to wynne his spurres	EFFORT 4

Edward VII (1841–1910)
King from 1901

treated as a brute	RACISM 6

Edward VIII (1894–1972)
King, 1936; afterwards Duke of Windsor

heavy burden of responsibility	ROYALTY 6
parents obey their children	UNITED S 8

Edwards, John

making you redundant	MANAGEMENT 3

Edwards, Jonathan (1703–58)
American theologian

made such a noise and tumult	DEATH 11

Edwards, Oliver (1711–91)
English lawyer

tried too in my time	PHILOSOPHY 5

Egan, Raymond B. (1890–1952)
see Kahn, Gus and Egan, Raymond B.

Ehrenreich, Barbara (1941–)
American sociologist and writer

nice four-colour catalogue	ROMANCE 3
yuppie version of bulimia	EXERCISE 2

Ehrlich, Paul Ralph (1932–)
American biologist

save all the parts	TECHNOLOGY 11

Ehrlichman, John (1925–99)
Presidential assistant to Richard Nixon

let him hang there	WAITING 2

Ehrmann, Max (1872–1945)

Go placidly amid the noise	PEACE 9

Eichmann, Adolf (1906–62)
German Nazi administrator

life of obedience	LAWS 8

Einstein, Albert (1879–1955)	between politics and equations	SCIENCE & SOC 3
German-born theoretical physicist	citizen of the world	PREJUDICE 2
	confronted with what exists	INTELLIGENCE 4
	degree of independence	CAREERS 7
	deposit of prejudices	PRACTICAL 6
	eternal mystery of the world	UNIVERSE 5
	God does not play dice	CHANCE 4
	grand aim of all science	THEORY 5
	he is not malicious	GOD 11
	keeping your mouth shut	SUCCESS 11
	militant pacifist	PACIFISM 4
	never think of the future	FUTURE 7
	past, present and future	TIME 9
	quaint and ceremonious village	UNIVERSITIES 6
	Science without religion	SCIENCE & REL 4
	stopped wearing socks	CLOTHES 7
	unleashed power of the atom	INVENTIONS 6
Eiseley, Loren (1907–77)	19th century beer bottles	ARCHAEOLOGY 2
American anthropologist, educator, and author	ghost continent	SELF 12
Eisenhower, Dwight D. (1890–1969)	Every gun that is made	WEAPONS 4
American general and Republican statesman, President 1953–61	No easy problems ever come	PRESIDENCY 7
	people want peace so much	PEACE 10
	planning is indispensable	ORGANIZATION 5
	plough is a pencil	FARMING 2
	row of dominoes	CAUSES 4
	sergeant is the army	ARMY 6
Eisenstaedt, Alfred (1898–1995)	brain is 30 years old	OLD AGE 3
German-born American photographer	click with people	PHOTOGRAPHY 5
	not the camera but the eye	SENSES 5
Ekland, Britt (1942–)	two months anniversary	RELATIONSHIPS 7
Elgar, Edward (1857–1934)	God was against art	ART 7
English composer	music in the air	MUSIC 7
Eliot, George (1819–80)	begin with liking or gratitude	FRIENDSHIP 12
English novelist	born i' the rotten cheese	FAMILIAR 4
	cannot love a woman so well	GREATNESS 7
	essence of real human love	MOTHERS 3
	exploring a closed basin	MARRIAGE 13
	foxes have a sincere interest	ELECTIONS 5
	Gossip is a sort of smoke	GOSSIP 3
	Half the sorrows of women	SPEECH 6
	happiest women	HAPPINESS 4
	know the sources of the Nile	IMAGINATION 5
	like every other vice	CRUELTY 7
	no despair so absolute	DESPAIR 4
	other side of silence	INSIGHT 6
	small hungry shivering self	DISCONTENT 2
	Speech is often barren	SILENCE 3
	strain on the affections	TASTE 2
	woman can hardly ever choose	CHOICE 7
Eliot, T. S. (1888–1965)	After such knowledge	FORGIVENESS 5
Anglo-American poet, critic, and dramatist	Any man has to, needs to	MURDER 6
	April is the cruellest month	SPRING 3
	arrive where we started	EXPLORATION 4
	bear very much reality	HUMAN RACE 8
	Birth, and copulation	LIFE 10
	Clear the air! clean the sky	POLLUTION 6
	dialect of the tribe	SPEECH 7
	do the right deed	MORALITY 6
	escape from emotion	POETRY 14

Eliot, T. S. (*cont.*)

fear in a handful of dust	FEAR 7
Footfalls echo in the memory	MEMORY 10
Hell is oneself	HELL 4
History is now and England	HISTORY 4
I gotta use words	WORDS 6
idea and the reality	REALITY 3
Life we have lost in living	LIFESTYLES 9
makes life worth living	CULTURE 7
mature poets steal	PLAGIARISM 2
measured out my life	LIFE 9
missed the meaning	EXPERIENCE 7
my end	BEGINNING 5
Naming of Cats	CATS 2
Not with a bang but a whimper	ENDING 7
patient etherized upon a table	EVENING 1
river is a strong brown god	RIVERS 3
saw the skull beneath the skin	DEATH 12
Success is relative	SUCCESS 12
surgeon plies the steel	MEDICINE 5
there's no one like Macavity	CATS 1
ticket to one's funeral	AWARDS 6
Time present and time past	TIME 10
unpleasant to meet Mr Eliot	POETS 10
We are the hollow men	FUTILITY 5
wisdom we have lost	INFORMATION 4
Words strain, crack	WORDS 7
yellow fog that rubs its back	FOG 2

Elizabeth I (1533–1603)
Queen of England and Ireland from 1558

for a moment of time	LAST WORDS 5
glory of my crown	GOVERNMENT 6
heart and stomach of a king	ROYALTY 7
to be addressed to princes	NECESSITY 1
windows into men's souls	SECRECY 10

Elizabeth II (1926–)
Queen of the United Kingdom from 1952

annus horribilis	MISFORTUNES 4
devoted to your service	ROYAL F 3
don't be too effusive	FLATTERY 4
for us older ones	CHANGE 10
My husband and I	WIVES 6
surfing the Net	PROGRESS 9
wearing a silver dress	ROYALTY 8

Elizabeth, Queen, the Queen Mother
(1900–2002)
Queen Consort of George VI

look the East End in the face	WORLD W II 8
small and selfish is sorrow	BEREAVEMENT 5

Elizabeth, Countess von Arnim
(1866–1941)
Australian-born British writer

get the upper hand	GUESTS 2

Ellington, Duke (1899–1974)
American jazz musician

all the vowels missing	JAZZ 3

Ellis, Alice Thomas (1932–)
English novelist

holding on to the sides	CHARACTER 8
she felt insignificant, plain	SELF-ESTEEM 9

Ellis, Havelock (1859–1939)
English sexologist

exchange of one nuisance	POLLUTION 7
volcano of revolution	CIVILIZATION 2

Ellman, Maud (1954–)

staged to trick the conscience	EATING 7

Elson, Andy
British balloon pilot

another way that doesn't work	FAILURE 6

Elton, Ben (1959–)
British writer and performer

how little possessions count	POSSESSIONS 8
never, ever try to look cool	LEADERSHIP 5
they've heard of Oasis	POLITICAL P 6
Uncool people	FASHION 2

Éluard, Paul (1895–1952)
French poet
Good-day sadness	SORROW 7
Hope raises no dust	HOPE 4

Elyot, Thomas (1499–1546)
English diplomatist and author
nothing but beastly fury	FOOTBALL 2

Elytis, Odysseus (1911–)
Greek poet
olive tree, a vineyard	GREECE 2

Emecheta, Buchi (1944–)
Nigerian writer
created like mistakes	CIRCUMSTANCE 6
I am a daughter of Nigeria	AFRICA 1

Emerson, Ralph Waldo (1803–82)
American philosopher and poet
Art is a jealous mistress	ART 8
boil at different degrees	ANGER 3
builded better than he knew	ARCHITECT 3
days never know	EXPERIENCE 8
Every hero becomes a bore	HEROES 8
faster we counted our spoons	HONESTY 2
glad to get asleep	CHILDREN 8
Hitch your wagon to a star	IDEALISM 6
hobgoblin of little minds	CONSISTENCY 1
Language is fossil poetry	LANGUAGE 6
make a better mouse-trap	ABILITY 2
no man is wanted much	VALUE 7
originator of a good sentence	QUOTATIONS 6
People wish to be settled	HABIT 6
Pythagoras was misunderstood	GREATNESS 2
schoolboys who educate him	SCHOOLS 5
sensible people are selfish	SELF-INTEREST 6
skating over thin ice	DANGER 3
stands on authority	FAITH 6
Tell me what you know	QUOTATIONS 5
Things are in the saddle	POSSESSIONS 9
three cannot take part	CONVERSATION 4
What is a weed	GARDENS 6
Whoso would be a man	CONFORMITY 5

Empson, William (1906–84)
English poet and literary critic
central function	FICTION 4

Engels, Friedrich (1820–95)
German socialist
State is not 'abolished'	GOVERNMENT 7
workers are perfectly free	UNEMPLOYMENT 2

Engels, Friedrich (1820–95)
see **Marx, Karl and Engels, Friedrich**

Ephron, Nora (1941–)
American writer and journalist
I'll have what she's having	SEX 15
Sex is always out there	FRIENDSHIP 13
what is controversial	ARGUMENT 5
what your uterus looks like	HAPPINESS 5

Epstein, Jacob (1880–1959)
British sculptor
leave art to us	SCULPTURE 2

Epstein, Julius J. (1909–2001) et al.
If she can stand it, I can	MUSIC 8
Of all the gin joints	MEETING 3
Round up the usual suspects	CRIME 8

Equiano, Olaudah (c.1745–c.1797)
African writer and former slave
nation of dancers, singers	AFRICA 2
white men with horrible looks	RACE 1

Erhard, Ludwig (1897–1977)
German statesman
remain only a torso	EUROPE 8

Ertz, Susan (1894–1985)
American writer
rainy Sunday afternoon	BOREDOM 4

Esher, Lord (1913–)
English architect and planner
feel for their blue pencils	CULTURE 8
gloomy bunkers	BUILDINGS 4

Essex, Robert Devereux, Earl of (1566–1601) *English soldier and courtier*	Reasons are not like garments	LOGIC 6
Estienne, Henri (1531–98) *French printer and publisher*	If youth knew	GENERATION 5
Euclid (fl. *c*.300 BC) *Greek mathematician*	no 'royal road' to geometry	MATHS 6
Eulalia, Infanta of Spain (1864–1958) *Spanish princess*	life might be put on parade	ROYALTY 9
Euripides (*c*.485–*c*.406 BC) *Greek dramatist*	My tongue swore stronger than Necessity	COMMITMENT 3 NECESSITY 2
Ewart, Gavin (1916–95) *British poet*	Mae West's hips Sex suppressed	ACTORS 6 EMPLOYMENT 6
Ewer, William Norman (1885–1976) *British writer*	gave my life for freedom How odd of God	SACRIFICE 6 RACISM 7
Eyre, Richard (1943–) *English theatre director*	addict rejecting the needle	TELEVISION 4
Fadiman, Clifton (1904–) *American critic*	archaeology of the future leap toward immortality mama of dada	SCIENCE FICT 3 FOOD 10 WRITERS 9
Fairbairn, Nicholas (1933–95)	*Recreations*: growling	LEISURE 5
Faisal	like the winds of the desert	SPEECHES 10
Faithfull, Marianne (1946–) *British singer*	relationship that goes bad	SINGING 6
Faldo, Nick (1957–) *English golfer*	Of course I want to win it	WINNING 6
Falkland, Lucius Cary, Lord (1610–43) *English royalist politician*	necessary not to change	CHANGE 11
Fanon, Frantz (1925–61) *French West Indian psychoanalyst*	murder men everywhere shape of Africa	EUROPE 9 AFRICA 3
Faraday, Michael (1791–1867) *English physicist and chemist*	integrity of my intellect path is strewed with flowers soon be able to tax it test of such consistency	TITLES 2 UNIVERSITIES 7 INVENTIONS 7 EXPERIMENT 1
Farjeon, Eleanor (1881–1965) *English writer for children*	Morning has broken	DAY 1
Farjeon, Herbert (1887–1945) *English writer and theatre critic*	man who's danced with a girl	ROYALTY 10
Farouk, King (1920–65) *King of Egypt 1936–52*	only five Kings left	ROYALTY 11
Farquhar, George (1678–1707) *Irish dramatist*	Poetry's a mere drug sinews of love, as of war	POETRY 15 MONEY 11
Farrow, Mia (1945–) *American actress*	discussed it with his shrink	COUNSELLING 2
Faulkner, William (1897–1962) *American novelist*	ain't still drunk tomorrow any number of old ladies fool with booze give gratitude constantly made the books past is never dead	DRUNKEN 2 LITERATURE/SOC 3 ALCOHOL 6 GRATITUDE 1 AUTOBIOG 3 PAST 4

Fawkes, Guy (1570–1606)
English conspirator
requires a dangerous remedy — NECESSITY 3

Feather, Vic (1908–76)
British trade unionist
two consenting parties — TRADE 5

Feinstein, Dianne (1933–)
American Democratic politician
come in a pinstripe suit — STRENGTH 10

Fenton, James (1949–)
English poet
didn't exist at Creation — GOD 12
what they knocked down — CITIES 5
where myths go when they die — MUSEUMS 3
Windbags can be right — QUOTATIONS 7

Ferber, Edna (1887–1968)
American writer
like death by drowning — CELIBACY 3
Roast Beef, Medium — FOOD 11

Ferdinand I (1503–64)
Holy Roman Emperor from 1558
though the world perish — JUSTICE 10

Fermi, Enrico (1901–54)
Italian-born American atomic physicist
ignorance is never better — INVENTIONS 8
names of all these particles — PHYSICS 6

Feynman, Richard Phillips (1918–88)
American theoretical physicist
nature cannot be fooled — TECHNOLOGY 12

Field, Frank (1942–)
British Labour politician
nailing his colours — INDECISION 3

Fielding, Helen (1958–)
British writer
dating in your thirties — COURTSHIP 6
not quite so hardworking — AMBITION 10
Oh God. Valentine's Day — ROMANCE 4

Fielding, Henry (1707–54)
English novelist and dramatist
best sweeteners of tea — GOSSIP 4
ravished this fair creature — SEDUCTION 4

Fields, Dorothy (1905–74)
American songwriter
fine romance with no kisses — KISSING 4
Hey! big spender — WEALTH 7
Start all over again — PERSISTENCE 5
sunny side of the street — OPTIMISM 4

Fields, W. C. (1880–1946)
American humorist
give a sucker an even break — FOOLS 6
I always vote *against* — ELECTIONS 6
I went to Philadelphia — AMERICAN CITIES 10
It ain't a fit night out — WEATHER 5
living in Philadelphia — EPITAPHS 15
Never cry over spilt milk — MISFORTUNES 5
never know why people laugh — COMEDY 3
took the cork out of my lunch — ALCOHOL 7
try again. Then quit — PERSISTENCE 6

Fierstein, Harvey (1954–)
American dramatist and actor
doin' all the talking — CONVERSATION 8

Filipovic, Zlata (1980–)
Bosnian child writer
We mix with the good — NATIONALITY 4

Finkielkraut, Alain
French philosopher
Fanaticism is indefensible — CULTURE 9

Firbank, Ronald (1886–1926)
English novelist
long enough for an angel — WAITING 3
world is disgracefully managed — UNIVERSE 6

Firth, Colin (1960–)
British actor
pacifist vegetarian — SPORTS 6

Fish, Michael (1944–)
British weather forecaster
hurricane on the way — WEATHER 6

Fisher, Carrie (1956–)
American actress and writer
sex, work, food, sports — RELATIONSHIPS 8

Fisher, H. A. L. (1856–1940) *English historian*	energetic mongrels	EUROPE 10
Fisher, John Arbuthnot (1841–1920) *British admiral*	best scale for an experiment Sack the lot	EXPERIMENT 2 CIVIL SERV 5
Fisher, Marve *American songwriter*	old-fashioned millionaire	GREED 5
Fisk, Robert (1946–) *British journalist*	prefer missiles to medicine	GOVERNMENT 8
Fitt, Gerry (1926–) *Northern Irish politician*	It is pure tribalism	NORTHERN 5
Fitzgerald, Edward (1809–83) *English scholar and poet*	Ah, fill the cup ball no question makes feminine of genius Morning in the bowl of night moving finger writes	PRESENT 7 CHANCE 5 TASTE 3 DAY 2 PAST 5
Fitzgerald, F. Scott (1896–1940) *American novelist*	backward a few inches a day different from you and me hold two opposed ideas I will write you a tragedy No grand idea was ever born our convictions are hills three o'clock in the morning youth of his own generation	WORLD W I 6 WEALTH 8 INTELLIGENCE 5 HEROES 9 COMMITTEES 3 MIDDLE AGE 8 DESPAIR 5 WRITING 13
Fitzgerald, Garret (1926–) *Irish Fine Gael statesman*	in a shuttered mansion no more a left-wing movement	HISTORY 5 POLITICAL P 7
Fitzgerald, Penelope (1916–2000) *English novelist and biographer*	pick up a spade what no-one else will do	ARCHAEOLOGY 3 DUTY 2
Flatley, Michael *Irish dancer*	do a hatchet job	CRITICS 8
Flaubert, Gustave (1821–80) *French novelist*	as God is in creation Human life is a sad show life-blood of thought like a cracked kettle number of his enemies rotten seat of a latrine they're just as useless	ART 10 ART 9 STYLE 5 SPEECH 8 VALUE 8 PROGRESS 10 BOOKS 8
Flecker, James Elroy (1884–1915) *English poet*	Golden Road to Samarkand pines are gossip pines serpent-haunted sea	KNOWLEDGE 10 TREES 5 SEA 6
Fleming, Ian (1908–64) *English thriller writer*	Shaken and not stirred subtract one from the other Twice is coincidence woman's flesh is clean	ALCOHOL 8 MARRIAGE 14 CHANCE 6 FAT 3
Fleming, Marjory (1803–11) *English child writer*	8 times 8 and 7 times 7	MATHS 7
Fleming, Peter (1907–71) *English journalist and travel writer*	I can feel the sharks' fins São Paulo is like Reading	FOOD 12 TRAVEL 8
Foch, Ferdinand (1851–1929) *French Marshal*	armistice for twenty years situation excellent	WORLD W I 7 WORLD W I 8
Foley, J. (1906–70) *British songwriter*	Old soldiers never die	ARMY 7
Fonda, Jane (1937–) *American actress*	man has every season spend all that money	MEN/WOMEN 10 COUNSELLING 3

Foot, Michael (1913–) *British Labour politician*	semi-house-trained polecat seraglio of eunuchs	PEOPLE 8 PARLIAMENT 8
Forbes, Miss C. F. (1817–1911) *English writer*	inward tranquillity	CLOTHES 8
Ford, Anna (1943–) *English journalist and broadcaster*	there are no plain women	TELEVISION 5
Ford, Gerald (1909–) *American Republican statesman, President 1974–7*	give you everything you want	GOVERNMENT 9
Ford, Henry (1863–1947) *American car manufacturer*	Exercise is bunk ignorance bumping its head more or less bunk so long as it is black	EXERCISE 3 EVIL 8 HISTORY 6 CHOICE 8
Forgy, Howell (1908–83) *American naval chaplain*	pass the ammunition	PRACTICAL 7
Forster, E. M. (1879–1970) *English novelist*	books that influence us coarseness and vulgarity emergencies of life feeling is bad form guts to betray my country half-alive things inverted Victorianism just a tiny night-light most sublime noise nothing but the blue sky nothing has value Nothing in India identifiable novel tells a story Only connect our gates to the glorious outer life of telegrams poor cannot afford it Remorse is the most wasteful see what I say so-called white races speak before you think those whom they want to love Two cheers are quite enough usually overpraised We are none of us safe Where there is officialism you've got to mind it	BOOKS 9 VULGARITY 4 FORESIGHT 6 ENGLAND 7 PATRIOTISM 8 GOSSIP 5 JOYCE 1 DYING 4 BEETHOVEN 2 ITALY 3 FUTILITY 6 ASIA 4 FICTION 5 WRITING 14 RAILWAYS 4 RELATIONSHIPS 9 TRUST 5 GUILT 4 THINKING 7 RACE 2 CREATIVITY 3 POVERTY 8 DEMOCRACY 4 BOOKS 10 LUCK 2 BUREAUCRACY 4 ADVICE 7
Forster, Margaret (1938–) *English novelist*	point of any memoir	BIOGRAPHY 8
Forsyth, Frederick (1938–) *English novelist*	heard Kennedy was dead keep a measly affair secret	MEMORY 11 SECRECY 11
Foster, Charles (1828–1904) *American politician*	billion dollar country	UNITED S 9
Fowler, H. W. (1858–1933) *English lexicographer and grammarian*	what a split infinitive is	GRAMMAR 5
Fox, Robin Lane (1946–) *English classicist*	Better Drains	GARDENS 7
Fox, Theodore (1899–1989) *English doctor*	refrain from doing things	MEDICINE 6
France, Anatole (1844–1924) *French novelist and man of letters*	adventures of his soul die for the industrialists	CRITICS 9 PATRIOTISM 9

France, Anatole (*cont.*)

it is the only sacred thing	WEALTH 9
majestic equality of the law	POVERTY 9
Make hatred hated	TOLERANCE 4
Never lend books	LENDING 1
perish of despair and boredom	LIES 4
state is like the human body	GOVERNMENT 10
who conforms to custom	CONFORMITY 6

Francis, St, de Sales (1567–1622)
French bishop

heart speaks to heart	SPEECH 9

Francis, St, of Assisi (1181–1226)
Italian monk

Lord, make me an instrument	PEACE 11
that I may not so much seek	COMPASSION 5

Frank, Anne (1929–45)
German-born Jewish diarist

go on living even after death	DIARIES 3

Franklin, Benjamin (1706–90)
American politician, inventor, and scientist

all hang separately	COOPERATION 6
at forty, the judgement	MATURITY 5
death and taxes	TAXES 4
die fasting	HOPE 5
made a good bargain	NECESSITY 4
never was a good war	WARFARE 12
time is money	TIME 11
tool-making animal	HUMAN RACE 9
use of a new-born child	INVENTIONS 9

Frayn, Michael (1933–)
English writer

feel really bad about	GUILT 5
reached the 'w' of 'now'	PRESENT 8

Frazer, James George (1854–1941)
Scottish anthropologist

untutored savage	IN-LAWS 3

Frederick the Great (1712–86)
King of Prussia from 1740

prejudices through the door	PREJUDICE 3
would you live for ever	ARMY 8

Freeman, E. A. (1823–92)
English historian

politics is present history	HISTORY 7

French, Marilyn (1929–)
American writer

all men are rapists	MEN 11
always the damned dishes	HOUSEWORK 4
insistent cheeriness	SICKNESS 5
largely in our own control	DYING 5
sorrows of the mothers	FAMILY 5

Freud, Sigmund (1856–1939)
Austrian psychiatrist

Anatomy is destiny	BODY 6
enjoyment from a contrast	CIRCUMSTANCE 7
Frozen anger	DEPRESSION 2
gigantic mistake	UNITED S 10
Intolerance of groups	PREJUDICE 4
love and work	LIFE 11
royal road to a knowledge	DREAMS 5
What does a woman want	WOMEN 13

Friday, Nancy (1937–)
American writer

I had men confused with life	MEN 12

Friedan, Betty (1921–)
American feminist

live through someone else	INDIVIDUAL 2
problem that has no name	WOMAN'S R 8

Friedman, Milton (1912–)
American economist

do not get all of the government	ADMIN 3
one form of taxation	ECONOMICS 3
political freedom	CAPITALISM 3

Friel, Brian (1929–)
Irish dramatist

images of the past	PAST 6

Frisch, Max (1911–91)
Swiss novelist and dramatist

Technology . . . the knack	TECHNOLOGY 13

Fromm, Erich (1900–80)
American philosopher and psychologist

I need you because I love you	MATURITY 6
supposed to want	DISCONTENT 3

Frost, David (1939–)
English broadcaster and writer

doing a grand job	ACHIEVEMENT 10
one child makes you a parent	PARENTS 3

Frost, Robert (1874–1963)
American poet

best way out	DETERMINATION 4
fences make good neighbours	NEIGHBOURS 5
ice on a hot stove	CREATIVITY 4
in and out of favour	CHANGE 12
I've broken Anne	CONFORMITY 7
listen to almost anything	EDUCATION 9
makes up in height	HAPPINESS 6
my little jokes on Thee	GOD 13
my own desert places	FEAR 8
never dared be radical	POLITICS 18
nothing to look backward to	DISILLUSION 3
play tennis with the net down	POETRY 16
remembers a woman's birthday	CELEBRATIONS 2
Secret sits in the middle	SECRECY 12
They have to take you in	HOME 2
took the one less travelled by	CHOICE 9
walling in or walling out	COOPERATION 7
Whose woods these are	SNOW 2
woods are lovely, dark	TREES 6
work twelve hours a day	CAREERS 8
world will end in fire	ENDING 8

Fry, Christopher (1907–)
English dramatist

circumambulating aphrodisiac	SKIES 5
life At a discount	BUREAUCRACY 5
longitude with no platitude	LANGUAGE 7
Look as much like home	HOME 3
sentimental value	BODY 7
What after all Is a halo	GOODNESS 4

Fry, Elizabeth (1780–1845)
English Quaker prison reformer

reform the criminal	PUNISHMENT 7

Fry, Roger (1866–1934)
English art critic

Art is significant deformity	ART 11
be a Christian	BACH 3

Fry, Stephen (1957–)
English comedian, actor, and writer

love affair with animals	ANIMAL RIGHTS 6
nickname for bikers: Donors	MEDICINE 7
pretty urban sort of person	CITIES 6
rather take their trousers off	MEN 13
used lavatory paper	NEWSPAPERS 8

Fuentes, Carlos (1928–)
Mexican novelist and writer

gringo in Mexico	MEXICO 3
tragic consciousness	TWENTY-FIRST 2

Fukuyama, Francis (1952–)
American historian

end of history as such	TWENTIETH 3
Florence of late 20th century	COMPUTERS 5

Fulbright, J. William (1905–95)
American politician

our greatest menace	COMMUNISM 7

Fuller, John (1937–)
English poet

when our days are done	PARTING 9

Fuller, R. Buckminster (1895–1983)
American designer and architect

God, it seems, is a verb	GOD 14
no instruction book	EARTH 4

Fuller, Sam (1912–)
American film director

survival is all there is	WARFARE 13

Fuller, Thomas (1608–61)
English preacher and historian

Light (God's eldest daughter)	ARCHITECT 4

Fuller, Thomas (1654–1734)	Care and diligence bring luck	LUCK 3
English writer and physician	He that plants trees	TREES 7
Funke, Alfred (b. 1869)	God punish England	WORLD W I 9
German writer		
Fyleman, Rose (1877–1957)	at the bottom of our garden	SUPERNATURAL 9
English writer for children		
Gabor, Zsa Zsa (1919–)	give him diamonds back	HATRED 3
Hungarian-born film actress	Husbands are like fires	HUSBANDS 8
	I've always been married	SEX 16
	Not hard enough	VIOLENCE 7
	taught me housekeeping	DIVORCE 5
	Then he's finished	BACHELORS 2
Gabriel, Peter (1950–)	core of English negativity	CELEBRATIONS 3
British rock singer and songwriter		
Gainsborough, Thomas (1727–88)	genius and regularity	PUNCTUALITY 4
English painter		
Gaitskell, Hugh (1906–63)	ditch between Subtopias	COUNTRY 5
British Labour politician	save the Party we love	POLITICAL P 8
	thousand years of history	EUROPEAN C 2
Galbraith, J. K. (1908–)	afflict the comfortable	HONESTY 3
American economist	bland lead the bland	CONFORMITY 8
	creates the wants	CONSUMER 2
	disasters we prevent	CRISES 6
	disastrous and the unpalatable	POLITICS 19
	firm anchor in nonsense	THINKING 8
	Himalayas to the heavens	MOUNTAINS 1
	immortality can be assured	MISTAKES 3
	In the affluent society	LUXURY 2
	necessary to advertise food	ADVERTISING 4
	private opulence	ECONOMICS 5
	salary of the chief executive	BUSINESS 6
	thicker will be the dirt	WEALTH 10
	Trickle-down theory	ECONOMICS 4
	wrong decision isn't forever	DELAY 3
Galileo Galilei (1564–1642)	But it does move	SKIES 6
Italian astronomer and physicist		
Gallagher, Noel (1967–)	Has God played Knebworth	ROCK 2
English pop singer	having a cup of tea	DRUGS 8
	We are lads	MEN 14
	we'll be a footprint	ROCK 3
Gallagher, Thomas	roots that started it all	FATHERS 1
Galsworthy, John (1867–1933)	looked on it as immoral	BEAUTY 9
English novelist	man of action forced	THINKING 9
	nobody tells me anything	IGNORANCE 6
Galt, John (1779–1839)	behold the Hebrides	SCOTLAND 7
Scottish writer	Fair these broad meads	EXILE 4
Galton, Ray (1930–) **and Simpson, Alan** (1929–)	It's red hot, mate	CENSORSHIP 6
English scriptwriters	nearly an armful	BODY 8
Gamow, George (1904–68)	Pauli [exclusion] principle	PHYSICS 7
Russian-born American physicist	profile of an elephant	THEORY 6
Gandhi, Mahatma (1869–1948)	ethical value of uncooked food	FOOD 13
Indian statesman	he will no longer be a slave	LIBERTY 5
	mad destruction is wrought	WARFARE 14

Gandhi, Mahatma (*cont.*)	my better half	BEREAVEMENT 6
	non-cooperation with evil	EVIL 9
	Non-violence is the first	PACIFISM 5
	would be a good idea	CIVILIZATION 3
Garbo, Greta (1905–90)	I want to be alone	SOLITUDE 10
Swedish film actress		
García Lorca, Federico (1899–1936)	Green how I love you	COLOURS 3
Spanish poet and dramatist		
Gardner, Ed (1901–63)	instead of bleeding, he sings	OPERA 3
American radio comedian		
Garner, John Nance (1868–1967)	pitcher of warm piss	PRESIDENCY 8
American Democratic politician		
Garrick, David (1717–79)	Heart of oak are our ships	NAVY 5
English actor-manager		
Gaskell, Elizabeth (1810–65)	I'll not listen to reason	LOGIC 7
English novelist	in the way in the house	MEN 15
Gates, Bill (1955–)	sleeping under the desk	COMPUTERS 6
American computer entrepreneur	teacher is the most important	TEACHING 6
Gay, John (1685–1732)	happy could I be with either	CHOICE 10
English poet and dramatist	Life is a jest	EPITAPHS 16
	lived comfortably so long	MARRIAGE 15
	pretended friend is worse	DECEPTION 3
Geddes, Eric (1875–1937)	until the pips squeak	REVENGE 8
British politician and administrator		
Geiger, Keith (1941–)	Our schools are improving	SCHOOLS 6
Geldof, Bob (1954–)	black Americans are African	RACE 3
Irish rock musician	disrespect it deserves	ROCK 4
	to get laid, to get fame	ROCK 5
Geldof, Bob (1954–) **and Ure, Midge** (1953–)	Feed the world	AID 3
Irish and Scottish rock musicians		
Gellhorn, Martha (1908–98)	unscathed tourist of wars	JOURNALISM 7
American journalist		
Genet, Jean (1910–86)	Are you there . . . Africa	AFRICA 4
French novelist, poet, and dramatist	ecstasy of betrayal	BETRAYAL 4
	What we need is hatred	IDEAS 4
George II (1683–1760)	I hope he will *bite*	MADNESS 2
King from 1727		
George V (1865–1936)	Bugger Bognor	BRITISH CIT 5
King from 1910	damned if I'm an alien	NATIONALITY 5
	I was frightened of my father	PARENTS 4
	more potent advocates of peace	PEACE 12
	that damned Mouse	CINEMA 9
George VI (1895–1952)	family firm	ROYAL F 4
King from 1936	no allies to be polite to	DIPLOMACY 5
George, Eddie (1938–)	giving him an aspirin	ECONOMICS 6
British banker		
Gershwin, Ira (1896–1983)	I like po-tah-to	SPEECH 10
American songwriter	laughed at Christopher Columbus	INVENTIONS 3
	Nice work if you can get it	COURTSHIP 7
	rhymed conversation	SINGING 7

Gershwin, Ira (1896–1983)
see **Heyward, Du Bose and Gershwin, Ira**

Getty, J. Paul (1892–1976) *American industrialist*	not really a rich man	WEALTH 11
Giamatti, A. Bartlett (1938–89) *American baseball player*	breaks your heart	BASEBALL 3
Gibbon, Edward (1737–94) *English historian*	common feelings of mankind	PUNISHMENT 8
	feeble can seldom persuade	ARGUMENT 6
	forgot that he had a duty	EMPLOYMENT 7
	licentious passages are left	LANGUAGES 3
	Our sympathy is cold	COMPASSION 6
Gibbons, Stella (1902–89) *English novelist*	long monotony of marriage	MARRIAGE 16
Gibran, Kahlil (1883–1931) *Syrian writer and painter*	has lost its temper	TRUTH 12
	Life's longing for itself	PARENTS 5
	raise hands together	INDIVIDUAL 3
	spaces in your togetherness	MARRIAGE 17
	Work is love made visible	WORK 7
Gibson, William (1948–) *American science fiction writer*	science fiction scenario	POLLUTION 8
Gide, André (1869–1951) *French novelist and critic*	Hugo—alas	POETS 11
	what she lacks: manure	EUROPE 11
Gilbert, W. S. (1836–1911) *English writer of comic and satirical verse*	blow your own trumpet	SELF-ESTEEM 10
	if it's only idle chatter	MEANING 6
	leave that brain outside	PARLIAMENT 9
	left shoulder-blade	BEAUTY 10
	Merely corroborative detail	FICTION 6
	never use a big, big D—	SWEARING 4
	no one's anybody	EQUALITY 6
	pass for forty-three	APPEARANCE 6
	policeman's lot	POLICE 1
	primordial atomic globule	ARISTOCRACY 3
	punishment fit the crime	PUNISHMENT 9
	sentimental passion	ART 12
	take this railway by surprise	RAILWAYS 5
	teems with hidden meaning	WORDS 8
	thought of thinking for myself	POLITICAL P 9
	What, *never*? Hardly ever	CERTAINTY 3
	you are sufficiently decayed	OLD AGE 6
Gill, A. A. (1954–) *British food critic*	mystical heart of Germany	EUROPE 12
	really want to please	GUESTS 3
	wife and a prostitute	COOKING 5
Gill, Eric (1882–1940) *English sculptor, engraver, and typographer*	man does what he likes to do	EMPLOYMENT 8
	obligation of gratitude	GRATITUDE 2
Gilliatt, Penelope (1933–93) *British writer*	nothing has to be better	DISCONTENT 4
Gilmore, Gary (1941–77) *American murderer*	Let's do it	EXECUTIONS 1
Ginsberg, Allen (1926–97) *American poet and novelist*	Aisles full of husbands	SHOPPING 3
	angelheaded hipsters	DRUGS 9
Giovanni, Nikki (1943–) *American poet*	response to error that counts	MISTAKES 4
	sex object if you're pretty	FAT 4
Giraldus Cambrensis (1146?–1220?) *Welsh cleric and historian*	Who dare compare the English	WALES 2

Giraudoux, Jean (1882–1944)	interpreted nature as freely	LAWYERS 1
French dramatist	Rhyme is the most effective drum	POETRY 17
Giuliani, Rudy (1944–)	discretion about what you do	LIBERTY 6
American politician and lawyer		
Gladstone, W. E. (1809–98)	I will back the masses	CLASS 8
British Liberal statesman, Prime Minister	not to govern the country	PARLIAMENT 10
1868–74, 1880–5, 1886, 1892–4	Swimming for his life	CRISES 7
	Time is on our side	FUTURE 8
Glass, George (1910–84)	if you ain't talking about him	ACTORS 7
Glencross, David (1936–)	reaches for a revolver	CULTURE 10
British television executive		
Glendinning, Victoria (1937–)	facts of life	BIOGRAPHY 9
English biographer and novelist	unblock your drains	PLEASURE 8
Gloucester, William Henry, Duke of (1743–1805)	Always scribble, scribble	WRITING 15
Godard, Jean-Luc (1930–)	beginning, middle and an end	CINEMA 12
French film director	just an image	CINEMA 11
	truth 24 times per second	CINEMA 10
Godwin, William (1756–1836)	illustrious bishop of Cambrai	CRISES 8
English philosopher and novelist		
Goebbels, Joseph (1897–1945)	effective means of opposition	ARGUMENT 7
German Nazi leader	with guns not with butter	WEAPONS 5
Goering, Hermann (1893–1946)	Jewish question	GENOCIDE 2
German Nazi leader	rather have butter or guns	WEAPONS 6
Goethe, Johann Wolfgang von (1749–1832)	best is good enough	ART 13
German poet, novelist, and dramatist	children still at heart	OLD AGE 7
	deed is all	FAME 11
	Eternal Woman draws us	WOMEN 14
	golden tree of actual life	REALITY 4
	hopes and desires of youth	MIDDLE AGE 9
	I do not know myself	SELF-KNOW 7
	More light	LAST WORDS 6
	poetry of life	SUPERNATURAL 10
	Talent develops	CHARACTER 9
	where a thought is lacking	WORDS 9
Gogol, Nikolai (1809–52)	Don't leave them on the road	EMOTIONS 6
Russian writer		
Golding, William (1911–93)	flying out as from a dustbin	SLEEP 3
English novelist	laughter in a language	HUMOUR 6
Goldsmith, Oliver (1728–74)	How happy he who crowns	OLD AGE 8
Anglo-Irish writer, poet, and dramatist	Laws grind the poor	POVERTY 10
	no arguing with Johnson	ARGUMENT 8
	one small head could carry	KNOWLEDGE 11
	scarce worth the sentinel	GOODNESS 5
	wants but little here below	LIFE 12
Goldwater, Barry (1909–98)	in the defence of liberty	FANATICISM 3
American Republican politician		
Goldwyn, Sam (1882–1974)	definite maybe	INDECISION 4
American film producer	delivered by Western Union	CINEMA 14
	Every Tom, Dick and Harry	NAMES 5
	hand that lays the golden egg	INGRATITUDE 1
	have his head examined	MENTAL 2
	Let's have some new clichés	ORIGINALITY 5
	make a copy of everything	ADMIN 4

Goldwyn, Sam (cont.)

pay to see bad movies	CINEMA 13
starts with an earthquake	CINEMA 15
verbal contract isn't worth	LAWS 9

Goodman, Amy (1957–)
American journalist

Go to where the silence is — JOURNALISM 8

Gorbachev, Mikhail Sergeevich (1931–)
Soviet statesman

Mitterrand has 100 lovers	KNOWLEDGE 12
restructuring [perestroika]	RUSSIA 7

Gorky, Maxim (1868–1936)
Russian writer and revolutionary

engineers of the soul — ART AND SOC 1

Gould, Stephen Jay (1941–2002)
American palaeontologist

grim reaper of extinction	LIFE SCI 7
integral part of culture	SCIENCE & SOC 4
status of Galileo	GREATNESS 3

Gowrie, Lord (1939–)
British Conservative politician

don't own a pair of trainers — ARISTOCRACY 4

Goya (1746–1828)
Spanish painter

One cannot look at this	CIRCUMSTANCE 8
reason produces monsters	DREAMS 6

Grace, W. G. (1848–1915)
English cricketer

Never read print — CRICKET 5

Grade, Lew (1906–98)
British television producer and executive

lower the Atlantic — FILMS 2

Graham, D. M. (1911–99)

fight for its King and Country — PATRIOTISM 10

Grahame, Kenneth (1859–1932)
Scottish-born writer

clever men at Oxford	INTELLIGENCE 6
messing about in boats	BOATS 3
poetry of motion	CARS 5

Graham, Martha (1894–1991)
American dancer, teacher, and choreographer

hidden language of the soul — DANCE 7

Graham, Philip (1915–63)
American newspaper publisher

first rough draft of a history — NEWSPAPERS 9

Graham, James , Marquess of Montrose
(1612–50)
Scottish general and poet

win or lose it all — RISK 3

Gramm, Phil (1942–)
American Republican politician

Balancing the budget — ECONOMICS 7

Grant, Ulysses S. (1822–85)
American Unionist general and statesman,
President 1869–77

I only know two tunes	SINGING 8
No personal consideration	DUTY 3
repeal of obnoxious laws	LAWS 10

Graves, Robert (1895–1985)
English poet

bright stain on the vision	LOVE 22
cool web of language	LANGUAGE 8
escaped from the drug factory	DRUGS 10
Grass-green and aspen-green	COLOURS 4
lost its virgin purity	SCIENCE 6

Gray, John Chipman (1839–1915)
American lawyer

matter out of place — POLLUTION 9

Gray, John (1951–)
American psychologist

I don't feel heard	RELATIONSHIPS 10
Martians do not offer advice	ADVICE 8
one point for a small gift	GIVING 4
show love by not worrying	WORRY 3

Gray, Patrick, Lord (d. 1612)

dead woman bites not — PRACTICAL 8

Gray, Thomas (1716–71)
English poet

Any fool may write	WRITING 16
born to blush unseen	FAME 12
curfew tolls the knell	EVENING 2

Gray, Thomas (*cont.*)	little victims play	CHILDHOOD 4
	mock their useful toil	POVERTY 11
	To each his suff'rings	SUFFERING 9
	Where ignorance is bliss	IGNORANCE 7
Gray, Tony (1928–)	Not an inch	CERTAINTY 4
Greaves, Jimmy (1940–) *English footballer*	swearing is part of it	SPORTS 7
Greeley, Horace (1811–72) *American newspaper editor*	Go West, young man	UNITED S 11
Green, Adolph (1915–) see **Comden, Betty and Green, Adolph**		
Green, Benny (1927–)	harmonies instead of oranges	JAZZ 4
Green, Michael (1927–) *British humorous writer*	colouring bits of the map red	BRITAIN 5
Greene, Graham (1904–91) *English novelist*	absolute ignorance	HAPPINESS 7
	Arrives like nursery tea	DYING 6
	evil can always find a home	HUMAN NATURE 7
	impossible aim	DESPAIR 6
	innocence is like a dumb leper	INNOCENCE 4
	lets the future in	CHILDHOOD 5
	nearly as God loved them	HUMAN RACE 10
	paper must imitate the tramp	JOURNALISM 9
	putting-off of unhappiness	DELAY 4
	rather have blood on my hands	INDIFFERENCE 3
	sentiment might uncoil	EMOTIONS 7
	those first fourteen years	READING 5
	victim demands allegiance	COMPASSION 7
	where we really belong	SORROW 8
Greene, Robert (*c.*1560–92) *English poet and dramatist*	Time is . . . Time was	TIME 12
Greer, Germaine (1939–) *Australian feminist*	how much men hate them	MEN/WOMEN 11
	huge rest home	AUSTRALIA 3
	lipstick must rot the brain	COSMETICS 4
	lonelier than any spinster	LONELINESS 2
	more central to our culture	FOOTBALL 3
	onto the board of Hoover	WOMAN'S R 9
	right to invent themselves	INDIVIDUAL 4
	see the Female Eunuch	WOMEN 15
	subhumanly ugly mate	BEAUTY 11
	when nothing can happen to you	SECURITY 3
Gregg, Hubert (1914–) *English songwriter*	because I'm a Londoner	LONDON 4
Gregory, Dick (1932–) *American comedian and civil rights activist*	call it a 'primitive society'	SOCIETY 5
	shake a bat at a white man	BASEBALL 4
Grellet, Stephen (1773–1855) *French missionary*	pass this way again	GOODNESS 6
Grenfell, Joyce (1910–79) *English comedy actress and writer*	dance it bust to bust	DANCE 8
Grey, Edward (1862–1933) *British Liberal politician*	lamps are going out	WORLD W I 10
Grierson, John (1888–1972) *English documentary film-maker*	discipline of public service	CINEMA 16
	not a mirror but a hammer	ART 14
Griffith-Jones, Mervyn (1909–79) *British lawyer*	wish your wife to read	CENSORSHIP 7

Griffiths, Philip Jones *Welsh photojournalist*	feet getting wet and cold	PRESS 3
Grigg, John (1924–) *British writer and journalist*	as common as adultery priggish schoolgirl	AUTOBIOG 4 ROYAL F 5
Grigson, Geoffrey (1905–85) *English critic*	minister on a pedestal	SCULPTURE 3
Grimond, Jo (1913–93) *British Liberal politician*	towards the sound of gunfire	CRISES 9
Grocott, Bruce (1940–) *British Labour politician*	rich would have kept more	WORK 8
Groening, Matt (1954–) *American humorist and satirist*	Don't have a cow	CRISES 10
Gromyko, Andrei (1909–89) *Soviet statesman*	he's got iron teeth	PEOPLE 9
Grossmith, George and Weedon (1847–1912, 1854–1919) *English writers*	caught my foot in the mat What's the good of a home	MISFORTUNES 6 HOME 4
Grove, Andrew (1936–) *American businessman*	Is steel good or bad Only the paranoid survive	TECHNOLOGY 14 BUSINESS 7
Guedalla, Philip (1889–1944) *British historian and biographer*	arrangement into three reigns beat a dogma	JAMES 1 ARGUMENT 9
Guevara, Ernesto ('Che') (1928–67) *Argentinian revolutionary*	forge his revolutionary spirit	REVOLUTION 8
Guibert, Hervé (1955–91) *French writer*	time to discover time	AIDS 2
Gulbenkian, Nubar (1896–1972) *British industrialist and philanthropist*	best number for a dinner party	PARTIES 4
Gunn, Thom (1929–) *English poet*	discussing if it existed My thoughts are crowded	RELATIONSHIPS 11 DEATH 13
Gurney, Dorothy Frances (1858–1932) *English poet*	nearer God's Heart	GARDENS 8
Guth, Alan (1947–) *American physicist*	Universe is a free lunch	UNIVERSE 7
Guthrie, Tyrone (1900–71) *English theatrical director*	religion-conscious city	BRITISH CIT 6
Guthrie, Woody (1912–67) *American folksinger and songwriter*	This land is your land	UNITED S 12
Hague, William (1961–) *British Conservative politician*	Titanic was going to set sail	FATE 5
Haig, Earl (1861–1928) *British Field Marshall*	very weak-minded fellow	INDECISION 5
Hailsham, Lord (1907–2001) *British Conservative politician*	by chance or inadvertence most of them have died unhappy prefer fox-hunting	GOVERNMENT 11 PRIME 5 POLITICAL P 10
Hakuin (1686–1769) *Japanese monk, writer and artist*	sound of the single hand	COOPERATION 8
Haldane, J. B. S. (1892–1964) *Scottish mathematical biologist*	composed of atoms I'd lay down my life NHS is quite like heaven preference for beetles	MIND 5 LIFE SCI 8 CANCER 2 STATISTICS 6

Haldane, J. B. S. (*cont.*)	queerer than we suppose	UNIVERSE 8
Haldeman, H. R. (1929–) *Presidential assistant to Richard Nixon*	toothpaste is out of the tube	SECRECY 13
Hale, Edward Everett (1822–1909) *American Unitarian clergyman*	pray for the senators	POLITICIANS 8
Hale, Nathan (1755–76) *American revolutionary*	but one life to lose	PATRIOTISM 11
Halifax, Lord (1633–95) *English politician and essayist*	get anything by their victory hanged for stealing horses never without an argument other use of their speech remember what is past	REVOLUTION 9 PUNISHMENT 10 ANGER 4 SPEECH 11 FORESIGHT 7
Hall, Jerry *American model*	whore in the bedroom	MEN/WOMEN 12
Hall, Radclyffe (1883–1943) *English novelist*	you're unexplained as yet	LESBIANISM 1
Halm, Friedrich (1806–71) *German dramatist*	Two hearts that beat as one	LOVE 23
Hamilton, Alex (1936–) *British writer and broadcaster*	fall for anything	CHARACTER 10
Hamilton, William (1788–1856) *Scottish metaphysician*	more it's shook it shines nothing great but man	TRUTH 13 MIND 6
Hamilton-Paterson, James (1941–) *British writer*	joinery with a chainsaw man's immemorial consolations Nothing aged one like loyalty	DIPLOMACY 6 GARDENS 9 LOYALTY 3
Hammerstein II, Oscar (1895–1960) *American songwriter*	alive with the sound of music Climb ev'ry mountain June is bustin' out last time I saw Paris nothin' like a dame Ol' man river Some enchanted evening you'll never walk alone You've got to be taught	MUSIC 9 DETERMINATION 5 SUMMER 3 FRANCE 4 WOMEN 16 RIVERS 4 MEETING 4 HOPE 6 RACISM 8
Hamnett, Katherine (1948–) *British fashion designer*	mystical and erotic	CLOTHES 9
Hampton, Christopher (1946–) *English dramatist*	thinking man's television	MASTURBATION 2
Hand, Learned (1872–1961) *American judge*	he did not pirate prefer a self-made name Words are chameleons	PLAGIARISM 3 NAMES 6 WORDS 10
Handy, Charles (1932–) *British businessman and economist*	goes out of fashion justifiably different profit is a means to be someone different	COMPROMISE 2 AGEING 6 BUSINESS 8 OLD AGE 9
Hannah, Sophie (1971–) *British poet*	queen of undercover loves	SECRECY 14
Hanrahan, Brian (1949–) *British journalist*	counted them all back	FALKLANDS 3
Hansberry, Lorraine (1930–65) *American dramatist*	young, gifted and *black*	RACE 4

Haran, Maeve (1950–)
British writer

itemised phone bill INVENTIONS 11

Haraucourt, Edmond (1856–1941)
French poet

To go away is to die a little ABSENCE 3

Harbach, Otto (1873–1963)
American songwriter

Smoke gets in your eyes SORROW 9

Harben, Susan

make do with ex-tennis players LESBIANISM 2

Harburg, E. Y. (1898–1981)
American songwriter

believes in me BELIEF 9
Brother can you spare a dime POVERTY 12
God who gave us flowers SICKNESS 6
good enough for Grandma WOMAN'S R 10
makes you feel a thought SINGING 9
retain our zones erogenous MEDICINE 8
throws a monkey wrench in NECESSITY 5
To let a fool kiss you KISSING 5

Harcourt, William (1827–1904)
British Liberal politician

We are all socialists now POLITICAL P 11

Harding, Gilbert (1907–60)
British broadcaster

potency of my voice SPEECH 12

Hardy, Thomas (1840–1928)
English novelist and poet

aged thrush, frail, gaunt BIRDS 3
clothes are hung up to dry SPEECH 13
courage with physical timidity PATIENCE 4
got as far as poison-gas PEACE 14
I am the family face FAMILY 6
Let me enjoy the earth EARTH 5
not religious-good GOODNESS 7
rattling good history PEACE 13
show the sorriness underlying WRITING 17
want their luck buttered LUCK 4
way to the Better PESSIMISM 5
weather the cuckoo likes WEATHER 7
Woman much missed BEREAVEMENT 7
woman to define her feelings LANGUAGE 9

Hare, David (1947–)
English actor and dramatist

before you count to five ANGER 5
single sheet of A4 CHURCH 5
sounds like propaganda PROPAGANDA 6
would like to be true CENSORSHIP 8

Hare, Maurice Evan (1886–1967)
English limerick writer

not even a bus, I'm a tram FATE 6

Harington, John (1561–1612)
English writer and courtier

Treason doth never prosper BETRAYAL 5

Harlech, Lord (1918–85)
British diplomat

disposed of an empire BRITAIN 6

Harman, Charles Eustace (1894–1970)
British judge

Accountants are witch-doctors BUSINESS 9

Harold II (*c.*1019–66)
King of England, 1066

seven feet of English ground DEFIANCE 4

Harris, Arthur (1892–1984)
British Air Force Marshal

bones of one British Grenadier WORLD W II 9

Harris, Joel Chandler (1848–1908)
American writer

Brer Fox, he lay low CAUTION 5
Licker talks mighty loud DRUNKEN 3

Harris, Thomas (1940–) **and Tally, Ted**
(1952–)
American writer; American screenwriter

I ate his liver FOOD 14
old friend for dinner EATING 8

Harrison, George (1943–2001)
English rock and pop guitarist

nothing to do with talent	ROCK 6
you can look at them	MUSICIANS 3

Harrison, Paul (1936–)
American dramatist and director

poor tread lightest	ENVIRONMENT 7

Harrison, Ted (1948–)
British broadcaster and writer

unique creatures of God	DISABILITY 4

Harrison, Tony (1953–)
British poet

Coal Board MacGregor	TRADE 6
Let them remember	GULF 2
ones we choose to love	LOVE 24

Hart, Josephine

Damaged people are dangerous	EXPERIENCE 9

Hart, Lorenz (1895–1943)
American songwriter

I wish I were in love again	LOVE 25
lady is a tramp	BEHAVIOUR 9

Harte, Bret (1836–1902)
American poet

It might have been	CIRCUMSTANCE 9
it's bound to change	LUCK 5

Hartley, Dorothy (1893–1985)
English writer

Hot on Sunday	COOKING 6

Hartley, L. P. (1895–1972)
English novelist

past is a foreign country	PAST 7

Haskins, Minnie Louise (1875–1957)
English teacher and writer

stood at the gate of the year	FAITH 7

Hattersley, Roy (1932–)
British Labour politician

adjust their principles	POLITICIANS 9
being ridiculous	POLITICS 20
slaughter ought not to be fun	HUNTING 2
to protect the Government	SECRECY 15

Havel, Václav (1936–)
Czech dramatist and statesman

art of the impossible	POLITICS 21
committing another evil	EVIL 10
Even a purely moral act	PROTEST 2
explain and conquer nature	NATURE 3
Gypsies are a litmus test	RACISM 9
something makes sense	HOPE 7
special time caught me up	REVOLUTION 10
under what circumstances	TRUTH 14

Hawking, Stephen (1942–)
English theoretical physicist

bother of existing	UNIVERSE 9
halve the sales	MATHS 8
redefined the task of science	SCIENCE 7
triumph of human reason	LIFE 13

Hay, Ian (1876–1952)
Scottish novelist and dramatist

Funny-peculiar or funny ha-ha	HUMOUR 7
his utter inability to spell	SCHOOLS 7
nuisances of peace-time	WARFARE 15

Hazlitt, William (1778–1830)
English essayist

art of pleasing	MANNERS 3
cannot miss an opportunity	WORDPLAY 5
child of ignorance	PREJUDICE 5
hate any one that we know	HATRED 4
I've had a happy life	LAST WORDS 7
nickname is the heaviest	NAMES 7
nothing good to be had	COUNTRY 6

Head, Bessie (1937–86)
South African-born writer

mutually feeding each other	LOVE 26
still smile with relief	RACISM 10

Healey, Denis (1917–)
British Labour politician

become the world's parson	DIPLOMACY 7
savaged by a dead sheep	INSULTS 4
when you're in a hole	POLITICS 22

Healey, Edna (1918–)
British writer

no sense of history	THATCHER 5

Heaney, Seamus (1939–) *Irish poet*	Here is the News	SPEECH 14
	huge nothing that we fear	WIND 1
	longed-for tidal wave	JUSTICE 11
	My passport's green	IRELAND 4
	oak would sprout in Derry	NORTHERN 6
	Of the 'wee six' I sing	NORTHERN 7
Hearst, William Randolph (1863–1951) *American newspaper publisher*	I'll furnish the war	JOURNALISM 10
Heath, Edward (1916–) *British Conservative statesman, Prime Minister 1970–4*	made the European tour	EUROPE 13
	stamina and good luck	PRIME 6
	unacceptable face	CAPITALISM 4
	under a cold shower	BOATS 4
Heath-Stubbs, John (1918–) *English poet*	Venerable Mother Toothache	SICKNESS 7
Hecht, Ben (1894–1964) *American screenwriter*	wonderful panic	CINEMA 17
Hedren, Tippi (1935–) *American actress*	looking like Cary Grant	SELF-KNOW 8
Hegel, G. W. F. (1770–1831) *German idealist philosopher*	experience and history teach	HISTORY 8
	Man owes his entire existence	SOCIETY 6
	philosophy's grey on grey	PHILOSOPHY 6
Heggs, Amanda	being untouchable	AIDS 3
Hein, Piet (1905–) *poet and cartoonist*	have their expert fun	EXPERTS 3
	Problems worthy of attack	PROBLEMS 8
	road to wisdom	MISTAKES 5
Heine, Heinrich (1797–1856) *German poet*	books will be burned	CENSORSHIP 9
	God will pardon me	FORGIVENESS 6
	soul Rousseau had created	REVOLUTION 11
Heiney, Paul	feed us cheaply	FARMING 3
	grow cash crops for export	AID 4
Heisenberg, Werner (1901–76) *German mathematical physicist*	some of the worst mistakes	EXPERTS 4
	Space is blue	SPACE 4
Heller, Joseph (1923–99) *American novelist*	as good as *Catch*-22	CRITICS 10
	country is a piece of land	NATIONALITY 6
	how to enjoy it	LITERATURE 5
	If Nixon was second-rate	MEDIOCRITY 2
	Kissinger brought peace	VIETNAM 2
	Some men are born mediocre	MEDIOCRITY 1
	that was Catch-22	MENTAL 3
Hellman, Lillian (1905–84) *American dramatist*	fit this year's fashions	CONSCIENCE 2
	way of saying the truth	CYNICISM 5
Helmsley, Leona (c.1920–) *American hotelier*	little people pay taxes	TAXES 5
Hemans, Felicia (1793–1835) *English poet*	stately homes of England	ARISTOCRACY 5
Hemingway, Ernest (1899–1961) *American novelist*	distinguished from panic	COWARDICE 1
	feel the earth move	SEX 17
	Grace under pressure	COURAGE 5
	man can be destroyed	DEFEAT 4
	Paris is a movable feast	FRANCE 5
	shock-proof shit detector	WRITING 18

Hemingway, Ernest (*cont.*)	Where do the noses go	KISSING 6
Hendrix, Jimi (1942–70) *American rock musician*	musician, if he's a messenger Purple haze is in my brain	MUSICIANS 4 MIND 7
Henley, Arthur W. D.	fairy when she's forty	MIDDLE AGE 10
Henley, W. E. (1849–1903) *English poet and dramatist*	bloody, but unbowed master of my fate	COURAGE 6 SELF 13
Henri IV (1553–1610) *King of France from 1589*	chicken in his pot well worth a mass	POVERTY 13 CYNICISM 6
Henry, Matthew (1662–1714) *English divine*	die by inches	FAMINE 1
Henry, O. (1862–1910) *American short-story writer*	all truly great swindles	DECEPTION 4
Henry, Patrick (1736–99) *American statesman*	liberty, or give me death	LIBERTY 7
Hepworth, Barbara (1903–75) *English sculptor*	always affirmative conveying an emotion I draw what I feel Man is only six foot tall	SCULPTURE 5 SCULPTURE 4 DRAWING 1 SENSES 6
Heraclitus (*c.*540–*c.*480 BC) *Greek philosopher*	man's character is his fate road up and the road down twice into the same river	CHARACTER 11 SIMILARITY 4 CHANGE 13
Herbert, A. P. (1890–1971) *English writer and humorist*	heart in his boots Nothing is wasted stop everyone from doing it suggests a lack of spirit There isn't any Trade We are not here for fun	FARMING 4 STRENGTH 11 ADMIN 5 ARGUMENT 10 CIVIL SERV 6 PLEASURE 9
Herrick, Robert (1591–1674) *English poet and clergyman*	Gather ye rosebuds liquefaction of her clothes	TRANSIENCE 8 CLOTHES 10
Hervey, Lord (1696–1743) *English politician and writer*	Whoever would lie usefully	LIES 5
Heseltine, Michael (1933–) *British Conservative politician*	handbag from an empty chair He who wields the knife intervene—before breakfast never stretch out the hand Polluted rivers, filthy streets	EUROPEAN C 3 BETRAYAL 2 BUSINESS 10 RELATIONSHIPS 12 SOCIETY 7
Hesse, Hermann (1877–1962) *German novelist and poet*	bourgeois prefers comfort hate something in him	CLASS 9 HATRED 5
Heston, Charlton (1924–) *American actor*	murder often three little words	DIVORCE 6 APOLOGY 5
Hewart, Gordon (1870–1943) *British lawyer and politician*	undoubtedly be seen to be done	JUSTICE 12
Hewison, Robert (1943–) *British historian*	golden age seems behind us	TWENTY-FIRST 3
Hewitt, C. W. *British police officer*	more moved by hatred	POLICE 2
Hewitt, John (1907–87) *Northern Irish poet*	heart of the race	NAMES 8
Hewson, John (1946–) *Australian Liberal politician*	call Paul Keating	INSULTS 5

Heyward, Du Bose (1885–1940) **and Gershwin, Ira** (1896–1983)
American songwriters

an' the livin' is easy	SUMMER 4
It ain't necessarily so	TRUTH 15
woman is a sometime thing	WOMEN 17

Hicks, J. R. (1904–)
British economist

| monopoly profits | ECONOMICS 8 |

Hicks, Seymour (1871–1949)
English actor-manager and author

| how young the policemen look | AGEING 7 |

Hightower, Jim
American politician

| dead armadillos | MODERATION 4 |

Hilbert, David (1862–1943)
German mathematician

| importance of a scientific work | SCIENCE 8 |
| We must know | KNOWLEDGE 13 |

Hill, Aaron (1685–1750)
English poet and dramatist

| Grasp it like a man of mettle | COURAGE 7 |

Hill, Christopher (1912–)
British historian

| Bunyan wanted the millennium | ACHIEVEMENT 11 |
| only extended privilege | LIBERTY 8 |

Hill, Damon (1960–)
English motor-racing driver

| only ones who remember you | WINNING 7 |

Hill, Geoffrey (1932–)
English poet

| no earthly weapon | INNOCENCE 5 |
| *sad and angry consolation* | POETRY 18 |

Hill, Joe (1879–1915)
Swedish-born American labour leader

| pie in the sky when you die | FUTURE 9 |
| waste any time in mourning | REVOLUTION 12 |

Hillary, Edmund (1919–)
New Zealand mountaineer

| knocked the bastard off | MOUNTAINS 2 |

Hillebrand, Fred (1893–)

| don't spare the horses | SPEED 5 |

Hillel 'The Elder' (c.60 BC– AD c.9)
Jewish scholar and teacher

| If not now when | SELF 14 |

Hillingdon, Lady (1857–1940)

| think of England | SEX 18 |

Hindenburg, Paul von (1847–1934)
German Field Marshal and statesman

| make him a postmaster | HITLER 4 |

Hippocrates (c.460–357 BC)
Greek physician

| Life is short, the art long | MEDICINE 9 |

Hird, Thora (1911–)
English actress

| mistaken for a prostitute | SEX 19 |

Hirohito, Emperor (1901–89)
Emperor of Japan from 1926

| to Japan's advantage | DEFEAT 5 |

Hirst, Damien (1965–)
English artist

| twisted imagination | ARTISTS 4 |

Hislop, Ian (1960–)
English satirical journalist

| I am a banana | JUSTICE 13 |

Hitchcock, Alfred (1899–1980)
British-born film director

Actors are cattle	ACTORS 8
If I made Cinderella	CINEMA 18
murder into the home	MURDER 7
no terror in a bang	FEAR 9

Hitler, Adolf (1889–1945)
German dictator

consolidating the attention	LEADERSHIP 6
fall victim to a big lie	LIES 6
If artists do see fields blue	COLOURS 5
night of the long knives	BETRAYAL 7
remembers the Armenians	GENOCIDE 4
way that Providence dictates	FATE 7

Ho, Mae-Wan

| *genetic determinism* | GENETIC 3 |

Hobbes, Thomas (1588–1679)	great leap in the dark	LAST WORDS 8
English philosopher	nasty, brutish, and short	LIFE 14
	nothing else but sudden glory	HUMOUR 8
Hobsbawm, Eric (1917–)	Middle Ages ended suddenly	TWENTIETH 4
British historian	produce victory parades	FALKLANDS 4
Hockney, David (1937–)	Art has to move you	ART 15
British artist	end up using scissors	TECHNOLOGY 15
	it's got to be organized	PAINTING 10
	they stare back, blankly	PHOTOGRAPHY 6
Hoddle, Glenn (1957–)	karma is working	DISABILITY 5
English footballer		
Hodgson, Ralph (1871–1962)	ring the bells of Heaven	ANIMAL RIGHTS 7
English poet	you old gipsy man	TIME 13
Hoffer, Eric (1902–83)	Originality is deliberate	ORIGINALITY 6
American philosopher		
Hogben, Lancelot (1895–1975)	age of the engineers	TECHNOLOGY 16
English scientist		
Holbach, Paul Henri, Baron d' (1723–89)	gave birth to the Gods	SCIENCE & REL 5
French philosopher		
Holbrooke, Richard (1941–)	Give us bombs for peace	WEAPONS 7
American diplomat	those already killed	DIPLOMACY 8
Holden, Patrick (1937–)	pollute now, pay later	GENETIC 4
British businessman		
Holiday, Billie (1915–59)	Black bodies swinging	RACISM 11
American singer	hell for those you love	DRUGS 11
	up to your boobies in white	RACISM 12
Holland, Henry Scott (1847–1918)	I have only slipped away	DEATH 14
English theologian and preacher		
Holloway, Richard (1933–)	language *about* mysteries	RELIGION 6
Bishop of Edinburgh		
Holmes, John H. (1879–1964)	It is simply indifferent	UNIVERSE 10
American Unitarian minister		
Holmes, Oliver Wendell Jr. (1841–1935)	man decides he is not God	FAITH 8
American lawyer	protection of free speech	LIBERTY 9
Holmes, Oliver Wendell (1809–94)	privilege of wisdom to listen	CONVERSATION 9
American physician, poet, and essayist	seventy years young	OLD AGE 10
	stick on conversation's burrs	CONVERSATION 10
	turn the other cheek	VIOLENCE 8
Holub, Miroslav (1923–)	ability to sort peas	PERSISTENCE 7
Czech poet		
Home, Lord (1903–95)	form of madness	FISHING 1
British Conservative statesman	fourteenth Mr Wilson	ARISTOCRACY 6
Homer (8th century BC)	generation of men	TRANSIENCE 9
Greek poet		
Hood, Thomas (1799–1845)	bread should be so dear	POVERTY 14
English poet and humorist	drive one from home	COOKING 7
	no leaves, no birds,—November	WINTER 3
Hoover, Herbert (1874–1964)	full garage	PROGRESS 11
American Republican statesman, President 1929–33	rugged individualism	UNITED S 13
	social and economic experiment	TEETOTALISM 2
	youth who must fight and die	WARFARE 16

Hope, A. D. (1907–)
Australian poet

second-hand Europeans | AUSTRALIA 4

Hope, Anthony (1863–1933)
English novelist

Economy is going without | MONEY 12
His foe was folly | EPITAPHS 17

Hope, Bob (1903–)
American comedian

If you watch a game | GOLF 1
prove that you don't need it | MONEY 13

Hopkins, Gerard Manley (1844–89)
English poet and priest

all is seared with trade | POLLUTION 10
all is seared with trade | WORK 9
All things counter, original | BEAUTY 12
beat upon my whorlèd ear | SILENCE 4
Cuckoo-echoing, bell-swarmèd | OXFORD 3
dapple-dawn-drawn Falcon | BIRDS 4
Long live the weeds | ENVIRONMENT 8
look, look up at the skies | SKIES 7
mind has mountains | MIND 8
not choose not to be | DESPAIR 7
This Jack, joke | HUMAN RACE 11
Time's eunuch | CREATIVITY 5
woman with a slop-pail | PRAYER 9
yet you *will* weep | SORROW 10

Horace (65–8 BC)
Roman poet

Force, unaided by judgement | VIOLENCE 9
I shall not altogether die | DEATH 15
it is your business | CRISES 11
Lovely and honourable it is | PATRIOTISM 12
Mountains will go into labour | EFFORT 5
Never despair | HOPE 8
poets being second-rate | MEDIOCRITY 3
Seize the day | PRESENT 9
short madness | ANGER 6
somehow, make money | MONEY 14
strive to be brief | STYLE 6
unmixed blessing | PERFECTION 5
We are just statistics | STATISTICS 7
word takes wing beyond recall | WORDS 11
written by drinkers of water | TEETOTALISM 3

Hornby, Nick (1957–)
British novelist and journalist

bitter disappointment | FOOTBALL 4
supporting the wrong team | FATHERS 2
what it means to be suburban | CITIES 7

Horne, Donald Richmond (1921–)

second-rate people | AUSTRALIA 5

Horowitz, Vladimir (1904–89)
Russian pianist

easiest instrument to play | MUSICAL INST 5

Housman, A. E. (1859–1936)
English poet

blue remembered hills | PAST 8
confirmed by the crash | RISK 4
European view of a poet | EUROPE 14
God abandoned, these defended | ARMY 9
handcuffs on his wrists | PREJUDICE 6
heartless, witless nature | NATURE 4
justify God's ways to man | ALCOHOL 9
my skin bristles | POETRY 19
On Wenlock Edge | WIND 2
photograph is not quite true | APPEARANCE 7
quarries to be used at will | QUOTATIONS 8
see the cherry hung with snow | SPRING 4
Wearing white for Eastertide | TREES 8
Written English is now inert | LANGUAGES 4

Howe, Geoffrey (1926–)
British Conservative politician

broken before the game | BETRAYAL 8

Howe, Julia Ward (1819–1910)
American Unitarian lay preacher

eyes have seen the glory	GOD 15

Howells, William Dean (1837–1920)
American novelist and critic

stay longer in an hour	GUESTS 4
tragedy with a happy ending	TRAGEDY 3

Howerd, Frankie (1922–92)
British comedian

either dead or deported	TELEVISION 6

Hoyle, Edmond (1672–1769)
English writer on card-games

When in doubt, win the trick	WINNING 8

Hoyle, Fred (1915–2001)
English astrophysicist

hour's drive away	SPACE 5
outrageous young fellow	GENERATION 6
There is a coherent plan	UNIVERSE 11

Hubbard, Elbert (1859–1915)
American writer

damned thing after another	LIFE 15
Little minds are interested	GENIUS 6
Never explain	APOLOGY 6
one extraordinary man	TECHNOLOGY 17

Hubbard, Frank McKinney ('Kin') (1868–1930)
American humorist

buried a hatchet	REVENGE 9
Classic music is th'kind	MUSIC 10

Hughes, Jimmy and Lake, Frank

Bless 'em all! Bless 'em all	ARMY 10

Hughes, Langston (1902–67)
American writer and poet

ancient as the world	RIVERS 5
bathed in the Euphrates	RIVERS 6
I am the darker brother	RACISM 13

Hughes, Simon (1951–)
British Liberal Democrat politician

in some mental hospitals	HEALTH 2

Hughes, Ted (1930–98)
English poet

Creation in my foot	BIRDS 5
flat As an old rough mat	CATS 3
Grey silent fragments	HORSES 2
her prostrate body, Science	NATURE 5
my mulatto mother	DRUNKEN 4
pink wool knitted dress	WEDDINGS 7
shock of your joy	DIARIES 4
surplus mental department	IMAGINATION 6
utility son-in-law	IN-LAWS 4

Hughes, Thomas (1822–96)
English lawyer, politician, and writer

his idea of a compromise	COMPROMISE 3
It's an institution	CRICKET 6

Hugo, Victor (1802–85)
French poet, novelist, and dramatist

daze with little bells	THINKING 10
invasion by an idea	IDEAS 5

Hull, Josephine (?1886–1957)
American actress

never get a chance to sit down	SHAKESPEARE 2

Hume, Basil (1923–99)
English cardinal

believe that God loves them	BELIEF 10
calm and at peace	DYING 7
could have been me	CELIBACY 4
especially precious to God	PRAYER 8
start where people are	CLERGY 3

Hume, David (1711–76)
Scottish philosopher

attended with miracles	CHRISTIAN 5
destruction of the whole world	SELF 15
enemies of liberty	CLERGY 4
exists merely in the mind	BEAUTY 13

Humphries, Barry (1934–)
Australian entertainer and writer

at four years of age	BEHAVIOUR 10
mass murderers or critics	CREATIVITY 6

Humphrys, John
British broadcaster and journalist

redemption through money	CONSUMER 3

Hunt, Leigh (1784–1859)
English poet and essayist

performance every thing	EXCELLENCE 3
stolen, be your apples	SECRECY 16
subject of eating	CONVERSATION 11

Hunter, Robert (1941–)
Canadian writer

ecology and antiwar	ENVIRONMENT 9

Hupfeld, Herman (1894–1951)
American songwriter

You must remember this	KISSING 7

Hurd, Douglas (1930–)
British Conservative politician

destroying experimental crops	GENETIC 5

Hussein, Saddam (1937–)
President of Iraq from 1979

mother of battles	GULF 3

Hutcheson, Francis (1694–1746)
Scottish philosopher

That action is best	MORALITY 7

Hutton, Will (1950–)
British newspaper editor

temptation to cut and run	CAPITALISM 5

Huxley, Aldous (1894–1963)
English novelist

Caesars and Napoleons	LEADERSHIP 7
choose to be Faraday	ARTS AND SCI 6
contrary to life	CONSISTENCY 2
easier to write ten sonnets	ADVERTISING 5
end cannot justify the means	MORALITY 8
exclusively in the right	ACHIEVEMENT 12
Facts do not cease to exist	FACTS 2
labour to write	BOOKS 11
less convincing than one	APOLOGY 7
man does with what happens	EXPERIENCE 10
million million spermatozoa	CHANCE 7
Official dignity	BUREAUCRACY 6
Parodies and caricatures	CRITICS 11
sexual perversions	CELIBACY 5

Huxley, Julian (1887–1975)
English biologist

cosmic Cheshire cat	GOD 16

Huxley, T. H. (1825–95)
English biologist

always think what is true	GOODNESS 8
beacons of wise men	LOGIC 9
customary fate of new truths	TRUTH 16
great tragedy of Science	THEORY 7
I am too much of a sceptic	DOUBT 4
Irrationally held truths	LOGIC 8
little knowledge is dangerous	KNOWLEDGE 14
no reason to be ashamed	SCIENCE & REL 6
organized common sense	SCIENCE 9

Hytner, Nicholas (1956–)
English theatre and film director

Mickey Mouse could direct	CINEMA 19

Ibarruri, Dolores (1895–1989)
Spanish Communist leader

better to die on your feet	LIBERTY 10
They shall not pass	DEFIANCE 5

Ibsen, Henrik (1828–1906)
Norwegian dramatist

have your best trousers on	CLOTHES 11
man who stands most alone	STRENGTH 12
people don't do such things	HUMAN NATURE 8
Take the life-lie away	DISILLUSION 4
terrible overwhelming majority	MINORITIES 3

Ice Cube (1970–)
American rap musician

look at yourself as a parent	FATHERS 3

Ice-T (1958–)
American rap musician

makes it a safer place	LOVE 27
take the system and rock it	ROCK 7

Ice-T (*cont.*)	talks good for a black guy	RACISM 14
Ignatius Loyola, St (**1491–1556**) *Spanish theologian*	not to count the cost	GIVING 5
Illich, Ivan (**1926–**) *American sociologist*	In a consumer society whether to be rich in things	CONSUMER 4 POSSESSIONS 10
Indiana, Gary *American writer*	How can we die like this	AIDS 4
Inge, Charles (**1868–1957**)	If you don't think you can't	ABILITY 3
Inge, William Ralph (**1860–1954**) *English writer; Dean of St. Paul's, 1911–34*	become a popular religion not of facts but of values one to make a quarrel repelled by man they shout and they shoot throne of bayonets	RELIGION 7 EDUCATION 10 ARGUMENT 11 HUMAN RACE 12 LIBERTY 11 VIOLENCE 10
Ingersoll, Robert G. (**1833–99**) *American agnostic*	there are consequences	NATURE 6
Ingham, Bernard (**1932–**) *British journalist*	Blood sport is brought conspiracy theory of government	GOSSIP 6 GOVERNMENT 12
Ingrams, Richard (**1937–**) *English satirical journalist*	bug-eyed serial killer publish and be sued regard the Law Courts	PRESS 4 JOURNALISM 11 LAWS 11
Ingres, J. A. D. (**1780–1867**) *French painter*	true test of art	DRAWING 2
Innes, Hammond (**1913–**) *English novelist*	accountants have moved in	PUBLISHING 4
Ionesco, Eugène (**1912–94**) *French dramatist*	doesn't make jokes	CIVIL SERV 7
Irving, John (**1942–**) *British novelist*	Your memory is a monster	MEMORY 12
Irving, Washington (**1783–1859**) *American writer*	bruised in a new place tart temper never mellows	CHANGE 14 SPEECH 15
Isaacson, Walter (**1952–**) *American editor*	symbol of the digital age	INTERNET 5
Isherwood, Christopher (**1904–86**) *English novelist*	camera with its shutter open	WRITING 19
Ishiguro, Kazuo (**1954–**) *Japanese-born British novelist*	only review that is no use very slowly to discover	REVIEWS 3 WRITING 20
Issigonis, Alec (**1906–88**) *British engineer*	camel is a horse	COMMITTEES 4
Jackson, Jesse (**1941–**) *American Democratic politician and clergyman*	real rainbow coalition	RACE 5
Jackson, Mahalia (**1911–72**) *American singer*	when you haven't got a thing	SELF-ESTEEM 11
Jackson, Michael (**1958–**) *American pop singer*	have you seen my childhood	CHARACTER 12
Jackson, Robert H. (**1892–1954**) *American lawyer and judge*	loyalties and ambitions stay the hands of vengeance	CORRUPTION 5 TRIALS 2
Jacobs, Joe (**1896–1940**) *American boxing manager*	We was robbed	BOXING 5

Jagger, Mick (1943–) **and Richards, Keith** (1943–) *English rock musicians*	fighting in the street, boy I can't get no satisfaction	PROTEST 3 COURTSHIP 8
James I (1566–1625) *(James VI of Scotland)*	custom loathsome to the eye Dr Donne's verses	SMOKING 6 POETS 12
James, Carwyn (1929–83) *Welsh Rugby Football coach*	retaliation in first	REVENGE 10
James, Clive (1939–) *Australian critic and writer*	crisis of the Church echoes the sails of yachts history worth bothering about powerless to change it verb chasing its own tail	CHURCH 6 BUILDINGS 5 AUSTRALIA 6 TELEVISION 7 GRAMMAR 6
James, Evan *Welsh bard*	sweet are thy hills	WALES 3
James, Henry (1843–1916) *American novelist*	all human life is there determination of incident discrimination and selection grant the artist his subject here it is at last I know what I like Live all you can Our doubt is our passion spoiled child of art Summer afternoon war has used up words	LIFE 16 FICTION 8 ART 17 CRITICS 12 DEATH 16 LIKES 4 LIFESTYLES 10 ART 16 FICTION 7 WORDS 12 WORLD W I 11
James, P. D. (1920–) *English writer of detective stories*	Did he fall or was he pushed form of linguistic fascism restoration of order	CRIME FICT 5 LANGUAGE 10 CRIME FICT 4
James, William (1842–1910) *American philosopher*	exceptional observations in whom nothing is habitual Man is polygamous preys on its own species worship of the bitch-goddess	FACTS 3 INDECISION 6 MARRIAGE 18 HUMAN RACE 13 SUCCESS 13
Jarrell, Randall (1914–65) *American poet*	In bombers named for girls obvious facts about grown-ups take it home to live with you there *are* no molehills To Americans, English manners wife is a girl playing house	AIR FORCE 3 MATURITY 7 IDEAS 6 DEPRESSION 3 MANNERS 4 WIVES 7
Jastrzebska, Maria (1953–)	Wears any trousers at all	LESBIANISM 3
Jay, Antony (1930–) see **Lynn, Jonathan and Jay, Antony**		
Jay, Douglas (1907–96) *British Labour politician*	gentleman in Whitehall used one syllable	CIVIL SERV 8 WORDS 13
Jean-Baptiste, Marianne *British actress*	no longer fish and chips	BRITAIN 7
Jeans, James (1877–1946) *English astronomer, physicist, and mathematician*	evidence of his creation future of the human race last breath of Julius Caesar Life exists in the universe	UNIVERSE 12 HUMAN RACE 14 PHYSICS 8 LIFE SCI 9
Jefferson, Thomas (1743–1826) *American Democratic Republican statesman, President 1801–9*	blood of patriots and tyrants friendship with all nations have the wolf by the ears himself as public property ignorant and free	LIBERTY 12 INTERNATIONAL 10 CRISES 12 RESPONSIBILITY 1 CIVILIZATION 4

Jefferson, Thomas (*cont.*)

little rebellion now and then	REVOLUTION 13
natural aristocracy among men	ARISTOCRACY 7
ploughman and a professor	MORALITY 9
possess their equal rights	MINORITIES 4
walking is best	EXERCISE 4
young gardener	GARDENS 10

Jenkins, David (1925–)
English theologian

conjuring trick with bones	GOD 17

Jenkins, Roy (1920–2003)
British politician

dead or dying beast	POLITICAL P 12
from their own party	PRIME 7

Jennings, Elizabeth (1926–2001)
English poet

fire from which I came	PARENTS 6
I hate a word like 'pets'	ANIMALS 14

Jerome, Jerome K. (1859–1927)
English writer

drink one another's healths	ALCOHOL 10
enjoy idling thoroughly	IDLENESS 6
everything has its drawbacks	ADVERSITY 2
exceptionally good liar	HONESTY 4
patent medicine advertisement	SICKNESS 8
sit and look at it for hours	WORK 10

Jerome, William (1865–1932)
American songwriter

place I can hang my hat	HOME 5

Jerrold, Douglas (1803–57)
English dramatist and journalist

laughs with a harvest	AUSTRALIA 7
Love's like the measles	LOVE 28
only athletic sport	SPORTS 8
Religion's in the heart	RELIGION 8

Jhabvala, Ruth Prawer (1927–)
German-born novelist and screenwriter

country as an experience	ASIA 5
make him into a better person	MEN/WOMEN 13

Joad, C. E. M. (1891–1953)
English philosopher

all depends what you mean	MEANING 7
fear I may be lonely	FRIENDSHIP 14
land of 'beauty spots'	COUNTRY 7

John, Elton (1947–)
English pop singer and songwriter

get goose bumps every time	SINGING 10

John, Elton (1947–) **and Taupin, Bernie**
(1950–)
English pop singer and songwriter; songwriter

candle in the wind	DIANA 7
	MONROE 2
Goodbye England's rose	DIANA 6
My gift is my song	GIVING 6

John XXIII, Pope (1881–1963)
Pope from 1958

Anybody can be pope	CLERGY 5
throw open the windows	CHURCH 7

John Paul II, Pope (1920–)
Polish cleric

Alleluia is our song	CHRISTIAN 6
It fell by itself	COMMUNISM 8

Johnson, Amy (1903–41)
English aviator

spirit found outlet in the air	AIR TRAVEL 1

Johnson, Dorothy (1905–84)

print the myth	HEROES 10

Johnson, Lyndon Baines (1908–73)
*American Democratic statesman, President
1963–9*

about to send American boys	VIETNAM 3
broadened into a brotherhood	INTERNATIONAL 11
fart and chew gum	FOOLS 7
I am a free man, an American	POLITICAL P 13
inside the tent pissing out	ENEMIES 7
kiss my ass in Macy's window	LOYALTY 4
not to be standing here today	BEREAVEMENT 8
to the Great Society	SOCIETY 8
write it in the books of law	HUMAN RIGHTS 7

Johnson, Philander Chase (1866–1939)

worst is yet to come	OPTIMISM 5

Johnson, Philip (1906–)
American architect

how to waste space	ARCHITECT 5

Johnson, Samuel (1709–84)
English poet, critic, and lexicographer

abuse a tragedy	CRITICS 13
all belief is for it	SUPERNATURAL 11
as good for nothing	FOOD 15
as inclination leads him	READING 6
aspires to be a hero	ALCOHOL 11
assuming a superiority	CONVERSATION 12
better to suffer wrong	TRUST 6
between a louse and a flea	EQUALITY 7
beyond the dreams of avarice	WEALTH 12
but the signs of ideas	WORDS 14
care for the child's rattle	TASTE 4
concentrates his mind	EXECUTIONS 2
cowardice keeps us in peace	COWARDICE 2
cut a Colossus from a rock	POETS 13
dignity of thinking beings	SENSES 7
enemy to human happiness	POVERTY 15
Excise. A hateful tax	TAXES 6
excite my amorous propensities	SEX 20
exclude the black dog	DEPRESSION 4
find you an understanding	INTELLIGENCE 7
first duty to serve society	RELIGION 9
flatter a man so grossly	FLATTERY 5
foolish thing well done	ACHIEVEMENT 13
from worse to better	CHANGE 15
happiness of an individual	GOVERNMENT 13
harmless drudge	DICTIONARIES 2
have his all neglected	EFFORT 6
I refute it *thus*	REALITY 5
if you are solitary	IDLENESS 7
Ignorance, madam	IGNORANCE 8
in constant repair	FRIENDSHIP 15
in the arms of a chambermaid	IMAGINATION 7
injustice of the cause	LAWYERS 2
knock him down first	COMPASSION 8
Knowledge is of two kinds	INFORMATION 5
last refuge of a scoundrel	PATRIOTISM 13
lasts so short a time	DYING 8
leads him to England	SCOTLAND 8
learned to play at cards	SPORTS 9
like a dog's walking	WOMAN'S R 11
man who exposes himself	DRUNKEN 5
Marriage has many pains	CELIBACY 6
Martyrdom is the test	OPINION 5
mind of large general powers	GENIUS 7
mind is actually employed	EMPLOYMENT 9
morals of a whore	BEHAVIOUR 11
No man but a blockhead	WRITING 22
not worth going to see	TRAVEL 9
paucity of human pleasures	HUNTING 3
pedigree of nations	LANGUAGES 5
Read over your compositions	WRITING 21
reading is right	CRITICS 14
sit and *growl*	ARGUMENT 12
soul of an advertisement	ADVERTISING 6
species of idleness	SORROW 11
species of revenge	GRATITUDE 3
stick and a string	FISHING 2
sting a stately horse	POWER 11
teach them [children] first	TEACHING 7
triumph of hope	MARRIAGE 19
vanity of human hopes	LIBRARIES 6
we will out-argue them	PARLIAMENT 11

Johnson, Samuel (*cont.*)

When a man is tired of London	LONDON 5
when his wife talks Greek	WOMAN'S R 12
When two Englishmen meet	WEATHER 8
wish to appear considerable	FAME 13
working or starving	LIBERTY 13
worst is better than none	DICTIONARIES 3
write the life of a man	BIOGRAPHY 10

Johnston, Jill (1929–)

fearful compromise	BISEXUAL 3

Johst, Hanns (1890–1978)
German dramatist

safety-catch of my Browning	CULTURE 11

Jolson, Al (1886–1950)
American singer

ain't heard nuttin' yet	SINGING 11

Jones, John Paul (1747–92)
American admiral

not yet begun to fight	DETERMINATION 6

Jones, Kennedy
British journalist

What sells a newspaper	NEWSPAPERS 10

Jones, Paul M.
see de Leon, Walter and Jones, Paul M.

Jones, Steve (1944–)
English geneticist

chance of winning the lottery	CHANCE 8
greenest political party	ENVIRONMENT 10
Sex and taxes	SEX 21
somewhat less Gadarene rush	AID 5
worry about GM soya beans	GENETIC 6

Jong, Erica (1942–)
American novelist

fun you *think* they had	JEALOUSY 4
measurements are being taken	GOSSIP 7
rhythm to the ending	DIVORCE 7

Jonson, Ben (*c.*1573–1637)
English dramatist and poet

He was not of an age	SHAKESPEARE 3
More in the cunning purchase	WEALTH 13
small Latin, and less Greek	SHAKESPEARE 4

Joplin, Janis (1943–70)
American singer

he had to die in my week	SELF-INTEREST 7

Joseph II (1741–90)
Holy Roman Emperor

too many notes, dear Mozart	MOZART 2

Joseph, Jenny (1932–)
English poet

doing nothing was a sin	IDLENESS 8
I shall wear purple	OLD AGE 11

Joseph, Keith (1918–94)
British Conservative politician

telling British management off	WORDS/DEED 4
telling people what to *think*	RESPONSIBILITY 2

Jospin, Lionel (1937–)
French statesman

No to the market society	CAPITALISM 6

Jowell, Tessa (1947–)
British Labour politician

all the women MPs	PARLIAMENT 12

Jowett, Benjamin (1817–93)
English classicist

nowhere worse taste	TASTE 5

Joyce, James (1882–1941)
Irish novelist

errors are volitional	GENIUS 8
hand that wrote *Ulysses*	JOYCE 1
heaventree of stars	SKIES 5
I fear those big words	WORDS 15
I will try to express myself	SELF 16
old sow that eats her farrow	IRELAND 5
paring his fingernails	ART 18
scrotumtightening sea	SEA 7
Tenors get women	SINGING 12
Terror is the feeling	SUFFERING 10

Jung, Carl Gustav (1875–1961) *Swiss psychologist*	afternoon of human life	MIDDLE AGE 11
	both are transformed	RELATIONSHIPS 13
	changed in ourselves	CHILDREN 9
	I do not believe . . . I know	BELIEF 11
	inferno of his passions	EMOTIONS 8
	morphine or idealism	DRUGS 12
	purpose of human existence	LIFE 17
	unlived lives of their parents	PARENTS 7
Junot, Marshal (1771–1813) *French general*	I am an ancestor	ARISTOCRACY 8
Justice, Donald (1925–) *American poet*	Men at forty learn	MIDDLE AGE 12
Juvenal (AD c.60–c.130) *Roman satirist*	Everything in Rome	CORRUPTION 6
	guard the guards themselves	TRUST 7
	makes men ridiculous	POVERTY 16
	no guilty man is acquitted	PUNISHMENT 11
	owed the greatest respect	CHILDREN 10
	paltry, feeble, tiny mind	REVENGE 11
	praised and left to shiver	HONESTY 5
	sound mind in a sound body	HEALTH 3
Kael, Pauline (1919–) *American film critic*	Kiss Kiss Bang Bang	CINEMA 20
Kafka, Franz (1883–1924) *Czech novelist*	often better to be in chains	LIBERTY 14
	trial if I recognize it	TRIALS 3
Kahn, Gus (1886–1941) **and Egan, Raymond B.** (1890–1952) *American songwriters*	poor get children	POVERTY 17
Kalmar, Bert (1884–1947) **et al.**	minute and a huff	PARTING 10
Kane, Sarah (1971–99) *British dramatist*	I write the truth	HONESTY 6
Kant, Immanuel (1724–1804) *German philosopher*	crooked timber of humanity	HUMAN RACE 15
	not an ideal of reason	HAPPINESS 8
	Two things fill the mind	THINKING 11
	Whoever wills the end	CAUSES 5
Kanter, Rosabeth Moss (1943–) *American management consultant and writer*	come from being employable	UNEMPLOYMENT 3
	innovate continually	BUSINESS 11
	people's desire to buy	CONSUMER 5
	world century is beginning	TWENTY-FIRST 4
Kapoor, Anish (1954–) *Indian sculptor*	life in the imagination	ART 19
Karr, Alphonse (1808–90) *French novelist and journalist*	abolish the death penalty	MURDER 8
	Plus ça change	CHANGE 16
Kaufman, Gerald (1930–) *British Labour politician*	House run by a philistine	CULTURE 12
	longest suicide note	POLITICAL P 14
Kaunda, Kenneth (1924–) *Zambian statesman*	Africans experience people	AFRICA 5
Kavanagh, Patrick (1904–67) *Irish poet*	Clay is the word	FAMINE 2
	clean place to die	TRAGEDY 4
Keating, Paul (1944–) *Australian Labor statesman, Prime Minister 1991–6*	back down the time tunnel	AUSTRALIA 8
	not about being nice	LEADERSHIP 8
	shiver looking for a spine	INSULTS 6
Keats, John (1795–1821) *English poet*	beaker full of the warm South	ALCOHOL 12
	Beauty is truth	BEAUTY 15

Keats, John (*cont.*)

cease upon the midnight	DEATH 17
do not christen him John	NAMES 9
flaw In happiness	DISCONTENT 5
flummery of a birth place	FAME 14
gordian shape of dazzling hue	APPEARANCE 8
I stand alone and think	VALUE 9
I would scarcely kick	DEPRESSION 5
impossible to live	RAIN 5
joy for ever	BEAUTY 14
leaden-eyed despairs	SUFFERING 11
like to be married to a poem	ROMANCE 5
magic casements	IMAGINATION 8
mists and mellow fruitfulness	AUTUMN 4
more concentrated in you	ABSENCE 4
name was writ in water	EPITAPHS 18
naturally as the leaves	POETRY 20
next to fine doing	LITERATURE/SOC 4
O for a life of sensations	SENSES 8
on tip-toe for a flight	FLOWERS 3
strengthening one's intellect	MIND 9
unravished bride of quietness	SILENCE 5
uproar's your only music	CHANGE 17
Was it a vision	DREAMS 7
would I were steadfast	FAITHFULNESS 8

Keats, John (1920–)

automobile changed our dress	CARS 6

Keeler, Christine (1942–)
English model and showgirl

lady with the moustache	FAME 15

Keenan, Brian (1950–)
Irish writer and teacher

my liberty, not my freedom	LIBERTY 15
you don't shut down	PRISON 3

Keillor, Garrison (1942–)
American humorous writer

never told bad news	REAGAN 1
problem to be overcome	MEN 16

Keith, Penelope (1940–)
British actress

egotism out of its depth	SELF-ESTEEM 12

Keller, Helen (1880–1968)
American writer and social reformer

apathy of human beings	INDIFFERENCE 4
daring adventure, or nothing	SECURITY 4
living word awakened my soul	LANGUAGE 11

Kelvin, Lord (1824–1907)
British scientist

when you cannot measure it	SCIENCE 10

Kennedy, Florynce (1916–2001)
American lawyer

If men could get pregnant	PREGNANCY 3

Kennedy, Jimmy and Carr, Michael
British songwriters

on the Siegfried Line	WORLD W II 10

Kennedy, John F. (1917–63)
*American Democratic statesman, President
1961–3*

city of southern efficiency	AMERICAN CITIES 11
finished in the first 100 days	BEGINNING 6
graveyards of battle	RACE 6
help the many who are poor	SOCIETY 9
I am a Berliner	INTERNATIONAL 12
Mankind must put an end	WARFARE 17
negotiate out of fear	DIPLOMACY 9
not engineers of the soul	ART AND SOC 2
pay for a landslide	ELECTIONS 7
salt in our blood	SEA 8
They sank my boat	HEROES 11
violent revolution inevitable	REVOLUTION 14
we shall pay any price	LIBERTY 16
what your country can do	PATRIOTISM 14
world safe for diversity	SIMILARITY 5

Kennedy, Robert (1925–68)
American Democratic politician

criminal it deserves	POLICE 3
dangerous about extremists	FANATICISM 4
One-fifth of the people	PROTEST 4

Kennedy, Rose (1890–1995)
wife of Joseph Kennedy

mother of a great son — ACHIEVEMENT 14

Kent, Princess Michael of (1945–)
Austrian-born British princess

cut ribbons and kiss babies — ROYALTY 12

Kerr, Jean (1923–2003)
American writer

adorable pancreas	BEAUTY 16
for other people to go on	AIR TRAVEL 2
haven't grasped the situation	CRISES 13

Kettle, Thomas (1880–1916)
Irish economist and poet

Liberals forget their principles — POLITICAL P 15

Key, Francis Scott (1779–1843)
American lawyer and verse-writer

star-spangled banner — UNITED S 14

Keyes, Marian
Irish writer

I want the M word	MARRIAGE 20
My biological clock	MIDDLE AGE 13

Keynes, John Maynard (1883–1946)
English economist

debauch the currency	ECONOMICS 9
Government I despise	GOVERNMENT 14
half-human visitor to our age	LLOYD 4
knew more about economics	EXAMINATIONS 3
Madmen in authority	IDEAS 7
we are all dead	FUTURE 10

Khrushchev, Nikita (1894–1971)
Soviet statesman, Premier 1958–64

catch the bird of paradise	COMPROMISE 4
history is on our side	CAPITALISM 7
Marx, Engels and Lenin	WAITING 4

Kierkegaard, Sören (1813–55)
Danish philosopher

must be understood backwards — LIFE 18

Kilmer, Joyce (1886–1918)
American poet

only God can make a tree	CREATIVITY 7
poem lovely as a tree	TREES 9

Kilmuir, Lord (1900–67)
British Conservative politician and lawyer

Tory's secret weapon — POLITICAL P 16

Kilvert, Francis (1840–79)
English clergyman and diarist

most noxious is a tourist	TRAVEL 10
out on the hills alone	MOUNTAINS 3

King, Benjamin Franklin (1857–94)
American poet

Nothing to do but work — PESSIMISM 6

King, Florence (1936–)

flee Family Man America — HOMOSEXUAL 8

King, Francis (1923–)
British writer

resembled a Baked Alaska — PEOPLE 10

King, Martin Luther (1929–68)
American civil rights leader

be the white man's brother	RACISM 15
I have a dream	EQUALITY 8
isn't fit to live	IDEALISM 7
language of the unheard	VIOLENCE 11
live together as brothers	COOPERATION 9
Nothing is more dangerous	IGNORANCE 9
outrun our spiritual power	SCIENCE & REL 7
threat to justice everywhere	JUSTICE 14

King, Stephen (1947–)
American writer

things are in the unmaking — FEAR 10

King, William Lyon Mackenzie
(1874–1950)
Canadian Liberal statesman

too much geography — CANADA 7

Kingsley, Charles (1819–75)	Be good, sweet maid	GOODNESS 9
English writer and clergyman	there's little to earn	WORK 11
	Welcome, wild North-easter	WIND 3
	work that's nearest	DUTY 4
Kingsmill, Hugh (1889–1949)	God's apology for relations	FRIENDSHIP 16
English man of letters		
Kington, Miles (1941–)	doesn't work any more	ARCHAEOLOGY 4
English humorist	know your place in the set-up	CLASS 10
Kinnock, Neil (1942–)	let my country die for me	PATRIOTISM 15
British Labour politician	Why am I the first Kinnock	UNIVERSITIES 8
Kinsey, Alfred (1894–1956)	that which you cannot perform	SEX 22
American zoologist and sex researcher		
Kipling, Rudyard (1865–1936)	all places were alike to him	CATS 4
English writer and poet	better man than I am, Gunga	CHARACTER 13
	constructing tribal lays	OPINION 6
	Every one is more or less mad	MADNESS 3
	For a little, little space	BEREAVEMENT 9
	giving your heart to a dog	DOGS 3
	Glory of the Garden	GARDENS 11
	He travels the fastest	SOLITUDE 11
	If you can keep your head	CRISES 14
	If you can trust yourself	CHARACTER 14
	It's clever, but is it Art?	ART 20
	Lest we forget	HUMILITY 4
	little grey shadow	DEPRESSION 6
	manage a clever man	MEN/WOMEN 14
	more deadly than the male	WOMEN 19
	most powerful drug	WORDS 16
	Mother o' mine	MOTHERS 4
	motto of the mongoose family	INFORMATION 6
	muddied oafs at the goals	SPORTS 10
	never the twain shall meet	EQUALITY 9
	Old England to adorn	TREES 10
	'Omer smote 'is bloomin' lyre	PLAGIARISM 4
	only four things certain	CAUSES 6
	prerogative of the harlot	RESPONSIBILITY 3
	road through the woods	PAST 9
	seldom walks up to the word	CANCER 3
	sin ye do by two and two	SIN 10
	sisters under their skins	WOMEN 18
	stay in a man's memory	SEX 23
	toad beneath the harrow	SUFFERING 12
	Tommy this, an' Tommy that	ARMY 11
	Watch the wall, my darling	CAUTION 6
	What and Why and When	KNOWLEDGE 15
	wrapped himself in quotations	QUOTATIONS 9
	you'll be a Man, my son	MATURITY 8
Kissinger, Henry (1923–)	great aphrodisiac	POWER 12
American politician	My schedule is already full	CRISES 15
	We are the President's men	LOYALTY 5
	wins if he does not lose	WARFARE 18
Kitchener, Lord (1850–1916)	Do your duty bravely	WORLD W I 12
British soldier and statesman		
Klee, Paul (1879–1940)	active line on a walk	DRAWING 3
Swiss painter	Colour has taken hold of me	COLOURS 6
	it makes visible	PAINTING 11
Knight, Laura (1877–1970)	few strokes of the pencil	DRAWING 4
English painter		

Knox, John (*c.*1505–72)
Scottish Protestant reformer

always in the majority

FAITH 9

Knox, Ronald (1888–1957)
English writer and Roman Catholic priest

After all, what was a paradox

LOGIC 10

blancmange and rhubarb tart

PARTIES 5

right to his own opinions

OPINION 7

tempering bigot zeal

MANNERS 5

Koestler, Arthur (1905–83)
Hungarian-born writer

receiver off the hook

GOD 18

ten readers in ten years' time

WRITING 23

Kohl, Helmut (1930–)
German statesman

policy of European integration

EUROPEAN C 4

Korb, Lawrence (1939–)
American government official

If Kuwait grew carrots

GULF 4

Krantz, Judith (1932–)
British writer

thrill was in the trying on

SHOPPING 4

Kraus, Karl (1874–1936)
Austrian satirist

brain has oozed out

SPEED 6

embrace a woman's shoe

SEX 24

tell lies to journalists

GOVERNMENT 15

Kray, Charlie (*c.*1930–2000)
English gangster

help an old lady

CRIME 9

Krishnamurti, Jiddu (1895–1986)
Indian spiritual philosopher

frozen thought of men

RELIGION 10

Truth is a pathless land

TRUTH 17

Kristofferson, Kris (1936–)
American actor

nothin' left to lose

LIBERTY 17

Kroc, Ray (1902–84)
American businessman

no pride in achievement

RISK 5

Kronecker, Leopold (1823–91)
German mathematician

God made the integers

MATHS 9

Krutch, Joseph Wood (1893–1970)
American critic and naturalist

ask for what you want

CATS 5

creates as she slumbers

SUMMER 5

Kubrick, Stanley (1928–99)
American film director

acted like gangsters

INTERNATIONAL 13

Kundera, Milan (1929–)
Czech novelist

man able to think

DEFEAT 6

Mankind's true moral test

ANIMAL RIGHTS 8

underrates toothaches

THINKING 12

Kuralt, Charles (1934–97)
American journalist and broadcaster

from coast to coast

TRAVEL 11

Kurtz, Irma

do great things with a woman

ROMANCE 6

Fathers don't curse

PARENTS 8

great fear is of failure

FEAR 11

one saintly virtue

CELIBACY 7

way cookery books do

PORNOGRAPHY 3

Laclos, Pierre Choderlos de (1741–1803)
French soldier and writer

enjoys the happiness he feels

PLEASURE 10

make blackguards of us all

GOODNESS 10

Lacroix, Christian (1951–)
French couturier

Haute Couture should be fun

FASHION 3

Lahr, John (1941–)
American critic

crazy with lust

ADVERTISING 7

exhilaration and exhaustion

TWENTIETH 5

Laing, R. D. (1927–89)
Scottish psychiatrist

It may also be break-through

MADNESS 4

live in an unlivable situation

MENTAL 5

obligation one owes to oneself

GUILT 6

without understanding despair

MENTAL 4

Lake, Frank
see **Hughes, Jimmy and Lake, Frank**

Lamb, Charles (1775–1834)	Archangel a little damaged	PEOPLE 12
English writer	child's strength	BELIEF 12
	endear Absents	GIVING 7
	going to leave off tobacco	SMOKING 7
	good action by stealth	PLEASURE 11
	I am disposed to harmony	SINGING 13
	importunity of business	WORK 12
	knock at the door	MEETING 5
	measured malice of music	MUSIC 11
	mutilators of collections	BOOKS 12
	Nothing puzzles me more	WORRY 4
	pistol let off at the ear	WORDPLAY 6
	primitive prison	GARDENS 12
	two distinct races	LENDING 2
	write for Antiquity	WRITING 24
Lamb, Lady Caroline (1785–1828)	Mad, bad, and dangerous	PEOPLE 11
wife of Lord Melbourne		
Lambert, Constant (1905–51)	trouble with a folk song	MUSIC 12
English composer		
Lamont, Norman (1942–)	green shoots of recovery	BUSINESS 12
British Conservative politician	in office but not in power	GOVERNMENT 16
Lampedusa, Giuseppe di (1896–1957)	Flames for a year	LOVE 29
Italian writer	things to stay as they are	CHANGE 18
Landor, Walter Savage (1775–1864)	give me rheumatics	ROMANCE 7
English poet	never was contented	IRELAND 6
Lang, Andrew (1844–1912)	drunken man uses lampposts	STATISTICS 8
Scottish man of letters		
Lang, Fritz (1890–1976)	Saga of the Nibelungen	CINEMA 21
Austrian-born film director		
Langer, Susanne (1895–1985)	objectification of feeling	ART 21
American philosopher		
Lao Tzu (*c.*604–*c.*531 BC)	hole that makes it useful	VALUE 10
Chinese philosopher	soft overcomes the hard	STRENGTH 13
	where one stands	BEGINNING 7
Larkin, Philip (1922–85)	began in nineteen sixty-three	SEX 25
English poet	Books are a load of crap	READING 7
	call myself a satirist	WIT 3
	concrete and tyres	ENVIRONMENT 11
	controls of Concorde	TECHNOLOGY 18
	daffodils were for Wordsworth	INSIGHT 7
	don't have any kids yourself	DISILLUSION 5
	first boredom, then fear	LIFE 19
	happens anywhere	BOREDOM 5
	let the toad *work* squat	WORK 13
	listen to money singing	MONEY 15
	London spread out in the sun	LONDON 6
	muddle, and an end	FICTION 9
	Never such innocence again	INNOCENCE 6
	not supposed to grow	GARDENS 13
	robed as destinies	CHURCH 8
	sentiments in short lines	POETRY 21
	They fuck you up	PARENTS 9
	What will survive of us	LOVE 30
	Where can we live but days	DAY 3

la Rochefoucauld, Duc de (1613–80) *French moralist*	accent of one's birthplace	HOME 6
	as unhappy as one thinks	HAPPINESS 9
	bear the misfortunes of others	COMPASSION 9
	diminishes commonplace passions	ABSENCE 5
	doubt one's friends	TRUST 8
	hope for greater favours	GRATITUDE 4
	misfortune of our best friends	MISFORTUNES 7
	tribute which vice pays	HYPOCRISY 3
Laski, Harold (1893–1950) *British Labour politician*	organize her own immortality	WRITERS 10
	respect fidelity to colleagues	LOYALTY 6
	These damned mystics	RELIGION 11
Latimer, Hugh (*c.*1485–1555) *English Protestant martyr*	drop of rain maketh a hole	PERSISTENCE 8
Lauder, Harry (1870–1950) *Scottish music-hall entertainer*	Keep right on to the end	PERSISTENCE 9
Laurel, Stan (1890–1965) *American film comedian, born in Britain*	Another nice mess	PROBLEMS 9
	do something to *help* me	COOPERATION 10
Laurier, Wilfrid (1841–1919) *Canadian politician*	fill the twentieth century	CANADA 8
Law, Andrew Bonar (1858–1923) *Canadian-born British Conservative statesman*	all great men are frauds	GREATNESS 4
Lawless, Emily (1845–1913) *Irish poet*	grip is tightening still	FAMINE 3
Lawrence, D. H. (1885–1930) *English novelist and poet*	all things are impure	INNOCENCE 7
	attempt to insult sex	PORNOGRAPHY 4
	Be a good animal	BEHAVIOUR 12
	great kick at misery	TRAGEDY 5
	heart of the North is dead	AUTUMN 5
	hoary sort of land	AUSTRALIA 9
	How beastly the bourgeois is	CLASS 11
	in 1915 the old world ended	TWENTIETH 7
	leave it alone, physically	SEX 26
	Never trust the artist	CRITICS 15
	such trivial people	SHAKESPEARE 5
	terror of the consequences	CAUSES 7
	They look on and help	DEATH 18
	try to nail anything down	FICTION 10
	white of egg in their veins	INSULTS 7
Lawrence, Frances *widow of Philip Lawrence*	value other human beings	VIOLENCE 12
Lawrence, T. E. (1888–1935) *English soldier and writer*	escape the life-sentence	CHOICE 11
	I hate furniture	COMMUNISM 9
	moved to folly by a noise	EMOTIONS 9
Lawson, Nigel (1932–) *British Conservative politician*	meaningless relic of Empire	INTERNATIONAL 14
Lazarus, Emma (1849–87) *American poet*	huddled masses	UNITED S 15
Leach, Edmund (1910–) *English anthropologist*	privacy and tawdry secrets	FAMILY 7
Leacock, Stephen (1869–1944) *Canadian humorist*	arresting human intelligence	ADVERTISING 8
	as a shark follows a ship	WORDPLAY 7
	borrows a detective story	READING 8
	form of moral effort	GOLF 2
	get out and kill something	FIELD 1

Leacock, Stephen (*cont.*)

no such thing as absolute rest | LEISURE 6

Leary, Timothy (1920–96)
American psychologist

invite to the last party | DYING 9
LSD of the '90s | COMPUTERS 7
Turn on, tune in and drop out | LIFESTYLES 11
wake up in fifty years | FUTURE 11
Why not, why not | LAST WORDS 9

Leavis, F. R. (1895–1978)
English literary critic

Self-contempt, well-grounded | POETS 14

Lebowitz, Fran (1946–)
American writer

answer to the servant problem | SCIENCE 11
aspiring male transsexuals | WOMEN 20
best fame is a writer's fame | FAME 16
hear from your sweater | CLOTHES 12
only nervousness or death | EMOTIONS 10
opposite of talking | CONVERSATION 13
part of a balanced Diet | DIETS 5
phone is for you | YOUTH 11
pleasant and safe to use | SLEEP 4
teach him to deduct | EDUCATION 11
you are leaking | APPEARANCE 9

Leboyer, Frederick

It is mortal combat | BIRTH 2

Le Corbusier (1887–1965)
French architect

machine for living in | ARCHITECT 6
materials of city planning | CITIES 8

Lec, Stanislaw (1909–66)
Polish writer

cannibal uses knife and fork | PROGRESS 12
multiply thoughts | CENSORSHIP 10

Lee, Gypsy Rose (1914–70)
American striptease artiste

get it in writing | GOD 19

Lee, Harper (1926–)
American novelist

sin to kill a mockingbird | SIN 11

Lee, Nathaniel (*c.*1653–92)
English dramatist

damn them, they outvoted me | MADNESS 5
When Greeks joined Greeks | SIMILARITY 6

Lee, Robert E. (1807–70)
American Confederate general

grow too fond of it | WARFARE 19
trading on the blood of my men | AUTOBIOG 5

Le Guin, Ursula K. (1929–)
American writer

holds a person inside it | HATRED 6
it has to be made, like bread | LOVE 31
make the world safer | SECURITY 5
myth of modern technology | SCIENCE FICT 4

Lehman, Ernest (1920–)
American screenwriter

Sweet smell of success | SUCCESS 14

Lehrer, Tom (1928–)
American humorist

Doing well by doing good | BUSINESS 13
Life is like a sewer | LIFE 20
say in front of a girl | WORDS 17
when Mozart was my age | ACHIEVEMENT 15

Leiber, Jerry (1933–)
American songwriter

ain't nothin' I can't do | WOMEN 21

Leigh, Fred W. (d. 1924) **and Arthurs, George**

little of what you fancy | LIKES 5

Leigh, Vivien (1913–67)
English actress

Shakespeare is like bathing | THEATRE 7

LeMay, Curtis E. (1906–90)
US air-force officer

back into the Stone Age | VIETNAM 4

Le Mesurier, John (1912–83)
British actor

conked out on November 15th | EPITAPHS 19

Lenin (1870–1924)
Russian revolutionary

Communism is Soviet power	COMMUNISM 10
good man fallen among Fabians	PEOPLE 13
it must be rationed	LIBERTY 18
monopoly stage of capitalism	CAPITALISM 8
One step forward	PROGRESS 13
subjection of the minority	DEMOCRACY 5
there can be no freedom	GOVERNMENT 17

Lennon, John (1940–80)
English pop singer and songwriter

Happiness is a warm gun	HAPPINESS 10
just rattle your jewellery	WEALTH 14
love is like a precious plant	RELATIONSHIPS 14
more popular than Jesus	FAME 17

Lennon, John (1940–80) **and McCartney, Paul** (1942–)
English pop singers and songwriters

All the lonely people	LONELINESS 3
All you need is love	LOVE 32
Give peace a chance	PEACE 15
He's a real nowhere man	FUTILITY 7
I get by with a little help	FRIENDSHIP 17
money can't buy me love	MONEY 16
She's got a ticket to ride	OPPORTUNITY 3
When I'm sixty four	OLD AGE 12
Yesterday, all my troubles	PAST 10

Leno, Jay (1950–)
American comedian and writer

Ken Starr report is now posted	INTERNET 6

Lenthall, William (1591–1662)
Speaker of the House of Commons

neither eye to see	PARLIAMENT 13

Lerner, Alan Jay (1918–86)
American songwriter

Accustomed to her face	FAMILIAR 5
Ah yes! I remember it well	MEMORY 13
English completely disappears	LANGUAGES 6
Oozing charm	CHARM 3
Thank heaven for little girls	WOMEN 22
to the church on time	WEDDINGS 8
up is where to grow	FLOWERS 4
With a little bit of luck	TEMPTATION 5
woman be more like a man	MEN/WOMEN 15

Le Saux, Graeme (1968–)
English football player

described as 'cerebral'	INTELLECTUALS 4

Lessing, Doris (1919–)
English writer

ambiguous month	AUTUMN 6
only one real sin	MEDIOCRITY 4
power thrown away	CHARM 4

Levant, Oscar (1906–72)
American pianist

Epigram: a wisecrack	WIT 4
this flabby exterior	CHARACTER 15

Lever, Harold (1914–95)
British businessman and politician

Loopholes are not always	LAWS 12

Leverhulme, Lord (1851–1925)
English industrialist and philanthropist

don't know which half	ADVERTISING 9

Leverson, Ada (1865–1936)
English novelist

last gentleman in Europe	PEOPLE 14

Levi, Primo (1919–87)
Italian novelist and poet

demolition of a man	GENOCIDE 5

Levin, Bernard (1928–)
British journalist

cure for mixed metaphors	LANGUAGE 12
persistence of public officials	BUREAUCRACY 7
remembered to turn the gas off	WORRY 5
Stag at Bay	PEOPLE 15

Lévis, Duc de (1764–1830)
French soldier and writer

govern is to choose	GOVERNMENT 18

Lewis, C. S. (1898–1963)
English literary scholar

Eunuchs boasting	TEMPTATION 7
form of every virtue	COURAGE 8
Future as a promised land	FUTURE 12
grief felt so like fear	SORROW 12
our experience of love	BEREAVEMENT 10
plate of ham and eggs	TEMPTATION 6
remain a sound atheist	ATHEISM 4
suggest a patient etherized	POETRY 22
their hunted expression	SACRIFICE 7
to a non-existent address	PRAYER 10

Lewis, George Cornewall (1806–63)
British Liberal politician and writer

Life would be tolerable	LIFE 21

Lewis, Sinclair (1885–1951)
American novelist

cold and pure and very dead	UNIVERSITIES 9
mind which reveres details	THINKING 13
motor car was poetry	CARS 7

Ley, Robert (1890–1945)
German Nazi

Strength through joy	STRENGTH 14

Liberace (1919–87)
American showman

cry all the way to the bank	REVIEWS 4
skip his spiritual struggles	MUSICIANS 5

Lichtenberg, Georg Christoph (1742–99)
German scientist and drama critic

call the Temple of Fame	JOURNALISM 12
still believing something	BELIEF 13

Lin Yutang (1895–1976)
Chinese writer and philologist

know where he is going to	TRAVEL 12

Lincoln, Abraham (1809–65)
American Republican statesman, President 1861–5

adherence to the old and tried	POLITICAL P 17
events have controlled me	POWER 13
fool all the people	DECEPTION 5
let us strive on	COMMITMENT 4
necessity of being *ready*	READINESS 3
new birth of freedom	DEMOCRACY 6
not bloody bullets	ELECTIONS 8
prefers common-looking people	APPEARANCE 10
who like this sort of thing	LIKES 6

Lindon, J. A.

Points have no parts	MATHS 10

Lindsay, Vachel (1879–1931)
American poet

Then I saw the Congo	RIVERS 7

Lineker, Gary (1960–)
English footballer

manager who gets the blame	FOOTBALL 5

Linley, George (1798–1865)
English songwriter

God bless the Prince of Wales	WALES 4

Linzey, Andrew (1952–)
British theologian

patenting animals	ANIMAL RIGHTS 9
right to be animals	GENETIC 7

Lipman, Maureen (1946–)
British actress

Awards are like piles	AWARDS 7
only surviving adjective	SWEARING 5

Lippmann, Walter (1889–1974)
American journalist

final test of a leader	LEADERSHIP 9

Liszt, Franz (1811–86)
Hungarian composer and pianist

pillars of smoke and fire	BEETHOVEN 3

Litvinov, Maxim (1876–1951)
Soviet diplomat

Peace is indivisible	PEACE 16

Lively, Penelope (1933–)
English novelist

most possessive of things	GIVING 8
We are walking lexicons	LANGUAGES 7

Livingstone, Ken (1945–) *British Labour politician*	If voting changed anything marathon, not a sprint	ELECTIONS 9 POLITICS 23
Livy (59 BC–AD 17) *Roman historian*	Down with the defeated	DEFEAT 7
Llewelyn-Davies, Jack (1894–1959)	I'll be sick tonight	GREED 6
Lloyd George, David (1863–1945) *British Liberal statesman, Prime Minister* *1916–22*	conscience well under control eleven o'clock this morning fully-equipped duke keep him straight most convenient time pick up mercury scent on a pocket handkerchief that which gets things done	POLITICIANS 10 WORLD W I 13 ARISTOCRACY 9 CONSCIENCE 3 TAXES 7 DIPLOMACY 10 TRANSIENCE 10 SPEECHES 11
Locke, John (1632–1704) *English philosopher*	positive in error as in truth show a man that he is in error suspected, and usually opposed	MISTAKES 6 TRUTH 18 IDEAS 8
Lodge, David (1935–) *English novelist*	human pack is shuffled and cut mostly about having sex should be élitist	EXAMINATIONS 4 CHILDREN 11 UNIVERSITIES 10
Logue, Christopher (1926–) *English poet*	he pushed and they flew	INSIGHT 8
Longfellow, Henry Wadsworth (1807–82) *American poet*	anniversaries of the heart cares that infest the day grave is not its goal men that women marry mills of God grind slowly patient endurance is godlike sands of time Ships that pass in the night soft words are like roses was a little girl	CELEBRATIONS 4 NIGHT 3 LIFE 22 HUSBANDS 9 GOD 20 SUFFERING 5 BIOGRAPHY 11 RELATIONSHIPS 15 HYPOCRISY 4 BEHAVIOUR 13
Longford, Lord (1905–2001) *British Labour politician and philanthropist*	It was a pioneering work young people haven't been old	HUMILITY 5 OLD AGE 13
Loos, Anita (1893–1981) *American writer*	diamond and safire bracelet no girl wants to laugh while you're looking good women are brighter than men	PRACTICAL 9 HUMOUR 9 PARTING 11 WOMAN'S R 13
Lorenz, Edward N. *American meteorologist*	flap of a butterfly's wings	CHANCE 9
Lorenz, Konrad (1903–89) *Austro-German zoologist*	discard a pet hypothesis	THEORY 8
Louis XIV (1638–1715) *King of France from 1643*	create a hundred malcontents	MANAGEMENT 4
Louis XVIII (1755–1824) *King of France from 1814*	carry the marshal's baton politeness of kings	AMBITION 11 PUNCTUALITY 5
Louis, Joe (1914–81) *American boxer*	He can run	BOXING 6
Love, Courtney (1965–) *American rock singer*	flush with your influence	FAME 18
Lovelace, Ada (1815–52) *English mathematician*	weaves algebraic patterns	COMPUTERS 8
Lovelace, Richard (1618–58) *English poet*	Loved I not honour more walls do not a prison make	DUTY 5 PRISON 4

Lovell, Bernard (1913–) *British astronomer*	fate of human civilization vivid rather than happy	SPACE 6 YOUTH 12
Lovell, James (1928–) *American astronaut*	Houston, we've had a problem	PROBLEMS 10
Low, David (1891–1963) *British political cartoonist*	anyone who wasn't against war	WARFARE 20
Lowe, Robert (1811–92) *British Liberal politician*	Chancellor of the Exchequer	TAXES 8
Lowell, Amy (1874–1925) *American poet*	dreams or swords want laurels for ourselves	BOOKS 13 ENVY 4
Lowell, James Russell (1819–91) *American poet*	arguing with the inevitable horny hands of toil	ARGUMENT 13 WORK 14
Lowell, Robert (1917–77) *American poet*	Black Widow, death light of the oncoming train What next, what next	DEATH 19 PESSIMISM 7 MIDDLE AGE 14
Lowndes, William (1652–1724) *English politician*	Take care of the pence	MONEY 17
Lowry, Malcolm (1909–57) *English novelist*	groans of love	LOVE 33
Lucas, E. V. (1868–1938) *English journalist, essayist, and critic*	often so much jollier	PUNCTUALITY 6
Luce, Clare Booth (1903–87) *American diplomat, politician, and writer*	think just with our wombs	WOMAN'S R 14
Lucretius (c.94–55 BC) *Roman poet*	created out of nothing	CREATIVITY 8
Ludendorff, Erich von (1865–1937) *German general*	words have become battles	PROPAGANDA 7
Lurie, Alison (1926–) *American novelist*	'friends' by compulsion	FRIENDSHIP 18
Luther, Martin (1483–1546) *German Protestant theologian*	Here stand I woman, wine, and song	DETERMINATION 7 PLEASURE 12
Lutyens, Edwin (1869–1944) *English architect*	Gentlemen!—Our mothers	MOTHERS 5
Luxemburg, Rosa (1871–1919) *German revolutionary*	one who thinks differently	LIBERTY 19
Lynes, Russell (1910–91) *American art critic*	mirror of taste	TELEVISION 8
Lynn, Jonathan (1943–) **and Jay, Antony** (1930–) *English writers*	administrative won't readmission to the human race those irregular verbs your statistics are facts	CIVIL SERV 9 EUROPEAN C 5 SECRECY 17 STATISTICS 9
Lynton, Michael *English publisher*	greatest interactive medium	BOOKS 14
Lyte, Henry Francis (1793–1847) *British hymn-writer*	abide with me	CHANGE 19
Lytton, Lady (1874–1971)	see all his faults	CHURCHILL 4
McAliskey, Bernadette Devlin (1947–) *Northern Irish politician*	that which is worth having	SACRIFICE 8

MacArthur, Douglas (1880–1964) *American general*	I shall return	WORLD W II 11
Macaulay, Lord (1800–59) *English politician and historian*	acre in Middlesex	VALUE 11
	beauty and power	BIBLE 4
	distant provinces	GOVERNMENT 19
	essence of war is violence	WARFARE 21
	Puritan hated bear-baiting	PLEASURE 13
	scarce forbear to cheer	PRAISE 4
	temple of silence	BUILDINGS 6
	they may indeed wait for ever	LIBERTY 20
	wings of an ostrich	IMAGINATION 9
McAuliffe, Anthony (1898–1975) *American general*	Nuts	DEFIANCE 6
McCabe, Patrick (1955–) *Irish writer*	hiss of the water	RAIN 6
	No more hanging	EXECUTIONS 3
McCaig, Norman (1910–96) *Scottish poet*	Who owns this landscape	SCOTLAND 9
McCarthy, Cormac (1933–) *American writer*	people to whom things happen	MISFORTUNES 8
	Scars have the strange power	SUFFERING 14
McCarthy, Mary (1912–89) *American novelist*	America is the proof	UNITED S 16
	Every word she writes	PEOPLE 16
	make a 'realistic decision'	CYNICISM 7
	we forget who we are	VIOLENCE 13
McCartney, Paul (1942–) *English pop singer and songwriter*	Ballads and babies	MUSICIANS 7
	reheat a soufflé	ENDING 9
McCartney, Paul (1942–) see **Lennon, John and McCartney, Paul**		
McCluskey, Lord (1914–) *Scottish churchman*	If you import cannabis	PUNISHMENT 12
McCourt, Frank (1930–) *Irish-born American writer*	dying for Ireland	PATRIOTISM 16
	miserable Irish childhood	CHILDHOOD 6
McCrae, John (1872–1918) *Canadian poet and military physician*	In Flanders fields	WORLD W I 14
McCrum, Robert (1953–) *British writer*	big fear in hospitals	SICKNESS 9
McCullough, Colleen (1937–) *Australian writer*	twenty-five-year-old men	MIDDLE AGE 15
MacDiarmid, Hugh (1892–1978) *Scottish poet and nationalist*	infinite Scotland *small*	SCOTLAND 10
	white rose of Scotland	FLOWERS 5
Macdonald, Dwight (1906–82) *American writer and film critic*	Götterdämmerung	WORLD W II 12
MacDonald, George (1824–1905) *Scottish writer and poet*	Hae mercy o' my soul	EPITAPHS 20
McDonald, Trevor (1939–) *West Indian-born broadcaster*	I am a West Indian peasant	SUCCESS 15
McEnroe, John (1959–) *American tennis player*	You cannot be serious	TENNIS 4
McEwan, Ian (1948–) *English novelist*	feeling of mild pride	CHILDREN 12
	good when it makes sense	GOODNESS 11
	It's always the present	CHILDHOOD 7

McEwan, Ian (*cont.*)

its leaders and the led	LEADERSHIP 10
know when to let them die	ARGUMENT 14
proud of knowing nothing	ARTS AND SCI 7
seemed a grey crew	GENERATION 7
what it was they thought	COMMITTEES 5

McGoohan, Patrick (1928–) **et al.**
American actor

I am not a number	SELF 17

McGough, Roger (1937–)
English poet

die a youngman's death	DEATH 21

McGregor, Jimmie (1932–)
Scottish singer and songwriter

Oh, he's football crazy	FOOTBALL 6

Machiavelli, Niccolò (1469–1527)
*Florentine statesman and political
philosopher*

conceal a fact with words	DECEPTION 6
do not end when you please	WARFARE 22
prince to be feared	GOVERNMENT 20
revenge for slight injuries	REVENGE 12

McInerney, Jay (1955–)
American writer

so they can sleep with them	MEN/WOMEN 16

McIntosh, John (1946–)
British headmaster

haircuts, holidays and homework	SCHOOLS 8

Mackenzie, Kelvin (1946–)
British journalist and media executive

We are surfing food	TELEVISION 9

McLean, Don (1945–)
American songwriter

day the music died	MUSICIANS 8

MacLeish, Archibald (1892–1982)
American poet and public official

fact that it exists	LIBRARIES 7
poem should not mean	POETRY 23

McLeod, Fiona (1855–1905)
Scottish writer

heart is a lonely hunter	SOLITUDE 12

McLeod, Irene Rutherford (1891–1964)

hunting on my own	DOGS 4

McLuhan, Marshall (1911–80)
Canadian communications scholar

become an article of dress	CARS 8
circuit learns your job	TECHNOLOGY 19
global village	EARTH 6
living rooms of America	TELEVISION 10
makes everybody a publisher	TECHNOLOGY 21
medium is the message	TECHNOLOGY 20
numbing blow	NAMES 11
psychiatrist's couch	MIND 10

Macmillan, Harold (1894–1986)
*British Conservative statesman, Prime
Minister 1957–63*

blowing through this continent	CHANGE 20
cliché and an indiscretion	POLITICIANS 11
Events, dear boy	POLITICS 24
Georgian silver goes	ECONOMICS 10
get it from their archbishops	MORALITY 10
like a Dead Sea fruit	POWER 14
never had it so good	PROGRESS 14
prophesying the imminent fall	CAPITALISM 9
sound and original ideas	POLITICAL P 18
thinking about themselves	YOUTH 13

McNamara, Robert (1916–)
American Democratic politician

McNamara's War	VIETNAM 5
We were terribly wrong	VIETNAM 6

MacNeice, Louis (1907–63)
British poet, born in Belfast

be the more together	MARRIAGE 21
Better authentic mammon	GOD 21
I am not yet born	PREGNANCY 4
Incorrigibly plural	SIMILARITY 7
let them not spill me	PREGNANCY 5
no go my honey love	FATE 8

MacNeice, Louis (*cont.*)

notes like little fishes	MUSICIANS 6
sunlight on the garden	TRANSIENCE 11
this is Sunday morning	LEISURE 7

McWilliam, Candia (1955–)
English novelist

After first confidences	TRUST 9
being no one but itself	INDIVIDUAL 5
comprehend other people	RELATIONSHIPS 16
impersonation of profundity	PESSIMISM 8
memory of happiness	MEMORY 14
there are no continuities	EXILE 5
unconsciousness of habit	GOODNESS 12
you lose two novels	CHILDREN 13

Madonna (1958–)
American pop singer and actress

artifice of being blonde	HAIR 2
incarnation of Satan	HEROES 12

Maeterlinck, Maurice (1862–1949)
Belgian poet, dramatist, and essayist

There are no dead	DEATH 20

Magee, John Gillespie (1922–41)
American airman

touched the face of God	AIR TRAVEL 3

Magna Carta (1215)
Political charter signed by King John

lawful judgement of his peers	HUMAN RIGHTS 8
To no man will we sell	JUSTICE 15

Magnusson, Magnus (1929–)
Scottish writer and broadcaster

started so I'll finish	BEGINNING 8

Mahaffy, John Pentland (1839–1919)
Irish writer

I'm a gentleman	AUTOBIOG 6
unexpected constantly occurs	IRELAND 7

Mahler, Gustav (1860–1911)
Austrian composer

Fortissimo at last	SENSES 9
It must embrace everything	MUSIC 13

Mahy, Margaret (1936–)
New Zealand writer for children

Americans with no Disneyland	CANADA 9

Mailer, Norman (1923–)
American novelist and essayist

argue with the Gods	HEROES 13
clean American backyards	MONROE 3
emotional promiscuity	EMOTIONS 11
four stages to a marriage	DIVORCE 8
insult to the ghetto	SELF-INTEREST 8
no sensitive heterosexual	HOMOSEXUAL 9
nothing safe about sex	SEX 27
security around the president	CAUTION 7
wise primitive	FASHION 4

Maine, Henry (1822–88)
English jurist

blind forces of Nature	GREECE 3

Major, John (1943–)
*British Conservative statesman, Prime
Minister 1990–7*

bicycling to Holy Communion	BRITAIN 8
condemn a little more	PUNISHMENT 13
If the policy isn't hurting	ECONOMICS 11

Malahide, Patrick (1945–)
British actor

you play rapists	ACTORS 9

Malamud, Bernard (1914–86)
American novelist and short-story writer

they offered spam	FRIENDSHIP 19
walks through a wall	DETERMINATION 8

Malcolm X (1925–65)
American civil rights campaigner

separate peace from freedom	PEACE 17

Mallarmé, Stéphane (1842–98)
French poet

eliminate chance	CHANCE 10
flesh, alas, is wearied	DISILLUSION 6

Mallory, George Leigh (1886–1924)
British mountaineer

Because it's there	MOUNTAINS 4

Mallory, John

come back alive	MOUNTAINS 5

Malory, Thomas (d. 1471)
English writer
Whoso pulleth out this sword — ROYALTY 13

Malraux, André (1901–76)
French novelist, essayist, and art critic
Neither revolution nor war — WARFARE 23
revolt against fate — ART 22

Malthus, Thomas Robert (1766–1834)
English political economist
in a geometrical ratio — LIFE SCI 10

Mancroft, Lord (1914–87)
British Conservative politician
conception of eternity — CRICKET 7

Mandela, Nelson (1918–)
South African statesman
ideal which I hope to live for — AFRICA 6
People must learn to hate — HATRED 7
True reconciliation — FORGIVENESS 7

Mankiewicz, Joseph L. (1909–)
American screenwriter, producer, and director
going to be a bumpy night — DANGER 4
I'm biting my knuckles — WORRY 6

Manley, Mrs (1663–1724)
English novelist and dramatist
No time like the present — READINESS 4

Mann, Herbie (1930–)
American jazz musician
you're labelled commercial — JAZZ 5

Mann, Thomas (1875–1955)
German novelist
best part of love — KISSING 8
more the survivors' affair — BEREAVEMENT 11
Speech is civilisation — SPEECH 16
Time has no divisions — CELEBRATIONS 5

Mansfield, Katherine (1888–1923)
New Zealand-born short-story writer
ain't going to be no tea — WRITERS 11
write to the people one loves — LETTERS 6

Mao Zedong (1893–1976)
Chinese statesman
barrel of a gun — POWER 15
reactionaries are paper tigers — POLITICS 26
war without bloodshed — POLITICS 25

Maradona, Diego (1960–)
Argentine football player
head of Maradona — FOOTBALL 7

Marchi, John (1948–)
American Republican politician
cottage industry — GENETIC 8

Marcy, William Learned (1786–1857)
American politician
politicians of New York — WINNING 9

Marguerite d'Angoulême (1492–1549)
French writer, Queen of Navarre
as ashes smother the flame — JEALOUSY 5

Margulis, Lynn (1938–)
American biologist
Gaia is a tough bitch — EARTH 7

Marlborough, Sarah, Duchess of (1660–1744)
pleasure me in his top-boots — SEX 28
share the heart and hand — LOVE 34

Marley, Bob (1945–81)
Jamaican reggae musician and songwriter
Stand up for your rights — DEFIANCE 7

Marlowe, Christopher (1564–93)
English dramatist and poet
launched a thousand ships — FACE 4
loved not at first sight — LOVE 35
religion but a childish toy — RELIGION 12

Márquez, Gabriel García (1928–)
Colombian novelist
face of a dog — NECESSITY 6
it ends every night — MARRIAGE 22

Marquis, Don (1878–1937)
American poet and journalist
always a comforting thought — MISFORTUNES 9
jamais triste archy — OPTIMISM 6
keeping up with yesterday — DELAY 5
profitable to its possessor — HONESTY 7
runs into accidents — LUCK 6
usually gets it all wrong — POLITICIANS 12

Marquis, Don (*cont.*)	want to cry into your beer	TEETOTALISM 4
Marshall, Arthur (1910–89) *British journalist*	life's rich pageant	LIFE 23
Martial (AD *c.*40–*c.*104) *Spanish-born Latin epigrammatist*	not just being alive with you—or without you	HEALTH 4 RELATIONSHIPS 17
Martin, Dean (1917–) *American singer and actor*	good as you're going to feel without holding on	TEETOTALISM 5 DRUNKEN 6
Marvell, Andrew (1621–78) *English poet*	at my back I always hear in a green shade world enough, and time	TIME 14 GARDENS 14 COURTSHIP 9
Marvell, Holt *English songwriter*	Remind me of you	MEMORY 15
Marx, Chico (1891–1961) *American film comedian*	whispering in her mouth	KISSING 9
Marx, Groucho (1895–1977) *American film comedian*	both were crazy about girls convulsed with laughter I'm breaking it in please accept my resignation	LESBIANISM 4 REVIEWS 5 NAMES 10 PREJUDICE 7
Marx, Karl (1818–83) *German political philosopher*	first time as tragedy I am not a Marxist only interpreted the world opium of the people to each according to his needs weighs like a nightmare	HISTORY 9 COMMUNISM 11 PHILOSOPHY 7 RELIGION 13 SOCIETY 10 TRADITION 3
Marx, Karl (1818–83) **and Engels, Friedrich** (1820–95) *Co-founders of modern Communism*	spectre is haunting Europe Workers of the world, unite	COMMUNISM 12 CLASS 12
Mary, Queen of Scots (1542–87) *Queen of Scotland, 1542–67*	In my end is my beginning	ENDING 10
Mary, Queen (1867–1953) *Queen Consort of George V*	what hay looks like you, as their King, refused	COUNTRY 8 SACRIFICE 9
Masefield, John (1878–1967) *English poet*	Dirty British coaster must go down to the sea again My mother's life made me a man Quinquireme of Nineveh	BOATS 6 SEA 9 PREGNANCY 6 BOATS 5
Mathew, James (1830–1908) *Irish judge*	justice is open to all	JUSTICE 16
Matisse, Henri (1869–1954) *French painter*	art of balance, of purity	PAINTING 12
Matlovich, Leonard (d. 1988) *American Air Force Sergeant*	medal for killing two men	HOMOSEXUAL 10
Maugham, W. Somerset (1874–1965) *English novelist*	another name for indifference eat wisely but not too well enjoyment of a good meal enough if he eats a cutlet form of self-indulgence go on a Government grant harm he does her However harmless a thing is humour of Dostoievsky Impropriety is the soul in its death throes like a sixth sense loop the loop on a commonplace	TOLERANCE 5 PARTIES 6 CHARITY 3 WRITING 25 SACRIFICE 11 UNIVERSITIES 11 MEN/WOMEN 17 LAWS 13 WRITERS 12 WIT 5 GRAMMAR 7 MONEY 18 WORDPLAY 8

Maugham, W. Somerset (*cont.*)

love that lasts longest	LOVE 36
makes men petty	SUFFERING 15
nerve-racking vice	HYPOCRISY 5
of unimaginable complexity	RUSSIA 8
passed the Victorian Era	CENSORSHIP 11
round a stately park	JAMES 2
sacrificed to expediency	MORALITY 11
see him in Baghdad	FATE 9
standpoint of pure reason	SACRIFICE 10
talked more and did less	WORDS/DEED 5
they are wiser	OLD AGE 14
they only want praise	CRITICS 16
very dull, dreary affair	DYING 10

Maxwell, Glyn (1962–)
English poet

May his anorak grow big	RAILWAYS 6

Maxwell, James Clerk (1831–79)
Scottish physicist

presented in different forms	SCIENCE 12

Mayakovsky, Vladimir (1893–1930)
Russian poet

cloud in trousers	MEN 17
eradication of conferences	COMMITTEES 6
heart's stalled motor	LOVE 37
resting a huge ear on its paw	UNIVERSE 13
rhyme is a barrel	POETRY 24

Mead, Margaret (1901–78)
American anthropologist

to wait for next week	CITIES 9
Women want mediocre men	MEDIOCRITY 5

Mead, Shepherd (1914–)
American advertising executive

How to succeed in business	BUSINESS 14

Medawar, Jean (1913–)
  see **Medawar, Peter and Medawar, Jean**

Medawar, Peter (1915–87)
English immunologist and author

art of the soluble	RESEARCH 3
bishop wrote gravely	IGNORANCE 10
scientist cut his ear off	ARTS AND SCI 8
to be clever *about*	ARTS AND SCI 9
willingness to be deceived	BELIEF 14

Medawar, Peter (1915–87) **and Medawar, Jean** (1913–)

find their way by a light	HUMAN RACE 16

Medici, Catherine de' (1518–89)
queen consort of Henri II of France

false report, if believed	PROPAGANDA 8

Medici, Cosimo de' (1389–1464)
Italian statesman and patron of the arts

forgive our friends	FORGIVENESS 8

Meehan, Paula (1955–)

I dreamt a robe	COLOURS 7

Megarry, Robert (1910–)
British judge

no-one knows what is permitted	EUROPEAN C 6

Meir, Golda (1898–1978)
Israeli stateswoman

They can't bear children	WOMAN'S R 15

Melbourne, Lord (1779–1848)
British Whig statesman

fools said would happen	FORESIGHT 8
men who will support me	POLITICIANS 13
Minister that meddles	ART AND SOC 3
sphere of private life	RELIGION 14
wish I was as cocksure	CERTAINTY 5

Melville, Herman (1819–91)
American novelist and poet

whaleship was my Yale College	UNIVERSITIES 12

Menander (342–*c.*292 BC)
Greek comic dramatist

We live, not as we wish to	LIFESTYLES 12
Whom the gods love	YOUTH 14

Mencken, H. L. (1880–1956)
American journalist and literary critic

authentic self into a letter	LETTERS 7
charm of a cryptogram	AUTOBIOG 7
forbidden to resort to physics	BIRTH CONT 2
formidable body of cannibals	ELECTIONS 10
get it good and hard	DEMOCRACY 7
God is a bore	CHRISTIAN 7
Injustice is relatively easy	JUSTICE 17
masses of the plain people	INTELLIGENCE 8
never to drink by daylight	ALCOHOL 13
occurrence of the improbable	FAITH 10
other party is unfit to rule	POLITICAL P 19
someone may be looking	CONSCIENCE 4
yields anything to theology	SCIENCE & REL 8
yours is a fake	COMPASSION 10

Menuhin, Yehudi (1916–99)
American-born British violinist

sing to the babies	MOTHERS 6
think of the poor trees	NEWSPAPERS 11

Menzies, Robert Gordon (1894–1978)
Australian Liberal statesman

to us the near north	AUSTRALIA 10

Mercer, Johnny (1909–76)
American songwriter

ac-cent-tchu-ate the positive	OPTIMISM 7
one more for the road	PARTING 12

Mercure, Jean (1909—98)
French actor and director

confront the Great Reaper	DEATH 22

Meredith, George (1828–1909)
English novelist and poet

hot for certainties	CERTAINTY 6
I play for Seasons	NATURE 7
inflict pain upon oneself	CHARITY 4
Kissing don't last	COOKING 8

Meredith, Owen (1831–91)
English poet and statesman

Talent does what it can	GENIUS 9

Merrill, Bob (1921–98)
American songwriter and composer

Clichés make the best songs	SINGING 14

Merrill, James (1926–)
American poet

collective unconscious	DICTIONARIES 4

Merritt, Dixon Lanier (1879–1972)

know how the helican	BIRDS 6

Metternich, Prince (1773–1859)
Austrian statesman

genuine point of arrival	LIBERTY 21
geographical expression	ITALY 4
what concessions to make	POLITICIANS 14

Meynell, Viola (1886–1956)
English poet

dust comes secretly	HOUSEWORK 5

Michelangelo (1475–1564)
Italian sculptor, painter, and architect

marble not yet carved	SCULPTURE 6

Midler, Bette (1945–)
American actress

Life is a Rare Entertainment	LIFESTYLES 13
still 1938 in London	PRESENT 10

Mies van der Rohe (1886–1969)
German-born architect and designer

God is in the details	ARCHITECT 7
Less is more	SIMPLICITY 3

Mikes, George (1912–)
Hungarian-born writer

English have hot-water bottles	SEX 29
forms an orderly queue of one	ENGLAND 8
good table manners	COOKING 9

Mill, John Stuart (1806–73)
English philosopher and economist

human being dissatisfied	DISCONTENT 6
justified in silencing	OPINION 8
not make himself a nuisance	LIBERTY 22
requires to be rebuilt	SOCIETY 11
whether you are happy	HAPPINESS 11

Millay, Edna St Vincent (1892–1950)
American poet

kingdom where nobody dies	CHILDHOOD 8
one damn thing over and over	LIFE 24
stricken, so remembering him	MEMORY 16
weeping of the rain	BEREAVEMENT 12

Miller, Alice Duer (1874–1942)
American writer

seen much to hate here	ENGLAND 9

Miller, Arthur (1915–)
American dramatist

attention must be paid	SUFFERING 16
birds came home to roost	CAUSES 8
car, the furniture, the wife	SHOPPING 5
claims on us of clan and race	RACE 7
comes with the territory	BUSINESS 15
exclusion and prohibition	ORGANIZATION 6
gullet of New York	AMERICAN CITIES 12
nation talking to itself	NEWSPAPERS 12
our neuroses just don't match	RELATIONSHIPS 18
suicide kills two people	SUICIDE 2
world is an oyster	EFFORT 7

Miller, Jonathan (1934–)
English writer and director

another way of *being*	SICKNESS 10
don't think about it	SUFFERING 17
equivalent of a condom	COMPUTERS 9
jack of all trades	ABILITY 4

Milligan, Spike (1918–2002)
Irish comedian

all conceivable occasions	BIRTH CONT 3
better class of enemy	MONEY 19
I am pretty cheerful	OLD AGE 15
We think sideways	IRELAND 8

Mills, Irving (1894–1985)

ain't got that swing	JAZZ 6

Milne, A. A. (1882–1956)
English writer for children

Bear of Very Little Brain	THINKING 14
good spelling but it Wobbles	WORDS 18
Hush! Hush! Whisper who dares	PRAYER 11
little something	EATING 9
lovely rice pudding for dinner	FOOD 16
more Piglet wasn't there	ABSENCE 6
Owl hasn't exactly got Brain	KNOWLEDGE 16
Tiggers don't like honey	LIKES 7
Where the wind comes from	WIND 4

Milner, Lord (1854–1925)
British colonial administrator

damn the consequences	DUTY 6

Milton, John (1608–74)
English poet

All is not lost	DEFIANCE 8
all passion spent	EMOTIONS 12
Better to reign in hell	AMBITION 12
Chaos umpire sits	SPORTS 11
Evil, be thou my good	EVIL 11
Fame is the spur	FAME 19
fresh woods, and pastures new	CHANGE 21
his tongue dropped manna	SPEECHES 12
how my light is spent	DISABILITY 6
joy is ever on the wing	HAPPINESS 12
justify the ways of God to men	WRITING 26
life-blood of a master spirit	BOOKS 15
Love's harbinger	SKIES 9
mind is its own place	MIND 11
Nothing is here for tears	SORROW 13
Of whom to be dispraised	PRAISE 5
On the light fantastic toe	DANCE 9
Opinion in good men	OPINION 9
ruin upon ruin	CHAOS 2
They also serve	PATIENCE 5
thy amber-dropping hair	RIVERS 8
What hath night to do	SLEEP 5

Mirren, Helen (1945–) *English actress*	quality of human life understand what you're saying	SOLITUDE 13 ACTORS 10
Missal, The	*Dies irae, dies illa*	ENDING 11
Mistinguette (1875–1956) *French dancer*	kiss can be a comma	KISSING 10
Mitchell, Adrian (1932–) *English poet, novelist, and dramatist*	poetry ignores most people	POETRY 25
Mitchell, George (1933–) *American politician*	Peace, political stability	SOCIETY 12
Mitchell, Joni (1945–) *Canadian singer and songwriter*	life's illusions I recall They paved paradise We are stardust	EXPERIENCE 11 ENVIRONMENT 12 INNOCENCE 8
Mitchell, Margaret (1900–49) *American novelist*	Death and taxes enough courage—or money My dear, I don't give a damn tomorrow is another day we'd have won the war	BIRTH 3 REPUTATION 6 INDIFFERENCE 5 HOPE 9 FILMS 3
Mitford, Nancy (1904–73) *English writer*	abroad is unutterably bloody aristocracy in a republic be civil to the girls Wooing, so tiring	TRAVEL 13 ARISTOCRACY 10 MANNERS 6 COURTSHIP 10
Mitterrand, François (1916–96) *French statesman*	mouth of Marilyn Monroe	THATCHER 6
Mizner, Wilson (1876–1933) *American dramatist*	if you steal from many meet 'em on your way down trip through a sewer what gets you an education	PLAGIARISM 5 PRACTICAL 10 AMERICAN CITIES 13 DOUBT 5
Mnouchkine, Ariane (1934–) *French theatre director*	cultural Chernobyl	CULTURE 13
Molière (1622–73) *French comic dramatist*	All that is not prose He who lives without tobacco I have been speaking prose knowledgeable fool look long at oneself sin in secret is not to sin	POETRY 26 SMOKING 8 LANGUAGE 13 FOOLS 8 CRITICS 17 SIN 12
Moltke, Helmuth von (1800–91) *Prussian military commander*	Everlasting peace is a dream	WARFARE 24
Monbiot, George *British writer and broadcaster*	old people are ostracized took root among nomads	OLD AGE 16 CITIES 10
Monnet, Jean (1888–1979) *French economist and diplomat*	create a nation Europe	EUROPEAN C 7
Monroe, Marilyn (1926–62) *American actress*	Chanel No. 5	CLOTHES 13
Montagu, Lady Mary Wortley (1689–1762) *English writer*	fall without shaking General notions give them the gout never had any great esteem	EFFORT 8 IDEAS 9 ENEMIES 8 WOMEN 23
Montague, John (1929–) *Irish poet and writer*	grow a second tongue	LANGUAGES 8
Montaigne (1533–92) *French moralist and essayist*	amusing herself with me bunch of other men's flowers little back shop, all his own	CATS 6 PLAGIARISM 6 SELF 18

Montaigne (*cont.*)

running of a family	HOME 7
serious-minded activity	CHILDREN 14
What do I know	KNOWLEDGE 17

Montesquieu (1689–1755)
French political philosopher

annals are blank	HISTORY 10
English are busy	ENGLAND 10
triangles were to make a God	GOD 22

Montessori, Maria (1870–1952)
Italian educationist

help the work going on	TEACHING 8

Montgomery, Lord (1887–1976)
British field marshal

Do not march on Moscow	WARFARE 25
increasingly under the sea	NAVY 6
We are British, thank God	HOMOSEXUAL 11

Montrond, Casimir, Comte de (1768–1843)
French diplomat

no truck with first impulses	IMPULSIVE 3
tell it to your friends	ENVY 5

Moore, Brian (1921–)
Northern Irish writer

years hang like old clothes	PAST 11

Moore, Clement C. (1779–1863)
American writer

night before Christmas	CHRISTMAS 7

Moore, George (1852–1933)
Anglo-Irish novelist

in search of what he needs	TRAVEL 14

Moore, Henry (1898–1986)
English sculptor and draughtsman

through a piece of stone	SCULPTURE 7

Moore, Marianne (1887–1972)
American poet

never make long visits	GUESTS 5
shining baubles	AWARDS 8
Spenser's Ireland	IRELAND 9

Moore, Oscar (1960–96)
English journalist

turn the lights back on	AIDS 5

Moore, Thomas (1779–1852)
Irish musician and songwriter

heart that has truly loved	FAITHFULNESS 9
never nursed a dear gazelle	TRANSIENCE 12
nothing half so sweet in life	LOVE 38
scent of the roses	MEMORY 17
ways to dress eggs	FRANCE 6

Moreau, Jeanne (1928–)
French actress

It's like a drug	ROCK 8

Morgan, John Pierpont (1837–1913)
American financier and philanthropist

how to do what I want to do	LAWYERS 3

Morgan, Piers (1965–)
British newspaper editor

cares if Le Saux is gay	FOOTBALL 8
put 'exclusive' on the weather	NEWSPAPERS 13

Morgan, Robin (1941–)
American feminist

Sisterhood is powerful	WOMEN 24

Morley, Lord (1838–1923)
British Liberal politician

you have silenced him	CENSORSHIP 12

Morley, Robert (1908–92)
English actor, director, and dramatist

French are a logical people	FRANCE 7

Morris, Bill (1938–)
British trade unionist

democracy in the workplace	TRADE 7
sums up the modern workforce	EMPLOYMENT 10

Morris, Desmond (1928–)
English anthropologist

Death may be inevitable	ANIMAL RIGHTS 10
elements of primeval hunting	SPORTS 12
human zoo	CITIES 11
meat on legs	FARMING 5
part of its beak	FARMING 6
wildlife will disappear	ENVIRONMENT 13

Morris, George Pope (1802–64) *American poet*	Woodman, spare that tree	TREES 11
Morris, William (1834–96) *English writer, artist, and designer*	believe to be beautiful counties overhung with smoke swinish luxury of the rich	POSSESSIONS 11 POLLUTION 11 LUXURY 3
Morrison, Blake (1950–) *British poet and critic*	culture without hope	FORGIVENESS 9
Morrison, Jim (1943–71) *American rock singer and songwriter*	done to our fair sister make your peace with authority revolt, disorder, chaos	ENVIRONMENT 14 POWER 16 PROTEST 5
Morrison, Toni (1931–) *American novelist*	decorating the house with guests Grab this land learns how to be a daughter People don't mix races problem of growing old try not to drop it turnips and no whipping world's beauty becomes enough	GUESTS 6 NATIONALITY 7 PARENTS 10 RACE 8 AGEING 8 OLD AGE 17 CHOICE 12 BEAUTY 17
Morrison, Van (1945–) *Irish singer, songwriter, and musician*	Music is spiritual	MUSIC 14
Morrow, Dwight (1873–1931) *American lawyer, banker, and diplomat*	people who do things	EFFORT 9
Morshead, Owen (1893–1977) *English librarian*	trample on their young	ROYAL F 6
Mortimer, Clifford (d. 1960) *English barrister*	art of cross-examination	TRIALS 4
Mortimer, John (1923–) *English novelist, barrister, and dramatist*	do you a decent death fault of the working classes No brilliance is needed silent, unfancied majority their astonishing reward	HUNTING 4 AMBITION 13 LAWYERS 4 APPEARANCE 11 BEAUTY 18
Morton, J. B. ('Beachcomber') (1893–1975) *British journalist*	must be seen to be believed Rolls body and a Balham mind	JUSTICE 18 MEDIOCRITY 6
Morton, Jelly Roll (1885–1941) *American jazz musician*	sweet, soft, plenty rhythm	JAZZ 7
Morton, Rogers (1914–79) *American public relations officer*	deck of the Titanic	FUTILITY 8
Moses, Edwin (1955–) *American athlete*	don't really see the hurdles	SPORTS 13
Motion, Andrew (1952–) *English poet*	own quick hounds poem about ice cream	DIANA 8 LITERATURE/SOC 5
Motley, John Lothrop (1814–77) *American historian*	Give us the luxuries of life	LUXURY 4
Mountbatten, Lord (1900–79) *British sailor, soldier, and statesman*	be jolly at my funeral Third World War is fought	BEREAVEMENT 13 WEAPONS 8
Mowlam, Mo (1949–) *British Labour politician*	can't switch on peace	PEACE 18
Mozart, Wolfgang Amadeus (1756–91) *Austrian composer*	Melody is the essence	MUSIC 15
Mugabe, Robert (1924–) *Zimbabwean statesman*	play cricket in Zimbabwe	CRICKET 8

Muggeridge, Malcolm (1903–90)	dead fish swim with the stream	CONFORMITY 9
British journalist	Good taste and humour	HUMOUR 10
	orgasm has replaced the Cross	SEX 30
	shape and direct events	HISTORY 11
Muir, Frank (1920–98)	thinking man's crumpet	PEOPLE 17
English writer and broadcaster		
Muldoon, Paul (1951–)	dumber than a fish	BEREAVEMENT 14
Irish poet	Volkswagen parked	TERRORISM 1
Muller, H. J. (1890–1967)	use him as a fertilizer	HUMAN RACE 17
American geneticist		
Mumford, Lewis (1895–)	concrete cloverleaf	UNITED S 17
American sociologist	revolts against its fathers	GENERATION 8
Munch, Edvard (1863–1944)	what someone has felt	PAINTING 13
Norwegian painter and engraver		
Murasaki Shikibu (*c.*978–*c.*1031)	memories of long love	MEMORY 18
Japanese writer and courtier		
Murdoch, Iris (1919–99)	arise from accusations	GUILT 7
English novelist	caught in mental cages	MIND 12
	discovery of reality	LOVE 39
	God was always doing geometry	UNIVERSE 14
	It's not a public conveyance	MARRIAGE 23
	planet without flowers	FLOWERS 6
	requirement of the good life	SELF-KNOW 9
	tooth is truly worshipped	RELIGION 15
Murdoch, Rupert (1931–)	editor did it	NEWSPAPERS 14
Australian-born American publisher	never sold a newspaper	AID 6
	paid far too much for them	PRESS 5
Murray, Les A. (1938–)	I s'pose you couldn't	COOPERATION 11
Australian poet	No centuries before these	TWENTIETH 6
	trouble with being best man	WEDDINGS 9
Murrow, Ed (1908–65)	Anyone who isn't confused	CIRCUMSTANCE 10
American broadcaster and journalist	circus was already there	TELEVISION 3
	mobilized the English language	CHURCHILL 5
Mussolini, Benito (1883–1945)	function to perfection	PUNCTUALITY 7
Italian Fascist dictator		
Muste, Rev. A. J. (1885–1967)	If I can't love Hitler	LOVE 40
American pacifist		
Nabokov, Vladimir (1899–1977)	active and creative reader	READING 9
Russian novelist	Discussion in class	TEACHING 9
	Life is a great surprise	DEATH 23
	life-quickening atmosphere	RAILWAYS 7
	Lolita, light of my life	SEX 31
	Satire is a lesson	WIT 6
	small-town bourgeois at heart	CONFORMITY 10
	two eternities of darkness	LIFE 25
Naidu, Sarojini (1879–1949)	setting him up in poverty	PEOPLE 18
Indian politician		
Naipaul, Shiva (1945–85)	construction of the west	AID 7
Trinidadian writer	Hopeless doomed continent	AFRICA 7
Naipaul, V. S. (1932–)	enormous amount of money	BEST-SELLERS 1
Trinidadian novelist and travel writer		
Napoleon I (1769–1821)	army marches on its stomach	ARMY 12
Emperor of France, 1804–15	career open to the talents	OPPORTUNITY 4

Napoleon I (*cont.*)

[Channel] is a mere ditch	SEA 10
character and relations	WARFARE 26
Europe to have one currency	MONEY 20
forty centuries look down	PAST 12
nation of shopkeepers	ENGLAND 11
Not tonight, Josephine	SEX 32
sublime to the ridiculous	FAILURE 7
that girls should think	WOMAN'S R 16
tormenting the people	INVENTIONS 12
two o'clock in the morning	COURAGE 9

Nash, Ogden (1902–71)
American humorist

billboard lovely as a tree	ENVIRONMENT 15
bone to pick with Fate	MIDDLE AGE 16
cheeks are covered with paint	COSMETICS 5
God in His wisdom	ANIMALS 16
got on too much lipstick	HUSBANDS 10
hating, my boy, is an art	HATRED 8
He watched the ads	CARS 9
keep your marriage brimming	MARRIAGE 24
liquor is quicker	PARTIES 7
little incompatibility	RELATIONSHIPS 19
lives 'twixt plated decks	ANIMALS 15
most exclusive club there is	ENGLAND 12
on the wrong side	DOGS 5
one's own kin and kith	FAMILY 8
Parsley Is gharsley	FOOD 17
products that people really want	ADVERTISING 10
roams the great Sahara	BIRDS 7
seen yourself retreating	APPEARANCE 12
tangled web do parents weave	PARENTS 12
test my bath before I sit	SENSES 10
they have no cares	EMPLOYMENT 11
trouble with a kitten	CATS 7
what parents were created for	PARENTS 11
Women would rather be right	WOMEN 25

Navratilova, Martina (1956–)
Czech-born American tennis player

victory is much too short	WINNING 10

Needham, Richard J. (1939–)

first child is made of glass	CHILDREN 15

Nehru, Jawaharlal (1889–1964)
Indian statesman

make the rich richer	CAPITALISM 10
our yearning for the sins	TEMPTATION 8

Neill, A. S. (1883–1973)
Scottish teacher and educationist

knowing what not to say	CHILDREN 16
make it one for humour	EXAMINATIONS 1
pale shadow of sex	MASTURBATION 3

Nelson, Horatio, Lord (1758–1805)
British admiral

England expects	DUTY 7
Kiss me, Hardy	LAST WORDS 10
peerage, or Westminster Abbey	AMBITION 14

Nemerov, Howard (1920–91)
American poet and novelist

invented the brake	INVENTIONS 13

Neruda, Pablo (1904–73)
Chilean poet

blank atlas of your body	BODY 9
form of my thin country	MEXICO 4
I shall go on living	BEREAVEMENT 15

Nesbit, Edith (1858–1924)
English writer

affection you get back	PARENTS 13
you are enjoying yourself	PLEASURE 14

Neumann, John von (1903–57)
Hungarian-born American mathematician

you don't understand things	MATHS 11

Newbolt, Henry (1862–1938)
English lawyer, poet, and man of letters

breathless hush in the Close	CRICKET 9
play up! and play the game	SPORTS 14

Newman, Andrea (1938–) *British dramatist*	if they get a better offer	DIVORCE 9
Newman, John Henry (1801–90) *English theologian and leader of the Oxford Movement; later Cardinal*	answerable for what we choose drink—to the Pope one single venial sin Ten thousand difficulties	BELIEF 15 CONSCIENCE 5 SIN 13 DOUBT 6
Newton, Isaac (1642–1727) *English mathematician and physicist*	boy playing on the sea-shore no arguing against facts shoulders of giants	INVENTIONS 14 EXPERIMENT 3 PROGRESS 15
Nicholas I (1796–1855) *Russian emperor from 1825*	Russia has two generals	RUSSIA 9
Nicholson, Norman (1914–87) *British poet and writer*	Give me weeds	FLOWERS 7
Nicholson, Vivian (1936–)	I want to spend	WEALTH 15
Nicolson, Harold (1886–1968) *English diplomat, politician, and writer*	did nothing at all like the masses in the flesh little snouty, sneaky mind treat disasters as incidents	ROYAL F 7 POLITICAL P 20 DIARIES 5 MARRIAGE 25
Niebuhr, Reinhold (1892–1971) *American theologian*	inclination to injustice Our gadget-filled paradise serenity to accept	DEMOCRACY 8 TWENTIETH 8 CHANGE 22
Niemöller, Martin (1892–1984) *German theologian*	standard of living When Hitler attacked the Jews	LIBERTY 23 INDIFFERENCE 6
Nietzsche, Friedrich (1844–1900) *German philosopher and writer*	epitaph of an emotion God's second blunder great source of comfort hears only those questions I teach you the superman live dangerously Morality is the herd-instinct shadow will be shown terrible explosive What does not kill me	WIT 7 WOMEN 26 SUICIDE 3 PROBLEMS 11 HUMAN RACE 18 LIFESTYLES 14 MORALITY 12 GOD 23 PHILOSOPHY 8 SUFFERING 18
Nightingale, Florence (1820–1910) *English nurse*	do the sick no harm	MEDICINE 10
Nin, Anaïs (1903–77) *French-born American writer*	strangle you with his panic very touch of the letter	FEAR 12 LETTERS 8
Nixon, Richard (1913–94) *American Republican statesman, President 1969–74*	Always give your best finished when he quits I brought myself down means that it is not illegal North Vietnam cannot defeat whitewash at the White House	HATRED 9 DEFEAT 8 GUILT 8 PRESIDENCY 10 VIETNAM 8 PRESIDENCY 9
Nkrumah, Kwame (1900–72) *Ghanaian statesman*	claim it as their own face neither East nor West	LIBERTY 24 INTERNATIONAL 15
Nobbs, David (1935–) *British comedy writer*	didn't get where I am	CAREERS 9
Nolan, Christopher (1965–) *Irish writer*	bounty of my mind's expanse	DISABILITY 7
Noonan, Peggy (1950–) *American writer*	battle for the mind	REAGAN 2
Norris, Steven (1945–) *British Conservative politician*	dreadful human beings	CARS 10

North, Christopher (1785–1854) *Scottish literary critic*	Laws were made to be broken	LAWS 14
	Minds like ours, my dear	SCOTLAND 11
Northcliffe, Lord (1865–1922) *British newspaper proprietor*	power of the press	NEWSPAPERS 15
	When I want a peerage	TITLES 3
Norton, Caroline (1808–77) *English poet and songwriter*	Not lost but gone before	DEATH 24
Norworth, Jack (1879–1959) *American songwriter*	out to the ball game	BASEBALL 5
Nuffield, Lord (1877–1963) *British motor manufacturer and philanthropist*	looks like a poached egg	CARS 11
Nunn, Sam (1938–) *American Democratic politician*	Don't ask, don't tell	HOMOSEXUAL 12
Nunn, Trevor (1940–) *British theatre director*	Soundbite and slogan	LANGUAGE 14
Nyerere, Julius (1922–99) *Tanzanian statesman*	let our people starve	DEBT 4
Oates, Captain Lawrence (1880–1912) *English polar explorer*	may be some time	LAST WORDS 11
O'Brien, Conor Cruise (1917–) *Irish politician, writer, and journalist*	wear a clove of garlic	POLITICIANS 15
O'Brien, Edna (1936–) *Irish novelist and short-story writer*	August is a wicked month	SUMMER 6
O'Brien, Flann (1911–66) *Irish novelist and journalist*	based upon licensed premises	WORDPLAY 9
	Book of Kells	BUSINESS 16
	defining what is unknown	DICTIONARIES 5
	I knew half of her	MOTHERS 7
	page 96—the secret page	BOOKS 16
	Waiting for the German verb	LANGUAGES 9
	wish they were small boys	RAILWAYS 8
O'Casey, Sean (1880–1964) *Irish dramatist*	keep it out of as many	RELIGION 16
	literature's performing flea	WRITERS 13
	never to lose me temper	ANGER 7
	worl's in a state o' chassis	CHAOS 3
Occam, William of (*c.*1285–1349) *English philosopher and friar*	presumed to exist	PHILOSOPHY 9
O'Connor, Joseph (1963–) *Irish writer*	always want to confess	GUILT 9
	English understand least	IRELAND 10
O'Connor, Sinéad (1966–) *Irish singer and songwriter*	big mouth and a shaved head	STRENGTH 15
	later in somebody's office	PARTING 13
O'Donoghue, Bernard (1945–) *Irish poet and academic*	Ceauşescus' execution	EXECUTIONS 4
O'Faolain, Sean (1900–91) *Irish writer*	punch and poetry	FICTION 11
	rain made the Irish	IRELAND 11
Ogilvy, David (1911–99) *British-born advertising executive*	consumer isn't a moron	ADVERTISING 11
	loudest noise in Rolls-Royce	CARS 12
O'Hara, John (1905–70) *American writer*	don't have to believe	BELIEF 16
O'Kelly, Dennis (*c.*1720–87) *Irish racehorse-owner*	Eclipse first	WINNING 11

Okpik, Abraham (d. 1997)
Canadian Inuit spokesman

improve on the igloo	ARCHITECT 8
just another mosquito	CANADA 10

Oldfield, Bruce (1950–)
English fashion designer

revisited ideas	FASHION 5

Olivier, Laurence (1907–89)
English actor and director

could not make up his mind	INDECISION 7
nearest thing in incarnation	SHAKESPEARE 6
occupation of an adult	ACTING 4

Omar, Caliph (d. 644)
Muslim caliph

writings of the Greeks	CENSORSHIP 13

Onassis, Jacqueline Kennedy (1929–94)
wife of John Fitzgerald Kennedy

bungle raising your children	PARENTS 14
sounds like a saddle horse	PRESIDENCY 11

Ondaatje, Michael (1943–)
Canadian writer

organ of fire	EMOTIONS 13
richness of lovers and tribes	DEATH 25

O'Neill, Eugene (1888–1953)
American dramatist

For de little stealin'	PUNISHMENT 14
keep diaries to remember	MEMORY 19
sea hates a coward	SEA 11

Ono, Yoko (1933–)
Japanese poet and songwriter

nigger of the world	WOMAN'S R 17

Oppenheimer, J. Robert (1904–67)
American physicist

atomic bomb	TECHNOLOGY 22
destroyer of worlds	PHYSICS 9
physicists have known sin	PHYSICS 10

Orbach, Susie (1946–)
American psychotherapist

feminist issue	FAT 5

Orbison, Roy (1936–88)
American singer and songwriter

Only the lonely	LONELINESS 4

O'Rourke, P. J. (1947–)
American humorous writer

bitten in half by a shark	COMPROMISE 5
discovered Caribbean vacations	EXPLORATION 5
God is a Republican	POLITICAL P 21
have a famous relation	FAME 20
idea behind foreign policy	INTERNATIONAL 16
intelligence, education, taste	MANNERS 7
long-term benefits	DIVORCE 10
No matter how liberated	HUSBANDS 11
now called publicity	REPUTATION 7
once every girlfriend	HOUSEWORK 6
party all by himself	PARTIES 8
realize what you spent	CHRISTMAS 8
resign your job as a human	SCIENCE 13
smell like a car	CARS 13
socks that match	BACHELORS 3
standing up for a principle	ARGUMENT 15
There is parody	WIT 8
threat of sex	COURTSHIP 11
vegetable with looks and money	FOOD 18
watch the critters scurry	JOURNALISM 13
Whose woods are whose	NEIGHBOURS 6
your American Express card	DEBT 5

Orpen, William (1878–1931)
British artist

Paint the Somme	WORLD W I 15

Ortega y Gasset, José (1883–1955)
Spanish writer and philosopher

I am I plus my surroundings	SELF 19

Orton, Joe (1933–67)
English dramatist

more familiar with Africa	INNOCENCE 9
thing is in good taste	TASTE 6
word in the Irish language	WORDS 19

Orwell, George (1903–50)
English novelist

always be judged guilty	SAINTS 2
better wages and shorter hours	POLITICAL P 22
BIG BROTHER IS WATCHING YOU	GOVERNMENT 21
biking to Holy Communion	ENGLAND 14
boot stamping on a human face	FUTURE 13
both honest and intelligent	ARGUMENT 16
brown bread and raw carrots	FOOD 19
deep sleep of England	ENGLAND 13
disbelieve in God	ATHEISM 5
Doublethink means	THINKING 15
face he deserves	FACE 5
food he has eaten	HEALTH 5
Four legs good, two legs bad	PREJUDICE 8
funny is subversive	HUMOUR 11
like a window-pane	WRITING 27
make lies sound truthful	POLITICS 27
make thoughtcrime impossible	CENSORSHIP 14
nothing to do with fair play	SPORTS 15
on the playing-fields of Eton	WATERLOO 2
quickest way of ending a war	WARFARE 27
sinking middle class	CLASS 13
some animals are more equal	EQUALITY 10
sort of gutless Kipling	POETS 15
stick inside a swill bucket	ADVERTISING 12
these blissful circumstances	MURDER 9
two plus two make four	LIBERTY 25
Who controls the past	POWER 17

Osborne, John (1929–94)
English dramatist

aren't any good, brave causes	FUTILITY 9
damn you England	ENGLAND 15
Don't clap too hard	THEATRE 8
either this world or the next	SAINTS 3
eternal flaming racket	WOMEN 27
in a mouthful of decay	ROYALTY 14
looking forward to the past	FUTURE 14
not even red brick	UNIVERSITIES 13
old beliefs are going up	DISILLUSION 7
ordinary human enthusiasm	EMOTIONS 14

O'Shaughnessy, Arthur (1844–81)
English poet

We are the music makers	MUSICIANS 9

Osler, Mirabel

find them smiling	GARDENS 15

Osler, William (1849–1919)
Canadian-born physician

One finger in the throat	MEDICINE 11
two primal passions	HUMAN NATURE 9

O'Sullevan, Peter (1918–)

racing people's Lourdes	HORSES 3

Otis, James (1725–83)
American politician

without representation	TAXES 9

O'Toole, Peter (1932–)
British actor

walking behind the coffins	EXERCISE 5

Ovid (43 BC–AD c.17)
Roman poet

devourer of everything	TIME 15
You will go most safely	MODERATION 5

Owen, David (1938–)
British Social Democratic politician

championing human rights	HUMAN RIGHTS 9

Owen, Wilfred (1893–1918)
English poet

All a poet can do today	POETRY 27
drawing-down of blinds	DEATH 26
for these who die as cattle	ARMY 13
I am the enemy you killed	ENEMIES 9
old Lie: Dulce et decorum est	WARFARE 29
Poetry is in the pity	WARFARE 28
undone years, The hopelessness	FUTILITY 10

Paderewski, Ignacy Jan (1860–1941)
Polish pianist, composer, and statesman

What a terrible revenge — JAZZ 8

Paget, Reginald (1908–90)
British Labour politician

sense of the ridiculous — FAT 6
source of brutality — BIBLE 5

Paglia, Camille (1947–)
American author and critic

emotion without sex — LESBIANISM 5
left in female hands — CIVILIZATION 5
madness of human life — TELEVISION 12
no female Jack the Ripper — WOMEN 28
part of the sizzle — SEDUCTION 5
ritual, religion, sport, art — BODY 10

Pagnol, Marcel (1895–1974)
French dramatist and film-maker

Honour is like a match — REPUTATION 8

Paige, Satchel (1906–82)
American baseball player

Don't look back — SPORTS 16

Paine, Thomas (1737–1809)
English political theorist

age going to the workhouse — GOVERNMENT 23
badge of lost innocence — GOVERNMENT 22
living to some purpose — REVOLUTION 15
My country is the world — RELIGION 17
shocks the mind of a child — RELIGION 18
teach governments humanity — PUNISHMENT 15
times that try men's souls — PATRIOTISM 17

Palden Gyatso
Tibetan monk

survived to bear witness — GENOCIDE 3

Paley, William (1743–1805)
English theologian and philosopher

refute a sneer — ARGUMENT 17

Palmerston, Lord (1784–1865)
*British statesman, Prime Minister 1855–8,
1859–65*

concurrence of atoms — COOPERATION 12
Die, my dear Doctor — LAST WORDS 12
how is the old complaint — MEETING 6
Humbug — EMOTIONS 15
Our interests are eternal — INTERNATIONAL 17
What is merit — REPUTATION 9

Pankhurst, Christabel (1880–1958)
English suffragette

claim our right as women — WOMAN'S R 18

Pankhurst, Emmeline (1858–1928)
English suffragette leader

broken window pane — ARGUMENT 18

Pankin, Boris (1931–)
Russian diplomat

tighten the belt — UNEMPLOYMENT 4

Paquin, Anna (1982–)
New Zealand actress

pretending to be someone else — ACTING 5

Parker, Charlie (1920–55)
American jazz saxophonist

Music is your own experience — MUSIC 16

Parker, Dorothy (1893–1967)
American critic and humorist

As artists they're rot — FICTION 12
assume that Oscar said it — WORDPLAY 10
emotions from A to B — ACTORS 11
Excuse My Dust — EPITAPHS 21
glorious cycle of song — DISILLUSION 8
Hollywood money isn't money — CINEMA 22
I'd have been under the host — DRUNKEN 7
It is our national joy — MEDIOCRITY 7
kiss and tell — GOSSIP 8
knew you had it in you — BIRTH 4

Parker, Dorothy (*cont.*)

Men seldom make passes	APPEARANCE 13
One of you is lying	LOVE 41
One perfect rose	GIVING 9
satin gown	CLOTHES 14
Scratch a lover	ENEMIES 10
see John Knox in Paradise	HEAVEN 1
thrown with great force	BOOKS 17
wise-cracking and wit	WIT 9
You might as well live	SUICIDE 4

Parker, Ross (1914–74) **and Charles, Hugh** (1907–)
British songwriters

There'll always be an England	ENGLAND 16
We'll meet again	MEETING 7

Parkes, Henry (1815–95)
English-born Australian statesman

crimson thread of kinship	AUSTRALIA 12
far more wicked	AUSTRALIA 11

Parkinson, Cecil (1932–)
British Conservative politician

better to be a has-been	AMBITION 15

Parkinson, C. Northcote (1909–93)
English writer

being unhappily married	POLITICS 28
decisions of importance	BUREAUCRACY 8
Expenditure rises	ECONOMICS 12
fill the time available	WORK 15
inverse proportion to the sum	COMMITTEES 7
Perfection of planned layout	MANAGEMENT 5

Parkinson, Michael (1935–)
British journalist and broadcaster

council estate in Sheffield	ROYAL F 8

Parks, Rosa (1913–)
American civil rights activist

mistreatment was not right	SELF-ESTEEM 13

Parnell, Charles Stewart (1846–91)
Irish nationalist leader

do what you think best	ADVICE 9

Parr, Doug

without industry connections	SCIENCE & SOC 5

Parris, Matthew (1949–)
British journalist and former politician

big cat detained briefly	THATCHER 7
Nice guys, when we turn nasty	CHARACTER 16
starves your self-respect	PARLIAMENT 14
vanilla-flavoured pixie	POLITICIANS 16

Parsons, Tony (1953–)
English critic and writer

bit him on his unwashed ass	POVERTY 18

Partridge, Frances (1900–)
English writer and diarist

long time to live alone	LONELINESS 5

Pascal, Blaise (1623–62)
French mathematician, physicist, and moralist

Cleopatra's nose	FACE 6
Continual eloquence is tedious	SPEECH 17
expected to see an author	STYLE 7
God is or he is not	GOD 24
he is a thinking reed	HUMAN RACE 19
heart has its reasons	EMOTIONS 16
self is hateful	SELF 20
these infinite spaces	SPACE 7
time to make it shorter	LETTERS 9
We shall die alone	DEATH 27
what to put first	WRITING 28

Pasternak, Boris (1890–1960)
Russian novelist and poet

bare, shivering human soul	SELF 21
Man is born to live	LIFESTYLES 15
Most people experience love	LOVE 42
run over by 'New Man'	PROGRESS 16

Pasternak, Boris (*cont.*)	That strapping dairymaid	SPRING 5
Pasteur, Louis (1822–95) *French chemist and bacteriologist*	applications of science favours only the prepared mind	SCIENCE 14 EXPERIMENT 4
Paterson, 'Banjo' (1864–1941) *Australian poet*	come a-waltzing, Matilda	AUSTRALIA 13
Paterson, Jennifer (1928–99) *British cook*	meat, drink and cigarettes	HEALTH 6
Patrick, St (fl. 5th cent.) *patron saint and Apostle of Ireland*	Christ beside me	PRAYER 12
Pattison, Mark (1813–84) *English educationist*	horizon recedes as we advance	RESEARCH 4
Patton, George S. (1885–1945) *American general*	good plan violently executed they are won by men	MANAGEMENT 6 WEAPONS 9
Pauli, Wolfgang (1900–58) *Austrian-born American physicist*	I mind your publishing	THINKING 16
Paulin, Tom (1949–) *English poet and critic*	juniper talks to the oak	TREES 12
Paxman, Jeremy (1950–) *British journalist and broadcaster*	let them die of neglect obsessed with public relations	IDEAS 10 JOURNALISM 14
Payn, James (1830–98) *English writer*	always on the buttered side	MISFORTUNES 10
Payne, J. H. (1791–1852) *American actor, dramatist, and songwriter*	there's no place like home	HOME 8
Paz, Octavio (1914–) *Mexican poet and essayist*	descended from the Aztecs stare death in the face	MEXICO 5 LOVE 43
Peake, Mervyn (1911–68) *British novelist, poet, and artist*	live at all is miracle enough live in a glass room	LIFE 26 SENSES 11
Pearse, Patrick (1879–1916) *Irish nationalist leader*	soldier's death for Ireland	EXECUTIONS 5
Pearson, Hesketh (1887–1964) *English actor and biographer*	he has read too widely no stronger craving	QUOTATIONS 10 TITLES 4
Pearson, Lester (1897–1972) *Canadian Liberal statesman*	we prepare for war	PEACE 19
Péguy, Charles (1873–1914) *French poet and essayist*	accomplice of liars sinner is at the heart Tyranny is better organized	TRUTH 19 CHRISTIAN 8 LIBERTY 26
Pelé (1940–) *Brazilian footballer*	It's the beautiful game	FOOTBALL 9
Penrose, Roger (1931–) *British mathematician*	universe's very existence whether a mechanical device	MIND 13 THINKING 17
Pepys, Samuel (1633–1703) *English diarist*	about hunting, in a dialect accompany my being blind And so to bed as cheap as other men conform, or be more wise hanged, drawn, and quartered	HUNTING 5 DISABILITY 8 SLEEP 6 ROYALTY 15 CONFORMITY 11 EXECUTIONS 6
Perelman, S. J. (1904–79) *American humorist*	irregular patch of nettles twang of the bedspring	FARMING 7 ROMANCE 8
Peres, Shimon (1923–) *Israeli statesman*	made dictatorship impossible	TELEVISION 13

Perón, Eva (1919–52)
wife of Juan Perón

use the money for the poor

CHARITY 5

Perot, H. Ross (1930–)
American businessman

running up a $4 trillion debt

EXPERIENCE 12

Perry, Jimmy
British songwriter

kidding, Mister Hitler

WORLD W II 13

Persaud, Rajen
English psychiatrist

new religion

COUNSELLING 4

Persons, Ted

ain't what they used to be

PAST 13

Perutz, Max (1914–)
Austrian-born scientist

does away with the hard lot

SCIENCE & SOC 6

Pétain, Henri Philippe (1856–1951)
French soldier and statesman

speak ill of everybody

AUTOBIOG 8

Peter, Laurence J. (1919–90)
Canadian writer

his level of incompetence
time left to be Canadian

MANAGEMENT 7
CANADA 11

Peters, Mike
American cartoonist

slime bucket

CHOICE 13

Peterson, Virgilia (1904–66)

no divorce from memory

DIVORCE 11

Pevsner, Nikolaus (1902–83)
German-born architectural historian

bicycle shed is a building

ARCHITECT 9

Pfeiffer, Michelle (1959–)
American actress

you can't do it all

WOMEN 29

Phelps, Edward John (1822–1900)
American lawyer and diplomat

man who makes no mistakes

MISTAKES 7

Philby, Kim (1912–88)
British intelligence officer and Soviet spy

first belong

BETRAYAL 9

Philip, John Woodward ('Jack')
(1840–1900)
American naval captain

poor devils are dying

NAVY 7

Philip, Prince, Duke of Edinburgh
(1921–)
husband of Elizabeth II

All I get is fancy stuff
go out in a bowler
[killing animals] for money
new car or a new wife
such extraordinary moods
tolerance in abundance
world does not owe us a living
You just got on with it

COOKING 10
TRAVEL 15
FIELD 2
CARS 14
SEA 12
ROYAL F 9
ACTION 9
COUNSELLING 5

Phillips, Arthur Angell (1900–85)
Australian critic and editor

Cultural Cringe

AUSTRALIA 14

Phillips, Julia (1944–)
British writer

we are not brave enough

RELATIONSHIPS 20

Phillips, Melanie
British journalist

believe in nothing

BELIEF 17

Phillips, Morgan (1902–63)
British Labour politician

owes more to Methodism

POLITICAL P 23

Phillips, Wendell (1811–84)
American abolitionist

as natural a growth as an oak

REVOLUTION 16

Picasso, Pablo (1881–1973)
Spanish painter

Art is a lie that makes
Cubism has not been understood
draw like these children

ART 23
INSIGHT 9
DRAWING 5

Picasso, Pablo (*cont.*)	offensive and defensive weapon	PAINTING 14
	only another artist	GOD 25
	positive value has its price	CAUSES 9
Piercy, Marge (1936–) *American novelist and poet*	Hope sleeps in our bones	HOPE 10
	rather die satiated	DIETS 6
Pimlott, Ben (1945–) *English historian*	genetic lottery comes up with	ROYAL 10
Pink, Janice	find a crippled man	DISABILITY 9
Pinter, Harold (1930–) *English dramatist*	cocktail cabinet	THEATRE 9
	could get down to Sidcup	OPPORTUNITY 5
Piron, Armand J.	I wish I could shimmy	DANCE 10
Pirsig, Robert M. (1928–) *American writer*	Buddha, the Godhead, resides	SCIENCE & REL 9
	classical mind at work	MIND 14
Pitt, William (1759–1806) *British Tory statesman*	infringement of human freedom	NECESSITY 7
Pitt, William, Earl of Chatham (1708–78) *British Whig statesman*	crime of being a young man	YOUTH 15
	parks are the lungs of London	LONDON 7
Pius VII, Pope (1742–1823) *Pope from 1800*	go to the gates of Hell	DIPLOMACY 11
Pius XII, Pope (1876–1958) *Italian cleric*	One Galileo	MISTAKES 8
Planck, Max (1858–1947) *German physicist*	its opponents eventually die	SCIENCE 15
Plath, Sylvia (1932–63) *American poet*	Dying, Is an art	DYING 11
	fat gold watch	BIRTH 5
	no way out of the mind	MENTAL 6
	woman adores a Fascist	MEN/WOMEN 18
	word consumes itself	BEREAVEMENT 16
Plato (429–347 BC) *Greek philosopher*	interest of the stronger	JUSTICE 19
Pliny the Elder (AD 23–79) *Roman statesman and scholar*	Always something new	AFRICA 8
Pohl, Frederik (1919–) *American science fiction writer*	see our world from outside	SCIENCE FICT 5
Poincaré, Henri (1854–1912) *French mathematician and philosopher*	Science is built up of facts	SCIENCE 16
Polanski, Roman (1933–) *French film director, of Polish descent*	great passion	CHILDREN 17
Pollitt, Harry (1890–1960) *British Communist politician*	Go to Spain and get killed	HEROES 14
Pollock, Jackson (1912–56) *American painter*	It was a fine compliment	PAINTING 15
Pompadour, Madame de (1721–64) *favourite of Louis XV of France*	After us the deluge	REVOLUTION 17
Pompidou, Georges (1911–74) *French statesman*	service of the nation	POLITICIANS 17
Pope, Alexander (1688–1744) *English poet*	as if you taught them not	TEACHING 10
	breaks a butterfly	FUTILITY 11
	Damn with faint praise	PRAISE 6
	devil's leavings	GOODNESS 13

Pope, Alexander (*cont.*)

Do good by stealth	CHARITY 6
fancy wit will come	INTELLIGENCE 9
Get place and wealth	WEALTH 16
God said, *Let Newton be!*	SCIENCE 17
hold sage Homer's rule	GUESTS 7
Hope springs eternal	HOPE 11
Know then thyself	HUMAN RACE 20
landscape-painting	GARDENS 16
little learning	KNOWLEDGE 18
makes the politician wise	FOOD 20
man who expects nothing	CYNICISM 8
Nature to advantage dressed	STYLE 8
noblest work of God	HONESTY 8
Not to admire, is all the art	HAPPINESS 13
Pleased with a rattle	CHILDREN 18
ruling passion conquers reason	EMOTIONS 17
think the last opinion right	OPINION 10
To err is human	FORGIVENESS 10
Whate'er is best administered	ADMIN 6
Whatever IS, is RIGHT	CIRCUMSTANCE 11
where angels fear to tread	FOOLS 9
wiser to-day than he was	APOLOGY 8
Words are like leaves	WORDS 20

Popper, Karl (1902–94)
Austrian-born philosopher

Science must begin with myths	ARTS AND SCI 10
tolerate the intolerant	TOLERANCE 6

Porter, Cole (1891–1964)
American songwriter

Birds do it, bees do it	LOVE 44
Brush up your Shakespeare	SHAKESPEARE 7
Every time we say goodbye	PARTING 14
heaven knows, Anything goes	MORALITY 13
I'm always true to you, darlin'	FAITHFULNESS 10

Portillo, Michael (1953–)
British Conservative politician

in one word what I am	CAREERS 10
You cannot ditch policies	SUCCESS 16

Postman, Neil (1931–)
American writer

away from the adult mind	TELEVISION 14

Potter, Beatrix (1866–1943)
English writer for children

eating too much lettuce	FOOD 21

Potter, Dennis (1935–94)
English television dramatist

lovely tube of delight	SMOKING 9
nowness of everything	PRESENT 11
saw Heathrow for myself	AIR TRAVEL 4
wound, not the bandage	RELIGION 19

Potter, Stephen (1900–69)
British writer

argument about any place	ARGUMENT 19
art of winning games	SPORTS 17
bouquet better than the taste	ALCOHOL 14

Pound, Ezra (1885–1972)
American poet

antennae of the race	ART AND SOC 4
give up verse, my boy	WRITING 29
left blanks in their writings	HISTORY 12
Lhude sing Goddamm	WINTER 4
like a cheque drawn on a bank	MEANING 8
news that STAYS news	LITERATURE 6
pleasures of middle age	MIDDLE AGE 17
too far from the dance	MUSIC 17

Poussin, Nicolas (1594–1665)
French painter

imitation in lines and colours	PAINTING 16

Powell, Anthony (1905–2000)
English novelist

crystallization of surnames	NAMES 12
don't fufil the promise	PARENTS 15
fell in love with himself	SELF-ESTEEM 14

Powell, Colin (1937–)
American general
we are going to cut it off	GULF 5

Powell, Dilys (1902–95)
English critic and writer
make a dress out of a curtain	FILMS 4

Powell, Enoch (1912–98)
British Conservative politician
end in failure	POLITICIANS 18
foaming with much blood	RACISM 16
History is littered	WARFARE 30
Judas was paid	BETRAYAL 10
returning to one's own vomit	DIARIES 6

Pratchett, Terry (1948–)
English science fiction writer
furniture in Tolkien's attic	FANTASY 4
Personal isn't the same	SELF 22

Prescott, John (1938–)
British Labour politician
branded, pigeon-holed	EDUCATION 12
pretty middle class	CLASS 14

Preston, Keith (1884–1927)
American poet
graves of little magazines	PUBLISHING 5

Price, Anthony (1928–)
English writer and editor
probably re-designed Hell	AIR TRAVEL 5

Priestland, Gerald (1927–91)
English writer and journalist
belong in the gutter	JOURNALISM 15

Priestley, J. B. (1894–1984)
English novelist, dramatist, and critic
American civilization	UNITED S 18
Conflict and Art	FOOTBALL 10
epic of Dunkirk	WORLD W II 14
God can stand being told	ATHEISM 6
it is a magical event	SNOW 3
school reports on our children	SCHOOLS 9
where the MCC ends	CRICKET 10

Prior, Matthew (1664–1721)
English poet
died of my physician	MEDICINE 12
I love thee in prose	COURTSHIP 12

Pritchett, V. S. (1900–97)
English writer and critic
our yawning Philistinism	CRIME FICT 6
procrastinated rape	BEST-SELLERS 2
What Chekhov saw	SOLITUDE 14

Protagoras (b. *c.*485 BC)
Greek sophist
measure of all things	HUMAN RACE 21

Proudhon, Pierre-Joseph (1809–65)
French social reformer
Property is theft	POSSESSIONS 12

Proust, Marcel (1871–1922)
French novelist
come to us from neurotics	GREATNESS 5
express his thought directly	CREATIVITY 9
horror of sunsets	EVENING 3
memory revealed itself	MEMORY 20
paradises that we have lost	HEAVEN 2
salutary to the body	HAPPINESS 14

Pulitzer, Joseph (1847–1911)
Hungarian-born American newspaper proprietor
demagogic, corrupt press	JOURNALISM 16

Punch (1841–1992)
English humorous weekly periodical
ain't got no zideways	FAT 7
'Eave 'arf a brick at 'im	PREJUDICE 9
Go directly	BEHAVIOUR 14
if this is coffee, I want tea	FOOD 22
Parts of it are excellent	TACT 3
put off till to-morrow	DELAY 6
Sometimes I sits and thinks	THINKING 18
this 'ere 'Tortis' is a insect	ANIMALS 17
What is Matter	MIND 15
worse than wicked, my dear	VULGARITY 5

Puntan-Galeo, Sarah-Louise *British student representative*	two classes of student	PROTEST 6
Pushkin, Alexander (1799–1837) *Russian poet*	hear November at the gate tumult in the Russian heart	WINTER 5 RUSSIA 10
Putnam, Israel (1718–90) *American general*	see the white of their eyes	AMERICAN WAR 2
Puttnam, Roger *British businessman*	top hats and crinolines	BUSINESS 17
Pu Yi (1906–67) *Chinese emperor*	never folded my own quilt	ROYALTY 16
Puzo, Mario (1920–99) *American novelist*	lawyer with his briefcase offer he can't refuse	LAWYERS 5 CHOICE 14
Pym, Barbara (1913–80) *English novelist*	cosiness and irritation	RELATIONSHIPS 21
Pyrrhus (319–272 BC) *King of Epirus*	One more such victory	WINNING 12
Quant, Mary (1934–) *English fashion designer*	Any failure seems so total belongs to Youth rather like being a blonde	YOUTH 16 TWENTIETH 9 WEALTH 17
Quarles, Francis (1592–1644) *English poet*	our midnight oil whole world is not sufficient	WORK 16 DISCONTENT 7
Quayle, Dan (1947–) *American Republican politician*	Space is almost infinite to lose one's mind	SPACE 8 MIND 16
Quennell, Peter (1905–) *English writer*	elderly fallen angel	PEOPLE 19
Quiller-Couch, Arthur (1863–1944) *English writer and critic*	best is the best Grief has no wings	EXCELLENCE 4 SORROW 14
Quindlen, Anna (1953–) *American columnist and novelist*	freeze-dried astronaut food multiple-personality cases	PRAYER 13 CLOTHES 15
Quine, W. V. O. (1908–) *American philosopher*	sages and cranks shape of identical elephants	PHILOSOPHY 10 LANGUAGE 15
Rabelais, François (*c.*1494–*c.*1553) *French humanist, satirist, and physician*	Do what you like fire to be lit going to seek a great perhaps	LIFESTYLES 16 CHILDREN 19 LAST WORDS 13
Rabin, Yitzhak (1922–95) *Israeli statesman*	Enough of blood and tears	PEACE 20
Racine, Jean (1639–99) *French tragedian*	burning within my veins I have loved him too much in a word, she's a woman	LOVE 45 HATRED 10 INDECISION 8
Rae, John (1931–) *English writer*	art of good manners everything your child tells me truth about the teacher	SWEARING 6 SCHOOLS 10 SCHOOLS 11
Ralegh, Walter (*c.*1552–1618) *English explorer and courtier*	but with age and dust deep are dumb Fain would I climb sharp remedy, but a sure one true love is a durable fire we die in earnest	TIME 16 EMOTIONS 18 AMBITION 16 EXECUTIONS 7 FAITHFULNESS 11 DEATH 28
Raleigh, Walter (1861–1922) *English lecturer and critic*	plums and orange peel those who do not wish to know wish I loved the Human Race	QUOTATIONS 11 EXAMINATIONS 6 HUMAN RACE 22

Ramey, Estelle (1917–)	short, brutal lives	MEN/WOMEN 19
Randi, James (1928–) *American magician*	old age stuck in a microwave	PRESENT 12
Ransome, Arthur (1884–1967) *English writer*	better drowned than duffers brats go on forever	RISK 6 BEST-SELLERS 3
Raphael, Frederic (1931–) *British novelist and screenwriter*	further away than anywhere more than one man in bed perspiring dreams	CITIES 12 FAITHFULNESS 12 BRITISH CIT 7
Ratner, Gerald (1949–) *English businessman*	cheaper than a prawn sandwich	BUSINESS 18
Rattigan, Terence (1911–77) *English dramatist*	be in the Horseguards le vice Anglais	CLASS 15 EMOTIONS 19
Rattle, Simon (1955–) *English conductor*	conducted a Beethoven performance	MUSICIANS 10
Ratushinskaya, Irina (1954–) *Russian poet and political dissident*	no one in that corrupt system	LITERATURE/SOC 6
Raverat, Gwen (1885–1957) *English wood-engraver*	do things themselves	CLASS 16
Raymond, Derek (1931–94) *English thriller writer*	psychopath is the furnace	MENTAL 7
Rayner, Claire (1931–) *English journalist*	It is a dead-end job You have the right to try	MOTHERS 8 HAPPINESS 15
Read, Herbert (1893–1968) *English art historian*	not just another amusing stunt This is the happy warrior	PAINTING 17 ARMY 14
Read, Piers Paul (1941–) *English novelist*	more subtle as you grow older	SIN 14
Reade, Charles (1814–84) *English novelist and dramatist*	reap a destiny	CAUSES 10
Reagan, Nancy (1923–) *American actress and wife of Ronald Reagan*	white glove pulpit woman is like a teabag	PRESIDENCY 12 ADVERSITY 3
Reagan, Ronald (1911–) *American Republican statesman, President 1981–9*	grasp and hold a vision hard work never killed anybody into the sunset of my life misfits, Looney Tunes second oldest profession way of eating jellybeans We will never forget them	LEADERSHIP 11 WORK 17 ALZHEIMER'S 3 TERRORISM 2 POLITICS 29 CHARACTER 17 SPACE 9
Reed, Henry (1914–86) *English poet and dramatist*	actually sitting up Modest? My word, no Today we have naming of parts	IDLENESS 9 SEX 33 ARMY 15
Reed, John (1887–1920) *American journalist and revolutionary*	Ten days that shook the world	REVOLUTION 18
Reed, Joseph (1741–85) *American Revolutionary politician*	King of Great Britain	CORRUPTION 7
Reeve, Christopher (1952–) *American actor*	play the hand you're dealt	DISABILITY 10
Reger, Max (1873–1916) *German composer*	smallest room of my house	REVIEWS 6
Reid, Keith (1946–) *English pop singer and songwriter*	whiter shade of pale	FACE 7

Reith, Lord (1889–1971)
British administrator and politician

give effect to a principle
CIVIL SERV 10

impartiality is bias
IMPARTIAL 2

Remarque, Erich Maria (1898–1970)
German novelist

quiet on the western front
WORLD W I 16

Renard, Jules (1864–1910)
French novelist and dramatist

bourgeois are other people
CLASS 17

Rendall, Montague John (1862–1950)
English headmaster

speak peace unto nation
TELEVISION 15

Renoir, Jean (1894–1979)
French film director

any act of betrayal
SUCCESS 17

disease called friendship
LETTERS 10

Renoir, Pierre Auguste (1841–1919)
French painter

with my brush I make love
PAINTING 18

Reuther, Walter (1907–70)
American labour leader

If it looks like a duck
FACTS 4

Revson, Charles (1906–75)
American businessman

we sell hope
COSMETICS 6

Reynolds, Joshua (1723–92)
English painter

been their own teachers
TEACHING 11

Could we teach taste
TASTE 7

industry will improve them
WORK 18

mere copier of nature
PAINTING 19

Reynolds, Malvina (1900–78)
American songwriter

Little boxes on the hillside
ARCHITECT 10

Reza, Yasmina (1969–)
Iranian-born French dramatist

writing a tragedy
COMEDY 4

Rhodes, Cecil (1853–1902)
South African statesman

prefer to be Englishmen
ENGLAND 17

So little done, so much to do
LAST WORDS 14

Rhys, Jean (*c.*1890–1979)
British novelist and short-story writer

doormat in a world of boots
PEOPLE 20

give or take sympathy
COMPASSION 11

real curse of Eve
WOMEN 30

We can't all be happy
SUFFERING 19

You poisoned it and stabbed
LOVE 46

Rice, Grantland (1880–1954)
American sports writer

how you played the Game
FOOTBALL 11

Rice-Davies, Mandy (1944–)
English model and showgirl

He would, wouldn't he
SELF-INTEREST 9

Richards, Ann (1933–)
American Democratic politician

silver foot in his mouth
SPEECHES 13

Richards, I. A. (1893–1979)
English literary critic

We believe a scientist
ARTS AND SCI 11

Richards, Keith (1943–)
English rock musician

I used to be a laboratory
DRUGS 13

Richards, Keith (1943–)
see **Jagger, Mick and Richards, Keith**

Richardson, Justin (1900–75)
British poet

all these surplus women
PARENTS 16

I'd not read Eliot, Auden
WRITERS 14

Richardson, Ralph (1902–83)
English actor

Acting is merely the art
ACTING 6

demented refrigerator
THEATRE 10

Rifkin, Jeremy (1945–)
American economist and environmentalist

alternative to formal work
WORK 19

from vice to virtue
CONSUMER 6

Rigg, Diana (1938–) *British actress*	one good scandal left	GOSSIP 9
Rilke, Rainer Maria (1875–1926) *German poet*	solitude of the other	RELATIONSHIPS 22
Ritz, César (1850–1918) *Swiss hotel proprietor*	customer is never wrong	BUSINESS 19
Rivarol, Antoine de (1753–1801) *French man of letters*	not clear is not French	LANGUAGES 10
Rivers, Joan (1939–) *American comedienne*	anger is 51 per cent	COMEDY 5
Robertson, George (1946–) *British Labour politician*	Serbs out, Nato in	BALKANS 5
Robespierre, Maximilien (1758–94) *French revolutionary*	inalienable rights of man	HUMAN RIGHTS 10
Robin, Leo (1900–84) *American songwriter*	diamonds are a girl's	WEALTH 18
Robinson, Gerry (1948–) *British businessman*	most excited voice I heard	COMMITMENT 5
Robinson, Jancis (1950–) *English journalist and broadcaster*	Wine is for drinking	ALCOHOL 15
Robinson, Sugar Ray (1920–89) *American boxer*	get him in trouble	BOXING 7
Rochester, Lord (1647–80) *English poet*	cowards if they durst great united what lies a great and mighty king	COWARDICE 3 BEGINNING 9 WORDS/DEED 6
Roddenberry, Gene (1921–91) *American film producer*	to boldly go	EXPLORATION 6
Roddick, Anita (1942–) *English businesswoman*	ennoble the spirit 'feminine' principles rear view mirror	COSMETICS 7 BUSINESS 20 BUSINESS 21
Rodriguez, Sue (1951–94) *Canadian euthanasia activist*	Who owns my life	SUICIDE 5
Rogers, Richard (1933–) *British architect*	able to read a building Form follows profit	ARCHITECT 11 BEAUTY 19
Rogers, Samuel (1763–1855) *English poet*	signify whom one marries while aught remains to do	MARRIAGE 26 ACHIEVEMENT 16
Rogers, Will (1879–1935) *American actor and humorist*	can kill the movies Communism is like prohibition Half our life is spent happening to Somebody Else kill you in a new way made more Liars met a man that I didn't like on different subjects shortest-lived professions what I read in the papers	CINEMA 23 COMMUNISM 13 TIME 17 HUMOUR 12 WEAPONS 10 TAXES 10 LIKES 8 IGNORANCE 11 HEROES 15 NEWSPAPERS 16
Roland, Mme (1754–93) *French revolutionary*	what crimes are committed	LIBERTY 27
Rolle, Richard de Hampole (*c.*1290–1349) *English mystic*	When Adam delved and Eve span	CLASS 18

Ronay, Egon
British publisher and journalist

missionary position — COOKING 11

Roosevelt, Eleanor (1884–1962)
American humanitarian and diplomat

make you feel inferior — SELF-ESTEEM 15

Roosevelt, Franklin D. (1882–1945)
American Democratic statesman, President 1933–45

arsenal of democracy — WORLD W II 15
date which will live in infamy — WORLD W II 16
four essential human freedoms — HUMAN RIGHTS 11
I have seen war — WARFARE 31
our son of a bitch — POLITICIANS 19
pledge myself, to a new deal — UNITED S 19
policy of the good neighbour — INTERNATIONAL 18
somnambulist walking backwards — POLITICAL P 24
these memoranda of yours — ADMIN 7
thing we have to fear — FEAR 13
weapons for man's freedom — BOOKS 18
work, my friend, is peace — PEACE 21

Roosevelt, Theodore (1858–1919)
American Republican statesman, President 1901–9

called 'weasel words' — LANGUAGE 16
carry a big stick — DIPLOMACY 12
hyphenated Americanism — UNITED S 20
stop raking the muck — JOURNALISM 17
such a bully pulpit — PRESIDENCY 13

Rootes, Lord (1894–1964)
English motor-car manufacturer

fulfils a man's ego — CARS 15

Ross, Eric

like a box of chocolates — LIFE 27

Ross, Martin (1862–1915)
see **Somerville, Edith Œ and Ross, Martin**

Rossetti, Christina (1830–94)
English poet

forget and smile — MEMORY 21
unrecorded did it slip away — MEETING 8

Rossini, Gioacchino (1792–1868)
Italian composer

awful quarters of an hour — MUSICIANS 11

Rostand, Edmond (1868–1918)
French dramatist

sign of an affable man — FACE 8

Rostand, Jean (1894–1977)
French biologist

frog remains — LIFE SCI 11
Kill millions of men — MURDER 10
To be adult is to be alone — MATURITY 9

Rosten, Leo (1908–97)
American writer and social scientist

hates dogs and babies — DOGS 6

Roth, Philip (1933–)
American novelist

Jew kids threw rocks at me — RACISM 17
Jewish man with parents alive — PARENTS 17

Rotten, Johnny (1957–)
British rock singer

squishing noises — SEX 34

Roupell, Charles

sign of an ill-spent youth — SPORTS 18

Rousseau, Jean-Jacques (1712–78)
French philosopher and novelist

Man was born free — LIBERTY 28

Routh, Martin Joseph (1755–1854)
English classicist

verify your references — INFORMATION 7

Rowland, Helen (1875–1950)
American writer

follies which a man regrets — FOOLS 10
Love the quest — DIVORCE 12
thing of beauty and a boy — BACHELORS 4
what is left of a lover — HUSBANDS 12

Rowland, Richard (c.1881–1947)
American film producer

lunatics have taken charge — CINEMA 24

Royden, Maude (1876–1956)
English religious writer
Conservative Party at prayer — CHURCH 9

Royde-Smith, Naomi (c.1875–1964)
English novelist and dramatist
one of them is rather coarse — HORSES 4

Rubens, Paul Alfred (1875–1917)
English songwriter
your King and your Country — WORLD W I 17

Rubinstein, Helena (1882–1965)
American beautician
no ugly women, only lazy ones — COSMETICS 8

Runcie, Robert (1921–99)
English Protestant clergyman; Archbishop of Canterbury
bridge of reconciliation — BEREAVEMENT 17
done my best to die — BIOGRAPHY 12
tourism is their religion — TRAVEL 16

Runyon, Damon (1884–1946)
American writer
try to rub up against money — MONEY 21

Rushdie, Salman (1947–)
Indian-born British novelist
freedom to offend — CENSORSHIP 10
halal portions of the past — FAMILY 9
say the unsayable — LITERATURE/SOC 7
voices talking about everything — LITERATURE 7
what matters in your life — ABSENCE 7

Rusk, Dean (1909–)
American politician
We're eyeball to eyeball — CRISES 16

Ruskin, John (1819–1900)
English art and social critic
cloud as a golden throne — IGNORANCE 12
hard and dirty work — EMPLOYMENT 12
Labour without joy is base — WORK 20
laws of life — COOPERATION 13
peacocks and lilies — BEAUTY 20
we build for ever — ARCHITECT 12

Russell, Bertrand (1872–1970)
British philosopher and mathematician
always proud of the fact — SORROW 15
beauty cold and austere — MATHS 12
examining his wives' mouths — EXPERIMENT 5
fatal to true happiness — CAUTION 8
fear love is to fear life — FEAR 14
fed the chicken every day — FORESIGHT 9
fundamental defect of fathers — FATHERS 4
I might have become a god — ATHEISM 7
lack of rational conviction — OPINION 11
last product of civilization — LEISURE 8
Machines are worshipped — TECHNOLOGY 23
Man is a credulous animal — BELIEF 18
moulding men's lives — IMPULSIVE 4
on the side of the Government — RELIGION 20
People wish to be liked — DUTY 8
'progress' is ethical — PROGRESS 17
shocks the magistrate — PORNOGRAPHY 5
vital problem for the moralist — BOREDOM 6
what we are saying is true — MATHS 13
why they invented Hell — CRUELTY 8
Work is of two kinds — EMPLOYMENT 13

Russell, Dora (1894–1986)
English feminist
how to prevent them — BIRTH CONT 4

Russell, Lord John (1792–1878)
British Whig statesman
proverb is one man's wit — QUOTATIONS 12

Rutherford, Ernest (1871–1937)
New Zealand physicist
done a better experiment — STATISTICS 10
fired a 15-inch shell — SURPRISE 4
physics or stamp collecting — SCIENCE 18
We haven't got the money — PROBLEMS 12

Sacks, Jonathan (1948–)
British rabbi

Values are tapes we play — MORALITY 14

Sackville-West, Vita (1892–1962)
English writer and gardener

greater cats with golden eyes — CATS 8
thing that wants Virginia — ABSENCE 8

Sagan, Carl (1934–96)
American astronomer

This is better than we thought — SCIENCE & REL 10

Sagan, Françoise (1935–)
French novelist

I said 'Yes' — WEDDINGS 10
Life is amorphous — LITERATURE 8
more frightful than laughter — JEALOUSY 6

Saint Laurent, Yves (1936–)
French couturier

don't really like knees — BODY 11

Sakharov, Andrei (1921–89)
Russian nuclear physicist

means of total destruction — SCIENCE & SOC 7

Saki (1870–1916)
Scottish writer

as cooks go — COOKING 12
Christmas box in February — TEMPTATION 9
discourage our better emotions — CHILDREN 20
leafy Kensington — COUNTRY 9
little inaccuracy sometimes saves — LIES 7
live beyond their incomes — DEBT 6
lives of the medieval saints — NAMES 13
mere restlessness — TRAVEL 17
produced green Chartreuse — CHRISTIAN 9
socks compelled one's attention — CLOTHES 16
wedded to the truth — PRIME 8
young have aspirations — GENERATION 9

Salinger, J. D. (1919–)
American novelist and short-story writer

all that David Copperfield — AUTOBIOG 9
terrific friend of yours — READING 10

Salisbury, Lord (1830–1903)
British Conservative statesman, Prime Minister 1855–6, 1886–92, 1895–1902

community of Europe — EUROPE 15
defend the moon — ARMY 16
give away his own money — CHARITY 7
insipid common sense — EXPERTS 5

Salisbury, Lord (1893–1972)
British Conservative politician

Too clever by half — PEOPLE 21

Samuel, Lord (1870–1963)
British Liberal politician

thought in cold storage — LIBRARIES 8

Samuelson, Paul A. (1915–)
American economist

consumer is the king — CONSUMER 7

Sand, George (1804–76)
French novelist

Art for the sake of the true — ART 24
difficult to love God — GOD 26

Sandburg, Carl (1878–1967)
American poet

City of the Big Shoulders — AMERICAN CITIES 14
comes on little cat feet — FOG 3
hyacinths and biscuits — POETRY 28
I am the grass; I cover all — NATURE 8
I don't know where I'm going — IDEALISM 8
nobody will come — WARFARE 32
past is a bucket of ashes — PAST 14
Slang rolls up its sleeves — LANGUAGE 17

Sanders, Henry 'Red'

Sure, winning isn't everything — WINNING 13

Sandwich, Lord (1718–92)
British politician and diplomat

turn over the sheet — ADMIN 8

Santayana, George (1863–1952)
Spanish-born philosopher and critic

condemned to repeat it — PAST 15
innovation without reason — FASHION 6
redoubling your effort — FANATICISM 5
saint out of a libertine — SAINTS 4

Santayana, George (*cont.*)

to be fashionable is ominous	IDEAS 11
young man who has not wept	GENERATION 10

Santer, Jacques (1937–)
Luxembourgeois politician

I am whiter than white	CORRUPTION 8

Sargent, John Singer (1856–1925)
American painter

Every time I paint a portrait	PAINTING 20

Saro-Wiwa, Ken (1941–95)
Nigerian author and environmentalist

but the struggle continues	LAST WORDS 15
My writing did it	LITERATURE/SOC 8

Sarraute, Nathalie (1902–)
French novelist

manufacture of banality	TELEVISION 16

Sartre, Jean-Paul (1905–80)
French philosopher, novelist, dramatist, and critic

condemned to be free	LIBERTY 29
disenchantment for truth	DISILLUSION 9
Don't lay the blame on men	FATHERS 5
Hell is other people	HELL 5
invented each day	HUMAN RACE 23
Nothingness haunts being	FUTILITY 12
on the far side of despair	DESPAIR 8
respect their executioners	EXECUTIONS 8
things with their names	BELIEF 19
too late or too early	TIME 18
transformed into an institution	LITERATURE/SOC 9

Sassoon, Siegfried (1886–1967)
English poet

bald, and short of breath	ARMY 17
filled with such delight	SINGING 15
intolerably nameless names	EPITAPHS 22
passing through this Gate	ARMY 18
splendid work for the blind	DISABILITY 11

Satie, Erik (1866–1925)
French composer

refuses the Legion of Honour	MUSICIANS 12

Saunders, Cicely (1916–)
English founder of St Christopher's Hospice, London

look at it with clear eyes	DYING 12

Sayers, Dorothy L. (1893–1957)
English writer of detective fiction

advertising we deserve	ADVERTISING 13
it is better fun to punt	PLEASURE 15
saves original thinking	QUOTATIONS 13
women were first	CHRISTIAN 10

Scanlon, Hugh (1913–)
British trade unionist

liberty is not licence	LIBERTY 30

Scarfe, Gerald (1936–)
English caricaturist

stretch the human frame	DRAWING 6

Scargill, Arthur (1938–)
British trades-union leader

castration of the trade union	TRADE 8
had people not defied the law	PARLIAMENT 15

Schelling, Friedrich von (1775–1854)
German philosopher

frozen music	ARCHITECT 13

Schiller, Friedrich von (1759–1805)
German dramatist and poet

gods themselves struggle	FOOLS 11

Schlesinger, Arthur M. Jr. (1917–)
American historian

Lenin had died of typhus	TWENTIETH 10
making the President a tsar	PRESIDENCY 14

Schnabel, Artur (1882–1951)
Austrian-born pianist

grown-ups avoid Mozart	MOZART 3
pauses between the notes	MUSICIANS 13

Schoenberg, Arnold (1874–1951)
Austrian-born American composer

another unplayable work	MUSIC 18

Schopenhauer, Arthur (1788–1860)
German philosopher

short-legged sex

WOMEN 31

Schroeder, Patricia (1940–)
American Democratic politician

Teflon-coated Presidency

REAGAN 3

Schulberg, Budd (1914–)
American writer

I could have had class

OPPORTUNITY 6

Schumacher, E. F. (1911–77)
German-born economist

disbelief of the Aztecs

DOUBT 7

inefficiency remains unnoticed

BUSINESS 22

production of deadly devices

TERRORISM 3

questioned its right to exist

ECONOMICS 14

Small is beautiful

ECONOMICS 13

Schumpeter, Joseph Alois (1883–1950)
American economist

theory is in Marx's pages

ECONOMICS 15

worth a thousand gadgets

TECHNOLOGY 24

Schurz, Carl (1829–1906)
American soldier and politician

My country, right or wrong

PATRIOTISM 18

Schwarzkopf III, H. Norman (1934–)
American general

can't get a plumber to come

POWER 18

consider myself hawkish

ARMY 19

get it over with

WARFARE 33

Schweitzer, Albert (1875–1965)
Franco-German missionary

don't drag wood about

INTELLECTUALS 5

Schwitters, Kurt (1887–1948)
German painter

nail my pictures together

PAINTING 21

Scott, C. P. (1846–1932)
British journalist

Comment is free

JOURNALISM 18

No good can come of it

TELEVISION 17

Scott, Robert Falcon (1868–1912)
English polar explorer

dead bodies must tell the tale

COURAGE 10

interested in natural history

SCHOOLS 12

look after our people

LAST WORDS 16

this is an awful place

EXPLORATION 7

we knew we took them

RISK 7

Scott, Sir Walter (1771–1832)
Scottish novelist and poet

Easy live and quiet die

INDIFFERENCE 7

exquisite touch

AUSTEN 3

ill taking the breeks aff

SCOTLAND 13

ministering angel thou

WOMEN 32

my own, my native land

PATRIOTISM 19

O Caledonia! stern and wild

SCOTLAND 12

O what a tangled web

DECEPTION 7

thinks the tither daft

FOOLS 12

tragedy of Hamlet

THEATRE 11

word, at random spoken

CHANCE 11

Scott-Maxwell, Florida

her middle-aged children

MOTHERS 9

Scruton, Roger (1944–)
British writer and philosopher

beyond an impassable barrier

ANIMALS 18

fulfilment of the person

HAPPINESS 16

not so as to enjoy himself

CHILDHOOD 9

respect the rights of others

ANIMAL RIGHTS 11

Searle, Ronald (1920–)
see Willans, Geoffrey and Searle, Ronald

Seeger, Pete (1919–)
American folk singer and songwriter

read the fine print

EXPERIENCE 13

Segal, Erich (1937–)
American novelist

having to say you're sorry

LOVE 47

Seikaly, Rony
American basketball player

unprotected sex

AIDS 6

Sei Shōnagon (*c.*966–*c.*1013) *Japanese diarist and writer*	strange form of lunacy what terrible depressions	ENEMIES 11 WRITING 30
Seitz, Raymond (1940–) *American diplomat*	majority may rule in Britain reinventing the wheel worth overdoing	MINORITIES 5 PROBLEMS 13 MODERATION 6
Selden, John (1584–1654) *English historian and antiquary*	Ignorance excuses no man intermission of pain Old friends are best	LAWS 15 PLEASURE 16 FAMILIAR 6
Seldon, Arthur (1916–) *British economist*	Government of the busy	GOVERNMENT 24
Self, Will (1961–) *British writer*	*éminence cerise* Some people are born slack	ROYAL F 11 IDLENESS 10
Sellar, W. C. (1898–1951) **and Yeatman, R. J.** (1898–1968) *British writers*	fear of Political Economy keen sense of humus person who wants to teach what you can remember write on both sides	DEBT 7 GARDENS 17 SCHOOLS 13 HISTORY 13 EXAMINATIONS 7
Seneca (*c.*4 BC–AD 65) *Roman philosopher and poet*	diseases are innumerable no wind is favourable stop a man's life while they teach, men learn	COOKING 13 IGNORANCE 13 DEATH 29 TEACHING 12
Sereny, Gitta (1923–) *Hungarian-born British writer and journalist*	If you looked away	GUILT 10
Service, Robert W. (1874–1958) *Canadian poet*	later than you think promise made is a debt unpaid This is the law of the Yukon What are WE fighting for	TIME 19 TRUST 10 STRENGTH 16 WARFARE 34
Seth, Vikram (1952–) *Indian poet, novelist, and travel writer*	chosen such a good boy	INGRATITUDE 2
Seward, William (1801–72) *American politician*	revolutions never go backward	REVOLUTION 19
Sewell, Brian *British art historian and critic*	I don't know what art is	ART 25
Sexton, Anne (1928–74) *American poet*	God owns heaven My sleeping pill is white tired of the gender of things want to know *which tools* who my father was	EARTH 8 MEDICINE 13 COSMETICS 9 SUICIDE 6 FATHERS 6
Shaffer, Peter (1926–) *English dramatist*	four bottles of Chianti Ordinary made beautiful	CULTURE 14 CONFORMITY 12
Shakespeare, William (1564–1616) *English dramatist*	a-bed after midnight all the perfumes of Arabia All the world's a stage And so beguile thy sorrow apparel oft proclaims the man Arm me, audacity borrower, nor a lender be bounded in a nut-shell Brevity is the soul of wit caviare to the general come before the swallow dares come not single spies Comparisons are odorous congregation of vapours constant as the northern star	SLEEP 7 GUILT 11 LIFE 28 LIBRARIES 9 CLOTHES 17 COURAGE 11 LENDING 3 DREAMS 8 WIT 11 TASTE 8 FLOWERS 9 SORROW 17 SIMILARITY 8 POLLUTION 12 FAITHFULNESS 13

Shakespeare, William (*cont.*)

Crabbed age and youth	GENERATION 11
cruel only to be kind	CRUELTY 9
devil can cite Scripture	BIBLE 6
divinity that shapes our ends	FATE 10
double toil and trouble	SUPERNATURAL 14
filches from me my good name	REPUTATION 10
find the mind's construction	FACE 9
Finds tongues in trees	NATURE 9
fling away ambition	AMBITION 18
Frailty, thy name is woman	WOMEN 33
Friends, Romans, countrymen	SPEECHES 14
furnace for your foe	ENEMIES 12
girdle round about the earth	SPEED 7
glib and oily art	HYPOCRISY 6
good deed in a naughty world	GOODNESS 14
great eater of beef	FOOD 23
hale souls out	MUSICAL INST 6
Hath not a Jew eyes	EQUALITY 11
he that moves my bones	EPITAPHS 23
help the feeble up	CHARITY 8
hold the mirror up to nature	ACTING 7
How weary, stale, flat	FUTILITY 13
I know how to curse	SWEARING 7
If it were done when 'tis done	ACTION 10
If music be the food of love	MUSIC 19
Ill met by moonlight	MEETING 9
in nothing else so happy	FRIENDSHIP 20
Is this a dagger	SENSES 12
Is this her fault or mine	TEMPTATION 10
joy's soul lies in the doing	EFFORT 10
know not what we may be	FUTURE 15
labour we delight in	WORK 21
less than horrible imaginings	FEAR 15
like the leaving it	DYING 13
local habitation and a name	WRITING 31
Macbeth does murder sleep	SLEEP 8
make cowards of us all	CONSCIENCE 6
man that's marred	MARRIAGE 27
manner of his speech	SPEECH 18
many years outlive performance	SEX 35
marriage of true minds	LOVE 50
Misery acquaints a man	MISFORTUNES 11
moon's an arrant thief	SKIES 10
More matter with less art	STYLE 9
most carefully upon your hour	PUNCTUALITY 8
Murder most foul	MURDER 11
My nature is subdued	CHARACTER 18
naked to mine enemies	RELIGION 21
never did run smooth	LOVE 48
never felt a wound	SUFFERING 20
newest kind of ways	SIN 15
Night's candles are burnt out	DAY 4
not bound to please thee	CONVERSATION 14
not only witty in myself	WIT 10
O! call back yesterday	PAST 16
O! let me not be mad	MADNESS 7
O polished perturbation	WORRY 7
O wonderful, wonderful	SURPRISE 5
Once more unto the breach	WARFARE 35
one half-pennyworth of bread	VALUE 12
paragon of animals	HUMAN RACE 24
parting is such sweet sorrow	PARTING 15
pluck this flower, safety	DANGER 5
prepare to shed them now	SORROW 16

Shakespeare, William (*cont.*)

primrose path of dalliance	WORDS/DEED 7
rest is silence	ENDING 12
Sans teeth, sans eyes	OLD AGE 18
screw your courage	FAILURE 8
sharper than a serpent's tooth	INGRATITUDE 3
Sigh no more, ladies	MEN 18
So long as men can breathe	FAME 21
some men are born great	GREATNESS 6
spirits from the vasty deep	SUPERNATURAL 13
stand up for bastards	DEFIANCE 9
Stands Scotland where it did	SCOTLAND 14
strong as proofs of holy writ	JEALOUSY 7
stuff will not endure	YOUTH 17
sweat but for promotion	CAREERS 11
takes away the performance	DRUNKEN 8
tale told by an idiot	· LIFE 29
taste of death but once	COWARDICE 4
tell him he hates flatterers	FLATTERY 6
that which we call a rose	NAMES 14
therefore may be wooed	COURTSHIP 13
things in heaven and earth	SUPERNATURAL 12
thinking makes it so	EVIL 12
This is the worst	SUFFERING 21
this sceptered isle	ENGLAND 18
thou cream-faced loon	INSULTS 8
thou shalt not escape calumny	GOSSIP 10
Throw physic to the dogs	MEDICINE 14
tide in the affairs of men	OPPORTUNITY 7
time is out of joint	CIRCUMSTANCE 12
To be, or not to be	CHOICE 15
To be wise, and love	LOVE 49
To sleep: perchance to dream	DEATH 31
to the manner born	TRADITION 4
to thine own self be true	SELF 23
To-morrow, and to-morrow	TIME 20
too rich for use	BEAUTY 21
Uneasy lies the head	ROYALTY 17
uses of adversity	ADVERSITY 4
wait on appetite	EATING 10
we owe God a death	DEATH 30
welcomest when they are gone	GUESTS 8
What is the city	CITIES 13
What news on the Rialto	NEWS 3
When shall we three meet	MEETING 10
whereon the wild thyme blows	FLOWERS 8
whips and scorns of time	SUICIDE 7
witching time of night	NIGHT 4
Within this wooden O	THEATRE 12
Words, words, words	READING 11
yet the pity of it, Iago	COMPASSION 12
yet there is method in't	MADNESS 6

Shanahan, Eileen	square of the number of people	COMMITTEES 8
Shankly, Bill (1914–81) *Scottish footballer*	more serious than that	FOOTBALL 12
Shapiro, Robert (1942–) *American lawyer*	play the race card	TRIALS 5
Sharpe, Tom (1928–) *British novelist*	even terror of their lives	POLICE 4
Shaw, George Bernard (1856–1950) *Irish dramatist*	adapt the world to himself	PROGRESS 18
	affection of the human animal	PARENTS 18
	always tell an old soldier	ARMY 20

Shaw, George Bernard (*cont.*)

as universal as sea sickness	COWARDICE 5
become famous without ability	FAME 22
blasted to eternal damnation	SWEARING 8
brandy of the damned	MUSIC 20
by the incompetent many	DEMOCRACY 9
champagne teetotaller	TEETOTALISM 6
Christ perish in torment	IMAGINATION 10
conspiracies against the laity	CAREERS 12
customs of his tribe	BRITAIN 9
despise so entirely	SHAKESPEARE 8
distinguish the mediocre	TITLES 5
divided by a common language	LANGUAGES 11
Do not do unto others	LIKES 10
does not return your blow	REVENGE 13
don't want to talk grammar	GRAMMAR 8
essence of inhumanity	INDIFFERENCE 8
Every man over forty	MEN 19
extreme form of censorship	CENSORSHIP 16
forgives itself nothing	GENERATION 12
furious secret rebellion	WOMAN'S R 19
get what you like	LIKES 9
get your heart's desire	ACHIEVEMENT 17
Government and public opinion	ENGLAND 19
great and blessed invention	FUTURE 16
He who can, does	TEACHING 13
He who has never hoped	HOPE 12
Home is the girl's prison	HOME 9
horizontal desire	DANCE 11
I enjoy convalescence	SICKNESS 11
I say 'Why not?'	IDEAS 12
If you strike a child	VIOLENCE 14
in the house three days	BEAUTY 22
knock the patriotism out	PATRIOTISM 20
know what to say	CRITICS 18
let his wife starve	ART AND SOC 5
Liberty means responsibility	LIBERTY 31
man wants to murder a tiger	FIELD 3
man without originality	CHARACTER 19
maximum of temptation	MARRIAGE 28
morals are like its teeth	MORALITY 15
never lightened the burden	REVOLUTION 20
No man alive could bear it	HAPPINESS 18
not a fraud, but a miracle	FAITH 11
Of all human struggles	MEN/WOMEN 20
One man that has a mind	DETERMINATION 9
only things that are true	REALITY 6
outdoes Nature herself	DEATH 32
perfect expression of scorn	INSULTS 9
photographer is like the cod	PHOTOGRAPHY 7
right to consume happiness	HAPPINESS 17
robs Peter to pay Paul	GOVERNMENT 25
sacrifice other people	SACRIFICE 12
Satisfaction is death	DISCONTENT 8
shake a man's faith in himself	SELF-ESTEEM 16
something he is ashamed of	DUTY 9
stimulate the phagocytes	MEDICINE 15
thinks he knows everything	POLITICIANS 20
treated as human beings	EMPLOYMENT 14
very important profession	PARENTS 19
Walk! Not bloody likely	LUXURY 5
working definition of hell	HOLIDAYS 4

| **Shaw, George Bernard** (*cont.*) | worst of crimes is poverty | POVERTY 19 |
| | you who are the pursued | COURTSHIP 14 |

| **Shawcross, Hartley** (1902–) | which is to be the master | POWER 19 |
| *British Labour politician* | | |

| **Shelley, Mary** (1797–1851) | Everywhere I see bliss | DESPAIR 9 |
| *English novelist* | think like other people | CONFORMITY 13 |

Shelley, Percy Bysshe (1792–1822)	blithe Spirit	BIRDS 8
English poet	buried in so sweet a place	DEATH 33
	can Spring be far behind	WINTER 6
	cloud-encircled meteor	POETS 16
	daughter of Earth and Water	SKIES 11
	dome of many-coloured glass	LIFE 30
	Let there be light	GREECE 4
	Monarchy is only the string	ROYALTY 18
	My name is Ozymandias	FUTILITY 14
	O wild West Wind, thou breath	WIND 5
	Sun-girt city	VENICE 3
	unacknowledged legislators	POETRY 29
	violet into a crucible	TRANSLATION 3

| **Sheppard, Dick** (1880–1937) | lying in the ditch | COMPASSION 13 |
| *British clergyman* | | |

| **Sheridan, Philip Henry** (1831–88) | only good Indian | RACISM 18 |
| *American cavalry commander* | | |

Sheridan, Richard Brinsley (1751–1816)	as headstrong as an allegory	DETERMINATION 10
Anglo-Irish dramatist	disinheriting countenance	APPEARANCE 14
	don't become a young woman	SIMILARITY 9
	indebted to his memory	SPEECHES 15
	individual calamity	CRISES 17
	interpreter is the hardest	MEANING 9
	maiden of bashful fifteen	WOMEN 34
	malice of a good thing	WIT 12
	nice derangement of epitaphs	WORDPLAY 11
	valour is certainly going	COURAGE 12
	very pineapple of politeness	MANNERS 9
	You write with ease	WRITING 32

Sherman, William (1820–91)	Hold the fort	AMERICAN CIVIL 4
American Union general	many a boy here to-day	WARFARE 36
	stand by each other always	LOYALTY 7

| **Sherratt, David** (1945–) | vitamin made by yeast | GENETIC 9 |
| *British microbiologist* | | |

| **Sherrin, Ned** (1931–) | | |
| see **Beaton, Alistair and Sherrin, Ned** | | |

Shields, Carol (1935–)	be like everyone else	INDIVIDUAL 6
Canadian writer and academic	slippery substance	INNOCENCE 10
	your life is going well	PARTIES 9

| **Short, Clare** (1946–) | golden elephants next | AID 8 |
| *British Labour politician* | They live in the dark | SECRECY 18 |

| **Sibelius, Jean** (1865–1957) | statue has never been set up | CRITICS 19 |
| *Finnish composer* | | |

| **Sidney, Philip** (1554–86) | My true love hath my heart | FAITHFULNESS 14 |
| *English soldier, poet, and courtier* | Shallow brooks murmur most | SILENCE 6 |

Smith, Cyril (1928–) *British Liberal politician*	longest running farce	PARLIAMENT 16
Smith, Delia *English cookery expert*	egg is a work of art Football and cookery	FOOD 24 FOOTBALL 13
Smith, Edgar (1857–1938) *American songwriter*	protect a working-girl	CLASS 19
Smith, F. E. (1872–1930) *British Conservative politician and lawyer*	extremely offensive, young man records of Somerset House stout hearts and sharp swords	INSULTS 10 HUMILITY 6 SUCCESS 18
Smith, Godfrey (1926–) *English journalist and columnist*	full of audio visual marvels	WORDS 21
Smith, Logan Pearsall (1865–1946) *American-born man of letters*	as big as they can pay for behave as the rich behave darken into nightmares far side of baldness fashionable and first-rate gilded tomb have to go out and enjoy it Most people sell their souls say that life is the thing straight into the gutter test of a vocation What music is more enchanting	HYPOCRISY 7 WEALTH 20 DREAMS 9 HAIR 4 FASHION 7 BEST-SELLERS 4 WEATHER 9 CONSCIENCE 7 READING 12 IDEALISM 9 CAREERS 13 YOUTH 18
Smith, Stevie (1902–71) *English poet and novelist*	best of opiates burnt at the stake as witches capacity women have Cross to be Borne Gallop about doing good I think you couldn't go on no bosom and no behind not waving but drowning When I am happy I live	MARRIAGE 30 PAST 17 PERSISTENCE 10 HUSBANDS 13 CHARITY 11 DEATH 34 BODY 13 LONELINESS 7 CREATIVITY 10
Smith, Sydney (1771–1845) *English clergyman and essayist*	almost always in the right barbarity of tyrants come down and littered distinguished from dying eating *pâté de foie gras* fiddling like madmen furniture so charming How can a bishop marry kind of healthy grave Let onion atoms lurk life without arithmetic men, women, and clergymen no very lively hope of success not further than dinner prejudices a man so resembles a pair of shears triangular person	MINORITIES 6 IRELAND 12 BUILDINGS 7 DEATH 35 HEAVEN 3 SINGING 16 BOOKS 19 CLERGY 7 COUNTRY 10 FOOD 25 MATHS 14 CLERGY 6 PRAYER 14 LIFESTYLES 18 REVIEWS 8 MARRIAGE 31 CIRCUMSTANCE 13
Snagge, John (1904–96) *English sports commentator*	either Oxford or Cambridge	SPORTS 19
Snow, Jon (1947–) *British journalist and broadcaster*	cheque-book journalism	JOURNALISM 19
Snyder, Gary (1930–) *American poet*	carefree, neat, and loving continually 'growing economy'	SIMPLICITY 4 ECONOMICS 16
Socrates (469–399 BC) *Greek philosopher*	fact of my ignorance things I can do without	KNOWLEDGE 19 POSSESSIONS 13

Socrates (*cont.*)

unexamined life is not worth	PHILOSOPHY 11
you cannot contradict	TRUTH 20

Solzhenitsyn, Alexander (1918–)
Russian novelist

crushed by the rubble	COMMUNISM 14
desire to have more things	POSSESSIONS 14
expect a man who's warm	SUFFERING 22
pillar of the State	PROPAGANDA 9
robbed a man of *everything*	POWER 20
thoughts of a prisoner	PRISON 5
today's mass living habits	TWENTIETH 11
truth cannot be told	CENSORSHIP 17
Work was like a stick	WORK 22

Somerville, Edith Œ (1858–1949) **and
Ross, Martin** (1862–1915)
Irish writers

Blood may be thicker	FAMILY 11
conscious of a nervous system	HUNTING 6

Somoza, Anastasio (1925–80)
Nicaraguan dictator

I won the count	ELECTIONS 11

Sondheim, Stephen (1930–)
American songwriter

Anything that is grey	AIR TRAVEL 6
Everything's coming up roses	OPTIMISM 8
Ev'ry day a little death	TRANSIENCE 13
I like to be in America	UNITED S 22

Sontag, Susan (1933–)
American writer

footprint or a death mask	PHOTOGRAPHY 8
identified with evil	AIDS 7
night-side of life	SICKNESS 12
other people's reality	REALITY 7
pornography is really about	PORNOGRAPHY 6
revenge of the intellect	CRITICS 20

Soper, Donald (1903–98)
British Methodist minister

evidence of life after death	PARLIAMENT 17
fizzy, explosive stuff	CHURCH 10
sex in Hyde Park	SPEECHES 16
What is morally wrong	POLITICS 30

Sophocles (*c.*496–406 BC)
Greek dramatist

mad and savage master	SEX 36
more wonderful than man	HUMAN RACE 25
Not to be born	LIFE 31

Sorley, Charles Hamilton (1895–1915)
English poet

no such thing as a just war	WARFARE 37

Soule, John L. B. (1815–91)
American journalist

Go West, young man	EXPLORATION 8

Sousa, John Philip (1854–1932)
American composer and conductor

hear it through their feet	JAZZ 9

Southey, Robert (1774–1843)
English poet and writer

in love with a cold climate	WINTER 7
longest half of your life	YOUTH 19
loves nothing but himself	HOME 10

Southgate, Colin (1938–)

downgrade the opera house	OPERA 4

Spark, Muriel (1918–)
British novelist

Beware of men bearing flowers	FLOWERS 10
candour in married life	HONESTY 9
crème de la crème	SCHOOLS 14
may as well be a Catholic	CHRISTIAN 11
One's prime is elusive	MATURITY 10

Sparrow, John (1906–92)
English academic

Hell would not be Hell	EPITAPHS 25
unsavoury engine of pollution	DOGS 7

Spector, Phil (1940–)
American record producer and songwriter

not a bona fide human being	ROCK 9

Spencer, Herbert (1820–1903)
English philosopher

clever theft was praiseworthy	CRIME 10

Spencer, Herbert (*cont.*)
effects of folly — FOOLS 13
Hero-worship is strongest — HEROES 16
How often misused words — THINKING 20

Spencer, Lord (1964–)
English peer
blood on their hands — PRESS 6
needed no royal title — TITLES 6

Spencer, Stanley (1891–1959)
English painter
saying 'Ta' to God — PAINTING 22

Spender, Stephen (1909–95)
English poet
gliding like a queen — RAILWAYS 9
good time to die — OLD AGE 19
perspective of the future — TECHNOLOGY 25
young Auden was someone — HUMOUR 13

Spenser, Edmund (*c.*1552–99)
English poet
Sweet Thames, run softly — RIVERS 9

Spice Girls, The
English pop singers
Yo I'll tell you what I want — AMBITION 17

Spielberg, Steven (1947–)
American film director and producer
live in the present — PAST 18
sky falls on my head — CINEMA 25

Spinoza, Baruch (1632–77)
Dutch philosopher
laugh at human actions — INSIGHT 10

Spring-Rice, Cecil (1859–1918)
British diplomat
I vow to thee, my country — PATRIOTISM 21

Springer, Jerry (1944–)
American chat-show host
My show is a circus — TELEVISION 18

Springsteen, Bruce (1949–)
American rock singer and songwriter
doesn't make *living* easier — SUCCESS 19
down in a dead man's town — POVERTY 20

Spurgeon, C. H. (1834–92)
English nonconformist preacher
lie to go round the world — LIES 8

Squire, J. C. (1884–1958)
English man of letters
'Good God!' said God — GOD 27
Ho! Let Einstein be — SCIENCE 19
I'm not so think — DRUNKEN 9

Staël, Mme de (1766–1817)
French writer
be totally understanding — INSIGHT 11
woman must submit to it — OPINION 12

Stalin, Joseph (1879–1953)
Soviet dictator
engineers of human souls — LITERATURE/SOC 10
million deaths a statistic — DEATH 36
sickness suffered by dogs — GRATITUDE 5
State is an instrument — COMMUNISM 15

Stanley, Henry Morton (1841–1904)
Welsh explorer
Dr Livingstone, I presume — MEETING 11

Stark, Freya (1893–1993)
English writer and traveller
pretend to be more stupid — WOMEN 35

Stark, John (1728–1822)
American Revolutionary officer
Molly Stark's a widow — AMERICAN WAR 3

Stassinopoulos, Arianna (1950–)
Greek-born American writer
striving for immortality — CREATIVITY 11

Stead, Christina (1902–83)
Australian novelist
all the rich people — GREED 7

Steele, Richard (1672–1729)
Irish-born essayist and dramatist
what exercise is to the body — READING 13
woman seldom writes her mind — LETTERS 11

Steffens, Lincoln (1866–1936)
American journalist
I have seen the future — COMMUNISM 16

Stein, Gertrude (1874–1946)
American writer

all a lost generation	WORLD W I 18
Complete disillusionment	DISILLUSION 10
more space where nobody is	UNITED S 23
Remarks are not literature	LITERATURE 9
Rose is a rose is a rose	SELF 24
what is the question	LAST WORDS 17

Steinbeck, John (1902–68)
American novelist

bellies of his children	FAMINE 4
boys who wanted the moon	GREATNESS 7
deep in its own filth	POLLUTION 13
dying for four thousand years	THEATRE 13
grows beyond his work	HUMAN RACE 26
man got to do	DUTY 10
Okie means you're scum	INSULTS 11
purpose is to get them off	WEDDINGS 11
We want to see tomorrow	FUTURE 17

Steinem, Gloria (1934–)
American journalist

fish without a bicycle	MEN/WOMEN 21
We are becoming the men	WOMAN'S R 20

Steiner, George (1926–)
American French-born critic and writer

day's work at Auschwitz	GENOCIDE 6
mutations in our experience	INTERNET 7
this breathtaking act	SPACE 10
to discard courtesy	CRITICS 21

Stendhal (1783–1842)
French novelist

novel is a mirror	FICTION 13
pistol-shot in a concert	ART AND SOC 6

Stengel, Casey (1891–1975)
American baseball player and manager

players who hate your guts	BASEBALL 6

Stephens, James (1882–1950)
Irish poet and writer

Finality is death	PERFECTION 6

Sterne, Laurence (1713–68)
English novelist

different name for conversation	WRITING 34
Digressions are the sunshine	READING 14
love is a thing below a man	LOVE 51
minded what they were about	PREGNANCY 7
They order this matter better	FRANCE 8
whistling half a dozen bars	ARGUMENT 20

Stevens, Anthony

nature turns girls into women	MEN/WOMEN 22

Stevens, Wallace (1879–1955)
American poet

beauty of inflections	BEAUTY 23
changed upon the blue guitar	REALITY 8

Stevenson, Adlai (1900–65)
American Democratic politician

does not live by words alone	WORDS 22
flattery hurts no one	FLATTERY 7
lies about the Democrats	POLITICAL P 25
no evil in the atom	SCIENCE & REL 11
platitudes and bayonets	POLITICIANS 21
take the politics out	POLITICAL P 26
they said, 'Let us march.'	SPEECHES 17
would rather light a candle	PEOPLE 22

Stevenson, Anne (1933–)
English poet

cellos of the deep farms	BIRDS 9

Stevenson, Juliet (1956–)
British actress

Motherhood is like sex	MOTHERS 10

Stevenson, Robert Louis (1850–94)
Scottish novelist

better thing than to arrive	TRAVEL 19
dreamed of cheese	FOOD 26
go the length of twopence	COLOURS 8
grand memory for forgetting	MEMORY 2
harmless art of knucklebones	SPORTS 20
have to go to bed by day	SLEEP 9
He sows hurry	EATING 12
hunter home from the hill	EPITAPHS 26

Stevenson, Robert Louis (*cont.*)	it is a field of battle	MARRIAGE 32
	I travel for travel's sake	TRAVEL 18
	long black passage up to bed	SLEEP 10
	often told in silence	LIES 9
	public and merited disgrace	PUNISHMENT 16
	What hangs people	GUILT 12
	Yo-ho-ho, and a bottle of rum	ALCOHOL 16
Stewart, Ian (1945–) *British mathematician*	like recipes in a cookbook	LIFE SCI 12
Sting (1951–) *English rock singer, songwriter, and actor*	burning the rain forest	ENVIRONMENT 16
	pointing at the moon	FAME 23
Stinnett, Caskie (1911–) *American writer*	tell you to go to hell	DIPLOMACY 13
Stinson, Joseph C. (1947–)	Go ahead, make my day	READINESS 5
Stone, Oliver (1946–) see **Weiser, Stanley and Stone, Oliver**		
Stopes, Marie (1880–1958) *Scottish pioneer of birth-control clinics*	lascivious gloating	BODY 14
Stoppard, Tom (1937–) *British dramatist*	bad end unhappily	TRAGEDY 6
	Blood is compulsory	THEATRE 14
	Eternity's a terrible thought	TIME 21
	facts are on expenses	JOURNALISM 20
	gamble at terrible odds	LIFE 32
	gatekeeper to the new age	INVENTIONS 15
	good just by being knowledge	KNOWLEDGE 20
	It is the third thing	KISSING 11
	its not being English	TRANSLATION 4
	It's not the voting	DEMOCRACY 10
	Last Chance Gulch	CHILDHOOD 10
	less than three days	CRICKET 11
	Life's a curse	POETS 17
	Papers are power	BUREAUCRACY 9
	prerogative of the eunuch	PARLIAMENT 18
	Save the gerund	GRAMMAR 9
	see past our invention	RELATIONSHIPS 23
	trick played on the calendar	SUICIDE 8
	War is capitalism	WARFARE 38
Stowe, Harriet Beecher (1811–96) *American novelist*	I s'pect I growed	BIRTH 6
Strachey, Lytton (1880–1932) *English biographer*	better part of biography	BIOGRAPHY 13
	I don't think much of it	LAST WORDS 18
	trying to violate your sister	PACIFISM 6
Strauss, William L. and Cave, A. J. E.	placed in a New York subway	HUMAN RACE 27
Stravinsky, Igor (1882–1971) *Russian composer*	entirely different from habit	TRADITION 5
Straw, Jack (1946–) *British Labour politician*	You have to pray daily	PRISON 6
Street-Porter, Janet (1946–) *English broadcaster and programme-maker*	nipping fun in the bud	TELEVISION 19
Streisand, Barbra (1942–) *American singer, actress, and film director*	having ten honeydew melons	SUCCESS 20
Strindberg, August (1849–1912) *Swedish dramatist and novelist*	hell for children	FAMILY 13

Strong, Roy (1935–)	death, sex and jewels	MUSEUMS 4
English art historian		
Stross, Randall E.	American anti-intellectualism	INTELLECTUALS 6
Studdert Kennedy, G. A. (1883–1929)	Waste of Glory, waste of God	WARFARE 39
British poet		
Suckling, John (1609–42)	fart Of every heart	LOVE 52
English poet and dramatist	Prithee, why so pale	COURTSHIP 15
Sullivan, J. W. N. (1886–1937)	easier to make measurements	EXPERIMENT 6
Sullivan, Louis Henri (1856–1924)	Form follows function	ARCHITECT 14
American architect		
Summerskill, Edith (1901–80)	Nagging is the repetition	SPEECH 19
British Labour politician		
Surtees, R. S. (1805–64)	all that's worth living for	HUNTING 8
English sporting journalist and novelist	Better be killed	FEAR 16
	fill hup the chinks	EATING 13
	flattered into virtue	GOODNESS 15
	I loves the 'ound more	HUNTING 7
	my 'oss, my wife, and my name	LENDING 4
Swaffer, Hannen (1879–1962)	Freedom of the press	NEWSPAPERS 17
British journalist		
Swenson, May (1919–89)	one summer that I was ten	CHILDHOOD 11
American poet		
Swift, Graham (1949–)	neither now nor here	PRESENT 13
British writer	Reality is uneventfulness	REALITY 9
Swift, Jonathan (1667–1745)	as if I had said it myself	SPEECH 20
Anglo-Irish poet and satirist	degree of persecution	CLERGY 8
	detest that animal called man	HUMAN RACE 28
	dunces are all in confederacy	GENIUS 10
	elephants for want of towns	MAPS 3
	flea hath smaller fleas	PLAGIARISM 7
	like cutting off our feet	DISCONTENT 9
	malice never was his aim	CRITICS 22
	no longer tear his heart	EPITAPHS 27
	no man would be old	AGEING 9
	no word in their language	LIES 10
	not enough to make us love	RELIGION 22
	Proper words in proper places	STYLE 10
	Satire is a sort of glass	SELF-KNOW 10
	sun-beams out of cucumbers	RESEARCH 5
	two blades of grass to grow	PRACTICAL 11
Sykes, Eric (1923–)	always at our expense	COMEDY 6
British comedian, actor, and writer		
Synge, John Millington (1871–1909)	give you the music of a poem	TRANSLATION 5
Irish dramatist	we do be afraid of the sea	SEA 13
Szasz, Thomas (1920–)	child becomes an adult	CHILDREN 21
Hungarian-born psychiatrist	forgive but do not forget	FORGIVENESS 11
	husbands shop for fame	WAITING 5
	if God talks to you	MENTAL 8
	imaginary condition	HAPPINESS 19
	minimal power	TEACHING 14
	mistook magic for medicine	MEDICINE 17
	primary sexual activity	MASTURBATION 4
	private, secretive activity	SEX 37
	Two wrongs don't make a right	REVENGE 14

Szent-Györgyi, Albert von (1893–1986)	life's *mater* and *matrix*	LIFE SCI 13
Hungarian-born biochemist	what nobody has thought	INVENTIONS 16
Tacitus (AD *c.*56–after 117)	gods are on the side	STRENGTH 17
Roman senator and historian	hate the man you have hurt	HUMAN NATURE 10
	They make a wilderness	PEACE 22
Tagore, Rabindranath (1861–1941)	keep truth safe in its hand	PREJUDICE 10
Bengali poet and philosopher	own clamour of silence	SOLITUDE 15
Talleyrand, Charles-Maurice de (1754–1838)	beginning of the end	ENDING 13
	not the slightest zeal	MODERATION 7
French statesman	question of dates	BETRAYAL 11
	What a sad old age	SPORTS 21
Tally, Ted (1952–)		
see **Harris, Thomas and Tally, Ted**		
Tangye, Derek (1912–96)	like a Christmas cake	TWENTIETH 12
English writer		
Tansi, Sony Labou (1947–95)	in an ocean of shit	JUSTICE 20
African writer		
Tarantino, Quentin (1963–)	more information than I needed	INFORMATION 8
American film director and screenwriter		
Taupin, Bernie (1950–)		
see **John, Elton and Taupin, Bernie**		
Tawney, R. H. (1880–1962)	dread a dead-level of income	EQUALITY 12
British economic historian	throwing away what you have	POSSESSIONS 15
	What harm have I ever done	TITLES 7
Taylor, A. J. P. (1906–90)	by railway timetables	WORLD W I 19
British historian	Extreme views, weakly held	OPINION 13
	History gets thicker	HISTORY 14
	Hitler's level of accuracy	HITLER 5
	magic of Shaw's words	WRITERS 16
	respect each other	POSSESSIONS 16
Teale, Edwin Way (1899–1980)	time of sowing	AUTUMN 7
Tebbit, Norman (1931–)	got on his bike	UNEMPLOYMENT 5
British Conservative politician	which side do they cheer for	PATRIOTISM 22
Tecumseh (1768–1813)	Where today are the Pequot	UNITED S 24
Shawnee leader		
Teilhard de Chardin, Pierre (1881–1955)	ever more perfect eyes	LIFE SCI 14
French Jesuit philosopher and palaeontologist		
Temple, William (1881–1944)	mistake to suppose that God	GOD 28
English theologian	most materialistic	CHRISTIAN 12
	organized loafing	CRICKET 12
Tennyson, Alfred, Lord (1809–92)	as sunlight drinketh dew	KISSING 12
English poet	as the strength of ten	GOODNESS 16
	better to have loved and lost	LOVE 54
	Break, break, break	SEA 14
	breaks the blank day	DAY 5
	Cannon to right of them	WEAPONS 11
	curse is come upon me	SUPERNATURAL 15
	dropping-wells of fire	TREES 14
	Every moment one is born	STATISTICS 11
	Faultily faultless, icily regular	PERFECTION 7
	find, and not to yield	DETERMINATION 11
	forward let us range	CHANGE 23
	haunts of coot and hern	RIVERS 10
	honour rooted in dishonour	FAITHFULNESS 15

Tennyson, Alfred, Lord (*cont.*)

How dull it is to pause	IDLENESS 11
jingling of the guinea	CORRUPTION 9
kiss again with tears	FORGIVENESS 12
know well I am not great	GREATNESS 8
lecture, rich in sentiment	UNIVERSITIES 15
makes no friend	ENEMIES 13
Man is the hunter	MEN/WOMEN 23
man's fancy lightly turns	LOVE 53
may not quit the post	SUICIDE 9
more faith in honest doubt	DOUBT 8
more than coronets	ARISTOCRACY 11
More things are wrought	PRAYER 15
Nature, red in tooth and claw	NATURE 10
not at all or all in all	TRUST 11
old order changeth	CHANGE 24
Ring out the old	CELEBRATIONS 7
roaming with a hungry heart	EXPLORATION 9
see my pilot face to face	DEATH 37
So many worlds, so much to do	FUTURE 18
Some one had blundered	MISTAKES 9
Tears, idle tears	SORROW 18
Theirs not to reason why	ARMY 21
warming his five wits	BIRDS 10
Willows whiten, aspens quiver	TREES 13
wisdom lingers	KNOWLEDGE 21
woman is so hard	WOMEN 36

Tenzing Norgay (1914–86)
Sherpa mountaineer

warm and friendly and living	MOUNTAINS 6

Terence (*c.*190–159 BC)
Roman comic dramatist

I count nothing human foreign	HUMAN RACE 29
not been said before	ORIGINALITY 7

Teresa, Mother (1910–97)
Roman Catholic nun and missionary

By blood and origin	NATIONALITY 8
feeling of being unwanted	SICKNESS 13
just a drop in the ocean	CHARITY 12

Teresa, St, of Lisieux (1873–97)
French Carmelite nun

doing good on earth	HEAVEN 4

Tertullian (AD *c.*160–*c.*225)
Latin Church father

because it is impossible	BELIEF 20
blood of Christians	CHURCH 11

Tessimond, A. S. J. (1902–62)

They slip, diminished, neat	CATS 10

Thackeray, William Makepeace (1811–63)
English novelist

living up to it	FAITH 12
nobody like a relation	FAMILY 14

Thatcher, Margaret (1925–)
*British Conservative stateswoman, Prime
Minister 1979–90*

European super-State	EUROPEAN C 8
Falklands Factor	FALKLANDS 6
get my own way in the end	PATIENCE 6
have nothing better to do	HOME 11
how much my Ministers talk	LEADERSHIP 12
humdrum issues	CRISES 18
If you want anything done	POLITICIANS 22
Just rejoice	FALKLANDS 5
lady's not for turning	DETERMINATION 12
living above the shop	PRIME 9
no real alternative	CHOICE 16
no such thing as Society	SOCIETY 13
oxygen of publicity	TERRORISM 4
Pennies don't fall from heaven	MONEY 22
Prime Minister needs a Willie	PRIME 10
remember the Good Samaritan	CHARITY 13
very good back-seat driver	ADVICE 10

Thayer, William Roscoe (1859–1923) *American biographer and historian*	Log-cabin to White House	PRESIDENCY 15
Theroux, Paul (1941–) *American novelist and travel writer*	it was always 1952 perfected good manners	TRAVEL 20 ASIA 6
Thomas à Kempis (*c.*1380–1471) *German ascetical writer*	spent one whole day well	GOODNESS 17
Thomas, Brandon (1856–1914) *English dramatist*	where the nuts come from	MEXICO 6
Thomas, Dylan (1914–53) *Welsh poet*	death shall have no dominion dying of the light everything about the wasp hand that signed the paper isn't life a terrible thing man you don't like mind it wipes its shoes My fathers can have it rather lie in a hot bath starless and bible-black through the green fuse	DEATH 38 AGEING 10 BOOKS 20 POWER 21 LIFE 33 DRUNKEN 10 HOUSEWORK 7 WALES 5 POETRY 30 NIGHT 5 YOUTH 20
Thomas, Edward (1878–1917) *English poet*	dead thing that smells sweet dust on the nettles	PAST 19 FLOWERS 11
Thomas, Gwyn (1913–81) *Welsh novelist and dramatist*	only to Rugby Union	WALES 6
Thomas, R. S. (1913–2000) *Welsh poet and clergyman*	Hate takes a long time sound of a man Breathing There is only the past	HATRED 11 FAITH 13 WALES 7
Thompson, E. P (1924–) *British social historian*	bedroom in a Brussels hotel	EUROPEAN C 9
Thompson, Francis (1859–1907) *English poet*	blundered into Paradise set lip to earth's bosom we are born in other's pain	HEAVEN 5 FLOWERS 12 SUFFERING 23
Thomson, David (1941–) *British film critic*	eternal, expensive and forsaken Fiction is the great virus wind tunnel at dawn	FILMS 5 FILMS 6 ACTORS 12
Thomson, James (1700–48) *Scottish poet*	Britannia, rule the waves rear the tender thought	BRITAIN 10 TEACHING 15
Thomson, Roy (1894–1976) *Canadian-born British newspaper proprietor*	licence to print money	TELEVISION 20
Thoreau, Henry David (1817–62) *American writer*	As if you could kill time Beware of all enterprises count the cats in Zanzibar desperate oddfellow society find a trout in the milk frittered away by detail hears a different drummer lives of quiet desperation once had a sparrow alight	TIME 22 CLOTHES 18 TRAVEL 21 SOCIETY 14 FACTS 5 SIMPLICITY 5 CONFORMITY 14 LIFE 34 BIRDS 11
Thorne, Robert (d. 1527) *English merchant and geographical writer*	no land unhabitable	EXPLORATION 10
Thorpe, Jeremy (1929–) *British Liberal politician*	lay down his friends	BETRAYAL 12
Thurber, James (1894–1961) *American humorist*	fall flat on your face healthy and wealthy and dead He who hesitates	TOLERANCE 7 SLEEP 11 DELAY 7

Thurber, James (*cont.*)

Humour is emotional chaos	HUMOUR 14
naïve domestic Burgundy	ALCOHOL 17
our *own* story *exactly*	ROMANCE 9
why did you answer the phone	MISTAKES 10

Thurlow, Lord (1731–1806)
English jurist

souls to be condemned — BUSINESS 25

Thwaite, Anthony (1930–)
English writer

caught on a drawn breath — BALKANS 6

Tillich, Paul (1886–1965)
German-born Protestant theologian

way of avoiding non-being — WORRY 8

Tipu Sultan (*c.*1750–99)

live two days like a tiger — HEROES 17

Titus (AD 39–81)
Roman emperor from AD 79

I have lost a day — CHARITY 14

Tocqueville, Alexis de (1805–59)
French historian and politician

most dangerous moment	REVOLUTION 21
this putrid sewer	BRITISH CIT 8

Tolstoy, Leo (1828–1910)
Russian novelist

desire for desires	BOREDOM 7
intellectual brothel	JOURNALISM 21
machine for living	BODY 15
making him carry me	HYPOCRISY 8
man cannot get accustomed	FAMILIAR 7
unhappy in its own way	FAMILY 15

Tolstoy, Sonya (1844–1919)
wife of Leo Tolstoy

I am a source of satisfaction — WIVES 8

Torke, Michael (1961–)
American composer

waste money on psychotherapy — COUNSELLING 6

Torrens, Robert (1780–1864)
British economist

origin of capital — CAPITALISM 11

Toscanini, Arturo (1867–1957)
Italian conductor

kissed my first woman — SMOKING 10

Toussenel, A. (1803–85)
French writer

more one gets to know of men — DOGS 8

Townsend, Sue (1946–)
English writer

perhaps seem more interesting — DIARIES 7

Townshend, Pete (1945–)
British rock musician and songwriter

Hope I die before I get old — AGEING 11

Toynbee, Arnold (1889–1975)
English historian

health of the whole human race — TWENTIETH 13

Toynbee, Polly (1946–)
English journalist

change in the human psyche	WOMAN'S R 21
talks to the vacuum cleaner	TELEVISION 21
unwilling to spend money	MENTAL 9

Traherne, Thomas (*c.*1637–74)
English mystic

hands are a sort of feet — BODY 16

Trapido, Barbara (1941–)
British novelist

like opposing football teams — WEDDINGS 12

Travis, Merle (1917–83)
American country singer

Sixteen tons — DEBT 8

Tree, Herbert Beerbohm (1852–1917)
English actor-manager

grave yawns for him	BOREDOM 8
just a little more virginity	ACTORS 13

Tremain, Rose (1943–)
British novelist and dramatist

private corner to weep — PUNISHMENT 17

Trevelyan, G. M. (1876–1962) *English historian*	cricket with their peasants easy prey to sensations world of voluble hates	FRANCE 9 EDUCATION 14 PEOPLE 23
Trevelyan, John *British film censor*	paid to have dirty minds	CENSORSHIP 18
Trevor, Claire *American actress*	pay the minister as much	WEDDINGS 13
Trevor, William (1928–) *Anglo-Irish novelist and short story writer*	disease in the family	NORTHERN 8
Trillin, Calvin (1935–) *American journalist and writer*	milk and the yoghurt	WRITING 35
Trollope, Anthony (1815–82) *English novelist*	dying out of the power fainéant government how to allure by denying Make all men equal today Nobody holds a good opinion preventing men from marrying so as to suit his wife Three hours a day wear and tear of practice	TEMPTATION 11 GOVERNMENT 26 COURTSHIP 16 EQUALITY 13 SELF-ESTEEM 18 BACHELORS 5 WIVES 9 WRITING 36 THEORY 9
Trollope, Joanna (1943–) *British writer*	such a tyranny for women	FOOD 27
Trotsky, Leon (1879–1940) *Russian revolutionary*	dustbin of history it must be applied boldly most unexpected of all things Not believing in force peasantry its pack animal	FAILURE 9 VIOLENCE 15 OLD AGE 20 PACIFISM 7 CLASS 20
Trudeau, Pierre (1919–2000) *Canadian Liberal statesman*	place in the nation's bedrooms sleeping with an elephant those who will build it	CENSORSHIP 19 INTERNATIONAL 19 TWENTIETH 14
Truffaut, François (1932–84) *French film director*	Airing one's dirty linen like cleaning women	ART 26 PROTEST 7
Truman, Harry S. (1884–1972) *American Democratic statesman, President 1945–53*	against the law for generals buck stops here can't stand the heat even if you don't mean it It's a recession matters of the mind and spirit politician who's been dead won't be a bit like the Army	ARMY 22 RESPONSIBILITY 4 STRENGTH 18 HONESTY 10 UNEMPLOYMENT 6 CENSORSHIP 20 POLITICIANS 23 PRESIDENCY 16
Trump, Donald (1946–) *American businessman*	Deals are my art form	BUSINESS 26
Truth, Sojourner (*c.*1797–1883) *American evangelist and reformer*	Christ wasn't a woman	WOMAN'S R 22
Tsvetaeva, Marina (1892–1941) *Russian poet*	all poets are Jews Live in my dreams	POETRY 31 BEREAVEMENT 18
Tuchman, Barbara W. (1912–89) *American writer*	prepare for the last war	WARFARE 40
Tucker, Sophie (1884–1966) *American vaudeville artiste*	From birth to 18 rich is better	WOMEN 37 WEALTH 21
Tupper, Martin (1810–89) *English writer*	best of friends	BOOKS 21

Turgenev, Ivan (1818–83)	Every prayer reduces itself
Russian novelist	not a temple, but a workshop
	not worth understanding
	share no one's ideas
	try and set death aside

Turgenev, Ivan (1818–83) *Russian novelist*	Every prayer reduces itself	PRAYER 16
	not a temple, but a workshop	NATURE 11
	not worth understanding	INSIGHT 12
	share no one's ideas	IDEAS 13
	try and set death aside	DEATH 39
Turgot, A. R. J. (1727–81) *French economist and statesman*	snatched the lightning shaft	PEOPLE 24
Turkle, Sherry (1948–) *American sociologist*	voyager in virtuality	COMPUTERS 10
Turner, J. M. W. (1775–1851) *English landscape painter*	blacker than black	COLOURS 9
	sees more in my pictures	CRITICS 23
Tusa, John (1936–) *British broadcaster and journalist*	change an institution	MANAGEMENT 8
Tutu, Desmond (1931–) *South African clergyman*	African Primates Meeting	NAMES 15
Twain, Mark (1835–1910) *American writer*	annoyance of a good example	GOODNESS 18
	as sudden as a massacre	EDUCATION 15
	barkeeper entering heaven	AUSTEN 4
	because it was forbidden	HUMAN NATURE 11
	between a cat and a lie	LIES 11
	concealing how much we think	MANNERS 9
	contempt—and children	FAMILIAR 8
	designs by Michael Angelo	ITALY 5
	freedom of the press's speech	JOURNALISM 22
	good thing Adam had	ORIGINALITY 8
	good walk spoiled	GOLF 3
	greatest of all the inventors	INVENTIONS 17
	hurt you to the heart	GOSSIP 11
	ignorance and confidence	SUCCESS 21
	keep your mouth shut	FOOLS 14
	learn to endure adversity	ADVERSITY 5
	makes horse-races	OPINION 14
	my father was so ignorant	GENERATION 13
	New England weather	WEATHER 10
	nothing but cabbage	FOOD 28
	Only Animal that Blushes	HUMAN RACE 30
	people praise and don't read	BOOKS 22
	prodigious quantity of mind	INDECISION 9
	report of my death	MISTAKES 11
	several good protections	TEMPTATION 12
	she edited everything I wrote	WIVES 10
	WATCH THAT BASKET	CAUTION 9
	When angry, count four	ANGER 8
	when in doubt, strike it out	STYLE 11
	when you've got an apple	INGRATITUDE 4
	wholesale returns of conjecture	SCIENCE 20
	You can't pray a lie	PRAYER 17
Tweedie, Jill (1936–93) *British journalist*	any job men willingly vacate	WOMAN'S R 23
	sacrificial instincts	CAREERS 14
Twiggy (1949–) *English model and actress*	sitcom in America	TELEVISION 22
Tynan, Kenneth (1927–80) *English theatre critic*	can't drive the car	CRITICS 24
	one sees in Garbo sober	PEOPLE 25
	secret you don't know	WORRY 9
	Sergeant Pepper	CIVILIZATION 6
Tyutchev, F. I. (1803–73) *Russian writer*	She has a nature all her own	RUSSIA 11

Unamuno, Miguel de (1864–1937) *Spanish philosopher and writer*	nothing but death	DOUBT 9
Updike, John (1932–) *American novelist and short-story writer*	America is a vast conspiracy	UNITED S 25
	centre is everywhere	ENGLAND 20
	mask that eats into the face	FAME 24
	move against the grain	ADVERSITY 6
	Neutrinos are very small	PHYSICS 11
	other people's patience	BOREDOM 9
	soggy little island	BRITAIN 11
	unreality of painted people	THEATRE 15
Ure, Midge (1953–) see **Geldof, Bob and Ure, Midge**		
Ustinov, Peter (1921–) *Russian-born actor, director, and writer*	bereaved if snobbery died	HUMOUR 15
	If Botticelli were alive	ARTISTS 5
	nothing but a head-waiter	DIPLOMACY 14
	Pavarotti is not vain	SELF-ESTEEM 19
	people who got there first	FRIENDSHIP 21
	used to have lots of questions	COMPUTERS 11
	we're all Generals	LEADERSHIP 13
Valéry, Paul (1871–1945) *French poet, critic, and man of letters*	feel his solitude more keenly	LONELINESS 8
Vanbrugh, John (1664–1726) *English architect and dramatist*	given you her heart	WOMEN 38
van Damm, Vivian (*c.*1889–1960) *British theatre manager*	We never closed	THEATRE 16
Vanderbilt, William H. (1821–85) *American railway magnate*	public be damned	BUSINESS 27
van der Post, Laurens (1906–96) *South African explorer and writer*	perhaps never more frightening	CERTAINTY 7
	watched the sun going down	MURDER 12
Van Dyke, Henry (1852–1933) *American Presbyterian minister and writer*	for those who love	TIME 23
Vaneigem, Raoul (1934–) *Belgian philosopher*	felt such a rage to live	TWENTIETH 15
	hellish cycle is complete	WORK 23
Van Gogh, Vincent (1853–90) *Dutch painter*	my pictures do not sell	VALUE 13
Vaucaire, Michel	*Non! je ne regrette rien*	GUILT 13
Vaughan, Janet-Maria (1899–1993) *English scientist*	trying to do science in hell	MEDICINE 18
Vaughan Williams, Ralph (1872–1958) *English composer*	it's what I meant	MUSIC 22
Veblen, Thorstein (1857–1929) *American economist and social scientist*	make two questions grow	RESEARCH 6
	sagacious use of sabotage	MANAGEMENT 9
Venturi, Robert (1925–) *American architect*	Less is a bore	ARCHITECT 15
Versace, Gianni (1949–96) *Italian designer*	like to dress egos	FASHION 8
Vespasian (AD 9–79) *Roman emperor from AD 69*	Money has no smell	TAXES 12
Vicious, Sid (1957–79) *British rock musician*	pick a chord, go twang	MUSIC 23

Victoria, Queen (1819–1901)
Queen of the United Kingdom from 1837

animal and unecstatic	BIRTH 7
as if I was a public meeting	CONVERSATION 15
bitter disappointment	CHILDREN 22
folly of 'Woman's Rights'	WOMAN'S R 24
I will be good	ROYALTY 19
possibilities of defeat	DEFEAT 9
they will pay for it	CLASS 21
We are not amused	HUMOUR 16

Vidal, Gore (1925–)
American novelist and critic

between consenting adults	PUNISHMENT 18
fact, no matter how suspect	REALITY 10
fast-forward button	PAST 20
IQ of a moron	ARTISTS 6
little something in me dies	SUCCESS 22
triumph of the embalmer's art	REAGAN 4

Vidor, King (1895–1982)
American film director

it's a *sentence*	MARRIAGE 33

Viera Gallo, José Antonio (1943–)
Chilean politician

only arrive by bicycle	POLITICAL P 27

Villon, François (b. 1431)
French poet

snows of yesteryear	PAST 21

Virgil (70–19 BC)
Roman poet

cursed craving for gold	GREED 8
Do not trust the horse	GIVING 10
expect no safety	DEFEAT 10
farmers excessively fortunate	FARMING 8
Love conquers all things	LOVE 55
meanwhile it is flying	TIME 24
mortality touches the heart	SORROW 19
one who has gone through it	EXPERIENCE 14
We can't all do everything	ABILITY 5

Voltaire (1694–1778)
French writer and philosopher

always have spoken French	LANGUAGES 12
best of possible worlds	OPTIMISM 9
Common sense is not so common	PRACTICAL 12
composition of a tragedy	TRAGEDY 7
defend to the death your right	CENSORSHIP 21
enemy of the good	EXCELLENCE 5
find something new	CHANGE 25
God is on the side	WARFARE 41
making new enemies	LAST WORDS 19
necessary to invent him	GOD 29
owe respect to the living	REPUTATION 11
shepherds and butchers	GOVERNMENT 27
superfluous, a very necessary	NECESSITY 8
tell everything	BOREDOM 10
to encourage the others	WAYS 5
whole world in flames	PHILOSOPHY 12

Vonnegut, Kurt (1922–)
American novelist and short-story writer

pistol pointed at my head	LOVE 56

Voznesensky, Andrei (1933–)
Russian poet

I am Goya of the bare field	WARFARE 42

Vreeland, Diana (1903–89)

navy blue of India	COLOURS 10

Vyazemsky, Prince Peter (1792–1878)
Russian poet

beggars, cripples by the yard	RUSSIA 12

Waite, Terry (1939–)
British religious adviser

try to extinguish life	TERRORISM 5

Walcott, Derek (1930–)
West Indian poet and dramatist

choose Between this Africa	AFRICA 9
desert is a moving mouth	FAMINE 5

Walcott, Derek (*cont.*)	I come from a backward place	WRITING 37
	Men are born makers	CREATIVITY 12
Wald, George (1904–97)	device to make Nature speak	EXPERIMENT 7
American biochemist	physicist is an atom's way	PHYSICS 12
	We are the products of editing	LIFE SCI 15
Waldegrave, William (1946–)	in the House of Commons	TRUTH 21
British Conservative politician		
Wałęsa, Lech (1943–)	search for love	CAPITALISM 12
Polish trade unionist and statesman	'Solidarity' means taking care	TRADE 9
Walker, Alice (1944–)	beautiful mother	EARTH 9
American poet	come to church to *share* God	GOD 30
	Live frugally on surprise	LIFE 35
	pacifist peaceful always die	PACIFISM 8
	walk by the colour purple	COLOURS 11
	woman is not a potted plant	WOMEN 39
Wallace, Edgar (1875–1932)	What is a highbrow	INTELLECTUALS 7
English thriller writer		
Wallace, George (1919–)	segregation forever	RACISM 19
American Democratic politician		
Wallace, Joe	cough in Washington	CANADA 12
Wallace, William Ross (d. 1881)	hand that rocks the cradle	MOTHERS 11
American poet		
Wallas, Graham (1858–1932)	How can I know what I think	MEANING 10
British political scientist		
Walpole, Horace (1717–97)	be overrun with nettles	MIND 17
English writer and connoisseur	comedy to those that think	LIFE 36
	ensure summer in England	SUMMER 7
	ink in my pen ran cold	FEAR 17
	made of Newcastle coal	WEATHER 11
	resolution on reflection	COURAGE 13
	totter into vogue	FASHION 9
	Virtue knows what it has lost	GOODNESS 19
	wisest prophets make sure	FORESIGHT 10
Walpole, Robert (1676–1745)	men have their price	CORRUPTION 10
English Whig statesman		
Walsh, John (1937–)	laugh at the Millennium Dome	BUILDINGS 8
British journalist		
Walton, Izaak (1593–1683)	blessing that money cannot buy	HEALTH 7
English writer	make friends ashamed	HUMOUR 17
	no man is born an angler	FISHING 3
Warburton, William (1698–1779)	Orthodoxy is my doxy	RELIGION 23
English theologian		
Ward, Ali	new rock'n'roll	GARDENS 18
Ward, Barbara (1914–81)	We cannot cheat on DNA	LIFE SCI 16
British author and educator		
Ward, Claire (1972–)	admit to being an MP	POLITICIANS 24
British Labour politician		
Warhol, Andy (1927–87)	famous for fifteen minutes	FAME 25
American artist	fascinating kind of art	BUSINESS 28
	like it to say 'figment'	EPITAPHS 28

Warhol, Andy (*cont.*)

Machines have less problems	TECHNOLOGY 26
more American than thinking	SHOPPING 6
most exciting attractions	IMAGINATION 12
personal sex is bad	RELATIONSHIPS 24
series of images	LIFE 37
Sex is more exciting	FICTION 14
there'll be more waste	POLLUTION 14
things that people don't need	ART 27

Warner, Jack (1892–1978)
Canadian-born American film producer

Reagan for his best friend	REAGAN 5

Warner, Sylvia Townsend (1893–1978)
English writer

fatal law of gravity	MISFORTUNES 12
good rancorous hatred	HATRED 12
grief is like a minefield	SORROW 20
old teapot, used daily	PAST 22
remember for ever	DIARIES 8
soup is chaos	COOKING 14
thought it would never end	MUSICIANS 14

Warren, Frank
British boxing promoter

Lead Plan Diet	DIETS 7

Washington, George (1732–99)
American general and statesman

decisive naval force	NAVY 8
I can't tell a lie, Pa	LIES 12

Waterhouse, Keith (1929–)
English novelist and dramatist

good a night as any to stay in	CELEBRATIONS 8
packet of biscuits	POLLUTION 15

Waters, Muddy (1915–83)
American blues singer and guitarist

kept writing those blues	MUSIC 24

Watson, James D. (1928–)
American biologist

No *good* model	THEORY 10
sue its parents	GENETIC 10

Watson, John
see **Densham, Pen and Watson, John**

Watson, Thomas Snr. (1874–1956)
American businessman

business in your heart	BUSINESS 29
Clothes don't make the man	CLOTHES 19

Watts, Alan (1915–73)
American teacher and writer

just to peel the potatoes	RELIGION 24

Watts, Isaac (1674–1748)
English hymn-writer

voice of the sluggard	SLEEP 12

Waugh, Evelyn (1903–66)
English novelist

among the under-dogs	ENGLAND 21
baying for broken glass	CLASS 22
Beware of writing to me	LETTERS 12
Britons alone use 'Might'	BRITAIN 12
chap who doesn't care much	NEWS 5
curiosity about the future	AUTOBIOG 10
disasters of English history	WALES 8
English public school	PRISON 7
great English blight	CHARM 5
hands of a chimpanzee	POETS 18
Impotence and sodomy	BIRTH CONT 5
indecent behaviour	TEACHING 16
Modern Churchman	CLERGY 9
need of the plain	MANNERS 10
through the plashy fen	STYLE 12
Up to a point	TACT 4
virtue of the bored	PUNCTUALITY 9
Without supernatural aid	CHRISTIAN 13

Webb, Sidney (1859–1947)
English socialist

waste-paper basket	MARRIAGE 34

Weber, Max (1864–1920) *German sociologist*	official secret	BUREAUCRACY 10
Webster, Daniel (1782–1852) *American politician*	always room at the top	AMBITION 19
	Law: It has honoured us	LAWYERS 6
Webster, John (*c.*1580–*c.*1625) *English dramatist*	stars' tennis-balls	FATE 11
	summer birdcage in a garden	DISCONTENT 10
	We think caged birds sing	SORROW 21
Wedgwood, Josiah (1730–95) *English potter*	man and a brother	RACISM 20
Weil, Simone (1909–43) *French essayist and philosopher*	attempts to fill voids	SIN 16
	enable it to make war	ECONOMICS 17
	right which goes unrecognized	HUMAN RIGHTS 12
Weir, Arabella *British actress*	Does my bum look big	CLOTHES 20
	I'd got 'pram eyes'	CHILDREN 23
	parent's raised eyebrow	PARENTS 21
Weir, Mary	deaf-related suffering	DISABILITY 12
Weiser, Stanley (1946–) **and Stone, Oliver** (1946–)	Greed is right	GREED 9
Weisskopf, Victor (1908–2002) *American physicist*	*all* questions were stupid	IGNORANCE 14
Weissmuller, Johnny (1904–84) *American film actor*	Me Tarzan, you Jane	MEN/WOMEN 24
Welch, Bruce and Bennett, Brian	all going on a summer holiday	HOLIDAYS 5
Weldon, Fay (1931–) *British novelist and scriptwriter*	God has become female	GOD 31
	if it's raining, apologizes	WIVES 11
	Men are so romantic	ROMANCE 10
	My children are ungrateful	INGRATITUDE 5
	OBE goes on for ever	AWARDS 9
	pleasanter to help the young	OLD AGE 21
	rape isn't the worst thing	VIOLENCE 16
	sex in yesterday's novels	PAST 23
	Who am I going to be	CLOTHES 21
Welles, Orson (1915–85) *American actor and film director*	biggest electric train set	CINEMA 26
	can't stop eating peanuts	TELEVISION 23
	only two emotions in a plane	AIR TRAVEL 7
	produced Michelangelo	CULTURE 15
Wellington, Duke of (1769–1852) *British soldier and statesman*	at the other side of the hill	WARFARE 44
	by God, they frighten me	ARMY 23
	does not make him a horse	NATIONALITY 9
	his presence on the field	LEADERSHIP 14
	misery is a battle gained	WARFARE 43
	on the playing fields of Eton	WATERLOO 5
	Publish and be damned	PUBLISHING 6
	scum of the earth	ARMY 24
	see who will pound longest	WATERLOO 4
	Up Guards and at them	WATERLOO 3
Wells, H. G. (1866–1946) *English novelist*	bit of primordial chaos	FACE 10
	education and catastrophe	HISTORY 15
	I told you so	FORESIGHT 11
	jealousy with a halo	MORALITY 16
	leviathan retrieving pebbles	JAMES 3
	Social Contract	SOCIETY 15
	tasted like weak vinegar	ALCOHOL 18

Wells, John (1936–) *British actor, comedian, and writer*	recognise one's own faults	SELF-KNOW 11
Welsh, Irvine (1957–) *Scottish novelist*	Cricket Test ambience	THEATRE 17
	They're just wankers	SCOTLAND 15
Welty, Eudora (1909–2001) *American writer*	daring starts from within	SELF 25
Wesker, Arnold (1932–) *English dramatist*	asking questions, all the time	EDUCATION 16
	Chips with everything	CHOICE 17
	murder the thought	CENSORSHIP 22
Wesley, John (1703–91) *English preacher; founder of Methodism*	convert the Indians	RELIGION 25
	death is not far behind	OLD AGE 22
	I am never in a hurry	SPEED 8
	no religion but social	CHRISTIAN 14
Wesley, Mary (1912–) *English novelist*	shock of sexual astonishment	HEALTH 8
	suck on a boiled sweet	SEX 38
Wesley, Samuel (1662–1735) *English clergyman and poet*	Neat, but not gaudy	STYLE 13
West, Mae (1892–1980) *American film actress*	better to be looked over	FAME 26
	come up sometime, and see me	MEETING 12
	Give a man a free hand	SEX 39
	gun in your pocket	SEX 40
	hard man is good to find	MEN 21
	It's not the men in my life	MEN 20
	It's not what I do	STYLE 14
	I've been in *Who's Who*	DICTIONARIES 6
	I've been things	EXPERIENCE 15
	never missed it	REPUTATION 12
	one I never tried before	CHOICE 18
	some day it'll keep you	DIARIES 9
	used to be Snow White	GOODNESS 21
	what beautiful diamonds	GOODNESS 20
	when I'm bad, I'm better	SIN 17
	When women go wrong	MEN/WOMEN 25
West, Nathaniel (1903–40) *American writer*	Lonelyhearts are the priests	ADVICE 11
West, Rebecca (1892–1983) *English novelist and journalist*	challenge of filling the space	JOURNALISM 23
	doormat or a prostitute	WOMAN'S R 25
	Hatred of domestic work	HOUSEWORK 8
	help with moving the piano	MEN 22
	hen picking at random	SHOPPING 7
	indefensible as infanticide	CENSORSHIP 23
	intersecting monologues	CONVERSATION 16
	It's a lout's game	BETRAYAL 13
	partly compensate people	LITERATURE 10
	smell of cooking cabbage	POVERTY 21
	special claim to virility	HAIR 5
	your hand concentrates	MEMORY 23
Westminster, Loelia, Duchess of (1902–93) *English aristocrat*	in a bus over the age of 30	FAILURE 10
Westwood, Vivienne (1941–) *British fashion designer*	contradiction in terms	CULTURE 16
Wetherell, Charles (1770–1846) *English lawyer and politician*	added a new terror to death	BIOGRAPHY 14
Wharton, Alan (1923–) *English cricketer*	best judge of a run	CRICKET 13

Wharton, Edith (1862–1937)	common symptom of immaturity	ART 28
American novelist	law of the musical world	OPERA 5
	pursue Culture in bands	CULTURE 17
	small change of his illusions	DISILLUSION 11
Whately, Richard (1787–1863)	not an honest man	HONESTY 11
English philosopher and theologian	pearls fetch a high price	VALUE 14
	reasonably be expected to do	EFFORT 11
	you have something to say	SPEECHES 18
Wheeler, Mortimer (1890–1976)	driest dust that blows	ARCHAEOLOGY 5
British archaeologist		
Whistler, James McNeill (1834–1903)	Had silicon been a gas	EXAMINATIONS 8
American-born painter	I am telling you	ARGUMENT 22
	knowledge of a lifetime	EXPERIENCE 16
	never was an artistic period	ART 29
	two and two would continue	ARGUMENT 21
	wish I had said that	QUOTATIONS 14
White, E. B. (1899–1985)	becomes a nudist	AUTOBIOG 11
American humorist	It's broccoli, dear	FOOD 29
	science of poll-taking	STATISTICS 12
	to and from his wife	TRAVEL 22
White, Edmund (1940–)	Aids epidemic has rolled back	AIDS 8
American writer and critic	movies spoil us for life	CINEMA 27
White, Patrick (1912–90)	least of possessions	AUSTRALIA 15
Australian novelist		
White, T. H. (1906–64)	best thing for being sad	EDUCATION 17
English novelist	not forbidden is compulsory	LAWS 16
White, Theodore H. (1915–86)	best time to listen	POLITICIANS 25
American writer and journalist	hopeful wanderers of Europe	UNITED S 26
	pollution of democracy	CORRUPTION 11
Whitehead, Alfred North (1861–1947)	all truths are half-truths	TRUTH 22
English philosopher and mathematician	capacity to act wisely	INTELLIGENCE 10
	Ideas won't keep	IDEAS 14
	perform without thinking	CIVILIZATION 7
	series of footnotes to Plato	PHILOSOPHY 13
	what is apparently useful	RESEARCH 7
Whitehorn, Katharine (1928–)	good at getting taxis	MEN 23
English journalist	mothers go on getting blamed	MOTHERS 12
	not having any money	YOUTH 21
	ones that grow like weeds	GARDENS 19
	scratching for the wrong fleas	PRESENT 14
	seen one Western	CINEMA 28
	something else to kick	SPORTS 22
	tea-girl's chance to kiss	PARTIES 10
Whiting, George	no place to go	CLOTHES 22
American songwriter		
Whitman, Walt (1819–92)	body electric	BODY 17
American poet	earth does not argue	EARTH 10
	essentially the greatest poem	UNITED S 27
	I contain multitudes	CONSISTENCY 3
	leaf of grass is no less	NATURE 12
	procreant urge of the world	CREATIVITY 13
	Seasons pursuing each other	CELEBRATIONS 9
	turn and live with animals	ANIMALS 19
	When I give I give myself	GIVING 11
Whittaker, Ben (1934–)	alter the suicide rate	DRUGS 14

Whittier, John Greenleaf (1807–92) *American poet*	sad words of tongue or pen	CIRCUMSTANCE 14
Whittington, Robert *English grammarian*	man for all seasons	PEOPLE 26
Whitton, Charlotte (1896–1975) *Canadian writer and politician*	do twice as well as men	MEN/WOMEN 26
Whyte-Melville, George John (1821–78) *Scottish-born novelist*	owe it to horse and hound	ANIMALS 20
Widdecombe, Ann (1947–) *British Conservative politician*	nanny state has decreed rather be round and jolly	RISK 8 FAT 8
Wiesel, Elie (1928–) *Romanian-born American writer*	murderers of Jewish children Neutrality helps the oppressor opposite of life is not death	FORGIVENESS 13 IMPARTIAL 3 INDIFFERENCE 9
Wilberforce, Samuel (1805–73) *English prelate*	his descent from a monkey	LIFE SCI 17
Wilbur, Richard (1921–) *American poet*	Mind in its purest play weapons, their force and range	MIND 18 WEAPONS 12
Wilcox, Ella Wheeler (1855–1919) *American poet*	just the art of being kind Weep, and you weep alone	RELIGION 26 SORROW 22
Wilcox, Toyah *British actress, and singer*	talk about quantum physics	SEX 41
Wilde, Oscar (1854–1900) *Anglo-Irish dramatist and poet*	absolutely fatal	HONESTY 12
	all existence in an epigram	WORDPLAY 12
	Anybody can be good	COUNTRY 11
	ask for a watercress sandwich	FOOD 30
	become like their mothers	MEN/WOMEN 27
	begin by loving their parents	PARENTS 22
	better to be beautiful	GOODNESS 22
	captivity was to the Jews	EXILE 6
	choice of his enemies	ENEMIES 14
	curse of the drinking classes	WORK 24
	death of Little Nell	EMOTIONS 20
	die beyond my means	MEDICINE 19
	education produces no effect	IGNORANCE 15
	ends with Revelations	BIBLE 7
	every sinner has a future	SAINTS 5
	flashes of lightning	POETS 19
	galloping after a fox	HUNTING 9
	get back my youth	HEALTH 9
	good ended happily	FICTION 15
	I can resist everything	TEMPTATION 13
	If one plays good music	PARTIES 11
	Judas writes the biography	BIOGRAPHY 15
	knows the price of everything	CYNICISM 9
	Life imitates Art far more	ART 30
	looking at the stars	IDEALISM 10
	Meredith's a prose Browning	WRITERS 17
	moral or an immoral book	BOOKS 23
	name every one gives	EXPERIENCE 17
	not being talked about	GOSSIP 12
	Nothing succeeds like excess	MODERATION 8
	nothing that is worth knowing	EDUCATION 18
	nothing to declare	GENIUS 11
	One of us must go	TASTE 9
	one's style is one's signature	STYLE 15
	pass on good advice	ADVICE 12
	pretending to be wicked	HYPOCRISY 9
	put my genius into my life	LIFESTYLES 19

Wilde, Oscar (*cont.*)	rage of Caliban	REALITY 11
	rarely pure, and never simple	TRUTH 23
	some sort of occupation	DEBT 9
	something sensational to read	DIARIES 10
	speak one's mind	DUTY 11
	tedious pack of people	FAMILY 16
	tells one her real age	WOMEN 40
	three is company and two none	MARRIAGE 35
	To lose one parent	MISTAKES 12
	tragedy of old age	AGEING 12
	type of a perfect pleasure	SMOKING 11
	Yet each man kills	LOVE 57
Wilder, Billy (1906–2002)	always twenty-twenty	PAST 24
American screenwriter and director	pay to see my Aunt Minnie	PUNCTUALITY 10
	something to look down on	TELEVISION 24
Wilder, Billy (1906–2002) see **Brackett, Charles and Wilder, Billy**		
Wilder, Thornton (1897–1975)	just to enjoy your ice cream	KNOWLEDGE 22
American novelist and dramatist	Marriage is a bribe	MARRIAGE 36
Wilensky, Robert (1951–) *American academic*	million monkeys banging	INTERNET 8
Will, George F. (1941–)	advertising blather	ADVERTISING 14
American columnist	only a game	BASEBALL 7
Willans, Geoffrey (1911–58) **and Searle, Ronald** (1920–)	As any fule kno	IGNORANCE 16
	Future is in yore Keeping	FUTURE 19
English humorous writers	i hope it will never die out	CHRISTMAS 9
	you hav various swots, bulies	SCHOOLS 15
Willard, Emma Hart (1787–1870) *American pioneer of women's education*	cradle of the deep	SEA 15
William III (1650–1702) *King from 1688*	bullet has its billet	FATE 12
Williams, Heathcote (1941–)	planet is blue	EARTH 11
British dramatist and poet	Whales play	ANIMALS 21
Williams, Hugo (1942–) *British writer and poet*	veil blows across my face	WEDDINGS 14
Williams, Kenneth (1926–88) *English actor*	often socially impressive	QUOTATIONS 15
Williams, R. J. P. (1926–) *British chemist*	search for the chemistry	LIFE SCI 18
Williams, Shirley (1930–)	frozen packet of semen	FAMILY 17
British politician	Madonnas or Mary Magdalenes	CHURCH 12
Williams, Ted (1918–) *American baseball player*	name of the game	BASEBALL 8
Williams, Tennessee (1911–83)	cat on a hot tin roof	PERSISTENCE 11
American dramatist	defence against betrayal	TRUST 12
	in the laboratory of God	HUMAN RACE 31
	inside our own skins	SOLITUDE 16
	kindness of strangers	CHARITY 15
	nature hates a vacuum	NATURE 13
	tell you what I want. Magic	REALITY 12
	We occupy the same cage	HOME 12
Williams-Ellis, Clough (1883–1978)	By God what a site	AUSTRALIA 16

Williamson, Marianne (1953–) *American writer and philanthropist*	powerful beyond measure	SELF-ESTEEM 20
Williamson, Roy (1936–90) *Scottish folksinger and musician*	when will we see your like	SCOTLAND 16
Willkie, Wendell (1892–1944) *American lawyer and politician*	second class citizens	EQUALITY 14
Willmot, Eric Paul (1936–)	secret beauty	AUSTRALIA 17
Wilson, Charles E. (1890–1961) *American industrialist*	good for General Motors	BUSINESS 30
Wilson, Edward O. (1929–) *sociobiologist*	born not as a blank tablet	MIND 19
Wilson, Harold (1916–95) *British Labour statesman, Prime Minister 1964–70, 1974–6*	appeals to the Dunkirk spirit	CRISES 19
	Get your tanks off my lawn	ARGUMENT 23
	like an old stage-coach	POLITICAL P 29
	middle-of-the-road muddle	CRISES 20
	party is a moral crusade	POLITICAL P 28
	pound here in Britain	MONEY 23
	week is a long time	POLITICS 31
	white heat of this revolution	TECHNOLOGY 27
Wilson, McLandburgh (b. 1892)	optimist sees the doughnut	PESSIMISM 9
Wilson, Sandy (1924–) *English songwriter*	thing called the Boy Friend	COURTSHIP 17
Wilson, Woodrow (1856–1924) *American Democratic statesman, President 1913–21*	Armed neutrality is ineffectual	INTERNATIONAL 20
	made safe for democracy	DEMOCRACY 11
	need a week for preparation	SPEECHES 19
	such a thing as tolerance	WARFARE 45
	writing history with lightning	FILMS 7
Windsor, Barbara (1937–) *English actress*	only as good as his parts	ACTING 8
Windsor, Duchess of (1896–1986) *wife of the former Edward VIII*	too rich or too thin	APPEARANCE 15
Winters, Shelley (1922–) *American actress*	hit them where they live	THEATRE 18
Winterson, Jeanette (1959–) *English novelist and critic*	absentee boss is best	CLERGY 10
	fenced in with posts	CRITICS 25
	weapon of the future	GENETIC 11
	your emotional role model	GOD 32
Wittgenstein, Ludwig (1889–1951) *Austrian-born philosopher*	everything that is the case	UNIVERSE 15
	I've had a wonderful life	LAST WORDS 20
	limits of my world	LANGUAGE 19
	Logic must take care	LOGIC 11
	show the fly the way out	PHILOSOPHY 14
	whereof one cannot speak	SPEECH 21
Wodehouse, P. G. (1881–1975) *English writer; an American citizen from 1955*	always a hellhound	CHARACTER 21
	as far as he could spit	TRUST 13
	Chumps make the best husbands	HUSBANDS 14
	far from being gruntled	DISCONTENT 11
	finished in half the time	COOPERATION 14
	forgotten to say 'When!'	CLOTHES 23
	good rule never to apologize	APOLOGY 9
	infallible test	GOLF 5
	my biggest armchair	BODY 18
	out pops the cloven hoof	FAMILY 18
	picking daisies on the railway	SURPRISE 6

Wodehouse, P. G. (*cont.*)

Scotsman with a grievance	SCOTLAND 17
shooting as a sport	FIELD 4
uproar of the butterflies	GOLF 4

Wogan, Terry (1938–)
Irish broadcaster

contracts the imagination	TELEVISION 25
magnificent foolishness	SINGING 17

Wolf, Naomi (1962–)
American writer

his own disillusion	BEAUTY 24
relinquish their sexuality	FAT 9

Wolfe, Humbert (1886–1940)
British poet

hope to bribe or twist	JOURNALISM 24

Wolfe, Tom (1931–)
American writer

liberal is a conservative	POLICE 5
now in the Me Decade	SELF-INTEREST 10
Radical Chic	FASHION 10

Wollstonecraft, Mary (1759–97)
English feminist

give a sex to mind	MIND 20
have power over men	WOMAN'S R 26
slavish bondage to parents	PARENTS 23

Wolpert, Lewis (1929–)
English biologist

had not written *Hamlet*	ARTS AND SCI 12
product of technology	INVENTIONS 18
unexpected provides the clues	RESEARCH 8

Wolstenholme, Kenneth (1920–2002)
English sports commentator

think it's all over	ENDING 14

Wood, Victoria (1953–)
British writer and comedienne

life-saving certificate	INTELLECTUALS 8
people who aren't intelligent	SPORTS 23
Reading it slower	TECHNOLOGY 28

Woodcock, George (1912–95)
Canadian writer

Canadians do not like heroes	CANADA 13

Woodhead, Chris (1946–)
British educationist

reject didactic teaching	TEACHING 17

Woods, Tiger (1975–)
American golfer

I'm a Cablinasian	RACE 9

Woolf, Virginia (1882–1941)
English novelist

bootboy at Claridges	JOYCE 3
Content is disillusioning	DISCONTENT 12
Each had his past shut in him	SELF 26
inability to cross the street	FRIENDSHIP 22
madness is terrific	MADNESS 8
mass of odds and ends	DIARIES 11
One likes people much better	MISFORTUNES 13
room of her own	WRITING 38
This great mind is hoarded	LIBRARIES 10
twice its natural size	MEN/WOMEN 28
wreckage of men	CRITICS 26

Woollcott, Alexander (1887–1943)
American writer

illegal, immoral, or fattening	PLEASURE 17
Little Nell and Lady Macbeth	PEOPLE 27

Wordsworth, Elizabeth (1840–1932)
English educationist

good are so harsh	GOODNESS 23

Wordsworth, Mary (1782–1859)
wife of William Wordsworth

thy inmost heart upon paper	LETTERS 13

Wordsworth, William (1770–1850)
English poet

Bliss was it in that dawn	REVOLUTION 22
Breathless with adoration	EVENING 4
Chatterton, the marvellous boy	POETS 20
Child is father of the Man	CHARACTER 22
Earth has not anything	LONDON 8
fair and shining youth	GENERATION 14
fled the visionary gleam	IMAGINATION 13
Heaven lies about us	YOUTH 22

Wordsworth, William (*cont.*)

impulse from a vernal wood	NATURE 14
must himself create the taste	ORIGINALITY 9
never see a flower	FLOWERS 14
Plain living and high thinking	IDEALISM 11
rainbow comes and goes	TRANSIENCE 14
recollected in tranquillity	POETRY 32
Scorn not the Sonnet	SHAKESPEARE 9
shares the nature of infinity	SUFFERING 24
trailing clouds of glory	BIRTH 8
unremembered, acts Of kindness	GOODNESS 24
wandered lonely as a cloud	FLOWERS 13
wandering voice	BIRDS 12
we lay waste our powers	LEISURE 9
We must be free or die	ENGLAND 22

Worrall, Terry
spokesman for British Rail

wrong kind of snow	SNOW 4

Wotton, Henry (**1568–1639**)
English poet and diplomat

honest man sent to lie abroad	DIPLOMACY 15
tried To live without him	BEREAVEMENT 19

Wran, Neville (**1926– **)
Australian politician

dagger in one hand	POLITICIANS 26

Wright, Frank Lloyd (**1867–1959**)
American architect

Art and Religion	CIVILIZATION 8
banking and prostitution	CITIES 14
bury his mistakes	ARCHITECT 16
necessities were going	LUXURY 6

Wu, Harry (**1937– **)
Chinese-born American political activist

word 'gulag' did not appear	PRISON 8

Wycherley, William (*c.***1640–1716**)
English dramatist

with faint praises	CRITICS 27

Wynette, Tammy (**1942– **)
American country singer

Stand by your man	LOYALTY 8

Xiao-Huang Yin

level of economic prosperity	DEMOCRACY 12

Yates, John (**1925– **)
English theologian and bishop

believing more in less	BELIEF 21

Yeatman, R. J. (**1898–1968**)
see **Sellar, W. C. and Yeatman, R. J.**

Yeats, W. B. (**1865–1939**)
Irish poet

best lack all conviction	EXCELLENCE 6
centre cannot hold	CHAOS 4
Dreading and hoping all	DYING 14
dried the sap out of my veins	PROBLEMS 14
foul rag-and-bone shop	EMOTIONS 21
glory most begins and ends	FRIENDSHIP 23
Great hatred, little room	IRELAND 13
Horseman, pass by	INDIFFERENCE 10
I will arise and go now	SOLITUDE 17
In balance with this life	AIR FORCE 4
knows death to the bone	DEATH 40
love you for yourself alone	HAIR 6
make a stone of the heart	SUFFERING 25
Never to have lived	LIFE 38
no enemy but time	INNOCENCE 11
O body swayed to music	DANCE 12
opinions are accursed	OPINION 15
Our stitching and unstitching	POETRY 33
Perfection of the life	PERFECTION 8
quarrel with others	POETRY 34
Slouches towards Bethlehem	CHRISTMAS 10
so shining loveliness	BEAUTY 25

Yeats, W. B. (*cont.*)

	tattered coat upon a stick	OLD AGE 24
	Tread softly	DREAMS 10
	We were the last romantics	IDEALISM 12
	When you are old and grey	OLD AGE 23
	woman can be proud and stiff	LOVE 58
	years like great black oxen	TIME 25

Yeltsin, Boris (1931–)
Russian statesman

last day of an era past	RUSSIA 13
plunging into a cold peace	EUROPE 16

Yeosock, John J. (1937–)

third of a million troops	ARMY 25

Yesenin, Sergei (1895–1925)
Russian poet

always the good feel rotten	PLEASURE 18
nothing new in dying	SUICIDE 10

Yevtushenko, Yevgeny (1933–)
Russian poet

Life is a rainbow	LIFE 39
rocking sky of '41	WORLD W II 17

Yokoi, Shoichi (1915–97)
Japanese soldier

terrible shame for me	DEFEAT 11

York, Sarah, Duchess of (1959–)

fresh, clean page	HOPE 13
I can almost *hear* food	ITALY 6

Young, Andrew (1932–)
American clergyman and diplomat

well-placed business men	BUSINESS 31

Young, Edward (1683–1765)
English poet and dramatist

Be wise with speed	FOOLS 15
man suspects himself a fool	SELF-KNOW 12
One to destroy, is murder	WARFARE 46
Tired Nature's sweet restorer	SLEEP 13

Young, George W. (1846–1919)

lips that touch liquor	TEETOTALISM 7

Young, G. M. (1882–1959)
English historian

married to a duchess	PUBLISHING 7

Young, Neil (1945–)
Canadian singer and songwriter

It's better to burn out	SUICIDE 11

Zamyatin, Yevgeny (1884–1937)
Russian writer

entropy of human thought	THINKING 21
madmen, heretics, dreamers	LITERATURE 11

Zangwill, Israel (1864–1926)
Jewish spokesman and writer

find the pagan—spoiled	CHRISTIAN 15
great Melting-Pot	UNITED S 28

Zappa, Frank (1940–93)
American rock musician and songwriter

act like an asshole	DRUGS 15
people who can't write	JOURNALISM 25

Zeno (333–261 BC)
Greek philosopher

two ears and only one mouth	SPEECH 22

Zephaniah, Benjamin (1958–)
British poet

be able to dance it	POETRY 35

Zhuangzi (*c.*369–286 BC)
Chinese philosopher

butterfly dreaming I am a man	SELF-KNOW 13

Zhvanetsky, Mikhail (1934–)
Russian writer

backward into the future	POLITICIANS 27

Zobel, Hiller B. (1932–)
American judge

decide the unknowable	TRIALS 6
follow their oaths	LAWYERS 7

Zola, Émile (1840–1902)
French novelist

I accuse	JUSTICE 21

Oxford Paperback Reference

The Concise Oxford Dictionary of Quotations
Edited by Elizabeth Knowles

Based on the highly acclaimed *Oxford Dictionary of Quotations*, this
paperback edition maintains its extensive coverage of literary and
historical quotations, and contains completely up-to-date material. A
fascinating read and an essential reference tool.

The Oxford Dictionary of Humorous Quotations
Edited by Ned Sherrin

From the sharply witty to the downright hilarious, this sparkling
collection will appeal to all senses of humour.

Quotations by Subject
Edited by Susan Ratcliffe

A collection of over 7,000 quotations, arranged thematically for easy
look-up. Covers an enormous range of nearly 600 themes from 'The
Internet' to 'Parliament'.

The Concise Oxford Dictionary of Phrase and Fable
Edited by Elizabeth Knowles

Provides a wealth of fascinating and informative detail for over 10,000
phrases and allusions used in English today. Find out about anything
from the 'Trojan house' to 'ground zero'.

OXFORD

Oxford Paperback Reference

The Concise Oxford Dictionary of English Etymology
T. F. Hoad

A wealth of information about our language and its history, this
reference source provides over 17,000 entries on word origins.

'A model of its kind'

Daily Telegraph

A Dictionary of Euphemisms
R. W. Holder

This hugely entertaining collection draws together euphemisms from all
aspects of life: work, sexuality, age, money, and politics.

Review of the previous edition
'This ingenious collection is not only very funny but extremely
instructive too'

Iris Murdoch

The Oxford Dictionary of Slang
John Ayto

Containing over 10,000 words and phrases, this is the ideal reference for
those interested in the more quirky and unofficial words used in the
English language.

'hours of happy browsing for language lovers'

Observer

OXFORD

Oxford Paperback Reference

The Concise Oxford Companion to English Literature
Margaret Drabble and Jenny Stringer

Based on the best-selling *Oxford Companion to English Literature*, this is
an indispensable guide to all aspects of English literature.

Review of the parent volume
'a magisterial and monumental achievement'

Literary Review

The Concise Oxford Companion to Irish Literature
Robert Welch

From the ogam alphabet developed in the 4th century to Roddy Doyle,
this is a comprehensive guide to writers, works, topics, folklore, and
historical and cultural events.

Review of the parent volume
'Heroic volume ... It surpasses previous exercises of similar nature in the
richness of its detail and the ecumenism of its approach.'

Times Literary Supplement

A Dictionary of Shakespeare
Stanley Wells

Compiled by one of the best-known international authorities on the
playwright's works, this dictionary offers up-to-date information on all
aspects of Shakespeare, both in his own time and in later ages.

OXFORD

Oxford Paperback Reference

The Kings of Queens of Britain
John Cannon and Anne Hargreaves

A detailed, fully-illustrated history ranging from mythical and pre-conquest rulers to the present House of Windsor, featuring regional maps and genealogies.

A Dictionary of Dates
Cyril Leslie Beeching

Births and deaths of the famous, significant and unusual dates in history – this is an entertaining guide to each day of the year.

'a dipper's blissful paradise … Every single day of the year, plus an index of birthdays and chronologies of scientific developments and world events.'

Observer

A Dictionary of British History
Edited by John Cannon

An invaluable source of information covering the history of Britain over the past two millennia. Over 3,600 entries written by more than 100 specialist contributors.

Review of the parent volume
'the range is impressive … truly (almost) all of human life is here'
Kenneth Morgan, *Observer*

OXFORD

More Art Reference from Oxford

The Grove Dictionary of Art

The 34 volumes of *The Grove Dictionary of Art* provide unrivalled coverage of the visual arts from Asia, Africa, the Americas, Europe, and the Pacific, from prehistory to the present day.

'succeeds in performing the most difficult of balancing acts, satisfying specialists while ... remaining accessible to the general reader'

The Times

The Grove Dictionary of Art – Online
www.groveart.com

This immense cultural resource is now available online. Updated regularly, it includes recent developments in the art world as well as the latest art scholarship.

'a mammoth one-stop site for art-related information'

Antiques Magazine

The Oxford History of Western Art
Edited by Martin Kemp

From Classical Greece to postmodernism, *The Oxford History of Western Art* is an authoritative and stimulating overview of the development of visual culture in the West over the last 2,700 years.

'here is a work that will permanently alter the face of art history ... a hugely ambitious project successfully achieved'

The Times

The Oxford Dictionary of Art
Edited by Ian Chilvers

The Oxford Dictionary of Art is an authoritative guide to the art of the western world, ranging across painting, sculpture, drawing, and the applied arts.

'the best and most inclusive single-volume available'

Marina Vaizey, *Sunday Times*

OXFORD

AskOxford.com

Oxford Dictionaries Passionate about language

For more information about the background to Oxford Quotations and Language Reference Dictionaries, and much more about Oxford's commitment to language exploration, why not visit the world's largest language learning site, www.AskOxford.com

Passionate about English?

What were the original 'brass monkeys'?   **Ask**Oxford.com

How do new words enter the dictionary?   **Ask**Oxford.com

How is 'whom' used?   **Ask**Oxford.com

Who said, 'For also knowledge itself is power?'   **Ask**Oxford.com

How can I improve my writing?   **Ask**Oxford.com

If you have a query about the English language, want to look up a word, need some help with your writing skills, are curious about how dictionaries are made, or simply have some time to learn about the language, bypass the rest and ask the experts at www.AskOxford.com.

Passionate about language?

If you want to find out about writing in French, German, Spanish, or Italian, improve your listening and speaking skills, learn about other cultures, access resources for language students, or gain insider travel tips from those **Ask**Oxford.com in the know, ask the experts at

OXFORD

Oxford Companions

'Opening such books is like sitting down with a knowledgeable friend. Not a bore or a know-all, but a genuinely well-informed chum ... So far so splendid.'

Sunday Times [of *The Oxford Companion to Shakespeare*]

For well over 60 years Oxford University Press has been publishing Companions that are of lasting value and interest, each one not only a comprehensive source of reference, but also a stimulating guide, mentor, and friend. There are between 40 and 60 Oxford Companions available at any one time, ranging from music, art, and literature to history, warfare, religion, and wine.

Titles include:

The Oxford Companion to English Literature
Edited by Margaret Drabble
'No guide could come more classic.'

Malcolm Bradbury, *The Times*

The Oxford Companion to Music
Edited by Alison Latham
'probably the best one-volume music reference book going'

Times Educational Supplement

The Oxford Companion to Western Art
Edited by Hugh Brigstocke
'more than meets the high standard set by the growing number of Oxford Companions'

Contemporary Review

The Oxford Companion to Food
Alan Davidson
'the best food reference work ever to appear in the English language'

New Statesman

The Oxford Companion to Wine
Edited by Jancis Robinson
'the greatest wine book ever published'

Washington Post

OXFORD

Oxford Paperback Reference

The Concise Oxford Dictionary of Art & Artists
Ian Chilvers

Based on the highly praised *Oxford Dictionary of Art*, over 2,500 up-to-date entries on painting, sculpture, and the graphic arts.

'the best and most inclusive single volume available, immensely useful and very well written'

Marina Vaizey, *Sunday Times*

The Concise Oxford Dictionary of Art Terms
Michael Clarke

Written by the Director of the National Gallery of Scotland, over 1,800 entries cover periods, styles, materials, techniques, and foreign terms.

A Dictionary of Architecture
James Stevens Curl

Over 5,000 entries and 250 illustrations cover all periods of Western architectural history.

'splendid ... you can't have a more concise, entertaining, and informative guide to the words of architecture'

Architectural Review

'excellent, and amazing value for money ... by far the best thing of its kind'

Professor David Walker

OXFORD

Great value ebooks from Oxford!

An ever-increasing number of Oxford subject reference dictionaries, English and bilingual dictionaries, and English language reference titles are available as ebooks.

All Oxford ebooks are available in the award-winning Mobipocket Reader format, compatible with most current handheld systems, including Palm, Pocket PC/Windows CE, Psion, Nokia, SymbianOS, Franklin eBookMan, and Windows. Some are also available in MS Reader and Palm Reader formats.

Priced on a par with the print editions, Oxford ebooks offer dictionary-specific search options making information retrieval quick and easy.

For further information and a full list of Oxford ebooks please visit: www.askoxford.com/shoponline/ebooks/

OXFORD

More Literature titles from OUP

Shakespeare: An Oxford Guide
Stanley Wells and Lena Cowen Orlin

This comprehensive guide to Shakespeare comprises over 40 specially commissioned essays by an outstanding team of contemporary Shakespeare scholars.

Literature in the Modern World
Dennis Walder

A unique perspective for students on literary studies from the 1920s to the present day.

The Poetry Handbook
John Lennard

A lucid and entertaining guide to the poet's craft, and an invaluable introduction to practical criticism.

VISIT THE HIGHER EDUCATION LITERATURE WEB SITE AT
www.oup.com/uk/best.textbooks/literature

OXFORD